CW00405815

HITS
OF THE
'60s

HITS
OF THE
'60s
THE
MILLION
SELLERS

DEMITRI CORYTON
& JOSEPH MURRELLS

B.T. Batsford Limited · London

This book is dedicated to my wife, Tracy Coryton, whose first experience of married life was having to put up with me writing my first book.

Opening Illustrations to Chapters:

Frontispiece	The Beatles
1960	Cliff Richard
1961	Elvis Presley
1962	The Shadows
1963	The Beatles
1964	The Rolling Stones
1965	The Supremes
1966	Beach Boys
1967	The Monkees
1968	Eric Clapton of Cream
1969	Creedence Clearwater Revival

© Demitri Coryton and Joseph Murrells, 1990
First published 1990

Part of this book is based on the 1960s section of *Million Selling Records From the 1900s to the 1980s*, by Joseph Murrells, 1984.

All rights reserved. No part of this publication may be reproduced, in any form or by any means, without permission from the publisher.

ISBN 0 7134 5851 8

Printed in Great Britain by
The Bath Press, Bath
for the publishers
B.T. Batsford Ltd,
4 Fitzhardinge Street,
London W1H OAH

CONTENTS

Preface   6

Explanatory Notes   8

Record Labels   10

Abbreviations and Terms   11

Acknowledgements   11

Million-selling Records 1960–69   12

Appendices   244
    British No 1s   244
    American No 1s   249
    British Silver Discs   255
    American Gold LPs   261
    Award Winners   268

Index of Artists   275

Index of Titles   279

PREFACE

The sixties was a great time in which to be young and into music. It was the decade of my teens, and many of the million-selling records described in this book bring back happy memories, as they will for anyone who was young at that time. It was not just the music. In a whole range of aspects of life the frontiers of the possible were pushed forward.

It was also an important decade for the history of rock music. Rock'n'roll had started in America in the mid-fifties, and soon crossed the Atlantic to Britain. By 1960 it had slowed down a bit, but then came the Beatles and the British beat boom that swept the world. By the end of the decade, rock music was progressing in new directions. The sixties was by far the most important decade of the rock era.

The origin of this book was the late Joseph Murrells' great work on million-selling records. He listed every million seller from the very first, Caruso's **On With The Motley** on Angel in 1903, to 1981. The first presentation for sales success by a record company to an artist was in 1905, when the Gramophone Company of Britain (now EMI) presented a bracelet to Marie Hall. The bracelet included seven tiny golden discs, representing each of her hit records. The first Gold Disc was presented by RCA to Glenn Miller on 10 February 1942, live on the Chesterfield Radio Show on CBS network radio, for over a million sales of his **Chattanooga Choo Choo**. By the mid-fifties RCA were presenting Gold Discs to all their artists who had million-selling records, and even after the RIAA took on this function in 1958 RCA continued, giving a second Gold Disc for the B side if the record sold over two million. This led to some confusion in the Murrells book about the number of million sellers that Elvis Presley had won, especially the number of Gold Discs awarded

(which included those for sales of a second million) and the smaller number of million sellers. These discrepancies have been put right in this volume.

We considered simply updating the Murrells book, but it was already so large that to have added another eight years' worth of records, mainly albums, would have created a very large and expensive book. We therefore decided to update his book on a decade by decade basis, starting with the sixties.

The bulk of this book is a description of every record released from 1 January 1960 to 31 December 1969 that has sold a million copies. Most of the entries for the main artists of the decade have been rewritten and updated. While the main story of each artist is told under their first entry, the progress of the major stars is followed throughout the decade. Since the last edition of Murrells' book, some more sixties records have passed the million mark, and are listed here for the first time.

Wherever possible the entries in the Murrells book were checked, and it is clear that a few had not sold a million copies after all. These have been withdrawn from this edition. It is very difficult to be sure about a record's sales figures unless it has won an award for million sales. In America the RIAA has certified million-selling singles since 1958, but million-selling albums only from 1976. However, not all US record companies were members of the RIAA, or were prepared to have their sales figures audited by the Association for a gold disc. In Britain those few records that sold a million copies were widely reported in the music press, though there was no uniform system of awards for million sales until the BPI took this on in the 1970s.

Record companies are normally very reluctant to issue sales figures. Some may not have paid full royalties on some records, while other companies of the sixties have gone out of business or have been taken over by others. In many cases the figures no longer exist. Royalty departments, which keep sales figures, exist to pay royalties and not to act as some sort of archive. Many companies saw no reason to keep information they no longer required from this pre-computer period, and simply threw the information away. In a few cases sales figures have been tracked down, and one or two have shown the difficulty that Joseph Murrells had in judging what had or had not sold a million.

Murrells relied largely on published reports of sales of a million. This could be dangerous. Artists and their management sometimes massaged their figures to help build up (or retain) their reputation. Lazy or gullible journalists would repeat in print a dubious claim, or simply make an honest mistake that once in print became accepted as fact. Two examples of the pitfalls will suffice. In 1979 Liberty Records in Britain put out a press release on Kenny Rogers that stated in the second paragraph that 'When he was only 19, Kenny first tasted fame and the special thrill of having a million selling hit single with **Crazy Feeling**.' This was duly reported, and the claim appeared as fact in many papers. Not only did this record, if it ever existed, not figure in the list of million sellers supplied to me by the RIAA, but it never made either the *Billboard* or *Cash Box* charts at even the lowest levels. Joseph Murrells did not fall for that one, and the record did not appear in his book. However, he did include the **Ask Me Why** EP by the Beatles, released by Vee Jay in America, stating that 'It sold a reputed million in the USA.' Most of the Beatles' sales figures do exist in the EMI Archives or Royalty departments. In fact this record sold only 49,617 copies net, and was nowhere near the million mark. I have withdrawn it from this edition.

Sometimes luck helped my research. As part of their preparations for marking the 30th anniversary of Cliff Richard's career, the Royalties department of EMI had worked out his sales figures for every record from 1958 to the present. A far larger number of Cliff Richard records had passed the million mark than had previously been thought. What this exercise showed was that over a period of many years, a record can quietly sell a very large number of copies without going back in the charts.

As well as the material on million sellers, this book also includes a review of each year of the decade. Singles that won a Silver Disc in Britain, and albums that won a Gold Disc in America (for million dollar sales) are listed, as are the No 1s from all the charts. Using up to five charts from Britain and four from America may seem confusing. It would certainly have been easier to have used only one, like the *Record Retailer* Top 50 used in the excellent Guinness chart books. However, the fact is that in the early sixties the *Record Retailer* chart did not count for much. EMI, for example, the biggest record company in the country, compiled its own chart by averaging out the music paper charts. It did not include the *Record Retailer* chart in its calculations until 1962. The fact is that in the sixties there was some confusion because of the number of charts. That was the reality of the time, so that is what is included here. An annual list of winners is also given, showing the popularity poll and award winners in Britain and America. Much of this information is listed together for the first time.

In checking the facts, details and dates of the hundreds of entries in this book I have gone to a number of sources, including many of the rock encyclopaedia published in recent years and the Orbis part-work *History Of Rock*, which I contributed to some years ago. The series of books about the American *Billboard* charts by Joel Whitburn are a mine of interesting information, and are highly recommended. Frank Hoffman's book on the *Cash Box* charts is also valuable. Much information about the recording career of the greatest group of them all, the Beatles, has been researched by EMI and is contained in the outstanding *The Complete Beatles Recording Sessions* by Mark Lewisohn, published by EMI and Hamlyn. This book is a must for anyone seriously interested in the Beatles.

While responsibility for the contents of this book lies with the late Joseph Murrells and myself, I would like to express my thanks to those who helped so much with the writing of this volume. All the sixties editions of the *New Musical Express*, *Melody Maker*, *Record Mirror*, *Disc* and *Record Retailer* were read, along with copies of other magazines that did not survive the whole decade. The American magazines *Billboard*, *Variety*, *Cash Box* and *Record Vendor/Record World* were read, and *Rolling Stone* and others were also consulted. I must express my gratitude to the staff of the British Library Newspaper Archive in Colindale, London, and to the Recorded Sound Reference Center of the Library of Congress in Washington DC. I am also grateful for the help of the vast EMI Archives at Hayes, London, the Capitol Archives, Los Angeles, and the CBS and RCA Archives in New York. While the research for this edition was carried out in Britain and the USA million sellers from other countries have not been ignored. I just hope that we have got them all, and have done justice to the many fine artists whose talent, along with that of their songwriters and producers, has brought so much enjoyment to us all.

Demitri Coryton, October 1989

EXPLANATORY NOTES

These notes explain the background to some of the areas covered in this book.

Million-Selling Records

For the purposes of this book, a million seller is a record that has sold a total of at least one million copies on a global basis. The world 'sold' means copies sold to members of the public, and not just bulk sales from record companies to wholesalers or dealers before returns. For singles, a record has to have had the same A side in all those countries where sales have contributed to the million total, though B sides may have varied from country to country. Different versions of the same song by the same artist do not count.

For albums whose million sale has been achieved from a number of countries, the content has to be broadly the same in each territory. There is a problem with the early and mid-sixties, in that the American version of many British albums differed from that released in Britain. In many cases it was simply a couple of tracks shorter, but sometimes the differences were greater. Inevitably it is an arbitrary matter where exactly to draw the line, but where there is a substantial difference the two versions have been counted as different albums, even if they have had the same name. For example, the Beatles' **Help!** album had seven tracks from the film on both the British and American versions. The British version also included seven other Beatles numbers, while the American one had six tracks from the George Martin Orchestra playing music from the film. These have been counted as two separate million sellers. On the other hand, the two versions of **Rubber Soul** had a core of ten tracks in common. The British version had four tracks not on the American one, and the American version had two tracks not on the British release. Both versions sold over a million copies, so should that give the Beatles one or two million sellers? Here, they have been counted as one as they were substantially the same.

Double albums had to sell one million units, not one million bits of plastic (i.e. not half a million units of two records per unit.) In a change from the Joseph Murrells editions, records that were released as EPs in Europe and as one or more singles in America are now counted as separate records.

Sales of all formats of a record count towards the million, provided that in the case of albums the content is broadly the same. Cassette and four and eight track cartridge sales only became significant in the late sixties, but tape and now CD sales of back catalogue over the years can mount up to an impressive total. There is no time limit on how long a record may take to qualify. The one format that is excluded is flexidiscs, which are usually given away free as a promotional tool.

In the sixties a record that sold a million copies won a Gold Disc for its artist. In fact the first edition of Joseph Murrells' book was called the *Book of Golden Discs*. In America these were awarded by the RIAA, and the information on which records won an RIAA Gold Disc and the date of the award comes from the RIAA. In Britain there was no consistent scheme. Sometimes the record company would present the award, sometimes *Disc* magazine would give it and sometimes both would.

The tiny number of British records that sold a million copies in Britain invariably got a Gold Disc, but those that sold a global million sometimes did and sometimes did not. If a record took several years to reach a global sale of a million it usually did not. Now a Gold Disc means a sale of half a million singles in Britain and America, and considerably fewer in those other countries that make such awards.

Silver Discs

In 1959 Gerald Marks, the editor and founder of *Disc*, started a scheme that he intended to be the equivalent of the RIAA Gold Discs for million-selling singles in America. Given that the population of Britain was only a quarter of that in the USA, Marks announced that *Disc* would present a Silver Disc for any record that sold a quarter of a million copies in Britain. He underestimated the number of records that would qualify, and as record sales soared he soon had to abandon the idea of giving a big presentation ceremony for every award.

The scheme was started and Russ Conway's **Side Saddle** on Columbia was the first record to win a Silver Disc. The award was made once the record company concerned wrote to the editor of *Disc* to claim the award. A senior executive had to state that sales were over the quarter million mark, but there was no independent audit. It was all taken on trust, but in 1959 there were only four record companies capable of winning Silver Discs in Britain. In the seventies *Disc* ceased publication, and the BPI took over the certification of records.

In 1959 no EP or LP had ever sold anywhere near 250,000 copies, so the question of whether the scheme covered those formats as well as singles was at first academic. EMI made a presentation to Russ Conway and Cliff Richard for sales of several albums that together reached the quarter million mark, but *Disc* did not make its first Silver Disc album award until 17 February 1962. This was to Elvis Presley for the *Blue Hawaii* film soundtrack, and was the first LP to sell 250,000 copies in Britain. After this *Disc* did not announce any further album awards, and certainly did not continue the practice in the late sixties when album sales really took off. There was a report in *Cash Box* that the Shadows and Cliff Richard had won Silver Discs for some of their albums, but this was not announced in Britain. The Beatles, the Rolling Stones and the Beach Boys also had LPs that sold over 250,000 copies, as did the *Sound Of Music* soundtrack which passed the million mark.

There was no consistent certification of albums in Britain until the BPI took over responsibility in the seventies. When the Beatles came along they had five EPs in a row which sold over 250,000 copies, and the scheme was extended to cover them and other EPs.

The date given for the awarding of Silver Discs is the date of *Disc* magazine that the award was announced in. Sometimes this would be a few days after the record sold the quarter million, but if the record company was slow in claiming, as for example Decca was with some Elvis Presley records, then the date of the award could be some while after the quarter million figure was passed. Those records that had achieved advance orders of 250,000 are indicated, but only where the record company had advised *Disc* that this was so. Again, Presley suffered from Decca's laggardly approach.

American Album Gold Discs

The RIAA began certifying million-selling singles in America in 1958. At the same time it introduced Gold Disc awards for albums that had sold one million dollars worth at manufacturers dollar volume (wholesale price) based on one third of the list price of the LP. This was well short of one million copies. On 1 January 1975 the system was changed to sales of half a million copies needed to qualify. Since 1 January 1989 this half million figure has also applied to singles. The information on which albums qualified for a Gold Disc and the date on which it was awarded is from the RIAA.

The British Charts

The first British singles chart was published by the *NME* on 14 November 1952. By January 1960 three other consumer music weeklies were publishing their own charts. *Melody Maker* had been second in the field, followed by *Record & Show Mirror* (which later changed its name to the present *Record Mirror*) and *Disc*. On 5 March 1960 the trade monthly *Record Retailer* (now called *Music Week*) changed its format to a weekly paper and published its own chart, a Top 50 which was 20 places more than in any other chart. This made five singles charts published each week, all of them differing slightly in the order in which records were listed. Over the next ten years the number was gradually reduced to three charts. *Record Mirror* scrapped its own Top 20 in favour of the more extensive *Record Retailer* charts on 24 March 1962. On 26 August 1967 *Disc* and the *Melody Maker*, both owned by the same company, began using the same chart (*Melody Maker*'s.)

The *Melody Maker* also published separate EP and LP charts, as did the *Record Retailer* as soon as it changed to publishing weekly. The *NME* did not introduce an album chart until 1962, nor did *Disc* until 1965. All British charts in the sixties were based only on record sales in shops. At first the number of shops used was very small. In 1960 *Melody Maker* were using a sample of only 14. The number soon increased to over a hundred. The BBC compiled its own chart from averaging out the published charts. The American trade paper *Cash Box* also produced a British chart, partly by averaging out the other charts but also by sampling shops themselves.

In the wake of the Beatles boom a few other music papers briefly flourished, and some of them published their own charts. One of them, *Music Echo*, was the first to produce a national singles Top 100. None of them lasted very long, either merging with the established papers or folding. Only the charts of those papers that published throughout the decade have been used.

In the annual lists of No 1 records, the date given is the Saturday at the end of each week that the papers compiling the charts were published. As up to five charts are involved, a standard date had to be used. The No 1s are listed in the order in which they first topped a chart. The date given for each record is that of the first chart the record topped. The exact date a record went to No 1 frequently varied between the different charts, especially in the earlier part of the decade, though the order was usually the same in all charts. If the order was different in one chart from that shown, a footnote indicates this. Not all records went to the top in all charts, but this is clear from the lists given in full in the appendices at the end of the book.

The American Charts

Unlike Britain the USA does not have a tradition of national newspapers. There were no equivalents to the British consumer music papers like the *NME*. In America the charts are compiled by record trade papers like *Billboard*, which produced the first singles chart on 20 July 1940. Until 1958 *Billboard* produced separate charts based on sales, juke box plays and radio plays. In 1958 these three charts were combined into the Hot 100. After 1961 this applied to all the other US singles charts as well, though album charts were based only on sales. The lower regions of the US charts in particular are based mainly on radio plays and not sales.

In 1960 there were at least eight record industry papers, many of which compiled their own charts. The four that have been used in this book are the ones that had by far the greatest influence. After *Billboard* it was *Cash Box* that was the main record industry paper, much more important in the sixties than it is now. *Record Vendor* was one of the also-rans at the start of the decade, but it grew in importance as the sixties wore on. It changed its name to *Record World* in 1964, and by the late sixties it had become an important trade paper, third behind *Billboard* and *Cash Box*. The fourth chart used in this book is that produced by the weekly edition of *Variety*. This was not a record industry paper, but one devoted to the entertainment business as a whole, with the emphasis on films followed by television. It had a lot of influence in the entertainment business, and was therefore an important chart for the record industry: While *Variety* did move to a Top 100 in 1960, when it combined its sales and airplay charts, it soon reduced that to a Top 50. On the album charts, from 1958 to 1963 *Billboard* published separate charts for mono and stereo sales, though most sales were in mono.

As well as the main pop charts, the American record industry papers also publish a number of specialist charts. In this book, *Billboard's* C&W and R&B charts are used where a record was a hit in either. Million sellers were usually hits on the main pop charts as well as the Country or R&B lists, in which case both sets of chart information are given.

International Chart Placings

The international chart placings are taken from a number of sources, including the EMI international chart lists produced by EMI throughout the decade. It has not been possible to obtain a complete run of the charts for all the countries of the world for the whole decade, so the list of countries where a record went to No 1, or was a hit, is not necessarily complete.

Charts Used In This Book

Unless otherwise stated, the *Record Retailer* charts have been used for British chart placings, and the *Billboard* charts for American chart placings. References to the 'Hot 100' indicate the *Billboard* charts, as the term is a *Billboard* trade mark. If a record reached No 1 in any of the five British or four American charts used, then it is reported as having made the top. The number of weeks (if any) spent at No 1 in each individual chart is given in the appendices on British and American No 1s at the back of the book.

The Award Winners

The annual winners section gives information about which artists won the various awards that are given each year. The number of awards that could have been listed is almost endless, so only the main British and American awards are listed. In Britian it was the consumer papers that were the main source of awards. The *NME* started a popularity poll among its readers in the mid-fifties, and gradually all the other papers followed. This involved tens of thousands of young people taking part in these postal polls each year, and gives a good barometer of popularity. Having a well organized fan club helped an artist a great deal, as Elvis Presley found out. The biggest of the polls, run by the *NME*, resulted in a major pop concert at the Empire Pool Wembley for the winning artists. By the end of the decade some of the sections in some polls were more for fun than anything, but they help to give a flavour of that era. Not all sections in every poll have been used.

In America, where there was no equivalent to the British national consumer papers, the prestigious NARAS Grammy Awards are given. Not all sections of these awards are listed — only the main awards are given. The Academy members who voted for the Grammies were often out of touch with the kids buying the records, as will be seen by some of the awards made, and those records left out. In 1964, for example, the year the Beatles hit America, was Stan Getz and Astrud Gilberto's **The Girl From Ipanema** really the best record of the year?

The top chart performers of the year are given. Success in this section measures consistency and not sales. The music papers compiled their annual chart lists using an inverted points system, giving (in the case of the *NME*) 30 points for each week at No 1 down to one point for one week at No 30. Acts like the Beatles, who sold vast numbers of records in a short period of time, did not do as well in these points leagues as others whose lower sales were spread over a longer period of time. An alternative to the points system was developed in America by the chart expert Joel Whitburn. He ranked records according to their length at the top of the charts, working downwards. Acts like the Beatles do better in this system, but it disadvantages a record like Frank Sinatra's **My Way**, which never made the top but stayed in the lower regions of the charts for a very long while. The Guinness team of Paul Gambaccini, Tim Rice and Jo Rice have done a similar job for the British charts. The winners of both systems are given, so you take your choice.

RECORD LABELS

For each million-selling record in this book, the label it was released on is given first, followed by its record number and the country of origin. For Anglo-American records, this is followed by the label of release on the other side of the Atlantic, but only if the record was a hit there. For records from other countries, label and number information for Britain and America is only given if the record was a hit in either country.

Some explanation needs to be given about some record labels. In a few cases the same label name was owned by different companies in different parts of the world. The main examples of this are given below.

Columbia

Columbia is the oldest record label in the world, formed in February 1888 in the United States. It set up a branch in Britain in 1900, and in 1923 this was sold to its British management. Two years later the Columbia Graphophone Company of Britain bought the Columbia Phonograph Company of America, reuniting the worldwide Columbia organization under British control. In 1927 Columbia bought the Nipponophone Company of Japan, which became Columbia Nipponophone. In 1931 Columbia merged with the other big British company of the day, the Gramophone Company (His Master's Voice) to form EMI. Because of American anti-trust legislation, EMI were forced to sell the Columbia Phonograph Company of New York, which they did in December 1931. From that time onwards the Columbia label in America was owned by a different company to that which owned the trade mark in Britain and the rest of the world. American Columbia passed through a number of owners including the CBS broadcasting company, and is now owned by the Japanese Sony Corporation. Sony own the Columbia trade mark in North and South America. EMI sold Columbia Nipponophone in 1938, and it remains an independent record company trading as Denon outside Japan and as Columbia Nippon inside Japan. English Columbia's Spanish licensee stole the trade mark in Spain in the 1930s, and as Columbia Espanol has been taken over by BMG (RCA/Ariola) who now own the Columbia trade mark in Spain. In Britain and every other country in the world the Columbia trade mark is owned by EMI, and was their primary pop label throughout the sixties. To this day (1989) Columbia has had more British No 1 singles than any other label. To distinguish between British and American Columbia, British Columbia records have the name (EMI) after Columbia. American Columbia is denoted by the name CBS in front of the Columbia label name. The Japanese and Spanish Columbia million sellers are identified as such.

His Master's Voice

As a label, His Master's Voice (or HMV as it is commonly known) is used and owned by EMI. When used by overseas EMI subsidiaries the name is sometimes translated into foreign languages, e.g. La Voix de son Maître for France. The HMV trade mark was first used by the Gramophone Company of Great Britain in December 1899. It is the reproduction of a painting by the English artist Francis Barraud. The Gramophone Company (now EMI) did not operate directly in America at that time, but had a licensing deal with the Victor Talking Machine Company. (Victor became RCA in 1928, and is now owned by the German BMG.) The Gramophone Company allowed Victor to use its Dog and Trumpet HMV trade mark in America, which they have done ever since. In Japan it is used by Japan Victor (JVC) which was once a subsidiary of RCA. The HMV trade mark is owned by EMI throughout the world except in the Americas and Japan.

Decca

Decca was originally used as the name of a gramophone made during the First World War. The Decca Record Company was started by Sir Edward Lewis in 1929. In 1934 he started an American subsidiary, but had to sell American Decca during the Second World War to raise money to pay for the development of radar. Thus the American and British branches of Decca were separated. American Decca was bought by MCA, though for many years it continued to use British Decca as its UK licensee. American Decca million sellers are denoted by the letters US in front of the Decca name. British Decca was taken over by the Dutch Polygram company in 1979.

London

After the Second World War, British Decca wanted to re-enter the American market. As the Decca name was no longer open to it, British Decca started London records in the US in 1949. In America, London signed local artists and released the records of British Decca artists. In Britain, British Decca used the London label as the outlet for American records licensed from small US indie companies. The artist rosta of British and American London was therefore quite different, even though the label was owned by British Decca on both sides of the Atlantic. Polygram gained the London label in Britain and America when it took over Decca in 1979.

Brunswick

The Brunswick label was one of the oldest in America. In the thirties it was taken over by Warner Brothers in their first, brief, foray into the record business. They soon sold it, and eventually the British end of the company was bought by British Decca and the American end by American Decca. In Britain the Brunswick label was used as the outlet for American Decca material, which is why the Who at one time appeared on it. They were signed via Shel Talmy to American Decca.

It is worth noting that a number of artists recorded for independent producers and not for the record label that their records appeared on. Artists like the Animals and Lulu, for example, were contracted to Mickie Most, who licensed their discs to EMI's Columbia label.

ABBREVIATIONS AND TERMS

ABC	Associated British Cinemas
ABC	American Broadcasting Company
AP	All Polls
A&R	Artist and Repertoire
BB	*Billboard*
BBC	British Broadcasting Corporation
BPI	British Phonographic Industry
BS	Band Stand
CB	*Cash Box*
CBS	Columbia Broadcasting System (American)
CBS/Col	CBS Columbia (i.e. American Columbia)
C&W	Country and Western
D	*Disc*
EMI	Electric and Musical Industries
FTC	Federal Trade Commission (American)
G	The Gambaccini/Rice/Rice chart listings published by Guinness
ITV	Independent Television (British)
Indies	Independent record companies
Majors	The largest, or major, record companies
MM	*Melody Maker*
NARAS	National Academy of Recording Arts and Sciences (American)
NARM	National Association of Record Merchandisers (American)
NBC	National Broadcasting Company (American)
NME	*New Musical Express*
R&B	Rhythm and Blues
RCA	Radio Corporation of America
RIAA	Recording Industry Association of America
RM	*Record Mirror*
RV	*Record Vendor*
RW	*Record World*
V	*Variety*
W	The chart listings published in America by Joel Whitburn

ACKNOWLEDGEMENTS

The compiler and publisher gratefully acknowledge the assistance of the following individuals and organizations, who in the latter case have either given permission to quote from their files or have supplied publicity photographs, which are copyright. In certain cases the publisher and compiler have not been able to trace the copyright holder; any omissions will be rectified in future editions.

ABC Television Ltd; A&M Records; American Society of Composers, Authors and Publishers; Apple Records; Arista Records; Asylum Records; Atco; Atlantic Records; Jacques Aubert-Philips; BBC Records; Tony Barrow International Ltd; *Billboard*; Broadcast Music Inc.; Brunswick; CBS Records; Capitol Records; *Cash Box*; Chess Records; Chrysalis Records; Columbia Pictures; Cotillion Records; Paul Cox; Syd Cullingham; *Current Biography*; Decca Record Co. Ltd; Deram Records; Deutsche Grammophon; *Disc*; *Down Beat*; N.V. Dureco; EMI Records; Roger Easterby; Electric and Musical Industries; Elektra Records; Epic Records; the late Brian Epstein; Leslie Gaylor; Philip Gotlop Photographic Ltd; H&L Records; Sue Harwood; Dezo Hoffmann Ltd; Island Records; James J. Konigsmann; Liberty Records; London Features International Ltd; Janet Lord; MCA; MGM; Major-Minor Records; J. Marcham; *Melody Maker*; Mercury Records; Metromedia Records; Monitor Press; Monument Records; Motown Records; Brian Mulligan; *New Musical Express*; Parlophone; Philips Records Ltd; Phonogram Ltd; Photo-Reportage Ltd; Pinnacle Records; Barry Plummer; Polar Music Int AB; Polydor Records; Patricia A. Pretty; Pye Records; RAK Records; RCA Records; Rann Productions Ltd; *Record Mirror*; *Record World*; Rex Features Ltd; G. Ricordi & Co. (London) Ltd; Bob Roberts; Rocket Records; Rockfield; Rogers & Cowan, Inc.; Roulette Records; Starshine Corporation; Stax Records; Tamla Motown Records; *Time*; United Artists; Universal Pictorial; *Variety*; Virgin Records; Vogue Records Ltd; WEA Records Ltd; Warner Brothers Ltd; Warner/Reprise; Clive Woods; P.F. Worger.

1 9 6 0

1960 was the year that rock'n'roll died, or at least so some people feared and others hoped. The Establishment launched a sustained attack on rock music. The Report of the BBC/IBA Joint Committee on 'The Effects of Television on Children' was published in July. It branded the lyrics of pop songs as 'drivel...degraded...and injurious'. BBC TV music programme producer Russell Turner agreed: 'Modern songs are musically and lyrically appalling.' The Report said that 'Too many of the lyrics broadcast are merely drivel and have a generally debasing tone which is to be deprecated.'

This view was supported by some of the older American pop singers who had been elbowed aside by the young rockers. Mel Tormé attacked rock'n'roll, claiming that '97% of the songs are bad...as we know them in the States, [they] have ruined the music game. I feel at this age kids are not old enough to make a choice between rock'n'roll and good music. It really bugs me to see, in my own country, the way that a bunch of grown men are catering to the whims of young children.'

The American showbiz paper *Variety* joined in the attack. On 2 March a headline screamed 'Rock'n'Roll's Global Wane: Strong Trend To Standards'. The paper reported that 'The de-emphasis of the rock'n'roll beat, which has been marked in the US since the start of the payola problems a few months ago, is being echoed in Europe as well. ... Among the Europeans themselves...the big beat never really established a firm hold on the market, except for a few stand-out artists like Elvis Presley or Bill Haley. Now the traditional European accent on melodic material is reasserting itself.'

Rock'n'roll had slowed down. When Elvis Presley got out of the US Army in March, after two years' military service, he came back as Elvis the ballad singer not Elvis the rocker. Especially in Britain, ballads like **It's Now Or Never** and **Surrender** sold far more copies than his rock records had ever done. In Britain, Cliff Richard had learned this lesson in 1959. None of his string of rock hits that followed **Move It** in 1958 went to No 1. Yet his first two ballads, **Living Doll** and **Travellin' Light**, roosted at the top for three months!

Cliff Richard and the Shadows

The success of these records helped Cliff Richard end the fifties by winning all the music paper popularity polls as Top British Male Singer. In the *Melody Maker* pop poll of March 1960, he won 40% of the vote compared to Frankie Vaughan, who came second with 7%. In both this and the *New Musical Express* poll of October 1959, **Living Doll** was voted Record of the Year. Cliff's performance in 1959 pointed the way to what would happen in 1960.

In Britain, Cliff Richard was by far the hottest property in the music world. He had five singles and an EP in the charts, with two of the singles going to No 1. His second film *Expresso Bongo* went down well, and he made what appeared at the time to be a successful tour of America. Just before their departure for the States, two of his backing group, the Shadows, were hurt in a car crash. Hank Marvin and Jet Harris, though injured, still made the American tour.

The Shadows started the year as the backing group for Cliff. On 20 August their first hit **Apache** knocked Cliff off the No 1 spot, and from then onwards they became the most successful beat group in the world until the Beatles. They were not the top act of 1960, for this was a time dominated by solo male singers. In Britain it was their 'lead singer' Cliff who was top, while in America the Shadows were (and would remain) virtually unknown. Even so, the emergence of the Shadows started a revolution. Thousands of young men all over Britain started imitating guitarists Hank Marvin and Jet Harris in particular, as countless amateur groups sprang up all over the country. In the mid-sixties many of these musicians turned professional, and formed the backbone of the British beat group invasion which conquered America and the world.

Britain later came to dominate pop music, a field that had always been an American preserve, and it has remained one of the two centres of pop repertory for the whole world ever since. The Beatles blazed the trail through America which so many followed from 1964, but the Shadows started the whole British group scene off in 1960.

Broadcasting — Records Banned

Rock on British television saw the end of Jack Good's 'Boy Meets Girl' series which had followed 'Oh Boy!'. Good had a new show called 'Wham!', which met with mixed reviews. Death discs were controversial, with the BBC banning the original version of **Tell Laura I Love Her** by Ray Paterson. This helped the slightly re-worded Ricky Valence cover shoot to No 1. In February, top DJ Pete Murray made a fool of himself by banning the Russ Conway instrumental **Royal Event**, claiming that it was in bad taste to name a record after the royal event of the moment, the birth of the Queen's second son, Prince Andrew. Rival DJ David Jacobs announced that he would not be banning the record as he knew it was named after the re-opening of the Royal Theatre in Lowestoft, and had nothing to do with the Royal Family.

Vera Lynn announced that she was leaving Decca after 25 years and over eight million records sold. June saw the tenth anniversary of Decca's introduction of LPs into Britain. Long Play records were invented by CBS, which then had strong ties with its former owner EMI, but EMI procrastinated and did not introduce LPs until 1952.

Cliff Richard published the first of many autobiographies (after a career of only two years!). *It's Great To Be Young* was a sell-out. His discovery Dave Sampson had a hit with his first record **Sweet Dreams**. The Madison dance craze arrived from America, but did not stay long. Actress Diana Dors, a sort of early sixties Samantha Fox, tried to launch a recording career but with less success than Sammy did a quarter of a century later. Teen idol Marty Wilde got married, and the screaming stopped. His career as a pop star was virtually over, though his marriage to Joyce produced a fruitful business partnership and a daughter Kim who was a more successful singer in the eighties.

Eddie Cochran Killed

Among the American stars visiting Britain in 1960 were Nat 'King' Cole; Johnny Ray, whose manager announced that in nine years with CBS he had sold 12 million records; the Everly Brothers, whose tour ended on a sour note when the popular press linked the name of 21-year-old Phil Everly with a 16-year-old girl from Doncaster; Gene Vincent, who spent five months in Britain; and Eddie Cochran. On Easter Sunday Eddie Cochran was killed in a car crash at Chippenham, Wiltshire. Gene Vincent was hurt in the same accident. Cochran had been living on borrowed time for the previous 18 months: he had been booked on the same flight that saw Buddy Holly, Ritchie Valens and the Big Bopper killed in a plane crash.

Outside America, British artists were already beginning to carve a major share of the market in many different countries. In December, EMI's chairman Sir Joseph Lockwood (knighted in the new year)

announced that, thanks mainly to the sales of Cliff Richard, Russ Conway and the Shadows, EMI sold one quarter of all the records then manufactured in the world.

The Record Industry

The British record industry was dominated by EMI and Decca, with Philips and Pye as the other two majors. There were very few record companies in Britain then, with only a handful of small independents like Oriole as competition. None of the American companies operated directly in Britain. Warner Brothers was launched as a new label in March, but within the Decca organization which also represented RCA and, via the London label, most of the smaller American indie companies. CBS was rumoured to be in talks with Philips, who released their product under licence, aimed at Philips launching the CBS label in Britain. Record sales reached a record high of over £36 million, with singles sales reaching £45 million by October.

On the independent front, producer Joe Meek launched his Triumph Records, the first attempt of the new decade to create a new record company. It later failed. The giant Rank Organization fared little better. Its Top Rank label had met with some success with Craig Douglas and John Leyton, but on 9 August a stunned record industry learned that after only 18 months Top Rank was being taken over by EMI.

On the world scene, the mighty EMI (which had moved into its new headquarters in Manchester Square in London in June) made a strategic move back into the Japanese record business by buying a minority stake in Toshiba Musical Industries, via its American subsidiary Capitol.

Ever since EMI sold it in December 1931, American Columbia had confined itself to operating on the American continent, with licensees in Europe and elsewhere. In May, CBS (as the company was known outside America) made its first move towards becoming a genuinely international operator. It bought the Australian Record Company, the biggest in that country.

The American industry continued to be dominated by RCA, CBS, Capitol and American Decca. Warner Brothers, which had started in 1958, signed up the Everly Brothers and Bill Haley. Payola remained a scandal.

America

In America the big news was the return of Elvis Presley. This resulted in his only visit to Britain. His plane stopped to refuel at Prestwich Airport, and Elvis signed autographs for an hour before resuming his journey home. Just before his return, his manager Col. Tom Parker had some spoof newspapers printed as a joke. The front page headline read: 'Elvis Re-enlists: Hal Wallis Suffers Total Collapse: Col. Parker Joins Circus'. (Wallis had Elvis under contract for films, and Parker had worked in the circus before entering the record business.)

Though Elvis was the most popular singer in America as far as young people were concerned, those who ran the music industry found it hard to recognize this. In Billboard's DJ poll, it was Frank Sinatra who was voted 'Top Male Singer'; Elvis was not even in the top 10. In another DJ poll, it was Jim Reeves who was voted 'Top Male Singer'. Connie Francis was the most successful female artist, with No 1s, poll awards and Gold Discs to prove it.

The Dutch company Philips, licensed to CBS in America, tried to enter the American market directly by bidding £4 million ($10 million) for Dot Records. The bid failed, and Philips later bought Mercury. Congress continued hearings into alleged payola scandals. Country-and-western star Johnny Horton was killed in a car crash. And just to show that it was not only rock'n'roll that could lead to violence, there was a riot at the Newport Jazz Festival in early July. The City Council vowed that there would be no more festivals at Newport.

1960 was the year that John F. Kennedy became the first Catholic to be elected President of the United States. He defeated Vice President Nixon, who made a come-back in 1968, only to resign in disgrace after the Watergate scandal in the early seventies. 1960 was one of the closest elections ever, with Kennedy owing much to the famous political machine of Mayor Richard Daley of Chicago. (One polling station reported a turn-out of over 100%, live over CBS radio.) In January the longest steel strike in American history was settled. Cuba seized American property worth £267 million. In September Hurricane Donna swept up the east coast of the USA. President Eisenhower visited the Far East, and was welcomed in South Korea, but there were riots in Japan against the security pact with the USA. At the request of the Japanese Prime Minister the President's visit was cancelled, as his security in Tokyo could not be guaranteed.

Around The World

In Britain Harold 'Supermac' Macmillan had won a landslide victory for the Conservatives in October 1959. He spent much time in 1960 working with President Eisenhower over nuclear test ban negotiations with the Russians. A conference with the Russians was torpedoed when an American U2 spy plane piloted by Gary Powers was shot down over Russia.

France became the fourth nuclear power in the world in February, and had to put down an army rebellion in Algeria. A number of French colonies in West Africa become independent, as did British colonies Nigeria and Cyprus. The Belgians pulled out of the Congo, and civil war and UN military intervention followed.

In South Africa, police opened fire on crowds in Sharpeville on 21 March, killing 70. The Government banned the African National Congress. An attempt by a white farmer to assassinate the South African Prime Minister Dr Verwoerd failed. Leading former Nazi Adolf Eichmann was captured by the Israelis in Argentina, smuggled out of the country and put on trial in Israel. In Ceylon, Mrs Sirima Bandaranaika became the world's first woman Prime Minister. In South America there were earthquakes in Chile, and Brazilia became the new capital of Brazil.

Films and Sport

Top films in 1960 included *Never On A Sunday*, *Psycho*, *The Alamo* and *The Apartment*.

The 17th modern Olympic Games were held in Rome. The Russians won the largest number of gold medals, with 43. America came next with 34. Britain had only two gold medallists, Donald Thompson in the 50km walk and Anita Lonsborough in the 200m breast stroke.

Wolverhampton Wanderers won the FA Cup and Burnley were top of League Division One. Rangers won the Scottish FA Cup. Hearts won the League Cup and were top of the Scottish First Division.

The Pittsburgh Pirates took the World Series from the New York Yankees. The Philadelphia Eagles beat the Green Bay Packers to win the NFL championship, while the Houston Oilers beat Los Angeles in the first AFL championship. (It was the only season that Los Angeles played in the AFL league, as in 1961 their franchise was transferred to the San Diego Chargers.)

End of An Era?

1960 was the year pop music quietened down, though in fact this trend really got under way in 1959. Rock'n'roll was not dead, however, it was just resting. In America it was the year of the clean cut, all-American-boy teenage idol who would not do anything to upset a teenager's parents. Elvis was out of the US Army his popularity intact, but he had quietened down too, and big ballads were the order of the day. In Britain Cliff Richard was the top teen idol though it was his backing group, the Shadows, who pointed the way to the future.

VARIOUS ARTISTS *American*

ORIGINAL THEATRE CAST WITH MARY MARTIN, THEODORE BIKEL, PATRICIA NEWAY, LAURI PETERS, BRIAN DAVIES, KURT KASZNER, MARION MARLOWE, KAREN SHEPARD, ELIZABETH HOWELLS, MURIEL O'MALLEY, CHILDREN, NUNS AND FRANK DVONCH ORCHESTRA

THE SOUND OF MUSIC (Album) CBS 5450 [USA] PHILIPS ABL 3370 [UK]. Here was another monumental stage musical success for Oscar Hammerstein (words), his last work, and Richard Rodgers (music). The album of the show became on million seller.

The contents of the disc: **The Sound of Music** (Mary Martin); **Do-Re-Mi** (Mary Martin and children); **The Lonely Goatherd** (Mary Martin and children); **Edelweiss** (Theodore Bikel); **So Long, Farewell** (the children); **Climb Ev'ry Mountain** (Patricia Neway); **Processional** (the nuns); **No Ordinary Couple** (Mary Martin and Theodore Bikel); **The Sound of Music** (Martin, Bikel and children); **My Favourite Things** (Mary Martin and Pat Neway); **Sixteen Going on Seventeen** (Brian Davies and Lauri Peters); **How Can Love Survive?** (Kurt Kaszner and Marion Marlowe); **No Way to Stop It** (Bikel, Kaszner and Marlowe); **Maria** (Eliz. Howells, Muriel O'Malley, Pat Neway and Karen Shepard); **Climb Ev'ry Mountain** (the company); **Laendler** (Frank Dvonch Orchestra); **Praedludium** (Frank Dvonch Orchestra).

The Sound of Music was first produced at the Lunt-Fontanne Theatre in New York on 16 November 1959 and ran for 1,443 performances to 15 June 1963. The London production at the Palace Theatre opened on 18 May 1961 with 2,385 performances (the most ever for an American musical in Britain) until its closing on 14 January 1967. The play was adapted from *The Trapp Family Singers*, originally written by Maria Augusta Trapp, which tells the story of the famous Austrian vocalists. This album sold half a million by 1960, reached the million towards the end of 1961, and two million by 1963. It was lyricist Oscar Hammerstein II's last musical — he died in 1960. His fabulous partnership with Richard Rodgers resulted in over 30 million albums of their various musicals (stage and film) being sold by 1970, a seemingly unbeatable record. This disc was No 1 for 12 weeks in the USA, and in the bestseller list for 277 weeks. Gold Disc award RIAA 1960. Grammy Award for Best Original Cast Album (1960).

PAUL ANKA *Canadian*

PUPPY LOVE ABC-Paramount 10082 [USA] Columbia (EMI) DB 4434 [UK]. Born on 30 July 1941 in Ottawa, Canada, the son of restaurant proprietors, Paul Anka has proved Canada's longest-lasting pop star. He started performing as part of a trio at the age of 12 at Fisher Park High School. When he left school, he went to stay with an uncle with film-world connections in Hollywood, California, and signed with a small local record company. His first release,

Blau Wildebeeste Fontaine, sold 3,000 copies. He then wrote **Diana**, on the strength of which Don Costa, A&R chief of ABC-Paramount, signed him to a long-term contract. **Diana** was released in 1957, went to No 1 for one week in the USA and No 1 for nine weeks in Britain, where it was released on EMI's Columbia label. The record sold over nine million copies, three million in America and one million in Britain. This was one of the few occasions when EMI chairman Sir Joseph Lockwood directly intervened in the signing of an act. The company were reluctant to pick up British rights to the song, but Lockwood had a gut feeling for it, and insisted. Anka was the first Canadian singer to achieve a million seller. He achieved three more in the fifties, and two in 1960. In 1969 he put English words to a French song which he called **My Way**. Frank Sinatra (in 1969) and Elvis Presley (in 1977) both sold over a million copies of what became a great classic.

Anka wrote **Puppy Love**, his fifth million seller, in 1959. Most of the million sales came from the USA, where the record held at No 2 for two weeks, with 14 weeks on the charts. The B side, **Adam and Eve**, from the film *The Private Lives of Adam and Eve*, also charted for two weeks, reaching No 90. This was Anka's 13th US hit, and the first where both sides charted independently. The record was a minor hit in Britain, reaching No 33.

MY HOME TOWN ABC-Paramount 10106 [USA]. The second of three double A side US hits in a row, Paul Anka wrote his sixth million seller himself. **My Home Town** was No 8 for two weeks with 13 weeks on chart, while its flip side **Something Happened** reached No 41 with nine weeks on the Top 100. Neither side was a hit in Britain.

HANK BALLARD AND *American*
THE MIDNIGHTERS

TEARDROPS ON YOUR LETTER/THE TWIST King 517 [USA]. Most artists are lucky to have one major claim to fame. Hank Ballard has two. He wrote **The Twist** which, thanks mainly to the Chubby Checker cover version, launched the dance craze that swept the world in the early sixties. He was also a highly original and successful R&B artist in the mid-fifties, writing and recording the **Annie** trio of earthy black teen anthems. Born in Detroit in 1936, Ballard grew up in Alabama. He returned to Detroit in 1950 and joined a local quartet, the Royals, in 1953. The Royals had sung in the Orioles' style, though without any success with their first six releases on King Records' Federal label. Henry 'Hank' Ballard changed their run of bad luck with the new line-up's first release, **Get It**, which he co-wrote. The group, which changed its name to the Midnighters early in 1954, had six hits on the US R&B charts in 1954 and 1955. Three of them sold over a million copies, though none of them made the main US national charts. The million sellers, all released in 1954, were **Work With Me Annie**, **Sexy Ways**, and **Annie Had A Baby**. The first two were written by Ballard.

Hank Ballard first made the US Top 100 in

1959, with **Teardrops On Your Letter**. This ballad also brought him back to the R&B charts for the first time in three years, where the B side also charted. This was a faster number Ballard had written, called **The Twist**. The following year this was covered by Chubby Checker and, although he had the bigger hit with it, the renewed interest in the song gave Ballard and the Midnighters a double A side hit. **Teardrops On Your Letter** reached No 87 in March 1959, staying three weeks on the chart. **The Twist** started a 16-week chart run in July 1960, reaching No 28. The record had sold a million by 1962. None of Ballard's records were ever hits in Britain.

FINGER POPPIN' TIME King 5341 [USA]. Hank Ballard and the Midnighters followed their minor pop hit **Teardrops On Your Letter** with **Kansas City**, which reached No 72. This was followed by their first Top 10 hit, **Finger Poppin' Time**, written by Ballard. It enjoyed by far their longest run on the Hot 100, charting for 26 weeks and peaking at No 7.

LET'S GO, LET'S GO, LET'S GO King 5400 [USA]. 1960 gave Hank Ballard two Top 10 million sellers in a row, with **Let's Go, Let's Go, Let's Go**, also written by him, the next release after **Finger Poppin' Time**. **The Twist** burst back into the charts in between these releases, making 1960 Ballard's best year since his debut in 1954. **Let's Go, Let's Go, Let's Go** gave Ballard and the Midnighters their highest-ever US chart placing. It went to No 6.

BELLE BARTH *American*

IF I EMBARRASS YOU, TELL YOUR FRIENDS (album) *Label unknown* [USA]. The sole million seller for comedienne and singer Annabelle (Belle) Barth (née Salzman) was achieved without the record entering the US album charts. The record sold two million copies without any radio exposure or much publicity. Born the youngest of nine children of a Manhattan merchant in 1912, she was soon working the Bortsch Circuit as a singer, piano player and teller of bawdy songs. She rose to the top of her field, and became an institution in Miami Beach from 1950 to 1970. She arrived there in 1945, establishing a reputation as an entertainer who used words on stage that no one else dared use. Belle was one of the better-known names on 'party disc' sex-angled comedy songs, which were sold *sub rosa* by less reputable record stores at that time.

Belle Barth was taken ill while performing in Las Vegas in May 1970, and did not work again. She died at her Miami home on 14 February 1971. The name of the offbeat label that produced this disc is unknown.

BROOK BENTON *See Dinah Washington with Brook Benton*

BILL BLACK AND HIS COMBO *American*

WHITE SILVER SANDS HI 2021 [USA] London HLU 9090 [UK]. Bill Black was the bass player on most of Elvis Presley's early records. Born in

Memphis on 17 September 1926, Black formed his own combo after Presley was drafted into the US Army. The other members were Carl McVoy (piano), Martin Wills (sax), Reggie Young (guitar) and Jerry Arnold (drums). The first of his 17 instrumental US hits was the million-selling **Smokie** of 1959. The follow-up was his biggest hit, **White Silver Sands**, which at No 9 gave him his only Top 10 hit. Black's version was written in 1957 by Chuck 'Red' Matthews and G. Reinhart, based on Matthews's 1949 piece **If I Knew**. The record spent 13 weeks in the Top 100, was No 1 on the R&B charts, and spent one week at No 50 in the British charts. Bill Black died on 21 October 1965, aged 39.

JOSEPHINE *HI 2022* [*USA*]. Bill Black's third million-selling instrumental was written by Gus Kahn, B. Rivens and Wayne King in 1937. It reached No 18 in the American charts, where it stayed for 10 weeks and was No 1 in the R&B charts for four weeks.

DON'T BE CRUEL *HI 2026* [*USA*] *London HLU 9212* [*UK*]. Bill Black's instrumental version of **Don't Be Cruel** was written in 1956 by Otis Blackwell. Elvis Presley, who sold over a million copies of the original version, is credited with co-writing it, though there is some doubt whether Elvis ever composed anything. This was the group's fourth million seller in a row, and also their last. It reached No 11 in the American pop charts, where it had a 13-week run. It was a big R&B hit, and gave Black his second, biggest, and last hit in Britain: reaching No 32 with seven weeks in the charts.

JEANNE BLACK — American

HE'LL HAVE TO STAY *Capitol 4368* [*USA*] *Capitol CL 15131* [*UK*]. The sole million seller for rock'n'roll singer Jeanne was written by J. and A. Alison and Charles Grean. Jeanne was born on 25 October 1937 and comes from Mount Baldy, California. She started singing duos with her sister Janie in the back seat of the

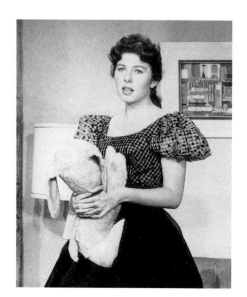

family car. Cliff Stone discovered her, then she made many appearances on his local TV show, 'Hometown Jamboree'. The disc was No 4 for two weeks in the USA and 11 weeks in the bestsellers, and No 41 in Britain.

THE BLUE DIAMONDS — Indonesian

RAMONA *Fontana F 2014* [*Netherlands*] *Decca T 2330* [*Germany*] *Decca CP 2216* [*UK*] *London 1954* [*USA*]. **Ramona** was the first million seller for this duo — the brothers Rudi (age 21) and Riem (age 19) de Wolff — who went to Holland from Indonesia in 1949. They started with a Hawaiian band. Both brothers play guitar and are rhythm-and-blues vocalists. Inspired by the Everly Brothers, the de Wolffs made their first disc in 1959 which was an immediate success. This disc of **Ramona** was the first ever to sell over 250,000 in Holland, and over one million in Germany when released on the Decca label, and it was also a hit in the USA. This disc sold the million by 1961. The song was written in 1928 by L. Wolfe Gilbert (words) and Mabel Wayne (music). The disc reached No 72 in the USA with five weeks in the charts.

BROTHERS FOUR — American

GREEN FIELDS *CBS-Columbia 41571* [*USA*] *Philips PB 1009* [*UK*]. The sole million seller for this quarter was written by Terry Gilkyson, Richard Dehr and Frank Miller in 1956. The 'brothers', all from Washington state, and then aged 20–22, are Bob Glick, Mike Kirkland, John Paine and Richard Foley. As fraternity brothers they met at the University of Washington, and made nightclub and personal appearances. The disc was No 2 for four weeks in the USA and 20 weeks in the bestsellers, and was No 40 in Britain with two weeks in the charts.

CHARLES BROWN — American

PLEASE COME HOME FOR CHRISTMAS *King 5405* [*USA*]. Recorded on 21 September 1960 at King Records' studio in Cincinnati, this disc sold a million by February 1968. A Gold Disc was presented to Gene Redd, artists and repertoire chief for King Records in early 1968, who both wrote the song and was responsible for its recording. It reached No 76 in the USA where it charted for only two weeks.

Charles Brown made a number of Christmas recordings including the popular **Merry Christmas Baby**.

HEIDI BRUHL — German

WIR WOLLEN NEIMALS AUSEINANDER-GEH'N (We will never part) (Ring of gold) *Philips 2217* [*West Germany*]. Here was the first million seller for the German actress-singer Heidi Bruhl who was born on 30 January 1942 in Munich. She started as a dancer and was a versatile entertainer from six years of age. Heidi became a skilled ballerina by 1956 and then started singing. In 1955 she had her first leading role in Germany, becoming very

popular there. She appeared in a number of films, became a popular magazine cover girl and received a major award in 1961 as the top TV personality of the year. In 1960, she sang **Wir wollen neimals** in the 'Song for Europe' TV contest and gained second place, and her subsequent disc of the song sold over a million in Germany. Heidi started her disc career in 1959, and then perfected a one-woman show which took Germany by storm. She has visited the USA and in 1962 was signed for a leading role in MGM's film *Captain Sinbad*. This song was written by Bruno Balz and Gloria De Voss (words) and Michael Jary (music). The English lyric was written by Al Stillman.

ANITA BRYANT — American

PAPER ROSES *Carlton 528* [*USA*] *London HLL 9144* [*UK*]. Ballad and beat vocalist Anita achieved her first million seller with a song written by Fred Spielman (music) and Janice Torre (words). Anita was born on 25 March 1940 in Barnsdale, Oklahoma, and started singing as a child, becoming popular at local functions. At nine she won a talent contest and became known as 'Oklahoma's Red Feather Girl' which led to appearances on the local TV station at Oklahoma City, then at the Tulsa station. Talent scout Arthur Godfrey heard her and booked her for his New York talent contest which she won. She then became in demand for guest spots on TV throughout the States and did tours. Anita had previously been 'Miss Oklahoma' in the Miss America Pageant and was second runner-up to 'Miss America' in 1958. This disc reached No 5 in the US charts with 17 weeks in the bestsellers, and was No 24 in Britain with four weeks in the Top 50.

IN MY LITTLE CORNER OF THE WORLD *Carlton 530* [*USA*] *London HLL 9171* [*UK*]. The second million seller for the beauty queen

Anita Bryant was written by Bob Hilliard (words) and Lee Pockriss (music). It was No 10 in the US charts and 14 weeks in the bestsellers, and was No 48 in Britain with two weeks in the charts.

PAPA BUE AND VIKING JAZZ BAND
Danish

SCHLAFE MEIN PRINZCHEN *Storyville 1003* [Denmark]. Papa Bue (real name Arne Bue Jensen) was born in 1931. He started an amateur band in the Copenhagen harbour district of Nyhavn, where his sextet was soon discovered by the Storyville-Sonet firm. This disc was his sole million seller by 1962. Papa Bue played the trombone. The tune on this disc is **Wiegenlied**, often attributed to Mozart, but actually written by one of his contemporaries, Bernard Flies, Bue's version is in the traditional jazz style.

JOHNNY BURNETTE
American

DREAMIN' *Liberty 55258* [USA] *London HLG 9172* [UK]. First million seller for Johnny Burnette, written by Ted Ellis and Barry De Vorzon. Rock'n'roll singer John Joseph Burnette was born in Memphis, Tennessee, on 25 March 1934, started playing the guitar at a very early age, and made appearances at local functions. He was also a Golden Gloves city champion for boxing in Memphis in his teens. In 1955 he formed his own rock'n'roll trio, himself as lead singer, his older brother Dorsey on bass vocals and Paul Burlison on electric guitar. They first played at a local fairground, then moved to California, won first place three times on Ted Mack's 'Original Amateur Hour' on TV, and went on a three-week tour with the show in South America. On return they found several contracts for recording awaiting them, and Johnny signed for Coral Records. Their first disc **Tear It Up** was not a success, and their second **The Train Kept A'rollin'** in 1957 was a hit only in Boston. In June 1958, Johnny disbanded the trio and started writing songs with his brother, and they were asked to write for Rick Nelson. They came up with three million-selling discs for Rick and subsequently Johnny signed for Liberty Records. Brother Dorsey became a hit disc artist on the Era label. Johnny's first discs for Liberty were not successful until July 1960 when, with 18 violins instead of his guitar backing him, he recorded **Dreamin'**. It reached No 11 with 15 weeks in the US bestsellers and was No 5 and 16 weeks in the British bestsellers. Other hits followed and in early 1964 he formed his own record label which had just one release before Johnny's death in a boating accident at Clear Lake, California, on 15 August 1964.

Before becoming a professional singer, Johnny was a deckhand on Mississippi tugboats. He entered show business aged 22 — his TV debut being on the Steve Allen Show.

Johnny's son Rocky Burnette had some success on EMI America in the early eighties. His debut **Tired of Toein' the Line** reached No 8 in the American charts, just as **You're Sixteen** had done for his father.

YOU'RE SIXTEEN *Liberty 55285* [USA] *London HLG 9254* [UK]. Johnny Burnette's second million-selling disc, the song written by Bob and Dick Sherman who later achieved fame with their Oscar-winning score of *Mary Poppins* (1964). **You're Sixteen** got to No 8 in the US charts with 15 weeks in the bestsellers, and No 3 with 12 weeks in Britain's charts.

RAY CHARLES
American

GEORGIA ON MY MIND *ABC-Paramount 10135* [USA] *HMV POP 792* [UK]. Ray Charles Robinson was born in Albany, Georgia, on 23 September 1932. He was blinded by illness at six and orphaned at 15, going to school just long enough to learn Braille. At 17, he formed his own trio, with himself playing piano, and toured America. He settled in Seattle, where he had his own TV show. At first he played in a Nat King Cole style, but then turned to a more original mixture of R&B, jazz and soul. He had six hits on Atlantic, starting in 1957 with **Swanee River Rock**. His first million seller was in 1959, when **What'd I Say?** reached No 6 in America.

In 1960, Ray Charles switched labels to ABC-Paramount. **Georgia On My Mind**, his second release on his new label, gave him his second million seller and first No 1 (for one week). The song was written in 1930 by Stuart Gorrell (words) and Hoagy Carmichael (music). The record won Grammy Awards as 'Best Male Vocal Recording' and 'Best Pop Singles Performance' of 1960. The record was his first British hit, on HMV, reaching No 24.

Ray Charles proved one of the most versatile and successful of America's popular singers. He has had over 80 hits on the American Top 100 singles charts and over 40 albums on the LP charts. Nichnamed 'The Genius', he has had numerous successes in the R&B/soul, pop, jazz and C&W fields.

CHUBBY CHECKER
American

THE TWIST *Cameo-Parkway 811* [USA] *Columbia (EMI) DB 4503* [UK]. Chubby Checker was born Ernest Evans on 3 October 1941 in Philadelphia. After school he worked in a chicken market whose owner, Henry Colt, was sufficiently impressed by his singing while he worked to contact songwriter Kal Mann. This led to a long-term contract with Cameo-Parkway. Mann wrote Checker's first hit, **The Class**, a novelty record originally recorded for famous American DJ Dick Clark's audio Christmas card. The card went down so well that Cameo-Parkway released the song commercially in 1959, and it reached No 38. Ernest Evans became Chubby Checker because Clark's then-wife Bobbie thought that he looked like a young Fats Domino.

Dick Clark played a crucial part in Chubby's next and biggest hit, **The Twist**. Hank Ballard wrote the song and used it as the B side of his **Teardrops on Your Letter** million seller. When the Twist became the big dance on Clark's 'American Bandstand' TV show, he tried to find someone to do a more upbeat cover of the Ballard number. Remembering the

singer of his Christmas card, Clark called Cameo-Parkway in Philadelphia. He also gave Checker valuable time on his show, and the result was a No 1 for one week in September 1960. A year later the Twist craze broke out all over again, and Chubby Checker took **The Twist** back up to No 1 for another two weeks in January 1962. This was the only time that a record has ever topped the American charts twice on two different chart runs. The record had 18 weeks on the Hot 100 in 1960, and a further 21 weeks the second time round when the B side **Twistin' USA** also reached No 68, separately spending three weeks on the charts.

In Britain **The Twist** was a minor hit in 1960, reaching No 44 and spending only two weeks on the charts. EMI's Columbia label had picked up rights to Chubby Checker, but at first did not look like reaping much success with him. His second British hit, the US No 1 **Pony Time**, only reached No 27. It was when the Twist really hit Britain in 1962 that Chubby Checker took off. His **Let's Twist Again** peaked at No 2. When Cameo-Parkway switched from EMI Columbia to Pye, **The Twist** and **Let's Twist Again** were re-released as a double A side, though initially without success. Over a decade later, in late 1975, the ailing Decca Records picked up rights to the songs and put out the same coupling. This time it reached No 5 and stayed 10 weeks in the charts.

In 1988 Chubby Checker teamed up with US rap act the Fat Boys, whose version of **The Twist** went back up the American charts. It peaked at No 16 for two weeks in August, spending 15 weeks on the charts.

PERRY COMO   *American*

DELAWARE *RCA Victor 7670 [USA] RCA Victor 1170 [UK]*. Perry Como was born Pierino Como, the son of Italian immigrants, in Canonsburg, Pennsylvania, USA, on 18 May 1913. He had his first hit in 1954 with **Long Ago (and Far Away)** and his first million seller the following year with **Till the End of Time**. He was one of the most successful singers of the fifties, and one of RCA's best-selling artists ever. In 30 years he amassed 103 US chart entries, including 11 No 1s.

Delaware was a novelty song written in 1959 by Irving Gordon. The lyrics made puns on the names of the American states, for example, 'What did Della wear?' The record gave Como his 89th and 90th US hits, as the B side **I Know What God Is** also charted for two weeks, reaching No 81.

Delaware peaked at No 22 in America, with 11 weeks on the charts. It did better in Britain, reaching No 3 with a 13-week chart run. Como had 28 British hits, including two No 1s.

SAM COOKE   *American*

WONDERFUL WORLD *Keen 2112 [USA] HMV POP 754 [UK, 1960] and RCA PB 49871 [UK, 1986]*. R&B singer Sam Cooke was born in 1937, one of eight sons of Rev. and Mrs S. Cooke of Chicago, USA. His first hit, **You Send Me**, was written by his brother Charles and reached No 1 for three weeks in 1957. It was Cooke's first million seller and the first hit for the fledgling Keen label. **Wonderful World** was Cooke's last hit for Keen, as he switched to RCA in 1960. The song was written by Barbara Campbell, with Lou Adler and Herb Alpert, in 1959. Its chart success was modest, it reaching No 12 with 15 weeks on chart in America, and No 27 with an eight-week chart run in Britain.

Sam Cooke was shot dead in an hotel incident in America on 11 December 1964. In a US chart career from 1957 to 1966 he achieved 42 different chart entries, only five of which made the Top 10. In Britain, he had eight chart entries between 1958 and 1963, three of which made the Top 10. In 1986 RCA re-released **Wonderful World**, giving Sam Cooke his biggest-ever British hit. Second time round, the record made No 2, staying 11 weeks in the charts.

As a follow-up, RCA re-issued his 1963 hit **Another Saturday Night** on 10 May 1986, giving Sam Cooke his last British chart place, No 75 for one week.

CHAIN GANG *RCA Victor 7783 [USA] RCA Victor 1202 [UK]*. **Chain Gang** was Sam Cooke's first million seller for RCA, following his switch from the small Keen indie label. Written by Sol Quasha and Herb Yakus in 1956, the record followed the million-selling **Wonderful World** into the charts, reaching No 2 for two weeks in America and No 9 in Britain. It lasted 16 weeks in the American charts, and 11 weeks in Britain. **Chain Gang** was Cooke's fourth of five million-selling records, and perhaps his best-known hit.

DON COSTA   *American*

NEVER ON SUNDAY *United Artists 234 [USA] London HLT 9195 [UK]*. The sole million seller for Don Costa was written in 1960 for the film *Jamais le Dimanche* (*Never On Sunday*) starring Melina Mercouri and Jules Dassin and composed by Manos Hadjidakis. Lyrics in English were written by Billy Towne. **Never On Sunday** won the Academy Award for Best Film Song of 1960, and was the first European song to do so. The original Greek title of the song was **Tu Pedea Topu Pirea** (The Children of Piraeus). The disc was No 19 and 26 weeks in the US bestsellers, and No 27 and 10 weeks in Britain's charts.

FLOYD CRAMER   *American*

LAST DATE *RCA Victor 7775 [USA]*. The first million seller for the rhythm pianist Floyd Cramer was his own composition. He was born in Shreveport, Louisiana, on 27 October 1933 and showed interest in music from the age of five. His family bought him a piano, and he actually began playing by ear before taking music lessons. After leaving school, he joined the 'Louisiana Hayride' and accompanied many leading artists. In 1955 he joined the Grand Ole Opry: His piano was featured on Elvis Presley's disc **Heartbreak Hotel** (1956).

He won a disc jockey poll in 1960 as 'The Most Promising Solo Instrumentalist', and in 1961 as 'Favourite and Most Played Solo Instrumentalist'. The disc was No 2 for four weeks in the US charts and 20 weeks in the bestsellers charts.

BOBBY DARIN   *American*

BEYOND THE SEA *ATCO 6158 [USA] London HLE 9034 [UK]*. Bobby Darin was born Waldon Cassotto on 14 May 1936, in the Bronx district of New York. His father died a few months before he was born and he was raised by his mother, a former professional entertainer. A versatile musician, he could play piano, drums, vibraphone, guitar and bass by the time he left school. He had a string of 40 American chart entries, starting with his first million seller **Splish Splash** in 1958. He wrote some of his own hits. His only US No 1 **Mack the Knife** (a Brecht/Weill composition) spent nine weeks at the top in 1959. He performed in films including *Pepe, Hell Is For Heroes* and *Come September*, for which he wrote the music.

Beyond The Sea was Darin's fifth of six million sellers. Originally written and performed by French singer Charles Trenet as **La Mer** in 1945, the English words of this version were written in 1947 by Jack Lawrence. The record was the follow-up to **Mack the Knife**, and reached No 6 with 14 weeks on the American charts. In Britain it reached No 8, listed as **La Mer (Beyond the Sea)**, and remained in the charts for 12 weeks. Darin had 18 British hits, including two No 1s.

Bobby Darin suffered from heart trouble stemming from rheumatic fever when he was eight years old. He underwent open-heart surgery in 1971. Two years later he entered hospital for surgery, and died of heart failure on 20 December 1973. He was 37 years old.

FATS DOMINO   *American*

WALKIN' TO NEW ORLEANS/DON'T COME KNOCKIN' *Imperial 5675 [USA] London HLP 9163 [UK]*. Fats (Antoine) Domino was one of the greatest influences on rock'n'roll, and by far the most successful black recording star of the fifties. 'The Fat Man' was born on 26 February 1928, in New Orleans. He had his first million seller, 'The Fat Man', in 1948 and his 23rd and last, this record, in 1960. Though he became one of the great rock'n'roll stars, he played the same basic R&B style throughout the fifties. Despite several R&B No 1s and nearly 70 hits on the pop charts, he never managed a pop No 1. He sold some 60 million records.

Walkin' to New Orleans was Domino's 10th and final US Top 10 hit. It was written by bandleader and arranger Dave Bartholomew (who was responsible for Lou Chudd signing Domino to Imperial in 1948), R. Guidry and Fats Domino. It reached No 6 in America, with a chart run of 14 weeks, while in Britain it went to No 19, staying 10 weeks in the charts. **Don't Come Knockin'**, written by Fats himself, gave him a double A side hit in America, where it reached No 21 with 11 weeks on the charts.

Walkin' reached No 2 during 11 weeks in the R&B charts. The flip side made No 28 during its three-week run.

LONNIE DONEGAN   *British*

MY OLD MAN'S A DUSTMAN *Pye 7N 15256 [UK]*. Lonnie Donegan started his chart career in 1956 when his **Rock Island Line** gave him Top 10 debut hits on both sides of the Atlantic, reaching No 8 in Britain and America. He made the record in 1953 when he was playing with

Chris Barber's Jazz Band. All he got from the recording was the £2.50 session fee and a Gold Disc when the record sold a million. Donegan was mainly responsible for the development of skiffle in Britain, popularizing a British version of the American music with a string of hits throughout the second half of the fifties.

When skiffle began to fade, Donegan turned to novelty records, with **My Old Man's a Dustman** giving him the biggest British hit of his career. The record was the first by a British artist to enter the charts at No 1 first week of release. It spent four weeks at the top, and 13 weeks in the charts, giving Donegan his third million seller. It was his first to sell a million in Britain alone. The words were written by Lonnie Donegan, his manager Peter Buchanan and Beverley Thorn, based on a traditional air sung by First World War troops on the march. In place of 'My old man's a farmer, and what do you think of that?' came 'My old man's a dustman, he wears a dustman's hat.' Fruitier lines like 'Water, water, water, water came at last. We don't want your water, you can stick it up your arse' were simply deleted. The song was recorded before a live audience. Though released in America on the Dot label, it failed to chart there.

Lonnie was born Anthony Donegan in Glasgow, Scotland, on 29 April 1931. He changed his name to Lonnie after appearing on the same bill as his idol, American blues artist Lonnie Johnson. He scored 31 British hits, charting every year between 1956 and 1962, and he has the rare distinction of having had a hit EP and LP on the singles charts. He had three American hits. His influence on British rock music was considerable. By leading the skiffle craze, he encouraged thousands of young people to take up playing music. Hank Marvin and Jet Harris of the Shadows started in the Vipers skiffle group and John Lennon and Paul McCartney first performed as part of the Quarrymen, a skiffle group that relied on Donegan hits for most of its repertoire.

THE DRIFTERS   *American*

SAVE THE LAST DANCE FOR ME *Atlantic 2071 [USA] London HLK 9201 [UK]*. Over the years the line-up of the Drifters has changed considerably, with over 50 singers drifting in and out of the group. They were formed in 1953 as back-up for Clyde McPhatter. Though rooted in R&B the Drifters have woven a number of musical styles into their records, from Latin-American rhythm to gospel. They were the first major black R&B act of the fifties to use a string orchestra, and recorded songs with socially relevant lyrics.

Save the Last Dance for Me was the group's fourth million seller, and their only American No 1. With three weeks at the top, the record was the biggest hit of their career. The group line-up when this was recorded was Ben E. King (lead vocals), Charles Thomas (tenor), Doc Green (baritone), Elsbeary Hobbs (bass) and Reggie Kimber (guitar). This line-up was originally known as the Crowns. Following a dispute between the Drifters and their manager George Treadwell in 1958, Treadwell had sacked the entire group. To

meet contractual performance obligations Treadwell had to find a new line-up, and Atlantic were keen to keep the valuable name in being, so the Crowns were signed up and their name changed to the Drifters. **Save the Last Dance for Me** was written by Jerome 'Doc' Pomus and Mort Shuman. It stayed 19 weeks on the American Top 100, and 18 weeks in Britain's Top 50 where it peaked at No 2. The song has become a standard, with many well-known artists recording their version of it over the last 30 years.

DUANE EDDY   *American*

BECAUSE THEY'RE YOUNG *Jamie 1156 [USA] London HLW 9162 [UK]*. Duane Eddy was born on 26 April 1938 in Corning, New York. He moved to Phoenix, Arizona when he was 13, and after leaving Coolridge High School in 1954 he played with various local dance bands. In 1955 he sat in with Al Casey's band, and began studying with well-known jazz guitarist Jimmy Wybele. It was at this point that he stumbled on the twangy sound that became his trade mark, made by playing the melody on the bottom instead of the top strings of his guitar. He had his first hit with **Movin' and Groovin'**, and from 1958 to 1964 had a continuous string of 27 mainly instrumental hits, most of them on Jamie until his appearance on RCA in 1962. His first big hit was **Rebel Rouser**, the follow-up to **Movin' and Groovin'**, which reached No 6 in America. This was also his first million seller.

Because They're Young was his second million seller, written for the film of the same name by Don Costa. Duane Eddy appeared in the film and played the title instrumental number. It became his biggest hit, going to No 4 in America and No 2 in Britain, with chart runs of 15 weeks in America and 18 weeks in Britain. (Like many rock'n'roll greats, he never achieved a No 1 on either side of the Atlantic.)

Though his string of hits dried up in 1964 with the desperate **Son of Rebel Rouser** peaking at No 97, Eddy had a considerable influence on rock music. He made a brief comeback in Britain with the 1975 Top 10 **Play Me Like You Play Your Guitar** on GTO. Despite a new recording contract with Capitol in the late 1980s, his only other chart appearance was in 1986, with the British techno-pop trio The Art Of Noise, whose **Peter Gunn** made No 50 in America on the China label.

THE EVERLY BROTHERS   *American*

CATHY'S CLOWN *Warner Brothers 5151 [USA] Warner Brother WB 1 [UK]*. Don and Phil Everly came from a show business family, singing on their parents' radio show in Virginia when they were only little children. Don (born in Brownie, Kentucky, on 1 February 1937) and Phil (born in Chicago on 19 January 1939) teamed up as a singing duo act while in their teens and in 1955 signed a contract with CBS. Only one single flowed from this, and **The Sun Keeps Shining** was not a hit. Two years later, with a more rock-orientated sound, their new contract with Cadence led to **Bye Bye Love** going to No 2. The follow-up, **Wake Up Little Suzie**, went to

No 1. Both were million sellers. This was the start of a string of big hits for the boys, featuring their highly distinctive country/rock harmonies.

In 1960 the duo switched labels, joining Warner Brothers. Their first release on the new label was **Cathy's Clown**, which the brothers had composed themselves. It went to No 1 for five weeks in America, where the flip side **Always It's You** also reached No 56 with six weeks on the charts. In Britain the record was an even bigger hit, staying at No 1 for nine weeks. It charted for 18 weeks in Britain, one week more than in America. The record was Warner Brothers' first release in Britain, where the label was licensed to Decca under Warner's own logo. This was something Decca had always resisted, preferring to put American records out under the famous London label. The Everlys' Cadence singles had appeared in Britain on London.

The Everlys enjoyed 37 American chart entries from 23 records between 1957 and 1964, including four No 1s. In Britain they lasted slightly longer, with 29 records (including five No 1s) charting from 1957 to 1968. The duo continued performing after their chart luck ran out, but as musical styles changed and personal friction developed it was a downhill trend. On Friday 13 July 1973, while giving an all-too typically poor performance at the John Wayne theatre in Buena Park, California, Phil smashed his guitar on the stage and stormed off, leaving a sad and surprised Don to tell the audience that the Everlys had been dead for years and would not be performing together again. Little was heard of them for the next 10 years.

In the early eighties, Phil Everly signed to Capitol. This did not lead to anything in America, but in Britain he scored a minor hit with **Louise** in 1982, and made the Top 10 the following year singing **She Means Nothing to Me** with Cliff Richard. On 22 and 23 September 1983 the Everly Brothers came together for a reunion concert at the Royal Albert Hall, London. The live double album of the concert was a minor hit on both sides of the Atlantic in 1984, released on Passport in America and Impression in Britain. After signing with Mercury, a studio album (**EB 84** in America, **The Everly Brothers** in Britain) did marginally better later the same year. A single specially composed by long-time Everlys' fan Paul McCartney, **On the Wings of a Nightingale**, was also a minor hit on both sides of the Atlantic. Their last appearance on the charts was with the **Born Yesterday** album, which reached No 83 in America in 1986.

PERCY FAITH AND   *Canadian*
HIS ORCHESTRA

THEME FROM A SUMMER PLACE *CBS-Columbia 41490 [USA] Philips PB 989 [UK]*. Musician Percy Faith was born on 7 April 1908 in Toronto, Ontario. He played with the Canadian Orchestra, later turned to arranging and conducting, and then became a staff arranger for the Canadian Broadcasting Corporation in the mid-1930s. In 1940 Faith went to the USA, specializing in 'middle-brow' arrangements of pop tunes. He later became musical director of CBS Columbia Records, recording with his studio orchestra. He had three million-selling records with Tony Bennett, and two on his own. His first was **The Song from Moulin Rouge** in 1953, which sold over two million and was No 1 in America for 10 weeks.

The second million seller for Faith was written for the film *A Summer Place* by Max Steiner in 1959. This disc sold over two million and was No 1 for nine weeks in the USA and 21 weeks in the bestsellers, and No 2 and 30 weeks in the British bestsellers. Grammy Award for 'Record of the Year' 1960. Gold Disc award RIAA 1962.

Percy Faith died in Los Angeles on 9 February 1976.

FERRANTE AND TEICHER   *American*

THEME FROM THE APARTMENT *United Artists 231 [USA] London HLT 9164 [UK]*. Here was the first million seller for this piano duo. The number was written in 1949 by the British composer Charles Williams, an instrumental work originally titled **Jealous Lover**, and used as the theme for the Jack Lemmon-Shirley MacLaine film *The Apartment* in 1960. Arthur Ferrante was born in New York (7 September 1921), and Louis Teicher in Wilkes-Barre, Pennsylvania (24 August 1924). They met at the age of six while students at Manhattan's Juilliard School of Music where they later taught. From around 1954 they recorded for Columbia, Westminster, ABC and MGM labels. In 1960 they were signed to United Artists with whom they began a string of film-theme hits. *The Apartment* theme was the first. From 1960 to 1970 they sold over 20 million records. Their biggest-selling album was **West Side Story**. *The Apartment* film received five Academy Awards. This disc reached No 10 in the US charts with 20 weeks in the bestsellers, and was No 44 in Britain in its only week in the charts.

EXODUS (main theme) *United Artists 274 [USA] London HLT 9298 and HMV POP 881 [UK] (UK release first on London, then on HMV when United Artists switched its UK licence from Decca to EMI)*. The second million seller for this duo was the tune from the film *Exodus*, composed by Ernest Gold, who received an Academy Award for his musical score and Grammy Award for 'Song of the Year' 1960. The disc was released in late 1960, reaching the million soon after in 1961. This disc reached No 2 in the USA with 21 weeks in the bestsellers, and No 6 with 17 weeks in Britain's charts.

CONNIE FRANCIS   *American*

MAMA/TEDDY *MGM 12878 [USA] MGM 1076 [UK] as Mama/Robot Man*. Connie Francis was by far the most consistent and successful female singer of the pre-Beatles rock era, though her records were hardly rock'n'roll at all. They were either ballads, remakes of old songs, or mildly up-tempo numbers as acceptable to mums and dads as to teenagers. Between 1958 and 1969 she had 56 chart entries in America, 12 of which were B sides that charted as well as the A sides. In Britain, she had 24 hits up to 1966. To a greater extent than almost any other American pop singer of the time, she went out of her way to build a successful international career, touring around the world and recording in many languages.

Born Concetta Rosa Maria Franconero on 12 December 1938 in Newark, New Jersey, she was always encouraged by her father to sing. He gave her an accordion when she was three years old, and later got her on a TV talent show. At 17 she signed with MGM, but her first 10 records failed to get anywhere. In 1957 she teamed up with Marvin Rainwater, and had a minor hit with **Majesty of Love**. Then in 1958 **Who's Sorry Now?** became her first solo hit on both sides of the Atlantic, reaching No 4 in America. In Britain, what was her debut disc went to No 1 for six weeks. She had three American No 1s and, with different records, two British chart toppers.

Mama was the sixth of her eleven million-selling records. The song was Italian, written in 1941 by B. Cherubini (words) and C.A. Bixio (music). English lyrics were added in 1955 by Harold Barlow and Phil Brito. Connie Francis recorded **Mama** in Britain, accompanied by Tony Osborne and his orchestra. In America, where **Mama** reached No 8 and had a chart run of 13 weeks, the double A side coupling was the 1959 Paul Anka composition **Teddy**. This reached No 17, with 11 weeks on the charts. In Britain, **Mama** was coupled with the upbeat **Robot Man**. This double A side reached No 2 and lasted 19 weeks in the charts.

With the changes in the music scene brought about by the Beatles and the British beat boom from 1964, Connie Francis gradually slipped out of the charts, though she continued to tour. In November 1974, after performing at the Westbury Music Fair in New York, she was brutally raped in her motel room. This attack shattered her emotionally and for many years she did not perform again. In March 1981 her brother was murdered in his New Jersey home. After these two personal tragedies, she

decided to try and make a come-back. While she has yet to return to the charts, her 1984 autobiography *Who's Sorry Now?* did receive wide media attention.

EVERYBODY'S SOMEBODY'S FOOL/ JEALOUS OF YOU *MGM 12899 [USA] MGM 1086 [UK]*. The seventh million seller for Connie comprised **Fool** by Jack Keller and Howard Greenfield and **Jealous of You**, originally **Tango della gelosia** from Italy (1930) by Peppino Mendes (words) and Vitorio Mascheroni (music). English words were by Marjorie Harper (1960). The latter was sung in part Italian, part English by Connie Francis. The accompaniments were by Joe Sherman's and Stan Applebaum's orchestras respectively for the two titles. **Fool** was No 1 in the USA for two weeks and 13 weeks in the bestsellers, and No 5 with 19 weeks in Britain's bestsellers. **Jealous of You** was No 19 and 11 weeks in the US bestsellers.

MY HEART HAS A MIND OF ITS OWN/ MALAGUENA *MGM 12923 [USA]/MGM 45-MGM-1100 [UK]*. The eighth million seller for Connie Francis was a country flavoured ballad written by Howard Greenfield and Jack Kelter, with orchestral accompaniment conducted by Joe Sherman. It went to No 1 for two weeks, with 17 weeks in the US Hot 100. It went to No 3 in Britain, with 17 weeks in the Top 50. In the USA the flip side also entered the charts. **Malaguena** was a Latin tempo song written by J. Lecuona, recorded with Geoff Love and his orchestra. Sung in Spanish, it reached No 42 with nine weeks in the *Billboard* charts. (It peaked at No 67 with seven weeks in the *Cash Box* charts.) This was an unusual success for a flip side in a foreign language.

MANY TEARS AGO *MGM 12964 [USA]/MGM 45-MGM-1111 [UK]*. The ninth million seller for Connie Francis was written by Winfield Scott. The accompaniment was by the Stan Applebaum Orchestra. The record reached No 7 in America, with 13 weeks in the charts. It reached No 12 with nine weeks in the British Top 50. In America the flip side, **Senza Mama**, also charted, spending one week in the *Billboard* charts at No 87.

FREDDY   *German*

UNTER FREEMDEN STERNEN *Polydor 2027 [West Germany]*. Freddy Quinn (real name Manfred Petz) was a major German-based, European pop star in the mid-fifties to early sixties. Born in 1932, his family fled Vienna in the face of the advancing Red Army in 1945. After travelling around the world, he returned to Germany in 1953. He changed his name to Freddy, signed a recording contract with Polydor (the pop label of DGG), and had his first big hit with a German-language version of **Memories are Made of This** in 1956. He had a string of big hits in Germany up to 1964, and made 11 films. He recorded in a number of European languages, had seven million-selling discs, and record sales of over 20 million. His fourth million seller, which translates to **Under Foreign Stars**, was written by Aldo Pinelli (words) and Lotar Olias (music).

ROCCO GRANATA   *Italian*

MARINA *Electrola 45-DW-5745 [West Germany]*
Laurie 3041 [USA]. **Marina** was a big success on
the Continent of Europe, and was written in
1959 by Italian pop ballad and rock vocalist
Granata himself. The English words are by Ray
Maxwell. The song was originally published
in Belgium. Rocco, born in 1939, lived at
Waterschei, Belgium. He played the accordion
and guitar in addition to writing songs. This
disc sold a million in Germany alone. It was No
31 and 11 weeks in the US bestsellers.

ROLF HARRIS   *Australian*

TIE ME KANGEROO DOWN, SPORT
Columbia (EMI) SEGO, 70119 [Australia]
Columbia (EMI) DB 4483 [UK] Epic 9596 [USA].
Rolf Harris certainly started a new craze when
he invented his now famous wobble board.
Rolf, a cabaret and TV artist who also aspired
to be a painter, was born in Australia, the son
of Welsh parents who emigrated there from
Cardiff. In 1958, Rolf had placed an oil painting
on Masonite board on an oil heater to dry. The
board got very hot, so he held it by the edges
and wobbled it back and forth to cool it. This
produced a resounding twang like the sound of
a tight-skinned bongo drum, and Rolf decided
the sound was just the background he required
for his kangaroo song. He recorded the number
and it soon rocketed to the top of Australia's
bestsellers. Rolf's wobbling of his oil painting
on a TV show resulted in the Masonite firm
turning out 200 boards as giveaways in a
promotion plan with Rolf's help. The demand
was so big that the company were obliged to
engage extra hands to produce them. They sold
over 55,000 in Australia alone. The craze

spread to England and the USA. Rolf's disc
was a big hit in Australia. It was his first British
hit, reaching No 9 with 13 weeks in the charts
and reached No 4 in the USA with 11 weeks in
the bestsellers, making an estimated million
combined global sale.

Rolf Harris was born 30 March 1930 in
Perth, Australia. Apart from being a very
talented entertainer, he is an artist, cartoonist,
sculptor, pianist and composer. He first
studied the piano at the age of nine and
eventually got a spot on the major Australian
talent show 'The Amateur Hour'. He saved
enough to give up teaching and sailed for
England. After two years in London, his
savings dwindled and things became rather
difficult. He then got his break through an
audition for Josephine Douglas, a TV producer,
who signed him for an appearance on one of
her shows. Thereafter, his TV appearances
increased, and he became widely known in
Britain for his cartoon characters on children's
TV shows.

Then came recording for Columbia with
further successes on disc including his **Sun
Arise** (based on an aboriginal chant) in 1962.
This was also a hit on both sides of the Atlantic.
In 1966, Rolf had his own BBC TV series 'Hey
Presto, It's Rolf', and a much-talked-about
Anglia TV wildlife series, 'Survival', on which
he was both singer and narrator. He had a
British No 1 in 1969 with **Two Little Boys**.

Rolf received the Royal accolade in 1968
when he was made a Member of the Order of
the British Empire (MBE), and again in 1977
when he was awarded the OBE.

THE HOLLYWOOD ARGYLES   *American*

ALLEY-OOP *Lute 5905 [USA] London HLU 9146*
[UK]. This was the sole million seller for this
septet which comprised Gary Paxton, Bobby
Rey (also a songwriter), Ted Marsh (bass
player), Gary Webb (drums), Deary Webb
(songwriter/guitarist), Deary Weaver and Ted
Winters, all from California. The song was
written for this rock'n'roll vocal group by
Dallas Frazier. This disc was a No 1 seller in the
USA for one week and 15 weeks in the
bestsellers. It was No 24 and 10 weeks in the
British bestsellers.

JOHNNY HORTON   *American*

NORTH TO ALASKA *CBS Columbia 41782*
[USA]/Philips PB 1062 [UK]. Johnny Horton
was born in Los Angeles on 3 April 1929, later
moving to Tyler, Texas. At Gallatin High
School he shone at basketball, and was offered
26 sports scholarships. He went to Lon Morris
Junior College, Jacksonville, Texas, where he
was voted Most Handsome Boy. He later
attended Baylor and Seattle universities,
majoring in geology and petroleum engineering with a minor in psychology. He began
songwriting as a hobby and later won a singing contest at the Harmony Park Corral in
Anaheim, California. Radio followed, including the 'Louisiana Hayride' on KWKH
Shreveport.

He wrote much of his own material,

combining folk, pop and country styles. His
first hit was **Honky-Tonk Man**, which made
No 9 on the Country Disc Jockey charts in 1956.
His first No 1 was in the country charts in 1959
with **When It's Spring Time In Alaska**. The
follow-up, **The Battle of New Orleans**, topped
the country charts for 10 weeks and the Hot 100
for six weeks, giving Horton his first pop hit.
That was also his first million seller.

North To Alaska was Horton's third and
last country chart topper, spending five weeks
at No 1 and 22 weeks in the C&W charts. It was
also his third and last Top 10 pop hit, reaching
No 4 with 23 weeks in the Hot 100. It reached
No 23 in Britain, with 11 weeks in the Top
50. This second Horton million seller was
written by Mike Philips, and sung by Horton
in the John Wayne film **North To Alaska**.
Horton had once worked in the fishing
industry in Alaska. During the four years
of his chart career, Johnny Horton was
a significant figure in American country
music. He married Billie Jean Jones, widow
of the famous country singer Hank Williams.
Johnny Horton was killed in a car crash on
5 November 1960.

BRYAN HYLAND   *American*

ITSY, BITSY, TEENIE, WEENIE, YELLOW
POLKA DOT BIKINI *Leader 805, later transferred*
to Kapp 342 [USA]/London HLR 9161 [UK]. Bryan
Hyland was born on 12 November 1943 in
Woodhaven, New York, and began singing in
his church choir at the age of nine. When he
was 12 he organized a vocal group, the
Delphis. They later made a demo record which
Bryan sent to New York record companies.
Dave Kapp of Kapp Records was impressed
and signed Hyland up. His first record was
Rosemary, and while that missed the charts the
follow-up **Bikini** disc was one of the biggest
novelty hits of the year. It made No 1 for one
week, with 15 weeks in the *Billboard* charts and
16 weeks in *Cash Box*. The record was originally
released on the small Leader label, and then
switched to Kapp when it started selling in
large numbers. The 16-year-old Hyland had an
international hit with this record, which
reached No 8 in Britain with 13 weeks in the
charts. It sold over two million copies globally.
Hyland signed to ABC Paramount in 1961,
where he had a big hit with **Sealed With A Kiss**
in 1962. Over the decade he had a string of hits
on Philips, Dot and Uni, scoring another
million seller in 1970 with **Gypsy Woman**.

JAN AND KJELD   *Danish*

BANJO BOY *Ariola 814 [West Germany]/Ember*
S 101 [UK]/Kapp 335 [USA]. This was the sole
million seller for Danish duo Jan and Kjeld,
12- and 14-year-old boys known as the Kids
from Copenhagen. The song was written by
Charlie Niessen in 1959 for the film *Kein Mann*
zum Heiraten. English words were written by
the American lyricist Buddy Kaye. The record
was picked up by the small indie label Ember in
Britain, where it reached No 36 with four weeks
in the charts. It went to No 58 in America, with
seven weeks in the charts.

MARV JOHNSON   American

(YOU'VE GOT TO) MOVE TWO MOUNTAINS *United Artists 241 [USA] London HLT 9187 [UK]*. Rock'n'roll singer Marv Johnson was born on 15 October 1938 and grew up in Detroit. At 13 he formed a vocal group, the Serenaders, performing at local functions and later at semi-professional dates throughout Michigan. He also directed and acted in amateur theatricals. Marv was spotted by Berry Gordy while his group sang on a lorry during a Detroit Carnival Parade. He signed him for his first recording, the disc released on the United Artists label. This song, his second million seller, was written by Berry Gordy, Jr., who subsequently signed Marv to his Tamla label. This disc was No 20 and 11 weeks in the US bestsellers.

JIMMY JONES   American

HANDY MAN *Cub 9049 [USA] MGM 1051 [UK]*. This first million seller for rock'n'roll singer Jimmy Jones was written by him and Otis Blackwell, in 1959. **Handy Man** reached No 2 in the US charts with 18 weeks in the bestsellers, and No 3 and 21 weeks in the British bestsellers. Born on 2 June 1937, Jimmy Jones came from Birmingham, Alabama.

GOOD TIMIN' *Cub 9067 [USA] MGM 1078 [UK]*. The second million seller for Jimmy Jones was written by Clint Ballard, Jr and Fred Tobias. This disc was a No 1 chart topper in Britain for three weeks, and No 3 for three weeks in the USA, with 15 weeks in the bestsellers of both countries.

BERT KAEMPFERT AND   German
HIS ORCHESTRA

WONDERLAND BY NIGHT (WUNDERLAND BEI NACHT) *Polydor [West Germany] Decca 31141 [USA]*. This first million seller for Kaempfert was written by Lincoln Chase (words) and Klauss-Gunter Neuman (music) in 1959. Kaempfert was born on 16 October 1923 in Hamburg, Germany. He became composer, arranger, producer and conductor for Polydor Records, Germany. He made his debut on radio with Hans Busch's orchestra in Danzig and after the last war formed his own band. As producer/arranger, he was responsible for **Die Gittare und das Meer** for Freddy, and **Morgen** for Ivo Robic. Both were million sellers. This disc was No 1 seller for three weeks in the USA in 1961 and 17 weeks in the bestsellers. It also sold another million copies outside the USA Kaempfert was the first man to record the Beatles when he hired them to back Tony Sheridan in Hamburg. (See Sheridan, 1961.) He died on holiday in Spain on 22 June 1980.

BRENDA LEE   American

I'M SORRY/THAT'S ALL YOU GOTTA DO *Decca 31093 [USA] Brunswick 05833 [UK]*. Brenda Lee enjoyed one of the longest careers of any of rock'n'roll's female singers. She started very young. Born Brenda Mae Tarpley in Atlanta, Georgia, USA, on 11 December 1944, she won a school talent contest when only five years old and never looked back. The talent contest win led to a regular spot on the Atlanta radio programme 'Starmakers Review'. This was followed by appearances on the 'TV Ranch' television show, and it was television that led to her main career in records. Country singer Red Foley saw her on TV, and signed her to his ABC-TV network 'Ozark Jubilee' show. This led to national press coverage, and more TV with people like Perry Como and Ed Sullivan.

She signed a recording contract with American Decca in 1956, when she was only 11. Her first record was **Jambalaya**, and her first (minor) hit came a year later with **One Step at a Time**. After a couple of misses, it was her third chart entry, **Sweet Nothin's**, that became her first big hit. It reached No 4 in Britain and America, and was her first million seller. (**Rockin' Around the Christmas Tree** was her first release to sell a million, but this failed when first released in 1958. It was a hit two years later, after **Sweet Nothin's** had established her as a major chart act.)

I'm Sorry was her first No 1 in America (she never made the top in Britain), written by Ronnie Self and Dub Albritton. Albritton managed Red Foley and, after her appearance on his 'Ozark Jubilee' show, he managed her as well, becoming her legal guardian as her father had died when she was nine. Brenda loved **I'm Sorry**, which was recorded in the few minutes left at the end of a recording session, but Decca did not think much of the song. It was put out as the B side of **That's All You Gotta Do**, written by J. Reed in 1958. In fact it gave her a Top 10 double A side. Produced by

Owen Bradley, **I'm Sorry** was No 1 for three weeks in America, spending 23 weeks on the charts. The flip side went to No 6, with 14 weeks on the charts. In Britain, **I'm Sorry** reached No 12, with a 16-week chart run.

Brenda Lee had 50 US chart entries, including another 1960 No 1, **I Want To Be Wanted**. In Britain, she had 22 hits between 1960 and 1965, seven of which made the Top 10. In America, her hits lasted on into 1973, when her last chart entry, **Nobody Wins**, also gave her a No 1 on the country charts. This opened up a new career for her in country music, taking her back to her roots in Nashville where she had first recorded.

HANK LOCKLIN   American

PLEASE HELP ME I'M FALLIN' *RCA Victor 7692 [USA]*. Written by Don Robertson and Hal Blair, Hank's disc of the song was No 1 for 14 weeks in the US C&W charts. It reached No 8 with 22 weeks in the US Hot 100. In Britain it reached No 19 with 19 weeks in the charts.

Lawrence Hankins Locklin was born in McLellean, Florida, on 15 February 1918. He played guitar for amateur contests in Milton, Florida, at the age of 10 and soon became featured at Pensacola's WCOA station. He then did mostly shipyard work and farming in his home state. At the age of 20 he made his first professional appearance at the Community Centre in Whistler, Alabama. In 1953 he started recording for 4-Star Records, his initial disc being **Let Me Be The One**. Two years later he signed with RCA Victor Records and recorded under famed guitarist Chet Atkins' direction in Nashville. **Please Help Me I'm Fallin'** is estimated to have sold a million by 1967 and was also a hit for Skeeter Davis.

From 1960, Hank became a member of the famous Grand Ole Opry just 10 years after deciding on a professional career. He has made several visits to Britain, Germany and other countries in Europe.

LOLITA   Austrian

SEEMANN (Sailor) *Polydor [Germany] Kapp 349 [USA]*. This sole million seller for Lolita (real name Ditta) was written by Werner Scharfenberger (of Vienna) with the German words by Fini Busch. An English lyric was written by David West — the pseudonym of Norman Newell, well-known artists' and repertoire manager of EMI in Britain. Lolita was born in St Poelten, about 40 miles from Vienna, and is the daughter of a civil servant. She worked as a children's nurse and as a secretary, and sang in the local church choir. After a radio spot on Radio Linz, her debut was such a success that she began working full time in cabaret.

Then came recording for Polydor, films, TV appearances and stage shows. **Seemann** was the first German song sung by a female artist to reach a high position in the US hit parade, reaching No 5 with 18 weeks in the bestsellers. The song was also a big hit for Petula Clark on the Pye label and Ann Shelton on the Philips label in Britain.

MANTOVANI   *British*

MANTOVANI PLAYS MUSIC FROM EXODUS AND OTHER GREAT THEMES (Album) *London 3231* [USA]. Until the Rolling Stones, Mantovani was Decca Records' biggest-selling and most consistent artist in America. Decca had sold its American subsidiary during the Second World War. In 1949 Edward Lewis decided to re-enter the American market and set up London Records. To help the new company get going, Mantovani was asked in 1951 to record some material especially for the American market. The result was **Charmaine**, which reached No 10 in the American charts (a considerable achievement for a non-American act before the Beatles) and became Mantovani's first million seller. In 1953 he scored his first album million seller with **Christmas Carols**, again mainly with American sales.

Born Annunzio Paolo Mantovani in Venice, Italy, on 15 November 1905, 'Monty' became one of the most popular orchestra leaders in the world. His father was first violinist at La Scala opera house, Milan, then under Arturo Toscanini. The family moved to England, where at 16 Mantovani became a professional violinist. In the 1930s he recorded for the EMI label Regal-Zonophone, and in 1940 signed with Decca.

While he had some success in England, it was in the USA that Mantovani had the biggest impact. He made several long tours that helped achieve a long string of hit albums, and between 1952 and 1972 he achieved 51 hits in the LP charts in America. In Britain, where album charts started later than in America, he had 11 LP hits from 1959 to 1979. He died on 30 March 1980, in Tunbridge Wells, Kent, England.

Exodus, the seventh million seller for maestro Mantovani, started with a half a million sale in the USA in 1961 on the London label, and built up to a global million by 1965. The contents of this disc are: Main theme from *Exodus*, by Ernest Gold (1960); **Karen** (from *Exodus*), by Ernest Gold (1960); Theme from *A Summer Place*, by Max Steiner (1960); **The Green Leaves of Summer** (from *The Alamo*), by P.F. Webster and Dimitri Tiomkin (1960); Theme from *The Sundowners*, by Dimitri Tiomkin (1960); **76 Trombones** (from *The Music Man*), by Meredith Willson (1957); **I Love Paris** (from *Can-Can*), by Cole Porter (1953); **Song Without End** (from *Song Without End*), by Ned Washington, Morris Stoloff and George Duning (1960); **Irma la Douce** (from *Irma la Douce*), by Marguerite Monnot (1958); **Carousel Waltz** (from *Carousel*), by O. Hammerstein and Richard Rodgers (1945); **The Sound of Music** (from *The Sound of Music*), by O. Hammerstein and Richard Rodgers (1959); **Mister Wonderful** (from *Mr Wonderful*), by Jerry Bock, Larry Holofcener and George Weiss (1956).

This disc was in the US album charts for 65 weeks and reached No 2. Gold Disc award RIAA, 1963.

MITCH MILLER AND THE GANG *American*

SENTIMENTAL SING ALONG WITH MITCH (Album) *CBS Columbia 1457* [USA]. This was the eight million seller for Mitch Miller (his sixth album million seller) with 107 weeks in the US bestseller charts, and a Gold Disc award from RIAA in 1962. It reached No 5.

The contents were: **Singin' in the Rain** (from film *Hollywood Revue of 1929*), by Arthur Freed and Nacio Herb Brown (1929); **All I Do is Dream of You** (from film *Sadie McKee*), by Arthur Freed and Nacio Herb Brown (1934); *****Toot, Toot, Tootsie, Good-bye** (from the show *Bombo*), by Gus Kahn, Ernie Erdman and Dan Russo (1922); **The Gang That Sang 'Heart of my Heart'**, by Ben Ryan (1926); **Little Annie Rooney**, by Michael Nolan (1889); *****Hello, Ma Baby**, by Joseph E. Howard and Ida Emerson (1899); **Our Boys Will Shine Tonight**, (traditional war song); **Give My Regards to Broadway** (from show *Little Johnny Jones*), by George M. Cohan (1904); **While Strolling Through the Park One Day**, by Ed Haley (1880); *****Ida, Sweet as Apple Cider**, by Eddie Leonard (1903); **When the Saints Go Marching In**, (traditional); **Jeannine, I Dream of Lilac Time** (from film *Lilac Time*), by L. Wolfe Gilbert and Nathaniel Shilkret (1928); **Just A-wearyin' for You**, by Frank Stanton and Carrie Jacobs-Bond (1901); *****I'll See You in My Dream**, by Gus Kahn and Isham Jones (1924); **When I Grow Too Old to Dream** (from film *The Night Is Young*), by O. Hammerstein and Sigmund Romberg (1935); **Jeannie with the Light Brown Hair**, by Stephen C. Foster (1854); *****Three O'clock in the Morning**, by Dorothy Terris and Julian Robledo (1922).

(*) denotes song was a million sheet music seller.

MEMORIES SING ALONG WITH MITCH (Album) *CBS Columbia 8342* [USA]. Mitch Miller's ninth million seller (his seventh album million seller). A Gold Disc was awarded by RIAA in 1962. It reached No 5 with 78 weeks in the album charts in America.

Contents of the disc: *****My Blue Heaven**, by George Whiting and Walter Donaldson (1927); **I'm Nobody's Baby**, by Benny Davis, Lester Santly and Milton Ager (1921); **You Were Meant for Me** (from film *Broadway Melody*), by Arthur Freed and Nacio Herb Brown (1929); **At Sundown**, by Walter Donaldson (1927); **Five Foot Two, Eyes of Blue**, by Sam M. Lewis, Joe Young and Ray Henderson (1925); **Meet Me in St Louis, Louis**, by Andrew B. Sterling and Kerry Mills (1904), arranged by Jimmy Carroll; **Bill Bailey, Won't You Please Come Home**, by Hughie Cannon (1902), arranged by Jimmy Carroll; **The Bowery** (from *A Trip to Chinatown*), by Charles H. Hoyt and Percy Gaunt (1892), arranged by Jimmy Carroll; **The Yankee Doodle Boy**, (from *Little Johnny Jones*), by George M. Cohan (1904), arranged by Jimmy Carroll; **I'm Going Back to Dixie (Dixie)**, by Dan D. Emmett (1860), arranged by L.L. Riker; **Honey**, by Seymour Simons, Haven Gillespie and Richard Whiting (1928); *****Sleepy Time Gal**, by J.R. Alden, Raymond B. Egan, A. Lorenzo and Richard A. Whiting (1925); *****Ramona** (from film *Ramona*), by L. Wolfe Gilbert and Mabel Wayne (1927); *****Peg O' My Heart**, by Alfred Bryan and Fred Fisher (1913); *****Peggy O'Neil**, by Harry Pease, Ed G. Nelson and Gilbert Dodge (1921); **I Love You** (from *Little Jessie James*), by Harlan Thompson and Harry Archer (1923); *****Home on the Range**, (traditional, *circa* 1873), arranged by Jimmy Carroll; **Battle Hymn of the Republic**, by Julia Ward Howe (1861), tune **Glory, Glory, Hallelujah** ascribed to William Steffe (*circa* 1856), arranged by Jimmy Carroll.

ROY ORBISON *American*

ONLY THE LONELY *Monument 421* [USA] *London HLU 9149* [UK]. Roy wrote his first million seller with the help of Joe Melson. He was born Roy Kelton Orbison in Vernon, Texas, on 23 April 1936 and was educated at Wink Texas High School and North Texas State College. His father, an oil-rig driller, taught Roy to play the guitar when he was six. He became extremely proficient with an instrument on which he might well have gained fame alone, if his vocal ability had not also been discovered. In his early teens, Roy was leading the *Wink Westerners* and conducting a talent show over the local radio station. At 16, he represented the Lone Star State at the International Lions Conclave in Chicago. While a student (and disc artist at the time) at college, Pat Boone advised him to look for disc hits instead of oil. In 1956 he was signed to Sun Records and in 1958 agreed to a writer/management pact with Wesley Rose, then over to Victor Records and subsequently to the Monument label and further big successes. Roy's radio debut was in Vernon in 1944, his first important stage appearance was in Richmond, Virginia, in 1956 and his TV debut in Dick Clark's 'American Bandstand' in 1960. Roy was a songwriter and also played the harmonica. The disc was No 2 in the USA with 21 weeks in the bestsellers, and a chart topper in Britain for three weeks with 24 weeks in the

bestsellers. He later recorded for MGM.

Roy Orbison enjoyed a long string of international hits during most of the sixties, and was one of the decade's great singers. With the exception of a 1980 duet with Emmylou Harris, Orbison's hits dried up in America in 1967. In Britain, where he retained a strong fan following, he had his last hit in 1969. In 1988 he got together with other rock legends George Harrison, Bob Dylan, Tom Petty and Jeff Lynne and formed the Traveling Wilburys. The group was flexible enough to allow its members to continue with solo projects, which Orbison did with a new recording deal with Virgin. Just as he seemed on the verge of a major come-back, he died of a heart attack on 7 December 1988. After his death the Traveling Wilburys self-titled LP made the top three in the US album charts. Two compilations of old Orbison material also charted, and his new album for Virgin, **Mystery Girl**, also made the Top 5. The **You Got It** single off the album reached No 9 in America and No 3 in Britain, where it won a Silver Disc for sales of 200,000 copies. (In January 1989 the sales qualification for a Silver Disc was reduced from 250,000 to 200,000.) Orbison had co-written the song with Jeff Lynne and Tom Petty.

BLUE ANGEL *Monument 425 [USA] London HLU 9207 [UK]*. This was the second million seller (globally) for Roy Orbison, also written by him with Joe Melson. It reached No 9 in the US charts with 14 weeks in the Hot 100 and also charted in Britain, at No 11 with 16 weeks in the charts.

I'M HURTIN' *Monument 433 [USA]*. Roy's third million seller was another collaboration with Joe Melson. The record was a relatively minor hit at first, reaching only No 27 in America with eight weeks on the charts. Though the record was not a hit in Britain, **I'm Hurtin'** finally sold a global million.

ELVIS PRESLEY   *American*

STUCK ON YOU/FAME AND FORTUNE *RCA Victor 47–7740 [USA] RCA 1187 [UK]*. Elvis Presley was the greatest of all rock'n'roll's solo singers, eclipsed in the pantheon of rock only by the Beatles. Between 1956 and his death in 1977, he racked up 62 million-selling records, including one EP and 14 albums, 28 of which sold a million in the USA alone. His long chart career included 149 entries in the US Hot 100, and 112 hits in Britain, including three EPs in the singles charts. A number of his earlier hits entered the charts again in 1977. On the album front, Elvis had 96 LPs charted in America, and 98 in Britain. He had 17 No 1 singles in both America and Britain, with nine No 1 albums in America and six in the UK.

Though Bill Haley was the first rock idol, he was soon overtaken by Elvis, who had a tremendous impact on the music scene. His music combined the country-and-western influence of Memphis, Tennessee, where his family moved when he was 13, with the more urban rhythm and blues of black America, plus a sprinkling of gospel music to produce classic rock'n'roll. When he first started, some people who heard him thought that he was black, because his voice had such a strong soul sound to it. He became the model that countless American singers tried to copy, and his influence spread far outside the United States. In Britain, Europe, South America and the Pacific from Australia to Japan, Elvis Presley appealed to teenagers to a degree that nobody had ever done before.

Elvis Aron Presley (he changed the spelling of his middle name to Aaron later in life) was the younger of twins born to Gladys and Vernon Presley, in East Tupelo, Mississippi, on 8 January 1935. His elder twin brother, Jesse Garon Presley, was stillborn. A great deal of myth surrounds Presley's life, starting with his birth. His mother claimed that Elvis was the first-born of identical twins, but the records of the doctor that delivered him show that he was not, nor was there any evidence that the twins were identical. Presley was always very close to his mother. Some of the peculiarities of his life can be traced back to his upbringing in penurious, conservative circumstances. His parents were very poor, superstitious hillbillies.

Elvis sang in his local church, the Pentecostal First Assembly of God. His first solo public performance was at the age of 11, when he won second prize at the Mississippi and Alabama Fair and Dairy Show singing **Old Shep**, an old-fashioned ballad about a dog. He did better at his next singing contest, coming first in a high school performance in 1953, singing the same song.

After he left school, Presley worked in a factory and then drove trucks for Crown Electric. It was at this time that he made his first recording. In 1953 he turned up at Sam Phillips' Sun Records studio in Memphis to make a private recording. The Elvis myth has it that this was a birthday present for his mother.

In fact, his mother's birthday had long passed and she did not have a record player. He probably just wanted to hear what he sounded like on disc. He recorded two Ink Spots numbers, **My Happiness** and **That's When Your Heartaches Begin**, which impressed Phillips' secretary and receptionist Marion Keisker. Phillips was not there at the time, but nine months later she persuaded her boss to give Elvis a chance.

Phillips was sceptical at first, but was interested enough to put Presley together with guitarist Scotty Moore and string bass player Bill Black for another session, and on 6 July 1954 the group made their first professional recordings. The 19-year-old Presley's first recording was a corny country balled called **I Love You Because**. The session also produced **That's Alright Mama** and **Blue Moon of Kentucky**, which became Elvis' first release on Sun 209. The record was a big local country hit, largely thanks to radio exposure.

Elvis released five singles on Sun, and all of them were regional country hits. But Sun did not have the clout, money or know-how to make him a national star. Colonel Tom Parker (born Andre van Kuijks in Breda, the Netherlands) took over as his manager, and soon after in November 1955 negotiated a deal with RCA, who paid $35,000 to Sun for the Presley contract and existing masters, and $5,000 to Elvis. Early the next year, RCA put out their first Elvis single. **Heartbreak Hotel** went to No 1 for 8 weeks, and the rest is history. . . .

Elvis Presley soon dominated rock'n'roll and the charts. From 1956 to his first release of 1961, he had 15 No 1s in America, with only four singles failing to hit the top (excluding EP tracks). After his second release in 1961, he topped the charts only twice. In Britain it was a somewhat different picture. He had only four No 1s in the fifties (two of which had failed to reach the top in America). He was a much bigger success with the soft, early sixties ballads than he ever had been with rock'n'roll, and 11 of his British No 1s were from the end of 1960 to 1965.

Presley's main objective had always been to be a film rather than a pop star, and he did make a series of films. Most of them were of poor quality, though they kept his fans happy and acted as a substitute for live tours, especially outside America as he never toured abroad. He was drafted into the US Army in 1958, serving two years in Germany. He survived this break in his career, coming back a ballad singer as by 1960 the music scene had changed. By the end of 1963 Cliff Richard had replaced him as the world's most popular pop star, and in 1964 the Beatles swept him from the top in America. From 1964 to the end of the decade, Presley released a string of mainly weak soundtrack songs that kept him in the lower reaches of the charts.

He became more and more of a recluse, living at his Gracelands home in Memphis with his family, friends and staff. He churned out the films and the records, and appeared in Las Vegas, but he seemed increasingly dated and out of touch with the music scene. Though he had never really been away, in 1969 he made a determined come-back and released three first-

rate non-soundtrack singles. **In the Ghetto**, **Suspicious Minds** and **Don't Cry Daddy** gave him his biggest hits in years and re-established him at the top of his profession.

In 1967 he married Priscilla Ann Beaulieu. He had first met her in 1959, when she had just turned 14. He was serving in the Army in Germany, where her stepfather was a captain. He dated her again when he got out of the Army, and after living with her for six years they married and a year later had their only child Lisa Marie. After her birth, the marriage fell apart and the couple were divorced in 1973. Priscilla took up a career as an actress and in the 1980s secured a part in the *Dallas* soap opera. The end of his marriage was a tremendous blow to Presley, who had already succumbed (as so many other rock stars did) to sexual excesses and drug abuse.

Despite earning a vast fortune, Elvis Presley had an extravagant life style. He also had a management team that cost a fortune. By 1974 he was back on the road again, earning huge fees for sell-out performances. The quality of the performances went downhill as fast as his health. He had put on a tremendous amount of weight. His dependence on drugs increased, and in the early hours of 16 August 1977 Presley's fiancée Ginger Alden found the star lying on the floor of his bedroom in Gracelands. He was dead on arrival at the Baptist Memorial Hospital, Memphis.

Elvis Presley made a tremendous contribution to the development of rock music. The King of Rock'n'Roll was not the first rock singer, nor necessarily the best, but the combination of his considerable singing talent, his personality and his electric stage presence meant that he did more than anyone else to propel the rock revolution around the world.

Though he ended his days in excess and drug abuse, he had a side of prodigious generosity to him throughout his life. He was 42 when he died, and though the world of pop and rock music had moved on by 1977, he was still a major figure right to the very end. In fact his record sales took off after his death, with many of his old hits enjoying another lease of life, and eight new releases (including four albums) passing the million mark.

Elvis Presley's first American hit of 1960 was the double A side **Stuck On You/Fame And Fortune**. It was Presley's 19th million-selling record. The disc had what at the time was a record advance order of 1,275,077, with global sales of over two million. (For some reason the record was never certificated Gold by the RIAA, though it is listed as a million seller in the RCA Archives.) **Stuck On You** was written by Aaron Schroeder and J. Leslie McFarland, and was No 1 in America for four weeks with a 16-week chart run. In Britain it went to No 3 with 14 weeks in the charts, Presley's second hit of the year following the **Strictly Elvis** EP. **Fame and Fortune** reached No 17 in America, with 10 weeks on the charts. It was written by Fred Wise and Ben Weisman.

Both sides were recorded in RCA's Nashville Studio B in the early hours of 21 March 1960 at the first session Elvis did after leaving the Army. Elvis and Scotty Moore played guitar, with Bob Moore and Hank Garland on bass. D. J. Fontana provided the steady beat on drums, with Buddy Harman providing additional percussion on a second drum set. Floyd Cramer played piano, with the Jordanaires providing vocal back-up. These were the musicians who backed Elvis on almost all his Nashville sessions in the early sixties. Producer credits for the record should be shared by Chet Atkins, who was the driving force behind RCA Nashville and who set the studio up, Steve Sholes and Elvis himself.

IT'S NOW OR NEVER *RCA 47-7777* [*USA*] *RCA 1207* [*UK*] *Teldec RCA* [*West Germany*]. **It's Now Or Never** gave Elvis Presley the biggest hit of his career, selling over 10 million copies around the world. His 20th million seller was a strong ballad adapted from the Italian song **O Sole Mio**, written in 1901 by G. Capurro (words) and Eduardo Di Capua (music). New lyrics were added by Aaron Schroeder and W. Gold. The record sold five million copies in the USA, and one million each in Britain and Germany. It entered the British charts at No 1 the first week of release, the second occasion that Presley had achieved this. (The first was in 1958, with **Jailhouse Rock**.) **It's Now Or Never** was No 1 in Britain for nine weeks, with 19 weeks in the charts.

The record was a double A side hit in America, coupled with **A Mess of Blues**. (In Britain, this record was released before **It's Now Or Never**, reaching No 2.) **It's Now Or Never** topped the US charts for five weeks, with 20 weeks on chart. At the same time **A Mess of Blues**, written by Doc Pomus and Mort Shuman, reached No 32 with an 11-week chart run. The massive success of this big ballad all over the world confirmed a change of direction for Presley. Gone was the surly rebel rocker, and in his place was the ballad-singing pop

star. Both sides were recorded at RCA Nashville on 4 April.

ARE YOU LONESOME TONIGHT?/I GOTTA KNOW *RCA 47-7810* [*USA*] *RCA 1216* [*UK*]. Another massive ballad hit for Presley, confirming his musical change of direction. **Are You Lonesome Tonight?** was written in 1926 by Roy Turk and Lou Handman, and was No 1 for six weeks in America and for five weeks in Britain when released in January 1961. The record spent 16 weeks in the American charts and 15 weeks in the British Top 50. **I Gotta Know** was written by Paul Evans and Matt Williams, and went to No 20 in America with an 11-week chart run. Global sales of four million were achieved. Elvis recorded **It's Now Or Never** on 3 April, again using Studio B of the RCA studios in Nashville. The record was produced by Chet Atkins and Steve Sholes.

G.I. BLUES (LP) *RCA LSP-2256* [*USA*] *RCA RD 27192* [*UK*]. Elvis Presley's 22nd million seller was the album soundtrack from the film *G.I. Blues*, his fourth album to sell a million. One of Presley's more successful films, it told the story of his two years in the American army in Germany, where he had been part of the 3rd Armoured (Spearhead) Division. It topped the American album charts for 10 weeks, with over two years on the charts. The 111-week run was easily his longest stay on the US charts of all his 96 hit albums. In Britain it gave him his second No 1 LP, remaining on top for 22 of its 53 weeks in the charts. The only single hit off the album was **Wooden Heart** which, though a massive success in Europe, was never released in America. The album sold over two million copies worldwide, winning an RIAA Gold Disc in March 1963 for US million dollar sales.

The contents were: **Tonight Is So Right For Love**, by Sid Wayne and Abner Silver (1960) (adaptation of Offenbach's **Bacarolle**); **What's She Really Like?**, by Sid Wayne and Abner Silver (1960); **Frankfurt Special**, by Sid Wayne and Sherman Edwards (1960); **Wooden Heart**, by Fred Wise, Ben Weisman, Kay Twomey and Bert Kaempfert (1960); **G.I. Blues**, by Sid Tepper, Roy C. Bennett and Aaron Schroeder (1960); **Pocketful of Rainbows**, by Fred Wise and Ben Weisman (1960); **Shoppin' Around**, by Sid Tepper, Roy C. Bennett and Aaron Schroeder (1960); **Big Boots**, by Sid Wayne and Sherman Edwards (1960); **Didja' Ever**, by Sid Wayne and Sherman Edwards (1960); **Blue Suede Shoes**, by Carl Lee Perkins (1955); **Doin' the Best I Can**, by Doc Pomus and Mort Shuman (1960). The music was recorded at two Hollywood studios, at RCA on 27 and 28 April, and at Radio Recorders on 6 May. The album was produced by Steve Sholes, with additional vocals, strings and horns added to the film soundtrack by Joseph Lilley.

WOODEN HEART *RCA 1226* [*UK*] *Teldec RCA* [*West Germany*]. Elvis Presley's 23rd million seller was his only one not to be released in the USA. Taken from the film soundtrack *G.I. Blues*, the record was a massive hit in Germany and the rest of Europe. The song was written by Fred Wise, Ben Weisman, Kay Twomey and Bert Kaempfert (a producer for the German Polydor label, and a major MOR album artist in

Germany). It was based on an old German folk song, **Muss I denn zum Stadtele naus**, and Elvis sang it partly in German and partly in English. It went to No 1 for three weeks in England, spending 27 weeks in the charts. This was the longest British chart run of his whole 21-year career. The record was also No 1 in Germany, and many other European countries. Though Elvis did not release the song as a single in America, Joe Dowell made his chart debut with a cover version in June 1961, going to No 1 for one week on the Smash label.

JOHNNY PRESTON   *American*

RUNNING BEAR *Mercury 71474 [USA] Mercury AMT 1079 [UK]*. This first million seller for rock'n'roll vocalist Johnny Preston is the story of an Indian brave and his love for a maiden of an enemy tribe. It was written in 1959 by J.P. Richardson, better known as 'The Big Bopper', who was killed in an air crash with Buddy Holly in early 1959. From Port Arthur, Texas, Johnny was born on 18 August 1939, and started singing with the school choir, later forming a combo called the Shades for local dances. He won a Certificate of Achievement and Richardson encouraged him to make his first recording. He signed a contract with Mercury, toured the USA and appeared on TV and on radio. This disc made him internationally known, and was No 1 in the USA for three weeks with 27 weeks in the bestsellers, and top of the charts in Britain for one week with 14 weeks in the bestsellers.

CHARLIE RICH   *American*

LONELY WEEKENDS *Philips International 3552 [USA]*. Pianist-vocalist Charlie Rich wrote this himself and his recording was reported to have sold the million. He was raised in Arkansas and was involved with music for most of his life. This disc was No 22 and 21 weeks in the US bestsellers.

CLIFF RICHARD AND   *British*
THE SHADOWS

EXPRESSO BONGO (EP) *Columbia (EMI) SEG 7971 [UK]*. The world of British pop music in the fifties was a pretty pallid affair, with local singers slavishly following American stars and American styles. Few had any real originality, and the result was that the Americans dominated the British charts. The first attempt at creating a British rock'n'roll star was made by Tommy Steele, whose **Rock with the Caveman** made the Top 20 in 1956. Steele did have talent as an entertainer but a rock king he was not, and by 1959 he was reduced to making novelty records like **Little White Bull**. He was only considered a rocker as long as there was no real competition around, and that competition arrived in September 1958.

Move It was by far the best fifties rock record ever made by a British artist. It was Cliff's first hit, and started him on an incredible career that took him from a moody rock'n'roll

singer, through being the country's leading teen idol, on to his role as an institution which 30 years later had the biggest-selling record of the year and was No 1 in the singles and album charts for Christmas 1988. All set to enter the fifth decade of the rock era, Cliff Richard remains the greatest solo singer Britain has ever produced.

Cliff Richard was born Harry Roger Webb on 14 October 1940 in Lucknow, then part of the British Indian Empire. India became independent in 1947, and a year later the Webb family moved 'home' to England, a country none of them had ever seen before. This move resulted in a dramatic drop in the family's standard of living. In India they had had four servants and a good income; In England they had no home, no money, and Cliff's father at first had no job. They lived in considerable poverty for some while, the family of six in one room. Eventually they moved to a council house in Cheshunt, Hertfordshire.

Cliff made his first public performance at a local dance in 1954, while still at secondary modern school in Cheshunt. He had formed a group of two boys and three girls called the Quintones. After leaving school at 15 he got a job in the same Enfield factory that his father worked in. In the evenings he played with a local skiffle group as vocalist, but soon left to form his own rock'n'roll band, the Drifters. This consisted of Cliff (guitar and vocals), Ian Samwell (bass) and Terry Smart (drums). It was this group that developed into the Shadows which, as well as backing Cliff on all his early records, developed a highly successful and long-lasting career for themselves. (See the Shadows, 1960.)

By the spring of 1958, the 17-year-old Harry Webb and his Drifters were still playing local pubs and clubs. Theatrical agent George Ganjou was persuaded to come and hear one of their performances, and liked what he saw as much as what he heard. He had them make a demo record, which he sent to Norrie Paramor, A&R manager of EMI's Columbia

Records. Like most A&R men at big record companies in the fifties, the middle-aged Paramor did not like rock'n'roll. He regarded it as something that should be left to the Americans, who he rightly thought did it best. However, he was looking for someone to do a cover of a fairly dreadful piece of typical American Tin Pan Alley pop called **Schoolboy Crush**. He called Cliff for a recording test at the Abbey Road studios, and signed him up for Columbia. He did not really want the Drifters as well, but Cliff insisted. They recorded **Schoolboy Crush**, and for the B side Paramor agreed to let them record a song of their own. Ian Samwell had written **Move It** on the top of a London double decker bus. It was the best British rock'n'roll record of the fifties, and with the help of appearances on Jack Good's new TV show 'Oh Boy!', it was **Move It** that made the charts, all the way to No 2. The record eventually sold over a million copies around the world. It also established Cliff as the country's leading rock star.

If **Move It** made Cliff the King of British rock, it was his first No 1, **Living Doll**, that established him as a superstar. Written by Lionel Bart for Cliff's first film *Serious Charge*, it was No 1 for six weeks and sold a million copies. It was also his first American hit, reaching No 30 — America was to be the one country that Cliff had only limited success in. The follow-up, another million-selling ballad called **Travellin' Light**, went to No 1 for seven weeks. The style of pop music was changing, and slowing down, though Cliff could still belt out the rockers. The flip side of **Travellin' Light** was a Samwell-written number, second only to **Move It** as a powerful rock song. **Dynamite** entered the charts in its own right, reaching No 16. Cliff's stage act was still pretty strong as well; The *New Musical Express* attacked his performance of **Dynamite** as 'the crudest exhibition ever seen on British television'.

Cliff's second film was *Expresso Bongo*, based on the London stage play of the same name. It was the story of a singer, Bongo Herbert (Cliff), who claws his way up through the corrupt and seedy world of the seamier side of showbiz. Set against the sleazy stripclubs of Soho, the film was directed and produced by Val Guest for British Lion Films. It starred Laurence Harvey, Sylvia Syms and Yolande Donlan, with the screenplay by Wolf Mankowitz. The film met with mixed critical reviews, though Cliff's supporting role was well received. It was released in November 1959, with four of the numbers featured in the film issued as an EP in January 1960.

It has always been extremely unusual for EPs to sell enough to get into the singles charts, and very few artists ever achieve this. On 15 January 1960 Cliff Richard joined the ranks of this select group when the **Expresso Bongo** EP entered the charts at No 25. It peaked at No 8 with six weeks in the Top 30. This feat is all the more remarkable as one of the tracks on the EP, **A Voice in the Wilderness**, was released as a single at the same time. This song was written by Cliff's recording manager Norrie Paramor and Bunny Lewis, who was manager and producer of Craig Douglas. Paramor and Lewis also wrote the other track on side one, **Love**.

On the second side was the Heneker-More-Norman composition **The Shrine on the Second Floor** and a Shadows instrumental, **Bongo Blues**, written by Paramor. The disc entered the EP charts at No 1 the first week of release, stayed at the top for 11 weeks, and remained in the EP charts for 32 weeks.

Within three months of release **Expresso Bongo** had sold 153,279 copies in the mono version and another 3,860 in stereo. By the end of the year, British sales were 178,138. This compares to sales of 30 to 40 thousand for an average hit EP, and around 60 thousand for a major success. The record achieved even higher sales on the Continent. France was entirely an EP and album market, with singles issued only for use in juke-boxes. By December 1963, Cliff Richard had sold 600,000 EPs in France, 283,472 were accounted for by sales from 16 EP releases, and the rest by **Expresso Bongo**. In Britain, the EP is one of the few Cliff Richard sixties releases that has been consistently available in the shops in various guises. From 1983 the Dutch-manufactured 12″ version was often to be found in major record stores as an import, and even in the eighties every time Cliff had a major hit and new fans were looking for something a bit exotic, sales of this EP perked up for a while. After nearly 30 years, it finally became the only Cliff Richard Extended Play record to sell a million copies, with that figure achieved from global sales.

The EP was recorded in 1959 in three sessions at EMI's Abbey Road Studio 2. On the evening of 8 September Cliff and the Shadows recorded **Love** (take five was used) and **A Voice In The Wilderness** (take 20). In the afternoon of 19 October they recorded **The Shrine On The Second Floor** (take 6) and the Shadows put down **Bongo Blues** (take 3). **A Voice In The Wilderness** proved the most difficult, and a remake had to be recorded around midday on Sunday 20 December. Norrie Paramor produced the EP, with engineers Peter Bown, Malcolm Addy and Stuart Eltham.

A VOICE IN THE WILDERNESS *Columbia (EMI) DB 4398* [*UK*]. **A Voice in the Wilderness** was Cliff's third ballad single in a row. Written by Norrie Paramor and Bunny Lewis, and produced by Paramor, it was one of the tracks on the **Expresso Bongo** EP from the Cliff Richard film of the same name. It entered the charts at No 8 the first week of release, the week after the EP. It climbed rapidly to No 2, but there it stayed for three weeks, stuck behind Anthony Newley's **Why**. Cliff was on his first American tour at the time, but had recorded a spot on the important BBC Radio show 'Saturday Club'. He did not think much of **A Voice in the Wilderness** (a view shared by many critics) so he recorded the B side instead. His manager Tito Burns was furios when he found out. Cliff learnt this lesson the hard way: at the crucial moment when he needed a final shove to get to the top and make it three No 1s in a row, he was out of the country and had wasted the equivalent of a 'Top of the Pops' plug on a B side.

A Voice in the Wilderness never did make the top. It spent 15 weeks in the Top 50, and won Cliff his third Silver Disc in a row on 20 February. It was his first hit in the land of his birth, India, and was also a hit in other countries like Norway, the Netherlands and Trinidad. A German version, **Die Stimme der Liebe**, was released as the flip side of a German version of **Fall in Love with You**. Over the years the record eventually sold a global million, the fourth Cliff Richard record to do so by 1989.

FALL IN LOVE WITH YOU/WILLIE AND THE HAND JIVE *Columbia (EMI) DB 4431* [*UK*]. Released in March 1960, this proved another massive hit for Cliff Richard and the Shadows. The record was an example of the policy Cliff had adopted from **Living Doll** onwards. He would usually release a ballad or medium-pace song as the A side, aimed to appeal to the widest-possible audience. He would then put a good upbeat number on the flip side, aimed to please his hard core of rock fans. The result was a string of eight flip sides that between 1959 and 1963 made the charts in their own right. It was part of the strategy of appealing to more people than any of the competition, and it worked. A central part of this strategy was the Shadows. They appealed to vast numbers of young men who could imagine themselves on stage with a guitar. (Many of them did more than just imagine it, copying the Shadows in groups of their own.) While the Shadows kept the fellas happy, Cliff appealed to the girls. Between them, Cliff and the Shadows had the best stage act in Britain, and beat the competition hands down.

Fall In Love With You was written by Ian Samwell, who had written all but one of Cliff's fifties rock hits. This was a world away from those numbers, a medium-paced ballad of the boy-girl, first romance type, with the Shadows twanging away in the background singing a 'baum, baum' chorus. It entered the Top 50 at No 6 the first week of release and peaked at No 2 (held off the top by Lonnie Donegan's million-selling **My Old Man's a Dustman**, one of the two biggest hits of the year). It had a chart life of 15 weeks. This side of the record was the international hit, with chart placings in Europe and India. A German version, **Bin Verliebt**, was Cliff's first foreign-language record and went to No 2 in Germany.

Willie and the Hand Jive was written by American Johnny Otis, whose R&B 'Caravan Show' had featured many top R&B artists of the fifties. It was a revival of the Otis hit of 1958, which in America had gone to No 9 in the pop charts, and No 5 in the R&B charts. Otis, real name John Veliotes, was a major R&B act throughout the fifties, and Cliff Richard had long wanted to record some of his songs. This he did in 1960, using another Otis hit, **Mumblin' Mosie**, as the B side of **Theme for a Dream**.

Both sides were recorded in 1959 at Abbey Road Studio 2, on 19 October, 17 and 18 November. Norrie Paramor was producer, with Malcolm Addy, Stuart Eltham and Peter Bown the engineers. The record won a Silver Disc for British sales of over a quarter of a million on 7 May, with British sales of 311,289 by the end of June. Over the years, world sales eventually passed the million mark.

PLEASE DON'T TEASE *Columbia (EMI) DB 4479* [*UK*]. Ex-Shadow Ian Samwell had written **Fall In Love With You**, and it was current Shadow rhythm guitarist Bruce Welsh who wrote the follow-up, **Please Don't Tease**, with comedian Charlie Chester's son Peter. This single was unique, being the only Cliff record chosen by his fans. Cliff had recorded 24 songs at Abbey Road, and he and his producer Norrie Paramor were not sure which tracks to

release as the next single. They decided on some market research, and in late May 80 young people were invited to the new EMI headquarters in Manchester Square, London, to listen to a tape of the recordings, and then vote for their favourite. The people were drawn from London youth clubs, Cliff's fan club and EMI's younger staff. Bruce's **Please Don't Tease** came out top with 758 points, followed by **Gee Whiz It's You** with 714 and **Nine Times out of Ten** with 708. Both Cliff and Norrie Paramor preferred **Nine Time out of Ten**, but the fans were right. **Please Don't Tease** went to No 1, which neither of the other two did.

The record was issued in the last week of June, entered the *Record Retailer* and *Melody Maker* charts at No 6 the first week of release (and the *New Musical Express* and *Record Mirror* charts at No 7), rose to No 2 the second week in, and in its fourth week went to No 1. It was Cliff's third chart-topper, staying at No 1 for four weeks and in the Top 50 for 18 weeks. It was knocked off the top by the Shadows' first hit **Apache**, on which Cliff played the bongo drums.

This was Cliff's biggest success of 1960, and his best seller since **Travellin' Light**. It had sold 505,252 copies in its first three months on sale in Britain, winning a Silver Disc on 13 August. Its global sales were over one and a half million copies. It was No 1 in New Zealand, Norway, The Netherlands and India, and a hit in many other countries. Cliff recorded a new version of the song for the B side of his 1978 single **Please Remember Me**.

Of the other tracks that did well in the fans' voting session at EMI, two were issued as singles. The best of the rest were issued on a 16-track LP, **Me And My Shadows**, which many considered the best Cliff and Shadows album of all. Most of the tracks were written by the Shadows and their friends. Released in October 1960, the album spent eight weeks at No 2, stuck behind the **South Pacific** soundtrack which was No 1 for most of the year. **Please Don't Tease** was recorded on the evening of 25 March 1960, and was produced by Norrie Paramor with Malcolm Addy as engineer.

NINE TIMES OUT OF TEN *Columbia (EMI) DB 4506* [*UK*]. Prior to release in September 1960, **Nine Times Out of Ten** achieved the highest advance orders for a Cliff Richard record ever up to that time. The order for 170,000 copies ensured that the record entered the charts at No 7 the first week of release. It peaked at No 2 for two weeks in the *Disc* charts, and at No 3 in three of the others, and spent 12 weeks in the Top 50. The Hall-Blackwell composition won Cliff's sixth Silver Disc in a row on 22 October, giving him twice as many of these trophies as any one else at the time. It was a hit in many countries, including Japan, India, The Netherlands, Norway Australia, New Zealand, South Africa and Ireland, and eventually sold a global million. It was recorded at Abbey Road Studio 2 on 15 and 16 March 1960 with Norrie Paramor as producer and Malcolm Addy as engineer.

I LOVE YOU/D IN LOVE *Columbia (EMI) DB 4547* [*UK*]. Cliff's second No 1 of the year and ninth million-selling record was another double A side. **I Love You** was written by Shadow Bruce Welsh, and again underlined the writing abilities of his own group. It was the quality of Cliff's material that helped him pull away from the rest of the pack, and the fact that he had an in-house writing team and did not have to rely on covering American songs was central to this. Six of the 11 singles up to **I Love You** were written by Ian Samwell or Bruce Welsh, and one by Cliff's producer Norrie Paramor. Samwell also wrote two of the four flip sides that charted in their own right. **I Love You** and **D In Love** were recorded at the same session at Abbey Road Studio 2 on Friday 9 September 1960, between 2.00 pm and 5.00 pm. As was the custom then, three tracks had to be recorded during the three hours in the studio, with **Catch Me** (destined for the **21 Today** album released a year later) as the third track. Norrie Paramor was the producer and Malcolm Addy the engineer.

I Love You entered the charts on 1 December at No 8. It gave Cliff his first Christmas No 1; he had to wait until 1988 for his second festive chart-topper **Mistletoe and Wine**. It was No 1 for three weeks, putting Cliff at the top for the first week of 1961 as well, and spent 16 weeks in the Top 50. It was his fourth record to go to No 1.

D in Love was written by the veteran American songwriting partnership of Sid Tepper and Roy C. Bennett, who were later commissioned to write the title song for the film *The Young Ones*. In the *Disc* charts, **D in Love** was listed instead of **I Love You** for the first week in the charts, and then as a double A side the next week. In the *New Musical Express*, **D in Love** had one week in the charts on its own, at No 26.

Both sides of the record were recorded at Abbey Road on 9 September 1960, produced by Norrie Paramor with Malcolm Addy as engineer. The record won the 50th Silver Disc to be awarded by *Disc* magazine on Christmas Eve, Cliff's fifth of 1960 and his seventh overall. (It would have been his ninth if the scheme had started in 1958 instead of 1959.) The record sold 564,399 copies in Britain within four months of release, and eventually sold just under one and a half million copies worldwide. **I Love You** was No 1 in The Netherlands (his first Dutch chart-topper) and a hit in New Zealand, South Africa, Ireland, Norway, Belgium, India and other countries. It was his first hit in Israel. **D in Love** was Cliff's first No 1 in South Africa.

This double A side brought to an end an incredible year for Cliff Richard and the Shadows. Cliff had eight chart entries in 1960, made up of five singles of which two had flip sides that also charted, and one EP. Two of the singles went to No 1, and three went to No 2. All five won Silver Discs and all five and the EP eventually sold over a million copies around the world. Cliff Richard triumphed in all the popularity polls conducted by the music papers. He had been voted 'Top New Singer' in 1958, and 'Top British Male Singer' in 1959. In the *Melody Maker* pop poll in March, Cliff was voted 'Top Male Singer' with 40% of the votes cast, compared to Frankie Vaughan in second place with 7%. At the end of 1960 he won the *New Musical Express* poll as 'Top British Male Singer' for the second time, and came second to Elvis Presley in the 'Top World Male Singer' section. This was the highest place that any British artist had ever reached in a world category of the poll. Cliff's **Please Don't Tease** came second as 'Record of the Year', beaten for the top place by the Shadows' **Apache**.

At the end of the year, the *New Musical Express* announced that Cliff Richard had been the most consistent chart artist of the year. The paper used a points system to log artist consistency, giving 30 points for each week at No 1 down to one point for one week at No 30. Cliff Richard moved up one place from No 2 in 1959 to No 1 artist of the year for 1960. The Shadows were 10th.

Cliff had started the year with his first visit to America, joining a package tour of young rock'n'roll singers and doing TV shows. The tour was a success, especially as far as the British press went. 'Cliff Sensational On Pat Boone Show' screamed the front page headline of *Disc* on 30 January, in a report that was typical of the tone of the British media. But, while he had made a good impression in America, this was the one country Cliff never really conquered.

In October, EMI Managing Director L.G. Wood announced that in his first two years Cliff Richard had sold five and a half million singles in Britain, an unprecedented feat. At the end of the year, EMI Chairman Sir Joseph Lockwood claimed that his company had a quarter of the global record market, with Cliff Richard and the Shadows leading the new penetration of world markets by British artists.

BOBBY RYDELL   *American*

WILD ONE/LITTLE BITTY GIRL *Cameo 171* [*USA*] *Columbia (EMI) DB 4429* [*UK*]. Robby Rydell was born Robert Louis Ridarelli on 26 April 1940, in Philadelphia, USA. He went to the same boys' club as his friends Fabian and Frankie Avalon. At the age of 12 he did a double act with Avalon, and appeared on a children's TV show hosted by Paul Whiteman. (It was Whiteman who suggested the name change.) In 1957, Bobby and Frankie Avalon were members of Rocko and His Saints, a rock group that played stints at a New Jersey nightclub, and from this came a recording contract with Cameo-Parkway Records. The deal included personal grooming in music, voice and dancing. Bobby played bass and drums, and composed as well as sang. He had his first hit in 1959 with **Kissin' Time**. His second hit later the same year, **We Got Love/I Dig Girls**, gave him his first Top 10 hit and million seller.

The follow-up was **Wild One/Little Bitty Girl**, which repeated the trick, **Wild One** was the biggest hit of Rydell's career, reaching No 2 in America in a 16-week chart run. It was also his biggest British hit and only Top 10 entry, reaching No 7 in its 15 weeks in the charts. The song was written by Bernie Lowe, Kal Mann and Dave Appell. **Little Bitty Girl** was written by Fred Tobias and Clint Ballard, and reached No 19 during its 15 weeks on the American charts.

SWINGIN' SCHOOL/DING-A-LING *Cameo 175 [USA] Columbia (EMI) DB 4471 [UK]*. Bobby Rydell's third million seller was another double A side. **Swingin' School** came from the film *Because They're Young* and, like **Wild One**, was written by Kal Mann (words), Bernie Lowe and Dave Appell (music). **Swingin' School** reached No 5 in America, with 12 weeks on the charts. It was only a minor hit in Britain, spending one week at No 44. **Ding-a-Ling**, also written by Mann-Lowe-Appell, reached No 18 with 11 weeks on the American charts.

VOLARE *Cameo 179 [USA] Columbia (EMI) DB 4495 [UK]*. Rydell's fourth million seller was **Volare**, an Italian song that was a massive hit for both its writer Domenico Modugno and Dean Martin. Modugno wrote the music and co-wrote the Italian words with Franco Migliacci; the English words were written by Mitchell Parish. Originally titled **Nel Blu Dipinto di Blu**, this was the third time that the song had sold a million records. Rydell's revival peaked at No 4 in America, with 15 weeks on the charts. It reached No 22 in six weeks in the British hit parade.

JACK SCOTT   *Canadian*

WHAT IN THE WORLD'S COME OVER YOU? *Top Rank 2028 [USA] Top Rank JAR 280 [UK]*. Jack Scott (real name Scafone) was born in Windsor, Ontario, Canada on 24 January 1938, moving to Detroit as a child. In 1958 he signed to Carlton and wrote his million-selling Top 3 debut hit called **Leroy/My True Love**. **What In The World's Come Over You?**, another self-written song, marked his debut for the new English Top Rank label. It reached No 5 in America, with 16 weeks on the charts, and went to No 11 during its 15-week British chart run.

THE SHADOWS   *British*

APACHE *Columbia (EMI) DB 4484 [UK]*. The Shadows were one of the most influential groups of the whole rock era. They revolutionized pop music with their classic line-up of three electric guitars and drums, the clean, clipped lead playing of Hank Marvin and the clear, firm bass of Jet Harris. They encouraged a whole generation of young British musicians, who copied Hank and Jet in particular. This generation came to the fore with the British beat boom that followed the Beatles in 1963. Many of these musicians, including the Beatles, Eric Clapton, Pete Townsend, and Roger Taylor and Brian May of Queen, were clearly influenced by the Shadows.

The group started off in 1958 as the Drifters, but as soon as their records were released by Capitol in America, Atlantic Records obtained an injunction stopping their sale. Atlantic had under contract the American group the Drifters, which had been disbanded in a blaze of bad publicity in 1958, but were re-formed with a completely different line-up later in the year. The British Drifters and EMI considered seeking an injunction in Britain to prevent the release of the American Drifters

material in the UK, but in the end the British group changed their name. Jet Harris came up with the name the Shadows, which they thought fitted their role as backing group to Cliff Richard. In fact, they nearly jumped from the frying pan into the fire, for there was already an American group called the Shadows. EMI had obtained world rights outside America to this group, licensing their disc from Del-Fi Records of Los Angeles in 1958 for an advance of $500. **Jungle Fever** was released on the HMV label in December 1958. Luckily for Cliff's group, **Jungle Fever** bombed, the American Shadows never had a hit anywhere and they eventually disbanded.

The original line-up was Cliff Richard (guitar and vocals), Ian Samwell (bass guitar), Terry Smart (drums), Ken Pavey (guitar) and occasionally Norman Mitham (guitar). Ian Samwell wrote nearly all Cliff Richard's early rock'n'roll hits. After the first of these, **Move It**, the line-up (October 1958) became Cliff Richard, Ian Samwell, Terry Smart, Hank Marvin (lead guitar) and Bruce Welsh (rhythm guitar).

Marvin and Welsh have remained the core of the group ever since. They both came from Newcastle in April 1958, and occasionally performed at the Two Is coffee bar in London where a number of famous British rockers (including Cliff Richard) got their start. They briefly joined the Five Chesternuts, then Hank went to the Vipers for a month before joining the Drifters with Bruce Welsh. The Shadows' most famous line-up was completed by January 1959 when Jet Harris replaced Ian Samwell on bass guitar, and drummer Tony Meehan replaced Terry Smart. Both had played with Hank in the Vipers.

Hank B. Marvin was born Brian Robson Rankin in Newcastle on 28 October 1941. Bruce Welsh was born on 2 November 1941 in Bognor Regis, moving with his mother to Newcastle three years later. (Welsh is his mother's name, his father's being Cripps.) The oldest of the Shadows at the time of **Apache** was Jet Harris, born Terence Harris in Kingsbury, London, on 7 July 1939. The youngest was Daniel Joseph Anthony (Tony) Meehan, born in London on 2 March 1942.

As well as backing Cliff Richard, the Shadows made records of their own. They featured three tracks on Cliff's first album, **Cliff**, in 1959, and released three singles before **Apache**. Two of these were vocals, but all three got nowhere. The group were on tour with Cliff in March 1960 when one of the other artists on the bill, singer Jerry Lordan, offered them an instrumental he had written. They recorded **Apache** for their next release, though their recording manager Norrie Paramor at first wanted to use it as a B side. **Apache** became their first hit, their first No 1 (for six weeks) and first million-selling record. They knocked themselves off the top of the charts, for they and Cliff Richard (who played bongos on **Apache** and arranged the record) were No 1 for four weeks with **Please Don't Tease**, written by Bruce Welsh.

Like Cliff Richard, the Shadows soon established a strong following all over the world except in the USA, where they suffered

from having a record company whose American subsidiary Capitol consistently failed to exploit British talent open to it. In the States the Danish guitarist Jorgen Ingmann took **Apache** to No 2 early in 1961. Three other versions of **Apache** have hit the American charts, the most recent a rap version by the Sugarhill Gang in 1982. Despite the Shadows' move to Atlantic in America, success there continued to elude them. Instead, they had a particularly strong following in France, Japan and Australia. **Apache** was a worldwide hit, and sold a million in Britain alone.

THE SHIRELLES   *American*

TONIGHT'S THE NIGHT *Scepter 1208 [USA]*. This female group comprised Addie Harris, Shirley Owens, Doris Kenner and Beverley Lee. They began their musical activities at their high school in Passaic, New Jersey, and were discovered while performing there in a talent show in late 1957, which brought them a Decca contract. Their first disc for Decca **I Met Him on Sunday** established them as a show-business

attraction. They then began to record with Scepter Records, a label formed by their manager Florence Greenberg, with great success.

This second million seller for the Shirelles was written by Owens, and Luther Dixon (artists' and repertoire manager and arranger for Scepter). The disc was recorded in late 1960, reaching No 39 with 12 weeks in the US charts.

WILL YOU LOVE ME TOMORROW? *Scepter 1211 [USA] Top Rank JAR 540 [UK]*. The third million seller for the Shirelles was written in 1960 by husband-and-wife Gerry Goffin and Carole King, one of USA's most successful songwriting teams. The disc was recorded in late 1960, and was a top seller for two weeks in the USA in 1961 with 19 weeks in the bestsellers. It was No 4 and 15 weeks in the British bestsellers.

RAY SMITH *American*

ROCKIN' LITTLE ANGEL *Judd 1016* [*USA*]. This was the sole million seller for both Ray Smith and the Judd label.

Ray Smith was born on 31 October 1938 in Paducah, Kentucky. He had his own local TV show and played guitar and piano in addition to singing. In 1969 he signed with the Celebrity label. The disc was No 22 and 16 weeks in the US bestsellers. Ray Smith died in November 1979, aged 41.

CONNIE STEVENS *American*

SIXTEEN REASONS *Warner Brothers 5137* [*USA*] *Warner Brothers WB 3* [*UK*]. Connie Stevens enjoyed a varied career as film, TV and music star. Born Concetta Ann Ingolia on 8 August 1938 in Brooklyn, she entered show business at 16. She made her film debut in *18 and Anxious* in 1957, and played leading lady to Jerry Lewis in *Rock-a-bye Baby* in 1959. She appeared in TV series like 'Tenderfoot', and with Ed Byrnes in '77 Sunset Strip'. Byrnes played the part of Kookie in the programme, and Connie teamed up with him to make a record for Warners based on the programme. **Kookie, Kookie, Lend Me Your Comb** went to No 4 in the US and sold a million copies.

After this and one other novelty hit with Byrnes, Connie Stevens enjoyed five solo hits from 1960 to 1965. The first of these, and the only big hit, was **Sixteen Reasons**. The four discs that followed were all minor hits in America, and did not chart in Britain. **Sixteen Reasons** was written by Bill and Doree Post in 1959. It reached No 3 in America, with 24 weeks on the charts, and No 9 in Britain with a 12-week chart run. Connie later played the part of Cricket Blake in the American TV series 'Hawaian Eye'.

JOHNNY TILLOTSON *American*

POETRY IN MOTION *Cadence 1384* [*USA*] *London HLA 9231* [*UK*]. The first million seller for Tillotson was written by Paul Kaufman and Mike Anthony. Johnny was born on 20 April 1939 in Jacksonville, Florida, and at the age of eight moved to Palatka, in the same state, and there developed his early musical interest — country music. He had earned a local reputation as a fine performer before he entered high school. Then came a three-year contract as a regular on a TV variety show, 'The Tom Dowdy Show'. Heard by Lee Rosenburg, who arranged an audition with Cadence, Johnny was immediately signed to the label, in 1958. He played ukulele and guitar as well as singing, and held two degrees as a graduate of the University of Florida. This disc was top seller in Britain for three weeks in 1961, and reached No 2 in the US charts with 15 weeks in the bestsellers and 15 weeks in Britain.

IKE AND TINA TURNER

A FOOL IN LOVE *Sue 730* [*USA*]. Ike and Tina Turner provided one of the most dynamic stage shows of the sixties. They had a string of R&B hits, many of which crossed over to the pop charts. After the couple broke up in 1976, Tina Turner went on to build a phenomenally successful solo career in the eighties.

Izear Luster Turner was born on 15 November 1931 in Clarksville, Mississippi, a town renowned as a centre of the delta blues. In his teens he joined a big swing band called the Tophatters. When the band broke up around 1948 some of its members became the Dukes of Swing, while Ike and the younger players formed the Kings of Rhythm.

Thanks to help from legendary blues guitarist B.B. King, Ike and his band went to Memphis in 1951 to record with King's producer Sam Phillips, owner of Sun Records. They cut **Rocket 88**, which when released by Chess Records went to No 1 in the R&B charts. Phillips later claimed this as the first rock'n'roll record. The disc was credited to Jackie Brenston (the main composer of the song, and lead singer on the disc) and the non-existent Delta Cats, and sold half a million copies.

In the early fifties Ike Turner combined keeping the Kings of Rhythm going with talent spotting for Joe Bihari's Modern/RPM Records. They recorded such blues greats as Howlin' Wolf, Elmore James and B.B. King.

The Kings of Rhythm continued to record, and had a regional R&B hit with **I'm Tore Up** in 1956. By then they were based in East St Louis, where their reputation as a wild live act had grown. It was here that in 1955 the 16-year-old Anna Mae Bullock first saw Ike perform. A year later she was singing with the band.

Anna Mae Bullock was born in Brownsville's Memorial Hospital on 26 November 1939. She lived not far from Brownsville, just up Highway 19 in Nut Bush, Tennessee, the small town about which she later wrote the Turners' last US hit, **Nutbush City Limits**. Her parents' marriage broke up and her mother Zelma abandoned the family when Anna was ten. Three years later her father Richard moved to Detroit, and Anna lived with relatives in Nut Bush and then nearby Ripley. In 1955 she was reunited with her mother, and went to live in St Louis.

In 1960 the Kings of Rhythm recorded **A Fool In Love**. Ike Turner wrote the song for singer Art Lassiter, but the two men fell out over money and Lassiter did not show up for the recording session. Ike got Anna Mae, who was pregnant by him at the time, to stand in for what was supposed to be a demo recording. Juggey Murray of Sue Records in New York picked up the record, and insisted on keeping the disc as it was. Ike decided that instead of being credited to the Kings of Rhythm, the record would go out as by Ike and Tina Turner, something that Anna Bullock was not, at first, very happy about.

Released in the summer of 1960, **A Fool In Love** was the couple's first pop and R&B hit. It reached No 19 for two weeks during a 16-week run in the *Cash Box* pop charts, though it reached only No 27 in *Billboard*. It made No 2 in *Billboard's* R&B charts, with 21 weeks in the Hot R&B Sides Top 30. The duo racked up 25 R&B hits from 1960 to 1975, hitting the pop charts 20 times during the same period. In 1964 they left Sue and up to 1970 recorded for a number of labels, with hits on Kent, Loma, Modern, Innes, Philles, Blue Thumb and Minit.

By 1965 the Turners were signed to Warner Brothers' R&B label Loma. The hits had dried up, so when Phil Spector indicated an interest in recording Tina, Loma agreed to their transfer to Spector's Philles label (which was released through London in Britain.) Though **River Deep — Mountain High** was credited to Ike and Tina Turner, part of Spector's deal with the Turners was that Ike was not even allowed in the studio, never mind on the record.

Released in 1966 it was only a minor hit in America, reaching No 88 in *Billboard* and failing to make the *Cash Box* and *Variety* charts at all. In Britain it was No 3, charting again in 1969 with a total of 20 weeks in the Top 50. The record made their reputation in Britain where it was recognized as a classic. Britain was also the launching place for Tina Turner as a solo star many years later, and the country she had settled in by 1989.

In 1970 the Turners signed to Liberty, with **Proud Mary** and **Nutbush City Limits** their biggest hits in the early seventies. This was also the period when the couple's marriage finally fell apart. Tina had become Ike's second wife at a wedding in Mexico in 1962. The marriage was stormy and, for Tina, violent. Ike was never faithful, and eventually Tina left him and in 1976 she obtained a divorce.

After the trauma of the divorce, Tina Turner started to build a solo career. When her record company Liberty/United Artists was taken over by EMI, she was transferred to EMI's Capitol label, and in the eighties had a string of multi-million-selling albums with **Private Dancer**, **Break Every Rule** and **Foreign Affair**. She had an American No 1 with the million-selling single **What's Love Got To Do With It** in 1984, and in 1989 entered the British album charts at No 1 first week of release with **Foreign Affair**. With a powerful and emotive voice and a body that a 20-year-old would have been proud of, Tina Turner established herself as one of the raunchiest and most exciting rock singers of the eighties, no mean achievement for a lady who turned 50 in 1989.

BOBBY VEE *American*

DEVIL OR ANGEL *Liberty 55270* [*USA*]. Bobby Vee was one of the most successful American pop singers of the sixties. He charted every year from his first hit in 1959 to **Sweet Sweetheart**, his final hit in 1970. He racked up a total of 38 chart entries in America, though he achieved only 10 hits in Britain from 1961 to 1963.

He was born Robert Thomas Velline on 30 April 1943, in Fargo, North Dakota. He came from a musical family, with both his father and uncle playing musical instruments as a hobby. His two elder brothers played guitar, and were part of a 15-member band that Bobby sometimes sat in with on practice sessions. He had his big break when a group his brothers had formed were asked to fill in for Buddy Holly after he was killed in an air crash on his way to Fargo. The boys bought identical sweaters, called themselves the Shadows, and put Bobby on as vocalist because he knew all

Crickets (1962), as well as with the Eligibles (1964) and the Strangers (1966–8).

Although he outlasted the Beatles, and had his biggest-selling hit in 1967, Bobby Vee did not outlast the decade. In the seventies he tried to re-launch his career, using his real name of Robert Velline. An album release in 1972 led nowhere. In 1978 he signed with United Artists records, which had taken over his old label Liberty, and which became part of EMI in 1979. Though EMI put out albums of his sixties material, his attempt at a come-back failed completely.

RUBBER BALL *Liberty 55287 [USA] London HLG 9255 [UK]*. Bobby Vee's follow-up to **Devil Or Angel** was **Rubber Ball**, written by Annie Orlowski and Aaron Schroeder. Both records peaked at No 6 in America. It was **Rubber Ball** that launched Bobby Vee as an international star. It was his first British hit, reaching No 4 with a chart life of 11 weeks. It was also a hit in many European countries.

THE VENTURES   *American*

WALK, DON'T RUN *Dolton 25 [USA] Top Rank JAR 417 [UK]*. The Ventures were America's most popular instrumental group. They were formed in 1958 by guitarists Don Wilson and Bob Bogle, with Nokie Edwards (guitar) and Howie Johnson (drums) completing the team. For a couple of years they played high school dates in their native Tacoma, Washington State, USA, and then came up with **Walk, Don't Run**, written by Johnny Smith. They tried to get record companies to give them a contract, but none were interested. They therefore formed their own label, Blue Horizon, and sent copies to local disc jockeys themselves. This generated enough interest for

the lyrics to the six numbers in their limited repertoire. (This group should not be confused with the much more successful English group of the same name who started backing Cliff Richard in 1958, and from 1960 had a long string of instrumental hits. (See the Shadows, p. 29.) The Shadows were Bobby's brother Bill Velline on guitar, Jim Stillman (electric bass) and Bob Korum (drums).

Bobby Vee and the Shadows were a big success deputizing for their idol Buddy Holly, and were soon booked for other local performances. They then went to Minneapolis where they recorded for Suma Records, a small local indie company. Their first disc was **Susie Baby**, written by Bobby and sung very much in the Buddy Holly style. The record had some local chart success, and was then picked up by Liberty Records for national distribution. It was a minor national hit in 1959. The follow-up was a cover of English singer Adam Faith's big British hit **What Do You Want?**, though this only just scraped into the US charts. Their third hit was **Devil Or Angel**, written by Blanche Carter in 1955. It gave Bobby Vee his first big hit, reaching No 6 and spending 19 weeks on the charts. The B side, **Since I Met You Baby**, also made the charts for one week at No 81. The record sold a global million, with most sales in the USA. Bobby Vee later recorded with the

local company Dolton to pick the disc up, with Liberty then taking it for national distribution.

Walk, Don't Run was the biggest hit of their career, reaching No 2 with 18 weeks on the American charts. In Britain, it reached No 8 with a 13-week chart run. They had another US Top 10 hit with a re-worked version of the tune in 1964. Once established in the USA, the Ventures set out to build an international following, achieving particular and long-lasting success in Japan. For a while, it looked as if the Ventures would challenge the Shadows as the most popular instrumental group in the world, but they never quite matched the presence, personality or talent of the British group.

The Ventures had 14 hits in the American singles charts, three of which made the Top 10 (the two versions of **Walk, Don't Run** and in 1969 the **Hawaii Five-O** TV theme on Liberty). They had two Top 10 singles in Britain and two other minor hits in 1960 and 1961. They switched most of their effort into albums, achieving 37 hit LPs in America between 1960 and 1972. While only one made the Top 10 three won RIAA Gold Discs for million dollar sales. None of their albums charted in Britain.

LARRY VERNE American

MISTER CUSTER *Era 3024* [USA]. This was a sole million seller for Larry Verne. He was born on 8 February 1936 and comes from Minneapolis. A country-and-western beat vocalist, he plays the guitar. This is a song with a historical flavour, written by Fred Darian, Al de Lory and Joe Van Winkle. The disc was a No 1 seller in the USA for one week and 13 weeks in the bestsellers.

DINAH WASHINGTON with American
BROOK BENTON

BABY (YOU GOT WHAT IT TAKES) *Mercury 71565* [USA]. This first million seller for Dinah was the second for Brook. The song was written in 1959 by Murray Stein and Clyde Otis. This disc is a conversational duet. Dinah (real name Ruth Jones), known as 'Queen of the Blues', was born 29 August 1924 in Tuscaloose, Alabama. She sang and directed the church choir in Chicago, and at the age of 19 became band vocalist with Lionel Hampton. She appeared in nightclubs and theatres, then as a solo artist — one of the best of the black jazz singers. She visited Britain in 1959 and appeared on TV and in the film *Jazz on a Summer's Day*. She died on 14 December 1963. This disc was No 5 in the US charts with 15 weeks in the bestsellers, and a No 1 in the R&B charts for 10 weeks in a 17-week chart run.

LAWRENCE WELK AND American
HIS ORCHESTRA

CALCUTTA *Dot 16161* [USA]. The first million

seller for the now famous Lawrence Welk orchestra was written by German composer Heino Gaze in 1958 with the title **Tivoli Melody**. The tune then appeared as **Take Me Dreaming**; next came the piano version called **Nicolette**; fourth it appeared as a song in 1960 in Germany titled **Kalkutta liegt am Ganges**; and finally as **Calcutta** in the USA. English words by Lee Pockriss and Paul J. Vance.

Lawrence Welk was born 11 March 1903 in Strasbourg, North Dakota. His parents and their family of four sons and four daughters left Alsace-Lorraine in 1878 fleeing Bismarck's invasion of their country. **Calcutta** was No 1 for two weeks in the USA with 17 weeks in the bestsellers, and No 1 in Germany. Gold Disc award RIAA 1961.

MAURICE WILLIAMS AND American
THE ZODIACS

STAY *Herald 552* [USA] *Top Rank JAR 526* [UK]. The first million seller for this group was written by Maurice Williams himself. The disc was No 1 in the USA for one week and 18 weeks in the bestsellers; No 14 and nine weeks in the British bestsellers.

The group comprised Maurice Williams (born 26 April 1938), Henry Gasten, Willie Bennet and Charles Thomas, all from Lancaster, South Carolina. The group won first prize in a talent show in 1955 at Barr High School in Lancaster. They were then known as the Charms. They travelled the South and came to Nashville where they hoped to be recorded. Williams, the leader-piano player and songwriter, had written **Little Darlin'** which he recorded for the Excello label. It was, however, the Diamonds' disc of this that made it a hit. The group at this time was called the Gladiolas. They also played under the names of the Royal Charms and the Excellos, and

finally the Zodiacs. A contract with Herald Records was signed and then came this big hit **Stay**.

JACKIE WILSON American

NIGHT/DOGGIN' AROUND *Brunswick 55166* [USA]. Jackie Wilson was a highly talented singer with an extremely versatile tenor voice. Despite a long chart career in America, poor management and an indifferent record company led to a somewhat directionless career.

Jack Leroy Wilson was born on 9 June 1934 in Detroit. He had a brief career as a boxer, winning the Golden Gloves welterweight title in 1950. He started his singing career with the Ever Ready Gospel Singers, though soon moved to a secular recording session for jazz trumpeter Dizzy Gillespie's Dee Gee label.

Wilson later joined the Dominoes before going solo in 1956. He signed to Brunswick and in 1957 had his first hit with **Reet Petite**. (The record was a bigger hit in Britain, where it reached No 6, than in his native America, where it reached No 62.)

1958 saw his first Top 10 hit and million seller with **Lonely Teardrops**. He went on to score 54 US chart entries (from 44 records, with 10 double A sides). In Britain he had eight hits, his last being a re-release of his first hit **Reet Petite**, which in 1986 gave him his only No 1 on either side of the Atlantic, two years after his death.

His music varied between upbeat numbers and ballads, with the material varying from the syrupy mediocre to the highly original. **Night/Doggin' Around** was his first double A side, and second Top 10 hit. It was also his second million seller. **Night** was written by Johnny Lehman and Herb Millier in 1959, and peaking at No 4 gave Wilson the highest US chart placing of his career. It spent 17 weeks on the Hot 100. **Night** was never released in Britain. **Doggin' Around** was written by Lena Agree, and went to No 15 with 16 weeks of chart action. It was this side that was released as the A side in Britain, coupled with **The Magic Of Love**. Released by Coral in April 1960, the record failed to chart. In the US R&B charts **Doggin' Around** was No 1 for 3 weeks of a 19-week chart run, while **Night** reached No 3 with 13 weeks in the charts.

In America the hits continued to roll, with **Alone At Last** (1960), **My Empty Arms** (1961), **Baby Workout** (1963) and **(Your Love Keeps Lifting Me) Higher And Higher** (1967) all making the Top 10. His last Hot 100 hit was in 1972, with his last soul chart hit the following year.

In 1961 a deranged female fan shot Wilson and nearly killed him. He recovered, but in September 1975 he had a heart attack while on stage at the Latin Casino, Camden, New Jersey. He hit his head when he fell, and suffered serious brain damage, leaving him completely helpless and unable even to speak. He finally died on 21 January 1984.

1 9 6 1

1961 was the year that Elvis Presley consolidated his grip as the world's leading pop star. In March he played his first concert in four years, at the Ellis Auditorium in Memphis. Later in the month, as the *NME* reported, 'Elvis Presley was honoured by the Tennessee State Legislature. He drove from Memphis to Nashville in his black Rolls Royce, addressed Members in the state capital, and was made an Honorary Tennessee Colonel.'

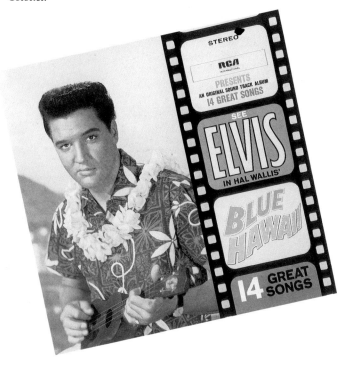

Elvis continued to perform in America, though the nearest that he got to an overseas date was in Hawaii. Giving his services free for the USS *Arizona* War Memorial fund raising concert, he gave a more subdued performance than in his rock'n'roll days, as the *NME* reported. 'Gone are all the actions that were dubbed vulgar by his critics. Presley's stage performance is now restrained.' Presley's manager Colonel Tom Parker claimed that Elvis had won 40 Gold Discs and RCA announced that he had sold $76 million worth of records. In September Elvis was hit by the bombshell that he might be redrafted back into the Army, if the Berlin crisis flared up.

Elvis was even more popular in Britain than in his native America. All five of his releases went to No 1 (though one of them only just — one week at the top in only one of the five charts.) He became the first artist ever to achieve more than two No 1s in a row. All his records racked up huge advance orders and sold in vast quantities. One of them, **Surrender**, gave Elvis his third single to enter the charts at No 1 first week of release. Despite press headlines of a Presley visit to Britain, Elvis never came. In fact he never performed outside the USA in his entire career.

Cliff On Top

Cliff Richard continued as the most popular British teen idol. With his backing group the Shadows, he was also the first British star to build a consistent following around the world. 1961 saw another hard schedule of world tours, with Cliff and the Shadows in America, South Africa, Australia, New Zealand, and various parts of Europe. His reception in South Africa was phenomenal, with tens of thousands of screaming fans everywhere he went. He fired his manager Tito Burns, was managed for a while by his father, and when he died later in the year Cliff took on the Shadows' manager Peter Gormley. In October Cliff got a Silver Disc from EMI chief Sir Joseph Lockwood, marking sales of a quarter of a million albums, only the second such award ever made. In a *Record Mirror* survey of the most successful chart records from 1958 to 1961,

Cliff's **Living Doll** was No 1. Cliff had three of the top five records, and two more in the top fifty. Elvis had four entries, Nos 11 to 14, and the Shadows had two. Cliff celebrated his 21st birthday with his first No 1 LP, titled **21 Today**.

The Shadows consolidated their position as the top group in Britain. Their leader, bass player Jet Harris turned photographer for *Record Mirror* on Cliff's Scandinavian tour, and all four Shadows wrote a column for *Disc* for several weeks. In October drummer Tony Meehan quit the Shadows, blaming the pressure of constant touring. He then did session work, joined Decca as an A&R man, teamed up with Jet Harris in 1962, and went on to be head of A&R for Shad-Rich, Cliff and the Shadows' production company. At the time of leaving the Shadows, he was still only 19. Other developments in the music press included a change in emphasis for Britain's *Record & Show Mirror*. In March the paper dropped its coverage of pantomimes, the theatre and other show elements and became the *New Record Mirror*.

A new pop paper started in Liverpool. *Mersey Beat* concentrated on the North West of England at first. After the Beatles and the other Liverpool groups broke nationally in 1963, it broadened its coverage to the whole country. The American record industry paper *Billboard* expanded its international coverage and became available in Britain via special Air Jet delivery for £5.50 a year. The present (1990) subscription is £165.

No Trends

1961 was a quiet year for rock'n'roll. There were no new trends of any importance on either side of the Atlantic. After the payola scandals that had destroyed the career of legendary rock DJ Alan Freed in 1960, American radio was turning away from the personality DJ who played what interested him towards the tighter Top 40 playlist format. This meant a more conservative, restricted pop radio. Payola had been a way by which the smaller indie record companies that pioneered rock'n'roll had successfully competed with the bigger majors. By paying DJs to play their records they ensured the vital air play essential to a hit record, and balanced the advantages of the majors with their better distribution and bigger publicity machines. Without payola the majors were less easy to challenge, and the sort of safer pop music they felt comfortable with dominated the airwaves and therefore the charts.

Not all the indies were pro rock. Mo Ostin, Vice President of Frank Sinatra's Reprise Records, said that his company would definitely never release any rock records. Ostin went on to become President of Warner Brothers, developing a rather different attitude. Sinatra's old record company Capitol sued him on the grounds that his new Reprise album was largely the same as his last LP for Capitol. Despite growing record sales, Lloyd Dunn (A&R Vice President of Capitol) described the state of the record business to *Variety* as: 'One of profitless prosperity. The profit picture has shrunk enormously. Singles and albums have become two distinct businesses. At the moment, the singles disk business is chaotic.' American Columbia continued with its plans to establish its own label identity throughout the world, something that RCA and Warner Brothers had already done. Their situation was complicated by the fact that EMI owned the Columbia trade mark virtually everywhere outside the Americas. The company adopted the logo of their broadcasting parent CBS instead.

In Britain Decca's chairman Edward Lewis was knighted. Decca suffered a brief strike at its record factory, but rumours of an EMI take-over were denied. Pye launched its new Piccadilly label on 14 April with Joe Brown's **Picture Of You**. Philips' American bid for Dot having failed, the Dutch company made a move to take over Mercury. At this time the only foreign owned record companies in America were Capitol (bought by EMI in 1955) and London (founded by British Decca in 1949.) The Rank Organisation, which had set up Top Rank Records in America in 1959, closed down early in 1961. They lost $2 million in their 18 months' existence. Rank had sold their British record company to EMI in 1960. Liberty Records switched their British licensee from Decca (where they went out on the London label) to their own label logo with EMI. The American quality jazz label Blue Note became available in Britain for the first time.

Sexual Revolution

1961 saw the first commercial introduction of the birth control pill in Britain. The sexual revolution that followed brought liberation to many women, and was a major factor in the increase in sexual freedom that was a feature of the swinging sixties. In reality it also brought greater pressure on women. The growing sexual permissiveness combined with other changes in society to create the Britain from which, after the Beatles, a new centre of worldwide youth culture emerged.

There were changes on the political front as well, though their main impact came later in the decade. With the staging of 'Beyond The Fringe', political satire returned to Britain. Other satirical offerings in 1961 included Joseph Heller's book *Catch 22* and the first issue of the magazine *Private Eye*. This was followed in 1962 by the BBC TV programme 'That Was The Week That Was'. Television was changing, reflecting a Britain that was becoming less staid and deferential.

Britain tried to join the European Economic Community, but was blocked by the French. Three new universities were opened as part of the biggest expansion of higher education this century. A judge declared the ballot of the Electrical Trades Union invalid as it was rigged by the Communists. In June Kuwait became independent of the British Empire. In July British troops were back to prevent an attack by Iraq. In January the one millionth Morris Minor ran off the production line, while in October the last steam train ran on the London Underground. Margaret Thatcher got her first Government job as Joint Parliamentary Secretary at the Ministry of Pensions.

World News

In America President Kennedy was sworn in, stating in his inaugural address 'Ask not what your country can do for you, ask what you can do for your country.' Kennedy began the escalation that trapped America in Vietnam. On 22 December James Davis became the first American soldier to die in the war. In April Kennedy suffered the Bay of Pigs fiasco when CIA backed Cuban exiles were easily rounded up by Fidel Castro after they landed to try and overthrow his Communist government. Kennedy formed the Peace Corps on 1 March. There was racial violence in Alabama as segregation laws were flouted.

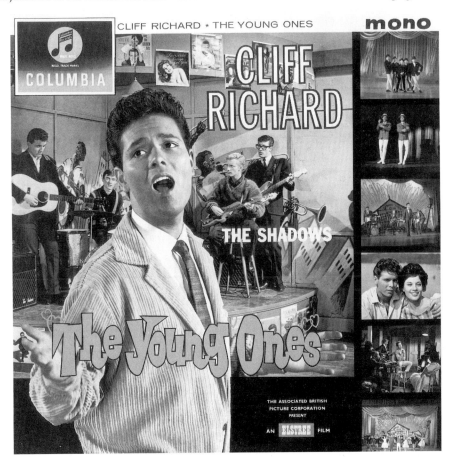

Relations with the Soviet Union remained difficult, with Berlin and nuclear weapons testing among the bones of contention. The East Germans began building the Berlin wall, and in the tension that followed British and American tanks faced Communist forces over the inner German border. The Russians put the first man into space, Yuri Gagarin's triumph emphasizing the Soviet lead in this area.

In Africa the French were still fighting in Algeria, and the Belgians sent troops to the war-torn Congo. UN forces defeated Katanga's attempted secession from the Congo. UN Secretary General Dag Hammarskjöld was killed in a plane crash in Northern Rhodesia on his way to meet Katanga leader Tshombe. The Portugese faced an uprising in Angola. In South Africa blacks called a general strike. The authorities arrested 10,000 people, though Nelson Mandela escaped. Albert Luthuli, Zulu Chief and respected black leader in South Africa, won the Nobel Prize for Peace.

1961 saw the 30th anniversary of Radio Luxembourg, then the only commercial radio station heard in Britain, while the Dutch pirate station Radio Veronica started test transmissions. Chubby Checker, Jo Stafford and Gene Vincent were among the Americans visiting Britain. The 14-year-old schoolgirl Helen Shapiro burst on the scene in a big way. The BBC banned Johnny Burnette's **God, Country And My Baby** ballad, and the Craig Douglas cover and Gene McDaniels original of **A Hundred Pounds Of Clay** for referring to Eve (of Adam and Eve) 'in a potentially offensive way'. They also banned Ricky Valence's death disc **Tell Laura I Love Her** (which promptly went to No 1, the first record banned by the BBC to do so) and Tony Bennett's **Stranger In Paradise**. The price of singles went up from 6/4 to 6/9.

Leading BBC DJ Pete Murray said, 'I hate rock'n'roll. It must be the only form of music which the majority of musicians who are playing it dislike, too. They only do it because it is popular among the kids. I reckon that the people who play rock are those who hate it more than anyone else. But all this business about it being on the way out is nonsense.'

Violent America

Singer Jackie Wilson of **Reet Petite** fame was shot by a girl fan in New York. Police arrested Miss Juanita Jones, who sobbed, 'I didn't want to hurt him. I'm all mixed up.' Wilson survived the incident, which was more than the Platters' 25-year-old pianist Rupert Branker did when he was attacked in Los Angeles. He was beaten to death with a Keep Left sign on the corner of 41st Street and Hoover Avenue at 4 o'clock in the morning.

Film

In America the top film of the year was the musical *West Side Story*, which won 11 Oscars. In Britain the British film *Swiss Family Robinson* was the top money-maker of the year. It starred John Mills, whose daughter Hayley was the top box office draw of the year. She was followed by Sophia Loren, Kenneth Moore, Elizabeth Taylor and her father John Mills. According to the *Motion Picture Herald*'s 1961 box office survey, *The Magnificent Seven* was the No 2 film of the year in Britain, with *101 Dalmatians, Pollyanna, Whistle Down The Wind* and *Carry On Regardless* also in the top ten. Seven of the top twelve were British films. Other movies released in 1961 included *The Guns Of Navarone* and Cliff Richard's *The Young Ones*.

Sport

Hampshire won the county cricket championship for the first time ever, while Tottenham Hotspur became the first football team this century to win the double of the FA Cup and the League championship. Their captain Danny Blanchflower was voted Footballer of the Year for the second time. In America, the New York Yankees won the World Series. The Green Bay Packers beat the New York Giants 37–0 for the NEL Championship. The Houston Oilers beat the San Diego Chargers (in their first year in the AFL) 10–3 for the AFL title.

In Between

1961 belongs to that period of rock history that lay between the original fifties rock and the Beatles, a more gentle time than either of them. It was a time of great teen idols like Elvis and Cliff, and of the beginnings of the group scene led by the Shadows. It was a time of great teen innocence compared to the drug-influenced free-sex image of the late sixties. Youth still knew its place. Of all the years of the sixties, there seemed to be less sense of direction in 1961 than in any other year. At the time, however, teenagers still had fun, even if it was in a less adventurous way than their younger brothers and sisters were to have later in the decade.

VARIOUS ARTISTS *American*

ORIGINAL THEATRE CAST WITH JULIE ANDREWS, RICHARD BURTON, ROBERT GOULET, ROBERT COOKE, RODDY McDOWALL, NEL DOWD

CAMELOT (Album) *CBS-Columbia 2031* [*USA*] *CBS APG 60001* [*UK*]. Another fine musical show by Alan Jay Lerner (lyrics) and Frederick Loewe (music) following their *My Fair Lady*. Further big laurels came the way of English actress/singer Julie Andrews. *Camelot* was produced on 3 December 1960 at the Majestic Theatre, New York, and ran into 1962. This album sold half a million by 1962 with a million by 1963. The contents of the disc are: **Overture; I Wonder What the King is Doing Tonight; The Simple Joys of Maidenhood; Camelot; Follow Me; The Lusty Month of May; C'est Moi; Then You May Take Me to the Fair; How to Handle a Woman; If Ever I Would Leave You; Parade; Before I Gaze at You Again; The Seven Deadly Virtues; What Do the Simple Folks Do?; Fie on Goodness; I Loved You Once in Silence; Guinevere; Camelot.**

Camelot cost $480,000 to produce, the money being put up by CBS. It was directed by Moss Hart. The disc was No 1 in the USA for six weeks, and in the bestsellers list for 265 weeks. Gold Disc award RIAA 1962.

VARIOUS ARTISTS *American*

ORIGINAL SOUNDTRACK WITH NATALIE WOOD, RICHARD BEYMER, RUSS TAMBLYN, RITA MORENO, GEORGE CHAKIRIS AND TUCKER SMITH

WEST SIDE STORY (Album) *CBS-Columbia 2070* [*USA*] *Philips BBL 7530* [*UK*]. For a second time this famous musical show of 1957 by Stephen Sondheim (lyrics) and Leonard Bernstein (music) sold a million discs. *West Side Story* won 10 Academy Awards including the 'Best Motion Picture' of 1961. The disc contains the following: **Prologue; Jet Song** (Russ Tamblyn and the Jets); **Something's Coming** (Richard Beymer); **Dance at the Gym** (orchestra); **Maria** (Richard Beymer); **America** (Rita Moreno, George Chakiris, Sharks and girls); **Tonight** (Richard Beymer and Natalie Wood); **Quintet** (Richard Beymer, Natalie Wood, Rita Moreno and the Jets); **I Feel Pretty** (Natalie Wood and girls); **One Hand, One Heart** (Beymer and Wood); **The Rumble** (orchestra); **Cool** (Tucker Smith and the Jets); **A Boy Like That** (Wood and Moreno); **I Have a Love** (Wood and Moreno); **Somewhere** (Beymer and Wood).

Natalie Wood's voice in these songs is not her own. The dubbing was by Marni Nixon, and some of Beymer's songs were also dubbed. Betty Wand dubbed for some of Rita Moreno's songs.

The stereo disc was No 1 for 54 weeks (May 1962–63); in the Top 10 for nearly two years in the USA; and in the bestsellers charts for 198 weeks. Gold Disc award RIAA 1963. Grammy Award, 'Best Original Cast Album Recording' (1961). In 1986, the RIAA certified

this album as multi-platinum, with sales of over three million in the USA alone. It sold over one million outside America.

THE ALLISONS *British*

ARE YOU SURE? *Fontana H 294* [*UK*]. This was the sole million seller for the 'Brothers' John and Bob — real names John Brian Alford born on 31 December 1939, London, and Bob Colin Day, born in Trowbridge 21 February 1942. Both were educated in London and first sang together in a church choir. They had a mutual passion for composing and singing, and, after perfecting their style by playing in coffee bars and local concerts, they won a talent contest in 1960 and an audition for Fontana Records. Fame came overnight when they took second place for Great Britain in the Eurovision Song Contest in March 1961 with their own composition **Are You Sure?** Prior to entering show business Johnny was an engineering draughtsman, and Bob a clerk. They made many guest appearances after the success of this song. This disc was No 1 in Britain for two weeks with 16 weeks in the bestsellers.

KENNY BALL AND HIS JAZZ BAND *British*

MIDNIGHT IN MOSCOW *Pye Jazz 7NJ 2049* [*UK*] *Kapp 442* [*USA*]. This first million seller for Kenny Ball, **Midnight in Moscow** is based on a song by the Russian writers Vassili Soloviev-Sedoi and M. Matusovosky, arranged by Kenny Ball. Kenneth Daniel Ball was born on 22 May 1931 in Ilford, Essex and started his career as a semi-professional with Charlie Galbraith's All Star Jazz Band in 1951, his former occupations being a salesman and working in an advertising agency. Lonnie Donegan heard them at a TV audition and was so impressed that he brought them to the attention of Pye Records who signed them up. Their first disc hit was **Samantha** (1961), then came the **Moscow** disc, which enjoyed tremendous sales all over the world, reaching No 2 position in the US hit parade in March

1962 with 14 weeks in the US bestsellers. It was No 2, and 21 weeks in the British bestsellers. In 1963 Kenny was the first British jazzman to become an honorary citizen of New Orleans. The original Russian title of the song was **Padmeskoveeye Vietchera**.

JOE BARRY *American*

I'M A FOOL TO CARE *Smash 1702* [*USA*] *Mercury AMT 1149* [*UK*]. Joe Barry (real name Joe Barious) came from Cut Off, Louisiana. He was educated at high school and started singing with gospel groups. He also studied music with the famed Al Hirt and Pete Fountain. Joe appeared at record hops and also on TV. He played guitar, drums and piano and wrote his own arrangements.

The song was written in 1948 by country-and-western artist/songwriter Ted Daffan. Barry's disc reached No 24 in the US charts with 12 weeks in the bestsellers, and No 49 in Britain, the million sale being reported in 1968. He was signed to Nugget records in 1968.

RALF BENDIX *German*

BABYSITTER BOOGIE *Electrola 45-DW-5880* [*West Germany*]. This first million seller for Ralf Bendix was an American song with German words written by Joachim Relin. Bendix was both a disc star and a director of TWA airlines in Dusseldorf, Germany. His first disc success was **Kriminal Tango** which sold over 750,000 in 1960, followed by **Babysitter Boogie**. In 1955 he appeared on a regular show for Pittsburgh TV in the USA. This disc sold its million on the Continent. This number was written by the American composer J. Parker in 1960.

BROOK BENTON *American*

BOLL WEEVIL SONG *Mercury 71820* [*USA*] *Mercury AMT 1148* [*UK*]. Brook Benton had a long run of hits on both the American Hot 100 and the R&B charts. Born Benjamin Franklin Peay on 19 September 1931 in Camden, South Carolina, he started singing with a local gospel group. He moved to New York and, while working in the garment industry and later as a truck driver, he wrote about 300 songs, did some minor nightclubs, and made some records for Epic and Vik. Some of his songs were recorded by stars like Nat King Cole and Clyde McPhatter. He then signed to Mercury and in 1958 had his first (minor) hit with **A Million Miles from Nowhere**. The follow-up, **It's Just a Matter of Time**, made No 3 in 1959 and became Benton's first million seller. In 1960 he teamed up with Dinah Washington and scored a second million seller with **Baby (You Got What It Takes)**.

The third million seller for Brook Benton, **Boll Weevil Song** was written in 1960 by Clyde Otis and Brook Benton himself. It is a new version of an old American song, telling the story of the farmer and the boll weevil bugs — the little eaters that devastate the cotton crops. The disc was No 2 for three weeks in the

US charts and 16 weeks in the bestsellers, and No 30 in Britain and nine weeks in the bestsellers.

ACKER BILK   *British*

STRANGER ON THE SHORE *Columbia (EMI) DB 4750* [*UK*] *Atco 6217* [*USA*]. This was Acker Bilk's first million seller. Its global sales were around four million by 1967, with the first million being sold by April 1962. The disc had the longest reign up to 1966 in the British bestsellers — 55 weeks, being No 1 for one week in 1962 — and was a No 1 chart hit in the USA also (for one week in 1962) with 21 weeks in their bestsellers. The tune was composed by Acker Bilk and issued by Atlantic Records in the USA as part of an album **Sentimental Journey**. Bilk named it **Jenny** after one of his children. About this time the BBC was planning to feature Bilk playing the signature tune for a children's TV series called **Stranger on the Shore**, so **Jenny** was retitled and issued in Britain as a single to tie in with the series.

Bernard Stanley Bilk was born on 28 January 1929, in Somerset. His father was a Methodist lay preacher, his mother a church organist. He took up the clarinet to pass the time while in an Army jail in Egypt for three months through falling asleep on guard (1947). After Army discharge, he gave up his job as a blacksmith and again took up the clarinet, forming his own group, the Paramount Jazz Band, in 1958. Gold Disc award RIAA 1 June 1967.

GARY 'US' BONDS   *American*

QUARTER TO THREE *Le Grand 1008* [*USA*] *Top Rank JAR 575* [*UK*]. The first million seller for Gary, whose real name is Gary Anderson, was

written by J. Royster, G. Barge, G. Anderson and F. Guida. Rock'n'roll singer Gary was born on 6 June 1939, in Jacksonville, Florida. He began singing at the age of nine in his church choir, and from 13 performing in different churches and choir groups. In 1952 he formed his own group the Turks, and became a solo artist after it disbanded. For some 12 years he was a resident of Norfolk, Virginia, singing in various local nightclubs. He then met Frank J. Guida, head of the Norfolk Recording Studio who felt he had great promise. His first disc **New Orleans** was a big hit, then came **Quarter to Three** followed by other hit singles. This disc was No 1 in the USA for two weeks and 15 weeks in the bestsellers, and No 7 and 13 weeks in Britain's charts.

In 1981 Bonds made a come-back with a new recording contract with EMI America, and new material written for him by long-time fan Bruce Springsteen. While he enjoyed hits with songs like **Jolé Blon**, the revival did not last, and without Springsteen material he once again faded away.

PAT BOONE   *American*

MOODY RIVER *Dot 16209* [*USA*] *London HLD 9350* [*UK*]. Pat Boone is a direct descendant of the American frontiersman folk hero Daniel Boone. He epitomized the clean-cut, white, middle-class, God-fearing all-American boy, an image that made him as acceptable to parents as to the young people who bought his records in huge numbers. He had enormous success, taking the R&B music of black America, knocking the stuffing out of it, and selling a bowdlerized and safe version to white kids. Though many of his early hits were with rock'n'roll records, he was never much of a rocker himself, always seeming more at home with ballads. He burst on to the scene in 1955, coming between Bill Haley and Elvis Presley, and for a while he gave Elvis a run for his money as America's leading teenage idol. He was as different to Elvis as it was possible to be, and though he soon ceased to compete directly with Presley he continued to make hit records. He chalked up 60 chart entries from 1955 to 1969.

Born Charles Eugene Pat Boone on 1 June 1934 in Jacksonville, Florida, his family later moved to Nashville, Tennessee, where country-and-western music and white gospel became major influences on him. It was not only in its music that the Church influenced Boone. Unusually for a fifties rock star, he publicly preached the virtues of church-going and respect for parents. He was an active church-goer himself, once refusing a film part because he had to portray a Catholic (he was a Protestant), and from the late sixties he concentrated on gospel recordings and tours.

While at school, he sang gospel songs on local radio and went on to win talent contests. It was also at school that he met Shirley Foley, the daughter of famous country star Red Foley (who also discovered Brenda Lee). They fell in love and eloped to Texas, where they married in 1953.

In 1955 Boone signed with Dot records, and began an amazing chart career. His first hit was

Two Hearts, which reached No 16. The follow-up, **Ain't That A Shame**, went to No 1 and sold a million. It was a cover version of the Fats Domino song, which also sold a million. This set a pattern of successful covers which usually outsold the originals. **I'll Be Home/Tutti Frutti**, **Long Tall Sally**, **I Almost Lost My Mind**, **Don't Forbid Me/Anastasia**, **Love Letters in the Sand/Bernadine** and **April Love** were some of his biggest fifties hits. In 1956 Boone signed a lucrative film contract with 20th Century Fox, which moved him further away from rock'n'roll.

After a string of only medium-sized hits from late 1958 to 1960, his second release of 1961 gave him his sixth and last American No 1. **Moody River** was written by Gary D. Bruce, and was Pat's 12th million seller. It was at No 1 for one week, with 15 weeks on the charts. Boone was also a big success in Britain, though his chart career was not quite as great as in America. He had 27 hits from 1955 to 1962, one of which (**I'll Be Home**) went to No 1. **Moody River** went to No 18, with 10 weeks in the British charts.

DAVE BRUBECK QUARTET   *American*

TAKE FIVE *CBS-Columbia 41479* [*USA*] *Fontana H 339* [*UK*]. Dave (David Warren) Brubeck was born 6 December 1920 in Concord, California.

Both this album and another, **Time Further Out**, had very big sales during 1962 and appeared in the Top 10 of the album charts. The uniqueness of **Take Five** resulted in its release as a singles disc in 1961 and it reached No 25 in the US charts with 12 weeks in the bestsellers, a high position for a jazz disc at a time when rock'n'roll still predominated. The disc was also a great favourite in Britain where it was No 5 for one week in 1961 and 15 weeks in the bestsellers. Sales around the world are said to be several million.

The Dave Brubeck Quartet was voted the 'Top Instrumental Group' of 1961 in America. It consisted of Dave Brubeck (piano), Paul Desmond (alto sax), Joe Morello (drums) and Eugene Wright (bass). Paul Desmond died on 30 May 1977, aged 52.

JERRY BUTLER   *American*

MOON RIVER Vee Jay 405 [USA]. This song, introduced by Audrey Hepburn in the film *Breakfast at Tiffany's*, received three Grammy Awards and had countless recordings. The biggest seller on disc was this version by Jerry Butler, which according to artist Andy Williams (who also had a big hit with it) sold over the million. Jerry's disc was released around October 1961, reached No 8 for two weeks and stayed in the US bestsellers for 17 weeks.

The song was written by Johnny Mercer (words) and Henry Mancini (music). Mancini, who scored the music for the film also had a hit with his version that reached No 11 and stayed in the US charts for 20 weeks.

RAY CHARLES   *American*

ONE MINT JULEP *Impulse 200 [USA].* Released in March 1961, this disc soon reached No 8 for two weeks on the US charts with 13 weeks in the bestsellers, subsequently selling a million, his third to do so. The song was a revival of a 1953 hit written by Rudolph Toombs who had a big success then with recordings by the Clovers and Louis Prima. It was No 1 for one week in the R&B charts during a 12-week chart run.

HIT THE ROAD, JACK *ABC-Paramount 10244 [USA] HMV POP 935 [UK].* The fourth million seller for Ray Charles was written by disc artist Percy Mayfield. The disc was No 1 in the USA for two weeks and 13 weeks in the bestsellers, and was No 6 in Britain with 12 weeks in the charts. Released 21 August 1961, it spent five weeks at No 1 in the R&B charts. It was Ray Charles' sixth R&B No 1 out of a subsequent total of 10 R&B chart toppers. It was in the R&B charts for 15 weeks.

CHUBBY CHECKER

PONY TIME *Parkway 818 [USA] Columbia (EMI) DB 4591 [UK].* Chubby's second million seller was written in 1960 by Don Covay and John Berry. This disc was No 1 in the USA for three weeks with 16 weeks in the bestsellers, and No 27 and six weeks in the British charts. No 1 in the R&B charts for two weeks, it is a rewrite of Pinetop Smith's famous **Boogie Woogie**.

LET'S TWIST AGAIN *Parkway 824 [USA] Columbia (EMI) DB 4691 [UK] re-released in Britain in 1975 as Let's Twist Again/The Twist, London HL 10512.* The third million seller for Chubby was written by Kal Mann and Dave Appell, both of Cameo's Artists and Repertoire Department. This disc was a top seller in Britain for two weeks in 1962, and got to No 8

in the US charts with 12 weeks in the bestsellers. Winner of NARAS Award for 'Best Rock and Roll Recording' 1961. With revivals up to 1975, it was 44 weeks in the British charts.

THE FLY *Parkway 830 [USA].* Chubby's fourth million seller was written by J. Madara and D. White. It got to No 7 in the US charts with 13 weeks in the bestsellers.

DEE CLARK   *American*

RAINDROPS *Vee Jay 383 [USA].* Dee wrote his own million seller **Raindrops**. He was born in Blythsville, Arkansas, on 7 November 1938, and is one of six children, having two brothers and three sisters. His family moved in 1940 to Chicago where he attended Farren Grammar School and, after moving again, graduated from Calhoun Grammar School. His musical interest stems from his mother, Delecta, a spiritual singer. In 1952, Dee joined a group, the Hambone Kids, and made a disc **Hambone** for Okeh Records. In 1955 he was with a group called the Goldentones, and they won first prize at Roberts Show Lounge in Chicago, a talent contest. This brought them to the attention of Herb Kent, a Chicago disc jockey who changed their name to the Kool Gents and took them to Vee Jay's studios. Their disc **The Convention** had Dee in the lead, and Vee Jay's artist and repertoire executive Calvin Carter saw tremendous potential in him as a singles artist. After a few discs, Dee's **Nobody But You**, a song he wrote, put him on the road to success, followed eventually by this hit **Raindrops**, which achieved No 2 in the US charts with 16 weeks in the bestsellers.

PETULA CLARK   *British*

ROMEO *Pye 7N 15361 [UK].* **Romeo** was reputedly the first million seller for Petula Clark, with its sale achieved in Europe in 1962. This song was originally published in Germany in 1920 under the title **Salome**, written by Robert Stolz, famous in Europe for his operettas. The English lyric for the new title **Romeo** was by Britain's Jimmy Kennedy (1961). (See 'Monsieur', 1962, for data on Petula Clark.) The disc was No 3 for two weeks in Britain and 15 weeks in the bestsellers.

THE COUSINS   *Belgian*

KILI WATCH *Palette 1001 [Belgium].* **Kili Watch** was both the first record for the Palette label and the first million seller (on the Continent) by this quartet of students: Adrien Ransy (drums), Gus Devon (lead guitar), Andre Vandemeerschoot (rhythm guitar) and Jacky (rhythm guitar). They were discovered at the club **Les Cousins** in Brussels, Belgium, from which they took their name. The disc got into the bestsellers list immediately and made the group one of the hottest combinations on the Continent. They appeared on TV and radio in Belgium, Holland, France, Sweden, Germany and Italy. This traditional tune was adapted by Gus Derse.

FLOYD CRAMER   *American*

ON THE REBOUND *RCA Victor 7840 [USA] RCA Victor 1231 [UK].* This second million seller for Floyd was his own composition. Written in 1960, it reached No 4 with 13 weeks in the US bestsellers, and No 1 and 14 weeks in the British charts.

THE CRYSTALS   *American*

THERE'S NO OTHER (LIKE MY BABY) — *Philles 100 [USA]* Phil Spector was working at music publishers Hill & Range when he heard the Crystals, and instead of signing them to his employers' Big Top label he signed them to his own fledgeling Philles Records instead. While this got him fired, it also resulted in the first hit for both of them and their first release to ultimately sell a million. It was written by the Crystals' friend Leroy Bates and produced by Spector at the Mira Sound Studios in New York. It reached No 20 with 11 weeks in the charts. (See the Crystals, 1962.)

JAMES DARREN   *American*

GOODBYE CRUEL WORLD *Colpix 609 [USA] Pye International 7N 25116 [UK].* This first million seller for Darren was written by Gloria Shayne. Darren (real name James Ercolani) was born in Philadelphia on 8 June 1936, and studied at the Epiphany and Southern High Schools there. His film debut was in *Rumble on the Docks* (1959), and later he starred in such films as *The Gene Krupa Story, The Guns of Navarone, Gidget* and many others. Columbia signed him to their record subsidiary Colpix, and Jimmy made discs in between making films, this disc being his biggest success. It was No 3 for two weeks in the US charts and 17 weeks in the bestsellers, and was No 28 in Britain, with nine weeks in the bestsellers.

JIMMY DEAN
American

BIG BAD JOHN *CBS-Columbia 42175 [USA] Philips PB 1187 [UK]*. This was a first million seller for country-and-western singer Dean, who wrote the song. He was born on 10 August 1928 on a farm outside Plainview, Texas, and began his musical career at the age of 10, first learning to play the piano, then mastering the accordion and guitar. Dean's musical and Air Corps careers developed simultaneously. He filled in as a replacement with the Tennessee Haymakers, a country-music quartet made up of Air Force buddies who played during off-duty hours in their Washington Base bars for $5 a night. In 1952, Dean caught the eye of Connie B. Guy who hired him to perform for the US troops in the Caribbean. After this tour Dean worked on radio and TV in Washington, and in 1957 began his CBS TV network show, winning many fans. In April 1957 he was signed to Columbia Records. **Big Bad John** was his first big pop hit, and was a top seller in the USA for five weeks and in the bestsellers for a total of 16 weeks. It was No 2 and 13 weeks in the British charts, Gold Disc award from RIAA 1961. Winner of NARAS. Award for 'Best Country-and-Western Recording' 1961. In the country charts it was No 1 for two weeks with a 22-week chart run.

JOEY DEE AND THE STARLITERS
American

PEPPERMINT TWIST PART 1 *Roulette 4401 [USA] Columbia (EMI) DB 4758 [UK]*. Joey Dee and his Starliters comprised Carlton Latimor (organist), Willie Davis (drums), Larry Vernieri and David Brigati (song and dance). **Peppermint Twist** was written by Joey Dee and Henry Glover. Dee was born on 11 June 1940 in Passaic, New Jersey. The group started in 1958, and played for over 12 months from 1960

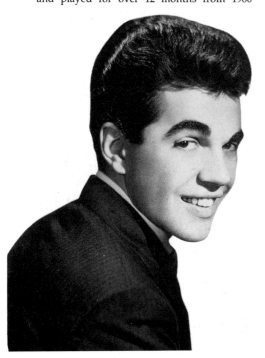

at New York's famous Peppermint Lounge, without doubt the home of Twist music, a nightclub that developed into a gold mine. They appeared in films including *Hey Let's Twist* and *Vive le Twist*. Roulette Records rapidly signed the group to record this, their first million seller and their biggest hit. They also had a hit with their album **Doing the Twist at the Peppermint Lounge**. **Peppermint Twist** was No 1 for three weeks in the USA in 1962 and 18 weeks in the bestsellers, and was No 33 in Britain, with eight weeks in the bestsellers.

DICK AND DEEDEE
American

THE MOUNTAIN'S HIGH *Liberty 55350 [USA] London HLG 9408 [UK]*. This first million seller for Dick and Deedee was written by Dick (real name Dick St John Gosting). Dick was 21 when he recorded the disc with an 18-year-old girl — Deedee. Dick had been recording for some time without success when he met the Wilder Brothers and Don Ralke who became managers and arrangers for them. They took Dick to a small California studio called Lama Records, to cut a song **I Want Someone** that Dick and Deedee (real name Sperling) had written. A female voice was needed for the flip side of the disc, so Dick called on Deedee whom he had known since junior high school for his song **The Mountain's High**. It was this side of the disc that broke first in San Francisco, spreading rapidly throughout the USA, when later released by Liberty Records. The duo did a tour of Texas with other disc stars, both returning to college and cutting more discs between studies, Dick at Los Angeles Art Center and Deedee at Santa Monica City College. This disc was No 2 for two weeks in the US charts and 15 weeks in the bestsellers. It reached No 37 in Britain during three weeks in the charts.

DION
American

RUNAROUND SUE *Laurie 3110 [USA] Top Rank JAR 586 [UK]*. Dion Di Mucci was born on 18 July 1939 in the Bronx district of New York, where he went to school. He was born into show business, as his father was a singer and his mother was in a stage act. He started singing when he was five, and made his first public appearance on the Paul Whiteman TV show in 1954. He made some records for the small Mohawk label, and then signed with Laurie. He teamed up with the Belmonts, and in 1958 they had their first hit with **I Wonder Why**. Their first million seller followed the next year, with **A Teenager in Love**. Dion made his film debut in *Teenage Millionaire*.

In 1960 Dion went solo, and after some minor hits came up with his first and only No 1, **Runaround Sue**, in 1961. He wrote the song with Ernie Maresca, and, though he married a woman named Sue, this was not about her. The record stayed 14 weeks in the American charts, and nine weeks in the British charts where it went to No 11. Dion toured Britain in 1961, undertaking radio, TV and live performances.

He almost made it two No 1s in a row, but the follow-up stalled at No 2. A string of Top 10

hits followed, and, though things were hard in the post-Beatles era, he scored a major hit in 1968 with **Abraham, Martin and John**. After a move to CBS, he went back to Laurie and had his last hit on Warner Brothers with **Your Own Back Yard**, which reached No 75 in 1970. The song was about drug addiction, which he had suffered from as a teenager. Though the hits had dried up, he continued to record. In 1975 he made an album produced by Phil Spector, which was only released in Britain. He now concentrates on gospel albums.

THE WANDERER/THE MAJESTIC *Laurie 3115 [USA] HMV POP 971 [UK] (re-released in Britain in 1976, on Philips 6146 700)*. **The Wanderer**, Dion's third million seller, was the follow-up to **Runaround Sue**, and was written by Ernie Maresca in 1960. The record was No 2 in America, with 18 weeks on the charts. In Britain the record gave Dion his only Top 10 hit, reaching No 10 with 12 weeks in the charts. The record was re-released by Philips in 1976, when it reached No 16 second time round, with another nine weeks in the charts. In America the B side, **The Majestic**, made No 36 with an eight-week chart run on its own.

LEE DORSEY
American

YA YA *Fury 1053 [USA]*. Irving Lee Dorsey was born on 24 December 1924 in New Orleans. His family moved to Portland, Oregon, when he was ten. In the early fifties he became a prizefighter known as Kid Chocolate, and developed into a contender for the World Lightweight Boxing Championship. He went into the US Navy for four years, and though he went back to boxing for a while he went on to work in a car repair shop in New Orleans. It was while underneath a car repairing it that he was discovered as a singer and given a recording contract by the small Fury label.

Ya Ya, which is slang for a boy or girl friend, was written by Lee Dorsey with C. Lewis and M. Robinson. Dorsey's first hit, it reached No 8 with 15 weeks in the *Cash Box* charts and No 7 with 13 weeks in *Billboard*. It spent 19 weeks in *Billboard*'s R&B charts, going to No 1 for one week. The song was also a British hit for Petula Clark in 1962. She sung it in a different style, in French as **Ya Ya Twist**.

Lee Dorsey had nine hits on the Hot 100, though only **Working In The Coal Mine** in 1966 made the Top 10. He had ten R&B hits, mostly on Amy, with five of them making the Top 10. In Britain his first hit was in 1966 with **Get Out Of My Life Woman**, which made No 22 when released on EMI's Stateside label. He had three further British hits, all in 1966, with **Coal Mine** and **Holy Cow** making the Top 10. Most of his major hits were produced by Allen Toussaint and Marshall Sehorn. A heavy smoker, he died of emphysema in New Orleans on 1 December 1986.

THE DOVELLS
American

BRISTOL STOMP *Cameo-Parkway 827 [USA]*. This vocal group comprised Len Barry, lead singer; Arnie Satin, baritone; Jerry Summers, first tenor; Danny Brooks, bass; and Mike Dennis, second tenor. They all came from Philadelphia, singing together from 1957 mostly for local and school functions. After their first disc, which was not a success, they went their separate ways, but got together again in December 1960. In the spring of 1961 they gave an audition for Dave Appell, a director of Parkway Records, and were signed to a contract. The Dovells then made this disc which quickly put them in the US limelight, following up with a string of hits. The Dovells' first million seller was written by Kal Mann and Dave Appell of Cameo Records. It was No 2 for two weeks in the US charts and 16 weeks in the bestsellers.

JOE DOWELL   American

WOODEN HEART Smash 1708 [USA]. The USA release of this version of the song also recorded by Elvis Presley in Europe, also sold a million. Joe Dowell's disc reached No 1 for a week and stayed in the US bestsellers for 16 weeks. It was released in June 1961.

Joe Dowell was born in 1943 in Bloomington, Illinois. He had a college education, and later made personal appearances. He is also a songwriter and plays guitar.

Wooden Heart is based on the German folk song **Muss I denn zum Stadtele naus** with words and adaptation by Ben Weisman, Kay Twomey and Bert Kaempfert (famous arranger/conductor). It was written in 1960.

JIMMY ELLEDGE   American

FUNNY (HOW TIME SLIPS AWAY) RCA Victor 7946 [USA]. Written by Willie Nelson, this disc is said to have sold a million through the years.

Born on 8 January 1943 in Nashville, Tennessee, Jimmy Elledge decided to become a recording artist, wrote a song, put it on tape and submitted it to Chet Atkins at RCA Victor. Chet signed him to a contract and **Funny How Time Slips Away**, his first record, became a bestseller. He later signed with the Hickory label. This disc reached No 22 with 14 weeks in the US bestsellers.

THE EVERLY BROTHERS   American

WALK RIGHT BACK/EBONY EYES Warner Brothers 5199 [USA] Warner Brothers WB 33 [UK]. **Walk Right Back** was written by Sonny Curtis in 1960, and **Ebony Eyes** was written by John D. Loudermilk. This disc, a No 1 seller in Britain for three weeks (with 16 weeks in the bestsellers), was the Everly Brothers' ninth million seller. **Walk Right Back** reached No 7 in the US charts and 13 weeks in the bestsellers. **Ebony Eyes** was No 8 and 12 weeks in the bestsellers.

FERRANTE AND TEICHER   American

TONIGHT United Artists 373 [USA]. This superb piano duet rendering of the hit song from the West Side Story musical of 1957 by Leonard Bernstein (music) and Stephen Sondheim (words) gave the wonderful team of Ferrante and Teicher their third million seller. It reached No 8 with 13 weeks in the US charts.

CONNIE FRANCIS   American

WHERE THE BOYS ARE/NO ONE [USA] — WHERE THE BOYS ARE/BABY ROO [UK] MGM 12971 [USA] MGM 1121 [UK]. **Where The Boys Are** was Connie Francis' 10th million seller, and came from the film of the same name, in which she made her acting debut. The song was written by Howard Greenfield

(words) and Neil Sedaka (music) in 1960. It reached No 4 for two weeks in America, with a 15-week chart run. In Britain the record reached No 5, with 14 weeks in the charts. This disc was a double A side on both sides of the Atlantic, but with different couplings in Britain and America. **Baby Roo** was listed in the British charts alongside **Where The Boys Are**. In America **No One** charted separately, reaching No 34 with eight weeks on the charts.

TOGETHER MGM 13019 [USA] MGM 1138 [UK]. **Together** is a revival of the 1928 song written by B.G. de Sylva, Lew Brown and Ray Henderson. Connie was accompanied by the Cliff Parman Orchestra on what was her 11th and final million seller. This record reached No 6 in Britain, with 11 weeks in the charts. This was exactly the same chart performance as in America, though there the B side also charted. **Too Many Rules** went to No 72 in two weeks of chart action.

FREDDY   German

LA PALOMA Polydor 2825 [West Germany]. The melody of **La Paloma** was written by Sebastian Yradier sometime before 1877. It is one of the world's best-known tango tunes. Freddy's vocal version was extremely popular on the Continent and produced a fifth million seller for him by 1962.

JUDY GARLAND   American

JUDY AT CARNEGIE HALL (Double Album) Capitol 1569 [USA] Capitol W 1569 [UK]. Judy Garland was born Frances Gumm on 10 June 1922, in Grand Rapids, Michigan, USA. Her family were vaudeville artists, and from three years old she began performing. She was signed to MGM at the age of 12, and made her first film for them, One Sunday Afternoon, in 1935. When she was 16 she starred in the film The Wizard of Oz, and in 1939 had her first million-selling record with **Over The Rainbow**, from the film. She also won an Oscar that year.

Starring roles in a series of musical films followed, together with performances on Broadway. Her second million seller was **The Man That Got Away**, from the 1954 film A Star is Born, in which she starred. She recorded first for Decca (then owned by British Decca), then CBS, MGM and Capitol. In 1961 she had her final million seller with this live double album. She died in London on 22 June 1969. Judy Garland was one of America's most celebrated performers. Her daughter Liza Minnelli has followed in her footsteps.

This two-disc album of Judy's sensational performance in New York's famous concert hall was recorded live in May 1961. The album was No 1 in the USA for 13 consecutive weeks, and in the US bestsellers lists for 85 weeks. It sold half a million by 1962 and the million subsequently. Gold Disc award RIAA 1962, and Grammy Awards for 'Best Engineering Contribution' (popular recording) and 'Best Album Cover', 1961. The contents of the discs are: Overture **The Trolley Song**, by Hugh Martin and Ralph Blane (1944); **Over the Rainbow**, by E.Y. Harburg and Harold Arlen (1939); **The Man That Got Away**, by Ira Gershwin and Harold Arlen (1954); **When You're Smiling**, by Mark Fisher, Joe Goodwin and Larry Shay (1928); Medley **Almost Like Being in Love**, by Alan J. Lerner and Frederick Loewe (1947); **This Can't Be Love**, by Lorenz Hart and Richard Rodgers (1938); **Do It Again**, by B.G. de Sylva and George Gershwin (1922); **You Go to My Head**, by Haven Gillespie and J.

Fred Coots (1938); **Alone Together**, by Howard Dietz and Arthur Schwartz (1932); **Who Cares?** by Ira Gershwin and George Gershwin (1931); **Puttin' on the Ritz**, by Irving Berlin (1929); **How Long Has This Been Going On?** by Ira Gershwin and George Gershwin (1927); **Just You, Just Me**, by Raymond Klages and Jesse Greer (1929); **The Man That Got Away**, by Ira Gershwin and Harold Arlen (1954); **San Francisco**, by Gus Kahn, W. Jurmann and B. Kaper (1936); **I Can't Give You Anything but Love**, by Dorothy Fields and Jimmy McHugh (1928); **That's Entertainment**, by Howard Dietz and Arthur Schwartz (1953); **Come Rain or Come Shine**, by Johnny Mercer and Harold Arlen (1946); **You're Nearer**, by Lorenz Hart and Richard Rodgers (1940); **A Foggy Day**, by Ira Gershwin and George Gershwin (1937); **If Love Were All**, by Noel Coward (1929); **Zing, Went the Strings of My Heart**, by James F. Hanley (1953); **Stormy Weather**, by Ted Koehler and Harold Arlen (1933); *Medley* **You Made Me Love You**, by Joe McCarthy and Jas. V. Monaco (1913); **For Me and My Gal**, by Edgar Leslie, E. Ray Goetz and George W. Meyer (1917); **The Trolley Song**, by Hugh Martin and Ralph Blane (1944); **Rock-a-bye Your Baby with a Dixie Melody**, by Sam M. Lewis, Joe Young and Jean Schwartz (1918); **Over the Rainbow**, by E.Y. Harburg and Harold Arlen (1939); **After You've Gone**, by Henry Creamer and Turner Layton (1918); **Chicago**, by Fred Fisher (1922).

JOHNNY HALLYDAY — French

LET'S TWIST AGAIN (Viens danser le Twist) *Phillips 4113 [France]*. Johnny Hallyday, the 'French Elvis', is reputed to have sold a million of his combined English and French versions of this American Twist song written by Kal Mann and Dave Appell in 1961, with French words by Gosset. Teenbeat vocalist/guitarist Johnny (real name Jean Philippe Smet) was born in

Paris in spring 1943 of a French mother and Belgian father. After his parents parted he was reared from the age of six by his aunt, wife of an American dancer in vaudeville named Lee Hallyday. With them he travelled the world from Cairo to Mexico City, eventually joining their song and dance act. He became France's first and most authentic rock'n'roller, the idol of the teenagers, by 1961 the highest paid pop singer on the Continent. He sold two-and-a-half million discs in 1961, a phenomenon in France. In his act, he sang about half the time in English. In 1961 he made a feature movie *Les Parisiennes*. By 1969 his disc sales totalled 12 million. He continued to have hits in France into the 1980s.

THE HIGHWAYMEN — American

MICHAEL (ROW THE BOAT ASHORE) *United Artists 258 [USA] HMV POP 910 [UK]*. The first million seller for this vocal quintet is a traditional song which is believed to have originated among slaves who travelled by boat each day between the mainland and their quarters on the islands dotted along the coast. This version was arranged by Dave Fisher. The group came into existence by mere coincidence. They got together to prepare an act for a party. It went over so well that they decided to continue with it, performing for their fellow students at college. In late 1960, they went to New York where they met Ken Greengrass, later their manager, who got the group signed to United Artists. They made an album that included **Michael** which, when released as a single, zoomed to the top of the US hit parade to become one of the top sellers of 1961. The quintet were Steve Butts, guitar and bass singer from New York City; Chan Daniels, guitar, charango and baritone singer; Bob Burnett, guitar, bongos, maracas and tenor singer, from Mystic, Connecticut; Steven Trott, guitar and tenor singer from Mexico City; and Dave Fisher, guitar, banjo, recorder, bongos, lead tenor, arranger and organizer from New Haven, Connecticut. The Highwaymen sang in English, French, Hebrew and Spanish, doing a spread of folk songs both American and foreign. This disc was No 1 for two weeks in the USA with 17 weeks in the bestsellers, and top seller in Britain for one week with 14 weeks in the Top 50.

JOHNNY HORTON — American

JOHNNY HORTON'S GREATEST HITS (album) *CBS-Columbia 8396 [USA]*. Johnny Horton died in a car crash on 5 November 1960, only 31 years old. Two months later CBS released a greatest hits album which over the next quarter of a century eventually sold over a million copies in America. Though Horton was a major star on the country charts, this album was his first pop LP hit, reaching No. 8 during a 34-week chart run. The RIAA certified the album Gold for million dollar sales in 1964, and Platinum for million unit sales on 21 November 1986. This was Horton's third and final million selling record, and his only million selling album.

All the tracks on the album were recorded in Nashville. The contents of the album (with the writer and the date of recording given in brackets) were as follows: **North To Alaska** from the 20th Century Fox film of the same name (M. Phillips, 9 August 1960), **Whispering Pines** (H. Halsey, 10 November 1958), **Johnny Reb** (M. Kilgore, 1 July 1959), **The Mansion You Stole** (J. Horton, 9 March 1960), **I'm Ready, If You're Willing** (V. Claud and J. Organ, 29 September 1959), **When It's Springtime In Alaska (It's Forty Below)** (T. Franks, 10 November 1958), **The Battle Of New Orleans** (based on the music of the traditional folk song **The Eighth Of January**, written in 1815, with words written by Jimmy Driftwood in 1955. Recorded by Horton on 27 January 1959), **All For The Love Of A Girl** (J. Horton, 27 January 1959), **Sink The Bismarck**, inspired by the 20th Century Fox film of the same name (J. Horton and T. Franks, 7 January 1960), **Comanche (The Brave Horse)** (F. Bandy and J. Horton, 11 March 1960), **Jim Bridger** (L. Payne, 10 March 1960) and **Johnny Freedom (Freedomland)** (G. Weiss and J. Styne, 11 March 1960.)

CHRIS KENNER — American

I LIKE IT LIKE THAT, PART 1 *Instant 3229 [USA]*. Chris Kenner was almost a one-hit wonder. His first hit was the million-selling **I Like It Like That, Part 1**, written by Kenner and Allen Toussaint. It reached No 2 for three weeks, and was 17 weeks on the charts. In 1963 Kenner had his second and final hit when **Land Of A Thousand Dances** climbed to No 77 in the US charts. He died on 21 January 1976.

GLADYS KNIGHT AND THE PIPS — American

EVERY BEAT OF MY HEART *Vee Jay 386 and Fury 1050 [USA]*. Gladys Knight and The Pips have had one of the most successful careers of any American group. Starting with **Every Beat of My Heart** in 1961, they have had a string of hits spanning the sixties, seventies and eighties. Gladys Knight was born on 28 May 1944 in Atlanta, Georgia. Both her parents were singers in the Wings Over Jordan gospel choir. She started singing as a young child, and followed the well-worn route of singing in her church and winning a radio talent contest. She teamed up with other members of her family to form the Pips. Apart from Gladys, the original line-up was her elder brother Merald, her sister Brenda, and her cousins William and Elenor Guest. Edward Patten, another cousin, then joined the group as a singer, and yet another cousin, James Wood, became their manager. As his nickname was Pip, he called the group the Pips.

The Pips recorded **Whistle My Love** for Brunswick in 1957. When this failed to take off, Brenda and Elenor decided that family life was a better bet than a singing career and left. The group later recorded for Huntom, Vee Jay, Fire and Maxx before signing to Motown's Soul label in 1965.

Every Beat of My Heart was first recorded for Huntom, a label formed to promote the song. This was taken up by Vee Jay, and reached No 6 in the charts with a 13-week chart run. By this time the group had signed to Fury, and re-recorded the song for them. The slightly different Fury version reached No 45, charting for seven weeks at the same time as the Vee Jay version. The song was written by Johnny Otis in 1952.

BOBBY LEWIS   *American*

TOSSIN' AND TURNIN' *Beltone 1002* [*USA*]. This was the first million seller for Bobby Lewis. It was written by Ritchie Adams and Malou Rene. Bobby was born on 17 February 1933 in Indianapolis and spent most of his early life in an orphanage. At the age of five, the orphanage board of directors sponsored him for piano lessons when he showed a remarkable talent for music. He was adopted at the age of 12, and taken to live in Detroit. Bobby began his career with an early morning radio show on a local station, then he travelled the usual round of local clubs and theatres. This disc was No 1 for seven weeks in the USA with 23 weeks in the bestsellers, and No 1 for 10 weeks in the R&B charts with a 19-week chart run.

GENE McDANIELS   *American*

ONE HUNDRED POUNDS OF CLAY *Liberty 55308* [*USA*]. This song was written by B. Elgin, L. Dixon and K. Rogers. Gene was born on 12 February 1935 in Kansas City, Kansas. At 13, Gene joined and toured with a gospel group playing the sax. After high school, Gene formed his own quartet, including everything from gospel to jazz in its repertoire. While touring with them he found time to attend Omaha University, Nebraska University and Omaha Conservatory of Music. He then signed with Liberty Records and gained attention with discs like **In Times Like These** and **The Green Door**, finally breaking through with his first million seller **One Hundred Pounds of Clay** (No 3 in the US charts and 15 weeks in the bestsellers), followed by other successes such as **Tower of Strength**.

HENRY MANCINI AND   *American*
HIS ORCHESTRA

BREAKFAST AT TIFFANY'S (Album) *RCA Victor 2362* [*USA*]. This was the second album to sell a million (by 1966) for composer/conductor Mancini. The stereo disc was No 1 for 12 weeks in early 1962 and the monaural disc was No 2 for two weeks. The album was in the US charts for 96 weeks. Tracks included **Breakfast at Tiffany's** (theme), **Holly, Something for the Cat, Moon River, Sally's Tomato, Mr Yunioshi, The Big Blow Out, Hubcap and Tail Lights, Latin Golightly, Loose Caboose, The Big Heist**, from the tremendously successful film that starred Audrey Hepburn and George Peppard, all composed by Mancini.

The song **Moon River** (with lyrics written by Johnny Mercer) won the Academy Award for 'Best Film Song' of 1961, and a second award went to Mancini for the best scoring of a dramatic or comedy picture. He also had two Grammy Awards for **Moon River** — 'Best Song of the Year' 1961, and 'Best Arrangement' 1961. By 1968, there were around 500 different recordings of **Moon River** and almost one million sheet music sales, the song earning Mancini $230,000 and Mercer over $100,000 by the end of March 1966.

This album received a Gold Disc award from RIAA in 1962, and Grammy Award for 'Best Film Soundtrack Album' (1961).

MANTOVANI AND   *British*
HIS ORCHESTRA

ITALIA MIA (Album) *Decca 0000* [*UK*] *London 3239* [*USA*]. This eighth million seller album for Mantovani achieved this figure by 1965. The tracks were: **Catari, Catari**, by S. Cardillo (1911); **Capriccio Italien** theme, by Tchaikovsky, arr: Milner; **Italia Mia**, by Mantovani (1961); **Vissi d'arte** (from *La Tosca*), by G. Puccini (1901); **Carnival of Venice** variations by Frosini; **Mattinata** ('Tis the day), by R. Leoncavallo (1904); **Bersaglieri March** by Eduardo di Capua; **Come Back to Sorrento**, by G.D. de Curtis and E. de Curtis (1911); **Return to Me**, by Danny Di Minno and Carmen Lombardo (1957); **Nessun Dorma** (from *Turandot*), by G. Puccini (1926); Italian fantasia medley — **Tarantella** (anon.); **O Sole Mio**, by G. Capurro and E. di Capua (1901); **A frangesa**, by Costa; **Santa Lucia**, by T. Cottrau (1849); **Maria, Mari**, by Russo and E. di Capua; **Funiculi, Funicula**, by Luigi Denza (1895).

This album was in the USA bestsellers' lists for 50 weeks, reaching No 8.

THE MARCELS   *American*

BLUE MOON *Colpix 186* [*USA*] *Pye International 7N 25073* [*UK*]. This quintet comprised Cornelius Hart, Fred and Allen Johnson (brothers), Ronald Mundy and Walter Maddox, all from Pittsburgh and then aged between 18 and 20. Their version of this famous song written by Lorenz Hart (words) and Richard Rodgers (music) in 1934 sold nearly two million. The quintet had formed and

disbanded several times before their manager, Julius Kruspir, thought them ready for Colpix Records. The Marcels appeared in the film *Twist Around the Clock* in 1961. **Blue Moon**, their first disc, was a No 1 in the USA for three weeks (with 14 weeks in the bestsellers) and in Britain for two weeks (with 13 weeks in the bestsellers). It also reached No 1 in the US R&B charts where it stayed for 11 weeks.

THE MAR-KEYS   *American*

LAST NIGHT *Satellite 107* [*USA*]. This novelty instrumental rhythm-and-blues group was made up by Jerry Johnson (drums), Steve Cropper (guitar), Don 'Duck' Dun (bass), Charles Axton (tenor sax), Don Nix (baritone), Wayne Jackson (trumpet), and Jerry Lee 'Smoochie' Smith (piano or organ). After being organized for three years, the group, which first consisted of four musicians, was in 1961 augmented by a brass section and an organist. These seven staff musicians for Satellite Records (now called Stax Records) of Memphis, decided to try a disc of their own, and helped by artists' and repertoire manager, 'Chips' Moman, they wrote and arranged **Last Night**. Teenagers took to their original sounding group and the disc zoomed into the hit parade, selling a million by 1962. It was No 3 in the US charts for two weeks and 14 weeks in the bestsellers.

THE MARVELETTES   *American*

PLEASE MISTER POSTMAN *Tamla 54046* [*USA*]. The girls of this vocal beat group, comprising Gladys Horton (lead singer), Katherine Anderson, Georgeanna Tillman, Juanita Cowart and Wanda Young, were all in their senior year at Inkster High School in Detroit when they recorded their first million seller. The Marvelettes were discovered by songwriter and Motown Records chief, Berry Gordy Jr at their school talent show early in 1961. He signed them to a disc contract. This, their first disc, soon got into the hit parade; the group then did a tour of theatre dates on the strength of its success in the USA. Further disc hits followed. The song was written by B. Holland, R. Bateman and F. Gorman. The disc was a No 1 seller in the USA for one week with 23 weeks in the bestsellers. It was No 1 in the R&B charts for seven weeks, with an R&B chart life of 23 weeks. Released 16 September 1961.

THE MIRACLES   *American*

SHOP AROUND *Tamla 54034* [*USA*]. The members of this major R&B group — Warren Moore, Robert Rogers, Ronald White, William 'Smokey' Robinson and Claudette Rogers (Smokey's wife), — came from Detroit and were around 21 years of age when the group was formed in 1958. This song was written by Bill Robinson and Berry Gordy, Jr (their manager and president of Motown Records). The disc, released 3 October 1960, sold a million by 1962. It was No 2 in the US charts and 16 weeks in the bestsellers, and No 1 in the R&B charts for eight weeks, with 16 weeks in that chart. It was the first of 48 R&B hits that lasted into 1978. Smokey Robinson went solo in 1972 and was replaced by William Griffin.

BOB MORE AND HIS ORCHESTRA
American

MEXICO *Monument 446* [*USA*]. Bob Moore (born Nashville, Tennessee, on 30 November 1932), living in the centre of the country music field, took up bass playing and after a few years of study obtained many studio dates. He made numerous cross-country tours of the USA accompanying the established artists including Connie Francis, Brenda Lee, Elvis Presley and Red Foley. Fred Foster, head of Monument Records, recognized his ability as a musical director and engaged him to head the orchestra on Roy Orbison's sessions. His band was so successful that it led to instrumental dates of his own. His first disc was **My Three Sons**, a fair hit, then came **Mexico** written by the famous songwriters Felice and Boudleaux Bryant. It is reputed to have sold a million to date. The disc reached No 7 in the US charts with 15 weeks in the bestsellers.

NANA MOUSKOURI WITH ORCHESTRA DIRECTED BY MANOS HADJIDAKIS
Greek

WEISSE ROSEN AUS ATHEN (THE WHITE ROSE OF ATHENS) *Fontana 412* [*West Germany*]. This disc reached the half million sale by January 1962 and the million later in the year. The song comes from the film *Traumland der Sehnsucht* (Dreamland of Desire), the tune being an adaptation of an old Greek song also known as **The Water and The Wine**. It was written and arranged for the film by Manos Hadjidakis. English words were written later by Norman Newell and Archie Bleyer. The voice of longing is the keynote of Nana

Mouskouri's success. She was born 10 October 1936 in Athens, Greece, and was already a success there before going to Germany. She got her biggest break when she met Manos Hadjidakis (composer of the sensational hit **Never on Sunday**) in 1958. He heard her sing and promised her material. In 1959 she made her first record in Greece and within one year was established as a top-disc artist. After winning several song contests, she went to Germany to record, her first disc there being this one of **Weisse Rosen aus Athen**, which earned her a Gold award. The Greek words were by Nikos Gatsas.

RICKY NELSON
American

HELLO MARY LOU/TRAVELLIN' MAN *Imperial 5741* [*USA*] *London HLP 9347* [*UK*]. Ricky Nelson was a nationally known star in America long before he made his first record. When he was eight, he joined his parents' long-running radio and TV show 'The Adventures of Ozzie and Harriet', playing himself. This family sitcom started in 1944, successfully transferred to television in 1952, and played until 1966. (When he married, his wife Kris played his wife on the show.) The family also made a film about themselves, *Here Come the Nelsons*.

Eric Hilliard Nelson was born on 8 May 1940 in Teaneck, New Jersey. When he was 16, he decided he would like to make a record. His father arranged a contract with Verve Records, who put out his first hit and million seller in 1957. The record company pushed **A Teenager's Romance** as the A side. Ricky preferred the more upbeat **I'm Walkin'**, a cover of the Fats Domino number, and this also made the charts. Verve and his parents saw his recording career as an extension and reinforcement of his family TV show, but Ricky wanted to be a rock'n'roll star. The result was that he soon left Verve for Imperial, where Lou Chudd was able to help him deliver a string of clean-cut late fifties hits mixing country music, rockabilly and rock'n'roll. They included **Be Bop Baby** (1957), **Stood Up/Waitin' in School** (1957), **Lonesome Town/I Got a Feeling** (1958) and the classic **Never Be Anyone Else But You** of 1959. His first No 1 was **Poor Little Fool** in 1958.

Travelin' Man was his second No 1, for two weeks. It was written by Jerry Fuller in 1960. The record spent 16 weeks on the charts, one week longer than the other side, which reached No 9. In Britain, the double A side reached No 2, with **Hello Mary Lou** the most popular side, and spent 18 weeks in the charts. **Hello Mary Lou** was written by Gene Pitney, who had recorded the song himself but without success. (Pitney would later have a highly successful career in both Britain and America.) This record was Nelson's ninth million seller.

Nelson tried to develop his career, dropping the 'y' from his Christian name in 1961, and signing to American Decca in 1963. Though Decca paid a million dollars for his services, the big hits almost completely dried up. He switched to Epic and then Capitol, but with little success. From 1957 to 1973, Rick

Nelson racked up 53 chart entries. This included 18 double A sides, with both sides charting. His penultimate hit, 1972's **Garden Party**, was his last Top 10 hit and million seller. In Britain he had 18 hits, only four of which made the Top 10. On 31 December 1985, Nelson, his fiancée Helen Blair and five members of his Stone Canyon Band were killed in an air crash in Texas.

SANDY NELSON
American

LET THERE BE DRUMS *Imperial 5775* [*USA*] *London HLP 9466* [*UK*]. Sandy Nelson was one of the most successful drummers in American rock. He had a string of instrumental hits, starting with **Teen Beat** in 1959. This was a Top 10 hit on both sides of the Atlantic, and his first million-selling record.

He was born Sander L. Nelson on 1 December 1938 in Santa Monica, California. He first performed as drummer in the local Kip Tyler Band, and later worked as a session musician. While working on a session with Original Sound Records he asked if he could record a drum solo, and **Teen Beat** was the result. His next hit came two years later with **Let There Be Drums**, written by Nelson himself and Richard Podolor. This second million seller for Nelson reached No 7 in America and No 3 in Britain. It was 16 weeks in the charts of both countries.

ROY ORBISON
American

RUNNING SCARED *Monument 438* [*USA*] *London HLU 9342* [*UK*]. Roy Orbison wrote this fourth million seller himself, with Joe Melson. It gave him his first American No 1, for one week, and at 17 weeks enjoyed the second-longest chart run of his career. (The longest was **Only the Lonely**, which was also his debut British hit and first UK No 1.) In Britain it made No 9 during 15 weeks in the charts.

CRYING/CANDY MAN *Monument 447* [*USA*] *London HLU 9405* [*UK*]. 1961 was a good year for Roy Orbison. The follow-up to **Running Scared** was the double A side **Crying**/**Candy Man**. **Crying** almost made it two No 1s in a row, but stalled at No 2. Like **Running Scared**, it was written by Orbison and Joe Melson, and sold a million copies. It charted for 16 weeks in America, and went to No 25 with nine weeks in the British charts. In America **Candy Man**, written by Beverly Ross and Fred Neil, went to No 25 and had a chart run of its own of 14 weeks.

EMILIO PERICOLI
Italian

AL DI LA *Ricordi 51202* [*Italy*]. *Warner Brothers 5259* [*USA*] *Warner Brothers WB69* [*UK*] **Al Di La** was the winner of the San Remo Song Festival in 1961, in which it was sung by Betty Curtis. The song, written by 'Mogol' (Guilio Rapetti) (words), and Carlo Donida (music), eventually amassed around 50 different recordings. An English lyric was written by Ervin Drake.

Pericoli's disc sold over 400,000 in the USA

on the Warner label (1961) and is said to have sold 1,300,000 globally by 1965, with particularly heavy sales in Latin American countries, despite only moderate sales in Italy itself. Emilio sang the song in the film *Rome Adventure* and this proved to be his international stepping stone to success. It was also used as the theme for Warner's film *Lovers Must Learn*, with shots of Emilio singing the song sparking off a rush for the disc, which achieved a position of No 6 in the US charts (1962) and 14 weeks in the bestsellers. It reached No 30 with 14 weeks in the British bestsellers.

Pericoli was born in 1928 at Cesenatico, Italy, the son of a sailor, the family living near Milan. He trained as an accountant, but developed his acting and singing abilities while at school.

GENE PITNEY   *American*

TOWN WITHOUT PITY *Musicor 1009 [USA] HMV POP 952 [UK]*. This was the theme song for the film of the same title sung by Pitney. The song was written by Ned Washington (words) and Dmitri Tiomkin (music). Gene was born on 17 February 1941 in Hartford, Connecticut, and was educated at Rockville High School, the University of Connecticut and Ward's Electronic School. He took guitar tuition for one year. Pitney began his career as a songwriter, supplying other performers with disc material, then with a disc rendition of his own song **I Wanna Love My Life Away** in which he produced all seven voices heard on the disc by means of electronics. This versatile singer/composer/arranger also plays the piano and drums in addition to guitar. His songs have been recorded by such artists as June Valli, Tommy Edwards, Steve Lawrence, Roy Orbison and Ricky Nelson. Gene has a voice that can reach such high notes that he does chorus bits of his own discs, aided by multi-tracking. He has made tours of Australia, New Zealand, Canada, Hawaii, England, Italy, Germany and France, and was particularly popular in England in 1963 when he came over to help promote his very popular disc of **24**

Hours from Tulsa. **Town Without Pity** is said to have sold a million by 1962. It was No 13 for two weeks in the US charts (1962) and 19 weeks in the bestsellers, reaching No 32 with six weeks in the British bestsellers.

ELVIS PRESLEY   *American*

HIS HAND IN MINE (Album) *RCA Victor LSP-2328 [USA] RCA Victor RD 27211 [UK]*. This LP was Presley's first full album of traditional sacred songs. Released in January 1961, the record reached No 13 with 20 weeks on the American album charts. It did better in Britain, where it went to No 3 with a 25-week chart run. The album was certified Gold by the RIAA (for million dollar sales) in April 1969, and Platinum (for sales of a million copies) in December 1977. This was Elvis' fifth album to sell a million, and his 24th million seller overall. The tracks on this album are: **His Hand in Mine, I'm Gonna Walk Dem Golden Stairs, My Father's House, Milky White Way, Known Only to Him, I Believe in the Man in the Sky, Joshua Fit the Battle, Jesus Knows What I Need, Swing Down Sweet Chariot, Mansion Over the Hilltop, If We Never Meet Again** and **Working on the Building**.

SURRENDER *RCA Victor 47-7850 [USA] RCA Victor 1227 [UK]*. The 25th million seller for Elvis had a reputed global sale of five million. The song was a new version of the 1911 Italian ballad **Torna a Sorrento** (**Come back to Sorrento**), originally written by G.D. de Curtis (words) and E. de Curtis (music). The English words and adaptation were by Doc Pomus and Mort Shuman in 1960. **Surrender** was No 1 in its first week in Britain and stayed there for four weeks. It was No 1 in the USA for two weeks and 12 weeks in the bestsellers, and 15 weeks in the British bestsellers. It was recorded on 30 October 1960, at the RCA studios in Nashville.

I FEEL SO BAD/WILD IN THE COUNTRY *RCA Victor 47-7880 [USA] RCA Victor 1244 [UK]*. The 26th million seller for Elvis Presley, **I Feel So Bad** was written by Chuck Willis. **Wild in the Country** was written by Hugo Peretti, Luigi Creatore and George Weiss. This disc was a top seller in Britain (with 12 weeks in the bestsellers) and a global million seller. **I Feel So Bad** was No 5 in the US charts with nine weeks in the bestsellers. **Wild in the Country** reached No 26. **I Feel So Bad** was recorded on 12 March 1961 at RCA Nashville. **Wild in the Country** was recorded in October 1960 by 20th Century Fox in Hollywood as the title track from the film of the same name.

LITTLE SISTER/(MARIE'S THE NAME) HIS LATEST FLAME *RCA Victor 47-7908 [USA] RCA 1258 [UK]*. These titles provided Elvis with his 27th million seller. Both songs were written by Doc Pomus and Mort Shuman. The disc was No 1 for three weeks in Britain and 13 weeks in the bestsellers, and a global million seller. It reached No 5 in the US charts with 13 weeks in the bestsellers. Both sides were recorded at the RCA studios in Nashville on 26 June 1961, and were produced by Steve Sholes and Chet Atkins.

CAN'T HELP FALLING IN LOVE/ROCK-A-HULA BABY *RCA Victor 47-7968 [USA] RCA 1270 [UK]*. Both sides of Elvis' 28th million seller came from the Presley film *Blue Hawaii*, the soundtrack of which also sold a million. **Can't Help Falling in Love**, adapted from **Plaisir d'Amour** by Giovanni Martini (1714–1816), was written by George Weiss, Hugo Peretti and Luigi Creatore (Gold Disc award on US sales). **Rock-a-Hula Baby**, written by Fred Wise, Ben Weisman and Dolores Fuller, achieved a global million sale. Both were taken from the filmtrack album **Blue Hawaii** and issued as a singles disc. **Can't Help Falling in Love** got to No 2 in the US charts with 14 weeks in the bestsellers. **Rock-a-Hula Baby** was No 23. The disc was No 1 and 20 weeks in the British bestsellers. Gold Disc award RIAA 1962.

BLUE HAWAII (Album) *RCA Victor LSP-2426 [USA] RCA RD 27238 [UK]*. The soundtrack album from the Presley film of the same name was Elvis' sixth million-selling album, and his 29th million seller in total. It was his biggest-selling album for RCA up to that time, going to No 1 in America for 20 out of the 79 weeks on the LP charts. In Britain it was No 1 for one week before being knocked off the top by the massive sales of Cliff Richard's film soundtrack **The Young Ones**. After six weeks at No 1, Cliff was in turn replaced by Elvis who had another 17 weeks at the top with **Blue Hawaii**. The album won a Gold Disc from the RIAA for million dollar sales in 1961.

Released in October 1961, the album sold 600,000 in three months in the USA and an eventual three million globally. All the songs on the disc were sung by Elvis in *Blue Hawaii*. The contents of the disc are: **Blue Hawaii**, by Leo Robin and Ralph Rainger (1937); **Can't Help Falling in Love** and **Ku-u-i-po**, by George Weiss, Hugo Peretti and Luigi Creatore; **Rock-a-Hula Baby**, by Fred Wise, Ben Weisman and Dolores Fuller; **Hawaiian Wedding Song**, by

Chas E. King (1926), English words: A. Hoffman and Dick Manning (1958); **Aloha Oe**, by Queen Liliuokalani (1878), arranged and adapted by Presley; **Almost Always True**, by Fred Wise and Ben Weisman; **No More**, by Don Robertson and Hal Blair; **Moonlight Swim**, by Sylvia Dee and Ben Weisman; **Ito Eats, Slicin' Sand, Hawaiian Sunset, Beach Boy Blues, Island of Love** (Kaui), by Sid Tepper and Roy C. Bennett. The film soundtrack was recorded by Paramount at the Radio Recorders studio in Hollywood between 21 and 23 March 1961. The album was produced by Steve Sholes, with Paramount's conductor Joseph Lilley doing the overdubbing for the film.

CLIFF RICHARD AND THE SHADOWS   *British*

THEME FOR A DREAM *Columbia (EMI) DB 4593* [*UK*]. 1961 started off with Cliff Richard at No 1 with **I Love You**, released at the end of the previous year. It was followed into the charts by his 10th million seller, **Theme for a Dream**, issued in February 1961. With advance orders of over 200,000 the record sailed into the charts at No 7 the first week of release in *Record Mirror* (and at No 11 in the *New Musical Express* and *Melody Maker*.) It peaked at No 2 in the NME and No 3 in the three other charts, with 14 weeks in the Top 50, winning Cliff his eighth Silver Disc in a row on 8 April. The Garson-Shuman composition was recorded at Abbey Road studios on 28 January 1961 and produced by Norrie Paramor. The record was, as usual, a big international hit, reaching No 1 in New Zealand and South Africa and hitting the charts in countries like Ireland, Denmark, Germany, Belgium, The Netherlands and India. On the B side, Cliff recorded **Mumblin' Mosie**, a 1960 American hit for leading R&B performer Johnny Otis.

GEE WHIZ IT'S YOU *Columbia (EMI) DC 756* [*Western Europe*]. **Gee Whiz It's You** was that rare event, a single that makes the charts without ever being released. Written by the Shadows' lead guitarist Hank B. Marvin and the group's former bass player Ian Samwell, the song had come second to **Please Don't Tease** in the teenagers' poll of 1960, when EMI invited 80 young people to choose Cliff's next record. EMI decided to issue this coupled with another Samwell song **I Can Not Find a True Love** as a single in Europe, pressed at the company's Hayes factory and exported to the Continent. Initial release was to be in Belgium and Holland to see how the record went. When it was a hit in both (No 2 in Belgium), it was made available in neighbouring countries.

Gee Whiz It's You was a big hit across Europe, but was never intended for British release. Both the tracks were on the **Me and My Shadows** album, and at that time in Britain tracks were not taken off albums for release as singles. Cliff Richard was then the most popular teen idol Britain had ever seen, with a huge army of fans eager for his every release. **Gee Whiz It's You** was the most popular track on the album, and though it was also released on an EP, when word got round that people could get the export single by ordering it from

their record shop, orders started pouring in. The record had already sold 40,000 copies by the time it made the charts on 30 March. It peaked at No 4 in *Record Retailer*, with 14 weeks in the charts. Though EMI did belatedly make sure that shops could order the record, it was never officially released in Britain. Its DC prefix denotes overseas release, as Columbia records issued in Britain had DB before the number.

After the disc's British success, it was released outside Europe. It made No 3 in Ireland, and was a hit in Australia, New Zealand, South Africa and India. As one of Cliff's upbeat numbers, it was a popular part of his stage act. As he toured the world in 1960 and 1961, playing in Europe, Australia, the Far East and South Africa, his global sales rocketed. Eventually **Gee Whiz It's You** passed the million mark on a worldwide basis. It was recorded on 17 March 1960.

A GIRL LIKE YOU *Columbia (EMI) DB 4667* [*UK*]. **A Girl Like You** was Cliff Richard's fifth British No 1, released in June 1961. It topped the *Disc* charts for one week on 15 July, and spent 14 weeks in the Top 50. It was written by Jerry Lordan, better known for writing instrumentals like **Apache** and **Wonderful Land** for the Shadows and **Diamonds** for Jet Harris and Tony Meehan. In fact, Lordan was a singer as well as a songwriter, and most of the songs he wrote had lyrics as well as music. **A Girl Like You** was produced by Norrie Paramor at EMI's Abbey Road studios on 28 January 1961. It was a big international hit, going to No 1 in South Africa and The Netherlands, and making the Top 10 in New Zealand, Australia, Eire, Sweden, and other countries.

WHEN THE GIRL IN YOUR ARMS IS THE GIRL IN YOUR HEART/GOT A FUNNY FEELING *Columbia (EMI) DB 4716* [*UK*]. This qualifies as the longest title of any of Cliff Richard's 100 hits to 1989. It was the first record from his fantastically successful film *The Young Ones*. **When the Girl in Your Arms** was the A side, and was one of two songs in the film commissioned from leading American song-writers Sid Tepper and Roy C. Bennett.

On 20 October 1961 **When the Girl in Your Arms** entered the *New Musical Express* charts at No 4 the first week of release, with **Got a Funny Feeling** also entering the Top 30 at No 23. The record peaked at No 2 the following week. It reached No 2 in four of the five British charts, with 15 weeks in the Top 50. This was the ninth Cliff single to be awarded a Silver Disc, on 11 November, four weeks after release. By the beginning of December, British sales had passed the 300,000 mark. **When the Girl in Your Arms** was Cliff's fourth No 1 in Norway and his sixth in The Netherlands. Among the other countries where it was a hit were Ireland, Australia, South Africa, Sweden, Denmark, Germany, Israel, India and the West Indies.

Got a Funny Feeling was written by Hank Marvin and Bruce Welsh of the Shadows. **When the Girl in Your Arms** was the first Cliff Richard single on which the Shadows did not play, the Norrie Paramor Orchestra providing the backing for this slow ballad. Both sides were produced by Norrie Paramor at Abbey

Road Studio 2, with Malcolm Addy and Norman Smith as engineers Smith went on to engineer records for the Beatles and produce Pink Floyd. It sold over a million copies around the world over the years.

With the exception of **Living Doll**, none of Cliff's records had been a hit in America. Cliff's management hoped that they could use *The Young Ones* film to have another go at breaking Cliff in the States. They were furious when they discovered that Connie Francis had covered the song, as it had been especially commissioned for Cliff. However, American law was such that nothing could be done to stop anyone covering it. The result was that Cliff's original was not released in America, while EMI, which distributed MGM in Britain under licence, did not release the Connie Francis cover in Europe. At the end of the year, Cliff again won all the popularity polls as 'Top British Male Singer'.

THE YOUNG ONES (Original film soundtrack album) *Columbia (EMI) 33SX 1384* [*UK*]. Cliff Richard released three albums in 1961. The first was **Listen to Cliff** which, like his two previous albums **Cliff Sings** (1959) and **Me and My Shadows** (1960), peaked at No 2 with 28 weeks in the album charts. In fact, the Shadows beat Cliff to the top of the album charts, their self-named debut LP going to No 1 for five weeks at the end of September. In a reversal of their role in the singles charts, where the Shadows knocked Cliff off the top three times, Cliff replaced **The Shadows** LP at No 1 on 4 November with his fifth LP and first No 1 album **21 Today**. Released to coincide with his 21st birthday, it was at the top for one week and in the charts for 16 weeks. Both these albums sold well by the standards of the day, but they paled into insignificance compared to the sales of his next release.

Cliff Richard's film career was designed to complement and support his role as a recording star. His first part was in the 1959 film *Serious Charge*, from which came the million-selling No 1 **Living Doll**. This was produced by Mickey Delamar, and Cliff signed a contract to make two more films for him. Later in 1959 Cliff got an offer to play a stronger supporting role in *Expresso Bongo*, from which came a million-selling EP and single. Delamar allowed Cliff leave to make *Expresso Bongo*, but by the end of 1960 it was clear that Cliff had become a much hotter attraction than he was before **Living Doll**, and was getting film offers that Delamar could not match. Delamar agreed not to stand in Cliff's way, and for a reported five figure sum he cancelled the contract. This paved the way for Cliff to take his first starring role, in *The Young Ones*.

The film was a musical in which Cliff played Nicky Black, leader of a youth club in Paddington threatened with closure by Nicky's property developer father Hamilton, played by comedian Robert Morley. The other star was the then 20-year-old South African dancer/actress Carol Gray, who played Cliff's girlfriend Toni. She joined the cast right at the last minute. The film was already a week into shooting and there was still no leading lady. Various names had been rumoured, including the young German singer/actress Heidi Bruhl.

seventies, imported copies were available from countries like The Netherlands and Australia where it was still in the EMI catalogue. It was re-released by public demand in 1983, and was one of the first Cliff Richard albums to be transferred to compact disc in 1988. It eventually sold a million copies worldwide, Cliff's first LP to do so.

In the US the film was re-titled *It's Wonderful to be Young*, with this title track added to the soundtrack. It was written by Burt Bacharach and Hal David, and was performed by Cliff, the Shadows and the Norrie Paramor Strings. Despite its release as a single, and a promotional coupling with *The Young Ones*, neither track was a hit in America. The version of *The Young Ones* in the film and on the soundtrack is not that on the single, which had an orchestral backing added.

The British version of the album, which was used throughout the world except in the USA, consisted of the following tracks: **Friday Night** (written by Peter Myers and Ronald Cass) performed by the Michael Sammes Singers and the Associated British Studio Orchestra; **Got a Funny Feeling** (Hank Marvin and Bruce Welsh), Cliff Richard and the Shadows; **Peace Pipe** (Norrie Paramor), the Shadows; **Nothing's Impossible** (Peter Myers and Ronald Cass), Cliff Richard and Grazina Frame with the Associated British Studio Orchestra; **The Young Ones** (Sid Tepper and Roy C. Bennett), Cliff Richard and the Shadows*; **All for One** (Peter Myers and Ronald Cass), Cliff Richard, the Michael Sammes Singers and the Associated British Studio Orchestra; **Lessons In Love** (Soloway-Wolfe), Cliff Richard and the Shadows; **No One for Me but Nicky** (Peter Myers and Ronald Cass), Grazina Frame and the Associated British Studio Orchestra; **What D'You Know, We've Got a Show** (Myers-Cass) and the Vaudeville Routine — **Have a Smile For Everyone You Meet** (Rule-Cunningham), **Tinkle, Tinkle, Tinkle** (Woods), **The Eccentric** (Cass-Myers), **Algy the Piccadilly Johnny** (Norris), **Captain Ginjah** (Leigh-Baston), **Joshua** (Lee Arthurs), **Where Did You Get That Hat?** (Rolmaz), **What D'You Know, We've Got a Show** (Myers-Cass) and **Living Doll** (Bart) — all performed by Cliff Richard, the Michael Sammes Singers and the Associated British Studio Orchestra; **When the Girl in Your Arms is the Girl in Your Heart** (Sid Tepper and Roy C. Bennett), Cliff Richard and the Norrie Paramor Orchestra*; **Mambo** — (a) **Just Dance** (Peter Myers and Ronald Cass), the Michael Sammes Singers and the Associated British Studio Orchestra, (b) **Mood Mambo** (Stanley Black), the Associated British Studio Orchestra; **The Savage** (Norrie Paramor), the Shadows; **We Say Yeah** (Peter Gormley, Bruce Welsh and Hank Marvin), Cliff Richard and the Shadows. In addition **The Savage** was a Top 10 hit for the Shadows, and **Peace Pipe** (the British flip side of **The Savage**) was issued as a single in some countries. **Lessons in Love** was also an overseas Cliff Richard hit, making the Top 10 in countries like South Africa, Denmark, The Netherlands and Poland. **We Say Yeah** (the British B side of **The Young Ones**) was a hit in Japan and Israel. *Indicates million-selling single.

The Shadows were also involved in the film, which was produced by Kenneth Harper and directed by Sidney J. Furie for Elstree Films through the Associated British Picture Corporation (which later became part of EMI). The original story and screenplay were by Peter Myers and Donald Cass, who also wrote some of the songs on the soundtrack. The background score, orchestration and musical direction were by Stanley Black, with music played by the Associated British Studio Orchestra with the Michael Sammes Singers and the Norrie Paramor Orchestra. The soundtrack was produced for records by Norrie Paramor with Malcolm Addy as engineer.

The Young Ones was a tremendous success. On the strength of just one film, Cliff Richard became the top box office draw of 1962. In the annual survey conducted by the *Motion Picture Herald*, Cliff was No 1, followed by Elvis Presley, though Elvis had three films on release in Britain in 1962. *The Young Ones* was also the second biggest money-maker of the year, behind *The Guns Of Navarone*.

The album did as well as the film had done. Released just before Christmas 1961, it was No 1 in the album charts for six weeks in early 1962, with six months in the Top 3. It spent 39 weeks in the *Melody Maker* LP Top 10, and 42 weeks in the *Record Retailer* Top 20. Its sales were obviously boosted by the success of the film, and by the title track which entered the singles charts at No 1 the first week of release in January 1962. It was by far the biggest-selling Cliff Richard album up to that date, and just as the film was a success all over the world, so also the album sold in unprecedented quantities. Though it was deleted in Britain in the

LINDA SCOTT · American

I'VE TOLD EVERY LITTLE STAR *Canadian-American 123* [USA] *Columbia (EMI) DB 4638* [UK]. The first million seller for teenage singer Linda Scott was a revival of the song written in 1932 for the US stage musical *Music in the Air* by Oscar Hammerstein II (words) and Jerome Kern (music). Linda (real name Linda Joy Sampson) was born on 11 June 1945 in Queens, New York and has been performing as a singer since she was four. She moved to Teaneck, New Jersey when 11 and enrolled at the high school there. In 1960–61 she divided her time between appearances at local functions and preparing for a disc career, which materialized with this recording. It got to No 3 in the USA charts with 14 weeks in the bestsellers, and No 7 and 13 weeks in the British bestsellers.

THE SHADOWS · British

FBI *Columbia (EMI) DB 4580* [UK]. After their first massive hit **Apache**, the Shadows released the double A side **Man Of Mystery/The Stranger** which reached No 2 in the charts. Their third release was **FBI**. This also peaked at No 2 (though it did not do so well in some charts). It spent 19 weeks in the Top 50. Released in February 1961, it won the Shadows their third Silver Disc on 29 April. Though it did not reach No 1, its sales were higher than other records that did. It also lasted longer as a seller once it was out of the charts. It has remained a favourite part of the Shadows' stage act right up to the late eighties, and was a big hit around the world. The Shadows were particularly popular in Japan, which is the second biggest record market in the world.

The writer credits on the record label indicate that **FBI** was written by the Shadows' manager Peter Gormley. In fact, it was written by Jet Harris, Hank Marvin and Bruce Welsh in Bruce and Hank's flat in Long Lane, Finchley. But, as there were some contractual problems following a less than advantageous publishing deal, Peter Gormley put his name on it, published it via a different company than the Shadows were contracted to, and passed the money over when he got paid.

The record sold 300,000 copies in Britain and a similar number abroad by the end of 1961. The record took over 20 years to sell the million globally. After **Apache** and **Wonderful Land**, it is probably the Shadows' best-known number. It was linked with these two massive No 1 hits when EMI issued a triple A side in 1975, and it was also included on the Shadows' **20 Golden Greats** album of 1977.

KON-TIKI *Columbia (EMI) DB 4691* [UK]. The Shadows' second No 1 was **Kon-Tiki**, an upbeat instrumental written by Michael Carr (who also wrote **Man Of Mystery**.) It was released in September as the follow-up to the film theme **The Frightened City**, which had followed **FBI**. It reached No 1 for one week on 30 September, had 12 weeks in the charts and won a Silver Disc. It also enjoyed considerable sales abroad, and was the Shadows' third global million seller.

DEL SHANNON · American

RUNAWAY *Big Top 3067* [USA] *London HLX 9317* [UK]. The first million seller for Shannon was a song written by him with the help of Max Crook. Del was born in Grand Rapids, Michigan on 30 December 1939. A successful songwriter and producer, he had a string of hits in the sixties, fought alcoholism in the seventies, and was back touring and charting in the eighties. This disc was No 1 for five weeks in the USA (with 17 weeks in the bestsellers) and four weeks in Britain (with 22 weeks in the bestsellers). Shannon's real name was Charles Westover. On 8 February 1990, at his Santa Clarita home, he shot himself.

HATS OFF TO LARRY *Big Top 3075* [USA] *London HLX 9402* [UK]. The second million seller for Del Shannon was entirely his own work. It reached No 5 in the US charts and was 13 weeks in the bestsellers, and No 6 and 12 weeks in the British bestsellers.

HELEN SHAPIRO · British

YOU DON'T KNOW *Columbia (EMI) DB 4670* [UK]. Helen Shapiro was the most sensational British discovery of 1961. She was born in London's East End on 28 September 1946, and started singing lessons in 1961, at the Maurice Berman School of Singing. John Schroeder of EMI called at the Berman School to find out whether there was any worthwhile talent, and heard Helen in the middle of her lesson. He was so impressed that he arranged for her to make some trial recordings. These were so good that the artists' and repertoire boss signed her up. John Schroeder wrote **Don't Treat Me Like a Child** specially for Helen, and

it became a hit. Then came **You Don't Know** which topped Britain's charts for three weeks with well over the quarter million sale, and a subsequent reputed million globally. By the end of the year her discs had sold over a million in Britain alone, at a time when she was still 14 and attending Clapton Girls' School. She became the only girl to make over a dozen radio and TV appearances before her 15th birthday. She was also featured in a documentary film *Look at Life*. After leaving school she made many tours and personal appearances round the globe. For a young singer she had dynamic drive and an inherent rhythmic sense, with confidence, assurance and personality quite outstanding for her age. She was voted 'No 1 Female British Singer' for 1961 and 1962. The disc was 23 weeks in Britain's bestsellers.

WALKING BACK TO HAPPINESS *Columbia (EMI) DB 4715* [UK] *Capitol 4662* [USA]. Helen Shapiro's second No 1 in a row was produced by Norrie Paramor, Columbia's director of A&R, who also directed the orchestral accompaniment. The record was No 1 for four weeks in Britain, with 19 weeks in the charts. It was her only American hit, though as small a hit as it is possible to have — it spent one week at No 100! The song was written by Mike Hawker (words) and John Schroeder (music), and sold half a million in Britain and over half a million in the rest of the world.

The follow-up to this, **Tell Me What He Said**, reached No 2, which meant that within her first year as a singing star she had racked up four Top Three hits, two of which had gone to No 1. Two had been million sellers, and all four had won Silver Discs for British sales of a quarter of a million. It was a tremendous start to her career, but it turned out to be over almost as quickly as it had begun. She had only one more Top 10 hit, and did not survive the change of style that followed the Beatles. She had 11 hits between 1961 and 1964, but made an impact that was remembered long after her hits had dried up.

TONY SHERIDAN AND THE BEATLES · British

MY BONNIE/WHEN THE SAINTS GO MARCHING IN *Polydor 0060* [West Germany] *Polydor NH 66833* [UK] *MGM 13213* [USA]. This sole million seller for Tony Sheridan reached its high sales figures only after the Beatles became famous. Though neither side is particularly good or representative of the Beatles, it was their first release to sell a million and is of interest for that reason alone.

Tony Sheridan, born Anthony Esmond Sheridan McGinnity in Norwich in 1941, went to art school in Norwich. Wanting to become a pop star, in 1961 he was one of a number of British hopefuls who felt that they could not get anywhere in England so tried their luck in Germany. He met the Beatles at the Top 10 Club in Hamburg. The group then comprised Paul McCartney, John Lennon, George Harrison, Stuart Sutcliffe (an artist friend of John Lennon who died in 1962) and Pete Best (who was replaced as drummer by Ringo Starr just as the group signed to EMI in 1962).

In 1961 the leading role model for aspiring pop stars was Cliff Richard and the Shadows. Tony Sheridan had a recording contract with the German record label Polydor and needed his own Shadows. As he had used the Beatles to back him at the Top 10 Club, it was a natural choice to ask them to help out at the recording session. Polydor were not very keen. Their producer Bert Kaempfert (who was also a successful recording artist himself) wanted Sheridan but did not think much of the Beatles. Sheridan insisted on the Beatles so they were signed up as well on 12 May 1961, but on a session fee not a royalty basis. All they got from the million sales of this record was £26. The recording session took place on 22 June 1961, on the stage of an infants' school where Polydor had set up mobile recording equipment. **My Bonnie** was the first number taped, followed by **When the Saints Go Marching In**, **Why** and **Nobody's Child**. They also recorded **Cry for a Shadow**, an instrumental written by George Harrison based on the Shadows' **Frightened City** which Bert Kaempfert liked. This was one of the tracks Brian Epstein later played to A&R men in England when he was trying to get the Beatles a recording contract of their own. It got the Beatles turned down as being a poor copy of the Shadows.

The first two songs recorded were chosen for release. Writer credits were given as 'traditional', though **My Bonnie** is believed to have been written by Charles T. Pratt under the pseudonyms of J.T. Wood and H.J. Fulmer in 1881. The record was released as being by Tony Sheridan and the Beat Brothers, because Polydor were not prepared to risk the German public mistaking the word Beatles for 'peedles', German slang for 'penis'. Two years later, EMI Electrola had no such qualms.

The record was a hit in Germany, where it sold over 100,000 copies. It was a minor hit in Britain, going to No 48 for one week in 1963. In America it reached No 26 in 1964, with six weeks on the charts. **Why** was another minor American hit (No 88 for one week) from the Sheridan Polydor session later in the same year. At a time when anything by the Beatles sold, this record eventually sold a global million.

Tony Sheridan went on to build a successful career in Germany, with a number of other hits to his credit. The Beatles went back to Britain, finally got a recording contract with EMI's Parlophone label, and went on to earn considerably more than £26 a record. Though they were to develop into a much more original and self-sufficient group, their time in Germany was very important. It transformed them from an amateur local group from Liverpool into a professional band capable of much more. This disc is the earliest recorded signpost along that route.

TROY SHONDELL   American

THIS TIME (WE'RE REALLY BREAKING UP) *Liberty 55353* [*USA*] *London HLG 9432* [*UK*]. Troy Shondell was born and raised in Indiana and was educated at Valparaiso University and Indiana University. He wrote his first song at the age of 14 (this was recorded by Little Anthony and the Imperials) and also learned to play five instruments. His recording career began in 1961 with **This Time**, which is said to have sold a million. It was written by Chips Moman in 1958. The disc, released in September 1961, reached No 6 for a week with 13 weeks in the US bestsellers. It was No 22 and 11 weeks in the British bestsellers.

From 1961, Troy toured the USA with many other top recording artists. In 1968 he became a songwriter for Acuff-Rose in Nashville and made the first recording for TRX Records, a branch of Hickory for whom he made some popular discs until 1969 when he went into the music publishing field. In October 1969, Troy was appointed as Assistant Regional Director of ASCAP's Southern Regional Office in Nashville.

THE STRING-A-LONGS   American

WHEELS *Warwick 603* [*USA*] *London HLU 9278* [*UK*]. This group comprised Jimmy Torres, lead guitar; Don Allen on drums; Aubrey Lee de Cordova on bass and guitar; Richard Stephens on guitar; and Keith McCormack on rhythm guitar, also vocalist. They started playing together in high school at local dances and parties. In late 1960, they auditioned and recorded for Norman Petty in Clovis, New Mexico. Petty liked the group and took their disc of **Wheels** to Warwick Records who signed them up. This tune was written by Jimmy Torres and Richard Stephens in 1960 in collaboration with Norman Petty. The disc was No 3 in the US charts for two weeks and 16 weeks in the bestsellers, and No 8 and 16 weeks in Britain's bestsellers.

SUE THOMPSON   American

SAD MOVIES (MAKE ME CRY) *Hickory 1153* [*USA*] *Polydor NH 66967* [*UK*]. The first reputed million seller for Sue was written by John D. Loudermilk. Her real name is Eva Sue McKee. She was born on a farm near Nevada, Missouri. From the age of seven she began singing and playing the guitar and entertaining at school and church functions. After the family moved to Sheridan, California, Sue kept singing while at high school and working at summer jobs. She entered a contest at the vaudeville theatre in San José, winning a fortnight's engagement there and a movie role. Local radio soon booked her, also TV, and then came recording for Mercury Records under Murray Nash. She also recorded for Columbia and Decca, eventually signing with the Hickory label and producing her first chart-topping disc **Sad Movies**. Many successful club and TV appearances followed, mostly in Las Vegas, where she lived with her artist husband Hank Perry. This disc reached No 5 in the US charts and was 14 weeks in the bestsellers, and was No 46 in Britain with two weeks in the charts.

NORMAN *Hickory 1159* [*USA*]. The second million seller for Sue Thompson was an even bigger success than **Sad Movies**. It was also written by John D. Loudermilk. This disc

achieved No 3 in the US charts and 16 weeks in the bestsellers.

THE TOKENS   American

TONIGHT I FELL IN LOVE *Warwick 615* [*USA*]. The Tokens comprised Mitchel Margo, Phillip Margo, Hank Medress, Jay Siegel and Joseph Venneri, all from Brooklyn, New York. They were originally a quartet formed by disc star Neil Sedaka around 1958.

Tonight I Fell In Love was their first hit, reaching No 15 in the American charts, where it had a 14-week run. Though released in Britain on the Parlophone label, it was not a hit. It was written by group members M. Margo and Hank Medress. Though the first Tokens' release to sell a million, this sale was achieved globally after the follow-up, **The Lion Sleeps Tonight**, had sold a million in America alone.

After this first hit, the Tokens moved to RCA. Later in the decade, they moved on to B.T. Puppy, Warner Brothers and Buddah, winning 11 hits betwen 1961 and 1970. Only one, **The Lion Sleeps Tonight**, made the Top 10; also their only record to chart in Britain.

THE LION SLEEPS TONIGHT *RCA Victor 7954* [*USA*] *RCA 1263* [*UK*]. **The Lion Sleeps Tonight** is a new version by Hugo Peretti, Luigi Creatore, George Weiss and Albert Stanton who revised the music and added new lyrics to the original song **Wimoweh**, a South African (Zulu) folk song **Mbube**, adapted and arranged by Paul Campbell, with English words by Roy Ilene, in 1951. This disc was No 1 for three weeks in the USA and 15 weeks in the bestsellers, and No 11 and 12 weeks in the British bestsellers. Gold Disc RIAA 1962.

In 1982, a revival of this record by the British male/female vocal group Tight Fit was No 1 for three weeks on the Jive label.

PHILIP UPCHURCH COMBO *American*

YOU CAN'T SIT DOWN, PART 2 *Boyd 3398 [USA] Sue WI 4005 [UK]*. Phil Upchurch recorded this disc (Parts 1 and 2) in Oklahoma City, and it was Part 2 that caught the fancy of the fans. It is said to have sold a million in the USA subsequently, and became a standard rave record. The disc was released five years later in Britain (1966) by Sue Records. It was written by Dee Clark, Cornell Muldrow and Kal Mann in 1960, and reached No 29 in the USA charts, and No 39 in Britain.

LEROY VAN DYKE *American*

WALK ON BY *Mercury 71834 [USA] Mercury AMT 1166 [UK]*. Leroy van Dyke was born on 4 October 1929 in Spring Fork, Sedalia, Missouri, and worked on his father's farm. He had a BSc from the University of Missouri, and intended to make farming his career. He took up the guitar while serving with the American Army in Korea. On his return, he attended the Auctioneering School in Decatur, Illinois, and went into livestock auctioneering and promotion. All this came together when, having entered various talent contests, he sang a composition of his own about auctioneering. He won the contest, got a recording deal with Dot Records, and **The Auctioneer** became his first hit and million-selling record in 1956. He developed into a successful country artist, though his next cross-over on to the national charts was not until 1961 with **Walk On By**. The song was written by Kendall Hayes. No 1 in the US C&W charts for a staggering 19 weeks with a country chart life of 37 weeks, it had an estimated one and a half million sale. It was No 5 for three weeks in the US national charts and 16 weeks in the bestsellers, and No 5 and 17 weeks in the British charts.

BILLY VAUGHN *American*

WHEELS/ORANGE BLOSSOM SPECIAL *Dot 16174 [USA]*. Billy Vaughn was musical director for Dot Records. As such, he and his orchestra appeared on many of the label's fifties hits, including million sellers like the Fontane Sisters' **Hearts of Stone** (1954) and a string of 1957 Pat Boone hits including **Love Letters in the Sand**.

Billy Vaughn was born in Bowling Green, Kentucky. At Western Kentucky College he became a member of the Hilltoppers who, from their formation in 1952, enjoyed a string of hits throughout the fifties. Their version of the 1934 hit **PS I Love You**, released in 1953, sold a million copies. Vaughn was both a singer with the quartet and their musical director.

He enjoyed a number of hits of his own, starting with the million-selling **Melody Of Love** in 1954. He had 28 entries in the American singles chart up to 1965 (23 records, on five of which both sides charted separately). He lasted longer on the album charts, with 36 hit LPs from 1958 to 1970. In Britain his success was much more limited, with two minor hit singles in 1956 and no hit albums.

Vaughn was very popular in Germany, with two million-selling singles licensed to British Decca's subsidiary Teldec. The first was **La Paloma** (1958) and the second was **Wheels**, Vaughn's fourth million seller in total. **Wheels** was written by Jimmy Torres, Richard Stevens and Norman Petty, and went to No 28 in the USA, with eight weeks on the charts. In America the flip side, **Orange Blossom Special**, also charted, reaching No 63 with a six-week run. It was written by E.T Rouse.

BOBBY VEE *American*

TAKE GOOD CARE OF MY BABY *Liberty 55354 [USA] London HLG 9438 [UK]*. This third million seller for Bobby Vee was another big song success for writers (husband and wife) Gerry Goffin and Carole King. The disc was No 1 for three weeks in the USA and 15 weeks in the bestsellers, and a chart topper in Britain for one week with 16 weeks in bestsellers.

RUN TO HIM *Liberty 55388 [USA] London HLG 9470 [UK]*. Million seller No 4 for Bobby Vee was written by Gerry Goffin and Jack Keller. It reached No 2 in the American charts, with a 15-week chart run. In Britain the record went to No 6 with 15 weeks in the charts. In the USA the flip side **Walkin' With My Angel** reached No 53 during nine weeks in the Hot 100.

THE VENTURES *American*

PERFIDIA *Dolton 28 [USA] London HLG 9232 [UK]*. The tune of this second million seller for the Ventures is a Latin American oldie of 1939 written by Alberto Dominguez. The disc was No 15 and 13 weeks in the USA bestsellers, and No 4 and 13 weeks in Britain's bestsellers.

FARON YOUNG *American*

HELLO WALLS *Capitol 4533 [USA]*. Faron Young was born on 25 February 1932 in Shreveport, Louisiana. His father bought a small dairy farm and moved away from the city, and it was here that Faron got his first guitar, and sang mostly to the cattle.

Later came an opportunity to sing on the 'Louisiana Hayride' on Shreveport's radio station KWKH. He did so well that they kept him for two years. In 1951 a talent scout for a small record label heard him on the show, and soon after he recorded **Tattle Tale Tears** for the Gotham label — his first hit.

His professional career began with this, and after a second Gotham release, Ken Nelson, Capitol Records' brilliant country producer who had heard Faron on this 15-minute morning radio show for KWKH, signed him to the label. Jack Stapp, programme manager for WSM's Grand Ole Opry, booked Faron for two guest appearances. Faron came for two weeks and stayed on the show for 11 years as a feature performer.

Hubert Long, a former record distributor, became Faron's manager, got bookings and helped get Faron in the movies. One of the movies Faron made in the early 1950s was *The Young Sheriff*, a label that stuck. Faron later called himself 'The Singing Sheriff'.

Throughout his career he had scores of hits for Capitol, the biggest being this disc of **Hello Walls** written by RCA artist Willie Nelson, one of the many people Faron befriended when in need. These also included Roger Miller, Johnny Cash and songwriter Kris Kristofferson. Faron later switched to Mercury Records, with most of his releases making the Top 10.

A successful business man, he became president of *Music City News*, a Nashville newspaper concerned solely with country music distributed throughout the world.

By 1971, Faron Young had recorded over 35 albums and nearly 500 songs, 57 of his songs making the Top 10 charts of the national trade publications.

Hello Walls was released in February 1961 and eventually sold over two million. It reached No 12 for two weeks in the US charts and was 15 weeks in the bestsellers.

Faron's other films were *Daniel Boone*, *Country Music Holiday* and *Hidden Guns*. He has appeared on network and syndicated TV programmes and has visited Europe, Canada and Mexico.

1 9 6 2

Cliff Richard started 1962 at the peak of his fame, thanks largely to his hugely successful film *The Young Ones*. The title track from the film entered the charts at No 1 first week of release with a record advance order of 524,000 copies, and sales of 830,000 four weeks after release. The album soundtrack sold 110,000 in six weeks, a then unheard of figure. Both single and album were also massive international hits. While Cliff had the biggest selling record of 1962, the Shadows had the biggest chart hit of the year with **Wonderful Land**.

Cliff undertook more touring around the world, with a major six-week push in the USA and a South American tour planned. Despite heavy promotion, *The Young Ones* film did not make it in America, where it was re-titled *Wonderful To Be Young*, though it did very well in Canada.

In March Cliff Richard was voted the Variety Club Show Business Personality of 1961. In April both the Shadows and Cliff received Ivor Novello Awards for outstanding services to British music during the previous year. In the music-paper polls Cliff was again voted Top British Male Singer, and runner-up to Elvis Presley in the World Male Singer section. No other British artist had ever reached such a high position in any world section of a poll.

After starring with Cliff at the *NME* Poll Winners concert at Wembley on 15 April, Jet Harris left the Shadows. In May Cliff won the 100th Silver Disc awarded, for **I'm Looking Out The Window/Do You Want To Dance**. The same month he started filming the follow-up to *The Young Ones*. *Summer Holiday* went on to be an even bigger box office hit in 1963. **The Next Time/Bachelor Boy** was his final release of the year, reaching No 1 as the new year dawned.

Cliff Richard has had the most remarkable career of any British solo rock star. He started in 1958, with the million-selling **Move It**, and by 1989 he had achieved 100 hits in Britain, with an additional eight B sides charting as well. He had 13 No 1s, and was the only artist ever to have No 1 singles in the fifties, sixties, seventies and eighties. He made the Top 3 31 times, and had 60 Top 10 hits. In 30 years only five of his records have failed to make the charts. He was Top British Male Singer in 1959 and for almost every year of the sixties, winning some award or another almost every year of his career. Thirty years after he started, Cliff had both the 1988 Christmas No 1 single and album, and in February 1989 picked up two prestigious awards in one week. He won the BPI Special Award for Outstanding Achievement (awarded only once in any artist's lifetime) and was voted Top Singer or Group for the fifth time in ten years by readers of *TV Times*. By 1989, Cliff Richard had sold over 77 million singles, 5 million EPs and 30 million albums.

The Media

A dispute between ITV and the actors' union Equity kept many pop stars off British TV. In the music press *Melody Maker* celebrated its 1,500th issue, boasting that most national newspapers used its charts. The *New Musical Express* had a bigger circulation than all the other music papers put together, and in March announced that in what was its tenth anniversary year its circulation had risen above 200,000 copies a week. By 1988 it had dropped to less than half that, at only 92,667. The *NME* started its first album chart, a Top 10, on 8th June. Elvis Presley was No 1 with the *Blue Hawaii* soundtrack.

America

1962 was an unusually good year for British records in America. For the first time ever two British records made No 1 in the States. Acker Bilk's **Stranger On The Shore** was the first. It reflected a resurgence for jazz, with Kenny Ball and Chris Barber also enjoying success. The Tornados' **Telstar** was the other, the first record by a British group to top the American charts.

A market research company announced that its survey of the pop scene showed that Chubby Checker had replaced Elvis Presley as the most popular male pop star in America, and Checker racked up three No 1 singles in the *Cash Box* charts. Elvis sold a million copies of his *Blue Hawaii* soundtrack album in America, and another half a million in the rest of the world. RCA announced that Presley had won his 30th Gold Disc for the album, somewhat to the embarrassment of his manager Col. Tom Parker who the previous year had announced that Presley had won 40 such discs.

A number of major artists switched labels in 1962. Paul Anka went from ABC to RCA, Anita Bryant from Carlton to CBS, Andy Williams from Cadence to CBS, Duane Eddy from Jamie to RCA, and Steve Lawrence and Eydie Gormé from United Artists to CBS. Warner Brothers signed Peter, Paul and Mary. CBS was also nurturing new talent for the future, with Bob Dylan making his second album for the company. CBS signed Barbra Streisand, who was described by *Variety* as the 'legit and nitery thrush'. The year saw the beginnings of greater things yet to come with the Beach Boys getting their first hit with **Surfin'** in February. The Beatles were turned down by Decca, and the Columbia and HMV divisions of EMI. The company's Parlophone label finally signed them, and in October the Beatles' first single, **Love Me Do**, entered the British charts.

The Twist came roaring back into fashion, giving Chubby Checker what remains to this day the unique distinction of being the only artist in the USA ever to go to No 1 one year, fall off the charts, and then return to the top in a second chart run in a subsequent year. He did it with **The Twist**. The dance was banned by some Catholic Church authorities in America. By September *Variety* were reporting that the Twist was being replaced by the Bossa Nova.

Crossing The Atlantic

As usual, a number of American stars crossed the Atlantic for promotional trips to Britain. Jerry Lee Lewis brought his wife Myra, and met a very different reception to their first visit in 1958. Myra was then only 14, and though the couple were married there was a public outcry about this child bride which led to the cancellation of the tour. This time, tragically, their three-year-old son Steve toddled into the family swimming pool and drowned just before the British tour. The couple still came, and were well received.

Frank Sinatra flew to Britain for concerts, Judy Garland came to record at EMI's Abbey Road studios, and Bruce Channel toured. The Everly Brothers also visited, though Don collapsed during the tour leaving Phil to finish on his own. (Billy Fury and Marty Wilde also collapsed, while on the Big Star Show of 1962.)

Connie Francis crossed the Atlantic, but to film in Italy. EMI took the opportunity to send Norman Newell and Geoff Love out to record some material for the European market. To the intense annoyance of EMI and Cliff Richard, she later covered Cliff's **When The Girl In Your Arms** from the film *The Young Ones*. Though it made No 10 in America, EMI would not release it in Europe.

The Record Industry

The most important events on the American record industry front both concerned small independent companies rather than the majors. Phil Spector, aged 21, bought out his partner to become sole owner of Philles, and launched the Crystals. He became the most famous record producer of all. Berry Gordy got Motown into gear, with the Tamla Motown rock'n'roll show touring America. Artists included the Supremes and 'Little Stevie Wonder, the 12 year old genius'. Motown had their first million seller, with the Miracles' **You've Really Got A Hold On Me**.

The FTC charged CBS with being a monopoly. The attack came from the dominant position that the company enjoyed in its record club activities rather than its chart share. CBS derived 60% of its record sales from its club. The FTC tried to force other record companies who licensed their product to the CBS club to withdraw from it.

In Britain, white Jamaican Chris Blackwell formed Island Records, initially as an outlet for West Indian recordings. His frontal assault on the majors was unusual. The big four (EMI, Decca, Philips and Pye) had 97% of the British market. Artists like Acker Bilk and producers like Joe Meek prefered to lease material to the majors rather than set up in competition with them. Island survived and prospered, being bought by PolyGram in 1989 for £200 million. A more typical story was that of 23-year-old Canadian Peter Snell. Who remembers his Aral label now? It folded soon after its launch in June.

EMI, which suffered a fire at its Manchester Square headquarters in April, launched its new Stateside label on 17 June. Designed as an outlet for American indies, it was meant to rival Decca's famous London label. It never did, for though it achieved some success, especially with Tamla

Motown product, it came at the wrong time. American labels wanted their own logos, which EMI and Decca were reluctant to agree to. Pye won a number of US labels for British distribution by offering them their own identity. CBS finally established their own label in Britain, though still under licence to Philips.

In April *Disc* asked 'Can Concrete Music Hit The Charts?' They reported the release of **Time Beat** by Ray Cathode, which was in fact a creation of Parlophone A&R man George Martin. He had recorded the BBC TV electronic interval signal and added a rhythm track. While electronic, or concrete, music was not new, it was new to pop music. The record went down like a lead balloon, though Martin had more success with a new group he had signed later in the year.

Two British record producers are worth mentioning. Columbia's Norrie Paramor produced records that spent half the year at No 1. Among his 26 weeks at the top were records by Cliff Richard, the Shadows, Helen Shapiro and Frank Ifield. His success with schoolgirl Shapiro led to a general scramble for girl singers, though to little avail. Joe Meek was the opposite to EMI's Paramor. He was an independent producer in an age dominated by the majors and their staff producers. He had founded his own label in 1960, and though it soon folded his independent product included smash hits by John Leyton (**Johnny Remember Me**) and Billy Fury's backing group the Tornados (**Telstar**). Like Phil Spector, he often wrote material for his acts to record.

Disc predicted that the Cinebox, an early video juke box, would revolutionize the music industry. It didn't. In their continuing feud, Frank Sinatra sued Capitol in America, claiming his former record company was trying to run him out of business. Sinatra lost the case. After the radio payola scandals of 1959 and 1960 came allegations of shop payola. While record companies paying shops to display their product and play it in store was not new, the practice had reached new heights in America in 1962.

When rock'n'roll burst out in the fifties, few senior executives with the major record companies either liked or understood the new music. The US majors continued to stick with the tried and trusted singers of the early fifties, referring to their style as 'good music'. In April 1962 Atlantic Vice President Nesuhi Ertegun attacked the practice. 'The term "good music" as it is used today in the trade is a hoax. It's a joke, a fallacy and an insult.' He went on to attack the suggestion that rock'n'roll and R&B were not good music.

In Europe, the Dutch electricals giant Philips merged its Phonogram records subsidiary with the DGG/Polydor records wing of the German company Seimens. It was to be ten years before the new PolyGram company adopted an integrated management structure combining the two record companies. In the seventies PolyGram acquired the record interests of MGM and British Decca, becoming one of the five global record industry majors. Originally owned 50/50 by Philips and Seimens, the Germans eventually sold out to Philips. In the late 1980s PolyGram went on to buy Island and A&M, making them one of the biggest record companies in the world.

World News

In Britain the Liberals won a spectacular by-election victory at Orpington. Four months later Premier Harold Macmillan sacked one third of his cabinet in a move that most commentators attributed to panic after by-election set-backs. The Commonwealth Immigration Act was passed in July, restricting black immigration into Britain. The British Antarctic Territory was created, and Malta, Jamaica, Trinidad and Uganda were given their independence. James Hanratty was hanged for the A6 murder, and in Israel former Nazi leader Adolf Eichmann was also hanged. The new Coventry Cathedral was consecrated. In May the last trolleybuses in London were retired.

In December Prime Minister Harold Macmillan met President Kennedy in the British colony of the Bahamas, and agreed the British purchase of the Polaris submarine-based nuclear deterrent. In London, Amnesty International was formed to campaign for human rights.

In October the world hovered on the brink of nuclear war as President Kennedy and Russian leader Nikita Khruschev argued over Russia's attempt to station missiles in Cuba capable of hitting the USA. After an American naval blockade of Cuba the Russians backed down.

Marilyn Monroe died of an overdose of sleeping pills at her Hollywood home. The American sex symbol had had a relationship with President Kennedy, and the exact details of her final hours have remained shrouded in mystery ever since her death.

In the American Deep South blacks continued their fight against racist segregation laws. Rev. Martin Luther King was arrested for the third time in August, while violence errupted at the University of Mississippi as the first black student was enrolled, protected by a large body of Federal Marshals led by the US Deputy Attorney-General.

In France violence continued until General de Gaulle gave independence to Algeria. China invaded India over a border dispute. After heavy fighting the Chinese won. In South Africa Nelson Mandela was jailed for five years for incitement. The army replaced democratic governments in coups in Argentina and Peru.

Films

Cliff Richard was the top film box-office draw in Britain, followed by Elvis Presley and Peter Sellers. All three of the biggest money-makers in Britain were British-made films. *The Guns Of Navarone* came top, followed by *The Young Ones* and *Only Two Can Play*. Other major films included *Doctor No*, *A Kind Of Loving*, *West Side Story* and *Ben Hur*. In America *Lawrence Of Arabia* won the Oscar as Best Film of 1962. David Lean was Best Director, Gregory Peck won the Oscar for Best Actor (*To Kill A Mockingbird*) and Anne Bancroft carried off the Oscar for Best Actress (*The Miracle Worker.*)

Sport

Sonny Liston won the World Heavyweight Boxing Championship from Floyd Patterson in spectacular style. For the first time this century, the reigning champion was knocked out by the challenger in the first round.

Brazil retained the football World Cup, beating Czechoslovakia 3–1 in the final. In England Tottenham won the FA Cup for the second year running, and Ipswich were top of League Division One. Rangers had the double of winning both the Scottish FA Cup and the Scottish League. Yorkshire won the Country Cricket Championship. In America the New York Yankees won the World Series for the second year in a row. The Green Bay Packers won the NFL championship, also for the second time in a row, while in their last year in the AFL Dallas won their championship.

The Lull Before The Storm

1962 belonged to Cliff Richard in Britain, with or without his Shadows, and to Elvis Presley in America. Thanks to his film *The Young Ones* Cliff Richard became the most popular British artist in the world, and outside America as big as Presley. The Shadows were the most popular instrumental group in the world, though most top groups were vocal acts like the Everly Brothers or the Crystals. Though it was predicted that the Shadows would break big in America, they never had a single chart entry there. It was the Tornados who became the first British group to top the American charts with **Telstar**, but then they faded away. Towards the end of 1962 the Beatles had their first, minor, hit. The following year they changed everything, and nothing was ever the same again.

HERB ALPERT AND HIS TIJUANA BRASS
American

THE LONELY BULL *A&M 703 [USA] Stateside SS 138 [UK]*. Herb Alpert was born 31 March 1937 of Jewish descent in Los Angeles, California, and was educated at the University of Southern California. An ex-Army trumpeter, he started experimenting with a tape recorder in his garage and found that by overdubbing one trumpet solo on top of another it produced the effect of a 'Spanish flare'. He achieved the most successful results from a song, **Twinkle Star**, written by his friend Sol Lake. At his first bullfight in Tijuana, he decided to add the roaring 'olés' of the crowd and the sounds of the mariachi band on to the beginning and end of **Twinkle Star**. With $200 he produced his disc, calling it **The Lonely Bull**, which eventually reached No 6 with 14 weeks in the bestsellers, selling over a million, and was No 22 in Britain with nine weeks in the bestsellers. Alpert's new quasi-Mexican music, part jazz, 'hot' mariachi and a touch of rock'n'roll soon became known as **Ameriachi** — a combination of American and mariachi. Alpert also composed, arranged and conducted his band which consists of trumpets, trombone, piano drums, mandolin (sometimes two electric guitars) and his voice.

Herb was also artists' and repertoire producer, partner and vice-president with Jerry Moss of A&M Records. Alpert's six sidemen (the Brass) were Lou Pagani (piano), Tonni Kalash (trumpet), John Pisano (guitar), Nick Ceroli (drums), Pat Senatore (guitar) and Bob Edmondson (trombone and band comic).

THE LONELY BULL (Album) *A&M 101 [USA]*. With the success of the singles disc of the same title, the newly formed A&M Records followed up with the release of this their first album in December 1962. It had a fair sale in early 1963 and came back with increasing sales in 1965 and 1966 through the big success of Herb Alpert and his **Whipped Cream and Other Delights** album, reaching No 10 in the US charts and a Gold Disc award from RIAA in 1966. By March 1966 it had sold 758,000 and passed the million sale by the end of 1967. It was in the bestsellers for 157 weeks.

The tracks on this album were: **The Lonely Bull** (El solo toro), by Sol Lake (1962); **El lobo** (The wolf), by Green and Sol Lake (1962); **Tijuana Sauerkraut**, by Jerry Moss and Herb Alpert (1962); **Desafinado**, by Newton Mendonca and Antonio Carlos Jobim (1959); **Mexico**, by Felice and Boudleaux Bryant (1961); **Never on Sunday** (film title number), by Billy Towne and Manos Hadjidakis (1960); **Struttin' with Maria**, by Herb Alpert (1962); **Let It Be Me**, by Pierre Delanoe and Gilbert Becaud (1955) (English words by Mann Curtis); **Acapulco 1922**, by Eldon Allan (1962); **Limbo Rock**, by Jon Sheldon and William E. Strange (1962); **Crawfish**, by Elsa Doran and Sol Lake (1962); **A Quiet Tear**, by Herb Alpert (1962).

RICHARD ANTHONY
French

J'ENTENDS SIFFLER LE TRAIN (500 MILES AWAY FROM HOME) (EP) *Columbia (EMI*

Pathé Marconi) S45: ESRF 1358 [France]. This French version of the American song **500 Miles Away from Home** (originally recorded by Peter, Paul and Mary) was written by Hedy West, Bobby Bare and Charles Williams and sold over one million. Richard Anthony Btesh, was born on 13 January 1938 in Egypt and was one of the first French singers with a rock'n'roll release — **Peggy Sue** in 1959. He had to wait, however, for three years before the Twist rage reached France, and after 1962 was Johnny Hallyday's main rival.

The French record market in the sixties, was almost entirely divided between EPs and LPs, with virtually no singles releases at all (Singles were only sold to juke box operators). The other tracks on this EP were **J'irai twister le Blues; Reviens vite mon amour; and J'irai pleurer sous la pluie''**.

THE BEATLES
British

LOVE ME DO/PS I LOVE YOU *Parlophone R 4949 [UK] Tollie 9008 [USA]*. Excluding the 1961 Polydor recordings of the group backing Tony Sheridan (see Tony Sheridan, 1961), this was the Beatles' first release. The record was a minor hit in Britain, but a No 1 in America in 1964 once Capitol had finally broken the group. It was the start of a recording career that made the Beatles the biggest-selling act of all time, with sales of over one billion records by 1988.

The roots of the Beatles go back to 1956, when John Lennon (born in Liverpool, England, on 9 October 1940) formed a skiffle group called the Quarry Men from his schoolfriends. John played guitar, Pete

Shotton played washboard and Bill Smith tried to play bass with a tea chest and broom handle. Smith did not last long, and his place was taken by Len Garry. Eric Griffiths joined on guitar, Rod Davis on banjo, and Colin Hanton came in on drums. The group's repertoire was limited to Lonnie Donegan skiffle numbers like **Rock Island Line** and **Cumberland Gap**. John Lennon was always the leader of the group, first called the Black Jacks, but soon changed to the Quarry Men after their school, Quarry Bank, in Liverpool. The line-up changed over the next couple of years, with Nigel Whalley and Ivan Vaughan coming in. Paul McCartney (born in Liverpool on 18 June 1942) joined in 1957, and he and John were soon writing songs together; **Love Me Do** was written at this time. George Harrison (born in Liverpool on 25 February 1943) joined them in 1958, Stu Sutcliffe in 1959 and Pete Best in 1960, and the group moved on from skiffle to rock'n'roll. In 1960 they went through a number of name changes, becoming Johnny and the Moondogs, then the Silver Beetles, and finally the Beatles. At this stage the group consisted of John Lennon, Paul McCartney, George Harrison, Stu Sutcliffe and Pete Best.

The Beatles entered a number of talent contests, but failed to win any of them. They played at venues in their native Liverpool, including the famous Cavern (originally a jazz club), but did not seem to be any nearer real success. In 1961, along with other Liverpool groups, they went to Germany to play in the clubs of Hamburg. Here they made their first recordings for Polydor. Stu Sutcliffe, a gifted artist, left the group to go back to art college. (See Tony Sheridan and the Beatles, 1961.)

In 1962 the Beatles were back in Britain, with a new manager. Brian Epstein, who became their manager on 13 December 1961, ran a record shop in Liverpool, though he had only a limited knowledge of the music business. Epstein tried desperately to get the Beatles a recording contract. He went first to EMI, then the biggest record company in the world. He submitted a Beatles Polydor record to Ron White, sales manager of EMI Records, who sent it on to the two main EMI labels, Columbia and His Master's Voice. In the words of a December 1963 memo from EMI Records' managing director L.G. Wood: 'Both turned it down on the basis that it sounded like a bad recording of the Shadows — and apparently it did!'. This was the **Cry for a Shadow** instrumental written by George Harrison.

The group next auditioned for Decca, as did Brian Poole and the Tremeloes. Decca's A&R manager Dick Rowe could only sign one of the groups, and decided to go for Brian Poole. On 8 May 1962, Epstein took a tape recording of Beatles' songs to the Private Recordings Department of the giant HMV record shop in London's Oxford Street, which in those days would transfer tape to disc for anyone for a small fee. The shop was owned by EMI, and the engineer there (Jim Foy) referred the tape to Sid Coleman, general manager of Ardmore & Beechwood, an EMI music publishing company which had an office above the HMV shop. He called George Martin, who was the A&R manager for Parlophone, and Martin agreed to hear the tape. Parlophone was very much the junior label of EMI. It had been formed in Germany by the Carl Lindstrom Organization, which also owned the Odeon label. In 1925 Britain's Columbia Records took over Lindstrom, and in 1931 merged with the Gramophone Company (HMV) to form EMI. Columbia and HMV were always the first-line marques, with Parlophone literally a joke label; apart from Adam Faith, Parlophone was mainly used for comedy records. George Martin therefore welcomed the chance to sign a pop group with potential. He liked Epstein's tape, and on 6 June gave the Beatles a recording test at EMI's Abbey Road studios. They performed **Love Me Do**, **PS I Love You** and **Ask Me Why**. George Martin then had to decide whether to sign the group and, on the grounds that he had nothing to lose, decided to go ahead, backdating the contract to 4 June.

On 4 September the Beatles returned to Abbey Road to record their first single. Between the recording test and this session, drummer Pete Best had been replaced by Ringo Starr (born Richard Starkey in Liverpool on 7 July 1940). Ringo was not a particularly good drummer, so George Martin decided that a second recording session was needed and he brought in session drummer Andy White on 11 September. Martin had intended **How Do You Do It?**, written by Mitch Murray, to be the group's first A side, but the Beatles preferred their own composition **Love Me Do**. In the end, Martin agreed and **Love Me Do** was recorded at both September sessions. (Columbia's Gerry and the Pacemakers then recorded **How Do You Do It?**, and took it to No 1 as their first hit.) The two takes of **Love Me Do** can be differentiated by the sound of a tambourine, played by Ringo Starr at the 11 September session as he had nothing else to do. When the record was first released, it was the Ringo version that was used. In 1963 a switch was made, and from then onwards (including the 1982 re-release) it was the White version of 11 September that was used.

On 4 October 1962 **Love Me Do** was released in England. It reached No 17, with an 18-week chart run, and sold 116,227 copies. This was a good start for a debut disc, though it was only with the release of their second hit **Please Please Me** in January 1963 that their career really took off. Twenty years later, EMI started to re-release the Beatles' singles, and in October 1982 **Love Me Do** started another seven-week chart run that took it to No 4.

Love Me Do was not released in the USA at first. Dave Dexter, Capitol's A&R man responsible for selecting overseas material for American release, did not think much of the record. He particularly disliked John Lennon's harmonica playing, and turned the disc down for American release. EMI had great difficulty persuading their American subsidiary Capitol to release the Beatles. As Capitol passed on all the early Beatles records, EMI placed them with other American companies. None were American hits until after Capitol broke **I Want to Hold Your Hand** in January 1964, but they then all made the charts. In 1964 the Beatles had 30 US chart placings, with 18 singles and an EP. (With 11 of the singles, both sides

charted separately.) **Love Me Do** and **PS I Love You** was a double A side put out by the Vee Jay subsidiary label Tollie. **Love Me Do** was the Beatles' fourth American No 1 (for one week) with 14 weeks on the charts, while the flip side reached No 10 with an eight-week chart run. It was their first double A side where both sides independently made the Top 10. It was American sales that made this record a million seller, though British sales finally passed the quarter-million mark.

TONY BENNETT   *American*

I LEFT MY HEART IN SAN FRANCISCO *CBS-Columbia 42332 [USA] CBS 201730 [UK]*. Tony Bennett was born Anthony Dominick Benedetto on 3 August 1926, in Queens, New York. He had his first hit, for American Columbia (CBS), in 1951 with the No 1 million-selling **Because of You**. His third hit of the same year, **Cold, Cold Heart**, was his second No 1 million seller. Tony Bennett had a long string of hits in America, lasting throughout the fifties and up to 1967. He also sold a lot of albums, with 24 of them landing on the Top 200 LP charts from 1957 to 1972. His second hit album, **I Left My Heart in San Francisco**, was his biggest, reaching No 5 in the charts. Released in 1962, it won an RIAA Gold Disc for million dollar sales in July 1963.

It was the title track from this album which won him his sixth million seller. It also won him Grammys for 'Best Male Vocal Performance' and 'Record of the Year' in 1962. The song was written by Douglas Cross and George Cory in 1954. The record was in the American charts for 21 weeks, though it only reached No 19. In Britain in 1962 CBS were planning to set up their own UK company, taking over the Oriole label as a base. With the change-over from a licensing deal with Philips to their own operation, CBS did not push this record into the charts until 1965. It spluttered around at the bottom of the Top 50 for a few weeks in May, then re-entered the charts in September and finally, on its third charts run, reached No 25. It spent a total of 14 weeks in the British charts, and continued to sell steadily once its chart life was over. It won a Silver Disc for British sales of a quarter of a million on 20 May 1967. Tony Bennett presented the Gold Record he won for global sales of over a million copies of **I Left My Heart in San Francisco** to the people of that city. The presentation was made to Mayor Joseph Alioto in his City Hall offices on 27 August 1970.

MARCIE BLAINE   *American*

BOBBY'S GIRL *Seville 120 [USA]*. Marcie Blaine was born on 21 May 1944, in Brooklyn, New York. She was discovered by Seville's A&R man Marv Holtzman and recorded this song, written by Henry Hoffman and Gary Klein. It got to No 2 in the US charts with 16 weeks in the bestsellers and sold an estimated million by 1963. The song also put Britain's Susan Maughan on the recording map, her disc reaching No 4 in Britain and selling over a quarter of a million.

PAT BOONE   *American*

SPEEDY GONZALES *Dot 16368 [USA] London HLD 9573 [UK]*. Far from unlucky, the 13th million seller for consistent Pat Boone enjoyed a reputed global sale of two million. This song was written by Buddy Kaye, David Hill and Ethel Lee in 1961. The disc was No 6 for three weeks in the US charts and 13 weeks in the bestsellers, and No 2 and 19 weeks in the British charts.

BOOKER T. AND THE MGs   *American*

GREEN ONIONS *Stax 127 [USA] Atlantic K 10109 [UK]*. This novelty pop instrumental group takes its title from the initials of 'Memphis Group'. Booker (real name Booker T. Jones) also hails from Memphis and was born on 12 November 1944. His instruments include string bass and organ. The number was written by the group, Booker T. Jones, Steve Cropper (guitar), Lewis Steinberg (bass) and Al Jackson (drums). The disc got to No 3 in the US charts with 16 weeks in the bestsellers, and was No 1 in the R&B charts for four weeks with 15 weeks in the R&B Top 30. It finally became a hit in Britain in 1979, when released on Atlantic. It reached No 7, with 12 weeks in the charts.

FREDDY CANNON   *American*

PALISADES PARK *Swan 4106 [USA] Stateside SS 101 [UK]*. This song was written to commemorate the opening of a huge American fun fair. The writer was Chuck Barris, manager of ABC TV's day-time programmes, and it provided Freddy with his third million seller. It was No 3 for two weeks in the US charts and 15 weeks in the bestsellers, and No 20 in Britain, with eight weeks in the bestsellers.

GENE CHANDLER   *American*

DUKE OF EARL *Vee Jay 416 [USA]*. The first million seller for Gene was written in 1961 by

Earl Edwards, Eugene Dixon and Bernice Williams. Gene Chandler (formerly Eugene Dixon) came from Chicago and was born on 6 July 1937. He began singing at the age of eight. He became a professional performer in 1960. The disc was No 1 for three weeks in the USA with 15 weeks in the bestsellers, and No 1 for five weeks with 13 weeks in the R&B charts, where he had a string of 36 hits up to 1986.

BRUCE CHANNEL   American

HEY! BABY *Smash 1731 [USA] Mercury AMT 1171 [UK]*. This first million seller for Bruce Channel was written by him and Margaret Cobb in 1961. Teenbeat singer Bruce was born on 28 November 1940, in Jacksonville, Texas, of a musical family. He was singing and playing the guitar from the age of five. His family moved to Dallas, and while in high school Bruce entertained at youth centres and local shows. His father took him to Shreveport, Louisiana, to seek an audition with Tillman Franks, producer of the famous 'Louisiana Hayride' show. Franks signed him for an appearance on the show and he became a regular on it for six months. In 1961 Smash Records signed him to an exclusive disc contract.

Hey! Baby reached the top of the charts. The disc was No 1 for three weeks in the USA with 15 weeks in the bestsellers and No 2 for three weeks in Britain with 12 weeks in the Top 50. It features the harmonica of Delbert McClinton.

RAY CHARLES   American

I CAN'T STOP LOVING YOU/BORN TO LOSE *ABC-Paramount 10330 [USA] HMV POP 1034 [UK]*. The fourth million seller for Ray Charles was one of the top discs of 1962 with a sale of over two million. The song for this singles disc, taken from Ray's big-selling album **Modern Sounds in Country-and-Western Music**, was written in 1957 by Don Gibson, who also had a million seller with it in 1958. It was the No 1 for 10 weeks in the R&B charts, where it had a 16-week chart run. It was also No 1 in the USA for five weeks with 18 weeks in the bestsellers, and for one week in Britain with 17 weeks in the British bestsellers. The backing of this disc was **Born to Lose** (written by Ted Daffan in 1943). It charted independently of **I Can't Stop Loving You** in America, reaching No 41 with nine weeks on the charts. Grammy award for 'Best Rhythm-and-Blues Recording' 1962. Gold Disc award RIAA 1962. Released 23 April 1962.

MODERN SOUNDS IN COUNTRY-AND-WESTERN MUSIC VOLUME 1 (Album) *ABC-Paramount 410 [USA] HMV CLP 1580 [UK]*. The fifth million seller for Ray Charles was his first album million seller. It sold half a million by September 1962. The contents of the album are: **Bye Bye, Love**, by Felice and Boudleaux Bryant (1957); **You Don't Know Me**, by Cindy Walker and Eddy Arnold (1955); **Half as Much**, by Curley Williams (1951); **I Love You So Much It Hurts**, by Floyd Tillman (1948); **Just a Little**

Lovin', by Eddy Arnold and Zeke Clements (1948); **Born to Lose**, by Frankie Brown (Ted Daffan) (1943); **Worried Man** (traditional); **It Makes No Difference Now**, by Floyd Tillman (1939); **You Win Again**, by Hank Williams (1952); **Careless Love**, traditional, arrangement by Ray Charles; **I Can't Stop Lovin' You**, by Don Gibson (1957); **Hey Good Lookin'**, by Hank Williams (1951).

This disc was No 1 for 14 weeks in the USA, and in their bestseller charts for 100 weeks. Gold Disc award RIAA 1962. In Britain, this was Ray Charles' first album hit. It reached No 6, with 16 weeks in the LP charts.

YOU DON'T KNOW ME/CARELESS LOVE *ABC-Paramount 10345 [USA] HMV POP 1064 [UK]*. The sixth million seller for Ray Charles, written in 1955 by Cindy Walker and Eddy Arnold, was also culled from Charles' big-seller album of **Modern Sounds in Country-and-Western Music**. It got to No 2 in the US charts with 11 weeks in the bestsellers; No 9 and 13 weeks in the British bestsellers. It was a top rhythm-and-blues seller. Released 10 July 1962, both sides charted in the US. **Careless Love**, written by Ray Charles from a traditional arrangement, reached No 60 in a four-week chart run.

CHUBBY CHECKER   American

SLOW TWISTIN' *Parkway 835 [USA] Columbia (EMI) DB 4808 [UK]*. The fifth million seller for Chubby was written by Jon Sheldon. It was No 3 in the US charts and 14 weeks in the bestsellers, and No 23 in Britain with eight weeks in the charts. The record was made with Dee Dee Sharp. In America the flip side, **La Paloma Twist**, also entered the charts for two weeks, peaking at No 72.

LIMBO ROCK/POPEYE THE HITCHHIKER *Parkway 849 [USA] Cameo-Parkway P 849 [UK]*. The sixth million seller and No 2 for two weeks for Chubby Checker comprised **Limbo Rock**, written by W.E. Strange and Jon Sheldon, and **Popeye**, the work of Kal Mann and Dave Appell, both on the staff of Cameo Records. **Limbo Rock** was 23 weeks in the US bestsellers; No 32 with 10 weeks in the British bestsellers. **Popeye** reached No 10 with 13 weeks in the US charts.

LOU CHRISTIE   American

THE GYPSY CRIED *Roulette 4457 [USA]*. This was the first (reputed) million seller for Lou Christie, the song written by him and Twyla Herbert. It achieved the No 18 chart position in the USA in early 1963 with 13 weeks in the US bestsellers.

Lou Christie (real name Geno Sacco) was born in Glen Willard near Pittsburgh, Pennsylvania. He won a state scholarship at Moon Township High School and studied classical music and singing. In 1963, Lou moved to New York and sang in backgrounds on other artists' discs after persistently asking record companies for a test. He eventually got a contract, with this disc as his first release. Lou

collaborated with Twyla Herbert, a mystic 20 years older than himself, who he says predicted his hits and often had visions of his future. After two years' Army service in the USA, Lou and Twyla came up with a big hit in late 1965 — **Lightnin' Strikes** — and Lou also signed with MGM for films.

JIMMY CLANTON   American

VENUS IN BLUE JEANS *Ace 8001 [USA]*. Jimmy Clanton came from a highly musical family. Born on 2 September 1940 in Baton Rouge, Louisiana, he studied guitar and played at local clubs while at high school. He formed a four-man group called the Rockets and travelled to New Orleans where he met studio owner Cosimo Matassa, who became his manager and got him a contract with Ace Records. Jimmy and Cosimo wrote his first hit and million seller, **Just a Dream**, in 1958. He appeared in a number of teenage music films including *Go, Jimmy, Go*.

Venus in Blue Jeans was Clanton's fourth million seller. It was written by Howard Greenfield and Jack Keller in 1961. It reached No 7 in the American charts, with 13 weeks in the Hot 100. The record was not a hit in Britain, where Mark Wynter had the biggest hit of his career with a cover version.

PETULA CLARK   British

MONSIEUR *Vogue 1903 [West Germany]*. This disc by Britain's actress-singer Petula Clark sold 250,000 in Germany alone by December 1962, and totalled two million on the Continent. Petula Sally Olwen Clark was born on 15 November 1932 in West Ewell, Surrey, and studied music from her earliest childhood. She first performed with a music chorus in Cardiff, later on local radio, from the age of

nine. During her teens, her career went into high gear, and between 11 and 18 she made more than 20 films and won an award in 1950 for the most outstanding TV artist. An experienced performer of stage, screen and radio, she signed a recording contract with Pye (Britain) in 1955, her first major hits being **Sailor** (1960) and **Romeo** (see 1961), then **My Friend the Sea**, followed by **Ya Ya Twist**, a Continental smash hit.

Petula married Claud Wolff, publicity director for Vogue Records in France, and has become one of the biggest disc stars and performers on the Continent, recording in English, French and German. **Monsieur** was her best-selling German disc. Her first film was *A Medal for the General* (1944) followed by *Strawberry Road, I Know Where I'm Going, London Town, Easy Money, Goodbye Mr Chips* and many others. She has appeared in TV plays in Britain and France, with her own series in Britain.

Petula's first recordings were for Columbia and Polygon. This song was written by Kurt Hertha (words) and Karl Goetz (music) in Germany. She was awarded the Grand Prix du Disque by the French Disc Academy for this record in 1963.

CHARIOT *Vogue 4340 [France] PYE 7N 15522 [UK].* This reputed million seller for Petula Clark (sung in French) achieved its sale on the Continent. It was written by Jacques Plant (words) and J.W. Stole and Del Roma (pseudonyms of famous French orchestra conductors Frank Pourcell and Paul Mauriat) (music). **Chariot** was also a million seller for Little Peggy March under the US title **I Will Follow Him** in 1963 (see 1963). This disc was No 39 in Britain and seven weeks in the bestsellers.

NAT 'KING' COLE   *American*

RAMBLIN' ROSE *Capitol 4804 [USA] Capitol CL 15270 [UK].* Nat 'King' Cole was one of America's all-time greatest singers. Nathaniel Cole was born on 17 March 1919 in Montgomery, Alabama, the son of a vicar. He started singing in nightclubs, and in 1937 formed the Nat King Cole Trio. He made some records for Decca, but it was after he signed with Capitol in 1943 that his career really took off. Capitol had only been formed the year before, and founders Johnny Mercer and Glen Wallichs signed him up as one of their first artists. They were encouraged by their teenage star Ella Mae Morse, whose **Cow Cow Boogie** was the label's first hit, who had heard Cole singing in a club.

His first hit was **Straighten Up and Fly Right** in 1944. His first No 1 was **(I Love You) For Sentimental Reasons** in 1946, and his first international hit and first million seller was **Nature Boy** in 1948. He entered the US charts 79 times between 1944 and 1966. In Britain, he had 30 hits from the very first week of the British charts published in the *New Musical Express* on 14 November 1952, to 1966. In 1958 he starred in the film *St Louis Blues*. He died on 15 February 1965. His daughter Natalie Cole also became a recording star on Capitol, with a string of hits in the eighties.

Ramblin' Rose was Nat 'King' Cole's sixth million seller, and was written by Joe and Noel Sherman. It was his biggest hit for years in America, and reached No 2 with 16 weeks on the charts. It peaked at No 7 during 11 weeks on the R&B charts. It was also a big hit in Britain, where it reached No 5, spent 14 weeks in the charts, and won a Silver Disc for British sales of a quarter of a million.

RAMBLIN' ROSE (Album) *Capitol 1793 [USA].* Capitol issued this disc in August 1963, following the great success of Nat 'King' Cole's disc of the same title. The album sold the half million by 1964, receiving a Gold Disc award from the RIAA. Since Nat's death, Capitol have had very big sales of his various albums, with this **Ramblin' Rose** album reaching the two million sale by 1968. The contents are: **Ramblin' Rose**, by Joe and Noel Sherman (1962); **Wolverton Mountain**, by Claude King and Merle Kilgore (1962); **Twilight on the Trail**, by Sydney Mitchell and Louis Alter (1936); **I Don't Want It That Way**, by Joe and Noel Sherman (1962); **He'll Have to Go**, by Joe and Audrey Alison (1959); **When You're Smiling**, by Mark Fisher, Joe Goodwin and Larry Shay (1928); **Goodnight Irene**, by Huddie Ledbetter and John Lomax (1950); **Your Cheatin' Heart**, by Hank Williams (1952); **One Has My Heart, the Other My Name**, by Eddie Dean, Dearest Dean and Hal Blair (1948); **Skip to My Lou,** by Hugh Martin and Ralph Blane (1944); **The Good Times**, by Ron Miller and Lee Porter (1962); **Sing Another Song (and We'll All Go Home)**, by Burke and Romoff (1962).

This album was in the US bestsellers for 162 weeks, and reached No 3.

THE CONTOURS   *American*

SO YOU LOVE ME? *Gordy 7005 [USA].* This vocal rhythm-and-blues sextet consisted of Bill Gordon, Billy Hoggs, Joe Billingslea, Sylvester Potts, Hubert Johnson and Huey Davis, all in their 20s. Around 1958, when The Contours were a quartet, Johnson joined and was instrumental in getting his distant cousin, disc star Jackie Wilson, to hear the group which led to an audition for Berry Gordy of Motown Records for whom they made their first disc **Whole Lotta Woman**. In early 1962, guitar player Huey Davies was added to their act, then came this hit disc. This first million seller for the Contours was written by Berry Gordy, Jr. Released on 18 August 1962, it reached No 3 with 18 weeks in the US Hot 100 and No 1 for 3 weeks during a 17-week stay in the US R&B charts.

SAM COOKE

TWISTIN' THE NIGHT AWAY *RCA Victor 7983 [USA] RCA 1277 [UK].* Sam wrote his own fifth seven-figure seller, which enjoyed a reputed global sale of over 1,500,000. It got to No 9 in the US charts with 15 weeks in the bestsellers and No 6 and 14 weeks in the British bestsellers. It was No 1 for 3 weeks during 15 weeks in the US R&B charts.

THE CRYSTALS   *American*

UPTOWN *Philles 102 [USA]* The Crystals' second hit was written by Barry Mann and Cynthia Weil, and produced by Phil Spector at the Mira Sound studio in New York. It reached No 13 during 13 weeks in *Billboard*, and No 10 during 14 weeks in *Cash Box*.

HE'S A REBEL *Philles 106 [USA] London HLU 9611 [UK].* The Crystals have the unique distinction of not having appeared on their first and only No 1 record. Though *Billboard* and *Cash Box* charts listed **He's a Rebel** as by the Crystals, 'their' first million-selling record was in fact by Darlene Love and the Blossoms. The key to this mystery lies in the record's producer, the brilliant but eccentric Phil Spector. Records by the Crystals and all the others he produced were really Phil Spector records; the singers merely actors singing their lines. It was the Spector production that made the difference.

Phil Spector was born in the Bronx, New York, on 26 December 1940. In 1949 his father died and in 1953 Spector and his mother moved to Los Angeles. He went to the local school, Fairfax High, and started a group called the Teddy Bears with fellow-students Marshal Leib and Annette Kleinbard. Spector wrote their first release, the theme of the song being based on the inscription on his father's tomb. 'To Have Known Him was to Have Loved Him' became **To Know Him is to Love Him**. The record went to No 1 for three weeks.

In 1961 Spector formed his own label with partner Lester Sill. Combining their two names, he called it Philles (Phil-Les). In the offices of Hill and Range Publishing in New York, he met five black schoolgirls from Brooklyn who sang together after school for fun. They were the Crystals, three 17-year-olds, Dee Dee Kennibrew, Barbara Alston and Pat Wright, and two 16-year-olds, Lala Brooks and Mary Thomas. Spector recorded the girls, and their first release **There's No Other (Like My Baby)** went to No 20.

Spector joined Liberty records, retaining

the right to go on producing his Philles acts. He then released a highly controversial Crystals' record, **He Hit Me (and It Felt Like a Kiss)**.

At Liberty, Spector heard a demo of a Gene Pitney song meant for Vikki Carr. He immediately resigned, flew out to Gold Star Studios in Los Angeles, brought in some experienced session musicians (including Sonny Bono who later found fame as half of Sonny and Cher) and, with the aid of arranger Jack Nitzsche, recorded **He's a Rebel** in record time. The only problem was that the Crystals (now a quartet after Mary Thomas left to get married) were still in New York. Whether he wanted to save the cost of flying them over or whether they did not like flying (as he claimed), or whether there simply was not time, the fact is that the Crystals were three thousand miles away from the studio when the record was made. Spector used local session singers the Blossoms instead (lead singer Darlene Love, with Fanita James and Gracia Nitzsche, wife of the arranger of the record). Though Liberty was a bigger company than Philles and had the original of the song, the Spector version beat them hands down. The record went to No 1 for two weeks in November 1962, and stayed in the charts for 18 weeks, the longest chart residency of the Crystals' career. In Britain, it gave them their first hit, reaching No 19 with 13 weeks in the charts. The record was The Crystal' third and biggest R&B hit, reaching No 2 with 10 weeks on the R&B charts.

The Crystals are better known for their two classic 1963 hits, **Da Do Ron Ron** and **Then He Kissed Me**, on which they did actually appear. Both were the result of Phil Spector developing his production techniques to an even higher level in the creation of his famous 'wall of sound'.

BOBBY DARIN   *American*

THINGS *Atco 6229* [*USA*] *London HLK 9575* [*UK*]. This six million seller for Darin was written by Bobby himself in 1961. It got to No 3 in the US charts with 12 weeks in the bestsellers, and No 2 and 17 weeks in the British bestsellers.

SAMMY DAVIS JR.   *American*

WHAT KIND OF FOOL AM I? *Reprise 20048* [*USA*] *Reprise R 20048* [*UK*]. Sammy Davis Jr has been appearing before the public since the age of two, when he made his professional debut. He was born on 8 December 1925 in New York City, into a family already well known to vaudeville audiences. His father, Sammy Davis Sr and his uncle Will Mastin were a popular act before he was born. He made a considerable number of singles, EPs and albums for Decca in the USA before switching to the Reprise label which was started by Frank Sinatra and sold to Warner Brothers in 1963. **What Kind of Fool Am I?** from the stage show *Stop the World — I Want to Get Off*, written by Leslie Bricusse (words) and Anthony Newley (music) and first produced in Britain in 1961, was his first hit disc by British

writers. It is said to have sold a global million, reaching No 7 with 15 weeks in the US bestsellers and No 26 and eight weeks in the British bestsellers. Sammy's follow-up was another British song **As Long as He Needs Me** from Lionel Bart's musical *Oliver*.

Grammy Award to the writers for 'Song of the Year' 1962. Davis died of throat cancer on 16 May 1990.

SKEETER DAVIS   *American*

THE END OF THE WORLD *RCA Victor 8098* [*USA*] *RCA 1328* [*UK*]. Skeeter Davis (real name Mary Frances Penick) was born on 30 December 1931 in Sparta, Kentucky, the eldest of six children. Her parents encouraged their talented daughters Skeeter and Bee Jay. After attending high school in Dixie Heights from 1945 to 1949, Skeeter sang with pop bands. Country music however was her real love. She appeared on Nashville's 'Grand Ole Opry' and the Ernest Tubb show. Skeeter became known for her disc of **I Forget More than You'll Ever Know** which she recorded with her sister, Bee Jay, in 1953. This was a very big hit for the Davis Sisters, as they were then known, as record artists. They received the *Cash Box* annual award that year for 'The Most Programmed Record of 1953'. This brief joint success ended when Bee Jay was killed in a car crash.

Steve Sholes, Victor's artists' and repertoire chief, persuaded Skeeter to do a solo session in 1957 — an important turning point in her career — and she received the 1958 *Cash Box* award as 'The Most Promising Female Country Vocalist'. She recorded **The End of the World** in late 1962, the disc staying at No 2 for three weeks in the US charts in 1963 with an eventual million sale by 1964. She was voted 'Favourite Female Country Artist' in the *Billboard* Disc

Jockey Poll of 1964.

The End of the World was written in 1962 by Sylvia Dee and Arthur Kent, Skeeter's disc becoming a hit also in Britain, reaching No 18 with 13 weeks in the bestsellers. It was 17 weeks in the US Hot 100 and 24 weeks in the C&W charts where it peaked at No 2.

JOEY DEE AND THE STARLITERS   *American*

SHOUT — PART 1 *Roulette 4416* [*USA*]. This song, written in 1959 by the Isley Brothers, was the second million seller for Joey Dee, and the second time the song produced a million-selling version. The disc got to No 6 in the US charts with 12 weeks in the bestsellers.

DUANE EDDY   *American*

(DANCE WITH) THE GUITAR MAN *RCA Victor 8087* [*USA*] *RCA 1316* [*UK*]. The third million seller for Duane Eddy was written by him in conjunction with Lee Hazlewood. It achieved No 12 in the US charts with 16 weeks in the bestsellers, and No 4 and 16 weeks in Britain's bestsellers.

SHELLEY FABARES   *American*

JOHNNY ANGEL *Colpix 621* [*USA*] *Pye International 7N 25132* [*UK*]. This song was written by Lee Pockriss (music) and Lyn Duddy (words). Shelly (real name Michele Fabares) hails from Santa Monica, California. Niece of Nanette Fabray, she started as a dancer, her first break coming in 1953 with an appearance on a Frank Sinatra TV show. She started her own showbiz career as an actress and moved into dramatic parts on several top-rating TV shows. Her film break came in 1955 with *Never Say Goodbye*, then featured parts in *Rock Pretty Baby* and *Summer Love*. Shelley subsequently played the role of Donna Reed's daughter in the US TV series 'The Donna Reed Show'. In 1962 she started her singing career with her first tune for Colpix Records, this disc of **Johnny Angel**. This first million seller for 19-year-old Shelley reached top place in the sellers charts almost overnight (two weeks in the USA with 15 weeks in the bestsellers, and reaching No 41 in Britain).

BENT FABRIC   *Danish*

ALLEY CAT *Metronome 4100* [*Denmark*] *Atco 6226* [*USA*]. Bent Fabric (real name Bent Fabricus Bjerre) was born on 7 December 1924 in Copenhagen. A multi-talented artist, Bent had a jazz band in his teens and made some early Danish jazz discs. He then went into the pop field and in 1950 took over Metronome Records in Denmark. He was also a successful artists' and repertoire man, composer, pianist and TV personality. As host and star of a popular Saturday night Danish TV show called 'Around A Piano' he presented guest stars and played piano. The tune of **Alley Cat** was written by Frank Bjorn (Fabric's pseudonym).

This disc sold a million when released on the Atco label in the USA, and was at No 12 in the charts with 18 weeks in the bestsellers. Jack Harlem's lyrics were written later for a song version. The disc was Denmark's first entry into the American bestseller charts to reach a high position. Winner of NARAS Award for 'Best Rock and Roll Recording' 1962.

LARRY FINNEGAN American

DEAR ONE *Old Town 1113* [*USA*]. Written in 1961 by Larry and Vincent Finnegan, this disc reached No 11 in the US charts with 14 weeks in the bestsellers, and is said to have sold a global million by 1966. It was Larry Finnegan's first recording.

John Lawrence Finnegan was born in New York in 1939, and was educated at Notre Dame. His musical interests were playing the guitar, piano, drums and songwriting. In 1966 Larry, who was by then living in Stockholm, Sweden, set up his own independent record company, Svensk-American.

He sings in the country style and is a successful songwriter in Denmark, Sweden, Norway and Germany.

THE FOUR SEASONS American

SHERRY *Vee Jay 456* [*USA*] *Stateside SS 122* [*UK*]. This teenbeat vocal quartet comprised Bob Gaudio (tenor singer, piano and organ, and composer of the song) born 17 November 1942; Franki Valli (leader and tenor) born 3 May 1937; Nick Massi (bass and vocal arrangements) born 19 September 1935; and Tommy de Vito (baritone and guitarist) born 19 June 1935. All four come from New Jersey. Except for Bob Gaudio, who joined the group after leaving the Royal Teens, the others had been working together for about six years under the name Four Lovers. After enjoying only mild success, they met record producer Bob Crewe in New York who changed their name to the Four Seasons and gave them fresh material. **Sherry** reached the top of the bestseller charts as did their second disc **Big Girls Don't Cry** (see below) to make the boys

a household name throughout the USA and achieve fame elsewhere. **Sherry** was top disc for five weeks in the USA with 14 weeks in the bestsellers, and No 8 and 16 weeks in the British bestsellers. The group previously recorded for the Gone label. **Sherry** was No 1 for one week during 11 weeks on the R&B charts.

BIG GIRLS DON'T CRY *Vee Jay 465* [*USA*] *Stateside SS 145* [*UK*]. Likewise this second million seller for the Four Seasons reached the top of the US charts for five weeks and was a bestseller for 16 weeks reaching No 13 with 10 weeks in the British bestsellers. The number was written by Bob Crewe and Robert Gaudio (of the group). It was also their second No 1 in a row on the R&B charts. It was top for three weeks during a 13-week chart run. They had two more R&B hits in 1963.

FREDDY German

JUNGE, KOMM BALD WIEDER (Son, Come Home Soon) *Polydor 4162* [*West Germany*]. This sixth million seller for Freddy was written by Walter Rothenburg (words) and Lotar Olias (music). The English version was released in late 1963 in the USA, with words by Charles Singleton and Quinn. The song was the hit number from the German musical *Homesick for St Pauli*, which starred Freddy Quinn. The disc sold two million by the end of 1967.

CONNY FROBOESS German

ZWEI KLEINE ITALIENER (Two Little Italians) *Electrola 45-DW-5944* [*West Germany*]. The first million seller for Conny was written by Christian Bruhn and George Buschor. Conny was born in Berlin on 28 October 1943 and made her first appearance and her first record there in 1950 when she was seven. After a career as a child star on discs and in films, she eventually established herself as Germany's top female teenage singer. She continued her career as a top star of stage, screen and TV. Her recording of this disc sold half a million by December 1962 in Germany and subsequently over the million with Continental sales (1,225,000 by June 1965). She won the 'Song for Europe' contest in Germany in 1962 and visited the USA in 1963.

STAN GETZ AND CHARLIE BYRD American

DESAFINADO (Slightly Out of Tune) *Verve 10260* [*USA*] *HMV POP 1061* [*UK*]. The music for this million seller was written in 1959 by Antonio Carlos Jobim, with the original text by Newton Mendonca, and was published in Brazil. The English lyrics were written by Jon Hendricks and Jessie Cavanaugh in 1962. Charlie Byrd, the talented jazz and classical guitarist, was born on 16 September 1925 in Chuckatuck, Virginia. He began on the guitar at the age of nine, learning from his father. Stan Getz was born on 2 February 1927, the son of Russian-Jewish immigrants (real name Gayetzsky), and comes from Philadelphia. A

veteran tenor sax player, and a mainstay of modern jazz, Getz has played with many top bands including Stan Kenton, Benny Goodman and Jimmy Dorsey. **Desafinado** was taken from the **Jazz Samba** album and issued as a single. It became a million seller in 1963, being the first Bossa Nova to climb the seller charts. Grammy Award for 'Best Jazz Performance (Small Group)' 1962. Sales were over 1,600,000 by 1967. The disc reached No 15 and was 16 weeks in the US bestsellers, and No 11 with 11 weeks in the British bestsellers.

JAZZ SAMBA (Album) *Verve 8432* [*USA*] *Verve SULP 9013* [*UK*]. This album is reputed to have sold a million by 1964; it was one of 1962's biggest sellers in the USA. It contained the famous **Desafinado** (see above). Titles on the album are: **Desafinado**, by Antonio Carlos Jobim (1959): **Samba Deese Days**, by Charlie Byrd; **O Pata**, by J. Silva and N. Teixeira (1962); **Samba triste**, by Baden Powell and Blanco; **Samba de una nota so**, by Antonio Carlos Jobim and Newton Mendonca (1959); **E luxo so**, by Peixota and Ary Barroso; **Baia**, by Ary Barroso (1939).

This disc was in the US bestsellers lists for 70 weeks, and was No 1 for one week. In the British album charts, **Jazz Samba** reached No 15 during seven weeks in the charts.

FRANÇOISE HARDY French

TOUS LES GARCONS ET LES FILLES (All The Boys And Girls) *Vogue V2365* [*France*] *Pye 7N 15653* [*UK*]. In the sixties, Françoise Hardy was one of France's biggest sellers on disc. She was born in Paris on 17 January 1944 and studied at Le Bruyère College. Given a guitar when she graduated, she taught herself to play and began writing songs. In April 1960 she began auditioning at various record companies and was immediately signed to Vogue. She continued however to study and obtained a degree in German. In addition she speaks English, Spanish and Italian as well as her native French.

In June 1962 her disc of **Tous les garçons et les filles** was released. Written by her, it became an international hit and was particularly big in France and in Italy. It stayed in the Continental charts for several weeks and subsequently amassed the million sale. By 1966 she was selling more discs than any other French singer. Apart from her singing, Françoise was in great demand as a model and a trendsetter. *Time* (30 December 1966) saw her as 'a symbol of the mystery of youth'. She appeared in several of Vadim's films, making her debut in Sagan's *A Castle in Sweden.* Her first major US film was *Grand Prix* (1966), co-starring with Yves Montand, James Garner and Genevieve Page.

The Italian version of the song was **Quelli della mia eta**. The disc was No 36 in Britain and seven weeks in the bestsellers.

BRIAN HYLAND   *American*

SEALED WITH A KISS *ABC-Paramount 10336* [*USA*] *HMV POP 1051* [*UK*] *(re-released in 1975 as ABC 4059).* This second million seller for Brian was written in 1960 by Peter Udell (words) and Gary Geld (music). The disc was No 3 for two weeks in the US charts and 14 weeks in the bestsellers. It was No 3 with 15 weeks in the British bestsellers in its first chart run, and No 7 with 11 weeks in the charts when re-released on ABC in 1975.

FRANK IFIELD   *British/Australian*

I REMEMBER YOU *Columbia (EMI) DB 4856* [*UK*] *Vee Jay 457* [*USA*]. Frank Ifield's sensational country-and-western style recording of this song sold two million. It sold 102,000 in one day, and 367,000 in five days after its release in June 1962. The song was written in 1942 by famed Johnny Mercer (words) and the late Victor Schertzinger (music) for the Dorothy Lamour, Bob Eberly, Helen O'Connell, Jimmy Dorsey and orchestra film *The Fleet's In.*

Frank was born on 30 November 1937 in Coventry, England. He actually began his career at the age of 15 in Australia. He was the first artist to appear on TV in Sydney when it was officially opened, and had several of his own TV and radio series 'down under'. To further his career, he travelled to England in 1959 and within a few months signed a disc contract with Columbia Records. He then won second place in the Eurovision TV contest with Britain's entry. He eventually became the first singer to get his first three hits to No 1 in Britain's charts. Ifield also plays guitar, ukulele, piano and bass as well as singing. This disc was No 1 for eight weeks in Britain with 28 weeks in the bestsellers, and a success in the USA where it reached No 5 with 11 weeks in the bestsellers.

LOVESICK BLUES *Columbia (EMI) DB 4913* [*UK*] *Vee Jay 477* [*USA*]. The second million seller for Frank Ifield was an oldie of 1922 written by Irving Mills (words) and Cliff Friend (music). It was No 1 disc for five weeks in Britain, and reached No 44 in the USA with

seven weeks in the bestsellers, and 17 weeks in the British charts.

THE ISLEY BROTHERS   *American*

TWIST AND SHOUT *Wand 124* [*USA*] *Stateside SS 112* [*UK*]. The Isley Brothers (Ronald, Rudolph and O'Kelly) were a black trio from Cincinnati, Ohio, who were discovered by RCA in Washington, DC in 1959. They had a minor chart hit with their first release, **Shout — Part 1**, which through steady sales and two chart runs (1959 and 1962) finally sold a million copies. They then switched labels to Wand and

recorded this Bert Russell and Bill Medley number, written in 1960. It reached No 17 in America with 16 weeks on the charts. In Britain

it was picked up by EMI and released on their Stateside label. It was their first British hit, but only just crept into the Top 50 at No 42 for one week. In 1963 the same song gave Brian Poole and the Tremeloes their first hit, and the Beatles a million-selling EP in Europe and (in 1964) a million-selling single in America.

CLAUDE KING   *American*

WOLVERTON MOUNTAIN *CBS-Columbia 42352* [*USA*]. A top country-and-western disc, this first million seller for Claude King was written by Merle Kilgore and King himself. Claude, country-and-western vocalist, was born in Shreveport, Louisiana. He bought his first guitar when he was 12 for 50 cents from a farmer, and began songwriting at an early age. He attended the University of Idaho and a business college at Shreveport. This disc got to No 7 in the US charts with 16 weeks in the bestsellers. The song is an adaptation of a traditional American mountain song and was No 1 for 9 weeks during its 26 weeks in the US country charts.

STEVE LAWRENCE   *American*

GO AWAY LITTLE GIRL *CBS-Columbia 42601* [*USA*]. The first million seller for Steve was another big success for husband and wife songwriting team Gerry Goffin and Carole King. Steve Lawrence (real name Sam Leibowitz) was born in New York on 8 July 1933. In 1952, he caught the public eye when he won an Arthur Godfrey 'Talent Scout' show, then appeared with it for a week on TV and radio, and later as a regular on the Steve Allen TV show. Through this latter association, he met Eydie Gormé, also a regular on the show. They married in 1957 and eventually became one of the most successful nightclub acts in the USA.

Steve was heard by King Records who signed him up and he had his first hit with **Poinciana** (1953). In 1954, he signed with Coral Records and enjoyed a hit with **Party Doll**. In 1959 he switched to ABC-Paramount and hits **Pretty Blue Eyes** and **Footsteps** followed. In 1961 came **Portrait of My Love** on the United Artists label, then this million seller on Columbia. Steve and Eydie have starred in their own TV shows . Eydie Gormé is also a disc star with hits **Yes My Darling Daughter** and **Blame It on the Bossa Nova**. This disc was No 1 for two weeks in the USA in 1963 and 17 weeks in the bestsellers.

BRENDA LEE   *American*

ALL ALONE AM I/SAVE ALL YOUR LOVIN' FOR ME *US Decca 31424* [*USA*] *Brunswick 05882* [*UK*]. This was Brenda Lee's fourth million seller. **All Alone Am I** was written by Jean Ioannidis (original Greek words) and Manos Hadjidakis (music), with English words added by Arthur Altman. It reached No 3 in America, with 15 weeks on the charts. It reached No 7 in Britain in 1963, with a 17-week chart run. The record was also a big hit in Japan, Brazil,

Mexico and Argentina. In America the flip side, **Save All Your Lovin' for Me**, also charted, reaching No 53 in six weeks on the Hot 100.

DICKEY LEE *American*

PATCHES *Smash 1758 [USA]*. Dickey Lee, talented singer-guitarist-composer, was born and raised in Memphis. He became a graduate of Memphis State University, where he participated in sports and majored in physical education. He is a former Golden Gloves champion.

Producer Jack Clement, who aided him in every phase of his career — writing, singing, confidence — was one of the major influences of his success. **Patches** was written in 1960 by Barry Mann and Larry Kolber. It got to No 6 and was on the US bestsellers for 14 weeks. It was reported that the disc subsequently sold over a million.

In 1965, Dickey had a hit with **Laurie** on the 20th Century-Fox-distributed TCF-Hall label, and later joined RCA Records.

KETTY LESTER *American*

LOVE LETTERS *Era 3068 [USA] London HLN 9527 [UK]*. The first million seller for Ketty was written in 1945 for the film *Love Letters* by Edward Heyman (words) and Victor Young (music). Ketty was born in Hope, Arkansas, and after college enrolled for training as a nurse at the City College, San Francisco. She joined the college choir which made her realize that it was music, not nursing, for which she was destined.

Miss Lester's disc chance came through two A&R men from Era Records hearing her nightclub act. They offered her **Love Letters** which racked up big sales through her rendering and the unique new treatment, particularly the original accompaniment. Era then signed her to a five-year pact. The disc was No 5 and 14 weeks in the US bestsellers, and No 4 and 12 weeks in the British bestsellers.

LITTLE EVA *American*

THE LOCOMOTION *Dimension 1000 [USA] London HL 9581*. The first million seller for teenbeat vocalist Little Eva was yet another big hit for husband-wife songwriters, Gerry Goffin and Carole King. Little Eva (Eva Narcissus Boyd) was born on 29 June 1945 in Belhaven, North Carolina, one of a family of 14. She moved to New York at 15 to stay with relatives and attend high school. Songwriters Goffin and King hired her in the evenings as their babysitter while they worked on new compositions. Eva sang as she went about the house. Her pleasant voice and easy style struck the trained ear of the Goffins as she sang a Dee Dee Sharp song, so they suggested she cut some demonstration discs. Dimension Records were impressed and let her record the Goffins' latest song **The Locomotion**. Little Eva demonstrated the dance on TV and for a while it superseded the Twist, from which it was a development. She later appeared in Britain. **The Locomotion** was No 1 for three weeks during 12 weeks in the R&B charts.

It went to No 1 for one week in the *Billboard* Hot 100 and three weeks in *Cash Box*. It stayed in the *Billboard* Hot 100 for 16 weeks. In Britain, the record went to No 2 and, although it spent 17 weeks in the charts, in one sense it never really went away. **The Locomotion** remains to this day a party favourite and, along with records like Chris Montez' **Let's Dance**, has been a consistent favourite whenever sixties records are played. In 1972 London re-issued **The Locomotion** and Little Eva went back up the charts again, reaching No 11 in an 11-week second chart run. In 1988 Australian TV actress-turned-pop star Kylie Minogue had a big international hit reviving the song again. Her Stock-Aitkin-Waterman-produced version also sold a million, and was the top-selling record in America for one week.

VAUGHN MEADER with NAOMI BROSSART *American*

THE FIRST FAMILY (Album) *Cadence 3060 [USA] London HAA 8048 [UK]*. This comedy disc by Vaughn Meader, assisted by Naomi Brossart, is a series of skits on the US President John F. Kennedy and his family. It was up to 1962 the disc industry's fastest and all-time bestseller comedy album with an estimated five and a half million sale in as many months. Released in mid-November 1962, this disc sold 1,600,000 in two weeks, and 3,250,000 in a month, continuing at the rate of 100,000 per day for some time thereafter. It was at No 1 for nine weeks.

Vaughn Meader was born on 20 March 1936 in Boston. He worked for a radio station in Boston prior to his four-year Army service. He started in show business as a pianist in the country field and switched to comedy while playing in clubs around New England. Eventually he came to New York and secured an engagement at the Phase 2 in Greenwich Village, and got his first big break on a 'Talent Scouts' TV show in 1962. From then he made numerous appearances on TV and played many of the top supper clubs throughout the USA. One of his assets was a resemblance to President Kennedy, and he even had the same kind of haircut. In his take off-of the President in the album, he perfectly captured his voice. Naomi Brossart impersonated Jackie Kennedy. After the President's assassination on 22 November 1963, all copies of the disc were withdrawn from the record stores. Gold Disc award RIAA 1962. Grammy Awards for 'Album of the Year' 1962 and 'Best Comedy Performance' 1962.

NED MILLER *American*

FROM A JACK TO A KING (originally released in 1957) *Fabor 114 [USA] London HL 9648 [UK]*. This disc was released in December 1962 and by July 1963 had sold an estimated two million. The song, written by Ned Miller in 1957, was recorded by him then on Fabor Records who leased it to Dot Records, but it failed to register. Then Fabor Robinson decided to try again and orders started to come in with spectacular results.

Ned Miller comes from Salt Lake City, Utah, where he was raised. (He was born in Rains, Utah, on 12 April 1925.) He bought his first guitar at the age of nine, his mother teaching him to play. At 16, he was writing songs. He served three years in the Marine Corps in the South Pacific, and after service studied for two years under the GI Bill and became a pipefitter. Miller then wrote **Dark Moon**, a hit for Gale Storm (1957), and, in all, 100 other songs. This disc reached No 6 with 13 weeks in the US bestsellers, and No 2 with 21 weeks in the British bestsellers.

MINA *Italian*

HEISSER SAND (Hot Sand) *Polydor 8136 [West Germany]*. This disc was a million seller, mainly in Europe, by 1965. The song was written by Kurt Feltz (a producer of operettas for Polydor since 1945) with music by Werner Scharfenberger. The song was specially recorded in Italy for release in Germany by Polydor, Mina's first disc in German.

Mina was born in Busto Arsizio, Italy in 1940, and became a very popular singing personality. She was discovered at a talent show. In addition to her disc success, she starred in films and on TV, and toured Europe, Japan and South America. Her first disc hit was **Il cielo in una stanza** (1961) which sold almost a million to win her nationwide acclaim. Then followed **Renato**, **Strigimi forte I polsi** and **Chihuahua** in 1962. In 1963 her disc of **Stessa piaggia stesso mare** was a big hit in Italy. Then came **Heisser Sand** and recording in several languages. Mina was later signed to RI.FI Records.

THE MIRACLES   *American*

YOU'VE REALLY GOT A HOLD ON ME *Tamla 54073 [USA]*. The second million seller for the Miracles was written by group leader William 'Smokey' Robinson. The disc was a big hit in early 1963. Released on 8 December 1962, it reached No 8 with 16 weeks in the US Hot 100, and No 1 for one week with 14 weeks in the R&B charts.

LOU MONTE   *American*

PEPINO THE ITALIAN MOUSE *Reprise 20106 [USA]*. The first million seller for Lou Monte was issued in late 1962 and reached a million sale by 1963. Comedy vocalist Lou was born on 2 April 1917 and comes from Oakland, New Jersey. **Pepino** was written by Ray Allen and Wanda Merrell. The disc was No 5 and 10 weeks in the US bestsellers.

CHRIS MONTEZ   *American*

LET'S DANCE *Monogram 505 [USA]* London HLU 9596 [UK]. The first million seller for teenbeat vocalist Chris was written by Jim Lee (chief of Monogram Records). It got to No 6 in the US charts and was 14 weeks in the bestsellers. It reached No 2 and was 18 weeks in the British charts. Chris was born on 17 January 1943 in Los Angeles. His brothers taught him to play guitar, and at 15 he began to sing and write songs. After high school in 1961, he met Jim Lee, a young impresario, who was looking for talent to start his Monogram Records. Chris first recorded one of his own songs **All You Had to Do Was Tell Me** which

got some attention, then came this million seller. His real name is Christoper Montanez.

SOME KINDA FUN *Monogram 507 [USA]* London HLU 9650 [UK]. The second million seller for Chris Montez was written by Jim Lee (of Monogram Records) and Montez himself. It reached No 43 and was nine weeks in the US charts. It was No 10 in Britain with nine weeks in the Top 50 chart.

ROY ORBISON   *American*

DREAM BABY *Monument 456 [USA]* London HLU 9511 [UK]. Roy's sixth million seller reached No 3 in the USA (with 12 weeks in the bestsellers), and No 2 and 14 weeks in the British charts. The song was written by Cindy Walker.

WORKIN' FOR THE MAN/LEAH *Monument 467 [USA]* London HLU 9607 [UK]. Roy Orbison wrote both sides of what in America was a double A side hit, with global sales eventually passing the million mark. This was his seventh record to reach this level. Though **Workin' for the Man** was meant to be the main side, and did reach No 33 with 11 weeks on the charts, **Leah** went higher. In its 10 weeks on the Hot 100, it reached No 25. In Britain, only **Workin' for the Man** charted, reaching No 50 for one week.

THE ORLONS   *American*

THE WAH-WATUSI *Cameo 218 [USA]*. The first million seller for the Orlons was written by Kal Mann and Dave Appell (of Cameo Records). This vocal group comprises Shirley Brickley (born 9 December 1944), Rosetta Hightower (born 23 June 1944), Marlena Davis (born 4 October 1944) and Steve Caldwell (born 22 November 1942). Originally the Orlons were a quintet who met in junior high school in Philadelphia and sang together for about five years at school assemblies and local functions. They disbanded and then Stephen Caldwell got the group together after locating two of the

original members to form this quartet. After about a year, they were signed up by Cameo and came up with this big hit which got to No 2 in the US charts and was 14 weeks in the bestsellers.

DON'T HANG UP *Cameo 231 [USA]* Cameo-Parkway C 231 [UK]. The second million seller for the Orlons was also written by Kal Mann and Dave Appell (of Cameo Records). It reached chart position No 4 in the USA with 15 weeks in the bestsellers, and was No 39 in Britain.

PAUL AND PAULA   *American*

HEY, PAULA *Philips 40084 [USA]* Philips BF 304012 [UK]. Issued in late 1962, this disc sold over one million in the USA and globally two million by 1963. The duo's real names are Ray Hildebrand, writer of the song, from Harlingen, Texas (born 21 November 1940), and Jill Jackson, from Brownwood, Texas. As students at Howard Payne College in Brownwood, Texas, they teamed up after singing for a Cancer Fund drive radio programme. They travelled to Fort Worth in November 1962 for an audition with Major Bill Smith, well-known star maker, only to learn he was scheduled to record an artist and could not hear them. Determined to get a hearing, they waited. The scheduled artist did not turn up. As Smith walked out, the duo began singing

Hey, Paula and within minutes Smith realized their talent and cut a demonstration disc the same day on the Lecam label as by Jill and Ray, Philips Records acquiring global rights. It soon zoomed to No 1 in the charts and stayed top for three weeks in the USA in 1963, as well as being 15 weeks in the Hot 100. It was No 1 for two weeks during 10 weeks in the R&B charts. It was No 8 and 17 weeks in the British bestsellers. Gold Disc award RIAA 1963.

PETER, PAUL AND MARY   *American*

PETER, PAUL AND MARY (Album) *Warner Brothers 1449 [USA] Warner Brothers WM 4064 [UK]*. Issued in March 1962, this album sold over a million in the USA by mid-1963, and two million by mid-1965. The trio's full names are Peter Yarrow (born in New York on 31 May 1938), Paul Stookey (born on 30 November 1937 in Baltimore, Maryland) and Mary Allin Travers (born on 7 November 1937 in Louisville, Kentucky). Peter holds a psychology degree from Cornell University where he was also an instructor on a folk ballad course. He was discovered at the Newport Folk Festival in 1960 after appearing as a single artist in his own very successful tour of various nightclub spots catering for folk music fans. He plays the guitar. Paul played an electric guitar for a high school rock'n'roll group on local TV and worked his way through Michigan State University, also doing stand-up comic routines in Greenwich Village, and helping Mary make a come-back as a singer after she had worked in a Broadway flop, *The Next President*, with Mort Sahl. Mary appeared with several teenage folk groups, and then twice at Carnegie Hall.

Life-long interest in folk music led the three to Greenwich Village where they formed a trio, touring the country from the Blue Angel to the Hungry I, after seven months working up their initial repertoire of 18 numbers with the assistance of Milton Okun (formerly with Harry Belafonte) to polish their arrangements. They developed their style and acquired a big following. Their fortunes began to rise with this album, one of the songs **Lemon Tree** issued as a single bringing the trio into the national limelight. **If I Had a Hammer** further enhanced their reputation. Their success was phenomenal both as recording artists and on personal appearances. The trio visited Britain in September 1963 and then appeared in other European countries.

This album was in the US bestsellers lists for 185 weeks, and spent seven weeks at No 1. In Britain the album did not chart until January 1964, when it made a brief appearance at No 18 for one week. The RIAA awarded it a Gold Disc in 1962, and a double Platinum Disc for US sales of two million on 13 October 1986.

The disc contained the following songs: **Early in the Morning**, by Paul Stookey; **Five Hundred Miles**, by Hedy West, Bobby Bare and Charlie Williams (1962); **Sorrow**, by Paul Stookey and Peter Yarrow; **This Train**, by Peter Yarrow; **Bamboo**, by Van Ronk and Weisman; **It's Raining**, by Paul Stookey; **If I Had My Way**, by Davis; **Cruel War**, by Peter Yarrow; **Lemon Tree**, by Will Holt (1960); **If I Had a Hammer**, by Lee Hays and Pete Seeger (1958); **Autumn to May**, by Peter Yarrow and Paul Stookey; **Where Have All the Flowers Gone?** by Pete Seeger (1961) (additional verses by Joe Hickerson).

ESTHER PHILLIPS   *American*

RELEASE ME *Lenox 5555 [USA] (re-released in 1967 on Atlantic 2411)*. Esther Phillips was born on 23 December 1935 in Houston. She made a number of R&B records in the forties and fifties. In 1962 she had her first hit on the national charts with the country-and-western favourite **Release Me**, written in 1954 by Eddie Miller and W.S. Stevenson. The record reached No 8 with 14 weeks on the charts. In 1967 Atlantic re-issued the record, and it made No 93 in its two-week return to the charts. Her last American hit, **What a Difference a Day Makes** in 1975, was her only British hit when released on both sides of the Atlantic by Kudu.

BOBBY 'BORIS' PICKETT AND   *American*
THE KRYPT KICKERS

MONSTER MASH *Garpax 44167 [USA] London HL 10320 [UK]*. Bobby Pickett himself and Leonard Capizzi wrote **Monster Mash**. It became a million seller by 1963, No 1 in the USA for two weeks with 14 weeks in the bestsellers, and No 3 and 13 weeks in the British bestsellers.

GENE PITNEY   *American*

THE MAN WHO SHOT LIBERTY VALANCE *Musicor 1020 [USA]*. The second reputed million seller for Gene Pitney took a title inspired by the film of the same name, and was written by Hal David (words) and Burt Bacharach (music). It was No 4 in the US charts and 13 weeks in the bestsellers.

ONLY LOVE CAN BREAK A HEART/IF I DIDN'T HAVE A DIME (TO PLAY THE JUKEBOX) *Musicor 1022 [USA]*. This third million seller for Gene Pitney consisted of the **Dime** song written by Bert Russell (Berns) and Phil Medley (with arrangement and conducting by Chuck Sagle. The **Heart** song was written by Hal David (words) and Burt Bacharach (music) with arrangement and conducting by the composer Bacharach. **Only Love Can Break a Heart** was No 2 and 14 weeks in the US bestsellers. **If I Didn't Have a Dime** was No 31 and eight weeks in the bestsellers.

ELVIS PRESLEY   *American*

GOOD LUCK CHARM/ANYTHING THAT'S PART OF YOU *RCA Victor 47–7992 [USA] RCA Victor 1280 [UK]*. Elvis Presley's 30th million seller was a result of global sales. **Good Luck Charm** was the main side, and was No 1 for two weeks in *Billboard*'s American charts. (It was No 1 for one week in *Cash Box*.) It was also in *Billboard*'s Hot 100 for 13 weeks. The song was written by Aaron Schroeder and Wally Gold. It spent five weeks at No 1 in Britain, winning Presley another Silver Disc for sales of a quarter of a million. It was in the British charts for 17 weeks, at the same time as his **Strictly Elvis** EP hit the singles charts. **Anything That's Part of You** was written by Don Robertson, and reached No 31 with eight weeks on the US charts. Both sides were recorded at RCA Nashville on 15 October 1961.

SHE'S NOT YOU/JUST TELL HER JIM SAID HELLO *RCA Victor 47–8041 [USA] RCA Victor 1303 [UK]*. Million seller No 31 for Elvis again came from global sales. The main side was **She's Not You**, written by the hit-writing team of Jerry Leiber, Mike Stoller and Doc Pomus. The record made No 5 in America, with a 10-week chart run. It was a bigger hit in Britain, where it went to No 1 for three weeks, with 14 weeks in the charts. In the US, **Just Tell Her Jim Said Hello** reached No 55 for five weeks, **She's Not You** made No 3 in the R&B charts where it stayed for five weeks. Both sides were recorded at RCA Nashville on 19 March 1962.

RETURN TO SENDER *RCA Victor 47–8100 [USA] RCA Victor 1320 [UK]*. Presley's 32nd million seller was the only one of the year to achieve the million in America alone, though it was April 1983, after his death, before it finally won an RIAA Gold Disc. The song was written by Otis Blackwell and Winfield Scott, and reached No 1 for one week in the *Cash Box* US charts. It was No 2 in *Billboard*, with 16 weeks on the charts. The song was from the Elvis film *Girls, Girls Girls* and, along with the rest of the soundtrack, was recorded for Paramount Pictures at the Radio Recorders studio in Hollywood in March 1962. As well as being a pop hit, it reached No 5 in the US R&B charts during a 12-week chart run. In Britain the record went to No 1 for three weeks, with a chart run of 12 weeks. Presley's was the only American record to reach No 1 in 1963, the first year since the charts began in 1952 that home-grown talent had been so dominant.

CLIFF RICHARD   *British*

THE YOUNG ONES *Columbia (EMI) DB 4761 [UK]*. **The Young Ones** entered the British charts at No 1 first week of release, on 12 January 1962. It had what was then a record advance order of 524,000 copies, thus qualifying for an immediate Silver Disc. It spent six weeks at No 1, and 21 weeks in the charts. Of all Cliff's 100 hits by 1989, only **Living Doll** spent longer in the charts. Sales of **The Young Ones** were enormous, bigger than any record he released until **We Don't Talk Anymore** in 1979. British sales passed the 900,000 mark by the end of February and the one million mark in March. It was also Cliff's biggest international hit until 1979. **The Young Ones** entered the Indian charts at No 1 first week of release, and was No 1 in Australia, New Zealand, South Africa, Ireland, Denmark, Belgium, The Netherlands and Japan. It was also a hit in Finland, Sweden, Norway, Germany, Austria, Spain, Israel, Venezuela and Chile.

The Young Ones was written for the Cliff Richard film of the same name by Sid Tepper and Roy Bennett. A slightly different version appeared in the film and on the soundtrack LP, which also sold a million copies. (See **The Young Ones** album, 1961.) For the singles version, producer Norrie Paramor added an orchestral backing to Cliff and the Shadows. The record was engineered by Malcolm Addy and Norman Smith. With global sales of two and a half million, it was Cliff's second biggest selling record ever. **We Say Yeah**, the British B side, was also a hit in Japan and Israel. It was written by Bruce Welsh and Hank Marvin

of the Shadows and their manager Peter Gormley, and produced by Norrie Paramor. It was also featured in the film.

1962 was another spectacular year for Cliff Richard, who reached new heights each year. The film made him the top box office attraction in Britain, and his records made him the No 1 pop star. He won an Ivor Novello Award and was named 'Show Business Personality of the Year'. At the end of the year, he again won all the music paper popularity polls as 'Top British Male Singer', for the fourth year running. The period from the release of **The Young Ones** in January 1962 to the chart dominance of tracks from *Summer Holiday* in the first quarter of 1963 marked the height of Cliff Richard's career.

I'M LOOKING OUT THE WINDOW/DO YOU WANNA DANCE? *Columbia (EMI) DB 4828* [*UK*]. Another double A-sided million seller for Cliff Richard, his 14th single and 16th record to achieve the seven-figure sale. Released in May 1962, **I'm Looking Out the Window** peaked at No 2, a position it held over a period of six weeks in the various charts. In the *New Musical Express* charts **Do You Wanna Dance?** charted separately, and reached No 10 in its own right. It was one of only two occasions when both sides of a Cliff record independently made the Top 10. (**The Next Time/Bachelor Boy** was the other.) It easily won another Silver Disc, and had 17 weeks in the Top 50.

I'm Looking Out the Window was the first oldie that Cliff had recorded as a single. A slow ballad written by John Jacob Niles, it had previously been recorded by Gracie Fields and Peggie Lee. **Do You Wanna Dance?** was a remake of the upbeat Bobby Freeman hit of 1958. The American singer composed it himself. Global sales were just over a million.

IT'LL BE ME *Columbia (EMI) DB 4886* [*UK*]. Cliff's next release was another rock'n'roll revival, this time of the old Jerry Lee Lewis rocker **It'll Be Me**. It had been written by Jack Clement, and though it was never a hit single for Lewis it was regularly featured in his fifties stage act. Cliff's version went to No 2 in all the charts, with 12 weeks in the Top 50. EMI claimed a Silver Disc on 19 October 1962. Overseas sales were particularly high: it went to No 1 in Australia and India (first week of release in both countries), South Africa, Denmark and Belgium, was No 2 in New Zealand, Ireland, Norway and The Netherlands, and a Top 10 hit in Sweden, Austria, Italy, Israel and Hong Kong. It was also his first hit in Canada for some while, reaching No 17. The record was produced by Norrie Paramor at the EMI Abbey Road studios in London on 17 May 1962.

BACHELOR BOY/THE NEXT TIME *Columbia (EMI) DB 4950* [*UK*] *Epic 9691* [*USA*]. In December 1962 Columbia released the first single from Cliff Richard's second major film, *Summer Holiday*. In the film, Cliff and the Shadows take a London double-decker bus on holiday to Greece. The film was a huge success, the top box office draw of 1963. The soundtrack album, released in 1963, went to No 1 for 14 weeks, knocking the Shadows' **Out of The Shadows** off the top. It was Cliff's longest period at No 1 in the LP charts. This single led to Cliff Richard and the Shadows completely dominating the top of the British charts for the first three months of 1963. The No 1s in *Record Retailer* from 3 January to 4 April were **The Next Time** and **Bachelor Boy** (Cliff), **Dance On** (Shadows), **Diamonds** (ex-Shadows Jet Harris and Tony Meehan), **Wayward Wind** (Frank

Ifield), **Summer Holiday/Dancing Shoes** (Cliff) and **Foot Tapper** (Shadows). The odd one out, Frank Ifield, had the same manager, promoter, producer and label as Cliff and the Shadows.

Bachelor Boy was written by Cliff Richard and Shadow Bruce Welsh in a few minutes as a filler for the film soundtrack. It was recorded on 16 November 1962 and proved one of the biggest hits of Cliff's whole career. **The Next Time** was written by Americans Buddy Kaye and Philip Springer and recorded on 10 May 1962. The Shadows backed Cliff on both records, which were produced by Norrie Paramor, who produced all Cliff's records at this time. The Norrie Paramor Strings also appeared on **The Next Time**. Both sides of the record were equally popular. The American paper *Cash Box* compiled a British chart which averaged out the other charts, and used some sales data of its own. In this chart both sides were listed as separate entries, and both went independently to No 1. This is the only time in the history of the charts that two sides of the same record have both separately topped the charts.

In the USA **The Next Time** was put out as the B side of **Lucky Lips** on Epic 5–9597. (See 1963.) **Bachelor Boy** was coupled with **True, True Loving** on Epic 5–9691, and made No 99 for one week. In the rest of the world, **The Next Time** was No 1 in Ireland, Belgium, India and Israel, while **Bachelor Boy** was No 1 in Israel, Japan, Canada, New Zealand, South Africa, Sweden and The Netherlands. The two sides were major hits in many other countries, chalking up 27 chart entries around the world. The record won a Silver Disc for British sales of over a quarter of a million, and sold one and a half million copies around the world.

TOMMY ROE   *American*

SHEILA *ABC-Paramount 10329* [*USA*] *HMV POP 1060* [*UK*]. The first million seller for teenbeat vocalist Tommy was his own composition. Thomas David Roe was born in Atlanta, Georgia, on 9 May 1942 and educated there, at Brown High School. At 16 he formed his own group — the Satins — for school and local dates. The group actually recorded **Sheila** on the Judd label in 1960 but it did not register then. Tommy then signed with ABC-Paramount. He has written over 125 songs. His singing style is based on Buddy Holly's. This disc was No 1 for two weeks in the USA with 14 weeks in the bestsellers, and No 3 and 14 weeks in the British bestsellers. Tommy was first recognized as a performer in Britain where he spent a great deal of his time. Gold Disc award RIAA 1969.

DAVE ROSE AND   *American*
HIS ORCHESTRA

THE STRIPPER *MGM 13064* [*USA*]. This third million seller for David Rose was his own composition. **The Stripper** was top seller in the US charts for two weeks, and 17 weeks in the bestsellers.

KYU SAKAMOTO   *Japanese*

SUKIYAKI (Ueo Muite Aruko) *Toshiba LR-1390 (Japan) Capitol 4945 [USA] HMV POP 1171 [UK].* **Sukiyaki** was the first million-selling Japanese disc in the USA. It was written in 1962 by pianist Hachidai Nakamura with lyrics by Rokusuke Ei entitled **Ueo Muite Aruko** (Walk with Your Chin Up) for an album. The disc was heard in December 1962 by Louis Benjamin, head of Pye Records (Britain) while on a business trip to Japan. He brought it back to England for Kenny Ball and his band to record it, dubbing it **Sukiyaki** for simplicity's sake. Kenny Ball's instrumental version was a hit in Britain. Capitol Records, therefore, released the original vocal version by Sakamoto under the title of **Sukiyaki** and it became the No 1 bestseller in the USA in 1963 for four weeks with 14 weeks in the bestsellers, selling a million there. In a bizarre twist it became the first and last Japanese-language disc to make the US R&B charts, where in its four weeks in the chart it peaked at No 18. It was No 6 and 13 weeks in the British bestsellers. Kyu Sakamoto was a big star in Japan for some years, with eight bestselling albums and 15 hit singles in that time, as well as acting in films and making TV appearances. His career started in the teahouses of Tokyo until, in 1960, the Toshiba label heard him and signed him up. His very first disc was a big hit. **Sukiyaki** is a lilting, melancholy song of nocturnal loneliness. It sold half a million copies in Japan when first released there. Kyu was a native of the industrial city of Kawasaki, and he first sang with a group, the Paradise Kings. It was disc jockey Rich Osborne of radio station KORD in Pasco, Washington, who introduced the original Japanese version from the Toshiba album to his night-time USA audience. He was immediately swamped with requests to repeat both the music and the announcement of the song's title and artist. Osborne repeated the song on his day-time programme with the same results, and it soon became immensely popular in Washington State, and eventually all over America. Kyu (pronounced 'Q') also registered with his follow-up disc **China Nights** in 1963. He was killed in the Japan Airlines 747 disaster on 12 August 1965, when a JAL jumbo crashed into a mountain near Tokyo killing 520 people.

NEIL SEDAKA   *American*

BREAKING UP IS HARD TO DO *RCA Victor 8046 [USA] RCA Victor 1298 [UK].* Neil Sedaka is an American of Turkish origin, born on 13 March 1939, in Brooklyn, New York. His taxi driver father encouraged his musical talent, and paid for him to study piano and composition. He won a scholarship to the Juilliard School of Music in New York, and made his radio debut in 1956 on a programme for school-age talent. He was a successful composer, with major stars like Connie Francis recording his songs. He then signed with RCA, and had his first hit in 1958 with **The Diary**. The follow-up was **I Go Ape**, which, though a minor hit at the time, sold steadily over the years and its much greater success abroad (it was his first British hit, reaching No 9), eventually made it his first global million seller.

    Breaking Up is Hard to Do was his first No 1, for two weeks with 14 weeks in the charts and was written by Sedaka and Howard Greenfield. In Britain the record reached No 7, with 14 weeks in the charts. Neil Sedaka had 28 records make the US charts, and 19 hits in Britain.

THE SHADOWS   *British*

WONDERFUL LAND *Columbia (EMI) DB 4790 [UK].* The Shadows' fourth million seller was written by Jerry Lordan, who also wrote their first Gold Disc **Apache** and other hits like **Atlantis**. The record was No 1 for nine weeks, and spent 19 weeks in the charts. It was a major international hit, and No 1 in many countries in Europe and the Commonwealth. It was the top record of the year in Britain in 1962.

    The Shadows' line-up underwent a number of changes in the sixties. Drummer Tony Meehan was replaced by Brian Bennett in October 1961. Bass guitarist Jet Harris left in April 1962. Harris' replacement was Brian 'Licorice' Locking, who only stayed just over a year. John Rostill took over on bass in 1963, remaining until the Shadows temporarily split up in 1969. He committed suicide in 1973. What brought the Shadows back together permanently was the release in 1977 of an EMI hits compilation album, **20 Golden Greats**. This went to No 1 for six weeks, and became their first album to sell over a million copies. They released a new LP in 1979, with **String of Hits** going to No 1 for three weeks in March 1980, with 48 weeks in the album charts. Their **Simply Shadows** LP went Platinum in Britain in 1988. In their 30-year career, the Shadows have been one of the most successful groups in the world. They have had 32 hit singles (plus one B side and an EP making the singles charts). Of these, five went to No 1 and six sold over a million copies. They have enjoyed huge album sales, with four of their 20 chart albums going to No 1 and two selling over a million copies. As with Cliff Richard, they show every sign of going on to the millennium.

DANCE ON *Columbia (EMI) DB 4948 [UK].* The Shadows' fourth No 1 and fifth million seller was **Dance On**. The composer credits on the record label read V. and E. Murtaguh-Adams. They were, in fact, the singing group the Avons, who had had a big hit in Britain with **Seven Little Girls Sitting in the Back Seat** in 1959. **Dance On**, an upbeat instrumental, went to No 1 in the *New Musical Express* in the first week of 1963, and stayed there for three weeks. The Shadows knocked Cliff Richard and themselves off the top, replacing **The Next Time/Bachelor Boy**. In an ironic twist, they were themselves knocked off the No 1 position by former Shadows Jet Harris and Tony Meehan and **Diamonds**.

    Dance On spent 15 weeks in the charts and won a Silver Disc. It was a major hit around the world, and after many years' global sales finally passed the million mark.

12   **DISC**, January 6, 1962

HANK MARVIN talks frankly about The Shadows' latest single

'The Savage' was mediocre —and a bad mistake

THERE has been a great deal of controversy over The Shadows' single—" The Savage." " We have had more conflicting opinions from the fans over this one than over any other record we have made," Hank Marvin told me. "Some say that it is the worst thing that they have heard and others say that it is the best single we have done.

" BUT WE KNOW HOW WE FEEL ABOUT IT. IT IS UNDOUBTEDLY A MEDIOCRE RECORD AND SHOULD NEVER HAVE BEEN RELEASED AS A SINGLE."

BRUCE WELCH, JET HARRIS and HANK MARVIN during a concert (DISC Pic)

DEE DEE SHARP — American

MASHED POTATO TIME *Cameo 212* [USA]. The first million seller for teenage vocalist Dee Dee was written by Jon Sheldon and Harry Land. Dee Dee (real name Dione LaRue) was born on 9 September 1945 and hails from Philadelphia. She started her rise to stardom after answering a newspaper advertisement for a girl singer when 15, and soon was doing backgrounds on recordings at various Philadelphia sessions. She eventually auditioned for Cameo and recorded as part of a group for a disc that was not released. Dee Dee then impressed the company's artists' and repertoire director Dave Appell who asked her to sing for him alone but the department was too busy at the time to record her. Several months later, Chubby Checker recorded **Slow Twistin'** which seemed to lack the punch of his previous efforts. Head man Bernie Lowe of Cameo suggested using a female vocalist to give the record added sound. Dee Dee was called in for the sessions, and Lowe was so overcome with her talent that he decided to record her first solo that same night. This disc **Mashed Potato Time** was the result. Dee Dee then went on to make more hit discs while still at Overbrook High School, and made radio, TV and personal appearances. This disc was No 2 for two weeks in the USA charts with 18 weeks in the bestsellers. It was No 1 for four weeks in the R&B charts where it stayed for 16 weeks. It was the first of 10 R&B hits up to **I Love You Anyway** in 1981.

RIDE! *Cameo 230* [USA]. This second million seller for Dee Dee Sharp was written by Jon Sheldon and Dave Leon. It achieved No 5 in the USA charts and 13 weeks in the bestsellers. Her third hit, it made No 7 with seven weeks in the R&B charts.

ALLAN SHERMAN — American

MY SON, THE FOLK SINGER (Album) *Warner Brothers 1475* [USA]. This exceedingly funny album sold a million in 10 weeks in the USA. Comedian Allan Sherman was born on 30 November 1924 in Chicago, raised by his mother, his father and three successive stepfathers in Los Angeles, Miami, Chicago and New York. He went to 21 schools and the University of Illinois. He created special material for many nightclub performers, worked in TV for some years, and devised and produced the panel game 'I've Got a Secret'. He then made this album to become a world famous comedian. His follow-up disc (1963) was **My Son, the Celebrity**. The **My Son** series of albums totalled three million sales. Gold Disc award RIAA 1962.

THE SHIRELLES — American

SOLDIER BOY *Scepter 1228* [USA] HMV POP 1019 [UK]. The fourth million seller for the Shirelles was No 1 seller in the US charts for three weeks, and 14 weeks in the bestsellers. It was No 23 and nine weeks in the British charts. The song was written in 1961 by Florence Green and Luther Dixon, the latter the Shirelles' artists' and repertoire manager and arranger at Scepter Records. **Soldier Boy** reached No 3 during 13 weeks on the US R&B charts.

THE SPRINGFIELDS — British

SILVER THREADS AND GOLDEN NEEDLES *Philips 40038* [USA]. The Springfields were formed in 1960 by Tom Springfield (born Tom O'Brien on 2 July 1934, in Hampstead, London), his sister Dusty (born Mary O'Brien on 16 April 1940, in Hampstead) and their friend Tim Field. The group had started after Tom Springfield, playing cabaret at Helen Cordet's London nightclub, substituted Tim Field for his then regular partner who had fallen ill. The new partnership worked so well that they decided to make it permanent, and added Tom's sister Dusty. (See Dusty Springfield, 1963.) During the spring of 1960, the group spent a lot of time rehearsing in a field, hence the name the Springfields (and the change of name for Tom and Dusty). In April 1961 the group auditioned for Philips. They played **Dear John** for A&R manager John Franz, who after the first chorus decided to sign them.

Dear John was their debut disc, though it failed to make the charts. On the last day of August 1961 their second record **Breakaway** entered the charts, reaching No 31. Their third disc **Bambino** peaked at No 16. On the basis of this rather slender chart activity, the Springfields were voted 'Top British Vocal Group' of 1961 in both the *New Musical Express* and *Melody Maker* reader polls. This was as much a reflection of the absence of competition in an era when most groups were instrumental acts copying the Shadows as a recognition of Tom Springfield's writing ability and Dusty's singing.

1962 was a quiet period for the group in England, where their only hit was **Island of Dreams**. It entered the charts in December, and reached No 5 early in 1963. Unusually for a British act at that time, they achieved success in America. Their version of the country standard **Silver Threads and Golden Needles** reached No 20 with 10 weeks on the charts. The song was written in 1956 by Dick Reynolds and Jack Rhodes. The record was produced in England by Johnny Franz, with accompaniment directed by Ivor Raymonde. Though the record was not a hit in England, it did make No 1 in Australia and New Zealand. It was also their only hit in the US country charts where it reached No 6 during a 10-week chart run.

The Springfields had one more hit in America, the 1962 follow-up **Dear Hearts and Gentle People**, which only reached No 95. In Britain **Say I Won't Be There** followed **Island of Dreams** to No 5 in 1963, and their final hit **Come On Home** reached No 31 later the same year.

Tim Field left the group in November 1962, and was replaced by Mike Hurst (formerly known as Mike Pickworth). The Springfields won more popularity polls in 1962, but in the summer of 1963 they decided to disband. Their final public performance was in September.

Though the Springfields had scored only a few hits, their commercial folk sound had made them very popular, and their decision to split came as a great surprise to the public. Tom Springfield successfully concentrated on songwriting and production, launching the Australian group the Seekers and writing many of their hits. Mike Hurst made some solo records, but sank without trace. Dusty Springfield launched a solo career that made her Britain's best and most popular female solo singer.

RAY STEVENS — American

AHAB THE ARAB *Mercury 71966* [USA]. The first million seller for Ray Stevens was his own composition. Ray, born 24 January 1941, is from Clarkdale, Georgia. He became a disc jockey at the age of 15, and had his own TV show at 16. He plays the piano, trumpet, sax, clarinet, bass drums, tube mellophone and violin in addition to being a songwriter. The disc got to No 5 in the US charts and 11 weeks in the bestsellers.

THE TORNADOS — British

TELSTAR *Decca F 11494* [UK] *London 9561* [USA]. This disc was No 1 seller for five weeks in Britain and for three weeks in the USA, and global sales were estimated at five million. The tune was composed by Joe Meek, then aged 29, an ex-junior studio engineer who started a hit-making factory in a small lounge in Holloway Road, North London. In early 1962, he advertised for a group and picked five applicants, groomed them and sent them out on tour with John Leyton and Don Charles, vocalists. He then took them to Decca and got them a disc contract, and a season backing Billy Fury at Great Yarmouth. Thrilled by the brilliant achievement of the first Telstar trans-Atlantic transmission (23 July 1962), Meek felt the strong urge to write a tune in his studio. He phoned the Tornados immediately he had finished it to tell them to come to London the following weekend. They arrived and within an hour had worked out an arrangement and in a further half hour had recorded it. The personnel of the Tornados was Clem Cattini (drums), born 28 August 1939 in London; Alan Caddy (violin and guitar), born 2 February 1940 in Chelsea, London; George Bellamy (guitar), born 8 October 1941 in Sunderland; Roger Jackson (piano and organ), born 11 November 1938 in Kidderminster; and Heinz Burt (bass), born 25 July 1942 in Hargin, Germany. It was 16 weeks in the USA bestsellers, and 25 weeks in the British bestsellers. Composer Meek died tragically on 3 February 1967.

BOBBY VEE — American

THE NIGHT HAS A THOUSAND EYES *Liberty 55521* [USA] *Liberty LIB 10069* [UK]. This fifth million seller for Bobby Vee was written by Ben Weisman, Dottie Wayne and Marilyn Garrett in 1962 for the film *Just for Fun* in which Bobby featured it. It reached No 3 with 14 weeks in the US bestsellers, and No 3 and 12 weeks in Britain's bestsellers.

BOBBY VINTON — American

ROSES ARE RED (MY LOVE) *Epic 9509* [USA] *Columbia (EMI) DB 4748* [UK]. The first big hit for Vinton produced a sale of nearly two million. The song was written in 1961 by Al Byron and Paul Evans. This disc was top seller for four weeks in the US charts and was 15 weeks in the bestsellers, and No 15 in Britain with eight weeks in the charts. Stanley Robert Vinton, from Canonsburg, Pennsylvania, was born on 16 April 1935. He organized his first band in high school and later began to sing with the band. Epic Records signed him to a contract after hearing some of his recorded tapes. After the success of this disc he won a poll as the 'Most Promising Male Vocalist' of 1962. Vinton appeared in London in 1962 on a promotional trip while filming *Just for Fun*. Gold Disc award RIAA 1962.

GERHARD WENDLAND — German

TANZE MIT MIR IN DEN MORGEN (Dance With Me In The Morning) *Philips 4667* [West Germany]. Wendland was born in Berlin in 1932. He started his career as a singer in 1952. He was a top stage star and also did much film work and TV work. This song was written by Karl Goetz (words) and Kurt Hertha (music).

ANDY WILLIAMS — American

'MOON RIVER' AND OTHER GREAT MOVIE THEMES (Album) *CBS-Columbia 8609* [USA]. This third million seller for Andy Williams was his first album in this category. Robert Mersey both arranged and conducted the songs. The disc includes five songs (marked *) that were winners of the Academy Award for best film songs of their year.

The contents of the disc are: *Side 1* — **Love is a Many-Splendored Thing** * (film of same title), by P.F. Webster and Sammy Fain (1955); **A Summer Place** (film, same title), by Mack Discant and Max Steiner (1959); **Maria** (film *West Side Story* 1962) by S. Sondheim and L. Bernstein (1957); **Never on Sunday** * (film, same title), by B. Towne and M. Hadjidakis (1960); **As Time Goes By** (film *Casablanca* 1943), by Herman Hupfeld (orig. 1931); **Exodus** (film *Exodus*), by Pat Boone (1961) and Ernest Gold (1960); *Side 2* — **Moon River** * (film *Breakfast at Tiffany's*), by J. Mercer and Henry Mancini (1961); **Tonight** (film *West Side Story* 1962), by S. Sondheim and L. Bernstein (1957); **The Second Time Around** (film *High Time*), by S. Cahn and J. Van Heusen (1960); **Tender is the Night** (film, same title), by P.F. Webster and Sammy Fain (1962); **It Might as Well Be Spring** * (film *State Fair*) (1945), by O. Hammerstein and R. Rodgers (1945); **Three Coins in the Fountain** * (film, same title), by Sammy Cahn and Jule Styne (1954).

This disc, a two million seller by 1967, was in the US bestsellers list for 176 weeks, reaching No 3 at the height of its stay. Gold Disc award RIAA 1963.

1 9 6 3

What a year! There have been few occasions when one year has seen a complete change of direction, but that is what happened in 1963. It was the year that the Beatles really happened, and after that nothing was ever quite the same again.

The year started off in much the same way as 1962. In Britain Cliff Richard and the Shadows were at No 1. They completely dominated early 1963. Helped by the phenomenal success of their *Summer Holiday* film, they each had two No 1s in a row, and the film soundtrack was top of the album charts for 14 weeks. In the first three months of the year seven records made No 1. Four were from Cliff and the Shadows, one from former Shadows Jet Harris and Tony Meehan, and one from Frank Ifield. He shared the same manager, promoter, producer and label as Cliff and the Shadows. Never before had there been such a complete domination of the charts by one group of artists, yet within a few weeks it was all to change, with new stars sweeping all before them. The seventh No 1 in that first quarter of 1963, the only outsider from the Cliff/Shadows machine, was **Please Please Me** by the Beatles.

The Beatles had built up a loyal following in their native Liverpool, and in the German city of Hamburg where they honed their act during three gruelling periods performing in beer and night clubs. Their manager Brian Epstein found it hard going getting them a recording contract. They eventually signed with the Parlophone division of EMI, and in October 1962 released their first record. **Love Me Do** stuck around the lower regions of the charts for a long time, reaching No 17. It sold 116,000 copies, a very respectable if unspectacular figure for a debut disc.

The follow-up was released in January 1963. **Please Please Me** topped three of the four charts for two weeks at the end of February. The Beatles were then thrown off the top by Cliff Richard's **Summer Holiday**, though the group got their revenge later in the year when they twice kept him off the top. On 6 April Gerry and the Pacemakers, another Liverpool group, replaced the Shadows at the top, and from then on it was the new groups all the way. During the first three months of the year the Beatles were the only new group to top the charts. For the rest of the year it was the other way round, with Elvis Presley the only act from the old order to go to No 1 — and he managed it for only one week in just one of the four charts.

As **Please Please Me** climbed the charts the Beatles were touring the country as support act to Helen Shapiro. They spent a lot of time on the road in 1963, headlining two tours of their own. As the year wore on the reaction from the fans, especially the girls, became greater and greater. Some queued all night for tickets to their concerts, and wild scenes met the group wherever they appeared. Beatlemania had arrived.

Brian Epstein had packaged the group well, smoothing off the rough edges of their Liverpool/Hamburg days. With their mop tops and matching collarless suits the Beatles looked quite cute. There was none of the smouldering rebelliousness of the Rolling Stones to frighten a young girl's parents. The press took to the Beatles as something that at last was new and refreshing. This, coupled with the originality of their music, propelled them past Cliff and the Shadows, past Elvis Presley, and to a position of influence and dominance unequalled before or since. Quite simply, they became the greatest recording act ever.

The Beatles' third single, **From Me To You**, spent six weeks at No 1. **She Loves You** became the group's first record to sell a million copies. Their fifth single. **I Want To Hold Your Hand**, entered the charts at No 1 the first week of release, the first of eight records in a row to do so. In fact eleven Beatles singles achieved this feat in at least one of the British charts before the group broke up in 1970.

The Mersey Sound

In the wake of the Beatles a number of other Liverpool acts emerged. Many of them were managed by Brian Epstein, and most were signed to EMI. It was EMI that had most to lose from the end of the old order. With the exception of Elvis Presley, who they had lost to Decca in the fifties, most of the leading artists of the early sixties were with EMI. They had helped make EMI the biggest record company in the world, with a market share of one quarter of the entire non-Communist world's disc sales. Yet it was EMI that snapped up an even bigger share of the new acts than they had had of the old ones. Of the 19 records that topped at least one of the British charts in 1963, all but four were on EMI's Columbia or Parlophone labels. Of the 38 Silver Discs awarded during the year, EMI collected 26.

This part of the sixties was a golden age for EMI. It had exceptionally good leadership in chairman Sir Joseph Lockwood and managing director L.G. Wood. At a time when the American majors CBS and RCA did not operate on a global scale, and with Warner Brothers and Atlantic still growing and competing independents, EMI reached the peak of its success. Only the failure of its American subsidiary Capitol to capitalize on the company's British artists marred the picture.

The Record Industry

RCA signed a licensing deal with Decca's German subsidiary Teldec for north and central Europe, and sold its Spanish factory to Philips. Motown switched its British licensee from Oriole to EMI. Warner Brothers made the first of its major moves towards becoming the biggest record company in America by buying Reprise from Frank Sinatra in a deal that involved films as well as music.

The American record merchants and distributors organization ARMADA, meeting in conference, was told to clean up its act or face Government intervention. Former FTC chairman Earl Kintner told them that they were ignoring the law and regularly cheating their customers. 'You need [the law] like pagan nations need God,' he told them.

In June *Variety* reported a growing row over gospel music. 'Gospel music's current swing into the nightclub field is stirring up a storm of controversy... The protests raised against the 'popularisation' of gospel music have come in the past week from Mahalia Jackson on the Coast... Miss Jackson's protest was a virtual declaration of war on the "greedy, blaspheming church folk who are getting rich the wrong way". She added, "You can make money and still have dignity. Gospel has been my hope and my staff. It's not here to entertain people, it's here to save people." Miss Jackson blames it all on money. "No sooner do these church folk learn to sing good than some fast talkin' promoter comes along and signs 'em up. They go right into the churches and hunt 'em out." Miss Jackson, who has sold about 8,000,000 records, admits that she has had some disks with some blues notes in them.'

In May *Variety* reported a British invasion of America led by Cliff Richard, who at last began to break into the American charts. He won his first US popularity poll, in *16* magazine in July, being voted 'Most Promising Singer', leading the paper to ask 'Can Cliff Richard Be The Next Elvis?' In August *Variety* reported the growing number of British hits in the States. It predicted that British music would be even bigger in America in the future — providing that English singers realized that they needed a gimmick to succeed. It was records like Lonnie Donegan's **Does Your Chewing Gum Lose Its Flavour On The Bedpost Over Night** and Rolf Harris's **Tie Me Kangeroo Down Sport** that the paper thought were where the future lay for British pop. In July the paper had noted the emergence in Britain of groups from the provinces, whose success was at the expense of American stars.

In fact 1963 was the year that British artists became the leading force around the world, though it was to be 1964 before they really broke through in the USA. At the end of the year *Billboard* carried out its annual survey of the world's record markets and listed the 78 artists who had achieved significant international success. 53 of these were Americans, but they dominated the lower reaches of the list. Of the top 20 stars, nine were British, six American, two French, and one each from Canada, Japan, and Belgium. Cliff Richard topped the list, followed by Elvis Presley, the Shadows and Frank Ifield. This was a triumph for Peter Gormley and Columbia's Norrie Paramor, who managed and produced three of the top four.

In America there was nothing particularly special about 1963. Capitol declined to release the Beatles, so EMI licensed their first four records to small indies who had no success at all with them (until Capitol broke **I Want To Hold Your Hand** in January 1964). Elvis Presley announced that at the end of 1962 he had re-signed with RCA for another ten years in a million-pound deal. Country singer Patsy Cline was killed when her light aircraft crashed. Dinah Washington died of an overdose of sleeping pills. Columnist Ralph Gleason predicted that a one-speed industry was imminent, with 45 rpm records about to die. He was wrong; they hit record sales levels the following year.

Hot Rods And Folk

Capitol announced that the Beach Boys, who had had some success with surfing records, were switching to hot rod music. Folk music continued to grow in popularity, with Peter, Paul and Mary scoring three Top 10 hits in a row with **Puff The Magic Dragon**, **Blowin' In The Wind** and **Don't Think Twice, It's Alright**. ABC TV's 'Hootenanny' folk show caused a storm by blacking Pete Seeger and others because of their radical political views. Bob Dylan walked out of the Ed Sullivan US TV show when they stopped him from singing his anti-segregationist **Talking John Birch Society Blues**. In January he had recorded a play for BBC Radio in which he played a tramp. He was a sensation at the Newport Folk Festival in July.

American stars visiting Britain included the Everly Brothers, supported on tour by the Rolling Stones, Bo Diddley and Little Richard. Also visiting were Nat Cole, Sam Cooke, Johnny Tillotson, Dinah Washington and Johnny and the Hurricanes.

Connie Francis toured South Africa, though it turned out to be a disaster. The organization was poor, and partly because of illness she failed to undertake all her performances, did not show for a major press reception, and did not attend the opening of her film *Follow The Boys*, as advertised.

Teenage Morals

At the beginning of March a worried *Melody Maker* asked its British readers, 'Should a pop singer discuss teenage sex problems in public?' The question arose because Adam Faith had been asked to give evidence to the British Medical Association committee looking into teenage morals. Opinions among the other singers questioned by the paper varied. One George Melly commented 'I am not against it in principle, but Adam Faith seems to have had a singularly dull sex life.' Three months later the leader of Faith's backing group the Roulettes was killed in a car crash. Jet Harris was injured in his second car crash, suffered a collapse, and withdrew from show business for several months through illness. He never fully recovered. Bruce Welsh temporarily left the Shadows suffering from exhaustion.

The BBC continued its hopeless quest of protecting the nation from hearing unsuitable music by banning the Cougars' **Red Square**, which was based on a theme from Tchaikovski's First Piano Concerto. A BBC spokesman said: 'The Cougars' **Red Square** is a distortion of a major classical work', and was not deemed suitable for broadcast. Joe Brown's remake of George Formby's **Little Ukelele** was banned by the Billy Cotton BBC TV show as being too smutty, but was played on the BBC children's show 'Crackerjack'. In January the BBC withdrew its ban on mentioning sex, religion, politics and royalty in comedy shows.

Cliff Richard toured South Africa with the Shadows and his 'new friend', dancer Jackie Irving, who performed a dance routine from *Summer Holiday*. The couple later got engaged, though Irving ended up marrying Adam Faith. John Lennon's wife Cynthia gave birth to their son Julian in April. They had married in August 1962, and at first had tried to keep the marriage secret in case it harmed the popularity of Lennon and the Beatles.

The Rolling Stones released their first single, **Come On**, at the end of May. It reached No 21. The Springfields broke up in October, paving the way for a highly successful solo career for Dusty Springfield. New television shows in Britain included 'Ready, Steady, Go!', 'Crane' and 'The Avengers' on ITV, and 'Dr Who' and 'Steptoe And Son' on BBC.

For the first time ever, British artists won in the international sections of a music paper popularity poll. In the *New Musical Express*, Cliff Richard was voted Top World Male Singer, knocking Elvis Presley out for the first time since 1957. The Beatles were voted Top World Vocal Group, replacing the Everly Brothers. In every previous poll, American artists had always won all the world titles.

World News

The political event that made the biggest impact in 1963 was the assassination of President John Kennedy in Dallas, Texas, on 22 November. He was succeeded by the Vice President, Lyndon B. Johnson. Lee Harvey Oswald was soon arrested and charged with the murder. Oswald was in turn shot dead by strip-club owner Jack Rubinstein. Despite a Commission of Inquiry into the President's assassination under the Chief Justice Earl Warren, mystery and rumour have continued to surround the case ever since. The police claimed that Oswald acted alone, though some evidence suggests that he did not. Some saw the hand of the Russians behind the murder, though the Mafia were most often mentioned as suspects.

Racial conflict was rife in America, as civil rights activists campaigned against apartheid-style segregation in the southern USA. The fight centred around Birmingham, Alabama, where the state Governor, George Wallace, led the fight to oppose federal desegregation laws. In April civil rights leader Dr Martin Luther King led a peaceful protest march in Birmingham, and was arrested for parading without a permit. In May a thousand people were arrested after another march in Alabama. In August over 200,000 people marched through Washington in the biggest ever civil rights protest. Stars like Judy Garland and Bob Dylan joined black civil rights leaders. On the steps of the Lincoln Memorial Martin Luther King made his famous 'I have a dream' speech, 'that the sons of former slaves and the sons of former slave owners would sit together at the table of brotherhood.' In September Governor Wallace ordered the Alabama National Guard to prevent blacks enrolling at Tuskegee High School. President Kennedy answered this by taking control of the National Guard and using them to enforce desegregation in schools. Five days later four young black girls were killed in an explosion during a service at a Birmingham church used by civil rights activists, which led to more riots.

In June President Kennedy had caused a sensation during his visit to Berlin with his stirring speech. He told a vast crowd by the Berlin wall, 'All free men, wherever they may live, are citizens of Berlin... I am a Berliner.' In August a 'hot line' was established between Washington and Moscow, in an attempt to improve communications between the superpowers during times of crisis.

1963 was a sensational year in Britain. The Government was rocked to its foundations by the Profumo affair. In 1961 War Minister John Profumo had had a relationship with sometime prostitute and society good time girl Christine Keeler. She had also been sleeping with the Russian military attaché Eugene Ivanov. Profumo broke the affair off as soon as MI5 warned him of Ivanov, but two years later Keeler and her friend Mandy Rice-Davies hit the headlines when Stephen Ward was accused of living off their immoral earnings. Profumo at first denied the affair and lied to the House of Commons. It was this that brought him down. The scandal gripped the public imagination, with rumours of sexual excess and depravity considerably greater than had in fact occurred. Lord Denning's official report on the affair was a bestseller. In October Harold Macmillan announced that owing to illness he would resign as Prime Minister. In an unseemly public scramble to succeed him, the Earl of Home became Prime Minister, renouncing his peerage to become plain Sir Alec Douglas-Home.

The Labour Party got a new leader too. With the death of Hugh Gaitskell in January, Harold Wilson was elected to succeed him. Sir Winston Churchill announced that he would retire from Parliament at the next election. In August £2.6 million pounds was stolen from a mail train; the Great Train Robbery was the biggest robbery in Britain up to that time. The publication of the Robbins Report lead to a massive expansion of higher education in Britain.

The Russians made Valentina Tereshkova the first woman in space. They also finally split with the other great communist power, China. The French got upset about the Anglo-American deal over the Polaris nuclear weapon submarines, and blocked Britain's entry to the EEC. The great French singer Edith Piaf died. In May the Organisation of African Unity was founded in Ethiopia. In June Pope John XXIII died. In December the treason trial of ANC leader Nelson Mandela began. In Iran the Shah ordered the arrest of Muslim leader Ayatollah Khomeini. He had organized protests against the Shah's programme of land reform and giving votes to women.

Films and Sport

For the second year running Cliff Richard was the top box office draw in Britain. He was followed by Peter Sellers, Elvis Presley and Sean Connery. It was Connery's first James Bond film *Dr No*, co-starring Ursula Andress, that was the biggest money-maker, followed by Cliff Richard's *Summer Holiday*. Other major films of the year included *The Great Escape*, *The Longest Day* and *Cleopatra*. In America *Tom Jones* won the Oscar as Best Film, and Tony Richardson was named Best Director. The Oscar for Best Actor went to Sidney Poitier for *Lilies Of The Field*, while Patricia Neal won the Oscar for Best Actress for her role in *Hud*.

Scottish racing driver Jim Clark became the youngest man ever to win the World Racing Championship. Manchester United won the FA Cup, and Everton were top of League Division One. Spurs won the European Cup Winners Cup. Sir Stanley Matthews of Stoke was voted Footballer of the Year for the second time. Rangers won the Scottish FA Cup and were top of the Scottish First Division. Hearts won the Scottish League Cup. Yorkshire again won the County Cricket Championship. The West Indies won the Test Series in England, and England and Australia drew the Series played in Australia. In America the Los Angeles Dodgers won the World Series. The Chicago Cardinals won the NFL championship, and the San Diego Chargers won the AFL title.

The Year Of The Beatles

1963 was obviously the year of the Beatles. It did not look like that at first, when Cliff Richard and the Shadows totally dominated the first three months of the year, but then the Beatles and the Liverpool sound changed everything with breathtaking speed. The new excitement generated boosted record sales across the board in Britain. EPs started selling in unprecedented numbers, with **Twist And Shout** selling over 800,000 copies in Britain and over a million in world sales. More EPs than ever before made the singles charts, though despite these increased sales the *Melody Maker* dropped its EP charts, the first in Britain, in May. Thereafter only the *Record Retailer* compiled a separate chart for EPs. For the first time British artists dominated their own charts as the new groups squeezed the Americans out. British acts also spread across the globe, with Cliff Richard rated the top artist in the world. Not much change happened in America, the greatest prize of all. Beatles' records sold only a few hundred copies there, but all that would change in 1964.

PRESIDENT JOHN F. KENNEDY *American*

JOHN FITZGERALD KENNEDY — A MEMORIAL ALBUM (Album) *Premier 2099 [USA]*. This disc — a recapitulation of a memorial tribute produced and broadcast by radio station WMCA-New York on 22 November 1963, the day of his assassination, with special recorded material from the files of Radio Press International — sold four million copies in six days (7–12 December 1963). Both Premier Records and WMCA Radio Station turned over all royalties to the Joseph Kennedy Jr Foundation for Mental Retardation.

The disc was the fastest seller of all time, and beat the previous record set by the satirical album **The First Family** made by Vaughn Meader for Cadence Records (see 1962). The disc is narrated by Ed Brown. It was sold at 99 cents, and included the inaugural address in its entirety as well as a collection of the late President's speeches. Gold Disc award RIAA 1964.

THE PRESIDENTIAL YEARS (1960 – 1963) (Album) *Pickwick 169 [USA]*. Close to one million copies of this album were sent out in the first six days of its release. Sales passed the million soon after. This disc was also sold at 99 cents.

VARIOUS ARTISTS *International*

ALL STAR FESTIVAL (Album) *United Nations*. This uniquely promoted album was produced by the United Nations High Commissioner for Refugees, and released in February 1963 on a worldwide basis for their benefit. The million sale was reached by June 1963. Presentations of the disc were made to numerous heads of state in Europe, to U Thant and to President Kennedy in America, and to numerous dignitaries throughout the world.

The contents of the disc were: **Lazy River** (Bing Crosby and Louis Armstrong) by Sidney Arodin and Hoagy Carmichael (1931); **The Everlasting Arms** (Doris Day) by Paul F. Webster and Martin Broones; **Ximeroni** (Nana Mouskouri) by Manos Hadjidakis; **La vie est une belle fille** (Maurice Chevalier) by Albert Willemitz and Joseph Kosma; **First Star I See Tonight** (Patti Page) by Corso, Otis and Hendricks; **All of Me** (Ella Fitzgerald) by Seymour Simons and Gerald Marks (1931); **Je m'imagine** (Edith Piaf) by Raya and Marguerite Monnot; **When You Belong to Me** (Nat 'King' Cole) by Merrick and Cochran; **Greensleeves** (Anne Shelton) traditional, arranged by Wally Stott; **Adonde Vas, Nino?** (Luis Alberto de Parano of Los Paraguayos) by Don Rafirio Camar; **Nobody but You Lord** (Mahalia Jackson) by M. Jackson; **La Golondrina** (Caterina Valente) by Narciso Serradell, arranged Flor.

All the artists, music publishers, disc companies and many others associated with the production of this disc contributed their services and waived royalties so that the maximum profits might be obtained for the refugees.

THE ANGELS *American*

MY BOYFRIEND'S BACK *Smash 1834 [USA] Mercury AMT 1211 [UK]*. This was the first million seller for this female trio, consisting of two sisters, Barbara and Jiggs, and another girl, Peggy. The song was written by Robert Fieldman, Gerald Goldstein and Richard Gottehrer. The disc was No 1 in the US charts for three weeks and 14 weeks in the bestsellers, and was No 50 in Britain. The trio got together in 1961 and had two hits with **Till** and **Cry Baby Cry** on the Caprice label. Jiggs went to college, but left to sing with the group when they recorded **Till**. She planned to become a teacher before she started her show business career. Barbara studied at the Juilliard School of Music and intended to be an arranger and producer. She arranged the trio's early hits. Peggy wrote and sang on commercials for WINS-New York before joining the sisters. She also appeared in *Do Re Mi* on Broadway. Barbara and Jiggs come from Orange, New Jersey, Peggy from Bellville, New Jersey.

CHARLES AZNAVOUR *French*

LA MAMA *Barclay 20205 [France]*. This first million seller for Aznavour achieved its sale in France alone. The song was written by Robert Gall (words) and Aznavour (music) and first recorded by the famous Les Compagnons de la Chanson in 1963. Aznavour's own version made it a big hit and France's No 1 by early January 1964, following his performances of it on a TV show 'Discorama'. The day after, it became the talk of France.

Aznavour was born on 22 May 1924 in Paris of Armenian parentage. His father was then running a restaurant on the Rue de la Huchette frequented by central European refugees

where young Charles heard many songs from his homeland. After leaving school he obtained various small parts in Shakespearean and other plays, and then a big part in the film *La guerre des gosses*. From 1940 and throughout the war he was able to continue his theatrical studies and went on several tours around France. Around 1942, he wrote his first songs **Il y a deux hiboux dans le beffroi** and **Père Noel est swing**, joined 'L'école du music-hall' and finally teamed up with Pierre Roche and wrote several hit songs with him. They were encouraged by Maurice Chevalier, Mistinguette and Raul Breton and began to make a reputation in the music hall world, becoming protégés of Edith Piaf. They went on to the Latin Quarter and Café Society in New York and triumphed at the Maison Doré in Montreal, Canada. On returning to France in 1950 from Montreal, Charles had a lean time until 1956 when his singing became the feature of the Olympic Theatre in Paris, making him a star. Then followed the lead in films, radio and TV and recording. His first songwriting success was **Sur ma vie**, 1955, and subsequent hits included **Il faut savoir, Alleluia** and **Je t'attends** which from 1961 helped to make him an international favourite. An English version of **La Mama** entitled **For Mama** was written in 1964, with words by Don Black. Aznavour made his first USA discs in English in 1965, and is said to have written around 500 songs. He was the highest paid French entertainer of 1965 and was presented with 12 Gold Discs on 17 July 1966, one for each of the big hits he had recorded for the Barclay label.

BOBBY BARE *American*

DETROIT CITY *RCA Victor 8183 [USA]*. Written in 1962 by Danny Dill and Mel Tillis, Bobby's disc is said to have sold a million by 1964. He was born on 7 April 1935 in Ironton, Ohio, and was left motherless at the age of 5. He became a farm worker by the time he was 15 and later started writing rock'n'roll songs. In 1958 he recorded **All-American Boy** which was released on the Fraternity label. It went to No 2, but a label error listed the record as by Bill Parsons. Earlier home town TV experience proved valuable and while in the US Army he appeared in an 'Ed Sullivan Show'. In 1961 he wrote three rock'n'roll songs for Chubby Checker's film *Teenage Millionaire* and the same year appeared in a movie *A Distant Trumpet*. Bobby was a regular member of WSM's 'Grand Ole Opry' radio programme.

This disc reached No 13 in the US charts with 12 weeks in the bestsellers, and was winner of NARAS Award for 'Best Country-and-Western Recording' 1963.

Bare was a major C&W artist. Compared to his seven Hot 100 hits, he made the country charts 70 times right up to the late 1980s. **Detroit City** spent 18 weeks in the C&W charts, peaking at No 6.

FIVE HUNDRED MILES AWAY FROM HOME *RCA Victor 8238 [USA]*. Bobby wrote this song with Hedy West and Charles Williams in 1962. It was a big hit for Peter, Paul and Mary, and also for French singer Richard Anthony. Bobby recorded it himself in 1963 when it reached No 10 in the US charts with 11 weeks in the bestsellers. On the country charts, it reached No 5 with a chart run of 16 weeks.

THE BEACH BOYS   *American*

SURFIN' USA/SHUT DOWN *Capitol 4932* [USA] *Capitol CL 15305* [UK]. The Beach Boys were the most successful American beat group of the sixties, and the only one which came near to meeting the British invasion that followed the Beatles. Like the Beatles in America, they were signed to EMI's subsidiary Capitol. They hold the record for the longest span of No 1 hits, from their first No 1 **I Get Around** in 1964 to their chart-topper **Kokomo** in November 1988. They also hold the record for the longest period between No 1s, 21 years 10 months between **Good Vibrations** in 1966 and **Kokomo** (from the *Cocktail* film soundtrack.)

The Beach Boys were a family affair, made up of the Wilson brothers Brian (born 20 June 1942), Dennis (born 4 December 1944) and Carl (born 21 December 1946), and their cousin Michael Love (born 15 March 1941.) Brian's close friend Alan Jardine (born 3 September 1942) completed the line-up which, until he was fired in 1964, was managed by the Wilson brothers' father Murry. All the group come from Hawthorne, California. The Beach Boys got going in 1961. They called themselves Carl and the Passions and then the Pendletons, before changing their name to the Beach Boys and making a record for the small local Candix label.

The group managed to capture a sound that projected the image of the sun-drenched life of the young in early sixties California. 'Surfing' records were the craze of summer 1962, and the Beach Boys capitalized on this with their first four singles. (In fact, only one of the five could surf.) Their style of close doo-wop harmonies with beat group instrumental backing caught the spirit of the times beautifully.

Their first of over 50 American hits was **Surfin'**, which reached No 75 in 1962. They then signed to Capitol, and had a Top 20 hit with **Surfin' Safari**. Their fourth hit **Surfin' USA** in 1963 gave them their first Top 3 single, their first million seller (for global sales) and their first international hit. The words were written by Brian Wilson to the tune of Chuck Berry's self-written **Sweet Little Sixteen**. Brian was the main creative force behind the group at this stage, producing their records and writing many of their songs, **Surfin' USA** reached No 3 with 17 weeks on the charts, while the flip side **Shut Down** reached No 23 with a chart run of its own of 13 weeks. This song was written by Brian Wilson and Roger Christian. **Surfin' USA** was their first British hit, reaching No 34 with seven weeks in the charts.

After their **Surfin' Safari** debut album in 1962, the Beach Boys produced three Top 10 LPs in 1963 which all won RIAA Gold Discs for million dollar sales. They produced three more Gold albums the following year, including their first No 1 LP, **Beach Boys Concert**. The band have had 38 hit albums in America, two

of which hit No 1. Both of the Beach Boys' British No 1 albums were Capitol hits compilations, including the million-selling **20 Golden Greats**, on which **Surfin' USA** appears.

Their album production was prolific, with three a year from 1963 to 1965. In the mid-sixties the group tried to progress from the 'surfing' sound, and the magnificent **Pet Sounds** album of 1966 was the result. Received with much critical acclaim, it did not sell as well as their earlier albums. It sneaked in to the Top 10 at No 10, and failed to go Gold. (In Britain it was the biggest non-hits album of their career, reaching No 2.)

Despite internal arguments which threatened to tear the group apart, and the depression, drug abuse and partial withdrawal of Brian Wilson, the Beach Boys have become an American institution. They left Capitol in 1967 for their own Brother Records, though they never recaptured the success of the Capitol years. Dennis Wilson drowned on 28 December 1983.

After their 25th anniversary celebrations in 1986, most people had written them off as history. Then came the film *Cocktail*, in which the group appeared singing **Kokomo**, and in 1988 they were back at the top of the charts.

SURFER GIRL/LITTLE DEUCE COUPE *Capitol 5009* [USA]. The Beach Boys' double A side follow-up to **Surfin' USA/Shut Down** combined songs about their favourite topics. **Surfer Girl**, written by Brian Wilson, was another beach-girls-and-surf song that went to No 7, with 14 weeks on the charts. **Little Deuce Coupe** was about cars, and was written by Brian Wilson and Roger Christian. It reached No 15 with 11 weeks on the charts.

Though the single was not a hit in Britain, **Little Deuce Coupe** in particular did become popular. Unlike the US A side, it was included in the **20 Golden Greats** album. The record eventually sold a global million.

BE TRUE TO YOUR SCHOOL/IN MY ROOM *Capitol 5069* [USA]. Three American singles releases in 1963, three double A sides, three Top 10 hits, and all three selling a global

million. Not a bad start for the Beach Boys' first full year as pop stars. **Be True to Your School** was written by Brian Wilson, and reached No 6 in the American charts with a residency of 12 weeks. This was one week longer than the more moody **In My Room**, also written by Brian with G. Usher, which peaked at No 23. As with the previous two singles, the record was produced by Brian Wilson.

THE BEATLES   *British*

PLEASE PLEASE ME *Parlophone R 4983* [UK] *Vee Jay 581* [USA]. **Please Please Me** was the Beatles' first record to reach No 1 in Britain. It was the follow-up to their debut disc **Love Me Do**, which had peaked at No 17 at the end of 1962. The song was written by Paul McCartney and John Lennon, and was the title track of their first album.

It was **Please Please Me** that really brought the Beatles to the attention of the British record-buying public. It was released in January 1963, and in its 18-week chart run had to compete at a time when the charts were completely dominated by Cliff Richard and the Shadows. (See Cliff Richard, 1962.) In the *Record Retailer/Record Mirror* charts the Beatles failed to break through this stranglehold and peaked at No 2, though in the *New Musical Express*, *Melody Maker* and *Disc* charts they made No 1 for one week.

To coincide with the release of their second record, the Beatles began their first British tour in January 1963. For the rest of the year they criss-crossed Britain, building support steadily as they went. Audience reaction was fantastic, with girls camping out on the streets days in advance of a concert to be sure of getting tickets. Beatlemania had arrived.

In the USA EMI's subsidiary Capitol passed on **Please Please Me**, claiming that the Beatles would never sell in America. EMI Records in the UK then placed the disc with Vee Jay, who got nowhere with it until after Capitol had made **I Want to Hold Your Hand** a massive No 1 hit in 1964. Vee Jay then re-promoted **Please Please Me**, which they coupled with the Beatles' third British hit, **From Me to You**, and got a double A-sided hit from it. **Please Please Me** reached No 3 in America in early 1964, staying 13 weeks on the Hot 100. Though **From Me to You** was by far the bigger hit in Britain, it played second to **Please Please Me** in America, only reaching No 41 with six weeks on the charts.

Please Please Me was the Beatles' first Silver Disc, selling a third of a million copies in Britain when first released. The record was re-released in January 1983, and after four weeks in the charts it reached No 29. The American release sold over a million copies in 1964.

PLEASE PLEASE ME (Album) *Parlophone PMC 1202 (mono) PCS 3042 (stereo)* [UK] *Parlophone-Capitol 46435 (CD)* [USA]. The Beatles' first album was released in April 1963, and spent 30 weeks at No 1 in the album charts, where it stayed for 67 weeks. It was a massive success, selling 600,000 copies in Britain alone by the end of 1965. The vast majority of these sales were of the mono version, with 30,715 in stereo and 24,442 on reel-to-reel tape (figures to September 1965). Incredibly, the Beatles recorded their first album in one day, in just under 10 hours, on Monday 11 February 1963. The final track to be recorded was **Twist and Shout**. This had to be done in one take as John Lennon's voice was completely shot through, and he was singing lead on this number. The album was produced by George Martin at EMI's Abbey Road Studio 2. Eight of the 14 tracks on the album were credited to McCartney-Lennon. The other six were mainly American songs featured in their stage act. The release of the album was timed to tie in with the launch of their third single **From Me to You**, though the single was not included on the album.

Please Please Me was not released in the USA until 1987, when all the Beatles' British albums were made available on compact disc, with their original British content and artwork. It then made No 2 for two weeks on the CD charts. Most of the tracks were issued in America on the **Introducing The Beatles** LP of 1964. With different Beatles tracks licensed to four American labels, a British pattern of 14 tracks to an album compared to 12 in America (the British soon adopted the American custom), and the one-year time lag between the Beatles' breakthrough in Britain and their launch in America, the early albums in America were different to those in the UK. In some cases the differences were small, but in others they were substantial.

The track order on the album was as follows, with songs written by Paul McCartney and John Lennon unless otherwise stated: **I Saw Her Standing There**, **Misery**, **Anna (Go to Him)** by Arthur Alexander, **Chains** by Gerry Goffin and Carole King, **Boys** by Wesley Farrell and Luther Dixon, **Ask Me Why**, **Please Please Me**, **Love Me Do**, **PS I Love You**, **Baby, It's You** by Mack David, Burt Bacharach and Barney Williams, **Do You Want to Know a Secret?**, **A Taste of Honey** by Rick Marlow and Bobby Scott, and **Twist and Shout** by Bert Russell and Phil Medley.

FROM ME TO YOU *Parlophone R 5015 [UK]*. It took three weeks for the Beatles' third single to go to No 1 in Britain, and this time there was no question of the record only topping some charts and not others. **From Me to You** spent seven weeks at No 1, and 21 weeks in the Top 50. It was the No 1 record of the year, selling 660,000 copies in Britain by the end of 1965. Sales from Europe and the Commonwealth took the total to over the million mark. Written by John and Paul, **From Me to You** was issued as the B side of **Please Please Me** by Vee Jay in America, where it was a minor hit in its own right.

TWIST AND SHOUT (EP) *Parlophone GEP 8882 [UK]*. **Twist and Shout** was the Beatles' first EP, released in England in July 1963. It entered the *New Musical Express* singles charts, and was No 1 in the *Record Mirror* EP lists for 21 of the 57 weeks it charted. It was the biggest-selling EP ever in Britain, with over 800,000 sales by 1965. With international sales, it became their first million-selling EP. The tracks on the EP were **Twist and Shout** by Bert Russell and Phil Medley, **A Taste of Honey** by Rick Marlow and Bobby Scott, and **Do You Want to Know a Secret?** and **There's a Place**, both by John Lennon and Paul McCartney. All but the last track had already been released on the **Please Please Me** album.

Twist and Shout was covered in England by Brian Poole and the Tremeloes, who had their debut hit with it, reaching No 4. **Do You Want to Know a Secret?** was the debut hit for fellow Epstein-managed Liverpudlian act Billy J. Kramer and the Dakotas, who took it to No 2. In America, where EPs were less common, Vee Jay released **Twist and Shout** with **There's a Place** as the first single for their new Tollie label in 1964. Both sides charted, with **Twist and Shout** reaching No 1. (See the Beatles 1964.) **Twist and Shout** is an adaption of the traditional Spanish song **La Bamba**, which was a hit for Ritchie Valens in 1958 and for Los Lobos in 1987. **Do You Want to Know a Secret?** was also released as a Beatles single in America, reaching No 2, on Capitol.

SHE LOVES YOU *Parlophone R 5055 [UK] Swan 4152 [USA]*. If **From Me to You** established the Beatles as one of the biggest pop acts in Britain, it was **She Loves You** that marked them out as head and shoulders above all the others. Released in August 1963, the record entered the charts at No 3 first week of release and went to No 1 the following week. It stayed there for four weeks. Ironically, the Beatles were knocked off the top by Brian Poole and the Tremeloes, the group that Decca had signed in preference to them after their 1962 recording test. After seven weeks, the Beatles came back up to No 1 for another two weeks with **She Loves You**, only to knock themselves off the top with their new release, **I Want to Hold Your Hand**. The record lasted 33 weeks in the charts when first released, and another three weeks when re-released in 1983, when it reached No 45.

She Loves You was written by John Lennon and Paul McCartney while on tour in Newcastle. They recorded it at the EMI Abbey Road studio on Monday 1 July 1963. The record was produced by George Martin, with the usual crew of Norman Smith as balance engineer and Geoff Emerick as assistant engineer/tape operator. Its famous 'Yeah, yeah, yeah' refrain became as well known as the Beatles' 'mop top' hair style and Mao suit collarless jackets. It sold one and a half million copies in Britain, the first Beatles record to reach seven figures. It sold a further three million in America, where EMI had licensed the record to Swan after Capitol had turned the Beatles down for the fourth time. **She Loves You** was the group's second No 1 in America, where it topped the charts for two weeks, with 15 weeks of chart action sandwiched between two other Beatles No 1s. It was preceded by **I Want to Hold Your Hand** on Capitol and followed by **Twist and Shout** on Tollie, which in turn was followed to the top by **Can't Buy Me Love**. Four No 1s in a row, on three different labels!

The song also has the unique distinction of being the only Beatles record in German ever to make the American charts. In January 1964 the Beatles were in Paris performing, and were booked into the studios of EMI's French subsidiary Pathé Marconi at the request of EMI's German company Electrola/Carl Lindstrom. The Germans insisted that they had to record in German to get big sales in that country. Though this had proved true for other artists, including Elvis Presley and Cliff Richard, the Beatles needed a great deal of persuasion from George Martin before they would reluctantly record **She Loves You** and **I Want to Hold Your Hand** in German. As it happened, they were right. Although the German records did sell well, so did the Beatles' English discs. What determined the Beatles never to record in anything but English again was when Swan, who had American rights to the English version under license from Parlophone, obtained the German version and released it. At a time when anything by the Beatles sold, **Sie liebt dich** made No 97 for one week. The Beatles were furious, and EMI terminated the Swan contract.

WITH THE BEATLES (Album) *Parlophone PMC 1206 (mono) PCS 3045 (stereo) [UK] Parlophone-Capitol 46436 (CD) [USA]*. The Beatles' second album was the most successful of their early releases, selling a million copies in Britain alone. It went to No 1 on its second week in the album charts, and stayed there for 21 weeks. Released at the end of November 1963, it had an album chart run of 50 weeks. It was also the only Beatles LP to make an appearance in the singles charts. (At this time, the singles charts listed the best-selling records of any kind. While the vast majority were singles, occasionally an EP or even an LP would sell fast enough to get in.) The Beatles spent more time recording this than they did **Please Please Me**, and it is a better album. As with their first LP, it was produced by George Martin at Abbey Road, assisted by engineers Norman Smith and Richard Langham.

The end-of-the-year release of this album and the **I Want to Hold Your Hand** single marked the Beatles' complete domination of the British music scene. In one incredible year, they had gone from a group with one minor hit single to four No 1 singles and two No 1 albums. In December the Beatles were Nos 1 and 2 on the singles, EP and album charts. Only nine albums topped the charts in 1963 and 1964, and four of them were by the Beatles, accounting for 64 out of 104 weeks.

The track order on the album was as follows, with songs written by Paul McCartney and John Lennon unless otherwise stated: **It Won't Be Long**, **All I've Got to Do**, **All My Loving**, **Don't Bother Me** by George Harrison, **Little Child**, **Till There Was You** (from 'The Music Man') by Meredith Willson, **Please Mr Postman** by B. Holland, F. Gorman and R. Bateman, **Roll Over Beethoven** by Chuck Berry, **Hold Me Tight**, **You Really Gotta Hold On Me** by William Robinson, **I Wanna Be Your Man**, **Devil in Her Heart** by Richard Drapkin, **Not a Second Time**, and **Money (That's What I Want)** by Berry Gordy Jr and J Bradford.

In what is a major difference between the early sixties and today, not one of these tracks was issued as a single. The EP **All My Loving** took two tracks from this and two from **Please**

Please Me, and went to No 1 in the EP charts for eight weeks, selling 300,000 copies. Some of the **With The Beatles** tracks were also released as singles overseas. **I Wanna Be Your Man** was recorded by the Rolling Stones and became their second hit.

With The Beatles was not issued in the USA until 1987, when all the group's British albums were released on compact disc. It then reached No 4 in the CD charts. Most of the tracks were used for the **Meet The Beatles** album put out by Capitol in 1964.

I WANT TO HOLD YOUR HAND *Parlophone R 5084* [*UK*] *Capitol 5112* [*USA*]. **I Want to Hold Your Hand** was released on Friday 29 November 1963. In some music papers, it entered the charts at No 1 first week of release, where it stayed for six weeks. In others, it came in while **She Loves You** was at No 1, taking over the following week. It had 21 weeks in the Top 50. When re-released in 1983, it peaked at No 62 with another two weeks in what by then had become the Top 100. **I Want to Hold Your Hand** was the first record to achieve an advance order prior to release of over one million. It sold one and a half million copies by the end of 1965. Coupled with **This Boy**, both sides were written by Paul McCartney and John Lennon, and were produced by George Martin at Abbey Road on Thursday 17 October 1963, assisted in studio 2 as usual by Norman Smith and Geoff Emerick. This was the first Beatles recording to take advantage of the new four-track recording equipment installed at Abbey Road.

This record is a very special part of the Beatles history. It was their first American hit, and turned them from being simply the biggest act in Britain into the spearhead of the British beat invasion of America. No previous British pop act had ever had more than fleeting success in America. Brian Epstein was advised not to bother about the States, and EMI's US company Capitol was initially not enthusiastic.

The man responsible for deciding which records from outside America Capitol would release was Dave Dexter. He liked British pop music, and had released a number of British hits (including Cliff Richard's earliest fifties releases), usually with no success at all. He did not like **Love Me Do** when he first heard it, in particular he did not like John Lennon's harmonica. (When he met Lennon in person in 1964, he took a dislike to the man as well as his music.) Dexter rejected all of the Beatles' first four releases, as did Tower, a new Capitol label. He was subsequently criticized for not recognizing the Beatles' talent straight away but, in fairness, the labels that EMI did place these records with achieved nothing until after Capitol had broken the group. Swan, for example, sold only 841 copies of **She Loves You** in the five months to Christmas 1963, but over three million in the first few months of 1964. America was simply not ready for the Beatles in 1963.

Looked at from the other side of the Atlantic, things appeared rather different. EMI was increasingly exasperated and embarrassed that its American subsidiary would not take its hottest home product. Since buying Capitol in 1955, EMI had taken great care not to try and run the company from London but to leave it in the hands of its American management. Eventually, his patience exhausted, EMI's managing director L.G. Wood telephoned Lloyd Dunn of Capitol in Los Angeles. Dunn got the message and ordered Dave Dexter to release the next Beatles single, whatever it turned out to be.

When Dexter heard **I Want to Hold Your Hand** he became very enthusiastic. The decision to release the Beatles having been taken, Capitol then did a superb job of launching the group. With the active support of Brian Epstein, Capitol planned a major campaign that in a matter of weeks made the Beatles the hottest act in the history of the American record industry. Within three weeks of release at the beginning of January 1964, the Beatles were at No 1 in both *Billboard* and *Cash Box* charts, where they stayed for two months. It was the fastest and biggest-selling record in Capitol's history; it sold a million in less than three weeks, and finally sold five million copies. It remained in the Hot 100 for 15 weeks, while the B side, **I Saw Her Standing There**, also charted for 11 weeks at the same time and reached No 14.

An avalanche of Beatles material then flooded onto the charts. Vee Jay/Tollie and Swan began re-promoting older material, and saw what had been stiffs turn into million-selling No 1s. The Beatles scored 30 chart entries in 1964, made up of 11 double A sides with both sides independently charting, two singles imported from Canada, both German and English-language versions of **She Loves You**, and an EP. Their old Polydor recordings with Tony Sheridan were dug up and became minor hits. This vast flood of material came out on seven labels — Capitol, Swan, Vee Jay, MGM, Capitol of Canada, Tollie and Atco.

Capitol contributed by pumping out singles from album tracks in addition to the official British releases. The Beatles and EMI had agreed to give Capitol freedom to release extra singles as they saw fit, but soon both Brian Epstein and George Martin were complaining about overkill and the number of Beatles records cluttering up the lower end of the charts. They were particularly horrified by the release of **Matchbox/Slow Down**, which they had never intended as a single. During a visit to America in August 1964, George Martin bluntly told Capitol Records president Alan Livingstone that Capitol's actions were irresponsible. The number of Beatles releases was duly reined in and, though extra singles were released, they were fewer in number and often went to No 1.

BOBBY BLAND   *American*

CALL ON ME/THAT'S THE WAY LOVE IS *Duke 360* [*USA*]. Bobby Bland was born on 27 January 1930 in Rosemark, Tennessee. He formed his own group at high school and joined the Duke label at the height of the rock'n'roll craze. His first big seller was **Turn on Your Lovelight**. In 1960 he was voted 'Best Rhythm-and-Bules Male Singer'. Both songs were written by D. Malone in 1962. **Call on Me** was No 22 and 12 weeks in the US bestsellers.

That's the Way Love Is was No 33 and 10 weeks in the bestsellers. It was No 1 in the R&B charts for two weeks, with an R&B chart life of 12 weeks. **Call on Me** was in the R&B charts for the same length of time, and peaked at No 6.

THE CASCADES   *American*

RHYTHM OF THE RAIN *Valiant 6026* [*USA*] *Warner Brothers WB 88* [*UK*]. This male quintet comprised John Gummoe, Eddie Snyder, Dave Stevens, Dave Wilson and Dave Zabo, all from San Diego, California. Before making this, their first million-selling disc, they had built up a reputation at teenage and school dances in and around San Diego, then throughout the southern California area, chiefly at the Peppermint Stick nightclub. The Cascades played a variety of instruments in addition to their fine ultra-smooth singing style. This song was written by John Gummoe in 1962. The disc was No 3 and 16 weeks in the US bestsellers and No 5 and 16 weeks in the British bestsellers.

JOHNNY CASH   *American*

RING OF FIRE *CBS-Columbia 42788* [*USA*]. On 1 August 1958, Johnny Cash, previously with Sun Records, with whom he had had a string of hits, signed with CBS. With his group the Tennessee Three (the original Tennessee Two, Marshal Grant and guitarist Luther Perkins, plus W.S. Holland on drums) he produced a number of hit discs for their new label. Suddenly a decline in Cash's popularity set in and a series of mediocre recordings followed. Then in 1963 he burst back on to the scene with **Ring of Fire**, a song written by Merle Kilgore and June Carter (who subsequently became his wife).

This recording enabled Johnny to 'experiment' with sounds while still retaining the rhythmic simplicity of Luther Perkins' lead-guitar. Defying all country music principles, Johnny dared to incorporate a Tijuana Brass sound on **Ring of Fire** and it provided him with his biggest hit since **I Walk the Line** in 1956. It established him in the US pop charts where it was No 14 for a week and in the bestsellers for 13 weeks. The million sale was reported in 1971. This disc was the true beginning of the Cash legend. The disc was a No 1 in the country-and-western charts also in 1963. Perkins died on 5 August 1968 as a result of burns received on 2 August. His place was subsequently taken by guitarist Bob Wooton.

RAY CHARLES   *American*

TAKE THESE CHAINS FROM MY HEART *ABC-Paramount 10435 [USA] HMV POP 1161 [UK]*. This seventh million seller for Ray was written in 1952 by Fred Rose and Hy Heath. Released on 27 March 1963, it was No 8 and 11 weeks in the US bestsellers; No 5 and 20 weeks in the British bestsellers. It was No 7 with eight weeks in the American R&B charts.

BUSTED *ABC-Paramount 10481 [USA] HMV POP 1221 [UK]*. Written in 1962 by Harlan Howard, this song was first introduced by Johnny Cash. Ray Charles' disc was released on 23 August 1963 and got to No 2 for a week in the US charts with 12 weeks in the bestsellers, and No 21 and 10 weeks in the British bestsellers, selling a reported million, his eighth. It was No 3 with nine weeks in the R&B charts.

The disc won a Grammy Award for the 'Best Rhythm-and-Blues Record' of 1963.

THE CHIFFONS   *American*

HE'S SO FINE *Laurie 3152 [USA] Stateside SS 172 [UK]*. This song was a No 1 seller in the USA for four weeks and 15 weeks in the bestsellers, and No 16 and 12 weeks in the British bestsellers. The Chiffons were a female quartet consisting of Barbara Lee, Patricia Bennet, Sylvia Peterson and Judy Craig (lead singer and comedienne), all then in their late teens and from the Bronx and Upper Manhattan districts of New York. This song was written by Ronald Mack (in 1962) who, with William Rigler, bought the girls together; Mack became their manager. Sylvia and Patricia had been singing for six or seven years whilst high school graduates. The record was No 1 for four weeks during 14 weeks in the US R&B charts.

LOU CHRISTIE   *American*

TWO FACES HAVE I *Roulette 4481 [USA]*. The second million seller for Lou, also written by him and Twyla Herbert. It achieved No 3 position on the US charts and 15 weeks in the bestsellers.

DAVE CLARK FIVE

DO YOU LOVE ME? *Columbia (EMI) DB 7112 [UK] Epic 9678 [USA]*. Dave Clark was one of the shrewdest of all the young men who burst on to the pop scene in the wake of the Beatles revolution. He had few pretensions, setting out to make good pop songs and to make money from doing it. Music as an art form was not what he was about. He was unusual in fronting a group from behind a drum hit. Drummers were not normally the most well-known member of a group, and most were hardly known at all outside the hard core of most devoted fans. The only other drummers who made much of an impact on the public consciousness were Ringo Starr (Beatles), Tony Meehan (Shadows and with Jet Harris), Keith Moon (Who), Charlie Watts (Rolling Stones) and the girl who drummed for the Honeycombs (Ann Lantree).

Dave Clark (born 15 December 1942) formed his group in 1958. He came from Tottenham, north London, and their sound was sometimes called the Tottenham Sound though Tottenham did not really have a distinctive sound of its own. Rick Huxley (bass guitar, born 5 August 1942, in Dartford, Kent) was with the group since the beginning. Other members were Mike Smith (keyboard and vocals, born 12 December 1943, In Edmonton, London), Denis West Payton (tenor sax and guitar, born 8 August 1943, in Walthamstow, London) and Leonard Davidson (guitar, born 30 May 1944, in Enfield, London).

The Dave Clark Five started out as an instrumental group and their first record, made for Ember Records in 1961, was the self-penned instrumental **Chaquita**. It was their only record for Ember, and did not get anywhere. Neither did the records they made for Pye's new Piccadilly label in 1962, the first of which was also instrumental. (Before the Beatles, the only successful groups were either instrumental groups based on the Shadows, or vocal harmony groups like the Springfields.) During this time the group all had regular jobs, and played music in the evenings. Dave was a film stunt man, Mike a finance correspondent, Denis an electronic engineer, Leonard a progress clerk, and Richard a light engineer.

In 1963 they signed with their third label, the Columbia Graphophone Company, part of EMI. Columbia had been the main pop label of EMI since the company was formed in 1931. It came as rather a jolt to find Parlophone, formerly the most junior of EMI labels and something of a joke, suddenly the No 1 label in Britain with most of Brian Epstein's Liverpool

artists signed to it. Like everyone else, Columbia was looking for another Beatles, and with the Dave Clark Five they thought they had the answer. Their first release was **Mulberry Bush**, which like all their other records was a miss. Their second was a cover of the Contours hit **Do You Love Me?**, and though the Brian Poole and the Tremeloes' cover beat the Dave Clark Five version up the charts, they did at least break into the Top 30 — even if only to No 30. In May 1964 their American record company Epic released this as their third official US release, in competition with one of their old Piccadilly discs. It reached No 11 with 10 weeks in the charts, and global sales finally passing the million mark.

GLAD ALL OVER *Columbia (EMI) DB 7154* [UK] *Epic 9656* [USA]. Their third Columbia release was **Glad All Over**, written by Dave Clark and Mike Smith. Released in November 1963, it went to No 1 on 16 January 1964. Its two weeks at the top toppled the Beatles from No 1, getting the Dave Clark Five a lot of national press coverage. The record stayed in the charts for 19 weeks, winning their first Silver Disc for British sales of a quarter of a million. Global sales reached two and a half million.

The Dave Clark Five were quick to transfer their success across the Atlantic where **Glad All Over** reached No 4, their American debut lasting 14 weeks in the Hot 100. Columbia had tried to interest their American affiliate, Capitol, in the group, but Capitol rejected them. Capitol had the most staggering record of failure in picking up British hit acts from the various labels owned by their EMI parent company. As well as the Dave Clark Five, those they passed on included Herman's Hermits, the Hollies, the Animals, Manfred Mann, the Yardbirds, Gerry and the Pacemakers, Lulu, the Move, and at first the Beatles. In the mid-sixties, EMI acts rejected by Capitol, which EMI then had to place with the competition, had 153 American hits including ten No 1s.

The Dave Clark Five had a run of 22 British hits from 1963 to 1970. In America they did slightly better, with 24 hits from 1964 to 1967. They had eight Top 10 hits on both sides of the Atlantic (not exactly the same eight). Their one US chart-topper came in 1965 with **Over and Over**. They spent a lot of time in America, and were frequent guests on the important 'Ed Sullivan Show' on TV. They were very popular in the States, with a string of successful albums far longer than their two entries in the British LP charts. They won two RIAA Gold Discs for albums achieving million dollar sales.

Though the Dave Clark Five were very much a sixties group, Clark himself remained active in the music business. In 1985 he masterminded the highly successful stage musical *Time*, originally starring Cliff Richard.

THE CRYSTALS   *American*

DA DO RON RON *Philles 112* [USA] *London HLU 9732 (re-released on Warner-Spector K 19010 in 1974).* [UK]. 1963 saw the Crystals sound reach its peak with the classic **Da Do Ron Ron** and **Then He Kissed Me**. Both were produced by Phil Spector and represented a new high in

the development of his famous 'wall of sound' technique. When the driving beat, full instrumental backing and the girls' vocal refrains were mixed in the studio by Spector, he created a totally original sound that was more Spector than the group.

In 1962 the Crystals had reached No 1 with **He's a Rebel** (see Crystals, 1962). They followed this with **He's Sure the Boy I Love**, which just missed the Top 10. **Da Do Ron Ron** was a far fuller sound than their earlier hits, and made No 3 with 13 weeks in the American charts. In Britain it reached No 5, with an initial chart run of 16 weeks. The record was revived in 1974, reaching No 15 with another eight weeks in the charts. It was also the title track of a minor EP hit in Britain in 1964. The song was written by Phil Spector with husband and wife songwriters Ellie Greenwich and Jeff Barry. This team wrote the best of Spector's productions in the mid-sixties.

THEN HE KISSED ME *Philles 115* [USA] *London HLU 9773* [UK]. **Then He Kissed Me** was another Spector-produced, Spector-Greenwich-Barry composition. Spector's 'wall of sound' was again the hallmark of one of the great classic, pre-Beatles sixties pop songs. It reached No 6 in the American charts, with a 12-week chart run. In Britain it was their biggest hit, with two weeks at No 2. Its 14 weeks in the charts in the last three months of 1963 coincided with the first full flush of the new Beatles-led British beat boom, with British charts being dominated by British records for the first time. In 1967, the Beach Boys had a British Top 5 hit with a remake **Then I Kissed Her.**

The Crystals' two big hits of 1963 marked the height of their career. Phil Spector, who managed them as well as producing their records, was losing interest in the group in favour of the Ronettes, one of whom he later married.

Pat Wright left the Crystals in October 1963 and was replaced by Frances Collins. They

toured Britain in February 1964, having a minor hit with the outstanding **I Wonder**. Unusually for a Spector record, this had a flip side of merit. (Spector usually put dreadful throw-away instrumentals on the B side of his records, keeping down costs.) In Britain, the flip side of **I Wonder** was the brilliant and underrated **Little Boy**, which only reached No 92 when released in America as the follow-up to **Then He Kissed Me**. Both songs were Spector-Greenwich-Barry specials. After one final minor American hit, **All Grown Up**, another good Spector-Greenwich-Barry composition. the Crystals switched to United Artists. Without Spector there was nothing very special about **My Place**, their first United Artists release, and the Crystals sank into obscurity.

DALE AND GRACE   *American*

I'M LEAVING IT UP TO YOU *Montel-Michele 921* [USA] *London HL 9807* [UK]. Written by Don Harris and Dewey Terry in 1957, this number was first recorded by the composers in that year. Dale (Houston) and Grace (Broussard) made this updated version which sold a million globally when released by the Jaimie-Guyden disc company in 1963, and was the No 1 seller for two weeks in the USA with 15 weeks in the bestsellers. It reached No 42 in Britain. Dale and Grace had sung in local bistros in Baton Rouge, Louisiana, for several years before teaming up. Grace first sang with brother Van, while Dale worked as a soloist. They met at producer Sam Montel's studio and did an impromptu session. Montel was greatly impressed with their version of **I'm Leaving It Up to You**. The disc was an immediate success in the southern States and a hit when Jaimie-Guyden released it for national distribution. It gave the new team a national hit with their first disc. Grace is from Prairieville, Louisiana, and Dale from Baton Rouge. Both were 19 when this disc was made.

THE DRIFTERS
American

UP ON THE ROOF *Atlantic 2162* [USA]. The fifth million seller for the Drifters was written by the ace husband-and-wife team Gerry Goffin and Carole King in 1962. It reached No 5 with 20 weeks in the US bestsellers. It reached No 14 with 15 weeks in the R&B charts.

DAVE DUDLEY
American

SIX DAYS ON THE ROAD *Golden Wing 3020* [USA]. Written by two Alabama truck drivers, Earl Green and Carl Montgomery, the success of this disc made truck drivers so keen on Dave's music that the Teamsters Union presented him with a gold permanent membership card.

Dave Dudley was born on 3 May 1928 in Stevens Point, Wisconsin, and played big league baseball before becoming a singer. In 1950 he was obliged to give up his professional baseball career through a serious arm injury. His next-door neighbour Vern Shepherd was a local disc jockey, and one morning in the studios Dave picked up Shepherd's guitar and started to play and sing along with the country records. The next day, Shepherd asked him to rush down to the studio and do some songs. The locals liked his singing and Dave became a professional musician/disc jockey/singer for a year in Stevens Point.

In 1963 his long-time friend Jimmy Key, a Nashville music publisher, sent a song called **Six Days on the Road**. Two months later the Golden Wing release made the C&W charts where it stayed for 21 weeks, reaching No 2. The disc reached No 32 in the Hot 100 with 11 weeks in the charts. Through the years it has sold over the million.

THE ESSEX
American

EASIER SAID THAN DONE *Roulette 4494* [USA] *Columbia (EMI) DB 7077* [UK]. This quintet (four men and one girl) comprised Walter Vickers from New Brunswick, New Jersey; Rodney Taylor from Gary, Indiana; Billie Hill from Princeton, New Jersey; Rudolph Johnson from New York; and Anita Humes from Harrisburg, Pennsylvania. All the boys were members of the United States Marine Corps and the group was started by Vickers and Taylor who met while stationed on Okinawa in the Pacific. On return to Camp Lejeune, North Carolina, they added Hill and Johnson to the partnership. They worked at perfecting their sound, but not until they heard Anita Humes singing at an NCO club and asked her to join them were they satisfied with their group. They decided to make the rounds of record companies while on short leave from Camp Lejeune, and their first and only stop was Roulette Records, which recorded their first two sides, including **Easier Said than Done**. Their first release was an immediate hit. The song was written by William Linton and Larry Huff, and the disc was top of the charts for two weeks in the USA with 13 weeks in the bestsellers; No 41 and five weeks in the British bestsellers.

THE FOUR SEASONS
American

WALK LIKE A MAN *Vee Jay 485* [USA] *Stateside SS 169* [UK]. The third million seller for this group was top of the sellers' charts for three weeks in the USA and 13 weeks in the bestsellers. It was No 12 and 12 weeks in the British bestsellers. The song was written in 1962 by Bob Crewe and Bob Gaudio. It was No 3 with 12 weeks in the R&B charts.

INEZ FOXX
American

MOCKINGBIRD *Symbol 919* [USA] *United Artists UP 2269* [UK]. **Mockingbird** was credited to Inez Foxx when released in America in 1963, and to Inez and her brother Charlie when a hit in Britain in 1969. The disc sold around 800,000 in the USA and over a million globally.

Inez was born in Greensboro, North Carolina, on 9 September 1942. She started singing in a church choir, her first public recital being with the Gospel Tide Chorus in Greensboro. She was discovered by Clarence Fuller who booked her at Greensboro's ABC Club. Inez appeared at other clubs in the district over following months. In 1959 she decided to try her luck on her own and went to New York. After three to four years of bad breaks, she caught the attention of Sue Records who signed her to their Symbol label. **Mockingbird** was her first release. It was No 7 in the US charts and 18 weeks in the bestsellers; No 34 and five weeks in the British bestsellers. It was No 2 with 19 weeks in the American R&B charts.

FREDDIE AND THE DREAMERS
British

I'M TELLING YOU NOW *Columbia (EMI) DB 7068* [UK] *Tower 125* [USA]. Freddie and the Dreamers were always more than just another pop group. They were very popular in their native Manchester, both for their clowning around stage act and their music. While Liverpool is remembered as the birthplace of the new British beat group revolution that followed the Beatles, Manchester had the second biggest impact. Like Liverpool, there were plenty of pubs, clubs and halls to provide work for the semi-professional and amateur groups that flourished in the north-west of England in the early sixties. Freddie and the Dreamers, the Hollies and Herman's Hermits all came from Manchester (and all were signed to EMI).

Freddie Garrity was born on 14 November 1940. He qualified as an engineer and then became a milkman. He taught himself to play the guitar, and became the vocalist with local skiffle group the Red Sox. He went on to join other local skiffle groups, the last of which was the Kingfishers. As skiffle died and Freddie became more central to the group's stage act, they changed their name to Freddie and the Dreamers. The Dreamers were Derek Quinn, (lead guitar and harmonica, born 24 May 1942; Roy Crewdson, rhythm guitar, piano and sometimes drums, born 29 May 1941; Pete Birrell, bass guitar and accordion, born 9 May

1941; and Bernie Dwyer, drums and piano, born 11 September 1940.

Freddie and the Dreamers made their broadcasting debut in 1961, on the 'Beat Show' radio programme broadcast by the BBC from Manchester, and, in October, on BBC TV's 'Let's Go'. They later did a number of appearances on children's television. They signed to Columbia Records in 1963, and their first record **If You Gotta Make a Fool of Somebody** made No 3. The follow-up was **I'm Telling You Now**, which gained them the highest chart placing of their fairly short career when it reached No 2. It spent 11 weeks in both the British and American charts, going to No 1 for two weeks in the States when released on Capitol's new Tower label in 1965. The record won a Silver Disc for British sales of a quarter of a million, sold over half a million in America, and reached the million from global sales. The song was written by Freddie and Mitch Murray.

Their comedy routine helped get them a part in the 1963 film *What a Crazy World*. Despite a world tour in 1964 and appearances in America, the early promise of Freddie and the Dreamers did not last. They had nine British hits from 1963 to 1965, four of which made the Top 10. They had five hits in America, all in 1965, with **'I'm Telling You Now** the only one to make the Top 10.

YOU WERE MADE FOR ME *Columbia (EMI) DB 7147* [UK] *Tower 127* [USA]. This next big hit for Freddie and the Dreamers was written by Mitch Murray. It sold over 250,000 in Britain in this year, and topped the million with continued sales when released in the USA in 1965 on the Tower label. It was No 17 for two weeks in the USA and seven weeks in the bestsellers and No 3 for one week in Britain and 15 weeks in the bestsellers.

JIMMY GILMER AND THE FIREBALLS
American

SUGAR SHACK *Dot 16487* [USA] *London HLD 9789* [UK]. The first million seller for Gilmer was written in 1962 by Keith McCormack and Faye Voss. Gilmer (born in Chicago in 1939) came from Amarillo, Texas, and began singing as a youngster in La Grange, Illinois. In 1951 he moved with his family to Amarillo where he studied the piano for four years at the Musical Arts Conservatory. In 1957, he organized his own rock'n'roll band, playing for schools and other teenage functions. While attending Amarillo College (for an engineering degree), he continued to perform. He met the Fireballs (Stan Lark, Eric Budd and George Pomsco) at Norman Petty's recording studios in Clovis, New Mexico. The Fireballs had already had some success on disc, and Jimmy teamed up with them as singer and rhythm guitarist. Their first hit was **Quite a Party**. Then came **Sugar Shack**, and subsequent tours of Canada and Europe. This disc was No 1 for five weeks in the USA with 15 weeks in the bestsellers; No 45 in Britain and eight weeks in the bestsellers. It was No 1 for one week with 10 weeks in the US R&B charts. Gold Disc award RIAA 1963.

GITTE   *Danish*

ICH WILL EINEN COWBOY ALS MANN (I Want To Marry A Cowboy) *Columbia (EMI Electrola/Carl Lindstrom) C 22 417 [West Germany]*. This song, written by Rudy von den Dovenmuhle and Nils Nobach, was winner of the 1963 German Song Festival in which it was sung by Gitte. The disc was No 1 for seven weeks in Germany, and sold over half a million there by the year's end and 1,050,000 by mid-1965.

Gitte Haenning was born on 29 July 1946 in Copenhagen, Denmark. She made her first record at the age of eight with her father Otto Haenning, a singer, teacher and composer, and her first solo disc in 1960. She became a top German and Scandinavian attraction on disc and TV, and was teamed with Rex Gildo, another teenage idol.

LESLEY GORE   *American*

IT'S MY PARTY *Mercury 72119 [USA] Mercury AMT 1205 [UK]*. This was the first million seller for Lesley Gore. From Tenafly, New Jersey, she was born on 2 May 1946, the daughter of a weathy American swimwear manufacturer, and was educated at an exclusive girls' school near her home. This song was written by Herb Wiener, Wally Gold and John Gluck Jr. Lesley first sang it at a friend's birthday party. She was discovered by Quincy Jones when she sang at a Manhattan hotel.

The disc was a No 1 seller in the US charts for two weeks, with 13 weeks in the bestsellers. It was No 9 and 12 weeks in the British bestsellers. It was No 1 for three weeks in the US R&B charts with an 11-week chart run. The final record was cut on the first take, Lesley performing like a seasoned professional. The record was produced by Quincy Jones.

YOU DON'T OWN ME *Mercury 72206 [USA]*. The second million seller for Lesley, this disc was released in December 1963, reaching No 2 for two weeks in the US charts by February 1964 and 13 weeks in the bestsellers. The song was written by John Madara and David White; the record was produced by Quincy Jones.

EYDIE GORMÉ   *American*

BLAME IT ON THE BOSSA NOVA *CBS-Columbia 42661 [USA] CBS AAG 131 [UK]*. This song was written in 1962 by the husband-and-wife team Barry Mann and Cynthia Weill. Eydie was born on 16 August 1933 and hails from the Bronx, New York. She came into prominence in the USA when she was a regular

performer on the Steve Allen 'Tonight' show where she met her husband-to-be, singer Steve Lawrence. Eydie also had a sizeable hit in 1962 with **Yes, My Darling Daughter**. **Blame it on the Bossa Nova** was No 7 and 15 weeks in the US bestsellers and was No 32 in Britain and six weeks in the bestsellers.

JET HARRIS AND TONY MEEHAN   *British*

DIAMONDS *Decca F 11563 [UK]*. Jet Harris and Tony Meehan were half of Cliff Richard's backing group the Shadows from 1959. At that time they were known as the Drifters, changing their name soon after Jet and Tony joined to avoid confusion with the re-activated American group of the same name. (See the Shadows, 1960.)

Jet Harris was born Terence Harris in London on 6 July 1939. He taught himself to play the double bass while at school, and later joined a jazz trio the Delinquents. From there he was invited to join Tony Crombie's Rockets, backing Wee Willie Harris. Crombie introduced him to the new American invention, the electric bass guitar, and Jet Harris was the first person in Europe to own and play this instrument. In the late fifties he toured Britain, backing a number of singers including Larry Page, who had much more success as a record company boss in the sixties than he did as a singer in the fifties.

During the day Jet Harris worked at the Two I's coffee bar in Soho, where Cliff Richard

and two other Shadows got started. He was spotted by leading skiffle group the Vipers, which included Hank Marvin (briefly) and Tony Meehan. The Vipers were booked to join the Most Brothers (Alex Murray and Mickie Most, who became a very successful record producer in the sixties) for a tour headlined by the American Karlin Twins. Also on the bill was a new singer, whose first record **Move It** entered the charts after the tour began. Cliff Richard and the Drifters at this time consisted of Cliff, Hank Marvin, Bruce Welsh, Ian Samwell and Terry Smart. By the end of the tour Jet Harris had replaced Ian Samwell on bass, and had got Tony Meehan in as replacement for Terry Smart on drums. Partly because he was the only one over the age of majority, and therefore old enough to sign contracts, Jet Harris became leader of the Shadows. (The 1959 recording contract with EMI was between the company and Jet Harris, not the Shadows as a whole.)

Tony Meehan was born in London on 2 March 1942, of Gaelic-speaking Irish parents. He got his first drum kit for Christmas 1953. He later joined a skiffle group, but soon became more interested in rock'n'roll. In 1958 he played his first date with Hank, Bruce and Jet at the Two I's coffee bar, though he did not join the Shadows permanently until the Karlin Twins' tour the following year.

After their first hit, the million-selling No 1 instrumental **Apache** in 1960, the Shadows became the most popular beat group in the world. They toured exhaustively, first Britain and then the world.

Inevitably tensions arose and the Shadows tended to split into two camps, with the two Newcastle friends Hank and Bruce on one side and the Londoners Jet and Tony on the other. Tony was the first to leave, in September 1961, and Jet followed soon after in April 1962.

After Tony Meehan left the Shadows, he combined work as a session musician with an A&R job at Decca. He signed Jet up when he left the Shadows, and both of them released solo records. Tony had one minor hit with **Song of Mexico**, while Jet had some success with **Besame Mucho** and **The Man With the Golden Arm**. Their real impact came after they teamed up in late 1962, releasing **Diamonds** at the beginning of January 1963. It soon reached No 1, knocking the Shadows' **Dance On** off the top in the *New Musical Express* charts and replacing Cliff Richard and the Shadows' **The Next Time/Bachelor Boy** at the top in *Disc*. The record was No 1 for four weeks, with 12 weeks in the charts. It won a Silver Disc for British sales, was a big hit around the world, and years later eventually passed the million mark from global sales. **Diamonds** was written by Jerry Lordan, who had also been responsible for some of the Shadows' biggest instrumental hits.

Jet and Tony had two more big hits, both in 1963. **Scarlett O'Hara** reached No 2, and **Applejack** No 4. A bad car crash put an end to the duo, and to Jet Harris' career. He had recovered from a smash in 1960 which badly injured his wife Carole and Hank Marvin, but he never fully recovered from this second accident. Despite a number of attempted comebacks, his career finished in 1963. The pressures of such enormous success, problems with his marriage and the accident all conspired to bring down an extremely talented bass player who was capable of so much more. Tony Meehan continued to build a career behind the scenes more than under the spotlight, remaining in the circle of the Shadows and their friends for the next couple of decades.

Although the recording career of Jet Harris and Tony Meehan as a duo was very brief, they made a major impact on the British music scene in the sixties. Jet and Tony made their last public appearance together in 1989, backing Cliff Richard on **Move It** during Cliff's 30th anniversary bash, The Event, before 150,000 people during two nights at the Wembley Stadium.

AL HIRT   *American*

JAVA *RCA Victor 8280 [USA].* This first million seller for Al ('The Monster') Hirt was written in 1958 by Allen Toussaint, Alvin O. Tyler and Freddy Friday (Murray Sporn). Al was born in 1923, the son of a New Orleans policeman, who gave him a trumpet when he was six. Hirt studied classical music at high school and then entered Cincinnati Conservatory on a scholarship. His nickname 'The Monster' derived from his huge stature and weight (6 ft 2 in, 300 lb). He played everything from Dixieland to modern jazz in an explosive and dynamic style. **Java** was released in late 1963 and became a million seller in 1964, reaching No 4 with 16 weeks in the US bestsellers. It was originally included on Al Hirt's album **Honey in the Horn**.

HONEY IN THE HORN (Album) *RCA Victor 2733 [USA].* This album made its debut in August 1963 and sold half a million by April 1964 and the million by February 1965. It included **Java** which was released as a single in late 1963 and sold a million in 1964. The contents of the album: **I Can't Get Started (With You)**, by Ira Gershwin and Vernon Duke (1936); **Java**, by Allen Toussaint, Alvin O. Tyler and Murray Sporn (1958); **Man with a Horn**, by Eddie De Lange, Lake and Jenney (1948); **Tansy**, by Norrie Paramor (1961); **Night Theme**, by Peterson and Cogswell; **Talkin' 'bout that River**, by Ray Charles; **Fly Me to the Moon (In other words)**, by Bart Howard (1954); **To Be in Love**, by Smith and Best; **Al Di La**, by Carl Donida and Mogol (Guilio Rapetti) (1962); **Malibu**, by Weiss and Attwood; **Theme from a Dream**, by Boudleaux Bryant; **I'm Movin' On**, by Hank Snow (1950). It was in the US bestsellers for 104 weeks and made No 3. Gold Disc award RIAA 1964.

JOHN LEE HOOKER   *American*

DIMPLES *Vee Jay 538 [USA] Stateside SS 297 [UK].* Hooker wrote his own third reputed million seller. It was originally included in a rhythm-and-blues album of various artists entitled **The Blues** in 1962. This disc was No 23 and 10 weeks in the British bestsellers.

JAN AND DEAN   *American*

SURF CITY *Liberty 55580 [USA] Liberty LIB 55580 [UK].* 'Surfing' music became a rage in the USA in 1963 and this is one of the million sellers in that idiom, and the first for Jan Berry and Dean Torrence. It was written by Jan Berry and Brian Wilson (of the Beach Boys).

Jan and Dean were from southern California. They went through high school together, Jan going to the University of Southern California, specializing in advertising art and design, and Dean to the University of California, Los Angeles, on a pre-medical course. They collaborated in songwriting, Dean as the writer, pianist and guitarist, and Jan also writing, playing and working on the arrangements. They cut their first record **Jennie Lee** in Jan's garage in 1958; it was a small hit. Then Dean was conscripted for six months' Army service, rejoining his partner on demob to make successful discs, including

Baby Talk, **There's a Girl** and **Clementine** on the Arwin label and **Heart and Soul** on the Challenge label. In 1961, they switched over to the Liberty label and came up with a success in **Linda**. Then surf music became a craze in the USA and the boys came in with the tide with **Surf City**. Their recording studio was a converted garage underneath their apartment in Bel Air, Hollywood. **Surf City** was No 1 seller for two weeks in the USA and 13 weeks in the bestsellers, and was No 26 and 10 weeks in the British bestsellers.

THE KINGSMEN   *American*

LOUIE LOUIE *Wand 143 [USA] Pye International 7N 25231 [UK].* This song, written by Richard Berry, provided a first million seller (by April 1964) for this quintet and for the Wand label. The Kingsmen are Lynn Easton (vocalist and saxophone); Gary Abbot (drums); Don Gallucci (organ); Mike Mitchell (lead guitar); and Norman Sundholm (guitar and bass). They were first organized by Lynn Easton in 1957 when he was a freshman in Portland's David Douglas High School, the group at that time consisting of three members — Lynn, Gary and Mike. They began to develop a distinctive hard-driving bluesy instrumental style, and over six years worked in a wide variety of media such as fairs, fashion shows, TV commercials, dances and one-night tours, developing an impressive reputation in northwest USA. The Kingsmen also had their own float in the annual Portland Rose Festival parade. Throughout 1963, they were the house band at Portland's popular teenage nightspot, The Chase, and their first album was recorded there by producer Jerry Dennon. In addition to their performing, Gary was a barber and Mike a clothing salesman. **Louie Louie** was a chart topper for two weeks in early 1964 in the USA with 16 weeks in the bestsellers plus two weeks in 1966; No 26 in Britain and seven weeks in the bestsellers.

BRENDA LEE   *American*

LOSING YOU *US Decca 31478 [USA] Brunswick 05886 [UK].* Brenda's fifth million seller was originally written by Pierre Havet and Jean Renard in France, in 1961. The US lyricist Carl Sigman wrote English words for it in 1963. The disc got to No 6 in the US charts with 13 weeks in the bestsellers; No 10 and six weeks in the British bestsellers. The original French title was **Un ange est venu**. In America the flip side **He's So Heavenly** also charted for three weeks, reaching No 73.

TRINI LOPEZ   *American*

IF I HAD A HAMMER *Reprise 20198 [USA] Reprise 20198 [UK].* This song was originally written in 1958 by Lee Hayes and Pete Seeger, members of the famous Weavers — a new version of a Negro folk song. The disc was Trini's first million seller. He was born in Dallas, Texas, on 15 May 1937. At 15, he began playing the guitar and singing Latin-American

songs in Dallas nightclubs. He visited Britain in 1963. This disc also sold half a million on the Ariola label in Germany, over a million in the USA, and globally four and a half million. It was No 3 for three weeks in the US charts and 14 weeks in the bestsellers, and No 4 and 17 weeks in the British bestsellers.

LOS INDIOS TABAJARAS   *Brazilian*

MARIA ELENA *RCA Victor 8216* [USA] *RCA 1365* [UK]. The presence of this disc in the hit parade (No 6 in the USA with 14 weeks in the bestsellers, and No 5 in Britain with 17 weeks in the bestsellers) of two Brazilian Indians playing the simplest-ever version of a 30-year-old Mexican tune on guitars without any electrical aid, and without even a change of key throughout the whole performance, astounded everyone in the disc business. Its success was also 1963's strangest hit parade story.

The two brothers, Musiperi and Herundy, sons of a Tabajaras Indian chieftain, were born in Ceara, in the isolated jungles of north-eastern Brazil. It is said that they found a guitar left by white men who had been exploring the jungle, and taught themselves to play. They travelled 1,200 miles to Rio de Janeiro and made their debut playing the guitar as an accompaniment to tribal folk songs. They were discovered by a theatrical agent who arranged instruction and bookings in Mexico, and the brothers eventually became completely schooled in folklore, literature and the classics, experts on Chopin, Bach and Beethoven as well as the contemporary Latin American music. They also speak six languages — Italian, German, Greek, Portuguese, Spanish and their native 'Tupi'. Their names were changed to Natalicio and Antenor Lima as their original Indian names were too difficult to pronounce. Following concerts in South America, they then toured Europe.

They made several albums for RCA Records, starting in 1943, mainly for the South American market, but **Maria Elena** was their

first single to be released in the USA, where it had a big sale. It also sold over 250,000 in Britain by 1964 and according to RCA Italiana, 536,350 by March 1966 in Italy alone, making it an indisputable global million seller.

Maria Elena was written in 1933 by Mexican composer Lorenzo Barcelata.

LITTLE PEGGY MARCH   *American*

I WILL FOLLOW HIM *RCA Victor 8139* [USA]. This song, originally **Chariot** from France, was written in 1962 by Jacques Plant (words) and J.W. Stole and Del Roma (*noms de plume* of Frederick Pourcell and Paul Mauriat) (music), and was a big hit there for Britain's Petula Clark (see 1962). This version has English lyrics by Arthur Altman and Norman Gimbel, and the disc was No 1 for three weeks in the USA with 14 weeks in the bestsellers.

Peggy March was born in Lansdale, Pennsylvania in March 1948, and began singing at the age of two, winning a talent contest at five. At six, she auditioned for Rex Trailer's TV show and became a regular member of his cast. Her career really started in a big way when she won a Children's House (a Sunday morning children's TV show) new faces contest a few years later. A relative heard her singing **Lazy River** at her cousin's wedding, became her manager and arranged an audition with RCA Victor Records. Little Peggy March has appeared at Atlantic City's Steel Pier, in Tony Grant's 'Stars of Tomorrow' and other contests. In 1963 she made a tour of Europe and did radio and TV work in Britain. The disc was her first million seller. Her real name is Peggy Battavio.

LONNIE MACK   *American*

MEMPHIS *Fraternity 906* [USA] *Lightning LIG*

9011 [UK]. Lonnie Mack (real name Lonnie McIntosh) was born in 1941 in Harrison, Indiana, and had his first guitar, a $10 Lone Ranger model, at the age of four. By the time he was six, Lonnie was playing country music and singing with his brother and sisters. At the age of 12 he was receiving fees for performing at a local hotel. As a teenager, he got his first electric guitar and worked clubs with his brother, Alvin. Then at 14 he had his own rock'n'roll band. He continued to make his living as a guitarist, and in 1963, caught the attention of Harry Carlson of Fraternity Records who was so impressed with the young instrumentalist that he recorded him immediately.

This first disc for the artist was a big success and reached No 5 for one week in the US charts and 13 weeks in the best-sellers. The composition is by famous composer/artist Chuck Berry who wrote it in 1959. A fine instrumental disc, it was released in May 1963, with a subsequent million sale. It reached No 4 during eight weeks in the R&B charts.

Memphis was not a hit in Britain when first released in 1963. Sixteen years later, the oldies' label Lightning coupled the song with **Let's Dance** by Chris Montez and put them out as part of their series of double A side revivals. Lonnie Mack finally made his only entry in the British charts on 14 April 1979. **Memphis** spent three weeks in the charts, peaking at No 47.

THE MARKETTS   *American*

OUT OF LIMITS *Warner Brothers 5391* [USA]. The Marketts were a group of five Hollywood high school graduates under the direction of Dick Glasser, all aged between 18 and 21 when they made their first records, **Start** and **Surfer's Stomp**, in 1962. The surfing craze was then popular in America. After recording **Balboa Blue** and **Stompede** in 1963, the group followed with **Out of Limits**, written by Michael Z. Gordon, an intriguing upbeat disc with a galloping rhythm. It reached No 3 in the US charts by early 1964 with 14 weeks in the bestsellers, and subsequently sold a million globally. It brought the group national prominence, and many radio, nightclub and personal appearances. They became professional musicians after graduating. The combination is three guitars, saxophone and drums.

MARTHA AND THE VANDELLAS *American*

HEATWAVE *Gordy 7022* [USA]. This was the first million seller for this trio, consisting of Martha Reeves (born 18 July 1941), Betty Kelly and Rosalind Ashford (born 2 September 1943). Martha became a secretary at the Tamla/Motown/Gordy Record Corporation. Part of her job was to sing lyrics on tape for artists to learn. One day an artist became ill and she was asked if she would like to sing on the session. The studio was pleased with the result and she then did some backing work with two other girls, Betty and Rosalind. Their first disc backing was for Marvin Gaye's **Stubborn Kind of Fellow**, and they were used on several of his subsequent discs. Tamla then gave the girls a disc contract of their own, and their second disc **Come and Get These Memories** got into the US charts. They then changed their style and **Heatwave** resulted, a vibrant rock number written by Eddie Holland, Lamont Dozier and Brian Holland. This disc was No 4 for two weeks in the US charts and 14 weeks in the bestsellers and No 1 for four weeks and 16 weeks in the R&B charts. It was released 27 July 1963.

GARNET MIMMS AND THE ENCHANTERS
American

CRY BABY *United Artists 629 [USA]*. The first million seller for this quartet was written by Bert Russell (Berns) and Norman Meade. Garnet Mimms and the Enchanters sang individually and collectively for a number of years. Garnet came from West Virginia, and sang in church choirs and small groups whenever it was possible to do so. Zola Pearnell, from Philadelphia, had much experience in her musical background. She travelled in Europe with a vocal group, sang with the Paul Roberts Choir and did solo work with Philadelphia orchestras. Samuel Bell, from Philadelphia, appeared with gospel groups all over the east of America before joining the group. He is also a successful songwriter. Charles Boyer, born in North Carolina, had extensive background experience with vocal groups including five years with a group called the Ambassadors. This disc was No 4 in the US charts with 14 weeks in the bestsellers, and No 1 in the R&B charts for three weeks with a 12-week chart run.

THE MIRACLES
American

MICKEY'S MONKEY *Tamla 54083 [USA]*. The third million seller for the Miracles, this song was written by the outstanding songwriting team of Eddie Holland, Brian Holland and Lamont Dozier. The disc got to No 8 for two weeks in the USA charts with 12 weeks in the bestsellers. Released 17 August 1963, it was No 3 and 11 weeks in the R&B charts.

THE NEW CHRISTY MINSTRELS
American

GREEN, GREEN *CBS-Columbia 42805 [USA]*. Randy Sparks conceived both the name and idea for his vocalist-instrumentalists from Edwin P. Christy who in 1842 formed the famous Christy Minstrels, America's foremost interpreters of the great Stephen Foster songs.

Randy was born on 29 July 1933 in Leavenworth, Kansas, and started in show business while in college. He sought a part-time job and made his first appearance at the Purple Onion in San Francisco. Subsequently he appeared at New York's Blue Angel, followed by the entire Playboy circuit, and often worked on TV. He planned the Christys as a recording group in 1961, but Columbia Records insisted they stayed together full-time.

Green, Green was written by Randy Sparks and Barry McGuire and is said to have sold a million to date. McGuire, who also wrote **Green Back Dollar** for the Kingston Trio, became a solo artist in 1964 when he left the group, and had a tremendous hit with **Eve of Destruction** in 1965.

Randy Sparks sold out his interest in the New Christy Minstrels in 1964 to a management company on the coast for $2,500,000 and went on to organize groups in the folk field, owning several music publishing concerns, and his own disc label — American Gramaphone. This song is based on fragments of traditional material. This disc was No 14 in the US charts and 12 weeks in the bestsellers.

ROY ORBISON
American

IN DREAMS *Monument 806 [USA] London HLU 9676 [UK]*. The eighth (global) million seller for Roy was his own composition. This disc was a sizeable seller in the USA (No 10 in their charts and 13 weeks in the bestsellers) and sold over a quarter million in Britain (No 5 in the charts and 23 weeks in the bestsellers).

FALLING *Monument 815 [USA] London HLU 9727 [UK]*. Written by Roy himself, this disc was a hit in both the USA and Britain and sold an estimated (global) million. It was Roy's 9th million seller, reaching No 22 with eight weeks in the US bestsellers; No 9 and 11 weeks in the British bestsellers.

MEAN WOMAN BLUES/BLUE BAYOU *Monument 824 [USA] London HLU 9777 [UK]*. **Mean Woman Blues** was No 5 in both the USA (with 13 weeks in the bestsellers) and Britain (with 19 weeks in the bestsellers). The song was written by Jerry West and Whispering Smith. **Blue Bayou**, written by Roy Orbison and Joe

Melson, was also high in the charts in both countries (No 29 for two weeks in the USA and 10 weeks in the bestsellers; No 3 in Britain).

The disc had big sales in the USA and sold over a quarter million with global sales being estimated at over the million. It was Roy's 10th disc to achieve a seven-figure sale.

THE ORLONS
American

SOUTH STREET *Cameo 243 [USA]*. This third million seller for the Orlons was written by Kal Mann and Dave Appell, both of Cameo Records. It was No 3 in the USA charts and 13 weeks in the bestsellers.

RITA PAVONE
Italian

LA PARTITA DI PALLONE (The Football Match) *RCA PM 45 3140 [Italy]*. Rita Pavone is probably the world's smallest singer (height 5 feet, weight 80 pounds) but she is certainly one of Italy's most powerful and successful vocalists.

She was born on 23 August 1945 in Turin, Italy, the daughter of a body worker at the Fiat plant. Her father entered her for a competition

organized by RCA in 1962. As she was the winner she was automatically signed by the label. **La Partita di Pallone** was her first recording and it immediately entered the charts, soon selling over a quarter of a million, and subsequently an estimated million globally. Her second disc **Come to non c'e' nessumo** sold half a million, and was top Italian disc of 1963. This was followed by **Cuore** backed with **Il ballo del Mattone**, another tremendous hit (see below).

Practically all Rita's discs became chart toppers, and her collective disc sales to the end of 1970 were estimated at over 10 million. Her extraordinary talent resulted in success in many countries including Spain, Germany, Brazil, Japan, Argentina and Holland. Her first British appearance was in October 1966 on TV. She also made several appearances on the famous Ed Sullivan show in the USA.

Rita records in English, French, German and Spanish and is also a talented performer on screen and stage. Her 1966 Italian film *Rita the Mosquito* became a top box office success. This song was written by Rossi and Vianello.

CUORE (Heart)/IL BALLO DEL MATTONE *RCA [Italy] PM 45 3232 RCA 1553 [UK]*. **Cuore** is the Italian version by Rossi of the American song **Heart**, written in 1962 by the USA husband-and-wife team Barry Mann and Cynthia Weill. The backing **Il ballo del Mattone** was written by Verde and Canfora. It was the second million seller globally for Rita Pavone. It was No 1 for nine weeks in Italy, and No 27 and 12 weeks in the British bestsellers.

PETER, PAUL AND MARY   *American*

PUFF (THE MAGIC DRAGON) *Warner Brothers 5348 [USA]*. Written by Leonard Lipton and Peter Yarrow (one of the trio), the disc was released in March 1963, reaching No 2 for a week and staying in the USA bestsellers for 14 weeks. The song tells of a little boy's friendship with a dragon and of its sadness when he does not appear any more. The disc had a great appeal for children and sales of over a million were reported through subsequent years.

BLOWIN' IN THE WIND *Warner Brothers 5368 [USA] Warner Brothers WB 104 [UK]*. Peter, Paul and Mary first sang this famous Bob Dylan song at the Newport Festival in 1963. It became one of the most powerful protest songs of America. The disc was released in June 1963, reaching No 2 for two weeks and staying in the US bestsellers for 15 weeks. It reached No 13 and 16 weeks in the British bestsellers. It also received two Grammy awards — 'Best Folk Recording' and 'Best Performance by a Vocal Group' of 1963.

MOVING (Album) *Warner Brothers 1473 [USA]*. This album by the famous folk trio was released in February 1963. It remained in the Top 10 in the USA for 40 weeks and reached No 2. The million sale was reported in December 1973. RIAA awarded a Gold Disc for $1 million sales on 27 August 1963.

The contents of the album are: **Settle Down (Goin' Down the Highway)**, by Mike Settle; **Gone the Rainbow**, by Stookey, Yarrow, Travers and Okun; **Flora**, by Stookey, Travers and Mizetti; **Pretty Mary**, traditional, arranged by Stookey, Mizetti and Okun; **Puff, the Magic Dragon**, by Leonard Lipton and Peter Yarrow (1963); **This Land is Your Land**, by Woody Guthrie (1956); **Man Come into Egypt**, by Hellerman and Minkoff; **Old Coat**, traditional, arranged by Stookey, Travers and Mizetti; **Tiny Sparrow**, traditional, arranged by Stookey, Mizetti and Okun; **Big Boat**, by Willie Dixon; **Morning Train**, traditional, arranged by Mizetti, **A-soulin'**, by Stookey, Batteaste and Mizetti.

IN THE WIND (Album) *Warner Brothers 1507 [USA] Warner Brothers WM 8142 [UK]*. Released towards the end of 1963, this album reached No 1 for five weeks in 1963 and was a bestseller for 80 weeks. A Gold Disc was awarded for $1 million sales by RIAA on 13 November 1973, and a Platinum Disc was awarded for million units sale in December 1973. The contents of the album are: **Very Last Day**, by Yarrow and Stookey; **Hush-a-bye**, traditional, arranged by Yarrow and Stookey; **Long Chain On**, by Jimmy Driftwood; **Rocky Road**, by Yarrow, Stookey and Grossman; **Tell It on the Mountain**, traditional, arranged by Yarrow, Stookey and Travers; **Polly Von**, traditional, arranged by Yarrow, Stookey and Travers; **Stewball**, traditional, arranged by Mizetti, Okun, Stookey and Travers; **All My Trials**, traditional, arranged by Yarrow, Stookey and Okun; **Don't Think Twice, It's All Right**, by Bob Dylan; **Freight Train**, by Elizabeth Cotton arranged by Mizetti, Travers, Yarrow and Stookey; **Quit Your Low-Down Ways**, by Bob Dylan; **Blowin' in the Wind**, by Bob Dylan.

GENE PITNEY   *American*

24 HOURS FROM TULSA *Musicor 1034 [USA] United Artists UA 1035 [UK]*. The fourth million seller for Gene Pitney was written by Hal David (words) and Burt Bacharach (music). The disc had a strong sale in the USA and sold over a quarter of a million in Britain (1964). It was No 17 in the USA and 11 weeks in the bestsellers; No 5 and 19 weeks in the British bestsellers.

ELVIS PRESLEY   *American*

ONE BROKEN HEART FOR SALE/THEY REMIND ME TOO MUCH OF YOU *RCA Victor 47-8134 [USA] RCA Victor 1337 [UK]*. Presley's first million seller of the year, his 33rd in all, was a double A side in America, with both sides taken from his film *It Happened at the World's Fair*. **One Broken Heart for Sale** was written by Otis Blackwell and Winfield Scott, and was the main side, reaching No 11 in America, with only nine weeks on the charts on both sides of the Atlantic. In Britain the record was a relatively minor hit, reaching only No 12. It followed a run of nine No 1s out of 10 releases. It reached No 21 in four weeks on the US R&B charts.

But this was 1963, the year British artists dominated both their own charts and those of the rest of the world. Elvis Presley was replaced as the most popular male singer in Britain by Cliff Richard, and by the end of the year the Beatles had taken over the pop scene.

(YOU'RE THE) DEVIL IN DISGUISE *RCA Victor 47-8188 [USA] RCA 1355 [UK]*. **Devil in Disguise** was Presley's biggest hit of the year. In America he reached No 3, managing 11 weeks in the Hot 100. In Britain the record peaked at No 2 in some charts and No 1 for one week in others. In those charts where he did go to the top, he was the only American artist to do so all year. He had 12 weeks in the British Top 50. As with the other Elvis million sellers of 1963, this (his 34th) made the million from

global sales. The record was a hit in The Netherlands, Hong Kong, Israel, South Africa and Sweden. In the US R&B charts it made No 9 during an eight-week chart run. The song was written by Bill Grant, Bernie Baum and Florence Kaye. It was recorded at Nashville on 26 May 1963.

BOSSA NOVA BABY/WITCHCRAFT *RCA Victor 47-8243 [USA] RCA Victor 1374 [UK]*. **Bossa Nova Baby** was from the Elvis film *Fun in Acapulco*, and was written by veteran American songwriters Jerry Leiber and Mike Stoller. It made No 8 for two weeks in the USA, with 10 weeks in the charts. In Britain it made No 13, with an eight-week chart run. In America the flip side **Witchcraft** also charted for seven weeks, reaching No 32. **Bossa Nova Baby** spent two weeks in the US R&B charts, peaking at No 20. It was the last Elvis disc to hit the R&B charts. He had had 35 R&B charts entries with six No 1s from 1956 to 1963.

Presley's 35th million seller was from global sales. Though Presley's popularity was slipping in America and falling fast in Britain, he remained extremely popular in a very large number of countries around the world. According to *Billboard* he was the second most popular recording artist in the world in 1963, following Cliff Richard.

CLIFF RICHARD & THE SHADOWS *British*

SUMMER HOLIDAY (Original soundtrack album) *Columbia (EMI) SX 1472 [UK]*. In 1963 Cliff Richard both reached the peak of his career and was eclipsed from the very top of it. By the end of the year the Beatles were clearly the No 1 recording act in Britain, but on the world scene it was a different story, for their main global success would come in 1964. *Billboard* ranked the world's top recording stars for 1963 as Cliff Richard, followed by Elvis Presley, the Shadows and Frank Ifield.

What boosted Cliff Richard's popularity at the start of the year was his second starring role on film. *The Young Ones* had made him the top box office draw in Britain in 1962, and *Summer Holiday* did the same for him in 1963. The film about a group of young people who take a London double-decker bus on holiday to Greece was a huge success, as was the music from the film. The soundtrack album was No 1 for 14 weeks, and spawned three No 1 singles from it which was a record at that time. All three sold over a million copies. The 36 weeks that the album spent in the LP charts was the longest chart run of Cliff Richard's career.

Though **Summer Holiday** was the second Cliff Richard album release to sell a million, it passed the million mark before the first, which was **The Young Ones**. The album was also a major seller throughout the world (except in the USA), boosted by the international success of the film. Much of the music for the show was written by the Shadows, who also performed on the album. The Norrie Paramor Strings and the Michael Sammes Singers were also featured on some tracks.

The contents of the album were as follows: **Seven Days To A Holiday**, by Peter Myers and Ronald Cass; **Summer Holiday**, by Bruce

Welsh and Brian Bennett; **Let Us Take You For A Ride**, by Peter Myers and Ronald Cass; **Les Girls ***, by Bruce Welsh, Hank Marvin and Brian Bennett; **Round And Round ***, by Hank Marvin, Bruce Welsh and Brian Bennett; **Foot Tapper ***, by Hank Marvin and Bruce Welsh; **Stranger In Town**, by Peter Myers and Ronald Cass; **Orlando's Mime**, by Stanley Black; **Bachelor Boy** by Cliff Richard and Bruce Welsh; **A Swingin' Affair** by Peter Myers and Ronald Cass; **Really Waltzing**, by Peter Myers and Ronald Cass; **All At Once**, by Peter Myers and Ronald Cass; **Dancing Shoes**, by Hank Marvin and Bruce Welsh; **Yugoslav Wedding** by Peter Myers and Ronald Cass; **The Next Time**, by Buddy Kaye and Philip Springer; and **Good News**, by Cliff Richard and Ronald Cass. The album was produced by Norrie Paramor assisted by engineer Malcolm Addy. It was recorded at Abbey Road during eight sessions in May, August, November and December 1962. * Performed by the Shadows.

SUMMER HOLIDAY/DANCING SHOES *Columbia (EMI) DB 4977 [UK]*. This was the second million-selling double A side from the film *Summer Holiday*, and was No 1 for three weeks. **Summer Holiday** has been a perennial radio summer-time favourite ever since. Both sides of this record were written by members of Cliff's backing group the Shadows. **Summer Holiday** was composed by Bruce Welsh and Brian Bennett, while **Dancing Shoes** was written by Bruce Welsh and Hank B. Marvin. **Summer Holiday** spent 18 weeks in the Top 50, while **Dancing Shoes** spent two weeks in the charts at the same time, peaking at No 25. Both sides were produced by Columbia's A&R manager Norrie Paramor.

The record was an enormous hit around the world. Some years after its release, it was even played by the Soviet Union to their cosmonauts while circling the earth. **Summer Holiday** was No 1 in Britain, Australia, Ireland, Norway, Denmark, The Netherlands, Israel, Japan and India. It was No 2 in Canada and Hong Kong, No 3 in New Zealand, South Africa and Belgium, and a Top 10 hit in

Finland, Sweden and Spain. It was No 20 in Turkey. **Dancing Shoes** was also a hit in at least six countries.

LUCKY LIPS *Columbia (EMI) DB 7034 [UK]/ Columbia (EMI Electrola/Carl Lindstrom) C 22 563 [West Germany]/Epic 9597 [USA]*. **Lucky Lips** peaked at No 4 in Britain, with 15 weeks in the charts. It was Cliff Richard's lowest chart placing for four years. It won a Gold Disc for million sales because of its success overseas, and in particular in Germany where it sold over half a million copies. Total sales were one and a quarter million. Cliff recorded the song in German, with the title **Rote Lippen sol man kussen**. It went to No 1 there for 11 weeks. It was a massive international hit, reaching No 1 in West Germany, South Africa, Norway, Denmark, Belgium, The Netherlands, Israel, India, Hong Kong and Switzerland. It was No 2 in Japan, Canada, New Zealand and Ireland, and a Top 10 hit in Australia, Spain and Finland. It was Cliff's second hit in the USA, where it reached No 62 with eight weeks on the chart. **Lucky Lips** was written by the American songwriting team of Jerry Leiber and Mike Stoller in 1957, when Ruth Brown had a million-selling American hit with it. Cliff's revival was produced by Norrie Paramor, and won a Silver Disc for British sales. As well as topping the singles and albums charts, Cliff Richard also landed a No 1 EP in 1963 with **Carnival**.

IT'S ALL IN THE GAME *Columbia (EMI) DB 7089 [UK]/Epic S 9633 [USA]*. Cliff Richard's 22nd million-selling record was his biggest American hit up to that time, reaching No 25 in *Billboard*, with 13 weeks in the Hot 100. In *Cash Box* he did even better, reaching No 24. Of all Cliff Richard's many million sellers, none was written by such a distinguished person as this one. The music was composed in 1912 by General Charles Gates Dawes, the Chicago banker, flute player and, from 1925 to 1929, Vice President of the United States in the Coolidge Administration. He called it **Melody In A Major**. In 1951 the American lyricist Carl

Sigman wrote the words to it, changing the name to **It's All In The Game**. A number of American singers recorded it in the fifties with versions by Dinah Shore, Sammy Kaye, Carmen Cavallaro and Tommy Edwards. Only the Tommy Edwards version charted, reaching No 18 in 1951. When he re-recorded it as a country rock ballad, it went to No 1 in 1958 and sold a million copies. The American B side of the Cliff Richard remake was **I'm Looking Out The Window**, which in the rest of the world had been coupled with **Do You Want To Dance?** and had been Cliff's 16th million seller.

In Britain **It's All In The Game** was another big hit, reaching No 2 with 13 weeks in the charts. It was kept off the No 1 spot by the Beatles. It won a Silver Disc on 26 October. The record was arranged and conducted by Norrie Paramor, who also produced it at the EMI studios in Abbey Road. Around the world it was a major hit, giving Cliff Richard No 1s in Canada, New Zealand, South Africa, Israel, India and Hong Kong. It was also a hit in Australia, Ireland, Sweden, Norway, Denmark, Belgium, The Netherlands and Italy and other countries.

DON'T TALK TO HIM *Columbia (EMI) DB 7150 [UK]*. Cliff Richard's 20th million-selling single (and 23rd million-selling record) was written by Cliff himself, with Shadow Bruce Welsh. It was Cliff's second composition to sell a million copies in just over a year, the other being **Bachelor Boy**. It was yet another No 2 for him in Britain (his tenth) and like his last hit was kept off the top by the Beatles. If it had not been for the phenomenal sales of the Liverpool foursome, Cliff would have had No 1s out of five releases in 1963. The record was in the Top 50 for 14 weeks and won Cliff his 17th Silver Disc. The record was produced by Norrie Paramor at EMI's Abbey Road studios. It was another big hit around the world, going to No 1 in Germany, New Zealand, Ireland, Norway, Belgium, Israel and India, and made the Top 10 in Canada, Australia, South Africa, Sweden, Denmark, Austria, Switzerland, The Netherlands, Spain and Italy. This record brought to an end a string of 19 million-selling singles in a row, plus one EP and two albums.

THE RONETTES *American*

BE MY BABY *Philles 116 [USA] London HLU 9793 [UK]*. The Crystals and the Ronettes were the main vehicle for brilliant producer Phil Spector and his 'wall of sound' in 1963. The Crystals had been his most successful act the year before, but as 1963 wore on he began to lose interest in them and transferred his attention to the sexier Ronettes. This was partly personal, as he later married their lead singer Veronica Bennett.

The Ronettes were sisters Veronica and Estelle Bennett (born on 10 August 1945 and 22 July 1944) and their cousin Nedra Talley (born on 27 January 1946.) They started singing together as the Dolly Sisters in 1959. By 1961 they were regular dancers at the famous New York nightclub, the Peppermint Lounge. They appeared in the film *Twist Around the Clock* and

signed to the Columbia Pictures record label Colpix.

In 1962 the Ronettes were doing session work for singers like Del Shannon. It is said that what brought the group and Phil Spector together was a crossed telephone line, with Spector chatting Estelle up and asking her to do some session work for him.

They signed to Philles, Phil Spector's label, in 1963. Their first and biggest hit, **Be My Baby**, was a typical Spector production. It was written by Spector with Ellie Greenwich and her husband Jeff Barry, the trio that wrote most of the Crystals' hits. Released at the end of August 1963, the record made No 1 in *Cash Box* for one week and No 2 in *Billboard*. It had a 13-week chart run both in America and in Britain, where it entered the Top 50 on 17 October. It reached No 4, and won a Silver Disc for British sales of a quarter of a million. In 1964 the Ronettes toured Britain with the Rolling Stones.

The girls followed their debut disc with two more classic Spector productions, **Baby, I Love You** and **(The Best Part of) Breakin' Up**, though neither made the Top 10 on either side of the Atlantic. Although their chart success declined, Spector still pulled some exceptionally good records out of the hat. Their chart career was limited to eight hits in America between 1963 and 1966, when **I Can Hear Music** made No 100 for one week. They had four hits in Britain, in 1963 and 1964. Other American black girl groups had longer careers, especially some of those on Motown, but the Ronettes and the Crystals epitomized in a very few records the brilliance and innovation that put Phil Spector so far ahead in 1963.

Spector married Ronnie (Veronica) Bennett in 1968. (They divorced in 1974.) Ronnie Spector made a number of attempts at a solo career but, despite critical acclaim, her only other hit was **Try Some, Buy Some**. This George Harrison song was produced by Phil Spector, and made No 77 with only four weeks on the charts in 1971.

Phil Spector went on to produce the Righteous Brothers and Ike and Tina Turner. The Turners' **River Deep, Mountain High** was another brilliant classic but, though a major hit in Britain, it failed to make much impact in America. After a period of retirement, Spector produced part of the Beatles' **Let It Be** album in 1970.

THE ROOFTOP SINGERS — American

WALK RIGHT IN *Vanguard 35017* [USA] *Fontana TF 271700* [UK]. This trio comprised Erik Darling, born 1933 (formerly of the Weavers), balladeer, guitarist and vocalist; Lynne Taylor, vocalist in leading Miami Beach and New York nightclubs and originally with the Benny Goodman Band for one year; and Bill Svanoe, graduate of Oberlin College and University of Minnesota, guitarist of seven years' standing.

Walk Right In was written in 1930 by Gus Cannon and Hosie Woods. When recorded by the Rooftop Singers, it was thought to be a traditional song until it was discovered to be an original composition by Gus Cannon (then 79), a yard man of Memphis, living in a little house near the railroad tracks. For years he had strummed the banjo, singing songs he wrote himself. Fifty years before, he had toured the South of the USA with a medicine show. In winter 1962, he had no work and no money and almost froze. He even had to 'hock' his banjo for $20 worth of coal. Then this disc was made and it walked right in among the USA's top hits. Gus was sought out and taken to Atlantic Records' studio to make an album for the Stax label. The Voice of America radio station broadcast its 'Gus Cannon Story' to Europe, Africa and the Near East in April 1963. This disc was No 1 for two weeks in the USA and 13 weeks in the bestsellers, and No 10 and 12 weeks in Britain's bestsellers. Gus Cannon's Jug Stompers first introduced the song on Victor Records around 1930.

BOBBY RYDELL — American

FORGET HIM *Cameo 280* [USA] *Cameo-Parkway C 108* [UK]. The fifth million seller for Bobby was written by Mark Anthony, real name Tony Hatch, the well-known musical director and songwriter of Pye Records, Britain. The disc reached No 4 for a week in the US charts in early January 1964 and 16 weeks in the bestsellers; No 13 and 14 weeks in the British bestsellers.

SHEILA — French

L'ECOLE EST FINIE (School Is Over) *Philips 7913* [France]. Two independent artists and repertoire men, Carrere and Plait, discovered teenage singer Sheila in France, selected her songs, made recordings and gave Philips Records the exploitation rights. Carrere wrote this song with André Salvet and it was a very big success, the disc holding the No 1 chart position in France for eight weeks, with a subsequent million sale. It was the first time a disc was put on the French market by independent producers.

Sheila (real name Anny Chancel), born in 1946, was the most surprising phenomenon the French disc world had ever known. She made 10 records for Disques Philips/Productions Carrere, from 1963 to 1966: all No 1s. She became an idol of French teenagers.

ALLAN SHERMAN — American

HELLO MUDDAH, HELLO FADDAH *Warner Brothers 5378* [USA] *Warner Brothers WB 106* [UK]. The second million seller for Allan was a comedy disc about a boy's first day at a summer camp and his letter to the folks back home. Set to the music of Poncielli's **Dance of the Hours**, it was written and adapted by Allan Sherman and Lou Busch (who is the artist Joe 'Fingers' Carr, and recording producer for Sherman). The disc was No 1 for one week in USA with 10 weeks in the bestsellers; No 14 and 10 weeks in the British bestsellers. Grammy Award for 'Best Comedy Performance' 1963.

THE SINGING NUN (SOEUR SOURIRE) WITH CHORUS OF FOUR NUNS — Belgian

DOMINIQUE *Philips 3891* (Belgium) *Philips BF 1293* [UK] *Philips 40152* [USA]. The extraordinary story of a Belgian nun singing in French having a hit in both America and Britain began in 1961, when Sister Luc-Gabrielle of the convent at Fichermont, near Brussels, began to entertain the young girls studying there. They asked the sister to make some recordings of her songs — private recordings just for them. With the Mother Superior's permission, Sister Luc-Gabrielle and a companion travelled to Philips Records' offices in Brussels to seek their aid. The nuns were politely turned down. Three months later (1962), Sister Luc-Gabrielle and four other nuns went again to the recording studios and this time were permitted to record some songs. When executives of Philips heard them, they liked them and instead of pressing just 200, pressed thousands and released them commercially. The discs were sent out as the songs of Soeur Sourire — 'Sister Smile' — and were an almost instant success throughout Europe.

An abum of the songs was released in the USA, but it meant nothing until publisher Paul Kapp took the song **Dominique** (which lauds the virtues of the Dominican Order) out of the album and transferred it to a single. This disc was sent to 360 radio stations and from the first broadcasts was an immediate success. Between October and December 1963 it sold over 750,000 in the USA, with a million by early 1964, and 250,000 in Britain by December 1963. The disc was No 1 for four weeks in the USA with 13 weeks in the bestsellers, and No 7 and 13 weeks in the British bestsellers, and both this and the album were No 1 sellers simultaneously in the USA, the first time such a double had been achieved. Grammy Award for 'Best Gospel or Religious Recording' 1963.

Soeur Sourire was so named by Philips Records after a poll was taken in France and Belgium. She played the guitar and most of the songs, all written by her, are in a religious vein. She was born in 1928. All the money earned from **Dominique** and her album (estimated at over £30,000) was spent on foreign missions. Soeur Sourire was also a very talented artist and designed and drew the cover for the sleeve of the album. She left the convent in October 1966. Her real name was Jeanine Dekers. She died in the late 1980s.

THE SINGING NUN (Album) *Philips (Belgium) Philips 203 [USA]*. All the songs on the disc were written by Sister Luc-Gabrielle (Soeur Sourire) and recorded by her, with a chorus of nuns, in Belgium in 1962. (See **Dominique** for data.) The disc sold over 750,000 by December 1963, with an eventual million by 1964, and was No 1 for 10 weeks in the USA. The contents are: **Plume de radis**; **Mets ton joli jupon** (Put on your pretty skirt); **Resurrection**; **Alleluia**, **J'ai trouvé le Seigneur** (I have found the Lord); **Entre les étoiles** (Among the stars); **Dominique** (Dominic); **Soeur Adele** (Sister Adele); **Fleur de cactus** (Cactus flower); **Complainte pour Marie-Jacques** (Lament for Marie-Jacques); **Je voudrais** (I would like); **Tous les chemins** (All the paths). Gold Disc award RIAA 1963.

JIMMY SOUL   American

IF YOU WANNA BE HAPPY *SPQR 3305 [USA] Stateside SS 178 [UK]*. Jimmy Soul, born James McCleese in Harlem in 1942, was a boy preacher at the age of seven and got his name from the church elders who whispered 'He's got soul' whenever Jimmy preached. His parents returned to their farm in North Carolina when he was young and Jimmy listened to the circuit-riding ministers in his rural area and soon became a circuit minister himself. Later his parents moved to Ports-mouth, Virginia, and Jimmy both preached and became a member of various local gospel-singing groups. For a year, he travelled with the famed gospellers the Nightingales all over the USA.

Jimmy then discovered his forte in singing pop tunes and rock'n'roll. He auditioned with a rock'n'roll combination for an engagement at the Azalea Gardens Club in Norfolk, Virginia, and the group had its week's engagement extended into several months. He formed his own group, taking the name 'Wonder Boy' from his days on the North Carolina preaching circuit. He and his manager approached Frank Guida, head of SPQR Records, and Jimmy made his first disc **Twisting Matilda** in 1962. **If You Wanna Be Happy** followed in 1963. The disc was No 1 in the USA for two weeks and 14 weeks in the bestsellers, and was No 39 in Britain with two weeks in the Top 50. It was No 1 for one week in the US R&B charts with a chart life of 12 weeks. Jimmy was also an excellent dancer and played the piano, drums and guitar.

The song was written by Frank Guida, Carmela Guida and Joseph Royster. A top rhythm-and-blues disc.

DUSTY SPRINGFIELD   British

I ONLY WANT TO BE WITH YOU *Philips BF 1292 [UK] Philips 40162 [USA]*. Dusty Springfield was Britain's most successful and admired female singer of the sixties. Born Mary O'Brien on 16 April 1940, in Hampstead, north London, she went to school at convents in High Wycombe and Ealing, and at 16 started working in a record shop. As a child she took part in her family's musical evenings, in a room which had been fitted out with an amplifier and microphone. She shared her brother Tom's interest in Latin American music, and learned to play the guitar. She started singing in public as an amateur folk singer in London and often joined her brother, who was starting to make a career as a performer. In 1958 she joined two other girls in the Lana Sisters. They enjoyed

some success and appeared in the influential BBC TV show '6.5 Special'.

In 1960 Dusty left the Lana Sisters and joined her brother Tom and his singing partner Tim Field to form the Springfields. In April 1961 they were signed to the Dutch record company Philips, who issued **Dear John** as their debut disc. It was a miss, but the follow-up was a hit and the group were voted 'Top British Vocal Group' of 1961 and 1962. A short string of hits followed on both sides of the Atlantic (see the Springfields, 1962) before the group decided to split up in 1963.

Of the three Springfields, it was Dusty whose solo career really took off. Her first solo single, **I Only Wanna Be With You**, reached No 4 in Britain. It won a Silver Disc, and spent 18 weeks in the charts. The record was also a hit in America, where it reached No 12 with a 10-week chart run. It was a global million seller. Written by Mike Hawker and Dusty's musical director Ivor Raymonde, it was produced by Johnny Franze. She went on to have a string of hits on both sides of the Atlantic. Between 1963 and 1979 she had 18 hits in Britain, including her only No 1 **You Don't Have to Say You Love Me**. In the USA she had the same number of chart entries (though from 16 discs, two of which were double A sides) from 1964 to 1970.

The Springfields had made a big impact in Britain with their highly commercial folk songs and country-and-western music borrowed from America. As a solo singer, Dusty moved away from this almost overnight to a soul sound no other British female singer could match. Her early recordings achieved a very full sound, her strong voice belting out over the orchestra, horns and all. She was voted 'Top British and Top World Female Singer' in the British music paper reader polls of 1965, 1966 and 1967.

In 1968 she switched labels in America to Atlantic, staying with Philips for the rest of the world. This resulted in the highly acclaimed

Dusty in Memphis album, from which **Son of a Preacher Man** became a Top 10 hit in Britain and America — her last in both countries. After one minor hit in 1970 (one hit on both sides of the Atlantic, but with different records), she took a long break from her career. She had been a great sixties star, but after that she did not seem to know where she wanted her career to go. She made the occasional attempt at a revival, and scored one more minor chart entry in Britain in 1979. It looked as if her career as a major star was over, and most commentators had written her off, then out of the blue she came back in 1987 with a million-selling smash with the Pet Shop Boys. **What Have I Done to Deserve This?** was utterly contemporary, as was to be expected from a collaboration with Britain's hottest act of the moment. It went to No 2 in Britain and No 1 in the *Cash Box* American charts. In 1989 she had her first big solo hit for 20 years with **Nothing Has Been Proved** from the film soundtrack of *Scandal*. The film was about the Profumo scandal that broke in 1963. As a result of this she signed a deal with EMI for the early 1990s.

THE SURFARIS   *American*

WIPE OUT *Dot 16479* [*USA*] *London HLD 9751* [*UK*]. 'Wipe out' is a surfing term, meaning that one has been knocked off the board while surfing or riding the waves. This disc was yet another million seller of the surfing craze that achieved such wide prominence amongst teenagers in the USA in 1963. **Wipe Out** was written by the Surfaris, all five of whom come from Glendora, California. The group comprises Jim Pash, saxophonist; Ron Wilson, drummer; Pat Connolly, leader and bass guitar; Jim Fuller, lead guitar; and Bob Berryhill, rhythm guitar. Because of their schooling, their personal appearances were restricted to local dances in and around Glendora. They later switched to the Decca label. This disc was No 2 for one week in the USA with 16 weeks in the bestsellers, and had a big revival in 1966 when it reached No 16 with 14 weeks in the bestsellers, and No 5 and 14 weeks in the British bestsellers.

In America the flip side **Surfer Joe** also charted. It peaked at No 62 during a six-week chart run. In 1987 the American rap group the Fat Boys reached No 2 in Britain with a remake of this song, which they did with the Beach Boys.

NINO TEMPO AND   *American*
APRIL STEVENS

DEEP PURPLE *Atco 6273* [*USA*]. **Deep Purple** was a big hit for brother and sister Nino and April, and chart topper for two weeks in the USA with 15 weeks in the bestsellers. It reached No 17 and 11 weeks in the British bestsellers. The song is the famous oldie of 1939 by Mitchell Parish (words) and Peter de Rose (music), originally composed by de Rose in 1934 for piano solo, and a great favourite for over 30 years with orchestras.

The duo are from Niagara Falls, New York. Nino has been a performer since the age of

three. By the time he was seven, he sang with the famous Benny Goodman orchestra and later with Glenn Miller's band. He is a skilled musician, and plays clarinet, saxophone, piano and guitar in addition to singing. He has also arranged and composed many songs for big name artists including Rosemary Clooney and Steve Lawrence. It was not until he teamed with April that he became a big name himself, although he had recorded one success, **Sweet and Lovely**. April had a hit with her first single disc **I'm in Love Again**, followed by two or three other successes including **Gimme a Little Kiss** and **And So To Sleep Again**. She first recorded for a small label, Society Recordings, in 1950. Their teaming together on **Deep Purple** produced a big success in the States and in several places around the world, the disc becoming a million seller by 1965. Grammy Award for 'Best Rock and Roll Recording' 1963.

THE TYMES   *American*

SO MUCH IN LOVE *Parkway 871* [*USA*] *Cameo-Parkway P 871* [*UK*]. This male quintet consisted of Donald Banks, Al Berry, Norman Burnett, George Hilliard and George Williams, Jr, then all in their early twenties. Banks and Hilliard hail from Franklin, Virginia, and Berry, Burnett and Williams from Philadelphia. This song was written by George Williams (of the group), William Jackson and Roy Straigie. The group

came into being when Burnett and Hilliard met at a summer camp in 1956 and started singing together for their own amusement. In the autumn, they teamed with Banks, Berry and Williams, singing and working together on the group's sound with the idea of a show business future. In April 1963 they appeared at a Philadelphia theatre on the WADS talent show, were spotted and asked to record for Parkway. **So Much in Love** was their first disc, and No 1 for one week in the US charts with 15 weeks in the bestsellers; No 21 and eight weeks in the British bestsellers.

BOBBY VINTON   *American*

BLUE VELVET *Epic 9614* [*USA*]. This second million seller for Bobby was No 1 in the USA for three weeks and 15 weeks in the bestsellers. The song was written in 1951 by Bernie Wayne and Lee Morriss.

THERE! I'VE SAID IT AGAIN *Epic 9638* [*USA*] *Columbia (EMI) DB 7179* [*UK*]. For a second time this song produced a million seller on disc. It was written by Redd Evans and Dave Mann in 1941. This version was the third million seller for Bobby Vinton. The disc was No 1 in the USA for four weeks in 1964 and 13 weeks in the bestsellers, with big sales there, and was No 34 and 10 weeks in the British bestsellers, additional sales elsewhere making it a global million.

DALE WARD   *American*

A LETTER FROM SHERRY *Dot 16520* [*USA*]. 'Pop' vocalist Dale Ward made this disc in 1963 when it was released in late December. By February 1964 it reached No 25 in the USA charts, was 11 weeks in the bestsellers and subsequently sold the million. The song was written by Kenneth R. Moffit, and the disc backed with another of his songs **Oh Julie** which he wrote in 1957 with Noel Ball — a million seller in 1958 for the Crescendos.

Dale joined the trend of pop stars gone country in 1971.

DIONNE WARWICK   *American*

ANYONE WHO HAD A HEART *Scepter A1262* [*USA*] *Pye International 7N 25234* [*UK*]. Dionne was born in East Orange, New Jersey, 12 December 1941, her family being gospel singers. She studied music from the age of six. After schooling in her native town, she studied at the Hartt College of Music in Hartford, becoming an accomplished singer and pianist, and still playing and singing in church every Sunday. She then sang in the background chorus in New York on several recording

sessions. Her unique style of singing greatly attracted the songwriter-producers Hal David (author) and Burt Bacharach (composer) who wrote this song. They introduced her to Scepter Records and a hit **Don't Make Me Over** followed. Then came **Anyone Who Had A Heart** which with big sales in the USA and abroad topped the million. It reached No 8 with 14 weeks in the US bestsellers; No 42 and three weeks in the British bestsellers. Dionne toured all over Europe and thus established a big international reputation with her audiences and on disc. **Anyone Who Had A Heart** was also a big hit for Britain's Cilla Black in 1964.

Dionne Warwick enjoyed a lengthy recording career from the sixties to the eighties. In 1985 she finally made No 1 in America with the help of a lot of recording star friends her record company Artista had put together. **That's What Friends are For** by Dionne Warwick and Friends was No 1 for four weeks.

MARY WELLS
American

TWO LOVERS *Motown 1035* [*USA*]. The first million seller for Mary Wells was written in 1962 by William 'Smokey' Robinson, vice-president of Motown. Mary was born in Detroit on 13 May 1943, and started singing at the age of 10. She was discovered by Motown during the firm's regular audition sessions and signed to a contract. Her first disc and own song **Bye Bye Baby** became a hit. Since then she has done many TV and club dates, and visited Britain in 1964. Her full name is Mary Esther Wells. Released in December 1962, **Two Lovers** reached No 7 with 13 weeks in the US Hot 100. It was No 1 for four weeks in the R&B charts where it had a chart run of 14 weeks.

ANDY WILLIAMS
American

CAN'T GET USED TO LOSING YOU/DAYS OF WINE AND ROSES *CBS-Columbia 42674* [*USA*] *CBS AAG 138* [*UK*]. This double A side was Andy Williams' fourth million seller. **Can't Get Used to Losing You** was No 1 for one week

in America in the *Cash Box* charts. It was No 2 for four weeks in *Billboard*, with 15 weeks on the charts, and with **Days of Wine and Roses** charting at the same time. It reached No 26, with 12 weeks of independent chart action. In Britain **Can't Get Used to Losing You** reached No 2, with 18 weeks in the charts. It was written by Doc Pomus and Mort Shuman. The flip side was written by Johnny Mercer and Henry Mancini for the film of the same name, and was the title of a million-selling album by Williams. Both songs were written in 1962.

DAYS OF WINE AND ROSES (*Album*) CBS-Columbia 8815 [*USA*] CBS BPG 62146 [*USA*]. This was the second million seller album for Andy Williams, with Robert Mersey's arrangements and conducting. It sold around 2,000,000 by end of 1967. The release in Britain was changed to **Can't Get Used to Losing You**, the title of his million-selling single included on the disc. This album was No 1 in the USA for 16 weeks in 1963 and stayed in the bestsellers lists for 107 weeks. It includes the Academy Award-winning film song of 1962 **Days of Wine and Roses** from the movie of the same title, which also gained a Grammy Award for Henry Mancini for 'Record of the Year' 1963. Gold Disc award RIAA 1963.

The contents of the disc are: *Side 1* — **Falling in Love with Love** (from *The Boys from Syracuse*), by Lorenz Hart/Richard Rodgers (1938); **I Left My Heart in San Francisco**, by Douglas Cross/George Corey (1954); **You Are My Sunshine**, by Jimmie Davis and Chas. Mitchell (1940); **What Kind of Fool Am I?** (from *Stop the World — I Want to Get Off*), by Leslie Bricusse/Anthony Newley (1961); **When You're Smiling**, by Mark Fisher, Joe Goodwin and Larry Shaw (1928); **Days of Wine and Roses** (from the film), by Johnny Mercer/Henry Mancini (1962); *Side 2* — **It's a Most Unusual Day** (from the film *A Date with Judy*), by Harold Adamson/Jimmy McHugh (1948); **My Colouring Book**, by Fred Ebb/John Kander (1962); **Can't Get Used to Losing You**, by Doc Pomus and Mort Shuman (1962); **I Really Don't Want to Know**, by Howard Barnes/Don Robertson (1953); **Exactly Like You**, by Dorothy Fields/Jimmy McHugh (1930); **May Each Day** (Andy Williams' theme song), by Morton J. Green/George Wyle (1963).

THE ANDY WILLIAMS CHRISTMAS ALBUM (Album) *CBS-Columbia CS 8887* [*USA*]. **The Andy Williams Christmas Album** made the special *Billboard* Christmas album charts for eight years, with a total of nine weeks at No 1. The RIAA finally awarded a Platinum Disc for sales of over a million copies on 21 November 1986. The album was a combination of traditional Christmas songs and newer material.

The contents of the album (with the writers given in brackets) is as follows: **White Christmas** (Berlin); **The Holiday Season** (Thompson); **The Christmas Song (Chestnuts Roasting On an Open Fire)** (Torme/Wells); **It's The Most Wonderful Time Of The Year** (Thompson); **A Song And A Christmas Tree (The Twelve Days of Christmas)** (traditional); **Kay Thompson's Jingle Bells** (traditional); **The First Noel** (traditional); **O Holy Night** (Adams); **Away In A Manager** (traditional);

Sweet Little Jesus Boy (MacGimsey); **The Little Drummer Boy** (Davis/Onorati/Simeone); and **Silent Night, Holy Night** (traditional).

STEVIE WONDER
American

FINGERTIPS PART 2 *Tamla 54080* [*USA*]. Stevie Wonder was one of the most successful and versatile artists ever to emerge from the United States. He recorded his first hit, **Fingertips — Part 2**, when he was only 12 years old. He survived the Motown conveyor-belt production line to emerge in the seventies as a highly talented and original artist with creative control over his own destiny.

Steveland Morris was born on 13 May 1950, in Saginaw, Michigan. As a result of a medical accident, he lost his sight soon after birth. His mother Lula Hardaway and his two brothers later moved to Detroit after his father J. Judkins had abandoned the family, settling in one of the East Side slums. Steve developed a keen ear for music, and an ability to sing and to play the piano, harmonica, bongos, organ and drums. He became friendly with Gerald White, whose elder brother Ronnie was a member of the Motown group the Miracles. When Ronnie heard Stevie sing, he was sufficiently impressed to take him to the Motown studios for an audition. Berry Gordy, owner of Motown, liked what he heard and signed the 11-year-old boy to his Tamla label. Given his age and wonderboy reputation, Gordy decided to change his stage name to Little Stevie Wonder, though 'Little' was later dropped.

Stevie's first release was **I Call It Pretty Music**, which failed to make much impact, as did his next two releases. Though his record sales were few, reaction to his live performances was excellent. Motown therefore recorded him live for his fourth single. The song was **Fingertips** which was over seven minutes long, so Motown simply put half the song on one side of the record, and the other half on the flip side. Public reaction made the second side the more popular. **Fingertips — Part 2** was released in June 1963, and soon went to No 1 for three weeks, spending 15 weeks in the Top 100. It was also No 1 in the R&B charts for six weeks, with a chart life of 15 weeks. The song was written by Clarence Paul and Henry Cosby, with Clarence also producing the record. It was the first live disc ever to go to No 1. The song was on Wonder's first hit LP, **Little Stevie Wonder — the 12-year-old Genius**. This also went to No 1 in the album charts, making him the first artist ever to top both American singles and album charts at the same time.

Fingertips was the first of over 50 American hits, spanning three decades. He has had eight No 1 singles in the USA. While at first a singles artist, in the seventies he developed as an outstanding songwriter and album act. His third No 1 album, the 1976 **Songs in the Key of Life**, topped the charts for 14 weeks in America. The double album and EP set spawned two No 1 singles in a row. Though **Fingertips** did not make it in Britain, Stevie Wonder has chalked up over 50 British hits from **Uptight** in 1966 to the present. He has made a number of successful duets with other major artists.

1 9 6 4

1964 was the year that the Beatles conquered America, closely followed by most of the newly successful British groups. There was much debate over who was Britain's No 2 group. The Shadows had started 1963 as top group, and ended that year as second to the Beatles at home, and still the top group in the world. Despite having their best year ever in 1963, they had faded a bit. Gerry and the Pacemakers started 1964 as the main challenger to the Beatles, just as they had been in Liverpool before they all made it nationally. Their first three records all made No 1, something that the Beatles had not achieved, but then they, too, started to fade. The Dave Clark Five looked like strong challengers, but though they had a lot of hits they were never really close to the Beatles.

The group that finally won the fight was the Rolling Stones. At first sight they were completely different from the Beatles. Their image was one of rebellion, notoriety and sexual provocation. Most parents would not have minded their daughter dating that nice Beatle Paul, but would have been horrified if she had got anywhere near Mick, Brian, or any of the other Stones. Musically, the Stones were heavily into R&B, and at first they were disdainful of straight pop. Yet despite a certain amount of professional rivalry the two groups became friends, and sometimes even appeared on each other's records.

The London-based Stones had their first hit with **Come On** in July 1962, and their second, **I Wanna Be Your Man**, later the same year. Neither made the Top 10. Then in February 1964 they released a remake of Buddy Holly's **Not Fade Away**, which made No 3. In July they released their first No 1, **It's All Over Now**, and in November **Little Red Rooster** entered the *NME* charts at No 1 first week of release. The Stones were only the fifth act in the history of the charts to do this. (The others were Elvis Presley three times, Lonnie Donegan, Cliff Richard and the Shadows, and the Beatles.) In two years the Stones had seven No 1s in a row.

The Beatles had an even more fabulous year. All three of their singles entered the British charts at No 1 first week of release, as did both of their albums. EPs and even LPs entered the singles charts. They could do no wrong. In March they won the Variety Club award as Show Business Personalities of 1963.

The British Are Coming

Their greatest success was in doing what no British pop stars had ever done before, and that was cracking the American market. After considerable pressure from EMI, the company's American subsidiary Capitol finally got behind the Beatles and mounted a brilliant campaign for the release of **I Want To Hold Your Hand**. All the Beatles' previous records had completely failed to sell in America, a country that had never really gone for British pop music. It was all the more remarkable, therefore, that on 18 January **I Want To Hold Your Hand** entered the *Billboard* Hot 100 at No 45 as the top new entry of the week. The following week it was the biggest mover on the charts, crashing up to No 3. It then hit No 1, on 1 February, and stayed there for seven weeks.

There followed an explosion the likes of which had never been seen before — or since. A vast amount of Beatles' product started pouring out. Every record company that had previously had rights to Beatles records

after Capitol turned them down started to re-promote them. All these old records made the charts, released by seven different record companies. Four Beatles singles hit the top one after another. On 28 February they became the first act ever to have the top two records in both the singles and album charts at the same time.

On 11 April the Beatles occupied the whole of the *Billboard* Top 5. At No 1 up from No 27 was **Can't Buy Me Love** on Capitol, at No 2 was **Twist And Shout** on Tollie, down from No 1 to No 3 was **She Loves You** on Swan, at No 4 **I Want To Hold Your Hand** on Capitol, and at No 5 **Please Please Me** on Vee Jay. On 18th April the Beatles had eleven records in the *Variety* Top 50 and an all-time record of 14 in the *Billboard* Top 100.

Capitol tried to stop the other companies from releasing Beatles' records, and while they finally won most battles it proved impossible to stem the flow completely. The Beatles had a staggering 30 US chart entries in 1964. This included double A sides, an EP, and a German language version of **She Loves You**. Their old Polydor recordings were dredged up and some made the charts. These did better in America than in Britain. They were given surprisingly good reviews for recordings so completely different from their new records. *Record Mirror*, for example, reviewed the instrumental **Cry For A Shadow** thus: 'The Harrison-Lennon composition is a good enough tune and performance, and sounds as though it was recorded while the Beatles were under the influence of the Shadows.' The Beatles were not disappointed when it failed to make the charts.

This phenomenal success in America did wonders for Capitol Records. In February the Beatles were responsible for 60% of all records sold in America, and nearly all of these were either on Capitol or under license from EMI. In January 1965 Capitol announced that 1964 had seen a 65% increase in their domestic record sales, due largely to the Beatles. The Beatles boosted sales everywhere. In Britain record sales in the first nine months of 1964 were up 30% on the same period of 1963. By April over a third of the records in the Top 30 had won Silver Discs for over a quarter of a million sales in Britain.

British Acts In America

Though the Beatles were the first British group to crack open the American charts, it was the Rolling Stones who were the first to perform there, in January. The Beatles arrived on 7 February to be met by thousands of screaming fans at Kennedy Airport. They appeared on the influential 'Ed Sullivan TV Show', and on 11 February played their first American concert, in Washington, DC.

An army of British acts then followed, with US record companies scrambling to sign anything British. An article in *Billboard* stated that 'Great Britain hasn't been as influential in American affairs since 1775.' The Dave Clark Five, the Searchers, Peter and Gordon, and the Animals were among other British groups touring America. The Beatles were back for a full tour in August, which met with a spectacular response from the fans. (*Variety* reported that 'Cities Gird For Teen Tempest.') A Washington woman predicted that the Beatles would all die in September, so just to be on the safe side extra security was imposed. The Beatles refused to play in Jacksonville, Florida, unless the normal custom of segregating blacks from whites was stopped. Segregation and apartheid in America and South Africa caused the cancellation of a number of performances and tours by British artists, with the Musicians Union taking a particularly strong stand on South Africa.

On a world basis, British artists consolidated the dominating position they had achieved in 1963. As well as touring America, British acts also visited Europe, Australia and South Africa, and the world's charts were full of British records to a greater degree than ever before. The biggest-selling artists in the world were reported as the Beatles, followed by Cliff Richard and the Dave Clark Five. All recorded for EMI.

Americans In Britain

In January the Ronettes were the opening act for the Rolling Stones' 'Group Scene 1964' British tour. Ben E. King arrived for media promotion in February. Chuck Berry and Bob Dylan both started tours in May. The Crickets toured in June, minus Jerry Naylor who was recovering from a heart attack. In September the grand-daddy of rock'n'roll, Bill Haley, arrived with his Comets for a British tour. In October the Supremes flew in for radio and TV dates. November saw Judy Garland giving a concert in London with her daughter Liza Minnelli.

The Beatles boom of 1963 had seriously eclipsed American artists in Britain, so long used to dominating the British market. The Americans began to fight back in 1964, when three American discs went to the top. Two of these were by Roy Orbison, who on 10 October was No 1 on both sides of the Atlantic with **Oh, Pretty Woman**, and one by the Supremes. For the first time ever, more British records topped the American charts (eleven of them) than American discs made No 1 in Britain.

Violent Deaths

Country singer Jim Reeves was killed in a plane crash near Nashville in July. His death generated a big increase in record sales in Britain, where he had the top two chart records of the year.

American rock singer Johnny Burnette was killed in an accident on Lake Clear, California, in August. He was out fishing with his family when their boat was hit by another craft. Burnette was knocked unconscious and drowned. He left a wife and two children, one of whom, Rocky Burnette, had a Top 10 hit on EMI America with **Tired Of Toein' The Line** in 1980.

In December leading R&B singer Sam Cooke was shot and beaten to death while attempting to rape a 22-year-old woman in Los Angeles. He had offered to take the girl home after a party, but took her to a motel room instead. She claimed that he had then ripped her clothes off. She escaped and called the police. Cooke broke down the door of the motel room demanding where the girl was. The 55-year-old manageress claimed that Cooke assaulted her, and in self-defence she shot him and beat him with a stick. He was dead by the time the police arrived.

Should A Pop Star Marry?

In May, *Record Mirror* ran a feature on pop stars and marriage. Did it harm their careers? They concluded that it did not matter for girl singers, and did not seem to for groups. Though John Lennon had tried to keep his marriage a secret, the Beatles' popularity was not affected when the news leaked out. Nor had the sudden announcement of Ringo Starr's marriage to Maureen Cox in February hurt them. (Even so, Rolling Stones drummer Charlie Watts kept his October wedding to Shirley Ann

Arnold a secret.) But the paper thought that it would be a different matter for Cliff Richard, Elvis Presley or Adam Faith.

The Record Industry

1964 was a wonderful year for the record companies. They were making money hand over fist, with disc sales at a record level. EMI reported profits were up by 40%. Yet by June there were worries that the boom would soon be over. Under the headline 'Redcoats Still Rocking US', *Variety* reported British Decca's Dick Rowe as saying that the British invasion of America was only a passing phase. Rowe said: 'The pop music business is really an American game. It is not cricket. I have little doubt that they will recapture their market before too long.' Rowe was the man who turned down the Beatles for Decca, preferring to sign Brian Poole and the Tremeloes instead.

The *New Musical Express* correctly predicted that CBS would buy Oriole Records in Britain, ending their ten-year licensing deal with Philips. CBS had made a similar move in Germany the year before. Both CBS and RCA were gradually setting up subsidiaries around the world, and would come to successfully challenge the European global majors EMI and Polygram.

In Britain, Pye launched their Top Six singles in January. They were TV advertised anonymous covers of six hits on one disc, for the price of a normal single. EMI followed in April with its Hot Six on Regal Zonophone. *Variety* reported that EMI had hired 'indie groover Robert Stigwood' to produce them.

A growing trend in the British industry was the move to independent producers. Mickie Most licensed the Animals and Herman's Hermits to EMI, while in February *Variety* reported that 50% of the output of British Decca came from independent producers.

In April RCA announced that Elvis Presley had sold more than 100,000,000 records around the world in the eight years that he had recorded for them. The Beatles passed this figure in February 1965, in just under two and a half years. Pretty well anything by the Beatles seemed to sell. W.H. Smith advertised imported singles from Europe featuring LP tracks not released as singles in Britain. Even the BBC's flagship current affairs TV programme 'Panorama' devoted a whole programme to Brian Epstein, with clips of the Beatles and his other acts. This success did not, however, extend to the Beatles former drummer Pete Best, who signed to Decca and desperately tried to cash in on the phenomenon he had so nearly been part of.

Top Of The Pops

On 1 January 1964 the BBC began broadcasting 'Top Of The Pops'. Based on the simple idea of playing the biggest hits of the week, the show has been a consistent hit for the last 25 years and is still going strong. The programme was initially produced by Johnny Stewart in Manchester, though it soon moved down to London. The show was hosted in turn by the BBC's leading DJs, with an early feature being a beautiful but silent girl appearing to spin the discs. The most famous of these (though not the first) was Samantha Juste. In 1968 she married Monkee Micky Dolenz, though the marriage did not last.

At the end of March Radio Caroline became the first of Britain's pirate radio stations. Apart from Radio Luxembourg in the evenings, there was no commercial or pop radio in Britain then. The BBC still had the Light Programme and the Home Service, but no Radio 1. Broadcasting from ships off the coast, these new stations brought a refreshing change to broadcasting, and were very popular. A number of other stations followed Caroline, the most successful being 'Big L' Radio London. They played a wider variety of pop music than the BBC had ever done, and this helped new acts and the growing number of new independent record labels. EMI's chairman Sir Joseph Lockwood later blamed the pirates for the substantial fall in record sales in 1965.

Survivors

Cliff Richard and the Shadows had a highly successful pantomime run at the London Palladium. Advance bookings for the 'Aladdin' show were the biggest ever at the theatre.

Not everyone was happy with the boom in rock music. It made veteran American singer Jo Stafford sad. He told *Variety*, 'A great, great thing has been lost — the American popular song... It's the Great God Money that rules the record industry today, not quality.'

Popularity Polls

For the first time all the British consumer music papers ran popularity polls. The *New Musical Express* ran the biggest and most important, though its poll contained no real surprises. It did include a new section for top R&B group, which the Rolling Stones won. This reflected the growing interest in this style of music in Britain. In April *Record Mirror* ran the country's first R&B poll, though relatively few people voted. For example, Mary Wells was voted Top Female Singer by 1,617 votes to second placed Etta James with 85. Chuck Berry got 543 votes as Top Male Singer. It still gave an interesting snapshot of the popularity of R&B artists, almost entirely American, whose records did not always feature high in the pop charts. The Top Male Group were the Miracles, the Top Female Group were the Shirelles, the Best Instrumental Group were Booker T and the MGs, and the Best British Artist was Georgie Fame. The All Time Best R&B Disc was **Smokestack** by Howling Wolf Burnette, with 168 votes. The paper later instituted separate charts for R&B singles and albums.

In the *Record Mirror*'s main poll in June the Rolling Stones beat the Beatles as Top British Vocal Group, though the Beatles won the Top World Group section. The Top Individual Group Members were Mick Jagger, followed by Hank B. Marvin of the Shadows, George, John, Paul and Ringo. In the *Melody Maker* poll in September, the top three in the World Group section were the Beatles, the Rolling Stones and the Shadows. In the Top British Musician section it was Shadows present and past, with Hank Marvin just ahead of Jet Harris. **Not Fade Away** beat **Can't Buy Me Love** as the Vocal Record of the Year. Like *Record Mirror*, *Disc* held its first pop poll. It had only one category, that of Top Pop Star. Elvis Presley won, followed by Cliff Richard, Mick Jagger and Paul McCartney.

World News

In October Britain had a general election, which after 13 years of Conservative rule the Labour Party won. Labour leader Harold Wilson promised to modernize Britain, talking of applying the 'white heat of technology', and won a narrow four-seat majority. Though he won a second and much bigger majority in 1966, Wilson largely failed to deliver.

The young British designer Mary Quant successfully took on the French fashion industry. She opened the country's first boutique in Chelsea, and within a year swinging London had for the first time become the centre of the fashion world for the young, with Carnaby Street full of boutiques and youth-orientated shops.

In January British troops flew in and crushed an army revolt in recently independent Uganda. In February a magistrate declared *Fanny Hill* obscene, and ordered all copies of the book to be destroyed. It had first been published in two volumes in 1748 and 1749. Written by John Cleland, it told the life story of a prostitute. In March the Government announced the mass closure of railway lines as Dr Beeching's axe fell. Later in the month Mods and Rockers clashed at Clacton in the first of a number of large-scale fights. In April the BBC started its second TV channel. In July the first Brook Advisory Clinic for family planning opened. In August three London women who had worn topless dresses were tried and convicted of indecency. In September the *Sun* newspaper was born out of the ashes of the old *Daily Herald*. In December the House of Commons voted to end the death penalty for murder, but not for treason or setting fire to a naval dockyard. On the last day of the year Donald Campbell set a new world water speed record in Australia.

In the American elections in November, the Democrats kept control of Congress and the Presidency. Lyndon Johnson talked of the Great Society during the campaign, and beat the far right Barry Goldwater by a landslide. Johnson escalated American involvement in Vietnam, with air strikes against the North in August. In July Johnson signed a major Civil Rights Act, though there were still race riots in Harlem and Rochester later in the month. In March the kidnappers of Frank Sinatra's

son were jailed for life. In June comedian Lenny Bruce was tried for obscenity.

In October Nikita Khrushchev was toppled from power in Russia. China became the fifth nuclear power the same month, exploding an atom bomb in Sinkiang. Cyprus and the Congo both suffered intercommunal violence. Indian leader Nehru died in May. The French withdrew the last of their troops from Algeria. French writer Jean-Paul Sartre refused the Nobel Prize for Literature, claiming that it would compromise his position as a writer.

Films

Sean Connery was the top box office draw in Britain in 1964, and his Bond film *Goldfinger* was the biggest money-maker. Cliff Richard, who had been top in 1962 and 1963, just failed to make it three years in a row and had to be content with second place. Elvis Presley, who had released his tenth film *Kissin' Cousins* during the year, was fourth and the Beatles came eighth. The five biggest money-makers were all British films. After *Goldfinger* came the Beatles' first film *A Hard Day's Night*, followed by *Zulu*, *A Stitch In Time* and Cliff Richard's *Wonderful Life*.

In America it was a great year for British stars when it came to the Oscars. It was also a great year for musicals. *My Fair Lady* won eight Oscars, including that for Best Film, Best Director in George Cukor, and Best Actor in Britain's Rex Harrison. *Mary Poppins* won five, including the Oscar for Best Actress which went to another British star, Julie Andrews.

Sport

The 18th Olympic Games were held in Tokyo. The Americans won the largest number of gold medals with 36, followed by the Russians with 30 and Japan with 16. Britain's four gold medallists were Kenneth Matthews (20km walk), Lynn Davies (long jump), Ann Packer (women's 800m) and Mary Rand (women's long jump). In February Cassius Clay defeated Sonny Liston to become the new heavyweight champion of the world. Clay had a combination of great speed and style in the ring, and a loud mouth outside it. West Ham United beat Preston North East for the FA Cup, while their Bobbie Moore was voted Footballer of the Year. Liverpool were top of League Division One, while Rangers won both the Scottish FA Cup and were top of the Scottish League Division One. Worcestershire were county cricket champions. In America, the St Louis Cardinals won the World Series. The Cleveland Browns won the NFL championship, and the Buffalo Bills the AFL crown.

Hope Of Things To Come

1964 was a unique year. For the first time since rock music burst on to the public consciousness in the mid-fifties, the American market was dominated by a British act. In the mid-sixties the American market accounted for half the world's total record sales, yet until the Beatles this vast market was denied to virtually all British artists except for the occasional one-off hit. The Beatles' performance in America in 1964 was fantastic by any standards, and has never been equalled since. The real test, however, was whether this level of success could be sustained, and whether the Beatles were a one-off phenomenon or whether Britain really did have something original to offer. As 1965 was to show, 1964 was only a foretaste of things to come.

VARIOUS ARTISTS *American*

ORIGINAL THEATRE CAST WITH ZERO
MOSTEL, MARIA KARNILOVA, BEATRICE
ARTHUR, JULIA MIGENES, MICHAEL
GRANGER, SUE BABEL, CAROL SAWYER,
BERT CONVY, AUSTIN PENDLETON,
LEONARD FREY, PAUL LIPSON, JOANNA
MERLIN, TANYA EVERETT, ORCHESTRA
CONDUCTED BY MILTON GREENE

FIDDLER ON THE ROOF (Album) *RCA-Victor
1093* [*USA*]. 1964 saw a new musicial which has
now become something of a theatrical legend.
Fiddler on the Roof, with book by Joseph Stein,
was based on stories by Sholom Aleichem, and
combines the elements of Jewish folklore with
those of a musical play. The lyrics are by Jerry
Bock and the music by Sheldon Harnick. This
saga from folk tales of a Jewish village in Russia
in 1905 was brilliantly directed by Jerome
Robbins, and Zero Mostel's performance as
Teyve the milkman added his name to the
small circle of really great stars. RCA-Victor's
album of the show became one of their hottest
sellers as early as 10 days after release and was
awarded a Gold Disc in 1965 by RIAA. It stayed
in the bestsellers for 206 weeks reaching No 7.
The show ran until 3 July 1972, with 3,242 performances, a record for a musical in the USA.

In Britain the show opened on 16 February
1967 at Her Majesty's Theatre with Topol in the
star part. His part was later taken over by
English actor Alfie Bass with great success. This
production closed in 1971 with 2,030
performances. Other productions were seen in
Israel, Holland, Finland and Denmark.

The album contents are: *Side 1 —* **Tradition**
(Zero Mostel and chorus); **Matchmaker,
Matchmaker** (Julia Migenes, Joanna Merlin
and Tanya Everett); **If I Were A Rich Man**
(Zero Mostel); **Sabbath Prayer** (Zero Mostel,
Maria Karnilova and chorus); **To Life** (Zero
Mostel, Michael Granger and men); **Miracle of
Miracles** (Austin Pendleton); *Side 2 —* **Teyve's
Dream** (Zero Mostel, Maria Karnilova, Sue
Babel, Carol Sawyer and chorus); **Sunrise,
Sunset** (Zero Mostel, Maria Karnilova and
chorus); **Now I Have Everything** (Bert Convy
and Julia Migenes), **Do You Love Me?** (Zero
Mostel and Maria Karnilova); **Far from the
Home I Love** (Julia Migenes and Zero Mostel);
Anatevka (Zero Mostel, Maria Karnilova,
Michael Granger, Beatrice Arthur, Leonard
Frey and Paul Lipson).

ORIGINAL FILM SOUNDTRACK *British*

GOLDFINGER (Album) *United Artists ULP
1076* [*UK*]. This James Bond film soundtrack
sold over 400,000 in its first three months and
over $2 million worth in six months, was No 1
for three weeks and stayed high in the charts
for 70 weeks in the USA.

Composer John Barry (surname Prendergast)
was born 3 November 1933 in York, England,
and grew up in Fulford, three miles outside the
city. He worked on the score for *Dr No*, the first
of the James Bond thrillers, which included
Monty Norman's **007** (1962), the now-famous
'Bond Theme' used in subsequent Bond films
— *From Russia with Love* (1963) *Goldfinger* (1964),

Thunderball (1965) and others. Lionel Bart wrote
the title song for *From Russia with Love*, but
Barry arranged it and composed the rest of the
score. In *Goldfinger* he wrote the entire musical
content, apart from the lyrics of the title song,
and similarly for *Thunderball*. For the latter two
films he composed the principal parts in only
two days. His scoring was a colossal worldwide triumph, particularly as the film music
domain had been virtually exclusive to
American writers until a few years before.

The *Goldfinger* film (starring Sean Connery
in the role of James Bond) grossed over $22
million in the USA and Canada alone by
January 1968, and with receipts from other
countries totalled £16 million in one year. The
title song from the film also sold a million as a
singles disc (see Bassey, 1964), while the
Goldfinger album was only outsold very
narrowly by the Beatles' **Hard Day's Night**
album in 1965.

The **Goldfinger** album comprises the
following, all the music composed by John
Barry: **Goldfinger** (title song) (sung by Shirley
Bassey) lyrics by Leslie Bricusse and Anthony
Newley; **Miama, Golden Girl, Alpine Drive,
Auric's Fancy, Death of Tilley, Odd Job's
Pressing Engagement, The Laser Beam, Bond
Back in Action Again, Pussy Galore's Flying
Circus, Teasing the Korean, Gassing the
Gangsters, Dawn Raid on Fort Knox, Arrival
of the Bomb, Count Down, Death of
Goldfinger.**

VARIOUS ARTISTS *Anglo-American*

ORIGINAL SOUNDTRACK OF FILM WITH
JULIE ANDREWS, DICK VAN DYKE,
DAVID TOMLINSON, GLYNIS JOHNS,
KAREN DOTRICE, MATTHEW GARBER,
ED WYNN (ARRANGED AND
CONDUCTED BY IRWIN KOSTAL)

MARY POPPINS (Album) *Buena Vista 4026*
[*USA*] *HMV CLP 1794* [*UK*]. This disc, released
in the USA on 6 July 1964, sold over four
million in the USA alone and over six million
globally by 1 January 1968 with sales still
mounting. **Mary Poppins** was No 1 for 16
weeks in the USA.

The film (biggest gross of 1965 in the USA
at $31 million), was based on the *Mary Poppins*
books by Miss P.L. Travers, premiered in the
USA in August 1964 and was undoubtedly
Walt Disney's greatest. (Disney accumulated
34 Oscars and won over 900 other awards and
five honorary doctorates.) A musical fantasy, it
mingled live action and animation. The dream-
world story of the English nanny (Julie
Andrews) arriving on the East Wind to take
over the household of a London banker (David
Tomlinson), his wife (Glynis Johns) and their
two young children, and changing their lives,
is sheer entertainment. It made Julie Andrews
a scintillating new film star and was also a
triumph for Dick Van Dyke. The film won five
Academy Awards for 1964: for 'Best Actress'
(Julie Andrews), 'Best Song' (**Chim Chim
Cher-ee**), 'Best Music Score', 'Best Visual
Effects' and 'Best Editing'. An additional
10-song album sold over 750,000 and a
storyteller album over 300,000 by the end of

1965. The songs were written by Richard M.
Sherman and Robert Sherman, sons of famed
US songwriter Al Sherman. Both were staff
writers for Disney.

The songs in the soundtrack were:
Overture (orchestra and chorus); **Sister
Suffragette** (Glynis Johns); **The Life I Lead**
(David Tomlinson); **Perfect Nanny** (Karen
Dotrice and Matthew Garber); **Pavement Artist
(Chim Chim Cher-ee)** (Dick Van Dyke); **A
Spoonful of Sugar** (Julie Andrews); **Jolly
Holiday** (Julie Andrews and Dick Van
Dyke); **Supercalifragilisticexpialidocious** (Julie
Andrews, Dick Van Dyke and Pearlies); **Stay
Awake** (Julie Andrews); **I Love to Laugh** (Ed
Wynn, Julie Andrews and Dick Van Dyke); **A
British Bank** (Julie Andrews and David
Tomlinson); **Feed the Birds (Tuppence a Bag)**
(Julie Andrews and chorus); **Fidelity,
Fiduciary Bank** (Dick Van Dyke, David
Tomlinson and Bankers); **Chim Chim Cher-ee**
(Dick Van Dyke, Karen Dotrice, Julie Andrews
and Matthew Garber); **Step in Time** (Chimney
Sweeps' Dance) (Dick Van Dyke and chimney
sweeps); **A Man has Dreams, Life I Lead**, and
Spoonful of Sugar (David Tomlinson and Dick
Van Dyke); **Let's Go Fly a Kite** (Tomlinson,
Van Dyke and Londoners).

Gold Disc award RIAA 1964 and Grammy
Awards for 'Best Original Film Song' 1964,
'Best Recording for Children' 1964. The disc
was in the US bestsellers for 114 weeks. By the
end of 1969 the film had grossed over $60
million (£25,000,000).

ORIGINAL FILM SOUNDTRACK *American*
**WITH AUDREY HEPBURN, REX
HARRISON, STANLEY HOLLOWAY AND
JEREMY BRETT**

MY FAIR LADY (Album) *CBS-Columbia 2600*
[*USA*] *CBS BPG 72237* [*UK*]. This film of the
stage musical, based on Bernard Shaw's play
Pygmalion, with lyrics by Alan Jay Lerner and
music by Frederick Loewe, can only be
described as a box office gold mine. In its first
year it grossed £16,300,000 at the box office, £10
million of it in the USA and Canada. Warner
Brothers paid the world record figure of
$5,500,000 for the film rights. Audrey
Hepburn, who had the star role of Eliza,
originally played by Julie Andrews in the stage
show, does not sing the songs in the film or on
the disc. These were dubbed by Marni Nixon
(soprano and wife of composer Ernest Gold of
Exodus fame) who could sing in the accents of
any unmusical star. Lerner and Loewe wrote
some new material for the film, and it was then
the most expensive musical and studio film
in the industry's history, costing in all
$17,000,000. *My Fair Lady* won eight Academy
Awards (1964).

This album was issued in the USA in
October 1964 and sold 500,000 before the film
opened with a one and a half million sale by
early 1966. The disc contained all the familiar
songs: **Wouldn't It Be Luverly?, I Could Have
Danced All Night, Just You Wait, Without
You, Show Me, The Rain in Spain, On the
Street Where You Live, Get Me to the Church
on Time, With a Little Bit of Luck, I've Grown
Accustomed to Her Face, I'm Just an Ordinary**

Man, **You Did It**, **The Ascot Gavotte**, **Why Can't the English?**, **A Hymn to Him**.

Gold Disc award RIAA 1964. This album was in the US bestsellers for 111 weeks, reaching No 4.

THE ANIMALS   *British*

HOUSE OF THE RISING SUN *Columbia (EMI) DB 7301 [UK] MGM 13264 [USA]*. After the Beatles and the Liverpool sound had broken in 1963, the next phase in the British beat boom was the emergence of R&B based groups from other parts of the UK. The Rolling Stones established themselves as the biggest of these groups; the Animals were not far behind.

The group started in 1960 as the Alan Price Combo, consisting of keyboard player Price (born 19 April 1942, in Fatfield, County Durham), bass guitarist Bryan 'Chas' Chandler (born 18 December 1938, in Heaton, Newcastle upon Tyne), lead guitarist Hilton Stuart Patterson Valentine (born 2 May 1943, in North Shields, Northumberland) and drummer John Steel (born 4 February 1941 in Gateshead, County Durham). In 1962 Eric Victor Burdon joined the group to take over the vocals from Alan Price. He was born on 19 May 1941, in Newcastle upon Tyne. The members of the group came from a number of different backgrounds. Alan had been an income tax officer, Bryan a ship's instrument maker, Hilton a machinist, John a technical illustrator and salesman, and Eric a designer, postman and draughtsman. After Burdon joined the group, their stage act became wilder, and their fans started calling them 'the animals', a name they later adopted. They started playing clubs in Newcastle, in the north-east of England, and by late 1963 had a resident spot at the Club-A-Go-Go, owned by their manager Michael Jeffery. It was here that independent record producer Mickie Most first heard them and offered Jeffery a production deal. Several record companies had already shown interest in the Animals following an EP they had made privately. Of the 500 copies they had had pressed, some were sold to fans and some sent to London in an attempt to get live work and a record contract. Most and Jeffery signed an agreement on 28 February 1964 that made Most responsible for recording and much of the promotion work, and gave him ownership of the recordings. Most, Jeffery and the Animals each got a royalty of 2%. This deal was to cause much resentment in later years, following the huge sales of **House of the Rising Sun**, when the Animals felt that they had not been given a fair deal. Jeffery died in an air crash in 1972.

Independent producers were a new part of the record industry in the early sixties, and Mickie Most was to become the most successful of them all. Born Michael Peter Hayes, he had tried to become a pop singer in 1957, though without much success in Britain. In 1958 he went to South Africa where he became a popular star. It was then the norm for singers in South Africa to produce their own records, which Most did, so when he returned to Britain in 1962 he decided to use his new skills to concentrate on producing records for others. The Animals were his first discovery.

The group moved to London in January 1964, having already made their radio debut on the BBC's 'Saturday Club' on 27 December 1963. Their first TV shows were both on ITV, on Tyne Tees 'Roundabout' (a local programme for the north-east) and Granada's 'Scene at 6.30'. In March 1964 Mickie Most took the Animals to the Kingsway Recording Studio in London where they recorded what was to be their first single **Baby Let Me Take You Home**. Most took the tape to Derek Everitt, label manager of Columbia Records, and negotiated a licensing deal with the EMI label. **Baby Let Me Take You Home** was a modest hit, reaching No 21. For the follow-up, Most selected a rather odd song. **House of the Rising Sun** was a slow number, originally recorded by veteran American folk singer Josh White in the 1940s, a world away from the brash R&B the Animals played in their live act. An old negro song, it tells the story of a man destroyed by prostitution. ('The House of the Rising Sun' was a brothel.) Columbia were not very keen on the idea, even though the words had been toned down from the bawdy original, not least because it ran to over four minutes. Most persuaded them to put it out, and it gave the Animals the biggest hit of their career. It went to No 1, with 12 weeks in the charts. In October 1972 Mickie Most re-released the record on his Rak label, and it went to No 25 with six more weeks in the charts. In 1982 it was a hit for the third time, reaching No 11 with 10 more weeks of chart action, making 28 weeks in all.

While Most had been able to overcome Columbia's doubts about the record, he was not able to convince Columbia's American company Capitol. Their international A&R manager Dave Dexter turned down the Animals, as he was to turn down most of the successful EMI acts offered to Capitol. Like the others, the Animals therefore went to Capitol's

competitors and made money for them instead. MGM picked up the Animals for America, and it was on their label that **House of the Rising Sun** went to No 1 for three weeks, with 11 weeks on the charts. The Animals followed **House of the Rising Sun** with five more Top 10 hits on Columbia, and then in early 1966 the contract with Mickie Most expired. Alan Parsons, who had arranged all their records and was therefore the group member who worked closest with Most, left the Animals in 1965 and was replaced by Dave Rowberry. This led to increasing friction between the remaining members of the group, now led by Eric Burdon, and Mickie Most. Rather than renew their contract with Most they signed with Decca, though they stayed with MGM for the USA. After only two hits with their new company, the Animals split up in June 1966.

Burdon then formed Eric Burdon and the Animals with a largely new line-up, and moved to America. There he got increasingly involved with the hippie life style of California and drugs. He continued to produce some excellent records and scored with hits like **San Franciscan Nights** (1967) and **Sky Pilot** (1968). In 1968 and again in 1976 the original Animals briefly reformed, but nothing much came of these reunions. The revivals of **House of the Rising Sun** only infuriated the Animals, and they twice threatened legal action against Mickie Most and EMI. On both occasions their case collapsed before reaching court. By early 1965 the controversial American businessman Allen Klein had become involved with the Animals making an agreement with Mickie Most for his ABKCO company to manage Most's affairs in America. Both Most and the Animals fell out with Klein, who went on to manage the Beatles and the Rolling Stones before falling out with them also. Global sales of this record over the years were reputed to be approaching nine million.

PAUL ANKA WITH ENNIO   *Canadian-Italian*
MORRICONI AND THE CANTORI
MODERNI

OGNI VOLTA *RCA 45N 1395 [Italy]*. This was a first million seller for Paul in the Italian market, and it was sung by him in Italian. He sang **Ogni Volta** at the San Remo Song Festival in February 1964, taking second place in the contest. The disc passed the million sale in Europe by mid-May. It sold a million in Italy alone, becoming the second disc to achieve such a figure in the country — the first being by Bobby Solo. The US title for the song was **Every Time**. The writers were Rossi and Robifer. This disc was Paul Anka's seventh million seller. He sold five million records in Italy alone by mid-1966.

LOUIS ARMSTRONG   *American*

HELLO DOLLY *Kapp 573 [USA] London HLR 9878 [UK]*. This song was originally written as a production number to get actress/singer Carol Channing on stage in the second act of the Broadway musical *Hello Dolly*, produced at

St James Theatre, New York, on 16 January 1964, with music and lyrics by Jerry Herman. *Hello Dolly*'s producer gave the tune exclusively to Lyndon B. Johnson for the Democratic campaign in the Presidential election of 1964 when it was sung everywhere as 'Hello Lyndon'.

After a long and successful career in the jazz world, it was Louis' first million seller at the age of 64, and was No 1 for one week in the USA and 22 weeks in the bestsellers. Total sales were over two million. It reached No 4 and 14 weeks in the British bestsellers.

Louis Armstrong was born on 4 July 1900 in New Orleans, and was destined to become one of the true immortals of jazz. He learned to play the cornet in a reform school where he had been sent in 1913 for firing a pistol on New Year's Day. On his release in 1917, he met the famed King Oliver who became his teacher, and the following year he replaced Oliver as trumpeter with Kid Ory's band, then joined Fate Marable's band on the Mississippi steamboats for two years. **Hello Dolly** received a Grammy Award in the USA for 'Song of the Year' 1964, and an award to Louis for 'Best Vocal Performance'.

Louis Armstrong died on 6 July 1971 in New York.

THE BACHELORS   *Irish*

DIANE *Decca F 11799* [*UK*] *London 9639* [*USA*]. The first million seller for this extremely popular trio came from the combined sales from Britain, the USA and other countries. The song was originally written in 1927 by Lew Pollack (words) and Erno Rapee (music). Rapee's tune was first entitled **Valse Dramatique** for the Janet Gaynor/Charles Farrell silent film *Seventh Heaven* for which it was used as the theme.

The Bachelors were all born in Dublin, Ireland, Con Cluskey on 18 November 1941, his brother Declan Cluskey on 12 December 1942, and John James Stokes on 13 August 1940. Con and Declan both studied piano, and John music theory. They were all educated in Dublin colleges, Declan becoming a design draughtsman, Con a heating engineer and John a builder. The trio came together in 1953

and formed a harmonica group, calling themselves the Harmonichords. They performed semi-professionally at dances and on radio and TV in Dublin. They became such a success that they were eventually asked to appear on the Ed Sullivan TV show in America, and also performed on a number of radio shows, playing mostly classical music. They changed their name to the Bachelors on the suggestion of Decca's artists' and repertoire producer Dick Rowe who auditioned them in late 1962.

Their first disc **Charmaine** soared to the top of the charts in 1963. Then followed this international hit, **Diane**. It reached No 10 with 13 weeks in US bestsellers, and No 1 and 19 weeks in Britain's bestsellers. The trio played several instruments: Con — piano, guitar, banjo and tin whistle; Declan — piano, guitar, banjo and harmonica; and John — guitar, double bass and harmonica.

I BELIEVE *Decca F 11857* [*UK*] *London 9672* [*USA*]. The second big seller for the Bachelors hit a 600,000 sale in Britain and 300,000 in the USA. Sales from other countries helped to make it a million. The song was written in 1952 by Ervin Drake, Irvin Graham, Jimmy Shirl and Al Stillman, and was previously a tremendous hit for Frankie Laine. The disc was No 33 and eight weeks in the US bestsellers. It was No 2 and 17 weeks in the British bestsellers.

BOBBY BARE   *American*

FOUR STRONG WINDS *RCA Victor 8443* [*USA*]. Another big hit through subsequent years for Bobby Bare with an estimated million sale. Written by Ian Tyson in 1963, the disc was No 3 in the American country charts where it had a 19-week chart life. In the Hot 100 it reached No 60 during a seven-week chart run.

SHIRLEY BASSEY   *British*

GOLDFINGER *Columbia (EMI) DB 7360* [*UK*] *United Artists 790* [*USA*]. This was the title song for the sensationally successful *Goldfinger* film, the third of the famous James Bond thrillers. It had a good sale in Britain but when released on the United Artists label in the USA in November 1964 it sold a fast million by May 1965. The music was by Britain's ace film composer John Barry, who became internationally famous for his scores of the James Bond films *Dr No*, *From Russia with Love*, *Goldfinger* and *Thunderball* (see p. 93). The soundtrack album of **Goldfinger** also sold over a million in the USA. The words of the song were by the famous British stage musical songwriting team of Anthony Newley and Leslie Bricusse.

Shirley Veronica Bassey was born on 8 January 1937 in the tough Tiger Bay area of Cardiff, Wales, the youngest of seven children. Her father died when she was two. She first worked in an enamel factory. Self-taught in music, she made her first appearance at Luton, Bedfordshire, in the chorus of a touring revue *Memories of Al Jolson* at the age of 16. In 1955, she was heard by the impresario Jack Hylton at London's Astor Club, and this led to her first

big break in the West End in the *Such is Life* review. Her first successful disc was **Banana Boat Song** (1956), then **As I Love You** (1958) and **Kiss Me Honey, Honey Kiss Me** (1959) for the Philips label. She then joined EMI's Columbia Records and became a consistent chart entrant with big hits including **If You Love Me** (1959), **As Long As He Needs Me** (1960), **Climb Ev'ry Mountain** (1961), **You'll Never Know** (1961), **Far Away** (1962), **What Now My Love?** (1962), **I (Who Have Nothing)** (1963).

This disc was No 7 in the US charts and 13 weeks in the bestsellers, and No 21 in Britain, with nine weeks in the bestsellers.

THE BEACH BOYS   *American*

FUN, FUN, FUN *Capitol 5118* [*USA*]. The Beach Boys' fourth global million seller was written by Brian Wilson and Mike Love, and produced by Brian Wilson. It reached No 5 in the American charts, where it stayed for 11 weeks.

I GET AROUND/DON'T WORRY BABY *Capitol 5174* [*USA*] *Capitol CL 15350* [*UK*]. **I Get Around** was the Beach Boys' first American No 1, and their first big hit in Britain. It took nearly 18 years to reach the million mark in America, with an RIAA Gold Disc awarded on 22 February 1982. **I Get Around** was written by Brian Wilson. It was No 1 for two weeks in *Billboard* and one week in *Cash Box*. It spent 15 weeks on the Hot 100, and 13 weeks in the British Top 50 where it peaked at No 7. The flip side **Don't Worry Baby** was written by Brian Wilson and Roger Christian, and reached No 24 during a 10-week American chart run of its own. The record was the group's fifth million-selling single in a row.

1964 was another good year for the Beach Boys on the album front. All four of their LP releases won RIAA Gold Discs for million dollar sales in America. **Shut Down, Volume 2** reached No 13 with 38 weeks on the album charts. **All Summer Long** peaked at No 4 with a 49-week chart run, and **Beach Boys Concert** went all the way to give them their first album No 1, for four weeks with 62 weeks on the charts. **The Beach Boys Christmas Album**, released at the end of the year, finally won a Gold Disc in April 1982.

THE BEATLES   *British*

TWIST AND SHOUT *Tollie 9001 and later Capitol 5624 [USA]*. 1964 was the year that the Beatles conquered America. With breathtaking speed they went from nowhere to become the most successful recording act in the history of the American music industry. In 1964 they had the longest run of consecutive No 1s ever in the history of the American charts. **I Want To Hold Your Hand** went to No 1 for eight weeks, and was followed to the top by **She Loves You**. In the *Cash Box* charts **Twist and Shout** replaced it at the top, with **Can't Buy Me Love** going to the top in both *Billboard* and *Cash Box*. The Beatles had 16 weeks in a row at No 1 in *Cash Box* and 14 weeks in *Billboard*.

Although the Beatles had become very big in Britain in 1963, no interest had been shown in the group in America. The Beatles' manager Brian Epstein managed to get a booking for two live appearances on the crucially important 'Ed Sullivan Show' on American TV. Sullivan had more faith in the Beatles than other Americans at that time as he had been held up at London's Heathrow Airport in 1963 because of the crowds who turned up to welcome the Beatles back from a European tour. In fact by the time the Beatles appeared on the Sullivan show, on 9 and 16 February, they were already at No 1 with **I Want To Hold Your Hand**. It was radio that proved more important in breaking the Beatles than TV, though the 'Ed Sullivan Show' was an important mark of respectability that indicated that the Beatles were here to stay.

Once Capitol had broken the Beatles with **I Want To Hold Your Hand**, other companies who had some Beatles product under license started to re-release it. **Twist and Shout** was part of the material from the British **Please Please Me** album that EMI had licensed to the Chicago based Vee Jay Records. They decided to put it out as the first release on their new Tollie label, and it went to No 1 for one week in the *Cash Box* and *Variety* charts, though it peaked at No 2 for four weeks in *Billboard*. It was in the *Billboard* charts for 11 weeks, and in *Cash Box* for 13 weeks. The B side, **There's A Place**, spent one week in the *Billboard* charts at the same time, at No 74, though it did not make any of the other US charts.

Though initial gross sales on Vee Jay were 1,140,998, returns and reserves reduced the net sales to 839,715. It was only when the record was re-issued by Capitol 22 years later that net sales finally passed the million mark. **Twist and Shout** was featured in the films *Ferris Bueller's Day Off* and *Back To School*, and the renewed interest that this sparked off resulted in the record re-charting, reaching No 23 with 15 weeks in the Hot 100 in 1986.

Both sides were taken from the British EP **Twist and Shout**, which also sold a million copies (see 1963). **Twist and Shout** was an adaptation of the traditional Spanish song **La Bamba**. This was something that EMI in Britain had to admit to when a flood of mail came in asking about the true origins of the song, which had been credited to Bert Russell and Phil Medley. **Twist and Shout** was on the **Please Please Me** album in Britain and the **Introducing The Beatles** album in America. **There's A Place** was written by John Lennon and Paul McCartney. Both sides were produced by George Martin at the famous EMI Abbey Road studios in North London.

INTRODUCING...THE BEATLES (Album) *Vee Jay 1062, 30 and 1092. [USA]*. This was the Beatles' first album release in America. When released in July 1963 it got nowhere, and only after Capitol had broken the band did it follow **Meet The Beatles!** into the album charts, getting stuck behind that Capitol LP for nine weeks at No 2. It spent 49 weeks in the LP charts.

Originally the album contained the same tracks as the **Please Please Me** LP in Britain, with the exception of **Please Please Me** and **Ask Me Why**, though the title and art work were different. (See the Beatles, **Please Please Me**, 1963 for track listing.) The version that made the charts in 1964 was different, as from the second pressing onwards it did not contain **PS I Love You** or **Love Me Do**, but did contain the two previously excluded tracks mentioned above.

Just as the singles charts had seen a flood of records put out by a number of labels, so 1964 saw a number of albums featuring the Beatles. The 1961 Polydor recordings with Tony Sheridan were released by MGM. A double album of interviews called **The American Tour With Ed Rudy** was released by RadioPulsebeat and reached the Top 20. EMI and Brian Epstein were very unhappy about the release of this album, and took joint legal action to stop it. They were constantly trying to prevent other companies cashing in on the Beatles. There were complaints to Liberty Records over a proposed 'The Chipmunks Sing The Beatles Hits' album, difficulties with groups who used Beatles soundalike names like the Beatle-ettes on Jubilee Records, and problems with United Artists over the soundtrack rights for the film *Help!*

Vee Jay made every effort to maximize sales for their Beatles product, though not always in a way beneficial to the Beatles. They put four Beatles tracks together with eight songs from Frank Ifield (also under license from EMI) and released an album called **Jolly What! The Beatles and Frank Ifield**. About the crassest marketing ploy was to couple the **Introducing...The Beatles** album with **Golden Hits Of The Four Seasons** as the double album **The Beatles vs The Four Seasons** (Vee Jay 30.) Vee Jay claimed that this was 'the international battle of the century' with 'each delivering their greatest vocal punches'. After picturing the heads of the group members and listing the album tracks, the Vee Jay hype screamed 'YOU BE THE JUDGE AND JURY!'

The album spent two weeks in the charts, reaching No 142.

The next attempt at repackaging the Beatles' first album was more successful. **Songs, Pictures And Stories Of The Fabulous Beatles** (Vee Jay 1092) contained the same music as **Introducing...The Beatles** but with additional materials included in the packaging. It reached No 63 in a ten-week chart run. All the various incarnations of **Introducing...The Beatles** were produced by George Martin at the EMI studios in Abbey Road, and were issued under license from EMI Parlophone in Britain. They sold over a million copies in the USA mainly in the format of the second pressing onwards of **Introducing The Beatles**.

CAN'T BUY ME LOVE *Parlophone R 5114 [UK]/Capitol 5150 [USA]*. **Can't Buy Me Love** was the Beatles' first release of 1964, entering some British charts at No 1 first week of release, and being at No 1 in all four main charts by its second week out. Another Lennon/McCartney composition, it was the third Beatles single in a row to sell over a million copies in Britain, and the second to achieve that figure on advance sales alone. It had sold 1,286,963 by the end of September 1965. It spent four weeks at No 1, and 14 weeks in the British charts.

It set a new record for advance sales in the United States, with orders for 2,100,000 copies. It achieved an RIAA Gold Disc on its first day of release. The record entered the charts at No 27 and went to No 1 the next week, where it stayed for five weeks. It spent ten weeks in the Hot 100, with the flip side **You Can't Do That** also charting for four weeks. This was a slightly different mix from the British B side, though both were recorded at the same time. This Lennon-McCartney song reached No 48 to give the Beatles another double A-sided hit. The record was also a major hit around the world. George Martin produced both sides of the record. **Can't Buy Me Love** was the only Beatles single not recorded in Britain. It was recorded at EMI's Pathé Marconi studios in Paris on Wednesday 29 January, while the Beatles were touring France. The B side was recorded later at Abbey Road.

February 1964 saw the Beatles' first US tour. It was a massive sell-out, though Capitol's intention of making a live recording of the Beatles in New York was scuppered by the American musicians' union. (The recording was subsequently made at the Hollywood Bowl in August.)

MEET THE BEATLES! (Album) *Capitol 2047 [USA]*. This was the first Beatles album to enter the American charts, which it did on 1 February 1964. The record went to No 1 for 11 weeks, and spent 71 weeks on the charts. All the tracks on the album were under license from the Parlophone division of EMI, and were produced by George Martin at the Abbey Road studios in London in 1963. Most of the material was first released in Britain on the Beatles' second 1963 album, **With The Beatles**, although the differences between these two albums were greater than those between **Please Please Me** and its American counterpart **Introducing...The Beatles**.

All songs on the album are by John Lennon

and Paul McCartney unless otherwise stated. The track listing is as follows: **I Want To Hold Your Hand; I Saw Her Standing There; This Boy; It Won't Be Long; All I've Got To Do; All My Loving; Don't Bother Me** by George Harrison; **Little Child; Till There Was You** from *The Music Man* by Meredith Willson; **Hold Me Tight; I Wanna Be Your Man;** and **Not A Second Time**. The first three tracks did not appear on **With The Beatles** in Britain, and five tracks that did appear on that album were not on **Meet The Beatles!** By 1987 the record had sold 1,716,000 copies in the USA and another 116,000 in Canada.

DO YOU WANT TO KNOW A SECRET?/ THANK YOU GIRL *Vee Jay 587* [*USA*]. Two more tracks licensed by EMI Parlophone to Vee Jay before Capitol picked up the Beatles, and issued once the group became successful in America. **Do You Want To Know A Secret?** reached No 2, with eleven weeks on the *Billboard* charts. (It reached No 3 with 12 weeks in the *Cash Box* charts.) The flip side charted independently at the same time, reaching No 35 in seven weeks on the Hot 100 and peaking at No 38 with nine weeks in *Cash Box*. Both sides were written by John Lennon and Paul McCartney and produced in 1963 by George Martin at Abbey Road. **Thank You Girl** was the British B side of **From Me To You**. US sales eventually passed the million.

THE BEATLES SECOND ALBUM (Album) *Capitol 2080* [*USA*]. This mis-named album (it was the fifth Beatles LP to make the American charts, but the second on Capitol) was something of a rag-bag of songs taken from British singles, EPs, and album tracks not released in the USA. Released on 10 April 1964 it was the Beatles' second album to top the American LP charts, which it did for five weeks. It spent 55 weeks on the charts, and was awarded an RIAA Gold Disc for million dollar sales on 13 April. This was twelve days before it entered the album charts! It sold a quarter of a million copies on its first day of release.

All tracks on the album were recorded for EMI Parlophone in Britain and licensed to Capitol. They were all produced by George Martin at the Abbey Road studios in London. All the songs were written by John Lennon and Paul McCartney unless otherwise stated. The album contained the following tracks: **Roll Over Beethoven**, by Chuck Berry; **Thank You Girl; You Really Got a Hold On Me** by William Robinson; **Devil in Her Heart** by Richard Drapkin; **Money (That's What I Want)**, by Berry Gordy Jr (the founder of Motown Records); **You Can't Do That; Long Tall Sally**, by E. Johnson, R. Blackwell and R. Penniman; **I Call Your Name; Please Mr Postman**, by B. Holland, F. Gorman and R. Bateman; **I'll Get You;** and **She Loves You**. This last track had originally been issued in America on the Philadelphia-based Swan label. Swan had failed to fully comply with the terms of the licensing agreement, thereby allowing EMI to transfer the material to Capitol in 1964.

A HARD DAY'S NIGHT *Parlophone R 5160* [*UK*]/*Capitol 5222* [*USA*]. The title track from the Beatles' first film was issued in Britain on 10 July 1964, and in America three days later. It was recorded at EMI's Abbey Road Studio 2 on Thursday 16 April, with George Martin producing, assisted by Norman Smith as engineer and Geoff Emerick as tape operator. The record was the first since **From Me to You** not to sell a million in Britain, though it did reach that figure in America and global sales were several million. The song won a Grammy Award for Best Vocal Group Performance of 1964.

As with all major pop stars before them, the Beatles and their manager Brian Epstein were keen to branch out into films. United Artists came up with a good offer, but wanted to release the soundtrack on their own record label. This gave EMI a problem. They had an exclusive recording deal with the Beatles, but did not want to upset the group or their manager (who was also responsible for a host of other EMI artists) by putting the film deal at risk by insisting on keeping the recording rights. Eventually L.G. Wood, Managing Director of EMI, skilfully negotiated a deal which gave United Artists the soundtrack album for North America (with a pressing fee to EMI) while EMI kept the rights for the rest of the world. He also got the film company to agree to allow Capitol to release the Beatles' tracks from the film providing the album was not called **A Hard Day's Night**.

The five new tracks were issued on **Something New** one month after the soundtrack was released. In the end EMI got their hands on everything connected with the film, when they bought United Artists Records in 1979.

A Hard Day's Night was written by John Lennon and Paul McCartney, though the title was thought up by Ringo Starr. It entered the British charts at No 1 the first week of release. It was at No 1 for four weeks in Britain, and for two weeks in America. It spent 13 weeks in the charts on both sides of the Atlantic. In America the B side also charted. **I Should Have Known Better** reached No 53 during four weeks in the *Billboard* charts, and No 43 during five weeks in

Cash Box. The British B side was **Things We Said Today**. Both B sides were Lennon-McCartney compositions. When re-released 20 years later in Britain, **A Hard Day's Night** reached No 52 with another three weeks in the British Top 100.

The film, the soundtrack album and the single were all tremendously popular all over the world. The film reinforced the Beatles' 1964 world tours of Europe, North America and Australia.

A Hard Day's Night was the Beatles' biggest international hit up to that time. It went to No 1 in Britain, the USA, Ireland, Australia, South Africa, Finland, Sweden, Norway, Germany, The Netherlands, Spain, Malaysia, Singapore, Hong Kong and Argentina. It was also a Top 5 hit in Australia, Switzerland, Belgium, the Philippines, Brazil, Peru and Uruguay. Having been the first British artists to conquer North America, this film helped the Beatles to conquer South America as well.

A HARD DAY'S NIGHT (Film soundtrack album) *United Artists UA 6366* [*USA*] *(later re-issued as Capitol SW 11921)*. The film soundtrack was issued in America by United Artists on 26 June 1964, two weeks before Parlophone issued an album of the same name in Britain. The two albums were in fact different. The American record is the film soundtrack, whereas the British release consists of the Beatles' recordings of songs featured in the film. Both albums were recorded at EMI's Abbey Road studios and produced by George Martin from the same takes, though the mixes were sometimes different as on the title track. The album went to No 1 for 14 weeks, keeping the Capitol album **Something New** (which contained five of the songs also on the soundtrack album) blocked at No 2 for nine weeks. The soundtrack spent 51 weeks on the charts. When EMI later bought United Artists Records, they re-issued the album on the Capitol label.

The soundtrack album contained four instrumental tracks by the George Martin Orchestra. (Martin had a personal recording contract with United Artists for America.) The rest of the album was eight tracks by the Beatles, all of them written by Lennon and McCartney: **A Hard Day's Night; Tell Me Why; I'll Cry Instead; I'm Happy Just To Dance With You; I Should Have Known Better; If I Fell; And I Love Her;** and **Can't Buy Me Love**. The last track had already been a big hit before the film was made. Originally **I Call Your Name** was to have been in the film, but was dropped in favour of the title track.

The film and soundtrack were enormously successful. The LP had an advance order of one million, and soon sold another million. The film reaped $5,800,000 in US rentals in six weeks, and around £4 million world gross. It had a print order of 800 prints for the USA and 1,000 for the rest of the world. The film was the second most profitable film of 1964 in Britain, just behind the James Bond film *Goldfinger*. The Beatles were the eighth most popular film stars of the year, behind Cliff Richard (second) and Elvis Presley (fourth). The film was released just prior to the Beatles' second US tour in August.

A HARD DAY'S NIGHT (Album) *Parlophone PMC 1230 (mono) PCS 3058 (stereo) [UK]/British version issued in America on CD was Parlophone-Capitol 46437 in 1987 [USA]).* The Beatles' third British album contained the songs from their first film *A Hard Day's Night* and other new material. In America the contents of this album appeared on the **A Hard Day's Night** soundtrack and the **Something New** LP. The album was produced by George Martin at Abbey Road. It went to No 1 in the album charts for 21 weeks, with 38 weeks in the charts. The record sold nearly 700,000 in Britain in its first year of release, with European sales well over the million. This disc was not released in the USA until 1987, when all the early British versions of the Beatles' LPs were issued on compact disc. The album went to No 1 in the American CD charts for three weeks, with eleven weeks on the chart.

This was the first Beatles album where all the tracks were written within the group, and the only time all the songs were written by John Lennon and Paul McCartney. They were **A Hard Day's Night; I Should Have Known Better; If I Fell; I'm Happy Just To Dance With You; And I Love Her; Tell Me Why; Can't Buy Me Love; Any Time At All; I'll Cry Instead; Things We Said Today; When I Get Home; You Can't Do That** and **I'll Be Back.**

SOMETHING NEW (Album) *Capitol 2108 [USA].* Released just after the **A Hard Day's Night** soundtrack, this album contained some of the songs that the Beatles sung in their film. Most of the material was from the British **A Hard Day's Night** album, which contained new material as well as songs from the film. All tracks were under license from EMI Parlophone in Britain, and were produced by George Martin at the Abbey Road studios in London (except for the German language version of **I Want To Hold Your Hand** which was recorded at the EMI Pathé Marconi studios in Paris.)

The album peaked at No 2 in the charts for nine weeks, kept out of the top spot by the Beatles' own **A Hard Day's Night** soundtrack album. The record was 41 weeks in the charts, won an RIAA Gold Disc for million dollar sales on 24 August 1964, a month after the disc was released on 20 July. Advance sales in the US were half a million, with eventual sales over the million mark.

The tracks on his album, all written by John Lennon and Paul McCartney unless otherwise stated, were as follows: **I'll Cry Instead; Things We Said Today; Any Time At All; When I Get Home; Slow Down** by Larry Williams; **Matchbox,** by Carl Perkins; **Tell Me Why; And I Love Her; I'm Happy Just to Dance With You; If I Fell;** and the German-language version of **I Want to Hold Your Hand, Komm, gib mir deine hand.**

Capitol released eight tracks from this and the **A Hard Day's Night** soundtrack as four singles. All eight charted, though apart from the title track from the film none achieved a particularly good chart placing. Nevertheless, the Beatles and Brian Epstein were particularly incensed by the release of **Slow Down/Matchbox.**

I FEEL FINE/SHE'S A WOMAN *Parlophone R 5200 [UK]/Capitol 5327 [USA].* The Beatles ended 1964 in brilliant style. **I Feel Fine** was released in Britain on 27 November, a week after its American release. It had a British advance order of three quarters of a million, and had sold the million by its second week on the market. It was the Beatles' fourth single to pass the million mark with sales in Britain alone, and by the end of September 1965 had sold 1,242,333 copies. It sold a million in America in its first week of release. It was also a massive hit around the world, with No 1s in Britain, the USA, Australia, Canada, Ireland, Norway, Denmark, The Netherlands, Spain and Hong Kong. Among the other countries where it made the Top 10 were South Africa, Finland, Germany, Austria, Switzerland, Belgium, Malaysia, Brazil and Argentina.

I Feel Fine was an immediate No 1 in Britain, where it had a six-week run at the top with 14 weeks in the charts. In America it was No 1 for four weeks, with an eleven-week chart run. The other side of this single, **She's A Woman,** was also a major hit reaching No 4 with a nine-week chart run of its own. Both songs were written by John Lennon and Paul McCartney, and produced at Abbey Road.

BEATLES FOR SALE (Album) *Parlophone PMC 1240 (mono) PCS 3062 (stereo) [UK]/Released in America as CD in 1987, Parlophone-Capitol 46438 [USA].* The Beatles' fourth album was released by EMI on 4 December 1964, just in time for the Christmas rush. Within two weeks it had taken over the No 1 album slot from the Beatles' own **A Hard Day's Night.** It had three spells at the top. After seven weeks it was replaced by the Rolling Stones' second album, which in turn was replaced after three weeks at No 1 by **Beatles For Sale.** After only one week at the top, the Beatles again gave way to the Stones and then Bob Dylan (for one week) before beginning their final three-week run on 1 May. A total of eleven weeks at No 1, with 46 weeks in the album chart in all. The album was not released in America until 1987, when all the original British Beatles albums were issued on CD. It then made No 3 in the CD charts, with eight weeks on the chart. Many of the tracks were issued on the **Beatles '65** album in America. As usual, the album was produced by George Martin at EMI's Abbey Road studios, with the Beatles working in Studio 2.

The tracks on this album, all of which were written by John Lennon and Paul McCartney unless otherwise stated, were as follows: **No Reply; I'm A Loser; Baby's In Black; Rock and Roll Music,** by Chuck Berry; **I'll Follow The Sun; Mr Moonlight,** by Roy Lee Johnson; **Kansas City/Hey-Hey-Hey-Hey!,** by Mike Stoller and Jerry Leiber; **Eight Days A Week; Words Of Love,** by Buddy Holly; **Honey Don't,** by Carl Lee Perkins; **Every Little Thing; I Don't Want To Spoil The Party; What You're Doing;** and **Everybody's Trying To Be My Baby,** by Carl Lee Perkins.

BEATLES '65 (Album) *Capitol 2228 [USA].* Though **Beatles '65** did not appear in the US album charts until the first week of January, it was actually released in time for the usual huge Christmas sales on 15 December 1964. Most of the material came from the British album **Beatles For Sale.** All the tracks were under license from the Parlophone division of EMI in Britain, and were produced by George Martin at the Abbey Road Studios.

The album was the huge success that every Beatles record was in America. It was their fourth No 1 album, topping the *Billboard* album charts for nine weeks with 71 weeks on the charts. This equalled the Beatles' previous longest album chart run, set by their first Capitol LP **Meet The Beatles!** It won an RIAA Gold Disc for million dollar sales the day it entered the charts, on 2 January 1965. **Beatles '65** had an advance order of three quarters of a million copies, sold over a million in the first week, 2,124,000 copies in the first four weeks and over three million in six weeks. It was the fastest selling album in history up to that time.

The tracks on this album, all of which were written by John Lennon and Paul McCartney unless otherwise stated, were as follows: **No Reply; I'm A Loser; Baby's In Black; Rock and Roll Music,** by Chuck Berry; **I'll Follow The Sun; Mr Moonlight,** by Roy Lee Johnson; **Honey Don't,** by Carl Lee Perkins; **I'll Be Back; She's A Woman; I Feel Fine;** and **Everybody's Trying To Be My Baby,** by Carl Lee Perkins. The difference in content between the Beatles' British and American albums at this time was partly caused by the British practice of putting more on an album. **Beatles For Sale,** for example, had 14 tracks while **Beatles '65** had only 11. British albums were also quite independent of singles, whereas in America singles were a marketing tool for the album. It therefore made no sense to Capitol to release **I Feel Fine** but not to put it on the album put out at the same time.

This album brought to an end a spectacularly successful year for the Beatles. They had achieved more than anyone could ever have dreamed would be possible. Everything they had touched had turned to gold, with No 1 singles, EPs and albums in every corner of the world. In just two years they had revolutionized the music industry, achieved unheard of sales, made their first film, conquered America and the rest of the world, and taken a host of other British groups with them to dominate the American and other charts.

CILLA BLACK
British

ANYONE WHO HAD A HEART *Parlophone R 5101 [UK].* Cilla Black (real name Priscilla Maria Veronica White) was born in Liverpool on 27 May 1943. After schooling at St Anthony's Junior and Secondary Schools and Anfield Commercial College, Liverpool, she became a typist and secretary with a local firm at the age of 15. In 1960 at The Iron Door, a well-known rock'n'roll club in Liverpool, she was singing along with the music when the bass player asked her to sing a song. She was then invited to join another well-known local group as vocalist, keeping her office job. She often sang at Liverpool's famous 'The Cavern' with then-unknowns like the Beatles and Gerry and the Pacemakers. In September 1963 she was spotted by Brian Epstein (manager of the

Beatles, Billy J. Kramer and others) who signed her up and persuaded her to become a full-time professional. She made her radio debuts on 'Friday Spectacular' on Radio Luxembourg, and on BBC's 'Easy Beat'. Her TV debut was on 'Ready, Steady, Go'. Epstein changed her name as so many people had said her voice sounded black rather than white.

Cilla's first recording was **Love of the Loved**, a John Lennon/Paul McCartney song. Then Billy J. Kramer brought back **Anyone Who Had a Heart** from the USA which he was certain was the right song for Cilla. It became No 1 in Britain for four weeks with 17 weeks in the bestsellers, selling over 800,000 in just over a month. This earned her a summer season at the London Palladium in 1964, where she was a great success. This song was written in 1963 by Hal David (words) and Burt Bacharach (music).

YOU'RE MY WORLD *Parlophone R 5133 [UK] Capitol 5196 [USA]*. Cilla Black's second million seller was No 1 for three weeks in Britain and 17 weeks in the bestsellers. It was also a success in the USA reaching No 26 with seven weeks in the bestsellers, and elsewhere. Combined British-US sales are estimated at 1,500,000. The song was written in 1963 in Italy, originally titled **Il mio mondo**, by Gino Paoli (words) and Umberto Bindi (music). The English lyrics were written by Carl Sigman in 1964.

GIGLIOLA CINQUETTI   *Italian*

NON HO L'ETA (PER AMARTI) (I'm Not Old Enough To Love You) *CGD (Compagnia Generale del Disco) N 9486 [Italy] Decca F 21882 [UK]*. **Non ho l'eta** was the biggest Continental pop hit of Europe in 1964. It was the Italian entry to the Eurovision Song Contest, which it won by a large margin. A beautiful, simple ballad, written by Nicola Nisa and Mario Panzer, it also won the San Remo Song Festival.

Gigliola was born in Verona on 20 December 1947 and started singing at the age of five. She won a local TV competition at 11, and beat 4,200 entrants in another contest. Talent contests and festivals are an important part of the music business in Italy, and Gigliola followed the traditional route of graduating from local events to national ones. She was only 17 at the time of the Eurovision Song Contest. She went on to develop a long-lasting career in Europe.

Non ho l'eta was a big hit throughout Western Europe. It was No 1 for four weeks in both Italy and France, for six weeks in Denmark, two weeks in Belgium, and one week in both The Netherlands and Spain. It was a minor hit in Britain, reaching No 17 with 17 weeks in the charts. This was quite an achievement for a Continental solo singer at a time when Britain's charts were dominated by British or American beat groups, and she had to compete with a cover version by veteran singer Vera Lynn. Gigliola had one other hit in Britain, when 10 years later she made the Top 10 with **Go (Before You Break My Heart)** on CBS.

Gigliola Cinquetti was presented with a Platinum Disc in August 1964 for global sales of two million copies of **No ho l'eta**. Final sales were over three million. She was accompanied on the record by Franco Monaldi and his orchestra.

THE DAVE CLARK FIVE   *British*

BITS AND PIECES *Columbia (EMI) DB 7210 [UK] Epic 9671 [USA]*. **Bits and Pieces** was the Dave Clark Five's third million seller. It was a pounding rocker very much in the style of their first two hits, **Do You Love Me?** and the chart-topping **Glad All Over**. Written by group members Dave Clark and vocalist Mike Smith, the record went to No 2 in Britain, where it lasted 11 weeks on the charts. In America it was their second hit, reaching No 4 with 11 weeks on the charts. It sold 605,000 in Britain, winning a Silver Disc, and half a million in the USA.

CAN'T YOU SEE THAT SHE'S MINE? *Columbia (EMI) DB 7291 [UK] Epic 9692 [USA]*. The Dave Clark Five's fourth million seller in a row was again written by Dave Clark and Mike Smith. It was a bigger hit in America than in Britain. At home, the record just made the Top 10, peaking at No 10 with 11 weeks in the Top 50. In America their first two Top 10 hits were followed by the release of older material. The Congress label put out a single from their Piccadilly time which only reached No 53. Epic countered with their first British hit, **Do You Love Me?** This had been a Top 3 hit in America for the Contours in 1962, and only reached No 11 for Dave Clark. Even so, American sales did mean that globally the group had another million seller. British sales were just over 160,000.

Can't You See that She's Mine? restored the group to the US Top 10, reaching No 4 with 10 weeks in the Hot 100. British and mainly American sales made it a million seller. It was produced by Adrian Clark.

BECAUSE *Epic 9704 [USA]*. **Because** was released by Epic in the USA at the height of the Dave Clark Five's popularity, at a time when British beat groups could do no wrong. The recording was released under licence from Columbia in Britain, where the song had been issued as the B side of **Can't You See That She's Mine?** **Because** was written by Dave Clark and produced by Adrian Clark at EMI's Abbey Road studios in London. It gave the group their then-highest chart placing in America, reaching No 3 with 10 weeks in the Top 100.

ANY WAY YOU WANT IT *Columbia (EMI) DB 7377 [UK] Epic 9739 [USA]*. After three Top 10 hits in a row, the Dave Clark Five ran into trouble. Their next five singles were only minor hits. **Thinking of You Baby**, released in August 1964, only reached No 26 in Britain and was not released in America. **Any Way You Want It** fared only marginally better, reaching No 25 in a short five weeks in the charts. In America it did better, peaking at No 8 in the *Cash Box* charts but only No 14 in *Billboard*. It spent 12 weeks in the Hot 100. It is a typical driving piece of Dave Clark rock'n'roll, with everything thrown in. The song was written by Dave Clark and produced by Adrian Clark. One feature of Dave Clark Five records in Britain was that producer credits were given on their singles. This was very unusual at this time. Not even George Martin was mentioned on Beatles singles. 1964 was a good year for the Dave Clark Five. This record brought to six the number of their million sellers.

PETULA CLARK   *British*

DOWNTOWN *Pye 7N 15722 [UK] Warner Brothers 5494 [USA]*. Petula's fourth million seller was her biggest hit. The song was written by Pye's musical director Tony Hatch. The disc was No 2 for two weeks in Britain (with 15 weeks in the bestsellers) with well over the quarter million sale, but when released on the Warner label in the USA in December 1964 it soon shot to the top of the charts in January 1965, and was No 1 for two weeks with 15 weeks in the bestsellers, selling over a million there.

Only one other female British artist had ever attained No 1 in America — Vera Lynn in 1952 — so this was a wonderful achievement, with global sales over three million. She received the 'Gramophone Academy Award' of the USA for this disc as the best rock'n'roll single of 1964. Gold Disc award RIAA 1965.

A modern remix, **Downtown '88**, was a British Top 20 hit in 1988. It brought Pet Clark back on 'Top of the Pops' for the first time in 20 years.

BILL COSBY   *American*

BILL COSBY IS A VERY FUNNY FELLOW, RIGHT! (Album) *Warner Brothers 1518 [USA]*. This was the first album of inimitable comedy material recorded by Bill Cosby (see 1966). It received a Gold Disc award from RIAA in 1966 and sold one and a half million units by 1968.

The album includes: **A Nut in Every Car, Superman, Hoof and Mouth, Karate, Planes, Wives, Baby.** It was in the US bestsellers for 128 weeks.

I STARTED OUT AS A CHILD (Album) *Warner Brothers 1567 [USA].* Bill Cosby's second album achieved a Gold Disc award from RIAA in 1966 and million units sale by July 1967. It was produced by his fellow comedian Allan Sherman and recorded **'live'** at Mr Kelly's in Chicago. (See 1966.)

The contents of the album were: **Sneakers, Street Football, The Water Bottle, Christmas Time, The Giant, Opps, The Lone Ranger, Ralph Jameson, Medic, My Pet Rhinoceros, Half Man, Rigor Mortis, The Neanderthal Man, TV Football, Seattle.** It was in the US bestsellers for 104 weeks and sold 1,200,000 up to then. Grammy Award for 'Best Comedy Performance', 1964.

THE DIXIE CUPS   *American*

CHAPEL OF LOVE *Red Bird 001 [USA] Pye International 7N 25245 [UK].* The Dixie Cups' **Chapel of Love** was the first release for the new Red Bird label founded by leading American songwriters Jerry Leiber and Mike Stoller. In its short two-year existence, Red Bird built up a strong reputation, especially for girl groups like the Shangri-Las and the Dixie Cups.

Singer Joe Jones discovered the Dixie Cups in their native New Orleans. The black trio consisted of Barbara Anne Hawkins, her sister Rose Lee Hawkins and Joan Marie Johnson. Jones took the girls to New York to see Leiber and Stoller, who signed them up and put them under the care of husband-and-wife songwriters Jeff Barry and Ellie Greenwich. They selected a track from a Ronettes album which they had written with Phil Spector, and produced **Chapel of Love.** The record was a great success, reaching No 1 for three weeks in America and knocking the Beatles' **Love Me Do** off the top spot in the *Billboard* charts. The record spent 13 weeks on the charts, with eight weeks in the British charts where it peaked at No 22. The reputation that this first No 1 smash earned them did not last long. The Dixie Cups had four more hits in America, none of which made the Top 10. Only the last, **Iko Iko,** was a hit in Britain.

PETE DRAKE   *American*

FOREVER *Smash 1867 [USA].* Pete Drake, the 'talking steel guitar man', achieved national limelight in the USA with this disc. Although only reaching No 22 with 11 weeks in the bestsellers, it was a steady seller and through the years is said to have sold a million. The composition is by Buddy Killen (1959). It was on this disc that Pete first featured the 'talking steel'.

Pete Drake was born on 8 October 1932 in Augusta, Georgia, and saved the money from his first job as a clerk in a grocery store to buy his first guitar, a cheaply made mail-order instrument. He saved for a further two years to buy a good steel guitar. He was encouraged by his two musician brothers and won his first professional job as a musician on WLMA-Atlanta while still a teenager. In 1959, his prowess became recognized throughout the South and he moved to Nashville, working with artists who came to record there. He soon played dates on the Grand Ole Opry where his popularity grew and earned him regular Saturday night dates with the show.

Pete became one of the busiest musicians in Nashville, recording with big names such as Elvis Presley, Perry Como and the Monkees in addition to all the top country stars. In 1968 he became President of his own Stop Records.

GEORGIE FAME AND   *British*
THE BLUE FLAMES

YEH YEH *Columbia (EMI) DB 7428 Imperial 66086 [USA].* This song was written in 1963 by Rodgers Grant, Pat Patrick and Jon Hendricks. Georgie Fame's disc achieved No 1 position in Britain's charts for one week in January 1965 with 12 weeks in the bestsellers, and sold over 250,000. It was also a success in the USA, reaching No 21 with eight weeks in the bestsellers, and elsewhere, making an estimated million global sale.

Georgie Fame (real name Clive Powell) was born on 26 June 1943 in Leigh, near Manchester, and took piano lessons when he was seven. At 15 he left Leigh Central County Secondary School and worked in a cotton-weaving factory, playing the piano at nights with a group called the Dominoes. In 1959 he sang in a Butlin's holiday camp contest at Pwllheli, Wales, and was offered a job in London by the bandleader Rory Blackwell. He was playing in Islington, north London, when composer Lionel Bart called and asked him to audition for Larry Parnes. Parnes changed his name to Georgie Fame and employed him as pianist in a group to accompany visiting American artists. One night one of the singers was missing, so Georgie took over and was given a solo spot in the show. The group eventually became the Blue Flames, and worked solely with artist Billy Fury. Later, the group decided to stay together and played weekend all-night dances at London's Flamingo Club, becoming the resident group. In 1962, Georgie switched to the electric organ and the club business trebled, attracting 1,000 people at the Saturday all-night sessions with his jazz-based rock'n'roll music and blues. His self-termed 'rockhouse' music became a cult among visiting West Indians and Americans; he sounded like the singers of America's Deep South. 'Live' recordings were made at the Flamingo, then came **Yeh Yeh.**

The Blue Flames consisted of Colin Green (guitar), Peter Coe (alto/tenor saxes and flute), Tony Makins (bass guitar), Bill Eyden (drums) and Speedy Acquaye (congo drums). Georgie Fame was generally considered to be the best rhythm-and-blues artist in Britain.

THE FOUR SEASONS   *American*

RAG DOLL *Philips 40211 [USA] Philips BF 1347 [UK].* Bob Crewe and Bob Gaudio of the Four Seasons wrote **Rag Doll,** which gave them their fourth million seller, and fourth US No 1. In the American charts, the record got sandwiched between EMI's two top groups. It replaced the Beach Boys' **I Get Around,** and was itself replaced by the Beatles' **A Hard Day's Night.** It spent two weeks at No 1 with 12 weeks on the charts. In Britain it reached No 2, with a chart run of 13 weeks. It won a Gold Disc for million sales from the RIAA on 24 August 1964. As well as helping Bob Gaudio to write the song, Bob Crewe also produced it.

The Four Seasons had started out on the Vee Jay label, and then switched to the Dutch company Philips, who in 1964 released two Top 10 hits before **Rag Doll** (their only No 1 on Philips). The group had 38 hit records in America from 1962 to 1980, and 17 in Britain. They were to have one more No 1, in 1976 on Warner Brothers, with **December 1963 (Oh What a Night),** their only British No 1.

THE FOUR TOPS   *American*

BABY, I NEED YOUR LOVE *Motown 1062 [USA].* Signed by the Tamla-Motown organization in 1964, this disc was the first release for the group (see 1965). The song was written by the famous team Eddie Holland, Lamont Dozier and Brian Holland. It reached No 11 in the USA with 12 weeks in the bestsellers, and was also a hit in Britain at No 15. The subsequent global sale was estimated at one million. It was released on 15 August 1964.

FREDDIE AND THE DREAMERS   *British*

I UNDERSTAND (JUST HOW YOU FEEL) *Columbia (EMI) DB 7381 [UK] Mercury 72377 [USA].* This third global million seller for Freddie was written by Pat Best in 1953. It sold around 500,000 in Britain and a further half million in the USA on the Mercury label when it was released there in 1965, following the group's sensational TV appearance in New York. In the USA the disc was No 36 and nine weeks in the bestsellers, and in Britain it was No 5 and 15 weeks in the bestsellers.

This song had been a previous million seller, when recorded by the Four Tunes in 1954.

FREDDY (QUINN)   *German*

VERGANGEN, VERGESSEN, VORUEBER *Polydor 5851 [West Germany].* This seventh million seller for Freddy was composed by Lotar Olias. It is said to have sold 1,800,000 by July 1965, mainly in Germany and other Continental countries. The literal translation of the title is **Gone, Forgotten, All Over.**

GALE GARNETT   *New Zealander.*

WE'LL SING IN THE SUNSHINE *RCA Victor 8388 [USA].* Gale Garnett was born in Auckland, New Zealand, on 17 July 1942, the eldest daughter of an English carnival pitchman, music-hall entertainer and a Russian émigrée. The family left the South Pacific for America when she was nine and travelled throughout the USA before going to New York. She began her career at 12 as a stage actress, and made her professional debut as an actress at 15, after having worked as a waitress and a janitress in an off-Broadway theatre. Thereafter she was featured in no fewer than 60 TV shows with acting leads in **Hawaiian Eye**, **77 Sunset Strip**, **Adventures in Paradise**, **Bonanza** and many others. She also appeared in the stage productions of *Threepenny Opera*, *Guys and Dolls*, *Showboat*, *World of Suzie Wong* and others.

Her singing debut was at Los Angeles' Garrett Club, followed by club dates across the country. Gale wrote songs as a hobby and took 25 of them to RCA Victor. Although primarily an actress up to that time, Victor signed her to a contract. She had only been singing professionally for three months before **We'll Sing in the Sunshine**, her own composition, got to No 1 for one week in the US charts and stayed in the Top 10 for two months and 17 weeks in the bestsellers, with an eventual estimated million sale.

This disc won the 1964 Grammy Award as the 'Best Folk Recording of the Year'. She became a full-time singer.

GERRY AND THE PACEMAKERS   *British*

DON'T LET THE SUN CATCH YOU CRYING
Columbia (EMI) DB 4987 [UK] Laurie 3251 [USA].
During 1962 and 1963, Gerry and the Pacemakers came second only to the Beatles in popularity, first in their native Liverpool and later in the country as a whole. Gerry

Marsden (born in Liverpool on 24 September 1942) formed the group in 1959. He had played guitar in a local skiffle group, then in 1958 formed his own group the Mars Bars with his brother Freddy. They played the clubs and pubs of Liverpool for six months before breaking up.

The original Pacemakers were Gerry, who handled lead vocals and lead guitar, brother Freddy (born in Liverpool on October 1940) on drums, and bass guitarist John Chadwick (born in Liverpool on 11 May 1943). In 1961 Leslie Maguire (born in Wallasey, Cheshire, on 27 December 1941) joined to play piano. At first the group kept their full-time jobs, confining their performances to evenings and weekends. Gerry worked for British Railways, Freddy was a clerk, John a bank clerk, and Leslie a joiner. In late 1961 they turned professional and left for their first visit to Germany, playing the same Hamburg club circuit as the Beatles. On their return to Liverpool, they were often to be found topping the bill, on one occasion playing together with the Beatles as the Beatmakers.

In June 1962 the Beatles' manager Brian Epstein signed the group to a management contract. He then persuaded EMI A&R man and Beatles' producer George Martin to come up to Liverpool and hear the group perform. Martin signed them up and put them on Columbia rather than on his own Parlophone label, though he continued to produce their records. Their first disc was a Mitch Miller number, **How Do You Do It?**, which Martin had originally wanted the Beatles to record for their second single to follow **Love Me Do**. (The Beatles' recording has never been released.) **How Do You Do It?** was the second Merseybeat No 1, following the Beatles' **Please Please Me**.

Until Frankie Goes To Hollywood in the 1980s, Gerry and the Pacemakers were unique in scoring three No 1 records with their first three releases. The other two were **I Like It** followed by **You'll Never Walk Alone**. This became the theme song for the Liverpool Football Club fans, and in 1985 went back up to No 1 when recorded by the Crowd, a group of pop personalities organized by Gerry Marsden to raise money for the victims of the Bradford Football Club stadium fire disaster. Marsden thus became the first singer to take the same song to No 1 with two versions, a feat which has only been achieved twice in the 36-year history of the charts. Cliff Richard and **Living Doll**, No 1 in 1959 with the Shadows, and in 1986 with the Young Ones and Hank Marvin, is the only other example.

Don't Let the Sun Catch You Crying was written by Gerry Marsden, and produced by George Martin at the EMI Abbey Road studios in London. It was the group's fifth British hit and, though it was their first to pass the million mark, it was at the time their lowest-placed hit. It reached No 6, with 11 weeks in the Top 50. It was their first American hit, reaching No 4 with 12 weeks in the Top 100. This was the biggest of their 11 US hits. Global sales made up the million. Despite being their biggest-selling record, this was the disc that marked the beginning of the end for the group. 1963 had been a fantastic year for them, with three No 1s in a row. 1964 started off well, with their fourth hit **I'm the One** peaking at No 2. While **Don't Let the Sun Catch You Crying** made the Top 10 and established them in America, it was followed in Britain by **It's Gonna Be Alright** which peaked at only No 24. **Ferry Across the Mersey**, their last major hit, made No 8. After two minor hits in 1965, they disappeared from the British charts for ever.

In America they never reached the same heights as in Britain, but they did last longer and had more hits than in their home country. EMI offered the group to its US company Capitol, which seemed completely incapable of recognizing hit records from Britain. In an all-too typical move, Capitol turned the group down and EMI licensed their records to Laurie. After the success of **Don't Let the Sun Catch You Crying**, Laurie put out their first British hit from 1963, **How Do You Do It?** This made No 9. **I'm the One**, **I Like It** and **I'll Be There** followed, though none made the Top 10. **Ferry Across the Mersey**, a song greatly admired by Paul McCartney, made the Top 10 on both sides of the Atlantic. The group had a few more minor hits in America, culminating with **Girl On a Swing** which charted in September 1966.

Gerry and the Pacemakers started out as a group to rival the Beatles. In their first year they were fantastically popular in Britain, but their success soon faded and other groups pushed them aside. The group was dominated by Gerry Marsden, who seemed content to move into the less demanding but steady work of cabaret and club dates. For a group that had started with such phenomenal success, they faded very fast and had little lasting impact. (Interestingly, the only other group to have three No 1s with their first three hits, Frankie Goes To Hollywood, faded out even faster in the eighties.)

ASTRUD GILBERTO AND STAN GETZ
American

THE GIRL FROM IPANEMA *Verve 10323* [USA] Verve VS 520 [UK]. The success of this disc was largely the result of an afterthought. Verve had planned an album to be built around the two bossa nova giants — Stan Getz, the American adaptor, and Joao Gilberto, designated 'father' of bossa nova in Brazil. It was decided to have the Portuguese lyrics to one of the tracks for the song **Girl from Ipanema** and to also have them sung in English. Astrud, wife of Joao, was invited to sing the English lyrics (written by Norman Gimbel). When the disc was issued as a single, Astrud came into her own. The shortened single version contained only the inspired tenor sax of Stan Getz and plaintive haunting voice of Astrud. The disc reached No 5 for two weeks in the USA with 12 weeks in the bestsellers, and became a global hit with an estimated over one million sale.

Astrud Gilberto (born 1941) comes from an area around Rio de Janeiro near the beach of Ipanema, of which she sings.

The original song was written by Vincius de Moraes (Portuguese words) and Antonio Carlos Jobim (music), who, working in company with singer Joao Gilberto, launched the bossa nova movement in pop music in Brazil. (See also Getz/Byrd, 1962.) Grammy Award for 'Record of the Year' 1964.

BOBBY GOLDSBORO
American

SEE THE FUNNY LITTLE CLOWN *United Artists 672* [USA]. Bobby comes from Maryanna, Florida, where he was born on 15 January 1941. His family moved to Dotham, Alabama, and after Bobby's graduation from high school there, he studied at Auburn University for two years. He learned to play the guitar and after a brief period of freelance work joined Roy Orbison as a guitarist in January 1962, also deciding to write his own songs. Orbison encouraged him to go solo.

In 1964, a friend took a recording of Bobby's voice to Jack Gold, an A&R director at United Artist Records in New York. Gold immediately took a plane to Dotham and signed Bobby to an exclusive contract. His first release was this disc which got to No 9 in the US charts with 13 weeks in the bestsellers, and an eventual million sale (by 1967). The song was written by Bobby in 1963, the arrangement and conducting for the disc by Garry Sherman.

Bobby has played various dates around the USA and Canada. He also toured Britain with Roy Orbison.

LORNE GREENE
Canadian

RINGO *RCA Victor 8444* [USA] RCA 1428 [UK]. At a time when pop groups and teenage music saturated the musical scene, Lorne Greene's disc created a big surprise. Born in 1914, he is best known as one of the stars of the TV series 'Bonanza', in which he played the role of Pa Cartwright. His interest in drama dates back to his days at Linger Collegiate Institute in Ottawa. He received a fellowship to study at New York's Neighbourhood Playhouse after being noticed in Canada's annual drama festival. Lorne did a few years of radio jobs in Canada and some acting in TV, then in the Hollywood films *The Silver Chalice* and *Tight Spot*, followed by acting assignments on Broadway and Stratford and then the immensely successful 'Bonanza' series.

In 1964, Lorne recorded some numbers for Victor although he had had no experience in this field. An album **Welcome to the Ponderosa** was the outcome, including **Ringo**. Sung in monologue style, it told the story of notorious gunman Johnny Ringo. Nothing happened to the album until a Texas disc jockey played it. The result was sensational. RCA Victor were obliged to release it as a single and it sold well over the half million very quickly, and got to No 1 for one week in the US charts and 12 weeks in the bestsellers. It was also popular in Britain (where it was No 22) and in many other countries, selling over a million globally.

Ringo was written by Don Robertson and Hal Blair in 1963.

HERMAN'S HERMITS
British

I'M INTO SOMETHING GOOD *Columbia (EMI) DB 7338* [UK] MGM 13280 [USA]. Herman's Hermits were one of the few British acts of the mid sixties to become much more successful in America than in their native Britain. The group were originally called the Heartbeats, and were formed in Manchester in 1963. Their line-up was process engraver Karl Anthony Green, born in Salford on 31 July 1947, who played bass guitar and harmonica and was the only member of the original group still there when they started making records; hairdresser Jan Berry Whitham, born in Manchester on 21 July 1946, who played drums; telephone engineer Keith Hopwood, born in Manchester on 26 October 1946, who played guitar; and student Derek Leckenby, born in Leeds on 14 May 1946, who also played guitar. Peter Noone (Herman) joined the group as vocalist in 1964. He was born in Manchester on 5 November 1967, and as a child actor had appeared on TV shows like 'Knight Errant', 'Saki' and in Britain's longest-running TV soap opera 'Coronation Street'. He was educated at St Bede's College and Stretford Grammar School, and took drama and singing lessons.

His TV fame and the Heartbeats' local popularity turned them into teenybopper celebrities in the Manchester area, and they came to the attention of independent record producer Mickie Most, who saw them performing in Bolton. He signed them up, and decided that he could market them better if he focused attention on Peter Noone. The group came up with the name 'Herman' as they thought Peter looked like Sherman, a character in the TV cartoon programme 'The Bullwinkle Show'. They added the Hermits as it fitted in so well with Herman.

Mickie Most had become a successful independent record producer with acts like the Animals and the Nashville Teens. He took Herman's Hermits to EMI, who signed them to their Columbia label. Most selected a song by American husband-and-wife composers Gerry Goffin and Carole King as their first record. Released on 7 August 1964, **I'm Into Something Good** was an immediate success, giving the group their first and only British No 1. Its 15-week chart run was also the group's longest. It sold nearly half a million in Britain, and another half million globally. The follow-up was disappointing, and only reached No 19. Their third release was **Silhouettes**, put out in early 1965, which made No 3. They had a string of hits that lasted to the end of the decade. All but two of their 21 British hits were released on Columbia, with the last two in 1970 going out on Mickie Most's Rak label (sold in the 1980s to EMI).

In Britain Herman's Hermits had been one of a number of successful beat groups, but their career in America was much more interesting. For a while they rivalled the Beatles, and in 1965 ended the year as *Billboard's* top singles act, ahead of the Beatles. (Beatles' records sold huge amounts in a short period of time, so had a shorter chart life than those of other artists whose records actually sold fewer copies.) The group had 18 American hits between 1964 and 1968, with one double A side, giving them 19 chart entries. **I'm Into Something Good** made No 13, with 13 weeks on the charts. The follow-up **Can't You Hear My Heartbeat?** became the first of three No 1 singles in 1965, when they also released three million-dollar Gold Disc albums. They made a number of records for the American market that were not released in Britain, like **Mrs Brown, You've Got a Lovely Daughter** and **I'm Henry VIII, I Am** which traded on their very English image.

In America their records were released by MGM, not EMI's American subsidiary Capitol. Capitol were offered the record before it was released by EMI in the UK. It took them three days to turn down one of the biggest-ever groups in America, yet another example of Capitol's hopeless inability to recognize potential hit material from their English parent company. Capitol's subsidiary label Tower (who considered it twice) also turned the disc down, and EMI then licensed the group to MGM. When the record became a hit in Britain, Capitol wanted to take the group on. To its horror, EMI found it had no written contract with Mickie Most, to whom Herman's Hermits were signed as an independent producer. There was a verbal understanding, which proved not to have the force of a legally binding contract.

In September 1964 the controversial American businessman Allen Klein came on to the scene. He went on to manage the Beatles and the Rolling Stones before falling out with both. He did a deal with Mickie Most to handle Most's affairs in America, and secured large financial guarantees from MGM and CBS for North America. CBS offered to sign a worldwide deal at a considerably higher figure than EMI had agreed, leaving EMI in a difficult position with no contract and no rights to go on releasing records. EMI managing director L.G. Wood made the best deal he could, and secured the group for the world, excluding North America. Interestingly, Capitol Records of Canada had picked up on the band. A more successfully run company than its American parent, it released a number of acts from EMI in Britain which had been turned down by US Capitol. But as a result of the Klein-MGM deal though, Canadian Capitol lost the group after the end of 1964.

The enormous success of the group in America caused a major row with EMI, who were increasingly fed up with Capitol consistently passing on its successful British artists. Capitol offered to take any EMI act that made the British Top 20, while EMI pressed for them to go with any act in the Top 50. In fact, EMI had grave doubts about whether Capitol could handle all their artists even if they did take them. In the end little was done until EMI purged Capitol's senior management in 1971.

JOE HINTON   *American*

FUNNY (HOW TIME SLIPS AWAY) *Back Beat 541 [USA]*. Originally a hit for Jimmy Elledge in 1961, this country song written by Willie Nelson was recorded by Joe Hinton in a gospel soul-flavoured style for the new Back Beat label, a subsidiary of Duke/Peacock Records in the USA. The disc reached No 12 with 12 weeks in the US bestsellers, and is said to have subsequently sold a million.

Joe Hinton was born in 1929, and died in Boston on 13 August 1968.

AL HIRT AND HIS BAND   *American*

COTTON CANDY *RCA Victor 8346 [USA]*. The second singles million seller for Al Hirt, written by Russ Damon, this was released in April 1964. It was No 15 for two weeks in the US charts and 12 weeks in the bestsellers. The title was used for another of Hirt's albums which became a million-dollar seller.

Al Hirt signed with GWP Records, a new label, in 1969.

SUGAR LIPS *RCA Victor 8391 [USA]*. Another big success for 'The Monster' Al Hirt, written by William D. (Buddy) Killen (executive vice president and co-owner of Tree Publishing Co., Inc and Dial Records) and Billy Sherrill. This disc was estimated to have sold a million by 1965. The composition was used as the title for Hirt's million-dollar-selling album. Released in July 1964, the disc was No 20 in the US charts and seven weeks in the bestsellers.

THE HONEYCOMBS   *British*

HAVE I THE RIGHT? *Pye 7N 15664 [UK] Interphon 7707 [USA]*. This new British group had a million seller with their disc debut. The song was written by their two managers Alan Blaikley and Ken Howard. It was No 1 for two weeks in Britain and 15 weeks in the bestsellers. The million sale came from the combined British (over 250,000), USA and other countries' totals. The line-up was Martin Murray (guitar), born on 7 October 1941 in the East End of London; Alan Ward (guitar, piano, organ), born on 12 December 1945 in Nottingham; Denis Dalziel (piano, guitar, harmonica, jews harp), born on 10 October

1943 in Whitechapel, London; John Lantree (bass), born on 20 August 1940 in Newbury, Berkshire; Ann ('Honey') Lantree (drums), born on 28 August 1943 in Hayes, Middlesex.

The group was formed in 1963 by Martin Murray. He started playing guitar in the skiffle era with various groups, but wanted a new 'sound' different from other groups. He finally advertised in a musical paper and met Ward, the group's lead guitar. Martin had known Honey Lantree for some time as they were both in the hairdressing business. She had an unusual hobby for a girl — drumming. He finally persuaded her to join the group and she became one of the few female drummers in Britain. Her brother John joined the group when Martin's previous bass player left. Martin then met Denis through a friend.

They submitted some of their original numbers to independent producer Joe ('Telstar') Meek. He chose **Have I the Right?**, recorded it and then took the disc to Pye. It soon put the Honeycombs' upbeat number into the hit parade, with subsequent radio, TV and personal appearances in Britain, France, Australia and New Zealand. In the USA it reached No 4 with 13 weeks in the bestsellers.

THE KINKS   *British*

YOU REALLY GOT ME *Pye 7N 15673 [UK] Reprise 0306 [USA]*. The Kinks were probably the most offbeat of all the major British groups of the sixties. Their style was always a little off the mainstream, sometimes well ahead of its time and sometimes just out of fashion, as in the late sixties. Their first two singles failed to make the charts for the simple reason that they were not very good. Their debut disc was a weak cover of Little Richard's **Long Tall Sally**. It was only when they started recording their own material that their career took off. Despite a questionable start, they became one of the longest-lasting of all British groups, with hits

on both sides of the Atlantic in the sixties, seventies and eighties.

The group were formed in 1961 by four art students in Muswell Hill, London. They were Ray Davies (born in London on 21 June 1944) who plays guitar, harmonica and piano; his brother Dave Davies (born in London on 3 February 1947) who plays guitar, piano and banjo; drummer Michael Avery (born in Hampton Court, London, on 15 February 1944) and Peter Quaife (born in Tavistock, Devon, on 31 December 1943) who plays bass and lead guitar and bongo drums. All except Michael Avery provided the vocals. The group got work backing singer Robert Wace at debutante parties and society balls, often dressed in a mock dandy style. Wace eventually moved over to managing the group in 1962. They had been known as the Ramrods and the Ravens, but by the time record producer Shel Talmy had discovered them and signed them to Pye they had changed their name to the Kinks.

Ray Davies wrote their third release, **You Really Got Me**. It marked the transition of the group from playing weak covers of other people's music to a strong style of their own. They played a hard rock'n'roll heavily influenced by R&B. **You Really Got Me** went all the way to No 1 for two weeks, and stayed in the charts for 12 weeks. It won a Silver Disc for British sales of a quarter of a million. It also gave the group their first hit in America, where Pye had licensed the record to the Reprise label, which had just been bought from Frank Sinatra by Warner Brothers in the first step of a long-term expansion that has made them the biggest record company in America. Reprise promoted the Kinks with a sensitivity never shown by Pye, and created something of a cult following for the group. The first of three US Top 10 hits in a row, **You Really Got Me** reached No 7 in the States, with 15 weeks on the charts. This was the longest chart run of their 20 American hits between 1964 and 1981, four of which made the Top 10. Shel Talmy produced the record which, with good sales in America, sold a global million.

The follow-up was another Ray Davies composition, **All Day and All of the Night**,

which reached No 2 in Britain and No 7 in America. That was followed by **Tired of Waiting for You**, which gave them their second British No 1 and made No 6 in America, their highest chart place there. In Britain a string of Top 10 hits followed, with one further No 1 in 1966, **Sunny Afternoon**. In America the hits kept coming, but of increasingly minor proportions. The late sixties saw this downward trend in Britain, though the brilliant 1970 hit **Lola** restored them to the Top 10 on both sides of the Atlantic.

In 1972 the group switched labels to RCA, and later had some success with Arista. They spent a lot of time touring in America, where they have enjoyed a longer line of hit albums than singles. Despite frequent rumours of splitting up, starting from the 1967 Dave Davis Top 3 solo single **Death of a Clown**, the Kinks have survived longer than almost all their original contemporaries.

BILLY J. KRAMER AND THE DAKOTAS
British

LITTLE CHILDREN/BAD TO ME *Parlophone R 5105 (Bad To Me R 5049)* [UK] *Imperial 66027* [USA]. Billy J. Kramer was born William Ashton, in Liverpool on 19 August 1943. The youngest of seven children, he went to St George of England Secondary Modern School, leaving school for an engineering apprenticeship with British Railways in Liverpool. In his spare time he sang in the clubs and pubs of Liverpool, where he was discovered by the Beatles' manager Brian Epstein who signed him to his NEMS company for a management contract in 1963. Epstein teamed him up with a leading Liverpool group the Dakotas, consisting of drummer Tony Mansfield, born in Salford on 28 May 1943; lead guitarist Mike Maxfield, born in Manchester on 23 February 1944; rhythm guitarist Robin Macdonald, born in Nairn, Scotland, on 18 July 1943; and bass guitarist Raymond Jones, born in Oldham on 20 October 1939.

In March 1963 Kramer and the Dakotas went to Hamburg to do a session at the Star Club. On their return from Germany they recorded their first disc, **Do You Want to Know a Secret?**, written by John Lennon and Paul McCartney. The record went to No 2. The follow-up was another Lennon-McCartney number **Bad To Me** which went to No 1 for two weeks, stayed 14 weeks in the Top 50 and won a Silver Disc. Their fourth release, in February 1964, was the delightful ballad **Little Children**, which netted another No 1 for one week, with 13 weeks in the charts. It also won a Silver Disc.

1964 was the year Billy J. Kramer was launched in America. His US record company Imperial selected his two British No 1s as a double A-sided debut disc for the American market. Both sides made the Top 10, with **Little Children** reaching No 7 with 15 weeks on the charts and **Bad To Me** going to No 9 with a 10-week chart run. American sales of **Little Children/Bad to Me** were considerable, and British sales of either side take total sales over the million mark. Billy had four more minor hits in America, none of them managing to reach the Top 10.

In Britain the Dakotas had one minor hit on their own with **The Cruel Sea** in 1963. With Billy, their follow-up to **Little Children** was **From a Window**, which made No 10, and in May 1965 their cover of **Trains and Boats and Planes** gave them their last hit, peaking at No 12. Despite a tremendous start, they faded very quickly. They had benefited considerably from the link with Brian Epstein, with Lennon-McCartney songs to sing and George Martin to record them, but at the end of the day they did not have what it took to last.

GARY LEWIS AND THE PLAYBOYS
American

THIS DIAMOND RING *Liberty 55756* [USA]. This disc was released in late December 1964, and by April 1965 had sold a million in the USA. It was No 1 for two weeks there and 12 weeks in the bestsellers. The song was written by Bobby Brass, Irwin Levine and Al Kooper.

Gary Lewis, born 1946, is the son of the famous comedian and film star Jerry Lewis, and made up his mind on a show business career early in life. In 1964, after many months of drum practice, he formed a small band just for parties and personal enjoyment. He took the group to Disneyland and auditioned for a summer job. They were engaged and completed their summer engagement by appearing in a Universal picture *Swinging Summer*. With his parents' and friends' encouragement, Gary asked Liberty Records for an audition, the result being this big hit on which he is the vocalist. The Playboys are Dave Costell, Dave Walker and Al Ramsey.

MAHINA STARS AND KAZUKO MATSUO
Japanese

OZASHIKI KOUTA *Victor 5655* [Japan]. This was the first local Japanese hit to sell well over one and a half million. A Gold Disc was awarded to Hiroshi Wada's Mahina Stars on 22 January 1965 in Tokyo. The disc was No 1 for 21 weeks in Japan from September 1964 into 1965.

The composer is unknown. Royalties are paid to the Japanese Bureau of Justice until the writer is established.

SIV MALMQUIST
Swedish

LIEBESKUMMER LOHNT SICH NICHT (Love Problems Are Not Worthwhile) *Metronome 5210* [West Germany]. Siv Malmquist's disc was No 1 in the German charts for 11 weeks in 1964, after running away with first prize in the German Pop Music Festival in Baden Baden on 13 July 1964. It sold 100,000 in a fortnight, and 880,000 in a year with an estimated million in Germany by the end of 1965. The song was written by Christian Bruhn and George Buschor, who also wrote the winning Festival song in 1962.

Siv Malmquist (Siw Malmkvist) was born in Landskrona, Sweden, on 31 December 1936 and made her debut on records for Metronome of Sweden in 1955 with **Tweedle Dee**. She is

also an actress and made films in Denmark. At the end of 1961, she was on the stage in Turku, Finland, in *Irma la Douce* and appeared later in other musicals. She made many tours in European countries and has been seen on TV all over Europe. Siv has recorded in Swedish, Danish, Norwegian, German, English, French and Dutch.

MANFRED MANN
British

DO WAH DIDDY DIDDY *HMV POP 1320* [UK] *Ascot 2157* [USA]. Manfred Mann were one of the most consistent hit-making groups of the sixties. Of their 17 hit singles, only four failed to make the Top 10, and two of those peaked at No 11. There was always something slightly different about the group. They had far greater musical versatility than most beat groups, with influences drawn from jazz as well as R&B.

The group was formed by Manfred Lubowitz. Born on 21 October 1940, in Johannesburg, South Africa, he received a thorough musical education at the renowned Juilliard School of Music, New York, and the Vienna State Academy. He played the piano and organ. When Manfred Mann later signed a recording contract with EMI, the contract was with Lubowitz and not the group as a whole. It was his responsibility to provide the musicians to form the group. Mike Hugg (born on 11 August 1942, in Andover, Hampshire) met Manfred who adopted the stage name of Mann after arriving in Britain in 1962, at a Butlin's holiday camp, and they teamed up as the Mann-Hugg Blues Brothers, progressing from jazz to R&B. Mike, then a trainee jeweller, played drums, vibes and piano. They were joined by bass player Dave Richmond, who was later replaced by Tom McGuinness, an insurance clerk born on 2 December 1941 in Wimbledon. Mike Vickers, a civil servant born on 18 April 1941, in Southampton, Hampshire, played guitar, alto saxophone, flute, clarinet and piano. Last to join the group was Oxford student Paul Jones, born Paul Pond in Portsmouth on 24 February 1942. He played the harmonica and provided the vocals.

The group had a regular spot at the Oxford Street club the Marquee, which had been the stamping ground of such R&B orientated groups as the Rolling Stones. A recording contract with the HMV division of EMI followed. Their first record was an instrumental **Why Should We Not?** which, like their second release, failed to make the charts. They made their TV debut on the ITV programme 'Ready, Steady, Go!' The programme-makers were so impressed that they asked the Manfreds to write a new theme song for the show. The result was **5-4-3-2-1**, which became their first hit in January 1964, reaching No 5. The follow-up, **Hubble Bubble Toil and Trouble**, was also used as a 'Ready, Steady, Go!' theme, and went to No 11.

Their third hit gave them their first No 1 and first million seller. **Do Wah Diddy Diddy** was written by American husband-and-wife songwriting team Jeff Barry and Ellie Greenwich, who had worked with Phil Spector on records by the Crystals and the Ronettes. It was No 1 for two weeks, with 14 weeks in the charts and a Silver Disc award. It sold 650,000 copies in Britain, three quarters of a million in America and a million in Europe, mainly in Germany when it was released there by EMI's Electrola. The record was produced by John Burgess at EMI's Abbey Road studios in London.

The group enjoyed two more British No 1s, **Pretty Flamingo** in 1966 and **Mighty Quinn**, after a label change to Fontana, in 1968. In America **Do Wah Diddy Diddy** was their first hit and went to No 1 for two weeks, with 13 weeks on the charts. They had five other American hits, only one of which made the Top 10. None of these were on EMI's US label Capitol, as Manfred Mann were another of the many successful British EMI acts that Capitol turned down.

As well as their highly successful singles, the Manfreds also released some acclaimed EPs and some promising albums. They had three No 1 EPs in a row. The first, **The One in the Middle**, stayed in the EP charts for 38 weeks, and had the extremely rare distinction of making the singles charts. It entered the *New Musical Express* Top 30 at No 18 the same week the Rolling Stones' **Got Live If You Want It** EP entered at No 13. The Manfreds overtook the Stones a couple of weeks later, peaking at No 6, a remarkable feat for an EP in the singles chart. As well as their regular albums, the group also recorded the soundtrack to the 1968 film *Up The Junction*. All the music was composed by Mike Hugg and Manfred Mann.

In 1965 Mike Vickers left to concentrate on solo work, and was replaced by Jack Bruce. This had little effect on the group, but they were more badly hit when Paul Jones left to go solo in 1966. He had two hits and then disappeared. He was replaced by Mike d'Abo. Jack Bruce stayed only a few months before joining Cream, leaving the Manfreds just after Paul Jones. His replacement was the Beatles' friend Klaus Voormann. In June 1969 the group split up. Tom McGuinness teamed up with drummer Hughie Flint to form McGuinness Flint, had the distinction of being the first act to be signed by the new British office of Capitol Records, EMI's US company. Manfred Mann went on to form Manfred Mann's Earth Band, which had a few hits in the 1970s.

SHA LA LA *HMV POP 1346* [UK] *Ascot 2165* [USA]. **Sha La La** was the follow-up to **Do Wah Diddy Diddy**, and gave the group their second million seller based on global sales. The song was written by Robert Mosley and Robert Taylor, and had been a hit for the Shirelles. It made No 3 in Britain, with 12 weeks in the Top 50. In America it made No 12 with 12 weeks in the Top 100. The record was produced by John Burgess at EMI's Abbey Road studios.

MARTHA AND THE VANDELLAS *American*

DANCING IN THE STREET *Gordy 7033* [USA] *Stateside SS 345* [UK]. The second estimated million seller for this trio, the song was written by disc artist Marvin Gaye and William Stevenson. It achieved the No 2 position in the US charts for two weeks and 14 weeks in the bestsellers.

Betty Kelly, born on 16 September 1944, replaced Annette Beard on this disc. It was released on 22 August 1964.

DEAN MARTIN *American*

EVERYBODY LOVES SOMEBODY *Reprise 281* [USA] *Reprise R 20281* [UK]. This song was written in 1948 by Irving Taylor (words) and Ken Lane (music), and first recorded by Frank Sinatra. This version sold a million in the USA and was No 1 for one week and 15 weeks in the bestsellers. It was Dean's fifth million seller, and constituted a major come-back for him. It was No 11 for two weeks in Britain and 13 weeks in the bestsellers. Gold Disc award RIAA 1964.

Subsequent research revealed the music was actually written by Sam Coslow, though attributed to Ken Lane.

ROGER MILLER *American*

DANG ME *Bang 1881* [USA]. The first million seller for C&W singer Roger Miller was his own composition and his first recording for the Smash label.

Roger Dean Miller was born on 2 January 1936 in Fort Worth, Texas, the son of poor parents. After his father died, he was raised in Erick, Oklahoma, by an uncle on a farm. At school, he was influenced by Hank Williams' singing and determined to go into show business. He saved to buy a guitar, started writing songs and earned prize money to get a violin. He spent three years in the US Army in Korea as a driver, then on discharge was a page-boy at the Andrew Jackson Hotel in Nashville. One night a disc executive heard him singing one of his own compositions and Roger got a contract, although his first three records didn't sell.

Ray Price wanted a comedian-singer for his travelling show and hired Roger, recording his

song **Invitation to the Blues** which was quite a big hit. He then joined C&W star Faron Young as a drummer in 1962 and started singing again.

Dang Me won three Grammy Awards for the best country-and-western performance, single disc and song of 1964 in the USA. It got to No 7 in the US charts with 11 weeks in the bestsellers, and was No 1 in the country charts for six weeks with a 25-week chart run.

CHUG-A-LUG *Smash 1926* [USA]. The second million seller for Roger Miller was also his own composition, reaching No 6 in the US charts and 13 weeks in the bestsellers. It made No 3 in the C&W charts with a chart life of 13 weeks.

MILLIE *Jamaican*

MY BOY LOLLIPOP *Fontana TF 449* [UK] *Smash 1893* [USA]. This song was written in 1965 by Robert Spencer and Johnny Roberts. It sold over 600,000 in Britain, where it reached No 2 with 18 weeks in the bestsellers, and nearly a million on the Smash label in the USA, where it reached No 2 with 12 weeks in the bestsellers. Millicent 'Dolly May' Small was born on 6 October 1948 in the parish of Clarendon, Jamaica. She started to take an interest in music at nine, and at 12 won a talent contest in Kingston, with a recording test as a prize. Her first disc **We'll Meet** (Island label) was No 1 there in six weeks and she became a big attraction in Jamaica. Further discs followed, with stage producers and carbaret managers competing for her.

Chris Blackwell ran the disc firm which released West Indian music on Island discs in England, and he went to Jamaica, signed her up, brought her back and introduced her work to artists' and repertoire manager Jack Baverstock of Fontana Records. This completely changed little Millie's life. She made her first disc **Don't You Know** (1963), then came **My Boy Lollipop** which Millie gave out with her native 'Ska' style, or 'Bluebeat' as it became known. (She was called 'Queen of the Bluebeat'.) Millie was enrolled at the Italia Conti Stage School to study dancing and diction soon after her arrival in Britain. In 1964 she became a great favourite with her bubbling explosive personality and powerful voice, appearing on radio, TV and at concerts around Britain.

The global sale of the disc was three and three-quarter million by 1969.

HARUO MINAMI *Japanese*

TOKYO GORIN ONDO (Tokyo Olympic Song) *Teichiku* [Japan]. This was written for the Olympic Games in Tokyo, 1964, by Takashi Miyata (words) and Masao Koga (music). The disc sold over 1,300,000, and was No 1 in Japan for 16 weeks.

THE MOODY BLUES *British*

GO NOW *Decca F 12022* [UK] *London 9726* [USA]. The Moody Blues started as a

America from the sixties to the present. Most of these are on their own Threshold label, which they started in 1970.

GIANNI MORANDI   *Italian*

IN GINOCCHIO DA TE (On My Knees to You) *RCA PM 45 3263* [*Italy*]. Gianni Morandi, a singer of extraordinary talent, was one of the top artists of 1964. This song won the Cantagiro Summer Song Contest, and topped the Italian charts for 14 weeks, the longest stay at No 1. By March 1966 the disc had sold almost 750,000 and the million was reported in 1968. The song was written by Franco Migliacci and Bruno Zambrini.

NON SON DEGNA DI TE (Not Good Enough for You) *RCA PM 3290* [*Italy*]. Gianni Morandi's follow-up song was as big a success as his former hit. It won the Festival Delle Rose, a televised show in Rome, in October 1964. It was a chart topper for many weeks, selling over 825,000 by March 1966, with the million reported by 1968. The song was written by Franco Migliacci and Bruno Zambrini.

THE NEWBEATS   *American*

BREAD AND BUTTER *Hickory 1269* [*USA*] *Hickory 1269* [*UK*]. This trio consists of Dean (Louis Al) Mathis, born on 17 March 1939, his brother Mark (Marcus F.) Mathis, born on 9 February 1942, both in Hahira, Georgia, and Larry Henley, born on 30 June 1941 in Arp, Texas. Their mother taught Dean and Mark the guitar as children, but they soon mastered the piano, bass and drums. They both played in the band at Bremen High School, Georgia, and decided on a show business career on leaving school. Dean joined Paul Howard's Western Swing Band in 1956 as pianist, then moved to Dale Hopkins' band where his brother Mark joined him on bass. They stayed with this band for two years and then recorded **Tell Him No** as a duo for the Chess label. They then started their own eight-piece band and played in their home town of Shreveport. Louisiana. Larry came up from the audience and asked to sing with the band, his first public appearance. After a time they went separate ways, Larry as solo artist, Mark and David as a duo, all recording independently for Wesley Rose.

After about 18 months, they met again, made a demonstration disc of **Bread and Butter** together and sent it to Wesley Rose (Hickory Records) who asked them to record it for the label. The trio did so under the name of the Newbeats. It soon shot up the US charts, reaching No 2 for two weeks and 12 weeks in the bestsellers, and was also a hit later in Britain where they appeared in 1964, reaching No 15. The song was written by Larry Parks and Jay Turnbow.

ROY ORBISON   *American*

IT'S OVER *Monument 837* [*USA*] *London HLU 9882* [*UK*]. Another global estimated million seller (Roy's 11th) was written again by him

Birmingham R&B group, had a No 1 single with their first hit, and ended up with a different line-up selling huge quantities of orchestra rock albums mainly in America.

The group was formed in 1964 by members of a number of different Birmingham groups coming together. Denny Laine (born Brian Hines in a boat off the coast of Jersey on 29 October 1944) was lead singer, played lead guitar and had fronted leading Birmingham group the Diplomats. He also played the ukulele, piano, organ and bass, and had played with the Crew Cats in Hamburg and Hanover. Graham Edge (born in Rochester, Staffordshire, on 30 March 1942) had played drums in three Birmingham groups. Ray Thomas (born in Stourport on 29 December 1942) played harmonica, had been a member of El Riot and the Rebels, and had worked with the Beatles on TV. Clint Warwick (born Clinton Eccles in Birmingham on 25 June 1949) was bass guitarist, and had played with the Rainbows at Ayr. Mike Pinder (born in Birmingham on 27 December 1942) was on keyboards, and shared vocals with the rest of the group. Soon after their formation, the Moody Blues landed a recording contract with British Decca. Their debut release, written by Denny Laine and Mike Pinder, was the aptly named **Lose Your Money**, and Decca did — the record was a flop. Sessions at the Marquee in London and TV and radio exposure helped to build them a following, and their second record went all the way to No 1.

Go Now was written by Larry Banks and Milton Bennett, and had been recorded by American blues singer Bessie Banks. The Moody Blues version was produced by Denny Cordell, and sold a million copies globally. It was No 1 for one week in Britain, where it spent 14 weeks in the Top 50. Decca's American subsidiary London also made a hit of it in America, where it reached No 14 with 14 weeks on the charts.

The huge success of **Go Now**, which won a British Silver Disc, was not repeated by the records that followed it. Though the Moody Blues did have a few minor hits, the early commercial promise soon faded. Clint Warwick and Denny Laine left in 1966, Laine later joining Paul McCartney's Wings. The group went through management changes, including a spell with the Beatles' manager Brian Epstein, tragically cut short by his suicide. Clint Warwick was replaced by John Lodge, who had played briefly with the group right at the beginning, but had left to complete his exams. Laine was replaced by Swindon guitarist Justin Hayward, who was also a gifted composer. These personnel changes resulted in a marked change of style and direction. With **Days of Future Passed**, the Moody Blues moved from R&B to classical-rock. They were lucky with their timing in making this change; their old record company Decca was launching a new progressive label, Deram, which was looking for something different. While Deram were keen to sign the group, their Decca bosses were not. The balance was tipped in their favour by the support of Decca's London Records people who thought the new Moody Blues would sell well in America. They were right.

Their first new concept album, **Days of Future Past**, was recorded with the London Festival Orchestra. It was a minor hit in Britain but went to No 3 in America, where it won a Gold Disc for million dollar sales. The 1968 hit single **Nights in White Satin** came from the album, and also did better in America than in Britain, though not until its re-release in 1972, when it went to No 1 for a week. In 1968 it reached No 19 in Britain, went to No 9 in 1972, and charted for a third time in 1979 when it reached No 14. This new direction proved much more successful, and the group have issued a long line of successful albums with a string of Gold and Platinum awards from and Bill Dees. The disc got to No 9 in the US charts with 11 weeks in the bestsellers and was No 1 in Britain for two weeks (and 18 weeks in the bestsellers) where it sold well over quarter of a million.

OH PRETTY WOMAN *Monument 851* [*USA*] *London HLU 9919* [*UK*]. Roy's 12th million seller was written by him with the help of Bill Dees. It sold a million by October in the USA and 680,000 in Britain, 350,000 in Germany and 180,000 in Canada. This disc was the first for many months to gain No 1 chart position for three weeks simultaneously in Britain (where it was 18 weeks in the bestsellers) and America, where it was 15 weeks in the bestsellers. The sale is estimated at four million. Gold Disc award RIAA 1964.

PETER AND GORDON   *British*

A WORLD WITHOUT LOVE *Columbia (EMI) DB 7225* [*UK*] *Capitol 5175* [*USA*]. The first million seller for this duo sold 550,000 in Britain and over 400,000 in the USA, as well as sales from other countries. The disc was No 1 in Britain for two weeks (with 14 weeks in the bestsellers) and for one week in the USA with 12 weeks in the bestsellers.

Peter Asher (born on 22 June 1944, in London) and Gordon Trueman Riviere Waller (born on 4 June 1945, in Braemar, Scotland) first met at boarding school in 1959. They both had piano tuition, and Peter also played the guitar and double bass, and Gordon the guitar. They began playing the guitar and singing together, performing at school concerts and in local coffee bars.

During a two-month booking at London's Pickwick Club, they were brought to the attention of EMI Records who sent an artists' and repertoire man to hear them. Next day they were summoned to EMI to record one of their own songs **If I Were You**. But a strong number was needed for the reverse side of the disc. Beatles John Lennon and Paul McCartney had written a song for them which was not complete, **World Without Love**. When finished it turned out to be a big hit. The duo then did radio, TV and personal appearances in Britain, Peter also appearing in such TV productions as

'Robin Hood' and 'Sword of Freedom'. They went to the USA in 1964 and did a long tour, becoming extremely popular there. Asher later became a prominent producer in the USA.

NOBODY I KNOW *Columbia (EMI) DB 7292* [*UK*] *Capitol 5211* [*USA*]. The second million seller for Peter and Gordon was also written by Beatles John Lennon and Paul McCartney. It was No 12 and nine weeks in the US bestsellers, and No 10 and 11 weeks in Britain's bestsellers.

PETER, PAUL AND MARY   *American*

PETER, PAUL AND MARY IN CONCERT (double album) *Warner Brothers 1555* [*USA*] *Warner Brothers WM 8142 (volume one only)* [*UK*]. This was another big success for the famous folk trio, with a Gold Disc award from RIAA on 21 January 1965. A million unit sale gave them a Platinum Disc award in December 1973, making this their fourth million seller album. The contents of the album are: **The Times They Are A-Changin'**, by Bob Dylan (1963); **A-soulin'**, by Paul Stookey; **500 Miles**, by Hedy West, Bobby Bare and Charlie Williams (1962); **Blue**, by Peter Yarrow, Paul Stookey and Mary Travers; **Three Ravens**, by Yarrow, Stookey, Travers and Okun; **One Kind Favor**, by Yarrow, Stookey and Travers; **Blowing in the Wind**, by Bob Dylan (1962); **Car, Car**, by Woody Guthrie; **Puff, the Magic Dragon**, by Leonard Lipton and Peter Yarrow (1963); **Jesus Met the Woman**, a traditional song arranged by Yarrow, Travers and Okun.

ELVIS PRESLEY   *American*

KISSIN' COUSINS/IT HURTS ME *RCA Victor 47-8307* [*USA*] *RCA Victor 1404* [*UK*]. Elvis Presley's 36th million seller was for global sales of another film song. **Kissin' Cousins**, from the Elvis film of the same name, was written by Fred Wise and Randy Starr. In Britain it was his biggest and only Top 10 hit of the year, reaching No 10 with 11 weeks in the charts. In America it reached No 12 with nine weeks on the charts. The flip side **It Hurts Me** also charted independently in America, reaching No 29 with a seven-week chart run of its own. The soundtrack album made No 6 in the American album charts and No 5 in Britain.

VIVA LAS VEGAS/WHAT'D I SAY? *RCA Victor 47-8360* [*USA*] *RCA Victor 1390* [*UK*]. Million seller No 37 came from yet another Elvis film. **Viva Las Vegas** was written by Doc Pomus and Mort Shuman, and reached No 29 in America with seven weeks on the charts, and No 17 in Britain with a 12-week chart run. All of Presley's 1964 million sellers were double A sides in America, and **What'd I Say** out-performed the main A side, reaching No 21 with six weeks on the chart. It was written by Ray Charles, who had a million-selling hit with the original version in 1959.

By 1964 Elvis had been overtaken by the Beatles and many other British groups, but he

still remained very popular. His **Viva Las Vegas** film soundtrack resulted in an EP from the film making the Hot 100, and for an EP to make the singles chart in America was an even rarer feat than in Britain. 1964 saw Elvis back at No 1 in the American album charts, where the soundtrack **Roustabout** went to the top for one week. It reached No 12 in Britain where it was released in 1965. It won an RIAA Gold Disc for million dollar sales on 20 May 1988.

AIN'T THAT LOVIN' YOU BABY?/ASK ME *RCA Victor 47-8440* [*USA*] *RCA Victor 1422* [*UK*]. Another American double A side for Elvis Presley, in Britain **Ain't That Loving You Baby?** went to No 15 with eight weeks in the charts. The song had been written by Clyde Otis and Ivory Joe Hunter in 1958, and was recorded by Elvis that year in Nashville, Tennessee. The fact that RCA had to dig into the vaults for Presley material at this time reflects the difficulty they had in getting the singer to record new material, partly due to his heavy filming schedule and a certain disenchantment with record-making after so many years of success. In America, **Ask Me** was the bigger side, reaching No 12 with 12 weeks on the charts. At the same time, **Ain't That Lovin' You Baby?** reached No 16 with 10 weeks of chart action. The record was a global million seller.

CLIFF RICHARD/SHADOWS   *British*

I COULD EASILY FALL (IN LOVE WITH YOU) *Columbia (EMI) DB 7420* [*UK*]. All Cliff Richard's 1964 hits sold well, with **I'm The Lonely One**, **Constantly** and **On The Beach** all close to the million sales. The only one of his hits that did pass the seven-figure mark was this, from the Cliff Richard and the Shadows London Palladium pantomime 'Aladdin'. The song was written by the four Shadows — Hank Marvin, Bruce Welsh, Brian Bennett and John Rostill — who wrote all the music for the show. The record was produced by Norrie Paramor at the Abbey Road studios of EMI. It went to No 6 in Britain, with 11 weeks in the Top 50. It won Cliff his 18th Silver Disc on 9 January 1965, giving him more of these awards than any other artist at that time. The record was a major hit in Europe and the Far East. Cliff was particularly popular in the major Japanese market. **On The Beach** had been a Japanese No 1, this record went to No 2, **Constantly** went to No 3 and **I'm The Lonely One** went to No 4. **I Could Easily Fall** went to No 1 in South Africa, India, Malaysia and Singapore, and was a Top 10 hit in Australia, Ireland, Finland, Sweden, Norway, Denmark, Germany, Austria, Switzerland, The Netherlands, Israel, Lebanon, Hong Kong and Japan, and in the Philippines the flip side **I'm In Love With You** was also a hit. Total global sales were over one and a half million.

THE ROLLING STONES   *British*

IT'S ALL OVER NOW *Decca F 11934* [*UK*] *London 9687* [*USA*]. Though 'the greatest rock and roll band in the world' are now very much part of the rock establishment, they started out as an R&B group, disdainful of rock, and with a carefully nurtured anti-establishment image which they have alway retained. In the sixties they were second only to the Beatles, though they have long since outlasted them — and every other British group except the Shadows. Uniquely, they have managed to last a quarter of a century and yet remain contemporary. Like Levi 501s, they will never be out of fashion.

The group came together in 1962, playing at various blues venues in and around London. The original line-up consisted of Brian Jones (born 28 February 1944, in Cheltenham) who played guitar, harmonica, and a variety of other instruments; Keith Richards (born 18 December 1943, in Dartford, Kent) who played guitar and who at first dropped the 's' from the end of his name in imitation of Cliff Richard; Charles Robert Watts (born 2 June 1941, in London) who played drums; and pianist Ian Stewart. Stewart soon left, to be replaced by Bill Wyman (born William Perks on 24 October 1936, in Penge, London) on bass guitar, and Michael Phillip Jagger (born 26 July 1943, in Dartford, Kent) as vocalist. Jagger and Richards had been at primary school together.

After a session at the Marquee Club in London, the Rolling Stones (the name is taken from a Muddy Waters song) moved to a residency at the Crawdaddy Club in Richmond, Surrey. It was here that the 19-year-old Andrew Loog Oldham and his partner Eric Easton saw them and signed them to a management contract. Oldham produced their early recordings and secured a contract with Decca, then the second largest record company in Britain. Decca had suffered the humiliation of turning down the Beatles, and correctly guessed that the Stones would be the next biggest thing.

Their first single, **Come On**, made the charts on 25 July 1963. It was a modest hit, reaching No 21. The follow-up, the Lennon-McCartney-written **I Wanna Be Your Man**, did better and peaked at No 12. The group went on their first national British tour in September 1963, and headlined another tour in January 1964, supported by the Ronettes.

In 1964 the Stones really broke through. Their first release of the year, **Not Fade Away**, was their first Top 10 hit and Silver Disc. It reached No 3 in Britain, and was their first American hit (reaching No 48) when released by Decca's US subsidiary London.

The Beatles had had great difficulty getting their early records released in America, as EMI's US subsidiary Capitol kept turning them down. Decca's chairman Sir Edward Lewis would never have tolerated such action from his admittedly smaller American company, and the Stones were assured of American release from the start.

It's All Over Now was the Stones' fourth release, and netted them their first No 1 for one week, with 15 weeks in the charts. It was written by Bobby and Shirley Womack and was a cover of the original hit by the American group the Valentinos. It was their third American hit, reaching No 26 with 10 weeks on

the charts. Produced by Andrew Oldham, it was their first million-selling record as a result of global sales. It was also the first of five British No 1s in a row.

Their next release was **Little Red Rooster**, the only Rolling Stones record ever to enter the British charts at No 1 first week of release. Their first album **The Rolling Stones** was released in 1964, went to No 1 for 12 weeks and spent 51 weeks in the album charts. In America their debut album was called **England's Newest Hit Makers: The Rolling Stones** and had a somewhat different content than the British album. The group also had two No 1 EPs in 1964: **The Rolling Stones**, which spent exactly a year in the EP charts, and **Five by Five**.

At this time, the leadership of the group revolved around Brian Jones and Mick Jagger. In Britain Mick fronted the group, though Jones took the lead in business negotiations. In some other countries, like Germany, it was Brian Jones who was the front man. When Jagger and Richards started writing material for the group, Brian Jones found himself increasingly isolated. A victim of drug abuse, he left the group in June 1969 and a month later he was found dead in his swimming pool. He was replaced by Mick Taylor (born 17 January 1948, in Hertfordshire) who was himself replaced in 1974 by Faces' guitarist Ron Wood.

The Stones have always been surrounded by controversy. In 1965 American businessman Allen Klein joined Andrew Oldham as manager, replacing him in 1967. Klein parted company with the Stones in some disagreement in 1970. When the group decided to leave Decca, they delivered **Cocksucker Blues** to fulfil their contractual obligations. They later got into trouble with Atlantic/WEA over the **Starfucker** track on the **Goat's Head Soup** album in 1973. (They eventually agreed to change the title to **Star Star**, though the lyrics remained the same.)

The Stones had more drug busts than any other group in history and their sexual exploits constantly made headlines, from the various girlfriends and their babies from the sixties, through Jagger's marriage and later divorce from Bianca in the seventies to Bill Wyman's relationship with the then under-age Mandy Smith in the eighties.

TIME IS ON MY SIDE *London 9708* [*USA*]. While Decca issued the No 1 **Little Red Rooster** as the British follow-up to **It's All Over Now**, their American company London Records prefered to put out **Time is on My Side**. A strong blues number written by Norman Meade (pseudonym of Jerry Ragovoy) in 1963, it was originally a track on the Stones' second British album **Rolling Stones No 2**. It was their first US Top 10 hit, reaching No 6 in a 13-week chart run. The record was not released in Britain, though in 1982 a live version was released on the Stones' own label (RSR 111). Taken from the **Still Life** live album of their 1981 US concerts, it reached No 62 in two weeks on the charts. It was produced by Andrew Oldham. Global sales of the original **Time is on My Side** had passed the million mark by 1966.

RONNY AND THE DAYTONAS   *American*

G.T.O. *Mala 481* [*USA*]. In addition to the surfing craze in the USA, the younger generation had a craze for 'hot rods' or 'stock cars' with souped-up engines for racing. **G.T.O.** was the first big hit in hot-rod music, and it established this group's reputation.

Ronny Dayton, leader of the group, was born in Tulsa, Oklahoma, on 26 April 1946. The Daytonas consist of his close musical friends, Lynn Williams (drums), Johnny Johnson (guitar) and Van Evans (bass).

When Ronny was 11 and living in Nashville, he had already had three years' guitar tuition. In his early teens he entered local talent shows and decided to pursue a musical career. He formed his group, the Daytonas.

G.T.O. was composed by John Wilkin. The disc got to No 4 in the US charts with 13 weeks in the bestsellers, and is estimated to have sold an eventual million.

In 1978 a new version of the song entitled **Little GTO** surfaced in Britain. Though theoretically by the New York Blondes featuring Madame X, it was in fact an illicit take of Blondie's Debbie Harry, who had been helping out at a recording session with some friends. She took court action against London Records who had licensed the record from Bomp in America. The record was soon withdrawn.

THE SEARCHERS   *British*

NEEDLES AND PINS *Pye 7N 15594* [*UK*] *Kapp 577* [*USA*]. The Searchers' sound was among the most distinctive of the mid-sixties, and in many ways they were ahead of their time. Formed in Liverpool in 1961, they were one of the few major Liverpool acts that had nothing to do with Brian Epstein's NEMS management company. The Searchers were Chris Curtis (born Christopher Crummey on 16 August 1941, in Oldham, Lancashire) who played drums, piano and guitar; Mike Pender (born Michael Pendergast on 3 March 1942, in Liverpool) on guitar, also able to play violin, piano and drums; Tony Jackson (born on 16 July 1940, in Liverpool) on bass guitar; and John McNally (born on 30 August 1941, in Liverpool) on lead guitar and harmonica. All but the drummer contributed to the vocals, in a highly distinctive harmony style which, together with their twangy guitar sound, became their trade mark.

The Searchers took their name from a John Wayne film, and originally formed the backing group for Liverpool singer Johnny Sandon. They soon broke with Sandon, and did not replace him nor did one member emerge as obvious leader. Chris, Mike and John had been friends since school, so a more collective style of leadership developed. The Searchers started as an R&B group doing the rounds of Liverpool gigs, including the Cavern, and, like the

Beatles, they performed in Hamburg, at the Star Club. There they made some records which Philips later released in Britain.

In 1963 Tony Hatch saw the group perform in Liverpool and signed them to a recording deal with Pye Records, the smallest of the four major companies which then dominated the British record industry. Their first Pye release was **Sweets for My Sweet**, which went to No 1 for two weeks in August 1963. The follow-up was **Sugar and Spice**, which sounded as much like their first release as possible and reached No 2. Their third release was **Needles and Pins**, which returned them to No 1 for three weeks and spent 15 weeks in the charts. It was also their first American hit, peaking at No 13 with 10 weeks on the charts. Unlike the other three majors (EMI, Decca and Philips), Pye did not have an American subsidiary, so they licensed the Searchers to the Kapp division of American Decca, which became MCA. **Needles and Pins** was written by Sonny Bono, later of Sonny and Cher, and Jack Nitzsche, who had arranged some of Phil Spector's records. It had originally been a minor US hit for Jackie de Shannon in 1963. The record was produced by Tony Hatch, and won a Silver Disc for British sales of a quarter of a million. Global sales made it the Searchers' only million-selling record.

At this stage of 1964, the Searchers were the second most popular group in Britain, behind the Beatles. Their next release, **Don't Throw Your Love Away**, gave them their third

No 1, but it also marked the end of their most popular period. Tony Jackson left the group in August 1964, and was replaced by Frank Allen. In 1966 Chris Curtis left and was replaced by Johnny Blunt. He in turn left in 1969, with Billy Adamson taking over the drummer's seat.

The Searchers released a number of highly acclaimed EPs. Their first, **Ain't Gonna Kiss Ya** in 1963, topped the EP charts for four weeks. **Sweets for My Sweet**, **Hungry for Love** and **Searchers Play the System** all did well in 1964, and the 1965 EP **Bumble Bee** was their biggest hit in this format. It not only topped the EP charts for two weeks in the middle of the No 1 residence of the **Beatles For Sale** EP, it also made the singles chart. On the album front, their first LP **Meet The Searchers** reached No 2. It was kept off the top spot by the lock the Beatles had on it at that time, but remained in the album charts for 44 weeks. The follow-up was released only three months later. **Sugar and Spice** reached No 5. In America they had more limited album success, with their first LP **Meet The Searchers/Needles and Pins** giving them their highest chart placing at No 22.

The Searchers had a string of British singles hits which lasted to the end of 1966. Their 15 hits (one a minor chart entry of old material from Philips) included three No 1s, three more records that made the upper echelons of the Top 10, and one EP. Their last Top 10 single was **Goodbye My Love**, which reached No 4 in 1965. In America their 14 hits included some tracks not released as singles in Britain. Their only Top 10 hit was **Love Potion No 9**, released in 1964, which made No 3 in early 1965.

In 1966 Pye declined to renew the Searchers' contract. They made two attempts to re-establish themselves. They signed to RCA, and in 1971 had a very small hit in America with **Desdemona**. At the end of the decade, they signed with the American record company Sire. Two albums came from this deal, including the highly acclaimed **Searchers**, but neither was a hit. From the end of the sixties, the Searchers have been highly successful on the cabaret circuit, replaying their old hits of 1963 to 1966 with some of their new material thrown in.

The group had started out with tremendous success from its first hit. It showed enormous promise, with a highly distinctive style often ahead of its time. Yet as a chart act it faded very quickly, with the hits lasting just over three years. Apart from the changes in personnel, the group had two main problems. One was the lack of a good songwriting team within the group, though others had survived with the same disability. Their greater problem was their record company. Pye ruthlessly exploited them for the maximum short-term gain, giving little thought to their long-term development. Singles, and in particular albums, were churned out at breakneck speed and, despite the abilities of the group and their producer Tony Hatch, the quality suffered. But, in spite of their relatively short chart life, the Searchers have remained one of the best-remembered sixties beat groups in Britain. Castle Communications are still mining their old catalogue material with success, which shows that the group still has a substantial following over 20 years after their last British singles hit.

THE SHANGRI-LAS *American*

REMEMBER (WALKIN' IN THE SAND) *Red Bird 008 [USA] Red Bird RB 10008 [UK]*. The Shangri-Las — Mary Ann and Margie Ganser (twins) and Betty and Mary Weiss (sisters) — started singing together while at Andrew Jackson High School in Queens, New York, around the beginning of 1964. The idea (and the song for the disc) came from George (Shadow) Morton, who discovered the group. He got them to make a demonstration disc for presentation to Artie Ripp, of Kama Sutra Productions. Ripp played this to writers Jeff Barry and Ellie Greenwich, and the group decided to produce the final master. They took it to George Goldner, head of Red Bird Records, and the Shangri-Las were immediately signed to a long-term contract. George Morton, a producer for Red Bird, included the cries of seagulls on the disc to add atmosphere to the plaintive love song with an offbeat, rapidly changing, hard-shuffling measure. The disc was No 5 for five weeks in the USA and 11 weeks in the bestsellers, and also a hit in Britain where it reached No 14 with 13 weeks in the bestsellers when the group visited in early 1965 and also toured Europe. Their very first disc is estimated to have sold well over a global million. They were still attending school when the disc was made, and later appeared on many top TV shows.

LEADER OF THE PACK *Red Bird 014 [USA] Red Bird RB 10014 (re-issues on Kama Sutra 2013 024 (1972), Charly CS 1009 (1976) and at the same time as the Charly release Contempo CS 9032) [UK]*. The second global million seller for the Shangri-Las was also written by George (Shadow) Morton, Ellie Greenwich and Jeff Barry. The song is a heartbreaking number about a girl in love with the leader of a motorcycle gang, of her parents'

disapproval, and how he loses his life in a crash. Sounds of motorcycle engines and screaming tyres gave the disc an extremely realistic backing. The disc was No 1 in all the US charts for one week with 14 weeks in the bestsellers, and it was also a big seller in Britain where it got to No 11 for two weeks. It was re-issued in Britain in 1972 and reached No 3. Subsequent re-issues 1974 and 1976 gave it a total of 44 weeks in the British charts.

DEL SHANNON *American*

KEEP SEARCHIN' (We'll Follow the Sun) *Amy 915 [USA] Stateside SS 368 [UK]*. The third million seller, globally, for Del was his own composition. It was a hit in the USA (No 9 in the charts with 14 weeks in bestsellers) and in Britain (No 3 in the charts with 11 weeks in the bestsellers).

BOBBY SOLO *Italian*

UNA LACRIMA SUL VISO (A Tear on Your Face) *Ricordi SRL 10-338 [Italy]*. Bobby Solo's disc of this song, written by 'Mogol' (Giulio Rappetti) (words) and Lunero (music), was one of the first discs to sell one million in Italy. Within 10 days of its release it had sold 600,000, and the total sale was three million, the top sale in the history of the Italian record market for a single disc. Bobby was born in 1946. In June 1963, he entered the 'Ribalta per San Remo', a competition to find new talent, which he won, and was immediately signed to a recording contract to wax the contest song **Ora che sei gia una donna**, following up with **Blue e blue/Marrone**. As a winner of the talent competition he automatically qualified to appear at the San Remo Song Festival in February 1964, and it was there that he first sang **Una lacrima sul viso**. The song did not win the contest but can be considered the real winner in so far as overall popularity was concerned. After the

success of his disc, Bobby Solo made a film of the same title. The disc was No 1 in Italy for nine weeks.

SOUNDS ORCHESTRAL *British*

CAST YOUR FATE TO THE WIND *Piccadilly 7N 35206 [UK] Parkway 942 [USA]*. Written in 1960 and composed by Vince Guaraldi and Frank Werber (words), this tune was a big success in the USA for modern jazz pianist Guaraldi and his trio at that time. It was brought to the attention of Piccadilly, a Pye label, who had been looking for material to create something orchestral, but at the same time totally different from most orchestral pieces and still within commercial boundaries. The disc, a quiet off-beat arrangement, features the brilliant piano playing of Britain's Johnny Pearson and was produced and directed by John Schroeder. Sales started quietly at first but the disc eventually got to No 5 in Britain's charts in 1965 with 16 weeks in the bestsellers and sold well over 250,000. Issued on the Parkway label in the USA, it got to No 9 in their charts and sold a million globally.

Johnny Pearson was born on 18 June 1925 in Plaistow, London.

TERRY STAFFORD *American*

SUSPICION *Crusader 101 [USA] London HLU 9871 [UK]*. Terry Stafford was born and educated in Amarillo, Texas, and started singing the songs of his two idols, Elvis Presley and Buddy Holly, at school dances. With the help of his mother, he went to Hollywood and, after two years of playing nightclubs and record hops, was heard by John Fisher and Les Worden, executives of the newly formed Crusader Record Company.

Suspicion, a song previously recorded by Elvis Presley, reached No 3 for two weeks in the US charts, the runner-up position to the Beatles who were at Nos 1 and 2 at that time, and had nine weeks in the British bestsellers. Terry's disc stayed in the charts for 15 weeks and the million sale was reported in 1970. It was No 31 in Britain. The disc was released in February 1964 and the song was written by Doc Pomus and Mort Shuman in 1962. In 1970 he signed with MGM Records.

LUCILLE STARR *Canadian*

THE FRENCH SONG *Almo 204 [USA]*. Lucille Starr, otherwise known as Fern Regan, and her husband Rob Regan (Robert Frederickson) were called the 'Canadian Sweethearts'. The song was written by Lucille and she first recorded it for a small Canadian label, Rodeo Records. In 1964 she recorded it for Almo, a label of A&M Records, Hollywood, and owned by the famous bandleader Herb Alpert with partner Jerry Moss. It was released in Canada on the Barry label, a subsidiary of Quality Records. Lucille's disc, sung in both English and French, soon topped the Canadian charts, and together with the US sales sold a million. It made her the first Canadian artiste to do so.

In the USA it reached No 54 with eight weeks in the bestsellers. In 1965, the disc was also very popular in Europe.

Lucille was born and raised in St Boniface, Manitoba.

THE SUPREMES   *American*

WHERE DID OUR LOVE GO? *Motown 1060 [USA] Stateside SS 327 [UK]*. The Supremes came out of the black ghetto of Detroit and became the most successful American vocal group ever. From 1962 to 1976 they scored 45 US chart entries from 44 records. This included one double A side, two records with the Four Tops and three with the Temptations. They went to No 1 a staggering 12 times, plus once with the Temptations. Only Elvis Presley and the Beatles had more No 1s. On the album front, they racked up 34 entries on the Top 200 from 1964 to 1976, three of which went to No 1. The group also enjoyed phenomenal success around the world, a first for a black female group. In Britain they were Motown's most successful group, next only to Stevie Wonder. In the mid-sixties they came to epitomize the Motown sound and the Motown image.

Diana Ross was born Diane Ross in Detroit, on 26 March 1944. Florence Ballard was also born in Detroit, on 30 June 1943. She went to school with Mary Wilson, who was born on 6 March 1944. Mary moved to Detroit as a child. She and Florence formed a singing trio with Betty Travis, calling themselves the Primettes, and sang in partnership with a male vocal group the Primes, out of which came the Temptations. Diane Ross joined the Primettes soon after Betty Travis, who was later replaced by Barbara Martin. The girls were all still at high school at this stage, in 1959. They tried to get a recording contract from Berry Gordy's Motown Records, but he was not interested in such a young group. They recorded some tracks for a very small Detroit independent, LuPine Records, and their debut disc **Pretty Baby** sold a few copies locally. The Primettes sang backing vocals for other LuPine acts and, when that label folded, they hung around Motown and picked up similar work there. They got a second audition from Berry Gordy, and this time he signed them to his Tamla label. He insisted on a name change, so Florence Ballard picked the Supremes from a list of names she was given. Although neither she nor Motown knew it at the time, this was the original name of the male group the Romantics, who with their female lead singer Ruby had a No 1 hit in 1963 with **Our Day Will Come**.

In March 1961, with the Supremes still schoolgirls, their first Motown disc was released. **I Want a Guy** was not a hit, and neither was the follow-up. By this time Barbara Martin had left, and was not replaced. For their next record, Gordy transferred the group to the Motown label, and **Your Heart Belongs to Me** became their first hit, though it only made No 95 in *Billboard* and No 90 in *Cash Box*.

Their next three releases gave them two minor hits and a miss, then in 1963 they released **When the Lovelight Starts Shining Through his Eyes**, which finally gave them a Top 30 hit. The follow-up only just made the charts, but **Where Did Our Love Go?** gave them their first No 1, for two weeks, with 14 weeks on the Hot 100. The song was written by the Motown in-house songwriting team of brothers Brian and Eddie Holland and Lamont Dozier, who also produced the record. They had originally offered the song to the Marvelettes, who turned it down. The Supremes did not think much of it either, but with such limited success behind them they were in no position to argue. The song became the first of five consecutive No 1s for the group in America, and was their first hit in Britain, where it reached No 3, with 14 weeks in the charts. They rapidly became the most important act in the Motown empire, and Berry Gordy took an increasing interest in every facet of their career. He had more than a professional interest in Diana Ross, and at one time rumour had it that they would marry. This helped her emerge as the leading member of the Supremes. Though she was not the best of singers, she had more ruthless ambition than the other two. This caused stress within the group, especially with Florence Ballard. In 1967 Florence left, claiming that she had been forced out. She sued Motown, claiming that she had never been paid anything but a pittance. Though she lost the case, she never seemed to see much of the money that the Supremes' million-selling records had made. Her husband later abandoned her and their children, and she died in great poverty in 1976, aged only 32.

Ballard was replaced by Cindy Birdsong (born on 15 December 1939). At the same time the name of the group was changed to Diana Ross and the Supremes, Diana Ross taking one more step towards a solo career. She finally left the group in 1970, being replaced by Jean Terrell. Still the hits came, especially in Britain where, until Bananarama charted in 1988 with a remake of the Supremes' own 1971 hit **Nathan Jones**, they had more hits than any other female group ever. Further personnel changes followed, with original Supreme Mary Wilson involved to the very end, when the Supremes were disbanded in 1977.

Diana Ross succeeded in launching a brilliant solo career. She achieved six more US No 1s on Motown (including one duet with Lionel Richie). Her chart success in America faltered when she finally left Berry Gordy and Motown. She signed with RCA for America, and though some hits still came they were not as big as before. For the rest of the world she signed with Capitol, who had much more success in countries like Britain than RCA did in America. This deal was unusual as Capitol did not operate directly outside America, being part of EMI. In the late 1980s she switched to the EMI label.

BABY LOVE *Motown 1066 [USA] Stateside SS 350 [UK]*. Of all their many hits, **Baby Love** was the only one the Supremes took to No 1 on both sides of the Atlantic. It was their second No 1 in a row in America, where it topped the charts for four weeks, their longest stay at No 1. It was in the Hot 100 for exactly three months. In Britain, Motown had signed a licensing deal with EMI, who released their product on the Stateside label. **Baby Love** was the Supremes' second UK hit and only No 1. It was two weeks at No 1 and spent 15 weeks in the charts.

Baby Love was written by the Holland-Dozier-Holland team, who also produced it. Though it was the biggest hit of their career, the Supremes never received an RIAA Gold Disc to mark its million sales. For most of Motown's existence, Berry Gordy would not let the RIAA audit his company's million sellers, so no Gold Discs were awarded.

COME SEE ABOUT ME *Motown 1068 [USA] Stateside SS 376 [UK]*. The third million seller in a row for the Supremes was also their third US No 1 in a row. As usual, the record was written and produced by Brian and Eddie Holland and Lamont Dozier. It was No 1 for two weeks in America, where it stayed in the charts for 14 weeks. In Britain it was a disappointing performance for a follow-up to a No 1. It only reached No 27 in a short six-week chart run.

All three of the Supremes' 1964 No 1 million sellers appeared on their first LP. **Where Did Our Love Go?** spent 89 weeks in the album charts, peaking at No 2 for four weeks. While the girls maintained a consistently high standard with singles releases at this time, their album material was highly variable. Their second 1964 album was **A Bit of Liverpool**, with covers of songs made famous by English beat groups. It only made No 21, with 21 weeks in the album charts. They put out four albums in 1965, the first two achieving very limited success for a group consistently hitting No 1 on the singles charts. These were **The Supremes Sing Country, Western and Pop** and **We Remember Sam Cooke**. It was only the **More Hits** package that put them back in the Top 10.

JOE TEX   *American*

HOLD WHAT YOU'VE GOT *Dial 4001 [USA]*. Joe Tex (Joseph Arrington, Jr) was born on 8 August 1936 in Baytown, Texas, and received musical training throughout his high school days there. His first step toward fame came in 1954 when he won an amateur talent contest in Baytown, the prize being a two-week expenses-paid trip to New York. Here he entered an amateur show at the Apollo Theatre, and took another first prize, returning to perform in the theatre. His early church training is evident in his emotional 'soul' performances of a semi-'preaching' style. Apart from his vocal talents, Joe wrote several hundred songs, including **Hold What You've Got**. Many have been recorded by famous disc stars including James Brown, Ernie K-Doe and Jerry Butler.

This disc was a hit in early 1965, achieving the No 5 chart position in the USA with 11 weeks in the bestsellers, and sold the million by 1966.

Joe appeared on TV, radio and club dates in Britain in December 1965, after successful personal appearances in the USA.

THE VENTURES   *American*

WALK — DON'T RUN '64 *Dolton 96 [USA]*.

This updated version of the Ventures' 1960 hit **Walk — Don't Run**, written by John H. Smith, Jr, was performed with a far more subtle relaxed feeling. It reached No 8 for two weeks in the USA and earned the group and song a second Gold Disc for a million sale, bringing their total of million sellers to three. The disc was recorded in July 1964.

The Ventures sold 20 million records in the USA and a further 10 million in Japan where they became immensely popular. By 1970 they had made 38 albums, and Don Wilson and Bob Bogle were still with the group. The original drummer Howie Johnson retired from music after an auto accident, and was replaced by Mel Taylor from New York some time after this disc was made. Nokie Edwards, the original guitarist, left in 1967 and was replaced by Jerry McGee, a noted guitarist, and an organist, Johnny Durrill from Houston (formerly with The Five Americans), joined in 1967. The group travelled more than a million miles in successful tours of Australia, Hawaii, Mexico and the Far East.

DIONNE WARWICK   *American*

WALK ON BY *Scepter 1274 [USA] Pye International 7N 25241 [UK]*. This second million seller globally for Dionne was another big hit for songwriters Hal David (words) and Burt Bacharach (music). The disc, besides being high in the US charts, was also a great favourite in Britain and Europe. In the USA it was No 6 for two weeks with 13 weeks in the bestsellers. In Britain it was No 9 for two weeks and 14 weeks in the bestsellers. The song was written in 1963.

MARY WELLS   *American*

MY GUY *Motown 1056 [USA] Stateside SS 288 [UK] (re-issued on Tamla Motown TMG 820)*. Mary Wells was Motown's first successful solo artist, with a long string of hits in America. **My Guy** was her second million seller, and was written and produced by Motown vice-president William 'Smokey' Robinson. It was her only No 1, and the biggest hit of her career. It was at the top for two weeks, with 15 weeks on the charts. Surprisingly for such a big star in America, where she had 21 chart entries from 17 records, Mary Wells had only one hit in Britain. **My Guy** reached No 5 when first released on Stateside, with 14 weeks in the charts. In 1972 the record was re-issued on Tamla Motown, reaching No 14 with an extra 10 weeks in the charts.

My Guy was Mary's last Motown hit. She was one of the first Motown stars to leave, getting a better offer from 20th Century Fox than from Berry Gordy when her contract expired in 1964. She had a few hits for her new label, but without the support of the Motown team of in-house writers and producers to sustain her they were not as big as those of her Motown days. In 1966 she switched to Atco for a couple more small hits, and made her final appearance in the charts with **The Doctor** for Jubilee in 1968.

J. FRANK WILSON AND   *American*
THE CAVALIERS

LAST KISS *Josie 923 [USA]*. This song, written in 1961 by Wayne Cochran, describes a young man and his girlfriend who are involved in a road accident in which the girl is killed. It was somewhat prophetic for in October, when the disc was at its highest (No 2) in the US charts, the group's manager was killed in a road crash and members of the group were injured.

J. Frank Wilson was born in 1941 in Lufkin, Texas, a lumber town. After graduation from high school there he joined the US Air Force, and was stationed at San Angelo, Texas, where he became lead vocalist with the Cavaliers. On discharge from the Forces, he decided to stay in show business but had a tough time for 18 months. Then in the spring of 1964 the independent producer Sonley Rush recorded some tunes with them. Major Bill Smith, an associate of their manager, took J. Frank Wilson's demonstration disc of **Last Kiss** to Josie Records and it soon got into the charts. The disc was 15 weeks in the US bestsellers, and sold a million by early 1965. The Cavaliers are Phil Trunzo from Geneva, New York, Jerry Graham from Flint, Michigan, Bobby Woods from Memphis, and Gene Croyle from San Antonio.

THE ZOMBIES   *British*

SHE'S NOT THERE *Decca F 11940 [UK] Parrot 9695 [USA]*. The Zombies were Colin Blunstone (vocalist-guitarist) born on 24 June 1945, Hatfield, Hertfordshire; Paul Atkinson (lead guitarist) born on 19 March 1946, in Cuffley, Hertfordshire; Rodney Argent (piano,

organ, harmonica, clarinet and violin) born in St Albans, Hertfordshire, on 14 June 1945; Hugh Grundy (drums) born on 6 March 1945, in Winchester, Hampshire; and Chris Taylor White (bass, guitar and double bass) born in Barnet, Hertfordshire, on 7 March 1943.

The quintet were all classmates at St Alban's School, the group being founded by Rod, Hugh and Paul. They began by playing for local clubs and school dances, and were joined later by Chris and Colin. Rod and Paul were set for university, Chris for teacher-training college, Hugh worked in a bank and Colin as an insurance broker. The group was in danger of breaking up, but after winning the *Evening News* Hearts Beat Competition their fortunes changed. Rod Argent then wrote **She's Not There** and submitted a demonstration disc to Decca. On release it became a hit in Britain, reaching No 12 for two weeks, with 11 weeks in the bestsellers. When released on the Parrot label in the USA, it got to No 1 in their charts for one week with 15 weeks in the bestsellers. The disc was estimated to have sold a global million.

1 9 6 5

1965 was a year of consolidation in Britain. The Beatles and the Stones confirmed their supremacy in the charts, but the old order they had largely replaced made a determined counter-attack. Cliff Richard, Elvis Presley and the Everly Brothers all had No 1 singles. In America the British invasion continued apace, with Herman's Hermits and the Dave Clark Five joining the Beatles and the Stones at the top. On 23 April the three Manchester groups the Mindbenders, Herman's Hermits and Freddie and the Dreamers held down the US top three. The following week British acts held the top six, and eight of the top ten. By 8 May it was nine British records in the US top ten.

After the shock of the initial invasion, America began to fight back. The Beach Boys had broken through with their surf music in 1963, before the Beatles arrived. Motown had also been on the move, bringing a fresh new R&B sound to a wider white pop audience than most black acts had ever reached. Motown were so sensitive to the race issue that at first no pictures of its singers appeared on Motown album covers. There were to be no black faces to put off white record-buyers.

The Supremes first made the charts in 1962, though their early records were only minor hits. In 1964 **Run, Run, Run** peaked at No 93. Then came **Where Did Our Love Go**, and that made No 1. It was the first of five No 1s in a row, and twelve No 1s in total, more than any other American group before or since. Between 1964 and 1967 they scored ten No 1s out of 13 releases. Three of their four 1965 releases made the top in America. **Stop! In The Name Of Love**, which was their biggest British hit of the year, **Back In My Arms Again** and **I Hear A Symphony**. All three (and nearly all their big early hits) were written and produced by the Motown team of Holland-Dozier-Holland. As their success grew, so did Diana Ross's ambition and this caused friction with the other two, and with Florence Ballard in particular. In 1967 Ballard was replaced by Cindy Birdsong. Diana Ross eventually left the Supremes in 1969 for a solo career that stretched out successfully to the present. After she left the Supremes, the group continued to have hits for most of the seventies, though not as big as when Diana fronted them.

Motown took its package tour to England in April. Despite the growing interest in R&B in Britain, the tour was a financial failure. People simply did not go to see the Supremes and Martha and the Vandellas among others. The concert halls in London were packed, but in the provinces they were empty. While Motown did win a considerable following in Britain, its stars never achieved anything like the success that they did in America.

Motown was one of the great American success stories of the sixties. It became the biggest black-owned business in America (though in 1988 Berry Gordy sold it to MCA). It was not just another label, but a large family of creative people working together, with writers and producers as important a part of the process as the singers. Motown had a number of very successful artists, including the Temptations, the Four Tops, Stevie Wonder, Marvin Gaye and the Miracles, but the Supremes were the most successful of them all.

British Stars Banned

The Americans fought the British invasion on two fronts. Their artists made some excellent music, and this won them the success it deserved, and their government used work permits and visas to keep British artists out. On 1 January 1965 the US Department of Labor announced that it would not issue any more H1 visas to British artists. These were the visas necessary to go and tour in America. H2 visas were still available, but this meant applying for a visa for each show in each state or city which in reality was impractical. Later in the year even these visas were denied to artists like Sandie Shaw and Twinkle.

The Hollies, Wayne Fontana and the Mindbenders, Freddie and the Dreamers, the Zombies, the Nashville Teens and the Animals all had trouble with visas. The American Embassy in London said that visas were being refused as 'The artists are insufficiently well-known in America to warrant them working here.' They said this about Wayne Fontana, who was No 1 in both *Billboard* and *Cash Box* charts at the time! This action was deeply resented in Britain, and was seen as grossly unfair.

For years America had dominated the world of pop music and American performers, stars and unknowns, had been free to come and work in Britain. Some, like the Walker Brothers, came to Britain to launch their careers. For the first time ever, it was the other way round.

For once, British singers and groups were dominating the USA, and the British media attacked the action of the American government as sour grapes and protectionism.

The Beatles

The Beatles were not affected by the visa problem, for they could hardly be described as 'insufficiently well-known in America'. In April the *New Musical Express* reported that a £1 million tour of America had been agreed, which started on 15 August, at the Shea Stadium, New York. Over 56,000 people came to see and scream at the Beatles, which was the largest attendance at a rock concert up to that time. Their pre-tour press conference was described by *Variety* as: 'Midway between nightmare and art.' It was a 'happening', in other words it was badly organized, with everything played for laughs.

Later in the month the Beatles were the guests of Elvis Presley. During their four hours together, Elvis played some records that he and the Beatles played along to. As the *NME* reported, 'Elvis, John and George providing the costliest ever backing to a selection of British and American discs, including one by the Shadows.' By the end of the year the Beatles' world sales had passed 115 million, while Elvis' had reached 110 million.

In the Queen's Birthday Honours list in June, each of the Beatles was awarded the MBE. They were the first pop stars to be so honoured, a move that caused some former recipients of the MBE to return their medals to the Queen in protest. John Lennon would return his MBE in 1969 in protest at Premier Harold Wilson's support for American policy in Vietnam, and the poor sales of his then current single **Cold Turkey**. In January Brian Epstein told the *Melody Maker*, 'I give the Beatles two or three years more at the top, but then they will become really established as film stars.' They started filming what turned out to be their last feature film, *Help!*, the next month.

Everyone was trying to jump on the Beatles bandwagon. Brian Epstein and EMI had a full-time job trying to protect the group as best they could. In December John's father Freddie Lennon, who had deserted his family years before, made a record for Pye's Piccadilly label. In October former Beatles drummer Pete Best sued Ringo Starr for libel for remarks that he had made in a *Playboy* article, and Brian Epstein for breach of contract.

Rolling Stones

The Stones had another great year. They did a number of major American TV shows, and started their third North American tour in Canada in April. They recorded some of their greatest million sellers in America, at the Chess studios in Chicago and at the RCA studios in Los Angeles. *Newsweek* described them as 'leering and obscene'. Back in London, the Stones were fined £5 each for urinating against the wall of a petrol station.

The Stones recorded a considerable amount of live material. Some of it was released in Britain on the **Got Live If You Want It** EP, which made the singles Top Ten, while other tracks were used for the album of the same name released in America and Germany. The group landed their first American No 1 single with **Satisfaction**, and first No 1 album with **Out Of Our Heads**. All three of their British releases made No 1. Their **Rolling Stones No 2** album had an advance order of 210,000 copies, entered the *NME* LP charts at No 1 first week of release, and also made the *Disc* singles Top 20.

September saw changes in the Stones' management. Andrew Oldham remained their co-manager, but his partner Eric Easton was replaced by the controversial American businessman Allen Klein. In a comment that was truer than he realized Oldham told the *Melody Maker*, 'I manage the Stones, and Allen Klein manages the Stones and me.'

The Stones would come to regret appointing Klein, who they hardly knew and who they had first met only days before they made him their manager. The group's contract with Decca expired in 1965, and CBS made a serious and substantial bid for them. They re-signed with Decca for the world outside America. Klein handled the negotiations for America, and in a separate deal, Decca's US subsidiary, London, continued to release the band.

The Girls

Female singers made good in Britain. Sandie Shaw followed fellow Pye artist Jackie Trent to No 1. Dusty Springfield became the first British star to win the World Female Singer title in the *NME* poll, though she collapsed due to overwork during the year. Cilla Black made No 2 with her cover of **You've Lost That Loving Feeling**. The then 16-year-old Twinkle had her second and last hit with **Golden Lights** in February, though she continued to get coverage in the pop press, often about who she was dating, for the rest of the year. Marianne Faithfull had three Top 10 hits, married John Dunbar in late May and had a baby in November. Ringo Starr also got married, to Maureen Cox in February. They had a baby in September. In June, the *NME* predicted: 'Expect Paul McCartney to marry Jane Asher *very* soon.' It later reported the happy couple flying off for a holiday in Shadow Bruce Welsh's villa in Portugal. French rock stars Johnny Hallyday and Sylvie Vartan married in May. Their attempt to break into the British market failed.

The Byrds

The Byrds' electric folk-rock version of Dylan's **Mr Tambourine Man** went to No 1 on both sides of the Atlantic, helped by tours in Britain and America. The rise of this group had a considerable influence in America, not least of all on Bob Dylan himself. In July, one month after the Byrds had topped the US charts, Dylan chose the Newport Folk Festival to debut his new electric guitar style. The folk enthusiasts were horrified, and booed him off the stage. The rest of the world loved it. Dylan's British concert tour was a great success, and resulted in two of his albums topping the British LP charts, ending two years of Beatles/Stones monopoly. The Beatles had helped launch Dylan in Britain by frequently mentioning him in interviews, and publicly associating with him when he arrived. His first British single, **The Times They Are A Changin'**, was also the first hit single for CBS, which had just broken from Philips and established an independent operation in Britain. English folk singer Donovan, who the press described as a rival to Dylan, made the Top 10 with his first two hits. He also made the British singles charts with his anti-war EP **Universal Soldier**.

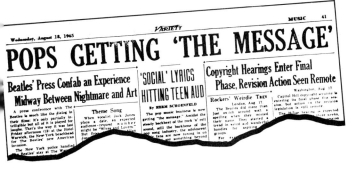

The Record Industry

In Britain record sales were down on 1964, which had been an exceptional year. EMI chairman Sir Joseph Lockwood, whose company's sales were down 40%, blamed the pirate radio stations, though Pye managing director Louis Benjamin claimed that his company had not experienced a drop in sales at all. EMI's Ron White said, 'I just do not know how to account for what is happening. It's the way the business goes.' Sir Joseph was bullish about the American market, where EMI had 20% to 25% of the singles and album charts. Just over half of this was via Capitol, but the rest came from records Capitol had turned down and EMI had then licensed to other companies. Capitol's consistent failure to recognize hit material from Britain was increasingly causing EMI concern.

EMI formed a new subsidiary in Mexico, and in October launched its budget rack label Music For Pleasure in Britain. With albums selling for 12/6 (62½p) it was a huge success. In August the company announced that it would expand its chain of HMV record shops.

Sir Edward Lewis, named by *Billboard* as Record Man Of The Year, again denied rumours that his Decca Record Company would be taken over by Philips. (They finally got Decca just after Sir Edward died in 1979.) As well as re-signing the Rolling Stones, Decca captured the Animals from EMI. They had fallen out with their recording manager Mickie Most, who had licensed their records to Columbia, so EMI were a casualty of the rift. Decca also signed Roy Orbison to a ten-year worldwide deal excluding America, where he signed with MGM. Orbison would continue to have his records released on the London label, which was also the British outlet for his old label Monument. The company also had another No 1 from Elvis Presley, as licensee for RCA. His **Crying In The Chapel**, recorded in 1960, was something of a surprise chart topper. In a *Melody Maker* article on the reaction of other pop stars, the Who's John Entwistle quipped, 'I didn't realise there were so many vicars in the country.'

For the second year running, more British records topped the American charts than US discs were No 1 in Britain. Seven British acts notched up 14 No 1s, compared to seven records by seven US artists that topped the British charts. (One of these, the Walker Brothers, were Americans living in Britain.)

In America, Cameo-Parkway Records was sold to Texan interests. It was eventually bought by Allen Klein, who changed its name to Abkco. The eight-track CARtridge, aimed at the in-car market, was launched by the Lear Jet Company. RCA were the first record company to endorse the new format, with 175 albums released on eight-track. CBS bought Fender Guitars in January.

In Britain the move towards independent production took a major step forward when four producers came together to form AIR — Associated Independent Recording. George Martin, John Burgess and Ron Richards of EMI and Peter Sulliven of Decca were the men involved. The EMI producers continued to work with their EMI artists, with EMI having first refusal of the new acts that AIR signed.

Rolling Stones manager Andrew Loog Oldham started the Immediate label with Tony Calder. He advertised it as Britain's first successful independent. In fact it wasn't the first, and in the end it wasn't successful. During its five-year life the company was mainly singles-orientated, with some classic sixties British pop from the Small Faces, Chris Farlowe, P.P. Arnold, the Nice and Amen Corner. Oldham and his label were very much part of Britain's swinging sixties scene, with its youth-orientated convergence of pop music, fashion and the media. The company went under in 1970, its catalogue bought by NEMS Records in 1975, and an anthology of the label licensed to Virgin and released in 1980.

The Media

Pop show TV ratings in Britain plummeted. ITV's 'Ready, Steady, Go!' changed to a live format in March, and it showed in more ways than intended. When Chris Farlowe appeared on 'Top Of The Pops' the following year, his **Out Of Time** was dedicated by the BBC show to the RSG dancers. Both the BBC and RSG banned the Shangri-Las' death disc **Leader Of The Pack**. For the same reason RSG banned Twinkle's **Terry**, though that did not stop it being a big hit. The BBC banned Barry McGuire's **Eve Of Destruction**, while the Corporation's 'Juke Box Jury' banned the Jonathan King-produced Hedgehoppers Anonymous disc **It's Good News Week** because it mentioned birth control. The practice of artists miming on TV shows was hotly debated, with the Musicians Union trying to get the practice banned.

In the USA TV programmes like 'The Ed Sullivan Show', 'Shindig', and NBC's new 'Hullabaloo' became a vital promotional route around the US Government's visa restrictions on British artists. The Rolling Stones, the Dave Clark Five, Dusty Springfield, Tom Jones and Kathy Kirby all appeared with Ed Sullivan. The first edition of 'Hullabaloo', broadcast on 12 January, included a segment from London featuring the Zombies and Gerry and the Pacemakers. Later in the month the rival ABC TV show 'Shindig!' also featured Gerry and the Pacemakers plus the Rolling Stones, the Dave Clark Five, Petula Clark and the Kinks.

Two great broadcasters died in 1965. In Britain the BBC's premier broadcaster Richard Dimbleby died in December. In America the veteran CBS reporter Ed Morrow passed away in April.

London-based American singer P.J. Proby received considerable press coverage when he split his trousers on stage in February. His act was described as obscene, and he was charged with lewd behaviour. Britain's two biggest theatre chains ABC and Rank banned him from their stages, and the BBC banned him from both their TV networks.

Dead and Buried

On 20 January Alan Freed died a poor and broken man in Palm Springs. He did more than any other DJ to bring R&B to white America, and was one of the biggest supporters of rock'n'roll. His career was broken by the payola scandals of 1959–60. On 15 February Nat King Cole died of cancer, at 45. From the 1940s he had been one of Capitol Records biggest stars. His daughter Natalie Cole recorded for Capitol from the mid-1970s. On 21 October Elvis Presley's old bass player Bill Black died of a brain tumour. He had a string of instrumental hits of his own, as leader of the Bill Black Combo. In March Buddy Holly's old group the Crickets disbanded. Jerry Allison kept the name, but signed a solo recording deal with Capitol.

Touring the World

As well as going to America, many British stars toured the rest of the world as well. The Who, whose seminal teen anthem **My Generation** reached No 2 during the year, toured Scandinavia. Cliff Richard and the Shadows became the first Western rock group to tour Poland, and Manfred Mann later toured behind the Iron Curtain as well. The Rolling Stones toured Ireland and were met by what they called a riot and what the Irish police called a normal crowd. The Beatles toured Europe.

World News

Britain's wartime Prime Minister Sir Winston Churchill died, aged 90, on 24 January. Sir Winston was the first commoner ever given a State funeral, and therefore the first whose funeral was attended by the reigning monarch.

Edward Heath became leader of the Conservative Party, replacing Sir Alec Douglas-Home, in the first leadership election in the party's near 300-year history. Previously leaders 'emerged' after soundings were taken within the party. Labour Prime Minister Harold Wilson faced the crisis of Rhodesia's Unilateral Declaration of Independence. In response to this illegal rebellion, Wilson imposed economic sanctions rather than using force. He claimed that they 'might well bring the rebellion to an end within a matter of weeks rather than months'. The rebellion lasted until 1979.

Cigarette advertising was banned from British television. BMC produced the one millionth Mini. In May the Queen welcomed President Kennedy's widow Jackie to Runnymede, where a monument to the late President had been erected close to where Magna Carta had been signed 750 years previously. Ian Brady and Myra Hindley were charged and later convicted of the Moors child murders.

America began the slide into active participation in the Vietnam war when President Johnson sent American combat troops into action against the Viet Cong for the first time in June. The President had earlier launched US bombing raids over North Vietnam. America also sent Marines into the Dominican Republic.

Racial tensions within the United States were still considerable. The worst race riots in half a century occurred in the Watts District of Los Angeles in an exceptionally hot August. Watts burned and snipers shot at the police and National Guard amid claims and counter claims of excessive police brutality and criminal elements as causes of the riots. The civil rights movement was growing in strength. It was supported by stars like Bob Dylan, and British groups like the Beatles and the Stones who refused to play before segregated audiences in the South. Dr Martin Luther King led another great civil rights march in Montgomery, Alabama, protected by troops.

India and Pakistan went to war over Kashmir, and India feared attack from China after troop movements near their border. De Gaulle

was re-elected President of France, but by a reduced majority. West Germany and Israel established diplomatic relations. Revolutionary Che Guevera left Cuba to foment Communist uprisings on the Latin American mainland.

Films

Sean Connery was the top box office draw in Britain and America, based on two James Bond films that were re-issued. *Dr No* and *From Russia With Love* were still very popular. For the first time in four years there was no new Cliff Richard film released, so in Britain Elvis Presley was the highest-placed pop star in films, coming in second to Connery. Presley's film career was one of commercial success and critical disaster. Julie Andrews came third, and her film musical *Mary Poppins* was the top money-making film in Britain. The Beatles were listed eighth in the *Motion Picture Herald*'s box office survey, though their film *Help!* was the second biggest money-maker, and the most profitable of the British-made films. Other major films included *Lawrence of Arabia*, the Frank Sinatra war film *Von Ryan's Express*, and Julie Christie playing the part of an amoral model in swinging London in *Darling*. One of the real-life characters of the swinging sixties, photographer David Bailey, married French model Catherine Deneuve in August. Mick Jagger was the best man.

Julie Christie won the Oscar for Best Actress for her part in *Darling*. She also won the British Variety Club award as Best Actress for the role. *The Sound of Music* won the Oscars for Best Film and Best Director (Robert Wise). Lee Marvin, whose **Wand'rin' Star** made No 1 in Britain in 1970, won the Oscar for Best Actor for his part in *Cat Ballou*.

Sport

Britain's greatest footballer Sir Stanley Matthews played his last match. Manchester United were champions of League Division One. Liverpool beat Leeds United for the FA Cup. Celtic won the Scottish FA Cup, Rangers won the Scottish League Cup, and Kilmarnock were top of Scottish League Division One. West Ham won the European Cup Winners Cup. Worcestershire again won the county cricket championship. In America, the Dodgers won the World Series. The Green Bay Packers won the NFL championship, while the Buffalo Bills easily won the AFL championship 23–0, their second win in a row.

At The End Of The Year

The British music press all ran popularity polls towards the end of the year. The Beatles were of course voted Top World Vocal Group, while the army of Elvis fans put their man on top as World Male Singer and Musical Personality. In the most important poll, run by the *NME*, Dusty Springfield was Top World Female Singer, the first British win in that section. Cliff Richard was Britain's Top Male Singer. In the *Melody Maker* poll, the top three in the British Group section were the Beatles, followed by the Rolling Stones and the Shadows. In *Disc*, Paul McCartney was voted the most popular Beatle.

That other survey of success, *Billboard*'s annual rating of international chart performance, showed British artists had increased their domination of the world's charts. The top three in the list of the 100 most successful artists in the world were all British. The Beatles were No 1, followed by the Rolling Stones and Cliff Richard. Six of the top ten were British, two American and two from Europe. In the 20 main markets that *Billboard* looked at in detail, British artists were No 1 in ten of them. The Beatles were the top act of the year in Australia, Hong Kong, Ireland, The Netherlands, Norway, Singapore and the UK. Herman's Hermits were No 1 in Canada and the USA and Cliff Richard was top in Malaysia. Against this American stars were top in two countries, and local artists in the other eight. The Ventures came out on top in the growing Japanese market, by 1965 the third biggest in the world after America and Britain, and Elvis Presley was top in the Philippines.

VARIOUS ARTISTS　　　　American

FAMOUS ORIGINAL HITS (Album) *Country Music Association* [USA]. This unique disc bears the distinction of being the first album to sell over a million through mail orders only without ever hitting the US charts. Advertising was restricted to mail order, radio and TV spots, amounting to one million from the time of release (27 September) for about a month, at a weekly rate of 7,000 on 300 TV and 35,000 on 500 radio stations, making it the largest radio-TV coverage ever known for a single record. Final sales of four million were anticipated in 18 months.

The disc features 25 of the top artists in country music. It was sponsored by Martin Gilbert, a local Hollywood disc executive, for the foundation of a museum in the country music centre of Nashville. With the help of CMA director Roy Horton, the co-operation of Capitol, Victor, Decca, Mercury, MGM, Hickory and Starday labels was solicited in borrowing material of their famous country artists — the labels, publishers and artists waiving their royalties to make the album possible. Martin Gilbert donated $25,000, and a guaranteed royalty of $85,000. In appreciation, CMA named a room in the museum after him. The building was officially opened on 31 March 1967.

The album contained the following: Roy Acuff, *Wabash Cannonball, trad. arr. A.P. Carter (1942); Bill Anderson, Still, by Bill Anderson (1963); Eddy Arnold, *Bouquet of Roses, by Steve Nelson and Bob Hilliard (1948); Bobby Bare, *Detroit City, by Danny Dill and Mel Tillis (1963); Johnny Bond, Cimarron (Roll On), by Johnny Bond (1942); Johnny Cash, *I Walk the Line, by Johnny Cash (1956); Patsy Cline, I Fall to Pieces, by Harlan Howard and Hank Cochran (1961); Dave Dudley, Six Days on the Road, by Earl Green and Carl Montgomery (1963); Red Foley, *Chattanooga Shoe Shine Boy, by Jack Stapp and Harry Stone (1950); Lefty Frizzell, If You've Got the Money, by Lefty Frizzell and Jim Beck (1950); Don Gibson, *I Can't Stop Loving You, by Don Gibson (1958); Pee Wee King, Tennessee Waltz, by Pee Wee King and Red Stewart (1947); Roger Miller, You Don't Want My Love, by Roger Miller (1964); George Morton, *Candy Kisses, by George Morgan (1948); Buck Owens, Act Naturally, by J. Russell and V. Morrison (1963); Ray Price, Heartaches by the Number, by Harlan Howard (1959); Jim Reeves, *He'll Have to Go, by J. and A. Allison (1959); Tex Ritter, Rye Whiskey, trad. arr. J. Bond; Marty Robbins, Singing the Blues, by Melvin Endsley (1954); Hank Snow, *I'm Movin' On, by Hank Snow (1950); Hank Thompson, *Humpty Dumpty Heart, by Hank Thompson (1948); Merle Travis, So Round, So Firm, So Fully Packed, by Merle Travis, Cliffie Stone and Eddie Kirk (1947); Ernest Tubb, *Walkin' the Floor Over You, by Ernest Tubb (1941); Kitty Wells, *It Wasn't God Who Made Honky Tonk Angels, by J.D. Miller (1952); Hank Williams, *Your Cheatin' Heart, by Hank Williams (1952). (Titles marked * were originally million seller discs for the artists concerned.)

A second album was released in 1966.

VARIOUS ARTISTS　　　　American

FILM SOUNDTRACK WITH JULIE ANDREWS, CHRISTOPHER PLUMMER, PEGGY WOOD, MARNI NIXON, DANIEL TRUHITTE AND THE SEVEN CHILDREN: CHARMIAN CARR, HEATHER MENZIES, NICHOLAS HAMMOND, DUANE CHASE, ANGELA CARTWRIGHT, DEBBIE TURNER, KYM KARATH; ORCHESTRA CONDUCTED BY IRWIN KOSTAL

THE SOUND OF MUSIC (Album) *RCA Victor 2005* [USA] *RCA Victor RB 6616* [UK]. This album, released in the USA on 2 March 1965, achieved Gold Disc status faster than any other soundtrack in record history, selling the half million in the first two weeks of release. According to *Time* magazine (23 December 1966) it had sold seven million, a sales record for all show or soundtrack albums, with sales continuing globally. Britain alone sold two million by October 1968, and there were big sales in Canada, Australia and Japan. It holds the record for the longest stay in Britain's charts at No 1 — 69 weeks. The album was No 1 in the USA for only two weeks in 1965 but stayed in the US charts for 233 weeks in all and in Britain for 381 weeks. Sales were reported at around 14 million globally. The film became one of the all-time money-makers in film history.

The film, a superb adaptation of the stage musical of 1959 by the late Oscar Hammerstein II and Richard Rodgers, starred Julie Andrews and Christopher Plummer in the famous story of the Von Trapp family singers. This was another tremendous triumph for Julie Andrews immediately following her *Mary Poppins* film. Marni Nixon, whose voice was used for Audrey Hepburn's in *My Fair Lady*, Natalie Wood's in *West Side Story* and Deborah Kerr's in *The King and I*, made her first film appearance. *The Sound of Music* received five Academy Awards (1965) for 'Best Picture', 'Best Director', 'Best Film Editing', 'Best Sound' and 'Best Scoring of Music'.

The Sound of Music was the first stereo eight-tape cartridge to become a million seller in the entire industry.

The contents of the disc are: Prelude (orchestra); Overture (orchestra); Morning Hymn and Alleluia (nuns' chorus); Maria (Marni Nixon, Peggy Wood and nuns' quartet); *I Have Confidence in Me (Julie Andrews); *Something Good (Julie Andrews and Christopher Plummer); Sixteen Going on Seventeen (Charmian Carr and Daniel Truhitte); My Favourite Things (Julie Andrews and children); Climb Every Mountain (Peggy Wood); Lonely Goatherd (Julie Andrews); The Sound of Muisc (Julie Andrews and Christopher Plummer); Do-Re-Mi (Julie Andrews and children); Processional (orchestra); Edelweiss (Christopher Plummer and Julie Andrews); So Long, Farewell (the children); Climb Every Mountain (the company).

Items marked * were specially written for the film version by Richard Rodgers, Hammerstein having died in 1960.)

Gold Disc award RIAA 1965.

JEWEL AKENS　　　　American

THE BIRDS AND THE BEES *Era 3141* [USA] *London HLN 9954* [UK]. Jewel Akens, born in Texas in 1940, had a million seller with this his first recording. The song was written by Herb Newman (of Era Records).

His unusual name came about because his mother wanted a daughter, and liked the name so much that she retained it even when she had a son. Jewel was one of 10 children. He began singing in church when he was only 11 years old.

The Birds and the Bees got to No 2 in the USA for two weeks with 14 weeks in the bestsellers, and was No 29 in Britain with eight weeks in the charts.

HERB ALPERT AND　　　American
THE TIJUANA BRASS

SOUTH OF THE BORDER (Album) *A&M 108* [UK]. Another big success for Alpert, this disc was issued in January 1965. It got to No 6 in the US charts in 1966 and was awarded a Gold Disc by RIAA, staying in the charts for 163 weeks. Sales by March 1966 were 770,000. It topped the million by the end of 1967.

The contents of the album are: **South of the Border**, by Jimmy Kennedy and Michael Carr (1939); **The Girl from Ipanema**, by Vincius de Moraes/Antonio Carlos Jobim (1963) (Eng. words by Norman Gimbel); **Hello Dolly** (from the stage musical), by Jerry Herman (1963); **I've Grown Accustomed to Her Face** (from *My Fair Lady*), by A.J. Lerner/Frederick Loewe (1956); **Up Cherry Street**, by Julius Wechter (1964); **Mexican Suffle**, by Sol Lake (1964); **El Presidente**, by Sol Lake (1964); **All My Loving**, by John Lennon and Paul McCartney (1963); **Angelito**, by Rene Herrera and Rene Ornellos

(1964); **Salud amor y dinero**, by Sol Lake (1964); **Numero cinco**, by Ervan Coleman (1964); **Adios, mi corazon**, by Sol Lake (1964).

WHIPPED CREAM AND OTHER DELIGHTS (Album) *A&M 110 [USA] Pye NPL 28058 [UK]*. Issued in the USA in April 1965, this album sold 1,100,000 by the end of the year. It was No 1 for eight weeks in the USA, with 2,283,000 sold by March 1966 and over 4,500,000 by the end of 1966. It remained in the US Top 200 for 185 weeks and in the British album charts for 42 weeks reaching No 2.

Herb Alpert's new 'Ameriarchi' sound made him world famous by the end of 1965. This album contained the following: **A Taste of Honey** (film title number), by Rick Marlow and Bobby Scott (1960); **Green Peppers**, by Sol Lake; **Tangerine**, by J. Mercer and V. Schertzinger (1942); **Bittersweet Samba**, by Sol Lake; **Lemon Tree**, by Will Holt (1960); **Whipped Cream**, by Naomi Neville (1964); **Love Potion No 9**, by Jerry Leiber and Mike Stoller (1959); **El Garbanzo**, by Sol Lake; **Ladyfingers**, by Toots Thielmans; **Butterballs**, by Mike Henderson; **Peanuts**, by Luis Guerrero (1965); **Lollipops and Roses**, by Tony Velona (1959).

GOING PLACES (Album) *A&M 112 [USA] Pye NPL 28065 [UK]*. This album sold 1,561,000 by 1 March 1966, just six months after release in the USA, where it also became No 1 for six weeks. It stayed in the charts for 164 weeks. It was in the British charts for 138 weeks reaching No 4.

It contained: **Tijuana Taxi**, by Ervan Coleman (1965); **I'm Getting Sentimental Over You**, by Ned Washington/George Bassman (1933); **More and More Amor**, by Sol Lake (1965); **Spanish Flea**, by Julius Wechter (1965); **Mae** (from the film *Yellow Rolls Royce*), by Riz Ortolani (1965); **Third Man** theme, by Anton Karas (1950); **Walk, don't Run**, by Johnny Smith (1960); **Felicia**, by John Pisano (1965); **And the Angels Sing**, by Johnny Mercer/Ziggie Elman (1939); **Cinco de mayo**, by Chris Montez (1965); **A Walk in the Black Forest**, by Horst Jankowski (1965); **Zorba the Greek** title number, by Mikis Theodorakis (1964). Gold Disc award RIAA December 1965.

SPANISH FLEA/WHAT NOW MY LOVE? *A&M 792 [USA] Pye International 7N 25335 [UK]*. Originally on Alpert's album **Going Places**, this novelty number was a big hit when issued as a singles disc, particularly in Britain where it sold over 250,000 and was No 3 for three weeks and 20 weeks in the bestsellers. Sales in Europe were also big.

In the USA **Spanish Flea** reached No 19 with seven weeks in the *Cash Box* Top 100. In *Billboard* the record was a double A side, with **Spanish Flea** (written by Julius Wechter) reaching No 27 with seven weeks on the Hot 100.

It was outperformed by the flip side, **What Now My Love?**, which at the same time made No 24 with eight weeks on the charts. This side, written by the Becaud/Sigman songwriting partnership, was a hit for Sonny and Cher in 1966. The record was a global million seller for Herb Alpert.

CHRIS ANDREWS   *British*

YESTERDAY MAN *Decca F 12236 [UK] Atco 6385 [USA]*. Christopher Frederick Andrews was born on 15 October 1942 in Romford, Essex, and started playing guitar and singing when he was 11. He made his TV debut on 'Oh Boy'. Chris formed his own group called Chris Ravell and the Ravers in late 1963, and started writing for the group rather than performing the current popular songs. After his return from Hamburg, Germany, he was introduced to Evelyn Taylor, manager for Britain's pop stars Adam Faith and Sandie Shaw. She asked to hear some of his songs. From then on his career as a professional songwriter started. Adam recorded his song **The First Time** and so one of the most successful composer/singer partnerships was formed. Chris then heard Sandie Shaw, who had been discovered by Adam, and was asked to write songs for her. He came up with **Long Live Love**, **Girl Don't Come** and **Message Understood**, all of which were big hits. He then recorded his song **Yesterday Man** himself, an immediate hit reaching a No 2 in the British charts for three weeks, 15 weeks in the bestsellers, and a Silver Disc. His disc was released in Germany on the Vogue label in 1966 and was No 1 for two weeks, No 1 in Austria and Switzerland, and No 94 in the USA. It sold half a million in Germany in two months and a million in four months, staying in their charts for 20 weeks. He received a Gold Disc award in May 1966.

Chris returned to Germany for a TV appearance in March 1966 and played Hamburg's famous Star Club. The tremedous success of **Yesterday Man** established him as one of the most in-demand stars in Germany, with his tours there becoming sell-outs.

LEN BARRY   *American*

1, 2, 3 *US Decca 31827 [USA] Brunswick 5942 [UK]*. Falling in love, Len Barry explains, is as

elementary as 1, 2, 3, or A-B-C. Len (real name Leonard Borisoff) wrote the song with John Madara and David White. The disc got to No 2 in the USA with 15 weeks in the bestsellers, and was No 1 for one week in Britain and 14 weeks in the charts. The record also made No 11 in the US R&B charts where it stayed for 14 weeks. The British sales were over 250,000 and the American sales 1,500,000.

Len was born in West Philadelphia on 6 December 1942. He studied at Temple University there and he and four friends formed a group, playing for over two years at local gatherings and school functions. Calling themselves the Dovells, they auditioned for Cameo-Parkway Records in 1961 and had a million seller hit with **Bristol Stomp** (see 1961). Later, Len left to become a solo artist. His first disc **Lip Sync** didn't become a hit but **1, 2, 3** did.

FONTELLA BASS   *American*

RESCUE ME *Checker 1120 [USA] Chess CRS 8023 [UK]*. Black singer Fontella Bass (born on 24 August 1942 in St Louis, Missouri) was educated at Golden High School, St Louis, and Lincoln University. Her mother sang with the

Clara Ward Singers and started coaching Fontella at the age of four. At five she was playing the piano and singing in a church choir in her native town. She eventually became the choir's director and an accomplished pianist and organist. Fontella made her first public appearance playing the piano and organ in the St Louis 'Gospel Blues Show'.

Chess Records' star Little Milton heard her singing in church in 1960 and was so impressed that he immediately engaged her to play the piano and sing in his band — a post she held for four years. In June 1964, Little Milton took her to Chess Records and introduced her to artists' and repertoire manager, Billy Davis, who in turn introduced her to a young singer Bobby McClure. Davis arranged for them to make their first disc together, **Don't Mess Up a Good Thing** which reached No 5 in the R&B charts and No 33 in the Hot 100. It was not, however, until August 1965 that she got her big chance for stardom. Sitting in the rehearsal studio with two of the Chess writers, Carl Smith and Raynard Miner, arranger Phil Wright called in. The outcome was the birth of **Rescue Me**, 'a sure-fire hit', said Marshall Chess. Fontella's rollicking rhythmic song about a love-sick girl begging her boyfriend for another chance got to No 4 in the US charts with 13 weeks in the bestsellers, and No 7 in Britain with 10 weeks in the bestsellers, selling a global million. It was 19 weeks in the US R&B charts, four weeks of which were spent at No 1.

Fontella visited Britain in December 1965 and again in January 1966.

THE BEACH BOYS   *American*

HELP ME, RHONDA *Capitol 5395* [*USA*] *Capitol CL 15392* [*UK*]. 1965 was another good year for the Beach Boys, who consolidated their position as the No 1 American beat group, indeed the only rock group standing up to the Beatles and the British invasion. The year started with the double A side **Do You Wanna Dance?/Please Let Me Wonder**. Though both sides charted, it was the old 1958 Bobby Freeman number **Dance** that was the bigger hit, just failing to make the Top 10. It stalled at No 12. (This record had been a million seller for Freeman, and again in 1962, as part of a double A side, for Cliff Richard.) In Britain **Do You Wanna Dance?** was the flip side of **All Summer Long**, released in March 1965, though neither side made it.

The Beach Boys followed this with their second American No 1, **Help Me, Rhonda**, written and produced by Brian Wilson. It spent two weeks at the top, and 14 weeks in the charts. In Britain the record was a minor hit. It only reached No 27, though it did last 10 weeks in the Top 50. It was their second British hit of the year, following the equally modest performance of **Dance, Dance, Dance**. The follow-up to **Help Me, Rhonda** on both sides of the Atlantic was **California Girls**. Though another minor hit in Britain, it reached No 3 in America.

On the album front, the Beach Boys put three more LPs into the charts, two of which went Gold (i.e. million-dollar sales status.) **The Beach Boys Today** made No 4 and spent almost a year (50 weeks) on the charts. **Summer Days (and Summer Nights!!)** made No 2, but charted for only 33 weeks. Both **Help Me, Rhonda** and **California Girls** were on this album. Surprisingly **Beach Boys Party**, which made No 6, was the one that did not bring home the precious metal. In Britain it was the biggest hit of the three, making No 3 when released the following year. The only Beach Boys album that charted in Britain in 1965 was **Surfin' USA**, which made No 17 with only seven weeks in the album charts. While the Beach Boys were established as a major act in the United States, it was not until **Barbara Ann** that they became really big in Britain.

BARBARA ANN *Capitol 5561* [*USA*] *Capitol CL 15432* [*UK*]. **California Girls** was followed by **The Little Girl I Once Knew**. This was a modest American hit, reaching No 20, though it failed to make the British charts at all. Then came **Barbara Ann**, a noisy fun disc that sounded as if it had been recorded live at a party. It was taken from the **Beach Boys Party** album, with suitable sound effects added. Released in December 1965, it made No 1 for one week in *Cash Box* early in 1966. It only made No 2 in *Billboard*, staying 11 weeks in the charts. The song was written by Fred Fassert in 1961, and produced by Brian Wilson. The Beach Boys did not think of **Barbara Ann** as a single and were astonished when it took off in the way it did.

In Britain it was the start of their most successful period, and a string of six Top 10 hits. In early 1966 it reached No 3, with 10 weeks in the charts. It won a Silver Disc for British sales of a quarter of a million, and sold 200,000 copies in Germany. It was very popular on the Continent, with European success making it the Beach Boys' seventh million seller, from global sales.

This was the first record that new Beach Boy Bruce Johnston played on. He was born on 27 June 1944, in Peoria, Illinois, and grew up in California. Brian Wilson had found the strain of writing much of the band's material, arranging and producing their records, and playing the live concerts too much. He decided to quit live performances and to concentrate on recording. The group first hired Glen Campbell for their live dates, but, not surprisingly, he did not quite fit in, and he was replaced by Bruce Johnston. Campbell went on to achieve major success with Capitol as a solo artist in the late sixties and seventies.

THE BEATLES   *British*

EIGHT DAYS A WEEK/I DON'T WANT TO SPOIL THE PARTY *Capitol 5371* [*USA*]. 1965 was another fantastic year for the Beatles. They were each awarded an MBE in the Queen's Birthday Honours List. They performed before what was at the time the largest ever crowd at a pop concert, at the Shea Stadium in New York, and continued their run of million-selling No 1 records all over the world. The popularity of the group was so great that most of EMI's overseas subsidiaries wanted to release more singles than the songs recorded as official British singles releases. A stream of petitions flowed in to EMI's London headquarters with requests to couple different album tracks for release as singles in different countries. EMI had to get the agreement of Brian Epstein in each case, and he was reluctant to agree to too many extra releases.

One of those recordings that did get past Epstein was **Eight Days A Week**, which was released as the Beatles' first recording of 1965 in North America and some countries in South America, Continental Europe and Asia. Both **Eight Days A Week** and its American B side **I Don't Want To Spoil The Party** were taken from the **Beatles For Sale** album (and from **Beatles '65** in Canada and the USA) and were written by John Lennon and Paul McCartney.

They were produced by George Martin at the Abbey Road studios in London.

In the USA **Eight Days A Week** went to No 1 for three weeks in *Cash Box* and *Variety* and two weeks in *Billboard*. It spent ten weeks in both the *Cash Box* and the *Billboard* charts. The flip side also charted, reaching No 39 during a six-week chart run in *Billboard*, but only No 83 during two weeks in the *Cash Box* charts. **Eight Days A Week** sold over a million copies in the USA alone, winning an RIAA Gold Disc on 16 September 1965. It was also No 1 in Malaysia, Hong Kong, Uruguay and Luxembourg, and in the Top 3 in Canada, Brazil, Lebanon and The Netherlands, and Top 10 in Belgium, Israel and Argentina.

On 1 February Capitol released the **Four By The Beatles** EP, which was not the same as that of the same title that Capitol had put out in 1964. EP releases were much more unusual in America than in Europe, for this format never really caught on in the States. The Beatles released only three EPs in the USA, the Vee Jay EP **The Beatles** being the first in 1964. Both the Capitol EPs made the US singles charts, with the 1965 release reaching No 68 in *Billboard* and No 74 in *Cash Box*. Compared to the Beatles' singles sales, their EPs did not do very well. That is why the **Magical Mystery Tour** double EP was released as an album in America in 1967. **The Beatles** EP, for example, sold only 49,617 copies at a time when in the smaller British market the Beatles had had five EPs in a row sell over a quarter of a million, and two pass the half million mark. (In previous additions of Joseph Murrells' million-sellers book, **The Beatles** EP was listed as a US million seller under the title **Ask Me Why**. In fact its sales were nowhere near that figure.)

TICKET TO RIDE/YES IT IS *Parlophone R 5265* [*UK*]/*Capitol 5407* [*USA*]. The Beatles' first official release of 1965 was another Lennon-McCartney number, as was the flip side which also charted in America. **Ticket To Ride** was from the Beatles' second feature film *Help!*, and entered the British charts at No 1 first week of release on 17 April, winning a Silver Disc two weeks later. It was their second Silver of the year, for the **Long Tall Sally** EP had passed the quarter million mark in February. (Previous editions of Murrells have listed this EP as a million seller. Its British sales were just over the quarter million, and there is no evidence in the EMI files of anything like three quarters of a million sales from Europe and the rest of the world.) **Ticket To Ride** spent 12 weeks in the British Top 50. Re-released 20 years later, it had another three weeks in the Top 100 reaching No 70.

In America the record was released ten days after it appeared in Britain. It made No 1 for one week in both *Billboard* and *Cash Box*, with 11 weeks in the *Billboard* charts and 12 weeks in *Cash Box*. The flip side, which was not from the film *Help!*, had a chart life of its own in *Billboard*, peaking at No 46 during four weeks in the Hot 100. It did not chart in *Cash Box*, *Variety* or *Record World*.

The record was the usual huge hit around the world. Among the countries in which it went to No 1 were Canada, Australia, New Zealand, Ireland, Sweden, Norway, The

Netherlands, Singapore and Hong Kong. It was also a major hit in Finland, Denmark, Germany, Switzerland, Belgium, Luxembourg, France, Spain, Lebanon, Malaysia, Brazil, Chile and Argentina. It achieved the million from global sales, with over half a million of those from Britain. Both sides were produced by George Martin at Abbey Road.

THE EARLY BEATLES (Album) Capitol 2309 [USA]. Released on 22 March 1965, this album was a collection of material that Capitol had originally passed on and which EMI had then licensed to Vee Jay. All the material on the album was produced by George Martin for Parlophone at EMI's Abbey Road studios in London.

All but two of the tracks (marked *) had already been released on the **Introducing The Beatles** Vee Jay album, the first Beatles LP released in America. Its chart performance was therefore unspectacular, reaching only No 43, with 34 weeks in the charts. Once the Vee Jay licence agreement ended, **Introducing The Beatles** was deleted, so **The Early Beatles** continued to sell steadily. Nine years after release it won an RIAA Gold Disc for million dollar sales on 8 January 1974. It continued selling over the years, and by the end of 1988 sales had finally passed the million mark in the USA alone.

The tracks on the album, all of which were written by Lennon and McCartney unless otherwise indicated and all of which had originally appeared on the **Please Please Me** album in Britain, were as follows: **Love Me Do**; **Twist And Shout**, by Bert Russell and Phil Medley; **Anna (Go To Him)**, by Arthur Alexander; **Chains**, by Gerry Goffin and Carole King; **Boys**, by Wesley Farrell and Luther Dixon; **Ask Me Why** *; **Please Please Me** *; **PS I Love You**; **Baby It's You**, by Mack David, Barney Williams and Burt Bacharach; **A Taste Of Honey**, by Rick Marlow and Bobby Scott; and **Do You Want To Know A Secret?**

HELP! Parlophone R 5305 [UK]/Capitol 5476 [USA]. **Help!** was the title track from the Beatles' second film. It was originally called **Eight Arms To Hold You**, and was released in July a week before the London premier of the film. **Help!** entered the British charts at No 1 the first week of release and qualified for a Silver Disc on advance orders alone. Within four weeks of release it had sold 815,874 copies in Britain. It was No 1 for four weeks, with 14 weeks in the Top 50. In America it was No 1 for four weeks in Variety and three weeks in the other charts. It spent 13 weeks in the charts in Billboard and 14 weeks in Cash Box. It won an RIAA Gold Disc on 2 September, just under two months after release. Boosted by the film, **Help!** was a major hit around the world, with No 1s in Canada, Australia, New Zealand, Ireland, Sweden, Norway, The Netherlands, Spain, Malaysia, Singapore, Hong Kong, Argentina and Brazil. It was No 2 in South Africa, Finland, Denmark and Chile, and in the Top 5 in Austria, Belgium, France and Italy.

Though credited as a Lennon-McCartney composition, most of the work was done by John Lennon. The song was recorded at Abbey Road on Tuesday 13 April, with producer

George Martin remixing on Sunday 18 April. The engineer for both sessions was Norman Smith, assisted by Ken Scott and Phil McDonald. The remixing session produced the mono version used in the film, with the single version being remixed on 18 June.

HELP! (Album) Parlophone PMC 1255 [UK]. The British **Help!** album contained the Beatles songs used in the film Help!, but was not the film soundtrack. The George Martin orchestral pieces from the film were not included on the British album, though they were on the American release. In their place, the British album had Beatles tracks not connected with the film. The tracks for this were all recorded at Abbey Road from February to June, under the direction of George Martin assisted by Norman Smith as engineer and Ken Scott, Jerry Boys and Phil McDonald as tape operators.

The album was released on 6 August and entered the LP charts at No 1 the first week of release. It stayed on top of the Record Retailer charts for nine weeks, with 37 weeks in the LP Top 20. In Melody Maker it also had an initial nine-week run at the top, being replaced by the Rolling Stones' **Out of Our Heads** on 16 October. One week later the Beatles were back on top, where they stayed for another six weeks until **The Sound Of Music** finally put an end to **Help's** run at the top on 4 December. One week after that and the Beatles' **Rubber Soul** crashed in to the charts at No 1 the first week of release, and so their domination of the album charts continued. In the third of the British LP charts, published by the New Musical Express, the Beatles entered the album Top 10 at No 1 and stayed there for 11 straight weeks in a row. The record had a British advance order of 280,000 copies, with 354, 161 sold by 25 August. This British version of **Help!** sold a million copies in the world outside North America, and was released in the USA in CD format in 1987.

The first side of the album, the first seven tracks, were songs from the film. The tracks on the album, all of which were Lennon-McCartney compositions unless otherwise stated, were as follows: **Help!**; **The Night Before**; **You've Got To Hide Your Love Away**; **I Need You**, by George Harrison; **Another Girl**; **You're Going To Lose That Girl**; **Ticket To Ride**; **Act Naturally**, by Van Morrison and John Russell; **It's Only Love**; **You Like Me Too Much**, by George Harrison; **Tell Me What You See**; **I've Just Seen A Face**; **Yesterday**; and **Dizzy Miss Lizzy**, by Larry Williams.

HELP! (soundtrack album) Capitol MAS 2386 [USA]. When the Beatles made their first film for United Artists, the film company had been able to insist that their record wing had rights to the soundtrack, at least in America. By the time the second film was made the balance of power had changed, for the Beatles were the hottest property on the entertainment stage. This time EMI insisted that the soundtrack could only be released on its labels, and so it went out on Capitol.

The film was a tremendous success throughout the world, making the Beatles the sixth most popular box office stars in Britain in 1965. The film was the second-biggest money-

maker in Britain, beaten only by Mary Poppins.

The album was No 1 for nine weeks in Billboard, with 44 weeks in the charts. It won a Gold Disc for million-dollar sales on 23 August, ten days after release. In fact the advance orders were well over the million-dollar mark. Final sales were 1,193,000 in the USA and 150,000 in Canada. This version of the album was not released in the rest of the world.

The Beatles numbers on the album, all but one of which were written by John Lennon and Paul McCartney, were as follows: **Help!**; **The Night Before**; **You've Got To Hide Your Love Away**; **I Need You**, by George Harrison; **Another Girl**; **Ticket To Ride**; **You're Going To Lose That Girl**. In addition, there were seven tracks composed by Ken Thorne and played by the George Martin Orchestra.

YESTERDAY Capitol 5498 [USA]/Apple R 6013 [UK]. **Yesterday** was a track off the British **Help!** album (though not from the film). In America it was released as a single, backed with **Act Naturally**, and both sides made the charts. **Yesterday** is one of the Beatles' best recordings, and their most successful composition. Over 2000 versions of the song have been recorded by other artists.

Although the record label stated that **Yesterday** was a Beatles record written by John Lennon and Paul McCartney, it was almost entirely a McCartney project. Recorded at Abbey Road on Monday 14 June 1965, the song was written by Paul. He sang lead, with backing from George Harrison. John Lennon and Ringo Starr were not even in the studio when the track was recorded. Paul had had the idea for the song in his mind for some while. After discussion with producer George Martin, they decided to use a classical string quartet. Those playing on the record were Paul McCartney (acoustic guitar), Tony Gilbert (first violin), Sidney Sax (second violin), Francisco Gabarro ('cello) and Kenneth Essex (viola.) This was the only occasion on which the quartet played together, as the members were session musicians and not a regular performing quartet.

The record was produced by George Martin at Abbey Road, assisted by engineer Norman Smith and tape operator Phil McDonald. The American flip side, **Act Naturally**, was another track off the British **Help!** album and featured Ringo Starr singing lead. The song was written by Van Morrison and John Russell in 1963, and was a country hit for Buck Owens. **Yesterday** was No 1 for four weeks in Billboard and three weeks in the other charts. It spent 11 weeks in the Billboard charts and 13 weeks in the Cash Box Top 100. **Act Naturally** also charted in America, reaching No 47 during seven weeks in the Billboard charts and peaking at No 28 during a similar chart run in Cash Box.

Yesterday was also released by various EMI companies around the world (though not always with **Act Naturally** on the flip side). It was No 1 in Canada, New Zealand, Finland, Norway, Denmark, The Netherlands, Belgium, Spain and Hong Kong. The record was No 2 in Australia, and a hit in Italy, France and Malaysia. After the Beatles had broken up, EMI released the track in Britain in 1976. It was the first Beatles single since the group had formally broken up in 1970, and reached No 8 during seven weeks in the charts. It won a Gold Disc for American sales on 20 October 1965, and sold over three million copies globally.

DAY TRIPPER/WE CAN WORK IT OUT

Parlophone R 5389 [UK]/Capitol 5555 [USA]. A major double A side for the Beatles, both sides were written by John Lennon and Paul McCartney. **Day Tripper** was recorded at Abbey Road on Saturday 16 October, and **We Can Work It Out** at the same studio four days later. George Martin produced both tracks, with Norman Smith as engineer and Ken Scott as tape operator.

The record was released on 3 December in Britain, and entered the charts at No 1 the first week of release, staying at the top for five weeks over the peak Christmas/New Year period. It qualified for a Silver Disc on advance sales alone. It spent 12 weeks in the Top 50. In America, where release was three days behind Britain, both sides made the Top 10. **We Can Work It Out** was No 1 for four weeks in early 1966. It was 12 weeks in the *Billboard* and *Cash Box* charts. **Day Tripper** peaked at No 5 in *Billboard* and No 10 in *Cash Box*, with a ten-week chart run in both papers. As usual the record was a massive international hit, with **We Can Work It Out** the more popular side. It was this side that gave the Beatles a big No 1 in Japan. The record sold a million copies in Britain and another million in the USA, with total world sales of several million. The RIAA Gold Disc was awarded on 6 January 1966, exactly one month after release and two days before the record hit No 1.

RUBBER SOUL (Album)

Parlophone PMC 1267 [UK]/Capitol T 2442 [USA]. On both sides of the Atlantic, the Beatles issued their new Christmas album **Rubber Soul** on the same day that their **Day Tripper/We Can Work It Out** single was released. In keeping with the British practice of the time, though in a move that would now be met with incredulity, neither side of the single was on the album. British fans still resented having to pay for an album that contained material already issued as a single, so British artists avoided putting singles on an album. American record companies were coming to view this as bizarre, as they were increasingly using singles as marketing tools for selling albums. Even without the promotional value of the single, **Rubber Soul** was still an enormous success, both artistically and commercially.

The album was recorded at the Abbey Road studios during October and November 1965. It was produced by George Martin, even though he had left EMI to form his own AIR production firm. The engineer was Norman Smith, performing this function for the last time, as he was promoted within the A&R department of EMI and went off to produce Pink Floyd for EMI's Columbia label. The tape operators used during the recording sessions were Jerry Boys, Ken Scott, Richard Lush and Graham Platt.

It was one of the most important albums the Beatles did, marking the transition from making albums as collections of pop songs to

thinking of them as musical entities in their own right. For three years the Beatles had pumped out two albums a year, increasingly recording their own material but also using good rock'n'roll classics made famous by others. **Rubber Soul** was the bridge between that and the new approach to albums represented by **Revolver** and **Sgt Pepper**.

The album did contain three tracks that were released as singles by various EMI companies around the world, though none were released in Britain. **Michelle** was probably the best known of these, with over a thousand cover versions. The Overlanders took it to No 1 in the UK. **Michelle** won the Grammy award as Song of the Year, 1966. The other two were **Norwegian Wood**, notable for George Harrison's sitar playing, and **Nowhere Man**, which Capitol released as a single in America. (EMI's Norwegian company were particularly keen to release **Norwegian Wood** as a single, but Brian Epstein would not agree. He tried to keep the number of 'unofficial' singles releases to a minimum, preferring all countries to wait for the next British release.) The album also included Ringo Starr's first composition, the country style **What Goes On**.

Rubber Soul entered the British album charts at No 1 the first week of release, and was at the top for nine weeks in the *Record Retailer* charts, 11 weeks in the *New Musical Express* (where it also entered the singles chart) and 13 weeks in the *Melody Maker*. It spent 42 weeks in the LP Top 20. In America the album went to No 1 for six weeks, with 59 weeks in the charts. It won an RIAA Gold Disc on Christmas Day 1965, and went on to sell over two and a half million copies in North America. Sales in the rest of the world, where the slightly different British version was released, were also over a million.

It was usual at that time for there to be some difference between the British and

American versions of an album, and that was so with **Rubber Soul**. The British version was eventually released in America, on CD in 1987. The tracks common to both, all written by Lennon and McCartney unless otherwise indicated, were as follows: **Norwegian Wood (This Bird Has Flown)**; **You Won't See Me**; **Think For Yourself**, by George Harrison; **The Word**; **Michelle**; **Girl**; **I'm Looking Through You**; **In My Life**; **Wait**; and **Run For Your Life**. The British version also contained **Drive My Car**; **Nowhere Man**; **What Goes On**, by John Lennon, Paul McCartney and Ringo Starr; and **If I Needed Someone**, by George Harrison. The American version included **I've Just Seen A Face** and **It's Only Love**.

JAMES BROWN AND THE FAMOUS FLAMES
American

PAPA'S GOT A BRAND NEW BAG — PART 1 *King 5999 [USA] London HL 9990 [UK].* James Brown was one of the most successful of all American black artists. He had 90 American chart entries from 1958 to 1977. On the album charts, his 47 hits from 1963 to 1980 failed to produce a pop No 1. As well as being a tremendous success as a singer and live performer, there was a time after the assassination of Dr Martin Luther King when Brown had a political presence as well.

Brown was born on 3 May 1933 in Barnwell, South Carolina, and later moved to nearby Augusta, Georgia. His parents separated when he was young, and he was brought up in great poverty by an aunt. He hardly attended school, spending his time on the streets.

At the age of 16, he was sent to prison for several years for car theft. In 1953 he was released on parole, and started singing in a gospel group called the Starlighters. Brown moved the group more into R&B and through various personnel changes the Starlighters became the Famous Flames. After a long hard slog, they finally secured a recording contract with the Cincinnati-based King-Federal Records, and in 1956 released their first record. This was **Please Please Please**, a slow number partly written by Brown. Though the record made the R&B Top 10, it did not reach the main pop Hot 100, until sneaking in to the bottom of the charts for a couple of weeks in 1964. This was Brown's first million seller. His second followed in 1958 with **Try Me**, which also gave him his first R&B No 1, at the top for one week, and his first Hot 100 chart entry.

There followed a long list of R&B successes, many of which were also minor pop hits. His first pop Top 10 entry was **Papa's Got a Brand New Bag**, which made No 8 with 13 weeks on the charts. It was No 1 for eight weeks on the US R&B charts. This was also his first British hit, reaching No 25 in a seven-week chart run.

The British beat group invasion of America, led by the Beatles, gave a great boost to many black R&B acts. The British groups had been greatly influenced by them, and gave them the public recognition that white American rock'n'roll singers never had. Brown wrote what was his biggest-selling record to that date himself, and also produced it. It was his third million seller, total sales passing the two million mark, with **Papa's Got a Brand New Bag** winning the Grammy Award for best R&B record of 1965.

I GOT YOU (I FEEL GOOD) *King 6015* [*USA*] *Pye International 7N 25350* [*UK*]. The follow-up to **Papa's Got a Brand New Bag** was another big chart hit written by James Brown. It was No 1 for five weeks on the US R&B charts, and reached No 3 on the Hot 100. In *Record World* it was No 1 for one week, the first chart topper of the year in January 1966. This was the highest position Brown ever made on the main pop singles chart. In Britain it made No 29 with six weeks in the charts, half the time it spent in the American Hot 100 and R&B chart.

The hits continued throughout the sixties and seventies and, on the black charts, into the eighties. In the late eighties James Brown increasingly ran foul of the law, and in December 1988 found himself back in prison.

THE BYRDS *American*

MR TAMBOURINE MAN *CBS-Columbia 43271* [*USA*] *CBS 201765* [*UK*]. The Byrds burst onto the American music scene in 1965. For a brief while, they looked as if they would stem the tide of the British invasion and restore American musical leadership with a new folk-rock style. But though they had a string of minor hits throughout the rest of the sixties, they never again achieved the heights of their two No 1s of 1965.

The main force behind the Byrds was Jim McGuinn (born in Chicago on 14 July 1942), who played 12-string guitar and banjo. His main influence had been folk music, and he had performed with the Limelighters and the Chad Mitchell Trio, and worked with Bobby Darin. Chris Hillman (born in Los Angeles on 4 December 1942) played bass guitar and mandolin. He came from a blue-grass background, and had formed his own band, the Hillmen, before joining the Byrds. Gene Clark (born in Tipton, Missouri, on 17 November 1941) played guitar, harmonica and tambourine, and had sung with the New Christy Minstrels. Mike Clarke (born in New York on 3 June 1944) played drums. David Crosby (born in Los Angeles on 14 August 1941) played guitar and had been in the Les Baxter Balladeers. He alone of the Byrds found major success when the group broke up, as part of Crosby, Stills, Nash and Young.

The origins of the Byrds go back to 1964. They made their first record for Elektra as the Beefeaters, though **Please Let Me Love You** flopped. CBS then picked the group up, with **Mr Tambourine Man** their first release on the (American) Columbia label. The highly distinctive sound of McGuinn's 12-string guitar and the group's harmonies, coupled with the strength of the Bob Dylan-composed song was an immense hit, and the record went to No 1 on both sides of the Atlantic. In fact, McGuinn was the only Byrd who actually played on the disc, the others singing the harmonies. A group of session men, including Glen Campbell, provided the music. In the USA the disc only survived at the top for one week, dethroned by the Rolling Stones' **Satisfaction**. In Britain the record stayed at No 1 for two weeks, winning a Silver Disc for UK sales of over a quarter of a milllion. The chart runs were 13 weeks in America and one week longer in Britain. The record was produced by CBS house producer Terry Melcher, the son of fifties CBS singer Doris Day.

TURN! TURN! TURN! *CBS-Columbia 43424* [*USA*] *CBS 202008* [*UK*]. For their second CBS record the Byrds recorded another Bob Dylan number, **All I Really Want to Do**. In America this proved disappointing, only reaching No 40, for Cher had also recorded the song as her solo debut disc and she won the chart battle. In Britain it was the Byrds who won, getting to No 4. The follow-up to this was **Turn! Turn! Turn!**, their biggest American hit. It spent three weeks at No 1, with 14 weeks on the charts, their longest-ever run. In Britain it only reached No 26 during its eight weeks in the charts.

The song was written by American folk singer Pete Seeger. He based the lyrics on the Old Testament Book of Ecclesiastes, making these the oldest set of words ever to top the charts! The disc was produced in Los Angeles by Terry Melcher. It was the Byrds' second and last million-selling single.

In August 1965 Gene Clark left the group, and over the next few years the line-up changed considerably. Gram Parsons spent five months with the group in 1967–8, and then teamed up with Chris Hillman (who had left soon after Parsons) to form the Flying Burrito Brothers. Parsons died in 1973. The original Byrds re-formed for a one-off album for Asylum (part of Warner Brothers) in 1973. Titled **Byrds**, it was their biggest album hit for years and reached No 20. After this, the group finally split up for good.

FREDDY CANNON *American*

ACTION *Warner Brothers 5645* [*USA*]. The fourth million seller for Freddy, this was his first on the Warner label. It was written by Tommy Boyce and Steve Venet. The disc reached the No 13 position in the USA with nine weeks in the bestsellers, and subsequent global million sale.

MEL CARTER *American*

HOLD ME, THRILL ME, KISS ME *Imperial 66113* [*USA*]. Mel Carter's recording of this 1952 song, written by Harry Noble, made it a million seller for the second time. His disc reached No 8 in the US charts and stayed in the charts for 15 weeks. It was released in June 1965.

Mel Carter was born on 22 April 1943 in Cincinnati. He made his first disc at the age of four, a Negro spiritual sung in a 25-cent recording booth in a penny arcade.

Mel first recorded in 1963 for Sam Cooke's Derby Records and came up with a successful disc, **When a Boy Falls in Love**. Then came a contract with the Imperial label, this big hit, and other successes such as **Band of Gold** and **My Heart Sings**. In 1968 he recorded for the Bell label.

LOU CHRISTIE *American*

LIGHTNIN' STRIKES *MGM 13412* [*USA*] *MGM 1297* [*UK*]. A third million seller for Lou, the song was again written by him with Twyla Herbert. The disc was issued in late 1965 and

was No 1 for two weeks in the USA in 1966 with 15 weeks in the bestsellers, and No 11 in Britain with eight weeks in the bestsellers. Gold Disc award from RIAA in March 1966. Sales were two million.

THE DAVE CLARK FIVE   *British*

I LIKE IT LIKE THAT *Epic 9811* [*USA*]. **Come Home** and **Reelin' and Rockin'** had been moderate American hits for the Dave Clark Five in early 1965, but like their last two releases of 1964 had failed to make the Top 10. All four of these records had been more successful in America than in Britain, and Epic decided to go for something different than the group's next British release. The Dave Clark Five's seventh million seller therefore came from a record only released in North America. **I Like It Like That** was written in 1961 by Chris Kenner (who had a million-selling hit with it himself) and Allen Toussaint. It was recorded by EMI Columbia at their Abbey Road studios in London, and licensed to Eros International Corporation of New York City for North America. The record went to No 6 in *Cash Box* and No 7 in *Billboard*. It was 11 weeks in both charts. Sales from Canada and the USA are reputed to be just over the million.

CATCH US IF YOU CAN *Columbia (EMI) DB 7625* [*UK*] *Epic 9833* [*USA*]. **Catch Us If You Can** was the only major hit the Dave Clark Five had in Britain in 1965. It reached No 5 and stayed 11 weeks in the charts. The song was from the film of the same name, which featured the group in the then-obligatory musical film most beat groups made. An EP from the film was a modest hit, reaching No 8 in the EP charts. The song was written by Dave Clark and Leonard Davidson of the DC5. In America it was their second Top 10 hit of the year, reaching No 4

during an 11-week chart run. This was another global million seller, with most sales coming from the USA.

OVER AND OVER *Columbia (EMI) DB 7744* [*UK*] *Epic 9863* [*USA*]. **Over and Over** was a great disappointment when released in Great Britain. As the follow-up to a big hit like **Catch Us If You Can**, more had been hoped for it than the No 45 position it peaked at during its brief four weeks in the Top 50. It was the lowest chart placing that the group had seen up to that time, though their next release **Look Before You Leap** managed the ultimate indignity of one week at the bottom of the chart (then No 50).

The American release, which took place at the same time, was a very different matter. **Over and Over** soared up the charts to give the Dave Clark Five the only US No 1 of their career. Although it spent only one week at the top, it was the maximum-sales Christmas week. The following week, the first of 1966, the Beatles took over the top spot with **We Can Work It Out** in the *Cash Box* charts (reversing the position in 1963, when the Dave Clark Five's only British No 1, **Glad All Over**, had knocked the Beatles off the top).

Over and Over was a remake of a song Bobby Day of the Hollywood Flames had taken into the charts in 1958. It reached No 41 as part of a double A side, the main half of which, **Rockin' Robin**, reached No 2. Day wrote the song himself, under his real name of Robert Byrd. The Dave Clark Five version was produced by Dave Clark at Columbia's Abbey Road studio in London.

PETULA CLARK   *British*

MY LOVE *Pye 7N 17038* [*UK*] *Warner Brothers 5684* [*USA*]. **My Love** was issued in December 1965. It sold a global million by March 1966, and was No 1 in the US charts for two weeks with 13 weeks in the bestsellers, and No 4 in Britain with nine weeks in the bestsellers. The song was written by Petula's recording manager Tony Hatch (of Pye Records, Britain) and the disc made history, being the first time a British female artist topped the US charts twice. The first was **Downtown**.

Tony Hatch completed **My Love**, one of three songs he wrote for Petula, on a transatlantic flight in November 1965. Pet recorded it in Los Angeles with an American studio orchestra.

BILL COSBY   *American*

WHY IS THERE AIR? (Album) *Warner Brothers 1606* [*USA*]. Bill Cosby's third album, about an expectant father, sold 951,000 by July 1967 with the million sale by the end of the year. It received a Gold Disc award from RIAA in 1966.

The album included **The Toothache**, **Kindergarten** and **Driving in San Francisco**. It stayed in the US bestsellers for 152 weeks. It was recorded at the Flamingo Hotel, Las Vegas, and produced by Roy Silver and fellow comedian Allan Sherman. Sales by end of 1967 were 1,400,000. (See 1966, for biography.)

Grammy Award for 'Best Comedy Performance', 1965.

DRAFI DEUTSCHER   *German*

MARMOR, STEIN UND EISEN BRICHT (Marble, stone and iron break) *Decca F 11683* [*West Germany*]. Written by Drafi himself in collaboration with Christian Bruhn, this disc sold 800,000 in Germany alone up to April 1966 and was No 1 there for 12 weeks from December 1965. It was issued in the USA in 1966 under the title **Marble Breaks and Iron Bends** on the London label with English lyrics by Marcel Stellman, and subsequently reached a million global sale.

Drafi Deutscher was born in Berlin on 9 May 1946, his father being Hungarian. At the age of 11, he won a talent contest on the accordion and two years later formed his first band, Charie and his Timebombs. A year later, Drafi formed another group called the Magics which won first prize in 1961 at a Twist festival in Berlin. They became firmly established in German beat circles over the following two years. In 1963, Drafi won another competition, this time for his vocal talents, resulting in an opportunity to record. His first disc was an overnight hit, and all his succeeding records followed the same pattern. In 1966, he was voted Germany's No 1 male vocalist.

KEN DODD   *Britain*

TEARS *Columbia (EMI) DB 7659* [*UK*]. With beat groups predominating in Britain, Ken Dodd's recording of this old sentimental song was the biggest surprise of 1965, and the year's greatest hit. By the end of November it passed the million mark to become Britain's biggest disc of 1965. Sales by August 1966 were 1,600,000.

The song, written by Frank Capano (words) and Billy Uhr (music), both Americans, was originally recorded by Rudy Vallee in 1929.

Ken Dodd was born in Liverpool, England, on 8 November 1932, the son of a coal merchant. He started entertaining when he was seven, giving backyard concerts to school friends. He later gave a show as a ventriloquist to pupils of local Knotty Ash School, and at 13 an audition at a Liverpool theatre which had advertised for dancers. He got the only vacant male role — leading Cinderella's coach. On leaving school, he worked with his father, then started selling pots and pans on the city's housing estates. In the evenings he entertained at clubs, and by 1954 was so busy with engagements he became a full-time professional comedian. Apart from comedy, he was a fine singer of romantic ballads, and this opened up a new career for him on discs. His first recording and first success was **Love is Like a Violin** issued in June 1960 on Decca label, and in 1964 came a hit with **Happiness** on Columbia.

It was No 1 for six weeks in Britain's charts with 24 weeks in the bestsellers. In 1989 he attracted much national publicity when he stood trial on tax fraud charges. He was acquitted.

EARLE DOUD AND ALEN ROBIN *American*

WELCOME TO THE LBJ RANCH (Album) *Capitol 2423* [*USA*]. Earle Doud, producer of the **First Family** album in 1962, teamed up with Alen Robin, head of the USA's 'Tonight' show, to produce this brilliant comedy disc. By matching interview questions with authentic but unrelated statements made by well-known political officials including President Lyndon B. Johnson, Dwight Eisenhower, Governor Nelson Rockefeller and Senator Barry Goldwater, their unique comedy idea resulted in an uproarious album with colossal sales in the USA. The clever tape editing involved some 40 lawyers employed by Capitol Records to clear the legal side before it was released on 2 November 1965. The disc sold half a million by 1 December and gained an RIAA Gold Disc award. It went on to sell an estimated million (1966), was No 3 for two weeks and stayed high on the US charts for most of its 25-week run.

The actual voices of prominent men in politics were used for this political spoof together with the voices of noted US commentator John Cameron Swayze, Westbrook Van Voorhis, John St Leger, and Doud and Robin themselves. The producers combed through 480,000 feet of tape to obtain the right answers to their questions. Other voices on the disc were Senator Robert Kennedy, Lady Bird Johnson, Senator Everett Dirksen and Vice-President Richard Nixon.

BOB DYLAN   *American*

LIKE A ROLLING STONE *CBS-Columbia 43346* [*USA*] *CBS 201811* [*UK*]. Bob Dylan has been one of the most influential people in the history of rock music. His own style of music

went through a number of changes, from folk to rock to C&W to gospel. His main talent was as a poet who reached his audience by singing his poems. Artists from the Beatles onwards were influenced by him.

Dylan was born Robert Allen Zimmerman in Duluth, Minnesota, on 24 May 1941. His family moved to Hibbing, a mining town near the Canadian border, when he was a child. He ran away from home seven times between the ages of 12 and 18, and dropped out of the University of Minnesota after only six months. At school he liked Little Richard, and listening to the music of black America on the radio; he was influenced by R&B. At college, he involved himself in folk music, and it was in this direction that he moved for the next few years. Dylan's first professional performance was playing piano in a strip club in Central City, Colorado, in 1960. His move to New York in January 1961 meant access to the more acceptable venues of Greenwich Village. Almost as soon as he arrived in New York, he went to see the legendary folksinger Woodie Guthrie, who had been ill with Huntington's chorea since 1954. As well as playing the folk circuit, he augmented his meagre income by doing session work. It was while he was playing harmonica at a session at the CBS studios that he was heard by producer John Hammond, who signed Dylan to CBS. Guthrie was clearly a great influence on him, though Dylan later denied this, claiming in 1965 that nobody had been an influence on him.

Dylan's first album **Bob Dylan** was released in early 1962. Though it failed to make the charts, other artists were beginning to record his songs with success. Peter, Paul and Mary took his **Blowing in the Wind** to No 2. His first single was released at the end of the year. Surprisingly, given his image as a folk singer, **Mixed-up Confusion** was an upbeat rock record. Perhaps luckily for Dylan, the record didn't sell, and his folk image remained

intact for the release of his much-acclaimed second album **The Freewheelin' Bob Dylan** in May 1963. This gave him his first album hit, reaching No 22 with 32 weeks on the LP chart. It won a Gold Disc for million dollar sales in December 1970. Soon after the release of this album, Dylan made a triumphant appearance at the Newport Folk Festival which established him as a major folk star.

Two more albums followed in 1964, each selling moderately well and building his career as a singer of folk and protest songs. The protest element was partly opportunistic, partly his own idealism and partly influenced by his then-girlfriend Suze Rotolo. His 1965 albums broke the Top 10 and won Gold Discs for million dollar sales. The first, **Bringing It all Back Home**, made No 6 and contained his first hit single. **Subterranean Homesick Blues** was a minor hit, reaching No 39 on the Hot 100. The second of these albums, **Highway 61 Revisited** included **Like a Rolling Stone**. It told the story of the fall of a young woman from wealth to prostitution. The album peaked at No 3, while the single went all the way to No 1 for a week in *Cash Box* and No 2 for two weeks in *Billboard*. It spent 12 weeks in both charts. This was Dylan's biggest ever hit in Britain, reaching No 4 with 12 weeks in the charts.

His first British hit had been **The Times They Are A-Changin'**, released earlier in 1965. It was also the first British hit for CBS, which had only just established a branch in Britain. Dylan came to England in April 1965 for a brief tour promoted by Tito Burns. The Beatles had helped build his reputation in Britain; John Lennon in particular was influenced by him, as songs like **Norwegian Wood** show.

Like a Rolling Stone was produced by Tom Wilson, and written by Bob Dylan. It was a global million seller. Its success was no mean achievement for such a long record (it lasted six minutes). Given the importance of radio in making hits in America (even the US charts are compiled in part from radio plays), Dylan and CBS took a risk in releasing a record that would normally be ignored by radio as too long as only Dylan's second hit. In a 1988 poll of *Rolling Stone* magazine critics, **Like a Rolling Stone** was ranked second (behind the Rolling Stones' **Satisfaction**) in a list of the 100 best singles of the previous 25 years.

POSITIVELY 4TH STREET *CBS-Columbia 43389* [*USA*] *CBS 201824* [*UK*]. The follow-up to **Like a Rolling Stone** was another composition by Dylan, which gave him two Top 10 hits in a row in America. It made No 7 with nine weeks on the charts. In Britain it had a longer chart life of 12 weeks, during which it reached No 8. This was his fourth British Top 10 hit.

After his British concerts, Dylan again played the Newport Folk Festival. His 1965 appearance had a very different effect from 1963, for he chose this venue to make his live debut as a rock rather than a folk singer. While his move to folk-rock marked an important change in his career, and influenced a whole generation of musicians like the Eagles, it appalled the traditional folk purists. This new phase in Dylan's career involved him in a great deal of touring, drugs, and a new backing outfit called the Band. Other artists had major hits with his compositions, in particular the Byrds with **Mr Tambourine Man** and **All I Really Wanna Do**, which was also a big hit for Cher.

In 1966 Dylan scored another Top 10 album with **Blonde on Blonde**, from which came **Rainy Day Women Numbers 12 and 35**. This reached No 2 in the US singles charts, and No 7 in Britain. 1966 was also the year Dylan had a serious motorbike accident, He had one more Top 10 single (on both sides of the Atlantic) with **Lay Lady Lay** in 1969. Though there were a number of minor singles hits continuing to 1979, Dylan was mainly an album artist and continued to produce major albums well into the eighties. He has had 19 Gold Discs for million dollar album sales in the USA with two of these selling over a million copies. These were the **Desire** and **Slow Train Coming** albums of 1976 and 1979. The first of these was No 1 for five weeks in America, his third and last No 1 LP. The first Dylan album to top the charts was his first on the Warner Brothers' label Asylum. This was **Planet Waves**, released in 1974, which had four weeks at the top. The link with Asylum was brief, for after one more album he returned to CBS, and in 1975 went back to No 1 with the first album of this new deal, **Blood on the Tracks**.

Dylan had an even more impressive album career in Britain. His debut British hit album was **The Freewheelin' Bob Dylan**, which went to No 1 for two weeks. It was knocked off the top by his own **Bringing It All Back Home**. He had four more No 1 albums in a row from 1968 to 1970. He had 29 hit albums in Britain from 1964 to 1986, of which 23 made the Top 10. This compares with 28 hit albums in America from 1963 to 1986, with 14 in the Top 10.

SHIRLEY ELLIS — American

THE CLAPPING SONG *Congress 234 [USA] London HLR 9961 [UK]*. Shirley's first million seller globally was written by her manager Lincoln Chase, Mrs James McCarthy and Mrs Larry Kent.

Shirley started in show business by winning an amateur contest at the Apollo Theatre, New York, her native city. She used her natural talents by gaining valuable experience performing whenever possible in clubs, charity affairs and dances, and then joined a group, the Metronomes, which played every type of music from rock'n'roll to calypso. In 1958 she met Lincoln Chase for whom she had made some demonstration discs for Decca some years previously. Chase signed her up to a management contract. After five years of intensive preparation, he wrote **The Nitty Gritty** for her (1963) and **The Name Game** (1964), both sizeable hits which got into the US Top 10. Then came **The Clapping Song**, which reached No 8 in the USA with nine weeks in the bestsellers. It was No 4 in Britain (on the London label) and 13 weeks in the bestsellers, with an estimated global million sale.

In 1978 **The Clapping Song** entered the British charts again, though this time as an EP containing other Shirley Ellis American hits of the mid-sixties. The EP spent four weeks in the singles charts on MCA, reaching No 59.

WAYNE FONTANA AND THE MINDBENDERS — British

GAME OF LOVE *Fontana TF 535 [UK] Fontana 1509 [USA]*. Wayne Fontana and the Mindbenders were one of the British beat group which burst on to the scene in the mid-sixties in the wake of the Beatles, had a few hits, made a splash in America, and then faded away as quickly as they had arrived.

Wayne Fontana was born Glyn Geoffrey Ellis on 28 October 1945, in Manchester. He became a telephone engineer after leaving school, though he had long had an interest in music. Originally Wayne Fontana and the Jets, formed in 1963, they played semi-professionally in the clubs and pubs of Manchester. When the group won an audition at the city's Oasis Club, only Wayne and bass guitarist Bob Lang (born on 10 January 1946) turned up. Jack Baverstock, A&R manager of Philips' Fontana label, was there so Wayne asked two other musicians to help out. They were lead guitarist Eric Stewart (born on 20 January 1945) and drummer Ric Rothwell (born on 11 March 1944.) Baverstock offered them a recording contract. When he asked them their name, Wayne picked the Mindbenders from a horror movie he had just seen.

In July 1963 their first release **Hello Josephine** reached No 46 in its two weeks in the Top 50. This was a cover of a Fats Domino song, and the group released other covers for their next two records, both of which failed. Their second hit, in May 1964, was a cover of Ben E. King's **Stop Look and Listen**, and made No 37. They then released a remake of **Um Um Um Um Um Um**, which had been an American Top 10 hit for Major Lance early in 1964. (The song would later be Johnny Rivers' 28th and last US hit, released at the end of 1977.) It was Wayne Fontana's big breakthrough, reaching No 5 in the British charts.

The follow-up did even better, giving them their biggest hit and only million seller. **Game of Love** was written by Clint Ballard Jnr in 1964, and took Wayne and the Mindbenders to No 2 and an 11-week chart run. The record was even more successful in America, where it was the group's first hit. It went to No 1 for one week, with 11 weeks on the chart. Combined British and American sales were around 900,000, with sales from the rest of the world taking the disc over the million mark.

The ever-increasing number of British acts that were dominating the US charts and wanting to perform in the United States led the Americans to react in a protectionist way. The US Government made it difficult to get work permits, and the American Musicians Union objected to British artists performing at all. Sandie Shaw and Twinkle were among those banned from performing in America. The Hollies, Zombies, Animals, Freddie and the Dreamers, and the Nashville Teens all had problems, as did Wayne Fontana and the Mindbenders. The American authorities at first claimed that the group was unknown in the States. They had to get *Billboard* and *Cash Box* magazines to confirm that they were at No 1 before the US embassy in Britain would give them a visa to enter America. Eventually an H-2 visa was granted, allowing Wayne to make initially one performance only.

After **Game of Love**, there were only two more modest hits before Wayne and the Mindbenders split up at the end of 1965. Wayne Fontana had four more hits, the biggest of which was **Pamela Pamela**, released in December 1966, reaching No 11. None of his records made it in America. The Mindbenders did better. They had four hits, keeping them in the British charts to the end of 1967. Their biggest hit was their first without Wayne. **A Groovy Kind Of Love** went to No 2 in both Britain and America. They had only one more hit in the USA. **Ashes to Ashes** made No 55, compared to No 14 in Britain in 1966.

They were an example of a group whose lead singer thought he could build a better career if he dumped his backing group after their initial success. Brian Poole made the same mistake when he sank after splitting with the Tremeloes, who went on to great success.

THE FOUR SEASONS — American

LET'S HANG ON *Philips 40317 [USA] Philips BF 1439 [UK]*. The fifth million seller for this outstanding group, the song was written by Denny Randell, Sandy Linzer and Bob Crewe. The disc was released in September 1965 and remained in the bestseller charts for 17 weeks, reaching No 1 for one week. It was also popular in Britain where it reached No 4 for one week with 16 weeks in the bestsellers.

THE FOUR TOPS — American

I CAN'T HELP MYSELF (SUGAR PIE HONEY BUNCH) *Motown 1076 [USA] Tamla Motown TMG 515 [UK]*. Unlike most of the young black acts Motown catapulted to fame in the early and mid-sixties, the Four Tops had a long

apprenticeship of years of performing together before their first hit. They were already a close-knit group of friends when success finally came, and, uniquely, the group has retained the same line-up throughout its 35-year existence.

The Four Tops are lead singer Levi Stubbs, Abdul Fakir, Renaldo Benson and Lawrence Payton, from the North End neighbourhood of Detroit. They came together in 1954, calling themselves the Four Aimes. They started doing the rounds of high school hops, then graduated to the club circuit and toured America as a cabaret act. In 1956 they signed with Chess Records of Chicago, changing their name to the Four Tops for the release of their debut single **Kiss Me Baby**. It failed to make the charts, and they had no better success with Red Top Records, CBS or on the Riverside label. By 1960 Berry Gordy had formed Motown Records, and the Four Tops signed with him in 1963. Their first release was a jazz album put out on the Workshop label. Before they had hits of their own, the Four Tops did backing vocals for most of the Motown stars. Their first hit came in 1964 with **Baby I Need Your Loving**, which reached No 11.

Their fourth hit, **I Can't Help Myself**, gave them their first American No 1 and million-selling record. On the main pop chart it spent two weeks at No 1, with 14 weeks on the chart. In the R&B charts it was No 1 for nine weeks during an 18-week chart run. In Britain **I Can't Help Myself** was their first hit, reaching a modest No 23 with nine weeks in the charts. The song was written by Motown's star writing team of Eddie and Brian Holland and Lamont Dozier, who also produced the record.

The follow-up single was **It's the Same Old Song**, which made No 5 in America and No 34 in Britain. **Ain't That Love**, an old track from their CBS days, surfaced at No 93 for one week.

Their next two official releases just made the Top 20, the one after that only reaching No 45. Then came the classic **Reach Out, I'll Be There** which in 1966 restored them to No 1 for the second and last time.

They continued to have a lot of usually minor hits throughout the sixties, though they were badly hit by the departure of the Holland-Dozier-Holland team from Motown. Eventually they decided to leave as well, and signed to Dunhill. Their first two records under this new deal were both Top 10 million-selling records, though after that the hits peaked in the lower reaches of the charts. In 1981 they signed to the disco-orientated Casablanca label, and had a hit from the film *Grease 2* on RSO. In 1983 they returned to Motown for their last hit, **I Can't Just Walk Away**, which made No 71 on the Hot 100 and No 36 on the black charts.

In their lengthy career, spanning four decades, the Four Tops developed from their gospel roots into a top R&B-based pop act. Their versatility encompassed a number of other styles, including C&W and jazz. They have always been an exciting live act, and had plenty of performing work both before and after the hits came. They have had 42 American chart entries (41 records including one double A side), of which only seven made the Top 10. They had two further hits with the Supremes, with whom they also co-operated on three LPs. Of their 26 hit albums, only one 'greatest hits' package made the Top 10 and ten did not even make the top half of the album Top 200.

Though their British album chart career was shorter, with nine hits, EMI (who had the Tamla Motown licence in Britain) put their first four albums into the LP Top 10 with the fourth, a 'greatest hits' compilation, going to No 1 for one week. (It was knocked off the top by another 'greatest hits' pack, from the Supremes on the same label.) On the singles front, the Four Tops had 27 British hits (including two hits re-issued). Of these, ten made the Top 10 and one, **Reach Out, I'll Be There**, made No 1 in 1966.

THE GENTRYS *American*

KEEP ON DANCING *MGM 13379* [USA]. The Gentrys were first organized in Memphis, Tennessee, in May 1963 as a rock'n'roll group for local dances, and were very successful playing for high school dates. In December 1964 the group were given a contract by a local record label and made their first disc **Sometimes**, which was very popular locally. Then came **Keep on Dancing**, which was leased for national distribution by MGM Records. It achieved No 3 for two weeks in the national charts with 14 weeks in the bestsellers, and subsequently sold a million.

The members of the group were Larry Raspberry (leader, guitar, vocalist), Larry Wall (drums), Jimmy Johnson (trumpet, organ), Bobby Fisher (tenor sax, electric piano), Pat Neal (bass guitar), Bruce Bowles (vocalist) and Jimmy Hart (vocalist).

Keep on Dancing was written by Allen A. Jones and Willie David Young. The group started recording for Bell Records in 1968.

BOBBY GOLDSBORO *American*

LITTLE THINGS *United Artists 810* [USA]. The second million seller (reported by 1967) for Bobby, the song was written by him in 1964. It reached No 12 in the US charts with 12 weeks in the bestsellers.

HERMAN'S HERMITS *British*

CAN'T YOU HEAR MY HEART BEAT? *MGM 13310* [USA]. 1965 was Herman's Hermits' most successful year in America, where the group had achieved a higher level of popularity than in their native Britain. They had seven singles in the Top 10, the first six of which sold over a million copies each. Three of them were American No 1s. The group ended the year being ranked by *Billboard* as the top singles artists of 1965, pushing the Beatles off the top spot after only one year. On the album front, *Billboard* ranked them fifth.

Can't You Hear My Heart Beat? was the American follow-up to their first hit **I'm Into Something Good**. It was written by John Carter and Ken Lewis (pseudonyms for John Shakespeare and Kenneth Hawker) and produced by Mickie Most in London for EMI's Columbia label. Columbia did not release it in Britain, putting out **Show Me Girl** instead. This was a mistake, as the record only made No 19. **Can't You Hear My Heart Beat?** was used as an album track in Britain. In America, where the Hermits' records were licensed to MGM, the record went to No 1 for one week in the *Cash Box* charts, and No 2 for two weeks in *Billboard*. It spent 15 weeks on the Hot 100, an all-time record for Herman's Hermits. The disc was also released in Canada and other countries, with global sales of a million, most US.

SILHOUETTES *Columbia (EMI) DB 7475* [*UK*] *MGM 13332* [*USA*]. **Silhouettes** was Herman's Hermits' third release on both sides of the Atlantic. It reached No 3 in Britain and No 5 in the USA, with a chart life of 12 weeks in Britain and 13 weeks in America. It was also a major hit in many European countries and in Canada, Australia and New Zealand. The record won a Silver Disc for British sales of a quarter of a million, sold well over half a million in America, with sales from other countries taking the total to over the million. It was the group's third million-selling record, and was produced by Mickie Most. Though Peter Noone (Herman) and the Hermits sang on their records, the music was actually provided by session musicians. Written by Bob Crewe and Frank Slay Jnr in 1957, it was a million seller for the American group the Rays.

MRS BROWN YOU'VE GOT A LOVELY DAUGHTER *MGM 13341* [*USA*]. The group's fourth million seller was released only in North America. **Mrs Brown You've Got a Lovely Daughter** was almost a novelty song. It fitted the very English image Herman's Hermits portrayed, and had something of a music-hall sound to it. The song was written by Trevor Peacock in 1963, and sung by actor Tom Courtenay in a British TV play. The Hermits' version was on their **Introducing Herman's Hermits** album, which sold over half a million copies in America and won an RIAA Gold Disc for million dollar sales. It was produced by Mickie Most. Public demand pushed MGM to release it as a single, and it went to No 1 for four weeks in *Cash Box* and three weeks in *Billboard*. It entered the Hot 100 at No 12, which was the highest position that any record had ever entered the charts. Released while the group

were on a spectacularly successful tour of America, it spent 11 weeks on the charts. Advance sales were over 600,000 and an RIAA Gold Disc was awarded for US sales of one million on 16 June 1965.

WONDERFUL WORLD *Columbia (EMI) DB 7546* [*UK*] *MGM 13354* [*USA*]. Million seller number five was the follow-up to **Silhouettes** in Britain and most of the world. It was a revival of Sam Cooke's 1960 hit, and was written by Cooke, Lou Adler and Herb Alpert in 1959 under the joint pseudonym of Barbara Campbell. As usual, the record was produced by Mickie Most. It went to No 7 in Britain, with nine weeks in the Top 50. In America it peaked at No 4 during a 10-week chart run. The record was a global million seller.

I'M HENRY VIII I AM *MGM 13367* [*USA*]. Herman's Hermits' sixth million seller was straight music-hall vaudeville. It was written in 1911 by Fred Murray and R.P. Weston, when it was performed by the great Cockney comedian Harry Champion. The track came from their second US album, **Herman's Hermits on Tour**, which won a Gold Disc for American sales of one million dollars. In America the record went to No 1 for one week in *Billboard* and *Cash Box*, two weeks in *Variety* and three weeks in *Record World* where it was in the charts for 10 weeks. The song might have been very cute for the American market, and have seemed typically English there, but Columbia realized it was not right for Britain and it was never released in the UK. The record was produced by Mickie Most, and won a Gold Disc from the RIAA for American sales of one million copies. Both the single and the album it was from were certificated Gold on 31 August 1965.

JUST A LITTLE BIT BETTER *Columbia (EMI) DB 7670* [*UK*] *MGM 13398* [*USA*]. The seventh million seller for Herman's Hermits was a more modest hit than any of their others at that time. **Just a Little Bit Better** followed **Wonderful World** into the British charts, and peaked at No 10 in the *New Musical Express* Top 30 (though in the *Record Retailer* industry chart it only made No 15, with nine weeks in their Top 50). In America it reached No 7, with 10 weeks on the charts. The song was written by Kenny Young in 1964, and Mickie Most produced the record in London. It sold a global million, with most of the sales coming from America.

The group had one more big hit in 1965, released just before Christmas. **A Must to Avoid** reached No 6 in Britain and No 8 in America. It had been a spectacular year but, though many more hits were to come, their 1965 level of success was unsustainable.

In an interview with *NME* in March 1965, Peter Noone was asked what sort of image he had. 'I'm the drinka-pinta-milka-day type,' he replied.

THE BEST OF HERMAN'S HERMITS (Album) *MGM 4315* [*USA*]. The third Herman's Hermits album to be released in America in 1965, and the third in a row to make the Top 10 and win RIAA Gold Discs for million dollar sales. The first two LPs, **Introducing Herman's Hermits** and **Herman's Hermits on Tour**, both had long stretches at No 2 in the album charts. Although **The Best of Herman's Hermits** only reached No 5 (for three weeks), it had a far longer stay in the album charts, lasting nearly two years. It spent 17 weeks in the Top 10. Its 105-week chart residency was by far the longest of the group's career. Released in mid-November, its million dollar sales were recognized by Gold Disc certification on 11 January 1966, with the million sales reached in 1967.

Herman's Hermits were far more successful on the album front in America than in Britain, and to a greater extent than with singles. They had 10 albums hit the US LP charts, of which five won Gold Discs for million dollar sales. Their first British hit, **Herman's Hermits**, was their only Columbia studio album to chart. It made No 16 in September 1965, and lasted only two weeks in the charts. Six years later, EMI put a hits package out on the budget Music For Pleasure label. **The Most of Herman's Hermits** reached No 14, and spent five weeks on a by then larger LP chart. Their final appearance in the charts was a K-Tel **Greatest Hits** compilation, which staggered to No 37 in a four-week chart run in 1977.

All the tracks on **The Best of Herman's Hermits** were produced by Mickie Most for release in Britain on the Columbia label, and licensed to MGM in North America.

The contents of the disc were: ***Just a Little Bit Better**, by Kenny Young (1964); ***I'm Henry VIII, I Am**, by R.P. Weston and Fred Murray (1911); ***Mrs Brown You've Got a Lovely Daughter**, by Trevor Peacock (1963); ***Silhouettes**, by Bob Crewe and Frank Slay, Jr (1975); ***I'm Into Something Good**, by Gerry Goffin and Carole King (1964); ***Can't You Hear My Heart Beat?**, by John Carter and Ken Lewis (1965); ***Wonderful World**, by Barbara Campbell (1959); **Mother in Law**, by Allen

Toussaint (1961); **The End of the World**, by Sylvia Dee and Arthur Kent (1962), **Sea Cruise**, by Frankie Ford and Huey Smith (1959); **I Gotta Dream On**, by Gordon (1965). Items marked * were million seller singles for the group.

HORST JANKOWSKI   *German*

A WALK IN THE BLACK FOREST *Philips 5311* [*West Germany*] *Mercury MF 861* [*UK*] *Mercury 72425* [*USA*]. Horst Jankowski was born in Berlin on 30 January 1936. His family moved from Berlin when the heavy bombing began. His father died when he was eight. In 1947, he and his mother moved back to Berlin where he attended the Conservatory of Music, his mother working and making sacrifices to pay for his tuition. Here he studied tenor saxophone, contra-bass and trumpet in addition to the piano. When he was 16, he met Caterina Valente who asked him to work with her for two years on a tour of Africa, Spain and France. He then joined a big band and started doing arrangements and composing. In 1960, he started a choir, made up of entirely amateur singers from all walks of life. He used this choir of 18 with his orchestra in a similar style to America's famous Ray Conniff. He certainly created something of a 'new sound' in instrumentals, and his fame spread rapidly throughout Germany, resulting in much recording and TV work.

A Walk in the Black Forest, his own composition written in 1962, sold over 250,000 in Britain and more in the USA, with big European sales, making a total of over a million.

Jankowski played a lot of jazz music apart from his choir and has worked with many famous musicians including Oscar Peterson, Ella Fitzgerald, Gerry Mulligan and Miles Davis. He also played in Benny Goodman's band in Brussels for four months. This disc was No 3 in Britain with 18 weeks in the bestsellers, and No 9 in the USA where it was 13 weeks in the charts.

THE GENIUS OF JANKOWSKI (Album) *Philips 10015* [*West Germany*] *Mercury 60993* [*USA*]. This album sold a global million by March 1966. It included the now famous Jankowski composition **A Walk in the Black Forest** which sold a million as a singles disc. In the USA it reached No 11 with a run of 31 weeks in the charts.

Jankowski received the Philips International Gold Record award in early 1966.

The contents of the disc are: **My Yiddishe Momma**, by Jack Yellen and Lew Pollack (1925); **Clair de lune**, by Debussy (1905), arr. Jankowski; **Eine Schwarzwaldfahrt** (A Walk in the Black Forest), by Horst Jankowski; **When the Girls Go Marching In**, by Jankowski and Rabe; *Donkey Serenade** (from *The Firefly*), by H. Sothart and Rudolf Friml (1937); **Sing-song**, by Lehn; **Serenata No 1**, by Enrico Toselli (1900), arr. Jankowski; **Simpel gimpel**, by Horst Jankowski; **Parles-moi d'amour**, by Bruce Sievier/Jean Lenoir (1930); **Caroline-Denise**, by Horst Jankowski; **Bald klopft das gluck auch mel an deine Tur** (Soon good luck will knock at your door), by Forell; **Nola**, by Felix Arndt (1915).

*Originally **Chanson — In Love**, by Rudolf Friml, a piano solo (1923).

CASEY JONES   *British*

DON'T HA HA *Golden Twelve* [*West Germany*]. Casey Jones was a Liverpool singer who followed the well-worn path to Germany in the early sixties. Unlike other Liverpool acts like the Beatles and the Searchers, he did not come back. He teamed up with Bristol group the Governors and made a successful career for himself in Germany. His **Don't Ha Ha** was No 1 in Germany for seven weeks, and was awarded a Gold Disc for million sales in that country alone. It was produced by Golden Twelve Record's A&R manager Reinhard Streit in Germany.

TOM JONES   *British*

IT'S NOT UNUSUAL *Decca F 12062* [*UK*] *Parrot 9737* [*USA*]. In a sense, Tom Jones was old-fashioned from the very start of his singing career. He was almost a throwback to the screen stars of the twenties, rather than one of the rock stars of the post-Beatles sixties. At a time of groups and folk rock, Tom Jones emerged as a solo male pop star. While the mainstream of pop followed the road of flower power, psychedelia and progressive rock, a group of ballad singers emerged during the mid- to late sixties who sold records by the warehouseful. Jim Reeves, Engelbert Humperdinck (who, like Jones, was managed by Gordon Mills) and comedian Ken Dodd (who had the biggest record of 1965 with **Tears**) were all examples of this, and Tom Jones was the most successful of them all.

He was born Thomas Jones Woodward on 7 June 1942 in Treforrest, Glamorgan, the son of a Welsh miner. He sang in his chapel choir, influenced by his father and uncle who also sang. Tom worked in several jobs, including a spell as a building labourer. He began playing drums in groups performing in South Wales men's clubs, and later formed his own group the Playboys. He recorded some material for Columbia, but nothing came of it. After appearing on the BBC TV show 'Donald Peers Presents', he got a contract from Decca. His first record for them, **Chills and Fever**, was released in August 1964 but was a failure.

The follow-up was **It's Not Unusual**, written by his manager Gordon Mills and songwriter-musical director Les Reed, and produced by Peter Sullivan. Released in January 1965, the record went to No 1 for one week in Britain, with 14 weeks in the charts. It was his first release in America, where Decca put the disc out on their Parrot label. It made No 10, with 12 weeks in the Hot 100. It won a Silver Disc in Britain, was a big hit in the English-speaking world, and achieved global sales of over a million. He then issued a highly successful EP **Tom Jones on Stage**, which went to No 3 in the EP charts, with a total of 28 weeks in the EP lists.

It was the start of a spectacular career for Tom Jones, especially in America where he ultimately went to live. For a while after **It's Not Unusual**, his records achieved only modest success, although **What's New Pussycat?** made No 3 in America. It was at this stage that EMI re-issued some of his old material. They released **Lonely Joe** on Columbia in Britain, which failed to chart, and **Little Lonely One** on Tower in America, which was a minor hit, reaching No 42. Then in November 1966 came his second No 1, **Green Green Grass Of Home**, and from then until 1970 almost all of his records made the Top 10. For a brief while he replaced Cliff Richard as Britain's favourite male singer, though by 1971

Cliff was again winning the annual popularity polls run by the music papers.

He enjoyed a long string of hits on Decca, with 25 from 1965 to 1974. He then switched labels, and had one more small hit on EMI in 1977. Although he never had a No 1 there, he did better in America where he enjoyed 29 hit singles, including three RIAA-certified million sellers. On the album front, he had 18 hit LPs in America. From 1967 to 1971, all 10 of his albums won RIAA Gold Discs for million dollar sales. Four of his LPs made the Top 10, though none went to No 1. In Britain he had nine hit albums from 1965 to 1969. One of them, **Delilah**, went to No 1 for two weeks in 1968.

From the early seventies the hits dried up but Tom Jones continued to be a major star in American cabaret, commanding huge fees in resorts like Las Vegas. His fine, powerful, Welsh voice and sexy stage act appealed more to mothers and grandmothers than to teenagers, but it enabled him to continue as a very successful entertainer after the pop star years had gone. He made a chart come-back at the end of 1988, when he teamed up with the Art Of Noise. Their disc **Kiss** peaked at No 5.

WHAT'S NEW PUSSYCAT? *Decca F 12203* [*UK*] *Parrot 9765* [*USA*]. **Once Upon a Time** was the follow-up to Tom Jones' No 1 debut hit, and disappointingly it reached only No 32 in Britain. **With These Hands** did better, reaching No 13, while his last release of 1965, **What's New Pussycat?**, made No 11 with 10 weeks in the charts. The theme song from the film of the same name, starring Peter Sellers, it was written by Hal David (words) and Burt Bacharach (music). Though a modest hit in Britain, it reached No 3 in America, with 12 weeks on the Hot 100. It eventually sold a global million, with high chart placings in Israel, New Zealand, Canada and South Africa.

BERT KAEMPFERT   German

RED ROSES FOR A BLUE LADY *US Decca 31722* [*USA*]. An outstanding revival of the 1948 song written by Sid Tepper and Roy Brodsky. Kaempfert's instrumental version was released in January 1965 and reached No 10 for two weeks in USA, subsequently selling a million. It was on the bestseller charts there for 14 weeks. It was also included in one of Kaempfert's bestselling albums **Blue Midnight**.

YUZO KAYAMA AND   Japanese
THE LAUNCHERS

KIMI TO ITSUMADEO (Forever With You or Love Forever) *Toshiba TP-10019* [*Japan*]. Yuzo Kayama, one of Japan's most brilliant film stars, is also well known as a composer under the name of Kosaku Dan. He made this record, his own composition (with lyrics by Tokiko Iwatani), with his band the Launchers in December 1965. It was No 1 in the Japanese charts for 16 weeks into 1966 and stayed in their charts for 24 weeks, and was reported to have sold over two million, the biggest selling disc

up to that time in the history of the Japanese recording industry.

It was released in the USA on Capitol under the title **Love Forever**, in July 1966.

Kayama and his group became Japan's top pop group as a result of this disc.

JONATHAN KING   British

EVERYONE'S GONE TO THE MOON *Decca F 12187* [*UK*] *Parrot 9774* [*USA*]. Jonathan King is one of the great personalities of the British music scene. He has made records, been a successful independent producer, owned his own record company, written a book and a regular newspaper column, hosted a successful television programme, and even stood for election to Parliament.

He was born Kenneth King in London on 6 December 1944, educated at Charterhouse, and read English at Trinity College, Cambridge.

His first venture into the record business was as a producer. He produced the Terry Ward single **Gotta Tell** which flopped, selling around 3,000 copies. He then teamed up with Ken Jones who produced **Everyone's Gone to the Moon**, which Jonathan wrote himself. This led to his TV debut on the BBC show 'Juke Box Jury' in July 1965.

The record went to No 3 with 11 weeks in the charts. At the end of September 1965 the record entered the American charts, where it peaked at No 17 during an 11-week chart run.

Jonathan King became one of the most successful independent producers in Britain. In 1972 he formed his own record company, UK Records, and created a number of hits for himself. As well as the nine hits under his own name on Decca, UK, GTO and Ariola, he scored under a number of other names. Bubblerock, 53rd and 3rd, Sakkarin, Shag, 100 Ton and A Feather, the Weathermen, Sound

9418, and Father Abraphart and the Smurps were all Jonathan King. He also produced the Hedgehoppers Anonymous 1965 Top 5 hit **It's Good News Week**.

In April 1978, King stood for Parliament in the Epsom and Ewell by-election. He intended it to be a stunt to publicize his latest record, but the stunt backfired. Under British election law, there has to be equality of radio and TV coverage to all candidates and, as none of the others had released a record, all that happened was that King's record was not played until the election was over! He issued a gold flexi disc as his election address, and fought a vigorous campaign, standing as a Monarchist candidate. He did very well for a 'joke' independent, polling 2,350 votes, 5.3% of the poll.

In the late eighties, King originated and hosted the highly successful 'Entertainment USA' television programme on BBC2. In this he showed British viewers a series of American cities, with clips of music, films, TV adverts and other snippets of American life.

THE KINKS   British

TIRED OF WAITING FOR YOU *Pye 7N 15759* [*UK*] *Reprise 347* [*USA*]. The Kinks' second million seller was also their second British No 1 single. Written by the group's Ray Davies and produced by Shel Talmy, it was their third hit in a row. It was No 1 for one week and in the charts for ten, winning a Silver Disc for British sales. In America it was the third of three Top 10 hits. Peaking at No 6, it gave them the highest American chart placing of their career. It was 11 weeks in the Hot 100. They had to wait another five years for their next and last entry into the US Top 10 with **Lola** in 1970. **Tired of Waiting for You** was a big international hit, with global sales passing the million mark.

BARBARA LEWIS   American

BABY, I'M YOURS *Atlantic 2283* [*USA*]. Barbara Lewis was born on 9 February 1945 in Detroit, where she grew up. She came from a family of musicians and, at the age of nine, wrote her first song. She later took some of her songs to Ollie McLaughlin who saw great possibilities in both her voice and her songs, and decided to record her.

She scored first with her own song **Hello Stranger**, a hit of 1963, and followed with her **Puppy Love**.

Baby, I'm Yours was written by Van McCoy in 1964 and Barbara's disc got to No 10 in the US charts with 14 weeks in the bestsellers, and an eventual million sale.

RAMSEY LEWIS TRIO   American

THE 'IN' CROWD *Argo-Cadet 5506* [*USA*]. Ramsey Lewis, born 27 May 1935 in Chicago, caught the fancy of the American record-buying public in a very big way with this disc. It got to No 5 in their charts with 16 weeks in the bestsellers, and sold over a million by the end of 1965.

The 'In' Crowd, written by Bill Page in 1964, was originally a success in early 1965 for singer Dobie Grey.

Ramsey Lewis began studying the piano at six. He graduated from school in 1948 after winning the American Legion Award as an outstanding scholar, and a special award for services as pianist at the Edward Jenner Elementary School plus a $150 scholarship. He began his musical career as piano accompanist for the choir at Chicago Zion Hill Missionary Baptist Church, and then went on to Chicago Musical College, aspiring to become a concert pianist. He married at 18 and left college, became a clerk in a record shop, and joined a seven-piece dance band, the Clefs. The rhythm section was bass player El Dee Young and drummer Isaac Holt with whom Ramsey formed a trio. They switched to jazz and played for 10 years together in some of the best-known jazz clubs in the USA.

In July, Ramsey heard a rock'n'roll version of The 'In' Crowd on a juke box and decided to put his version on the market. He insisted it should be recorded in a nightclub where he would have the infectious handclapping and enthusiastic 'Yeah Yeah' cries from the audience. This disc was originally released by Argo, the label being changed later to Cadet. Grammy Award for 'Best Instrumental Jazz Performances (Small Group)'.

HANG ON SLOOPY Cadet 5522 [USA]. Ramsey Lewis' version of the McCoys' big hit of this year was also a success, selling a reported million. The disc reached No 11 in the US charts with eight weeks in the bestsellers. The composition was by Bert Russell (Berns) and Wes Farrell in 1964.

THE McCOYS   American

HANG ON SLOOPY Bang 506 [USA] Immediate IM 001 [UK]. This song, written in 1964 by Bert Russell (Berns) and Wes Farrell, was also a hit in Canada with Little Caesar and the Consuls. It was No 1 in the USA for two weeks with 14 weeks in the bestsellers, and got to No 4 in Britain with 13 weeks in the charts. American sales alone were a million.

The McCoys first started as a duo, Rick Zehringer (then aged 17) and his brother Randy (aged 16), when they lived in Ohio. Later in Indiana, Dennis Kelly, a neighbour, made it a trio as bass guitarist. The brothers then met Ronnie Brandon (aged 18), a pianist

who learned the organ and joined the group. After Dennis left for college, Randy Hobbs (aged 17) joined them. On an engagement in Dayton, Ohio, they met the Strangeloves band who were greatly impressed with their performance, and brought the McCoys to New York to meet their producers at Bang Records. Within two days of their arrival they were signed to the label and cut their first disc Hang on Sloopy, a tremendous hit.

Ricky was lead vocalist and lead guitarist; his brother Randy was the drummer; Hobbs was bass guitarist and vocalist. Ronnie was also the comedian of the group in addition to his organ playing. Randy's other instruments were bass, piano and harmonica.

Recorded versions of Hang on Sloopy have sold an estimated 10 million copies globally. It was first recorded in 1964 by the Vibrations on Atlantic.

BARRY McGUIRE   American

EVE OF DESTRUCTION Dunhill 4009 [USA] RCA Victor 1469 [UK]. The year 1965 was notable for the popularity of protest songs and this, written by 19-year-old P.F. Sloan and Steve Barri as an anti-war song, was a tremendous hit in the USA where it sold over the million (nearly two million globally).

Barry McGuire, born 15 October 1935 in Oklahoma City, made his first public appearance as an amateur at the Frankenstein Coffee House, Laguna Beach, in 1960. His first professional appearance was at Ye Little Club, Beverly Hills, 1961, and his TV debut was in a 'Route 66' episode. He worked with another singer Barry Kane for a while as Barry and Barry and was then hired by Randy Sparks when Randy formed the New Christy Minstrels (1962). He became a lead singer with them and made a tour of Europe with the group, including Britain. Leaving the group in 1964 to become a solo singer, he met Lou Adler of Dunhill Records in June 1964 and told him about Sloan's song, and it was then recorded. Although the disc was banned by some US stations and by the BBC, it was aired by pirate radio stations. In the USA it was a chart topper for one week with 14 weeks in the bestsellers, and reached No 3 in Britain with 12 weeks in the charts.

THE MAMAS AND THE PAPAS   American

CALIFORNIA DREAMIN' Dunhill 4020 [USA] RCA Victor 1503 [UK]. The Mamas and the Papas epitomized the California image of the late sixties, and at the same time they had a strong following among other rock musicians. They were involved in the drug abuse and excesses endemic in the Californian rock world at the time.

John Phillips was the main force behind the Mamas and the Papas. He was born on Parris Island, South Carolina, on 30 August 1935. He later moved to New York and from 1957 performed in folk clubs in Greenwich Village, both solo and with the Journeymen. This folk group included Scott McKenzie, for whom Phillips later wrote the million-selling San

Francisco (Be Sure to Wear Some Flowers in Your Hair). He married Holly Michelle Gilliam in 1962. She was born in Long Beach, California on 6 April 1944, and had been a model before getting involved in the music business. They teamed up with two folk singers they had met in New York. Both Cass Elliot (born Ellen Naomi Cohen in Baltimore, Maryland, on 19 September 1943) and Canadian Denny (Dennis) Doherty (born in Halifax, Nova Scotia, Canada, on 29 November 1941) had been members of the Mugwumps. The four came together after a holiday in the US Virgin Islands. Moving to Los Angeles, they met up with Barry McGuire (singer of Eve of Destruction) and he introduced them to his producer Lou Adler, who signed them to Dunhill. When they were asked what their name was, they said that they had jokingly been calling each other Mamas and Papas, so they took that name as their own. Released in December 1965, California Dreamin' entered the US charts on 8 January 1966, where it stayed for 17 weeks (the longest chart duration of their career) and went to No 4. It won an RIAA Gold Disc for US sales of over a million on 10 June 1966. In Britain the record reached No 23 during nine weeks in the charts. The song was written by John Phillips, and the record was produced by Lou Adler.

1966 was the biggest year of the group's career. Behind the scenes, relationships within the group were frequently not good and the Phillips' marriage was disintegrating. (The couple later divorced.) In 1968 the group split up, with Cass Elliot following a solo career. On 29 July 1974 she performed a highly successful show at the London Palladium. In the evening, while eating a sandwich in bed, she suffered a massive heart attack and died.

In 1971 John Phillips briefly re-formed the Mamas and the Papas, though with a different line-up. In place of his wife he brought in his daughter Mackenzie Phillips, with Elaine McFarlane (Spankey of Spankey And Our Gang) taking over from Cass Elliot. The People Like Us album of 1972 was a disaster, both critically and commercially, and the group soon split up again.

This failure should not detract from the achievements of the original group in 1966 and 1967. The carefree, happy image of the beautiful Michelle balanced by the overweight Cass, articulate Michael and the tanned Canadian Denny was largely hype, but there was something of value. Behind the beautiful harmonies lay the outstanding songwriting ability of John Phillips. The group had a sound that influenced many American bands of the early seventies, to say nothing of all the two-boys-two-girls groups like Abba and Bucks Fizz which followed in Europe.

With Cass Elliot dead and John Phillips' considerable talent going to waste through drug abuse, it was only Michelle Phillips who survived, turning her talent to a career as an actress with some success in the late seventies and eighties. Her daughter Chynna teamed up with Beach Boy Brian Wilson's daughters Carnie and Wendy as Wilson Phillips, who in 1990 had a US No 1 hit with their debut disc Hold On.

AL MARTINO   *American*

SPANISH EYES *Capitol 5542 [USA] Capitol CL 15430 [UK]*. Although Al Martino had his second million seller at the height of the Beatles pop era, he really belongs to the pre-rock period of the early fifties.

He was born Alfred Cini in South Philadelphia on 7 October 1927. As a first-generation Italian American, he was brought up very much in the environment of the Caruso style of Italian opera, and was a boyhood friend of Mario Lanza. His big break came in 1952 when he recorded **Here in My Heart**. His main claim to fame is that this record was the first No 1 in the history of the British charts. On 14 November 1952 the *New Musical Express* (which had only just taken over from the defunct *Musical Express*) published the first British chart. It was a Top 10, but consisted of 12 records as there were two records tying for two places. Martino stayed at No 1 for the rest of 1952, his nine weeks at the top taking him into January 1953. As it also went to No 1 for three weeks in America, it became the first record to top the charts on both sides of the Atlantic.

Martino enjoyed a long string of hits right the way through to the late seventies. **Spanish Eyes** was originally recorded by the German conductor Bert Kaempfert, who was also the A&R man for the German Polydor label, which first recorded the Beatles. His **Moon Over Naples** was an instrumental on his **Magic Music of Faraway Places** Polydor album, and was also successful when released as a single. Charles Singleton and Eddy Snyder wrote lyrics to the tune and gave it the new title of **Spanish Eyes**. It reached No 11 for two weeks in the *Cash Box* charts, though only No 15 in *Billboard*. It was 12 weeks in both American charts. An album of the same name, released at the beginning of 1966, won an RIAA Gold Disc for million dollar sales on 30 December 1966.

In Britain it was to be five years before **Spanish Eyes** made the charts. In 1970 it was No 49 for one week. Three years later EMI re-released the Capitol record, and this time it took off. It peaked at No 5, his highest UK chart placing since **Wanted** made No 4 in 1954. This re-release had a lengthy chart run of 21 weeks. Eventually the record sold about one and a half million copies, of which 800,000 were achieved by EMI's German subsidiary Electrola.

ROGER MILLER   *American*

KING OF THE ROAD *Smash 1965 [USA] Philips BF 1397 [UK]*. Roger Miller was a successful country singer, and wrote this C&W song himself in 1964. The record showed considerable cross-over potential, for as well as being a big country hit, it also made No 3 in the American pop charts, with 13 weeks in the Hot 100. It was No 1 for five weeks with 20 weeks in the US country charts.

In Britain it was Miller's first hit. Though country music was not particularly popular in Britain then, the record went to No 1 for one week, with 15 weeks in the charts. It sold 550,000 copies within 18 days of release in America, with sales ultimately reaching the two million mark. It won an RIAA Gold Disc for American sales of one million on 19 May 1965. Miller also won a Gold Disc for million dollar sales of his album **The Return of Roger Miller** the same year.

This was Miller's third million-selling record, and did particularly well in the 1965 Grammy Awards. Apart from winning the 'Best C&W Recording', 'Best C&W Song' and 'Best C&W Performance' awards, it also won in the 'Best Rock'n'Roll Recording' and 'Best Rock'n'Roll (Male) Performance' categories. (This just showed how ludicrous the Grammys could get. **King of the Road** may have been a nice song and was a highly successful record, but by no stretch of the imagination could it be called rock'n'roll.)

THE MIRACLES   *American*

TRACKS OF MY TEARS *Tamla 54118 [USA] Tamla Motown TMG 696 [UK]*. Though not their biggest chart hit, **Tracks of My Tears** has proved one of the most enduring of the Miracles' records. In the 1988 *Rolling Stone* magazine critics' poll, it came 12th in the list of the 100 best records of the previous quarter century.

The song was written by three members of the Miracles, William 'Smokey' Robinson, Warren Moore and Marvin Taplin. The record was produced by lead singer Smokey Robinson. Though it only reached No 16 in the Hot 100, it sold steadily long after its 12 weeks in the charts were over. It made No 2 in the R&B charts with an 18-week chart life. When the record was first released in Britain in July 1965, it failed to chart. It was only when EMI re-released it in 1969 that it took off, giving Smokey Robinson and the Miracles (as the group were billed in Britain) their first Top 10 hit. It reached No 9 with 13 weeks in the charts. Their next British hit, **Tears of a Clown**, gave them their only British No 1 in 1970 and charted again in 1976. **Tracks of My Tears** was the Miracles' fourth million seller, with global sales eventually passing the million mark.

Smokey Robinson's wife Claudette, who took Warren Moore's place when he was called up for 21 months' service with the US Forces, left the group in December 1964 to devote her time to youth clubs and the Church. The group then consisted of Smokey Robinson, Bobby Rogers, Ronnie White and Warren Moore. Lead guitarist Marv Taplin and drummer Donald White completed the personnel.

GOING TO A GO-GO *Tamla 54127 [USA] Tamla Motown TMG 547 [UK]*. **My Girl Has Gone** was the American follow-up to **Tracks of My Tears**, and reached No 14. The next US release was **Going to a Go-Go**, issued in December 1965. This went to No 11, with 12 weeks on the Hot 100. In the R&B charts it made No 2 for two weeks during a 15-week chart run while the flip side **Choosy Beggar** had two weeks in the R&B charts, reaching No 35. It was written by group members Smokey Robinson, Warren Moore, Robert Rogers and Marv Taplin, and produced by Smokey Robinson.

Though the Miracles paid their first visit to Britain in November 1964, it was only when EMI released **Going to a Go-Go** in February 1966 that the group had their first British hit. Their initial success was modest, the record reaching No 44, with five weeks in the Top 50. It eventually sold a global million, their fifth to sell the million, with most sales coming from the USA.

YUKIKO NINOMIYA   *Japanese*

MATSUNOKI KOUTA *King 4908 [Japan]*. This disc was issued in Japan in January 1965 and sold a million by April. The song is a type of Ozashiki melody. The disc was No 1 for 10 weeks in Japan from 3 April to 5 June 1965. The composer is unknown, so under Japanese law a certain sum in royalties has to be paid into the Bureau of Justice until the composer is established.

PETER AND GORDON   *British*

TRUE LOVE WAYS *Columbia (EMI) DB 7524 [UK] Capitol 5406 [USA]*. Another big hit for this very popular duo made it their third million seller from combined British and American sales. The disc was No 2 in Britain with 15 weeks in the bestsellers, and No 14 in the USA with 11 weeks in the bestsellers. The song is an oldie of 1958 written by Norman Petty and Buddy Holly.

WILSON PICKETT   *American*

IN THE MIDNIGHT HOUR *Atlantic 2289 [USA] Atlantic AT 4036 [UK]*. Wilson Pickett was born in Prattville, Alabama, on 18 March 1941, his family moving to Detroit when Wilson was in his teens. For four years he was a spiritual singer and performed with groups

and as a soloist in and around Detroit. In 1959 he became a singer with the Falcons, a top group in the area, where he became aware for the first time of the rhythm-and-blues music that was to have a profound effect on his future. He found he had a talent for song-writing and composed many songs for the group including their first hit **I Found a Love**. His solo career was sparked off by an audition in 1963 for artist Lloyd Price's label Double L, and his first self-written solo **If You Need Me** became a hit and eventually a rhythm-and-blues standard. His second self-written song **It's Too Late** was also a hit for Double L.

In 1964, Pickett signed with Atlantic Records and continued his string of hits on his new label, including his own compositions **For Better or Worse**, **I'm Gonna Cry**, **In the Midnight Hour** and **Mustang Sally**.

Wilson Pickett appeared in Britain for the first time in November 1965 to promote **In the Midnight Hour** and other songs.

This disc was No 19 for two weeks in the USA with 21 weeks in the bestsellers, and reached No 12 for a week in Britain with 11 weeks in the bestsellers. The song was written by Wilson Pickett and Steve Cropper and first released in the USA in July 1965. The disc sold over the million globally.

GENE PITNEY   *American*

LOOKING THROUGH THE EYES OF LOVE *Musicor 1103* [*USA*] *Stateside SS 420* [*UK*]. Gene Pitney's fifth million seller was written by the husband and wife team of Barry Mann and Cynthia Weill. It was a moderate hit in America, reaching No 23 with seven weeks in *Cash Box* and No 28 with eight weeks in *Billboard*. It was a much bigger hit in Europe. In Britain it reached No 3 during 12 weeks in the Top 50. Global sales took the record past the million mark.

ELVIS PRESLEY   *American*

CRYING IN THE CHAPEL *RCA Victor 47-0643* [*USA*] *RCA Victor 1455* [*UK*]. The mid- to late sixties were not a good time for Elvis Presley. The Beatles had changed for ever the music world he had dominated for so long. His lengthy string of No 1s petered out in 1962, and the big hits stopped coming the year after. Presley was losing interest in making records, and RCA found it increasingly difficult to get him into the studio. From 1964 to 1967, almost every Presley hit was either from a film soundtrack or, like **Crying in the Chapel**, an old recording from the vaults. It was recorded on 31 October 1960 for an album, though in the end the track was not included on the LP. It was his thirty-ninth million seller.

The song was written by Artie Glenn in 1953, when it was a million-selling hit for the Orioles. **Crying in the Chapel** made No 3 in the American charts, being Presley's only Top 10 hit from **Bossa Nova Baby** in 1963 to **In the Ghetto** in 1969. It spent 14 weeks in the Hot 100, his longest run since **Return to Sender** in 1962. The situation was slightly better in Britain, where the record went to No 1 for two

weeks in the June 1965, with 15 weeks in the Top 50. As in America, most of Presley's records from 1963 to his revival in 1969 were minor hits in Britain, though **Kissin' Cousins** (1964) and **Love Letters** (1966) both made the Top 10. **Crying in the Chapel** won a Silver Disc for British sales of a quarter of a million, which when added to American and other sales gave Elvis another global million seller. It was produced by Steve Sholes.

On the album front, Elvis put three LPs in the US Top 10 in 1965. The **Girl Happy** film soundtrack reached No 8. **Elvis for Everyone!** was a compilation of recordings from 1957 to 1964 which made No 10. The **Harum Scarum** soundtrack made No 8, and was the last in his long run of Top 10 LPs. There were to be four more isolated Top 10 entries in the years ahead, and many more Gold Discs for million dollar sales, but, as with the singles charts, the years of Presley as a major force were rapidly fading. In Britain the **Roustabout** soundtrack charted in January 1965, making No 12. **Girl Happy** was his biggest hit of the year, making No 8 with 18 weeks in the LP charts. **Flaming Star and Summer Kisses** (not released in the USA) made No 11, and **Elvis for Everyone** made No 8. **Harem Holiday** was not released in Britain until January 1966. On the EP charts, two records from the *Tickle Me* film were hits.

1965 was still a good year for the King of Rock'n'Roll, even if it was not quite as good as previous years. In their end-of-year surveys, *Billboard* ranked Elvis seventh singles artist of 1965 and 17th LP artist, and **Crying in the Chapel** ninth top single of the Year. On the international charts, *Billboard* ranked Elvis the fourth most popular artist in the world (and No 1 in the Philippines.) But the British were now masters of the pop world. The top three were all from the UK — the Beatles, the Rolling Stones and Cliff Richard.

CLIFF RICHARD   *British*

THE MINUTE YOU'RE GONE *Columbia (EMI) DB 7496* [*UK*] *Epic 9757* [*USA*]. Alone of the British pre-Beatles stars, Cliff Richard (and, to a lesser extent, his backing group the Shadows) had survived the pop revolution of the mid-sixties. By 1965 Cliff was still in a very strong position. At the end of the year, *Billboard* ranked him as the third most popular recording artist in the world, and No 1 in a number of countries. The *NME* ranked him as sixth in their end-of-year chart survey, with four hit singles during 1965. Cliff was again voted 'Top British Male Singer' in the music press popularity polls, a position he had won every year since 1959.

His biggest hit of the years was **The Minute You're Gone**, which gave him his first British No 1 since **Summer Holiday** in 1963. It was his ninth No 1 single, topping the charts for one week in April 1965. It spent 14 weeks in the Top 50. It was also one of Cliff's few American hits, though only just. It spent one week at No 98 in *Cash Box*, and did not make the *Billboard* Hot 100 at all. It was a very big hit in the rest of the world, going to No 1 in India (first week of release), Malaysia and Singapore. It made the Top 10 in Australia, New Zealand, South

Africa, Ireland, Norway, Denmark, Austria, The Netherlands, Hong Kong, Lebanon and Israel, and the Top 20 in Sweden. In South Africa and Malaysia it was a double A side, with the flip side **Just Another Guy** (composed by Neil Diamond) also making the charts independently of the A side. It won a Silver Disc in Britain, and sold one and a quarter million copies around the world.

The Minute You're Gone was written by Jimmy Gateley, and produced by Billy Sherrill and Bob Morgan in Nashville, USA, in the summer of 1964. It had originally been a hit in 1963 for American country singer Sonney James. Cliff recorded this and other material in America, at sessions in Nashville and New York organized by his American record company CBS, who licensed his records for the USA alone from EMI. As the records would be owned by EMI, the British company had to pay the recording costs. EMI thought them astronomical compared to recording costs in London but, as they got two million-selling records out of the Nashville session, they presumably thought the investment worth-while. Most of the material recorded in America ended up on the **Cliff Richard** album, which made No 9 in the LP charts. His two other 1965 hit albums were the pantomime soundtrack **Aladdin** and **More Hits by Cliff**. On the EP charts, he had three hits. The biggest was **Take Four**, which peaked at No 4 during 16 weeks in the EP lists. The other two were **Look In My Eyes Maria** and an EP from the pantomime **Aladdin**.

The Minute You're Gone marked one first and one last. It was Cliff's first No 1 without the Shadows. It was also the last in an incredible run of 26 Top 10 hits in a row. Of his then 29 singles, only one had failed to make the Top 10, when **Livin' Lovin' Doll** peaked at No 17 in 1959. No other artist before or since has ever achieved such a run.

The follow-up that broke this long trend was **On My Word**, which peaked at No 12. It started something of a trend of its own, for the follow-up to each of Cliff's subsequent No 1s was also a relative disappointment. **I'll Love You Forever Today** (which followed **Congratulations** in 1968) made No 27, **Hot Shot** (following **We Don't Talk Anymore** in 1979) peaked at No 46, and **Born to Rock and Roll** (following the remake of **Living Doll** in 1986) peaked, if that is the right word for such a low position, at No 78. This jinx was only broken when **The Best of Me**, the follow-up to Cliff's 1988 Christmas No 1 **Mistletoe and Wine**, entered the charts at No 2 first week of release.

WIND ME UP (LET ME GO) *Columbia (EMI) DB 7745* [*UK*]. Cliff Richard's second million seller of 1965 was his fourth and final release of the year. The Talley-Montgomery composition was another ballad, described as a country waltz. It was recorded during Cliff's sessions in Nashville at the same time as **The Minute You're Gone**, and was produced by Billy Sherrill and Bob Morgan. Though released in America on the Epic label, it failed to chart there. In Britain it reached No 2, with 16 weeks in the charts. This was his longest chart run since **Summer Holiday** in 1963, and has not been equalled. It was another big international hit for Cliff, going to No 1 in South Africa, India and Malaysia, and making the Top 10 in New Zealand, Ireland, Germany, The Netherlands, Singapore and Hong Kong. **Wind Me Up** won a Silver Disc in Britain, with global sales of 1,200,000.

THE ROLLING STONES   *British*

THE LAST TIME *Decca F 12104* [*UK*] *London 9741* [*USA*]. If 1964 was the year the Beatles took the world by storm, in 1965 it was the turn of the Rolling Stones. By the end of the year they had achieved six more million-selling records, including two albums, and were firmly placed as the No 2 rock act in the world.

The Last Time was the third Stones record to sell a million. It was the first singles release from the group written by their songwriting team of Mick Jagger and Keith Richard, and was produced in London by their manager, Andrew Loog Oldham. It was their third No 1 in a row in Britain, with three weeks at No 1 and 13 weeks in the charts. In America, London Records (the US subsidiary of British Decca) released **Heart of Stone** as the follow-up to **Time is on My Side**, which they had put out in 1964 after **It's All Over Now** in preference to the British release, **Little Red Rooster**. **Heart of Stone** made No 19 in the US Hot 100, and **The Last Time** gave them their second Top 10 hit, peaking at No 9 with 10 weeks on the charts. The B side also charted, reaching No 96 for just one week. This was **Play with Fire** which, like the A side, was produced by Oldham and written by Jagger and Richard, using the pseudonyms of Nanker and Phelge.

The record won a British Silver Disc. It was also the Stones' first really big international hit. It was No 1 in Australia, Ireland, Finland and Hong Kong, and a hit in Canada, New Zealand, Sweden, Norway, Denmark, Germany Switzerland, Belgium, The Netherlands, France, Lebanon, Malaysia, Singapore and Ireland. Global sales were well over the million.

(I CAN'T GET NO) SATISFACTION *Decca F 12220* [*UK*] *London 9766* [*USA*]. The Rolling Stones have been making great hit records for a quarter of a century, and the greatest of them all is **Satisfaction**. In its 1988 critics poll of the 100 best singles of the last 25 years, *Rolling Stone* magazine put **Safisfaction** at the top of the list, describing it as 'the rock'n'roll equivalent of the opening notes of Beethoven's Fifth'. In the same article, Keith Richards outlined the song's influence on subsequent Stones material: He said 'I hear **Satisfaction** in **Jumping Jack Flash**. I hear it in half the songs that the Stones have done. I'm almost to the point now, after writing songs for so many years, that there is only one song — it's just the variations you come up with.'

Keith Richards and Mick Jagger wrote **Satisfaction** during the group's spring 1965 tour of the States. Produced by Andrew Oldham, it was recorded at the Chess studios in Chicago and the RCA studios in Los Angeles. It was their first American No 1, and their first American RIAA-certificated million seller.

It was the biggest hit of the group's career up to that time. It was their fourth No 1 in a row in Britain, where it topped the charts for two weeks during a 12-week chart run. It won a Silver Disc for British sales. In America it was No 1 for four weeks, with 14 weeks on the Hot 100. The RIAA certified the record Gold on 19 July 1965, signifying the million sale just over a month after its release. **Satisfaction** was the Stones' biggest-ever international hit. It went to No 1 in Britian, the USA, Canada, Australia, Ireland, Finland, Sweden, Norway, Denmark, Austria, The Netherlands and Malaysia. It was a Top 10 hit in New Zealand, South Africa, Germany, Belgium, France, Singapore, Hong Kong, the Philippines, Mexico, Bermuda and Peru, and a Top 30 hit in Brazil. Global sales were over five million. In 1990 Allan Klein, whose Abcko Records owned the Stones' sixties catalogue, negotiated a record one and three quarter million-dollar fee from a sweet manufacturer for the right to use **Satisfaction** in a TV advertisement.

GET OFF OF MY CLOUD *Decca F 12263* [*UK*] *London 9792* [*USA*]. Released in Britain on 22 October 1965, **Get Off of My Cloud** was the Stones' fifth No 1 in a row, on top for three weeks and in the charts for 12. It won a Silver Disc for British sales. It was their second No 1 in a row in America, where it stayed at the top for two weeks and on the charts for 12. It was written by Keith Richards and Mick Jagger, and produced by Andrew Oldham while the group were in Hollywood, California. It was a big hit in at least a dozen countries, and sold well over a million around the world.

AS TEARS GO BY *London 9808* [*USA*]. Written by Mick Jagger, Keith Richards and Andrew Oldham, **As Tears Go By** was issued by London Records in America just in time for Christmas 1965. The record reached No 6, with nine weeks on the charts. It was not released as a single in Britain, where Mick Jagger's then-girlfriend Marianne Faithfull launched her career with it. Decca did issue the song as a Rolling Stones single in some other countries, and global sales finally gave the Stones their sixth million-selling record. It was produced by Andrew Oldham.

OUT OF OUR HEADS (Album) *Decca LK 4733* [*UK*] [*British version*] *London 429* [*USA*] *Decca LKD 5336* [*UK*] [*American version*]. The Rolling Stones issued their first album, called **The Rolling Stones**, in April 1964. Its 51 weeks in the British album charts was their longest stretch ever, with 12 weeks at No 1. Issued in January 1965, the follow-up **Rolling Stones No 2** also went to No 1, for 10 weeks. On 24 September 1965 Decca issued **Out of Our Heads**, which reached No 2 during 24 weeks in the album charts.

As with the Beatles, album titles, content and artwork of early Rolling Stones LPs differed on either side of the Atlantic. Decca's London Records subsidiary released **England's Newest Hit Makers/The Rolling Stones** as their American debut album in June 1964. It reached No 11 and spent 35 weeks in the US album charts. While it had much in common with the British **Rolling Stones** LP, it also included the hit single **Not Fade Away**. (It was still the custom in Britain for albums not to

contain hit singles released at the same time. As singles were more of a marketing tool for albums in America, American record companies could see little point in following the British practice.) The Stones' second American album was **12 × 5**, issued in November 1964. Much of the content matched their second British album, though the American version included **It's All Over Now**. This made No 3, and was the first of 26 Top 10 albums in a row, the line being broken by the 1981 hits package **Sucking in the Seventies**, which peaked at No 15. (However, the following studio album, **Tattoo You**, went to No 1 for nine weeks.)

Out of Our Heads was their third American release, in July 1965, and went to No 1 for three weeks. It spent over a year on the charts, with 65 weeks of chart activity in total. The album was produced by Andrew Oldham for Impact Sound. The engineers were Dave Hassinger, Ron Malo and Glyn Johns. The cover photo on the album was shot by David Bailey. The tracks for the album were recorded in Hollywood (at the RCA studios) and Chicago (at Chess), and for the American version one track was recorded in London.

While the title of the third Stones album was the same on both sides of the Atlantic, the content was not. Many years later the American version was digitally re-mastered and released in Britain and Europe. It is this American version that sold a million copies. The RIAA awarded a Gold Disc for American sales of a million dollars on 12 October 1965. (The RIAA did not certificate sales of a million copies for albums in the sixties.)

The contents of the US album are (Nanker and Phelge are pseudonyms for Jagger and Richard): *Mercy, Mercy, by Don Covay and Ronnie Miller (1964); *Hitch Hike, by Marvin Gaye, William Stevenson and Paul (1965); **The Last Time**, by Mick Jagger and Keith Richard (1965); *That's How Strong My Love Is, by Jamison (1965); *Good Times, by Sam Cooke (1964); **I'm All Right**, by Nanker and Phelge (1965); **Satisfaction**, by Mick Jagger and Keith Richard (1965); *Cry to Me, by Bert Russell (1961); *The Under Assistant West Coast Promotion Man, by Nanker and Phelge (1965); **Play with Fire**, by Nanker and Phelge (1965); **The Spider and the Fly**, by Nanker and Phelge (1965); **One More Try**, by Mick Jagger and Keith Richard (1965).

The British album contained the following extra to the six titles marked * above: **She Said 'Yeah'**, by Jackson and Christy (1965); **Gotta Get Away**, by Mick Jagger and Keith Richard (1965); **Talkin' 'Bout You**, by Chuck Berry (1961); **Oh Baby (We Got a Good Thing Tonight)**, by Ozen (1965); **Heart of Stone**, by Mick Jagger and Keith Richard (1965); **I'm Free**, by Mick Jagger and Keith Richard (1965).

Three other musicians, Jack Nitzsche (the group's road manager in the USA), Ian Stewart and J.W. Alexander, assisted in organ, piano and percussion work.

DECEMBER'S CHILDREN (AND EVERY-BODY'S) (Album) *London 451* [USA]. **December's Children** was released in America just in time for the peak Christmas sales period in December 1965. It reached No 2 in the *Cash Box* album charts and No 4 in *Billboard*, with 33 weeks in the LP charts. The RIAA awarded a Gold Disc for million dollar sales a month after release, on 15 January 1966. The record was also a big hit in Canada, though it was not released in Britain.

The album was a collection of tracks taken mainly from previous British albums, which had not been released on their American equivalents. The album also included the Jagger-Richard composition **Blue Turns to Grey** which, though not released in Britain, was a hit single for Cliff Richard.

The contents of the album are: **She Said 'Yeah'**, by Jackson and Christy (1965); **Talkin' 'Bout You**, by Chuck Berry (1961); **You Better Move On**, by Arthur Alexander; **Look What You've Done**, by Margonfield (1965); **Get Off My Cloud**, by Mick Jagger and Keith Richard (1965); **The Singer not the Song**, by Green (1965); **Route 66**, by Bob Troup (1965); **As Tears Go By**, by Mick Jagger, Keith Richard and Andrew Oldham (1964); **I'm Free**, by Mick Jagger and Keith Richard (1965); **Gotta Get Away**, by Mick Jagger and Keith Richard (1965); **Blue Turns to Grey**, by Mick Jagger and Keith Richard (1965); **I'm Movin' On**, by Hank Snow (1950).

NINI ROSSO — Italian

IL SILENZIO (The Silence) *Durium DRS 54000* [UK]. This disc became a big hit all over Europe, No 1 in Italy (for six weeks), West Germany (five weeks), Austria, Holland, Belgium and Switzerland. It sold over 750,000 in Italy and two million in Germany. Global sales were estimated at five million by end of 1967. The tune, written by Nini Rosso and Guglielmo Brezza, is a trumpet solo — a variation of **The Last Post**.

Nini (real name Celeste Rosso) was born in Turin on 19 September 1926 and ran away from home at the age of 19 to follow a musical career instead of an academic one — against his parents' wishes. He was found playing a trumpet in a Nice nightclub by the police and sent back to his family. They allowed him to continue playing, and he formed a small orchestra, touring all over Italy, the rest of Europe and India. On their return he was engaged by Radio Turin, later going to Rome where he soon became known as one of Italy's best jazz players. His first disc was **La ballata della tromba**, an instant hit. Then came **Concerto disperato**, another of his compositions (1963) that became the theme of Stewart Granger's film *The Legion's Last Patrol*, a hit in Italy and other countries including Japan.

Il silenzio was also a success in Britain, reaching No 8 with 14 weeks in the bestsellers; it was additionally recorded there by Eddie Calvert, and in the USA by Al Hirt.

MITCH RYDER AND THE DETROIT WHEELS — American

JENNY TAKE A RIDE *New Voice 806* [USA] *Stateside SS 481* [UK]. The first recording for this group took their disc to No 10 in the US charts within as many weeks from date of release in December 1965 with 12 weeks in the bestsellers, and was reported to have sold the million. It was No 33 in Britain, and five weeks in the Top 50.

The group was first called Billy Lee and the (Detroit) Rivieras, the name being changed to Mitch Ryder and the Detroit Wheels by their manager Alan Stroh. Mitch Ryder formerly sang with rhythm-and-blues groups in the Detroit area. When the Dave Clark Five appeared in Detroit in 1965, the group appeared on the same bill under their original name. They were scheduled to sing only two numbers, but were on stage for almost an hour and a half. Famous producer Bob Crewe, notified by WXYZ Detroit's disc jockey Dave Prince, was in the audience and immediately signed them. Under his guidance, this disc resulted plus five consecutive top records, and personal appearances through the USA.

Besides Mitch Ryder, the group consisted of 'Little' John Badenjek (drums), Jimmy McCartney (lead guitarist), Earl Eliot (bass guitarist) and Joe Cubert (rhythm guitarist).

The composition is by E. Johnson and R. Penniman (the real name of Little Richard).

SAM THE SHAM AND THE PHARAOHS — American

WOOLY BULLY *Initially Penn label, then MGM 13322* [USA] *MGM 1269* [UK]. Sam the Sham (real name Domingo Samudio) was born and raised in Dallas, Texas. After graduation he joined the US Navy for four years. He then worked on building sites and saved enough money for the entrance fee to Arlington State College in Texas, and began singing with various groups. Moving to Louisiana, he joined a friend's band which became popular in many clubs in and around Memphis until its leader returned home. Sam and the bass player David Martin stayed on, added guitarist Ray Stinnet and drummer Jerry Paterson, and later saxophonist Butch Gibson, adopting the name Sam the Sham and the Pharaohs. Stan Kessler, a producer for Penn Records, invited them to the studios for an audition. They arrived in their black hearse which they used for transportation.

Their first disc was **Haunted House** in May 1964. Then came **Wooly Bully**, written by Sam in 1964 — a thudding beat number with a tongue-twisting chorus and nonsense lyrics, which when released on MGM label became a big hit, reaching No 2 in the US charts in June 1965 with 18 weeks in the bestsellers, and an eventual two million sale with another million abroad. It was No 11 in Britain with 15 weeks in the bestsellers.

Sam explains the term 'sham' as rhythm-and-blues jargon for shuffling, twisting or jiving around to music. Before he started playing the organ, Sam 'shammed' while he sang.

Gold Disc award RIAA 1965.

THE SEEKERS — Australian

I'LL NEVER FIND ANOTHER YOU *Columbia (EMI) DB 7431* [UK] *Capitol 5383* [USA]. This first big hit for the Australian group was a million seller for the Seekers in their very first recording in Britain. Over 700,000 copies in Britain plus big sales from the USA and elsewhere totalled 1,750,000.

The quartet was one girl and three boys: Judith Durham, born in Melbourne on 3 July 1943, who also plays the piano, guitar, the harmonica, castanets and tambourine; Bruce Woodley, born in Melbourne, 25 July 1942, plays Spanish guitar and five-string banjo; Keith Potger, born in Columbo, Ceylon, 2 May 1941, plays guitar, banjo and recorder; and Athol Guy, born in Victoria, Australia, 5 January 1940, double bass and zimbuka. Keith's family moved to Australia when he was six. The quartet met in 1964 in Australia and was started purely as a hobby after their day jobs (Bruce and Athol worked for an advertising agency in Melbourne, Judith was a pathologist's secretary, and Keith a radio producer). They appeared on local TV shows around Melbourne, and becoming very popular decided to give up their jobs and try their luck in Britain. After some work on board ships, one of the trips finished in Britain. Within three weeks of arriving in London they made their first TV appearance on 'Sunday Night at the Palladium'. They then made their first disc in Britain, **I'll Never Find Another You** which was No 1 for two weeks and 23 weeks in the bestsellers. In the USA the disc was No 4 and 13 weeks in the bestsellers. This song was written in 1964 by Tom Springfield (of the Springfields).

The Seekers were unusual in that their style was more folk song than electronic, and they were the first Australian group to become successful abroad. They held the Australian record for crowds, drawing 200,000 at Melbourne's Myer Music Bowl in 1967.

A WORLD OF OUR OWN *Columbia (EMI) DB 7532 [UK] Capitol 5430 [USA].* The second million seller for the Seekers, the song was again by Tom Springfield. The disc was No 2 in Britain with 18 weeks in the bestsellers and duplicated the success of their first disc, with big sales in Britain (half a million or more), the USA, and elsewhere around the world, making well over the magic seven figures. In the US charts it was No 19 for two weeks with a 10-week in chart run.

THE CARNIVAL IS OVER *Columbia (EMI) DB 7711 [UK].* Issued in October 1965, this disc soon achieved the No 1 spot in Britain for three weeks with 17 weeks in the charts and sold a million by the year's end. An 'end of a romance' song, it was Tom Springfield's third consecutive big hit for the group. The composer adapted the melody from an old Russian folk song **Stenjka razin**, but half the tune is his own composition and the lyric entirely his own work. A million sale was achieved in Britain alone.

SIMON AND GARFUNKEL · *American*

THE SOUND OF SILENCE *CBS-Columbia 43396 [USA].* The influence of folk music on rock was an important trend in 1965. It saw the emergence of Simon and Garfunkel, and the Byrds, and the breakthrough of Bob Dylan to mass appeal after his change of style from folk to folk-rock. All this was very important to CBS Records, as these three acts were all on their Columbia label in America (though on CBS outside America, where the Columbia label is owned by EMI). CBS had been one of the major US record companies all along, but it had an image of establishment stuffiness in the fifties and early sixties that the company was keen to shake off. It had never got into rock'n'roll in the fifties, and had missed out on the British groups of the sixties. In *Billboard's* survey of best-selling records of 1963, CBS had only two in the Top 30. If CBS were to compete and grow successfully, they had to position themselves more in the mainstream of pop and rock, and by 1965 they had gone a long way to doing this.

CBS were hungry for new, contemporary pop signings when Paul Simon, who worked for a music publisher, offered some of his own songs to CBS producer Tom Wilson in 1964. Wilson liked what he heard and signed Simon

and Art Garfunkel up. The duo had known each other since their school days, and started singing together when they were 13. Performing together as Tom (Graph) and Jerry (Landis), they had a minor hit in 1957 with their own composition **Hey Schoolgirl**, which reached No 49 on the Big label. Two follow-ups failed, so the duo split up and went back to college. Paul Simon (born in Newark, New Jersey, on 13 October, 1941) studied music at New York University and English at Queen's College. After six unhappy months at law school, he fled to London. Art Garfunkel (born in New York City on 5 November, 1942) studied mathematics and education at Columbia University. Both continued to make the odd record. Paul Simon achieved minor chart success as Tico of Tico and the Triumphs (**Motorcycle** reached No 99 for one week, on Amy in 1962), and as Jerry Landis (**The Lone Teen Ranger** reached No 97 with three weeks on the chart, on Amy in January 1963).

At university, both Simon and Garfunkel were influenced by the folk boom. Once they left they continued to sing folk songs together in the coffee houses of Greenwich Village. Their first album for CBS, **Wednesday Morning, 3 a.m.,** was a combination of Bob Dylan folk songs, protest songs and Paul Simon originals. Released in November 1964, it did not make the album charts until January 1966, reaching No 30. It won an RIAA Gold Disc for million dollar sales on 4 March 1969. This album contained the original, accoustic, version of **Sounds of Silence**. A Boston radio station generated positive public response to this track when they gave it considerable air play. CBS felt that it could be a successful single, though a stronger electric backing was needed. Producer Tom Wilson added this new backing rhythm track, and the single version was released in November 1965. In the *Billboard* charts it became the first No 1 of 1966, dropped off the top after one week when the Beatles **We Can Work It Out** went to No 1 for two weeks, then returned to the top for one more week. In the *Cash Box* charts it followed the Beatles to No 1 as the second chart topper of the year, staying there for one week. It spent 14 weeks on the Hot 100. Unusually for an American No 1, the record was not a hit in Britain, where the Bachelors' cover version made No 3.

The Sound of Silence was written by Paul Simon and produced by Tom Wilson at the CBS studios in New York City. It sold over a million copies in the USA alone, winning an RIAA Gold Disc on 14 February 1966. The singles version was included on the **Sound of Silence** album, released in 1966, which reached No 21 in the LP charts during a 143-week residency. It won a Gold Disc for million dollar sales in August 1967.

Simon and Garfunkel followed up with two Top 10 singles in 1966. **Homeward Bound** made No 5, and was also their first British hit, reaching No 9 on the CBS label. **I Am a Rock** made No 3 in America, and No 17 in Britain. There then followed a number of relatively minor hits until in 1968 the film theme **Mrs Robinson** gave them their second No 1 million-selling single. 1966 saw their first Top 10 album, **Parsley, Sage, Rosemary and Thyme**, which made No 4 and won a Gold Disc for million dollar sales — as did all eight of their US album releases. In Britain **Sounds of Silence** was their first of 10 hit LPs. Although it only reached No 13, it stayed exactly two years in the album charts.

SONNY AND CHER · *American*

I GOT YOU BABE *Atco 6359 [USA] Atlantic AT 4035 [UK].* In the summer of 1965, Sonny and Cher seemed to come from nowhere right to the top of the pop world. Their first hit **I Got You Babe**, written and produced by Sonny, went to No 1 for three weeks in America and one week in Britain. Their Bohemian dress and hippy (but married) life style caught the imagination of the media and the teenagers who bought their records by the million.

While this was overnight success for Cher, Sonny had been in the music business almost all his adult life. He was born Salvatore Philip

Bono, on 16 February 1935 in Detroit, Michigan, the son of Italian immigrant parents. After working as a lorry driver and waiter, he got a job in 1957 with Specialty Records. He was involved in A&R work, and wrote songs for the label's artists. (He co-wrote **She Said 'Yeah'** for Larry Williams, which was later covered by the Rolling Stones, and **Needles and Pins** for Jackie De Shannon, also a worldwide smash hit for the Searchers.) He also worked in the recording studios, producing and recording for others and himself. He continued to make records after he left Specialty in 1959, though none of them were hits. In 1963 he joined Phil Spector and his arranger Jack Nitzsche (with whom he had written **Needles and Pins**), doing a variety of jobs for Spector's Philles label.

It was at this time that Bono met 16-year-old Cherilyn Sarkasian La Pierre, of Armenian and Cherokee Indian heritage. She was born in El Centro, California, on 20 May 1946. Her mother had been a Hollywood actress, and had arranged for Cherilyn to be tutored by Jeff Corey, a prominent Hollywood acting teacher. She met Sonny in a Los Angeles coffee shop, and he introduced her to Phil Spector. Spector was not keen to record her, though he did use both of them as backing for the Crystals, the Ronettes and the Righteous Brothers. Sonny's first marriage was breaking up at the time he met Cher, and in 1964 he married her. The image of a happily married couple singing love songs to each other only added to their appeal. Sonny continued to try and break Cher, both as a solo singer and with him as the duo Caesar and Cleo, but without success. As Sonny and Cher they then had a local hit with **Baby Don't Go** on Reprise. This was intended to be a solo performance by Cher, but she had an attack of nerves so Sonny sang along with her. This led to a recording contract with Atlantic, who released **I Got You Babe** on their Atco subsidiary in America. The record was

produced by Sonny, with arrangement by Harold Battiste. The transatlantic chart topper spent 14 weeks in the American charts and 12 weeks in the British Top 50. **Baby Don't Go** then broke out nationally, and was a No 8 hit in America and No 11 in Britain. The Atco follow-up was **Just You**, which made No 20 in the USA. That was followed by **But You're Mine**, which made No 15 and was also the duo's next British hit, reaching No 17.

Sonny and Cher had 18 hits in the USA between 1965 and 1973, five of which made the Top 10. In Britain they had nine Top 50 hits up to 1972, three of which made the Top 10. **I Got You Babe** was easily their biggest hit (and only No 1 on either side of the Atlantic). It sold three million copies around the world, half a million in Britain, where the record won a Silver Disc. The RIAA awarded a Gold Disc for American sales of a million copies on 17 September 1965, just over two months after its release.

At the same time as the Sonny and Cher hits, both artists also had solo releases. Sonny had only two hits in America and one in Britain, with **Laugh at Me** going into the Top 10 in both countries. Cher was much more successful. Her version of Bob Dylan's **All I Really Wanna Do** beat the Byrds' interpretation up the American charts. She had a string of hits on Imperial, the biggest of which was **Bang Bang (My Baby Shot Me Down)**, which reached No 2 in 1966. In the 1970s she changed to Kapp/MCA, which netted her three No 1s in America. These were **Gypsies, Tramps and Thieves** in 1971, and back-to-back No 1s with **Half Breed** (1973) and **Dark Lady** (1974). After one small hit on Warner Brothers in 1977, she moved to Casablanca. Her first hit on her new label was the Top 10 million-selling **Take Me Home** of 1979. The hits kept coming, and her highly acclaimed 1987 **Cher** album on Geffen spawned hits with **I Found Someone** and **We All Sleep Alone**. In Britain her chart career was more restricted, with six hits in the sixties and seventies (three of them making the Top 10, of which the most successful was the No 3 **Bang Bang**.) **Dark Lady** was a minor hit in 1974, and **I Found Someone** made it in 1988 and **If I Could Turn Back Time** in 1989.

Cher's initial training had been as an actress, and she put these talents to good use. As well as their records, Sonny and Cher hosted a successful television series for CBS-TV from 1971. When their marriage broke up in 1974, they both hosted their own shows. Cher pursued a parallel acting career, appearing on Broadway in 'Come Back to the Five and Dime, Jimmy Dean, Jimmy Dean', and in films like *Good Times* and *Chastity*. She won an Oscar nomination for 'Best Supporting Actress' for her role in *Silkwood*, and finally won an Oscar as 'Best Actress' in *Moonstruck*.

LOOK AT US (Album) *Atco 177 [USA] Atlantic ATL 5036 [UK]*. Soon after the release of the **I Got You Babe** single, Atco released Sonny and Cher's debut album **Look at Us**. It was a tremendous success, holding at No 2 for eight weeks, with 44 weeks in the US album charts. It won an RIAA Gold Disc for million dollar sales on 30 September 1965, just over a month after its release. It went on to sell over three quarters of a million copies in the USA, with

European and Far Eastern sales putting it over the million. It reached No 7 in Britain, with 13 weeks in the album charts.

Between 1965 and 1974 the duo had 12 hit albums in America, though only two in Britain (in 1965 and 1966). Of the American albums, only **Look at Us** made the Top 10, but **Sonny and Cher Live** (1971) and the follow-up **All I Ever Need is You** (1972) both won Gold Discs. As a solo artist, Cher enjoyed a longer string of hit albums, with 17 making the charts from **All I Really Want to Do** in 1965 to **Cher** in 1987. While none of them made the Top 10, three did win Gold Discs. In Britain Cher had two hit albums on Liberty in 1965–6, and one with **Cher** in 1987–8.

I Got You Babe and the **Look at Us** album did wonders for Sonny and Cher's finances. They went from an income of $3,000 in 1964 to an estimated $3,000,000 in 1965. Much of that came from the **Look at Us** album, the contents of which were: **I Got You Babe**, by Sonny Bono (1965); **Unchained Melody** (from the film *Unchained* 1955), by Hy Zaret/Alex North (1955); **Then He Kissed Me**, by Jeff Barry, Ellie Greenwich and Phil Spector (1963); **Sing C'est La Vie**, by Bono, Greene and Stone (1965); **It's Gonna Rain**, by Sonny Bono (1965); **500 Miles Away From Home**, by Bobby Bare, Hedy West and Charles Williams (1962); **Just You**, by Sonny Bono (1965); **The Letter**, by Don Harris and Dewey Terry (orig. **Je t'appartiens** in France, 1955), by Pierre Delanoe and Gilbert Becaud (English words: Mann Curtis, 1960); **You Don't Love Me**, by Raye; **You Really Got a Hold on Me**, by William 'Smokey' Robinson (1962); **Why Don't They Let Us Fall in Love?**, by Jeff Barry, Ellie Greenwich and Phil Spector (1965).

BARBRA STREISAND   *American*

MY NAME IS BARBRA, TWO (Album) *CBS-Columbia 9209 [USA] CBS BPG 62603 [UK]*. Barbra Streisand started her show-business career as an actress, a profession that she returned to with great success as her recording career also took off. She was born on 24 April 1942 in Brooklyn, New York, and attended acting classes at Erasmus High School. On leaving school, she moved to Manhattan and covered as many auditions as she could. She entered and won a Greenwich Village nightclub contest, and was soon singing in some of the best showcase nightclubs in New York.

Producer David Merrick saw her act, and signed her to play the leading role in his 1962 production 'I Can Get it for You Wholesale'. The original cast recording of this Broadway show crept into the album charts for five weeks, reaching No 125. Another star role in the Broadway show 'Pins and Needles' won her a contract with CBS Records, who released her first single **My Colouring Book**, though it failed to make the charts. Her tie-up with CBS also ensured her major television exposure on the CBS TV network.

Streisand became a major album artist before it became fashionable to do so, and before LP sales made it a form so much more rewarding than singles. Her first LP **The**

Barbra Streisand Album made the LP charts in 1963, reaching No 8 during its 101-week run. It won a Gold Disc, as did her first eight albums. It also won the NARAS award as 'Best Album of the Year', and Barbra was named 'Best Vocalist of the Year'. In 1964 she landed the leading role in the hit Broadway musical 'Funny Girl'. With the release of the score's most powerful ballad, **People**, she also secured her first singles hit. The record made No 5, though the follow-up **Funny Girl** only made No 44. Barbra also played the star role in the 1968 film version of 'Funny Girl', as she did in the 1969 film of the Broadway musical 'Hello Dolly'. It was the film *The Way We Were* that gave her her first million-selling single for the title song, and an Oscar for her performance in the film.

If her singles performance was patchy, her success on the album front was considerable and consistent. In 1964 she had her first No 1 album with **People**, followed in 1965 with **My Name is Barbra** which spent three weeks at No 2. **My Name is Barbra, Two** also spent two weeks at No 2. With 48 weeks in the charts, it won a Gold Disc on 4 January 1966. Subsequent sales of over a million in the USA resulted in Platinum certification on 21 November 1986. In Britain this was Barbra's first hit album, entering the LP charts on 22 January 1966. It reached No 6, with 22 weeks in the charts.

The album was produced by Robert Mersey. The tracks were arranged and conducted by Peter Matz, except those marked * which were arranged and conducted by Don Costa. The tracks on the album (with songwriters in brackets) were: ***He Touched Me** from 'Drat! The Cat!' (I. Levin/M. Schafer); ***The Shadow of Your Smile**, the love theme from *The Sandpipers* (P. F. Webster/J. Mandel); **Quiet Night** (R. Rodgers/L. Hart); **I Got Plenty Of Nothin'** (I. Gershwin/D. Heyward/G. Gershwin); ***How Much Of The Dream Comes True** (J. Barry/T. Peacock); **Second Hand Rose** (G. Clarke/J. F. Hanley); **The Kind Of Man A Woman Needs** from 'The Yearling' (M. Leonard/H. Martin); **All That I Want** (N. Welte/F. Forest); **Where's That Rainbow?** (L. Hart/R. Rodgers); ***No More Songs For Me** (R. Maltby Jr/D. Shire); and the following medley, **Second Hand Rose** (G. Clarke/J. F. Hanley) **Give Me The Simple Life** (H. Ruby/R. Bloom); **I Got Plenty Of Nothin'** (I. Gershwin/D. Heyward/G. Gershwin); **Brother Can You Spare A Dime** (E.Y. Harburg/J. Gorney); **Nobody Knows You When You're Down And Out** (J. Cox); **Second Hand Rose** (G. Clarke/J. F. Hanley); and **The Best Things In Life Are Free** (B.G. DeSylva/L. Brown/R. Henderson).

THE SUPREMES   *American*

STOP! IN THE NAME OF LOVE *Motown 1074* [*USA*] *Tamla Motown TMC 501* [*UK*]. **Stop! In the Name of Love** was the fourth million seller for the Supremes and gave them their fourth American No 1 in a row. It was written by Brian and Eddie Holland and Lamont Dozier, and produced by Brian Holland and Lamont Dozier. This team wrote and produced all their 1965 million sellers. It was No 1 for two weeks,

with 12 weeks in the American Top 100 and No 2 for four weeks and 14 weeks in the R&B charts.

In Britain EMI was the licensee for Motown, and had achieved some success for the Supremes, though nothing like as much as in the USA. **Where Did Our Love Go?** had gone to No 3 in 1964, and **Baby Love** had topped the British charts for two weeks later the same year. January 1965 saw the release of **Come See About Me**, which only reached No 27. **Stop! In the Name of Love** reached No 7, with 12 weeks in the charts. It is in fact a very important record, though not because it restored the Supremes to the Top 10. When EMI obtained the licence for Motown Records, they issued all the American company's product on the Stateside label. This had been set up on 15 June 1962 as a vehicle for recordings to be picked up from American independents and smaller companies. EMI hoped that it would do for them what the phenomenally successful London label had done for their great rivals Decca. Motown's first recordings had appeared in Britain on London, before a brief spell on Philip's Fontana label from 1961 to 1962. For the next year, Motown switched its licence to the small independent Oriole company, which was then taken over by CBS. In late 1963 Motown moved to EMI, where it was to remain until the late seventies. In 1965 EMI agreed to give Motown their own logo, and in March **Stop! In the Name of Love** became the first release on the new Tamla Motown label. (see 1964).

BACK IN MY ARMS AGAIN *Motown 1075* [*USA*] *Tamla Motown TMG 516* [*UK*]. This was the fifth consecutive record by the Supremes to go to No 1 in America (for one week) and to sell a million copies. It spent 11 weeks in the Hot 100, and was No 1 for one week on the American R&B charts where it had an 11-week run. In Britain it did less well, reaching No 40 during five weeks in the charts. It was another success for the Holland-Dozier-Holland songwriting team, and was produced by Brian Holland and Lamont Dozier at the Motown studios in Detroit.

NOTHING BUT A HEARTACHE *Motown 1080* [*USA*]. After the amazing success of five No 1 singles in a row, **Nothing But a Heartache** was something of a disappointment. It reached No 8 in *Cash Box*, though in *Billboard* it did not even make the Top 10, stalling at No 11. It spent nine weeks on the Hot 100. Though this was the Supremes' least successful hit between **Where Did Our Love Go?** in 1964 and **In and Out of Love** at the end of 1967, and was not a hit in Britain when it was released in August 1965, it finally sold a global million. It reached No 6 during 10 weeks in the US R&B charts. As usual, a Holland-Dozier-Holland composition and Brian Holland/Lamont Dozier production.

I HEAR A SYMPHONY *Motown 1083* [*USA*] *Tamla Motown TMG 543* [*UK*]. The Supremes' seventh million seller restored them to No 1 in America, where **I Hear a Symphony** spent two weeks of its 10-week chart run at the top. During 13 weeks in the R&B charts it peaked at No 2 for two weeks. It was a minor hit in

Britain, reaching No 39 with five weeks in the charts. It was another hit for Holland-Dozier-Holland, and like their other hits was produced at Motown by Brian Holland and Lamont Dozier. Released in America on 23 October 1965, and in Britain in November, global sales were over two million copies.

THE TEMPTATIONS   *American*

MY GIRL *Gordy 7038* [*USA*] *Stateside SS 398* [*UK*]. One of America's greatest R&B groups, the Temptations were formed in Detroit in 1960. They were originally known as the Elgins, a group formed by Milton Jenkins from two groups that he managed. Both the Primes and the Distants had lost members, so Jenkins merged them together. In 1961 the Elgins were signed to Berry Gordy's new Miracle label, though they changed their name to the Temptations just before the release of their first disc, **Oh Mother Of Mine**.

The group were soon switched the new Gordy label, and in 1962 had their first, modest, R&B hit with **Dream Come Home**. In 1964 they had their first pop hit with **The Way You Do The Things You Do**, which reached No 11 in the Hot 100.

My Girl was written and produced by William 'Smokey' Robinson and Ronald White and was originally intended for the Miracles. The Temptations heard it first and badgered Robinson to let them have it. The Temptations recorded it on 21 December 1964 at the Motown studios in Detroit. **My Girl** went to No 1 for one week on 6 March 1965. It spent 13 weeks in both the Hot 100 and the R&B charts, where it went to No 1 for six weeks. It was the group's first hit in Britain, where it reached No 43 in its one week in the Top 50.

The Temptations had a long string of hits on both sides of the Atlantic. In America they had two more No 1 pop hits with **I Can't Get Next To You** (1969) and **Papa Was A Rolling Stone** (1972). Both pop and R&B hits continued

into the eighties, with 14 R&B No 1s among the 76 hits in that specialist chart up to 1988. In Joel Whitburn's chart book on US R&B singles from 1942 to 1988, the Temptations ranked fourth in his list of all time top R&B acts. In Britain the Temptations have had 22 hits up to 1988, though only three of them made the Top 10.

Over the years the line-up of the Temptations has changed. The members of the group when this disc was made were Melvin Franklin, born David English on 12 October 1942 in Montgomery, Alabama; Eddie Kendricks, born on 17 December 1939 in Birmingham, Alabama; Paul Williams, born on 2 July 1939 in Birmingham, Alabama; Otis Williams, born Otis Miles on 30 October 1941 in Texarkana, Texas; and David Ruffin, born on 18 January 1941 in Meridian, Mississippi. Ruffin enjoyed a lengthy and successful solo career after he left the Temptations in 1968.

THE TOYS   American

A LOVER'S CONCERTO *Dyno Voice 209 [USA] Stateside SS 460 [UK]*. This million seller was the very first recording by the Toys, a black female trio consisting of Barbara Harris (lead singer), born on 18 August 1945 in Elizabeth City, North Carolina; June Montiero, born 1 July 1946 in Queens, New York; and Barbara Parritt, born 10 January 1944 in Wilmington, North Carolina.

They all went to the Woodrow Wilson High School in Jamaica, New York, where they discovered that they all liked to sing. They teamed up and rehearsed for a few weeks, then contacted a US disc company Genius Inc., making an appointment with Vince Marc. Greatly impressed, Marc called in his songwriting producers Sandy Linzer and Denny Rendell, who went to work on a Bach five-finger exercise and wrote **A Lover's Concerto** for their first session. Within three months the disc got to No 1 in *Record World* for two weeks. It was No 1 for one week in *Cash Box*, where it had 14 weeks in the charts. In *Billboard* it peaked at No 2 for three weeks with 15 weeks in the Hot 100, and at No 4 with 12 weeks in the R&B charts. It was a major international hit through EMI, reaching No 5 in Britain with 13 weeks in the Top 50. It was awarded a Gold Disc from the RIAA on 7 December 1965, with global sales of two million. The Toys were later featured in the film *The Girl In Daddy's Bikini*.

THE WALKER BROTHERS   American

MAKE IT EASY ON YOURSELF *Philips BF 1428 [UK] Smash 2009 [USA]*. The remarkable fact about this American trio is that it was not until they came to Britain in 1965 that they became a big success. This disc got them to No 1 in the British charts for one week with 14 weeks in the bestsellers. It was also a hit (No 16) in the USA later on the Smash label and was 10 weeks in the bestsellers.

The Walkers are not actually brothers. Gary Walker (real name Gary Leeds) was born 3 September 1944, in Glendale, California (drummer); John Walker (real name John Maus), was born 12 November 1943 in New York City (guitarist); and Scott Walker (real name Scott Engel) was born 9 January 1944 in Hamilton, Ohio (bass guitarist). Gary had been to England on a tour with the US artist P.J. Proby, and on his return to the States found John and Scott playing in Gazzarri's in Hollywood. They decided to leave for England at this time and try for their big break there, rightly assuming that three Americans with long hair would be something entirely new. They were firstly a success at novelties, but English audiences began to notice they had good voices when they sang **Make It Easy on Yourself**. Their disc soon sold over 250,000 in Britain where it was 14 weeks in the bestsellers, and sales in the US and elsewhere eventually made a global million. The song was written by Hal David (words) and Burt Bacharach (music) in 1962.

WE FIVE   American

YOU WERE ON MY MIND *A&M 770 [USA]*. This song, a folk-influenced ballad written in 1964 by Sylvia Fricker, was the debut disc for the group and achieved the No 2 spot in the US charts for two weeks. It sold a million by the end of 1965.

The We Five story began in 1962 when Mike Stewart, brother of John (a member of the Kingston Trio), formed the Ridge Runners, a mainly folk singing group. John brought his brother's group to the attention of Frank Werber, the Kingston Trio manager. Werber urged them to abandon the folk idiom and search for their own unique sound. For the following two years they perfected their sound, and Werber became convinced of their potentiality after auditioning them at this newly formed Trident Productions. Werber groomed them for eight months, rehearsing, developing new ideas and polishing tunes, etc., and finally on 20 April 1965 took the group to a recording studio and produced **You Were on My Mind**. A deal was made for A&M Records to release the singles disc. It stayed in the US charts for 15 weeks.

The group consisted of Mike Stewart, leader and arranger, writer of several songs for the Kingston Trio, who comes from Riverside, California, and was educated at San Francisco University and Mt San Antonio College; Beverly Bivens, the only female member and lead singer, born in Orange, California, and educated at Santa Anna High School where she was a member of the school's glee club; Bob Jones, a keen jazz guitarist from Honolulu, educated at St Louis High School, Hawaii, then at the same university and college as Mike Stewart in San Francisco; Jerry Burgan, born in Kansas City and raised in San Diego, California, who also attended the same colleges as Mike and Bob, a versatile guitarist who highlighted the group's driving, rhythmic beat; Pete Fullerton, a native of Pomona, California, star football athlete at Clarmont High School, then a graduate of Mt San Antonio College, the drummer of the group.

(LITTLE) STEVIE WONDER   American

UP TIGHT (EVERYTHING'S ALL RIGHT) *Tamla 54124 [USA] Tamla Motown TMG 545 [UK]*. The second big hit for (erstwhile 'Little') Stevie was written by Henry Cosby, Sylvia Moy and Stevie Judkins (Stevie Wonder). Released on 11 December 1965, it achieved the No 3 position in 1966 in the US charts, and a run of 14 weeks in the bestsellers. The disc was also a success in Britain where it was No 13 in 1966 with 10 weeks in the bestsellers. It is estimated to have sold a million globally. The record was No 1 in the US R&B charts for five weeks with a chart run of 15 weeks. It was Stevie's second out of 19 R&B No 1s. His 60 R&B hits rank him sixth in Joel Whitburn's list of the all-time Top 200 R&B acts from 1944 to 1988.

THE YARDBIRDS   British

FOR YOUR LOVE *Columbia (EMI) DB 7499 [UK] Epic 9790 [USA]*. Personnel of this group were Keith Relf (harmonica and vocalist) born in Richmond, Surrey, 22 March 1943; Eric Clapton (guitar) 30 March 1945, Chris Dreja (rhythm guitar) born in Surbiton, Surrey, 11 November 1945; Paul Samwell-Smith (bass guitar) born in south-west London, 8 May 1945; and Jim McCarty (drums) born in Liverpool, 25 July 1943. They had all played with various groups before joining up and becoming the Yardbirds. The group were offered the residency of the Crawdaddy Club, Richmond, replacing the Rolling Stones in 1963. With the Rolling Stones so popular, it took the Yardbirds a few months to win back the fans to the club, but this they did, beating the crowds the Stones had brought in. Further appearances at London's Marquee Club and in Liverpool were also big successes.

For Your Love was their third disc and in a few weeks got to No 1 in one of the four British charts. It was equal No 1 with Cliff Richard's **The Minute You're Gone** for one week, in *NME*. It had 12 weeks in the *Record Retailer* Top 50 where it peaked at No 3. On release in the USA, it reached No 6 position with 12 weeks in the bestsellers, and sold a global million. Eric Clapton left the group just after this disc was released and was replaced by Jeff Beck (lead guitar) who was born 24 June 1944.

For Your Love was written by Graham Gouldman.

1 9 6 6

1966 was the year that the Beach Boys reached their peak. The California quintet had their first hit in 1962, when **Surfin'** made No 75 on the Candix label. Capitol then signed them up, and a string of surfing records followed. **Surfin' USA** was their first US Top 10 hit in 1963, and **I Get Around** their first No 1 single in 1964. By 1965 they had become the leading American beat group, with the Supremes the only American group of any kind to out perform them. They had their second No 1 single that year, with **Help Me, Rhonda**.

In 1966 they had two No 1 singles in America, with **Barbara Ann** and **Good Vibrations**. Both of them, and **Sloop John B**, sold over a million copies. They also received three Gold Discs for albums. **Summer Days** won the award for million dollar sales in February, while **Little Deuce Coup** and **Shut Down, Volume 2** went Gold in December, bringing their total of Gold albums to eight.

Despite their considerable success in America, prior to 1966 the Beach Boys had made only limited headway in the rest of the world. In Britain **Surfin' USA** had been a minor hit in 1963, though **I Get Around** made the Top Ten in 1964. There followed four minor hits until EMI launched a massive campaign for the group early in 1966. **Barbara Ann** made No 3, **Sloop John B** and **God Only Knows** both made No 2, and **Good Vibrations** hit the top.

The group toured Europe towards the end of the year, with Peter and Gordon as support act. In early November the Beach Boys tour hit Britain, with one sell-out concert after another. The Beach Boys became so popular that they actually toppled the Beatles in the end of year music paper popularity polls, and were voted 'Top World Vocal Group'.

Their time at the very top was surprisingly short. After the massive success of **Good Vibrations**, on which producer Brian Wilson had spent the sort of money most groups normally spent on a whole album (it was the most expensively produced single up to that time) the Beach Boys did not make the US Top 10 again for another decade. Despite this, they did become something of an American institution, a fact underlined by their unexpected 1988 No 1 **Kokomo**. It came from the film *Cocktail*, which featured the group because of their place in the pantheon of American popular music.

The Beatles and Jesus Christ

While the Beach Boys may have won the popularity polls, the Beatles in fact sold more records. Both their 1966 worldwide releases made No 1 and sold millions. As well as **Paperback Writer** and **Yellow Submarine**, Capitol also released **Nowhere Man** in the United States. It also made No 1, and sold over a million copies.

Brian Epstein had sold the Beatles to the world as four sweet, harmless, mop tops. That image had never been accurate, and by 1966 the mask was slipping. What destroyed it for ever in America were the remarks that John Lennon made to the London *Evening Standard* newspaper in March. During a long interview John told the paper, 'We're more popular than Jesus Christ right now.' The statement did not get that great a reaction in Britain, where religion was less important to most people than in the USA and some other countries. Lennon later apologized for any offence that the remark had caused, but as London's *Catholic Herald* pointed out, however arrogant it may have been for a Beatle to have said it, the claim was probably true.

Reaction around the world grew in August. The South African authorities banned the playing of all Beatles records because of Lennon's remark. Many American radio stations took the same course of action, and in a number of countries (including the USA) there were public burnings of Beatles' records. When the Beatles arrived in America for their last tour of the country in August, there was some negative reaction from a few fans, though in the main Lennon's remarks did not appear to have affected their record sales, which remained huge. In April the *Daily Express* claimed that the Beatles had sold 159,000,000 records around the world.

The Beatles' flight from innocence was given a further boost by John Lennon's public support for draft dodgers, made at a press conference in Toronto in August, at the height of his Jesus Christ controversy. American involvement in the Vietnam war was increasing, and American conscripts were being sent to fight in ever larger numbers. While opposition to the war was still a minority view at this time, it was beginning to grow. In October John Lennon met Yoko Ono, a development that was ultimately to be a major factor in the breakup of the Beatles.

Drugs and Psychedelia

The music industry had always had an element of drug abuse about it, certainly from the 1940s. By 1966 concern was beginning to grow on both sides of the Atlantic that too many pop singers were publicly supporting the use of illegal drugs. In June the problem made the lead story on page one of *Variety*. The paper's headline read 'Pop Music's Moral Crisis: Dope Tunes Fan DJ's Ire'. Complaining that the issue had caused the worst moralistic outcry since Elvis Presley had swivelled his hips in public in the fifties, the paper reported that: 'A recent wave of pop songs contains references to getting high on dope or liquor, suicide, prostitution, and sundry other way out, off beat and taboo subjects. The freedom of today's young songwriters and performers to tackle any subject is resulting in a rising tide of DJ protest.'

In Britain, 25-year-old Birmingham City councillor Colin Beardwood appealed to Home Secretary Roy Jenkins to ban Bob Dylan's **Rainy Day Women Numbers 12 and 34** and the Byrds' **Eight Miles High**, claiming that they both encouraged drug taking. Both had been banned by many radio stations in America.

The Beatles, the Rolling Stones and many other groups were experimenting with drugs, and would get increasingly public about their use. Their American tours had opened them up to new experiences, for the drug problem was greater in America than in Britain. The American federal government declared LSD (also called 'acid') illegal in October, but that did not stop its increasing use by musicians and artists, especially in California. It was this year that psychedelia broke ground, and the Haight-Ashbury district of San Francisco was an important centre of psychedelia right from the start.

In Britain groups like Columbia's Pink Floyd were moving in a new psychedelic direction. (EMI moved them from Columbia to the new Harvest label in 1969.) As with any new trend, there was a certain amount of hype involved, but one feature of this development was the increased quality of musicianship demanded. Many of the beat groups of the mid-sixties were not very talented musicians, yet that did not stop

them having hits. In the late sixties artists like the Floyd and the Jimi Hendrix Experience showed very considerable expertise.

An important move in this direction occurred in July. That was when Eric Clapton, Jack Bruce and Ginger Baker formed Cream. Though the group itself did not stay together for long, its influence, and that of Blind Faith which followed it, was considerable.

Another element of the move to psychedelia was a growing interest in things Eastern. George Harrison and Brian Jones were both experimenting with the sitar, which Jones in particular used with great effect on the Stones' **Paint It Black**. Harrison followed his interest in Indian music to Eastern mysticism. In September he went to India to see spiritual guru the Maharishi Mahesh Yogi.

Breakups, Deaths and Injuries

A number of groups underwent personnel changes. The Yardbirds lost Paul Samwell-Smith in July, replacing him with Jimmy Page. In October the group made their first tour of America, but their new line-up did not survive it. By December the group announced that Jeff Beck had left due to ill health. He had replaced Eric Clapton in 1964, and in fact had ceased playing with the group in October. The Hollies sacked their bass player Eric Haydock for unreliability. Mike D'Abo replaced Paul Jones as lead singer of Manfred Mann. Jill Gibson replaced Michelle Philips in the Mamas and the Papas. Michelle had found it increasingly difficult to work with her husband John, from whom she was estranged. After three weeks they had worked their personal problems out sufficiently for Michelle to rejoin the group.

Tragedy struck Roy Orbison in June when he saw his wife Claudette killed in a motorbike crash. The couple had separated the previous year, then come back together again. In fact Roy was always extremely close to her. Further disaster was to come later when two of their three sons were killed in a fire at Orbison's home. In July Bobby Fuller, leader of the Bobby Fuller Four who had a hit with **I Fought The Law**, was found dead in his car in Los Angeles. The exact circumstances of his death were never established. In October British singer Alma Cogan died of cancer, and Johnny Kidd (second only to Cliff Richard as an authentic British rocker) was killed in a car crash.

In January Manfred Mann and Paul Jones were hospitalized after a car accident. In June Tom Jones crashed his car after skidding, and needed stitches in his head. In August Scott Walker of the Walker Brothers was found unconscious in a gas-filled room; he recovered in hospital. All these incidents were in Britain. In America Bob Dylan was seriously injured at the end of July in a motorbike crash near New York. In December Ike and Tina Turner's tour bus was involved in a crash in Topeka, Kansas, that injured Ike and seven of his band and wrecked all their equipment. Tina Turner escaped unhurt.

Touring

The Beatles spent much of the year touring the world. They made their first visit to Japan and the Philippines, as well as touring in Europe and Britain. In May they made their last appearance at the *NME* popularity poll winners concert. This was the biggest and most successful concert that the paper had ever organized. As well as the Beatles the concert boasted the Rolling Stones, Cliff Richard, the Shadows, Dusty Springfield, Roy Orbison, Herman's Hermits, the Who, the Walker Brothers, the Yardbirds, the Spencer Davis Group, the Small Faces, the Seekers and many more. Held at the Empire Pool, Wembley, over 10,000 people saw Cliff Richard close the first half and the Beatles finish the second. The show was televised in two parts later in the month.

In March the Rolling Stones started a European tour. They also visited Australia, and in June started their third American tour. They were refused entry by 14 New York hotels, who they then sued for £1,786,000 on the grounds of racial discrimination. The Dave Clark Five completed their fifth US tour, and the Seekers and the Animals also visited America. In July the Kinks toured Europe, both East and West. The Jimi Hendrix Experience made their debut in Paris in October. Bob Dylan returned to the Royal Albert Hall in London in June. The first half of his concert was folk music with Dylan playing his acoustic guitar, and was well received. The second half was the new electric Dylan, backed by a rock group. This caused an uproar, partly because the group were so poor and played so loud. The folk audience did not like it, with a result similar to that at the Newport Folk Festival in America.

The Record Industry

In Britain EMI announced major changes in its organization in June. The company was split into two, with Columbia's Norrie Paramour made general manager of the larger half dealing with the company's own product, including the Capitol label. Rex Oldfield headed the licensed repertoire division, covering both British and American material. In October the company released its first batch of musicassettes.

In January, EMI's big British rival Decca was absent from the Top 10 for the first time since the British charts began in 1952. In February Decca lost British rights to Atlantic, which had been with the company for the previous 15 years. Atlantic signed a cross licensing deal with Polydor, giving Atlantic rights to Polydor material in America. In August Decca announced plans for the launch of their new Deram label. At the end of the year Decca re-signed their hottest property, Tom Jones. He had been dissatisfied with the company until **Green Green Grass Of Home** proved such a massive hit. He turned down an offer to sign with Motown, though seriously considered it, telling *Melody Maker* that 'You can't get a good sound [recording] in the UK.'

In October Brian Epstein denied rumours that he was joining the Board of Directors of the American company CBS, or that he was starting a new label with them and signing Georgie Fame as the first artist. In fact CBS in Britain did lure Fame away from Columbia, though there was to be no link up with the Beatles or their manager. CBS also signed the Tremeloes, following their split from Brian Poole. Philips finally agreed to allow Larry Page his own Page One label for his independent productions. Radio Caroline boss Philip Soloman, whose wife Dorothy was agent for the Bachelors, founded his own Major Minor indie label, to be pressed by CBS and distributed by Decca's Selecta.

In America the Righteous Brothers left Phil Spector's Philles label. They had proved impossible to dominate in the same way as Spector's female groups the Crystals and the Ronettes, and unlike those groups the male duo did have life after Spector. They signed with MGM in a deal that included films. MGM made a determined effort to increase their stake in the record business by making similar record and film deals with Roy Orbison, the Animals and Herman's Hermits. In each case the deals were for the American market only. In December MGM made a fantastic offer for Bob Dylan, but he stayed with CBS.

In March A&M, owned jointly by Herb Alpert and Gerry Moss, turned down an offer of $5 million from Warner Brothers. In June A&M turned down a takeover bid from RCA. The company has remained one of the few consistently successful independents, though in October 1989 they agreed a takeover by Polygram.

The GPO, who then ran Britain's telephone service, started their 'Dial-A-Disc' service, with a different record played over the phones each night. In April the Discatron was launched in Britain. A bulky machine for playing singles in cars, it arrived on the market just too late to catch on, for the Philips tape cassettes had just arrived and they proved more versatile.

Who Records The Who?

One of the great mysteries of the year was who was recording the Who. The group had been turned down by EMI in October 1964. They then signed a deal with American independent producer Shel Talmy, who in turn brought the group to American Decca. They had a deal with British Decca, who released their product outside America on the Brunswick label. It was therefore on this label that the Who's early hits were issued. The Who were the only major British group launched in the mid-sixties via an American record company.

In January, British independent producer Robert Stigwood signed a deal with Polydor to issue his Reaction label. The following month Stigwood announced that he had signed the Who to Reaction, thus switching the band from Decca to Polydor. The Who were involved in a dispute with American Decca over money at the time, and the result was a writ from British Decca (US Decca's licencee) preventing further Who releases on Reaction. At the same time Shel Talmy sought to prevent the end of what he claimed was a legal producers agreement with him. In July the NME reported that the Who had signed a recording contract with the Stones producer/manager Andrew Oldham, in a deal negotiated by the ubiquitous Allen Klein which involved the buying out of Shel Talmy. In August this deal collapsed, due to difficulties between Klein and Talmy. In October the dispute finally ended, with the Who going out on a new label, Track, distributed by Polydor.

The Media

In Britain the Musicians Union successfully campaigned for a ban on artists miming on TV shows. In June NME reported that 'The Musicians Union is tightening its stranglehold on pop music. It has successfully ordered an all out ban on TV shows (such as ''Top Of The Pops'', ''A Whole Scene Going'' and ''Thank Your Lucky Stars'') on which artists mime to records, and prevented groups taking part in taping shows for pirate radio stations. Both the BBC and ITV have given in to the Union's ''no miming'' demands.' The immediate result of the Union's action was that the BBC axed 'A Whole Scene Going', which they had previously announced would get a second series. 'Thank Your Lucky Stars' was scrapped in June. It was a bad year for pop on television. 'Ready, Steady Go!' came off the air for the last time on 23 December.

It was a mixed story in America. 'Shindig!' was taken off in January, while its rival 'Hullabaloo' saw its final broadcast in April. But in September a new programme aired featuring a Beatles-like group called the Monkees. 'The Monkees' show put together two actors and two musicians, and was a huge success on both television and disc.

In the traditional pop papers in Britain, the NME celebrated its 1,000th issue. It had the biggest circulation of any music paper in the world, and outsold all its British rivals put together. Melody Maker was 40 years old. Its sister paper Disc took over and absorbed the Liverpool-based Music Echo, which had been the first paper in Britain to compile a Top 100 singles chart. In a new and psychedelic vein, the year had seen the launch of the youth culture periodical the International Times, which had to shorten its name to IT when the publishers of The Times took legal action. Its creation followed that of Crawdaddy in the United States.

Rock's Vicar

Cliff Richard was widely rumoured to be on the verge of retiring from pop music to teach religion. His Christian commitment was well known, and had cost him some support as a rock star. The closure of his massive 42,000 member fan club in June fuelled the rumours, but after 10,000 fans signed a petition 120 feet long asking him not to quit, he decided to remain in the rock business. He made his sixth film, Finders Keepers, and in December won the Radio Luxembourg Credit To Showbusiness Award.

In January the NME reported that in the first half of the decade, Cliff Richard had been the most consistent chart star. Using its inverted points system to measure chart consistency, the paper listed the top five of the first half of the sixties as: 1 — Cliff Richard (4,841 points), 2 — Elvis Presley (4,344), 3 — the Beatles (3,737), 4 — the Shadows (3,107) and 5 — Billy Fury (2,458). In the NME popularity poll at the end of the year, Cliff improved his performance on 1965. He was runner-up to Elvis Presley in the World Male Singer and Musical Personality sections, easily beat Tom Jones as Top British Male Singer, and defeated John Lennon to win back his Top British Vocal Personality crown.

Soaps And Stars

George Harrison became the third Beatle to marry when in January he wed model Patti Boyd. They had first met on the set of the Beatles' film A Hard Day's Night. The couple later divorced after Harrison's best friend Eric Clapton became infatuated with Patti and pursued her. He eventually married her, though that marriage did not last either. The 21-year-old star of 'Peyton Place' Mia Farrow married 50-year-old Frank Sinatra in July. It was his third marriage. Sinatra was in Britain during the year, and bought a flat in London. Looking across the Atlantic from the other direction, Dusty Springfield demanded a change of label in the United States, claiming that Philips' Mercury subsidiary had done nothing to promote her there. She got her way in 1968 when for America only she switched to Atlantic. In fact they never equalled the success Mercury had with her **You Don't Have To Say You Love Me**, which reached No 4 on the Philips label. This 1966 hit gave her the only British No 1 of her career.

World News

In Britain Harold Wilson led the Labour Party to a major election victory in October. He had won the 1964 election with an overall majority of only four, but this time came back with a majority of 96. The country was shocked in October when a coal slag heap engulfed the school and part of the village of Aberfan in Wales, killing 116 children and 28 adults. For the first time in 400 years, the leaders of the Anglican and Catholic churches met when the Archbishop of Canterbury visited the Pope in Rome. Britain won its three-year jungle war against Indonesia, and unveiled the world's first vertical-take-off jet, the Harrier. The Canadian Lord Thompson bought The Times.

In America it was a year of continuing racial tension at home and escalating involvement in Vietnam abroad. Dr Martin Luther King led civil rights marches in the South, while race riots exploded in the cities of the North. The year started with the biggest American offensive against the Viet Cong seen up to that time. In June America bombed Hanoi for the first time, and in November the Viet Cong bombarded Saigon. Australian troops were sent to Vietnam for the first time. Former film star Ronald Reagan won the Republican nomination for Governor of California. The former Democrat would go on to greater things...

In China Mao Tse Tung proclaimed the Cultural Revolution. He sent hundreds of thousands of young Red Guards into the countryside, and turned the country upside down for years. In Russia Leonid Brezhnev became sole leader of the Soviet Union. Following the death of Lal Shastri, Nehru's daughter Indira Gandhi became Prime Minister of India. Ghana's President Kwame Nkrumah was overthrown by the army while away on a peace mission to South-East Asia and China.

Films

Sean Connery was again the most popular film star in Britain, followed by Michael Caine. In third place came the Man From UNCLE duo Robert Vaughn and David McCallum. Their TV series was successfully transferred to film. Julie Andrews was the top female singing star at number eight, and Elvis Presley slipped to tenth. There was continuing debate in the press about the quality of his films. The James Bond film Thunderball was the biggest money-maker in Britain, followed by Alfie and The Battle Of The Bulge. Other major films were Those Magnificent Men In Their Flying Machines, and Richard Burton and his then-wife Elizabeth Taylor in Who's Afraid Of Virginia Woolf?

In America *A Man For All Seasons* won the Oscar for Best Film of 1966, and the Oscar for Best Director in Fred Zinnemann. The film picked up another Oscar when Paul Scofield won the Best Actor award. The Best Actress Oscar went to Elizabeth Taylor for *Who's Afraid Of Virginia Woolf*, a role that also won her the same award from the British Film Academy. (Her husband Richard Burton won the British Academy's award for Best Actor as well.)

Sport

On Saturday 30 July England won the World Cup for the first time, beating West Germany 4-2 at the Wembley Stadium. West Ham's Geoff Hurst was the first to score for England, followed by his clubmate Martin Peters. Hurst scored two more goals to give England victory in football's most prestigious competition. Earlier in the year the World Cup itself had been stolen. It was recovered after a man out walking his dog, a mongrel called Pickles, saw the hound tearing away at something. The something was the solid gold cup.

Everton beat Sheffield Wednesday in the FA Cup, Liverpool were top of League Division One, and West Bromwich Albion were the League Cup winners. Rangers beat Celtic in the Scottish FA Cup final, and Celtic beat Rangers for the Scottish League Cup. Celtic were also top of the Scottish League Division One. Manchester United's Bobby Charlton was Footballer of the Year. Yorkshire won the County Cricket Championship. In America, English racing driver Graham Hill won the Indianapolis 500. The Baltimore Orioles won the World Series. The Green Bay Packers won the NFL championship for the second year running, while the Kansas City Chiefs were AFL champions.

Swinging England

London strengthened its position as the youth capital of the world. The Beatles and the Rolling Stones remained the biggest-selling recording artists globally, with many other British stars selling in almost every country where records were freely available. Britain's EMI was the biggest record company in the world by a very long way. As well as the music, London had taken over from Paris as the fashion capital of the world, at least as far as young people were concerned. Designers like Mary Quant and models like Twiggy put Carnaby Street and the King's Road firmly on the map. This was also the era of hair stylist Vidal Sassoon. The most popular female hair style was long and straight, with men's hair also lengthening. As well as mini skirts for the girls, men's fashions were shaken up and became more fun and eye catching.

The media focused on the life style of the young, and the social revolution that was under way. The contraceptive pill was helping to change sexual attitudes. The emphasis of the youth revolution was on freedom and talent. Rock musicians, artists, designers, models, photographers, writers and media people all set the pace, and for millions of young people in Britain and around the world, the sixties were a great time to be young.

ORIGINAL FILM *American/French*
SOUNDTRACK: MGM STUDIO
ORCHESTRA (conducted by Maurice Jarre)

DOCTOR ZHIVAGO (Album) *MGM 6 [USA] MGM C 8007 [UK]*. The music for this outstanding film was written by Maurice Jarre, one of France's leading modern composers, who won an Oscar for the score for the film *Lawrence of Arabia* (1962).

Jarre began work on the *Zhivago* score — one of the most monumental ever undertaken for a motion picture — while the film was being shot in Spain. The film is a multi-million production of the Nobel Prize-winning novel by the Russian author Boris Pasternak. The novel was banned in Russia and political pressure made it impossible for the author-poet to accept the Nobel Prize for Literature. The film was directed by David Lean who won an Oscar for directing *Lawrence of Arabia*. *Doctor Zhivago* was awarded five Oscars, and the film was made in 22 foreign-language versions.

The dramatic story of Doctor Zhivago evokes the whole experience of Russia, and its Revolution, over the past 50 years. The film had an international cast, with Omar Sharif as Zhivago, Julie Christie as Lara, and Alec Guinness, Geraldine Chaplin, Tom Courtenay, Siobhan McKenna, Ralph Richardson, Rod Steiger and Rita Tushingham.

The album was released in January 1966. The contents are: **Overture** from *Doctor Zhivago*; **Main title** from *Doctor Zhivago*; **Lara Leaves Yuri**; **At the Student Café**; **Komarovsky and Lara's Rendezvous**; **Revolution**; **Lara's theme** from *Doctor Zhivago*; **The Funeral**; **Sventyski's Waltz**; **Yuri Escapes**; **Yonya Arrives at Varykino**; **Yuri Writes a Poem for Lara**.

The song version of **Lara's theme**, **Somewhere My Love** (words by Paul Francis Webster) was subsequently published.

Sales by 1967 were two million. The album was 157 weeks in the US bestsellers, where it reached No 1 for one week. In Britain it reached No 3 with 106 weeks in the charts. Grammy Award for Best Film Soundtrack, 1966.

ORIGINAL FILM SOUNDTRACK: *French*
PIERRE BAROUCH AND NICOLE
CROISELLE

UN HOMME ET UNE FEMME (A Man and a Woman) (Album) *United Artists 5147 [USA] United Artists SULP 1155 [UK]*. The first French film soundtrack to sell a million, with a Gold Disc award from RIAA in 1967, it was put out in the USA by United Artists. The film starred Anouk Aimée and Jean Trintignant, and featured Pierre Barouch, Valerie Legrange and Simone Paris. It was directed and filmed by the French film-maker Claude Lelouch. The film won the Grand Prize at the Cannes Film Festival in 1966 and then became a great international success.

The music was composed by Francis Lai. The author was Pierre Barouch, who sings on the disc and appeared in the film. He and Nicole Croiselle sing the following (in French): **A Man and A Woman**; **Samba Saravah**; **Today It's You**; **Stronger Than Us**; **In Our Shadow**; **124 Miles an Hour**.

The million sale was reported in September 1967 and the disc was in the bestsellers for 93 weeks, reaching No 10 in the US album charts. In Britain it reached No 31 with 11 weeks in the LP charts.

VARIOUS ARTISTS *American*

ORIGINAL THEATRE
CAST WITH RICHARD KILEY, IRVING JACOBSON, RAY MIDDLETON, ROBERT ROUNSEVILLE, JEAN DIENER, ELEANOR KNAPP, MIMI TURQUE, GINO CONFORTI, HARRY THEYARD; ORCHESTRA CONDUCTED BY NEIL WARNER
MAN OF LA MANCHA (Album) *Kapp 4505 [USA]*. This musical adaptation of Miguel de Cervantes-Saavedra's world-famous novel, *Don Quixote*, written in 1605 (part 1) and 1615 (part 2) — with book by Dale Wasserman, lyrics by Joe Darion and music by Mitch Leigh — had its first try out in the summer of 1965 at the Goodspeed Opera House, and was then produced at the ANTA Washington Square Theatre, New York, on 22 November 1965. It was composer Mitch Leigh's first Broadway musical and earned both the composer and Richard Kiley (cast as 'Don Quixote') the top awards in the New York drama critics poll of 1965-1966. When the ANTA Theatre was demolished, the show moved to New York's Beck Theatre (spring 1968) and played a total of 2,329 performances, making it one of the top 20 long-runners on Broadway. The London production opened on 24 April 1968 at the Piccadilly Theatre for 253 performances with Keith Michell as Don Quixote, and then a revival there from 10 June 1969.

This album was released in January 1966 and stayed on the charts in USA for 167 weeks, receiving a Gold Disc award from RIAA in 1967. It sold the million units by 1969.

The contents of the album are: **Overture**; **Man of La Mancha (I, Don Quixote)** (Richard Kiley, Irving Jacobson); **It's All the Same** (Jean Diener); **Dulcinea** (Richard Kiley); **I'm Only Thinking of Him** (Mimi Turque, Robert Rounseville, Eleanor Knapp); **I Really Like Him** (Irving Jacobson and Jean Diener); **What Do You Want of Me?** (Jean Diener); **Barber's Song/Golden Helmet** (Gino Conforti, Kiley and Jacobson); **To Each His Own Dulcinea** (Robert Rounseville); **The Impossible Dream** (Richard Kiley); **Little Bird, Little Bird** (Harry Theyard); **Dubbing** (Ray Middleton, Kiley, Diener and Jacobson); **Abduction** (Harry Theyard); **Aldonza** (Jean Diener, Richard Kiley); **Little Gossip** (Irving Jacobson); **Dulcinea/Impossible Dream** (Jean Diener, Kiley, Jacobson, Rounseville and entire company); **Man of La Mancha/Psalm/Finale**.

HERB ALPERT AND *American*
THE TIJUANA BRASS

WHAT NOW MY LOVE? (Album) *A&M 4114 [USA] Pye NPL 28077 and later A&M AMLS 977 [UK]*. Another tremendous success for Alpert and his disc firm A&M, this album had initial orders of close to one million. It was released in

early May, reached No 2 in its second week and then No 1 for 12 weeks in the US charts. By the end of May it had sold 1,600,000 and subsequently passed the two million mark. The disc received an immediate Gold Disc award from RIAA and the first 'Gold Cartridge' Award (from ITCC) for record-breaking retail sales of their stereo tape cartridge release of the same song selection. In its first three weeks, the cartridge sales exceeded $250,000.

The album contains the following: *Side 1* — **What Now My Love?** (originally **Et maintenant** 1962 in France), by P. Delanoe/Gilbert Becaud (English words Carl Sigman, 1962); **Freckles**, by Ervan Coleman; **Memories of Madrid**, by Sol Lake; **It Was a Very Good Year*, by Ervin Drake (1961); **So What's New?**, by John Pisano; **Plucky**, by Herb Alpert and John Pisano; *Side 2* — **Magic Trumpet**, by Bert Kaempfert; **Cantina Blue**, by Sol Lake; **Brasilia**, by Julius Wechter; **If I Were a Rich Man** (from the show *Fiddler on the Roof*), by Sheldon Harnick/Jerry Bock (1964); **Five Minutes More**, by Sammy Cahn/Jule Styne (1946); **The Shadow of Your Smile** (from the film *The Sandpiper* — song was Oscar winner of 1965), by P.F. Webster/Johnny Mandel (1965).
*From Frank Sinatra's CBS TV special show.

This disc was in the US charts for 128 weeks and received Grammy Awards for 'Best Performance by an Orchestra', and 'Best Arrangement', 1966. In Britain the album reached No 18 with 17 weeks in the charts.

SRO (Album) *A&M 4119 [USA] Pye NSPL 28088 [UK]*. An extremely appropriate title for this album, 'SRO' is short for **Standing Room Only**. It had the incredible advance order of 1,700,000, a record up to the end of 1967. Alpert was voted 'The Record Man of the Year', his seven albums dominating the album charts in 1966. The album was No 1 for three weeks and stayed in the Top 10 in the USA for six months from its release in late 1966 through 1967.

Its contents were: *Side 1* — **Our Day Will Come**, by Mort Garson/Bob Hilliard (1962); **Mexican Road Race**, by Sol Lake; **I Will Wait for You** (from the film *Umbrellas of Cherbourg*), by Jacques Demy/Michel Legrand (English words N. Gimbel) (1964); **Bean Bag**, by John Pisano, Julius Wechter and Herb Alpert; **The Wall Street Rag**, by Ervan Coleman; **Work Song**, by Oscar Brown Jr/Nat Adderley (1960); *Side 2* — **Mame** (from show *Mame*), by Jerry Herman (1966); **Blue Sunday**, by Julius Wechter; **Don't Go Breaking My Heart**, by Hal David/Burt Bacharach; **For Carlos**, by John Pisano, Nick Ceroli and Herb Alpert; **Freight Train Joe**, by John Pisano; **Flamingo**, by Ed Anderson/Ted Grouya (1951).

By the end of 1967 sales of this album were well over the 2,500,000 figure. The disc was in the US charts for 85 weeks. In Britain the album reached No 5 with 26 weeks in the charts. RIAA Gold Disc award February 1967.

THE ANIMALS *British*

THE MOST OF THE ANIMALS (in Britain) THE BEST OF THE ANIMALS (in the USA) (Album) *Columbia (EMI) 33SX 6035 [UK] MGM 4324 [USA]*. This album of the group's big hits recorded by them up to the end of 1965 was issued in the USA in early 1966 and sold over 800,000 by the end of the year, with sales continuing into 1967. It was also issued in Britain on the Columbia label as **The Most of The Animals** in April 1966, the combined global sales being over the million mark. A Gold Disc was awarded by RIAA on 28 July 1966.

The contents were: **We've Gotta Get Out of This Place**, by Barry Mann and Cynthia Weill (1965); **Don't Let Me Be Misunderstood**, by Bernie Benjamin, Sol Marcus and Gloria Caldwell (1965); **Boom, Boom**, by John Lee Hooker; **Baby, Let Me Take You Home**, by Bert Russell and Wes Farrell (1963); **Bright Lights, Big City**, by J. Reed (1961); **I'm Crying**, by Alan Price and Eric Burdon (1964); **House of the Rising Sun**, traditional, arranged Alan Price (1964); **It's My Life**, by Roger Atkins/Carl Derrilo (1965); **Mess Around**, by 'Nugetre' (Ahmet Ertegun) (1954); **Dimples**, by John Lee Hooker; **Bring It on Home to Me**, by Sam Cooke (1962); **Gonna Send You Back to Walker**, by J. Matthews and Jake Hammonds, Jr (1963); **I'm Mad Again** by John Lee Hooker; **Talkin' 'Bout You**, by Ray Charles (1959).

The recordings were originally made on Columbia in Britain. The disc was in the bestsellers for 113 weeks in the USA and for 20 weeks in Britain. It reached No 6 in the American album charts and No 4 in Britain. When the record was re-issued in Britain on the budget label Music For Pleasure (MFP 5218) in 1971, it reached No 18 with a further three weeks in the charts.

THE ASSOCIATION   *American*

CHERISH *Valiant 747* [USA]. The Association's success with this disc helped to put the small Valiant label on its financial feet. The disc was No 1 for three weeks in the USA with 14 weeks in the bestsellers, and sold a million in two months. The song was written by group member Terry Kirkman.

The group was formed in February 1965 and made their debut in July the same year. They first played in Los Angeles nightclubs and folk clubs, then Disneyland and the college and university circuit. Bob Dylan's **One Too Many Mornings** was their first record, followed by **Along Comes Mary**, which reached No 7 in the US charts. **Cherish** became the first major hit for the Valiant label, with Gold Disc award RIAA. The Association quickly became a top attraction in America with their unique vocal blending.

The group comprised Gary Alexander (first lead guitar, composer-arranger); Ted Bluechel (drummer, third rhythm guitar); Brian Cole (bass); Russ Giguere (lead singer, second rhythm guitar); Terry Kirkman (lead singer, composer); and Jim Yester (first rhythm guitar, lead singer).

THE BEACH BOYS   *Capitol*

SLOOP JOHN B *Capitol 5602* [USA] *Capitol CL 15441* [UK]. The Beach Boys' two 1966 million sellers were at opposite ends of the musical

spectrum, and showed just how versatile the group had become. **Sloop John B** was a traditional folk song, while **Good Vibrations** employed all the latest technology of the recording studio to produce what at the time was a masterpiece of progressive pop music. They had moved on from their surfing and 'hot rod' hits, and 1966 was the most successful year of their career.

Sloop John B is a song about an old ship that came to grief. The song originated in the West Indies, and has long been popular in the Bahamas. It was first published as **The John B Sails** in a collection by American folk specialist Carl Sandburg. The sloop lies embedded in the sand of Governor's Harbour, Nassau. In 1926 an expedition salvaged two items from the craft, a knee of horse bone and a ring-bolt. Both are preserved in the Watch Tower on the southern coast.

Lee Hayes wrote an adaptation of the song, calling it **I Wanna Go Home (Wreck of the John B)**, in 1951. He formed the Weavers with Pete Seeger, Ronnie Gilbert and Fred Hellerman, and in the early fifties they did more than anyone to popularize folk music in America. In 1960 Lonnie Donegan had a No 5 hit with **I Wanna Go Home** in Britain. Donegan had pioneered skiffle music in the mid-fifties.

The Beach Boys' version was a magnificent record, their fine harmonies giving the song a haunting beauty, tinged with sadness, that made it one of their finest singles. It was arranged and produced by Brian Wilson. It made No 3 in America, with 11 weeks on the charts. In Britain it peaked at No 2, with a longer chart run of 15 weeks. It was a big success in Europe, going to No 1 in Norway and The Netherlands. Global sales gave the Beach Boys their eighth million-selling record, with American sales reputedly the fastest of their career up to that time.

GOOD VIBRATIONS *Capitol 5676* [USA] *Capitol CL 15475* [UK]. Although released in

time for Christmas 1965, the Beach Boys' first big hit of 1966 was the million-selling **Barbara Ann**. It was followed by **Sloop John B**, which in turn was followed by what in America was the double A side **Wouldn't It be Nice?**/**God Only Knows**. **Wouldn't It be Nice?** was the bigger hit, reaching No 8. Though **God Only Knows** reached only No 39 in America, it was the A side in Britain and went to No 2.

Then came the Brian Wilson masterpiece **Good Vibrations**. Wilson spent the sort of time, money and effort producing this single that other bands would not even have spent on an album. The basic plan for the disc came to Wilson in a Hollywood recording studio in April 1966. An instrumental track was completed after two sessions, but the vocal tracks proved much more difficult to get right, and Wilson used five different recording studios before he was satisfied. These were Western Recorder, Gold Star (where Phil Spector had made many of his records), CBS, RCA and Sunset Sound. As well as pushing the electronics of the recording equipment to their limit, Wilson also used a theremin, an electronic instrument first used in the film *Spellbound*. Track after track of the Beach Boys singing the harmonies was overlaid, with Carl Wilson singing lead. The disc also featured Bruce Johnson (born in Chicago on 24 June 1944) who was standing in for Brian Wilson on the Beach Boys' live dates. Johnson played lead, bass guitar and the organ, singing the difficult falsetto harmonies on stage and sometimes on record. It took over six months to record **Good Vibrations**, but it resulted in the biggest hit of their career.

Released on 24 October 1966, the record went to No 1 six weeks later, staying at the top for one week. It spent 14 weeks on the Hot 100, and was awarded an RIAA Gold Disc for US sales of over one million on 21 December 1966. In Britain it gave the Beach Boys their first No 1, topping all the British charts for two weeks in November. It spent 13 weeks in the Top 50,

and was awarded a Silver Disc for British sales of a quarter of a million on 3 December 1966. When re-released in the UK in 1976, it made No 18 with a further seven weeks in the charts. It was also featured as part of the **Beach Boys Medley** single that was a minor British hit (but No 12 in America) in 1981. **Good Vibrations** was a big international hit, going into the Top 3 in Canada, Australia, New Zealand, South Africa, Ireland, Finland, Malaysia (No 1) and Singapore. It also made the charts in many other European countries. In Britain the single had **Wendy** as its B side, from the highly successful **Four by The Beach Boys** EP of 1964. Two of the tracks from it (including **Wendy**) had made the *Billboard* singles charts then, while the EP made the *Cash Box* charts.

Good Vibrations was an outstanding record, both for the Beach Boys and for pop music at the time. In its 1988 critics poll of the 100 best singles of the previous 25 years, *Rolling Stone* magazine ranked it 11th. Both Brian Wilson and the Beach Boys reached a height of excellence with this single that they were not to repeat. They made many more fine records, and had plenty more hits over the next 20 years, but none as successful as **Good Vibrations**.

In America the group had only one more Top 10 hit until their 1988 No 1 **Kokomo**, and that was **Rock and Roll Music** which reached No 5 in 1976. In Britain they had two top 10 hits in 1967 with **Then I Kissed Her** (a version of the old Crystals/Spector hit **Then He Kissed Me**, which was not released in America) and **Heroes and Villains**. They had one more British No 1 with **Do It Again** in 1968, and a few more Top 10 hits after that.

On the album front, 1966 was a disappointment. Though critically acclaimed, the **Pet Sounds** album was not as big a commercial success as their previous LPs. It was the album equivalent of the **Good Vibrations** single, and influenced the Beatles in the making of their **Sergeant Pepper** album in 1967. It reached No 10 in the US album charts, and failed to win a Gold Disc. It did better in Britain, where it peaked at No 2. The **Best of the Beach Boys** hits compilation reached No 8 in the States, with an RIAA Gold Disc for million dollar sales, and No 2 in Britain (with 142 weeks in the LP Top 40, compared to 78 weeks in the larger American Top 150). The group had two entries in the British EP Top 10 in 1966. **Hits** went to No 1 for 32 weeks in 1966 and 1967, with 82 weeks in the chart. **God Only Knows** made No 3, with 17 weeks in the EP Top 20.

Decline was just around the corner as 1966 came to a close, but that is not how it looked at the time. The Beach Boys ended the year with sensational victory over the Beatles, knocking the British group off the top spot in the *New Musical Express* and *Record Mirror* readers' polls to take the title of 'Top World Vocal Group'. The *NME* listed the Beach Boys as top singles act of the year, based on its Top 30 chart. *Record Mirror* also listed them as 1966's No 1, based on their larger British Top 50. The Beach Boys just beat the Beatles as top album act, and were the year's No 3 EP performers. In America, a similar survey of the *Cash Box* Top 50 for 1966 put the Beach Boys fifth. (All these surveys

were based on a points system, and measured chart consistency and not actual sales, although there was a strong link between the two.) **Good Vibrations** was to be their last sixties' million-selling single. They also had three million-selling albums in the 1970s.

In 1987 the Beach Boys teamed up with American rap trio the Fat Boys, and took a re-make of the 1963 Surfaris' surfing song **Wipe Out** to No 2 in Britain and No 12 in America. The following year the Beach Boys were featured on the soundtrack of the film 'Cocktail', taking **Kokomo** to No 1 in America and No 25 in Britain. 1989 saw a new record deal with their old company EMI-Capitol, a sold out European tour, and a new hit single and album, **Still Cruisin'**. After over a quarter of a century of hits, one of rock's greatest groups were '. . . still cruisin' after all of these years'.

THE BEATLES   *British*

NOWHERE MAN *Capitol 5587* [USA]. After three full years as major recording stars, the Beatles had racked up an incredible 29 million-selling records, including one EP and 13 albums. In 1966 the group slowed down a little, producing one new studio album. It was the year that saw them move irrevocably from their initial image of cute mop tops to more serious and outspoken musicians. It was a year of considerable controversy, especially in the United States. John Lennon's remarks about the Beatles being bigger than Jesus Christ did not go down well in the Bible belt, or many other parts of America, and he did not help his cause in the eyes of conservative America by following that comment up by ever stronger anti-Vietnam war statements.

The Beatles' first official release was **Paperback Writer**, but as that was not available until June Capitol issued **Nowhere Man** off the **Yesterday...And Today** album in February. The record was No 1 for two weeks in *Record World* and reached No 2 in *Cash Box* and No 3 in *Billboard*, with nine weeks in all charts. The flip side, **What Goes On**, also charted in *Billboard*, reaching No 81 in two weeks on the chart. The disc won an RIAA Gold Disc on 1 April 1966. Both sides were written by Paul McCartney and John Lennon, and produced by George Martin at the Abbey Road studios.

YESTERDAY...AND TODAY (Album) *Capitol T 2553* [USA]. The Beatles' 14th million-selling album was an American-only release put together by Capitol from material already released by EMI in Britain. The tracks were mainly those from Parlophone LPs that had been left off the American versions. All the tracks were produced by George Martin at the Abbey Road studios. The album went to No 1 for five weeks with 31 weeks in the charts. It included four records that had been hit singles, three of which had gone to No 1. The record ran into controversy over the original album cover. This showed a picture of the Beatles with bits of meat draped over them. As a result of the fuss, an alternative cover was designed. The picture was used as a publicity shot in Britain, and appeared on the front page of *Disc*.

The LP won an RIAA Gold Disc on 8 July, some three weeks after its release on 20 June. It went on to sell one and a half million copies in North America.

The tracks on the album, all of which were written by Lennon and McCartney unless otherwise indicated, were as follows: **Drive My Car**; **I'm Only Sleeping**; **Nowhere Man**; **Doctor Robert**; **Yesterday**; **Act Naturally**, by Van Morrison and John Russell; **And Your Bird Can Sing**; **If I Needed Someone**, by George Harrison; **We Can Work It Out**; **What Goes On**, by John Lennon, Paul McCartney and Ringo Starr; and **Day Tripper**.

PAPERBACK WRITER *Parlophone R 5452* [UK]/ *Capitol 5651* [USA]. **Paperback Writer** was the first new release of the year, six months after their last British hit. What it showed was the progress of both the Beatles and the EMI studios. Abbey Road had obtained some new equipment, and the Beatles experimented with it to the full. The track was recorded on Thursday 14 April, but it was not released until 10 June in Britain, and 30 May in America. It was produced by George Martin at Abbey Road, with Geoff Emerick as engineer and Phil McDonald as tape operator.

It had the lowest sale of any Beatles record since **Love Me Do** in Britain, but still made No 1 for two weeks in three of the four charts. This was a sign of things to come. All their singles since **I Want To Hold Your Hand** had entered at least three of the British charts at No 1 first week of release. This one achieved that only in the *Melody Maker*, and from this record onwards immediate number ones were the exception and no longer the rule.

Paperback Writer spent 11 weeks in the British Top 50, and ten weeks in the American charts where it was No 1 for two weeks. The flip side **Rain** also charted in America, reaching No 23 during seven weeks on the *Billboard* charts and No 31 during five weeks on the *Cash Box* Top 100. It won an American Gold Disc on 14 July 1966. It was a big hit around the world, going to No 1 in The Netherlands, Denmark, Norway, Germany, Austria, Ireland, New Zealand, Australia, Hong Kong, Malaysia and Singapore.

YELLOW SUBMARINE/ELEANOR RIGBY *Parlophone R 5493* [UK]/*Capitol 5715* [USA]. Both tracks of this double A side were on the **Revolver** album released on the same day, 5 August in Britain and 8 August in America. The Beatles were spending more time in the studio recording than previously, and both sides of this single were recorded between April and June 1966. Both were Lennon-McCartney compositions. George Martin produced both sides at Abbey Road.

Eleanor Rigby was very much a Paul McCartney masterpiece, with a considerable contribution from George Martin's scoring. As with **Yesterday**, Paul wanted a different, classical, sound for the record. George Martin brought in eight session musicians, using a double string quartet. The result was a piece of pop music of great beauty, and it won a Grammy as Best Contemporary Rock'n'Roll Solo Male Performance of 1966.

Despite the quality and complexity of

Eleanor Rigby, it was **Yellow Submarine** that the public really took to. Each Beatles album had at least one track featuring each Beatle. In the case of Ringo Starr it was usually only one track, and that one a bit of a problem. As Ringo had not written anything usable himself, John and Paul put together a nice, simple sing-along number for Ringo to sing lead on. It ended up at No 1 for four weeks in Britain and one week in America. In the USA **Eleanor Rigby** charted separately, reaching No 11 in *Billboard* and No 12 in *Cash Box*. **Yellow Submarine** was nine weeks in the *Billboard* charts and ten weeks in *Cash Box*. **Eleanor Rigby** lasted eight weeks in both charts. The double A side spent 13 weeks in the British Top 50. An RIAA Gold Disc was awarded on 12 September 1966. The record was a big international hit, going to No 1 in Canada, Australia, New Zealand, Germany, Switzerland, Norway, Sweden and The Netherlands.

REVOLVER (Album) *Parlophone PMC 7009* [*UK*]/*Capitol T 2576* [*USA*]. **Revolver** was a Beatles milestone, the first Beatles LP of their new recording era. It was full of experimentation, using the newly enhanced facilities of the Abbey Road studios to the full. It took longer to make than the earlier Beatles albums, but the result was their best album to date. The recording team was producer George Martin, engineer Geoff Emerick and tape operator Phil McDonald.

The album topped the British LP charts for seven weeks in the *Record Retailer*, where it stayed for 34 weeks, and nine weeks in *Melody Maker* where it entered the album charts at No 1 the first week of release. In America it went to No 1 for six weeks, with 77 weeks in the Top 150. It won an RIAA Gold Disc on 22 August 1966, going on to sell two and a half million in North America.

For the last time with a Beatles studio album, there were some differences between the British and American releases, with the British version eventually released in America on CD in 1987. The tracks on both versions of the album, all of which were written by Lennon and McCartney unless otherwise indicated, were as follows: **Taxman**, by George Harrison; **Eleanor Rigby**; **Love You To**, by George Harrison; **Here, There And Everywhere**; **Yellow Submarine**; **She Said She Said**; **Good Day Sunshine**; **For No One**; **I Want To Tell You**, by George Harrison; **Got To Get You Into My Life**; and **Tomorrow Never Knows**. The British album also included **I'm Only Sleeping**; **And Your Bird Can Sing** and **Doctor Robert**.

A COLLECTION OF BEATLES OLDIES (Album) *Parlophone PMC 7016* [*UK*]. The Beatles' first hits compilation was released on 9 December 1966. At first sales were disappointing, the album peaking at No 7 with 18 weeks in the Top 20. It was the first Beatles LP that failed to top the charts, though of course most Beatles fans had already bought every track on the album. Over the years global sales have eventually passed the million mark. The album was not released in the United States or Canada.

The tracks on the album, all but one of which were written by Lennon and McCartney, were as follows: **She Loves You**; **From Me To You**; **We Can Work It Out**; **Help!**; **Michelle**; **Yesterday**; **I Feel Fine**; **Yellow Submarine**; **Can't Buy Me Love**; **Bad Boy**, by Larry Williams; **Day Tripper**; **A Hard Day's Night**; **Ticket To Ride**; **Paperback Writer**; **Eleanor Rigby**; and **I Want To Hold Your Hand**.

ROY BLACK   *German*

GANZ IN WEISS (All in White) *Polydor 6024* [*West Germany*]. Roy Black, a teenage singer from Augsburg, Germany, first appeared with a beat band but gave up these activities to become one of Germany's most popular ballad singers. He entered the German Pop Music Festival and this resulted in a two-sided hit disc with both sides high on the German charts. His first big hit was **Du bist nicht allein** (You are not alone) in 1965 which sold half a million and established him in his native country. He then became a firm favourite on tours and TV. Each of his disc releases racked up big sales and made top positions in the German charts.

Ganz in weiss, written by Arland and Hertha, sold half a million by mid-1966 and achieved the million sale by the end of 1967. The disc was No 1 for six weeks.

His first album was a bestseller at Christmas 1966 and his **Roy Black II** album (November 1967) had advance orders of 50,000.

GRAHAM BONNEY   *British*

SUPER GIRL *Columbia (EMI) DB 7843* [*UK*]. Graham Bonney was born on 2 June 1945 in Stratford, East London, and at the age of four attended a dancing school. A few years later he was appearing in pantomime, on TV and in films, both acting and dancing. Around 1961 he became interested in popular music and played semi-professionally with various groups including the well-known Riot Squad. He also did session work for prominent artists including the Ivy League, Julie Rogers and Jet Harris. After a trip to Paris in 1965, playing with Michael Chaplin, Graham switched to solo singing, songwriting and record production. He wrote both the songs for his first solo disc, released in November 1965, and collaborated with Barry Mason on **Super Girl**, his second disc, released in February 1966. This was only a minor success in Britain reaching No 19 with eight weeks in the Top 50, but when released in Germany later it went to the top of their charts for six weeks with an estimated million sale. Bonney would subsequently build up an enormous following across the channel in Germany, where he appeared on many local TV and radio shows.

Super Girl was one of Germany's 'Top 10 Hits of 1966'.

THE BUCKINGHAMS   *American*

KIND OF A DRAG *USA 890* [*USA*]. A million seller for their first recording was achieved by this new American teenage group of five vocalists, and their 'Chicago' sound. Written

by J. Holvay, it sold the million by 1967 and was No 1 in the USA for two weeks with 13 weeks in the bestsellers. In early 1967, the group signed an exclusive contract with CBS Records.

CATERINA CASELLI   *Italian*

NESSUNO MI PUO GUIDICARE (No one Can Judge Me) *CGD N 9608* [*Italy*]. Caterina Caselli, a young Italian singer born in 1948, was quite unknown until she sang this song in the San Remo Song Festival in February 1966. Although placed second in the contest, it proved to be the biggest seller of the entries. Caterina was discovered and introduced on the disc market by CGD (Compagna Generale del Disco) in 1965. This disc became one of the biggest sellers in Italy during the winter of 1966 and reached a 650,000 figure in early 1967, with subsequent million sale and a Gold Disc award on 26 April 1967 by CGD. It was No 1 for nine consecutive weeks in Italy, and a success in Argentina.

In 1966, Caterina won the Juke Box 'Festival Bar' with **L'uomo d'oro** which sold half a million. By 1967 she was performing in concerts all over Italy and partnered Giorgio Gaber in a weekly TV series 'Diamoci del Tu — one of the most popular Italian TV musical shows.

Nessumo mi puo giudicare was written by M. Panzeri, D. Pace, Beretta and Prete, and is a pulsating up-tempo romantic ballad with a contagious repeating riff.

RAY CONNIFF   *American*

SOMEWHERE MY LOVE (Album) *CBS-Columbia 9319* [*USA*] *CBS SBPG 62740* [*UK*]. Ray Conniff was born on 6 November 1916 in Attleboro, Massachusetts. After graduation in

1934 he went to Boston and got his first engagement as a professional with Dan Murphy's society orchestra, the Musical Skippers. In late 1953 he was introduced to CBS's Mitch Miller and in 1954 was arranger for Don Cherry's **Band of Gold**, an eventual million seller, which was followed by a string of Conniff-arranged sessions and chart toppers for Johnnie Ray, Guy Mitchell, Frankie Laine, and later Marty Robbins and Johnny Mathis. CBS then decided to give Ray a session of his own, the result being his first album. This was **S'wonderful** (1956) which sold half a million. Many more big-selling albums followed.

By 1970 he had been awarded nine Gold Discs by RIAA for million-dollar-selling albums, including this album of **Somewhere My Love** which sold a million units by February 1967. The Gold Disc award for this was on 20 September 1966, with an RIAA Platinum Disc for sales of one million copies in the USA on 21 November 1986.

The contents of the album are: *Side 1* — **Red Roses for a Blue Lady**, by Sid Tepper and Roy C. Bennett (1948); **Downtown**, by Tony Hatch (1964); **Charade** (from the film *Charade*), by Johnny Mercer/Henry Mancini (1963); **King of the Road**, by Roger Miller (1964); **Edelweiss** (from *Sound of Music*), by O. Hammerstein II/Richard Rodgers (1960); **Young and Foolish** (from *Plain and Fancy*), by Arnold B. Horwitt/Albert Hague (1954); *Side 2* — **Somewhere My Love** (**Lara's theme** from the film *Doctor Zhivago*), by Paul Francis Webster/Maurice Jarre (1965); **Days of Wine and Roses** (from the film *Days of Wine and Roses*), by Johnny Mercer/Henry Mancini (1962); **Tie Me Kangaroo Down Sport**, by Rolf Harris (1960); **Wouldn't It be Luverly?** (from *My Fair Lady*), by Alan J. Lerner/Frederick Loewe (1956); **So Long, Farewell** (from *Sound of Music*), by O. Hammerstein/Richard Rodgers (1960).

This album was 18 weeks in the Top 10, and reached No 2 in the USA. It was in the bestsellers for 90 weeks. Conniff was the first American pop performer to record in the USSR.

BILL COSBY   *American*

WONDERFULNESS (Album) *Warner Brothers 1634* [*USA*]. Bill Cosby has the distinction of hitting the Gold album jackpot (1966) with four RIAA awards at the same time. This album went over the million mark on 4 April 1967, just under one year after its release in May 1966, selling 1,400,000 by the year's end. Cosby had to wait until the RIAA changed its certification rules in 1986 before he received a Platinum Disc to mark a million sales in the USA.

Cosby is one of America's funniest comedians and could have become a big name in the athletic field. After service in the US Navy medical corps, he attended Temple University on a football scholarship, but somewhere along the line decided on show business as a career. He gave up both football and college after two years and took a part-time job as a bartender, the customers being highly amused with his unusual brand of comedy. He soon had a big following and was eventually

booked into the Gaslight Café in Greenwich Village, New York, where he was 'discovered' by one of the city's journalists with subsequent tremendous publicity. In New York he met fellow comedian Allan Sherman who speedily introduced him to the Warner Brothers label, for whom he made his first album **Bill Cosby is a Very Funny Fellow** (1964). The same year he co-starred with Robert Culp in the popular 'I Spy' TV series and in 1965 came to fame through his many TV appearances on the Jack Paar, Jimmy Dean and Andy Williams shows. His second album **I Started Out as a Child** (1964) was followed by **Why is There Air?** (1965), with **Wonderfulness** amassing the largest initial order ever garnered on a comedy album in single day — 200,000. It got to No 7 in the US charts.

Bill Cosby, born on 12 July 1937, is a native of Philadelphia. **Wonderfulness** contains some of his funniest material including **Tonsils**, **Go Carts**, **Chicken Heart** and **The Playground**. All four albums were in the Top Sellers lists for most of 1966 continuing into 1967, earning him a Grammy Award as 'Best Comedy Artist' of 1966. This album was a US bestseller for 106 weeks.

THE BOB CREWE GENERATION   *American*

MUSIC TO WATCH GIRLS BY *Dynovoice 229* [*USA*]. Written by Tony Velona and Sid Ramin, this was the campaign theme of Diet Pepsi. Bob Crewe's disc got to No 9 in the US charts with 12 weeks in the bestsellers, and sold an estimated million by mid-1967. The disc is a 'brass-filled thumper' played by the Generation — an aggregation of 17 instrumentalists (seven brass, three saxophones, three guitars, piano, drums, tympani and xylophone) headed by Bob Crewe, the famous songwriter. It also proved to be a big hit for Andy Williams as a song.

Bob Crewe, born 12 November 1937, was one of New York's top male models. He also became a noted artist, some of his canvases selling for as much as $1,200. He was a talented all-rounder. As well as songwriting and making records, he produced other artists like the Four Seasons and the Highwaymen. He also built a business empire that included music publishing, film and video companies and Dynovoice Records.

THE CYRKLE   *American*

RED RUBBER BALL *CBS-Columbia 43589* [*USA*]. The Cyrkle, originally the Rondells, were renamed by Brian Epstein, manager of the Beatles, and John Lennon contributed the unique spelling of the name. It was Epstein's sole American group. The song was written by Paul Simon (of Simon and Garfunkel) and Bruce Woodley (of the Seekers), a hard-driving rhythmic ode about a boy who has just got over an unhappy romance and finally sees the light of day. The Cyrkle's disc was released in the USA in April 1966 and in Britain on 12 August 1966. It was not a success in Britain, but in the USA reached No 2 with 13 weeks in the bestsellers, and went on to sell a million.

The group originally began as a three-man unit at Lafayette College, later becoming a quartet. Each of the Cyrkles is a college graduate, their music sometimes having a folk-like campus flavour. They became exceedingly popular on the Gotham discotheque scene, and in addition to their own sound had an amazing talent for imitating sounds of other groups such as the Four Seasons and the Beach Boys, and performing favourite older tunes. They appeared on 14 of the dates in the US Beatles tour in 1966.

The members are Tom Dawes, born 25 July 1944 in Albany, New York, who plays 12-string guitar, five-string banjo, bass guitar and sitar; Don Danneman, born 9 May 1944 in Brooklyn, New York, who plays piano and guitar; Marty Fried, born 1944 in Wayside, New Jersey, who plays drums; Earl Pickens, who plays organ.

THE SPENCER DAVIS GROUP   *British*

GIMME SOME LOVIN' *Fontana TF-623* [*UK*] *United Artists 50108* [*USA*]. The Spencer Davis Group became one of Britain's leading R&B bands. It was formed by Birmingham University student Spencer Davis (born in Swansea, South Wales, on 17 July 1941), who became interested in R&B playing guitar with the university jazz band. He also played the harmonica and the piano accordion. While with the band, he heard the Muff-Woody Quartet, who at that time had 13-year-old Stephen Winwood (born in Birmingham on 12 May 1948) playing piano. He also played the organ and guitar. A few months later Spencer formed his group, getting Stephen Winwood, his brother Mervyn (Muff) Winwood (born in Birmingham on 15 June 1943) who played bass guitar, and Peter York (born in Redcar, Yorkshire, on 15 August 1942) to join him. York played drums and vibraphone, and all four shared the vocals, with Steve taking the lead.

Their first professional appearance was at the Golden Eagle in Birmingham in 1964. Chris Blackwell, then with the Fontana division of Dutch record company Philips, heard the group and signed them, becoming their recording and personal manager. They made their film debut in *Pop Gear* in 1964, which also included appearances by the Beatles, the Animals, Herman's Hermits, Billy J. Kramer, Peter and Gordon, the Honeycombs and Susan Maughan.

The group had their first hit with **I Can't Stand It**, which crept into the Top 50 for three weeks in November 1964, peaking at No 47. They had two more similarly small hits in 1965, and then released **Keep On Running** at the end of November. On 15 January 1966 it made No 1 in the *NME* Top 30, where it stayed for three weeks. (It was No 1 for one week in the *Record Retailer* Top 50.) It was also their first, though minor, American hit, released on Atco. It was followed by **Somebody Help Me**, which in Britain gave them back-to-back No 1s. Far from making it three chart toppers in a row, the follow-up did not even make the Top 10. **When I Come Home** peaked at No 12.

Their last release of 1966 was **Gimme Some Lovin'**, which almost made it to the top. It stalled at No 2, with 12 weeks in the Top 50,

though it won a Silver Disc for British sales of over a quarter of a million. It was also their biggest hit in America, reaching No 7 with 13 weeks on the charts. Combined British, American and other international sales easily pushed the record over the million mark. The song was written by Stevie and Muff Winwood and Spencer Davis, and produced by Chris Blackwell.

The Spencer Davis Group had one more Top 10 hit in Britain, when the follow-up to **Gimme Some Lovin'**, **I'm a Man**, reached No 9 early in 1967. In April of that year Stevie and Muff Winwood left the group, and, though they had two more minor hits, the Winwoods' departure in effect marked the end of the Spencer Davis Group. They had had 10 British hits between 1964 and 1968, of which four had made the Top 10 and two had gone to No 1. They had put three albums in the LP Top 10, all in 1966. In America they had had five hits in 1966 and 1967, two of which made the Top 10. Three albums made the lower regions of the LP charts in 1967 and 1968. Stevie Winwood went on to form Traffic in 1967 and Blind Faith in 1969, before going solo from the 1970s. In the 1980s Muff Winwood became senior A&R executive with CBS Records UK.

DAVE DEE, DOZY, BEAKY, MICK AND TICH
British

BEND IT *Fontana TF 746* [*UK*]. Written by Howard Blaikley (joint pseudonym of Ken Howard and Alan Blaikley who managed the group), this disc was No 2 in Britain and 12 weeks in the bestsellers with over 250,000 sale. It was a particularly big hit on the Continent, No 1 in Germany and high up other European charts. In order to obtain the bouzouki sound, an electrified mandola was used. With deliberate tempo accelerations, the disc caught the flavour of Greek music. The combined British and European sales were over a million.

The group came from Salisbury, Wiltshire, and first gained recognition through their disc **You Make It Move** and then their quarter-million seller **Hold Tight** (1966), also written by Howard Blaikley. This also was a hit in Germany where the group performed. They became musical globe-trotters and visited Greece, Africa and Australia. The name of the group was partly taken from the nicknames of three of them. They became noted for their dazzling colour combinations in stage clothing.

The personnel of the group were Dave Dee (David Harman), born 17 December 1943, Salisbury, Wiltshire (jews harp); Dozy (Trevor Leonard Ward Davies), born 27 November 1944, Enford, Wiltshire (bass guitar, drums, bongos); Beaky (John Dymond), born 10 July 1944, Salisbury, Wiltshire (guitar, drums, bass accordion); Mick (Michael Wilson), born 4 March 1944, Amesbury, Wiltshire (drums); Tich (Ian Frederick Stephen Amey), born 15 May 1944, Salisbury, Wiltshire (lead guitar).

NEIL DIAMOND
American

CHERRY, CHERRY *Bang 528* [*USA*]. Neil's first million-selling disc was a song written by him. It was released in August 1966 and reached No 5 in the US charts for one week with 12 weeks in the bestsellers. He switched to the Uni label in 1969 after having written big hits for the Monkees, and became a major artist for that label. (See 1969 for biographical data.)

DONOVAN
British

SUNSHINE SUPERMAN *Pye 7N 17241* [*UK*] *Epic 10045* [*USA*]. Donovan (Donovan Phillips Leitch) is one of the few British artists to appear on TV before making his first record, and achieved national recognition through his appearance on the 'Ready, Steady, Go' programme. His new and refreshing approach to folk music singing brought him prominence.

He was born on 10 May 1946 in Maryhill, Glasgow. He was educated at St Audrey's Secondary School, Hatfield, and attended the Campus, Welwyn Garden City, for a year. He left college to roam, and travelled throughout Britain, often in the company of a kazoo player named Gypsy Dave. He sang and wrote on the beaches of St Ives, Cornwall, for a while. He had purchased a guitar and taught himself to play. He worked in hotels occasionally and did a few jobs in art clubs.

Donovan met his manager, Peter Eden, at Southend, Essex; he later recorded some tapes, for him in London. This resulted in a meeting with Bob Bickford of the 'Ready, Steady, Go' TV programme and his first appearance thereon, also an eventual Pye Records contract (1965). His first recording, **Catch the Wind**, his own composition, sold over 200,000 (No 4 in the British charts), followed by another self-penned hit **Colours** and then his biggest success, a US song **Universal Soldier** (on an EP of the same title) which was No 1 for eight weeks in the EP charts. Donovan made his first American appearance on the 'Shindig' TV shows in the summer of 1965, after a tour in Britain with pop groups. He again appeared in the USA in November 1965 for several concerts and TV shows, and became an international name with appearances in France, Norway, Sweden, Finland, Denmark and Belgium.

Sunshine Superman was written by him and recorded specially for the American market. It sold 800,000 in six weeks and soon passed the million mark, achieving the No 1 chart position for one week in USA with 13 weeks in the bestsellers.

His album of the same title had an advance order of a quarter million and quickly sold half a million.

This disc also sold over 250,000 when released in Britain (Pye label) where it was No 3 and 11 weeks in the bestsellers.

MELLOW YELLOW *Pye 7N 17267* [*UK*] *Epic 10098* [*USA*]. The second million seller for Donovan, this off-beat rock number was again written by him for the American market. It was No 1 for two weeks in the US charts and 12 weeks in the bestsellers, and No 8 in Britain. RIAA Gold Disc award February 1967.

THE EASYBEATS   *British/Australian*

FRIDAY ON MY MIND *Parlophone GEPO 70041* [*Australia*] *United Artists UP 1157* [*UK*] *United Artists 50106* [*USA*]. Although designated as an Australian group, all the Easybeats are sons of European parents who emigrated to Australia. They met in a hostel in Sydney and played at various clubs in the vicinity. After a year or so they made their first disc, **For My Woman**, which had only small success. Their second disc **She's So Fine** got them the No 1 position in the Australian charts and established them. By July 1966, four of their six discs had reached the top chart position, making them the most popular group 'down under', with riots wherever they appeared, and several awards — 'Best Group', 'Most Original Group' and 'Best Vocal Group in Australia'. The Easybeats made their first big impact on the pop music scene in April 1965 when they appeared at the Village, Sydney, receiving plaudits that started to gain them recognition further afield in the US.

Friday on My Mind was the group's first English-produced disc by United Artists. It was issued on Parlophone in Australia and stayed No 1 there for eight weeks. It got to No 6 in Britain with 15 weeks in the bestsellers, and No 16 in the USA staying 14 weeks in the charts. Sales in Britain were over 250,000 and a Gold Disc for a global million was presented to them in May 1967 in Australia.

They made a short tour of America and toured Germany in 1967, in addition to British appearances.

The group consisted of George Young, born 6 November 1947 in Glasgow, Scotland; Gordon 'Snowy' Fleet, born 16 August 1945 in Bootle, Lancashire; Dick Diamonde, born 28 December 1947 in Hilversum, Holland; Harry Vanda, born 22 March 1974 in The Hague, Holland; Little Stevie Wright, born 20 December 1948 in Leeds, Yorkshire. Vanda and Young play guitar, Wright plays drums and guitar, Diamonde plays bass and Fleet plays drums.

Friday on My Mind was written by Young and Vanda who wrote most of the group's songs.

THE FOUR TOPS   *American*

REACH OUT I'LL BE THERE *Motown 1098* [*USA*] *Tamla Motown TMG 579* [*UK*]. **Reach Out I'll Be There** was a Motown classic, and the biggest hit of the Four Tops' career. It was written and produced by the Motown house team of Eddie and Brian Holland and Lamont Dozier. The Tops did not rate it very highly at first, but the record gave them their second US No 1 and third million-selling record. It was at the top for one week in *Cash Box* and two weeks in *Billboard*, with 15 weeks on the Hot 100. In Britain it was the group's first big hit, going all the way to No 1 for three weeks (four weeks in the *Disc* charts) with 16 weeks in the Top 50. It was awarded a Silver Disc for British sales on 12 November 1966. The record was also a major R&B hit, with two weeks at No 1 in the American R&B charts and six weeks at the top of the British R&B Top 20.

STANDING IN THE SHADOWS OF LOVE *Motown 1102* [*USA*] *Tamla Motown TMG 589* [*UK*]. The Four Tops' fourth million seller **Standing in the Shadow of Love** was written and produced by the same Motown team of Holland-Dozier-Holland which created the classic **Reach Out I'll Be There**, which it followed into the US Top 10. Both it and its follow-up, **Bernadette** (which made the Top 10 in 1967), bore a remarkable resemblance to **Reach Out**. Those Motown boys certainly knew how to milk the most out of a big hit when they had one. It was No 6 for two weeks in America, and No 5 in Britain. It spent 10 weeks in the American charts and eight weeks in the British charts. The record was also an R&B hit on both sides on the Atlantic, topping the British R&B charts for one week at the end of January 1967. It was No 2 with 12 weeks in the US R&B charts.

BOBBY GOLDSBORO   *American*

IT'S TOO LATE *United Artists 980* [*USA*]. Bobby's third million seller, also written by him. The disc achieved No 22 position in the US charts and eight weeks in the bestsellers. The million sale was reported by 1967.

THE HAPPENINGS   *American*

SEE YOU IN SEPTEMBER *B.T. Puppy 520* [*USA*]. The members of this group, Dave Libert (lead baritone and arranger), Tom Juliano (tenor and second lead), Bob Miranda (lead singer) and Ralph Divito (baritone, high falsetto and comedian), all hail from Paterson, New Jersey. They spent the three years from 1964 in planning, training and practising. After the usual rounds of one record company to another, they had a recording session produced by the successful recording group the Tokens. Their second session was much more successful and included **See You in September** (written in 1959 by Sid Wayne, author, and Sherman Edwards, composer). The recording on the B. T. Puppy label (owned by Jubilee Records) was finally a big success in Boston, Massachusetts, and quickly spread thoughout the USA. It was No 1 for a week and in the *Variety* and *Record World* charts and 14 weeks in the Hot 100. It had an eventual million sale and Gold Disc award by Jubilee Records.

GO AWAY LITTLE GIRL *B.T. Puppy 522* [*USA*]. This revival of the 1962 hit song by Gerry Goffin and Carole King made it the second time it was a million seller for the husband-and-wife songwriter team. The disc was produced by the Tokens, and the Happenings' version reached No 9 in the US charts with nine weeks in the bestsellers, a successful follow-up to their **See You in September**, with a seven-figure sale subsequently.

BOBBY HEBB   *American*

SUNNY *Philips 40365* [*USA*] *Philips BF 1503* [*UK*]. Bobby Hebb started songwriting in 1958 He wrote **Sunny** in the dawn of the day following President Kennedy's assassination in 1963, his sleep having been disturbed by the event, and this no doubt accounts for the rather poignant lyrics. It took over two years to get the song on disc, but when released it opened up a promising career for Bobby. The disc got to No 1 in the USA for one week in *Cash Box* and *Record World* with 15 weeks in the US bestsellers, also reaching No 11 in Britain, with nine weeks in the bestsellers.

Bobby Hebb was born 26 July 1941, one of seven children, in Nashville and started performing at the age of four. Both his parents are blind. When he was 12, Roy Acuff invited him to be the first Afro-American to appear on the Grand Ole Opry show. On leaving high school in Nashville, he learned to play the trumpet. He graduated from a dental technician's course in Chicago, resuming his music studies and on occasion played spoons at Bo Diddley's recordings. He played trumpet with a jazz combo during his US Navy service and on discharge moved on to other brass instruments, then guitar studies with famous Chet Atkins whom he credits with launching him on a recording career. He also plays four-string banjo and drums, and is virtually a 'one-man band'. Bobby then joined the Mickey and Sylvia team in New York which finally became just Bobby and Sylvia for a while (1961), working together for two years. Bobby then sang in New York and local clubs on his own. The success of **Sunny** earned Bobby a booking as a supporting attraction with the Beatles' 1966 US tour.

Many famous artists have recorded Bobby's material including Percy Sledge, Mary Wells, Marvin Gaye, Billy Preston and Herb Alpert. **Sunny** was also recorded by many other artists including Cher, Georgie Fame and Gloria Lynne.

HERMAN'S HERMITS   *British*

LISTEN, PEOPLE *MGM 13462* [*USA*]. Herman's Hermits' ninth million seller was from the film *When the Boys Meet the Girls*, in which the group starred. It was a remake of the 1930 George Gershwin musical 'Girl Crazy'. Columbia did not release the record as a single in Britain or Europe, though EMI did put it out in the Far East. In North America, where EMI's Capitol Records had passed on the group, their records were licensed to MGM. They did release **Listen, People** as a single, and it went to No 3, with nine weeks on the charts. It had an advance order of 600,000 with Canadian and Australian sales, where it was a Top 10 hit, taking the total to over the million. **Listen, People** was written by Britain's Graham Gouldman for the film, and was produced by Mickie Most.

THE HOLLIES   *British*

BUS STOP *Parlophone R 5469* [*UK*] *Imperial 66186* [*USA*]. The Hollies were one of the most consistent of all British groups, with 30 hit singles in the charts from 1963 to 1988. Twenty of these were in the sixties, a total beaten by only two other groups — the Shadows and the Beatles. The Hollies were formed in 1962. Their membership, drawn from Manchester groups the Dolphins and the Deltas, consisted of Graham Nash (born in Blackpool, Lancashire, on 2 February 1942) on guitar, Allan Clarke (born in Salford, Greater Manchester, on 15 April 1942) on guitar and harmonica, Tony Hicks (born in Nelson, Lancashire on 16 December 1943) on guitar, Don Rathbone (born in Manchester in 1942) on drums, and Eric Haydoc (born in Lancashire on 3 February 1943) on bass guitar. Rathbone was soon replaced by Bobby Elliott (born in Burnley, Lancashire, on 8 December 1942), while in 1966 Heycock was replaced by Bernie Calvert (born on 16 September 1944.)

In 1963 the group signed a recording deal with EMI, who put their records out on the Parlophone label. Their first release was **(Ain't That) Just Like Me?** which like most of their early records was a cover of an American R&B

song. It reached No 25 in the charts. Their third hit, **Stay**, was released at the end of 1963. It gave them the first of 17 Top 10 hits, reaching No 3. The follow-up did even better. **Just One Look** reached No 2 early in 1964. **I'm Alive** gave them their first No 1 the following year, and **I Can't Let Go** their second chart topper in March 1966.

The Hollies followed this with **Bus Stop**, which went to No 5 in Britain with nine weeks in the Top 50. The song was written by Graham Gouldman, who also wrote the Herman's Hermits' million seller **Listen, People**, a major hit in the USA. This may have been the factor that helped break the group in America. **Bus Stop** was their first big hit there, reaching No 5 with 14 weeks on *Billboard*'s Hot 100. Their first US chart entry had been in 1964, when **Just One Look** spent just one week in the charts at No 98.

Two other minor hits followed, but, almost alone of the big British groups, the Hollies did not seem able to make it in the biggest record market in the world. The group and their management were increasingly upset by this, and blamed their American record company. (The fact that all their early records were covers of American songs was clearly a factor as well.) The Hollies were signed to EMI for the whole world, but when Capitol passed on them EMI licensed their material to Liberty Records, who put the Hollies' discs out on their Imperial label. In an attempt to resolve the problem, EMI managing director L.G. Wood promised to get Liberty to release the Hollies from their commitment if **I'm Alive**, which after all had been a No 1 in Britain, did not do well. It bombed completely, and L.G. Wood soon had both the Hollies' manager and agent writing to him seeking a switch of label to Capitol. Capitol were not that interested, and the follow-up, **Look Through Any Window**, was a minor hit.

The problem was shelved when **Bus Stop** finally put the Hollies in the Top 10.

Bus Stop was produced by Ron Richards at the EMI studios at Abbey Road, London. It was the Hollies' first million-selling record, based on world sales. It was a hit in Europe and South America, reaching No 3 in Brazil.

STOP, STOP, STOP *Parlophone R 5508* [*UK*] *Imperial 66214* [*USA*]. The follow-up to **Bus Stop** was **Stop, Stop, Stop**, which was written by Graham Nash, Tony Hicks and Allan Clarke. At last the group had developed its own songwriting ability, and with that came more sustained success in America. It was produced by Ron Richards at Abbey Road, and was the Hollies' second global million seller. In their home market, the Hollies took this record to No 2 and 12 weeks in the charts. In America it reached No 7 during a ten week chart run.

The American success of this record took the heat off Liberty, who had worked hard to break the Hollies. When their recording contract with EMI expired on 31 December 1966, it was replaced by a licensing deal restricted to Britain, South America, and certain other territories.

In the USA the Hollies switched to licensing their records to CBS via their Epic label. In 1973 they switched to Polydor in Britain, and had a number of hits in the early seventies. They later returned to EMI, and in 1981 had a moderate hit with **Holliedaze**, a segued collection of their sixties hits. In the late eighties EMI released a number of their records on Columbia, though it was the re-issue of **He Ain't Heavy, He's My Brother** on the EMI label that brought them back into the charts with a vengeance in 1988.

The song was used in a Miller Lite beer television commercial, and with this extra boost the Hollies were back at No 1.

TOMMY JAMES AND THE SHONDELLS
American

HANKY PANKY *Snap, then Roulette 4686 [USA] Roulette RK 7000 [UK]*. Written by the famous US husband-and-wife songwriters Jeff Barry and Ellie Greenwich, **Hanky Panky** did not sell when first issued in 1963 on Snap label. A job lot of the disc was bought up in 1966 and some action was obtained on Pittsburgh radio when it was aired by a disc jockey. It then sold 28,000 in ten days, with other broadcasts in Cleveland and Memphis. A scramble to obtain the master disc ended with the rights going to Roulette Records for $10,000. When subsequently nationally promoted by them, it shot to No 1 position on the charts for two weeks with 12 weeks in the US bestsellers, and sold a million. The disc was No 38 in Britain. The group were given a Gold Disc in August 1966 by RIAA.

Lead singer Tommy James, born 29 April 1947 in Dayton, Ohio, originally started a group in Niles, Michigan, called Tommy and the Tornados when he was 13. All the Shondells come from Greensboro, a small town in the Pittsburgh suburbs. Three of them,

Joe, Ronnie and George, went to the same college, St Vincent's in Latrobe, Pennsylvania. Tommy James met the Shondells (six members) one night in Pittsburgh and decided to join them. They were managed by Bob Mack of Pittsburgh, who negotiated the deal with Roulette Records, and who operated 11 teen-type nightclubs in the city.

The Shondells were Joe Kessler, guitarist; George Magura, saxophonist, bass and organist; Vinnie Pietropaoli, drummer; Ronnie Rosman, piano and organ; and Mike Vale, bass, piano and vocalist.

TOM JONES
British

GREEN GREEN GRASS OF HOME *Decca F 22511 [UK] Parrot 40009 [USA]*. Tom Jones' **Green Green Grass of Home** was the biggest-selling record in Britain in 1966, topping the charts over Christmas and the New Year during its seven weeks at No 1. It won a Gold Disc for British sales of over one million; only Elvis Presley, Lonnie Donegan, Cliff Richard, the Shadows and the Beatles had done it before. It was the only British record in Decca's history to have sold the million in Britain alone. It was the biggest hit of Tom Jones' career.

It marked Tom's triumphant return to the Top 10 after a disappointing 18 months. He had

gone to No 1 with his first hit, the million-selling **It's Not Unusual**, in early 1965. There then followed six minor hits and one miss. **Green Green Grass of Home** marked the beginning of his peak period as a pop star. While the record was at No 1, he came second to Cliff Richard in the 'Top British Male Singer' section of the *New Musical Express* and *Record Mirror* readers' polls, repeating the performance early in 1967 in a similar poll in *Disc*.

Tom Jones picked this hit himself, the first time he had selected a record for release. He was a big fan of Jerry Lee Lewis, who by the mid-sixties had moved into the country field. He bought Lewis's **Country Songs for City People** album as soon as it came out, and **Green Green Grass of Home** was the first track on it. Long a C&W favourite, it had previously been recorded by American country singers like Ferlin Husky and Porter Wagoner. Tom included the song on his TV show, and had a lot of requests from viewers asking how they could get hold of it. He had never had such a reaction before, so he insisted on recording the song. It was written by American Curley Putman, and produced by Peter Sullivan.

Tom Jones spent a lot of time in the United States in 1966, following the big success of **It's Not Unusual** and **What's New Pussycat?** the year before. Yet **Green Grass** was not one of his big hits there, peaking at No 11. It spent 12 weeks in the American Top 100, compared to 22 weeks in the British Top 50. The record was a big international hit, making the charts in South Africa (No 1), Australia, New Zealand, Ireland and Norway (No 2 in all of them), and in Finland, The Netherlands and Malaysia, among others.

UDO JURGENS
Austrian

MERCI CHÉRIE *Vogue 2136 [West Germany]*. This song, a dreamy romantic ballad with an 'Ave Maria'-like lilt, won for Udo Jurgens and Austria the Grand Prix of the 1966 Eurovision Song Contest at the Villa Louvigny, Luxembourg, on 5 March. The words are by Thomas Hoerbiger with music by Udo Jurgens. It was the third time Udo had entered for the contest and the first time he won. He accompanied himself at the piano, and was heard and seen by 200 million throughout Europe and North Africa.

Udo Jurgen Beckelman was born on 30 September 1934 in Klagenfurt, Austria, and spent his childhood in his parents' 800-year-old home, Ottmanach Castle, once Napoleon's Austrian residence. He learned to play the harmonica at five and, soon after, the accordion. He studied music in 1948 at the music college in Klagenfurt, and took a five-year course in composition, music theory and singing. During this course, his composition **Je t'aime** won a national competition and this award resulted in his directing the big band of Radio Klagenfurt, in 1951. At the age of 20, Udo made his first record which was unsuccessful. In 1960 at the Knokke (Belgium) Song Festival he gained a prize for the best solo singer, and immediately afterwards had a hit in Belgium with his own song **Jenny**. During 1961 and 1962, he became well known through a series of

films he made, and in 1963 his song **Warum nur warum** got fifth place in the 1964 Eurovision Contest. This became a big hit all over Europe and was a success for Britain's Matt Munro under its English title of **Walk Away**. Udo then became a top export item in Germany, and an established European star both as artist and composer all over Europe.

Merci chérie sold over 350,000 in France and over 250,000 in Germany plus big sales in his native Austria (No 2 in the charts) and in Holland. It sold over the million globally and Deutsche Vogue presented him with a Gold Disc.

KEITH
American

98.6 Mercury 72639 [USA] Mercury MF 955 [UK]. Keith was American singer James Barry Keefer. He had his first hit with **Ain't Gonna Lie** in September 1966, reaching No 39 in the *Billboard* Hot 100. The follow-up was **98.6** (the normal body temperature in degrees Fahrenheit), which gave him his only Top 10 hit. It reached No 7 with 14 weeks on the charts. He had two more minor hits in 1967 and then disappeared. **98.6** was his first British hit, reaching No 24 with seven weeks in the Top 50 in 1967. The follow-up hit on both sides of the Atlantic was **Tell Me to My Face**. It was only just a hit in Britain, reaching No 50 for one week in March 1967.

98.6 was written by Tony Powers (words) and George Fischoff (music). It was produced by Jerry Ross, who was responsible for a number of hits in the mid-sixties. It sold a million globally.

THE RAMSEY LEWIS TRIO
American

WADE IN THE WATER *Cadet 5541 [USA] Chess 6145 004 [UK]*. **Wade in the Water** was arranged by Ramsey Lewis, and was based on a pre-American Civil War slave song. It reached No 19 in America, with 13 weeks in the Hot 100. This was the Ramsey Lewis Trio's sixth instrumental hit. With and without his trio, Lewis was to have 15 American hits, all but one of them instrumentals. Pianist Lewis also teamed up with Earth, Wind And Fire for two more instrumental hits in 1975. He was not a chart act in Britain, where **Wade in the Water** was his only hit, and only after it was put out by Chess in 1972. It reached No 31 with eight weeks in the charts. Global sales of a million were subsequently reported.

LOS BRAVOS
Spanish

BLACK IS BLACK *Decca F 22419 [UK] Press 60002 [USA]*. Los Bravos were the first Spanish group to have a major hit in Britain. They had been voted No 1 group in Spain, where they recorded for Columbia Espanol an independent Spanish company no longer connected with EMI, who owned the Columbia trademark in the rest of Europe and most of the world.

Spanish Columbia had a matrix exchange agreement with British Decca, which usually meant that Columbia acted as licensee for Decca in Spain. For once the relationship was not a one-way street, for when Columbia sent Decca some Los Bravos records musical director Ivor Raymonde was sufficiently impressed to go to Madrid to hear the group. He took a number of British songs with him for the group to play, and one of them was **Black is Black**. Los Bravos came to London and recorded the song at the Decca studios in West Hampstead in April 1966. The record was released in Britain on 17 June, and went to No 2, with 13 weeks in the charts. It was a big hit in Europe, and reached No 4 in the USA, where Decca released it on their new Press label. It was 12 weeks in the American charts. Global sales were over a million. **Black is Black** was written by Tony Hayes and Steve Wadey from the village of Hoo, near Rochester, Kent, where the duo had their own recording studio. It was their very first song, but no British artist wanted it.

Los Bravos consisted of Antonio Martinez (born in Madrid on 3 October 1945) on guitar, Manuel Fernandez (born in Seville on 29 September 1943) on electric organ, Miguel Vicens Danus (born in Mallona, Palma, on 21 June 1944) on bass, Pablo Gomez (born in Barcelona on 5 November 1943) on drums, and Mike Kogel, the one German in this otherwise Spanish group (born in Berlin on 25 April 1945) who played the guitar and was the lead vocalist. The group was formed in 1965 from an amalgamation of two other Spanish groups, Los Sonor and the Runaways. They made their radio debut in Madrid, and soon became popular throughout Spain.

Their time as international stars was brief. In Britain they followed **Black is Black** with **I Don't Care**, which reached No 16. It was their last hit, for the next single, the prophetically titled **Going Nowhere** released in December 1966, failed. So did **I'm All Ears** the following May, **Like Nobody Else** in October 1967, **Bring a Little Loving** in 1968 and **Save Me, Save Me** in 1969. It was a similar story in America, where **Going Nowhere** made No 91 with two weeks in the charts in December 1966. Their only other US hit was in 1968, with **Bring a Little Loving** from the film *Bravos II*. It reached No 51. Though their time on the world stage was soon over, they were very popular in Spain for the rest of the decade, and they remain the only Spanish group ever to storm the British and American charts.

THE LOVIN' SPOONFUL   *American*

DAYDREAM *Kama Sutra 208* [*USA*] *Pye International 7N 25361* [*UK*]. This group with its extraordinary name first met in New York's famed Greenwich Village where they became friends through a mutual love of music and were teamed by their manager Bob Cavallo and producer Erik Jacobson. After their formation, they obtained a booking at Greenwich Village's Night Owl Café, but the manager wasn't too impressed and said they needed more practice. The group took his advice and literally went underground, to the basement of a nearby hotel and emerged two months later professionally polished. The Night Owl Café

owner then engaged them for an indefinite period and many famous personalities in the entertainment world came to hear them. They made their first disc **Do You Believe in Magic?** which hit the US charts in August 1965. It achieved the No 4 position for two weeks in October and was the start of a quick rise to fame. **You Didn't Have to Be So Nice** followed with a high chart position, and in early 1966 their **Daydream** got to No 1 for a week with 12 weeks in the bestsellers, and to No 2 for two weeks in Britain with 13 weeks in the bestsellers (over 250,000 sale). With big US sales, the disc is estimated to have sold a global million. The song is an easy-going blues-tinged happy-go-lucky item, somewhat reminiscent of the idiom of the 1930s.

The group members are Zal Yanovsky (lead guitarist), born 19 December 1944; John Sebastian (guitar, harmonica and autoharp),

born 17 March 1943; Steve Boone (electric bass), born 23 September 1943; and Joe Butler (drums), born 16 September 1943. **Daydream** was written by John Sebastian. Most of their songs are written by members of the group.

The Lovin' Spoonful visited Britain in April 1966 for TV and club appearances, then Sweden and Ireland.

SUMMER IN THE CITY *Kama Sutra 211* [*USA*] *Kama Sutra KAS 200* [*UK*]. The second million seller for the the Lovin' Spoonful, with Gold Disc award from RIAA for a million sale in the USA alone. This infectious hard-driving blues beat number rocketed to No 1 for three weeks in America with 11 weeks in the bestsellers, and was also a hit in Britain (No 7 with 11 weeks in the bestsellers) and in Germany. It was written by Steve Boone, John Sebastian and M. Sebastian.

THE MAMAS AND THE PAPAS   *American*

IF YOU CAN BELIEVE YOUR EYES AND EARS (Album) *Dunhill 50006 [USA] RCA Victor RD 7803 [UK]*. This first album by the group, following their tremendous success with their first singles disc, proved to be a gold mine. It contained **Monday, Monday**, issued as a singles disc, and is said to have sold three million by early 1967, just 12 months after release in February 1966. It achieved the No 1 position for one week and was in the Top 10 for 20 weeks, staying in the bestsellers for 105 weeks.

More than half the songs on the album were written by the group's John Phillips. Gold Disc award RIAA 10 June 1966.

Contents of the disc: *Side 1* — **Monday, Monday**, by John Phillips (1966); **Straight Shooter**, by John Phillips (1966); **Got a Feelin'**, by Denny Doherty and John Phillips (1966); **I Call Your Name**, by John Lennon and Paul McCartney (1963); **Do You Wanna Dance?**, by Freeman; **Go Where You Wanna Go**, by John Phillips (1966); *Side 2* — **California Dreamin'**, by John Phillips (1965); **Spanish Harlem**, by Jerry Leiber and Phil Spector (1961); **Somebody Groovy**, by John Phillips (1966); **Her Girl**, by John and Michelle Phillips (1966); **You Baby**, by P.F. Sloan and Steve Barri (1966); **The 'In' Crowd**, by Billy Page (1965).

The British release was titled **The Mamas and The Papas**, and should not be confused with the group's second American album of the same name (see below).

MONDAY MONDAY *Dunhill 4026 [USA] RCA Victor 1516 [UK]*. The second big hit for this group this was an even bigger success than their first. Written by the group's lead singer John Phillips, the disc was No 1 for three weeks in the US charts and 12 weeks in the bestsellers, and was No 3 for three weeks in Britain with 13 weeks in the bestsellers, and also a success in Europe and abroad.

With a Gold Disc for million dollar sales of their first and second albums, this made four Gold Discs from RIAA for the group.

The disc was released on 24 March 1966. Grammy Award for 'Best Contemporary Rock'n'Roll Group Performance', 1966.

THE MAMAS AND THE PAPAS (Album) *Dunhill 51101 [USA] RCA Victor SF 7639 [UK]*. This second album by America's most successful group of 1966 had an estimated two million sale by early 1967. Again most of the songs were written by the group's John Phillips. It was No 4 for seven weeks, in the Top 10 for 11 weeks and in the bestsellers for 76 weeks. The disc was released in September 1966. Gold Disc award RIAA 1 December 1966.

The group were reported to have sold six million singles and five million albums in just over a year, making a gigantic success for themselves and the Dunhill label, which was bought up by ABC-Paramount in May 1966.

The contents of disc are: *Side 1* — **No Salt on Her Tail**, by John Phillips (1966); **Trip, Stumble and Fall**, by John Phillips and Michelle Gilliam (1966); **Dancing Bear**, by John Phillips (1966); **Words of Love**, by John Phillips (1966); **My Heart Stood Still**, by Lorenz Hart/Richard Rodgers (1927); **Dancing in the Street**, by William Stevenson and Marvin Gaye (1964); *Side 2* — **I Saw Her Again**, by Denny Doherty and John Phillips (1966); **Strange Young Girl**, by John Phillips (1966); **I Can't Wait**, by John Phillips (1966); **Even if I Could**, by John Phillips (1966); **That Kind of Girl**, by John Phillips (1966); **Once Was a Time I Thought**, by John Phillips (1966).

The British album was titled **Cass, John, Michelle, Denny**.

THE MINDBENDERS   *British*

A GROOVY KIND OF LOVE *Fontana TF 644 [UK] Fontana 1521 [USA]*. The first big hit for the Mindbenders (see 1965) who, after being with Wayne Fontana (see 1965), went out on their own. The song was written by American teenager Toni Wine with Carole Bayer in 1965. The disc was No 1 for one week in Britain with 14 weeks in the bestsellers, and sold over 250,000. With the release on the Fontana label in the USA where it was also No 1 for a week in *Cash Box* and *Record World* and 13 weeks in the bestsellers with big sales, the disc reached an estimated million.

Eric Stewart, the group's lead guitarist, doubles as lead vocalist on the disc. The Mindbenders made a long personal appearance tour throughout the USA in 1965.

THE MONKEES   *American*

LAST TRAIN TO CLARKSVILLE *Colgems 1001 [USA] RCA Victor 1547 [UK]*. The idea for the Monkees came from two TV producers — Robert Rafelson and Bert Schneider of Raybert Productions. They advertised in *Variety* and the *Hollywood Reporter* on 8 September 1965 for 'four insane boys, aged 17 to 21' to form a group for a TV show, to reflect the 'adventures of an unknown young group and its dreams on the way to fame and fortune. These 'dreams' actually came true.

Mickey (George Michael) Dolenz, born 8 March 1945 in Los Angeles, the son of famous actor George Dolenz, had been TV's 'Circus Boy' for three years and had had other acting appearances in 'Peyton Place', 'Route 66' and 'Mr Novak'. He became drummer of the group. Peter Halsten Tork (real name Thorkelson), born 13 February 1942 in Washington, DC, the son of H.J. Thorkelson, an Associate Professor of Economics at the University of Connecticut, had been training for a career as a teacher but decided on singing instead. He became vocalist/guitarist of the group, and was also a pianist and French horn player. Robert Michael Nesmith, born 30 December 1942 in Dallas, Texas, first appeared in San Antonio folk clubs, becoming performer-composer in California cafés known as 'Wool Hat' Nesmith. He became second vocalist/guitarist. David Thomas Jones, born 30 December 1946 in Manchester, England, had been a TV actor with parts in 'Coronation Street', 'Z Cars', 'Ben Casey' and 'Farmer's Daughter', and on stage in the USA as the Artful Dodger in *Oliver* and Sam Weller in *Pickwick*. He was third guitarist of the group.

Don Kirschner, president of Colgems spent two months grooming them in singing and supervised their disc sessions as well as their TV series. **Last Train to Clarksville** was written and produced by Tommy Boyce and Bobby Hart, exclusive writers for Screen Gems, the Columbia Music Publishing Company. The song, a hard-driving, pulsating number with a catchy repeating 'riff', was the group's first disc for the newly formed Colgems label. It was released on 16 August 1966 with extensive promotion, and just prior to the filmed Screen Gems TV show 'The Monkees', a comedy-fantasy series especially created for them, with the debut on 12 September. Their first album **The Monkees** was also released on this date to coincide with the series.

The single reached No 1 in the US charts in nine weeks with 15 weeks in the bestsellers, and sold nearly two million, with RIAA Gold Disc award on 31 October. It stayed at the top for two weeks. It was No 23 in Britain with seven weeks in the bestsellers. The album also received a Gold Disc award from RIAA at the same time (setting a precedent) after only five weeks in the charts, and was No 1 for 15 weeks. The success of the TV series and the disc made the group the rage of the USA, emulating the Beatles' success. The TV series became a tremendous hit in Britain from January 1967. Monkee merchandise from guitars to comic books and Monkee pants grossed $20 million by the end of 1966 in America. The group's quick rise to fame is an outstanding example of American show business co-ordination and planned promotion.

The backing of this disc was **Take a Giant Step** by husband-and-wife team Gerry Goffin and Carole King. Due to pressure of work, the group do only the singing on the disc.

THE MONKEES (Album) *Colgems 101 [USA] RCA Victor SF 7844 [UK]*. This first album by the group was issued on 12 September to coincide with the first showing of their TV series. It sold over 3,200,000 in just over three months on the

US market, faster than the Beatles did at their launching there in 1964. It was No 1 in the USA for 15 weeks, and in Britain for eight weeks in 1967. RIAA Gold Disc award in December 1966.

By 1 January 1968, it had sold around five million and was in the US bestsellers for 78 weeks.

The album contained two songs written by group member Mike Nesmith and six by their writer-producers Tommy Boyce and Bobby Hart.

The contents were: Side 1 — Theme from 'The Monkees', by Tommy Boyce and Bobby Hart; **I Wanna be Free**, by Tommy Boyce and Bobby Hart; **Tomorrow's Gonna be Another Day**, by Tommy Boyce and Steve Venet Gates; **Saturday's Child**, by Gates; **Papa Jean's Blues**, by Mike Nesmith; **Take a Giant Step**, by Gerry Goffin and Carole King; Side 2 — **Last Train to Clarksville**, by Tommy Boyce and Bobby Hart; **This Just Doesn't Seem to be My Day**, by Tommy Boyce and Bobby Hart; **Let's Dance On**, by Tommy Boyce and Bobby Hart; **I'll be True to You**, by Gerry Goffin and Russ Titelman; **Sweet Young Thing**, by Mike Nesmith, Gerry Goffin and Carole King; **Gonna Buy Me a Dog**, by Tommy Boyce and Bobby Hart.

I'M A BELIEVER *Colgems 1002 [USA] RCA Victor 1560 [UK]*. This second single by the Monkees had an advance order of 1,051,280 before release on 26 November and was awarded an immediate Gold Disc by RIAA. It was the first time that RCA Victor (manufacturers and distributors of the Colgems label) had advance orders in excess of one million on a single record release, with the exception of Elvis Presley.

The song was written by Neil Diamond, and produced by Jeff Barry.

The disc was No 1 in the USA for seven weeks (with 15 weeks in the bestsellers) and in Britain for four weeks — four weeks simultaneously with USA — and was 17 weeks in the bestsellers. It sold over three million in America in its first two months on the market, and over 750,000 in Britain in two weeks to March 1967. Global sales are estimated at around 10 million. It was No 1 in Australia, Eire, Finland, New Zealand, Norway and South Africa in early 1967.

The backing of this disc was **(I'm not Your) Steppin' Stone**, written by Tommy Boyce and Bobby Hart. Here again, only the singing is by the group on this disc.

In Britain **I'm a Believer** was the Monkees' first hit, followed by **Last Train to Clarksville**. The TV series, produced by Bob Rafelson, generated enormous interest from the pop press, which was supported by sporadic personal appearances from the individual Monkees. Mickey Dolenz even married Samantha Juste, the beautiful girl who silently spun the records on 'Top of the Pops' in the sixties. (The couple later divorced.)

As their records took off, selling by the million, the Monkees wanted to increase their involvement with the musical side of their affairs. But they had been hired as actors for a TV series and not primarily as musicians. Clashes with Don Kirschner led to his departure, but the Monkees could not adequately replace him. Their material varied enormously, as did the musical tastes and abilities of the group.

By 1968, after five highly successful albums, the group began to fade. By the end of the decade they were no more. In 1976 Arista had a moderate hit in America with a 'greatest hits' package, but the main Monkees revival came in the 1980s. In 1980 Arista had a hit in Britain with **The Monkees** EP, which made No

33 during nine weeks in the singles charts. It included both **Last Train to Clarksville** and **I'm a Believer**. In 1986 three of the group re-formed (without Mike Nesmith). They had a very small British hit with **That Was Then, This Is Now** which spent one week in the Top 75 at No 68, though it reached No 20 in America. In the USA, a 'greatest hits' album from 1976 re-charted, and a new album **Then & Now... The Best of The Monkees** made No 21 and sold over a million copies. Both these LPs were on Arista, but from August six of the Monkees old sixties albums re-charted on Rhino, most reaching the middle of the album Top 200.

NAPOLEON XIV — American

THEY'RE COMING TO TAKE ME AWAY HA-HAAA! *Warner Brothers 5831 [USA] Warner Brothers WB 5831 [UK]*. Napoleon XIV is in reality a New York recording engineer, producer and composer named Jerry Samuels, who wrote and recorded this number himself. He hired a studio for $15 and made the record in one and a half hours, then took the tape to George Lee, a top executive of Warner/Reprise, who immediately signed him to the company.

When the disc was released, it sold over half a million in five days, the bestselling single in the history of the company, and proved to be the novelty single of the decade. In one month it had sold 775,000, was No 1 in the US charts for one week and six weeks in the bestsellers, and sold an eventual million plus.

Jerry Samuels decided to write a comedy song that would be entirely different. The completed song is about a man going mad because his dog leaves him, but this is not apparent at the beginning. Most of the American radio stations banned it on the grounds of bad taste, believing it to refer to a man who had lost his girl. This, however, did not stop the disc selling in huge quantities. It also turned out to be quite a big seller in Britain and reached No 4 in the charts with ten weeks in the bestsellers.

The song is recited, more than sung, with a catchy martial backing consisting of drum, tambourine and hand clapping plus Napoleon's voice getting higher and higher.

An additional novelty is the reverse side of the disc — **Aaah-Ah Yawa Em Ekat Ot Gnimoc Er-Yeht** — the complete song played backwards.

AARON NEVILLE — American

TELL IT LIKE IT IS *Par-lo 101 [USA]*. This disc sold a million after being in the US charts for five weeks to the end of 1966, and was the No 1 rhythm-and-blues number for five weeks in early 1967. It reached No 2 for one week in the US national charts and was 14 weeks in the bestsellers.

Aaron Neville hails from New Orleans where he was educated, and studied vocal and instrumental music and manuscript writing. His compositions include **Every Day** and **Humdinger**. Aaron literally grew up in show business, having made his debut at the age of five. His first public appearance was at the

YMCA in New Orleans as an amateur, and his first professional appearance at the Roosevelt Hotel there when he was 13.

This song was written by Lee Diamond (words) and George Davis (music).

THE NEW VAUDEVILLE BAND   *British*

WINCHESTER CATHEDRAL *Fontana TF 741 [UK] Fontana 1562 [USA]*. The New Vaudeville Band came into being through the keen interest of composer Geoff Stevens in old recordings of the 1920s and the sounds of vaudeville. After working as a schoolteacher in Southend, Essex, he became a training executive in an advertising agency. He then helped to write a fairly successful amateur revue and started writing short sketches for the BBC. An advertisement by a London music publisher landed him a job with them for two years, resulting in big successes with **Tell Me When** for the Applejacks and **The Crying Game** for Dave Berry in 1964. He also discovered Donovan whose first three records he produced.

Geoff decided to write a simple tuneful song as he was convinced other writers were trying to make popular music too complicated. He organized a group of musicians for a recording session of **Winchester Cathedral**, a song about a boy who is deserted there by his girl. He named the group the New Vaudeville Band and decided to sing on the record himself in order to obtain the interpretation he wanted. It made No 4 with 19 weeks in the bestsellers with a sale of over 200,000. In the USA it sold over one and a half million in six weeks and became No 1 there for three weeks; America's biggest British hit of 1966, and an unprecedented feat for a group playing ordinary band instruments in a style devoid of modern rock'n'roll.

Geoff Stevens, born in New Southgate, London, on 1 October 1934, sang only on the disc and did not tour with the band, being replaced by Alan Klein who adopted the title of 'Tristram, seventh Earl of Cricklewood'. The group projected a nostalgic image of the late 1920s. None of them played on the original recording, which was made by session musicians. The rest of the group are Mick Wilsher (lead guitar) born 21 December 1945 in Sutton, Surrey; Bobby 'Pops' Kerr (trumpet, saxophone and French horn) born 14 February 1943 in Kensington, London; Hugh Watts (trombone) born 25 July 1941 in Watford,

Hertfordshire; Neil Korner (bass) born 6 October 1942 in Ashford, Middlesex; Henry Harrison (drums) born 6 June 1943 in Watford, Hertfordshire; Stan Heywood (piano, organ, accordion) born 23 August 1947 in Dagenham, Essex; Alan Klein born 29 June 1942 in Clerkenwell, London

Global sales of this disc were over three million. Grammy Award for 'Best Contemporary Rock'n'Roll Recording'. Gold Disc award by RIAA.

CHIYO OKUMURA   *Japanese*

HOKKAIDO SKIES *Toshiba CA-30-1428 [Japan]*. Written by the US group the Ventures, who became extremely popular in Japan during the mid- and late 1960s via their personal tours and disc sales. They wrote many songs about Japan, with recordings by popular Japanese singers.

This song was a million seller for female singer Chiyo Okumura, who followed up with another hit **Ginza Lights**.

THE OUTSIDERS   *American*

TIME WON'T LET ME *Capitol 5573 [USA]*. The Outsiders' first single was virtually an immediate hit for them. The song was written by the group's leader-guitarist-composer-arranger Tom King.

Tom became interested in music when he transposed the zither part of the 'Third Man' theme to guitar. He formed the Outsiders, and played in various night spots in Cleveland where he met Sonny Geraci, a young singer. The duo invited Bill Bruno, a Pittsburgh university student to join them as a lead guitarist, then Rick Baker (real name Biagiola) from Cleveland on drums, and Mert Madsen, a native of Denmark, on bass. After a four-hour recording session, they took this song to a Capitol executive who immediately signed them to a contract. The disc was released in February in the USA and reached No 5 for two weeks in the national charts with 15 weeks in the bestsellers, and a subsequent million sale.

The group consisted of Tom King (guitar-composer-arranger-leader), born in Cleveland 1944; Bill Bruno (lead guitar), born in Pittsburgh 1946; Sonny Geraci (lead vocalist), born in Cleveland 1948; Rick Biagiola (drums), born in Cleveland 1949; Mert Madsen (bass, accordion, harmonica and guitar), born in Denmark. Later, Madsen was replaced by Ritchie D'Amato, born in Cleveland 1949.

ROBERT PARKER   *American*

BAREFOOTIN' *Nola 721 [USA] Island WI 286 [UK]*. Robert Parker's disc reached No 7 for two weeks in the USA and was a consistent seller for 14 weeks in their charts, selling (it is claimed by the Nola company) over a million there.

Robert was born in New Orleans in 1942 and the recording was his first. The song, a raunchy blues novelty, was written by him. It was released on the Island label in Britain

where it was No 24, with eight weeks in the bestsellers.

Parker started his musical career as a tenor sax player and gained experience playing with Sonny Stitt, Miles Davis and Gene Ammons in jam sessions in New York. On his return to New Orleans, he started playing on backing session for other artists. He then wrote his first song **All Night Long** followed by **Across the Tracks**, the discs of these becoming local New Orleans hits. Nola Records then signed him up and **Barefootin'** became a big success very quickly, with resultant bookings and a tour of the USA.

PETER AND GORDON   *British*

LADY GODIVA *Columbia (EMI) DB 8003 [UK] Capitol 5740 [USA]*. The fourth million seller for this popular British duo, the song was written by Mike Leander and Charles Mills. The disc reached No 16 for two weeks in Britain with 16 weeks in the bestsellers, and was released in September 1966. It was an even bigger success in the USA, achieving No 5 for two weeks with 14 weeks in the bestsellers, the combined sales totalling the million by 1967.

WILSON PICKETT   *American*

LAND OF A THOUSAND DANCES *Atlantic 2348 [USA] Atlantic 584039 [UK]*. Originally a bestseller in 1963 for the writers Kris (Chris) Kenner and Fats Domino on the Instant label, Wilson Pickett's recording was released in July 1966. It was No 6 in the USA charts for two weeks and 11 weeks in the bestsellers, and achieved No 22 in Britain with nine weeks in the bestsellers to make a million global sale. It was No 1 for one week in the US R&B charts during a 12-week chart run.

MUSTANG SALLY *Atlantic 2365 [USA] Atlantic 584066 [UK]*. Written by Wilson Pickett, his disc was released in the USA in November 1966 and was No 16 for one week with nine weeks in the bestsellers. In Britain it reached No 22 for a week with seven weeks in the bestsellers and global sale estimated at one million. It peaked at No 6 during 12 weeks on the US R&B charts.

SANDY POSEY   *American*

BORN A WOMAN *MGM 13501 [USA] MGM 1321 [UK]*. Sandy Posey was born in 1945 in Jasper, Alabama, and began singing when she was five years old, harmonizing to the music of the radio. In her late teens she moved to West Memphis, Arkansas, just across the Mississippi River from Memphis, a top recording centre in the South. While working as a receptionist at the American studios, she filled in as a background singer for many famous artists including Tommy Roe, Bobby Goldsboro, Bobby Bare, Joe Tex, Percy Sledge and Skeeter Davis.

In mid-1965 she signed a recording contract with Chips Moman, an independent hit record producer. He found a great piece of material for her first recording in **Born a Woman** written by

Martha Sharp. The demo disc, released by MGM, got to No 9 for two weeks and stayed in the bestsellers for 14 weeks, and subsequently sold the million. Release was in July 1966 in the USA and 19 August 1966 in Britain, where it was No 22, with 11 weeks in the bestsellers.

SINGLE GIRL *MGM 13612* [*USA*] *MGM 1330* [*UK*]. Sandy Posey's second big hit was also written by Martha Sharp and released in the USA in November 1966. It reached No 10 in 1967 and stayed in the bestsellers for 12 weeks.

In Britain it reached No 15 and was 13 weeks in the bestsellers, in 1967.

ELVIS PRESLEY

FRANKIE AND JOHNNY/PLEASE DON'T STOP LOVING ME *RCA Victor 47-8780* [*USA*] *RCA Victor 1509* [*UK*]. Both sides of this record were from the Elvis film *Frankie and Johnny*. The title track was the bigger hit of the two in America, where the record was a double A side hit. It reached No 25 in a short eight-week chart duration, the same chart life as **Please Don't Stop Loving Me**, which peaked at No 45. In Britain, **Frankie and Johnny** reached No 21 with nine weeks in the charts. Despite these low chart placings, the record was said to have finally passed the million mark from global sales. It was his fortieth record to sell one million.

Frankie and Johnny was a version of the classical American gutter song about Frankie and her man. It was written by Gottlieb, Fred Karger and Ben Weisman. The song was originally called the 'Frankie and Albert' song, and was well known along the Mississippi River and among railroad men of the Middle West as early as 1888.

LOVE LETTERS *RCA Victor 47-8870* [*USA*] *RCA Victor 1526* [*UK*]. **Love Letters** was written by Edward Heyman (words) and Victor Young (music) in 1945, originally for the film of the same name. Elvis' version of the ballad was released in America in June 1966, reaching No 19, with seven weeks in the Hot 100. It did better in Britain, where it reached No 6 with 10 weeks in the Top 50. Global sales were said to have passed the million.

JAMES AND BOBBY PURIFY · American

I'M YOUR PUPPET *Bell 648* [*USA*] *Mercury 6167 324* [*UK*]. James Lee Purify and Robert Lee Dickey are the real names of this duo who are cousins. James was born in Pensacola, and Bobby in Tallahassee, Florida. James left Pensacola and was raised in Chicago, and Bobby on a farm outside Tallahassee. From 1963 until 1966 they played the school and nightclub road circuit throughout Florida, Georgia and Alabama. They first started out in the music field by forming a group called the Dothan Sextet.

This disc by the talented duo was No 5 for two weeks in the USA and 14 weeks in the bestsellers. It reached No 12 with 10 weeks in the British bestsellers and sold an estimated million. It was released in September 1966. The song was written by Lindon Oldham and Dan Penn.

? (QUESTION MARK) AND · American
THE MYSTERIANS

96 TEARS *Cameo 428* [*USA*] *Cameo Parkway C 428* [*UK*]. This quintet was a Mexican/American group out of Detroit via Acapulco. The Mysterians were discovered by Bob Dell, a programme director of WTAC in Flint, Michigan. Lead singer Question Mark joined the group one night when they were playing at Michigan's Mount Holly Ski Lodge. Not even the group were said to know his real name or anything about his past. He lived alone and never removed his sunglasses. The Mysterians were Bobby Balderamma (lead guitar), Frank Lugo (bass guitar), Eddie Serrato (drummer) and Frank Rodriguez (organist).

96 Tears was written by Rudy Martinez. The disc, their first, reached the No 1 spot in the US charts for two weeks with 15 weeks in the bestsellers, and was also a top seller in Canada. It reached No 37 with four weeks in the British bestsellers.

Cameo-Parkway Records presented the group with an RIAA Gold Disc for a million sale in November 1966, just 12 weeks after its release.

THE RIGHTEOUS BROTHERS · American

(YOU'RE MY) SOUL AND INSPIRATION *Verve 10383* [*USA*] *Verve VS 535* [*UK*]. The second million seller for this duo, the song was again written by the husband-and-wife team Barry Mann and Cynthia Weill. The disc sold 750,000 in the USA in two weeks, and the million in six weeks, with a Gold Disc award from RIAA in May 1966, just 12 weeks after its release.

The disc was No 1 in the US charts for three weeks and 13 weeks in the bestsellers. It made No 13 during nine weeks in the R&B charts. It reached No 15 and was ten weeks in the British bestsellers.

JOHNNY RIVERS · American

SECRET AGENT MAN *Imperial 66159* [*USA*]. This song was written by P.J. Sloan and Steve Barri, who also had a tremendous hit with **Eve of Destruction**. Johnny Rivers' recording reached No 2 in the US charts with 11 weeks in the bestsellers, and he was presented with a Gold Disc on his return visit to Hollywood's Whiskey à Go Go, the scene of his initial triumph in 1964.

The 'bluesy' song was sung by Johnny over the credits on the popular CBS TV series of the same title. The disc was issued in March 1966.

TOMMY ROE · American

SWEET PEA *ABC-Paramount 10762* [*USA*]. Another self-penned success for singer Tommy Roe with consistent sales over 16 weeks in the US charts and reaching the No 5 position.

Subsequent sales made this the second million seller for him, with a belated Gold Disc award by RIAA in March 1969.

THE ROLLING STONES · British

NINETEENTH NERVOUS BREAKDOWN *Decca F 12331* [*UK*] *London 9823* [*USA*]. 1966 was another great year for the Rolling Stones. Two of their three singles went to No 1 in Britain, and two of their four American singles also topped the charts. On the album front, they had a No 1 on both sides of the Atlantic. All their releases, both singles and LPs, sold over a million copies.

Nineteenth Nervous Breakdown was in the same mould as its two predecessors, **Satisfaction** and **Get Off of My Cloud**. It was loud, raucous rock'n'roll at its best. The song was written by Mick Jagger and Keith Richards, the words containing more social comment from Jagger. It was recorded in Hollywood, produced by Andrew Oldham, and arranged by the Rolling Stones.

The record was released in Britain on 4 February 1966, and went to No 1 in the *NME* charts on 19 February, where it stayed for three weeks. (It peaked at No 2 in the *Record Retailer* charts.) It spent seven weeks in the *NME* Top 30, eight weeks in the *Record Retailer* Top 50, and won a Silver Disc for British sales of a quarter of a million. In America, it was also a case of topping some but not all charts. It was No 1 for one week in *Cash Box*, but No 2 for three weeks in *Billboard*, where it spent 10 weeks on the charts. This was the Stones' ninth million seller, with a seven-figure total achieved from global sales.

AFTERMATH (Album) *Decca SKL 4786* [*UK*] *London 476* [*USA*]. The Stones' tenth record to sell a million was an album. **Aftermath** was released in Britain on 15 April 1966. The following week it entered the album charts at No 2, replacing **The Sound of Music** at the top the week after that. It was No 1 for nine weeks in the *NME* Top 10, and eight weeks in the *Record Retailer* Top 30, where it stayed a total of 28 weeks. **The Sound of Music** reclaimed the top spot in both charts. In America the record was released in July, and went to No 1 for two weeks in *Cash Box*, and No 2 for two weeks in the *Billboard* charts where it stayed for 50 weeks. It was awarded an RIAA Gold Disc for million dollar sales on 9 August, one month after its release, with global sales well over the million mark.

Aftermath marks an important landmark in the Rolling Stones' career. It was the first album where Jagger and Richards had written all the material. On their previous album **Out of Our Heads**, only three of the tracks had been credited to Jagger and Richards, with another four under their pseudonym of Nanker and Phelge. The other tracks were covers of mainly American R&B songs. (These figures apply to the million-selling American version; the position on the British version was broadly similar.) There were to be no pseudonyms or cover versions on this album, or on any other from then on.

The album was recorded at the RCA Studios in Hollywood. Their record company Decca was the licensee in Britain for RCA, and so had close links with RCA. Even so, unlike the Beatles, the Stones were beginning to record where they chose and refused to be confined to their record company's own studios, as was the custom at the time. The album was produced by Andrew Oldham, engineered by Dave Hassinger and arranged by the Rolling Stones. Apart from their normal instruments, Brian Jones, Charlie Watts and Bill Wyman provided the marimbas and bells; Brian Jones played the dulcimer and sitar; Jones, Wyman, Jack Nitzsche and Ian Stewart played piano, organ and harpsichord on various tracks, and Nitzsche also helped out occasionally with the percussion.

The tracks on the album are: **Mother's Little Helper†**; **Stupid Girl**; **Lady Jane**; **Under My Thumb**; **Doncha Bother Me**; **Goin' Home**; **Hight SOS**; **High and Dry**; **Out of Time†**; **It's Not Easy**; **I Am Waiting**; **Take It or Leave It†**; **Think**; **What to Do†** and **Paint It Black***. († Tracks only on the British version; * only on the American version.)

PAINT IT BLACK *Decca F 12395* [UK] *London 901* [USA]. Million seller number 11 was another pounding rock classic, with Brian Jones adding the sitar to great effect. It was written by Mick Jagger and Keith Richards while touring Australia, and produced by Andrew Oldham at the RCA studios in Hollywood. It entered the *NME* charts at No 5 the first week of release, and went to No 1 the following week, 28 May. This time it also topped the *Record Retailer* charts, for one week, staying in the Top 50 for 10 weeks. It won a Silver Disc for British sales, their eighth, on 4 June. This was the Rolling Stones' seventh British No 1 in a row. It also went to No 1 in a number of other countries around the world.

MOTHER'S LITTLE HELPER/LADY JANE *London 902* [USA]. With no official British Stones release due for some months, Decca's American subsidiary London decided to pull a couple of tracks off the **Aftermath** album and put them out as a stop-gap single in July. Both sides made the charts, with **Mother's Little Helper** being the bigger hit. It reached No 8 during a nine-week chart stay, while **Lady Jane** made No 24 during its six weeks on the charts. Both tracks were written by Jagger and Richards and produced by Andrew Oldham in Hollywood. The record was not released in Britain, nor in most other countries as most of the world followed the British pattern of releases. It was a big hit in Canada, and with large sales in the USA it finally sold a million copies.

HAVE YOU SEEN YOUR MOTHER, BABY, STANDING IN THE SHADOW? *Decca F 12497* [UK] *London 903* [USA]. This was the Rolling Stones' least successful single in Britain since their days struggling to establish themselves in 1963. It did not even get near No 1, peaking at No 5 with only eight weeks in the charts. In America it reached No 9 with only seven weeks in the Hot 100. It was written by Mick Jagger and Keith Richards, and produced by Andrew Oldham. Global sales finally pushed it over the million.

BIG HITS (HIGH TIDE AND GREEN GRASS) (Album) *Decca TXS 101* [UK] *London 1* [USA]. The Stones' first hit album was lavishly packaged in a gate-fold sleeve with full-page colour pictures of each member of the group, and three more pages of photographs by Gered Mankowitz, Guy Webster and Jerrold Schatzberg. The British version contained all their hits except **I Wanna Be Your Man**, while the American version (which was almost the same) included all their US chart entries except **Mother's Little Helper**. The tracks were all recorded in London, Hollywood or Chicago, produced by Andrew Oldham and arranged by the Rolling Stones. Various singles had been engineered by Dave Hassinger, Bill Farley, Ron Malo, Glyn Johns and Roger Savage. Writing the credits on the album liner notes, Andrew Oldham said, 'For the most part, the mastering was done by Dominic (his second name escapes me).' Ian Stewart and Jack Nitzsche had helped out with various instruments. Nitzsche also arranged the brass on **Have You Seen Your Mother**... and Mike Leander arranged the strings on **As Tears Go By**.

The album contained gems by the Stones at the height of their creativity and youthful vitality. They still had some great records to make, but the period from 1963 to 1966 was in many ways their best. The album was a massive success. It was released in Britain in November, and reached No 4 with 43 weeks in the album Top 30. In America, where it had been released much earlier, in April 1966, it went to No 3 with 99 weeks in the charts. It easily won an RIAA Gold Disc for million dollar sales, awarded on 27 April. It sold over five million copies in America.

The contents of the British release were; ***Have You Seen Your Mother, Baby, Standing in the Shadow?†** by Mick Jagger and Keith Richard (1966); ***Paint It Black†**, by Mick Jagger and Keith Richard (1966); ***It's All Over Now**, by B. and S. Womack (1964); ***The Last Time**, by Mick Jagger and Keith Richard (1965); **Heart of Stone**, by Mick Jagger and Keith Richard (1965); **Not Fade Away**, by Charles Hardin and Norman Petty (1957); ***(I Can't Get No) Satisfaction**, by Mick Jagger and Keith Richard (1965); ***Get Off My Cloud**, by Mick Jagger and Keith Richard (1965); ***As Tears Go By**, by Mick Jagger, Keith Richard and Andrew Loog Oldham (1964); ***19th Nervous Breakdown**, by Mick Jagger and Keith Richard (1966); ***Lady Jane**, by Mick Jagger and Keith Richard (1966); ***Time Is On My Side** by J. Meade and A. Norman (1963), **Come On†** by Chuck Berry (1961), **Little Red Rooster†** by Willie Dixon (1961). Items marked * were million seller singles. The American version did not contain tracks marked†, but included **Tell Me** by Mick Jagger and Keith Richard (1964), **Good Times, Bad Times** by Mick Jagger and Keith Richard (1964) and **Play With Fire** by Nanker and Phelge (pseudonyms for Jagger and Richard) (1965).

GOT LIVE IF YOU WANT IT (Album) *London 493* [USA] *Teldec SHZT 547* [West Germany]. The Stones' fifteenth million seller, **Got Live If You Want It**, was recorded live at the Royal Albert Hall, London. Decca had put out an EP of the same name, recorded at Stones' concerts in London, Manchester and Liverpool, in 1965. That had sold well enough to make the singles charts Top 10. London released this live album in December. It reached No 6, with 48 weeks in the American album charts, and won an RIAA Gold Disc for million dollar sales on 19 January 1967. This album was not released in Britain, but Decca's German subsidiary Teldec (a joint venture with Telefunken, hence the name Tel-Dec) did release it via a tie-up with the record promotional activity of *Hor Zu* magazine. The album was produced by Andrew Oldham and engineered by Glyn Johns.

The track listing was **Under My Thumb**; **Get Off of My Cloud**; **Lady Jane**; **Not Fade Away** (Petty-Hardin); **I've Been Loving You Too Long (To Stop Now)** (Redding); **Fortune Teller** (Neville); **The Last Time**; **Nineteenth Nervous Breakdown**; **Time is on My Side** (Meade-Norman); **I'm Alright** (Nanker-Phelge); **Have You Seen Your Mother, Baby, Standing In The Shadow?**; and **(I Can't Get No) Satisfaction**. All tracks were composed by Jagger-Richards unless otherwise stated. (Nanker-Phelge was a pseudonym for Jagger-Richards.)

THE ROYAL GUARDSMEN   *American*

SNOOPY VERSUS THE RED BARON *Laurie 3366* [USA] *Stateside SS 574* [UK]. Evolved from the popular US comic strip 'Peanuts' by Charles Schulz in which the hero's dog Snoopy imagines himself to be a World War I pilot hunting the skies for the Red Baron from Germany, this gimmick song proved to be a big hit. The Royal Guardsmen, six American cowboy-booted singers and instrumentalists, give a highly individual telling of the story, written by Phil Gernhard and Dick Holler. The Red Baron was actually the famous World War I aviator Baron Maurice von Richthofen (born 1888) who between 1917 and 1918 brought down over 80 Allied machines and then met his match in April 1918 when he was shot down behind the British lines by Captain Roy Brown of the Royal Flying Corps. Richtofen's exploits were told in a film entitled *The Blue Max* (1966).

This disc was first broadcast in early December 1966 over the Tampa, Florida, and Abilene, Texas, airwaves. It spread to Pittsburgh, Albany, Providence and then right across the USA, selling over 360,000 in a few days. It soon reached No 2 in the charts, remaining in that position for five weeks with 12 weeks in the bestsellers, with an eventual million sale in early 1967 and a Gold Disc award from RIAA in February 1967. Global sales were over three million.

It was also quite a success in Britain in 1967 when released on the Stateside label, reaching No 6 position in the charts with 13 weeks in the bestsellers.

The Royal Guardsmen were all from Ocala, Florida, and were all at high school or university when they made this disc. The line-up was John Burdett (drums), Bill Balogh (bass), Barry Winslow (rhythm guitarist/vocalist), Tom Richards (lead guitarist), Billy Taylor (organist) and Chris Nunley (vocalist/percussionist). They came to the attention of Phil Gernhard, a producer, who groomed them until he decided they were ready to make their first record **Baby Let's Wait** for the Laurie label. This was not a success, but the label decided to give the group a second try at the end of 1966 with **Snoopy**, with sensational results.

STAFF SERGEANT BARRY SADLER
American

THE BALLAD OF THE GREEN BERETS *RCA Victor 8739* [*USA*] *RCA Victor 1506* [*UK*]. Barry's disc was released on 11 January 1966, selling the million in a fortnight, with an RIAA Gold Disc award. The song was inspired by Robin Moore's bestseller book *The Green Berets*, and was written by Robin Moore with music by Barry Sadler. The disc was No 1 in the USA for five weeks and 13 weeks in the bestsellers, and sold over five million. A German version by Freddy (Quinn) on Polydor titled **100 mann und ein befehl** was No 1 for nine weeks there and sold over 600,000. Sadler's disc was No 24 in Britain, with eight weeks in the bestsellers.

Staff Sergeant Barry Sadler was born in New Mexico in 1941, his father, a plumber, died when Barry was seven. His mother was a barmaid. After leaving school at 15, he tramped around for three years before joining the US Air Force at 18 for four years. On discharge in 1962 a friend taught him the drums and guitar, and they formed a group which was unsuccessful. Barry then joined the US Army and after about a year's rigorous training qualified for his green beret as a combat medic. Along the way, at Fort Sam Houston, he started writing songs. A few months later, while on patrol in Vietnam, he fell into a man-trap and a pungi stake (a poisoned spear made of sharpened bamboo) plunged into his leg. He operated on himself between fainting spells and was ultimately found and carried to safety. This ended his combat career and left him with

one leg scarred and partially numb.

He had written a number of songs during his Army career and during off-duty hours in Vietnam, mostly about men at war, and once back in America he contacted the publisher to whom he had given his first song **The Ballad of the Green Berets**. He was then brought to the attention of RCA Victor who put him under contract immediately, and he recorded the song in his raw tenor voice. With America deeply involved in the Vietnam conflict, his disc made a tremendous impact and rocketed him to fame and fortune, with so many demands for personal appearances that the Army assigned a lieutenant colonel to handle his bookings. Barry's earnings as writer and performer from the song and the album brought him well over $500,000 for himself alone.

BALLADS OF THE GREEN BERETS (Album) *RCA Victor 3547* [*USA*]. All the arrangements for this album of songs, written and sung by Barry Sadler, were by Sid Bass. Released on 19 January 1966, it was No 1 for seven weeks (four of these simultaneously with the single) and sold well over two million. Both this album and the single were certified simultaneously for Gold Disc awards, the second time in the history of RIAA (the first being **Help!** by the Beatles). The album was also one of the fastest selling in RCA Victor's history. It stayed in the bestseller charts for 32 weeks and sold the first million in five weeks.

The contents of the disc were all written by Barry Sadler unless otherwise indicated: **Ballad of the Green Berets**, by Robin Moore/Barry Sadler; **Letter from Vietnam; Saigon; The Soldier has Come Home; I'm Watching the Raindrops Fall; Trooper's Lament; Bamiba; Badge of Courage; Salute to the Nurses; I'm a Lucky One; Garet Trooper; Lullaby**.

SAM AND DAVE
American

HOLD ON, I'M A COMIN' *Stax 189* [*USA*]. Sam and Dave's first million seller was composed by Isaac Hayes and David Porter, who produced this record and wrote many of the duo's hits. Samuel David Moore was born on 12 October 1935 in Miami, Florida, and was the son of a Baptist deacon. His early musical experience was in his father's church. His interest in gospel and pop music was encouraged by his grandfather, who was also a Baptist minister. David Prater was born on 9 May 1937 in Ocilla, Georgia, the son of a labourer. As with so many black artists, his earliest musical experience was also singing in church. Both men were following solo singing careers when they met at the King of Hearts Club in Miami, where Sam was performing.

They decided to form a duo and in 1962 signed to the Alston label, though without success. They later moved to Stax, and in 1965 recorded **You Don't Know Like I Know**. It gave them their first hit, entering the R&B charts on 1 January 1966. Two weeks later it entered the Hot 100. It was a sizeable R&B hit, reaching No 7 during a 14-week chart run. On the pop charts it did less well, reaching No 90

during only two weeks on the Hot 100.

The follow-up was **Hold On! I'm A Comin'** which gave them their first of two No 1s in the R&B charts. It was top for one week, and its 20-week chart run was the longest of their career. It reached No 15 in *Cash Box*, and No 21 in *Billboard* during 13 weeks in the Hot 100. Though international sales were limited at first, Sam and Dave did enjoy success in Britain in the late sixties. **Sooth Me** was a hit in 1967, and was followed by **Soul Man** (also 1967). **I Thank You** (1968) and **Soul Sister, Brown Sugar** (1969). Global sales finally pushed **Hold On! I'm A Comin'** over the million mark.

Sam and Dave enjoyed a string of 15 R&B hits, the last of which was **The Sam and Dave Medley** in 1985. They had 13 US pop hits up to 1969. Their biggest hit came in 1967 with **Soul Man**, which sold a million copies. Dave Prater was killed in a car crash on 11 April 1988.

SAM THE SHAM AND THE PHARAOHS
American

LI'L RED RIDING HOOD *MGM 13506* [*USA*]/*MGM 45-MGM-1315* [*UK*]. The second million seller for Sam the Sham was No 1 in the USA for one week in the *Cash Box* and *Record World* charts. It peaked at No 2 for two weeks in *Billboard*, with 14 weeks in the Hot 100. It reached No 46 during three weeks in the British charts. The song was written by Ronald Blackwell, and won an RIAA Gold Disc on 11 August 1966.

THE SEEKERS
Australian

GEORGY GIRL *Columbia (EMI) DB 8134* [*UK*] *Capitol 5756* [*USA*]. The fourth million seller for the Seekers was composed by Tom Springfield, with words by Jim Dale. It was written for the film *Georgy Girl* (starring James

Mason, Alan Bates and Lynn Redgrave as 'Georgy') as a replacement for another song, and sung for the film by the Seekers. The disc was a compilation of the two sets of lyrics written for the opening and closing of the film, which was a tremendous success. The disc was first released in the USA and became No 1 there for one week with 16 weeks in the bestsellers. It was issued in Britain in early 1967 on the Columbia label and reached No 1 for one week in *Disc* with 11 weeks in the *Record Retailer* Top 50. It was also a big hit in the group's native Australia (No 1 for two weeks) where they received a Gold Disc in March 1967 for a million global sale, and appeared before an audience of 200,000 at the Myer Music Bowl in Melbourne. Total sales of this disc were subsequently three million.

The song was nominated for an Academy Award, 1966. Gold Disc award RIAA 1967.

THE SHADOWS OF NIGHT   *American*

GLORIA *Dunwich 116* [*USA*]. The first big hit for the Dunwich label (distributed in the USA by Atlantic) was also the first million seller for this group.

The quintet, all high school graduates, began their swift rise to the top in the summer of 1965 at the Cellar in Arlington Heights, a suburb of Chicago. They played teenage clubs and dances in and around Chicago for a year. Then came this disc which reached No 6 in the US charts with 12 weeks in the bestsellers, with eventual sales of a million.

The song was written by Van Morrison in 1965. The group consisted of Jim Sohns (lead singer), born 23 August 1949, Prospect Heights, Illinois; Warren Rogers (lead guitar); Jerry McGeorge (rhythm guitar); Tom Schiffour (drums); Joe Kelly (bass). In 1968 the group was assigned to Team Records.

SIMON AND GARFUNKEL   *American*

PARSLEY, SAGE, ROSEMARY AND THYME (Album) *CBS-Columbia 9363* [*USA*] *CBS 62860* [*UK*]. This was Simon and Garfunkel's third album, and the first to make the Top 10. All the songs on it were written by Paul Simon, with help from Art Garfunkel, a folk song for **Scarborough Fair/Canticle**, and a traditional carol for **7 O'clock News/Silent Night**. Like all eight of their albums released in America, **Parsley, Sage, Rosemary and Thyme** won an RIAA Gold Disc for million dollar sales on 6 July 1967, some eight months after its release. It went on to sell over three million copies in the USA with multi-platinum RIAA awards certificated on 21 November 1986. It was their second record to finally pass the million mark, following the **Sound of Silence** single in 1965.

The album spent 145 weeks in the US album Top 200, peaking at No 4. In Britain it did not chart until 1968, finally making it on the back of **Bookends**, which became their first British No 1 three weeks after entering the charts on 3 August. **Parsley, Sage, Rosemary and Thyme** followed it into the charts on 31 August, and stayed in the Top 40 for 66 weeks. Its highest chart position was No 13.

The tracks on the album were **Scarborough Fair/Canticle**, **Patterns**, **Cloudy**, **The Big Bright Green Pleasure Machine**, **The 59th Street Bridge Song (Feelin' Groovy)**, **The Dangling Conversation**, **Flowers Never Bend with the Rainfall**, **A Simple Desultory Philippic (or How I was Robert McNamara'd into Submission)**, **For Emily, Whenever I May Find Her**, **A Poem on the Underground Wall** and **7 O'clock News/Silent Night**.

FRANK SINATRA   *American*

STRANGERS IN THE NIGHT *Reprise 0470* [*USA*] *Reprise R 23052* [*UK*]. A great triumph for Sinatra, this disc was No 1 for one week in the USA and No 1 for three weeks in Britain (one week of these simultaneously with the USA). Sinatra had only topped Britain's charts once before — in 1954 with **Three Coins in the Fountain** — but this time it was to the tune of over half a million sale. The disc was released on 11 April 1966 and stayed in the US charts for 15 weeks and in Britain for 20 weeks. Combined US/British sales were over a million.

The tune was written by famous German conductor-composer Bert Kaempfert as part of the score of the Universal picture *A Man Could Get Killed*, Kaempfert's first musical assignment for an American film. The publisher realized its potentialities as a hit song for Sinatra and lyrics were written by Charles Singleton and Eddy Snyder.

Frank Sinatra's big hit with this disc immediately followed his daughter Nancy's success with **These Boots are Made for Walkin'**, making a 1966 'double' No 1 for the Sinatras.

Strangers in the Night was also No 1 in Argentina, Italy, Switzerland, Austria, Belgium, France (over 600,000 sold), Australia and Eire and thus created a worldwide resurgence for the Sinatra 'magic'. His album of the same title also won a Gold Disc award. In 1966, there were four Grammy Awards for **Strangers in the Night** — 'Record of the Year', 'Best Vocal (Male) Performance', 'Best Engineering Contribution (Popular Recording)' and 'Best Arrangement'.

NANCY SINATRA   *American*

THESE BOOTS ARE MADE FOR WALKIN' *Reprise 0432* [*USA*] *Reprise R 20432* [*UK*]. Written by Lee Hazlewood (composer of many hits for guitarist Duane Eddy), Nancy's disc sold a million in the USA in eight weeks and received an RIAA Gold Disc award on 25 February 1966. It was No 1 there for one week, with 14 weeks in the bestsellers and for four weeks in Britain (one week of these simultaneously with the USA) and 14 weeks in the bestsellers. British sales were well over 250,000, Germany over 400,000, and this disc was No 1 also in Australia, New Zealand, Germany, Holland, South Africa, Eire and Singapore, with global sales estimated at four million.

Nancy, daughter of Frank Sinatra, was born in Jersey City, New Jersey, in 1941. When she moved to Los Angeles, she attended University High and studied economics at the University of Southern California. She decided to develop her own talents rather than bask in her father's fame, and spent many years studying the arts — 11 years of piano, five years' voice and singing lessons, eight years of dance and five years of dramatics. She first attracted attention when she sang on a TV show with her father and Elvis Presley in 1959. Since then she has appeared on many TV shows as singer and dramatic actress. In 1961, she signed exclusively with Reprise Records and began to build an international reputation. Her first disc **Cuff Links and a Tie Clip** was quite a success, and by 1963 such discs as **Tonight You Belong to Me**, and **Like I Do** were hits in Japan, Italy, South Africa, Holland and Belgium. She appeared in four movies, including *Marriage on the Rocks* which starred Frank Sinatra and Dean Martin and, in 1966, *The Last of the Secret Agents*.

With **These Boots are Made for Walkin'**, Nancy was the first US girl singer since Connie Francis (in 1958) to top the British charts, and followed her father in the golden disc route. With his **Strangers in the Night** success, it was a memorable year for the Sinatras and the Reprise label.

SUGAR TOWN *Reprise 0527* [*USA*] *Reprise 20527* [*UK*]. Another big success for Nancy and the composer Lee Hazlewood, this disc achieved the No 4 position in early 1967 in the US charts and a run of 13 weeks. It also had a good sale in Britain where it was No 8 in 1967, with 10 weeks in the bestsellers.

US sales were over a million. Gold Disc RIAA in 1967.

PERCY SLEDGE   *American*

WHEN A MAN LOVES A WOMAN *Atlantic 2326* [*USA*] *Atlantic 584 001* [*UK*]. The very first disc for Percy Sledge became No 1 after seven weeks in the US charts. It stayed there for two weeks in all, in early June 1966, was 13 weeks in the bestsellers, and won a Gold Disc award from RIAA on 15 July 1966. The disc also got to No 4 in Britain with 17 weeks in the bestsellers.

Percy Sledge, born in 1941, hails from Muscle Shoals in the Deep South of Alabama. He began singing at the age of 15. After leaving school, he became a male nurse at Colbert County Hospital near his home town, and also devoted' some of his time to singing in the choirs of Galilee Baptist Church and other churches near his home. He also managed to eke a living as member of a group called the Esquires Combo. Percy finally met Quin Ivy, a former disc jockey, at his 'Ivy's Tune Town Record Shop' in Sheffield, Alabama. Quin and a man named Greene, guitarist and A&R man, recorded Percy at a small studio in Sheffield. Manager-agent Phil Walden — closely associated with Otis Redding's success — flew to Sheffield to hear the result of the session. With very little promotion and even less publicity, the virtually unknown singer was a success in a very short time.

The song, written by C. Lewis and A. Wright, is an easy-going, moving, blues-based song. In the US R&B charts the record was No 1 for four weeks during a 16-week chart run.

THE SPIDERS   *Japanese*

YUHI GA NAITEIRU (Sad Sunset) *Philips 3347* [*Japan*]. The Spiders, one of Japan's top recording groups, had an advance order of 150,000 for this disc which sold half a million in six months and the million by eight months (July 1967). The composition was by Kuranosuke Hamaguchi.

The group was formed by drummer Sochi Tanabe in 1962, and made its debut at a jazz tea-house in Kinshico, Tokyo. Their reception was mild, but they kept pace with American pop styles such as the Twist and surfing music, adapting them to their own fashion. Their popularity gradually increased by playing in tea-houses and at American military camps. They finally became national favourites in 1964

when the group's arrangements of Beatles-type sounds began to make an impact with their fans. They were then invited to appear with visiting artists such as the Animals, Beach Boys, Peter and Gordon, etc., and made their film debut in *Seishun-à-Go-Go*. They made their first promotional tour of Europe in 1966, and a personal appearance tour in Hawaii and America in 1967.

Their beat music, known in Japan as 'eleki', remains recognizably oriental in flavour. This disc was No 1 for 14 weeks from November 1966 to February 1967 and stayed in the charts in Japan for 20 weeks.

The group were Sochi Tanabe (drummer), born 1942; Katsuo Ohno (steel guitar and organ), born 1943; Takayuki Inoue (lead guitarist and vocalist), born 1944; Hirochi Kamayatsu (rhythm guitarist and vocalist), born 1942; Masaaki Sakai (tambourine and vocalist), born 1947; Mitsuru Kato (bass), born 1939; Jun Inoue (vocalist), born 1948.

DUSTY SPRINGFIELD   *British*

YOU DON'T HAVE TO SAY YOU LOVE ME *Philips BF 1482* [*UK*] *Philips 40371* [*USA*]. This song came from the Italian San Remo Song Contest in 1965. The original title was **Io che non vivo (senzate)**, by V. Pallavicini (words) and P. Donaggio (music). The English lyrics were by Vicki Wickham and Simon Napier-Bell.

Dusty's disc sold over 250,000 in Britain where it was No 1 for two weeks. It had a big sale in the USA where it reached No 3 in their charts and stayed high up for six weeks with 13 weeks in the bestsellers. It had 18 weeks in the British bestsellers. The global sale reached a million by 1967.

THE SUPREMES   *American*

MY WORLD IS EMPTY WITHOUT YOU *Motown 1089* [*USA*]. This was the eighth million seller for the Supremes, and for the writers Eddie Holland, Brian Holland and Lamont Dozier. It was released on 15 January 1966, the disc reaching No 4 for a week in the US charts with 11 weeks in the bestsellers. It reached No 10 with 10 weeks in the R&B charts.

YOU CAN'T HURRY LOVE *Motown 1097* [*USA*] *Tamla Motown TMG 575* [*UK*]. In 1964 and 1965 the Supremes had had a string of six No 1s in America out of seven releases. Their first two releases of 1966 made the Top 10, but did not get near No 1. **You Can't Hurry Love** restored them to the top, being the first of another run of four No 1s in a row. No American group has ever equalled the Supremes' record of 12 No 1 singles, or 10 chart toppers out of 13 releases scored by the group in the mid-sixties.

As usual, the song was written by Eddie Holland, Lamont Dozier and Brian Holland. It was produced by Brian Holland and Lamont Dozier at the Motown studios in Detroit, and was their strongest record for some time. Released on 13 August 1966, the record entered the *Billboard* charts at No 66. Four weeks later

it was at No 1 in the Hot 100, the week after it had topped the R&B charts. It was No 1 on both charts for two weeks and spent 13 weeks in both charts. It was also a big hit in Britain, reaching No 3 with 12 weeks in the Top 50. It spent four weeks at No 1 in the British R&B charts. The song was revived in 1982, when Phil Collins had a British No 1 and US Top 10 hit with it.

YOU KEEP ME HANGIN' ON *Motown 1101* [*USA*] *Tamla Motown TMG 585* [*UK*]. The Supremes' eighth No 1 and tenth million seller was again a Holland-Dozier-Holland composition, produced by Brian Holland and Lamont Dozier at the Motown studios in Detroit. The song had a harder rock edge to it than previous Supremes records, and shot up the charts faster than most. It took four weeks to reach No 1 in the pop charts, where it stayed for two weeks with 12 weeks on the charts. This was one week longer than the record took to top the R&B charts, where it was No 1 for four weeks. This was their second No 1 of 1966 on both the American and British R&B charts. Although it only reached No 8 in the main British chart, with 10 weeks in the Top 50, it was No 1 for four weeks in the R&B Top 20.

On the album front, the Supremes put out two LPs in 1966. The first was **I Hear a Symphony**, which went to No 8 and spent 55 weeks on the album charts. Their next release gave them their first No 1 album. **The Supremes A-Go-Go** was on top for two weeks, with 60 weeks of chart action. The album contained both **You Can't Hurry Love** and the Top 10 **Love is Like An Itching in My Heart**. It was only **Supremes A-Go-Go** that charted in Britain, reaching No 15 during a chart life of 21 weeks.

B.J. THOMAS WITH   *American*
THE TRIUMPHS

I'M SO LONELY I COULD CRY *Scepter 12129* [*USA*]. The first big hit for B.J. Thomas. It was

recorded in late 1965 and by 1966, after release in February, reached No 5 for two weeks on the US charts and was 13 weeks in the bestsellers. The song was written in 1949 by singer Hank Williams, one of his own personal favourite numbers. Release in Britain was 25 March 1966. The million sale was reported in 1970.

The Triumphs, a seven-piece band from Rosenberg, Texas, made 15 recordings with B.J. Thomas before he became a solo artist in 1966. (See 1968 for B.J. Thomas biography.)

THE TROGGS   *British*

WILD THING *Fontana TF 689 [UK] Fontana 1548 and Atco 6415 [USA]*. The Troggs were the most promising new group in Britain in 1966, the year of their formation. **Wild Thing** was written by Chips Taylor who had also had hit songs recorded by the Hollies and Peggy Lee. An outstanding feature of this disc is Reg Presley's ocarina playing.

The group was fronted by Reg Presley, born in Andover, Hampshire, 12 June 1943, formerly a bricklayer. He was bass guitarist with his previous group but became lead vocalist with the Troggs. Chris Britton, born in Watford, Hertfordshire, 21 June 1945, studied classical guitar for four years, joined a local group at 16 and was an apprentice lithographic camera operator. Peter Staples, born in Andover, Hampshire, 3 May 1944, was an electrician. He learned to play guitar at 14, played in various local groups from 15, and was with Chris prior to the Troggs' formation. Ronnie Bond was born in Andover, Hampshire, 4 May 1943. All were educated at Andover schools.

The group got its biggest break when they met Larry Page who became both their personal and recording manager. They made their radio debut on 'Saturday Club' and TV debut in 'Thank Your Lucky Stars'. Ronnie played drums, Chris the guitar, Reg the bass and ocarina, Peter bass and rhythm guitar. The

group adopted their name from the shortened form of the word 'troglodyte' (cave-dweller) because they liked it.

Wild Thing became a very fast-moving hit, and two American labels Atco and Fontana claimed the US distribution rights. It was released there on both*, the Fontana label backed with **From Home** and the Atco with **With a Girl Like You** (see below). The song was No 1 in the USA for two weeks with 11 weeks in the bestsellers, and No 1 for one week in Britain with 12 weeks in the bestsellers. A Gold Disc for global million sale was presented by Page One Records, the independent company which produced their discs. **Wild Thing** was released on 22 April 1966.

*Dual-label releases had occurred only once before in the USA — in 1950 with Eileen Barton.

WITH A GIRL LIKE YOU *Fontana TF 717 [UK] Fontana 1552 (and on the B side of Atco 6415 above) [USA]*. Written by the Troggs' member Reg Presley, this was also released by both Atco and Fontana in the USA. It reached No 29 with eight weeks in the US bestsellers, and sold a global million. It was No 1 for two weeks in Britain and 12 weeks in the bestsellers, with over 250,000 sales. The disc was backed by **I Want You** on the Fontana label in the USA.

MAO TSE TUNG   *Chinese*

THE THOUGHTS OF CHAIRMAN MAO (Album) *China Record Company*. Sales figures from Communist China during the Mao era are obviously difficult to come by. The country was served by one record company, based at the EMI Pathé factory in Shanghai. Though taken over by the Government when the Communists came to power in 1949, the China Record Company (itself once part of EMI) continued to pay EMI a nominal rent for the Pathé factory. Records produced in the sixties were almost entirely political propaganda,

tedious songs or revolutionary operas (some written by Mao's second wife Jiang Jou) extolling how grain yield or oil production had been increased by 20% thanks to the thought of Chairman Mao. Sales would have been largely in the cities, as few of the 90% of Chinese living in rural areas would have had a record player.

Red China's Chairman Mao Tse-Tung made this disc in late November 1966. It contains excerpts from his quotations which he chants, 'live' recordings of his three meetings with the Red Guards, and recordings of speeches by Defence Minister Lin Piao and Premier Chou En-lai at Red Guard rallies in Peking.

The disc is said to have easily gone over the million mark and replaced the former No 1 favourite disc in China, **The East is Red**, a collection of revolutionary opera music.

JACKY YOSHIKAWA AND   *Japanese*
HIS BLUE COMETS

AOI HITOMI (Blue Eyes) *CBS 647 [Japan]*. Jacky Yoshikawa and his Blue Comets formed in May 1965, became extremely popular in their native Japan in 1966, and made their debut with this disc released on 20 March. It sold half a million by July and the million sale was reported in May 1967. The disc stayed in the Japanese bestseller charts for six months, was No 2 for eight weeks and No 1 for one week.

The song, a Japanese folk-rock original, was written by Jun Hashimoto (words) and Tadao Inoue (music). The disc was also released on the Epic label in the USA.

THE YOUNG RASCALS   *American*

GOOD LOVIN' *Atlantic 2321 [USA]*. The Young Rascals were first formed in January 1965, and their first engagement was the Choo Choo Club, Garfield, New Jersey. Then came an engagement on The Barge, a real barge lying in the waters off Southampton, Long Island, where they performed for some months. Here they were tremendously popular and were discovered by Sid Bernstein, a New York promoter who signed them to Atlantic Records against bids from practically every other major US recording company. Their first release was **I Ain't Gonna Eat My Heart Out Any More** (1965) which got into the national charts. Then came **Good Lovin'** written by Rudy Clark and Arthur Resnick, which put them at No 1 for two weeks in the charts with 14 weeks in the US bestsellers, with a Gold Disc award from Atlantic for the million sale of this hard-pounding rhythmic number.

The group consisted of Eddie Brigati (lead vocalist) of Garfield, New Jersey; Felix Cavaliere (organ) of Pelham, New York; Gene Cornish (guitar) of Rochester, New York; Dino Danelli (drums) of Jersey City. The group did their own arrangements for recording.

1 9 6 7

1967 was a year of transition and expansion. Rock music was progressing in one direction to greater musical virtuosity, while in other directions it was the year of old-fashioned ballad singers and teenybopper pop. There was more variety to music, from the fashion concious mod fans of the Who to the country and western lovers of Jim Reeves. The Beatles remained the biggest selling act in the world, and launched their **All You Need Is Love** single before a global satellite TV audience of 600,000,000 people. This was also the year of **Sgt Pepper**. For the Rolling Stones, they will remember 1967 more for their drug busts and the famous Redlands trial than for their music. The Monkees dominated the pop music press, with saturation coverage almost every week of the year. Yet the biggest-selling act in Britain, with two million-selling singles in the UK alone, was the least hip star on the whole scene — Englebert Humperdinck.

The teenage rage on both sides of the Atlantic was the Monkees. They had been invented in 1965 as characters for a TV show that Colgems (the TV production wing of Columbia Pictures) wanted to make, modelled on the Beatles and their antics in the *A Hard Days Night* film. They placed an advertisement in *Variety*, and nearly five hundred hopeful young actors and musicians applied. Some of these people later went on to be accomplished musicians, but Screen Gems chose their cast on the basis of how they would look on television.

Two of the four Monkees were actors with limited if any musical ability. Micky Dolenz had been an actor since he was ten. He had played the part of Corky in the American TV series 'Circus Boy' for three years, and appeared in 'Naked City', the 'Peyton Place' soap, and 'Playhouse 90'. He had played guitar before, and had briefly performed as vocalist for an obscure group called the Missing Links, but he ended up on drums for the Monkees. The one British member of the group, Davy Jones, had been a child actor in the 'Coronation Street' TV soap, and had appeared on Broadway in both *Oliver* and *Pickwick*. The musicians in the group were Peter Tork and Mike Nesmith, both of whom came from a folk background. Tork had once been a member of the Mugwumps with Mama Cass Elliot, and Nesmith had recorded some unsuccessful protest songs and played in the L.A. folk scene. Neither had been successful musicians before joining the group.

'The Monkees' was first shown on NBC in September 1966, and was a success from the start. Just before the first screening of the programme, Columbia Pictures' records division Colgems released the group's first single, **Last Train To Clarksville**, which went to No 1 in the first week of November. The follow-up, **I'm A Believer**, topped the American

charts at the end of December, staying at No 1 for seven weeks. Both singles and their first few albums sold over a million copies.

Though the Monkees were seen playing their songs on the TV series, they did not in fact play their instruments on the records. This was partly because their heavy filming commitment left little time for recording, and partly because their record company rightly did not rate their musical ability. Colgems used some of the best session men in Los Angeles to lay down the backing tracks, while the Monkees supplied the vocals. The company also got music publisher Don Kirshner to use some of the top song writers in America to come up with songs.

As the Monkees became increasingly successful as a pop group and not just a TV show, so some members of the group wanted more musical involvement with making their records. The row that ensued with their record company led to the departure of Kirshner, the Monkees playing on their own records, and even recording some of their own songs. Despite their success on disc, their dependence on the TV series was apparent when in 1968, after 59 episodes, NBC cancelled it. The Top Ten hits dried up once the series was off the air.

The Monkees broke in Britain in January 1967. The BBC aired the TV series and record sales took off, with **I'm A Believer** as their first hit, and first and only No 1. In February the group achieved the extremely rare distinction of topping the singles and album charts in both Britain and America the same week. In April there was talk of Davy Jones being drafted into the American military. Even though he was British, his American residence made him elligible. He appealed, and was not called up.

In July the Monkees toured America with Jimi Hendrix as support act. This was not a successful combination, for the Monkees' fans, many of whom were pre-teens from 7 to 12, were not ready for the sound volume, style or stage act of Hendrix. He was asked to tone down his act, which had been criticized as too erotic by the Daughters of the American Revolution, but refused and left the tour. The Monkees were so far removed from what Hendrix was doing that the whole idea of putting the two together was doomed. As Hendrix commented after his departure, 'I think they're replacing me with Micky Mouse.'

In the main the group avoided controversy, for that was not their TV image. When there was an outcry over the title of one of their singles, which they planned to call **Randy Scouse Git** after a catch phrase from the BBC TV series 'Till Death Us Do Part', they changed the name to **Alternate Title**. Despite all the packaging and the deception, the Monkees had a fantastic year. They were the top singles group in America, Mexico, New Zealand and Norway, and were just pipped at the post in Britain by Englebert Humperdinck.

The Beatles

The Beatles had another fabulous year. All three of their singles made No 1 on both sides of the Atlantic. On the album front they released the seminal theme album **Sgt Pepper's Lonely Hearts Club Band**, which made the British singles charts as well as topping the LP lists on both sides of the Atlantic. In May it was announced that Beatles' sales had topped the 200,000,000 mark, well ahead of their nearest rival Elvis Presley whose sales had considerably slowed down.

At the end of August the Beatles were studying transcendental meditation with the Maharishi Yogi in North Wales when the devastating news of Brian Epstein's death hit them. His suicide was a tremendous blow, and opened up the way for Allan Klein, the growing John — Paul split and the eventual breakup of the Beatles. A few months after his death the Beatles suffered their first failure with the showing of the *Magical Mystery Tour* film on television over Christmas. Though the double EP in Britain and the LP in America were big successes, the film was slammed by the critics and given the thumbs down by the fans.

Drugs

The **A Day In The Life** track from **Sgt Pepper** was banned by the BBC as 'it might encourage a permissive attitude to drug taking.' The track was also banned by many radio stations in the USA for similar reasons. Paul McCartney denied that there was any link between the song and drugs. At the end of July the Beatles signed a full-page advertisement in *The Times* which stated that 'the law against marijuana is immoral in principle and unworkable in practice'. While with the Maharishi Yogi in August, McCartney announced that the Beatles had given up the use of drugs. 'We don't need it anymore', he claimed, though in fact various Beatles continued to use drugs for many years.

The increasing way in which drugs were linked with rock stars caused growing concern among those musicians who were not involved. The Troggs' lead guitarist Chris Britton quit the group in April because of it. 'I am fed up with the connection between pop groups and drugs', he said. 'It is so bad now, you cannot move without being searched. My guitar was pulled to pieces last week when we came back from the continent... I can't stand the way people look at you and immediately think that because you're in a group you're drugged to the eyebrows.'

The press took an increasing interest in the rock and drugs connection. The British Sunday tabloid the *New Of The World* ran a number of stories linking pop stars to drugs. In one report they quoted Mick Jagger as claiming he had used LSD and other drugs. Jagger sued for libel, for the paper had got the wrong Stone, mistaking Brian Jones for Mick. The *News Of The World* got their revenge a few days later when they tipped off the police to raid Keith Richards' home, Redlands, in Sussex. Mick Jagger and Keith Richards were later arrested on drugs charges. Both were sentenced to prison, Richards for a year, at their trial in June. Even the staid old *Times* came to their defence, with a famous editorial under the headline 'Who Breaks A Butterfly On A Wheel?' Richards' sentence was later quashed, and that of Jagger reduced to a fine. It was widely believed that George Harrison and his wife had left the Redlands party just before the police raid began. Another person caught up in the raid was Marianne Faithfull, who was naked when the police burst in. In October Brian Jones pleaded guilty to drugs charges and got nine months in prison, suspended on appeal.

The BBC became increasingly sensitive to lyrics that referred to drugs. In January a discussion of **The Addicted Man** by the Game was cut from 'Juke Box Jury'. As *NME* pointed out in a strong editorial attack on the BBC, while the record should never have been released, 'Directly or indirectly, drugs are playing an increasingly prominent part in pop lyrics,' and this problem needed discussion.

The Record Industry

With Brian Epstein dead and the Rolling Stones said to be increasingly distant from their manager Andrew Oldham, there were rumours in October of the Beatles and the Rolling Stones merging their business activities. In fact Paul McCartney and Mick Jagger had discussed a joint venture to build and run a recording studio, though nothing came of this. The Stones then announced that they were considering plans to launch their own Mother Earth label, with Marianne Faithfull as the first signing.

The year began well for EMI, who in January renewed their contract with the Beatles for another nine years. EMI bought the huge Grade Organisation talent agency in March, and later bought their Dutch licensee Bovema. In August the company reactivated the Regal Zonophone label as an outlet for independent producer Denny Cordell. He then switched his acts the Move and Procul Harum from Decca's Deram to the new EMI label. The Move immediately ran into a law suit from the Prime Minister, Harold Wilson, who took exception to them promoting their first EMI release with postcards depicting him in bed in the nude. The Labour Prime Minister hired the leading Tory politician and future Lord Chancellor Quintin Hogg (Lord Hailsham) to represent him. He won the case. Regal Zonophone had previously been reserved for the Salvation Army, and the Joy Strings continued to be released on it.

Decca lost the valuable RCA licence. The two companies signed a termination agreement in October that gave Decca rights to RCA records until RCA set up in Britain on its own in 1969. Decca had represented RCA from the time they had split with EMI in 1956. Decca picked up the much smaller Hickory label from Pye. In America, Warner Brothers bought Atlantic Records, the most important move in the strategy that led the company to become the biggest in the USA. Clive Davis became President of American Columbia (CBS).

In January Brian Epstein's NEMS had taken over the Robert Stigwood Organization, including the Reaction label. This was distributed through Polydor, who also had the UK rights to Stax, and gave that label its own logo in Britain. Its main star was Otis Redding, who in March toured Britain with the Stax Review. This included Sam & Dave, Arthur Conley, Eddie Floyd and Booker T. & the MGs.

Pirates Walk The Plank

On 15 August the Marine Offences Act came into force, making the pirate radio stations illegal. All except Radio Caroline came off the air. Caroline continued defiantly, broadcasting on 259m from its two ships Caroline North and South. Earlier in the year Caroline had admitted to a payola scandal, accepting £100 for a week's plug of any record not in their Top 50. The BBC reorganized its radio services, killing off the old

Light, Home and Third networks and replacing them with Radios 1, 2, 3 and 4. Radio 1 hired the best DJs from the old pirates, and though it was not as good as the pirates it was better than most people had dared hope.

Some big record companies had blamed the pirates for the slump in record sales that occured in 1966, but sales in 1967 were booming. In March, for example, the Beatles' **Penny Lane** sold 400,000 copies in its first two weeks of release, yet was still stuck at No 3 in its second week in the charts. British record production increased by ten million in 1967, to 94,234,000. Only in the peak year of 1964 had production been higher. Behind this figure lay a small recovery in singles sales and a steady and larger increase in album sales. In America sales had increased to 187,000,000 singles and 192,000,000 LPs, with album sales overtaking those of singles for the first time. On the international front, of the 25 major markets that *Billboard* surveyed at the end of 1967, British and American acts were the top singles artists in seven countries each. The main winners were the Beatles, the Monkees and Cliff Richard.

Marriages and Mods

On 1 May Elvis Presley married Priscilla Beaulieu, an army colonel's daughter he had first met when serving with the US Army in Germany when she was 14 years old. Sadly, the marriage did not last. Gene Pitney married his childhood sweetheart Lynn Gayton on the Italian Riviera in February. John Entwistle of the Who married his childhood sweetheart Alison Wise in July. In August Adam Faith married Cliff Richard's ex-fiancée Jackie Irving, and Jackie Trent married Tony Hatch. Eric Burdon married Angie King in September. Sandie Shaw was involved in a messy divorce case in March, winning the Eurovision Song Contest in April with **Puppet On A String**, which later went to No 1.

Marianne Faithfull was estranged from her recently married husband John Dunbar, and was dating Mick Jagger. His ex-girlfriend

Chrissie Shrimpton went from Mick to dating Steve Marriott of the Small Faces. Her sister, top model Jean, branched out into films, playing the leading role opposite ex Manfred Mann singer Paul Jones in *Privilege*. The film was directed by Peter Watkins, whose *The War Game* about nuclear war had been the most controversial film of 1966.

The fashion scene continued to centre on London. Mini skirts were still in, with bright colours for both sexes and psychedelic gear increasingly in vogue. 'Top Of The Pops' girl and top model Samantha Juste wrote a column for *Disc*. She described American fashion as a real let-down. 'New York is probably the biggest fashion disappointment I've had,' she wrote in April. 'The fashion scene in New York is practically non-existent. You hardly ever see anyone in a mini skirt... It's all very depressing... the only place in New York that swings at all, fashion-wise, is Greenwich Village. In the heart of hippy country...California fashion [is] a much happier scene.' Sammy left 'Top Of The Pops' in November, going to Australia on a modelling job, and then to America and marriage to Monkee Micky Dolenz. (Sadly, the marriage did not last.) *Disc* selected 17-year-old Jayne Harries, of Ewhurst, Surrey, as its Miss Mod Britain 1967, and she had a whale of a time for the rest of the year, going to all the 'in' functions and meeting the stars to report for *Disc*.

Splits and Disputes

In March Steve and Muff Winwood announced that they were leaving the Spencer Davis Group. The departures pretty well killed off the band. In April Cliff Richard denied that he would be splitting from the Shadows, and both continued to have hits throughout the year. In May the Walker Brothers split up, and Gerry and the Pacemakers parted. In September the Mamas and the Papas announced that they were splitting, and then denied it.

Procul Harum sacked their manager in July, and the Troggs got rid of Larry Page, who had been their manager, agent and producer. The Beach Boys settled their dispute with Capitol in July. They had sued for $225,000, claiming under-payment of royalties, and sought an end to their contract. The settlement gave them their own Brother label for America, though they remained on Capitol for the rest of the world. Beach Boy Carl Wilson was held for avoiding the draft in May. He was released on bail, and appealed against his call up. Former Shadows leader Jet Harris tried a come-back in July, but his Tony Meehan produced **My Lady** failed to restore him to the charts.

Deaths

Britain's first successful independent producer Joe Meek shot himself in the head in February. He had produced for Lonnie Donegan in the fifties, and John Leyton and the Tornados in the early sixties. A man ahead of his time, the beat boom of the mid-sixties had left him behind. His suicide brought to an end the life of one of the most talented pioneers of British pop music.

In July Jayne Mansfield was killed in a car crash on her way to do a TV programme in New Orleans. In December Otis Redding and four members of his group the Bar Kays were killed when his light plane crashed into a lake in Wisconsin. He had his biggest hit, **(Sitting On) The Dock Of The Bay** after his death.

Touring

A large batch of American stars made appearances in Britain. Apart from the Stax tour, Roy Orbison, Gene Pitney, the Beach Boys, the Monkees, the Mamas and the Papas, Stevie Wonder, the Four Tops, Vikki Carr, the Turtles and the Lovin' Spoonful were all in Britain. The Beach Boys won a special Silver Disc for a quarter of a million British sales of their 'Best of...' album.

The Who made their first tour of America. Keith Moon was mugged in the South by a group of whites who did not appreciate his long hair and 'way out' looks. Other British acts crossing the Atlantic included the Troggs, Cream and, for the first time, Pink Floyd. Japan was recognized as a growing and important market. Cliff Richard and Dusty Springfield toured there.

DISC and MUSIC ECHO 9d

MAY 13, 1967   USA 20c

BEACH BOYS BOOM TOUR
Pictures and stories—centre pages

WIN SEATS for the MONKEES!

ELVIS WEDS CILLA!

FIRST COLOUR PICTURE from Las Vegas of Elvis Presley and his bride, Priscilla Beaulieu. And their wedding has coincided with the release in Britain of a new Presley single—"The Love Machine."

But there were no wedding congratulations from last Saturday's "Juke Box Jury."

panel. Disc-jockey Alan Freeman described the record as "draggy." And Val Doonican criticised it, too, joking: "I suppose he needs the money now he's married!"

In Disc today, top British stars offer some advice to Presley in his new role as a married King. Turn to page 11.

The Media

Two new youth-orientated magazines were founded in 1967. In Britain the underground paper *Oz* began publication in February. It did not last. In America *Rolling Stone* became the first national consumer music paper in November. The US did not have the sort of pop consumer papers that Britain had enjoyed for many years. *Rolling Stone* went further than the British music papers, and covered the life style of a generation. It is still going strong.

World News

The major event of the year was war in the Middle East. In six days the Israelis triumphed over the Arabs and occupied all Jerusalem, the West Bank, the Gaza Strip and the Golan Heights. The Israelis were jubilant, feeling that that had increased their security. In part this was true, but they also became prisoners of their own occupation, and the present uprising in the West Bank and Gaza is a reflection of this. A month after the June war in the Middle East civil war broke out in Nigeria, as the Eastern States tried to break away as Biafra. After a bloody war, they failed. After an army coup in Greece, a junta of colonels seized power and the King of Greece fled abroad. Australian Prime Minister Harold Holt drowned while surfing. Che Guevara, the Latin American revolutionary and ally of Cuba's Fidel Castro, was killed by the Bolivian army in October, the same month as the coronation of the Shah of Iran.

In Britain a private member's bill introduced by Liberal MP David Steele made abortion legal. The Liberal Party, with 12 MPs, elected 34-year-old Jeremy Thorpe as leader. His career would later crash into the ground as a result of a bizarre homosexual scandal with Thorpe accused (and aquitted) of plotting to kill gay male model Norman Scott. The Labour Government ran into increasing economic problems and devalued the pound. France again vetoed Britain's second attempt to join the European Economic Community. General De Gaulle called for an end to the Anglo-American special relationship before Britain could be considered truly European. Aden became independent after 128 years as a British colony. In a 95% turnout, 12,138 people in Gibraltar voted to keep the colony British and 44 voted for joining Spain.

In America opposition to the Vietnam War grew. President Johnson visited his troops in South Vietnam, where their combat role had been stepped up. American bombing of North Vietnam and Viet Cong positions in the South was also increased. With the increase in American involvement came an increase in American dead and wounded. Ronald Reagan, Governor of California, called for the war to be substantially escalated to ensure a quick victory. In October a major anti-war demonstration at the Lincoln Memorial in Washington turned violent when the crowd attempted to advance on the Pentagon. Race riots erupted again in America's cities, the most serious being in Detroit in July. The year had started badly for America when in January a fire had burned three astronauts to death as they practised a launch. In April a Russian cosmonaut died trying to bring his spaceship back to earth.

Films

Sean Connery was the most popular film star in Britain for the fourth year running. His James Bond film *You Only Live Twice* was the biggest money maker in the country. After Connery, Lee Marvin, Michael Caine and Julie Christie were the most popular stars in Britain. Other major films of the year were *The Blue Max*, *Bonnie And Clyde*, *My Fair Lady* and Raquel Welch in *One Million Years B.C.* In America the Oscar for Film Of The Year went to *In The Heat Of The Night*, Rod Steiger won the Best Actor Oscar for his part in the same movie, while Katharine Hepburn carried off the Best Actress prize for her part in *Guess Who's Coming To Dinner*. The Oscar for Best Director went to Mike Nichols, for *The Graduate*.

Sport

The year started with a tragedy on the water for Britain. Donald Campbell died when his Bluebird craft somersaulted and crashed on Lake Coniston as he neared his own world water speed record. In May, 65-year-old yachtsman Francis Chichester returned home to Plymouth after his 119-day lone voyage around the world. He was later knighted.

In Britain, Yorkshire were the County Cricket Champions for the second year in a row. England won test matches against both India and Pakistan. In the FA Cup Tottenham Hotspur beat Chelsea, while Queens Park Rangers were the League Cup winners. Manchester United were top of League Division One, while Celtic beat Rangers at the top of the Scottish equivalent. It was a good year for Celtic. The Glasgow club also won the Scottish League and FA Cups, and were European Cup Winners.

In America the 1966–7 season was the first in which the National and American Football Leagues were merged. The Green Bay Packers won the NFL championships for the third time in a row, and the fifth time in the decade. The Oakland Raiders had an easy win in the AFL championship final. The 1966 champions of the two leagues met for the first Super Bowl contest in January 1967. The Green Bay Packers (NFL) beat the Kansas City Chiefs (AFL) by 35 to 10. The decision of the two leagues to merge and the excitement of the new Super Bowl contest matched the baseball World Series final, and made American football the country's most popular sport. The St Louis Cardinals won the World Series for the second time in the decade.

Festivals Of Love

Rock music in 1967 took on a more political role than it had previously done. Most of the pop scene had not been remotely political, but especially in America, where the reality of the military draft and fighting in Vietnam was a very real threat for young American men, the message of love and peace of the hippy psychedelic scene began to take on some real meaning. As Cassius Clay said when refusing to enlist in the American army, 'No Vietnamese ever called me nigger.' A combination of folk music, rock protest songs and psychedelia came together in the era of the massive music festival, mainly in the United States.

In January 20,000 people gathered in the Golden Gate Park in San Francisco for the first Human Be-In and Gathering Of The Tribes. The Grateful Dead, Jefferson Airplane and the Quicksilver Messenger Service provided the music. In June another large crowd attended the Fantasy Fair and Magic Mountain Music Fest in Mount Tamalpais, California, and heard the Doors, the Byrds and Country Joe and the Fish. The big pop festival of the year was at Monterey, California. Michelle and John Phillips of the Mamas and the Papas and Lou Adler organized the three-day June event that brought 50,000 people to Monterey. Acts appearing included the Who, Jimi Hendrix, Janis Joplin, Otis Redding, the Association, Buffalo Springfield, the Byrds, Canned Heat, and many more. In Britain the Festival Of The Flower Children took place at the end of August on the Duke of Bedford's estate at Woburn Abbey, with Eric Burdon and the Animals.

The year saw a number of groups emerge that would later become important. Peter Green's Fleetwood Mac made their first appearance, while the Doors released their first album in January. After leaving the Spencer Davis Group, Stevie Winwood got together with Jim Capaldi, Chris Wood and Dave Mason and formed Traffic. The Bee Gees had their first British hit with **New York Mining Disaster 1941**.

In many ways it was an enigmatic year. The front page of the final 1967 edition of *NME* rather summed it up. It listed the top ten chart artists for the year, and within that group lay the full variety of acts that had made 1967 such a varied year. Britain's top ten were Englebert Humperdinck, followed by the Monkees, Tom Jones, the Beatles, the Tremeloes, Diana Ross & the Supremes, Cliff Richard & the Shadows, Dave Dee, Dozy, Beaky, Mick and Tich, the Move and Traffic.

ORIGINAL FILM SOUNDTRACK *American*

CAMELOT (Album) *Warner Brothers 1712 [USA] Warner Brothers WS 1712 [UK]*. In 1961 the Broadway musical *Camelot* had been a great success. It was written by Alan Jay Lerner (lyrics) and Frederick Loewe (music) and followed their outstanding success with *My Fair Lady*. Starring Richard Burton, Julie Andrews and Robert Goulet, **Camelot** had been a hit on the stage and on record. The CBS-Columbia album logged six weeks at No 1 in the US album charts, and sold a million copies. (See 1961 for details.) Canadian conductor-arranger Percy Faith also had a hit instrumental album with music from the show the same year.

The 1967 film version starred Richard Harris and Vanessa Redgrave. The conductor on the soundtrack was Alfred Newman. The album reached No 11 in the American album charts, with a chart life of 87 weeks. It was a great deal more successful in America than in England, where it managed only one week in the LP charts, at No 37 on 23 November 1968.

It won an RIAA Gold Disc for million dollar sales on 17 September 1968, and a Platinum Disc for sales of a million copies on 13 October 1986.

THE AMERICAN BREED *American*

BEND ME, SHAPE ME *Acta 811 [USA] Stateside SS 2078 [UK]*. The American Breed's disc produced in Chicago was No 1 for one week in the US in early 1968 with 14 weeks in the bestsellers, and went over the million mark. The song was written by Scott English and Laurence Weiss, and the disc was released in late 1967.

It was also a hit in Britain in early 1968 when released there on the Stateside label. It reached No 24, and stayed six weeks in the charts. RIAA Gold Disc award, January 1968.

The group became especially popular in the Chicago area at dance dates, originally as Gary and The Nite Lights. Their discovery was a 'fortunate accident'. Kenny Myers, Acta's general manager, was caught in a blizzard in the winter of 1966 and forced to stay in Chicago. He wandered down to one of the recording studios and ran into Bill Traut of Dunwich Productions who played him some tapes of a new group he was producing called the Mauds. Sandwiched between their takes was a foursome from Cicero who had previously recorded for MGM — a number titled **I Don't Think You Know Me** by Gary and The Nite Lights. Myers signed them immediately for the new Acta label (a division of Dot Records) and the song was the label's first release, under the group's new name of the American Breed. This got into the US charts and their second disc got to No 10. A successful album followed.

The personal of the group were Gary Loizzo (lead singer, lead guitarist) born 16 August 1945; Charles 'Chuck' Colbert (bass guitarist) born 29 August 1944; Alan Ciner (12-string guitarist) born 14 May 1947; Lee Anthony Graziano (drummer, trumpet) born 9 November 1943.

LOUIS ARMSTRONG *American*

WHAT A WONDERFUL WORLD *A&M 3010 [USA] HMV Pop 1615 [UK]*. **What a Wonderful World** was the biggest hit of Louis Armstrong's career in Britain. It was his only No 1, and the last No 1 single on the HMV label before EMI switched it to a classical-only marque in 1968. (This policy lasted until 1988, when the company added Morrissey to the otherwise all-classical catalogue. His debut album on the label went to No 1 in the LP charts, but Louis Armstrong remained the last artist to have a chart-topping single on the world-famous 'His Master's Voice' label.)

EMI had picked up British rights to the record from ABC, for whom this was Armstrong's first record. When it was issued in America in September 1967, it did nothing. It was released in Britain on 27 October, and proved something of a sleeper. Three months later, on 7 February 1968, it entered the charts, and 11 weeks after that 'Satchmo' knocked Cliff Richard off the top and scored his first and only British No 1. It stayed at the top for two weeks, and in the Top 50 for a lengthy 29 weeks. For all but its first week in the charts, it was listed in some charts as a double A side, with **Cabaret** as its flip side.

What a Wonderful World was written by George David Weiss and George Douglas (pseudonym for Robert Thiele) and produced by Thiele and D. Anderle. The record sold half a million copies in Britain, winning a Silver Disc. It eventually sold a million copies outside America, but remained unloved in the land of its birth.

In 1971 Louis Armstrong died. Then, 17 years later, the makers of the film *Good Morning Viet-Nam* included the song on their soundtrack. On 20 February 1988, **What a Wonderful World** by the late Louis Armstrong at last entered the American Hot 100, at No 67. It gradually rose up the charts, and peaked at No 32 during its 11 weeks on the charts. It was one of the greatest 'sleepers', with about the longest period of time between initial release and making the charts.

In 1986 the American chart expert Joel Whitburn published a book called *Pop Memories 1890–1954*. He had researched music charts going back to 1890, and, although they were not really comparable to the charts published by *Billboard* since 1940, he created a series of charts going back to the last century. In these, Louis Armstrong had had his first hit in 1926, when **Muskrat Ramble** went to No 8. This gave him a chart career of 62 years, clearly an all-time record. During this time he had 79 hits, of which only two went to No 1. These were **All of Me** (from the film *Careless Lady*) in 1932 and **Hello Dolly** in 1964. This 32-year span was also a record for the longest time between No 1s.

THE ASSOCIATION *American*

WINDY *Warner Brothers 7041 [USA]*. This was the second million seller for this group and another RIAA Gold Disc award. The disc was No 1 in the USA for four weeks and 14 weeks in the bestsellers. The song was written by 19-year-old Ruthann Friedman.

NEVER MY LOVE *Warner Brothers 7074 [USA]*. This beautiful, slow-paced ballad featuring the Association's brilliant harmony was written by Don and Dick Addrisi, and released in August 1967. By November it sold a million and was awarded a Gold Disc by RIAA. It was No 1 for one week in the US charts and 14 weeks in the bestsellers.

The flip side **Requiem for the Masses** just made the charts as well. It was No 100 for two weeks.

AL BANO *Italian*

NEL SOLE (In the sun) *VOP (Italian HMV) MQ 2085 [Italy]*. Al Bano was awarded La Maschera d'Argent in Rome (October 1967) as the most popular young singer of that year. He also won the fourth International Roses Festival with the song **L'oro del mondo**.

Nel sole was written by Vito Pallavicini and Pino Massara, Bano's producer. The disc sold over 600,000 in its first three months on the Italian market, with the million reported in July 1968 plus a Gold Disc award. It stayed in a high position in the Italian charts for 22 weeks after release in July 1967, and was No 1 for 11 of those weeks. The song was first introduced on the TV-radio contest 'A Disc for the Summer' in Italy.

Al Bano was born in southern Italy in 1943. His real name is Albano Carrisi.

THE BEATLES *British*

STRAWBERRY FIELDS FOR EVER/PENNY LANE *Capitol 5810 [USA] Parlophone R 5570 [UK]*. The Beatles' 36th million seller was another double A side, released on 17 February in Britain and four days earlier in America. Both sides were Lennon-McCartney compositions, and were produced by George Martin at the Abbey Road studios in London. The titles of both songs were named after parts of the Beatles' native Liverpool.

Strawberry Fields Forever was mainly the work of John Lennon. The Beatles had reached that stage in their development where the touring had stopped and the music was that which could be created in the studio rather than played live at a gig. The Beatles continued to experiment and push the frontiers of recording to their limits. On **Strawberry Fields Forever** the Beatles took further the techniques they had developed when recording **Revolver** and would use for **Sgt Pepper**. The playing of tape backwards, the varying of the speed of the tape, and the use of an ever-increasing number of instruments, all pulled together into ever-lengthening recording sessions a world away from the one day it took to record their first album **Please Please Me**. On this track John Lennon used his new Mellotron for the introduction. The sessions for this were in November and December 1966. **Penny Lane** was a more simple and commercial song, recorded in December 1966 and January 1967.

The record topped only one of the four British charts, spending three weeks at No 1 in *Melody Maker*. It was 11 weeks in the Top 50. In America **Penny Lane** topped the *Cash Box* and

Record World charts for two weeks and the others for one week. It was 10 weeks in both the main US charts. **Strawberry Fields Forever** also charted, reaching No 8 in *Billboard* and No 10 in *Cash Box*, with nine weeks in both charts. It won a Gold Disc for US sales on 20 March 1967. It was No 1 in Australia, New Zealand, Germany, Malaysia, and, entering the charts at No 1 the first week of release, in Denmark and the Netherlands. It was Top 5 in Ireland, Finland, Norway, Switzerland, France, Italy, Singapore and Argentina.

SGT PEPPER'S LONELY HEARTS CLUB BAND (Album) *Parlophone PMC 7027* [*UK*]/ *Capitol MAS 2653* [*USA*]. **Sgt Pepper** is probably the most famous album of all. With it, the Beatles reached the height of their creativity as a group. The album was packed full of new ideas, helped along by the drugs that the Beatles were taking. The recording equipment and the Abbey Road studios were stretched to their limits, as was the ingenuity of all those involved in the project. All the tracks were linked up together so that there were no gaps of silence between songs, a first for a pop album. Each track flowed into the next. Even small points of detail did not escape the attention of the group. There was even a recording of jumbled sounds recorded backwards put on the run out groove, and a high pitched whistle that only dogs could hear on the groove leading to it.

The album took five months to record, with EMI allowing the group unlimited studio time at Abbey Road. They started in December 1966, and finished in May the following year. The album was produced by George Martin, who also played a leading musical part, scoring the album and playing some of the instruments on some tracks. Geoff Emerick was the engineer, and Richard Lush tape operator. Almost every session took place at Abbey Road. The album encompassed a wide variety of different sounds, from the 40 musicians brought in for the orchestral accompaniment of **A Day In The Life** to the music hall of **When I'm 64**.

The packaging of the album was also special, with its gatefold sleeve and distinctive art work. EMI were terrified that half the

people depicted in the photomontage on the cover would sue the company for millions. EMI chairman Sir Joseph Lockwood insisted that the Beatles guarantee EMI against this. The group eventually agreed to take Gandhi and Jesus Christ off, but despite EMI's fears none of the others ever complained.

For the first time with a Beatles record, the British and American versions were the same, in both content and packaging design. Capitol had been resisting this for years, but finally gave way and agreed to the EMI UK version being used unaltered in America.

The album was released in Britain on 1 June, and in America the day after. It entered the British album charts at No 1 the first week of release, staying on top for 27 weeks, just over half its 52-week chart life. It also made the singles Top 20. It charted again 20 years later, reaching No 3 in 1987 with an extra 16 weeks in the charts.

In America it was No 1 for 15 weeks with a then-record 168 weeks on the LP charts.

This was the longest stretch at the top of any Beatles record. An RIAA Gold Disc was awarded on 15 June 1967, with total American sales of six million.

Sgt Pepper remains the biggest selling Beatles album in America. It sold 600,000 copies in Canada, and several million around the world.

Sgt Pepper was more than just another successful Beatles record. It epitomized its age, that part of the sixties when psychedelia, love, peace and a little acid seemed to offer hope for a better future.

The Beatles poured everything into this album, and it seemed to drain them. They were never to perform as effectively again, and in fact the process of disintegration began soon after the project was completed.

The tracks on the album, all of which were written by Lennon and McCartney unless otherwise indicated, were as follows: **Sgt Pepper's Lonely Hearts Club Band**; **With A**

Little Help From My Friends; **Lucy In The Sky With Diamonds**; **Getting Better**; **Fixing A Hole**; **She's Leaving Home**; **Being For The Benefit Of Mr Kite!**; **Within You Without You**, by George Harrison; **When I'm 64**; **Lovely Rita**; **Good Morning Good Morning**; **Sgt Pepper's Lonely Hearts Club Band (Reprise)**; and **A Day In The Life**.

ALL YOU NEED IS LOVE *Parlophone R 5620* [*UK*]/*Capitol 5964* [*USA*]. **All You Need Is Love** was the British contribution to the international satellite TV programme 'Our World', which linked up 600,000,000 people in 26 countries on Sunday 25 June. The BBC broadcast their segment of the programme from the large Abbey Road Number One studio, where the Beatles had assembled a number of their friends to help them. Various Rolling Stones, Marianne Faithfull, Eric Clapton, Keith Moon and others all joined in, and held up placards with slogans like 'Peace' and 'Love' written on them. The recording was produced by George Martin, with Geoff Emerick as engineer assisted by Peter Lush and Martin Benge. The song was another Lennon-McCartney composition.

The record was a major international hit, going to No 1 in Britain, the USA, Canada, Australia, New Zealand, Ireland, Denmark, Germany, Switzerland, Spain, Poland, Israel and Argentina. It was Top 10 in Finland, Norway, Belgium, Netherlands, France, Malaysia, Singapore and Mexico. It was in the British Top 50 for 13 weeks, and in the American Top 100 for 11 weeks. It won an RIAA Gold Disc on 11 September 1967.

HELLO GOODBYE *Parlophone R 5655* [*UK*] /*Capitol 2056* [*USA*]. After **All You Need Is Love** the Beatles turned to a harder rock style for their next few singles. **Hello Goodbye** was the group's 39th million seller, and was written by Lennon and McCartney. It was produced by George Martin at Abbey Road, and released on both sides of the Atlantic at the end of November.

The record was their biggest hit for some while. It was No 1 for seven weeks in Britain, with 12 weeks in the Top 50. It was also a No 1 in America, with 12 weeks in the charts. The flip side, another Lennon-McCartney composition **I Am The Walrus**, also charted. It made No 46 in *Cash Box* during six weeks in that chart, and No 56 during its four weeks in the *Billboard* charts. The B side was taken from the group's *Magical Mystery Tour* TV film. **Hello Goodbye** sold well over half a million in Britain, and won an RIAA Gold Disc for American sales of over a million on 15 December 1967. It was a major international hit, going to No 1 in Canada, Australia, New Zealand, South Africa, Ireland, Sweden, Norway, Denmark, Switzerland, Belgium, Netherlands, Malaysia and Singapore, and was also a hit in Germany, Austria, France, Spain, Italy, Poland, Israel, the Philippines, Japan, Argentina and Brazil.

MAGICAL MYSTERY TOUR (Album) *Capitol MAL 2835* [*USA*]/*Parlophone PCTC 255* [*UK*]. Released in America on 27 November, this album was the Beatles' 40th million-selling record. The first half contained the tracks from the British double EP from the TV film **Magical Mystery Tour**. The second half contained a collection of odds and ends that had not been released on album in America at that time. George Martin produced all the tracks at Abbey Road.

The album was a tremendous commercial success, selling five million copies mainly in America. It was No 1 for eight weeks, with 87 weeks in the charts. Import copies put the album in the British charts at No 31. The album was finally released in Britain twenty years later, when in 1987 it made No 52 for one week. It won an RIAA Gold Disc on 15 December 1967.

The tracks on the album, all of which were written by Lennon and McCartney unless otherwise indicated, were as follows: **Magical Mystery Tour; The Fool On The Hill; Flying**, an instrumental by all four Beatles; **Blue Jay Way**, by George Harrison while on holiday in Los Angeles and near a highway called Blue Jay Way; **Your Mother Should Know; I Am The Walrus; Hello Goodbye; Strawberry Fields Forever; Penny Lane; Baby You're A Rich Man**; and **All You Need Is Love**.

MAGICAL MYSTERY TOUR (double EP) *Parlophone MMT 1* [*UK*]. In Britain EMI put all the songs from the Beatles produced and directed TV film *Magical Mystery Tour* on a double EP, lavishly packaged in a double gatefold sleeve with a free 32-page booklet that included the words to all the songs. And all this for under a pound. The record went to No 1 for one week, kept off the top in some charts by their own **Hello Goodbye**, and spent 12 weeks in the singles charts. The EP was released the week after the last EP chart ceased publication. The double EP was also released in the rest of the world outside North America, making the singles charts in New Zealand, Ireland and Norway. It was the first EP to sell a million copies in Britain, the first to top the singles charts, and remains the only double EP ever to do so. It was the Beatles sixth EP to win a Silver Disc for British sales of a quarter of a million, and their 21st Silver Disc overall. The records were produced by George Martin using the EMI studios at Abbey Road and the Chappell Recording Studios in London. Though the film was a critical failure, it and the records from it were another huge commercial success.

The tracks on the double EP, all of which were written by Lennon and McCartney unless otherwise indicated, were as follows: **Magical Mystery Tour; The Fool On The Hill; Flying**, an instrumental by all four Beatles; **Blue Jay Way** by George Harrison; **Your Mother Should Know**; and **I Am The Walrus**.

THE BEE GEES   *British/Australian*

NEW YORK MINING DISASTER 1941 (Have You Seen My Wife, Mr Jones?) *Polydor 56 161* [*UK*] *Atco 6487* [*USA*]. The Bee Gees were originally a trio — twins Robin and Maurice Gibb plus their brother Barry. They began as amateurs in Manchester, England, in 1956 when they were very young, and in 1958 the

family emigrated to Australia. By 1960, when the average age of the group was just 10 years, they were starring in their own weekly half-hour TV series from Brisbane, and during the following eight years became one of Australia's top pop acts.

They made their first disc there in January 1963, and their own song **Coal Man** got to No 1. They returned to Britain in February 1967 and established a big reputation for themselves with their song **New York Mining Disaster**, which entered the charts on both sides of the Atlantic. It sold over 350,000 in America alone in three weeks, reaching No 14 for two weeks. It was actually written on the stairs in the dark at Polydor's studios before going into a recording session. They had sent a couple of their records to Brian Epstein when they returned to Britain, and were signed by his agency prior to the recording. They had added Colin Petersen to the group, and a fifth member, Vince Melouney, also joined. **New York Mining Disaster** was the Bee Gees' first British release (April 1967), the song by Maurice, Barry and Robin Gibb of the group. A global million sale was reported by the end of the year. It was released in the USA in May 1967 and reached No 14 for two weeks there with seven weeks in the bestsellers, and over half a million sales. In Britain, the disc was No 12 for a week with 10 weeks in the bestsellers, and it was also big seller in six other countries including Australia, New Zealand and Holland.

The Bee Gees consisted of Barry Gibb (guitar, piano, harpsichord) born 1 September 1947; Robin Gibb (guitar, piano, melodia and autoharp) born 22 December 1949; Maurice Gibb (bass guitar) born 22 December 1949 (birthplace of all three Douglas, Isle of Man); Colin Petersen (drums) born 24 March 1946 in Kinearoy, Queensland, Australia; Vince Melouney (lead guitarist) born 18 August 1945 in Sydney, Australia.

MASSACHUSETTS *Polydor 56 192* [*UK*] *Atco 6532* [*USA*]. **Massachusetts** was released in Britain on 1 September 1967 and soon raced up the charts, becoming No 1 for four weeks with 17 weeks in the bestsellers, selling over 250,000. It was No 11 for two weeks in the USA with eight weeks in the bestsellers and big sales, and a No 1 in many other countries including Germany (three weeks), Japan (six weeks) with over 500,000 sold, Malaysia, South Africa, New Zealand, Singapore and Australia. The million sale was reported in mid-January 1968. The song was written by Barry, Robin and Maurice Gibb.

The group went to the USA in June 1967 for a promotional visit, and a million dollar tour there in 1968.

Sales of this disc were over five million.

WORLD *Polydor 56 220* [*UK*]. Release in Britain on 17 November 1967, **World** proved another outstanding song for the group, again written by the three group member brothers, Barry, Robin and Maurice Gibb. It achieved No 7 in Britain with 16 weeks in the bestsellers, selling over 250,000, and then became a No 1 hit in Holland, Germany and Switzerland with big sales elsewhere in Europe and abroad. The

final sales tally was two million.

The group's promotional tour of the USA in this year was a tremendous success. In the USA they were voted the 'World's Most Promising Group' by one magazine and had other 'Top Musical Group' awards from Britain, Germany and Australia. In just over 12 months (to May 1968) their discs were No 1 27 times in 15 countries, with collective sales of over 10 million.

The international career that started in 1967 lasted on into the eighties, boosted in the late seventies by the disco craze. From 1977 to 1979, the group had six US million-selling No 1s in a row, four of which won Platinum Disc awards for sales of over two million copies in the USA alone. The first three were from the film *Saturday Night Fever*. The six chart-toppers included **Stayin' Alive**, **Night Fever** (eight weeks at No 1 in America, two weeks at the top in Britain) and **Tragedy** (No 1 for two weeks on both sides of the Atlantic).

THE BOX TOPS   *American*

THE LETTER *Mala 565* [*USA*] *Stateside SS 2044* [*UK*]. The first record for this group sold almost three million (of its four million global sales) in the USA where it was No 1 for four weeks with 16 weeks in the bestsellers, and received a gold disc award from RIAA. It reached No 5 and was 12 weeks in the British bestsellers. The song was written by Wayne Carson Thompson.

The Box Tops were five young men from Memphis: Alex Chilton (lead guitar), Danny Smythe (drums), Bill Cunningham (bass guitar), Gary Talley (lead guitar) and John Evans (organ). They met while at college and formed the group in 1965. Their particular interest was in 'soul' music.

TOMMY BOYCE AND   *American*
BOBBY HART

I WONDER WHAT SHE'S DOING TO-NIGHT? *A&M 893* [*USA*]. The talented American songwriting team, Tommy Boyce and Bobby Hart, wrote, sang and produced this disc which was released in early December 1967. The million sale was reported in February 1968, the disc having reached No 6 for two weeks in the USA charts with 14 weeks in the bestsellers.

Tommy Boyce, born in Charlottesville, Virginia, in 1944, went to Los Angeles with his parents when he was 12. His parents were both singers, and his father once had his own C&W band. While at school he wrote his first song, and later Fats Domino recorded **Be My Guest** (1959) which he wrote with Fats and John Marascalco. This became a No 1 in the USA.

Bobby Hart, born in Phoenix, Arizona, in 1944, is the son of a preacher, and became influenced by the music of the Church. He met Tommy in Hollywood and they began working together at weekends. After a car accident in which they were both injured, Tommy went to New York for treatment where he was joined by Bobby. Their song **Come a Little Bit Closer** (1964) was a hit for Jay and the Americans. They then returned to Hollywood and a prior exclusive writers contract with Screen Gems landed them the music assignment for the Monkees project for whom they wrote and produced 80 per cent of the music and lyrics (1966).

In May 1967 they decided to form a duo and record their own material, released by A&M Records. **I Wonder What She's Doing Tonight?** proved to be a big personal hit.

JAMES BROWN   *American*

COLD SWEAT (Part 1) *King 6110 [USA]*. Written by the dynamic Brown himself and A. Ellis, this throbbing, pounding disc proved another million seller for James Brown. It got to No 4 for two weeks in the national charts with 12 weeks in the bestsellers, and No 1 for four weeks with 16 weeks in the R&B charts. Brown's backing group on this record was the Famous Flames.

BUFFALO SPRINGFIELD   *America*

FOR WHAT IT'S WORTH (STOP, HEY WHAT'S THAT SOUND) *Atco 6459 [USA]*. This top group from Los Angeles were born in the West Coast rock revolution of 1966–7 and survived for two years, during which stormy time they produced some of the most distinctive and enjoyable sounds to come out of that whole scene. They took their name from an American tractor company. Their soft country rock, tight playing and more relaxed approach never received the acclaim given to the heavier and flashier groups such as The Doors and Iron Butterfly, despite the fact that they cut three albums with moderate success. The group's greatest strength — and the eventual cause of its dissolution in 1968 — was the strongly contrasting musical personalities of its three writers, Steve Stills (writer of this recording), Richie Furay and Neil Young. Stills mostly wrote up-tempo songs, Furay quiet romantic numbers, and Young songs of love, despair and regret. The other members of the group were Dewey Martin (drums) and Jim Fielder (bass), plus occasional vocals by the group's engineer Jim Messina.

Their break-up makes interesting pop history. Fielder, once with the Mothers of Invention, left to join Blood, Sweat and Tears. Messina and Furay formed the country group Poco. Stills joined Al Kooper and Mike Bloomfield on the legendary **Supersession**, and then formed an alliance with Crosby and Nash. Young teamed with a trio called Crazy Horse and eventually with Crosby, Stills and Nash.

For What It's Worth reached No 7 in the US charts for two weeks with 15 weeks in the bestsellers. The million sale was reported in 1970.

THE BYRDS   *American*

THE BYRDS' GREATEST HITS (Album) *CBS-Columbia CS 9516 [USA]*. This **Greatest Hits** package was the Byrds' fifth album to make the charts, and reached No 6 during 29 weeks in

the LP Top 200. (*Billboard* had expanded its album charts from a Top 150 at the beginning of the year to a Top 175 in April, and then to its present size of a Top 200 in May.) The album contained all their biggest hit singles up to that time, with tracks produced by Terry Melcher, Allen Stanton and Gary Usher. It won a Gold Disc from the RIAA for million dollar sales on 13 March 1968, and a Platinum Disc for sales of a million units on 21 November 1986.

The tracks on the album (with song writers in brackets) were: **Mr Tambourine Man** (Bob Dylan); **I'll Feel A Whole Lot Better** (Gene Clark); **The Bells of Rhymney** (Pete Seeger/I. Davies); **Turn! Turn! Turn! (To Everything There Is A Season)** (words from the Old Testament Book of Ecclesiastes, with adaptation and music by Pete Seeger); **All I Really Want To Do** (Bob Dylan); **Chimes Of Freedom** (Bob Dylan); **Eight Miles High** (Gene Clark/Jim McGuinn/David Crosby); **Mr. Spaceman** (Jim McGuinn); **5 D (Fifth Dimension)** (Jim McGuinn); **So You Want To Be A Rock'n'Roll Star** (Jim McGuinn/Chris Hillman) and **My Back Pages** (Bob Dylan).

VIKKI CARR   *American*

IT MUST BE HIM (Seul sur son etoile) *Liberty 55986 [USA] Liberty LIB 55917 [UK]*. Vikki Carr (real name Florencia Bisenta de Casillas Martinez Cardona) was born on 19 July 1942 in El Paso, Texas, the eldest of seven children. She made her public debut at the age of four, singing **Adeste Fideles** and **Silent Night** in Latin at a Christmas programme. She moved to Los Angeles, where she attended the San Gabriel Parochial and Rosemead High Schools, taking music courses and the leading roles in the school musical productions. After graduation, she became a bookkeeper in a local bank. She was chosen for an engagement in Palm Springs' Chi Chi Club with the Pepe Callahan Orchestra, a Mexican-Irish band, travelling to Reno, Las Vegas, Lake Tahoe and Hawaii over a period of three years. During her appearances in Reno with the Chuck Leonard Quartette, she staged a solo act and worked for nine months in Elko, Nevada. After a considerable time in club work, she made a demo disc, and was signed by Liberty Records to a long-term contract. Her first disc was so successful in Australia that she toured that continent.

It Must Be Him, written by Maurice Vidalin (words) and Gilbert Becaud (music), and originally published in France, had English words supplied by Mack David. Vikki's disc was No 3 for two weeks in the USA with 15 weeks in the bestsellers, and No 2 for one week in Britain with 30 weeks in the bestsellers, subsequently selling a global million.

JOHNNY CASH   *American*

GREATEST HITS — Volume 1 (Album) *CBS-Columbia 9478 [USA] CBS 63062 [UK]*. Johnny Cash's great success in 1968 brought renewed interest to this album, with a resurgence in sales in 1969 along with his other albums. **Greatest Hits**, a collection of his former disc

successes, became a consistent seller and by February 1970 sold over one million in albums and tapes. It received a Gold Disc award from RIAA in 1969 and was in the bestsellers for 71 weeks.

The album contained **Jackson** (sung by Johnny Cash and June Carter), by G. Rodgers and B. Wheeler (1967); **I Walk the Line**, by Johnny Cash (1956); **Understand Your Man**, by Johnny Cash (1964); **Orange Blossom Special**, by E.T. Rouse (1965); **The One on the Right is on the Left**, by Jack Clement (1966); **Ring of Fire**, by Merle Kilgore and June Carter (1962); **It Ain't Me Babe**, by Bob Dylan (1964); **Ballad of Ira Hayes**, by Peter La Farge (1962); **Johnny Yuma** (theme from *The Rebel*); **Five Feet High and Rising**, by Johnny Cash (1959); **Don't Take Your Guns to Town**, by Johnny Cash (1958).

ADRIANO CELENTANO   *Italian*

LA COPPIA PIU' BELLA DEL MONDO (The most beautiful couple in the world) *ACC 24051 [Italy]*. Adriano was one of Italy's most popular male singers. He was discovered by Guertler, and made his disc debut on Guertler's label, SAAR, in 1959, adopting Elvis Presley's style at the time of rock'n'roll. His debut appearance was at Milan's Ice Palace where he sang **Rock Around the Clock** at the **Rock and Roll Festival**. Other appearances elsewhere followed, with regular six-monthly disc releases, all appearing high on Italy's charts. His biggest seller for SAAR was **Nata per me** ('Born for me') which sold over 450,000 in 1962.

He then formed his own disc company, Clan Celentano, and had an astonishing debut on the new label with the Italian version of **Tower of Strength**, which sold over 600,000. It was followed by **Preghero** ('Stand by me') which sold over 700,000 between 1962 and 1963. Adriano was the top-selling artist of 1961, 1962, 1963 and 1964, and he was also very popular in Argentina, France, Spain and Germany, where his discs over the subsequent years have been consistent sellers.

This disc was released in July 1967 and after only five weeks on the Italian market sold 500,000, with the million by the beginning of 1968. It was No 1 for four weeks and stayed in the Italian charts for 18 weeks.

Adriano has starred in a number of films. He was born in Milan in 1938.

PETULA CLARK   *British*

THIS IS MY SONG *Pye 7N 17258 [UK] Warner Brothers 7002 [USA]*. A great tribute to the composing talents of the celebrated Charles Chaplin, who at the age of 77 was probably the oldest writer of a new hit song. Chaplin wrote it for his film *A Countess from Hong Kong* (starring Sophia Loren and Marlon Brando). Petula Clark first recorded the song in French ('C'est ma chanson' with French lyrics by Pierre Delanoe) and in Italian and German for the European market while she was in Hollywood. Claude Wolf, Petula's husband and manager, recorded the original English version (adding a second voice track) at the end of the session, there being some time to spare.

The tape was sent to England and, although Petula was not impressed with the song when she first heard it, her disc made an explosive impact in Britain and gave her her first-ever No 1 there (for two weeks with 14 weeks in the bestsellers), selling over 500,000. Her Continental versions sold over 700,000 in five months and topped the charts in France, Belgium, Holland and Eire, as well as being a big hit in Germany, Italy and Scandinavia. There were also big sales in the USA, the disc reaching No 3 in their charts with 12 weeks in the bestsellers. The arrangement for the recording was by Ernie Freeman.

England's Harry Secombe recorded the song prior to Petula Clark, and his version reached No 1 for one week in Britain and sold over 250,000. World sales of Petula's versions are estimated at well over two million.

The disc was released in Britain on 16 January 1967.

CLASSICS IV   American

SPOOKY *Imperial 66259 [USA] Liberty LIB 15051 [UK]*. Classics IV, a group of four young men, were discovered by Bill Lowery of Lowery Productions in Atlanta who produced this disc for Imperial Records. It was the group's first disc, released in November 1967, and in 1968 it got to No 2 for one week in the USA charts with 15 weeks in the bestsellers, and subsequently sold a million. It was No 46 in Britain. The disc was started off in Louisville over the radio to break into national popularity. It was written by Sharpe and Middlebrook.

The group (expanded to five members) consisted of James Cobb (lead guitar), Dennis Yost (lead vocals), Wally Eaton (rhythm guitar), Kim Venable (drums) and Joe Wilson (bass guitar and vocals).

Cobb, who arranged **Spooky**, was born in Birmingham, Alabama. He was a studio musician before joining the group. Yost is from Jacksonville, Florida, and was formerly an usher in a movie theatre. Eaton also comes from Jacksonville. Venable, from Alabama, first played at teenage dances and was a musician from the age of 14. Wilson wrote many tunes for the group.

ARTHUR CONLEY   American

SWEET SOUL MUSIC *Atco 6463 [USA] Atlantic 584 083 [UK]*. Arthur Conley got his start through a demo record called **I'm a Lonely Stranger** played to Otis Redding in Baltimore in 1965. Redding, who became Conley's record producer, was instrumental in getting him to record it on the Jotis label. Conley had previously recorded for NRC as Arthur and the Corvets. Subsequent recordings were made for Jotis and Fame labels, then Redding produced Conley's **Sweet Soul Music** on his own on the Atco label and Arthur Conley was on his way. The disc sold over the million, with a RIAA Gold Disc award. It got to No 2 in the USA charts for two weeks with 15 weeks in the bestsellers, and to No 7 in Britain with 14 weeks in the bestsellers. It was No 2 for five weeks in the US R&B charts and

charted in Britain at No 1 for six weeks in the British R&B Top 20.

The song was jointly written by Otis Redding, Sam Cooke and Arthur Conley, based on Sam Cooke's tune **Yeah Man**. Arthur Conley was born on 14 January 1946 in Atlanta, Georgia.

BILL COSBY   American

REVENGE (Album) *Warner Brothers 1691*. This hit comedy disc for Bill Cosby sold a million units by the year's end. It was No 1 in the USA for one week with 73 weeks in the charts.

Cosby's five comedy albums over the past four years grossed $30 million for Warner's, a record sales figure for spoken-word discs. Grammy Award for 'Best Comedy Performance', 1967 — the fourth in a row.

LITTLE OLE MAN (Uptight — Everything's Alright) *Warner Brothers 7072 [USA]*. Bill Cosby's first singles disc for the Warner label and his first as a singer, the recording is a volatile version of the Stevie Wonder hit of 1965 written by Henry Cosby, Sylvia Moy and Stevie Wonder.

It reached No 4 in the USA charts with 11 weeks in the bestsellers, and sold a million.

THE COWSILLS   American

THE RAIN, THE PARK AND OTHER THINGS *MGM 13810 [USA]*. The Cowsills were a complete family unit consisting of father, mother, daughter and six sons. Chief Petty Officer Bud Cowsill retired from the US Navy after 20 years' service in 1963, and decided that his four singing, drumming, guitar-playing youngest sons were destined for better things

than just local and family concerts. He teamed them with their 'mini-mom', Barbara, and took on his other sons Dick and Paul as road managers and sound engineers. With their then four-year-old sister Susan, they set out into the world of professional music. Artie Kornfeld, a producer and writer, brought them to Leonard Stogel's personal management firm, who introduced the group to MGM. An album resulted which included **The Rain, the Park and Other Things** (written by S. Duboff and Artie Kornfeld who also produced the disc). Released as a single in September 1967, it soon climbed the US charts and reached No 1 for one week with 16 weeks in the bestsellers. It was a consistent seller for over three months and awarded a Gold Disc on 19 December by RIAA.

The personnel of the group were Bill Cowsill (vocal), born 9 January 1948, also writer of own lyrics; Bob Cowsill (vocals), born 26 August 1949; Barry Cowsill (vocals and bass guitarist), born 14 September 1954; John Cowsill (drums), born 2 March 1956; Susan Cowsill born 1959; Barbara Cowsill, born 1928, who lends her voice to the quartet's close-harmony whenever it is needed.

CREAM   British

DISRAELI GEARS (Album) *Reaction 594-003 [UK] Atco 232 [USA]*. It was London agent Robert Stigwood who got together in 1966 three of Britain's top musicians — Eric Clapton (lead guitar), Jack Bruce (bass) and Peter 'Ginger' Baker (drums) — and called them Cream. Stigwood produced the new outfit's first hit disc, **Wrapping Paper**. All three had previously played with some of Britain's top bands — Clapton with the Yardbirds, Bruce with Manfred Mann, and Baker with the Graham Bond Organization.

Cream spent most of their time in the USA where their blues and psyche-orchestral flavour became exceedingly popular with teenagers, young adults and a mass of 'underground' listeners, a far less important audience hitherto. They became one of the rock world's biggest names through their sheer, outstanding musical talent. Their first album **Fresh Cream** in 1967 achieved a Gold Disc for

group made for America and was produced by Jimmie Miller, the American who also produced their first million seller **Gimme Some Lovin'**. The disc had a lengthy introductory riff, building to an intense swinging atmosphere with the crashing chords of Stevie Winwood's organ, plus banshee-like wailing by the group.

THE DOORS   *American*

LIGHT MY FIRE *Elektra 45615* [*USA*] *Elektra EKSN 45014* [*UK*]. The Doors collectively wrote this. They all became influenced by jazz, blues and rock music, welding these influences into they own style. Jim Morrison's vocals ring out over the striking electric sound that the group made their own.

This disc was No 1 for three weeks in the USA and 17 weeks in the bestsellers, and was awarded a Gold Disc by RIAA. It was No 49 in Britain. Their first album (also a No 1) **The Doors** received an RIAA. Gold Disc for million dollar sales at the same time. **Light My Fire** was Elektra's first-ever Top 10 after 18 years of successful record production. The group comprised Jim Morrison (vocal) born 8 December 1943, in Melbourne, Florida; Ray Manzarek (organ and piano) born 2 December 1942, in Chicago; Bobby Krieger (guitar) born 1 August 1946 in Los Angeles; John Densmore (drums) born 1 December 1944 in Santa Monica, California. Morrison died in Paris, France, on 3 July 1971.

THE DOORS (Album) *Elektra 74007* [*USA*]. By 1972, The Doors had reportedly sold over four million albums and almost eight million singles. This album was their biggest with a sale of 1,234,919 by that year. After release in March 1967, it stayed in the US bestsellers for 104 weeks and during that time was No 1 for three weeks and in the Top 10 for 23 weeks, and certified gold by RIAA in November 1967. Release in Britain was on Polydor label in September 1967. The album was certificated Double Platinum for over two million US sales on 10 June 1987, though sales passed that figure well before 1987.

The album contained their great hit **Light My Fire**, an eventual million seller as a single for the group, and later for Jose Feliciano.

The contents of the album were: *Side 1 —* **Break On Through (to the other side)**, by The Doors; **Soul Kitchen**, by The Doors; **The**

million dollar sales from RIAA in 1968. Their second album, **Disraeli Gears** for Atco, was their biggest success and received a similar award, plus Platinum Disc award for sales of $2 million of their third (double) album **Wheels of Fire**. This also received a Gold Disc award from RIAA.

Disraeli Gears was produced by Felix Pappalardi in Atlantic City, and the group's discs were released in Britain on Polydor's Reaction label. In the USA, it stayed in the Top 10 for eight months during 1968.

In 1968, Cream decided to go their individual musical ways. They gave their final US performances at Madison Square Garden, New York, on 2 November 1968 before a capacity audience of 21,000 young patrons, and in Baltimore (3 November) and Providence (4 November). A farewell performance took place in Britain on 26 November 1968 in London's Royal Albert Hall before a rapturous audience of 5,000.

Each of the trio developed into individual virtuosi on their respective instruments. Bruce, in addition, is a vocalist and harmonica player of equally high status.

The group wrote most of their own material. **Disraeli Gears** comprised the following: **Strange Brew**, by Collins, Pappalardi and Clapton; **Sunshine of Your Love**, by Bruce, Brown and Clapton; **World of Pain**, by Collins and Pappalardi; **Dance the Night**, by Bruce and Brown; **Blue Condition**, by Baker; **Tales of Brave Ulysses**, by Clapton and Sharp; **Swlabu**, by Bruce and Brown;

We're Going Wrong, by Bruce; **Outside Woman Blues**, by Reynolds; **Take It Back**, by Bruce and Brown; **Mother's Lament**, traditional, arr. Cream.

A notable first million-selling 'underground' album. It was in the USA bestsellers for 69 weeks.

SUNSHINE OF YOUR LOVE *Atco 6544* [*USA*] *Polydor 56 286* [*UK*]. Written by Eric Clapton, Jack Bruce and Peter Brown, this was originally inluded on Cream's **Disraeli Gears** album, and released in the USA in December 1967 as a single through popular demand. It stayed on the USA bestseller charts for 26 weeks in 1968, achieving No 4 for one week. Release in Britain was on 27 September 1968 on Polydor label but it only reached No 25.

The disc sold a million in the USA and was awarded a Gold Disc by RIAA in September 1968.

THE SPENCER DAVIS GROUP   *British*

I'M A MAN *Fontana TF 785* [*UK*] *United Artists 50144* [*USA*]. The second million seller for this group, the song was written by Jimmie Miller and the group's Stevie Winwood. The disc was released in Britain on 20 January 1967, and reached No 2 for two weeks with seven weeks in the bestsellers, then No 6 for one week in the USA with 10 weeks in the bestsellers, with a subsequent estimated million combined sale. The record came from a promotional film the

Crystal Ship, by The Doors; Twentieth Century Fox, by The Doors; *Alabama Song, by Bertolt Brecht and Kurt Weill (1928); Light My Fire, by The Doors; Side 2 — Back Door Man, by Dixon and Burnett; I Looked at You, by The Doors; End of the Night, by The Doors; Take It as It Comes, by The Doors; The End, by The Doors.

*Also known as Moon of Alabama, this was originally published in Germany and introduced by Lotte Lenya in Rise and Fall of the City of Mahagonny (opera, 1930).

BOB DYLAN   American

BOB DYLAN'S GREATEST HITS (Album) CBS-Columbia 9463 [USA] CBS SBPG 62847 [UK]. Dylan's only album release of 1967 was this 'greatest hits' package. It included some of his own singles hits, and self-composed album tracks that had been big hits for others. His 1965 million-selling single Like a Rolling Stone is included, as are two songs that were million sellers for others. Mr Tambourine Man was a No 1 for The Byrds in 1965. Blowin' in the Wind sold a million in 1963 for Peter, Paul and Mary, and was a US Top 10 hit for Stevie Wonder in 1966. This was the third Bob Dylan record to sell a million copies, and his first album to do so.

After his major success in 1965, he had a slightly quieter chart year in 1966. Rainy Day Women Nos 12 & 35 was his one Top 10 hit on both sides of the Atlantic, reaching No 2 in America and No 7 in Britain. It is on this album, as are two more modest 1966 hits I Want You and Just Like a Woman (which was covered by Manfred Mann). While Bob Dylan made the singles charts throughout the rest of the decade, he had only one more Top 10 hit, again on both sides of the Atlantic, with Lay Lady Lay in 1969.

On the album front, which was more important to Dylan, this hits album reached No 10 with 94 weeks on the LP charts. It won an RIAA Gold Disc for million dollar sales on 5 January 1968. A consistent good seller, it sold over two million copies in the USA, and was also a big hit in Britain and other parts of the world. The album was certificated for Platinum and Double Platinum by the RIAA on 21 November 1986. This followed a change in the certification rules, allowing the RIAA to mark the sale of one and more million units. The album had passed this figure before 1986. In Britain it reached No 6, and spent a lengthy 28 weeks in the charts. All the songs on the album were written by Bob Dylan.

In 1968 Dylan released the John Wesley Harding album, which reached No 2 and stayed exactly a year in the American charts. In 1969 Nashville Skyline made No 3 on the US album charts. Both won Gold Discs for million dollar sales, as did the two 1970 releases Self Portrait and New Morning.

The tracks on the Greatest Hits album are Blowin' in the Wind, It Ain't Me Babe, The Times They are A-Changin', Mr Tambourine Man; She Belongs to Me, It's All Over Now, Baby Blue, Subterranean Homesick Blues, One of Us Must Know, Like a Rolling Stone, Just Like a Woman, Rainy Day Women Nos 12 & 35 and I Want You.

GEORGIE FAME   Britain

THE BALLAD OF BONNIE AND CLYDE CBS 3124 [UK] Epic 10283 [USA]. Georgie Fame had a dozen hits in Britain, all of them in the sixties. Only three made the Top 10, and each of them went all the way to No 1. From 1964 to 1966 he racked up seven hits on Columbia, two of which went to the top. In 1967 he switched to CBS, and after one modest and one small hit came up with this in December 1967. It was No 1 for one week in January 1968, and stayed in the British Top 50 for 13 weeks. In America it was his biggest and only Top 10 hit, reaching No 7 with 14 weeks on the Hot 100. It was also his last American hit. During his Columbia days, EMI had licensed his records to Imperial for America, and he had scored one modest and two minor hits with them. After the switch to CBS, who released his discs on their Epic label in America, The Ballad of Bonnie and Clyde made the charts in February 1968, but nothing else followed.

The song was written by leading British songwriters Peter Callander and Mitch Murrey. It was inspired by the immensely successful film Bonnie and Clyde, based on the true story of Texas gangsters, Bonnie Parker and Clyde Barrow in the American South-West and Mid-West in the early 1930s.

The record sold under a million in the USA, but sales from Canada, Australia, Europe and Britain (where it won a Silver Disc) made it a second million seller for Georgie Fame.

THE FIFTH DIMENSION   American

UP, UP AND AWAY Soul City 756 [USA]. This song was written by America's outstanding young writer Jim Webb, the son of a Baptist minister. Webb started to play piano and organ at 11, and to compose at 13. Raised in Oklahoma and Texas, he started music studies at California's San Bernardino Valley College in 1966 at the age of 18, then went to Hollywood to become a songwriter. After disappointments, he wrote a wistful ballad By the Time I Get to Phoenix which when recorded by Glen Campbell won a Grammy Award for the singer for 'Best Male Vocal Performance' of 1967. In the meantime, Webb and a friend planned a movie about a balloon trip, but the only thing that soared was the title song which when recorded by the Fifth Dimension got to No 4 in the USA charts with 12 weeks in the bestsellers. It sold 875,000 and by 1968 topped the million, and put the group on the map (see 1968). Jim Webb was also up, up and away. Trans World Air Lines bought the rights to use the song in its TV and radio commercials, to make it a universal standard song.

The disc was issued in May 1967.

THE FOLK CRUSADERS   Japanese

KAETTE KITA YOPPARAI (I only live twice) Express ETP-10228 [Japan]. I Only Live Twice was the first 'underground' record to be released in Japan by the Toshiba Record Co. in December 1967. It proved to be so popular with college students that it sold 1,200,000 by mid-February 1968, and was No 1 for five weeks in Japan.

The Folk Crusaders, an unknown student group, recorded this song at their own expense, created a sensation in the Kansai area and started an 'underground music' trend in Japan. Toshiba Records then obtained the recording rights.

THE FOUNDATIONS   British

BABY, NOW THAT I'VE FOUND YOU Pye 7N 17366 [UK] Uni 55038 [USA]. The unusual feature of this group was the difference in their ages, ranging from 19 to 38. They were discovered by Barry Class, a London record dealer who had been listening to the group playing in a basement club, The Butterfly, underneath his office in Westbourne Grove, London. Intrigued by their sound, he contacted Tony Macauley, one of Pye's young recording managers, who agreed to record the group. With his partner John MacLeod, Tony wrote this song for their first recording which was released on 25 August 1967. It eventually got to No 1 for three weeks with 16 weeks in the bestsellers and sold between a quarter and a half million. It was released in the USA on the Uni label and got to No 9 in their charts in February 1968 with 13 weeks in the bestsellers. Sale of a combined million was reached in January 1968. Global sale was three and a half million.

Three of the group were born in London — Tim Harris (drums) on 14 January 1948 in St

John's Wood, a musician since leaving school; Peter Macbeth (bass guitarist) born 2 February 1943 in Marylebone, formerly a teacher and in book publishing; Alan Warner (lead guitarist) born 21 April 1947 in Paddington, formerly a printer then with various groups. Five members were from the Commonwealth — Eric Allan Dale (trombonist) born 4 March 1936 in Dominica, West Indies, formerly with the Hammersmith Brass Band, then his own band and member of the Terry Lightfoot and Alex Walsh bands; Clem Curtis (lead singer) born 28 November 1940 in Trinidad, formerly a metal worker and professional boxer who came to England in 1956; Tony Gomez (organist) born 13 December 1948 in Colombo, Ceylon, formerly a clerical officer at London's County Hall; Pat Burke (tenor sax and flute) born 9 October 1937 in Jamaica, a musician with various groups since his arrival in Britain in 1952; Mike Elliot (tenor sax) born 6 August 1929 in Jamaica, formerly with the Colin Hicks group. He came to Britain in 1955.

The group was formed in January 1967.

ARETHA FRANKLIN   *American*

I NEVER LOVED A MAN (The way I love you) *Atlantic 2386 [USA] Atlantic 584084 [UK].* Aretha Franklin, the 'Queen of Soul', is one of the greatest of all R&B singers. In a survey of America's R&B singles charts from 1942 to 1988, the chart expert Joel Whitburn ranked Aretha Franklin second to James Brown as the most popular R&B chart act of the last half-century. She has had 71 R&B hit records between 1960 and 1987, 20 of which have gone to No 1; more R&B chart-toppers than any other artist. As well as her own hits, she has been a great example to, and influence on, many others.

Aretha was born on 25 March 1942 in Memphis, Tennessee, one of five children of the Rev. C.L. Franklin. The family moved to Detroit when she was two years old. Her mother, gospel singer Barbara Siggers, deserted the family when Aretha was six and died four years later. Aretha sang in the choir of her father's pastorate, New Bethel Baptist Church in Detroit. Some recordings were made there from 1956, and released on the small JVB label. At the age of 14, she joined her father's evangelical tours, singing in churches all over America for the next four years. Gospel music was an essential influence on her, and a central strand in her own music in later life.

By 1960 she had begun to move towards the blues, and Major 'Mule' Holly, bass player for pianist Teddy Wilson, helped get her an audition with CBS A&R executive John Hammond. He signed her up to her first recording deal with a major company. At this time CBS were a rather staid and conservative company. They had completely missed out on rock'n'roll and were not really interested in R&B. They catered very successfully for middle-of-the-road white America, and did not do much with Aretha, though they did get her into the charts. Her first hit was **Today I Sing the Blues**, which reached No 10 in the R&B charts. It did not cross over into the pop charts, but her next hit, **Won't Be Long**, entered the

R&B charts on 13 February 1961, and gave her a debut Hot 100 hit two weeks later. It peaked at a respectable No 7 in the R&B charts, but in its three-week run on the main pop charts it only reached No 76.

Aretha's biggest hit at CBS was her next chart entry, in October 1961. CBS used a clever marketing ploy to maximize her appeal. They issued a double A side, one side aimed at the R&B market and the other a more pop-orientated sound. Both sides charted. **Operation Heartbreak** made No 6 on the R&B charts, her highest place until her switch to Atlantic, and **Rock-A-Bye Your Baby with a Dixie Melody** reached No 37 on the pop charts. None of her other CBS releases made the Top 50 in the USA.

Her undoubted talents were clearly being wasted at CBS, so she and her husband-manager Ted White decided to switch labels. She went to Atlantic, a company with strong roots in R&B. It had been the most successful of the fifties independents, and was on its way to being part of the biggest record company in America. Atlantic was run by Ahmet and Nesuhi Ertegun and Jerry Wexler, and in 1967 they sold it to the Canadian company Seven Arts, who had bought Warner Brothers the year before. In 1968 Seven Arts was taken over by Kinney National Services, which later changed its name to Warner Communications Inc. Through all these corporate manoeuvres, the Erteguns and Wexler ended up running what became WEA Records. In 1967 Jerry Wexler was Atlantic's leading producer, and it was to him that Aretha Franklin turned next to help build her career.

The change of labels in November 1966 resulted in a change of fortune that was immediate and spectacular. Her first release on Atlantic was **I Never Loved a Man**.

The song had a much stronger soul feel to it than anything CBS had put out. It was recorded at Rick Hall's Fame Studio in Muscle Shoals, Alabama, and produced by Jerry Wexler. The song was written by Ronny Shannon. Released in February 1967, it entered the Hot 100 at the beginning of March and gave Aretha her first Top 10 hit, peaking at No 9 during an 11-week chart run. In the R&B charts she scored the first of three No 1s in a row. During 14 weeks on the R&B Top 50, she was at No 1 for seven of them. The flip side also charted. **Do Right Woman — Do Right Man** made No 37 during its own R&B chart life of four weeks. In Britain the record did not make the national Top 50, but it did get into the R&B Top 20. On 29 April it entered that chart at No 14 equal, peaking at No 3 during eight weeks in the R&B charts.

The record was awarded a Gold Disc for American sales of over a million on 13 June 1967, three months after release. The **I Never Loved a Man the Way I Love You** album went Gold (for million dollar sales) on the same day. Her four CBS LPs had only made the bottom part of the album charts, but this Atlantic debut album reached No 2.

1967 was a fantastic year for Aretha Franklin. It was the year she broke through to the front rank. She released five records on Atlantic (with some old material from CBS also charting). Of these five, four were million

sellers and topped the R&B charts. All five made the pop Top 10, with one, **Respect**, going to No 1. At the end of the year *Billboard* ranked her as 'Top Female Singles Artist', 'Top R&B Singles Artist', third 'R&B Album Artist' and fourth overall 'Singles Artist'. She also won a couple of Grammys for **Respect**.

RESPECT *Atlantic 2403 [USA] Atlantic 584 115 [UK].* Despite her 20 R&B No 1s, Aretha Franklin has topped *Billboard*'s main Hot 100 only once, with **Respect**, in June 1967. It was her second release on Atlantic, and proved to be the biggest record of her career. It was written in 1965 by fellow soul singer Otis Redding (see 1968), who had originally recorded the song. It was engineered by Tom Dowd and produced by Jerry Wexler at the Atlantic Records studio in New York, with the Muscle Shoals musicians used for **I Never Loved A Man** flown up from Alabama for the recording session. They included Roger Hawkins, Spooner Oldham, Chips Maman, Jimmy Johnson, and renowned sax player King Curtis in the horn section. It was also one of the tracks on her Gold album **I Never Loved a Man**.

Respect entered the Hot 100 on 29 April 1967, and the R&B Top 50 the following week. It spent two weeks at No 1 on the pop charts and eight weeks at the top of the R&B lists, where it was her biggest No 1. It spent 12 weeks on the Hot 100 and 14 weeks on the R&B Top 50.

Respect was also Aretha's first pop hit in Britain, entering the main Top 50 on 10 June at No 47, one place above Cilla Black's new entry and two places below Cliff Richard. The following week it entered the British R&B Top 20 at No 5, the highest of the seven entries of the week, and went to No 1 the week after. It stayed there for six weeks, and reached No 10 in the pop Top 50. It spent 14 weeks in the pop charts, and 15 weeks in the R&B lists.

While **I Never Loved a Man** broke Aretha as a top disc star, **Respect** established her as the leading lady of soul. The words of the song had deep political and sexual significance, especially as sung by a black woman. It was not only the different arrangement that made her version a bigger hit than Otis Redding's earlier original. Every woman, regardless of race, could identify with her dignified demand for 'a little respect'.

In the 1988 *Rolling Stone* magazine critics' poll of the 100 best singles of the previous quarter century, **Respect** came sixth. It won an RIAA Gold Disc on 1 June 1967, and two Grammies. It was voted the 'Best R&B Recording' and 'Best R&B Female Solo Performance' of 1967.

BABY I LOVE YOU *Atlantic 2427 [USA] Atlantic 584 127 [UK].* Written by Ronny Shannon and produced by Jerry Wexler, **Baby I Love You** was Aretha's third million-selling record in a row. It reached No 3 in the *Cash Box* Top 100, and No 4 in the *Billboard* pop charts, where it had an 11-week chart run. In *Billboard*'s R&B charts it was No 1 for two weeks, with 13 weeks on the chart. The single was on **Aretha Arrives**, her second Atlantic album, which went to No 5 in the LP charts. In Britain the record was only a minor pop hit, reaching No 39 with four weeks in the Top 50. It did much better in the R&B charts, entering at No 6 the first week of release, while **Respect** was three places lower. It reached No 4, and spent seven weeks in the R&B Top 20. **Baby I Love You** won an RIAA Gold Disc on 5 September 1967.

CHAIN OF FOOLS *Atlantic 2464* [*USA*] *Atlantic 584 157* [*UK*]. After **Baby I Love You**, Aretha Franklin's next hit was an old recording put out by CBS. **Take a Look** made No 56 in the pop charts. Her official Atlantic follow-up was **A Natural Woman (You Make Me Feel Like)**. Though the record did well, reaching No 8 on the pop charts and No 2 on the R&B charts, it was not as big as her other Atlantic hits of 1967. It failed to make the British Top 50, though it did creep into the R&B charts, entering at No 20 on 28 October. It reached No 5, with 10 weeks in the R&B Top 20. It broke her run of million sellers, with sales short of seven figures.

The next Atlantic release restored her to No 1 in the American R&B charts and gave her a fourth million seller. **Chain of Fools** was written by Don Covay and produced by Jerry Wexler. Background vocals were added by songwriter Ellie Greenwich, who with her husband Geoff Barry had worked with Phil Spector on Crystals' and Ronettes' hits earlier in the decade. The guitar intro was provided by Joe South, who later had a string of hits on Capitol, including **Games People Play**. The track was included on the **Aretha: Lady Soul** album, released early in 1968. It went to No 2 in the album charts, and won an RIAA Gold Disc for million dollar sales. It entered the Hot 100 on 9 December and the American R&B Top 50 the following week. In *Billboard* she reached No 2 on the pop charts and No 1 for four weeks on the R&B Top 50, with 12 and 14 weeks respectively on the two charts. In *Cash Box*, **Chain of Fools** went to No 1 on both the R&B and the Top 100 charts. This was her second *Cash Box* No 1, staying on top for one week.

In Britain the record entered the Top 50 on 23 December 1967 at No 45, as the double A side **Chain of Fools/Satisfaction**. It rose two places for the final week of the year, and then fell out of the charts for 6 January 1968. The same week it entered the British R&B Top 20 at No 6, but with only **Chain of Fools** listed. The following week Aretha was back in the Top 50, but with only **Satisfaction** listed. For the next few weeks the record continued to progress on both charts, but with different sides listed on each. **Satisfaction** peaked at No 37, with five more weeks in the Top 50. **Chain of Fools** reached No 3 on the R&B charts, lasting eight weeks in the Top 20.

The RIAA Gold Disc for American sales of over a million came on 10 January 1968, just over a month after the record was released. **Chain of Fools** also won Aretha her second Grammy in a row in the 'Best R&B Female Solo Performance' category.

JOHN FRED AND HIS PLAYBOY BAND
American

JUDY IN DISGUISE (WITH GLASSES) *Paula 282* [*USA*] *Pye International 7N 25442* [*UK*]. This

group of eight instrumentalists was formed in high school. After starting college at Louisiana State University, they concentrated more on recording. John Fred (6ft 5ins tall) made his first record in 1962. He is lead vocalist and harmonica player, the rest of the group consisting of Charlie Spinoza and Ronnie Goodson (trumpets), Andrew Bernard (baritone sax), Jimmy O'Rourke (guitar), Harold Cowart (bass), Joe Micelli (drums), and Tommy Dee (organ). The ensemble did its own writing, recording, arranging and producing, and had a big sound.

Their first hit was **Agnes English**. **Judy in Disguise** (a play on the Beatles' **Lucy in the Sky with Diamonds**) was first included on their album of **Agnes English**. When released as a single in November 1967, it soon rocketed to the top of the US charts and stayed No 1 for two weeks with 16 weeks in the bestsellers. By mid-January 1968 it sold a million with RIAA Gold Disc award. It was written by John Fred and Andrew Bernard of the group, and has a hard rock beat with much humour and solid dance appeal.

The disc was also a success in Britain where it reached No 3 in the charts for one week with 12 weeks in the bestsellers.

The group members were Ron Goodson, born 2 February 1945 in Miami, Florida; Tommy Dee, born 3 November 1946 in Baton Rouge, Louisiana; Andrew Bernard, born 1945 in New Orleans, Louisiana; Harold Cowart, born 12 June 1944, in Baton Rouge; Joe Micelli, born 9 July 1946 in Baton Rouge; Charlie Spinoza, born 29 December 1948 in Baton Rouge; Jimmy O'Rourke, born 14 March 1947 in Fall River, Massachusetts; John Fred, born 8 May 1945 in Baton Rouge.

GENE AND DEBBE
American

PLAYBOY *TRX 5006* [*USA*]. Gene Thomas and Debbe Nevills had only been together for eight weeks when they made their first disc **Go with Me** in their home town, Nashville, Tennessee. It was an instant hit around October 1967. The boy-girl duo then became a much-sought-after act in the USA, appearing on top TV shows and in nightclubs.

Playboy, their next disc, released on 17 November 1967, was first broadcast on 15 November from WMAK Nashville, a 'grass roots' station, and sold 18,000 immediately. WMAK kept playing the disc for around three months and it sold 250,000 before being taken

up by the major markets, starting with 6,500 from Cleveland in January 1968. It then became a national success and got to No 11 for two weeks in the charts, with 16 weeks in the bestsellers, with an eventual million sale in 1968. Gene and Debbe received a Gold Disc in June 1968.

Playboy was written by Gene Thomas.

BOBBIE GENTRY
American

ODE TO BILLIE JOE *Capitol 5950* [*USA*] *Capitol CL 15511* [*UK*]. Bobbie Gentry, of Portuguese descent, was born on 27 July 1944 on a farm in Chicasaw County, Mississippi. She first appeared as a performer at the age of 11 on stage, strumming the guitar while accompanying a singer from Chicasaw County. Since then she has become proficient on piano, banjo, vibraphones and electric bass.

She studied philosophy at UCLA, and counterpoint and composition at Los Angeles Conservatory of Music. She worked in various San Diego and Las Vegas night spots dancing as well as singing, and at the age of 13 acted in 'little theatre' locally and in the South.

In mid-1967, she recorded this song, her own composition, backed with **Mississippi Delta** in Capitol's Studio C in less than half an hour, accompanied by half a dozen violins, two cellos and her own guitar, under the supervision of recording manager Kelly Gordon. After only two weeks, the disc shot into the Top 30, sold 750,000 in three weeks and was No 1 in the charts for four weeks and 14 weeks in the bestsellers. Soon after, this her very first recording was awarded a Gold Disc by RIAA and went on to sell two million (three million globally). It reached No 17 in the country charts where it stayed for 8 weeks. A film based on the song was made in 1976 following which the record re-charted for 6 weeks reaching No 54. A new version from the film made No 65 charting for 4 weeks at the same time.

She writes all her own material, the first one when she was only seven called **My Dog Sergeant is a Good Dog**. Her first album, containing 10 of her own compositions, was also issued in 1967 and soon went to No 1 in the album charts with a fast RIAA Gold Disc award, completing a double for her very first recordings.

Bobbie appeared in Britain on TV in October 1967 and made her first extensive personal tour the same year. The disc reach No 13 in Britain with 11 weeks in the bestsellers.

1967 Grammy Awards for 'Best Solo (Female) Performance', 'Best Arrangement', 'Best Contemporary (Rock'n'Roll) Vocal Performance', 'Best New Artist'.

The disc was released in the USA on 10 July 1967. Bobbie's real name is Roberta Streete, she changed it to Gentry after seeing the movie *Ruby Gentry*. She married singer Jim Stafford in 1978.

THE GRASS ROOTS
American

LET'S LIVE FOR TODAY *Dunhill 4084* [*USA*]. The Grass Roots were Warren Entner (lead singer, guitar and piano), Rob Grill (joint lead singer, bass guitar), Rickey Coonce (drums) and Creed Bratton (guitar, sitar and banjo).

Entner and Bratton met by accident while travelling through Israel in 1966. Both were originally folk artists. They teamed with Coonce and Grill in Los Angeles on their return to America and formed the group. Entner, born in Boston, grew up in Los Angeles and holds a BA in theatre arts from UCLA where he specialized in film-making. He is self-taught on guitar and has been a singer and musician from the age of 12. Bratton, a native of California, played guitar during an extensive trip through virtually the whole of Europe, and while in Israel worked on the film *Cast a Giant Shadow* with Kirk Douglas. Grill was born in Hollywood and studied at Los Angeles City College and has been a professional musician and singer since his college days. Coonce, the group's drummer, has played in every sort of musical group from symphony orchestras to Dixieland bands. A native of Los Angeles, he was educated at Ventura College.

Let's Live for Today, the English version of the Italian hit **Piangi con me** written by Shel Shapiro, Mike Shepstone (both members of the Rokes) Mogol (Guilio Rapetti) and Julien, was their first recording. It reached No 3 in the USA charts with 12 weeks in the bestsellers, and is said to have sold a million. The disc was released in May 1967.

The group combined an exciting sound with a driving beat, expert musicianship and professionalism. British release of the disc on Pye Records was on 2 June 1967.

ARLO GUTHRIE   *American*

ALICE'S RESTAURANT (Album) Reprise 6267 [*USA*] *Reprise RSLP 6267* [*UK*]. Arlo Guthrie is the son of famous American folksinger Woody Guthrie. He was born in Coney Island, New York, on 10 July 1947. He grew up under the influence of his father's folk music and political activity in support of such causes as the rights of migrant workers. Both made their impact on Arlo's adult life, for though he developed a highly individual musical style, he also followed in his father's footsteps. He became a major figure in the folk world after performing the 18-minute long **Alice's Restaurant Massacree** at the 1967 Newport Folk Festival, and became a political activist in causes like the anti-Vietnam war movement and environmental issues.

The **Alice's Restaurant** track tells the true story of how in 1965-6 he was refused for the Vietnam draft because of a criminal record. He had once dumped garbage illegally and been fined. In a delightfully ironic way, the song pokes fun at the Army, the police and the Establishment in one of the most memorable anti-war songs of the year. In 1970 the story was expanded into a film, which satirized the American Establishment and gave a positive view of the alternative society. The film starred Arlo Guthrie, who also wrote a cookery book full of alternative recipes. While he never repeated the success of **Alice's Restaurant**, he continued as a significant force in the folk/alternative field. He performed live and on

record with other acts like Pete Seeger and the Doobie Brothers. He continued to write, record and perform, living with his family on a farm near Alice's Restaurant.

The title track of this album took up the whole of Side 1. The tracks on Side 2 were all written by Arlo Guthrie (as was **Alice's Restaurant**): **Chilling of the Evening, Ring around A Rosy Rag, Now and Then I'm Coming Home, The Motor Cycle Song** and **Highway in the Wind**. The album reached No 17 with 99 weeks on the American album charts. It reached No 44 for one week in Britain. It won an RIAA Gold Disc for million dollar sales on 29 September 1969, and a Platinum Disc for US sales of over a million copies on 13 October 1986. In 1969 the film soundtrack charted; released on United Artists, it made No 63. Arlo sang two of the songs on the album.

THE HAPPENINGS   *American*

I GOT RHYTHM *B.T. Puppy 527* [*USA*] *Stateside SS 2013* [*UK*]. An updated version of the famous song by Ira Gershwin (words) and George Gershwin (music), written in 1930 for the musical *Girl Crazy* in the USA. It reached No 1 for one week with 13 weeks in the US bestsellers, and got to No 28 in Britain with nine weeks in the bestsellers. It was released in April 1967.

MY MAMMY *B.T. Puppy 530* [*USA*] *Pye International 7N 25501 and B.T. Puppy BTS 45530* [*UK*]. Another updated version by this group of the famous song written by Joe Young and Sam Lewis (words) and Walter Donaldson (music) in 1920, it was featured in the first talkie *The Jazz Singer* by the great Al Jolson in 1927.

The disc was released in the USA in July 1967 and reached No 12 in the national charts with eight weeks in the bestsellers. It was No 34 in Britain with five weeks in the bestsellers. The million sale was reported in 1969.

ANITA HARRIS   *British*

JUST LOVING YOU *CBS 2724* [*UK*]. Anita Madeleine Harris was born on 3 June 1944 in the small village of Midsomer Norton, Somerset. When quite young she started to sing and dance, and at the age of eight took up ice-skating. Just before her 16th birthday the manager at a London ice rink was impressed with Anita's skating ability and offered her her first professional job in Naples followed by six weeks in Las Vegas. On return to Britain she lived in Bournemouth, Hampshire, and worked locally. She then joined the Grenadiers and sang with the Cliff Adams Singers in **Song Parade** on TV. In 1961 she decided to go solo and for four years worked on TV, radio, stage, cabaret and in recording. She represented Britain as vocalist in three European song festivals at Montreux, Knokke-le-Zoute and San Remo. In late 1964 she met Mike Margolis and John Lane, and decided they should jointly manage her.

Anita has recorded for the Parlophone, Vocalion and Pye labels, and in 1966 made her first important public appearance at the

London Palladium — an eight-and-a-half months' run.

In June 1967, CBS released **Just Loving You** which got to No 6 in the British charts, was 30 weeks in the bestsellers and was a consistent seller for over six months with 625,000 sales in Britain and 200,000 in South Africa (where it was No 1). Sales from other European countries and Australia took the total over the million.

The song was another great success for British writer Tom Springfield whose compositions helped the Seekers to fame. It was inspired by a theme from Chopin's **Fantaisie Impromptu**.

HEINTJE   *Dutch*

MAMA *CNR 2064* [*The Netherlands*] *Ariola 3177* [*West Germany*]. **Mama** was a big hit in Holland in 1967 and reached the Top 10 there very quickly. When released on the Ariola label in February 1968 in Germany, it sold over a million and was No 1 there for 12 weeks, only equalled by Drafi Deutscher. It was also in Germany's Top 10 for six months and, with another Heintje disc **Du sollst nicht weinen**, the two discs held the No 1 and No 2 positions for a week. At the same time, Heintje's Dutch release of **Ich bau dir ein Schloss** was also No 1 in Holland. It is not surprising that he became known as Holland's 'Wonder Boy'. His disc sales were over two million in a few months. He was also a phenomenal seller in Switzerland.

Heintje was discovered by Addy Klyngeld, CNR's A&R representative, in 1967. Born in Bleijerheide, South Holland, on 12 August 1956, Heintje was only 11 years of age when he recorded **Mama**, one of the youngest hit makers in the industry.

The song was originally published in 1941 in Italy under the title **Mamma**, words by B. Cherubini and music by C.A. Bixio, and was a big hit for Connie Francis in 1960. It has been sung and recorded by most of the world's famous operatic tenors including Gigli, Tino Rossi, Sergio Franchi and a great number of pop tenor vocalists.

Heintje recorded in German and his recordings were made in Germany. His singing was not in contemporary style, but straightforward and often unabashedly sentimental.

By mid-1970 he had sold over six and a half million singles and over four million albums.

JIMI HENDRIX   *American*

ARE YOU EXPERIENCED? (Album) *Track 612-001 [UK] Reprise 6261 [USA]*. Jimi Hendrix was born the son of a gardener in Seattle, Washington State, on 27 November 1942. His first job was as a paratrooper in the 101st Airborne Division of the US Army, but he was discharged after a back injury caused by a bad jump. He then went into the music business, playing guitar with a number of R&B acts. He was one of James Brown's Famous Flames for a while, and also played with Little Richard.

In 1966 Chas Chandler of the Animals saw him perform in a Greenwich Village café in New York. Impressed, he later persuaded Hendrix to come to Britain where Chandler launched his career. To support the psychedelic blues guitarist they brought in two other musicians. Mitch Mitchell, born the year before Hendrix, had been a child actor, and had appeared in various TV commercials, before turning to music as a drummer. He did session work and had played in the background of the Rediffusion TV show 'Ready Steady Go!' before joining Georgie Fame's backing group the Blue Flames. Noel Redding was the same age as Hendrix, and was a highly talented musician who dropped out of Folkstone Art College and moved to London playing with various groups. He usually played lead guitar, though was capable of playing a number of other instruments. After a spell playing in Germany, he returned to England and tried to get into the Animals. While he failed that audition, he was taken on as bass player by Hendrix. Both Mitchell and Redding were British. The three of them formed the Jimi Hendrix Experience.

The group made their debut at the Paris Olympia in late 1966, and continued to tour Europe into 1967. They signed to Track Records, and on 5 January 1967 made their British chart debut with **Hey Joe**. This was actually released on the Polydor label, as Polydor had a promotion, manufacturing and distribution deal with the small Track company. After the record's success (it reached No 6), Polydor put Track out on their own logo. A string of hits followed, including **Purple Haze** (No 3), **The Wind Cries Mary** (No 6), **All Along the Watchtower** (No 5 in 1968), and in 1970 their one No 1, **Voodoo Chile**.

Hendrix made his reputation by a combination of brilliant guitar work and a flamboyant stage act. He was seen by the Monkees on one of their visits to Britain in early 1967. They booked him to support them on their next American tour, though this proved a serious mistake. Hendrix was not a success with the Monkees' teenybopper fans. Eventually one night he gave the finger to the unappreciative audience, walked off the stage and off the tour. What finally made Hendrix in his native America was his appearance at the 1967 Monterey Pop Festival. This was an audience more in tune with his music, and they also loved his style. His notoriety spread fast, and he became known as much for his foul language, sexually suggestive lyrics and flashy stage show as for his brilliant musicianship. His American tours became sell-outs, and his records also began selling. None of his seven hit singles were very big. **All Along the Watchtower** made No 20, but none of the others made the Top 50.

His albums, however, sold very well, and he was one of the leading artists who began the trend of those who could generate huge album sales without worrying about singles chart success. His style was much more suited to albums, and it was via albums that his reputation was sustained. **Are You Experienced?** was his first LP. It was a massive hit on both sides of the Atlantic. In Britain it made No 2, with 33 weeks in the album charts. In America it made No 5, with 106 weeks in the charts. It won an RIAA Gold Disc for million dollar sales on 19 March 1968. After changes in RIAA rules to allow for the certification of multi-million-selling albums, **Are You Experienced?** went Double Platinum (signifying US sales of over two million copies) on 13 October 1986.

A number of other Gold albums followed, 10 in all. **Axis: Bold as Love** was the follow-up, followed by **Electric Ladyland**, his only American No 1 album. In England a No 1 eluded him, but between 1967 and 1983 17 of his albums hit the charts. In the year-end popularity polls in the British pop papers, Hendrix won 'Top World Musician' awards in 1967, 1968 and 1969. He was named 'Artist of the Year' by *Billboard* in 1968. In their December 'Record Talent' supplement they said: '1968 was the year of the underground, the year of progressive rock, the year of blues rock, the year of Jimi Hendrix and the Jimi Hendrix Experience.' *Playboy* named him 'Artist of the Year' in 1969.

The accolades piled up, but time was running out for Jimi Hendrix. Very much part of the drug scene that ultimately brought him down, he had sowed the seeds of his own destruction. His heroin adiction undermined his talent, and in 1970 his performance at the Isle of Wight Festival went down badly. On 18 September 1970 he was found dead in his London rooms, having choked on his own vomit after a drug overdose.

Are You Experienced? was produced and written by Jimi Hendrix. The tracks on the album were **Foxy Lady**, **Manic Depression**, **Red House**, **Can You See Me?**, **Love or Confusion**, **I Don't Live Today**, **May This Be Love**, **Fire**, **Third Stone from the Sun**, **Remember** and **Are You Experienced?**

AXIS: BOLD AS LOVE (Album) *Track 613-003*

[UK] Reprise 6281 [USA]. After the outstanding **Are You Experienced?** debut album, the Jimi Hendrix Experience followed up at the end of 1967 with **Axis: Bold as Love**. It made No 5 in the British album charts, with 16 weeks in the Top 40. In America, where the album was released in early 1968, it made No 3, with 53 weeks in the Top 200.

Just at the time **Axis** was released in Britain, Capitol put out the **Get That Feeling** album with Jimi playing guitar, backing singer Curtis Knight. Although the latter was originally released without much success in 1964, the interest in Hendrix generated by the **Are You Experienced?** album helped promote this one. It reached No 75. In Britain it was released by London Records, and briefly made the album charts in May 1968.

The tracks on **Axis** were **Up From the Skies**, **Spanish Castles Magic**, **Wait Until Tomorrow**, **Ain't No Telling**, **Little Wing**, **If Six was Nine**, **You've Got Me Floating**, **Castles Made of Sand**, **She's So Fine**, **One Rainy Wish**, **Little Miss Lover** and **Bold as Love**.

HERMAN'S HERMITS   *British*

THERE'S A KIND OF HUSH/NO MILK TODAY *Columbia (EMI) DB 8123 [UK] MGM 13681 [USA]*. **There's a Kind of Hush** was released on both sides of the Atlantic in February 1967. It followed the less than successful **East West**, which was only a minor hit, reaching No 37 in Britain and No 27 in America. As that had followed different Top 10 hits in both countries, the group had hoped for something better. They got something better with **A Kind of Hush**, though it was to be their last Top 10 hit in America, where they had become more popular than in their native Britain. Written by British composers Geoff Stevens and Les Reed and produced by Mickie Most, it made No 7 in Britain with 11 weeks in the Top 50.

In America it reached No 4, with 12 weeks on the Hot 100. MGM used a different flip side for America than Columbia had used in Britain. They used **No Milk Today**, written by Graham Gouldman and also produced by Mickie Most, which had made No 7 with 11 weeks in the charts when released in Britain as an A side in September 1966. It had also been a hit in Europe. In America it made No 35 during a 10-week chart life independent of its A side.

The double A side won an RIAA Gold Disc for American sales of over a million on 14 April 1967. It was their 10th million-selling disc. Their album **There's a Kind of Hush All Over the World**, which included both sides of this single, also went Gold in America, on 13 June 1969. It reached No 13 during 35 weeks on the album charts. It continued to sell steadily even after it dropped off the charts, which during its chart life were increased to a Top 175, and again in May 1967 to the present Top 200.

THE HOLLIES   *British*

ON A CAROUSEL *Parlophone R 5562 [UK] Imperial 66231 [USA]*. The third million seller for the Hollies was issued in Britain on 11

February 1967. It was the second million seller for the writers, Allan Clarke, Tony Hicks and Graham Nash, members of the group. The disc sold its million in the USA by the end of the year, and was No 7 for two weeks with 14 weeks in the bestsellers. It got to No 4 in Britain, with 11 weeks in the bestsellers.

CARRIE ANNE *Parlophone R 5602* [*UK*] *Epic 10180* [*USA*]. The fourth million seller for the Hollies, the song was again by group members Clarke, Hicks and Nash (their third). The disc was issued on 27 May 1967, in Britain, and was No 3 for two weeks with 11 weeks in the bestsellers. In the USA it climbed to No 5, staying in the bestsellers for 13 weeks, and sold a million there by the year's end.

ENGELBERT HUMPERDINCK *British*

RELEASE ME *Decca F 12541* [*UK*] *Parrot 40011* [*USA*]. Engelbert Humperdinck (real name Arnold George Dorsey) was born on 2 May 1936 in Madras, India where his father was a leading engineer. He had two brothers and seven sisters. In 1947 the family came to England, his father having retired and taken a house in Leicester, where 'Gerry' was educated at secondary school, and learned to play piano and saxophone by night. On leaving school he started out as an apprentice engineer for a short time, but the urge to make music proved too strong. He started to sing in local clubs and then did his National Service in the Army Corps of Signals. On discharge in 1956

he resumed his semi-professional singing in working men's clubs and won a contest in the Isle of Man while on holiday. This resulted in a London agent getting him a recording contract in London, and Decca released his first disc **Mister Music Man** in 1958.

After a solo spot on the TV 'Song Parade' he went out with top pop package tours, but by 1960, with no recordings and only occasional work, found himself engaged in a struggle both to eat and gain recognition. Then came a six months' sojourn in hospital with a chest complaint and six months to recuperate. In 1965 he met up again with a former flatmate, Gordon Mills, who had become Tom Jones' manager. Mills decided to manage Gerry and suggested he change his name to Engelbert Humperdinck, borrowed from the famous German composer. He got a new chance with Decca and recorded **Stay**, and was sent with the Decca team to the Knokke-le-Zoute Song Festival in Belgium (1966). He was a big success and his disc of **Dommage, Dommage** sold over 100,000 on the Continent. On 13 January 1967 his disc of **Release Me** was issued. Soon after, he was asked to deputize for Dicky Valentine for TV's 'Sunday Night at the Palladium', and included **Release Me** in his programme. Record shops were inundated the next day with orders for his disc which rocketed to No 1 and stayed there for six weeks, with a run of 56 weeks in the bestseller charts. In the USA this disc was No 4 and 14 weeks in the bestsellers. Sales in Britain alone went over the million, and globally it sold over five million. Engelbert had definitely arrived. He started his own TV

series 'The Engelbert Humperdinck Show' in November 1967.

Release Me was written in 1954 by US songsmiths Eddie Miller and Dub Williams (W.S. Stevenson) when it was a success for country-and-western artists including Ray Price. It was acclaimed by the Music Operators of America as 'the most popular record of the year in coin-operated phonographs'. The song is also the world's most performed country music composition with collective disc sales of 12 million.

THERE GOES MY EVERYTHING *Decca F 12610* [*UK*] *Parrot 40015* [*USA*]. Engelbert's second big success of the year was a country-and-western number written by US composer Dallas Frazier in 1965. The disc has a choir and string backing with a gentle beat. It soon sold over 250,000 in Britain where it was No 2 for four weeks with 29 weeks in the bestsellers, and then topped the 750,000 sales mark. In the US it reached No 20 with six weeks in the bestsellers. The combined sales well exceeded a global million. The disc was released on 19 May.

The song was also a great hit in 1966 for US country artist Jack Greene.

THE LAST WALTZ *Decca F 12655* [*UK*] *Parrot 40019* [*USA*]. A continuation of the Humperdinck success story, and his third million seller in a row. This is a British song written by Barry Mason and Les Reed; the latter also provided the arrangement. Released on 18 August it sold a million in Britain alone in two months and was No 1 for six weeks with 27 weeks in the bestsellers. In the USA it was No 21 for two weeks and nine weeks in the bestsellers.

The song was also recorded by several prominent disc artists including Petula Clark and Mireille Mathieu for the French market under the title **La dernière valse**, with French lyrics by Hubert Ithier.

Global sales for the record were over three million, two million of these being in Europe alone.

RELEASE ME (Album) *Decca SKL 4868* [*UK*] *Parrot 71012* [*USA*]. Engelbert Humperdinck's tremendous success with his single **Release Me** was followed by this album of the same title released in Britain on 12 May 1967 and soon after on the Parrot label in the USA. It became a big seller on both sides of the Atlantic and the forerunner of several other successful albums. This album stayed in Britain's bestsellers for 57 weeks, reaching No 6 for one week, and in the USA for 116 weeks, reaching No 7 for three weeks. By the end of 1969 it had sold well over a million, by which time Engelbert was established as a world star and, along with Tom Jones, a big money earner for Britain with sell-out performances in the USA. A Gold Disc was awarded by RIAA in December 1967.

The contents of the album were: *Side 1 —* **Release Me**, by Eddie Miller and Dub Williams (1954); **Quiet Night**, by Jobim, Kaye and Lees; **Yours Until Tomorrow**, by Gerry Goffin and Carole King (1967); **There's a Kind of Hush**, by Les Reed and Geoff Stephens (1967); **This is My Song**, by Charles Chaplin (1967) (from the

film *Countess from Hong Kong*); **Misty Blue**, by Bob Montgomery (1967); *Side 2 — ***Take My Heart**, by Gordon Mills (1967); **How Near Is Love**, by Ivor Raymonde, Marcel Stellman and Dix (1967); **Walk Through This World**, by Seamons and Savage; **If I Was You**, by Crewe and Rambeau; **Talking Love**, by Werner Scharfenberger and Kurt Feltz (Eng. words: Marcel Stellman); **El mondo** ('My world'), by Pes, Fontana, Meccia and Mellin; **Ten Guitars**, by Gordon Mills (1967).

TOMMY JAMES AND THE SHONDELLS　　*American*

I THINK WE'RE ALONE NOW *Roulette 4720* [*USA*]. This was the second million seller for this group in the USA, where the disc got to No 3 with 17 weeks in the bestsellers. The song, an easy-paced 'rocker', was written by Ritchie Cordell.

MIRAGE *Roulette 4736* [*USA*]. A fast-driving rock number, written by Ritchie Cordell who also produced the disc. It registered No 7 for two weeks in the US charts with 10 weeks in the bestsellers, and was No 10 for a week in Britain. Global sales are estimated at over a million.

The arrangement was by Jimmy Wisner, and the disc was released in the USA in April 1967.

JAY AND THE TECHNIQUES　　*American*

APPLES, PEACHES, PUMPKIN PIE (Ready or not) *Smash 2086* [*USA*]. Written by Maurice Irby, Jr., the group's recording reached No 6 and was in the US bestsellers for 17 weeks, with a million reported sale.

Jay Proctor, a Philadelphia-born vocalist, has been in close touch with music almost all his life. He sang occasionally on WAEB-Allentown, Pennsylvania, with a group he formed with several friends in the late 1950s. He played in other groups in the Pennsylvania area, and then formed The Techniques with fellow member Karl Landis. Besides Proctor, the other members of the group are Landis, Chuck Crowl, George Lloyd, Ronnie Goosly, Dante Dancho and John Walsh. All of them lived in Allentown and its environs. They all got together one night with guitars, drums, trumpets and saxophones and tried to form a symphony orchestra, but ended up starting a rock group instead. **Apples, Peaches, Pumpkin Pie**, their first single for Smash records, was a hit, as was **Keep the Ball Rollin**.

KEEP THE BALL ROLLIN' *Smash 2124* [*USA*]. This second reported million seller for Jay and the Techniques was written by Denny Randell and Sandy Linzer. It reached No 14 and stayed 12 weeks in the US bestsellers.

JEFFERSON AIRPLANE　　*American*

SURREALISTIC PILLOW (Album) *RCA Victor 3766* [*USA*]. Jefferson Airplane was formed in 1966 by Martin Balin, with Signe Anderson (vocals), Skip Spence (drums), Paul Kantner (vocals and guitar), Jorma Kaukonen (guitar) and Jack Casady (bass). When Signe Anderson left she was replaced by Grace Slick. Spence also left the group and was replaced by Spencer Dryden. The band subsequently included Papa John Creach (violin) and Johnny Barbata as a replacement to Dryden on drums. They first appeared at the Matrix Club in San Francisco where the group became one of the premier bands. Their first albums were quite extra-ordinary, with Balin, Slick and Kantner's vocal use of unorthodox musical intervals and Kaukonen's unusual and unpredictable guitar lines.

Their first album, **Jefferson Airplane Takes Off**, was released in 1966, followed by **Surrealistic Pillow** which, by 1975, was reported as having sold one and a half million. RIAA awarded a Gold Disc in 1967. It is notable for two of Grace Slick's songs, **White Rabbit** and **Somebody to Love**, which were also released as a single, giving the group their first US success.

Balin was replaced by David Freiberg in 1972, and Kaukonen and Casady formed their own group, Hot Tuna, while Slick and Kantner began recording solo albums. In 1974, the group changed their name to Jefferson Starship with the release of their **Dragonfly** album, and in 1975 their **Red Octopus** album reached No 1 in the charts.

TOM JONES　　*British*

I'LL NEVER FALL IN LOVE AGAIN *Decca F 12639* [*UK*] *Parrot 40018* [*USA*]. Tom Jones had the Christmas No 1 in 1966, and looked set to dominate 1967. As it turned out, he was rather overshadowed by his stable-mate Engelbert Humperdinck, who was also managed by Gordon Mills. His one million seller of the year only reached the seven-figure sale when re-released in America in 1969. When first released in July 1967 it did well enough in Britain, reaching No 2 with 25 weeks in the Top 50 and winning Jones his third Silver Disc, but in America it only made No 49 with seven weeks on the Hot 100.

British Decca's American subsidiary London re-issued the record again in 1969. It took off and went all the way to No 6, with 16 more weeks of chart action on London's Parrot label. American sales alone were over the million as a result of this second chart outing, with an RIAA Gold Disc awarded on 3 October 1969. It was Jones' fourth million seller. This re-release also helped sales of two more of his albums released in 1967. **Green Green Grass of Home** and **Tom Jones Live!** both won RIAA Gold Discs for million dollar sales in 1969. The **Live!** album had not even charted when it was first released in America in 1967. **I'll Never Fall in Love Again** was written by British writers Jim Currie and Lonnie Donegan.

GLADYS KNIGHT AND THE PIPS *American*

I HEARD IT THROUGH THE GRAPEVINE *Soul 35039* [*USA*] *Tamla Motown TMG 629* [*UK*]. Written by N. Whitfield and B. Strong, this disc

sold one and a half million by the end of 1967, the first million seller for the Soul label, put out by Motown. The recording was one of the biggest hits in the history of the company and a great triumph for Gladys Knight and the Pips since their first million seller of 1961. The disc was No 1 for one week in the US national charts with 17 weeks in the Hot 100 and R&B charts where it was No 1 for six weeks. In Britain it reached No 47. Release was on 21 October 1967. A sale of two million was reported by 1969.

FAUSTO LEALI　　*Italian*

A CHI *RI FI RF NNP 16171* [*Italy*]. This is an Italian version of an American hit **Hurt**, originally written in 1953 by Jimmy Crane and Al Jacobs, and a big success for singer Timi Yuro in 1963.

Fausto Leali's disc, released in April 1967, was No 1 for three weeks and stayed in the Top 15 for 26 weeks in Italy. By mid April 1968 it had sold over 800,000, and went on to pass the million mark.

THE LEMON PIPERS　　*American*

GREEN TAMBOURINE *Buddah 23* [*USA*] *Pye International 7N 25444* [*UK*]. The Lemon Pipers were five young men based in New York: Bill Albaugh (drummer), Reg Nave (organist, tambourine), Bill Bartlett (lead guitar), born in South Harrow, Middlesex, England, Steve Walmsley (bass guitar), born in New Zealand, and Ivan Brown (lead singer, rhythm guitar).

Issued in late 1967, this disc reached No 1 in the US charts in February 1968 for two weeks with 13 weeks in the bestsellers, and subsequently sold two million. The number was written by S. Pinz and Paul Leka (producer of the disc). The disc also achieved popularity in Britain where it got to No 7 in 1968 and was 11 weeks in the bestsellers.

RIAA Gold Disc award, February 1968.

LITTLE TONY
Italian

CUORE MATTO (Crazy heart) *Ld A 7500* *[Italy]*. Little Tony (real name Antonio Ciacci) was born in 1940 in San Marino, Italy. He formed a trio with his two brothers, and in 1959 they were discovered by Jack Good, the British producer of the TV series **Boy Meets Girl**. Good brought Tony to Britain in spite of the fact that he could not speak English, and he appeared on TV and toured the country with Cliff Richard, staying in Britain for a year. His disc of **Too Good** got into Britain's Top 10. In 1961, Little Tony won second prize in the 1961 San Remo Festival with the song **24,000 Kisses**, and again appeared in the Festival in 1964. In 1967 he sang **Cuore matto** in the contest which, although not the winner, proved to be the bestselling song of the entries, reaching the million sale in three months. It was No 1 for 10 weeks in Italy.

The song was written by Ambrosino and Toto Savio. The English version by Jackie Trent and Tony Hatch, titled **Long is the Lonely Night**, was issued by Pye on 24 March 1967.

Little Tony received a Gold Disc award in Italy in May 1967 for the million sale.

LULU
British

TO SIR, WITH LOVE *Epic 10187* *[USA]* *[under licence from Columbia (EMI) in Britain]*. Marie McDonald McLaughlin Lawrie, professionally known as Lulu, was born on 3 November 1948 at Lennox Castle, Lennoxtown, north of Glasgow, and began to sing at a very early age. She won a competition on holiday in Blackpool at the age of five and by the time she was nine appeared regularly with a local accordion band. In 1963 she was singing with a group originally called the Gleneagles, which was re-named Lulu and the Luvers (a six-piece band). Her impact on the audience at Glasgow's Le Phonographe Club inspired the owner Tony Gordon to invite his sister Marian Massey, a

show-business woman in London, to hear Lulu. Marian was greatly impressed by this young dynamic singer and became her manager.

Lulu's first disc was **Shout**, recorded while she was still at school in 1964, which entered the British charts. Then came another success with **Satisfied**. She subsequently appeared on TV, radio and in pantomime and made British and Continental tours. She was the first British girl artist to perform behind the Iron Curtain in Poland (March 1966). In 1967 Lulu had a hit with **The Boat that I Row** and was chosen for a top acting role in the film *To Sir, With Love* starring Sidney Poitier. She was a tremendous success in this, the film breaking many box office records in the USA. Her song of the same title written by Don Black (words) and Mark London (music) was released as a single in the USA and soon reached No 1 there, staying top for five weeks and selling over two million, the first time in recording history a British disc topped the US charts without entering the British charts. Gold Disc award RIAA in November 1967.

This diminutive (5 ft 2 ins) redhead possesses a very powerful voice and projects her songs with infinite clarity.

She first recorded for Decca, switching to Columbia in 1967. This disc was first recorded for Columbia (Britain) and released on 23 June 1967.

VICTOR E. LUNDBERG
American

AN OPEN LETTER TO MY TEENAGE SON *Liberty 55996* *[USA]*. This controversial record, projecting Lundberg's opinions and advice concerning the world situation and the youth of the day, became one of the fastest-selling discs in the USA selling over the million within a month.

Victor E. Lundberg was born in 1923 in Grand Rapids, Michigan, when he was the owner of an advertising firm. He served for five years during World War II in the Infantry and Psychological Warfare Department. After the War, he started a broadcasting career and was an announcer and newsman at stations in Grand Rapids, Tulsa and Phoenix. He then moved into sales and management with the Imperial Broadcasting System of Hollywood and later started his own company.

This disc achieved No 6 for two weeks in the US charts and was six weeks in the bestsellers.

SCOTT McKENZIE
American

SAN FRANCISCO (Be sure to wear some flowers in your hair) *Ode 103* *[USA]* *CBS 2816* *[UK]*. The 'hippies' emerged on the American scene in a big way by 1967. They preached 'altruism, mysticism, honesty, joy and non-violence, finding an almost childlike fascination in beads, blossoms and bells, ear-shattering music, exotic clothing and erotic slogans' (*Time*, 7 July 1967). They also popularized a new word, 'psychedelic'. San Francisco became the major musical centre, spawning dozens of new groups.

Scott McKenzie, born in Alexandria, Virginia, recorded this song with charm and simplicity. It was written by John Phillips, leader of the Mamas and the Papas, who also produced the disc, playing guitar himself with Mama Michelle playing bells.

Scott had originally sung with John Phillips in the Journeymen group some years before, when his range stretched from jazz to folk to blues.

The disc was No 3 for three weeks in the USA with 12 weeks in the bestsellers, and a big success in Britain where it was No 1 for four weeks and 17 weeks in the bestsellers with over 250,000 sales on the CBS label. The disc was also No 1 in Germany, Belgium, Denmark and Norway and a big seller elsewhere abroad. It was re-released in 1977 with great success.

Global sales were over seven million.

THE MAMAS AND THE PAPAS
American

DEDICATED TO THE ONE I LOVE *Dunhill 4077* *[USA]* *RCA Victor 1576* *[UK]*. This great revival of the Shirelles hit of 1960 was written by L. Pauling and R. Bass in 1957. Performed by the Mamas and Papas in a harmonic soft rock style, it soon reached the No 2 position for three weeks in the USA with 10 weeks in the bestsellers, and was also No 2 for two weeks in Britain and 17 weeks in the bestsellers, with a subsequent million global sale.

PAUL MAURIAT AND HIS ORCHESTRA
French

LOVE IS BLUE (L'amour est blue) *Philips 7012* *[France]* *Philips BF 1637* *[UK]* *Philips 40495* *[USA]*. The background of this instrumental hit is one of the most surprising stories to come out of France. The song, by André Popp (music) and Pierre Cour (words), was written in early 1967 and chosen to represent Luxembourg in the 1967 Eurovision Song Contest. Polydor artist Vicky (real name Vicky Leandros) sang it and came fourth. Her recording was not, however, a sales success.

Paul Mauriat's instrumental version, released in late 1967 in the USA, raced to the top of their charts in early 1968 and stayed No 1 for seven weeks with 18 weeks in the bestsellers, sparking off other instrumental versions and many vocal versions (with lyrics by Bryan Blackburn). This singles disc reached No 12 in Britain with 14 weeks in the bestsellers. Sheet music copies went over the million mark, and Paul's disc (featuring the harpsichord) sold well over four million in the USA. Vicky's disc then became a hit in Canada.

Paul Mauriat, born in 1925, conductor-arranger, studied music from the age of four.

He made his first appearance on US TV in February 1968. An album titled **Blooming Hits**, including **Love is Blue**, was a very big seller in the USA in early 1968, and reached No 1 for seven weeks. Gold Disc award from RIAA, March 1968.

BLOOMING HITS (Album) *Philips 21104* [*France*] *Philips 248* [*USA*]. Originally recorded in France, this album was released in December 1967 in the USA and sold 750,000 in three months with the million passed during 1968, and two million by mid-1968.

The disc, with its distinctive Mauriat sounds and arrangements played by his orchestra of soaring lush strings and horns with rocking rhythms, includes the million-selling **Love is Blue** and other great international hits.

The content of the album were: *****Puppet on a String**, by Bill Martin and Phil Goulter (1967) (winner of Eurovision Song Contest, 1967); *****This is My Song**, by Charles Chaplin (1967) (from the film *Countess from Hong Kong*); *****Penny Lane**, by John Lennon and Paul McCartney (1967); *****L'amour est bleu** ('Love is Blue'), by Pierre Cour/André Popp (1967); **Adieu à la nuit** ('Adieu to the night'), by M. Vidalin/Maurice Jarre (1967); **Mama (when my dollies have babies)**, by J. Monty and Sonny Bono (1967); *****Somethin' Stupid**, by C. Carson Parks (1966); **Inch Allah**, by Adamo (1967); *****There's a Kind of Hush**, by Geoff Stevens and Les Reed (1967); **Seul au monde** ('Alone in the world'), by A. Pascal and Paul Mauriat (1967).

Titles marked * were million seller discs for various artists.

Additional titles of the British release were: **Ta, Ta, Ta-Ta**, by Michel Polnareff and Gerald (1967); **L'important c'est la rose**, by Louis Amade/Gilbert Becaud (1967).

A Gold Disc was awarded by RIAA in March 1968 and the record was No 1 for seven weeks in the USA, staying in the charts for 50 weeks.

SMOKEY ROBINSON AND THE MIRACLES   *American*

I SECOND THAT EMOTION *Tamla 54159* [*USA*] *Tamla Motown TMG 631* [*UK*]. The famous Miracles added William 'Smokey' Robinson to the name of the group, and this song, written and produced by 'Smokey' and A. Cleveland, was a big hit in the USA where it reached No 3 for two weeks in their charts and 15 weeks in the Hot 100. It was No 1 for 1 week in the R&B charts with a 15-week chart run. It was also a hit in Britain where it achieved No 27 and was 11 weeks in the bestsellers.

THE MONKEES   *American*

MORE OF THE MONKEES (Album) *Colgems 102* [*USA*] *RCA Victor SF 7868* [*UK*]. The second tremendous seller for this group had an advance sale of one and a half million, the biggest ever for a vocal album. The disc was No 1 for 18 weeks in the USA and two weeks in Britain. US sales were reported at around five million. It was awarded an instant Gold Disc by RIAA.

It was released in the USA on 1 February and in Britain on 31 March. The disc includes two songs written by Mike Nesmith of the group. Contents: **She**, by Tommy Boyce and Bobby Hart; **When Love Comes Knockin** (at your door), by Neil Sedaka and Carole Bayer; **Mary, Mary**, by Mike Nesmith; **Hold on Girl**, by Jack Keller, Raleigh and Carr; **Your Auntie Grizelda**, by Jack Keller and Diana Hilderbrand; **(I'm not your) Steppin' Stone**, by Tommy Boyce and Bobby Hart (1966); **Look Out (here comes tomorrow)**, by Neil Diamond; **The Kind of Girl I Could Love**, by Sandy Linzer and Denny Randell; **Sometime in the Morning**, by Gerry Goffin and Carole King; **Laugh**, by Medress, Seigel, P. and M. Margo; **I'm a Believer**, by Neil Diamond (1966).

The disc was in the US bestsellers for 70 weeks.

A LITTLE BIT ME, A LITTLE BIT YOU *Cologems 1004* [*USA*] *RCA Victor 1580* [*UK*]. This was the third million seller single for the Monkees and second for writer Neil Diamond. Advance orders were over one and a half million at the time of release in mid-March with a simultaneous Gold Disc award by RIAA. Sales in Britain (RCA label) were over 250,000 and the global well over two million.

The disc was No 1 for two weeks in the USA and 10 weeks in the bestsellers, and No 3 for three weeks in Britain with 12 weeks in the bestsellers.

HEADQUARTERS (Album) *Colgems 103* [*USA*] *RCA Victor SF 7886* [*UK*]. Issued on 16 May, advanced orders were well over the million copies, the group's third consecutive album to achieve the seven-figure sale, plus a Gold Disc award from RIAA on 23 May. The disc was recorded in Hollywood, and was No 1 for one week and No 2 for 11 weeks in the USA. In Britain it was No 2 for five weeks. Half of the songs on the album were written by members of the group, Mike Nesmith, Peter Tork, Mickey Dolenz and Davy Jones: **You Told Me**, by Mike Nesmith; **Forget that Girl**, by Chip Douglas (Douglas Farthing Hatlelid); **Band 6**, by Mike Nesmith, Peter Tork, Davy Jones and Mickey Dolenz; **I'll Spend My Life with You**, by Tommy Boyce and Bobby Hart; **You Just May Be the One**, by Mike Nesmith; **Shades of Grey**, by Barry Mann and Cynthia Weill; **I Can't Get Her Off My Mind**, by Tommy Boyce and Bobby Hart. **For Pete's Sake**, by Peter Tork and Joe Richards; **Mr Webster**, by Tommy Boyce and Bobby Hart; **Sunny Girlfriend**, by

Mike Nesmith; **Nilch**, by Mike Nesmith, Peter Tork, Davy Jones and Mickey Dolenz; **No Time**, by Hank Cicalo; **Early Morning Blues and Greens**, by Diane Hilderbrand and Jack Keller; **Alternate Title** (Randy S.), by Mickey Dolenz.

Sales by 31 December 1967 were estimated at over two million and continued into 1968. The disc was in the bestsellers for 50 weeks.

PLEASANT VALLEY SUNDAY/WORDS *Colgems 1007* [*USA*] *RCA Victor 1620* [*UK*]. The fourth singles million for the popular Monkees, the song was written by ace American husband-and-wife team Gerry Goffin and Carole King.

The disc was No 2 for a week in the USA and 10 weeks in the bestsellers, selling a million with an RIAA Gold Disc award. It also sold well in Britain, reaching No 10 in the charts.

Release in Britain was on 11 August. By October 1967, the Monkees' TV series was being screened in 39 different countries.

DAYDREAM BELIEVER *Colgems 1007* [*USA*] *RCA Victor 1645* [*UK*]. This fifth singles million seller for the Monkees, written by John Stewart, was awarded a Gold Disc from RIAA a fortnight after the disc was released in November 1967. Davy Jones takes the vocal honours in this beautifully constructed ballad, with strings and brass lending atmosphere to the group's harmonization.

It was No 1 in the US charts for five weeks with 12 weeks in the bestsellers, and No 2 in Britain for one week with 17 weeks in the bestsellers where it was released on 10 November. The disc sold over two million by end of 1967.

PISCES, AQUARIUS, CAPRICORN AND JONES LTD (Album) *Colgems 104* [*USA*] *RCA Victor SF 7912* [*UK*]. The Monkees' fourth album was another huge success, with an RIAA Gold Disc award for advance sales presented on 2 November. The disc was recorded in Hollywood in the summer of 1967 following the group's highly successful tour of the USA and Britain, and released on 25 October. The title of the album incorporates the Zodiac signs of the members of the group, plus

Davy Jones who is also a Capricorn. The album got to No 1 in its second week on the market and stayed top for five weeks, soon passing the million units sale. Sales continued into 1968.

Group members Davy Jones, Mike Nesmith and Peter Tork contributed their own songs to the album: **Salesman**, by Nesmith; **She Hangs On**, by Jeff Barry; **Door into Summer**, by Douglas and Martin; **Love is Only Sleeping**, by Barry Mann and Cynthia Weill; **Cuddly Toy**, by Nilsson; **Words**, by Tommy Boyce and Bobby Hart; **Hard to Believe**, by Davy Jones, Capli and Brick; **What Am I Doing Hangin' Round?** by Travis Lewis and Boomer Clarke; **Peter Percival Patterson's Pet Pig Porky**, by Peter Tork; **Pleasant Valley Sunday**, by Gerry Goffin and Carole King; **Daily Nightly**, by Mike Nesmith; **Don't Call on Me**, by Mark London and Mike Nesmith; **Star Collector**, by Gerry Goffin and Carole King.

It stayed in the US bestsellers for 47 weeks. The disc was released in Britain on the RCA label on 5 January 1968.

THE MOODY BLUES   *British*

NIGHTS IN WHITE SATIN *Deram DM 161* [*UK*] *Deram 85023* [*USA*]. After their first hit **Go Now**, released in 1964, went to No 1 and sold a million copies, the Moody Blues hit a lean period. They had three minor hits in 1965, and then disappeared from sight. Seeing little future in continuing with their original R&B style, they decided on a dramatic change of direction. **Nights in White Satin** was the first example of their new and very different classical rock sound. Written by Justin Hayward, it was taken from the **Days of Future Past** album, recorded with the London Festival Orchestra. Released in Britain on 10 November 1967, it finally restored the Moody Blues to the Top 50 on 27 December. It was a modest hit at first, reaching No 19 with 11 weeks in the charts.

In America the group had had less success than in Britain. **Go Now** had done well, reaching No 10, but after that they could manage only two very small hits. **From the Bottom of My Heart**, their third British hit released in 1965, made No 22 in Britain, but only reached No 93 during its three weeks on the US charts. **Stop!**, which was not a hit in Britain, made No 98 for one week in the USA in 1966. **Nights in White Satin** did not make it in America when first released, though the **Days of Future Past** album, released in 1968, did chart.

What turned this record from a minor hit into the Moody Blues' second million seller was its re-release in 1972. The second time around, it reached No 9 in Britain, with another 11 weeks of chart activity. In America it made No 1 for one week in November, with 18 weeks on the charts. It won an RIAA Gold Disc for US sales of a million copies on 18 December 1972. The record also went to No 1 in France and was a big hit in Germany and the Netherlands.

The personnel of the group for this disc were three original members — Graeme Edge, Mike Pinder and Ray Thomas — plus two others: John Lodge (bass guitar/cello) born 20 July 1945 in Birmingham, and Justin Hayward (guitar, piano, sitar) born 14 October 1946 in Swindon, Wiltshire. Both joined the group in 1965, replacing Denny Laine and Clint Warwick.

DAYS OF FUTURE PAST (Album) *Deram SML 707* [*UK*]/*Deram 18012* [*USA*]. **Days Of Future Past** was a new beginning for the Moody Blues. By marrying their rock music to a full orchestra they created a classical rock style that has sustained them ever since. The group had been hired by Decca to record some Dvorak with the London Festival Orchestra to demonstrate the range and excellence of the company's new Deram Sound System. They managed to convince the orchestra's conductor Peter Knight to let them record their own theme album instead.

In fact the group had only enough material for about half an album, and it was Knight who extended the material by writing the classical sounding links between the songs, the orchestral introduction to the first track **The Day Begins**, and the two and a half minutes of strings after the last track **Nights In White Satin**. He composed the whole orchestral score. The melodies were written by Redwood, which was the collective name for Moody Blues John Lodge and Justin Hayward. The lyrics were written by those members of the group indicated in brackets in the track listing below.

Peter Knight was born on 23 June 1917 in Exmouth, Devon. During a long and distinguished career he was the first Musical Director of Granada TV, starting just after the company won an ITV franchise in 1956. He also worked for the BBC, conducting the music for the very last 'Goon Show', a TV special in the early seventies. The music for every episode of the regular TV series had been arranged and conducted by Walley Stott, but he had just become Angela Morley and the BBC feared ridicule if he/she was involved in, of all things, a 'Goon Show', so Peter Knight was brought in instead. As well as conducting the London Festival Orchestra, he worked on a number of records and did the arrangement for many of the Carpenters discs. He died on 30 July 1985.

Knight was instrumental in getting this album off the ground. Decca's senior management was not keen on the project, but Knight and the enthusiasm of Decca's American subsidiary London Records prevailed.

In January 1968 this became the Moody Blues first album to make the British LP charts. It reached No 27 during 16 weeks in the charts. It was also their debut on the American album charts, where it stayed for 102 weeks. It peaked at No 3 in the *Billboard* charts, but made No 1 for one week in *Cash Box*. It won an RIAA Gold Disc for million dollar sales on 10 October 1970, and passed the million in world sales in 1972. The album was produced by Michael Dacre-Barclay assisted by Tony Clarke, with Derek Varnals as engineer. Hugh Mendl is credited on the album cover as Executive Producer, but apart from writing the liner notes he had very little to do with producing the album. He was the senior executive at Decca responsible for the new Deram Sound System, and was therefore more involved with the new recording technique in general than with the details of this particular album.

This was the first of a string of hit albums for the Moody Blues. The follow-up **In Search Of The Lost Chord** (1968) reached No 5 in Britain and No 23 in America, and their third successful album **On The Threshold Of A Dream** (1969) made No 1 in Britain. They topped the American album charts in 1972 with **Seventh Sojourn** and in 1981 with **Long Distance Voyager**. This and 1978's **Octave** both went Platinum in America, while the group's first eight hit albums all won RIAA Gold Discs.

The tracks on **Days Of Future Passed** were: **The Day Begins** (John Lodge/Justin Hayward); **Dawn: Dawn Is A Feeling** (Mike Pinder); **The Morning: Another Morning** (Ray Thomas); **Lunch Break: Peak Hour** (John Lodge); **The Afternoon: Forever Afternoon (Tuesday?)** (Justin Hayward) and **Time To Get Away** (John Lodge); **Evening: The Sun Set** (Mike Pinder) and **Twilight Time** (Ray Thomas); **The Night: Nights In White Satin** (Justin Hayward).

VAN MORRISON   *British*

BROWN-EYED GIRL *Bang 545* [*USA*]. Van Morrison is acknowledged as one of Britain's foremost 'blueswailers', due to the influence of his father's big collection of blues records. He was born on 31 August 1945 in Belfast, Northern Ireland. At the age of 11 he sang with a skiffle group at the local *palais de danse* and in 1960 went to Germany, playing at US bases for four months. On his return to Belfast he formed a group called Them (1964) which was signed to Decca, their first disc being released in September 1964. The group's second disc got into the charts and their third **Here Comes the Night** was a global hit followed by TV, national tours and much acclaim. Trouble over music policy caused the group to break up. Van returned to Belfast from London and formed a new Them group. One of the group's discs, **Gloria**, written by him, was a 1965 US hit.

Van was subsequently signed to an exclusive contract by Bang Records in New York. **Brown-Eyed Girl** was his first release, in March 1967, a song he wrote himself. It got to No 7 in the US charts and was 16 weeks in the bestsellers, with an eventual million sale. He made a tour of the USA following the success of this disc.

It was released on the London label in Britain on 28 July.

THE MUSIC EXPLOSION   *American*

A LITTLE BIT O'SOUL *Laurie 3380* [*USA*]. Another success for the Laurie label and their new group. The Music Explosion were five youngsters: James Lyons (lead singer, ocarina) from Galion, Ohio; Don (Tudor) Atkins (lead guitar) from Mansfield, Ohio; Richard Nesta (rhythm guitar) from Mansfield, Ohio; Burton Stahl (bass guitar, organ) from Mansfield, Ohio; Bob Avery (drums, harmonica) from Cohoes, New York.

This disc was No 1 for one week in the USA with 16 weeks in the bestsellers, and received an RIAA Gold Disc award for a million sales.

The song was written in the early 1960s by Britain's John Carter and Ken Lewis (members of the Ivy League vocal trio), who also wrote **Can't You Hear My Heartbeats?** for Herman's Hermits.

PETER, PAUL AND MARY   *American*

ALBUM 1700 (Album) *Warner Brothers 1700* [*USA*]. The fifth million seller album for Peter, Paul and Mary, with a Gold Disc award for a million dollar sale on 27 January 1969. The million units sale was reported in December 1973. The contents of the album were: **I Did Rock and Roll Music**, by Stookey, Mason and Dixon; **Bob Dylan's Dream**, by Bob Dylan; **Great Mandella**, by Peter Yarrow; **The House Song**, by Stookey and Bannard; **If I Had Wings**, by Yarrow and Yardley; **I'm in Love with a Blue Frog**, by Bernstein; **No Other Name**, by Paul Stookey; **The Song Is Love**, by Dixon, Kniss, Stookey, Yarrow and Travers, **Weep for Jamie**, by Peter Yarrow; **Whatsername**, by Stookey, Dixon and Kniss; **Rolling Home**, by Andersen; ***Leaving on a Jet Plane**, by John Denver (1966).

* This was released as a singles disc in 1969 and sold a million. John Denver wrote it in 1966 when he was a member of the Mitchell Trio.

WILSON PICKETT   *American*

FUNKY BROADWAY *Atlantic 2430* [*USA*] *Atlantic 584-130* [*UK*]. This was first recorded by Dyke and the Blazers in early 1967. Pickett's recording was released in July 1967 and reached No 6 for one week with 12 weeks in the Hot 100. It was No 1 for one week during its 13 weeks in the R&B charts. It reached No 43 during 3 weeks in the British Top 50 and had a total estimated million sale.

The song was written by Lester Christian.

PROCUL HARUM   *British*

A WHITER SHADE OF PALE *Deram DM 126* [*UK*] *Deram 7507* [*USA*]. The Procol Harum story started around September 1966, when vocalist/pianist Gary Brooker found himself out of a job after a German tour with the Paramounts, a group from Southend, Essex. Gary met Keith Reid through a mutual friend and they decided to write songs together, although Keith had nothing to do with the pop business except the desire to write. Keith had shown his poem **A Whiter Shade of Pale** to publisher David Platz of Essex Music who was greatly impressed and told Reid to get it set to music, which was done by Gary.

The writers then decided to form a group, recruiting Matthew Fisher (a classical organist at the Royal Guildhall School), guitarist Ray Royer, bassist Dave Knights and drummer Bobby Harrison. Platz assisted with a loan of £100 ($280). Denny Cordell, an old friend of Gary's, produced the disc just prior to the group's first appearance at London's Speakeasy Club. The release of the disc on Decca's newly formed (September 1966) label Deram on 12 May 1967 had dynamic reactions. Within days it was No 1 in the national charts and became a sensational success all over

Europe. There were also huge sales in the USA. In Britain the disc was No 1 for six weeks with 15 weeks in the bestsellers, selling 380,000 in 16 days and soon easily passing the half million. In France it was No 1 for 11 weeks and went on to sell over half a million — a rarity for that country. In the USA it got to No 3 with 12 weeks in their bestsellers. Global sales were reported at six million.

The lyrics of the song are set against a baroque organ riff or rock organ version based on one of the movements of Bach's Suite No 3 in D Major (Air on the G String). Garry Brooker provided the soulful vocal, Matthew Fisher dominating with his celestial organ playing and Bach-inspired chords. Keith Reid became manager of the group.

Procol Harum took their name from a rare breed of Burmese cat. It is also Latin-derived, meaning 'beyond these things'.

Drummer Harrison did not play on the disc 'take' that was used owing to illness. Session drummer Bill Eyden deputised.

The line-up on the disc was: Gary Brooker (vocal, piano, organ) born 29 May 1945, in Hackney, London; Matthew Charles Fisher (organ, piano, bass, guitar) born 7 March 1946, in Croydon, Surrey; Ray Royer (lead guitar, violin) born 8 October 1945, in London; Dave Knights (guitar, bass) born 28 June 1945, in Islington, London; Bobby Harrison (drums, vibraphones) born 28 June 1943, in East Ham, London. Royer and Harrison left the group in July 1967 and were replaced by Robin Trower and Barrie J. Wilson.

HOMBURG *Regal Zonophone RZ 3003* [*UK*] *A&M 885* [*USA*]. The second million seller (globally) for Procol Harum was again written by Gary Brooker and Keith Reid. It was released on 29 September, on the revived Regal-Zonophone label. The group then comprised: Gary Brooker, Matthew Charles Fisher, Dave Knights (original members) and newcomers Robin Trower and Barrie J. Wilson. The disc was No 5 in Britain, with 10 weeks in the bestsellers, but only achieved No 34 in the USA with five weeks in the charts. It sold well in many other countries.

ROCKY ROBERTS AND   *American*
THE AIREDALES

STASERA MI BUTTO (Tonight I'll jump) *Durium CN A 9237* [*Italy*]. Rocky Roberts was born in the USA but started a career in Italy. He arrived in Europe as a Marine on board the ship *Enterprise*, a member of its jazz band. In Europe he got his first contract to record on the Barclay label. He returned to the USA after his military service, then in 1965 came back to Europe and began to perform with his group the Airedales (six members) in Rome's popular 'beat' club the Piper. He then signed a long-term contract with Durium.

Early in 1967 they were given a 12-week series as leading group in the Italian TV show 'Sabato Sera' ('Saturday night'). This tune **Stasera mi butto** was used as the show's theme music. Rocky became one of Italy's most popular beat stars and his disc of the theme tune became a No 1 in the charts, selling 100,000 in three weeks. In three months it had sold 600,000 and went on to sell a million for which he received a Gold Disc award at the Whiskey à Go Go in Cannes in October 1967. It is said to have sold around four million by 1970.

The American version was made by dubbling English lyrics onto the original Continental recording. It was released by United Artists in the USA.

The composition is by Amurri, B. Canfora and Doug Fowlkes.

THE ROKES   British

PIANGI CON ME (Cry with me) ARC AN 4081 [Italy]. The Rokes became the best beat group in the Italian pop world, their story somewhat similar to that of the Beatles. The group are all English: Shel Shapiro, born 16 August 1944 in London; Johny, born 3 April 1944 in Walthamstow, London; Bobby Posner, born 6 May 1945 in Harrow, Middlesex; and Mike Shepstone, born 29 March 1944 in Weymouth, Dorset. Shel and Johny play guitar, Bobby the bass, and Mike on drums.

Shel, Bobby and Mike all went to Harrow County School and after leaving joined with a boy called Malcolm. At the end of 1961 they left for Hamburg and were invited to make a four-week tour of Italy. Malcolm returned to England, his place being taken by Johny (originally with a group called the Londines in Paris). They made their first appearance at the Alcyone Theatre in Milan, and won a national contest for unknown pop singers in 1963. Teddy Reno, a noted Italian talent scout, liked them and invited them to appear with Rita Pavone on two big package tours. In August 1963 they recorded Un' anima pura, an old melodic Italian song.

It was, however, in February 1965 that the group had their first very big success when they appeared at Rome's first-ever beat club, the Piper, which had just opened. They played there for two months and became the symbols for Italy's teenagers. Most of their subsequent disc releases hit the top of the Italian charts, the group becoming Italy's top-selling disc makers on the beat scene for three years with four million sales.

Piangi con me, written by Shel and Mike with Mogol and Julien, sold over 800,000 — an enormous figure for the Italian market — and with sales elsewhere totalled the million. The English version was entitled **Let's Live for Today** and was released on 21 April 1967 in Britain. The song also achieved No 3 in the USA with the Grass Roots' recording.

Shel and Mike wrote nearly all the songs for the group. The Rokes also co-starred with Rita Pavone in the film La Figlia Americana, and had their own TV show in Italy.

THE ROLLING STONES   British

LET'S SPEND THE NIGHT TOGETHER/ RUBY TUESDAY Decca F 12546 [UK] London 904 [USA]. With **Let's Spend the Night Together**

the Rolling Stones were at their most outrageous. There is nothing subtly suggestive about this record and, as intended, it caused an outcry though it got good reviews in the music press. In Britain it was the lead A side, and entered the NME charts on 21 January 1967 at No 17. **Ruby Tuesday**, which was the bigger side in America, entered the Top 30 the same week at No 29. The following week, the two sides stood at No 5 and No 20 respectively. **Let's Spend the Night Together** peaked at No 2 with eight weeks in the Top 30, while **Ruby Tuesday** got no higher than No 20 for two weeks during its four-week run. In the Record Retailer Top 50, where the two sides were listed together as one entry, it only reached No 3 with 10 weeks in their charts. The double A side won a Silver Disc for British sales of a quarter of a million, the Stones' ninth, on 25 February.

In America **Ruby Tuesday** gave the Rolling Stones another No 1, something that eluded them in Britain in 1967. In Billboard it was No 1 for one week in March, with 12 weeks on the Hot 100. The flip side reached No 55 during its chart life of eight weeks. In Cash Box, **Ruby Tuesday** went to the top the last week in February, was knocked off the following week by the Supremes' **Love is Here and Now You're Gone** (this was the week they were No 1 in Billboard), and then returned to the top for one last week the week after that. Thus they were No 1 in one of the main trade paper charts for three weeks, though never at the top in both papers at the same time! It was their fifth American No 1 single. It won an RIAA Gold Disc for sales of a million copies on 1 May 1967.

As usual, the record was a big hit around the world. **Ruby Tuesday** charted in Canada, Australia, South Africa, Ireland, Italy and Malaysia. **Let's Spend the Night Together** was a hit in Norway, Demark, Germany, the Netherlands, France, Italy and Malaysia. Both sides were written by Mick Jagger and Keith Richards, and produced by Andrew Loog Oldham.

1967 had its ups and downs for the Stones. They had two singles out and, though neither made No 1 in Britain, they both sold a million. (In America London also issued **She's a Rainbow**, which did not do so well.) They had two big studio albums, and in America the **Flowers** hits package. All three won Gold Discs for million dollar sales. In February they won a special trophy at the Cannes Music Festival in France for being 'the best-selling British record recording act from 1 July 1965 to 30 September 1966.' They later toured Europe in the spring. There was also the inevitable controversy. They ran foul of the Musicians' Union ban on the use of backing tapes for TV shows, and Jagger issued a writ against the News of the World sensational Sunday newspaper alleging defamation. (Their story got the wrong Stone. They should have named Brian Jones.) The start of the year was not a good time for Mick Jagger. His romance with model Chrissie Shrimpton ended in January.

BETWEEN THE BUTTONS (Album) Decca SKL 4852 [UK] London 499 [USA]. The Rolling Stones' 17th million seller was also their sixth LP to reach seven-figure sales. All the tracks

on **Between the Buttons** were written by Mick Jagger and Keith Richards, and it was the last Stones album to be produced by Andrew Oldham. The album was recorded in London and Los Angeles. The cover photograph was by Gered Mankowitz, who had taken the photos used in the montage on the cover of the **Got Live If You Want It** album, and also some of the shots used in the packaging of **Big Hits**. On the back of **Between the Buttons** was a series of cartoon drawings and verses by Charlie Watts.

The album was released in Britain in January 1967. It made No 3 in the album charts, kept off the top by the Monkees and the **Sound of Music** soundtrack. It spent 22 weeks in the charts. In America it made No 2 for four weeks, with 47 weeks on the Top 200. It won an RIAA Gold Disc for million dollar sales on 24 February 1967, one week after release. Global sales were over a million.

The track order was: **Yesterday's Papers**, **My Obsession**, **Back Street Girl**, **Connection**, **She Smiled Sweetly**, **Cool, Calm and Collected**, **All Sold Out**, **Please Go Home**, **Who's Been Sleeping Here?**, **Complicated**, **Miss Amanda Jones**, and **Something Happened to Me Yesterday**. On the American version **Back Street Girl** and **Please Go Home** were replaced by **Let's Spend the Night Together** and **Ruby Tuesday**.

WE LOVE YOU/DANDELION Decca F 12654 [UK] London 905 [USA]. **We Love You** was released in Britain in August, just after the infamous drugs trila of Mick Jagger and Keith Richards. From 1966 the use of drugs among rock musicians had spread widely, in particular LSD. There had always been an element of drug-taking among jazz and pop musicians, from the fifties and even earlier. What was new was the increasingly blatant and public way pop stars talked about it, with seeming impunity. The authorities became increasingly concerned, fearing that young fans would soon follow their idols. In California LSD was made illegal in 1966, and in Britain the popular press and the police took an increasing interest in the activities of rock stars. The Stones were on the receiving end of a number of 'busts'.

On 12 February 1967 Keith Richards' Sussex house Redlands was raided by the police, and Jagger, Richard and art dealer Robert Frazer were arrested. George Harrison had left the party before the raid began. Others present included Jagger's girlfriend Marianne Faithfull, referred to in the trial as Miss X. Stories of nudity, sexual licence and drug abuse were manna from heaven for the popular press.

Keith Richards was charged with allowing his house to be used for smoking cannabis. Mick Jagger was accused of having four amphetamine tablets which had been bought prefectly legally in Italy. At the trial in June 1967 Richards was jailed for a year, and Jagger got six months. There was a public outcry. Even the The Times, in a famous editorial 'Who Breaks a Butterfly on a Wheel?' attacked the injustice of the case and the severity of the sentence. On appeal Jagger's sentence was changed to a conditional discharge, which meant that he spent only two days in prison during the whole affair, and Richards' conviction was quashed. In celebration of their release, Jagger and Richards wrote **We Love You**, recorded with the intro sound of a banging prison door. The double A side was the Stones' move into psychedelia. Commercially it was their least successful single since 1963, the million coming from global sales. On 26 August **We Love You** entered the *NME* Top 30 at No 13, the top new entry of the week. It was one place ahead of Engelbert Humperdinck, with the Beach Boys, Frankie Vaughan and Jimi Hendrix lower down the list as the other new entries. It entered the *Record Retailer* Top 50 at No 17 the same week, with both sides listed together. In this chart the record peaked at No 8 with eight weeks in the chart. In the *NME* it did better, reaching No 4.

In America both sides charted independently. There **Dandelion** was the lead side, reaching No 14 with eight weeks on the charts. **We Love You** made No 50 during its six-week chart life. It was their lowest American chart placing since **Heart of Stone** was released in January 1965. Worse was to come. London released **She's a Rainbow**, which, though about the best track from the **Satanic Majesties** album, only managed to make No 25 in the Hot 100. 1967 was something of a low for the Stones, but they were far from ready to be written off.

THEIR SATANIC MAJESTIES REQUEST (Album) *Decca TXL 103* [*UK*] *London 2* [*USA*]. Just as the Beach Boys had their **Pet Sounds** album and the Beatles had **Sgt Pepper**, so the Rolling Stones had **Satanic Majesties**. It was the album of the psychedelic era, and its variable quality owed as much to the drugged state of the people who made it as to their intuitive genius.

The album was the Stones at their most experimental, and a world away from their R&B roots. **2000 Man** and **She's a Rainbow** were among the tracks that stood out, but, like any experiment, there were some ideas that simply did not come off. All but one of the tracks were written by the Jagger/Richards team. **In Another Land** was written by Bill Wyman, who sang lead on it. The album was produced and arranged by the Rolling Stones. It was recorded at the Olympic studios in London and the Bell Sound studios in New York, with Glyn Johns as engineer. Nicky Hopkins played piano on most of the tracks, and J.P. Jones provided the strings on **She's a Rainbow**.

The artwork of the album cover was unusual. It was a three-dimensional picture of the Stones in theatrical dress, with Mick Jagger dressed as a wizard in the middle. In the background was a science fiction, magic and space backdrop. This was put together and photographed by Michael Cooper, working with the Stones in a warehouse in New York. The idea for the title came from the first page of a British passport: 'Her Britannic Majesty's... Requests and requires....' **Their Satanic Majesties Request** entered the *Record Retailer* album charts at No 23 on 23 December 1967, though it entered the *NME* album charts at No 10 the same week. It peaked at No 3, with 13 weeks in the album Top 40. In

America it made No 2 for six weeks, with a chart life of 30 weeks. It won an RIAA Gold Disc for million dollar sales on 6 December 1967, the day before its release. World sales were well over the million.

SAM AND DAVE   *American*

SOUL MAN *STAX 231* [*USA*]/*STAX 601-023* [*UK*]. Sam and Dave's biggest hit was with **Soul Man**, which was written and produced by Isaac Hayes and David Porter. Released in September 1967, it had sold the million within two months, receiving a Gold Disc from the RIAA on 22 November 1967. It was No 1 in America for one week in *Cash Box* and *Record World*, and peaked at No 2 for three weeks in *Billboard*. It was 15 weeks in all three charts. In *Billboard*'s R&B charts it went to No 1 for 7 weeks, with 18 weeks in the then recently expanded R&B Top 50. It reached No 24 during its 14 weeks in the British Top 50, and was No 1 for 9 weeks in the British R&B Top 20. Sam and Dave won a Grammy for Best R&B Group of 1967.

SANDIE SHAW   *British*

PUPPET ON A STRING *Pye 7N 17272* [*UK*]. After winning the British section, this song won the Eurovision Song Contest in 1967, the first ever for Britain, putting both the writers, Bill Martin and Phil Coulter, and Sandie Shaw, the singer, in the spotlight. Sandie's disc was No 1 for four weeks in Britain with 18 weeks in

the bestsellers, and No 1 in practically every country in Europe. She received a Gold Disc for million plus combined British and European sales on 9 May. Global sales were estimated at four million plus. The disc was released on 10 March 1967.

Sandie Shaw (real name Sandra Goodrich) was born on 26 February 1947 in Dagenham, Essex, and educated at the Robert Clack Technical School there. She decided to become a singer and at the age of 17 went backstage at a theatre where pop singer Adam Faith was appearing and sang for him. Adam was so impressed, as was his agent Eva Taylor, that within a few weeks the young singer who always sings with her shoes off was auditioned and signed to a contract by Pye Records. Her first release was **As Long as You're Happy, Baby** followed by **There's Always Something There to Remind Me** (No 1 for three weeks) and **Girl Don't Come**, both 250,000-plus sellers in 1964, and **Long Live Love** selling as many in 1965 (also No 1 for three weeks). She was then chosen by the BBC to represent Britain in the Eurovision contest which, in the finals on 8 April in Vienna, proved to be her greatest success.

The outstanding arrangement for the disc was by Kenny Woodman whose orchestra accompanies her. With three No 1 chart toppers, Sandie became one of Britain's outstanding female singers.

This disc sold over 500,000 in Britain and 750,000 in Germany.

FRANK AND NANCY SINATRA   *American*

SOMETHIN' STUPID *Reprise 0561* [*USA*] *Reprise RS 23166* [*UK*]. A unique recording by a famous father and famous daughter, their first duet disc, the song was written by C. Carson Parks in 1966.

This beautiful ballad with its captivating arrangement by Billy Strange sold over the million in the USA and received a Gold Disc award from RIAA. It was No 1 there for five weeks with 13 weeks in the bestsellers. It also sold over 250,000 in Britain where it was No 1 for two weeks simultaneously with the USA and had 18 weeks in the bestsellers.

The recording was made 'off the cuff' a few days before Nancy left the States to entertain troops in Vietnam and took only 35 minutes, one of the easiest recordings ever for Nancy's disc producer Lee Hazlewood, in collaboration with Jimmy Bowen (Frank's producer).

THE SMALL FACES   *British*

ITCHYCOO PARK *Immediate IM 057* [*UK*] Immediate 501 [*USA*]. This group was formed in early 1965 by Ronnie 'Plonk' Lane. After leaving school he started working in a fairground and took up playing guitar in his spare time. He decided to form a group, and his brother suggested Kenny Jones, a drummer he had heard playing in a local pub. Soon after, they recruited Steve Marriott who had appeared in the show *Oliver* for 18 months from the age of 12, and he brought in the fourth member Jimmy Winston, a guitarist-organist.

Their first week together was at a club in Sheffield, then to Manchester, and then London, working in an East Ham London pub. A 'one-night stand' at the Cavern in Leicester Square resulted in a five-week booking there, and their popularity induced Don Arden, a top agent, to sign them up. Their first disc **Watcha Gonna Do About It?** on Decca was released on 6 August 1965 only a few weeks after the group's formation, and they were also signed for parts in a film. This included a song **Sha-La-La-La-Lee** which got to No 2 in the charts. On 5 November, Winston left the group and was replaced by Ian McLagan. They made two highly successful nationwide tours in 1966 and had their first No 1 hit with **All or Nothing**. Thereafter came a Scandinavian tour, and a tour with Roy Orbison (1967), a radio and TV promotion tour of Europe, and appearance in Germany's first TV colour transmission.

In May 1967 the group switched to the new Immediate label and were later managed by Andrew Oldham, manager of the Rolling Stones.

Itchycoo Park, released on 4 August 1967, reached No 3 in Britain with 14 weeks in the bestsellers, and got to No 12 in the USA (February 1968) with 17 weeks in the bestsellers, the global sales totalling over a million. The song was written by group members Steve Marriott and Ronnie Lane who together wrote most of the band's hits.

The group comprised Steve Marriott (guitar, drums, organ, harmonica) born 30 January 1947 in Bow, East London; Ronnie 'Plonk' Lane (bass and guitar) born 1 April 1946 in Plaistow, East London; Kenny Jones (drums) born 16 September 1948 in Stepney, London; Ian McLagan (organ) born 12 May 1946 in Hounslow, Middlesex.

The disc was re-released in 1977 reaching No 9 with an extra 11 weeks in the British charts.

WHISTLING JACK SMITH   *British*

I WAS KAISER BILL'S BATMAN *Deram DM 112* [UK] *Deram 85005* [USA]. The name of Whistling Jack Smith for this disc is somewhat misleading. The recording was said to have been made as a 'laugh' originally by the Mike Sammes Singers, a popular TV singing group, and Smith didn't exist at the time. When the disc hit the British charts, a singer named Billy Moeller who had previously recorded for the Decca organization under his professional name of Coby Wells was given the name of Whistling Jack Smith to promote the disc on tour throughout Britain.

The recording got to No 5 in Britain with 12 weeks in the bestsellers, and No 14 in the USA with seven weeks in the bestsellers, where the tune also had several other recordings and became an international hit, the first in this idiom to do so for many years. This catchy tune subsequently sold a global million of the so-called Whistling Jack Smith version.

Billy Moeller was born on 2 February 1946 in Liverpool. The tune was written by Roger Greenaway and Roger Cooke, a talented pair of songwriters and recording artists known as David and Jonathan.

SONNY AND CHER   *American*

THE BEAT GOES ON *Atco 6461* [USA] *Atlantic 584-078* [UK]. Released in January 1967, this disc is said to have sold four million globally for the husband-and-wife team. It reached No 3 for a week in the US charts with 11 weeks in the bestsellers. It reached No 29 with eight weeks in the bestsellers in Britain. The song was written by Sonny Bono.

THE SOUL SURVIVORS   *American*

EXPRESSWAY TO YOUR HEART *Crimson 1010* [USA]. Written by K. Gamble and L. Huff, who also produced the disc, this song first broke big in Philadelphia, then New York. Three months after appearing in the US charts it sold a million, after climbing to No 4 with 15 weeks in the bestsellers.

The Soul Survivors were a group of six youngsters.

SPANKY AND OUR GANG   *American*

SUNDAY WILL NEVER BE THE SAME *Mercury 72679* [USA]. Written in 1966 by Gene Pistilli and Terry Cashman, Spanky and Our Gang's recording in 1967 reached No 9 and was eight weeks in the the the US bestsellers, with a reported million sale.

Spanky McFarlane had been known for some years in folk singing circles. She had sung with the New Wine Singers and had gained an excellent musical reputation, particularly in the Chicago area. In early 1966 she left the group and moved to Florida. One night a hurricane struck the Miami area in which Spanky was living in a one-room converted chicken coop. Two young men named Nigel Pickering and Oz Bach took shelter in her quarters. While they waited for the winds to subside, the three passed the time by singing. Thus was born the idea for Spanky and Our Gang. They finally got together in Chicago and worked as a trio. They recruited a fourth member, Malcolm Hale, a folk singer who had also worked with the New Wine Singers. Pickering, before joining Spanky, had done a lot of singing, particularly country-and-western. Bach was at one time a well-known performer in Miami coffeehouses. Hale participated in a US State Department tour of Vietnam while playing with the New Wine Singers.

Spanky and Our Gang first broke into the charts with **Sunday Will Never Be the Same**. Bob Dorough and Stu Scharf took over production reins of the group in late 1967. Several personnel changes took place in the group when Oz Bach left to form his own unit. Malcolm Hale died of pneumonia late in 1968 and was not replaced.

LAZY DAY *Mercury 72732* [USA]. The second reported million seller for Spanky and Our Gang, the song was written by Tony Powers (words) and George Fischoff (music). The disc reached No 14 and was in the US bestsellers for 11 weeks.

THE STRAWBERRY ALARM CLOCK   *American*

INCENSE AND PEPPERMINTS *Uni 55018* [USA]. This sextet, exponents of jazz-rock, was composed of Mark Weitz (leader), organ; Randy Seol, vocalist, drums and vibraphones; Lee Freeman, rhythm guitar and lead vocalist; Ed King, lead guitar; Gary Lovetro, bass guitar (lead); and George Bunnell, special deffects bass guitarist.

The group was a combination of two successful Southern Californian bands and had been together for less than a year when this disc hit the US charts. It reached No 1 within two months and stayed on top for two weeks with 16 weeks in the bestsellers. A Gold Disc for a million sale was awarded by RIAA on 19 December. The group not only developed an unusual sound, but built themselves a top visual act. Randy Seol, drummer, developed a technique whereby he performed on bongos with his hands on fire during shows. They appeared all over the West Coast of America.

Incense and Peppermints shows the influence of jazz and Oriental music. It was written by J. Carter and T. Gilbert.

BARBRA STREISAND   *American*

A CHRISTMAS ALBUM (Album) *CBS-Columbia CS 9557* [USA] *CBS 31850* [UK]. Barbra Streisand's second record eventually to sell a million was released for Christmas 1967, and sold well over the next 20 years. *Billboard* used to have special charts for Christmas records, and this disc made No 1 in that chart in 1967. It made the chart again in 1968, 1970, 1971, 1983 and 1984. It also spent five weeks in the main LP charts in 1981, reaching No 108. It won a Gold Disc for million dollar sales on 21 January 1976. It went on to sell over two million copies in the United States, with a double Platinum award on 21 November 1986. Though the record did not chart in Britain, it was a steady seller at Christmas time.

All the songs on the album were traditional Christmas songs. The tracks were **Jingle Bells, Have Yourself a Merry Little Christmas, The Christmas Song, Chestnuts Roasting on an Open Fire, White Christmas, My Favourite Things, The Best Gift, Sleep in Heavenly Peace (Silent Night), Ave Maria, O Little Town of Bethlehem, I Wonder as I Wander** and **The Lord's Prayer**.

THE SUPREMES   *American*

LOVE IS HERE AND NOW YOU'RE GONE
*Motown 1103 [USA] Tamla Motown TMG 597
[UK]*. Million seller number 11 for the
Supremes was another Holland-Dozier-
Holland composition, produced by Brian
Holland and Lamont Dozier. It was also their
ninth American No 1. It topped the charts for
one week in March, sandwiched between the
Beatles and the Rolling Stones in the *Billboard*
charts where it hit the top on 11 March, and
caught between the first and last week at No 1
for the Stones' **Ruby Tuesday** in *Cash Box*,
where it was No 1 on 4 March. It was the sixth
of their eight R&B No 1s, with two weeks at the
top and 11 weeks on the R&B charts.

The Supremes tried a new technique on
this record. They had Diana Ross talk through
part of the record rather than sing it. The idea
worked well, and the record spent 11 weeks on
the charts. Supremes records never did as well
in Britain as in America, and this one only
reached No 17 with 10 weeks in the charts. It
reached No 2 in the British R&B charts.

THE HAPPENING *Motown 1107 [USA] Tamla
Motown TMG*. **The Happening** was rather a
special No 1 for the Supremes, for reasons not
all of which were positive. It was their 10th No
1, and their fourth chart-topper in a row. It was
the last record until 1970 released under the
name of the Supremes, for their next record
went out as Diana Ross and the Supremes.
Diana's star billing caused resentment among
the other two Supremes, especially Florence
Ballard. Florence had been increasingly
unhappy with the way Diana Ross was
pushing her way to the front, and she began to
miss live performances. She was accused of
being overweight and drunk. In the end she
was sacked from the Supremes, and this was
the last record on which she sang. After an
attempted solo career failed, her marriage
broke up and she died of a heart attack on 21
February 1976. She was only 32 years old.
The Happening was written by Holland-
Dozier-Holland and Frank de Vol, who
composed the soundtrack music for the film of
the same name. It was the first time the
Supremes had recorded a film theme. It was
produced by Brian Holland and Lamont
Dozier, and was the last Supremes No 1 that
the Holland-Dozier-Holland team would work
on. Later the Supremes left Motown after a
disagreement with Berry Gordy over royalty
payments. Though Diana Ross and the
Supremes had two more No 1s to come, their
recording career suffered from the loss of three
such talented writers and producers.
The Happening was No 1 for one week in
America, with 11 weeks on the pop charts. It
did badly on the R&B charts, only reaching No
12. It was the Supremes' first record not to
make the R&B Top 10 since they made it big
with **Where Did Our Love Go?** in 1964. In
Britain it reached No 6, with 12 weeks in the
Top 50.

REFLECTIONS *Motown 1111 [USA] Tamla
Motown TMG 616 [UK]*. **Reflections** was the
first release under the new group name of
Diana Ross and the Supremes, and the first
record to feature new group member Cindy
Birdsong. She was born on 15 December 1939,
and came from Camden, New Jersey. She had
been with Pattie La Belle and the Bluebelles
before acting as a stand-in for Florence Ballard
just before she finally left the group.

The new line-up almost made it to the top,
but the record stalled at No 2 with 11 weeks on
the pop charts. It made No 4 with 10 weeks on
the R&B Top 50. It was a big hit in Britain,
where it reached No 4 in some charts and lasted
14 weeks in the Top 50. In the British R&B
charts it was No 1 for seven weeks. The record
was their last million seller to be written by
Eddie and Brian Holland and Lamont Dozier
and produced by Brian Holland and Lamont
Dozier at the Motown studios in Detroit. It was
the group's 13th million seller, though as Berry
Gordy would not let the RIAA audit his sales
figures there was no RIAA Gold Disc to prove
it.

DIANA ROSS AND THE SUPREMES'
GREATEST HITS (Album) *Motown 663 [USA]
Tamla Motown STML 11063 [UK]*. A superlative
album containing all the million sellers to date
by the world's greatest female group, and a
remarkable tribute to their songwriters Eddie
Holland, Brian Holland and Lamont Dozier
who wrote every song (except the music for
The Happening, written by Frank de Vol). The
album was issued as a two-disc set in the USA
in September 1967. It soon climbed to No 1 and
was top for five weeks. The British issue as a
single album was released in January 1968, and
was No 1 for six weeks.

Contents: ***Stop, in the Name of Love**
(1965); ***Nothing but Heartaches** (1965); **When
the Lovelight Starts Shining Thru' his Eyes**
(1963); ***My World is Empty Without You**
(1966); ***Where Did our Love Go?** (1964); **Love
Is Like an Itching in my Heart** (1966); ***Come
See about Me** (1964); ***I Hear a Symphony**
(1965); ***Reflections** (1967); ***Back in my Arms
Again** (1965); ***You Keep Me Hangin' On**
(1966); **Whisper You Love Me, Boy** (1965);
*The Happening (1967); ***Love is Here and
Now You're Gone** (1967); ***You Can't Hurry
Love (1966)**; ***Baby Love** (1964).

* Indicates million seller single in year
given.

This album soon sold half a million and
went to the million mark in 1968. It was in the
US bestsellers for 89 weeks.

JOE TEX   *American*

SKINNY LEGS AND ALL *Dial 4063 [USA]*.
This was the second million seller for Joe Tex,
the song written by him. Issued in October, it
reached No 7 for one week in the US charts
with 15 weeks in the bestsellers, and sold the
million with RIAA Gold Disc in January 1968.

THE TREMELOES   *British*

HERE COMES MY BABY *CBS 202519 [UK] Epic
10139 [USA]*. The Tremeloes were originally a
backing group for Brian Poole, the three
original Tremeloes (Alan Blakely, Rick West
and Dave Munden) breaking away in 1964 to go
out on their own, spending most of their time
of the road throughout England and Scotland.
Chip Hawkes was added to make the
foursome.

Brian Poole and the Tremeloes first came
into prominence in 1963 through their
recording of **Twist and Shout**, and their
quarter million seller **Do You Love Me?**. They
toured with Roy Orbison and appeared at the
Paris Olympia. In 1964 they made tours of
South Africa and Australia, and also recorded
their second quarter million seller **Someone**,
followed by a film musical in Ireland *A Touch of
Blarney*, and a concert tour in Sweden. 1965
saw them on a British tour, and Irish and
Scandinavian tours. Up to 1966 the Tremeloes
recorded for British Decca, afterwards going
over to CBS.

Here Comes My Baby was their first hit on
their new label, reaching No 4 for two weeks in
Britain with 11 weeks in the bestsellers, and No
11 in the USA with 12 weeks in the bestsellers.
The song was written by recording artist Cat
Stevens and the disc achieved a million global
sale by the end of the year.

The group consisted of Rick (Richard
Charles Westwood) West (lead guitar, banjo)
born 7 May 1943, in Dagenham, Essex; Dave
(Dave Charles) Munden (drums) born 2
December 1943, in Dagenham, Essex; Chip
(Leonard Donald) Hawkes (bass guitar) born 11
November 1946, in Shepherd's Bush, London;
Alan Blakely (rhythm, organ, piano, drums)
born 1 April 1942, in Bromley, Kent. Rick, Dave
and Alan were all educated in Dagenham, Chip
in Slough, Buckinghamshire.

SILENCE IS GOLDEN *CBS 2723* [*UK*] *Epic 10184* [*USA*]. The Tremeloes' revival of the song by American writers Bob Crewe and Bob Gaudio (1963) with its beautiful recording and falsetto singing proved to be the group's biggest hit. It sold well over 250,000 in Britain where it was No 1 for three weeks with 15 weeks in the bestsellers, and also reached No 9 in the USA with big sales there (14 weeks in the bestsellers) and around the globe. Released on 22 April 1967, it soon racked up a million-plus sale. The Tremeloes made an American tour during summer 1967 following this disc's success.

EVEN THE BAD TIMES ARE GOOD *CBS 2930* [*UK*] *Epic 10233* [*USA*]. This was the third global million seller for the Tremeloes. This disc was released on 28 July 1967, and the song was written by two of Britain's top pop songsmiths Peter Callender (words) and Mitch Murray (music). It got to No 4 for a week in Britain and 13 weeks in the bestsellers, and had good sales in the USA (No 28 and seven weeks in the bestsellers) plus additional sales from other countries.

THE TROGGS   *British*

LOVE IS ALL AROUND *Page One POF 040* [*UK*] *Fontana 1607* [*USA*]. Written by the group's Reg Presley, this disc reached No 4 in Britain with 14 weeks in the bestsellers, and No 7 in the USA where it was a hit on the Fontana label with 16 weeks in the bestsellers. The million sale globally was reached by May 1968, and the disc first released in Britain in October 1967.

The group made successful tours of the USA.

THE TURTLES   *American*

HAPPY TOGETHER *White Whale 244* [*USA*] *London HL 10115* [*UK*]. Formed in early 1965, the group commenced their career at Reb Foster's Rebelaire Club in Redondo Beach, California, although they were still at high school. They were immediately signed as the club's regular band, adopting the name The Turtles soon afterwards.

Foster then invited them to headline his celebrity night at Hollywood's Red Velvet Club. They were so successful that a new label, White Whale, signed them to a contract. Their first release **It Ain't Me Babe** a Bob Dylan composition was a big hit for the label's initial issue. **Happy Together** was No 1 in the USA for three weeks with 15 weeks in the bestsellers, and sold over a million with RIAA Gold Disc award. It reached No 12 in Britain with 12 weeks in the bestsellers.

The song was written by Garry Bonner and Alan Gordon. The group actually changed bass players and drummers a couple of times after its formation. The personnel on this recording was: Howard Kaylan (sax, clarinet, harmonica, lead singer) born 22 June 1947, New York; Mark Volman (clarinet, sax, vocals) born 19 April 1947, Los Angeles; Al Nichol (guitar, piano, organ, bass, trumpet, harpsichord, vocals); Jim Pons (bass, vocals) born 14 March 1943, Santa Monica, California; John Barbata (drums) born 1 April 1946, New Jersey; Jim Tucker (guitar, harmonica).

SHE'D RATHER BE WITH ME *White Whale 249* [*USA*] *London HLU 10135* [*UK*]. A pulsating

rock number, again written by Garry Bonner and Alan Gordon for the Turtles, and their second million seller (globally). The disc was No 1 for one week in the USA and 11 weeks in the bestsellers, and got to No 4 in Britain with 15 weeks in the bestsellers.

THE UNION GAP   *American*

WOMAN, WOMAN *CBS-Columbia 44297* [*USA*] *CBS 3365* [*UK*]. Dressed in Civil War uniforms and named after the historic town of Union Gap, Washington, this group attracted a very large following in the USA, playing at clubs and colleges.

Their leader, vocalist and guitarist 'General' Gary Puckett, an accomplished songwriter, was born in Minnesota in 1942. 'Sergeant' Dwight Bement (tenor sax) was a former music major at San Diego State. Canadian-born 'Corporal' Kerry Chater was bass-guitarist. 'Private' Gary ('Mutha') Withem played woodwind and piano, and 'Private' Paul Whitbread was drummer.

The group was organized in January 1967 in San Diego, California. **Woman, Woman**, written by J. Grosen and J. Payne, got to No 2 in the USA charts with 17 weeks in the bestsellers, and sold the million by mid-February 1968, with an RIAA Gold Disc award for their very first CBS recording. It was No 48 in Britain. The personnel were: Bement, born in San Diego, California, 1944; Withem, born in San Diego, California, 1945; Whitbread, born in San Diego, California, 1945; Chater, born in Vancouver, British Columbia, 1944.

FRANKIE VALLI
American

CAN'T TAKE MY EYES OFF YOU *Philips 40446* [*USA*]. Frankie Valli, as lead singer to the famous group the Four Seasons, always wanted to make solo discs and the success of this one, his first, certainly justified the effort. It was No 1 for two weeks in the USA and 16 weeks in the bestsellers, and sold a million with an RIAA Gold Disc award. The song was written by record producer Bob Crewe and the Four Seasons' Bob Gaudio.

Frank Valli was born on 3 May 1937 in Newark, New Jersey and started singing while still at high school. He was also a skilled though self-taught drummer. It was his fine tenor voice that gave the Four Seasons their characteristic and easily distinguishable sound.

BOBBY VEE AND THE STRANGERS
American

COME BACK WHEN YOU GROW UP *Liberty 55964* [*USA*]. Bobby's first big seller since 1962 achieved an RIAA Gold Disc award for the million sale in the USA. The disc got to No 2 for a week there with 16 weeks in the bestsellers. The song was written by Martha Sharp.

DIONNE WARWICK
American

I SAY A LITTLE PRAYER/VALLEY OF THE DOLLS *Scepter 12203* [*USA*] *Pye International 7N 25445* [*UK*]. **I Say a Little Prayer** was written by Hal David (words) and Burt Bacharach (music) who also produced both sides of the disc. In late 1967, this side reached No 4 for two weeks in the USA charts, the disc selling over 700,000. With the release of the film *Valley of the Dolls*, the reverse side became a big hit in early 1968 and took the sales to well over the million mark. Both sides were 13 weeks in the US bestsellers.

The songs were written by Dory Previn (words) and her composer/musical director then-husband André Previn who scored the music for the film. It reached No 1 for 2 weeks in *Record World* in March 1968 in the USA. In Britain the reverse side charted, reaching No 28 with eight weeks in the bestsellers. RIAA Gold Disc award, February 1968.

STEVIE WONDER
American

I WAS MADE TO LOVE HER *Tamla 54151* [*USA*] *Tamla Motown TMG 613* [*UK*]. The third million seller for Stevie was written by him with Lula Hardaway, Henry Cosby and Sylvia Moy. It was No 2 for two weeks in the USA with 15 weeks in the bestsellers, plus No 5 for one week in Britain with 15 weeks in the bestsellers. It spent 15 weeks in the US R&B charts reaching No 1 for 4 weeks. It also topped the British R&B charts for 2 weeks. Release in the USA was on 3 June 1967.

BRENTON WOOD
American

GIMME LITTLE SIGN *Double Shot 116* [*USA*] *Liberty LBF 15021*. Brenton Wood (real name Alfred Smith) was born on 26 July 1941 in Shreveport, Louisiana. He took his stage name from a district in Beverly Hills called Brent Wood. He went to California at the age of two and attended high school and college there. In Compton College he became lead singer of the Quotations group, but left later to become a solo singer. In early 1967 he was signed to Double Shot Records and scored immediately with his own song **The Oogum Boogum Song** which was a hit. Then came **Gimme Little Sign**, another self-written song which reached No 6 in the US charts with 15 weeks in the bestsellers, and also got to No 8 in Britain when released there in 1968 with 14 weeks in the charts.

Gimme Little Sign was the first million seller for the small Double Shot Record company in the USA. It was also in the Top 10 in Australia, Canada, Mexico, Italy and Germany.

JACKY YOSHIKAWA AND HIS BLUE COMETS
Japanese

BLUE CHATEAU *CBS 909* [*Japan*]. Released in Japan on 15 March 1967, this disc sold 500,000 in a month. By year's end the sales were over 1,300,000. It was awarded the Disc Grand Prize of Japan for 1967.

The group became one of the most popular in Japan and, in just over two and a half years after its formation, sold 8,180,000 discs by 31 December 1967.

The song was a second million-selling success for the writers Jun Hashimoto (words) and Tadao Inoue (music) who also wrote the group's **Aoi hitomi** ('Blue eyes') in 1966.

This disc was No 1 for four weeks in Japan and stayed in their charts for six months.

THE YOUNGBLOODS
American

GET TOGETHER *RCA Victor 9752* [*USA*]. The Youngbloods were four young men: Jesse Colin Young (leader), Jerry Corbitt (harmonica, guitar), 'Banana' Lovell Levinger (comedian) and Joe Bauer (drums) born Memphis, Tennessee.

Get Together, written by Chet Powers, was originally a track from the group's first album issued in 1967, and released then in September as a single when it had a fair sale, reaching a minor position in the US charts. RCA Victor re-issued the disc in July 1969 when it achieved No 4 for two weeks, and sold the million with an RIAA Gold Disc award on 7 October. Although the group had made many recordings from 1967, this re-issue was their first big hit. It stayed in the US bestsellers for 17 weeks making 25 weeks in all. They had only one more hit when **Darkness, Darkness** reached No 86 in 1970.

THE YOUNG RASCALS
American

GROOVIN' *Atlantic 2401* [*USA*] *Atlantic 584-111* [*UK*]. This was the second million seller for this group, with RIAA Gold Disc award. This disc was No 1 for four weeks in the US charts with 13 weeks in the bestsellers, and was also a success in Britain where for two weeks it reached No 8 with 13 weeks in the Top 50. It was written by Eddie Brigati and Felix Cavaliere of the group.

1 9 6 8

The year 1968, like 1967, saw rock and pop music go in several directions at once. In America it was a year when Motown did very well, with four No 1 singles, and Aretha Franklin had four million-sellers and was the top singles artist of the year. The West Coast came alive, but it was also the year that Tiny Tim surfaced, Paul Mauriat topped the charts with **Love Is Blue**, and Herb Alpert and the Tijuana Brass were the top album artists. It was a similar picture in Britain, where Julie Driscol and the Brian Auger Trinity were among the new acts to emerge, and Louis Armstrong had his first No 1 with **What A Wonderful World**.

One of the most talented groups to emerge from Britain in the late sixties was Cream. Formed in 1966 by Eric Clapton, Jack Bruce and Ginger Baker, they were at the forefront of the development of progressive rock. All three came from an R&B background, and went on to develop into musicians of exceptional ability. They combined blues and elements of jazz and rock into a unique style that included long instrumental improvisations that pushed rock music to new frontiers. They built their reputation steadily through 1967, and by 1968 were generally considered to be the best live rock group in the world.

Unlike most pop stars, they built their reputation by word of mouth, personal appearances and coverage in the underground press on both sides of the Atlantic. Though they released a few singles, none of them were big hits in Britain, though in 1968 two of them made the Top Ten in America. In January they announced that they would not be releasing any more singles. Though in fact they did not keep to this policy, the announcement underlined that Cream was an album act, and singles were only incidental to them. This was very unusual for the sixties. However, 1968 was the first year that album sales were greater than singles sales in Britain, a situation that had first occured in America only the year before. Every album Cream made sold over a million copies.

At the height of their fame rumours began to circulate that the group had decided to split. In May these rumours were denied, but in July their manager Robert Stigwood announced that in fact the group would break up at the end of the year. In August it was rumoured that Eric Clapton was to join the Rolling Stones, though that was one rumour about Cream that was not true. In October and November Cream did a farewell tour of America, where they had been particularly well received. Their final concert in New York was sold out well in advance. Cream then came home for two final performances at the Royal Albert Hall, London, playing their last concert on 26 November.

The West Coast

While Cream were the best of British rock, in 1968 most of the interesting developments in music came from the American West Coast. It was in California that a whole range of groups and singers had emerged that showed where American rock was going. These included Country Joe and the Fish, the Strawberry Alarm Clock, Grace Slick and Jefferson Airplane, Janis Joplin and Big Brother and the Holding Company, and Linda Ronstadt and the Stone Poneys. Jim Morrison and the Doors were very big with what one American paper called their 'total theatre' music, and the Grateful Dead and Buffalo Springfield were also important acts.

The Beatles

The Beatles dumped the giggling guru, Maharishi Yogi, in May. The final straw for them was his concert tour of America with the Beach Boys (which was a financial disaster.) George Harrison, who had got the Beatles into this in the first place, said: 'The Maharishi's main trouble was a tendency to spread something subtle in a gross way.' Ringo Starr was more blunt: 'Visting the Maharishi was like being at Butlins on the Ganges.' Paul McCartney said: 'It was just a phase we went through. He's still a nice fella, but we don't got out with him anymore.'

The Beatles began to branch out into various business activities via their Apple Corps companies headquartered in Savile Row, London. In May they launched the Apple Tailoring boutique in the Kings Road. In August the first four singles on their Apple record label were released, with Mary Hopkin's **Those Were The Days** following the Beatles' own **Hey Jude** to No 1. (Although the Beatles' records were released on Apple, the recordings were still owned by EMI with whom the group were contracted.) In March Ringo Starr wound up his building business,

started soon after the Beatles became big as a way of investing his royalties. 'It was no good', he said. 'Nobody could afford to buy any houses since Harold [Wilson, Labour Prime Minister] came to power.'

In November Cynthia Lennon finally divorced John, who had left her for the twice-married Yoko Ono. Yoko was into art films. Her *Film No 4* consisted of 365 bare bottoms paraded across the screen for one and a half hours. She planned to follow this with a shorter film, 45 minutes of John Lennon standing absolutely still, smiling. The film had been shot in three minutes, and then slowed down, a technique Yoko Ono was pioneering. The couple also released the **Two Virgins** LP. Of little musical merit, the album cover aroused considerable controversy. Yoko was quoted as saying of the album, 'even the process of distribution will, in its own way, be artistic and tactful.' Apple's distributor EMI did not see it that way, and refused to handle the album with its picture of John and Yoko naked on the front cover. EMI sent a telex to all their overseas subsidiaries forbidding them to handle it either.

On the record front the Beatles maintained their position as the biggest-selling act in the world. They started the year with the **Magical Mystery Tour** double EP at No 1 in one of the British charts, and **Hello Goodbye** at the top of the other two and No 1 in America. **Lady Madonna** made No 1 in two British charts, though it failed to reach the top in America. **Hey Jude** made up for this, spending seven weeks as America's No 1 as well as topping all the British charts (entering one of them at No 1 in its first week of release.) On the album front the group released their only studio double album, **The Beatles**. Known as the **White Album** because of its plain white cover, on its first week of release it entered the LP charts at No 1 and the singles charts at No 20. In April EMI announced that total Beatles sales had passed 230 million. The Beatles cartoon film *Yellow Submarine* was screened in July, and was met with greater acclaim than the *Magical Mystery Tour* film had been, though that was not saying much.

Rock'n'roll

The great British rock'n'roll revival got under way early in the year. MCA re-released Buddy Holly's **Peggy Sue** and Bill Haley's **Rock Around The Clock**. Both made the charts again. Bill Haley's *Rock Around The Clock* film was also re-released. In May Haley and his Comets returned to Britain and played a concert at the Royal Albert Hall with Duane Eddy. The Everly Brothers visited Britain, as did Carl Perkins, Johnny Cash and his wife June Carter.

Cliff Richard and the Shadows celebrated ten years at the top, and Cliff had his tenth British No 1 with his Eurovision song **Congratulations**, which was also his 50th chart entry. Though he came second in the contest to Spanish singer Massiel, it was Cliff who had the bigger hit throughout Europe. He even knocked Massiel off the top of the charts in Spain. The Shadows announced that they would split up in December, though a decade later they were to reform.

Cliff Richard played a dramatic role in the *Two A Penny* film for the Billy Graham Organization, having decided not to quit the pop world but further his Christian beliefs as a rock singer. He also made his debut acting in a TV play, in *A Matter Of Diamonds*. He was recruited to help an anti-drugs campaign similar to that later launched in New York. There, Performers Against Drugs was headed by Neil Diamond, who had written hits for the Monkees and then become a successful singer himself. He tied with Frank Sinatra in the *Cash Box* 1967 DJ poll as Top Male Singer.

Love and Marriage

There was much speculation about Lulu's love life. She blamed this press attention for breaking up her romance with Bee Gee Maurice Gibb. She then dated Monkee Davy Jones for several months, before getting back with Gibb, whom she later married and later still divorced. Shadow Bruce Welsh was sued for divorce by his wife, who cited Olivia Newton-John. Though Olivia and Bruce later got engaged, the romance cooled and Bruce subsequently married someone else. Shandie Shaw married fashion designer Jeff Banks. In May Cliff Richard's manager Peter Gormley married dancer Audrey Bayley. In July the Bee Gees' drummer Colin Peterson married Joanne Newfield in Nassau, and Monkee Micky Dolenz married 'Top Of The Tops' girl Samantha Juste in California.

Peter Noone (Herman of Herman's Hermits) married Mireille Strasser in November.

Who drummer Keith Moon announced that he had been married for two years, and had a child. Though other members of the Who knew, he had kept the marriage a secret from the fans. Elvis and Priscilla Presley had a daughter, Lisa Marie, on 1 February. One rock couple who were not planning to get married were Mick Jagger and Marianne Faithfull, even though Marianne announced that she was expecting Mick's baby.

The Rolling Stones had a better year than in 1967. They hired Jimmy Miller to produce their records, and in June fled the Olympic Sound Studios in London when a fire started during a Stones session. They had only one worldwide single release, **Jumping Jack Flash**. It was a transatlantic No 1, and 20 years later is still regarded as a Stones classic. In some countries, including the USA and Germany, Decca issued **Street Fighting Man**. Though a hit in much of Europe and Asia, it got so little radio exposure in the States (where most radio stations banned it) that it barely made the Top 50 there.

America Fights Back

By 1968 the British invasion of America had slowed down, and the Americans had counter-attacked. As well as the exciting developments on the West Coast, many American stars visited Britain. The Association, Aretha Franklin, Reparata and the Delrons, Bobby Goldsboro, Edwin Starr, Tommy James and the Shondelles, Canned Heat, the Doors and Judy Collins all came. Old American stars making return visits included the Beach Boys, Bruce Channel, Gene Pitney, Bobby Vee and Roy Orbison. Tragedy struck Orbison only a year after his wife was killed in a motorbike accident. While he has in Britain, two of his three young sons were burned to death in a fire at his American home.

Among those British acts crossing the Atlantic in the other direction were Procul Harum, Eric Burdon and the Animals, Status Quo (who never really made it in America), the Move, the Hollies, the Herd, the Who, Amen Corner and the British blues group Fleetwood Mac. A major campaign was organized to launch the Bee Gees in America. Dusty Springfield made three visits to the States in 1968, and signed a new recording deal that tied her to Atlantic in America, where her records were produced by Jerry Wexler. For the rest of the world she remained with Philips under the direction of Johnny Franz.

In May the *New Musical Express* organized their annual popularity poll winners concert, which again proved a major success. Lulu, Scott Walker, Status Quo, the Love Affair, the Association, the Paper Dolls, the Herd, Amen Corner, the Tremeloes, the Move and Dusty Springfield were among the artists performing. Cliff Richard closed the first half, and the Rolling Stones the second.

In August it was reported that the highly successful British-based Australian group the Seekers were to split up. They had had three UK No 1 singles. In November Graham Nash left the Hollies, and Vince Meloaney left the Bee Gees. The following month Traffic split up, and Eric Burdon announced than the Animals were disbanding.

The Media

Diana Ross and the Supremes played three nuns in the jungle in the NBC TV series 'Tarzan'. They turned in a rather different performance in a highly successful cabaret act at the Talk Of The Town in London. They were less successful at the Royal Variety Show, when Diana Ross caused much embarrassment by stopping half way through a number and giving a monologue in praise of Dr Martin Luther King and the struggle of black Americans. The problem of racism in America was highlighted in May when Petula Clark sparked a row when in her American-made TV spectacular she took the arm of her guest on the programme, the leading black entertainer Harry Belafonte. The gesture, which seemed natural to the English star, caused a furore in America.

In Britain the franchises for the commercial ITV channels changed, with some new companies joining the network. In the biggest region, London, two companies shared the franchise. Thames, which broadcast during the week, would end up half-owned by EMI. Tom Jones did a major TV deal with Lew Grade, to make 17 hour-long shows a year for

five years aimed at the American market. Jones claimed that he was paid £9 million for the deal.

Two new pop music shows started in Britain in January. On the BBC 'All Systems Freeman' was a fast moving magazine programme introduced by veteran DJ Alan Freeman. As soon as it finished on a Saturday evening, most ITV regions showed 'New Release', hosted by DJ Tony Blackburn, who had made a name for himself on pirate radio. His show was criticized for being little more than a re-hash of the BBC's old 'Juke Box Jury', which had also featured new releases. Though neither show lasted very long, it was Freeman's that came out on top of the inevitable comparisons that were made between the two.

Simon Dee had the scoop of his career when Jane Asher announced on his 'Dee Time' Saturday BBC television show on 20 July that her seven-month engagement to Paul McCartney was off, and that she had not broken it. Paul and Jane had been going steady for over five years, throughout the whole period of his time as a famous Beatle, and had got engaged on Christmas Day 1967. Tony Palmer made his 'All My Loving' pop documentary for the BBC, featuring interviews with the Beatles and performances by the Animals, Cream, Donovan, Jimi Hendrix, Lulu, Manfred Mann, Pink Floyd and the Who.

In America Don Kirshner was working on creating a new TV series centred around a pop group. After his troubled times on 'The Monkees' project which he had done so much to create, he played it safe with his new venture. The new group were to be a cartoon, though he also put together session musicians for the accompanying records which were issued under the cartoon group's name, the Archies. Their **Sugar Sugar** would be one of the biggest hits in the world in 1969.

Manfred Mann won critical aclaim though few sales for their soundtrack from the *Up The Junction* film. Manfred Mann and Mike Hugg wrote the music for the film, as well as recording the soundtrack with the group.

Marianne Faithfull made her film debut in *Girl On A Motorcycle*. Mick Jagger was filming *Performance* with Anita Pallenberg, girlfriend of Brian Jones and then fellow Rolling Stone Charlie Watts. The Rolling Stones filmed their 'Rock'n'Roll TV Circus' with guests the Who, Eric Clapton, John Lennon and Yoko Ono. Yoko embarrassed everyone when, during an impromptu super-group session involving Lennon, Clapton and a couple of Stones, she walked onto the stage and started wailing. Things slightly improved when she climbed into a large white bag (it was her 'bagism' phase) and carried on wailing. The Herman's Hermits film *Mrs Brown, You've Got A Lovely Daughter* was released. The title track had given the group a million selling US No 1 in 1965.

On the radio front, despite many promises that it was about to return, Radio Caroline remained silent. The only pirate left afloat was the original one, the Dutch station Radio Veronica. Caroline's boss Ronan O'Rahilly became a business adviser to the Beatles' Apple. Former pirate DJ Kenny Everett had his BBC Radio 1 show axed. He claimed that this was because he spoke his mind about the BBC. In the eighties the BBC gave him a highly successful television comedy programme. The veteran 'Saturday Club' was also axed by BBC Radio 1 after over 500 shows.

The Record Industry

There was an increase in new record labels. The American company MCA, which included American Decca and Uni (Universal Studios), set up in Britain. So did RCA, one of the three biggest companies in America. In March records from the Bell, Amy and Mala labels were issued in Britain on Bell. They were licensed through EMI, which also captured British rights to Dunhill from RCA and Stax/Volt from Polydor. Brian Epstein's old company NEMS launched its own label in March, distributed via CBS. Britain's biggest-selling album, **The Sound Of Music**, passed the two-million sales mark in Britain alone.

World News

In what was a particularly violent world in 1968, Britain had a relatively tranquil year. In January five London typists started the I'm Backing Britain campaign that soon caught the public's immagination. There was a violent demonstration outside the American Embassy in Leicester Square, with left-wing demonstrators attacking the police and attempting to storm the Embassy in protest at America's involvement in the Vietnam War and the support given to America by Britain's Labour Government. The Foreign Secretary and Deputy Leader of that Government, the erratic George Brown, resigned after another row with his colleagues in March. In April leading Tory politician Enoch Powell made his famous 'river of blood' speech attacking coloured immigration. Conservation leader Edward Health considered the speech racist and promptly sacked Powell from the Shadow Cabinet.

The Grosvenor Square riot was nothing compared to student unrest in other parts of Europe, especially France. Vast numbers of students threw up barricades in Paris and threw petrol bombs at the police. The students were supported by half the work force of France, with strikes paralysing the country. After weeks of unrest a general strike forced President De Gaulle to act. He dissolved Parliament and called a general election. For a short while France hovered on the brink of civil war, and De Gaulle prepared to flee to Germany. The army remained loyal, De Gaulle stood his ground and then won a landslide in the election. France's worst violence since the wartime occupation was then over.

In Czechoslovakia a more liberal Communist regime came to power under Alexander Dubcek. The Prague Spring of reforms followed, which caused considerable alarm in the Soviet Union. On 22 August the Russian Army invaded, and the short lived reform was snuffed out. The Russians invoked the Brezhnev Doctrine, claiming a right to intervene in any East European country if they felt their interests required it.

In Rome the Pope issued the Humanae Vitae encyclical banning birth control. This order to Roman Catholics throughout the world to avoid any form of artificial birth control, which the Pope said was against God's will, was met with considerable opposition from within the Catholic Church, especially those from Latin America where Catholic countries had huge overpopulation problems.

1968 was a year of unusual violence in America, with the twin issues of Vietnam and racism that bedevilled America throughout the sixties reaching a new peak of divisiveness. In January the Viet Cong launched the Tet Offensive against South Vietnamese cities, temporarily occupying the American Embassy in Saigon. The Americans and South Vietnamese Army hit back in February, recapturing the city of Hue from the Communists. In March Robert Kennedy announced that he would run for the Democratic Party's nomination for the Presidency, against this party's sitting candidate Lyndon Johnson. Two weeks later Johnson astonished America by announcing on television that he would not seek re-election as President in the November election.

On 4 April the civil rights leader Dr Martin Luther King was gunned down in Memphis, Tennessee. His assassination sparked off serious rioting in cities across America. On 6 June Bobby Kennedy was shot dead in Los Angeles. In one of the bitterest primary campaigns in the Democrats' history, they picked the liberal Vice President Hubert Humphrey as their nominee for President, but their Chicago Convention was turned into a disaster by the violence of Mayor Richard Daley's Chicago Police. What Democrat Senator Ribicoff called the 'gestapo tactics' of the police against anti Vietnam War demonstrators outside the Convention were televised coast to coast, projecting a dreadful image to the voters. In November the Republican Richard Nixon was elected President with Spiro T. Agnew as Vice President, though the Democrats retained control of both Houses of Congress.

Sport

Even the 1968 Mexico City Olympics were dominated by violence and controversy. A student riot in the city was brutally crushed before the games began. South Africa was invited to take part, then the invitation was withdrawn to avoid a walk-out from Third-World countries. Black American athletes like Tommie Smith gave the Black Power clenched-fist salute on the medal podium, causing embarrassment to America. The USA won the largest number of gold medals with 45, followed by the Russians with 29 and the Japanese with 11. Britain came eighth in the gold list with five, the same number as West Germany and Australia though they both won more silver and bronze medals.

Cricket was badly shaken when the South African Government banned the MCC from touring the country after they picked Basil d'Oliveira to play for England. Before emigrating to Britain d'Oliveira had been a South African Cape Coloured. England and Australia drew their Test Match series in England, while England beat the West Indies when touring there. Yorkshire were County Cricket Champions for the third year running, and their outstanding bowler Fred Truman retired from cricket at the end of the season.

Manchester United won the European Cup, and their Georgie Best was voted footballer of the year. He lent his support to an anti-smoking campaign, which followed from a major report linking smoking with cancer published in 1967. It was a good year for Manchester. Manchester City were top of League Division One, with Manchester United second. West Bromwich Albion beat Everton for the FA Cup, and Leeds United won the League Cup. In Scotland Celtic were top of the First Division and won the League Cup. Dunfermline won the Scottish FA Cup.

In America the Detroit Tigers won the World Series. The Green Bay Packers won the second Super Bowl, just as they had won the first championship the year before. The Baltimore Colts won the NFL championship and the New York Jets won the AFL title.

Films

Veteran actor John Wayne was the most popular film star in Britain in 1968, followed by Julie Christie and Steve McQueen. *The Jungle Book* was the biggest money maker of the year. Other major films were *Barbarella*, *The Good, The Bad, And The Ugly*, *Poor Cow*, *Planet Of The Apes*, *Up The Junction* and *Rosemary's Baby*, which starred Frank Sinatra's wife Mia Farrow.

Oliver! won the Oscar for Best Film, with its director Sir Carol Reed picking up the Oscar for Best Director. The Best Actor award went to Cliff Robertson for his performance in *Charly*. The Best Actress Oscar was shared by two women. Katharine Hepburn's performance in *The Lion In Winter* was honoured, as was Barbra Streisand for her part in *Funny Girl*. The Best Film in the British Film Academy Awards was *The Graduate*, a film that did much for Simon and Garfunkel who wrote and performed the music for the soundtrack.

Bubblegum and Hair

Though Britain remained an important repertoire source in 1968, it was America that made most of the running in pop music. The parameters of American rock ranged from the bubblegum of the 1910 Fruitgum Company and the Ohio Express's **Yummy, Yummy, Yummy** to the stage performance of the rock musical *Hair*. That arrived across the Atlantic just in time to benefit from the abolition of stage censorship by the Lord Chamberlain.

It was somehow appropriate that the first challenge to the establishment after abolition should have been this celebration of hippy values. With its nudity, anti-authority message, liberal use of the word *fuck*, deafening volume and psychedelic lighting, it seemed to sum up the latest message of youth. But things change fast in the music world. As 1968 drew to a close, a very different and far simpler sound was heard from a new American group, drawing its inspiration from a more traditional source than flower power. However, the story of Creedence Clearwater Revival belongs to 1969.

VARIOUS ARTISTS
American

ORIGINAL THEATRE CAST WITH GEROME RAGNI, JAMES RADO, SHELLEY PLIMPTON, RONALD DYSON, LYNN KELLOGG, LAMONT WASHINGTON, MELBA MOORE AND COMPANY; ORCHESTRA CONDUCTED BY GALT MacDERMOT

HAIR (Album) *RCA Victor 1150 [USA] RCA SF 7959 [UK]*. Hair, billed as America's first 'tribal love-rock musical', became a Broadway landmark overnight and made producers realize that rock music could be successful on the legitimate stage. The story concerns the activities of a number of freaky contemporary youths, the music a potpourri of modern pop sounds linked together in composer Galt MacDermot's individual style. The book and lyrics were written by two actors, Gerome Ragni and James Rado, who between 1965 and 1967 had spent two years listening to rock sounds among the devotees of 'underground' music.

In 1967 they showed their first draft of the script of *Hair* to well-known author Nat Shapiro who suggested the wild and weirdly creative Galt MacDermot, a Canadian and son of a diplomat, musically educated in South Africa, to write the music. MacDermot had composed 'African Waltz' in 1961, a modern jazz work that was a sizeable hit (two Grammy Awards 1961), and was well equipped to undertake the score of *Hair*, being one of the few musicians who understood the roots and dynamics of the new popular music.

Hair was chosen by Joseph Papp for the launching of his part-subsidized New York Shakespeare Public Theatre (October 1967). The eight-week run was a sell-out and RCA recorded an original cast album. The show was then moved to the Cheetah, a Broadway *palais de danse*, but this proved unsatisfactory. Eventually, Michael Butler brought the show to Broadway and presented it at the Biltmore Theatre on 29 April 1968 after substantial revision of the book, music and lyrics. It became an important contribution to Broadway, a revolution both in theatre and in music. The London production opened on 27 September 1968 at the Shaftesbury Theatre, with productions following in Copenhagen, Stockholm, Acapulco, Munich, Los Angeles, Paris, Milan, Sydney, Tokyo, Belgrade, Amsterdam and every major city in the USA and Canada. By April 1969, three of its tunes — the title song, **Aquarius, Let the Sunshine In** — were Nos 1 and 2 on the US singles charts and the album of the Broadway version was No 1 on the album charts. The album of the Broadway theatre cast was issued in June 1968 and received a Gold Disc award in early 1969 from RIAA. It subsequently went on to sell over five million copies by mid-1971 and in due course was to receive a Grammy Award for 'Best Score from an Original Cast Show Album' of 1968.

The Broadway cast album comprised: **Aquarius** (Ronald Dyson and the Company); **Donna** (Gerome Ragni and the Company); **Hashish** (the Company); **Sodomy** (Steve Curry and the Company); **Coloured Spade** (Lamont Washington and the Company); **Manchester, England** (James Rado and the Company); **I'm Black** (Washington, Curry, Ragni and Rado); **Ain't Got No** (Curry, Washington, Melba, Moore and the Company); **Air** (Sally Eaton, Shelley Plimpton, Moore and the Company); **Initials** (the Company); **I Got Life** (Rado and the Company); **Hair** (Rado, Ragni and Company); **My Conviction** (Jonathan Kramer); **Don't Put It Down** Ragni and the Company); **Frank Mills** (Shelley Plimpton); **Be-in** (the Company); **Where Do I Go** (Rado and the Company); **Black Boys** (Diane Keaton, Suzannah Nostrand, Natalie Mosco); **White Boys** (Moore, Lorri Davis, Emmaretta Marks); **Easy To Be Hard** (Lynn Kellogg); **Walking in Space** (the Company); **Abie Baby** (Washington, Dyson, Donnie Burks and Davis); **Three-Five-Zero-Zero** (the Company); **What a Piece of Work Is Man** (Dyson and Walter Harris); **Good Morning Starshine** (Kellogg, Moore, Rado and Ragni); **The Flesh Failures — Let the Sunshine In** (Rado, Kellogg, Moore and the Company).

This album was No 1 in the USA for 20 weeks and in the bestseller charts for 151 weeks, into 1971.

HERB ALPERT AND THE TIJUANA BRASS
American

THIS GUY'S IN LOVE WITH YOU *A&M 929 [USA] A&M AMS 727 [UK]*. This song, with its unusual range of an octave and a fifth, was written by ace songwriters Hal David (words) and Burt Bacharach (music) for trumpeter Herb Alpert to sing on a CBS-TV special on 22 April 1968.

Alpert wanted something different for the programme so he sang the number to his wife Sharon. He had no intention of releasing the record as a single, but after the TV show was flooded with calls the following morning he put it out right away. It shot to No 1 within six weeks and stayed there for four weeks with 14 weeks in the USA bestsellers, and a Gold Disc award for million sale (August) from RIAA. In Britain, the disc was released on 14 June and reached No 1 for one week, selling over 250,000 with 16 weeks in the bestsellers.

The disc was the first No 1 ever for the David-Bacharach team in the USA.

Although this was the first big hit for Alpert as a singer, he had actually made two vocal records in 1960 while under contract for a year to RCA with the name of Dore Alpert, and in 1962 made his first vocal disc **Tell It To the Birds** for A&M, one of the label's first records.

THE BEAT OF THE BRASS (Album) *A&M 4146 [USA] A&M AMLS 916 [UK]*. Another colossal success for Herb Alpert, his 10th album contained numbers from his CBS-TV special on 22 April 1968. It was No 1 for four weeks in the USA and stayed in the charts for 54 weeks. Advance order pressings were over a million and an RIAA Gold Disc award was made at the beginning of August.

The album contains **Monday, Monday**, by John Philips (1966); **A Beautiful Friend**, by Sol Lake (1968); **Cabaret** (from the show *Cabaret*), by Fred Ebb and John Kander (1966); **Panama**, by Julius Wechter (1968); **Belz mein shtetele belz** ('My home town'), by Jacob Jacobs and Alexander Olshanetsky; **Talk to the Animals** (from the film *Dr Doolittle*), by Leslie Bricusse (1967); **Slick**, by Herb Alpert and John Pisano (1968); **She Touches Me**, by Sol Lake (1968); **Thanks for the Memory** (from the film *Big Broadcast of 1938*), by Leo Robin and Ralph Rainger (1938); **The Robin**, by John Pisano (1968); **This Guy's in Love with You**, by Hal David and Burt Bacharach (1968).

ANTOINE
French

LA TRAMONTANA (The bearings) *Vogue-Saar 2022 [Italy]*. Another big success for Italian songwriters D. Pace (words) and Mario Panzeri (music), Antoine's disc was No 1 for 10 weeks in Italy and also a big hit in France. Italian sales reached a million.

The song was first sung by Antoine in the 1968 San Remo Song Festival, with French and German versions being recorded later. It is an amusing song expressly made in Antoine's 'Italian' style of direct folk inspiration with a catchy melody and samba rhythm.

Antoine (real name Pierre Antoine Muraccioli) was born in 1945 in Tamatave, one of Madagascar's main ports. He was the son of a Corsican public works engineer who took his family to Canada, America and Africa before settling in Paris when Antoine was 16. Antoine quickly became one of France's leading pop-folk singers and he was awarded the Prix d'Honneur for his performance of this song. His discs were said to outsell those by Charles Aznavour, Johnny Hallyday and Yves Montand combined. He first achieved success in early 1966 with his particular brand of protest songs such as **La guerre**. **Antoine's Lucubrations**, in a lighter vien, was a big seller in France. Maurice Chevalier observed, 'Never in French show business has an artist reached the top so fast.' It took Antoine four months to do so in 1966, after fantastic scenes at the Paris Olympic Music Hall.

The disc was released in Britain on 5 April 1968 on the Vogue label.

APHRODITE'S CHILD
Greek

RAIN AND TEARS *Philips 7164 [France] Mercury MF 1039 [UK]*. **Rain and Tears** is an old tune originally written by the seventeenth-century German organist-composer Johann Pachelbel (1653-1706). It was arranged by Vangelis Papathanassiou of the group with B. Bergman.

The group started working and recording in Greece around 1963, playing English and American songs. They found it difficult to get real success with this type of music and decided to try their luck in England. Being held up by a transport strike in Paris during the student demonstrations proved to be lucky for them. They were heard by Philips Records producer Pierre Sberre who was greatly impressed and signed them to the label immediately. Their success with this song, sung in English, was almost instantaneous in France. It got into the charts there within three days and soon after was No 1, staying top for a record 14 weeks, and was also a huge hit right across the Continent and Scandinavia. It also achieved No 27 in Britain with seven weeks in the bestsellers.

Each of the trio are accomplished musicians. Evangelos Papathanassiou, born in Valos, Greece, on 29 March 1943, Demis Roussos was born in Alexandria of Greek parents on 15 June 1947. Lucas Sideras was born in Athens on 5 December 1944. After the group split up in the mid-1970s, Demis Roussos became an internationally successful solo singer. Evangelos Papathanassiou teamed up with Jon Anderson, formerly of Yes, as Jon and Vangelis, Vangelis then became a successful composer and had a major hit with the *Chariots of Fire* film soundtrack.

THE ASSOCIATION   *American*

GREATEST HITS (Album) **Warner Brothers-7 Arts 1967** [*USA*]. This Californian soft rock six-piece band enjoyed a number of big hits in the mid to late sixties. Their first million seller was *Cherish* (see 1966). After three million-selling singles, their fourth disc past the seven-figure sales mark was a 'greatest hits' package. Of their 10 hit albums, this was the most successful. It reached No 4, with 75 weeks in the Top 200. It won an RIAA Gold Disc for million dollar sales on 3 March 1969, and was certificated Platinum for million unit sales on 13 October 1986. As the Association had hardly any hits in Britain (only **Time for Living** made the charts, in 1968, peaking at No 23), there was not much demand for a 'greatest hits (or hit?)' album, and the record did not sell in Britain.

The tracks on the album were: [1]**Time It Is Today** (written by Russ Giguere); [1]**Everything That Touches You** (Terry Kirkman); [1]**Like Always** (Larry Ramos/Bob Alcivar/Tony Ortega); [1]**Never My Love** (Don and Dick Addrial); [1]**Requiem For The Masses** (Terry Kirkman); [2]**Along Comes Mary** (Tandyn Almer); [3]**Enter The Young** (Terry Kirkman); [4]**No Fair At All** (James Yester); [1]**Time For Livin'** (Don and Dick Adrial); [1]**We Love** (Ted Bluechel); [2]**Cherish** (Terry Kirkman); [1]**Windy** (Ruthann Friedman); and [3]**Six Man Band** (Terry Kirkman). (Tracks were produced by 1) Bone Howe, 2) Curt Boetticher, 3) the Association and 4) Jerry Yester.)

THE BEATLES   *British*

LADY MADONNA *Parlophone R 5675* [*UK*]/ *Capitol 2138* [*USA*]. The Beatles' 42nd million seller was the Lennon-McCartney **Lady Madonna**, a record whose style was a return to rock'n'roll a world away from the psychedelia of **Sgt Pepper**. It was produced by George Martin at Abbey Road in February 1968, with Ken Scott as engineer and Richard Lush as tape operator. Though John and Paul continued to label all their songs as combined compositions they were increasingly working apart, and this was really the work of Paul.

The record gave the Beatles their third British No 1 of 1968 (**Hello Goodbye** and the **Magical Mystery Tour** double EP being the

others) and topped the charts for two weeks. It spent only eight weeks in the Top 50, the shortest chart duration of their whole career (prior to their break-up) except for an old Polydor release from their German days, **Ain't She Sweet**, which managed only six weeks in 1964. It won the Beatles their 22nd Silver Disc for British sales. In America it failed to make the top, peaking at No 2 for three weeks in *Cash Box* and No 4 in *Billboard*. It brought to an end a run of 12 records that had made No 1 in at least one of the four main American charts. It remained in the *Cash Box* and *Billboard* charts for 11 weeks.

In *Billboard* the George Harrison composed flip side **The Inner Light** made a chart appearance for one week, at No 96. This had been recorded in January at EMI's Gramophone Company of India studios in Bombay, with further work done later at Abbey Road. George Harrison produced the track with Vijay Dubey, using Indian musicians. The engineers were J.P. Sen and S.N. Gupta. The team for the Abbey Road work was George Martin, Geoff Emerick, Ken Scott and Richard Lush.

Lady Madonna won the Beatles their 15th RIAA Gold Disc single on 8 April 1968. The record was the usual big hit around the world, though with rather fewer No 1s than usual. It made the charts in Canada, Australia, New Zealand, South Africa, Ireland, Finland, Sweden, Norway, Denmark, Germany, Austria, Switzerland, Belgium, the Netherlands, France, Spain, Italy, Israel, Lebanon, Malaysia, Singapore, Japan, Mexico, Argentina and Brazil.

HEY JUDE *Apple (Parlophone) R 5722* [*UK*]/*Apple (Capitol) 2276* [*USA*]. **Hey Jude** was the first Beatles record issued on their own record label Apple. In fact the Beatles were never signed to Apple. They had a long term contract with EMI, which agreed to release their records with an Apple logo on them, but they remained EMI-owned recordings and in Britain retained the Parlophone R prefix in their catalogue number.

Hey Jude was written by John Lennon and Paul McCartney, with Paul taking the lead. It was produced by George Martin at the end of July and the beginning of August, assisted by Ken Scott as engineer and John Smith as tape operator. They used the Abbey Road studios and the new independent Trident Studios, which had the advantage of an eight-track tape recorder. (Abbey Road had an eight-track machine, but it had not yet been fully installed.) **Hey Jude** was a beautiful ballad recorded with a 40-piece orchestra, and was the longest of all the Beatles singles, lasting seven minutes and eleven seconds.

Released on 30 August in Britain (and 26 August in America) it was another transatlantic No 1. It did particularly well in America. Critics who said that **Lady Madonna** failing to top the charts showed that the Beatles were on the way down had to eat their words as **Hey Jude** sat at the top for nine weeks, the longest run at the top of their entire career. It was in the *Billboard* and *Cash Box* charts for 19 weeks, and was followed to the top on both sides of the Atlantic by a second Apple record, Mary Hopkin's

Those Were The Days. The flip side **Revolution** also charted. This was a John Lennon composition, recorded at Abbey Road in May and June. It reached No 11 in *Cash Box* and No 12 in *Billboard*, with 10 and 11 weeks on each of those charts. An RIAA Gold Disc was awarded on 13 September 1968. The record was a massive hit around the world, entering the British, Irish and Danish charts at No 1 the first week of release, and topping the charts in Canada, Australia, New Zealand, South Africa, Finland, Sweden, Norway, Germany, Austria, Belgium, the Netherlands, Spain, the Philippines, Mexico and Brazil, and made the Top 10 in Switzerland, France, Italy, Lebanon, Japan, Argentina and Chile.

THE BEATLES (Double Album) *Apple (Parlophone) PMC 7067/7068* [*UK*]/*Apple (Capitol) SWBO 101* [*USA*]. **The Beatles**, commonly known as the White Album from the all-white album jacket, was the only studio double album that the group made. In fact it was more a collection of solo efforts than a genuine group effort, though all members of the group did contribute something to most of the tracks. Although this reflected the fact that the Beatles were beginning to fall apart as a group, the album was their biggest-selling LP ever. Its content was simpler than their two previous LPs, many of the tracks harking back to the Beatles' earlier style. It was produced by George Martin, though the individual Beatles were increasingly involved with the production of their songs. Most of the work was done at Abbey Road, though the Trident Studio was also used.

Released on 22 November 1968 the double album entered the British LP charts at No 1 (and also made the singles Top 20.) It spent eight weeks at the top, and 22 weeks in the charts. In America it was No 1 for nine weeks, and in the charts for 144 weeks. It won an RIAA Gold Disc on 6 December 1968. It was the group's biggest album in the USA, with North American sales of over six and a half million.

The tracks on the album, all of which were listed as Lennon-McCartney compositions unless otherwise indicated, were as follows: **Back In The USSR**; **Dear Prudence**; **Glass Onion**; **Ob-La-Di Ob-La-Da**; **Wild Honey Pie**; **The Continuing Story Of Bungalow Bill**; **While My Guitar Gently Weeps**, by George Harrison; **Happiness Is A Warm Gun**; **Martha My Dear**; **I'm So Tired**; **Blackbird**; **Piggies**, by George Harrison; **Rocky Racoon**; **Don't Pass Me By**, by Ringo Starr; **Why Don't We Do It In The Road**; **I Will**; **Julia**; **Birthday**; **Yer Blues**; **Mother Nature's Son**; **Everybody's Got Something To Hide Except Me And My Monkey**, by all four Beatles; **Sexie Sadie**; **Helter Skelter**; **Long Long Long**, by George Harrison; **Revolution 1**; **Honey Pie**; **Savoy Truffle**, by George Harrison; **Cry Baby Cry**; **Revolution 9**; and **Good Night**.

OB-LA-DI OB-LA-DA *Apple (Various national Parlophone numbers)/Capitol 4347* [*USA*]. This track off the **Beatles** double album was the only Beatles single to sell a million copies before it was released in either Britain or America. The group's 45th million seller was an overseas release put out by many EMI subsidiaries, but not released in Britain or (until 1976) the USA. It was listed as a Lennon-McCartney composition, though in fact it was Paul's. It went to No 1 in Australia, New Zealand, South Africa, Germany, Austria, Switzerland, the Philippines, Japan, Brazil, Chile and Argentina. It made the Top 10 in Finland, Sweden, Belgium, the Netherlands, France, Spain, Italy, Israel and the Lebanon. It was the most commercial track on the whole double album, a fact many other artists recognized by covering it. Marmalade got a British No 1 with their version. Once the Beatles had broken up, Capitol belatedly put the record out in 1976. By then the Beatles were no longer the force they had once been, and the disc made No 49 with six weeks in the *Billboard* charts, and No 47 with seven weeks in *Cash Box*. If it had been released with the album in 1968, it would have been a different story.

THE BEE GEES   *British/Australian*

WORDS *Atco 6548* [*USA*] *Polydor 56 229* [*UK*]. This million-seller was written by the three brothers Barry, Robin and Maurice Gibb of the group. The disc was released in mid-January in the USA and in Britain on 26 January. It achieved No 8 in Britain for one week with 10 weeks in the bestsellers and No 15 In the USA for one week with 11 weeks in the bestsellers, but was even more successful in Europe where it was No 1 in Germany, Holland and Switzerland with big sales. It sold two million globally.

I'VE GOTTA GET A MESSAGE TO YOU *Poldor 56 273* [*UK*] *Atco 6603* [*USA*]. Another big hit for the Bee Gees, written by the three brothers Barry, Robin and Maurice Gibb. The disc was released in Britain on 2 August 1968, and in the USA a week later. Sales in Britain were over 250,000 where it was No 1 for a week and 15 weeks in the bestsellers. In the USA it was No 3 for one week with 13 weeks in the bestsellers. The record was a global million seller by the end of September 1968.

ARCHIE BELL AND THE DRELLS *American*

TIGHTEN UP *Atlantic 2478* [*USA*]. Archie Bell and the Drells made this disc in Texas where it was broadcast by Don Sundeen, programme director for station KCOH-Houston and the station's disc jockey. Atlantic then picked up the master. The disc was released at the end of March 1968 and sold the million by May, with an RIAA Gold Disc award. It was No 1 for two weeks in the USA and 15 weeks in the bestsellers.

The song was written by Archie Bell and Billy Buttier.

BIG BROTHER AND   *American*
THE HOLDING COMPANY
WITH JANIS JOPLIN

CHEAP THRILLS (Album) *CBS-Columbia CS 9700* [*USA*]. Big Brother and the Holding Company comprised Sam Andrew (guitars), James Gurley (guitars), Pete Albin (bass) and David Getz (drums). They played regularly at the Avalon Ballroom, San Francisco, and went out on the road in January 1966. Pete Albin was vocalist at the time, but they needed another singer. Their manager decided on Janis Joplin. A small Chicago company, Mainstream, offered Big Brother a chance to record, but their first album was not released until the group got rave reviews and audience reaction at the Monterey Pop Festival in the summer of 1967. The album was not very good but Clive Davis of CBS Records was impressed with Janis' performance. The group were then signed with Albert Grossman as manager in 1968, and in the spring they recorded the album **Cheap Thrills**. This was a colossal success after release in September, and received a Gold Disc award from RIAA for a million dollar sale on 15 October with a subsequent million units sale. It was No 1 for eight weeks in the US charts.

By the end of 1968, Janis Joplin's star status far outweighed the rest of the group, and she went solo.

Janis Joplin was born on 19 January 1943 in Port Arthur, Texas. She listened to Bessie Smith and Leadbelly records, and in the early 1960s began singing country-and-blues music with a blue-grass band. She worked in Austin, Texas, in 1961, and San Francisco in 1962. She also attended the University of Texas for a while and was in and out of college from 1962-6. On her return to San Francisco in 1966, she joined Big Brother and the Holding Company in June. Her performance on stage was very powerful, frantic and passionate. She made three other albums — **I Got Dem Ol' Kozmic Blues Again Mamma** (1969), **Pearl** (1971) (a very big hit), and **In Concert** (1972), the last two released after her death from a drug overdose in a hotel room in Hollywood on 4 October 1970. Her last few years were full of excesses. An album of her greatest hits was released in 1973.

The contents of **Cheap Thrills** were **Combination of the Two**, by Sam Andrew; **I Need a Man**, by Janis Joplin and Sam Andrew; **Summertime** (from *Porgy and Bess*), by DuBose Heyward and George Gershwin (1935); **Piece of My Heart**, by J. Ragovoy and B. Berns; **Turtle Blues**, by Janis Joplin; **Oh, Sweet Mary**, by Janis Joplin; **Ball and Chain**, by Mama Willie Mae Thornton.

THE BOX TOPS   *American*

CRY LIKE A BABY *Mala 593* [*USA*] *Bell 1001* [*UK*]. The second million seller for the Box Tops, the song was written by Dan Penn (producer of the disc for Bell Records) and Spooner Oldham. The disc was released in the USA in mid-February and sold the million by mid-May. It was No 2 for two weeks in the USA with 15 weeks in the bestsellers, and No 14 for one week in Britain with 12 weeks in the bestsellers. British release was on 1 March 1968 on the Bell label. It featured a new hybrid instrument, the electric sitar. The composition is a mid-speed rock-blues. In 1968, Rick Allan took over the bass guitar duties in the group.

RIAA Gold Disc award, 1968.

THE BROOKLYN BRIDGE   *American*

THE WORST THAT COULD HAPPEN *Buddah 75* [*USA*]. The Brooklyn Bridge, a complete, self-contained show band, was formed in 1968 by four singers, each from different groups, with the idea of creating a totally unique musical organization. The four singers were present at the first audition of a newly formed seven-piece band which they liked, and they joined forces to build the Brooklyn Bridge group to play 'blue-eyed soul', hard rock, progressive contemporary sounds and everything in between.

The personnel of the group, 10 men and one woman, were Johnny Maestro (solo vocals), Fred Ferrara, Les Cauchi and Mike Gregorie (solo vocals and harmonic backing), Tom Sullivan (bandleader/arranger/saxophonist), Carolyn Wood (organ), Jimmy Rosica (bass), Richie Macioce (guitar), Artie Catanzarita (drums), Shelly Davis (trumpet and piano) and Joe Ruvio (saxophone).

The group's recording of this brilliant song by Jim Webb was released in November 1968 in the USA, and by mid-March 1969 sold over 1,250,000, with a Gold Disc award from RIAA. The disc was produced by Wes Farrell and reached No 3 for two weeks in the US charts and spent 12 weeks in the bestsellers.

THE CRAZY WORLD OF   *British*
ARTHUR BROWN

FIRE *Track 604 022* [*UK*] *Atlantic 2556* [*USA*]. Arthur Brown's stage routine was one of the most dynamic. He appeared in flowing multi-coloured robes, his face streaked with colourful make-up and a helmet on his head with flames leaping from it. With a band backing him in a mixture of rock, rhythm and blues, jazz and pop, he electrified his audiences with shrieks, jumps, growling and singing.

Arthur Brown was born in Whitby, Yorkshire, on 24 June 1944. He studied law at London University but failed his exams after one year. He then studied philosophy at Reading University, where he formed a college group in the area. Before entering show business he had various occupations such as teacher, dishwasher, road-digger, etc. His fire stage act stemmed from his preoccupation with fire in his youth, and his hobby of going to funfairs.

Fire was written by him with Vincent Crane. It achieved No 1 for one week in Britain and 14 weeks in the bestsellers, and was No 2 for two weeks in the USA with 13 weeks in the bestsellers. It was awarded a Gold Disc from RIAA for the million sale in the USA alone and also had big sales elsewhere. It was released in Britain on 7 June.

GLEN CAMPBELL   *American*

WITCHITA LINEMAN *Capitol 2302* [*USA*] *Ember EMBS 261* [*UK*]. Glen Campbell, the seventh son of a seventh son in a family of 12 children, was born on 22 April 1936 on a farm near Delight, Arkansas. His entire family played musical instruments, so he was sur-

where it reached No 5 for one week with 13 weeks in the bestsellers on the Ember label. Campbell had been offered to Capitol's parent company EMI, but they turned him down. Glen's album of the same title had a 450,000 advance sale, the largest ever for the artist.

WALTER CARLOS AND BENJAMIN FOLKMAN
American

SWITCHED ON BACH (Album) *CBS-Columbia CS 7194* [*USA*]. Released in late 1968, this album was in the bestseller US national charts for 58 weeks and on their best classical sellers chart for the whole of 1969, 1970 and 1971 reached No 10 in the US album charts and was No 1 classical seller for 94 weeks. The disc received three Grammy Awards for 1969 — 'Best Engineered Recording Classical' (Engineer's award to Walter Carlos), 'Best Performance by Instrumental Soloist' (to Walter Carlos on the Moog synthesizer), and 'Best Classical Album of the Year' (performed on the Moog synthesizer by Walter Carlos). It was in the US classical charts for 310 weeks to the end of 1974.

The album used a Moog synthesizer to play Bach. The synthesizer was played by Walter Carlos (born 1941) advised by noted musicologist Benjamin Folkman.

Dr Robert A. Moog of New York (born 1934) began work on the synthesizer in 1964. This piece of electronic wizardry was used in commercials, films and on record to produce a seemingly endless variety of sound effects and music. The synthesizer allows the player to predetermine and reconstitute not only any known sound but also entirely new sounds, never before heard.

Dr Moog took his PhD in engineering before he became interested in setting up the synthesizer in 1964 during his last year at college, and had a team of 20 people working with him, including composers.

The album contained: Side 1 — **Sinfonia to Cantata No 29**; **Air on the G string**; **Two-part Invention in F major**; **Two-part Invention in B flat major**; **Two-part Invention in D minor**; **Jesu Joy of Man's Desiring**; **Prelude and Fugue No 7 in E flat major** (from Book 1, *Well-Tempered Klavier*); Side 2 — **Prelude and Fuge No 2 in C minor** (from Book 1, *Well-Tempered Klavier*); **Chorale Prelude — Wachet auf**; **Brandenburg Concerto No 3 in G major** (1st, 2nd and 3rd movements).

A Gold Disc was awarded by RIAA in August 1969. It was released in Britain on 21 February 1969 on the CBS label.

CLARENCE CARTER
American

SLIP AWAY *Atlantic 2508* [*USA*]. Written by W. Armstrong, W. Terrell and M. Daniel, this song was recorded by Carter in Muscle Shoals, Alabama and produced by Rick Hall in his Fame Recording Studios.

The disc was released in the USA in May 1968 but did not begin attract attention until July. It then climbed the charts steadily, reaching No 6 for one week in October with 16 weeks in the bestsellers, and a Gold Disc award

from RIAA. It was No 2 in the R&B charts for 2 weeks with 19 weeks in the R&B Top 50.

Clarence Carter was originally a gospel singer and made his first recording with his partner Calvin Thomas for Rick Hall. Clarence, who had a degree in music from an Alabama college, was blind. He was a talented arranger, writer and musician, and played guitar, piano and organ. He wrote his arrangements in Braille which were then transposed for the studio musicians.

TOO WEAK TO FIGHT *Atlantic 2569* [*USA*]. A similar type of love song to Clarence Carter's previous big seller **Slip Away**, this disc was released in October 1968. It sold over a million by mid-March and received a Gold Disc award from RIAA. It was No 7 for 2 weeks in the US charts and 13 weeks in he bestsellers. It had 13 weeks in the R&B charts peaking at No 3. The song was written by Clarence Carter, G. Jackson and J. Keyes, and arranged by Rick Hall (producer of the disc).

JOHNNY CASH
American

JOHNNY CASH AT FOLSOM PRISON (Album) *CBS-Columbia 9639* [*USA*] *CBS 63308* [*UK*]. Because of Johnny Cash's great compassion for outcasts, he insisted that this album be recorded 'live' at a concert he gave at California's Folsom Prison. The collection of old and new Cash songs was released in May 1968 in the USA and in Britain on 28 May 1968 (No 7 for one week). It was a colossal success, reaching No 1 on the USA country charts for 10 weeks and staying in the Top 10 for eight months. In the US national charts it reached No 11. The disc sold over the million units by June 1969. Johnny Cash, a solid country-and-western success since 1955, was finally discovered by the US pop world in 1969.

rounded with music from birth. By the age of six he was singing and strumming the guitar on his local radio and at barn dances. He joined a western band in his teens, led by his uncle Dick Bills, in Albuquerque, New Mexico, and appeared with the band on radio and TV for five years. Glen then had his own band for several years before heading for the West Coast. He arrived in Hollywood in 1960 and started to record for the Crest label there, and worked with a vocal and instrumental group, the Champs. He then cut **Turn Around, Look at Me** for Crest Records and the disc brought him national popularity (1961). This success resulted in an exclusive contract with Capitol Records (1962). A proficient artist on drums, bass, violin, mandolin and harmonica, this helped Glen to find work as a studio musician, and he played on sessions for many star artists including Nat 'King' Cole and Frank Sinatra in addition to making some recordings himself. He was briefly a member of the Beach Boys.

It wasn't until he recorded **Gentle on My Mind** (1967) that his name was noted seriously in America. This disc was a hit and the subsequent **By The Time I Get to Phoenix** achieved No 1 in the US charts plus three Grammy Awards. By 1968, Glen was the toast of the American music scene with three million dollar albums simultaneously certified by RIAA in November 1968.

Witchita Lineman, a melancholy love ballad with an eerie production atmosphere, was released in October 1968 and sold over 700,000 in two months, reaching the million by March 1969 plus a Gold Disc award by RIAA and a Grammy Award for the 'Best Engineered (Popular) Recording' of 1968. The song was written by America's Jim Webb, and the disc was No 2 for one week and in the US bestsellers for 15 weeks. It was also a success in Britain

The contents of the album are: **Folsom Prison Blues**, by Johnny Cash (1956); **Dark as the Dungeon**, by Merle Travers (1968); **I Still Miss Someone**, by R. Cash and Johnny Cash (1958); **Cocaine Blues**, by T.J. Arnall (1968); **25 Minutes to Go**, by Shel Silverstein (1962); **Orange Blossom Special**, by E.T. Rouse (1965); **Long Black Veil**, by Danny Dill and Marijohn Wilkin (1959); **Send a Picture of Mother**, by Johnny Cash (1968); **Wall**, by Harlan Howard (1968); **Dirty Old Eggsucking Dog**, by J.H. Clement (1966); **Flushed from the Bathroom of Your Heart**, by J.H. Clement (1968); **Jackson**, by G. Rodgers and B. Wheeler (1967); **Give My Love to Rose**, by Johnny Cash (1957); **I Got Stripes**, by Charlie Williams and Johnny Cash (1959); **Green, Green Grass of Home**, by Claude (Curly) Putman, Jr. (1965); **Greystone Chapel**, by G. Shirley (1968).

This album stayed in the bestseller charts in the USA for 122 weeks. It was awarded a Gold Disc for million dollar sales on 30 October 1968, and a Double Platinum award for sales of two million units on 21 November 1986.

CLASSICS IV *American*

STORMY *Imperial 66328* [*USA*]. Written by B. Buie and J. Cobb, **Stormy** was No 2 for one week in the USA and 15 weeks in the bestsellers. The disc, issued in mid-September, features Dennis Yost and was taken from the Imperial album **Mammas and Papas/Soul Train**. The disc sold a million, the second to do so for the group. It won an RIAA Gold Disc award.

CREAM *British*

WHITE ROOM *Polydor 56 300* [*UK*] *Atco 6617* [*USA*]. Written by Jack Bruce and Ginger Baker of the trio, this song was first included in their album **Wheels of Fire** which was itself a very big seller. When this track was issued as a single by popular demand, it got to No 6 for three weeks in the US charts with 11 weeks in the bestsellers, was No 28 in Britain with eight weeks in the bestsellers, and sold an estimated million globally.

CREEDENCE CLEARWATER REVIVAL *American*

CREEDENCE CLEARWATER REVIVAL (Album) *Fantasy 8382* [*USA*]. The first album by this outstanding group was released in spring 1968. It was awarded a Gold Disc by RIAA on 16 December 1970 for a million dollar sale and subsequently sold a million units. The album contained one of their big hits, **Susie Q**, which lasted eight and a half minutes. (See 1969 for biographical data.)

The contents of the album are: **I Put a Spell on You**, by Screaming Jay Hawkins; **99½ Won't Do**, by Wilson Pickett and S. Cooper; **Susie Q**, by Dale Hawkins, Stanley Lewis and Eleanor Broadwater (1957); **Walk on the Water**, by John Fogerty; **Get Down Woman**, by John Fogerty; **Working Man**, by John Fogerty; **Porterville**, by John Fogerty; **Gloomy**, by John Fogerty.

TYRONE DAVIS *American*

CAN I CHANGE MY MIND? *Dakar 602* [*USA*]. Blues singer Davis came from Chicago and once served as a chauffeur for soul-singer Freddie King who also recorded for Cotillion Records, a new subsidary label started by Atlantic Records in 1968. Cotillion distributed Dakar products, and this disc was its first million seller (by February 1969) released in November 1968. It reached No 5 for two weeks in the US charts with 13 weeks in the bestsellers, and was awarded a Gold Disc by RIAA in February 1969. It was also No 1 for three weeks in the rhythm-and-blues charts.

The song was written by Barry Despenza and Carl Wolfolk.

DAVE DEE, DOZY BEAKY, MICK AND TICH *British*

THE LEGEND OF XANADU *Fontana TF 903* [*UK*]. Another success for British writers Ken Howard and Alan Blaikley, and second million seller for the group. The disc was released on 9 February 1968 in Britain and in March in the USA. It sold over 250,000 in Britain and sales from Europe and the Commonwealth and elsewhere made it a global million. The disc was No 1 for a week in Britain and 12 weeks in the bestsellers.

DEEP PURPLE *British*

HUSH *Parlophone R 5708* [*UK*] *Tetragramaton 1503* [*USA*]. Deep Purple made their recording debut with this disc for the Parlophone label on 21 June 1968 in Britain. In the USA the disc became a million seller in 1968, reaching No 4 there for two weeks via the Tetragrammaton label, with 10 weeks in the bestsellers.

One of Britain's top progressive rock bands, Deep Purple were a big attraction all over Europe, making a name for themselves with their powerful, exhibitionist and musically rock. Though **Hush** was a hit in the USA with two other high-placed albums there, it wasn't until the autumn of 1969 that the group made any impact in Britain. They performed organist Jon Lord's **Concerto for Group and Orchestra** at London's Royal Albert Hall with the London Philharmonic Orchestra,

after which they returned to America for a third tour, climaxing in a 'Concerto' date at the Hollywood Bowl with the Los Angeles Philharmonic.

The members of the group were Rod Evans (lead singer) born in Edinburgh and a professional since the age of 15, lyric writer for the group's originals together with Jon Lord; Nicky Simper (bass guitar and vocal harmony) from Norwood Green, Southall, London; Jon Lord (organ and vocal harmony) from Leicester, born 9 June 1941, studied piano at nine and was an accomplished organist at 11, switched from classics to jazz and pop music in his late teens; Ian Paice (drummer) from Nottingham, born 29 June 1948; Ritchie Blackmore (lead guitar) from Weston-super-Mare, born 14 April 1945. These constituted the group for the **Hush** recording, but Evans and Simper were later replaced by Roger Glover and Ian Gillan.

Hush was written by US composer Joe South, a well-known studio guitarist for several years in Atlanta. He received the Grammy Award for his **Games People Play** — the 'Song of the Year' (1969).

THE DELFONICS *American*

LA LA (MEANS I LOVE YOU) *Philly Groove 150* [*USA*] *Bell 1165* [*UK*]. The Delfonics were a trio from Washington, Pennsylvania. Brothers Wilbert and William Hart and Randy Cain began singing together in 1961. They later moved to Philadelphia.

La La (Mean I Love You) was their first single, and gave them the biggest chart success of their career. It reached No 4 in the American charts, with 15 weeks on the Hot 100. It was followed by a string of minor hits until in 1970 they had their only other major success, the million-selling **Didn't I (Blow Your Mind This Time)?** Of their 16 US hits, these were the only two to make the Top 10. In Britain **La La** did not take off at first. It was only after the moderate success of **Didn't I?** in 1971 that **La La** was re-released. This time it clicked, and made No 19 with 10 weeks in the Top 50. It was the biggest of their three British hits, all of which charted in 1971.

La La was written by William Hart (words) and Thom Bell (music), with Bell producing the record. A global sale of over one million copies was reported in 1974.

DION *American*

ABRAHAM, MARTIN AND JOHN *Laurie 3464* [*USA*]. This disc sparked a new career for Dion (Dion Di Mucci), the former teenybopper rock star, who had recorded for the Laurie label from 1958 to 1962. Producer Phil Gernhard was anxious to be involved in more contemporary projects, and when Dick Holler, his songwriter, showed him this song he liked it.

Holler wrote the song the day after the assassination of Senator Robert F. Kennedy in Los Angeles (June 1968), expressing the tragedy personally in his own medium, a ballad equating Abraham Lincoln, Dr Martin Luther King and John F. Kennedy.

Gernhard's search for a sensitive artist to sing the song ran into several months, until Gene Schwartz, Laurie's A&R chief, contacted Gernhard to ask him to arrange a meeting with Dion as Schwartz was interest in resuming what had once been a highly successful relationship between the artist and Laurie. Gernhard expected to find the old Dion, a rock'n'roll singer, but discovered that the artist was tuned to the style of the day. The disc was released in September 1968, got to No 2 for one week in the US charts with 14 weeks in the bestsellers, and by Feburary 1969 sold the million with a Gold Disc award by RIAA.

The disc was released in Britain on 8 November 1968.

THE DOORS   *American*

HELLO, I LOVE YOU *Elektra 45631 [USA] Elektra EKSN 45037 [UK]*. The first of three million-selling records for the Doors in 1968 was their biggest hit since their debut **Light My Fire** the year before. Written by the group, **Hello, I Love You** was released in America in late June, and went to No 1 after five weeks. It stayed at the top for 3 weeks in *Variety*, 2 weeks in *Billboard*, and 1 week in *Cash Box* and *Record World*, and on the charts for 12 weeks. It won an RIAA Gold Disc on 28 August 1968. In Britain it was the Doors' second hit, entering the charts almost exactly one year after **Light My Fire**. It reached No 15, with 12 weeks in the Top 50. It was re-released in 1979, and in what by then was an expanded chart made No 71 with an additional two weeks in the Top 100.

WAITING FOR THE SUN (Album) *Elektra 74024 [USA] Elektra EKS7 4024 [UK]*. **Waiting for the Sun** was the Doors' only No 1 album in America. It was their third release, following the million-selling **The Doors** and the million dollar **Strange Days** albums of 1967. They had made No 2 and No 3 respectively, but **Waiting for the Sun** went to No 1 for four weeks with 41 weeks on the album charts. It won a Gold Disc on 6 August 1968, and a Platinum Disc on 10 June 1987.

The Doors never enjoyed the level of popularity in Britain that they achieved in their native America. **Waiting for the Sun** was their first album to make the LP charts in the UK, where it reached No 16. Its 10 weeks in the Top 40 was the longest stay any Doors album had in the British charts. Only the follow-up **Morrison Hotel** went higher, reaching No 12. Seven Doors albums appeared in the British charts over a period of 20 years, each lasting a few weeks at the lower end of the charts (two of them having a chart life of only one week). It was a similar story in the singles charts, where the Doors had only three modest British hits. However, both **Hello, I Love You** and **Riders on the Storm** charted twice with a gap of several years between each issue.

The tracks on **Waiting for the Sun** were Hello, I Love You, Love Street, Not to Touch, The Earth, Summer's Almost Gone, Wintertime Love, The Unknown Soldier, Spanish Caravan, My Wild Love, We Could Be So Good Together, Yes, the River Knows, Five to One. All songs were by the Doors.

TOUCH ME *Elektra 45646 [USA]*. The Doors' fifth million-selling record was also their third and last single to sell a million in the USA. Written by the group, it was released in December 1968 and in *Cash Box* it went to No 1 for one week on 8 February 1969. It spent 13 weeks in the US charts and won a Gold Disc on 13 February 1969. The single was released in Britain, but it was not a hit.

Though **Love Her Madly** made No 11 in 1971, the Doors were not to enjoy a major singles success again. They made the charts a total of 16 times, their last entry being in 1983-4 with **Gloria**, recorded in 1969 as a sound check. They were mainly an album act, winning eight Gold Discs in a row for their first eight LPs. With Morrison's death on 3 July 1971 (from a heart attack) soon after the release of the eighth album **L.A. Woman**, the Doors effectively came to an end as a major force in rock. The remaining members put out a couple more albums, but they did not do particularly well. Only the Gold **Weird Scenes Outside the Goldmine** 1972 double-album compilation and the Platinum 1981 **Greatest Hits** package sold really well.

THE EQUALS   *British/West Indian*

BABY COME BACK *President PT 135 [UK] RCA Victor 9583 [USA]*. The Equals' disc of this song was originally released in Britain in late 1966 as the secondary number and did not register there until the summer of 1968.

Pat Lloyd, John Hall and Eddie Grant all went to school together at Acland Burghley School, north London, and decided to form a group. Twin brothers Derve and Lincoln Gordon asked if they could join. Eddie, the only one who could play an instrument, began to teach them. They first started rehearsing on a council estate at Hornsey Rise, north London, around 1965, Eddie writing most of their material. They later spent six months of each year on the Continent, building their popularity, and appeared in TV shows. A friend wanted to make a demo disc of this song and took the group to President Records. The label liked the song so much they suggested the group record it themselves. The disc — issued on Ariola in Germany — was a big hit there in 1967 and became a No 1 in Belgium and Holland in early 1968. Then quite quickly it began to climb the British charts and within eight weeks was No 1 for three weeks plus over 250,000 sale.

A Gold Disc was presented to the group in June 1968 for a combined million sale. In the USA it reached No 26 for one week with nine weeks in the bestsellers.

Eddie Grant, who wrote the song, has also written material for other groups including the blue-beat spoof **Train Trip to Rainbow City** and **Wedding in Peyton Place**.

The group were Derve Gordon (lead singer) born 29 June 1948 in Jamaica; Eddie Grant (lead guitarist) born 5 March 1948 in Guyana; Lincoln Gordon (rhythm guitar) born 29 June 1948 in Jamaica; John Hall (drummer) born 25 October 1947 in Holloway, London; Patrick Lloyd (rhythm guitarist) born 17 March 1948 in Holloway, London.

Eddie Grant later enjoyed a highly successful solo career. His first solo hit was **Living on the Front Line** in 1979. He hit No 1 with **I Don't Wanna Dance** in 1982, and had a big international hit with **Gimme Hope Jo'anna** in 1988. After a career with small independent record companies, Grant signed with EMI after the success of **Jo'anna**, his record going out on Parlophone with his Blue Wave Records logo also on the label. He recorded **Baby Come Back** again as a solo singer; it was released as a single in 1989.

DON FARDON   *British*

INDIAN RESERVATION (The Lament of the Cherokee) *GNP Crescendo 415 [USA] Youngblood YB 1015 [UK]*. Famous US songwriter John D. Loudermilk originally copyrighted this song in 1963. It is a lament concerning the plight of the Cherokee Indians, who in 1791 were moved from their home in Georgia, when gold was found on the land, to Oklahoma. It was never recorded as a protest song, but when the record became a hit in the USA, the Indians in Salt Lake City used it as a publicity song in their struggle for civil rights.

The disc was released in August 1968 in the USA and reached No 20 in the charts. It was issued in Britain by Pye in October 1968, but did not become popular until re-issue on the Youngblood label in 1970 in Britain, reaching No 2 with 17 weeks in the bestsellers. The disc was also a No 1 on the Continent. The global sale is estimated at over the million.

Micki Dallon, Don Fardon's producer, made a deal with Crescendo Records in Hollywood for a number of masters including **Indian Reservation**, resulting in its US release.

Don Fardon from Coventry, England, was managed by Micki Dallon from 1965 when Don was a member of the Sorrows group. He promoted Don as a solo artist after the group broke up. Don spent much of his time working in cabaret both on the Continent and in Britain with his backing band A Touch of Raspberry — a six-piece Scottish group with two vocalists. His discs were also successful in Canada, Australia, Germany, Italy, France and Brazil.

JOSE FELICIANO   *American*

LIGHT MY FIRE *RCA Victor 9550 [USA] RCA Victor 1715 [UK]*. José Monserrate Feliciano was born in Puerto Rico in 1945 and has been blind since birth. One of a family of nine children, they moved to New York when José was very young and he displayed a talent for music at a very early age. His first performance in public was at the Teatro Puerto Rico in the Bronx as an accordionist when he was nine. José then discovered the guitar, an instrument on which he has become a virtuoso. He made his professional debut in Detroit's Retort Coffee House, and received wider exposure when he appeared in Gerde's Folk City in New York's Greenwich Village. He was discovered there quite accidentally when an RCA-Victor A&R man called in to see another act. He was so impressed by José that he forgot about the other artist, and signed José to a recording

contract (1963). His first single was released in the autumn of 1964 — his own composition **Everybody Do the Click** — and he also cut two albums for Victor. From then on he enjoyed great popularity with his Latin American records and successful radio, TV and nightclub appearances. After hearing the Doors' recording of their own composition **Light My Fire**, José decided to record it in a slower tempo as a 'soul' number, with himself singing and playing guitar plus bass and conga drums, special string arrangements and a jazz flautist improvising. The result was a disc that reached No 3 for three weeks in the USA with 12 weeks in the bestsellers, and No 6 for one week in Britain with combined sales of over the million, and 16 weeks in the bestsellers.

His album **Feliciano** was a No 1 seller later in the year, and earned a Gold Disc award from RIAA.

The disc was issued in the USA in July 1968. José received two Grammy Awards for 'Best New Artist' and 'Best Contemporary Pop Vocal (Male) Performance' of 1968. In the 1980s he signed with EMI and achieved more success in South America and the US Latin market.

THE FIFTH DIMENSION   *American*

STONED SOUL PICNIC *Soul City 766* [USA]. The Fifth Dimension quintet was formed in 1965, and at that time was called the Versatiles, later the Vocals when they were on tour for six months with Ray Charles. During this tour they received high praise for their performances. Their first successful disc was **Go Where You Wanna Go** and then, after meeting songwriter Jim Webb, they recorded in 1967 his **Up, Up and Away** which achieved No 4 in the US charts. This proved an immensely popular item with disc jockeys everywhere and resulted in the group becoming internationally known, gaining them five Grammy Awards for 'Record of the Year', 'Song of the Year', 'Best Vocal Performance', 'Best Contemporary Single' and 'Best Contemporary Group Performance'. By 1968 they had reached the top of their profession.

Marilyn McCoo (born 1944) graduated from UCLA with a BA degree in business administration after switching from theatre arts. She made her TV debut at 15. She also plays piano. Florence LaRue (born 1943), a BA in elementary education at Cal State in Los Angeles, and a school-teacher for a short time before joining the group in 1966, also plays violin and viola. Ron Townson (born 1933), a singer with choirs and spiritual groups from the age of six, toured with Nat 'King' Cole and Dorothy Dandridge as a teenager, later joined the Wings Over Jordan Gospel Singers, and also played a small part in the film version of *Porgy and Bess*. LaMonte McLemore (born 1939) was a former member of the US Army Drum and Bugle Corps. Billy Davis, Jr. was owner of a cocktail lounge in his hometown, St Louis. He used the lounge as an entertainment workshop.

Stoned Soul Picnic was written by Laura Nyro, then a promising new artist. The disc was released in mid-May 1968 and in Britain on 5 July (Liberty label). It was No 3 for three weeks in the USA, spent 16 weeks in the bestsellers, and sold a million by October with a Gold Disc award from RIAA.

FLEETWOOD MAC   *British*

ALBATROSS *Blue Horizon 57 3145 re-issued as CBS 8306* [UK]. Originally known as Peter Green's Fleetwood Mac, this group had its origins in the legendary John Mayall's Bluesbreakers. In fact the first reference to Fleetwood Mac was the name on an unreleased instrumental track in 1967 recorded by Mayall and his then-Bluesbreakers Peter Green, Mick Fleetwood and John McVee. Over two decades Fleetwood Mac have changed their style and personnel, but have retained an astonishing consistency. Their **Tango in the Night** album was No 1 in 1988, 20 years after their first No 1 single, the million-selling **Albatross**.

The line-up of the first group to perform as Fleetwood Mac was Peter Green (born in Bethnal Green, East London, on 29 October 1946) who played guitar and harmonica as well as being lead vocalist; Mick Fleetwood (born in London on 24 June 1947) on drums; Jeremy Spencer (born in London on 4 July 1948) on guitar and piano; and Bob Brunning on bass. They made their debut at the Windsor Jazz and Blues Festival in August 1967, and then performed at London's Marquee Club where they broke all previous box office records. They made their radio debut on the BBC's **Top Gear**. Bob Brunning was soon replaced by John McVie (born in London 26 November 1945) on bass guitar. In August 1968 the group were joined by a third guitarist, Danny Kirwan (born in London on 13 May 1950.)

In February 1968 the group released their first album **Fleetwood Mac** which reached No 4 during its 37 weeks in the album Top 40. Their first hit single was **Black Magic Woman** which was a minor hit, reaching No 37. **Need Your Love So Bad** did better, making No 31 in the *Record Retailer* Top 50, and No 28 in the *NME* Top 30. On 4 December **Albatross** entered the charts, hitting No 1 for one week at the end of January 1969. It spent 20 weeks in the charts, plus another 15 weeks when re-released on CBS in 1973 when it reached No 2. It was their first Silver Disc, and went on to sell a global million.

Albatross was unusual in being an instrumental. Apart from Hugo Montenegro's film theme from *The Good, The Bad And The Ugly* which went to No 1 at the end of 1968, you had to go back to the string of Shadows' chart-toppers from 1960 to 1963 to find another instrumental No 1. It was written by Peter Green, and produced by Mike Vernon. All Fleetwood Mac's other hits have been vocals.

Fleetwood Mac did a tremendous amount to make the blues popular in Britain. In a feature in *NME* in January 1969, they cited the artists who had most influenced them as John Mayall, Eric Clapton and Elmore James, plus B.B. King, Django Reinhardt and Leadbelly through the Beatles and the Rolling Stones to Cliff Richard and the Troggs. Though their main influence was the blues, there was also input from rock'n'roll, folk and classical music.

Their early success with albums and **Albatross** was very important for the new and very small Blue Horizon label, distributed by CBS. They later switched briefly to Immediate, before signing a long-term contract with Warner Brothers who initially put their records out on their Reprise label. It was said that the profits from signing Fleetwood Mac paid the entire start-up costs of Warners' British subsidiary, which was founded at this time.

The group toured America in 1968 and 1969, and were critically acclaimed. Their first three albums made the US charts, but only just. **Fleetwood Mac** made No 198, with three weeks on the charts in 1968. The US follow-up **English Rose** made No 184 in 1969, and **Then Play On** made No 109. It was only in the mid-seventies, when the membership of the group bcame part-American, that they really took off there.

Their second British album, **Mr Wonderful**, started an 11-week chart run in September 1968 and made No 10. Their third British LP, the 1969 **Pious Bird of Good Omen**, only made No 18 but the next album did much better. **Then Play On** was the first LP of the Warner-Reprise deal, and this made No 6. On the singles front, the follow-up to **Albatross** was the very different **Man of the World**. Released on the Immediate label, it made No 2, as did **Oh Well** on Reprise.

Over the years the composition of the group has changed considerably. Founder Peter Green left in May 1970, to be replaced by John McVie's then-wife Christine Perfect. She had been with Chicken Shack, and was voted 'Top British Female Singer' in the *Melody Maker* readers' poll of 1969. (Fleetwood Mac had been voted No 2 new group and No 2 R&B group in the *New Musical Express* poll the year before.) During a tour of America in 1971, Jeremy Spencer joined the Children of God religious cult in California, and was replaced by American Bob Welsh. Danny Kirwan was fired in 1972. He had joined Fleetwood Mac as a blues band when he was 18, and was increasingly unhappy with his role as an American-based rock star. Bob Weston replaced him. Singer Dave Walker joined soon after, though he did not last long, leaving in 1973. Bob Weston and Bob Welsh both left in 1974. At this point the group almost packed up, but instead the band embarked on their most commercially successful period, thanks to the energizing addition of American couple Stevie Nicks and Lindsay Buckingham. Recorded in early 1975, **Fleetwood Mac** (not to be confused with their first LP, which had the same name) gave them their first US No 1. That topped the charts for one week, but **Rumours**, released in 1977, went to No 1 for 31 weeks. To promote these albums, the group toured the USA extensively, and the hectic schedules added to the strain on personal relationships within the band. Stevie Nicks parted from Lindsay Buckingham, the McVies' divorced, as did Mick Fleetwood and his wife Jenny (the sister of Eric Clapton's wife Patti Boyd, the ex-Mrs George Harrison). Mick and Jenny were twice married to each other and twice divorced. Solo efforts by Lindsay Buckingham, Stevie Nicks and Mick Fleetwood in the eighties ran alongside further personnel changes, with Buckingham leaving in 1988. When Fleetwood Mac, now long-resident in America, returned to play the London Wembley Arena and other dates in May 1988, their **Tango in the Night** album was No 1 in Britain. The band line-up was Mick Fleetwood, John and Christine McVie, Stevie Nicks, Billy Burnette and new guitarist Rick Vito from Philadelphia. Their 1990 album **Behind the Mask** entered the British charts at No 1 in the first week of release, set to win over a new generation of fans to take them into their fourth decade.

THE FOUNDATIONS   *British*

BUILD ME UP, BUTTERCUP *Pye 7N 17638* [*UK*] *Uni 55101* [*USA*]. Written by Tony Macauley (of Pye Records) and Mike D'Abo (of Manfred Mann group), this infectious rhythmic number reached No 2 for a week in Britain with 15 weeks in the bestsellers and sold over 250,000 by early January 1969, just two months after release on 8 November 1968. The disc was released in the USA in late December on the Uni label and got to No 1 for two weeks in 1969 with 15 weeks in the bestsellers. Global sales totalled four and a half million by April 1969, over one million of this total in the USA alone.

The lead singer for this recording was Colin Young, born 12 September 1944 in Barbados, West Indies, who replaced Clem Curtis. Mike Elliot had left the group, making it a septet.

RIAA Gold Disc award, March 1969.

ARETHA FRANKLIN   *American*

(SWEET, SWEET BABY) SINCE YOU'VE BEEN GONE/AIN'T NO WAY *Atlantic 2486* [*USA*] *Atlantic 584 172* [*UK*]. This song was written by Aretha Franklin and Ted White, the disc being released in February 1968 with a million sale by the end of March plus a Gold Disc award from RIAA. It was Aretha's fifth million seller single. It was No 4 in the charts for four weeks and 12 weeks in the US bestsellers. It was also the No 1 rhythm-and-blues disc for three weeks in the USA with 13 weeks in the R&B Top 50. In Britain it achieved No 4 for three weeks.

The song, highly emotional, is rendered in a most powerful manner, with a tingling orchestral backing. Aretha, who had earned the name of 'Lady Soul', was named by *Billboard* as the 'Top Female Vocalist' of 1967. The disc was released in Britain 1 March 1968 on Atlantic label.

In America the flip side also charted. **Ain't No Way** reached No 16 with eight weeks on the pop charts, and No 9 with 10 weeks on the R&B charts. It was written by Aretha's sister Carolyn Franklin.

THINK *Atlantic 2518* [*USA*] *Atlantic 584 186* [*UK*]. The sixth million seller for Aretha Franklin, the song was again written by her with Ted White. The disc was released in May 1968, was No 7 for two weeks in the US charts with 10 weeks in the bestsellers, and sold the million by July, with an RIAA Gold Disc award. In Britain it reached No 26 and was nine weeks in the bestsellers.

It was the No 1 R&B disc for three weeks in the USA and No 1 for five weeks in Britain's R&B charts. The disc was released in Britain on 10 May 1968 on the Atlantic label.

In America it was another double A side, with the flip side **You Send Me** making No 56 with six weeks on the pop charts, and No 28 with nine weeks in the R&B charts compared to 13 weeks for **Think**.

I SAY A LITTLE PRAYER/THE HOUSE THAT JACK BUILT *Atlantic 2546* [*USA*] *Atlantic 584 206* [*UK*]. Million seller single No 7 for Aretha was another Gold Disc RIAA award. **I Say a Little Prayer** (written in 1967 by Burt Bacharach and Hal David) had been a million seller for Dionne Warwick in 1967. This version was taken from Aretha's album **Aretha Now** and released in August. It was No 10 for one week in the USA with 11 weeks in the bestsellers, and No 4 for two weeks in Britain and 14 weeks in the bestsellers. The backing **The House that Jack Built** (written by Bob Lance and Fran Robins) got to No 6 for two weeks in the USA with nine weeks in the bestsellers.

Prayer was released in Britain on 2 August with a different backing. In the US R&B charts **The House that Jack Built** was No 2 for 2 weeks during a 10-week chart run. **I Say A Little Prayer** had 12 weeks in the R&B charts peaking at No 3.

SEE SAW/MY SONG *Atlantic 2574* [*USA*]. Released in mid-November, this double hit disc sold a million by early January 1969 with an RIAA Gold Disc award. Both songs are revivals. **See Saw** written by Steve Cropper and Don Covay was originally a hit for Don Covay in 1965. **My Song** was written by Arthur Alexander in 1952 and was then a hit for Johnny Ace. The disc was produced by Atlantic's Jerry Wexler and made the eighth million seller for Aretha. She was voted 'Top Female Vocalist' of 1968 by all the major polls, making it two years running for 'Lady Soul'.

See Saw was No 11 for one week, and **My Song** No 31 for one week in the USA. The titles were respectively 14 and seven weeks in the US bestsellers. In the R&B charts **See Saw** made No 9 and **My Song** made No 10 with both sides having a chart life of nine weeks.

MARVIN GAYE   *American*

I HEARD IT THROUGH THE GRAPEVINE *Tamla 54176* [*USA*] *Tamla Motown TMG 686* [*UK*]. A million seller for the second time, this song was written in 1967 by Norman Whitfield and Barrett Strong and was a hit then for Gladys Knight and the Pips. This version was No 1 in the USA for seven weeks and 15 weeks in the bestsellers, and sold over three million, by early 1969. The disc was released on 9 November and was also No 1 for 7 weeks in the R&B charts where it stayed for 14 weeks. The record was produced by Norman Whitfield, who had also produced the Gladys Knight version, at the Motown studios in Detroit. In the *Rolling Stone* magazine critics' poll of the best singles of 1963-88, this record was ranked fourth out of 100.

This disc was also No 1 in Britain in 1969 for three weeks where it was released on 7 February, and 15 weeks in the bestsellers.

Marvin Pentz Gay Jr, born in 1939 in Washington, DC, was the son of a church minister. He made his debut as a solo vocalist at the age of three, and later both sang and played organ in church every Sunday. He continued singing religious music until his early teens, and in high school used his talents in popular music as vocalist-pianist-guitarist-drummer with the school orchestra.

His first break came when he was on tour with the Moonglows. He was heard by Tamla-

Motown president Berry Gordy, Jr, who persuaded Marvin to become a solo performer and signed him to a long-term contract. His first hit was **Stubborn Kind of Fella** (1962) followed by **Pride and Joy**, **Hitch Hike** and **Can I Get a Witness?**. He later teamed up with Kim Weston. Marvin became better known to the British public from 1965 onwards when the Tamla-Motown label was launched here. Following problems with drugs and taxes he lived in Europe for 3 years. He was married to Berry Gordy's sister Anna from 1961 to 1975.

He was shot dead by his father in Los Angeles on the eve of his forty-fifth birthday on 1 April 1984.

BOBBY GOLDSBORO   *American*

HONEY *United Artists 50283 [USA] United Artists UP 2215 and later UP 35633 [UK]*. **Honey** was the biggest hit of Bobby Goldsboro's career. The country ballad was written by Bobby Russell, arranged by Don Tweety, and produced by Bob Montgomery and Bobby Goldsboro. It had originally been recorded by Bob Shane, one of the founders of the Kingston Trio, but his version never took off. Released in March 1968, the Goldsboro cover took four weeks to get to No 1, where it stayed for five weeks, with 15 weeks on the Hot 100. It was the first of 22 solo hits on the country charts where it reached No 1 for 3 weeks during a 15-week chart run. It was the fastest-selling record United Artists had ever released. It sold its first million in just over three weeks, winning a Gold Disc on 4 April 1968, and went on to sell three million copies.

In Britain it was Bobby's first hit, and reached No 2 with 15 weeks in the charts. It won a Silver Disc for British sales of over a quarter of a million on 22 June 1968. Seven years later, on 29 March 1975, United Artists re-released **Honey**. On its second chart outing it again peaked at No 2, with another 12 weeks in the Top 50. Goldsboro did not make the British charts again, so this was his first and last British hit.

THE GRASS ROOTS   *American*

MIDNIGHT CONFESSIONS *Dunhill 4144 [USA]*. This disc was No 3 for a week and stayed in the USA charts for 18 weeks, subsequently amassing a million sale by early December plus an RIAA Gold Disc award. It was released in August. The song was written by Lou Josie, and arranged by Jimmy Haskell.

The group's first hit was **Let's Live for Today** (No 3 in the USA), a former hit for the Italian group the Rokes (see 1967).

RICHARD HARRIS   *Irish*

MacARTHUR PARK *RCA Victor 1699 and then Probe GFF 101 [UK] Dunhill 4134 [USA]*. Richard Harris was born on 1 October 1933 in Limerick, Ireland and attended the Royal Academy of Dramatic Art, London. He first became known to the public for his performance in the film *This Sporting Life* which earned him an Academy Award nomination, and appeared in other films — *The Red Desert, Hawaii, Mutiny on the Bounty, The Guns of Navarone* and the star role as King Arthur in the film version of *Camelot* (1967).

In January 1968, American songwriter Jim Webb came to Britain to record an entire album of his songs all sung by Harris entitled **A Tramp Shining**, which included **MacArthur Park**. When issued as a single, the disc swept up the US charts and was No 2 for four weeks with 13 weeks in the bestsellers, selling over a million. In Britain it reached No 4 for two weeks and 12 weeks in the bestsellers. The record extends for over seven minutes as against the normal three for most singles. MacArthur Park does exist — at the end of Wilshire Boulevard in Los Angeles. Harris first met composer Jim Webb (then aged 21) in California in early 1967, where he was presenting a charity show. Webb's first big hit was the multi-award-winning **Up, Up and Away** (six Grammy Awards, 1967), then **By the Time I Get to Phoenix** (three Grammy Awards, 1967). **MacArthur Park** was awarded a Grammy for 'Best Arrangement Accompanying Vocalist(s)' of 1968.

In 1972 the record was re-issued in Britain on the Probe label. The second time around it reached No 38 with six more weeks in the charts, making 18 weeks in all.

HEINTJE   *Dutch*

HEINTJE (Album) *CNR 912 [Netherlands] Ariola 2115 [West Germany]*. Heintje's first album, this included his big first hit **Mama**, **Ich bau dir ein schloss** and 12 other songs, was a fantastic success for the singing youngster from Holland. It sold 1,250,000 in its first year on the market, probably a record for Germany. 68,000 were sold in Switzerland, a phenomenal figure for that country where sales of 6,000 are considered excellent. Total sales were over two million by 1970 when Heintje was presented with a Platinum Disc award. His disc sales 1968-9 totalled over 10 million.

DU SOLLST NICHT WEINEN (You shouldn't cry) *CNR UH 100 70 [Netherlands] Ariola 14101 [West Germany]*. Boy-wonder Heintje's second million seller was released in Germany in May 1968 and was No 1 there for 11 weeks, staying in the Top 10 for over eight months (36 weeks). The disc also sold over 90,000 in Switzerland, a figure seldom if ever reached for a single there. It was additionally a big seller in Denmark in 1969.

The song is based on the famous Mexican air **La golondrina** ('The Swallow') composed many years ago by Narciso Serradell, with new German lyrics. The backing of the disc was **Ich bau dir ein schloss**.

HEIDSCHI BUMBEIDSCHI (Album) *CNR UH 100 83 [Netherlands] Ariola 14 114 [West Germany]*. The third million seller in a row for Heintje was released in Germany in October 1968. By mid-January 1969 it had sold over 800,000 and soon easily achieved the million. The disc was an immediate No 1 in Germany and for 16 weeks, the most for any in that country, staying in their Top 10 for over six months. It was also No 1 for four weeks in Holland and a hit in Denmark (1969).

Heidschi Bumbeidschi is based on an old German folk song, the title of which is untranslatable into English. This new version had new German lyrics.

By the end of 1968, Heintje was the most successful artist ever to have hit Germany, and his discs accounted for around 20 per cent of the country's total record sales at that time. By 1969 he had been awarded 12 Gold Discs in Germany, and a total of 27 by mid-1970 from various countries. The backing of the disc was **Ich sing ein lied fur dich**.

WEIHNACHTEN MIT HEINTJE (Christmas with Heintje) (Album) *CNR 955 [Netherlands] Ariola 2451 [West Germany]*. Another collosal seller for Holland's boy wonder, this album of songs for Christmas had an initial pressing of one million in Germany and was soon completely sold out. Swiss advance orders were 20,000, a large amount for that country. Heintje sold around two million of his already released albums, the biggest Christmas sales ever for the Ariola label.

JIMI HENDRIX   *American*

SMASH HITS (Album) *Track 613-004 [UK] Reprise 2025 [USA]*. The third Hendrix release to eventually pass the million mark was this **Smash Hits** compilation. It was released in Britain in April 1968, and went to No 4 with 25 weeks in the album charts. The **Electric Ladyland** double album followed it into the British charts in November 1968, though in America release of these albums was the other way round — while **Electric Ladyland** was released at the same time as in Britain, **Smash Hits** was not put out until July 1969. Coming after a No 1 album, the hits package did well, reaching No 6 with 35 weeks on the album charts. It won a Gold Disc on 14 October 1969, and eventually sold over two million copies in the USA alone. It was certificated Double Platinum on 13 October 1986. This followed a change in the certification rules of the RIAA that allowed awards for back product. Reprise submitted sales figures for all the Hendrix albums that had sold one or more million copies, and picked up Platinum or Double Platinum Discs for four Hendrix albums on the same day.

The tracks on the album were **Purple Haze**, **Fire**, **The Wind Cries Mary**, **Can You See Me?**, **51st Anniversary**, **Hey Joe**, **Stone Free**, **The Stars that Play the Laughing Sam's Dice**, **Manic Depression**, **Highway Chile**, **Burning of The Midnight Lamp** and **Foxy Lady**.

ELECTRIC LADYLAND (Album) *Track 613-008/9 [UK] Reprise 6307 [USA]*. The fourth million seller for the British-based American guitarist-singer was, like the other three, an album. As with the others, Mitch Mitchell and Noel Redding joined Hendrix on this double album as the Jimi Hendrix Experience.

Electric Ladyland made No 6 in the British album charts, with 12 weeks in the Top 40. Years later it was made available as two single albums. In America **Electric Ladyland** gave Hendrix his only No 1 album, topping the charts for two weeks in November 1968. The album spent 37 weeks on the charts. It won a Gold Disc for million dollar sales on 18 November 1968, and a Platinum Disc in recognition of American sales of one million copies on 13 October 1986.

The tracks on **Electric Ladyland**, divided into the two volumes (subsequently made available separately), were: *Volume 1* — **Still Raining, Still Dreaming, House Burning Down, All Along the Watchtower, Voodoo Chile, Rainy Day Dream Away 1983** and **Moon Turn the Tide**. *Volume 2* — **And the Gods Made Love, Have You Ever Been?, Cross Town Traffic, Voodoo Chile, Little Miss Strange, Long Hot Summer Night, Come On-part 1, Gipsy Eyes, The Burning of the Midnight Lamp** and **Foxy Lady**.

MARY HOPKIN   *British*

THOSE WERE THE DAYS *Apple 2* [*UK*] *Apple 1801* [*USA*]. The melody for this song is based on a Russian folk song **Darogoi Dlimmoyo** ('Dear for me'), the first known recording of the original being made in the 1920s by Alexander Wertinsky. Another recording was made in 1958 in Finland by Mrs Annikki Tahtiand, and the song was also recorded in 1966 by Finnish singer Martti Caram in tango rhythm. American composer and nightclub performer Gene Raskin wrote the popular version in 1962, and it was first recorded by the Limeliters folk group in 1963.

Mary Hopkin was born in Pontardawe, Wales, on 3 May 1950, daughter of the housing officer there. She began singing at the age of four and later took singing lessons every Saturday. She got engagements at working men's clubs and elsewhere from a local agent for around £6 ($15) per show and in 1968

appeared in the TV show 'Opportunity Knocks'. Top model Twiggy told Beatle Paul McCartney about Mary's performance. At this time Apple Records were looking for singers, so Paul asked her to come to London. He remembered Gene Raskin and his wife Francesca singing **Those Were the Days** in the Blue Angel in London around 1966. A demo of the song was obtained from America by the English publishers and Mary recorded the song. The disc was released on 30 August along with three other discs (including the Beatles' **Hey Jude**) and gave the new Apple Records a second huge hit. In four weeks it sold 360,000 and around 750,000 in three months. In the USA the disc was issued in September and sold a million in two months with an RIAA Gold Disc award. The disc became a No 1 all round the world and by year's end had sold over five million. It was No 1 for six weeks in Britain with 21 weeks in the bestsellers, and No 1 for four weeks in USA with 14 weeks in the bestsellers. Mary Hopkin gave a gentle, swaying, lyrical performance, singing in a high, clear soprano reminiscent of Joan Baez.

Those Were the Days is regarded as Mary's first single, but this is not correct. She made her first recording for a small independent label in Wales — Cambrian — but in her own language, Welsh. She also sang folk songs on Welsh TV programmes before her big disc success.

By February 1969 the cumulative sales of this song in Mary Hopkin's recordings in English, French, German, Italian, Spanish and Hebrew topped the eight million mark. Of this figure USA sales were over one and a half million.

THE INTRUDERS   *American*

COWBOYS TO GIRLS *Gamble 214* [*USA*]. First million seller for this group and for the Gamble label, the disc was issued in March 1968 and was awarded an RIAA Gold Disc for million sales in mid-May. It reached No 5 for one week with 14 weeks in the US bestsellers. Release in Britain was on the Ember label.

The group consists of Sam (Little Sonny) Brown (lead singer), Eugene Daughtry, Robert Edwards and Philip Terry. All come from Philadelphia.

The song was written by K. Gamble and L. Huff (producer of the disc).

IRON BUTTERFLY   *American*

IN-A-GADDA-DA-VIDA (Album) *Atco 250* [*USA*]. Released in July 1968 in the USA, this sold over three million by the end of 1970, and stayed in the Top 10 for 12 months. It achieved No 4 for two weeks in November 1968, and was in the charts for 140 weeks. A Gold Disc was awarded by RIAA in December 1968.

The Iron Butterfly consisted of Doug Ingle (group leader and lead vocalist), composer of most of the group's numbers, born 1947; Ron Bushy (drums) born 1946; Lee Dorman (bass guitar) born 1946; Erik Keith Brann (lead guitar) born 1951.

Ingle, who spent most of his spare time composing, had played the organ for two

years. Bushy had been drumming since school days. Dorman, who also played drums and piano, was the group's comedian. Brann was another versatile performer, and also played violin and drums. The group, noted for their incredible blending of light, airy sounds with a 'heavy' blues blend, broke into the charts with their first album **Heavy**, but it was **In-A-Gadda-Da-Vida** that established them as a leading act in the USA. The album includes the tune of the same title, a 17-minute composition that became a showcase for the group on its personal appearances. This, together with a contracted version of the work that was a hit single in 1968, greatly increased their following. They performed with Cream and others in the film *Savage Seven*, for which Ingle wrote the Iron Butterfly's first Atco single **Possession** backed with **Unconscious Power**.

The contents of the album are **Most Anything You Want**, by Doug Ingle; **Flowers and Beads**, by Doug Ingle; **My Mirage**, by Doug Ingle; **Termination**, by Eric Brann and Lee Dorman; **Are You Happy?** by Doug Ingle; **In-A-Gadda-Da-Vida**, by Doug Ingle.

Release in Britain was in 1968 on the Atlantic label.

TOMMY JAMES AND   *American*
THE SHONDELLS

MONY MONY *Routlette 7008* [*USA*] *Major Minor MM 567* [*UK*]. This disc was written by B. Bloom, Tommy James (of the group), Ritchie Cordell and Bo Gentry (producers of the disc). Released in March 1968, the disc was No 3 for two weeks in the USA and 17 weeks in the bestsellers, and a big hit in Britain where it was No 1 for five weeks and 18 weeks in the bestsellers, winning a Silver Disc.

Tommy James and Ritchie Cordell got the title for the song when they were writing one night. Outside the apartment was a sign 'Mutual of New York' which when lit up spelled MONY.

The personnel for this disc were Ronnie Rosman, Mike Vale, Tommy James, Peter Lucia and Eddie Gray.

Global sales were over one and a half million.

CRIMSON AND CLOVER *Routlette 7028* [*USA*]. This teen-type balled was written by P. Lucia and Tommy James (of the group) and issued in early December 1968. It sold 700,000 in its first four weeks and over two and a half million by mid-June 1969, Roulette's biggest seller. The disc was No 1 for two weeks in US charts with 16 weeks in the bestsellers, and another triumph for Tommy James and the Shondells, their fifth million seller. The global sales totalled four million.

JAY AND THE AMERICANS   *American*

THIS MAGIC MOMENT *United Artists 50475 [USA]*. This group was formed in the autumn of 1961 and made its first recording in 1962 with **She Cried** which achieved No 5 in the charts, followed by other charts hits **Only in America**, **Let's Lock the Door and Throw Away the Key** and **Think of the Good Times**. In 1965 their disc of the British song **Cara Mia** got to No 4 and was also instrumental in making a name for the group with this updated version in Britain.

The group worked steadily in and around New York for some time then got an audition and a recording contract with United Artists. They all come from Brooklyn.

Jay and the Americans were a quintet in 1965, comprising Jay Black (lead singer) born 2 November 1941, originally a show salesman; Kenny Vance, born 9 December 1943; Sandy Deane (real name Sandy Yaguda) born 30 January 1943; Marty Sanders, born 28 February 1941; Howie Kane, born 6 June 1942, a mortician.

This Magic Moment was originally a hit for the Drifters in 1960, written by Doc Pomus and Mort Shuman. Jay and the the Americans' disc was released in November 1968 and reached No 4 for two weeks in the USA with 14 weeks in the bestsellers, and the certified million sale in early 1969 with an RIAA Gold Disc award on 16 May. The group for this disc was a quartet and excluded Howie Kane.

TOM JONES   *British*

DELILAH *Decca F 12747 [UK] Parrot 40025 [USA]*. This song was written by the enormously successful British composers Les Reed and Barry Mason. Released on 23 February 1968, it sold well over half a million in Britain, and was No 2 for three weeks with 17 weeks in the bestsellers. It was No 1 in France, Israel, Switzerland, Germany (14 weeks), South Africa, Belgium, Eire, Spain and Finland, with big sales in the USA where it achieved No 15 chart position with 14 weeks in the bestsellers. Global sales totalled five million.

The song has a big-sounding backing devised by Les Reed, plus Tom Jones' fiery, emotional vocal.

13 SMASH HITS [IN BRITAIN] THE TOM JONES FEVER ZONE [IN AMERICA] (Album) *Decca SKL 4909 [UK] Parrot 71019 [USA]*. Released in the USA in May 1968, this album sold the million by the end of 1970. A Gold Disc was awarded by RIAA in May 1969.

The album contained **Don't Fight It**, by Wilson Pickett and Stephen Cropper (1965); **You Keep Me Hanging On**, by B. Holland, E. Holland and Lamont Dozier (1966); **Hold on, I'm Coming**, by David Porter and Isaac Hayes (1966); **I Was Made to Love Her**, by H. Crosby, S. Moy, L. Hardaway and Stevie Wonder

(1967); **Keep on Running**, by Jackie Edwards (1965); **Get Ready**, by Smokey Robinson (1966); **Delilah**, by Les Reed and Barry Mason (1968); **I Know**, by Barbara George (1961); **I Wake Up Crying**, by Hal David and Burt Bacharach (1964); **Funny How Time Slips Away**, by Willie Nelson (1961); **Danny Boy**, by F.E. Weatherly (1913), arr. Blackwell (tune **Londonderry Air**); **It's a Man's Man's World**, by James Brown (1966).

The British release was titled **13 Smash Hits** and included **I'll Never Fall in Love Again**, by Lonnie Donegan and Jim Currie (1967), **Yesterday**, by John Lennon and Paul McCartney (1965), plus all the songs on **Fever Zone** except **Delilah**.

British release was in December 1967, and the disc was No 4 for two weeks and in the bestsellers for 42 weeks. In the USA it was No 14 in 1969 for one week, but was a consistent seller for 82 weeks into 1970 by which time Tom Jones had became an international star, with several albums and singles becoming big hits in the USA after his 1969 tour there. He was named 'Entertainer of the Year' (1970) and voted 'World's No 1 Male Vocalist' (1970) by a *Playboy* international poll.

GLADYS KNIGHT AND   *American*
THE PIPS

THE END OF OUR ROAD *Soul 35042 [USA]*. The third million seller for this group, the song was written by N. Whitfield, B. Strong and Roger Penzabene. The disc reached No 11 in the USA with 10 weeks in the bestsellers. It reached No 5 with 11 weeks in the R&B charts.

It was released in the USA on 10 February 1968.

LEAPY LEE   *British*

LITTLE ARROWS *MCA MU 1028 [UK] US Decca 32380 [USA]*. Leapy Lee (real name Lee Graham) was born on 2 July 1942 in Eastbourne, Sussex, England and educated there. He became active in school amateur dramatics and later formed his own rock group. At 15 he left school, and after working for a year in a factory the group became professional.

Leapy's career became highly diversified. He acted, was an entertainment manager, antique dealer, songwriter and singer. he made his TV debut in 'State Your Case', was one year at the London Palladium in *Large as Life* (1958). He also started a bingo hall in Shepherd's Bush, London.

In 1968 he found the song **Little Arrows**, written by Albert Hammond and Mike Hazlewood, and recorded it for the new MCA label. It reached No 2 in Britain's charts for two weeks with 21 weeks in the bestsellers and was No 12 in the *Cash Box* US charts and No 16 in *Billboard* with 14 weeks in both charts. It had a combined global sale of three million.

The origin of Leapy Lee's stage name was, as he said himself when asked, 'I was always a leaper.'

The disc was released in August 1968 in Britain.

MANFRED MANN   *British*

MIGHTY QUINN *Fontana TF 897 [UK] Mercury 72770 [USA]*. Released on 19 April 1968, this disc was No 1 for two weeks in Britain and 11 weeks in the bestsellers winning a Silver Disc and also a hit in the USA where it reached No 4 with 11 weeks in the bestsellers. A fine version of a Bob Dylan composition, a writer much favoured by the group who recorded many of his songs. It was also a huge hit in Germany, a No 1 there, and global sales totalled two million.

The group included singer Mike D'Abo (born 1 March 1944 in Bletchworth, Surrey) who replaced Paul Jones in 1969 when Paul became a solo artist, and Klaus Voormann who replaced Mike Vickers.

Other countries in which the disc reached No 1 included Singapore, Sweden and Denmark.

MARMALADE   *British*

OB-LA-DI OB-LA-DA *CBS 3892 [UK]*. Written by John Lennon and Paul McCartney, this West Indian-type number with an infectious melody and rhythm was first recorded by them on their double album **The Beatles**. This recording by Marmalade sold around half a million or more in Britain and the million globally by April 1969. It was released in Britain in November 1968.

The group were originally called the Gaylords and were exceedingly popular in Scotland where they were voted No 1 group from 1964 to 1966. They then decided to cross the border to England and appeared at the Windsor Jazz Festival in 1967, nearly stealing the show. This resulted in a regular Thursday-night residency at London's Marquee Club, where other British groups such as Manfred Mann, the Yardbirds, Traffic, Spencer Davis, the Herd, the Rolling Stones and the Animals acquired fame. Their first disc success was **Lovin' Things**, No 6 in Britain in 1968, followed by **Ob-la di, Ob-la-da** (No 1 for three weeks and 20 weeks in the bestsellers).

Marmalade were Alan Whitehead (drums) born 24 July 1946, originally a work-study

trainee; Graham Knight (bass guitar) born 8 December 1946; Junior Wullie Campbell (guitar, piano, drums) born 31 May 1947, originally a plasterer; Patrick Fairley (six-string bass and rhythm guitar) born 14 April 1946, originally an industrial chemist; Dean Ford (real name Thomas McAleese) (lead vocalist, guitar, harmonica) born 5 September 1946, originally an office worker and apprentice plater.

HUGH MASEKELA   South African

GRAZING IN THE GRASS *Uni 55066* [*USA*]. Hugh Masekela is the son of a famous sculptor and was born in Witbank, Johannesburg, South Africa in 1939. He was raised by his grandmother until he was old enough to attend school. At the age of 13 he saw the film *Young Man with a Horn* which gave direction to his future. The school headmaster got him a trumpet and after a few months he began playing in the clubs and streets of Johannesburg, later travelled the country with a band, and eventually fled from the South African apartheid repressions. He won a scholarship to study at London's Royal Academy of Music and Guild Hall School, then went to the USA to study at the Manhattan School of Music. It was there he met Harry Belafonte who was impressed with his talent and sponsored him in America. Hugh worked in various New York clubs during his four years of study and in 1966 formed Chisa Records, his product later being released on the Uni label.

Hugh was an extremely exciting performer, his style a combination of traditional South African and contemporary pop, while his vocal numbers were mostly South African. He was usually assisted in his playing by a tenor/soprano sax, pianist, drummer and bass.

Grazing in the Grass was written by Philemon Hou and achieved No 1 in the USA charts for three weeks with 12 weeks in the bestsellers, with an RIAA Gold Disc award for a million sale in July 1968 within three months of release.

JUN MAYUZUMI   Japanese

TENSHI NO YUWAKU *Toshiba CA30-1374* [*Japan*]. Written by Rei Nakanishi (words) and Kunihiko Suzuki (music), this disc was released through EMI's Toshiba Records (Japan) in May 1968. It was No 2 for two weeks in Japan and by the year's end sold 1,700,000, with a 16 weeks' stay in their charts. The recording was awarded the Japan Gold Disc Prize of 1968.

Jun Mayuzumi was one of Japan's top female disc stars of the year.

THE MONKEES   American

VALLERI/TAPIOCA TUNDRA *Colgems 1019* [*USA*] *RCA Victor 1967* [*UK*]. The Monkees 10th million-selling record was another double A side. Released in March 1968, it was also the last of their string of massive hits. All of their first six singles sold a million in America and made the US Top Three, and four of them (including the first three) made No 1. After **Valleri** they never made the Top 10 again, and only its follow-up, **D.W. Washburn**, scraped into the Top 20. It made No 19 in July 1968. The Monkees' bubble burst almost as quickly as it had arisen.

Valleri was written by American writers Tommy Boyce and Bobby Hart. It was the side that made the British charts, reaching No 12 in its eight weeks in the Top 50. In America it made No 1 for 2 weeks in *Cash Box* and *Record World*, spent 11 weeks in the *Cash Box* charts, and 10 weeks in *Billboard* were it peaked at No 3. **Tapioca Tundra**, written by Mike Nesmith, was No 34 with six weeks on the *Billboard* charts and No 37 with eight weeks in *Cash Box*.

HUGO MONTENEGRO,   American
HIS ORCHESTRA AND CHORUS

THE GOOD, THE BAD AND THE UGLY *RCA Victor 9423* [*USA*] *RCA Victor 1727* [*UK*]. Hugo Montenegro's disc of the theme from the Italian-made 'Spaghetti' Western film of the same title starring Clint Eastwood was an outstanding instrumental recording, reaching No 2 for one week in the USA and a consistent seller for 22 weeks. It sold a million there and over 250,000 in Britain where it was No 1 for four weeks and 24 weeks in the bestsellers. The tune was composed by Ennio Morricone. The disc was released in the USA in March and later in the year in Britain.

Hugo Montenegro was born in 1925 and raised in New York City where he attended city schools. After two years in the US Navy he graduated from Manhattan College. His arranging for Service bands was but a stepping stone to later success. He moved to California with his family and wrote and conducted the scores for Otto Preminger's *Hurry Sundown* and *The Ambushers* (1967).

THE 1910 FRUITGUM COMPANY American

SIMON SAYS *Buddah 24* [*USA*] *Pye International 7N 25447* [*UK*]. An old children's

play song **Simon Says** was the inspiration for this disc debut by the extraordinarily named 1910 Fruitgum Company.

The group consisted of Floyd Marcus (drums) born 1949; Pat Karwan (lead guitar) born 1949; Mark Gutkowski (organ) born 1950; Steve Mortkowitz (bass guitar) born 1949; Frank Jeckell (rhythm guitar) born 1947.

The quinter, all from Lynden, New Jersey, went to the same high school and formed the group in January 1967. They played under several names including Jeckell and Hyde, the Odyssey and the Lower Road. Frank Jeckell coined the name 1910 Fruitgum Company after discovering an old bubble-gum wrapper while going through a trunk in an attic.

Simon Says, written by Elliot Chiprut, is pure 'bubble-gum' pop. It was issued in early January 1968 and sold a million by March with an RIAA Gold Disc award. In the USA the disc was No 1 for one week with 14 weeks in the bestsellers, and in Britain No 2 for two weeks and 16 weeks in the charts, winning a Silver Disc. It also sold a million in Canada, the global sales totalling around three and a half million. It was released in Britain on 3 May 1968.

In April 1968, Bruce Shaw and Dave Peck replaced Marcus and Mortkowitz.

This disc sparked a trend for 'bubble-gum music' in the USA, the formula being set by actor and rock'n'roll singer Neil Bogart, general manager of the newly formed Buddah label in 1967.

1, 2, 3, RED LIGHT *Buddah 54* [*USA*]. The second million seller for the 1910 Fruitgum Company, the song was written by S. and Bobbi Trimachi. The disc was released in the USA in July 1968 and achieved No 3 chart position for three weeks with 13 weeks in the bestsellers, with a Gold Disc award from RIAA in October.

CLIFF NOBLES & CO.   American

THE HORSE *Phil-LA of Soul 313* [*USA*]. A unique instrumental disc, written by Jesse

James who also produced the disc, and arranged by Bobby Martin. The song is unusual in the way it was put together, although no unusual instruments were used, the instruments being two bass guitars, drums, piano, baritone sax, tenor sax, three trumpets and trombone. A new dance was fashioned around **The Horse**.

The disc was No 2 for three weeks in the USA with 14 weeks in the bestsellers, and sold the million within three months of release plus a Gold Disc award from RIAA in August 1968. Nobels was born in Mobile, Alabama, in 1944.

ESTHER AND ABI OFARIM   *Israeli*

CINDERELLA ROCKEFELLA *Philips BF 1640* [UK] *Philips 40526* [USA]. Esther and Abi Ofarim first met when Esther was a student in Abi's dance studio in Haifa, Israel. Esther served four months in the Israeli Army and was released on her marriage to Abi. They started singing at home for fun and then decided to try to make it as a duo in Israel. Their first album (1961) went to No 1 and the same year, Frank Sinatra, who was touring the Orient doing shows for youth relief, choose Esther to perform in his Israeli concerts. She then did other dates with Sinatra in Europe and the Ofarims settled in Geneva. In 1961 Esther won a prize in a festival in Poland. She represented Switzerland in the 1963 Eurovision Contest in London, was announced the winner but was deposed when a judging mistake was discovered. The recorded version of her contest song, however, attained international popularity. In 1964, Esther won the Dutch prize at the Grand Gala du Disque and a top award came for the duo in Rome in 1967. In 1967 they released their **2 in 3** album in London.

This album included **Cinderella Rockefella**, a nonsense song written by Mason Williams and Nancy Ames of the USA in 1966. Williams, writer for the Smothers Brothers TV show in the USA, was a personal friend of the singers. In December 1967, the duo appeared on the 'Eamonn Andrews Show' on TV in Britain and introduced the song. It was the start of their success in Britain and Philips issued it as a single on 9 February 1968. In six weeks it sold a million and was No 1 for four weeks with 13 weeks in the bestsellers, and No 1 in

Holland and Sweden. In the USA the disc was No 68 and six weeks in the bestsellers.

Esther Ofarim (real name Esther Zaled) was born on 13 June 1943 in Safed, Israel and educated in Haifa. Abi Ofarim (real name Abraham Reichstadt) was born on 5 October 1939 in Tel Aviv, Israel, and educated there, studying dancing and music.

THE OHIO EXPRESS   *American*

YUMMY, YUMMY, YUMMY *Buddah 38* [USA] *Pye International 7N 25459* [UK]. The Ohio Express consists of Douglas Grassel (rhythm guitar) born 1949; Dale Powers (lead guitar) born 1948; Jim Pfahler (organ) born 1948; Tim Corwin (drums) born 1949; Dean Kastran (bass guitar) born 1949.

The group was formed in 1965 in Mansfield, Ohio, and was brought to the attention of Super K Productions' Jerry Kasenetz and Jeff Katz by Jamie Lyons, lead singer of the Music Explosion who also lived in Mansfield. Katz and Kasenetz gave the group a recording session, during which they cut **Beg, Borrow and Steal** (1967) which was a sizeable hit. They then made their first big public appearance opposite the Beach Boys in Cleveland and were a huge success with an audience of over 10,000 teenagers.

Yummy, Yummy, Yummy, written by K. Resnick and J. Levine, was first played on WMCA-New York station. After two months it sold a million and was awarded a Gold Disc by RIAA in June. It was No 4 for three weeks in the USA with 14 weeks in the bestsellers, and No 4 for two weeks in Britain with 15 weeks in the bestsellers.

Dean, Jim and Dale wrote most of the group's material, Jim doing the quintet's arrangement. Dale performed most of the singing with Jim occasionally joining in. Tim, Dean and Jim added the background harmony.

It was released in Britain on 17 May 1968. The disc was another big success for the new Buddah label and the 'bubble-gum music' market.

CHEWY, CHEWY *Buddah 70* [USA]. The second million seller for the Ohio Express was again written by J. Levine and K. Resnick. Released in October, it sold 875,000 in two months and finally went on to a seven-figure sale. The disc was another 'bubble-gum' hit

and reached No 8 for one week in the USA charts and 13 weeks in the bestsellers. RIAA Gold Disc award, March 1969.

THE O'KAYSIONS   *American*

GIRL WATCHER *ABC 11094* [USA]. This group comprised Donnie Weaver (lead vocals and organ), Wayne Pittman (lead guitar), Jim Hinnant (bass), Bruce Joyner (drums), Ronnie Turner (trumpet) and Jim Speidel (saxophone). The song was written by Pittman with B. Traill.

Weaver and Hinnant started playing together in 1963, but although they knew all the other members of the group they only got together in the latter part of 1967.

Girl Watcher was No 4 for two weeks in the USA. It was released in mid-August and received a Gold Disc award for a million sale from RIAA in December. The disc stayed in the charts for 15 weeks.

PEPPERMINT RAINBOW   *American*

WILL YOU BE STAYING AFTER SUNDAY? *US Decca 32410* [USA]. Written by A. Kasha and J. Hirschhorn and arranged by Paul Leka who also produced the disc, it was released in December 1968 with a reported million sale in 1969. The disc was No 20 for two weeks in the USA and stayed in the bestseller charts for 20 weeks.

PINKY AND THE KILLERS   *Japanese*

KOI NO KISETSU *King 6106* [Japan]. This group received an award as 'The Most Promising New Group' in Japan in 1968. Their disc first entered the Japanese charts in September 1968 and stayed there right up to March 1969, holding the No 1 position for 17 weeks. It is estimated to have sold well over the million.

PATTY PRAVO   *Italian*

LA BAMBOLA *Arc AN 4155* [Italy]. Released in May, Patty's disc was No 1 for nine weeks of its 20 weeks' stay in the Italian charts. It sold well over the half million in four months and achieved the million by the end of the year.

Patty Pravo, born in 1948, made her debut in 1965 when she was 17 at Rome's Piper Club as vocalist with a band. She was discovered there by an RCA Italiana talent scout and signed to a long-term agreement in 1967. Her first disc **Ragazzo triste** ('Sad boy') brought her much popularity and appearances in song contests. Patty is a native of Venice.

ELVIS PRESLEY   *American*

IF I CAN DREAM *RCA Victor 47-9670* [USA] *RCA Victor 1795* [UK]. Released in November 1968, this disc reached the million sale by the end of 1969. The song, written by W. Earl Brown, is a ballad with a message lyric — a plea for 'peace and understanding'. In the USA it

was No 9 for a week with 13 weeks in the bestsellers, and in Britain No 11 for two weeks with 10 weeks in the bestsellers. This made million seller No 42 for Elvis.

THE RASCALS   *American*
(formerly The Young Rascals)

A BEAUTIFUL MORNING *Atlantic 2493 [USA]*. Written by Felix Cavaliere and Eddie Brigati of the group, this disc was released at the beginning of April 1968. It sold a million by July with a Gold Disc award from RIAA, achieving the No 2 chart position in the USA for three weeks, with 13 weeks in the US bestsellers.

PEOPLE GOT TO BE FREE *Atlantic 2537 [USA]*. Also written by Felix Cavaliere and Eddie Brigati of the Rascals, this disc achieved No 1 in the USA in a month from its release in mid-July and stayed top for five weeks with 14 weeks in the bestsellers. By mid-September it had sold over one and a half million, and was awarded a Gold Disc by RIAA in August 1968. The disc was released in Britain on 16 August.

OTIS REDDING   *American*

(SITTIN' ON) THE DOCK OF THE BAY *Volt 157 [USA] Stax 601 031 [UK]*. Otis Redding, born 9 September 1941 in Dawson, Georgia, was one of the best exponents of soul music — the American blend of blues, gospel and pop that began in the late 1940s via the dedicated pioneers of rhythm-and-blues discs, put out by Atlantic, Savoy, Chess, King, Specialty, Imperial and Modern labels with a flock of new labels in the early 1950s and over 40 by the mid-1960s. The pioneer labels filled a long-felt need due to the larger labels having practically abandoned the R&B field during World War Two. By 1967, the R&B field became one of the most exciting and lucrative in the disc industry.

Otis' family moved to Macon, Georgia, while he was still young and he attended the high school there. The enormous success of Little Richard (also from Macon) inspired him to embark on a singing career. He entered local talent contests and won most of them. Then Otis joined forces with Phil Walden, another high school student who had been booking a local band in his spare time. Walden recognized Redding's talent and became his manager, and Otis cut several discs for various labels including **Shout Bamalama** for Sue label and **Fat Girl** for Bethlehem (a subsidiary of the King label). He then became vocalist with Johnny Jenkins and the Pinetoppers, their disc **Love Twist** becoming a regional success on the Atlantic label. The group became established favourites in Southern colleges and universities. More discs were cut and then the group were scheduled for a session in Memphis, Tennessee for the Volt label. After the session, Otis asked if he could cut a demo disc and in less than an hour recorded **These Arms of Mine**, a self-written song. When issued by Volt and distributed by Atlantic, it sold around 750,000 and Redding's career was on its way.

His next disc **Pain in My Heart** (1963) was later recorded by Britain's the Rolling Stones. Otis reciprocated with a hit recording of their song **Satisfaction**. In 1965 he recorded the self-penned **Respect** which sold a million when recorded by Aretha Franklin in 1967. In the same year Arthur Conley had a Gold Disc hit with Redding's **Sweet Soul Music**.

Otis formed his own disc company Jotis Records and his own Redwal Music Publishing Co.

In 1967 he came to Britain with the famous 'Hit the Road Stax' tour of Stax-Volt artists.

The Dock of the Bay was recorded on 7 December 1967. Three days later his plane crashed into icy Lake Monona, Madison, Wisconsin, killing Otis, four members of his musical revue, his valet and the pilot. The sole survivor was Ben Cauley, also with the Redding Show. The US record-buying public made it up to Redding with an almost two million sale of the disc which was No 1 for four weeks with 16 weeks in the bestsellers, and was awarded a Gold Disc by RIAA in March 1968.

The song was written by Steve Cropper (producer of the disc) and Otis Redding. The disc was No 3 in Britain for one week with 15 weeks in the bestsellers, and top R&B disc in the USA for three weeks, and Britain for eight weeks.

It was released in Britain on 9 February 1968 on the Stax label.

The disc also sold over 400,000 in Japan. It received two Grammy Awards for 'Best Rhythm-and-Blues, Vocal Performance (Male)' and 'Best Rhythm-and-Blues Song' of 1968.

In the *Rolling Stone* magazine 1988 critics' poll of the 100 best singles of the previous quarter century, this record was ranked seventh.

CLIFF RICHARD   *British*

CONGRATULATIONS *Colbumia (EMI) DB 8376 [UK]/Uni 55069 [USA]*. Cliff Richard's 27th million seller, the last of the decade for him, was the British Eurovision Song Contest entry. It lost by one point to the Spanish entry, **La La La**, sung by Massiel. On the sales front Cliff Richard beat Massiel hands down, and even knocked her off the top of the Spanish charts with **Congratulations**. The song was written by Phil Coulter and Bill Martin, who had written the 1967 Eurovision winner for Sandie Shaw with **Puppet On A String**. It was arranged, conducted and produced by Norrie Paramour at the EMI studios in Abbey Road. **Congratulations** was No 1 in Britain for two weeks, with 13 weeks in the Top 50. Released on 13 March 1968, it won a Silver Disc for British sales of a quarter of a million on 27 April and a Gold Disc for British sales of a million on 22 June. It was his first British-only million seller since 1963, and his first No 1 since 1965.

Cliff Richard had survived the Beatles onslaught better than any other pre-Beatles stars had done. His international career had become even stronger. Yet from 1966 he began to lose ground, especially when he went public over his Christianity, and talked of leaving the rock business to teach religion. This was a very unfashionable image to project, though he managed to survive it. **Congratulations** was a massive hit in Europe and the Far East. It went to No 1 in Japan, South Africa, Ireland, Sweden, Norway, Denmark, Germany, Switzerland, Belgium, the Netherlands, Spain, Israel, Lebanon, India, Malaysia and Singapore. It was also a hit in the USA (No 99), Australia, New Zealand, Finland, Austria, France, Italy, Poland, Yugoslavia, the Philippines and Argentina. It sold over two million copies worldwide.

Cliff Richard is the most consistent rock star in Britain. Although there were some leanish times for him in the seventies (only three million sellers and one No 1) he was still in the Top 10 of most charted artists of the decade. Only seven artists had more weeks in the charts during the seventies than Cliff, and in the eighties his career took off again with two more No 1s and many more million sellers. He had the second largest number of hits of the decade. He looks all set to conquer the 1990s in much the same way that he has buried the competition in each of the last four decades.

JEANNIE C. RILEY   *American*

HARPER VALLEY P.T.A. *Plantation 3 [USA] Polydor 56 148 [UK]*. 'Judge not lest ye be judged' is the story line of this unique song. It tells of a widowed wife criticized by the Harper Valley Parent-Teacher Association for her high skirts and low life in a note brought home by her teenage daughter. The mother attends a meeting of the P.T.A. and exposes the hypocritical behaviour of her accusers.

Jeannie C. Riley recorded the song on 26 July 1968 and it launched the new Plantation label for Shelby S. Singleton, Jr., who also produced the disc, in Nashville. It sold 1,750,000 in two weeks after hitting the turntables when it became No 1, and stayed top for three weeks with a total of 13 weeks in the US Hot 100. The record was No 1 in the country charts for 3 weeks with a chart run of 14 weeks, bestsellers. The song was written by her friend Tom T. Hall, son of a Kentucky minister. A former disc jockey, he progressed into a top songwriter and entertainer.

Jeannie C. Riley, from Anson, Texas (born Jeanne Carolyn Stephenson on 19 October 1945), made this multi-market monster after having been in Nashville only a few months. Her only previous show business experience had been routine song-demo sessions for various Nashville firms. Her superb performance of the song resulted in the inevitable nationwide round of TV shows and disc jockeys.

Sales in the USA were four million, a further million in Canada and big sales elsewhere, making an estimated tally of five and a half million globally. A Gold Disc award was made by RIAA in August, four weeks after the disc's release. Release in Britain (Polydor label) was on 20 August, the disc reaching No 10 for one week with 15 weeks in the bestsellers.

The first artist to record this song was Alice Joy who toured with the Marty Robbins Show. Her disc was never released, but it was after hearing her version that Jeannie Riley decided to record the song. It earned her a Grammy Award for 'Best Country Vocal Performance (Female)' of 1968. On the pop charts she had a short career. This was her only Top 50 hit in the USA, though she had four minor hits between 1968 and 1971. On the country charts it was different, with 23 chart entries over the next eight years.

HARPER VALLEY P.T.A. (Album) *Plantation PLP 1* [*USA*]. Jeannie C. Riley's phenomenal success with her single disc of this title sparked

the inevitable follow-up of an album. This was released in the USA in September 1968 and reached No 6 for two weeks, with a Gold Disc award from RIAA in December. It stayed in the bestsellers for 27 weeks but consistent sales throughout 1969 made it a million copy seller by the end of that year. In Britain, the album was released in 1968 on the Polydor label.

The album was produced by Shelby S. Singleton and Jerry Kennedy, and engineered by Neal Wilbern, at the Columbia studios in Nashville. The tracks on the album were **Harper Valley P.T.A.**, by Tom T. Hall; **Widow Jones**, by Tom T. Hall; **No Brass Band**, by Lenny Groah, Lu Groah and Steve Singleton; **Mr Harper**, by Tom T. Hall; **Run, Jeannie, Run**, by Clark Bentley and Jerri Clark; **Shed Me No Tears**, by Steve Singleton; **The Cotton Patch**, by Myra Smith and Margaret Lewis; **Sippin' Shirley Thompson**, by Tom T. Hall; **The Little Town Square**, by Ben Peters; **Ballad Of Louise**, by Naomi Martin; and **Satan Place**, by Ben Peters and Clark Bentley.

TOMMY ROE   *American*

DIZZY *ABC 11164* [*USA*] *Stateside SS 2143* [*UK*]. Tommy's disc, released in December 1968, was No 1 for four weeks (1969) with 15 weeks in the US charts, and sold two million by mid-April 1969 with a Gold Disc award from RIAA.

The song was written by Tommy Roe and F. Weller. **Dizzy** was also a big hit in Britain where it was No 1 for two weeks and 19 weeks in the Top 50.

THE ROLLING STONES   *British*

JUMPIN' JACK FLASH *Decca F 12782* [*UK*] *London 908* [*USA*]. After the psychedelic experimentation and relative commercial failure of **We Love You**/**Dandelion** the Stones went back to basics for their only worldwide singles release of 1968. (In America and some other territories, local Decca companies issued **Street Fighting Man** from the **Beggars Banquet** album, but this was not an official global release.) **Jumpin' Jack Flash** is a classic piece of hard, driving, Rolling Stones rock, and though it failed to win either a Gold Disc for American sales of a million or a Silver Disc for British sales of a quarter of a million, it has remained for 20 years one of the two or three best-love Stones singles. It was the first of three classic Stones singles in a row, being followed by **Honky Tonk Women** and **Brown Sugar**.

Jumpin' Jack Flash was the first single recorded with the Stones' new producer Jimmy Miller. It was also the last single recorded with Brian Jones.

Mick Jagger and Keith Richards wrote **Jumpin' Jack Flash**, which remained a high point of their stage act over the next couple of decades. It was released in Britain on 24 May, and in America a week later. It entered the British charts at No 12 the first week of release. (This was in the *NME* Top 30. It came in at No 17 in the *Disc* charts and No 18 in the *Record Retailer* Top 50.) It went to No 1 for two weeks, with 11 weeks in the Top 50. In America it made No 1 for one week, with 12 weeks on the

charts. The record also went to No 1 in New Zealand, Germany and Singapore, and was a hit in Canada, Australia, South Africa, Ireland, Norway, Denmark, Spain, the Lebanon, Malaysia, Japan and Rhodesia.

BEGGARS BANQUET (Album) *Decca LK 4955* [*UK*] *London 539* [*USA*]. **Beggars Banquet** was the first Stones album produced by Jimmy Miller. It was recorded at the Olympic Studios in London with Glyn Johns as engineer. Jagger and Richard wrote all the songs on the album, and though Brian Jones was still a member of the band his contribution was limited. The sleeve credits pointedly say 'We are deeply indebted to (guitarist) Nicky Hopkins.' The album found the Stones at the centre of controversy again, this time over the design of the album cover. The Stones wanted a picture of a grafitti-covered lavatory wall, but Decca were horrified at the very thought. Despite public statements from Mick Jagger that the Stones would stick to their guns, Decca refused to release the album with the offending picture on it. After several weeks of delay, the Stones caved in, and the album went out with a 'tasteful' design in the form of an official invitation to the Beggar's Banquet.

The album entered the British LP charts at No 3, where it stayed for five weeks stuck behind the Beatles' white album and the Seekers. (This was in the *NME* charts. In the *Record Retailer* Top 40 it entered at No 9, dropped to 10 the following week, then up to four and then No 3.) It spent 12 weeks in the Top 40. In America it reached No 5 with 32 weeks on the charts. It won a Gold Disc for million dollar sales on 23 December 1968, a couple of weeks after release. While not one of the Stones' biggest-selling albums, world sales eventually passed the million mark.

In some countries Decca released one of the tracks, **Street Fighting Man**, as a single. In America this proved a mistake. With its exhortation that 'the time is right for fighting in the street, boys', it hardly endeared itself to American radio. It staggered up the charts to No 48. It lasted six weeks in the Hot 100. Decca eventually released **Street Fighting Man** in Britain, but only after the Stones had left the label. It reached No 21 in 1971, with eight weeks in the Top 50.

The tracks on **Beggars Banquet** are **Sympathy for the Devil**, **No Expectations**, **Dear Doctor**, **Parachute Woman**, **Jig-Saw Puzzle**, **Street Fighting Man**, **Prodigal Son**, **Stray Cat Blues**, **Factory Girl** and **Salt of the Earth**.

MERRILEE RUSH   *American*

ANGEL OF THE MORNING *AGP then Bell 705* [*USA*]. This disc was released in April 1968, reached No 3 for three weeks on the USA charts and was in the bestsellers for 16 weeks. The million sale was reported in 1970.

Merrilee Rush studied classical piano for 10 years, and also played organ with her backing group the Turnabouts, a quartet of saxophone, drums, bass and guitar. They made numerous TV appearances together. All were managed by Paul Revere and the Raiders.

This disc was Merrilee's first single. The song was written by C. Taylor.

BARRY RYAN   *British*

ELOISE *MGM 1442* [*UK*] *MGM 14010* [*USA*]. Barry Ryan's recording of a song written by his twin brother Paul achieved No 1 in Britain for one week with 12 weeks in the bestsellers and was also No 1 in Holland, Italy, Austria, Belgium, Switzerland and Germany, with prominent chart positions in most other European countries. In the USA it reached No 50 for one week. The disc was released in Britain in October and by January 1969 had sold a global million, with over three million by April 1969.

Paul and Barry Ryan (real name Sapherson) are the twin sons of British singer Marion Ryan and were born on 24 October 1948 in Leeds. It took the twins three years to persuade their mother to let them make a record. Their first was **Don't Bring Me Your Heartaches** (October 1965) which was a success. They continued recording for Decca until 1968 when they were signed to MGM who also signed them to a £100,000 film contract. **Eloise** was the first disc for MGM with Barry who had turned solo performer, brother Paul having decided to concentrate on writing.

SAM AND DAVE   *American*

I THANK YOU *Stax 242* [*USA*] *Stax 601 030* [*UK*]. The third million seller for leading R&B duo Sam and Dave was written and produced by Isaac Hayes and David Porter, as were their two previous million sellers. In the American pop charts **I Thank You** reached No 9, with 13 weeks on the charts. It followed their only other Top 10 record, the million-selling 1967 release **Soul Man**. In the R&B charts it went to No 4, with 14 weeks on the Top 50. Sam and Dave had 15 hits on the R&B charts between 1966 and 1985. In Britain the record made No 34 with nine weeks in the Top 50. It did much better in the British R&B Top 20, which it entered at No 3 on 2 March 1968, three weeks before it made the main charts. It spent 11 weeks in the UK R&B Top 20.

THE SCAFFOLD   *British*

LILY THE PINK *Parlophone R 5734* [*UK*]. The Scaffold were first formed in the summer of 1962. John Gorman, a post office engineer, was invited to assist in organizing the Merseyside Arts Festival and was introduced to Roger McGough, a teacher and part-time poet. Poetry readings for the festival were later supplemented by duologues and comedy sketches which called for the addition of Mike McGear, then an apprentice hairdresser. The Scaffold thus came into being. In December 1963 while appearing at Liverpool's Everyman Theatre, an ABC-TV talent scout spotted them and signed them to a six-months' contract to supply humorous content to the late night TV show 'Gazette'. Their success in this and other shows encouraged them to turn professional in 1964.

They first started using musical items at a show at the Everyman Theatre, with a number called **Today's Monday**. In 1967, Mike McGear wrote **Thank U Very Much** which when recorded by the trio was a big hit. It was only then that it was revealed that Mike McGear was actually Michael McCartney, brother of the Beatles' famous Paul. Mike had wanted to work without using the Beatles, and that was why he changed his name.

Lily the Pink was released on 18 October 1968 and was written by the Scaffold, based on an old traditional rugby song, telling the story of Lily who invented a medicinal compound 'most efficacious in every case'. It was an enormous success and sold 825,000 in three months and was No 1 for five weeks, staying in the British charts for 24 weeks. It was also popular in Norway, New Zealand and Malaysia in 1969, and subsequently went over the million mark. Despite the popularity of their songs, the Scaffold were basically a highly original humorous group. They were John Gorman, born 4 January 1937 in Birkenhead, educated at St Anselm's College, Liverpool; Mike McGear (Michael McCartney), born 7 January 1944 in Walton; Roger McGough, born 9 November 1937 in Liverpool, educated St Mary's College, Crosby and Hull University (where he obtained a BA degree in French and geography). McGough wrote much of the group's material.

A French version of the song, **Le sirop typhon** recorded by Richard Anthony, also sold around 800,000. The original traditional version was known as **Lydia Pinkham**.

SIMON AND GARFUNKEL   *American*

BOOKENDS (Album) *CBS-Columbia 9529* [*USA*] *CBS 63101* [*UK*]. 1968 was the best year yet for Simon and Garfunkel. The film *The Graduate*, which became as famous for its Simon and Garfunkel music as for Dustin Hoffman's acting, gave them a No 1 soundtrack album in America, a No 1 single, and in Britain a Top 10 EP. That was followed by another US No 1 album with **Bookends**.

The Graduate was about a college graduate (Hoffman) seduced by his next-door-neighbour Mrs Robinson (Anne Bancroft) whom he rejects to pursue and eventually win her young daughter (Katharine Ross). The film was one of the most successful of 1968. The soundtrack, which was No 1 for nine weeks, included a number of previously released Simon and Garfunkel tracks like **Sounds of Silence**, and two cuts of **Mrs Robinson** from which the hit single version later evolved.

In April 1968, a month after **The Graduate** hit the album charts, came the release of **Bookends**. This went to No 1 for seven weeks in America, with 66 weeks on the charts. In Britain it was Simon and Garfunkel's second hit album, and gave them their first No 1. It spent seven weeks at the top, and 77 weeks in the charts altogether. All the songs were written by Paul Simon. It won an RIAA Gold Disc on 18 April 1968, and a Double Platinum Disc for American sales of over two million on 21 November 1986. In 1970 Simon and Garfunkel made it three US album No 1s in a row, as their next LP was the mega-hit **Bridge Over Troubled Waters**.

The tracks on the album were **Bookends Theme**, **Save the Life of My Child**, **America**; **Overs**, **Voice of Old People**, **Old Friends**, **Bookends Theme**, **Fakin' It**, **Punky's Dilemma**, **A Hazy Shade of Winter**, **At the Zoo** and **Mrs Robinson**.

MRS ROBINSON *CBS-Columbia 44511* [*USA*] *CBS 3443* [*UK*]. After their first three singles had made the US Top 10 in 1966, the next couple of years proved slightly quieter on the singles chart. The hits came, but did not quite make it into the Top 10. In March 1968 **Scarborough Fair/Canticle** entered the Hot 100 and eventually peaked at No 11. It had been featured in *The Graduate* and was on the soundtrack album, although it had originally appeared on the **Parsley, Sage, Rosemary and Thyme** LP of 1966. The following month **Mrs Robinson** was released. Also from **The Graduate**, it was the music played over the film credits. It reached No 1 for four weeks in *Cash Box* and three weeks in *Billboard*, with 13 weeks in the charts. An RIAA Gold Disc for American sales of a million was awarded on 10 June 1968. **Mrs Robinson** won a Grammy Award as 'Best Contemporary Pop Performance by a Vocal Duo or Group' in 1968.

In Britain **Homeward Bound** had been their first hit single, entering the charts on 24 March 1966 and reaching No 9. Later in the year **I Am a Rock** made No 17, but other singles failed to make the charts. On 13 July 1968 **Mrs Robinson** entered the *Record Retailer* chart at No 42, eventually peaking at No 4 with 12 weeks in the Top 50. It entered the *NME* Top 30 at No 27 the same week, and also peaked at No 4 in that chart. On 11 January 1969 Simon and Garfunkel achieved something very few artists managed in Britain. They entered the singles charts with an EP. The **Mrs Robinson** EP included the title track and three other songs from the film — **Scarboro Fair/Canticle**, **The Sound of Silence** and **April Come She Will**. It was the highest new entry in the Top 50, coming in at No 31. After five weeks it had reached No 9, but then a decision was taken to exclude EPs from the singles charts, so the following week it was absent from the Top 50. In the *NME* Top 30, which continued to feature EPs, it peaked at No 19. **Mrs Robinson** was written by Paul Simon and produced by Simon, Art Garfunkel and Roy Halee.

FRANK SINATRA   *American*

FRANK SINATRA'S GREATEST HITS! (Album) *Reprise 1025* [*USA*] *Reprise RSLP 1025* [*UK*]. Frank Sinatra had enjoyed something of a renaissance in the mid-sixties. His **Somethin' Stupid** duet with his daughter Nancy had given him a No 1 on both sides of the Atlantic in 1966. **Strangers in the Night** (only his second solo No 1 in Britain) gave him a second transatlantic chart-topper later the same year. He had four records in the US charts in 1966, two more in 1967 and another three in 1968. While the 1966 No 4 **That's Life** was the only major hit, it all added up to more interest in Sinatra's music than at any time since the late fifties. It was the ideal time to put out a 'greatest hits' package. Though it reached only No 55 in the album charts, where it stayed for 25 weeks, it continued to be a steady seller long after it had left the charts. It won an RIAA Gold Disc on 19 November 1970, and a Platinum Disc on 13 October 1986. In Britain the album reached No 8 with a lengthy 38 weeks in the LP Top 40.

Sinatra is one of the all-time greatest American performers. In a career that has spanned half a century and touched most aspects of the entertainment world, he has had 167 hits in America, including seven No 1s. His first hit was in 1942, singing **Night and Day** with Alex Stordahl and his Orchestra. His next hit the following year was his first No 1, though **All or Nothing** had been recorded with Harry James and his Orchestra in 1939. His last appearance in the singles charts was in 1980 with the **Theme from New York, New York**, and in the album charts in 1984 with **L.A. is My Lady**. Since the British charts started in 1952 he has had 37 entries in the singles charts, including the extremely rare feat of an LP making the singles Top 20 in the 1950s. On the British album front, he has had 50 hits between the first LP chart of 1958 and 1986.

The tracks on his **Greatest Hits** album were **Stranger in the Night**, **Summer Wind**, **It Was a Very Good Year**, **Somewhere in Your Heart**, **Forget Domani**, **Somethin' Stupid** (with daughter Nancy), **That's Life**, **Tell Her (You Love Her Each Day)**, **The World We Knew**, **When Somebody Loves You**, **This Town** and **Softly As I Leave You**.

SIR DOUGLAS QUINTET PLUS TWO   *American*

MENDOCINO *Smash 2191* [*USA*]. The Sir Douglas Quintet was formed in the early 1960s by Doug Sahm, born in Texas in 1943. Sahm himself started in music at the age of six, playing steel guitar, and at nine was a featured performer on the 'Louisiana Hayride' country show. He was a graduate of San Antonio's Sam Houston High School and leader of the group which also included four boys from the Lone Star State: August Meyers, Jackson Barber, John Perez and Franklin Morin. They had their first hit with **She's About a Mover** (Tribe label) in 1965. The group moved to San Francisco and became caught up in the musical scene there.

They signed with Smash Records, calling the group Sir Douglas Quintet Plus Two as by that time the personnel had changed and increased. It became a front for the talents of writer-singer-producer Doug Sahm who also produced other acts for Smash Records.

Sahm wrote **Mendocino**, and the group's disc was released in December 1968. It reached No 14 by early 1969 in the US charts with 15 weeks in the bestsellers, but was much more successful in Europe, selling over three million and making the group one of the relatively few American bands to attain international acclaim. It was particularly successful in Germany and Belgium.

The line-up of the group for this recording was Doug Sahm (vocalist/guitarist), Franklin Morin (tenor), Wayne Talbert (piano), Martin Fierro (alto sax), Bill Atwood (trumpet), Mel Barton (baritone sax), Terry Henry (trumpet), Whitney Freeman (bass) and George Rains (drums). All came from Texas except Freeman who was a Californian.

SLY AND THE FAMILY STONE   *American*

EVERYDAY PEOPLE *Epic 10407* [*USA*] *Direction 58 3938* [*UK*]. This group was formed in 1966 by Sly Stone who was a rhythm-and-blues disc jockey at KSOL-San Francisco and at KDIA-Oakland. It comprised Sly Stone (leader, composer, organ) born 15 March 1944, Freddie 'Pyhotee' Stone (guitar, vocals), Rosemary Davis (Stone) (electric piano), Cynthia 'Ecco' Robinson (trumpet); Larry Graham (bass guitar, vocals), Jerry Martini (saxophone) and Greg 'Handfeet' Errico (drums). Freddie and Rosemary are Sly's brother and sister. Sly wrote for and produced the Beau Brummels, the Mojo Men and Bobby Freeman for the Autumn label in Los Angeles at the age of 20.

The group rehearsed in Sly's basement before performing on the local club circuit, then appeared at the Fillmore Auditorium, and thence to New York, Los Angeles, Chicago and Las Vegas. Their first disc **Dance to the Music**, issued in February 1968, was a big hit in the USA (No 5 for one week) and also in Britain (No 7). **Everyday People** was released in the USA in November 1968 and was No 1 for four weeks in early 1969 with 19 weeks in the bestsellers, passing the million sale by February 1969 plus an RIAA Gold Disc award. The disc was also No 1 for 2 weeks in the US R&B charts where it stayed for 15 weeks. The flip side **Sing a Simple Song** made No 28 in a 10-week chart life of its own. It also made No 89 during 4 weeks on the Hot 100. In Britain it reached No 36 and was five weeks in the bestsellers. The song was written by Sylvester Stewart (Sly's real name), who wrote much of the group's material. He made his first recording at the age of four, and in his senior year at high school was a member of the Viscanes group. He studied music theory and composition in college and led several groups, playing guitar and bass around the San Francisco nightclub circuit. He then became producer for Autumn Records, and a radio disc jockey.

Sly described the group as 'a dance and concert combination', and their sound as 'the first fusion of psychedelia and rhythm-and-blues'.

O.C. SMITH   *American*

LITTLE GREEN APPLES *CBS-Columbia 44616* [*USA*]. This tender ballad was first recorded in February by country artist Roger Miller, then by Patti Page. It was written by Bobby Russell who was also to enjoy a huge hit with **Honey** in 1968.

O.C. Smith's version was completely different in that he gave the song a bluesy approach rather than country-and-western. It proved to be a tremendous hit and two months after its release in August got to No 2 for a week in the US charts with 17 weeks in the bestsellers, and a Gold Disc award from RIAA for a million sales.

Smith was raised in Los Angeles, and instructed in music by his mother. He attended high school and college there and performed whenever possible. He gained his first full-time semi-professional experience during his four years in the US Air Force. His popularity there made him decide to become professional after discharge. He obtained a singing job in New York's Club Baby Grand and was later hired by Count Basie with whom he worked for three years, making five trips to Europe. His recording of **Son of Hickory Holler's Tramp** earlier in the year brought him prominence in both Britain and America. **Little Green Apples** gave him global recognition.

The song received two Grammy Awards for 'Song of the Year' and 'Best Country Song' of 1968. It made No 2 for ten weeks during 14 weeks in the US R&B Top 50.

STATUS QUO   *British*

PICTURES OF MATCHSTICK MEN *Pye 7N 17449* [*UK*] *Cadet Concept 7001* [*USA*]. Along with the Shadows, the Rolling Stones and the Bee Gees, Status Quo are among the longest-lasting of all British groups. Starting in the sixties, they are still going strong into the nineties. Their origins go back to a Shadows sound-a-like instrumental group called the Spectres, formed in 1962 by two London schoolboys. Francis Dominic Michael Nicholas Rossi (born in Forest Hill, south London, on 29 May 1949) played guitar, and Alan Lancaster (born in Peckham, south London, on 7 February 1949) played bass guitar. They both went to the same south London comprehensive school, as did Jess Joworski whom they roped in to play organ. In 1963 they recruited drummer John Coghlan (born in West Norwood, south London, on 19 September 1946). When the group turned professional in 1965, Joworski left, as he wanted to continue his studies. He was replaced by Roy Lynes (born in Redhill, Surrey, on 25 October, 1943). The last to join the group, in 1967, was guitarist Rick Parfitt (born in Woking, Surrey, on 12 October 1948). All the members of the group started in show business very young. Parfitt made his first public performance at the age of 10, and had been on the 'Midwinter Music' TV show singing Cliff Richard's **Travelin' Light** at 11. Francis Rossi and Alan Lancaster started performing together at the age of 13, and Roy Lynes and John Coghlan at 16.

With the coming of the Beatles, the Spectres changed their style from playing instrumentals to vocal beat music, and gigged their way around London. In 1966 they secured a recording deal with Pye, who released a cover of the old Shirley Bassey number **I (Who Have Nothing)** as their first single. That and the records that followed it flopped, so in 1967 the group decided on another change of style. This was the era of flower power and psychedelia, so they donned Carnaby Street gear and changed their name to Traffic. That clashed with Stevie Winwood's new group, and as he was better known than they were they amended the new name to Traffic Jam. That lasted for one more failed single, then came the final change to Status Quo. (Originally it was the Status Quo, but the 'The' was dropped after their first hit.)

At last they had a break, with **Pictures of Matchstick Men**, written by Francis Rossi and produced by John Schroeder of Pye. On 27 January 1968 their first hit entered the Top 50 at No 49. It was their fifth attempt at a hit single, **Matchstick Men** spent 12 weeks in the Top 50, reaching No 7 (and No 6 in the *NME* Top 30). The record was a major international hit, with global sales of over a million. It made No 12 in America with 17 weeks on the charts there. This early American success proved a false dawn, for after one more minor hit with **Ice in the Sun** later in 1968, the Quo never again made the American charts. Despite a number of tours there, America did not take to their later change of style.

This final change of direction came about after the sixties psychedelic hits dried up. Flower power and the like did not last, and though they had a couple more hits with Pye Status Quo were soon back to square one. In going back to their roots, to the rock'n'roll they had enjoyed as kids, in the early seventies they turned towards simple 12-bar boogie and heavy metal. Exhaustive touring built up an entirely new following, the 'Quo Army' as it was known, and with one hit single and album after another they cruised on effortlessly through the years. Some of their seventies' albums entered the charts at No 1 the first week of release and, though the band temporarily disbanded in the mid-eighties, Rick Parfitt and Francis Rossi re-formed with Rhino Edwards (bass), Jeff Rich (drums) and Andrew Bown (keyboards). They were soon back with the highly successful **In the Army Now** (1986) and **Ain't Complaining** (1988) albums.

STEPPENWOLF — Canadian

BORN TO BE WILD *Dunhill 4138* [USA] *Stateside SS 8017* [UK]. Steppenwolf were formerly a Canadian group called Sparrow who migrated to Los Angeles and San Francisco during the West Coast rock rush. As Steppenwolf, they emerged as a major force in rock. Their name was taken from Herman Hesse's novel, an immensely popular work with college students.

The group comprised John Kay (lead singer), Michael Monarch (lead guitar), Jerry Edminton (drummer), Nick St Nicholas (bass and harmony), Galdy McJohn (organ).

Rushton Moore was originally bassist in early 1967 and John Russell Morgan in late 1968.

The group were discovered at midnight in a coffee-house at Venice Beach in California. Their performances consist of hard blues, sinister pyschedelics and rip-roaring rock numbers.

Born to Be Wild, written by Mars Bonfield, is played in the rock style. The disc was released in July 1968 and was No 2 for three weeks in the US charts and 13 weeks in the bestsellers, selling over a million with a Gold Disc award from RIAA. It was No 30 in Britain and nine weeks in the charts.

John Kay is also second guitarist, harmonica player and a composer.

MAGIC CARPET RIDE *Dunhill 4161* [USA]. Released in the USA in October 1968, this disc reached No 2 in the charts and was a steady seller for 16 weeks into 1969 with subsequent reported million sale. The song was written by John Kay (of the group) and Rushton Moore (formerly bassist of the group).

BARBRA STREISAND — American

FUNNY GIRL (Album) *CBS-Columbia CS 3220* [USA] *CBS 70044* [UK]. Barbra Streisand's third release to eventually sell a million was another album. Like **My Name is Barbra, Two** and the **Christmas Album**, **Funny Girl** took many years to reach seven-figure sales. In fact, some of her subsequent releases got there before these did.

This album was the screen soundtrack from the film *Funny Girl*, which itself was based on the successful Broadway musical about the early life of Fanny Brice. Barbra Streisand and Sydney Chaplin starred in the Broadway show, and the original cast album on Capitol had given Barbra her fourth Gold Disc album in a row after its release in 1964. She then got a second bite of the cherry with the film soundtrack on CBS four years later. In the film, Barbra shared star billing with Omar Sharif.

The music for *Funny Girl* was written by Jule Styne, with words by Bob Merrill. The Broadway cast album made No 2 for three weeks in the American album charts, where it stayed for 51 weeks. It won its Gold Disc on 21 September 1964.

In chart terms, the film soundtrack did not do so well. It only made No 12, though its chart life was twice as long, with 108 weeks on the Top 200. (This was a larger chart than the album Top 150 that existed in 1964.) The film soundtrack album won a Gold Disc on 23 December 1968 and a Platinum Disc on 21 November 1986.

In Britain the Broadway cast album did not make the charts. The film soundtrack did in May 1969, reaching No 11 during its 22 weeks in the album charts.

The tracks on the film soundtrack are **Overture, I'm the Greatest Star, If a Girl Isn't Pretty, Roller Skate Rag, I'd Rather Be Blue Over You (than Happy with Somebody Else), His Love Makes Me Beautiful, People, You are Woman, I am Man, Don't Rain on My Parade, Sadie Sadie, The Swan, Funny Girl, My Man** and **Finale**.

DIANA ROSS AND THE SUPREMES — American

LOVE CHILD *Motown 1135* [USA] *Tamla Motown TMG 677* [UK]. Another tremendous disc for the Supremes, the song was written by Pam Sawyer, Dean Taylor, Frank Wilson and Deke Richards. It was released on 19 October and marked a new turn in Supreme sound. It sold 500,000 in its first week, and by year's end had reached two million. The disc was No 1 for four weeks in the USA with 16 weeks in the Hot 100. During 13 weeks in the R&B Top 50, it spent three weeks at No 2. It and reached No 11 in Britain for one week with 14 weeks in the bestsellers.

DIANA ROSS AND THE SUPREMES with THE TEMPTATIONS — American

I'M GONNA MAKE YOU LOVE ME *Motown 1137* [USA]. Diana Ross and the Supremes first joined forces with the Temptations on the Ed Sullivan Show. The result was as though they had been together for years. Motown issued an album of the two groups together in November 1968, and one of the tracks was **I'm Gonna Make You Love Me**, written by K. Gamble, J. Ross and Jerry. A Williams. On 7 December this was issued as a single and sold an astonishing 900,000 in its first two weeks on the market, thereafter quickly passing the million mark. It became No 1 at the beginning of 1969 and stayed top for three weeks with a total of 13 weeks in the bestsellers. It peaked at No 2 for 3 weeks during 12 weeks in the R&B charts. RIAA Gold Disc award, March 1969. The disc was also No 3 for two weeks (1969) in Britain with 11 weeks in the bestsellers, where it was released on 24 January.

On 9 December 1968, the two groups presented their first joint TV special in colour 'Takin' Care of Business' (T.C.B.) and the original soundtrack was released by Motown, resulting in very big sales.

T.C.B. (Taking Care of Business) (Album) *Motown 682* [USA]. The advance orders for this original soundtrack of the combined group's first television special in colour on NBC-TV on 9 December 1968 poured in at the fastest rate in Motown's history. The album was released immediately after the show and by April 1969 had easily passed the million sale, reaching No 1 in the US charts for one week.

The complete programme was **Somewhere** (from *West Side Story*) (Diana Ross) by Stephen Sondheim and Leonard Bernstein (1957); **Stop in the Name of Love** (Diana Ross and the Supremes) by E. Holland, L. Dozier and B. Holland (1965); **You Keep Me Hangin' On** (Diana Ross and the Supremes) by E. Holland, L. Dozier and B. Holland (1966); **Mrs Robinson** (from the film *The Graduate*) (Diana Ross and the Supremes) by Paul Simon (1967); **I Hear a Symphony** (Diana Ross and the Supremes) by E. Holland, L. Dozier and B. Holland (1965); **With a Song in My Heart** (from *Spring is Here*) by Lorenz Hart and Richard Rodgers (1929) and **Without a Song** (from *Great Day*) (medley — Diana Ross and the Supremes) by W. Rose, E. Eliscu and V. Youmans (1929); **Come See**

About Me (medley — Diana Ross and the Supremes) by E. Holland, L. Dozier and B. Holland (1966); **Baby Love** (medley — Diana Ross and the Supremes) by E. Holland, L. Dozier and B. Holland (1964); **Eleanor Rigby** (Diana Ross) by John Lennon and Paul McCartney (1966); **Reflections** (excerpt) (Diana Ross) by E. Holland, L. Dozier and B. Holland (1967); **Do You Know the Way to San Jose?** (Diana Ross) by Hal David and Burt Barcharach (1968); **Pata Pata** (The Temptations) by Ragavoy and Mackeba; **Get Ready** (The Temptations) by William 'Smokey' Robinson (1966); **A Taste of Honey** (The Temptations) by Ric Marlow and Bobby Scott (1960); **Ain't Too Proud to Beg** (The Temptations) by E. Holland and N. Whitfield (1966); **Hello Young Lovers** (from *The King and I*) (The Temptations) by O. Hammerstein II and Richard Rodgers (1951); **For Once in My Life** (The Temptations) by Orlando Murdon and Ron S. Miller (1965); **I'm Losing You** (The Temptations) by Grant, N. Whitfield and E. Holland (1967); **My Girl** (except) (The Temptations) by William 'Smokey' Robinson and Ronald White (1964); **The Way You Do the Things You Do** (Diana Ross and The Temptations) by William 'Smonkey' Robinson and Bobby Rodgers (1964); **Respect** (The Supremes and The Temptations) by Otis Redding (1965); **The Impossible Dream** (from *Man of La Mancha*) (The Supremes and the Temptations) by Joe Darion and Mitch Leigh (1966).

The Temptations were Paul Williams, Eddie Kendricks, Otis Williams (Miles), Melvin Franklin and Dennis Edward (who replaced David Ruffin). The Supremes were Mary Wilson, Cindy Birdsong and Diana Ross (lead singer).

T.C.B. was a US bestseller for 34 weeks.

JOHNNY TAYLOR   *American*

WHO'S MAKING LOVE? *Stax 0009* [*USA*]. Johnny Taylor was born in 1940 in Memphis, Tennessee, and, like so many other popular singers, became interested in music in his local church where he sang in the choir. Although a deeply religious man, a show business career prompted him to take up more commercial material than gospel songs.

He became professional in 1956 at the age of 16, and had quite a success with his first single for the Galaxy label — **You'll Need Another Favor**. In 1963, he had another hit on Galaxy with **Part Time Love**.

Who's Making Love? was written by Homer Banks, Betty Crutcher, Don Davis and Raymond Jackson, and the disc got to No 4 for two weeks in the USA with 14 weeks in the bestsellers, and had a Gold Disc award from RIAA for a million sale.

The disc was released in October 1968.

Johnny became a solo artist after joining the Soul Stirrers in 1960 as a replacement for Sam Cooke, the group's leader.

THE TEMPTATIONS   *American*

I WISH IT WOULD RAIN *Gordy 7068* [*USA*] *Tamla Motown TMG 641* [*UK*]. Written by B.

Strong, Roger Penzabene and Norman Whitfield (producer of the disc) this disc achieved No 2 for one week in the USA and 14 weeks in the Hot 100. In the R&B Top 50 it was No 1 for three weeks with a 14-week chart run. The flip side **I Truly Truly Believe** also charted, reaching No 41 in a six-week R&B chart life. On the pop charts it bubbled under at No 116. It was No 45 in Britain. Released in early January 1968, the million sale was reported in February.

CLOUD NINE *Gordy 7081* [*USA*] *Tamla Motown TMG 707* [*UK*]. This disc was issued at the beginning of November and in four weeks sold 800,000, passing the million mark by early January 1969. It achieved No 4 for two weeks in the US charts and was 12 weeks in the Hot 100. In the R&B charts it reached No 2 for three weeks during a 13-week chart life. It was No 15 and 10 weeks in the British bestsellers. The song, written by B. Strong and Norman Whitfield (producer of the disc), is a dual-level narrative that has been interpreted as either dealing with narcotic addiction or a dream world. The listener is left to decide which.

The Temptations received a Grammy Award with this disc for 'Best Rhythm-and-Blues Performance by a Duo or Group' of 1968.

THE TEMPTERS   *Japanese*

EMERALD — NO DENSETSU (Legend of the Emerald) *Phillips 4891* [*Japan*]. The Tempters were one of Japan's top selling rock'n'roll groups of 1968 and consisted of She-kan (real name Ken-ichi Hagiwara) (leader) born 1948, Y. Matsuzaki (guitar), Kireshi Oguchi (drums), Toshio Tanaka (guitar and organ) and Noboru Takaku (bass).

The group had several million-sellers (three albums and seven singles up to 1968). They had a near million seller with **Kamisama enegai**, released in Arpil 1968, which was No 1 for four weeks and in the Top 10 for 14 weeks. Their following release in July 1968 of **Emerald — no densetsu** was No 1 for two weeks and in the Top 10 for 13 weeks, selling over the million.

In October 1969, She-kan went to the USA as he wanted to be the first from Japan to try and get the Memphis Sound. He recorded 10 songs brought from Japan and two written by Memphis songwriter Bob McDill. He sang the album in both Japanese and English.

B.J. THOMAS   *American*

HOOKED ON A FEELING *Scepter 12230* [*USA*]. Billy Joe Thomas was born in Houston, Texas, in 1946 and joined the church choir and subsequently the high school choral group. His admiration for Roy Head led him to make a career in singing. While in high school, he became lead singer with a group called the Triumphs, a seven-piece outfit which subsequently provided the instrumental backing to many of his records. Thomas began performing with the Triumphs at teenage functions in and around Houston at weekends. His popularity soared after a performance at a state park in Texas, where he sang his own

song **The Lazy Man**, a single he had recorded months previously and which became a local hit. Here he was 'discovered' by independent producer Charlie Booth who became his manager and started his rise to national prominence. His first record **I'm So Lonesome I Could Cry**, a Hank Williams song, brought him to the attention of Scepter Records who bought the master and signed Thomas to a contract. The disc became a national hit and Thomas was on his way. Other hit tunes followed: **Mama**, **Billy and Sue** and **Tomorrow Never Comes**.

Hooked on a Feeling was written by Mark James. The disc was released in the USA in October 1968, was No 5 for two weeks and stayed in the charts for 16 weeks. A Gold Disc for a million sale was awarded by RIAA in February 1969. The disc was released in Britain on 3 December 1968.

THE THREE MECKYS   *Austrian*

GEN ALTE SCHAU MI NET SO TEPPART AN *WM Produktion WM 5002* [*Austria*]. This record was the first single to be issued on the WM Produktion label founded in 1968, and owned by the Austrian music publisher Wien Melodie. By 1971, there were 68 versions of this Viennese song in existence, 18 from the Netherlands. An instrumental version by famous orchestra leader James Last was very successful, the **Non-Stop Dancing '70** album containing it selling 422,000.

The Three Meckys, an Austrian folk trio who made this first Austrian million seller, were awarded a Gold Disc in October 1971. It was by then the most successful Viennese song ever recorded. The group's disc was released on the Elite Special label in Germany and reached the Top 10 there in 1969.

The song was written by Szälot and Ull.

THE UNION GAP   *American*
(featuring Gary Puckett)

YOUNG GIRL *CBS-Columbia 44450* [*USA*] *CBS 3365* [*UK*]. The second million seller for this group, the composition is by Jerry Fuller, arranged by Al Capps. Issued at the end of February 1968, it reached the magic figure by 13 April with a Gold Disc award from RIAA. The disc was No 1 for one week in the USA and 15 weeks in the charts and No 1 for five weeks in Britain with 17 weeks in the charts. It features the group's leader Gary Puckett.

Young Girl won a Silver Disc in Britain.

LADY WILLPOWER *CBS-Columbia 44547* [*USA*] *CBS 3551* [*UK*]. The third million seller and RIAA. Gold Disc award (July 1968) in a row for Gary Puckett and the Union Gap, the song was again written by Jerry Fuller and arranged by Al Capps. The recording is on the same lines as their previous million sellers.

The disc was No 1 for one week in the US charts with 13 weeks in the bestsellers, and No 5 for two weeks in Britain with 16 weeks in the Top 50.

It was released at end of May 1968 in the USA.

OVER YOU *CBS-Columbia 44644* [*USA*]. The fourth million seller and RIAA Gold Disc award (December 1968) for Gary Puckett and the Union Gap, and another triumph for writer Jerry Fuller. The disc was released in September 1968 and reach No 5 for two weeks with 11 weeks in the charts. An exceptional ballad with the arrangement and power of their previous great successes.

BOBBY VINTON   *American*

I LOVE HOW YOU LOVE ME *Epic 10397* [*USA*]. A come-back for Bobby with an oldie written by Barry Mann and Larry Kolber in 1961. The disc was released in mid-October 1968 and got to No 4 for one week in the US charts with 14 weeks in the bestsellers. A consistent seller for over three months, it sold a million by the end of the year and was awarded a Gold Disc by RIAA.

THE VOGUES   *American*

TURN AROUND, LOOK AT ME *Reprise 0686* [*USA*]. This song was written in 1961 by Jerry Capehart and provided the Vogues with their first million seller and a Gold Disc award from RIAA. The disc was released in June 1968 and attained No 4 chart position in the USA for one week with 15 weeks in the bestsellers.

The group, all then in their early twenties, comprised Bill Burkette (lead baritone), Don Miller (baritone), Hugh Geyer (first tenor), and Chuck Blasko (second tenor). They all grew up together in Turtle Creek, near Pittsburgh, and formed a working partnership in 1960. They were originally called the Val-Aires, but changed the name to the Vogues, an apt choice since they all dressed very stylishly. They had several chart hits including **Five o'clock World**, **Magic Town**, **You're the One** and **Please Mr Sun** before this hit with **Turn Around, Look at Me**. They were known almost as much for their club act as for their recordings.

MASON WILLIAMS   *American*

CLASSICAL GAS *Warner Brothers-Seven Arts 7190* [*USA*] *Warner Brothers WB 7190* [*UK*]. Mason Williams was born in Abilene, Texas, on 24 August 1938 and learned to play guitar while studying mathematics at Oklahoma City University. He played at night after classes and toured with his folk music group the Wayfarers Trio. After service in the US Navy during which he wrote songs commemorating every event, he began singing in folk clubs around Los Angeles where he met Glenn Yarborough of the Limeliters. Glenn introduced him to the Smothers Brothers who were appearing at Glenn's club. They used Mason's material on a new album they were recording and he wrote for them from then on, also appearing on stage with them playing guitar. Many of his songs have been recorded by the Smothers Brothers, the Kingston Trio, Gale Garnett, Johnny Desmond, Claudine Longet and Glenn Yarborough in addition to his own versions on Warner-7 Arts label. He also wrote for a Petula Clark TV spectacular. His name became widely known when his song **Cinderella Rockefella** became an international hit for the young Israeli duo Esther and Abi Ofarim. He wrote **Classical Gas**, a dreamy orchestral instrumental that includes a dose of everything from classical rock and blue-grass, for his first major album **The Mason Williams Phonograph Record**. Classical Gas was issued on 19 April 1968 as a single in Britain and reached No 9 for one week. In the USA it got to No 1 for a week with 14 weeks in the bestsellers, and sold a million. In Britain it was 13 weeks in the charts.

The instruments used were 10 violins, four cellos, one baritone sax, two tubin horns (Wagnerian tubin horn — a very rare instrument), two trombones, two pianos, one percussion, three guitars and a bass. This instrumental record was produced by Mike Post.

The disc achieved three Grammy Awards for 'Best Instrumental Arrangement', 'Best Contemporary-Pop Performance' and 'Best Intrumental Theme' of 1968. It was re-released in 1978.

STEVIE WONDER   *American*

FOR ONCE IN MY LIFE *Tamla 54174* [*USA*] *Tamla Motown 697* [*UK*]. The fourth million seller for Stevie, the song was written by Orlando Murdon and Ron S. Miller (composer of special material for nightclubs) in 1965. The recording of this ballad was No 1 for one week and 14 weeks in the *Cash Box* Top 100. In *Billboard* it made No 2 in both the pop and R&B charts with 14 weeks in the Hot 100 and 13 weeks in the R&B Top 50. It was released 2 November 1968. The million sale was reached in March 1969. It was also a hit in Britain (released 29 November 1968) where it was No 3 for four weeks and 13 weeks in the bestsellers.

TAMMY WYNETTE   *American*

STAND BY YOUR MAN *Epic 10398* [*USA*] *Epic EPC 7137* [*UK*]. Tammy Wynette's first big hit was written by her and Epic's producer, Billy Sherrill. It reached No 19 and was 16 weeks in the US charts. It was reported in 1975 that the disc had sold over two million.

Tammy was awarded the Grammy for this song, the 'Best Country-and-Western Solo Vocal Performance (Female)' for 1969.

Stand by Your Man had a tremendous success in 1975 when Tammy performed in Britain, her disc selling over 500,000 there. It reached No 1 and was 12 weeks in the charts.

YOUNG-HOLT UNLIMITED   *American*

SOULFUL STRUT *Brunswick 55391* [*USA*]. This trio consisted of Eldee Young (bass) and Isaac 'Red' Holt (drums), formerly two-thirds of the Ramsey Lewis Trio, plus Ken Chaney (piano).

Young studied at the American Conservatory of Music in Chicago, and started his professional career as a guitarist, later switching to bass. He recorded an album on which he made his debut as a cellist, and was the first to introduce the cello to soul sounds effectively. Holt also studied music at the same conservatory as Young, and played professionally with the late Lester Young, Wardell Gray and James Moody. He is said to have introduced the tambourine to jazz. Chaney is a self-taught artist who began his career as a vocalist and then went over to piano. Before going to Chicago where he teamed with Young and Holt, Chaney resided in Detroit and played with such famous jazz artists as Donald Byrd and Kenny Burrell.

Soulful Strut, written by E. Record and Sonny Sanders, was a jazz-rock flavoured disc. It was No 1 for one week with 13 weeks in the US charts, and sold a million with an RIAA Gold Disc award by the end of January 1969, just two months after its release in November 1968.

1 9 6 9

The year 1969 was the year rock festivals blossomed, especially in the USA, and then received a mortal blow at Altamont. Progressive rock flourished, even though Cream were no more. Drugs, free sex and rock'n'roll appeared to be ever more closely linked in the way the popular press portrayed the pop world. Drug busts, nudity at festivals and on album covers, and ever more explicit lyrics all added to the image.

There was growing concern about the effects of this on the morality of the young. In America there was much media discussion about the groupie phenomenon, defined by *Variety* as 'young girls who chase after the rock combos, even into their hotel rooms.' *Time* and *Rolling Stone* devoted much space to the subject, and David Susskind made a television programme on the issue. Alan Lorber made a documentary album on the history of groupies. *Cash Box* reported that: 'Subjects discussed by the various groupies that Lorber found include the status ladder, the groupies' attitude towards group sex, towards themselves and towards the record business; their views of their general futures, marriage, the drug scene; and the seeming dominance of English groups on the groupie scene.'

While progressive rock moved increasingly centre stage, with massive album sales in America, 1969 was also the year that Henry Mancini topped the American charts and Rolf Harris had the Christmas No 1 in Britain. Elvis had a chart topper on both sides of the Atlantic, as did the Rolling Stones. In their case, it was to be their last in Britain.

Creedence Clearwater Revival

The most consistent group in America was Creedence Clearwater Revival. They released four singles in 1969, three of which were double A-sides. Two of them made No 1. In Britain all four made the charts, with **Bad Moon Rising** going to No 1. All the singles sold over a million copies, three of them in America alone, as did all three of the albums they released during the year.

The success of Creedence was something of a reaction against the ever more complicated underground music. Their tight, traditional rock'n'roll had an appealing simplicity about it that swept the world. Creedence were no overnight success. They had been going ten years before they finally made it big, and had been playing pretty well the same music all that time.

The California band developed a style of country blues rock that drew its inspiration from the roots of American rock'n'roll. In John Fogerty they had an extremely talented musician, a song writer of outstanding ability, and a lead singer with a firm voice. Creedence were the Top Singles Artists in America in 1969, and were named by *Rolling Stone* as the Best American Band. At the end of 1970 they toppled the Beatles as Top World Vocal Group in the *New Musical Express* popularity poll in Britain.

The Beatles

If any act can be said to have epitomized a decade as varied as the sixties it was the Beatles. As the decade drew to a close the Beatles were falling apart, though they did not formally split up until 1970. As John Lennon said after the World Peace Show in London in December, where he had appeared with the Plastic Ono Band, 'I'm not the Beatles anymore.'

The Beatles had started the year with business problems. In a January interview with *Disc*, Lennon commented on their Apple experiment: 'Like one or two Beatles things, it didn't work because we aren't practical and we weren't quick enough to realize that we need a businessman's brain to run the whole thing... It's been pie in the sky from the start. Apple's losing money every week...We did it all wrong...It doesn't need to make vast profits but if it carries on like this, all of us will be broke within the next six months.'

His remarks made headlines in the national press, and led to the Beatles bringing in American Allen Klein as their business manager. This exacerbated the tension between John and Paul, for McCartney did not trust Klein and wanted to bring in his new in-laws the Eastmans. The 34-year-old Klein already acted as business manager for the Rolling Stones, Donovan and Mickie Most, though he ultimately fell out with all of them.

Despite all his skills, Klein could not help the Beatles beat off Associated Television, owners of Pye Records, from gaining control of Northern Songs. Northern controlled all the Lennon-McCartney compositions. At one point Warner Brothers entered the battle, but in the end the Beatles admitted defeat and sold their shares to ATV.

The Beatles also sold out of another piece of their heritage. NEMS was the company that Brian Epstein had formed, centred around his management activities. After his death, his mother Queenie inherited his 70% of the company, with the Beatles together owning 10%. At the end of February Triumph Investment bought Mrs Epstein's 70%, buying out the Beatles in July.

Despite all these business set backs, the core of their activity, making music, continued successfully. In April Apple reported that their global disc sales since their formation six months previously had passed 16 million, with sales by the Beatles standing at 8,449,040. Their first single of the year was **Get Back**. Despite some criticism in the music press, the record was No 1 for five weeks on both sides of the Atlantic. The follow-up, **The Ballad Of John And Yoko**, was really a Lennon project with a Beatles name on it. That ensured that it spent a couple of weeks at No 1 in Britain, but it only just made the Top 10 in America.

Lennon was increasingly working on his own, or rather with Yoko Ono in preference to the other Beatles. They let him put his **Ballad** out under the group name, but drew the line at **Give Peace A Chance**, which Lennon released as by the Plastic Ono Band. Lennon seemed increasingly idiosyncratic in his music and in his peace campaign. As well as the commercial singles, Lennon released a couple of avant garde albums that were slammed by the critics. In May came **Unfinished Music No 2, Life With The Lions**. The *New Musical Express* described it thus: 'Side one is... the recording of what Yoko screeched at students in Cambridge... it sounds as if some dreadful torture is being used on Yoko.' In November came the Lennons' **Wedding Album**. *Disc* described this as nicely packaged, but musically 'a terrible bore'.

The individual members of the group were moving in different directions. They no longer enjoyed being Beatles as they had in their earlier days, and in particular they no longer enjoyed touring. In March the group turned down an offer of $4 million for four American concerts from Sid Bernstein, who had promoted their Shea Stadium New York dates in 1965 and 1966.

Lennon in particular was breaking away. In his January interview with *Disc* he said: 'We never were moptops except in other people's minds, and I don't remember us ever being thought of as nice... I think now, people are beginning to realize we don't set any of these trends, and never did. We're just part of the whole thing.' He consciously distanced himself from the old Beatles image. When asked about his reading habits, for example, he jokingly replied: 'The only thing I want to read is pornographic books but they're hard to get hold of.' His peace efforts often drew ridicule, causing the *New Musical Express* to ask of him: 'Bore, Saint or Fool?' While most people recognized his sincerity, it was increasingly clear that it implied that the days of the Beatles were numbered. In December the Beatles released what was to be their last Christmas disc for their fan club. The *NME* described it as their worst ever. December was also the last issue of the *Beatles Monthly*, which had been published every month since August 1963. The editor explained that the group were no longer co-operating in its production.

Family Affairs

The Bee Gees got more publicity for their feuding and matrimonial activity than for their music. In May Robin Gibb fell out with his brothers Maurice and Barry and left the group. Their sister Lesley came in as a temporary replacement. Robin launched his solo career with the highly successful **Saved By The Bell**, though some while later he rejoined the Bee Gees. In August the remaining two Gibb Brothers fired Bee Gees drummer Colin Petersen, leading to Colin and Robin sueing Maurice and Barry in September. Colin lost, and Robin largely won.

Tensions within the group were not helped when in February Barry publicly criticized Maurice as being too young to marry Lulu. He also claimed that Robin had been too young when he had married Molley Hullis a few days before his 19th birthday. At the time his remarks seemed rather unkind, for the 20-year-old Lulu and her new husband seemed idyllically happy. However Barry spoke from experience, for he had married at 20, and was being sued for divorce by his wife Maureen one year later. Barry proved right, for the Maurice/Lulu marriage did not last.

Lulu had the biggest British hit of her career with the Eurovision Song Contest entry **Boom Bang-A-Bang**. It made No 2 in the charts, though it won the contest. To be exact it came top equal with three other entries, all sung by female singers, from France, the Netherlands and Spain. Then things suddenly went badly wrong. She parted company with her producer Mickey Most, and moved from EMI's Columbia to the Atlantic division of Warner Brothers, appearing on their Atco label. This proved a mistake, for the hits dried up. Her first Atco release, **Oh Me, Oh My**, made the Top 50 for only two weeks, peaking at No 47. It was her only Atco hit in Britain, and she did not make the charts again until 1974.

Woodstock

1969 was a great year for festivals. It was mainly in America that this type of concert flourished, for there is something about a brilliantly sunny hot summer's day in California that does not quite translate into a wet and windy London evening. Over 400,000 people came to the three-day Woodstock Music and Art Fair in Bethel, New York, in August. A host of leading rock acts performed. The list included Joan Baez, Joe Cocker, Canned Heat, Country Joe and the Fish, Crosby Stills Nash and Young, the Grateful Dead, Jimi Hendrix, Jefferson Airplane, Janis Joplin, Santana, Sly and the Family Stone, Ten Years After and the Who. The event was relatively trouble-free — there were only three deaths, and two births — and the image of peace, love and rock'n'roll seemed to epitomize what American rock thought it was all about.

Other major three-day festivals included the Texas International Pop Festival with a 120,000 attendance, the Newport '69 Rock Festival seen by 150,000, the Atlantic City Pop Festival with a 110,000 crowd, and the Seattle Pop Festival which drew 70,000. And then there was Altamont. In December the Rolling Stones put on a hastily and badly organized free thank-you concert at the Altamont Speedway in Livermore, California.

Some 300,000 people turn up to see the Stones and a number of other top acts perform. The event was marred by drug abuse and violence, with one fan killed by the Hell's Angels, who had been hired as security for the concert, while the Stones were performing.

Both Woodstock and Altamont were the subject of feature films, with the Altamont picture *Gimme Shelter* actually showing the fan murder. While rock fans viewed Woodstock as a cultural high, many other Americans did not like what they saw. The clear association with drugs and sex caused a backlash. In March Catholic youth groups organized a Rally for Decency in Florida, while in Washington State the Catholic Church called for criminal prosecutions against 'rock festivals and their drug-sex-rock-squalor culture.'

In Britain a free concert in London's Hyde Park drew 120,000 fans to listen to what the *NME* called the 'adult, thinking pop music' of the first performance by Blind Faith, with Donovan and Jimi Hendrix among the others appearing. There were no violent incidents at the concert. Two days after the death of Brian Jones in July, the Rolling Stones gave a free concert in Hyde Park. A quarter of a million people attended. Two other rock events that July were the Bath Pop Music Festival, with John Mayall's Bluesbreakers, Nice and Ten Years After, and the Pop Proms at the Royal Albert Hall. This drew a full house for Led Zeppelin, Blodwin Pig and Fleetwood Mac, but was only one third full for Amen Corner and Marmalade.

August saw the Plumton 9th National Jazz and Blues Festival. The Who and the Nice stole the show. In September 200,000 people attended the Isle of Wight Festival and saw Bob Dylan and the Band. After a long delay, Dylan finally came on stage at 11.00 pm. After only an hour he finished his act, which was shorter than had been expected. Other acts at the three-day event were Marsha Hunt, the Moody Blues and the Who. In October the first Carribean Music Festival, at the Empire Pool, Wembley, starred Johnny Nash.

Globetrotters

Status Quo left for a South American tour in January, later touring the USA, Eastern Europe, Scandinavia and Australasia. The Move and the Hollies did world tours as well. British acts performing in America included Joe Cocker, Julie Driscoll, Herman's Hermits, Mary Hopkin, Humble Pie, Englebert Humperdinck, Led Zeppelin, Lulu, Clodagh Rodgers, the Rolling Stones, Dusty Springfield, Jethro Tull, Thunderclap Newman and the Who. Tom Jones continued to have a lot of success in America with his TV show.

American stars crossing the Atlantic in the other direction included the Beach Boys, Judy Collins, Fats Domino, the Drifters, the Flying Burrito Brothers, Inez and Charlie Foxx, Bill Haley, Janis Joplin, Gene Pitney, the Platters, the Rascals, Little Richard, the Ronettes, Jimmy Ruffin, the Sandpipers, O.C. Smith, Joe South, Tiny Tim, the Toys, Vanilla Fudge, Gene Vincent and Stevie Wonder.

Ins And Outs

Hardly a week seemed to go by without a group splitting up. This was also the age of the supergroup, with band members constantly splitting and forming new outfits. When Traffic broke up, Jim Capaldi and Chris Wood teamed up with Dave Mason and Wynder K. Frog to form Mason, Capaldi, Wood and Frog. As supergroups went, this held some sort of record, for they split up after only 60 days. In May Eric Clapton, Stevie Winwood, Ginger Baker and Ric Grech formed the somewhat longer-lasting Blind Faith. They ran into trouble with their first album cover, which showed a naked 11-year-old girl holding a plane. American dealers complained that it was salacious, so in the States the LP was available in an alternative cover for those who wanted it. May was also the month that Steve Marriott, free after the Small Faces split up in March, joined ex-Herd Peter Frampton in Humble Pie. In June Manfred Mann broke up, with Mann and Mike Hugg forming the nucleus of Manfred Mann Chapter III. It was also in June that Brian Jones left the Rolling Stones.

In October Amen Corner announced that they were splitting, and the music press reported that Christine Perfect was leaving Chicken Shack to spend more time with her husband John McVie. She would later join him in his band Fleetwood Mac, thus playing in two of the most important bands responsible for the rise of British blues. October was also the month that Diana Ross finally left the Supremes, a move that had long been predicted. She was replaced by Jean Terrell. One group that briefly re-formed was the Shadows, who came together for TV dates in December. While this reunion was short lived, the group did finally get back together again in the mid-seventies, and were still going strong into the nineties. In one of the more unlikely moves in the group scene, when Trevor Burton left the Move in February the group asked Shadows lead guitarist Hank Marvin to join them. Understandably he declined.

Hatch, Match And Despatch

The birth, marriage and death columns of the press as usual reported the comings and goings of the pop world. In January ex 'Top Of The Pops' girl Samantha Juste, by then married to Monkee Mickey Dolenz, had a daughter, Anie Bluebell. Janet Bruce, wife of ex-Cream Jack, had baby boy Joey in February.

Two Beatles got married in March. Paul McCartney married Linda Eastman, the second time for her, and they had a daughter Mary on 28 August. A couple of week's after Paul's wedding, John Lennon wed for the second time. He and Yoko Ono married in Gibraltar, and then proceeded to Amsterdam for their honeymoon and a public bed-in for peace.

Lulu married Maurice Gibb in February, the same month that Roy Orbison married his second wife, the German Barbara Wellhoemer. The couple visited England just after their wedding. Roy's first wife Claudette had been killed in a road accident. The tackiest wedding of the year was in February, when Tiny Tim married 17-year-old Vicky Budinger on prime-time TV, on the Johnny Carson Show! DJ Kenny Everett married Lee Middleton in June.

Gerald Marks, who founded *Disc* in 1958, died in January. Shorty Long, whose records included **Function At The Junction** and **Here Comes The Judge**, drowned in Canada in June. Brian Jones also drowned, in his swimming pool in England, on 3 July. Chess Records founder Leonard Chess died in October.

One person who did not die, despite constant rumours to the contrary of an ever more bizarre nature, was Paul McCartney. The 'Paul is dead' hoax was fuelled by 'evidence' as varied as the claim that the hand that appeared over Paul's head on the **Sgt. Pepper** album cover was a symbol of death, to Paul's barefoot appearance on the cover of **Abbey Road**.

The Record Industry

Two trends that surfaced in 1969 were portents of things to come. In America RCA were the first major to announce a move to stereo for all future singles releases. The other American majors soon followed, though in Britain it was the independents who led the way, with the British majors (except Pye) a lot more cautious.

Pye were the most innovative of the four British majors. Internationally they were by far the smallest, with none of the vast world-wide chain of subsidiaries that the mighty EMI or the heavyweight Philips/Polygram had. Alone of the British majors, they had no direct stake in the huge American market. In July Pye and the American tape company GRT, which had bought Chess, formed Janus as a US-based joint venture.

Warner Brothers, which included Atlantic/Atco and Reprise, was owned by the Canadian company Seven Arts. In February an attempted take-over was thwarted when the US Justice Department objected to a bid from the National General Corporation of the US. The next month another American company, Kinney National Services, was more successful. To gain complete control, Kinney bought the 20 per cent of Warner Brothers-7 Arts owned by former Reprise founder Frank Sinatra for $22,500,000. Kinney later changed its own name to Warner Brothers.

On 30 June Warners set up its own branch in Britain, signing a manufacturing and distribution deal with its former licensee Pye. Warner's first release was Kenny Rogers and the First Edition's **Ruby, Don't Take Your Love To Town**. Though this gave them their first No 1, it was the signing of Fleetwood Mac that recouped the entire start-up costs of the new company.

The Warner takeover was not the only one to attract the attention of the US Justice Department. In May the attempt of the giant Westinghouse company to take over MCA (American Decca) was abandoned in the face of objections from Justice. Further restructuring in the American record industry occured when in November Gulf and Western consolidated all their music interests into one concern, the Famous Music Company. This included the Paramount, Dot, Steed and Stax/Volt labels and three music publishing companies.

Other corporate moves in America saw Columbia Pictures buy Bell/Amy/Mala Records and Polydor set up in the US. Shelby Singleton, whose Plantation label had had a massive hit with Jeannie C. Riley's **Harper Valley PTA**, bought the Sun label from Sam Phillips. Sun had launched Elvis Presley, Johnny Cash, Jerry Lee Lewis, Charlie Rich, Roy Orbison, Bill Justice and Carl Perkins. In August Singleton bought the Red Bird catalogue, though not the label itself. This included classics by the Shangri-Las and the Dixie Cups.

In January EMI took over the Associated British Picture Corporation. This included the ABC chain of cinemas and 50 per cent of Thames Television. This made EMI the biggest entertainment company in Britain. EMI was also the biggest record company in the world, a position it enhanced by increasing its stake in the Japanese record company Toshiba from 10 per cent to 50 per cent. This joint venture followed a similar deal between Sony and CBS the year before. EMI also re-established a branch in Norway, the 32nd country in which it had a subsidiary, and CBS opened in Sweden. CBS was blacked by the Arab League because of its support for Israel.

In June EMI launched their underground label Harvest. The first batch of releases included a Deep Purple album and an Edgar Broughton Band single. Pink Floyd were transferred from EMI's Columbia label to Harvest, which also boasted the Pretty Things. Philips started their progressive rock label Vertigo in November. By the mid-seventies its musical style had broadened sufficiently to give a home to Status Quo. The Moody Blues launched their own Threshold label. Motown's success and growth meant a change from its style as a small family unit into a large and diversified organization. It even signed the occasional white act like Kiki Dee. The budget album concept pioneered by Pye blossomed in Britain, with EMI launching the Regal Starline label, and Decca Eclipse.

EMI expanded its music publishing by buying Keith Prowse Music in Britain, and, via Capitol, the major American country and western publisher Central Songs. It was a good year for EMI, with sales up 32 per cent and profits up 36 per cent. Capitol's half-yearly results showed a sales increase of 62 per cent. At the end of the year, the company's boss Sir Joseph Lockwood stepped down as Chief Executive in favour of John Read, though the stayed on as Chairman. It was Read who lead EMI into the brain scanner fiasco that cost it its independence in 1979.

The management agency Chrysalis launched its own label in October. It lasted twenty years as an independent, with acts like Jethro Tull and Blondie, and was bought by EMI in 1989.

In America CBS and RCA were vying with each other to produce the video system of the future. CBS launched its film-based EVR, which was obsolete as soon as it hit the market. RCA invented a holography-based system they called Selectavision. In fact the Japanese JVC beat both of them out of the market with their magnetic tape VHS video recorders. The four-inch pocketdisc was test marketed in Seattle, but despite encouraging results it did not catch on.

World News

The greatest event of the year was the first moon landing. On Monday 21st July American astronaut Neil Armstrong, the commander of Apollo 11, became the first man to set foot on the moon. Later in the month the Americans also received close-up pictures of Mars from Mariner 6.

Richard Nixon took over the White House, and there was growing opposition to the Vietnam War, fuelled by the announcement in April that the American death toll had exceeded that of the Korean War. In October a nationwide Vietnam Moratorium was the biggest protest organized up to that time. In November it was announced that Lt. William Calley, the commander of the US Army platoon that had killed 109 Vietnamese civilians in the My Lai massacre of 1968, would stand trial for murder. The North Vietnamese Communist leader Ho Chi Minh died in September.

In July Senator Edward Kennedy drove his car off a bridge from Chappaquiddick Island, and though he escaped his passenger, 27-year-old Mary Jo Kopechne, was drowned. Kennedy did not report the accident for eight hours. The incident effectively ended his chances of the Presidency. In August pregnant actress Sharon Tate, wife of film director Roman Polanski, and her house guests were brutally murdered by a gang of hippies led by Charles Manson.

It was also a violent year in the United Kingdom, in particular in Ulster. The start of the most recent round of 'troubles' began in Londonderry in January when the police clashed with Catholic civil rights marchers who had trapped the Protestant leader Ian Paisley in the town's Guildhall. In August British troops were sent in to protect Catholics after fierce inter-communal fighting.

In February President Nixon visited Prime Minister Harold Wilson in London. Wilson would be replaced by the Conservatives in the 1970 election. In March the Anglo-French supersonic plane Concorde made its first flight. Oil was discovered in the North Sea in June. The Queen crowned Charles Prince of Wales in July. The Divorce Reform Act was passed in October, making divorce possible after two years if both parties agreed that the marriage had broken down.

The Nigeria Biafra War staggered towards its bloody close, with starvation in defeated Biafra. The civil war finally ended in 1970. Colonel Gaddafi seized power in Libya. General de Gaulle risked one referendum too many, and lost a vote on constitutional reform. He resigned as President of France. Yassar Arafat became leader of the Palestine Liberation Organization.

The Media

'Rowan And Martin's Laugh In' on BBC 2 achieved cult status. On 30 August, the 18-month-old BBC 2 late-night show 'Colour Me Pop' was axed, though it returned for two Christmas specials. During the year 'Top Of The Pops' and other BBC programmes switched from black and white to colour. In November the BBC caused a stir by dropping Simon Dee. The corporation banned **Desdemona** by John's Children, and the No 1 single **Je T'Aime...Moi Non Plus** by Jane Birkin and Serge Gainsbourg. The record was a huge international hit, and when Jane Birkin heard the Japanese version she described it as 'the most terrible noise I've ever heard.' In October, 'Monty Python's Flying Circus' started on BBC 2.

After two years of Radio 1, Disc conducted an opinion poll on radio among its readers. Some 82 per cent thought Radio 1 was an unsatisfactory replacement for the pirate radio stations, while only 15 per cent thought that it was better. The most popular programmes were 'Top Gear' introduced by John Peel, who was also the top DJ, 'Foreverett' centred around the No 2 DJ Kenny Everett, the 'Tony Blackburn Breakfast Show', Alan Freeman's 'Pick Of The Pops' and Johnny Moran's 'Scene And Heard'.

Films

The Rolling Stones released the Jean Luc Godard directed *Sympathy For The Devil*, and it was slammed by the critics. *Disc* reviewed it thus: 'It is a mind boggling mixture of sex, music, black power and politics — and its entertainment value is less than nil...complete and utter rubbish...a clumsy cinematograph catastrophy.'' Mick Jagger starred as Ned Kelly in an Australian film about the famous outlaw. Marianne Faithfull had been hired for the film, but was dropped after she attempted suicide while filming.

Clint Eastwood was the most popular film star in Britain, followed by Omar Sharif, Michael Caine and Steve McQueen. Julie Andrews, ranked eighth, was the only female in the Top Ten. *Oliver!* was the top money maker of the year. Other big films were *Baby Love*, *Candy* and *The Virgin Soldiers*. *Midnight Cowboy* won the Oscar for Best Film, with John Schlesinger getting the Oscar for Best Director. John Wayne won the Best Actor Oscar for his part in *True Grit*, and Maggie Smith won the Best Actress award for *The Prime Of Miss Jean Brodie*.

Sport

Britain's Jackie Stewart won the World Motor Racing Championship. For only the second time since 1945, Britain won a Wimbledon singles tennis championship when Ann Jones beat American Billy Jean King in the Women's Finals. Tony Jacklin became the first British golfer to win the British Open since 1951.

Manchester City beat Leicester City for the FA Cup. Swindon Town beat Arsenal for the League Cup, and Leeds United were top of League Division One. In Scotland Celtic beat Rangers for the SFA Cup, won the League Cup and were top of League Division One. Whatever trouble football hooligans caused in Britain, they never matched the results of violence at an El Salvador versus Honduras match. Passions were so inflamed that the two countries went to war.

Glamorgan were County Cricket Champions, and England won Test Matches against both the West Indies and New Zealand. Both series were played in England.

In America the New York Mets won the World Series. New York also won the Super Bowl, when the Jets beat the Baltimore Colts by 16 to 7. The Minnesota Vikings won the NFL championship, and the Kansas City Chiefs were AFL champions.

End Of The Decade

In 1969 rock music thought it knew where it was going. The Who produced *Tommy*, Led Zeppelin went from strength to strength, and in America Chicago and Blood Sweat and Tears became very big. From the past, Phil Spector returned as a record producer with the Checkmates and Elvis Presley had his best year since the Beatles.

Pete Townsend of the Who detected an anti-British feeling in America. 'They're disenchanted with the Beatles', he told *Disc*, 'and disappointed that groups they want to see, like the Kinks, the Small Faces and the Zombies, never appear.' In fact a new generation of groups had taken America by storm. Cream, Blind Faith, Led Zeppelin and Humble Pie had all been well received.

Some of the biggest stars of the seventies emerged in 1969. In August George Martin's AIR launched a new group called Sweet. After five years of trying, David Bowie got his first hit with **Space Oddity** in September. Marc Bolan had surfaced as half of Tyrannosaurus Rex the

year before, in May 1968. In October ex-Animals guitarist Chas Chandler, who had discovered Jimi Hendrix, launched a skinhead group originally called the In Betweens. They then changed their name to Ambrose Slade, and then dropped the Ambrose bit. They made their debut on the front page of *Disc* the same week as David Bowie did.

The seventies did not turn out as many people expected. There was more glam rock than progressive rock, Creedence did not last, Phil Spector never really made his comeback, the Beatles formally split in 1970 and Elvis Presley died in 1977. Only Cliff Richard went on for ever. 1969 was more than just the end of the decade. It was the end of an era.

ORIGINAL FILM SOUNDTRACK *American*

EASY RIDER (Album) *Dunhill 50063* [USA] *Stateside SSL 5018* [UK]. Columbia Films' release of *Easy Rider* was winner at the Cannes Film Festival, May 1969. It was a directorial debut for Dennis Hopper who teamed with Peter Fonda and Terry Southern to write the script. The story concerns two motorcyclists looking for freedom. Their jaunt takes them across America from California to Louisiana during which the two dropouts' search for freedom is thwarted by the bigoted violence in modern America. The film employed recorded music tracks with rare aptitude, brilliantly edited to the film. Peter Fonda and Dennis Hopper were the two motorbike stars of the film. This soundtrack was a big seller on both sides of the Atlantic and the USA reported a million sale by July 1970. The disc got to No 6 in the USA and stayed in their Top 20 for 33 weeks. It was in the bestsellers for 72 weeks. In Britain it was No 2 for two weeks in 1970, in the Top 20 for 42 weeks and the bestsellers for 71 weeks.

The contents of the album are: **The Pusher** (Steppenwolf), by Hoyt Axton; **Born to Be Wild** (Steppenwolf), by Mars Bonfield (1968); **The Weight** (Smith), by Robbie Robertson; **Wasn't Born to Follow** (The Byrds), by Gerry Goffin and Carole King; **If You Want to Be a Bird** (Holy Modal Rounders), by Antonia; **Don't Bogart Me** (Fraternity of Man), by Elliott Ingber and Larry Wagner; **If 6 Were 9** (Jimi Hendrix Experience), by Jimi Hendrix; ***Kyrie Eleison — Mardi Gras** (The Electric Prunes), by David Axelrod (1969); **It's Alright, Ma** (Roger McGuinn), by Bob Dylan; **Ballad of Easy Rider** (Roger McGuinn), by Roger McGuinn.

*From **Mass in F Minor**, a 'rock' work using extended classical forms by rock musicians, composed by Los Angeles record producer David Axelrod and recorded by the Electric Prunes in 1967.

A Gold Disc award was presented by RIAA on 19 January 1970.

ORIGINAL FILM SOUNDTRACK *British/American*

ROMEO AND JULIET (Album) *Capitol 2993* [USA]. This beautiful film of Shakespeare's play was first released in 1968 and had its US premiere in October at the Paris Theatre in New York. The film was directed by Franco Zefferelli and starred Leonard Whiting (then aged 17) and Olivia Hussey (aged 16), allegedly the youngest performers over to play Shakespeare's 'star-crossed lovers' professionally. An album was released in January 1969, strictly dialogue. It was enormously successful, stayed in the Top 10 from May to September for 16 weeks and achieved the No 1 position for one week. By 3 July it received a Gold Disc award for million dollar sale from RIAA and by the year's end had passed the million units sale. The film's beautiful 'Love Theme' became a million seller as a singles disc for Henry Mancini and his orchestra.

The contents of the album are: **Prologue, Romeo's foreboding and feast at the house of Capulet; Song 'What is Youth?'; Balcony scene; Romeo and Juliet are wed; Death of Mercutio and Tybalt; Farewell love scene; Likeness of death; In Capulet's tomb; All are punished**.

A vocal version of the theme, **A Time for Us** with lyrics by Eddie Snyder and Larry Kusik, was also published.

The album stayed in the US bestseller charts for 74 weeks.

Capitol issued a second album which was a combination of Nino Rota's lovely musical score and dialogue, on four discs. A third version of the entire Nino Rota score without dialogue was issued in January 1970, the first time the label had issued three albums from the same film.

VARIOUS ARTISTS *German*

STUNDE DER STARS (Hour of the stars) (Album) [West Germany]. This album was marketed specifically to raise funds for the 'Altershilfe' (old age relief) and the 'Mutter-genesungswerk' (maternity homes). It sold over two million and produced a net profit of $540,000 (two million Deutschmarks) by February 1970.

VARIOUS ARTISTS *British/American*

WORLD STAR FESTIVAL (Album) *Philips for the United Nations*. Sixteen top disc artists and 12 British and US record companies waived all fees and copyright royalties on the sales of this magnificent album, released in March 1969, in aid of the United Nations fund for refugees, the second of its kind (see also 'All-Star Festival', 1963). It was marketed through Philips Records and sold over 1,250,000 in over 130 different countries in four months. It was launched through the United Nations via the UN High Commissioner for Refugees, Prince Sadruddin Aga Khan.

Contents: **The Happening** (Diana Ross and the Supremes), by E. Holland, L. Dozier and B. Holland (1967); **What the World Needs Now Is Love** (Dionne Warwick), by Hal David and Burt Bacharach (1966); **Georgia on My Mind** (Ray Charles), by S. Gorrell and Hoagy Carmichael (1930); **Cowboys and Indians** (Herb Alpert and the Tijuana Brass), by Sol Lake (1967); **Homeward Bound** (Simon and Garfunkel), by Paul Simon (1966); **For the First Time in My Life** (Tom Jones), by E. Greines (1969); **The Beat Goes On** (Sonny and Cher), by Sonny Bono (1966); **The Singer Sang His Song** (The Bee Gees), by Maurice, Barry and Robin Gibb (1968); **I've Got a Song for You** (Shirley Bassey), by L. Holmes and Al Stillman (1968); **May Each Day** (Andy Williams), by Morton J. Green and George Wyle (1963); **Thoroughly Modern Millie** (from the film) (Julie Andrews), by Sammy Cahn and James van Heusen (1967); **I'll Go On Loving Her** (Je l'aimerai toujours) (Paul Mauriat and his Orchestra), by Charles Aznavour (1968); **Talk to the Animals** (from the film *Doctor Doolittle*) (Sammy Davis, Jr), by Leslie Bricusse (1967); **I Think It's Going to Rain Today** (Dusty Springfield), by Randy Newman (1968); **September of My Years** (Frank Sinatra), by Sammy Cahn and James van Heusen (1965); **He Touched Me** (Barbra Streisand), by M. Schafer and I. Levin (1965).

ADAMO *Belgian*

PETIT BONHEUR *La Voi De Son Maitre (French HMV) C006-23104M* [France]. Another million seller for Belgian star Adamo, whose sales had increased every year of the sixties since his first hit in 1962. Salvatore Adamo wrote nearly all his own material, including **Inch Allah**, his biggest hit of 1968. He also wrote **Petit Bonheur**, which in 1969 reached No 7 in Belgium and No 5 in France. World sales totalled a million by April 1970.

THE APOLLO 11 *American*
ASTRONAUTS (narrated by Hugh Downs)

FIRST MAN ON THE MOON *MGM* [USA]. The successful lunar landing on 20 July 1969 was one of the greatest events in human history.

Apollo 11 with astronauts Neil Armstrong, Edwin Aldrin and Michael Collins blasted off from Cape Kennedy on 16 July 1969 for the over 250,000-mile journey to the moon. On 20 July, the lunar module 'Eagle' separated from the command ship 'Columbus' for the descent to the moon's surface with Armstrong and Aldrin, while Collins orbited the moon in 'Columbus' to await their re-docking. 'Eagle' touched down on the moon's surface in the Sea of Tranquillity. Neil Armstrong became the first man ever to set foot on the moon, saying as he planted his white left boot in the moon's grey dust, 'That's one small step for a man — a giant leap for mankind. The moon walk was seen by millions of people on television around the world and the voices of the astronauts were clearly heard.

Each of the three astronauts was born in 1930: Neil Alden Armstrong in Wapakoneta, Ohio on 5 August, Col. Edwin Eugene Aldrin in Montclair, New Jersey on 20 January, and Lt.-Col. Michael Collins in Rome, Italy, on 31 October.

This successful lunar landing launched a great outpouring of documentary discs. And the first to hit the US market was this 45 rpm disc aimed at the chain stores and supermarkets. It traces the history of the US space programme and features the actual voices of the astronauts. MGM released the disc on 22 July and it quicky passed the million and a half mark with sales thereafter rapidly accelerating. Prices of the various discs and albums ranged from 39c to as high as $19.95 and aggregate sales ran into many millions.

In Britain, Philips manufactured a special disc sold exclusively to readers of the *News of the World*, Britain's largest-selling Sunday newspaper.

THE ARCHIES *American*

SUGAR SUGAR *Calendar 1008* [USA] *RCA Victor 1872* [UK]. Written by Jeff Barry (producer of the disc) and Andy Kim, this disc was released in the USA in July 1969 and by 30 August had sold a million with an RIAA Gold Disc award. It got to No 1 for four weeks with 22 weeks in the bestsellers, and by October passed the three million sale in the USA. The Archies were cartoon characters — Archie Andrews, Mr Weatherbee, Betty Cooper, Veronica Lodge, Reggie Mantle and Jughead Jones — who topped the TV ratings all over the USA with their Saturday morning CBS series. The series was based on a newspaper strip, originated in 1942 by the American cartoonist John L. Goldwater, which first appeared in the late 1940s. Don Kirschner, who made the Monkees famous, was responsible for the music in the series.

This single was cut by studio singers who remained anonymous with the exception of Ron Dante (born 1948) who was later named as the lead singer.

In Britain the disc was No 1 for eight weeks and sold over a million. It was also No 1 in many other countries including Spain, Denmark, Norway, Belgium, Germany, and Mexico, and sales brought the global tally up to six million. Don Kirschner received the Carl-Alan Award in Britain for Sugar, Sugar — the most popular disc of the year.

JINGLE JANGLE Kirschner 5002 [USA]. The second million seller for the Archies, again written by Jeff Barry and Andy Kim, was released in November and taken from the Jingle Jangle album. The disc reached No 4 for a week with 13 weeks in the bestsellers, and received a Gold Disc award from RIAA in February 1970.

THE BEATLES   British

YELLOW SUBMARINE (Album) Apple (Parlophone) PMC 7070 [UK]/Apple (Capitol) SW 153 [USA]. Yellow Submarine was the soundtrack album from the Beatles cartoon film of the same name, inspired by the group's 1966 hit single. Unlike the 'Magical Mystery Tour' film, the cartoon was a critical as well as a financial success. Though the album sold well enough, the Beatles did not regard it as one of their better recordings. For a start, only half of it was the Beatles. Side two was the George Martin Orchestra with incidental music from the film. Of the six Beatles tacks, two had already been released and the other four were old recordings as the release of the LP had been delayed because of the White Album project. George Martin had had overall producer responsibility, and had scored the music for Yellow Submarine.

The Yellow Submarine album was not, therefore, a milestone between the White Album and Abbey Road. It was really a case of tidying up a project that they were committed to as best they could. Of the Beatles tracks, Yellow Submarine had been recorded in 1966. Only A Northern Song was written by George Harrison for Sgt Pepper, but had not been used. It was recorded in February 1967 at Abbey Road, and produced by George Martin. Its All Too Much was another Harrison song recorded in May 1967, at the De Lane Lea Music Studios in London. George himself and

Dave Siddle handled the production work. All Together Now was recorded in May 1967 at Abbey Road. George Martin was absent for this, and Geoff Emerick took control of the session. Hey Bulldog was written by John Lennon for the Yellow Submarine film, and was recorded in February 1968 in Abbey Road's Studio 3. George Martin produced the track. All You Need Is Love had been recorded as a single in 1967. The George Martin tracks were all recorded at Abbey Road in January 1969, with Martin producing and conducting his 41 piece orchestra.

Released in Britain on 17 January, the album reached No 3 during 10 weeks in the LP charts. In America, where release was on 13 January, the album spent two weeks at No 2, with 24 weeks in the charts. It won an RIAA Gold Disc on 5 Feburary 1969, and went on to sell over a million copies in America.

Of the Beatles tracks on side one, four were credited to John Lennon and Paul McCartney two, marked *, were written by George Harrison. All the music on side two was written by George Martin. The track listing was as follows: Side 1: Yellow Submarine; *Only A Northern Song; All Together Now; Hey Bulldog; *It's All Too Much; and All You Need Is Love. Side 2: Pepperland; Sea Of Time/Sea of Holes; Sea Of Monsters; March Of The Meanies; Pepperland Laid Waste; and Yellow Submarine In Pepperland.

GET BACK Apple (Parlophone) R 5777 [UK]/ Apple (Capitol) 2490 [USA]. The Beatles's 47th million seller was the Lennon-McCartney rocker Get Back. Originally meant as the title track of an album of the same name, it comes from a particularly difficult period of the Beatles career. The Beatles were falling apart. Ringo Starr had already walked out of the group once, and George Harrison briefly did the same. John Lennon, working increasingly with Yoko Ono, had suggested that the group disband. Only Paul McCartney wanted to keep going. He thought that the answer to the group's malaise was to get back to their roots and perform to a live audience. The last thing that the other three wanted to do was to go back to touring, so they all compromised and agreed to make a film of them making a live album. That album was to be Get Back, but the whole project proved a disaster and the album never materialized. The title track, however, did and was released as a single on 11 April 1969 (and on 5 May in the USA.)

Get Back featured black American organist Billy Preston, who the Beatles had signed to Apple. He was not the first musician to appear on a Beatles record, but he was the first to be credited on the record label. Born in Houston, Texas, in 1947, he first came across the Beatles in their Hamburg days. He was included in the Get Back album recording sessions by George Harrison partly to ease the tension in the studio caused by the internal group politics.

Get Back and its flip side Don't Let Me Down were both recorded at the new Apple studios in Savile Row on 28 January. This was the first Beatles single not to be recorded at Abbey Road. It is not entirely clear who the producer was, for the whole Get Back album project had descended into confusion. Though

George Martin was involved, he did not have the clear control of the old Abbey Road days. Glyn Johns had also been involved, and he was given the task of trying to produce the album once the recording was finished. Eventually the Get Back album was shelved, though some of the material was used for the 1970 album Let It Be.

The record entered the Record Retailer Top 50 at No 1 first week of release, and spent 17 weeks in the charts. In America it entered the Billboard Top 100 at No 10 five days after release, on 10 May. This equalled the record for the highest debut position set by the Beatles' Hey Jude the year before. In fact up to the end of 1988, six of the ten highest entries in the Billboard chart since the Hot 100 began in 1958 were by the Beatles, including all three that debuted in the Top 10. Of the remaining four, one was by John Lennon. Get Back shot up to No 3 in its second week in the charts and made the top in its third week. It won a Gold Disc on 19 May 1969.

Around the world Get Back hit No 1 in Canada, Australia, New Zealand, South Africa, Ireland, Sweden, Norway, Denmark, Germany, Austria, Switzerland, Belgium, the Netherlands, France, Spain, Yugoslavia, Singapore, the Philippines, Mexico and Brazil. It also made the Top 10 in Finland, Italy, Turkey, Malaysia, Hong Kong, Japan, Peru, Chile and Argentina. The flip side, Don't Let Me Down, also charted in the USA, Canada, Australia, Switzerland and Spain. In Israel, the EMI licensee coupled Get Back with The Ballad Of John And Yoko, creating a double A side which went to No 2.

THE BALLAD OF JOHN AND YOKO Apple (Parlophone) R 5786 [UK]/Apple (Capitol) 2531 [USA]. The Ballad Of John And Yoko was really a John Lennon project with a Beatles name on it. It was the first in the line of records that included Give Peace A Chance and Happy Xmas, War Is Over, which were credited to the Plastic Ono Band. George Harrison and Ringo Starr had nothing to do with making the record, for George was abroad and Ringo was filming. Paul McCartney did help out, playing drums as well as guitar. Though credited as a Lennon-McCartney composition it was actually written by John Lennon, who sang lead on the record. It was produced by George Martin in Studio 3 at Abbey Road on 14 April.

The song is the story of John Lennon's recent life and his marriage to Yoko Ono. The lyrics caused a storm in America because of the line 'Christ, you know it ain't easy' and the later reference to crucifixion. A number of radio stations refused to play the record. This harmed its chart performance, both because fewer people heard it and because the American charts are compiled partly from radio plays as well as sales. The record reached only No 8 in America, with 9 weeks in the charts. Apart from Lady Madonna, it was the only Beatles single from the end of 1964 to their break up in 1970 that did not go to No 1 in at least one of the four main American charts. It was also the first Beatles record since Help!, twelve releases previously in 1965, where the flip side did not also chart in Billboard. It still sold over a million copies in America, winning a Gold Disc on 16 June 1969.

In Britain the record was released on 30 May, while the group's **Get Back** was still at No 1. The Beatles were soon back at No 1 with this, with a total of 14 weeks in the Top 50. It spent three weeks at the top, and was the last occasion on which the Beatles went to No 1 in Britain. Around the world the record was almost as successful as **Get Back**. It was No 1 in Canada, Australia, Norway, Denmark, Germany, Austria, Switzerland, Belgium, the Netherlands, Spain, Malaysia, Hong Kong, the Philippines, Japan and Mexico. It was also a hit in New Zealand, Sweden, France, Italy, Israel, Turkey, Argentina, Brazil, Chile and Peru.

ABBEY ROAD (Album) *Apple (Parlophone) PCS 7088* [UK]/*Apple (Capitol) SO 383* [USA]. The *Abbey Road* album was, of course, named after the EMI studios where most of the Beatles' material had been recorded. Its famous cover, of the group walking across the zebra pedestrian crossing outside the studios in Abbey Road, has been copied by groups as varied as the Shadows, whose **Live At Abbey Road** set even had the same Volkswagen car parked in the same place as on the Beatles cover, and the Red Hot Chilli Peppers, whose infamous version had the group posing in the same way as the Beatles, but competely naked except for a single strategically worn sock.

Recorded in July and August 1969, **Abbey Road** was the last Beatles album and one of their best. (**Let It Be** was the last Beatles LP to be released, but it was really a continuation of the **Get Back** album saga.) It was released in Britain on 26 September 1969, and on 1 October in America. It was produced by George Martin at EMI's Abbey Road Studios, with Phil McDonald, Tony Clark and Geoff Emerick as engineers and Chris Blair, John Kurlander and Alan Parsons (later of the Alan Parson Project) as tape operators.

On the first side of the album John Lennon was the main influence, as the harder rock feel about it suggests. Paul McCartney was the dominant force on the softer second side, where tracks were segued into each other in what *Time* described as a 'long, interlocked, medley — a kind of odyssey from innocence to experience.' George Harrison contributed his best ever Beatles song with the beautiful **Something**, which the other Beatles rated the best song on the album.

In more ways than one **Abbey Road** was in part a return to an earlier Beatles era. After the fiasco of **Get Back/Let It Be**, George Martin was firmly back in charge as producer. The music harked back to **Rubber Soul** and **Revolver** rather than **Sgt Pepper**. Yet the Beatles themselves had not returned to a happier time. The divisions were still there during the recording of this album, exacerbated by John's insistence on bringing Yoko along all the time — she even moved a double bed into the studio. The Beatles were all pursuing solo projects. John had already released records as the Plastic Ono Band, George had the **Wonderwall Music** album out, Paul was planning his first solo album and Ringo was

increasingly looking to films, though he was also to have solo recording success. Though these divisions were contained for the making of this album, and further Beatles records would be released in 1970, in the creative sense this was the end of the road for the greatest recording artists of all time. The Beatles formally broke up in 1970.

The album went to No 1 in Britain for 17 weeks, and was in the LP charts for 81 weeks. In America it was No 1 for 11 weeks, with 116 weeks in the charts. It won an RIAA Gold Disc for million dollar sales on 27 October 1969, and also won a Grammy for Best Engineered Album of the Year. It was the biggest selling of all Beatles albums in North America. It sold over eight million copies in the USA, and just under a million in Canada.

The tracks on the album, all of which were credited to Lennon and McCartney unless otherwise stated, were as follows: **Come Together**; **Something** by George Harrison; **Maxwell's Silver Hammer**; **Oh! Darling**; **Octopus's Garden** by Ringo Starr; **I Want You (She's So Heavy)**; **Here Comes The Sun** by George Harrison; **Because**; **You Never Give Me Your Money**; **Sun King/Mean Mr Mustard**; **Polythene Pam/She Came in Through The Ballroom Window**; **Golden Slumbers/Carry That Weight**; **The End**; **Her Majesty**.

SOMETHING/COME TOGETHER *Apple (Parlophone R 5814* [UK]/*Apple (Capitol) 2654* [USA]. The Beatles' 50th million selling record, their last of the decade, was the double A side **Something/Come Together**. It was the first time that the Beatles had released a single in Britain from material already available on an album, for both sides came from **Abbey Road**. This practice was still frowned upon in Britain, and sales of the record were appreciably lower than other Beatles singles. It was the only Beatles record released while the group were still in existence that did not qualify for a Silver Disc for British sales of a quarter of a million. (**Love Me Do** did not qualify at first, but passed the quarter million mark in 1982 when EMI re-released it.)

The two sides were recorded from April to August 1969, using a number of studios and recording people. The recording was done mainly at EMI's Abbey Road Studios 2 and 3, with the Olympic Sound Studios also used. George Martin, Chris Thompson and George Harrison were the producers at various sessions. The engineer on duty, depending on the session, was either Jeff Jarratt, Glyn Johns or Phil McDonald. The tape operators were Richard Lush, Nick Webb, Steve Vaughan, John Kurlander and Alan Parsons.

Something was the A side in Britain, written by George Harrison and featuring him as lead singer. It was released on 31 October, but failed to go to No 1. It stalled at No 4 in the *Disc/Melody Maker* and *Record Retailer* charts, with 12 weeks in the Top 50. In *NME*, still the most widely read pop paper in the world at that time, it entered the Top 30 at No 17, which was the lowest Beatles debut position since the group broke big in 1963. Its chart progress over the next seven weeks was 10, 5, 5, 9, 14, 21 and 20. Though **Something** was a high quality

beautiful ballad, it was not as commercial a song as the other Beatles records.

In America radio stations were playing both sides of the record, and both therefore featured in the US charts. It was released on 6 October. **Something** entered the *Billboard* Hot 100 as the highest new entry of the week at No 20 on 18 October. The Lennon-McCartney **Come Together**, a more up-beat number with John Lennon as lead vocalist, entered the charts just behind it. The two sides raced each other up the charts, with **Come Together** soon overtaking **Something**, though never by much. On 15 November **Come Together** was at No 2 and **Something** at No 3. On 29 November *Billboard* changed its policy on listing double A sides separately, and from that week onwards the two sides had one chart placing. This put the record straight up to No 1, something that the previously split sales had prevented. The record spent 16 weeks in the charts, and was the 60th and 61st Beatles entries in the *Billboard* singles Hot 100. It won an RIAA Gold Disc on 27 October 1969.

As usual the record sold well around the world. With sales split between the two sides there were fewer No 1 placings than usual, though one side or the other (and frequently both sides) made the charts in 30 different countries.

Something was No 1 in the USA, Canada, Australia, New Zealand, Israel, Malaysia and Singapore. **Come Together** reached the top in New Zealand (as a separate chart entry to **Something**), South Africa, Austria and the Philippines. The record was also a hit in Ireland, Finland, Sweden, Norway, Denmark, Germany, Switzerland, Belgium, the Netherlands, France, Spain, Italy, Poland, Lebanon, Hong Kong, Japan, Mexico, Brazil and Chile.

The Beatles would go on to have more million sellers in the 1970s and 1980s as EMI repackaged their material. Their 50 million sellers of the sixties, 49 of which were with EMI, were a tremendous achievement: 27 of them were singles, 21 were LPs (including one double album) and two were EPs (one a double EP.)

No other artists came anywhere near this. The sixties were an exciting decade in which to live and enjoy music. Pop and rock changed a great deal during the decade, and many great records (and not a few duff ones) were made. Some very talented artists were at work. Standing head and shoulders above them all were the Beatles.

BROOK BENTON   *American*

RAINY NIGHT IN GEORGIA *Cotillion 44057* [USA]. Released in late December 1969, this disc achieved No 2 in the US charts for a week in March 1970, by which time it had sold a million with an RIAA Gold Disc award. The song, written by disc artist Tony Joe White, proved powerful material for Benton. It was recorded at the Criteria Studio in Miami, Benton being backed by the promising new Florida Rhythm Section 'Cold Grits' (a quartet) plus Cornell Dupree on guitar and Dave Crawford on piano.

JANE BIRKIN AND SERGE GAINSBOURG
British/French

JE T'AIME...MOI NON PLUS *Fontana TF 1042 and then Major Minor MM 645* [*UK*] *Fontana 1665* [*USA*]. **Je t'aime** was the most controversial record of the decade, banned by most broadcasting organizations as too erotic. It is a love song in the fullest sense, with Jane Birkin and Serge Gainsbourg cooing to each other as they make love, with heavy breathing, orgasm and all. Though sung in French, it proved too much for the BBC. How many people actually understood the French words is debatable, but the heavy breathing sound effects left little doubt about the general drift of its meaning.

Jane Birkin (born in London on 14 December 1947) was an actress who first came to public attention with a small part in the film *Blow Up*. She later had parts in *Wonderwall* and *Pashion Flower Hotel*. She met Frenchman Serge (born 1929) while auditioning for the film *Slogan*, for which she had moved to France. The couple were soon living together. Serge, a singer, actor, film music and pop composer, originally wrote **Je t'aime** for Brigitte Bardot, who recorded it but on reflection she considered the song too erotic and would not agree to its release. In early 1969 Serge and Jane came to Britain to record the album **Jane Birkin & Serge Gainsbourg**, and included **Je t'aime** as one of the tracks.

The Dutch record company Philips released the record in France in the spring, and in Britain on its Fontana label on 27 June 1969. A month later it entered the Top 50, and then the controversy really began. After eight weeks in the charts the record stood at No 3, and then Philips withdrew it. They withdrew it throughout Europe, claiming that they did not intend that any of their products should be the centre of controversy. However, in the lucrative American market their company was pushing it with full-page press advertising.

In France Philips passed the controversial record on to Disque AZ, a small independent company. When Philips withdrew the record in Britain, AZ licensed it to Major Minor, and within two days the record was back on sale with a terrific publicity boost. On 11 October **Je t'aime** made No 1. It spent one week at the top, and 25 weeks in the charts. It was re-issued in 1974, when it reached No 31 with another nine weeks in the Top 50. Although it sold well over a quarter of a million copies in Britain, it did not win a Silver Disc as the sales were split between two different record companies.

The record generated similar controversy throughout Europe, and was a major hit all over the world. It went to No 1 in Sweden, Norway, Denmark, Austria, Switzerland, France and Israel, and was a Top Four hit in Germany, the Netherlands, Belgium, the West Indies, Mexico, Brazil and Peru. The one country it was not a big hit in was America. There had not been anything like the controversy there, and though there was hardly any airplay the record was not such a big issue. Philips continued to promote it throughout its 10 weeks on the charts. Its highest position was No 58.

Jane Birkin's first and only hit record did wonders for her career. Though her impact in Britain was not long-lasting, she became the new sex symbol of France where she lived with Serge. They were voted France's most exiting couple of 1969.

ROY BLACK
German

DEINE SCHONSTES GESCHENK *Polydor 3411* [*West Germany*]. Another big success for Roy Black, this disc was released in November 1969. By mid-January 1970 it sold over half a million, with the million sale plus Gold Disc by May 1970. It stayed at No 1 for nine weeks in Germany between January and March.

BLOOD, SWEAT AND TEARS
American

BLOOD, SWEAT AND TEARS (Album) *CBS-Columbia 9720* [*USA*] *CBS 63504* [*UK*]. The nucleus of this group was born in New York in the summer of 1967, the brainchild of Al Kooper, an organist and singer previously a member of the Blues Project. He also gave the group its name. Kooper recruited guitarist Steve Katz from his old band, Katz brought in drummer Bobby Colomby, and Colomby discovered sax-pianist-arranger Fred Lipsius. Classical-trained trombone-organist-arranger Dick Halligan and rock bass player Jim Fielder completed the band. They made a debut album **Child is Father to the Man** for CBS (an early 1968 chart success) by which time trumpeters Randy Brecker and Jerry Weiss had made the group an octet. After about a year, Kooper left to become a soloist and record producer, followed by Weiss and Becker. The group found new blood in vocalist David Clayton-Thomas and three seasoned brass men, trumpeters Lew Soloff and Chuck Winfield and trombonist Jerry Hyman, making a nine-piece band.

In late December 1968 the new group's album entitled **Blood, Sweat and Tears** was released and sold 600,000 in four months, and received a Gold Disc award from RIAA within three months. It was No 1 in the charts for seven weeks and stayed in the Top 10 for several months, selling two million by the year's end.

David Clayton-Thomas, born 1944 in London, was raised in Toronto and previously led his own band in Canada; Steve Katz, born 1945 in Brooklyn, was originally with the Blues Project; Fred Lipsius born 1944 in New York, was a graduate of the High School of Music and Art, also studied at Berklee Music School, Boston; Jim Fielder, born 1948 in Texas, was taught music by his father, and then worked with the Mothers of Invention and Buffalo Springfield; Dick Halligan, born 1944 in New York, studied at Manhattan School of Music where he received an MA in music, going on to lead his own trio; Bobby Colomby, born 1945 in New York City, has a BA in psychology; Chuck Winfield, born 1943 in Pennsylvania, gained BA and Master's degrees in music at the Juilliard School of Music, New York; Jerry Hyman, born 1947 in Brooklyn, studied at New York School of Music, and is also a pianist and flugel horn player; Lew Soloff, born Brooklyn, 1944, studied at the Juilliard School of Music, New York for six years, then at Eastman School of Music, Rochester, New York.

The contents of this exciting, progressive album were: *****Trois Gymnopedies** — 1st and 2nd Movements, by Erik Satie (1866-1925); **Smiling Phases**, by Steve Winwood; Jim Capaldi and Chris Wood (all members of Traffic); **Sometimes in Winter** (sung by Steve Katz), by Steve Katz; **More and More**, by P. Vee and D. Juan; **And When I Die**, by Laura Nyro; **God Bless the Child**, by Arthur Herzog, Jr., and Billie Holiday (1941); **Spinning Wheel**, by David Clayton-Thomas; **You've Made Me So Very Happy**, by Berry Gordy, Jr., B. Holloway, P. Holloway and F. Wilson; **Blues Part 2**, by David Clayton-Thomas, Steve Katz,

Fred Lipsius and Bobby Colomby; **Trois Gymnopedies** (reprise) by Erik Satie.

This disc received the Grammy Award for 'Album of the Year' (1969) and the Erik Satie variations (*) a Grammy Award for 'Best Contemporary Instrumental Performance' (1969).

It was in the US bestsellers for 109 weeks. In Britain it made No 15 during 8 weeks in the charts.

YOU'VE MADE ME SO VERY HAPPY *CBS-Columbia 44776 [USA] CBS 4416 [UK]*. Taken from the group's album **Blood, Sweat and Tears** this track was issued as a single in the USA in March 1969. It was No 2 for three weeks with 13 weeks in the US bestsellers, and sold a million by 12 June with an RIAA Gold Disc award. It was No 35 in Britain. The song was written by Berry Gordy, Jr., B. Holloway, P. Holloway and F. Wilson.

SPINNING WHEEL *CBS-Columbia 44871 [USA]*. This disc was also taken from their album and released as a single in May 1969. It sold a million by 23 July 1969 with an RIAA Gold Disc award. The disc was No 2 for three weeks in the US charts with 13 weeks in the bestsellers. The song was written by David Clayton-Thomas, lead singer of the group. Grammy Award (1969) for 'Best Arrangement Accompanying Vocalist(s)'.

AND WHEN I DIE *CBS-Columbia 45008 [USA]*. An easy-going arrangement of the tune by Laura Nyro, this was the third single taken from the album **Blood, Sweat and Tears** to sell a million. It was released in October 1969 and was No 2 in the US charts for two weeks with 13 weeks in the bestsellers. A Gold Disc was awarded by RIAA in January 1970.

JERRY BUTLER   *American*

ONLY THE STRONG SURVIVE *Mercury 72898 [USA]*. Jerry Butler's recording of this song was released in the USA in February 1969, and in Britain on 11 April 1969. It reached No 4 in America with 13 weeks in the bestsellers, and by 24 April sold the million with an RIAA Gold Disc award. The song was written by Jerry with the producers of the disc, K. Gamble and L. Huff.

Jerry Butler was born on 8 December 1939 in Sunflower, Missouri, his family moving to Chicago in 1942 where his father was a railroad fireman for the Northwestern railroad. Jerry sang spirituals as a child on a Chicago radio station, and was active in choir singing from 12. He then joined the Northern Jubilee Gospel Singers. After graduation from Washburn School in Chicago he found singing was his main interest and sang with his own group, the Impressions. Eventually, the group came to the attention of Vee Jay Records' Ewart Abner, Jr. Their first hit was **For Your Precious Love** written by Jerry with Arthur and Richard Brooks in 1958, now a standard evergreen. Soon after, Jerry decided to become a soloist and made several hits including **Aware of Love, He Will Break Your Heart, Love Me, Let It Be Me** and in 1961 **Moon River**.

GLEN CAMPBELL   *American*

GALVESTON *Capitol 2428 [USA] Ember EMBS 263 [UK]*. The second million seller singles disc for Glen, the song was again written for him by Jim Webb, the disc was released in February 1969 and was awarded a Gold Disc by RIAA on 14 October. It was No 3 in the charts for two weeks in the USA with 12 weeks in the bestsellers. The title was also used for a million-dollar-selling album by Glen.

Release of this single in Britain was in May 1969 where it reached No 11 for one week and spent 10 weeks in the charts.

GLEN CAMPBELL — LIVE (Double Album) *Capitol 0268 [USA]*. This two-record release on 29 August 1969 was Glen Campbell's first 'live' album of his sell-out concert at the Garden State Art Center, New Jersey, on 24 July 1969. it contained 18 'on stage' recordings — nine of his previous hits and nine songs he had never before recorded — and was produced by Al deLory. It sold over 600,000 in one month and was awarded a Gold Disc by RIAA on 19 September for million dollars sale, and easily sold a million units before year's end.

This US release contained: **More** (from the film *Mondo Cane*), by M. Cioriolini, Riz Ortolani and N. Oliviero (1963) (English words by Norman Newell); **Somewhere** (from *West Side Story*), by Stephen Sondheim and Leonard Bernstein (1957); **Didn't We**, by Jim Webb (1969); **Dreams of the Everyday Housewife**, by Chris Gantry (1969); **By the Time I Get to Phoenix**, by Jim Webb (1968); **For Once in My Life**, by Orlando Murdon and Ron S. Miller (1965); **Gentle on My Mind**, by John Hartford (1968); **Where's the Playground, Susie?** by Jim Webb (1969); **Dock of the Bay (Sittin' on)**, by Steve Cropper and Otis Redding (1967); **If You Go Away** (Ne me quitte pas), by Rod McKuen and Jacques Brel (1969); **Walk Right In**, by Gus Cannon and Hosie Woods (1930); **The Impossible Dream** (from *Man of La Mancha*), by Joe Darion and Mitch Leigh (1966); **The Lord's Prayer**, music by Albert Hay Malotte (1935); **Mountain Dew**; and four other titles.

It reached No 7 in the US charts for two weeks, and was in the bestsellers for 29 weeks. The British release was a single disc album and contained the first 12 titles as above.

JOHNNY CASH   *American*

A BOY NAMED SUE *CBS-Columbia 44944 [USA] CBS 4460 [UK]*. A very amusing song about the disadvantages of a boy being saddled with a girl's name, it was one of the tracks from his album recorded at San Quentin, performed against a background of cheers and laughter from the prisoners.

The song was written by Shel Silverstein and the disc released in July 1969. It was No 1 in the USA for one week with 12 weeks in the bestsellers, and sold a million with an RIAA Gold Disc award on 14 August. It was also a No 1 country disc for five weeks. In Britain it reached No 3 for one week.

The song received Grammy Awards (1969) for 'Best Country Vocal Performance' and 'Best Country Song'.

JOHNNY CASH AT SAN QUENTIN (Album) *CBS-Columbia CS 9827 [USA] CBS 63629 [UK]*. A tremendous selling album for Johnny Cash, it was released in June 1969 in the USA and was awarded a Gold Disc for million dollar sales on 12 August. By the year's end it had sold over two million in records and tapes. In the USA it achieved No 1 for four weeks and was in the Top 10 for 20 weeks with sales continuing strongly into 1970. In Britain it was No 1 for two weeks and in the Top 10 for 25 weeks into 1970. British release was in August 1969. The album contained the song **A Boy Named Sue**, a million seller as a single (see above).

It was the second album recorded by Johnny at a US prison. Johnny was awarded five of the 10 awards at the Country Music Association Festival in October 1969 — 'Entertainer of the Year', 'Male Vocalist of the Year', 'Singles Disc of the Year', 'Vocal Group (with wife June Carter) of the Year' and 'Album of the Year' (**At San Quentin**).

The contents of the album are: **Wanted Man**, by Bob Dylan; **Wreck of the Old '97**, traditional: arr. Cash, Johnson and Blake; **I Walk the Line**, by Johnny Cash (1956); **Darling Companion**, by John Sebastian; **Starkville City Jail**, by Johnny Cash; **San Quentin**, by Johnny Cash; **A Boy Named Sue**, by Shel Silverstein (1969); **Peace in the Valley**, by Thomas A. Dorsey (1939); **Folsom Prison Blues**, by Johnny Cash (1956).

This album was in the US album charts for 70 weeks. In Britain the record made No 2, with 114 weeks in the album charts.

CHAIRMEN OF THE BOARD   *American*

GIVE ME JUST A LITTLE MORE TIME *Invictus 9074 [USA] Invictus INV 501 [UK]*. Produced by the great songwriting team of Holland, Dozier and Holland for their new label Invictus, the song was written by R. Dunbar and E. Wayne. The disc was released in late December 1969, and reached No 3 for a week in the USA with million sale plus an RIAA Gold Disc award by May 1970. It reached No 8 during 13 weeks in the R&B charts. In Britain it made No 3 with 13 weeks in the Top 50. This was the first million seller for the Invictus label. The group were General Johnson (formerly with the Showmen) lead singer, Harrison Kennedy, Denny Woods and Eddie Curtis.

CHICAGO TRANSIT AUTHORITY *American*

CHICAGO TRANSIT AUTHORITY (Double Album) *CBS-Columbia 8 CBS 66221 [USA]*. Chicago Transit Authority came into being as a club band around 1968, performing in local clubs in the Chicago area under the name of the Big Thing, probably to describe their booming sound. Jim Guercio, a producer for CBS, met the group while they were attending De Paul University, Chicago. Having been associated with Chad and Jeremy and the Buckinghams, he was so impressed with the Big Thing that he devoted most of his time and energy towards making the group a success. The name of Chicago Transit Authority came later, when the group signed with CBS. Their first outing for the label was this now classic two-record set which initially was not a success but, after the release of their second double album in 1970, began to sell until it subsequently received a Gold Disc RIAA award and went on to Platinum status for a million units sale. It reached No 25 for two weeks in the US charts. It finally won a Double Platinum award for sales of two million on 21 November 1986.

The group had its first singles success with **I'm a Man** written by Stevie Winwood of Britain's Spencer Davis Group.

Chicago Transit Authority were Dan Seraphine (drums); Robert Lamm (organ, electric piano, vocals); Terry Kath (guitar, vocals); James Pankow (trombone); Peter Cetera (bass, vocals); Walter Parazaider (woodwinds); Lee Loughnane (trumpet, flugel horn).

This first album contained 12 tracks, the most outstanding being **Beginnings**, **Does Anybody Really Know What Time It Is?** and **Questions 67 & 68**. Other tracks were **Introduction**, **Listen**, **Poem 58**, **South California Purples**, **I'm a Man**, **Someday** and **Liberation**. It was 148 weeks in the US bestsellers, released in April 1969.

CLASSICS IV *American*

TRACES *Imperial 66352 [USA]*. A beautiful romantic ballad featuring Dennis Yost, lead vocalist of the group, it was written by James Cobb (of the group) with B. Buie and E. Gordy.

The disc was released in January 1969 and was No 2 for a week in the USA with 12 weeks in the bestsellers. It is estimated to have sold a million by April 1969, the third for the group.

Originally a quartet, they became an octet (see 1967) and the personnel for this recording had two changes, Auburn Burrell (lead guitar) and Dean Daughtry (organ) in place of James Cobb and Joe Wilson. Cobb left to remain in Atlanta as a writer.

BILL COSBY *American*

THE BEST OF BILL COSBY (Album) *Warner Brothers 1798 [USA]*. By the time **The Best of Bill Cosby** was released in August 1969, America's most successful comedian on record had already notched up seven Gold Discs for million-dollar-selling albums. This hits package, taken from the best of his previous albums, was his sixth million-selling record.

It only made No 51 in the American album charts, with 25 weeks in the Top 200, but it remained a steady seller over the years. When the RIAA changed their rules about the certification of albums, allowing awards for million units as well as for million dollar sales, Warner Brothers checked Cosby's royalty payments and found that this album qualified for both Gold and Platinum. Both awards were made on 13 October 1986.

In the July 1969 disc jockey poll conducted by the American trade paper *Record World*, the highly successful black comedian was voted 'Top Comedy Artist of the Year'.

THE COWSILLS *American*

HAIR (from *Hair*) *MGM 14026 [USA]*. The Cowsills' version of **Hair** was rearranged and recorded by Bill and Bob Cowsill of the famous family group and released in March 1969. By the following month (24 April) it had passed the million mark (24 April) and was awarded a Gold Disc by RIAA. The disc was No 1 for three weeks with 15 weeks in the US bestsellers. Bill Cowsill, the oldest member of the group, left in May 1969 to pursue a career in composing.

The disc was the second million seller for the Cowsills. The song was written by Gerome Ragni and James Rado (words) and Galt MacDermot (music).

CREEDENCE CLEARWATER REVIVAL *American*

PROUD MARY *Fantasy 619 [USA] Liberty LBF 15223 [UK]*. Early in 1969 a new, refreshingly simple sound spread around the pop world. Creedence Clearwater Revival looked back to the roots of rock'n'roll and combined country blues with rock, with a bayou feel about it. Though they came from San Francisco their music had little in common with other West Coast bands who were into psychedelia, drugs and social comment.

In fact Creedence had been around for a long while. They started playing around 1959 when they were school kids in El Cerrito, in the East Bay area of San Francisco. Originally known as the Blue Velvets, the group consisted of John Fogerty (born in Berkeley, California, on 28 May 1945) on guitar; Doug Clifford (born in Palo Alto, California, on 24 April 1945) on drums; and Stuart Cook (born in Oakland, California, on 25 April 1945) on bass and piano. They were soon joined by John's brother Tom Fogerty (born in Berkeley on 9 November 1941) on guitar. The group drew their inspiration from fifties rock, R&B and country music, influenced by artists like Muddy Waters, Jerry Lee Lewis and Chuck Berry.

After the Beatles' invasion of America, the Blue Velvets adapted their act to include hits by British groups. They made one record for the Orchestra label, which failed, then in 1964 signed with local record company Fantasy. They became the Golliwogs as Fantasy thought this sounded more contemporary, and released a number of records, none of them a success.

At the end of 1967 they changed their name again, and spent months working on their debut album **Creedence Clearwater Revival**. It contained standards like Dale Hawkins' **Suzie Q**, their first hit single which reached No 11, and original John Fogerty material. The album reached No 52, spent 73 weeks in the LP charts, and carried on selling long after it had dropped off the Top 200. It eventually sold a million copies. Another track off the album, a cover of Screamin' Jay Hawkins **I Put a Spell on You**, was released as the follow-up to **Suzie Q** but reached only No 58.

The disappointing performance of **I Put a Spell on You** proved a blessing in disguise. It encouraged Fantasy and Creedence to risk a John Fogerty song as their next release, part of the outcome of a row within the group that saw John Fogerty take control. The risk payed off handsomely, for **Proud Mary** proved a classic. It entered the American charts in January 1969 and went to No 1 for three weeks. It spent 14 weeks on the charts and won an RIAA Gold Disc on 28 January 1976. It was also their first international hit. It made No 8 in Britain, with 13 weeks in the Top 50. It was a No 1 in South Africa, Austria and Poland (where the charts were compiled by a computerized public voting system rather than by sales) and was a hit in Canada, Australia, New Zealand, Norway, Denmark, Germany, Switzerland, Belgium, the Netherlands, Hong Kong, the Philippines, Japan, Mexico, Brazil and Argentina. It was written, produced and arranged by John Fogerty. Many other artists recorded the song, including a Checkmates version produced by Phil Spector and a cover by former Spector act Ike and Tina Turner.

BAYOU COUNTRY (Album) *Fantasy 8387 [USA] Liberty LBS 83261 [UK]*. The second Creedence album built on the reputation of the first and the singles success of **Proud Mary**, which was on the album. It made No 7 in the American album charts, with a chart run of 87 weeks. It won an RIAA Gold Disc for million dollar sales on 16 December 1970. The album did not take off in Britain at first, but did make the charts, for one week at No 62, in May 1970. This was after both **Green River** and **Willie and the Poor Boys** had made it.

The album was produced and arranged by John Fogerty, who played lead guitar and harp and provided the vocals. He also wrote all the tracks on it except **Good Golly Miss Molly**, which was written in 1957 by Robert Blackwell and John Marascalco. The other tracks were **Born on the Bayou**, **Bootleg**, **Graveyard Train**, **Penthouse Pauper**, **Proud Mary** and **Keep on Chooglin'**.

BAD MOON RISING/LODI *Fantasy 622 [USA] Liberty LBF 15230 [UK]*. The second massive international hit single for Creedence was **Bad Moon Rising**, written by the group's John Fogerty who also produced and arranged it. In America it reached No 1 for one week in the *Record World* charts, and No 2 in *Billboard* and *Cash Box*, with 14 weeks on the charts. The flip side **Lodi** also charted, reaching No 52 in *Billboard* during a four-week chart life of its own. It was also written by John Fogerty. The record won an RIAA Gold Disc for million sales on 16 December 1970, their first record to actually pass the million sales mark.

In Britain it was the biggest hit of their career. It went to No 1 for three weeks in all charts, with 15 weeks in the Top 50. It was No 1 in Canada and the Lebanon, and a Top 10 hit in Australia, New Zealand, South Africa, Ireland, Sweden, Norway, Denmark, Germany, Austria, Switzerland, Belgium, the Netherlands, Israel, Singapore, the Philippines and Argentina.

GREEN RIVER/COMMOTION *Fantasy 625* [USA] *Liberty LBF 15250* [UK]. The title track from Creedence's third album was their next single release at the end of July. Both sides of the single, which were the first two tracks on the album, made the Hot 100. **Green River** entered the *Billboard* charts at No 70 on 2 August, moving up rapidly to 48, 15, 7 and 7, peaked at No 2 to the Archies' **Sugar Sugar** at No 1, and then back down to No 7. It spent 13 weeks on the charts while **Commotion** peaked at No 30 during its independent chart life of eight weeks. This was the only one of their first eight Top Five hits not to win an RIAA Gold Disc, but it did achieve global sales of over a million. In Britain **Green River** was a bit of a disappointment for a follow-up to a No 1. It reached No 19 with 11 weeks in the Top 50. It was also a more modest international hit, reaching No 2 in Canada and the Top 10 in Australia, South Africa, Switzerland, the Netherlands, Spain, the Lebanon, the Philippines and Mexico. Both sides were written, produced and arranged by John Fogerty.

GREEN RIVER (Album) *Fantasy 8393* [USA] *Liberty LBS 83273* [UK]. The third million-selling album in a row for Creedence was their most successful to date, and finally landed them an American No 1. It was released in September 1969, went to No 1 for four weeks, spent 88 weeks on the LP charts, and was finally certificated a Gold Disc winner on 16 December 1970. It included both the **Bad Moon Rising** and **Green River** hits. In Britain **Green River** was the group's first hit album, though it did not make the LP charts until 1970. It went to No 20 with six weeks in the charts.

As with the previous albums, this one was produced and arranged by John Fogerty. He followed the same pattern as with **Bayou Country**, including one old number from the fifties with otherwise all new material. On this album the Herman-written minor R&B standard **The Night Time is the Right Time** was added to the following Fogerty tracks: **Green River**, **Commotion**, **Tombstone Shadow**, **Wrote a Song for Everyone**, **Bad Moon Rising**, **Lodi**, **Cross-Tie Walker** and **Sinister Purpose**.

DOWN ON THE CORNER/FORTUNATE SON *Fantasy* [USA] *Liberty LBF 15283* [UK]. For their fourth million-selling single of the year the band came up with another outstanding double A side. *Billboard* had changed its policy on listing double A sides by the time this was released in October, so both sides were listed together in the charts. It reached No 3 with 14 weeks on the Hot 100. (**Fortunate Son** was listed for all but one of those weeks.) In *Cash Box* the two sides chased each other up the Top 100. **Fortunate Son** peaked at No 6 in December 1969, while **Down on the Corner** stalled at No 10 for two weeks in January 1970. Fogerty's songs were so good and the group's delivery of such quality that, of their nine Top 10 hits, seven in a row were listed as double A sides.

Down on the Corner was a slow bayou blues number, **Fortunate Son** a faster and harder track with biting lyrics. At the time of the Vietnam war, when many fortunate sons avoided the draft thanks to their parents' money and influence, such a song had particular relevance to young Americans. Such socially aware lyrics were a new departure for a Creedence single.

Both sides were written by John Fogerty, who arranged and produced the record at Wally Heider's studio in their home town of San Francisco. **Down on the Corner** was certified an RIAA Gold Disc on 16 December 1970. Fantasy submitted a batch of Creedence records for RIAA audit all at the same time, and they received 10 Gold Discs for singles and albums on the same day, most of them having qualified for Gold status some while before.

Internationally **Down on the Corner** was the more popular side. In Britain it reached No 31 with six weeks in the charts. It was No 1 in South Africa, Malaysia and Argentina, and one side or the other was a Top 10 hit in Australia, New Zealand, Denmark, Germany, Austria, Switzerland, the Netherlands, Belgium and Spain (where in both countries both sides charted separately), France, the Philippines and Mexico.

In the 1988 *Rolling Stone* magazine critics' poll of the 100 best singles of the previous 25 years, **Fortunate Son** was ranked eighth, the only Creedence record in the Top 50.

WILLIE AND THE POOR BOYS (Album) *Fantasy 8397* [USA] *Liberty LBS 83338* [UK]. Released in December 1969, **Willie and the Poor Boys** brought to an end a fantastic year for Creedence Clearwater Revival. They had released four singles and three albums during the year, and all eventually sold over a million copies. A year earlier they had been a minor league group with a couple of modest hits behind them, but by December 1969 they were one of the most popular rock bands in the world. *Rolling Stone* named them 'Best American Band' of 1969. *Billboard* gave them a Trendsetter award for combining two heritages of the past — blues and country into a fresh, funky, and influential sound that scored with the popular market in an unprecedented way. The group were Top Singles Act of 1969 in America and 'No 2 Singles Act' in Canada. (These two awards were based on chart activity during the year.) John Fogerty was ranked No 5 in the 'Top Producer of 1969' category. While Creedence were the 12th most popular album act, they ranked second in sales of cassettes and 8-track cartridges, and were the No 1 sellers of the soon-to-be-doomed 4-track cartridges.

The **Willie and The Poor Boys** album served up another quality helping of swamp rock. It contained the **Down on the Corner** and **Fortunate Son** hits and **It Came Out of the Sky**, which was a hit in Europe and in South America though it was not released in Britain or America. The album reached No 3 in the United States with 60 weeks on the Top 200. In Britain it went to No 10 with 24 weeks in the LP charts.

1970 would prove another fantastic year, with three more Top Five million-selling singles and two more smash albums, including the outstanding transatlantic No 1 **Cosmo's Factory**. But the rest of the group were increasingly resentful of John Fogerty's dictatorial ways, and in early 1971 Tom Fogerty left. The rest of the group tried to carry on, and produced an excellent single in **Sweet Hitch Hiker** in July 1971. John Fogerty finally gave the other two members of the group more involvement in what proved to be their final album, but **Mardi Gras** (1972) proved to be a disappointment.

The group finally disbanded in October 1972, though two live albums and three hits packages kept them on the US charts until 1980. All the group members sought to pursue solo careers, but in the seventies none met with much success. In 1985 John Fogerty re-emerged after a long period of absence with the US No 1 album **Centrefield**. It met with much media excitement and sold over a million copies. Though the 1986 follow-up **Eye of the Zombie** won a Gold Disc, its content and performance were something of a disappointment.

Creedence Clearwater Revival took a very long time to arrive, and then lasted at the top for only two years before coming apart at the seams. However, during those two years they produced some outstanding rock'n'roll. At a time when 'progression' and psychedelia were the direction many West Coast groups were taking, Creedence Clearwater Revival went back to rock's roots and came up with a simple but effective sound that actually lasted far longer than the group itself.

CROSBY, STILLS AND NASH
British/American

CROSBY, STILLS AND NASH (Album) *Atlantic 8229 [USA] Atlantic 588-189 [UK]*. Crosby, Stills and Nash, three formidable members of the royalty of rock, were formed as a group in the spring of 1969. Each had separated from the groups in which they had become famous — David Crosby, formerly of the Byrds; Stephen Stills, formerly of Buffalo Springfield; and Graham Nash, formerly of the Hollies. All three are writers, singers and guitarists. They signed as a group with Atlantic Records and together produced this album, a magnificent debut and showcase for their combined talents.

Crosby, Stills and Nash was completed after many weeks of intensive work and released in the USA in June 1969. It was one of the most eagerly awaited albums of the year and got to No 5 for three weeks, and stayed in the Top 10 for 31 weeks into 1970 with sales of two million reported by March 1970. A Gold Disc was awarded by RIAA and the group received the Grammy Award for 'Best New Artists of 1969'. The drummer with the group was Dallas Taylor. **Marrakesh Express**, written by Nash, was a hit as a single in the USA (No 17 for a week).

The album contents were: **Suite: Judy Blue Eyes**, by Stephen Stills; **Marrakesh Express**, by Graham Nash; **Guinevere**, by David Crosby; **You Don't Have to Cry**, by Stephen Stills; **Pre-Road Downs**, by Graham Nash; **Wooden Ships**, by David Crosby and Stephen Stills; **Lady of the Island**, by Graham Nash; **Helplessly Hoping**, by Stephen Stills; **Long Time Gone**, by David Crosby; **49 Bye-Byes**, by Stephen Stills.

The album was released in Britain in August 1969, and was No 19 for two weeks. In the USA it stayed in the bestsellers for 100 weeks.

THE CUFF LINKS
American

TRACY *US Decca 32533 [USA] MCA MU 1101 [UK]*. **Tracy** was written by Paul Vance and Lee Pockriss. It was released in the USA in July 1969, shot up the charts to No 4 for two weeks with 12 weeks in the bestsellers, and subsequently sold a million. In Britain it was released in November 1969 and reached No 2 for two weeks with 16 weeks in the bestsellers, and won a Silver Disc by early 1970.

The line-up was Pat Rizzo (sax, flute) ex-member and former child star with Joey Dee and the Starlighters, and the Riverboat Soul Band; Danny Valentine (drums); Rich Dimino (organist); Bob Gill (trumpet, flugel horn and flute); Dave Lavender (guitar); Andrew 'Junior' Denno (bassist); Joe Cord (vocalist).

DESMOND DEKKER AND THE ACES
Jamaican

ISRAELITES *Pyramid PYR 6058 and later Cactus CT 57 [UK] Uni 55129 [USA]*. Desmond Dekker was a major star in his native Jamaica before he came to Britain to promote **007** in 1967. His presence helped push that record to No 14 in the charts, but subsequent records failed to make it. Two years later, Dekker was back with a new reggae record that took him right to No 1. Though **Israelites** was his first British chart-topper, it was his 40th No 1 in Jamaica.

Desmond Dekker was born Desmond Dacres on 16 July 1941 in Kingston, Jamaica. He made his first amateur appearance there in a church choir and his first professional appearance in 1962. He made his British TV debut on 'Top of the Pops', and then starred in his own Jamaican TV series 'Action'.

Israelites was arranged and produced in Jamaica by Leslie Kong, and written by Kong and Dekker (who used his real name Dacres for songwriting.) The record entered the Top 50 on 19 March 1969. One month later it was No 1, staying at the top for two weeks in the *NME* and one week in the other two charts. It spent 15 weeks in the Top 50. The record won Desmond his first Silver Disc for British sales of a quarter of a million on 26 April 1969. In America it was his only hit, reaching No 9 during its 10 weeks on the charts.

Later in 1969 the Trojan label issued a maxi disc with **Israelites** on the A side and **It Mek** and **007** on the flip side. In 1975 Cactus Records re-issued **Israelites** and it was a hit all over again. The second time around it reached No 10 with an extra nine weeks in the charts. It finally sold a global million.

IT MEK *Pyramid PYR 6068 [UK]*. **It Mek** was originally released before **Israelites**, but withdrawn when **Israelites** took off. Re-released as the follow-up in June 1969, it made No 7 in Britain with 11 weeks in the Top 50. The title is Jamaican *patois* for 'That's why'. The song was written by Desmond Dekker and Leslie Kong, and was produced and arranged in Jamaica by Leslie Kong, with the brass section added in Lodon. By September 1970 the record had sold a global million, will a Gold Disc presented to Dekker by Ember Records, who were the British licensee for Dekker.

Dekker had three more hits in Britain. **Pickney Gal** was a minor hit in January 1970, but **You Can Get It If You Really Want** went to No 2 later in the year. After the 1975 re-release of **Israelites**, Dekker had his last British hit, on Cactus, with **Sing a Little Song** which made No 16. Dekker continued to be a mjaor artist in Jamaica. By 1969 he had won the Jamaican Golden Trophy for the best song of the year five times. As well as ska, his stage act included Tamla and soul numbers. He played guitar, piano and drums.

THE DELLS
American

OH WHAT A NIGHT *Cadet 5649 [USA]*. The Dells were a leading American R&B group formed at Thornton Township High School in Harvey, Illinois, in the early fifties. They first recorded as the El Rays for Chess in 1953, then as the Dells for Vee Jay for whom they recorded **Oh What a Night** in 1956. It made No 4 during 11 weeks on the R&B best-selling records chart.

The Dells were Johnny Funches (lead), Chuck Barksdale (bass), Michael McGill (baritone), Marvin Junior (tenor) and Verne Allison (tenor). In 1960 Funches left and was replaced by ex-Flamingoes Johnny Carter.

After their initial R&B chart success with **Oh What a Night**, they spent the next few years doing the club circuit and touring with people like Ray Charles and the late Dinah Washington. In 1962 they had their first pop hit on Argo with **The (Bossa Nova) Bird**. It spent three weeks in the Hot 100, climbing no higher than No 97. It did not make the R&B charts. In 1963 they backed Barbara Lewis on her first hit **Hello Stranger**. Released on Atlantic, it went to No 3 on the Hot 100 and No 1 for two weeks on the R&B charts. Two years later the Dells were back on the R&B charts with **Stay in My Corner**. It was a minor R&B hit when first released on Vee Jay, but when re-recorded by Cadet in 1968 it gave them their first solo R&B No 1. The re-recording of **Oh What a Night** gave them their second R&B chart-topper, and reached No 10 with 11 weeks on the Hot 100. The song was written by Johnny Funches and Marvin Junior.

Both the 1956 original and the 1969 re-make sold a million copies. The Dells made the R&B singles charts 43 times between 1956 and 1984. The American chart expert Joel Whitburn ranked them as 35th most successful R&B chart act of the last half century.

JACKIE DE SHANNON
American

PUT A LITTLE LOVE IN YOUR HEART *Imperial 66385 [USA]*. Jackie De Shannon's (real name Sharon Myers) career has embraced acting, singing and songwriting. She was born on 21 August 1945 in Hazel, Kentucky. At the age of six she had her own radio show. She toured with the Platters, and with a group called the Cookies, early in her career. When Imperial Records heard she was both performing and producing her own radio show at the age of 12, they signed her to a contract.

She is a prolific songwriter. Artists who have recorded her songs include the Byrds,

Brenda Lee, Rick Nelson, Bobby Vee, the Searchers and Helen Shapiro.

Put a Little Love in Your Heart was written by Jackie with Jimmy Holiday and Randy Myers. It was released in June 1969, reached No 3 in the US charts with 14 weeks in the bestsellers, and was a certified RIAA million seller by 29 September.

NEIL DIAMOND   *American*

SWEET CAROLINE (Good times never seemed so good) *Uni 55136 [USA] Uni UN 531 [UK]*. Neil Diamond was born in Coney Island, New York, on 24 January 1945. At the age of seven, he moved to Memphis and at 10 played with the Memphis Backstreet Boys who earned a living by singing in the streets. At 13, Neil ran away from home and landed in Kansas City, Missouri, where he got together a folk group called the Roadrunners. They travelled the Midwest for a few years, during which time Neil absorbed various styles of folk music and also met the legendary Woody Guthrie. Neil subsequently left the Midwestern nightclub circuit for New York, and in 1964 was discovered by the songwriting team of Jeff Barry and Ellie Greenwich who put him on the road to fame as a songwriter. He wrote for Sonny and Cher, the Ronettes, Jay and the Americans, and the Monkees, with two million sellers for the later — **I'm a Believer** and **A Little Bit Me, A Little Bit You**.

Barry and Greenwich induced him to record, and he made his first vocal disc **Solitary Man** in 1966, for the Bang label. Several of his discs on this label were chart items. In 1968, Neil signed with the Uni label and made an album **Brother Love's Travelling Salvation Show** for them, released in 1969. This included **Sweet Caroline** released in June 1969 as a single. It got to No 3 in the US charts for two weeks with 14 weeks in the bestsellers, and by 18 August sold a million with an RIAA Gold Disc award. The song, a fine love ballad, was written by Neil.

HOLLY HOLY *Uni 55175 [USA]*. A great follow-up disc for Neil Diamond, again written by him. This was released in October 1969 and got to No 4 for two weeks in the US charts with 14 weeks in the bestsellers, with million sale and a Gold Disc award from RIAA in January 1970.

THE DOORS   *American*

THE SOFT PARADE (Album) *Elektra 75005 [USA]*. **The Soft Parade** was the Doors' fourth Gold album in a row. Released in America in late July 1969, it reached No 6 with 28 weeks in the album charts. It did not make the British charts at all. It was the Doors' sixth million-selling record, three of them being albums and three singles. An RIAA Gold Disc was awarded for million dollar sales on 5 August 1969, and a Platinum Disc signifying sales of one million copies on 10 June 1987.

The Doors got four hit singles off the album, an unusually large number at the time. **Touch Me** was released in December 1968, went to No 3 in America, and sold a million

copies. The three tracks released as singles in 1969 were only minor hits. **Wishful Sinful** made No 44 during its six weeks on the charts, **Tell All the People** made No 57 though it lasted nine weeks on the Hot 100, and **Runnin' Blue** made No 64 with a six-week chart life. None of the Doors' records made the British singles charts in 1969.

The songs on the album were written by the Doors. The tracks were **Tell All the People**, **Touch Me**, **Shaman's Blues**, **Do It**, **Easy Ride**, **Wild Child**, **Runnin' Blue**, **Wishful Sin** and **The Soft Parade**.

DIMITRI DOURAKINE   *French/Russian*
AND HIS ORCHESTRA

CASATSCHOK *Philips 4424 [France]*. Released in early 1969, **Casatschok**, a new dance craze created by François Patrice Saint-Hilaire, sold over a million via Dourakine's disc throughout Europe. It was No 1 for 10 weeks in France, and a big seller in Denmark (No 1), Italy (No 5), Holland (No 3), Spain, Germany, Belgium (sold 150,000) and Mexico (No 1). A near million by Philips artist Rika Zaraï was also sold, this disc reaching No 2 in France.

Dourakine was born in Russia. **Casatschok** was written by Boris Rubashkin.

BOB DYLAN   *American*

NASHVILLE SKYLINE (Album) *CBS-Columbia CS (9825) [USA] CBS 63601 [UK]*. Released in America at the end of April 1969, **Nashville Skyline** was Bob Dylan's ninth hit album, and the seventh to win a Gold Disc for million dollar sales. It was the sixth in a row both to go Gold and make the Top 10, where it made No 3 with 46 weeks on the charts. In Britain it was No 1 for four weeks, with 42 weeks in the charts. It was the second of a string of four No 1 albums in a row. This was Dylan's fourth record to sell a million copies, and his first studio album to do so.

Three of the tracks off the album charted in America as singles. **I Threw It All Away** made the Hot 100 in May 1969, reaching No 85 during its five weeks chart run. The big hit off the album was **Lay Lady Lay**, which made No 7 during 14 weeks on the charts. At the end of the year **Tonight I'll Be Staying Here With You** made No 50 with seven weeks on the singles charts.

All the songs on the album were written by Bob Dylan. The tracks were **Girl of the North Country** with Johnny Cash, **Nashville Skyline Rag**, **To Be Alone With You**, **I Threw It All Away**, **Peggy Day**, **Lay Lady Lay**; **One More Night**, **Tell Me That It Isn't True**, **Country Pie** and **Tonight I'll Be Staying Here With You**.

FERRANTE AND TEICHER   *American*

MIDNIGHT COWBOY *United Artists 50554 [USA]*. The theme of the film of the same title was written by British composer John Barry (a three-time Academy Award winner) this disc was released in the USA in October, reaching No 10 and staying in the charts for 15 weeks. It

is said to have sold a million, making the fourth for the famous piano duo.

The film received the Academy Awards for 'Best Picture', 'Best Director of 1969', and 'Best Instrumental Theme'.

THE FIFTH DIMENSION   *American*

THE AGE OF AQUARIUS (Album) *Soul City 92005 [USA]*. A superlative album, released in the USA in May 1969, this was in the Top 10 for 10 weeks and reached No 2 for two weeks, with a Gold Disc award by RIAA on 14 July. By early January 1970 it had sold over a million units. It contained two titles that sold a million as singles by the group.

The contents of the album were: **Aquarius** (from *Hair*), by Gerome Ragni, James Rado and Galt MacDermot (1968); **Blowing Away**, by Laura Nyro; **Skinny Man**, by Kollander and Kollander; **Wedding Bell Blues**, by Laura Nyro; **Don'tcha Hear Me Callin' to Ya**, by Stevenson; **The Hideaway**, by Jim Webb; **Workin' On a Groovy Thing**, by Roger Atkins and Neil Sedaka; **Let It Be Me** ('Je t'appartien') by Pierre Delanoe and Gilbert Becaud (1955) (English words: Mann Curtis); **Sunshine of Your Love**, by Eric Clapton, Jack Bruce and Peter Brown (1967); **The Winds of Heaven**, by Dorough and Landesman; **Those Were the Days**, by Gene Haskin (1963); **Let the Sunshine In** (from *Hair*) by Gerome Ragni, James Rado and Galt MacDermot (1968).

This album was in the US bestsellers for 72 weeks.

In Britain, the disc was released on the Liberty label.

AQUARIUS/LET THE SUNSHINE IN (medley from the musical *Hair*) *Soul City 772 [USA] Liberty LBF 15198 [UK]*. The Fifth Dimension first saw the show *Hair* in the summer of 1968 and decided that the song **Aquarius** would be a great one for them to record. Their vocal arranger Bob Alcivar and the group's producer Bones Howe worked out the rhythm arrangement and cut the basic track in Los Angeles in October 1968. The group's vocals were overdubbed in a studio at Las Vegas in December. The disc was released at the end of February 1969 and soon zoomed to No 1 where it stayed for six weeks with 17 weeks in the Hot 100. It made No 6 with 11 weeks in the R&B Top 50. It won an RIAA Gold Disc award for a million sale by 30 April. By mid-May it had sold over two million. The disc rose to No 11 for a week in Britain where it was released on 3 April 1969 with 11 weeks in the bestsellers.

This was the first big seller of the show's 26 songs written by Gerome Ragni and James Rado (words) and Galt MacDermot (music).

Grammy award (1969) for 'Best Contemporary Vocal Performance' by a group.

WEDDING BELL BLUES *Soul City 779 [USA] Liberty LBF 15288 [UK]*. Released in September 1969 and taken from the Fifth Dimension's enormously successful album **Age of Aquarius**, this song by Laura Nyro became No 1 in the US charts for three weeks with 15 weeks in the bestsellers, and sold the million by 5 December 1969 with a Gold Disc award from

RIAA. It reached No 23 on the R&B charts with an eight-week chart run. It was No 16 in Britain.

FLEETWOOD MAC   *British*

OH WELL *Reprise RS 27000 [UK] Reprise 0883 [USA]*. **Oh Well** was Fleetwood Mac's second million-selling No 1 single, following the 1968 instrumental **Albatross**. Both words and music were written by the group's Peter Green. Following **Albatross**, the group had three records in the charts in 1969, on three different labels. **Man of the World**, issued on Immediate, made No 2 in Britain. Their old label Blue Horizon then re-promoted **Need Your Love So Bad**, which had been a minor hit in 1968, reaching No 31. It was a minor hit the second time round, reaching No 32. Then came **Oh Well**, their first record under their long-lasting deal with Warner Brothers. Issued on Warner's Reprise label, the record made No 1 on 15 November, with 16 weeks in the Top 50. In the USA it was Mac's first hit, reaching No 55 with 10 weeks on the Hot 100. Global sales were eventually over the million mark.

FLYING MACHINE   *British*

SMILE A LITTLE SMILE FOR ME *Congress 6000 [USA]*. This disc, by five talented musicians with several years of combined experience, was released in Britain on 11 April 1969 but did not register as a hit. When released in the USA by Congress in June, it rose to No 4 for two weeks with 14 weeks in the bestsellers, and by 12 December had sold a million with an RIAA Gold Disc award. The song was the work of British writers Tony Macauley and Geoff Stevens.

Tony Newman (born 1947 in Rugby) 'vocalist' and Sam Kempe (born 1946 in Rugby) first played together in local groups, then with the Pinkertons for nearly five years, and later became friends with Stuart Colman (born 1945 in Rugby), bass guitarist and electric piano player. When the Pinkertons split up, they formed their own group. They met guitarist Steve Jones (born 1946 in Coventry) and Paul Wilkinson (born 1948 in Coventry) when they were sharing a bill in Coventry, and then formed Flying Machine. They developed a soft and provocative style. **Smile a Little Smile** was their debut on the Pye label.

FRIENDS OF DISTINCTION   *American*

GRAZIN' IN THE GRASS *RCA Victor 0107 [USA]*. The personnel of this group, two women and two men, were Harry Elson, Floyd Butler, Jessica Cleaves and Barbara Jean Love. Elson was previously a professional baseball player for a time with the Los Angeles Angels, and then decided on a singing career when he joined a rock group in the early 1960s. When this group was a touring troupe with soul singer Ray Charles, Elson met Butler and formed the nucleus of Friends of Distinction. Butler brought Jessica Cleaves into the group when they met in the Los Angeles Urban League, Butler being its assistant project director for two years. Barbara Jean Love, daughter of West Coast disc jockey Reuben Brown, joined the group about six months before the act made its debut at the Daisy, a top Hollywood discotheque, in the summer of 1968.

The group was brought to the attention of RCA-Victor by actor Jim Brown who signed them after hearing them sing in their first professional engagement.

Grazin' in the Grass, originally a million seller for trumpeter Hugh Masekela who composed it, was an instrumental number. Harry Elston, writer for Friends, wrote lyrics for the tune and the result was the group's initial RCA recording. This was released in March 1969, rose to No 3 for one week on the US charts with 16 weeks in the bestsellers, and sold the million by 10 June, with an RIAA Gold Disc award.

LET YOURSELF GO/GOING IN CIRCLES *RCA Victor 0204 [USA]*. **Let Yourself Go** was the original A side of Friends of Distinction's follow-up to **Grazing in the Grass**, but although it did make the charts for five weeks and reached No 63, it was the flip side that turned out to be the major hit. That climbed to No 15 during 20 weeks on the charts. It was written by Anita Poree and Jerry Peters in 1968. It was a steady seller, and despite its relatively low peak position it eventually won the group their second RIAA Gold Disc in a row on 12 December 1969.

The group followed this in 1970 with **Love or Let Me Be Lonely**, which reached No 6. Two more minor hits followed and then Friends of Distinction disappeared. They never had any hits in Britain.

ROBIN GIBB   *British*

SAVED BY THE BELL *Polydor 56-337 [UK]*. The Bee Gees temporarily broke up in 1969, and Robin released this solo recording on 4 July 1969. It went to No 2 for four weeks with 17 weeks in the Top 50. It won a Silver Disc on 6 December. **Saved by the Bell** was also a hit on the Continent, making No 1 in Denmark and the Top 10 in the Netherlands, Belgium and Germany. The song was written by Robin Gibb himself, and sold a global million. After such a big first solo hit, he looked set to become a major solo star, but the follow-up, **August October**, only made No 45, and the Bee Gees re-formed. Robin Gibb had one further British hit in 1984, when **Another Lonely Night in New York** made No 71 for one week. His only solo hit in America was **Oh Darling**, which made No 15 in 1978.

R.B. GREAVES   *American*

TAKE A LETTER, MARIA *Atco 6714 [USA]*. R.B. Greaves was born at a US Air Force Base in South America, the son of a captain in the Air Force. He moved to a Seminole reservation in Samona, California, where, being half Indian, he was raised by his stepmother from the age of four. As a youngster, he learned to play guitar in his spare time. He also acquired cowboy techniques, rode Indian style, and learned how to track in the wilderness. He became an accomplished songwriter and wrote this song himself. The vocal impact of this disc rocketed him to instant stardom and it was No 2 in the USA for a week with 15 weeks in the bestsellers, selling the million with a Gold Disc award from RIAA on 11 December, just three months after its September release.

Greaves' singing is said to be 'an uncanny echo of his uncle, the late Sam Cooke'.

GARLAND GREEN   *American*

JEALOUS KIND OF FELLA *Uni 55143 [USA]*. Written by singer Garland Greene, R. Browner, M. Dollison and Joe Armstead (producer of the disc), this was released in the USA in August 1969 and reached No 19 for a week with 10 weeks in the bestsellers. It was reported to have sold the million by March 1971. Garland Greene had previous hits on the Uni label with **Ain't That Good Enough** and **Don't Think I'm a Violent Guy**. He signed with the Cotillion label in March 1971.

GUESS WHO   *Canadian*

THESE EYES *RCA Victor 0102 [USA]*. Guess Who, all of whom are from Winnipeg, Manitoba, consisted of Randy Bachman (leader and lead guitarist); Burton Cummings (lead singer, piano, organ, rhythm guitar, flute and harmonica); Garry Peterson (drummer); Jim Kale (bassist).

Garry made his debut at four in a show with Gisele Mackenzie and has also appeared on CBC radio and TV, and in concert with the Winnipeg Symphony. Jim gave voice recitals as a youngster at Shinn Conservatory of Music. Randy was composer of all the group's material with Burton, including this song.

The group had been in and around the Canadian music scene since 1960 and won a silver record for their first single **Shakin' All Over**. **These Eyes** was turned down for several weeks by a leading pop radio station in Canada as being not suitable commercially. Guess Who then became the first group in Canadian history to top the charts from Newfoundland to British Columbia. Through this success, the disc got wide exposure in the USA where it rose to No 3 for two weeks after release in

March 1969 with a subsequent 14 weeks in the bestsellers. By 25 June it sold over the million and was awarded a Gold Disc by RIAA.

The disc was produced by Jack Richardson and arranged by Ben McPeek for Nimbus 9 Productions, cut at the A&R Studios in New York and released through RCA-Victor. Randy Bachman later formed Bachman-Turner Overdrive.

LAUGHING/UNDUN *RCA Victor 0195 [USA]*. This disc was the second million seller for Guess Who, again written by the group's Randy Bachman and Burton Cummings. It was released in July 1969 and sold the million by October, reaching No 5 for a week in the USA with 11 weeks in the bestsellers. RIAA Gold Disc award, 28 October 1969.

Undun also made an appearance in the charts, making No 22 during a 10-week chart run of its own.

NO TIME *RCA Victor 0300 [USA]*. The third million seller in a row for this Canadian group was also written by its two members Randy Bachman and Burton Cummings. It was released in December 1969 and sold the million by early 1970, reaching No 3 in the US charts for one week with 14 weeks in the bestsellers.

MERLE HAGGARD   *American*

OKIE FROM MUSKOGEE (also known as 'The Only Hippie in Muskogee') *Capitol 2626 [USA]*. Merle Haggard was born on 6 April 1937 and raised in Bakersfield, California. At the age of 14 he ran away from his Bakersfield home and embarked on a riot of vagrancy and wild living. By 1960 he had spent seven years of his life in reform school or jails, including a three-year term in San Quentin. He then decided to change direction. While in San Quentin, he began to write and pick guitar for himself, and

he was there when Johnny Cash came to record his **Live at San Quentin** album. On release, his music showed no compromise. **Mama Tried** tells of his rift with home, and **Hungry Eyes** is from life. He entered the recording business when he signed with Tally Records, where he gained his first recognition among country music fans with a country hit called **Strangers**. Merle Haggard then came to the attention of Capitol Records, and in 1965 was signed by them.

In February 1966 his talent was recognized by the Academy of Country-and-Western Music, which named him at its first Annual Awards Show, the 'Most Promising Male Vocalist' of that year.

With the continued global interest in country-and-western singers, Merle became one of the 'greats'.

In addition, he and his then wife Bonnie Owens received the Academy's award for Best Vocal Group. After his marriage to Owens ended in breakup and divorce, he later married and then divorced country singer Leona Williams.

Okie was written by Merle Haggard and Roy Edward Burris. It reached No 41 in the pop charts, with 13 weeks in the Hot 100, his first pop hit. His impact on the pop charts was limited, though on the country charts he has been one of the most successful artists of all time. From the time *Billboard's* country charts began in 1944 to the end of 1988, Merle Haggard ranks as the fourth most successful country act, with 98 chart entries including 38 No 1s. This was his eighth country No 1, and the third of four in a row. His first country hit had been **Sing A Sad Song**, which hit No 19 in 1963, and he is still making country hits today (1989).

Merle got the idea for the song while driving into a small western town with his band the Strangers when someone looked out of the window and commented, 'I bet they don't smoke marijuana in Muskogee.' One line led to another and very quickly the whole song was put together. The song was adopted by the 'silent majority' and became the redneck's battle song.

ROLF HARRIS   *Australian*

TWO LITTLE BOYS *Columbia (EMI) DB 8630 [UK]*. **Two Little Boys** is one of the oldest pop songs to have topped the record charts. It was written way back in 1903 by the American songwriters Edward Madden (words) and Theodore Morse (music) who had already had many hits such as **Blue Bell** and **Down in Jungle Town** to their credit in the early part of this century.

Rolf Harris was on a four-months' working holiday around Northern Australia and met Ted Egan, a member of the Aborigine Welfare Department. At a sing-song after the meal, Ted sang a song his father had taught him. Rolf didn't think such a weepy song of boyhood friendship about an incident in the American Civil War would really suit him, but after singing it a few times it began to attract him. Egan put the song on tape and Rolf brought it back to England. Stewart Morris, producer of

his British TV show, was keen, but Rolf found the tape had been over-recorded and phoned Egan in Australia and taped it across 13,000 miles as Egan sang it. Rolf featured it on his TV show, was inundated with requests, and made a commercial recording which shot up the British charts and stayed at No 1 for six weeks with 25 weeks in the bestsellers. The disc was released in Britain on 7 November 1969 and by 31 February 1970 sold over 900,000 in Britain, sales elsewhere easily making it a global million seller. It was the bestselling British made record of 1969.

THE EDWIN HAWKINS   *American*
SINGERS FEATURING DOROTHY
COOMBS MORRISON

OH HAPPY DAY *Pavilion 20001 [USA] Buddah 201 048 [UK]*. The Edwin Hawkins Singers were originally the Northern California State Youth Choir, founded in April 1967 by soprano Betty Watson and Edwin Hawkins, the members' ages ranging from 17 to 25. It was formed by drawing upon leading singers from Pentecostal choirs throughout the San Francisco area.

In 1967, the choir director of the Ephesian Church of God in Christ, Edwin Hawkins of Oakland, California, also a pianist and music arranger, sent the 46-strong ensemble into the church with eight traditional gospel songs arranged by himself to make an album to raise funds for the choir. It was done on an ordinary two-track tape recorder.

At a cost of $750 (£250) the choir decided to make 1,000 records from the tape, and the album titled **Let Us Go into the House of the Lord** was recorded by an Oakland company that specialized in church sales. It sold about 600 in the limited gospel market at the Annual Youth Congress in Cleveland in June 1968, and the choir was placed first in the singing competition. The disc was then forgotten, but in February 1969 a copy was unearthed by John Lingel, rock promotion director at Chatton

Distributors in Oakland, and given to a local radio station KSAN-FM. Disc jockey Abe Keshishian played the record heavily, especially the track **Oh Happy Day**. Record companies started bidding for the album but New York's Buddah Records got the distribution right by paying a $55,000 advance plus a $25,000 bonus and changed the name of the choir to The Edwin Hawkins Singers. **Oh Happy Day** was released as a single on Pavilion label in April. In two weeks the disc sold over a million and rose to No 2 on the US charts with 10 weeks in the bestsellers. Release in Britain was on the Buddah label on 18 May 1969, the disc being No 2 for two weeks with 12 weeks in the bestsellers. RIAA awarded a Gold Disc on 3 June.

Oh Happy Day dates back to 1755, when it was written by Phillip Doddige. E.F. Rimbault revised it in 1855 and it is included in the Baptist Standard Hymnal. Edwin Hawkins' arrangement became one of the most recorded of 1969. The album, also released on the new Pyramid label owned by Edwin Hawkins and producer/engineer Lamont Beech, soon passed the million dollar sale. US sales of **Oh Happy Day** were over two million.

Grammy award (1969) for 'Best Soul Gospel'.

THE HOLLIES   British

HE AIN'T HEAVY — HE'S MY BROTHER *Parlophone R 5806 then EMI EM 74 [UK] Epic 10532 [USA]*. Tony Hicks of the Hollies heard this song in a British publisher's office and was charmed by its beauty. The song came about through Father Flanagan, of Boys' Town, who saw one of his little boys carrying a much bigger but crippled boy in his arms. Father Flanagan asked the little boy if that wasn't a heavy load, to which he replied, 'He ain't heavy, he's my brother.' A Jesuit priest who knew the Boys' Town story, heard the song on the radio and contacted the disc jockey to tell him about it. The D.J. then related the story every time he played the disc and it soon became a hit, spreading to all the big cities in the USA where it was released on the Epic label in December 1969. It sold a million there by March 1970 and reached No 7 in the US charts for two weeks with 19 weeks in the bestsellers. In Britain, the disc was released earlier — on 19 September 1969 — reaching No 2 for two weeks.

The lead vocal is by Allan Clarke, with the large orchestral accompaniment arranged and conducted by Johnny Scott. On this disc, Terry Sylvester replaced Graham Nash who had left to join the new supergroup of Crosby, Stills and Nash. The song was written by US songwriters Bob Russen and Bobby Scott.

The Hollies' career carried on into the seventies. **He Ain't Heavy** was followed in 1970 by **I Can't Tell the Bottom from the Top** which made No 7 in Britain (though only No 82 in America.) It was their last UK Top 10 hit until 1974 when **The Air That I Breathe** made No 2, their last British chart entry until 1980. In America they had two small hits in 1975, and then nothing until **Stop in the Name of Love** just made the Top 30 on Atlantic in 1983.

The eighties started with one small British hit in 1980, and an EMI single of a medley of their earlier hits. **Holliedaze** made No 28. In the late eighties the Hollies were back with EMI with a string of singles on Columbia. While **Reunion of the Heart** got some attention, none of them made the charts. Then the advertising agency for Miller Lite beer decided to use **He Ain't Heavy** in a TV advertising campaign. EMI re-released the song on the EMI label and it went to No 1 for two weeks in September 1988. This gave it another 11 weeks in the Top 100, making 26 in all.

It won a second Silver Disc in 1988, the only record to win two such awards. When it was first a hit in 1969, *Disc* magazine made the Silver Disc awards for British sales of over a quarter of a million. By 1988 *Disc* had long gone out of business and the British Phonographic Industry (a trade body made up of the record companies) awarded the Silver Discs. As **He Ain't Heavy** had got its first Silver before the BPI awards began, it was entitled to a BPI Silver Disc. The Hollies therefore collected two for the same record.

MICHAEL HOLM   German

MENDOCINO *Ariola 14 346 [West Germany]*. A big success for Michael Holm who wrote the German lyrics, the disc was released in September 1969. It reached No 3 for five weeks in 1970 in Germany and stayed in the Top 10 for over three months, selling over a million. Ariola presented a Gold Disc award in October 1970. Doug Sahm (of Sir Douglas Quintet) composed the tune.

EDDIE HOLMAN   American

HEY THERE, LONELY GIRL *ABC 11240 [USA] ABC 4012 [UK]*. Originally **Hey There, Lonely Boy** was written by Earl Shuman (words) and Leon Carr (music) in 1963, when it was a hit for Ruby and the Romantics. Eddie Holman's version was released in early November 1969. By February 1970, the disc was No 2 for three weeks with 14 weeks in the US bestsellers, and received a Gold Disc award from RIAA for million sale in March 1970.

THE ISLEY BROTHERS   American

IT'S YOUR THING *T. Neck 901 [USA] Major Minor MM 621 [UK]*. Released in February 1969, this disc sold half a million in its first three weeks on the market, and two million by June, the first big hit for the three Isleys (Rudolph, Ronald and Kelly) since 1962. It was the first release on their own T. Neck label, which they had planned for a year and a half after several years of hit records, extended tours and fame since their rock hit of 1959, **Shout. It's Your Thing** was thus written, produced and performed by the brothers with the help of their band which included two other Isley brothers. Ernest (who arranged and played a variety of instruments) and Marvin (who played bass and contributed arrangement ideas). The disc was No 2 for two weeks in the US charts and 14 weeks in the Hot 100. It was No 1 for 4 weeks in the R&B Top 50 with a 14-week chart life. It was No 25 for two weeks in Britain. RIAA Gold Disc awarded on 9 April 1969.

Grammy Award for 'Best Rhythm-and-Blues Vocal Performance' 1969.

THE JACKSON FIVE   American

I WANT YOU BACK *Motown 1157 [USA] Tamla Motown TMG 724 [UK]*. Diana Ross of the Supremes discovered this talented quintet in Gary, Indiana, at a talent show to which she had been invited by the city's black mayor. She was so impressed that she immediately took them back to Detroit where Motown chief Berry Gordy, Jr, rushed them into the recording studio. **I Want You Back** became one of the label's biggest hits, selling two million in its first six weeks after release in October. It achieved No 1 for a week and stayed in the US charts for 19 weeks. On the Soul charts (as *Billboard* re-christened the R&B Top 50 in August 1969) it was No 1 for 4 weeks. The flip side was also a soul hit. **Who's Loving You** was listed with **I Want You Back** as a double A side for 7 of the record's 18 weeks in the Soul Top 50. In Britain it was No 1 for one week where it was released on 16 January 1970 and won a Silver Disc.

The personnel were lead singer Michael (then aged 10), Marlon (aged 12), Jermaine (aged 14), Toriano (aged 15) and Sigmund Jackson (aged 18), all brothers. These new 'soul-kings' had the old Supremes/Four Tops flair with a bit of Sly Stone added. Their performance of the song, written by the Corporation is certainly dynamic. The Corporation was the team of Freddie Perren, Fonso Mizell, Deke Richards and Berry Gordy, Jr.

DIANA ROSS PRESENTS THE JACKSON FIVE (Album) *Motown 700 [USA] Tamla Motown STML 11142 [UK]*. This was the Jackson Five's first album, released in the USA on 18 December 1969. It was No 5 for a week and stayed in the bestsellers for 32 weeks, amassing a reported million sale by the end of December 1970. The British release was on 6 March 1970. The contents of the album were: **Zip-A-Dee Doo Dah** (from the film *Song of the South*, 1946), by Ray Gilbert and Allie Wrubel (1945); **Nobody**, by the Corporation (1969); **I Want You Back**, by the Corporation (1969); **Can You Remember?**, by Thom Bell and William Hart; **Standing in the Shadows of Love**, by E.

Holland, B. Holland and L. Dozier (1966); **You've Changed**, by Reese; **My Cherie Amour**, by S. Wonder, H. Cosby and S. Moy (1968); **Who's Lovin' You?**, by Smokey Robinson; **Chained**, by Reese; **My Cherie Amour**, by S. Wonder, H. Cosby and S. Moy (1968); **Who's Lovin' You?**, by Smokey Robinson; **Chained**, by Frank Wilson (1967); **(I Know) I'm Losing You**, by Whitfield, Holland and Grant; **Stand**, by Sly Stewart; **Born to Love You**, by Hunter and Stevenson.

JAGGERZ   *American*

THE RAPPER *Kama Sutra 502* [*USA*]. Released in late December 1969, this disc got to No 1 for two weeks in the USA in March 1970 and sold over the million with an RIAA Gold Disc award. It was written by D. Ierace, and performed with a belting bass line by the group with their hard rock sound. The song fuses bayou and 'bubble-gum'.

The group played local dates around Pittsburgh for five years before making this, their first disc.

TOMMY JAMES AND   *American*
THE SHONDELLS

SWEET CHERRY WINE *Roulette 7039* [*USA*]. This disc was released in mid-March 1969 and was No 5 for two weeks in the USA with 10 weeks in the bestsellers. The million sale was reported in June. The disc also sold another half million abroad. The song was written by Tommy James with Richie Grasso.

CRYSTAL BLUE PERSUASION *Roulette 7050* [*USA*]. The fifth million seller for Tommy James and the Shondells was written by Tommy James and M. Vale (both of the group) with Ed Gray. It was released in May 1969 and was No 1 for one week in the USA and 15 weeks in the bestsellers, with the million sale reported in July. The song is a soft ballad. With this hit, the group had achieved seven Top 10 chart hits, plus an aggregate of 19 hits in a row.

TOM JONES   *British*

WITHOUT LOVE (There is nothing) *Decca F 12990* [*UK*] *Parrot 40045* [*USA*]. This song was written in 1957 by Danny Small of the USA. It was originally a hit for the Platters. The disc was first released in Britain on 28 November 1969 and reached No 9 in the charts. US release was in December 1969, and Tom's great popularity in 1970 over there resulted in the disc reaching No 3 for a week in February 1970 and 11 weeks in the bestsellers, with a Gold Disc award from RIAA for million sale in March.

THIS IS TOM JONES (Album) *Decca SKL 5007* [*UK*] *Parrot 71028* [*USA*]. Released in both Britain and the USA in June 1969, this disc reached No 4 for four weeks and was in the bestsellers for 42 weeks in the USA, selling a million there by end of 1970. A Gold Disc was awarded by RIAA almost immediately on release. In Britain the disc was No 1 for four weeks and in the bestsellers for 16 weeks.

The contents of the album were: **Fly Me to the Moon (in other words)**, by Bart Howard (1954); **Little Green Apples**, by Bobby Russell (1968); **Wichita Lineman**, by Jim Webb (1969), **Dock of the Bay (Sittin' on the)**, by Steve Cropper and Otis Redding (1968); **Dance of Love**, by Charles Rich (1969); **Hey Jude**, by John Lennon and Paul McCartney (1968); **Without You** (orig. ''Non ce' che lei' in Italy), Rossi and Tersi (English words by Barry Mason); **That's All Any Man Can Say**, by Tony Macauley and John Macleod (1969); **That Wonderful Sound**, by Les Reed and Geoff Stephens (1969); **Only Once**, by Clive Weslake (1969); **I'm a Fool to Want You**, by Jack Wolf, Joel Herron and Frank Sinatra (1951); **Let It Be Me** (orig. 'Je t'appartiens' in France), by Pierre Delance and Gilbert Becaud (1955) (English words by Mann Curtis).

Sales were around two million by January 1971.

TOM JONES LIVE IN LAS VEGAS (Album) *Decca SKL 5032* [*UK*]/*Parrot 71031* [*USA*]. Tom Jones started out as a mid-sixties pop star in Britain, but soon moved on to the lucrative cabaret circuit in America. In July 1969 he performed for four weeks at the Flamingo Hotel in Las Vegas. The performance was recorded, and became his biggest selling album, with nearly two million copies sold by early 1971.

Released in October 1969, the album reached No 2 for a week in Britain, with 23 weeks in the album charts. It also reached No 2 in America, with 51 weeks in the US album charts. It won an RIAA Gold Disc for million dollar sales on 27 October 1969.

The album contained: **Turn on Your Love Light**, by Deadric Malone and Joseph Scott (1961); **The Bright Lights and You Girl**, by Shepard; **I Can't Stop Loving You**, by Don Gibson (1958); **Hard to Handle**, by Isbell, Jones and Redding; **Delilah**, by Les Reed and Barry Mason (1968); **Danny Boy**, by F.E. Weatherly (tune 'Londonderry Air') (1913) arranged: Blackwell; **I'll Never Fall in Love Again**, by Lonnie Donegan and Jim Currie (1967); **Help Yourself** (orig. 'Gli occhi miei' in Italy), by

Mogul and C. Donida (1968) (English words by Jack Fishman); **Yesterday**, by John Lennon and Paul McCartney (1965); **Hey Jude**, by John Lennon and Paul McCartney (1968); **Love Me Tonight** (orig. 'Alla fine della, strada' in Italy) by D. Pace/Pilat and M. Panzer (1969) (English words by Barry Mason); **It's Not Unusual**, by Gordon Mills and Les Reed (1965); **Twist and Shout**, by Bert Russell (Berns) and Phil Medley (1961).

ANDY KIM   *Canadian*

BABY, I LOVE YOU *Steed 716* [*USA*]. The first million seller (by September 1969) for Andy Kim and for the Steed label, the disc was released in May 1969. It rose to No 5 in the US charts for two weeks with 16 weeks in the bestsellers. The song written by American songwriters Jeff Barry, Ellie Greenwich and Phil Spector and was originally a hit for the Ronettes.

Andy Kim was born in Montreal on 5 December 1946, the third of four sons in a Lebanese family. He left high school and hitchhiked to New York, where he continually made the rounds of record companies. He learned to play the guitar in order to accompany himself on his self-written songs. His older brother became his manager. The disc was produced by writer Jeff Barry.

RIAA Gold Disc award, 14 October 1969.

B.B. KING   *American*

THE THRILL IS GONE *Blues Way 61032* [*USA*]. Written by Arthur H. Benson and Dale Pettie, this disc was released in the USA in December 1969 and reached No 13 for two weeks in early 1970 with 14 weeks in the bestsellers, selling a million by April 1970. It entered the Soul charts on 3 January 1970 and reached No 3 during a 14-week chart run. 1969 was the year in which 'King of the Blues' B.B. King was recognized as one of the world's great artists, after some 20

years in comparative anonymity to white audiences. B.B. King received a Grammy Award for this disc — 'Best Rhythm-and-Blues Vocal Performance (Male) 1970'.

LED ZEPPELIN   British

LED ZEPPELIN (Album) *Atlantic 588-171* [*UK*] *Atlantic 8216* [*USA*]. Led Zeppelin, a British rock group, consisted of Jimmy Page (lead guitar, pedal steel guitar, acoustic guitar) born Heston, Middlesex, 9 January 1944; John Paul Jones, real name John Baldwin, (bass, organ, piano) born Sidcup, Kent, 3 January 1946; John Bonham (drums) born Redditch, Worcs., 31 May 1948, died Windsor, Berks., 25 September 1980; and Robert Plant (lead vocals, harmonica, occasional bass) born Bromwich, Staffs, 20 August 1939. Their success story stems mainly from Jimmy Page's drive and initiative. Jimmy, a brilliant young session player who had backed such artists as the Rolling Stones, Donovan and Jeff Beck on sessions, became lead guitarist of the Yardbirds in 1966 until the group dissolved in 1968. In October 1968, Led Zeppelin was born. At that time Cream, who had pioneered the heavy instrumental rock band, were breaking up, and although Led Zeppelin was not created to take over their role, this did in fact happen. Britain was the last to hear about it. America made them the hottest act to come from Britain in some time. Their hard rock and blues sound established them as one of the supergroups, and their Carnegie Hall debut in New York in the autumn of 1969 was hailed as the biggest happening since the Beatles. Their first album was released in February 1969. Within two months it was No 8 in the charts, and stayed in the Top 20 for six months with sales continuing into 1970. It received a Gold Disc award from RIAA for million dollar sales on 22 July 1969 and sold over a million units by the year's end. In Britain the disc reached No 5.

The album contained **Good Times, Bad Times**, by Jimmy Page, John P. Jones and John Bonham; **Babe I'm Gonna Leave You**, traditional: arr. Jimmy Page; **You Shook Me**, by Willie Dixon; **Dazed and Confused**, by Jimmy Page; **Your Time Is Gonna Come**, by Jimmy Page and John Paul Jones; **Black Mountain Side**, by Jimmy Page; **Communication Breakdown**, by J. Page, John P. Jones and John Bonham; **I Can't Quit You Baby**, by Willie Dixon; **How Many More Times?**, by J. Page, John P. Jones and John Bonham.

By April 1970, sales were around the two million mark in the USA alone. It was in the US bestsellers for 73 weeks.

LED ZEPPELIN 2 (Album) *Atlantic 588-198* [*UK*] *Atlantic 8236* [*USA*]. The second big seller for this exciting group had the same driving instrumental and vocal power. It was released in the USA in October 1969. It received a Gold Disc award for million dollar sales from RIAA on 10 November within three weeks of release and the disc was No 1 at year's end, and for a further six weeks in 1970 (seven weeks in all). It was also No 1 in Britain for four weeks in 1970. The numbers on the album were all composed by the group's members.

US sales swiftly reached the million, and both the group's albums gained Gold and Platinum awards for collective sales of over six million by mid-February 1970.

The album contained **Whole Lotta Love** which was a big seller as a single when released in November 1969.

Album contents: **Whole Lotta Love**, by Jimmy Page and Robert Plant; **What Is and What Should Never Be**, by Jimmy Page and Robert Plant; **The Lemon Song**, by J. Page, R. Plant, John Bonham and John Paul Jones; **Thank You**, by Jimmy Page and Robert Plant; **Hearbreaker**, by J. Page, R. Plant, John Boham and John Paul Jones; **Livin' Lovin' Maid (She's just a woman)**, by Jimmy Page and Robert Plant; **Ramble On**, by Jimmy Page and Robert Plant; **Moby Dick**, by J. Bonham, J. Page and John Paul Jones; **Bring It on Home**, by Jimmy Page and Robert Plant.

A million sale was also achieved in Europe.

WHOLE LOTTA LOVE/LIVING LOVING MAID (She's just a woman) *Atlantic 2690* [*USA*]. Released in November 1969 as a single from the group's **Led Zeppelin II** album, **Whole Lotta Love** made No 2 for two weeks in *Cash Box* and No 4 in *Billboard*, with 15 weeks on the Hot 100. It won the group's only RIAA Gold Disc for a million-selling single on 13 April 1970. Though it was a No 1 hit in Germany and Belgium, it did not make the charts in Britain. In fact, Led Zeppelin never made the singles charts in their own home market. The song was written by the group's Jimmy Page and Robert Plant.

In the USA the flip side **Living Loving Maid** also made the charts, reaching No 65 during a five-week chart run of its own.

MARK LINDSAY   American

ARIZONA *CBS-Columbia 45037* [*USA*]. Written by Kenny Young and released in November 1969, the disc was No 9 for two weeks in the USA in early 1970 and sold a million, with an RIAA Gold Disc award by April 1970, after 16 weeks in the bestsellers.

Mark Lindsay was born in Idaho. He was originally a bread delivery boy until he asked to be allowed to sing for Paul Revere, a drive-in hotel proprietor who played electric piano on local dates. Mark became lead singer and doubled on sax for Paul Revere and the Raiders (around 1963). This disc was his second solo single.

KARUMEN MAKI   Japanese

TOKINIWA HAHA NO NAIKO NO YOHNI (Sometimes I feel like a lonely baby) *CBS/Sony 1824* [*Japan*]. This was first million-selling disc for the CBS/Sony label. Singer Karumen (Carmen) Maki's disc, her first recording, was No 2 in the Japanese charts for six weeks and in the bestsellers for three months. It was released in Japan in April 1969 and sold the million by July. CBS/Sony awarded her a Gold Disc in July.

HENRY MANCINI AND   American
HIS ORCHESTRA

LOVE THEME FROM 'ROMEO AND JULIET' *RCA Victor 0131* [*USA*]. Mancini's beautiful arrangement of the love theme from the Franco Zeffirelli production of the film *Romeo and Juliet* was released on 4 April 1969, was No 1 for two weeks in the US charts with 14 weeks in the bestsellers, and sold the million by 25 June with an RIAA Gold Disc award. The theme is based on Nino Rota's score for the film which starred Leonard Whiting and Olivia Hussey.

Grammy Award (1969) for 'Best Instrumental Arrangement'.

MARMALADE   British

REFLECTIONS OF MY LIFE *Decca F 12982* [*UK*] *London 20058* [*USA*]. The Marmalade's first recording for Decca, written by W. Campbell and T. McAleese (both members of the group), this disc reached No 1 for a week in Britain in early 1970 with 12 weeks in the bestsellers. Release was on 14 November 1969. In the USA it was No 7 for a week and stayed on their bestseller charts for 15 weeks.

Sales were quite big in both countries, and the million was reported in November 1971 when the group was presented with a Gold Disc for global sales.

MEL AND TIM   American

BACKFIELD IN MOTION *Bamboo 107* [*USA*]. The disc was released in September 1969 and reached No 10 for a week in the US charts with 14 weeks in the bestsellers, selling a million with an RIAA Gold Disc award by the end of the year. This overnight success for Mel and Tim (real names Melvin Harden and Tim McPherson) who wrote the song was their debut disc for the Bamboo label. A soul-singing duo, they were originally employed as bus drivers in St Louis until the demo disc of their song was played to producer Gene Chandler who was so impressed that he cut it for his Scepter-distributed Bamboo label.

MERCY   American

LOVE (Can make you happy) *Sundi 6811* [*USA*]. This was the first hit both for this new group and the small Sundi label. The song was written by J. Sigler, Jr., and the disc released through Jamie Records in April 1969, with million sale and RIAA Gold Disc award on 15 July. The disc was No 2 for three weeks in the USA and 13 weeks in the bestsellers. The group subsequently signed with Warner Brothers-Seven Arts.

Mercy was the brainchild of Jack Sigler, Jr. who at the age of nine started learning guitar and then came into contact with members of what became Mercy. In Brandon High School he formed his own group, all graduates at the school, and they gained experience by appearing at schools around Florida. Mercy underwent changes of personnel that eventually brought them to the attention of producer George Roberts. Roberts introduced the group to its future hit as part of his film *Fireball Jungle*, and their performance led to recording for Sundi in Florida.

OSAMU MINAGAWA   Japan

KURO NEKO NO TANGO (Black cat tango) *Victor 10782* [*Japan*]. Osamu Minagawa is the youngest artist to achieve a million sale of a recording. A native of Tokyo, he made this disc at the age of six in 1969. It was released there in November and swiftly leapt to No 1 in the Japanese charts, staying in that position for 15 weeks. By February 1970 it had sold two million, mostly on the basis of Osamu's imitation of a mewing cat.

The song is a Japanese version of **Volveo un gatto nero** ('I wanted a black cat') from Italy where it was featured in the Golden Sequin Festival of Bologna. The disc sold 840,000 in its first 18 days on the Japanese market where Italian children's songs were becoming important on their disc scene. Total sales were around three million.

Osamu Minagawa was born in Tokyo on 22 January 1963, and started singing at the age of three.

Reiko Okiai assisted Osamu on the recording. She was born in Tokyo on 28 October 1964.

GIANNI MORANDI   Italian

SCENDE LA POGGIA (It's raining) *RCA PM 3476* [*Italy*]. This is the Italian version of the 1968 American hit 'Elenore' written by the Turtles (H. Kaylan, M. Volman, J. Pons, A. Nichel and J. Barbata). It was the winner of the top popular contest called 'Canzonissima' (The Best Song) organized by the Italian State Television by postcards sent to the TV company. Of the 20 million sent in, Morandi won with six million votes. The disc was issued in early January 1969 and sold 800,000 in a month, was No 1 for five weeks in the Italian charts and subsequently sold the million, making Morandi the most popular singer in Italy.

RYOKO MORIYAMA   Japanese

KINIJIRARETA KOI (Unpermitted love) *Philips 5056* [*Japan*]. Ryoko Moriyama describes herself as a pop folk singer. By this year she had eight albums released in Japan, also her own radio and TV programmes. This disc was released in April 1969 and stayed at No 1 in the Japanese charts for 12 weeks with over a million subsequent sale (by October 1969).

In October 1969 she visited Nashville to record with local musicians to get the authentic Nashville sound.

GIORGIO MORODER   Italian

LOOKY LOOKY *Hansa 14 280* [*West Germany*]. Giorgio Moroder was born in 1942 in St Ulrich, South Tirol, Italy, where he studied at the local Academy of Fine Arts. He started playing guitar when at school, and when he was 19 left school and home to play in a dancing group. He toured Europe for five years, then in 1967 he quit touring to concentrate on writing. Six months after this change of direction, in 1968, he wrote his first hit, a very Eurovision-style song that made it in Germany.

A year later he recorded the bubble-gum style **Looky Looky** in Berlin. This was the first time he had been writer, producer and performer on a record. It sold well in France, Italy, Spain and West Germany, with European sales finally passing the million mark. His stage name for this record was just Giorgio.

In 1970 he met Englishman Pete Bellotte and formed a writing and producing partnership that was a key element in the 1970s disco craze. Their first big hit song as writers was **Son of My Father**, which Giorgio took to No 46 in America, his first hit as an artist there. Chicory Tip took a cover version to No 1 in Britain. Moroder and Bellotte formed a production company, Say Yes Productions, based in Munich, the nearest city with good recording studios to where Moroder lived in northern Italy. They shared the same office building as the Musicland Studios, where they recorded many of the Eurodisco hits of the seventies. In 1974 they started recording an expatriate American black singer separated from her Austrian actor-husband Helmut Sommer. She slightly Anglicized her name, and in 1975 Donna Summer had a huge international hit with the 17-minute erotic epic **Love to Love You Baby**. The record was written by Summer, Bellotte and Moroder and produced by Moroder and Bellotte. A string of Donna Summer disco hits followed, with US No 1s like **Hot Stuff** and **Bad Girls**.

Moroder also turned his attention to film scores. He produced Blondie's **Call Me**, from the film *American Gigolo*, which went to No 1 in Britain and America. The same year (1980) saw Donna Summer with another Moroder-produced hit with **On the Radio** from the film *Foxes* for which he won an Oscar for best film score.

1910 FRUITGUM COMPANY   American

INDIAN GIVER *Buddah 91* [*USA*]. The third million seller for this 'bubble-gum' band was released in January 1969. The disc received a Gold Disc award from RIAA on 31 March. The song, written by B. Gentry, R. Cordell and B. Bloom, features heavy drumming. It rose to No 3 for one week on the US charts with 13 weeks in the bestsellers.

OLIVER   American

GOOD MORNING STARSHINE *Jubilee 5659* [*USA*] *CBS 4435* [*UK*]. William Oliver Swofford was born on 22 February 1945 in North Wilkesboro, North Carolina, and started playing guitar at the age of 15. While at the University of North Carolina he sang with a group called the Virginians, and they moved to New York subsequently touring with the Mitch Ryder Show for a year in Canada. They had a regional hit **Long Walk Back to Paradise** on the Epic label. Bill Cash, the group's manager, took them to Bob Crewe who signed them to a disc contract, and he changed the act's name to the Good Earth Trio. The group soon disbanded and Oliver joined Jim Dawson to form a duo called Good Earth. A song written by Oliver **I Can See the Light** was a success for them.

Dawson then left to form a new group and Oliver decided to be a soloist. He chose **Good Morning Starshine**, one of the hit songs from the musical *Hair* written by Gerome Ragni and James Rado (words) and Galt MacDermot (music). The disc was produced and directed by Bob Crewe.

This version was released in May 1969 and achieved No 3 for two weeks on the US charts with 13 weeks in the bestsellers. In Britain it was No 6 with 16 weeks in the bestsellers. By August it had sold the million with an RIAA Gold Disc award. It was the third song from *Hair* in this year to sell a million or more on disc.

JEAN *Crewe 334* [USA]. With the success of **Good Morning Starshine**, an album of the same title by Oliver was released at the end of July 1969 on Bob Crewe's label. This included the song **Jean** from the film *The Prime of Miss Jean Brodie* written by Rod McKuen which was released as a single in August. It sold the million by October with an RIAA Gold Disc award on 10 October. The disc was No 1 for one week in the US charts and 14 weeks in the bestsellers.

PETER, PAUL AND MARY   *American*

LEAVING ON A JET PLANE *Warner Brothers-7 Arts 7340* [USA] *Warner Brothers WB 7340* [UK]. A beautiful ballad written by John Denver with an especially fine arrangement, the disc, released in October 1969, highlights Mary as lead singer, and brought the trio even greater national prominence. It reached No 1 for two weeks with 17 weeks in the bestsellers, and sold the million by December 1969 with an RIAA Gold Disc award.

British release was in January 1970, the disc reaching No 2 for one week with 16 weeks in the bestsellers.

THE PLASTIC ONO BAND   *British*
(JOHN LENNON)

GIVE PEACE A CHANCE *Apple 13* [UK]/*Apple 1809* [USA]. In 1969 the Beatles were clearly falling apart, with John Lennon increasingly thinking of his future being with Yoko Ono rather than as part of the Fab Four. **Give Peace A Chance** was recorded in room 1472 of the Queen Elizabeth's Hotel in Montreal on 2 June 1969, during a week long bed-in following Lennon's marriage to Ono. Among the cast of 40 who made the record were Tommy Smothers on guitar, LSD advocate Dr Timothy Leary, the Beatles' press officer Derek Taylor, a Toronto rabbi and various journalists, photographers, TV crews and friends.

As John Lennon and Paul McCartney had agreed that all songs written by either of them would be published as Lennon-McCartney songs, that is the author credit on this record. In fact it was written by John Lennon alone. Lennon wanted the record to go out as a Beatles disc, but the others refused, so John thought up the Plastic Ono Band name instead.

The record was very cheap to produce. A portable eight track recording machine was

hired at £3,300 ($8,000) for five hours, the cost of the crew included. The hotel costs were around £400 ($1,000) a day, considerably cheaper than a recording studio. The record sold around two million copies globally, of which 800,000 were sold in America. The record won a Silver Disc for British sales of over a quarter of a million. During its 13 week British chart run it went to No 2 for two weeks. In America it peaked at No 10 for two weeks, with a chart life of nine weeks.

THE POPPY FAMILY   *Canadian*

WHICH WAY YOU GOIN' BILLY? *London 129* [USA] *Decca F 22976* [UK]. Released initially in Canada in the summer of 1969 and in the USA on 30 September 1969, this disc reached No 2 for two weeks in the USA in June 1970, stayed on the bestsellers for 16 weeks and sold a million by July with an RIAA Gold Disc award. Release in Britain was 31 October 1969 where it reached No 5 for one week in 1970 with 14 weeks in the bestsellers.

The song was written by Terry Jacks (of the group), and is sung on the disc by his wife Susan. The group is Canadian, comprising Susan Jacks (vocals), Terry Jacks (rhythm guitar, composer, arranger), Craig MacCaw (guitar, sitar and harp) and Satwan Singh (tabla, percussion, violin, organ).

The Poppy Family made their first appearance in the small town of Blubber Bay to an audience of 150 people, and subsequently played in Western Canada for four years.

ELVIS PRESLEY   *American*

IN THE GHETTO *RCA Victor 47-9741* [USA] *RCA Victor 1831* [UK]. The mid to late sixties was a frustrating time for Elvis fans. The King of Rock'n'Roll churned out one dreadful film after another, while RCA despaired of the man who had once been their all-conquering star and had to make do with releasing a combination of awful soundtrack material and old recordings. Elvis lost interest in making records; the process simply bored him.

Then in 1969 he came back with a vengeance, showing what the King could do if he really tried. With strong material and some effort on his part, Elvis surprised many in the music business who had written him off. The Presley revival started with an NBC-TV special in 1968. Two performances were recorded before a live audience at NBC's Burbank (California) studios on 29 June 1968, and broadcast on 3 December. The programme's producer Steve Binder built the special as a showcase to Elvis, with old hits and some good new material. The show rekindled both Elvis's interest in his recording career and the public's interest in him. He began touring again, but only in the United States. (His manager Col. Tom Parker persuaded him against any overseas performances.) His recording career perked up with the release of **If I Can Dream**, the closing number from the TV special. It reached No 12 in America, giving him one of his four best hits since 1963. The follow-up **Memories**, also from the TV show, did not do

so well, though its No 35 chart placing was better than many Presley records in the late sixties. The soundtrack album from the programme also did very well, reaching No 8 in the album charts and winning a Gold Disc for million dollar sales.

The next move was a return to Memphis for his first recording session since his Sun days in 1955. This 10-day return to his roots in January 1969 proved highly productive. All three of Presley's 1969 million sellers were recorded then, at the American Recording Studios. The first was the powerful **In the Ghetto**. Written by Scott Davis (pseudonym for Mac Davis and Billy Strange), the record was produced by Chips Moman and Felton Jarvis. In a new departure for Elvis, **In the Ghetto** was something of a protest song. On 28 June 1969 Elvis Presley was back at No 1, with his first American chart-topper since 1962. In *Cash Box* he was No 1 for one week, though **Ghetto** peaked at No 3 in *Billboard*, where it stayed in the Hot 100 for 13 weeks. It won an RIAA Gold Disc, his third for a single, on 25 June 1969. (As Presley pre-dates the start of RIAA Gold Discs in 1958, more than three of his singles sold a million copies in America. Papers in the RCA Archives in New York show another eight singles that sold a million from 1955 and 1956. Other Elvis singles released in the years before **In the Ghetto** also finally passed the million mark, with a number winning an RIAA award in 1983. However, RIAA files show that **In the Ghetto** was only the third Presley single to actually receive an RIAA Gold Disc. Most of Presley's early sixties hits sold a global million fairly soon after release.)

In Britain **In the Ghetto** went to No 1 for one week in the *NME* and *Disc/Melody Maker* charts, but stalled at No 2 in the *Record Retailer/Record Mirror* Top 50. This was Presley's first British No 1 since **Crying in the Chapel** in 1965. The 16 weeks it spent in the Top 50 was a longer chart run than any Elvis hit since **Good Luck Charm** in 1962. He won his 15th Silver Disc for British sales of over a quarter of a million on 13 September 1969. The record was also his biggest international hit for years. Apart from topping the British and American charts, it was No 1 in Australia, New Zealand, South Africa, Sweden, Norway, Germany, Belgium and Malaysia, No 2 in Canada, Switzerland and Israel, and a Top 10 hit in Ireland, Denmark, Austria, the Netherlands, France, Spain, Poland, Singapore and Hong Kong.

SUSPICIOUS MINDS *RCA Victor 47-9764* [USA] *RCA Victor 1900* [UK]. After the excellent **In the Ghetto** came a return to the bad old days when Elvis released another film soundtrack as his next single. **Clean Up Your Own Back Yard** came from the film *The Trouble With Girls*, and peaked at No 35 in America and No 21 in Britain. Then Elvis went back to his new-found form with another strong single from the Memphis session. **Suspicious Minds** entered the US charts in September 1969 and rose to No 1 for two weeks in *Cash Box* and for one week in *Billboard*. It spent 15 weeks on the Hot 100, and won Elvis his second RIAA Gold Disc of the year on 28 October 1969. The song was written by Mark James, and the record was produced by Chips Moman and Felton Jarvis at the American Recording Studios in Memphis.

It also won Presley his second Silver Disc of the year in Britain, awarded on 7 February 1970. This record peaked at No 2 in the *Record Retailer* charts, at No 4 in the *NME* and No 6 for six weeks in *Melody Maker*. It was 14 weeks in the Top 50. Internationally, it was No 1 in Canada and New Zealand, and a hit in Australia, South Africa, Ireland, the West Indies, Norway, Denmark, Germany, Austria, Belgium, the Netherlands and Spain.

DON'T CRY DADDY/RUBBERNECKIN' *RCA Victor 47-9768* [USA] *RCA Victor 1916* [UK]. Another double A side for Elvis, and a strong follow-up to **Suspicious Minds**, the King's third million seller of the year was released in December 1969 in America and February 1970 in Britain. The main side was **Don't Cry Daddy**, written by Scott Davis (pseudonym for Mac Davis and Billy Strange.) This ballad was recorded at the Memphis session, and was produced by Chips Moman and Felton Jarvis at the American Recording Studios. It won a Gold Disc on 21 January 1970 and was his 45th million seller.

Don't Cry Daddy reached No 5 in *Cash Box* and No 6 in *Billboard*, where it charted for 13 weeks. In *Billboard* the flip side **Rubberneckin'** was also listed with **Don't Cry Daddy**. In *Cash Box* the two sides were listed separately, and **Rubberneckin'** (*Cash Box* listed the title as two words) had three weeks in the Top 100, entering at No 80, going up to a peak of No 69, and falling back to No 70 for its last week on the charts. It was from the film *Change of Habit* and was written by Dory Jones and Bunny Warren.

In Britain **Don't Cry Daddy** reached No 8 with 11 weeks in the Top 50. It was not such a big hit around the world as Presley's other two 1969 smashes, but it was a Top 20 hit in Australia, New Zealand, South Africa, Norway, Denmark, Germany, Belgium, Malaysia and Hong Kong.

1969 was a good year for Elvis. On the album front his first LP of the year was a budget compilation on RCA Camden. **Elvis Sings Flaming Star** included the title track from the film *Flaming Star* and previously recorded material from 1963 to 1968. It reached No 96 in the American album charts. The first album of new material was **From Elvis in Memphis**, recorded at the American Recording Studios in Memphis at the same January session that produced Presley's three 1969 million sellers. (One of them, **In the Ghetto**, was on the album.) It reached No 13 in the American album charts, where it stayed for 34 weeks. It won an RIAA Gold Disc for million dollar sales on 28 January 1970, some six months after release. In Britain it went to No 1 for one week on 30 August 1969. It was Elvis' first UK No 1 album since **Pot Luck** in 1962.

The next Presley release was the double album **From Memphis to Vegas/From Vegas to Memphis**. The first was a live recording of Elvis at the International Hotel in Las Vegas, while the second was more studio material from the January session in Memphis. Released in November 1969 in America, the double set reached No 12 with 24 weeks on the album Top 200. It won an RIAA Gold Disc for million

dollar sales on 12 December 1969. In Britain, where it was released in March 1970, it reached No 3 with 16 weeks in the charts. Two weeks before it entered the charts an Elvis European import, **Portrait in Music**, had sold enough copies to make the charts for one week at No 36.

Elvis ended the sixties in triumph. In the annual *Record World* American disc jockeys' poll in July 1969, he was voted fifth world male singer. In the British consumer paper polls at the end of the year, he did even better, winning the 'Top World Male Singer' title in every paper. He had won this award every year of the decade except one, coming second to Cliff Richard in 1963. At the end of the year, two of the three American trade papers gave awards for success based on chart activity in the previous year. Elvis was the No 1 solo male singer in the singles category according to *Cash Box*, and No 2 behind James Brown in *Billboard*. (The *Billboard* awards were for the first 10 months of the year, and would not have reflected the success of **Don't Cry Daddy**.) Elvis was sixth in *Billboard*'s overall singles artists category, and 19th in the albums section. He was also sixth albums male vocalist (and seventh in *Cash Box*).

The year's end edition of *Cash Box* reported that by the end of 1969 Elvis had achieved 21 million-selling singles, three of which had won RIAA Gold Discs. (In fact, the total was 22 million sellers with a fourth RIAA award for **Suspicious Minds**, which *Cash Box* had forgotten. In January 1970 another RIAA award went to the 1969 release **Don't Cry Daddy**.) Of these, 20 were released up to 1962 and the others in 1969. On the album front Elvis had won nine RIAA Gold Discs for million dollar sales. Over the years many of Presley's discs continued to sell, and his death in August 1977 only added to the demand for his records. By the summer of 1988, he had won 16 RIAA Gold Discs for singles that sold a million copies in America, eight Platinum Disc awards for million-selling albums, and 32 Gold Discs for albums that sold a million dollars' worth at factory prices. (This figure includes the eight that went on to sell a million copies.) He had also had three records that sold a million copies in Britain, and one that sold a million in Germany. Taking into account world sales, Elvis Presley has had 39 singles and 6 albums that have sold over a million copies. In both the sixties and in total, only the Beatles have had more million sellers than Presley.

The contribution that Elvis Presley made to popular music has been enormous. Together with the Beatles, he had more influence than anyone in the history of rock music.

CHARLEY PRIDE   *American*

THE BEST OF CHARLEY PRIDE (Album) *RCA Victor 4223* [USA]. From an early age, Charley Pride spent several years working towards a baseball career. He played with the Los Angeles Angels, but after several seasons decided to try his luck as a singer in Nashville, the home of country-and-western music. Here he met famous guitarist and RCA artist/executive Chet Atkins who signed him up.

Charley made several albums for RCA and in 1967 had two singles **I Know One** and **Just Between You and Me** in the Top 10 US country charts. In 1968 he had three more singles and two albums in the charts, with more successes in 1969 and 1970 by which time he won the *Billboard* award for 'Best Male Country Vocalist' and for the 'Best Album' — 'The Best of Charley Pride', originally released in the USA in October 1969. By March 1971 it had sold over the million (seven million dollars at retail) and a Gold Disc was awarded by RIAA in 1970. Charlie had a further three Gold Disc awards from RIAA for albums in March 1971.

The Best of Charley Pride album was produced by Chet Atkins who also produced all the singer's other discs. It contained the following: **Just Between You and Me**, by Jack Clement (1967); **Does My Ring Hurt Your Finger?** by Robertson, Crutchfield and Clement; **Kaw-Liga**, by Fred Rose and Hank Williams (1952); **The Snakes Crawl at Night**, by Mel Tillis and Fred Burch; **All I Have to Offer You (is me)**, by A.L. Owens and Dallas Frazier (1969); **The Easy Part's Over**, by Jerry Foster and Bill Rice (1968); **The Day the World Stood Still**, by Jerry Foster and Bill Rice (1968); **I Know One**, by Jack Clement (1967); **Gone, on the Other Hand**, by Jack Clement; **Before I Met You**, by Seitz, Lewis and Rader (1957); **Too Hard to Say I'm Sorry**, by Clement and Johnson; **Let the Chips Fall**, by Jack Clement.

Release of the album in Britain was on 7 August 1970. In the USA it was No 25 for two weeks and was a bestseller for 65 weeks.

Pride was born on 18 March 1938 at Sledge, Mississippi. He was the first black artist ever to appear at Nashville's Grand Ole Opry (1967).

LOU RAWLS   *American*

YOUR GOOD THING (is about to end) *Capitol 2550* [USA]. Lou Rawls was born on 1 December 1937, a native of Chicago, and began singing in the choir of Greater Mount Olive Baptist Church there at seven. He graduated from Dunbar High School and later joined the Pilgrim Travelers, a gospel group, leaving the gospel field in 1958 following a car accident. After two years in the US Army he played service clubs, and then on the backwater Midwestern nightclub circuit from around 1959, earning about 10 dollars a night. He moved on to Los Angeles where he began singing blues. This pushed him into the jazz field, and he did a series of recordings that at various times labelled him as a jazz, pop, gospel and even folk singer. He appeared with Dick Clark on a 'Hollywood Bowl' show, also the 'Steve Allen', 'Johnny Carson', 'Mike Douglas' and 'Jack Benny' TV shows. In 1964 he was a success at the Monterey Jazz Festival.

In early 1966, Lou decided to make a recording of his old 'chitlin' circuit' style, singing and soliloquizing, and invited a number of friends to the studio for the finger-clicking, hand-clapping accompaniment. The resultant album Lou Rawls LIVE was a big hit and sold around 500,000, followed by the Soulin' album, another big seller. Both received Gold Disc awards from RIAA for million dollar sales. In a few months he was commanding $5,000 for a one-night stand.

Your Good Thing, a powerful ballad, was written by Isaac Hayes and David Porter, who had provided big hits for Sam and Dave. The disc was released in July 1969 and by November sold over 900,000, subsequently reaching the million. It was No 15 for one week in the USA and in the bestsellers for 14 weeks.

MIGUEL RIOS (with orchestra and chorus conducted by Waldo De Los Rios) — *Spanish*

HIMNO A LA ALEGRIA (Song of Joy) *Hispavox 3915 [Spain] A&M AMS 790 [UK] A&M 1193 [USA]*. This disc, commemorating the bicentennial of Beethoven (born 1770), was first a big hit in Spain where it achieved No 3. The song is based on the last movement of Beethoven's Ninth ('The Choral') Symphony, the words by Orbe and musical adaptation by Waldo De Los Rios. It was released in the USA in May 1970 where it got to No 9 for a week and by July sold a million combined US/Canada sales and was awarded a Gold Disc by RIAA. The English words were written by Ross Parker. **Song of Joy** was a hit in Canada before the USA, and then got into the charts in Portugal, Holland, France, Belgium, South America and Germany (No 1). Release in Britain was on 13 February 1970 but it was not a hit there until its US success, when the disc was re-released and reached No 16 with 16 weeks in the bestsellers.

Miguel Rios was born in 1944 in Granada and started singing at six. At eight he was soloist in his school choir. After school he formed a rock group in Granada, playing local clubs. He then met a record man who invited him to make a disc, and **Song of Joy** resulted in December 1969. The enormous choir and symphony orchestra that made the disc in Madrid gave a tasteful modern pop treatment and a fresh meaning to Beethoven's immortal melody, 200 years after his birth.

Conductor Waldo De Los Rios is also the composer of **South American Suite**.

TOMMY ROE — *American*

JAM UP JELLY TIGHT *ABC 11247 [USA]*. Written by Tommy Roe with F. Waller, the disc was released in November 1969, reaching No 4 for a week in the US charts with 14 weeks in the bestsellers. It was a big hit for the 'bubble-gum' devotees and sold a million by January 1970 with an RIAA Gold Disc award.

KENNY ROGERS AND THE FIRST EDITION — *American*

RUBY, DON'T TAKE YOUR LOVE TO TOWN *Reprise 0829 [USA] Reprise RS 20829 [UK]*. Kenny Rogers, leader and lead singer of the group, was born on 21 August 1938 in Houston, Texas, and was formerly a bass man with the Bobby Doyle Trio, a jazz group which toured the USA and recorded for CBS. They performed in nightclubs and concerts frequently with the Kirby Stone Four. On leaving the trio, Rogers joined the New Christy Minstrels for a year (1966) and then left to form the First Edition. Thelma Camacho, who had four years of classical voice training, had played roles in San Diego opera and light opera. She was with the New Christy Minstrels when she met Mike Settle (rhythm guitar), Kenny Rogers, and Terry Williams (guitar) and formed the First Edition. Terry, whose father played first trombone for Tommy Dorsey, and whose mother was vocalist with the band, took up the guitar at 14. Settle, while a member of the Cumberland Three, worked with John Stewart, later of the Kingston Trio. He wrote much of the First Edition's music. Mickey Jones (drummer) had played with Trini Lopez, Johnny Rivers and Bob Dylan.

Ruby, Don't Take Your Love to Town was written in 1966 by Mel Tillis and is now considered to be a country classic. It tells the story of a war cripple and has a deeply moving tune. The First Edition's disc was released in the USA in June 1969 and achieved No 6 for two weeks with 13 weeks in the charts. In Britain, release was in October and it went to No 1 there for a week with 23 weeks in the bestsellers, selling over 250,000. Together with the US sales and other countries it sold over a million.

The song caused some controversy, with its criticism of that crazy Asian war coming at a sensitive time in the Vietnam conflict. In fact the song refered to the Korean war. Kenny Rogers later developed a highly successful solo career, both as a Country artist with 20 C&W No 1s, and as a pop artist with several Hot 100 hits, two No 1s and a collection of million sellers in the late seventies and early eighties.

THE ROLLING STONES — *British*

HONKY TONK WOMEN *Decca F 12952 [UK] London 910 [USA]*. 1969 was a year of transition for the Rolling Stones. Brian Jones left the group in June, and was found dead in his swimming pool on 3 July. He was replaced by ex-John Mayall's Bluesbreakers rhythm guitarist Mick Taylor (born in London on 17 January 1941). On 5 July the Stones gave a free concert in Hyde Park, London, to introduce Taylor, though the concert became a tribute to Jones. A quarter of a million people attended. In late November the Stones did four performances at New York's Madison Square Gardens, which later provided the material for the live **Get Yer Ya-Yas Out** album of 1970. Their American tour was their first in three years. The final live show of the year turned out to be a hastily put together disaster. It was a free show at the Altamont Speedway, in Livermore, California. Hells Angels were hired as security guards, but they only made the violence worse. A black spectator, Meredith Hunter, waved a gun at the stage and was stabbed to death by the Angels. The incident was filmed by David and Albert Maysles who had been hired to film the concert. The killing featured in the opening shots of their *Gimme Shelter* film, which is more than the ill-fated 'Rolling Stones Rock'n'Roll TV Circus' did. Made in London on Saturday 12 December 1968, the film was never shown.

The group's only single of the year was their biggest British No 1. It was also their last, topping the charts a month after **The Ballad of John and Yoko** became the Beatles' last No 1. It was written by Mick Jagger and Keith Richards while they were on holiday in Brazil. They were on a ranch miles from the nearest recording studio, with only an acoustic guitar. The original version had a strong country feel to it, and the **Country Honk** on the **Let It Bleed** album (complete with country fiddle) is much closer to the original than the more upbeat rocker that went to No 1. The singles version was on the **Through the Past Darkly** hits package.

This was the first Stones single to be produced by Jimmy Miller, at the Olympic Studios in Barnes, London, in May 1969. Having fallen out with their original recording and personal manager Andrew Oldham, they were also falling out with their new manager Allen Klein. They would soon take greater control of their financial affairs. This was the first and only UK No 1 single on which Mick Taylor played. It was also the group's last official single for the Decca Record Company. Among those that the group had fallen out with was Decca's authoritarian chairman Sir Edward Lewis. From 1970 onwards they released their records on their own Rolling Stones Records label.

Honky Tonk Women was released in Britain at the beginning of July, and on 26 July reached the top spot. It was No 1 for five weeks on all three British charts, with 17 weeks in the Top 50. It was their second No 1 in a row, following **Jumpin' Jack Flash** the year before, and won them their 10th Silver Disc for British sales of a quarter of a million on 2 August. British sales were nearer half a million, with massive sales all over the world. It was No 1 in Britain, the USA, Canada, Australia, New Zealand, Denmark, Switzerland, and Malaysia, a Top 10 hit in Ireland, Finland, Sweden, Norway, Germany, Austria, Belgium, the Netherlands, France, Spain, Poland, the Lebanon, Hong Kong and Mexico, and a Top 20 hit in the Philippines. It was their biggest international hit since **Satisfaction**.

In America it was No 1 for four weeks in *Billboard* and *Cash Box*, with 15 weeks on the Hot 100. It won the Stones their third RIAA Gold Disc for US sales of a million on 26 August 1969, just over a month after its release. The flip side, **You Can't Always Get What You Want**, charted four years later. By then the Stones had long left Decca and its American subsidiary London. Unpromoted by the group, it peaked at No 42 with eight weeks on the charts. It was the last singles appearance by the Stones on the London label. The flip was also listed as a double A side in Australia.

THROUGH THE PAST, DARKLY — BIG HITS VOLUME 2 (Album) *Decca SKL 5019* [*UK*] *London 3* [*USA*]. The Rolling Stones' second 'greatest hits' album was released on both sides of the Atlantic in September, and dedicated to the late Brian Jones. There were two versions of the album, with a slightly different track listing in the United States from that in Britain. Canada followed the American version, and the rest of the world followed the British pattern. All the tracks on both versions were produced by Andrew Oldham, except **Honky Tonk Women** which was produced by Jimmy Miller.

The album reached No 2 in Britain, with 37 weeks in the LP charts. In the USA it went to No 2 for two weeks, with 32 weeks on the charts. It won an RIAA Gold Disc for million dollar sales on 9 September 1969, based on advance sales. The album was also a major seller throughout Europe, and in Australia, New Zealand and South Africa.

Contents (British release): *****Honky Tonk Women**, by Mick Jagger and Keith Richards (1969); *****Ruby Tuesday**, by Mick Jagger and Keith Richards (1967); *****Jumpin' Jack Flash**, by Mick Jagger and Keith Richards (1968); **Street Fighting Man**, by Mick Jagger and Keith Richards (1968); *****Let's Spend the Night Together**, by Mick Jagger and Keith Richards (1967); **2,000 Light Years from Now**, by Mick Jagger and Keith Richards (1967); *****Mother's Little Helper**, by Mick Jagger and Keith Richards (1966); **She's a Rainbow**, by Mick Jagger and Keith Richards (1967); *****Dandelion**, by Mick Jagger and Keith Richards (1967); **You Better Move On**, by Arthur Alexander (1964); *****We Love You**, by Mick Jagger and Keith Richards (1967); **Sitting on the Fence**, by Mick Jagger and Keith Richards (1967).

The American release contained the first nine titles plus: *****Paint It Black**, by Mick Jagger and Keith Richards (1966); *****Have You Seen Your Mother, Baby, Standing in the Shadow?** by Mick Jagger and Keith Richards (1966).

Items marked * were million seller singles.

LET IT BLEED (Album) *Decca SKL 5025* [*UK*] *London 4* [*USA*]. **Let It Bleed** was the Stones' last studio album for Decca. Like all their albums, it contained songs about sex, drugs and violence. In style the album ranged from hard rock'n'roll to a couple of tracks with a strong country flavour to them. The album was produced by Jimmy Miller, who had previously produced hits for the Spencer Davis Group and Traffic. The album included the first Keith Richardss lead vocal, **You Got the Silver**. Both Brian Jones and Mick Taylor played.

London Records released the album in America in November. It reached No 3 with 44 weeks on the charts. It won an RIAA Gold Disc for million dollar sales on 24 November, based on advance orders. It was their 11th Gold Album in a row. Decca released it in Britain in December, where it went to No 1 for one week on 20 December, breaking into the middle of a 17-week run at the top for the Beatles' **Abbey Road** album. It was their fourth No 1 British album, and was to be followed in 1970 by another, the live **Get Yer Ya-Yas Out**. The Stones would enjoy three more No 1 albums in the seventies, with **Sticky Fingers** (1971), the **Exile on Main Street** double album (1972) and **Goat's Head Soup** (1973). Their final No 1 album in Britain was **Emotional Rescue** in 1980. In America the Stones were more successful on the album charts in the seventies than they had been in the sixties. Compared to the one chart-topping album of the sixties (*****Out of Our Heads**), they notched up six in the seventies and two in the eighties.

The contents of the album were as follows with all the songs written by Mick Jagger and Keith Richards except Payne's **Love in Vain**. **Let It Bleed**; **Love in Vain**; **Midnight Rambler**; **Gimme Shelter**; **You Got the Silver**; **You Can't Always Get What You Want**; **Live with Me**; **Monkey Man**; **Country Honk**.

The album includes many artists on the various songs such as Mary Clayton (vocalist), Ray Cooper (mandolin), Byron Berline (blue-grass violin), Ian Stewart (piano), Jimmy Miller (tambourine), Nicky Hopkins (piano), Jack Nitzche (arrangements for London Bach Choir), Madeline Bell (vocalist), Doris Troy (vocalist) and Nanette Newman (vocalist).

For a quarter of a century the Rolling Stones have kept on rocking, outraging the establishment even when they became part of it. In 1976 Ron Wood replaced Mick Taylor, but apart from that the line-up has remained the same. After their years signed direct to Decca, the band kept to their own label from 1970 onwards, licensing it first to Warner Brothers, then EMI. Finally, as the Stones were pushing 50, they screwed $15 million out of CBS in a deal that the company will not make money out of. In the mid-eighties various Stones got involved in solo projects, and Mick Jagger in particular had some success. As a new decade dawns and the **Steel Wheels** album storms the charts, the greatest rock'n' roll band in the world is still one of the world's biggest acts.

DIANA ROSS AND THE SUPREMES
American

SOMEDAY WE'LL BE TOGETHER *Motown 1156* [*USA*] *Tamla Motown TMG 721* [*UK*]. It is somehow fitting that the last American No 1 of the sixties should have been by the most successful American group of the decade. It was also the Supremes' last No 1. They had topped the US charts 12 times, a record beaten only by the Beatles and Elvis Presley. It was also the last Supremes disc to feature Diana Ross, who left to follow a solo career. She was replaced by Jean Terrell.

The song was written by Jackey Beavers, Johnny Bristol and Harvey Fuqua in 1961, and produced by Johnny Bristol at the Motown studios in Detroit. Beavers and Bristol had recorded the song for Fuqua's Tri-Phi label in 1961 before they all joined Motown, though the record was not a hit then. By 1969 Bristol was a successful writer and producer with Motown. When he told Berry Gordy he wanted to re-record the song himself, Gordy persuaded him that it would be much more successful as the next Diana Ross and the Supremes single. In fact, the Supremes did not sing on the record. Diana Ross was supported by two session singers, Julia and Maxine Waters.

It entered the US charts at the beginning of November, and reached No 1 in both *Billboard* and *Cash Box* for the last week of the year. In *Cash Box* it had a second week at the top as the first No 1 of the seventies. In *Billboard* it had only one week at the top, with 16 weeks on the charts. It was No 1 for four weeks on the R&B charts, with 15-weeks chart duration. It sold well over a million copies in America, but because Motown did not apply for RIAA certification for million sellers until the 1980s no RIAA Gold Disc was ever awarded. Despite 18 million sellers in the sixties, and another four in the early seventies, the only RIAA Gold Disc the group ever got was for the **Anthology** album released when the group broke up in 1974. It was awarded for million dollar sales (not for the sale of a million units) on 21 January 1986; and sold three million copies worldwide.

In Britain **Someday We'll Be Together** was not as big a hit as it had been in America. It reached No 10 in the *NME* and No 13 in the *Record Retailer* Top 50, where it stayed for 13 weeks. On 13 December it entered the British R&B charts at No 3, moving up to No 1 for two weeks in January 1970. It spent 12 weeks in the R&B chart, and would have spent longer there if the chart had not been abandoned. The American trade paper *Billboard* had bought *Record Mirror*, which published the British R&B charts. The R&B singles chart had already been reduced to a Top 10 before **Someday We'll Be Together** was released. On 7 March 1970 *Record Mirror* announced, 'We are overhauling the R&B charts in order to present a more accurate picture of national sales.' It never appeared again.

BARRY RYAN
British

LOVE IS LOVE *MGM 1464* [*UK*]. Written by Barry himself, and released in Britain during February 1969, his disc was not a success in his own country. Although Barry had never performed any live dates outside Britain, his discs were extremely popular on the Continent, particularly in Germany, Austria and Holland, and did in fact win a poll by several European papers as the most popular in that territory. **Love is Love** sold a million globally by August 1969, the second for Barry. It was No 25 in Britain.

SANTANA
American

SANTANA (Album) *CBS-Columbia 9781* [*USA*] *CBS 63815* [*UK*]. Santana's first album was released in September 1969. In 12 months it sold two million and earned the group $300,000 in royalties. It reached No 2 for a week in 1970 in the USA.

The group started in San Francisco around 1966. It included Gregg Rolie (pianist-organist), Carlos Santana (guitarist), Dave Brown (bass guitarist) and two others since departed. They first called themselves the Santana Blues Band and were immensely popular in San Francisco's Spanish Mission District. In early 1969 they were joined by Jose Areas (conga drums, trumpet, timbales), Mike Carrabello (conga drums) and Mike Shrieve (drums), the group being managed from the beginning by Stan Marcum, a music-struck local barber. Marcum even sold his clothes for the group's benefit and went out to cut hair while the group stayed home and played music.

The contents of the album were written by the group unless otherwise credited: **Waiting**; **Evil Ways**, by J. Zach; **Shades of Time**; **Savor**; **Jin-go-lo-ba**, by Michael Olatunje; **Persuasion**; **Treat**; **You Just Don't Care**; **Soul Sacrifice**.

The album was in the Top 10 for 28 weeks, and in the bestsellers for 108 weeks in the USA. Gold Disc award by RIAA in December 1969.

Release in Britain was on 14 November 1969. The album did not make the charts until May 1970 when in an 11-week chart run it peaked at No 26.

BOBBY SHERMAN   *American*

LITTLE WOMAN *Metromedia 121* [*USA*]. Bobby Sherman became one of Metromedia's first successful artists. This disc released in August 1969 was No 1 for a week and 13 weeks in the US bestsellers, and sold the million by October with an RIAA Gold Disc award on 7 October. The song was written by D. Janssen.

In 1965, Bobby Sherman was a high school football star and engineering student, but in his spare time he was a songwriter, record producer, and singer. He was discovered by Natalie Wood and Sal Mineo, resulting in an audition and then an appearance on the ABC-TV network 'Shindig' show. When the series ended he became a featured character in the TV series 'Here Come the Brides'. **Little Woman** was his first recording on the Metromedia label.

LA LA LA (If I had you) *Metromedia 150* [*USA*]. The follow-up hit for Bobby Sherman, again written by D. Janssen, was released in November 1969. It was No 8 for one week in the USA and 11 weeks in the bestsellers, and sold the million by January 1970 with a Gold Disc award from RIAA.

SHOCKING BLUE   *Dutch*

VENUS *Pink Elephant 304* [*Netherlands*] *Penny Farthing PEN 702* [*UK*] *Colossus 108* [*USA*]. Towards the end of the sixties it looked as if the Anglo-American domination of the pop world might be successfully challenged by the Netherlands. A number of Dutch groups had considerable international success, with many records being hits all over the world. The

biggest group in Holland in the late sixties and early seventies was the Cats. Signed to EMI's Imperial label, they had a string of 32 Dutch hits between 1966 and 1984. Their first international hit was **Lea** in 1968, and their biggest world hit was **Marian** the year after. This went to No 1 in countries as far afield as Malaysia and the Lebanon. While they enjoyed long-lasting success in Europe, including major markets like Germany (eight big hits), their style of big ballads with lush orchestral backing did not go down so well in the English-speaking world.

Here it was the No 2 Dutch group that broke through. Shocking Blue were formed by lead guitarist Robert van Leeuwen (born in 1944), who had previously led local group the Motions for three years. After a year working as a producer he decided to go back to performing, and in 1968 formed Shocking Blue with bass guitarist Klasse van der Wal, drummer Cornelius van der Beek, and the beautiful Mariska Veres whose powerful vocals skilfully complemented the simple, driving country-rock style of the other three. Born in 1949, Mariska was the daughter of a gipsy violinist, and was discovered in an Amsterdam club.

Shocking Blue based themselves in the Hague, and sang in English. Their first Dutch hit was **Send Me a Postcard** in 1968. **Venus** was their third Dutch hit, and reached No 3 for three weeks in their native country. It had two runs in the Dutch Top 40, with 26 weeks in the charts in all. It was written and produced by Robert van Leeuwen. It went to No 1 in the USA, Canada, New Zealand, South Africa, Sweden, Austria, Switzerland, Belgium, France, Spain, Italy, Israel, Lebanon, Singapore, Argentina and Chile. It was Top Three in Australia, Finland, Norway, Germany, Holland, Japan, Mexico, Brazil and Peru, and a hit in Britain, Denmark, Poland, Turkey, Yugoslavia, Hong Kong and the Philippines. This massive hit sold eight million copies around the world. It was the first Dutch record ever to top the American charts. Released in 1969, it went to No 1 in *Cash Box* on 31 January 1970, and stayed there for three

weeks. It topped the *Billboard* charts for only one week, on 7 February 1970, staying in the Hot 100 for 14 weeks. It won an RIAA Gold Disc, the first awarded to a Dutch act, on 28 January 1970.

Compared to the huge success **Venus** enjoyed in the rest of the English-speaking world, its performance in Britain was positively restrained. It only reached No 8, with 11 weeks in the Top 50. This was in spite of a tremendous campaign by the group's British record company, Larry Page's Penny Farthing.

MIGHTY JOE *Pink Elephant 322* [*Netherlands*] *Penny Farthing PEN 713* [*UK*] *Colossus 111* [*USA*]. On 29 November 1969 Shocking Blue entered their native Dutch Top 40 at No 29 with **Mighty Joe**, the eagerly awaited follow-up to **Venus**. It leapt to 14 the following week and then up to No 8. The same week the Cats' **Marian** entered the charts at No 16 its first week of release and was at No 1 its second week in the charts. **Mighty Joe** was No 2 for Christmas, but looked as if it would be locked out of the top spot by the five weeks the Cats spent at No 1. After four weeks at No 2, and 16 No 1s in other countries in all six continents, Shocking Blue finally got their first No 1 at home. **Mighty Joe** spent two weeks at the top and 18 weeks in the Top 40. Its success saw **Venus** re-enter the Dutch charts for a second time, though it got no higher than the No 3 it had reached when first released.

Mighty Joe was produced by Robert van Leeuwen who, as with most of their singles, also wrote the song. It was a hit in a number of countries, though on nothing like the same scale as **Venus**. It was released in Britain and America in 1970, reaching No 43 in both countries. It had only three weeks in the British Top 50, and was their second and last hit. It had seven weeks on the American Hot 100, and was followed by one more hit. **Long and Lonesome Road** was released in Holland before **Venus**, being their second domestic hit. It was their final American chart entry, reaching No 75 during its five-week chart life.

Their third and final million-selling single came later, in 1970, with **Never Marry a**

Railroad Man, the follow-up to **Mighty Joe** everywhere but America, and their second No 1 in a row in the Netherlands.

Shocking Blue were a talented group. They had a good producer and songwriter in Rob van Leeuwen, and Mariska Veres was more than just a beautiful front girl. However, the unprecedented success of **Venus** proved impossible to sustain. While they continued to have hits in the Netherlands well into the seventies, their days as international stars were fairly brief. The Dutch threat proved to be a false dawn for Continental pop, though other Dutch groups like Focus and the George Baker Selection also had international hits. Europe had to wait for Abba in 1974 before a Continental act really made it.

On 6 September 1986, British female trio Bananarama took their revival of the song back up the American charts to No 1 for the second time.

JOE SIMON   American

THE CHOKIN' KIND *Sound Stage 7 2628* [*USA*]. Soul singer Joe Simon's disc was written by Harland Howard. The disc was released in March 1969 and rose to No 11 in the US charts for a week with 12 weeks in the bestsellers. By 16 June it sold a million and was awarded a Gold Disc by RIAA.

Joe Simon was born in Simmesport, Louisiana, on 2 September 1943. At the age of 15 he moved to California, and later gained an introduction to Sound Stage 7 Records, a subsidiary of Monument Records, which signed him to a contract in 1966. His first release **Teenager's Prayer** got into the charts and he followed up with a string of hits. Joe made a successful European tour in 1968 which took in Britain, France, Italy and Germany.

Grammy award (1969) for 'Best Rhythm-and-Blues Vocal Performance (Male)'.

FRANK SINATRA   American

MY WAY *Reprise 0817* [*USA*] *Reprise RS 20817* [*UK*]. Written in 1967 by the French songwriters Gilles Thibaut (words) and Claude François and Jacques Revaux (music) with the title **Comme d'habitude**, the English lyrics were written by famous disc artist Paul Anka in 1969. The disc only reached No 27 in the USA (with eight weeks in the bestsellers) but got to No 4 in Britain. The million sale in Britain was reported in early 1970. It was released in the USA in March 1969 and Britain on 21 March 1970. The song was the No 1 sheet music seller in Britain in 1969.

The disc holds the then record for the longest stay in Britain's bestseller charts — 122 weeks into 1971.

SLY AND THE FAMILY STONE   American

THANK YOU (Falettin me be mice elf again)/ EVERYBODY IS A STAR *Epic 10555* [*USA*]. A big double-sided hit for this group, both songs were written by their leader Sly (Sylvester Stewart). It was released in late December 1969

and was No 1 for two weeks in the USA. **Thank You** entered the soul charts on 10 January 1970 and was No 1 for 5 weeks during a 14-week chart run. The million sale Gold Disc was awarded in mid-February 1970 by RIAA.

STAND! (Album) *Epic 26456* [*USA*]. **Stand!** was the third hit album from this San Francisco funk-rock band. Their first had been **Dance to the Music** in 1968, which reached No 142 in the American album charts. Their second album of the year, **Life**, did even less well, reaching No 195 during five weeks on the main pop LP charts. At the same time the inter-racial 'psychedelic soul' group had two major hits on the pop and R&B Top 10, including the No 1 **Everyday People**.

In April 1969 **Stand!** entered the charts at the start of a two-year stint on the LP Top 200. It peaked at No 13, but with 102 weeks on the charts it sold a lot better than many albums that got to a higher position. It went Gold on 4 December 1969, went on to pass the million mark, and was awarded a Platinum Disc on 21 November 1986.

The contents of the album were: **Stand!**; **Don't Call Me Nigger, Whitey**; **I Want To Take You Higher**; **Somebody's Watching You**; **Sing a Simple Song**; **Everyday People**; **Sex Machine** and **You Can Make It If You Try**. All the tracks on the album were by Sly Stone, who wrote nearly all the material recorded by the group.

SMITH   American

BABY IT'S YOU *Dunhill 4206* [*USA*]. Smith quintet comprised one girl and four men: Gayle McCormick (lead singer) born in St Louis, Missouri, Larry Moss (organ and kazoo); Jerry Carter (bass); Robert Evans (drums); Rich Cliburn (lead guitar).

Baby It's You, a song written in 1961 by Mack David, Burt Bacharach and Barney Williams, was originally a hit for the Shirelles in 1962. Smith's disc was released in July 1969 and by October sold a million with an RIAA Gold Disc award. It reached No 3 for two weeks and stayed in the US bestsellers for 15 weeks.

Smith was managed by disc artist Del Shannon who selected the song from their repertoire for recording.

THE SPIRAL STAIRCASE   American

MORE TODAY THAN YESTERDAY *CBS-Columbia 44741* [*USA*]. This group began in January 1964 at a nightclub in Sacramento, California. After a few years of name and personnel changes they were signed to CBS Records. This was their second disc for the label and it rose to No 7 for a week in the US charts with 15 weeks in the bestsellers after release in March 1969. By the end of August it had sold almost a million and reached the magic figure subsequently.

The Spiral Staircase consisted of Pat Upton (lead singer, guitar), writer of the group's material; Richard Lopes (organizer, leader of the act, saxophone and vocals); Bob Raymond

(bass); Harvey Kaye (keyboards); Vinnie Panariello (drums).

The song for this disc was written by Pat Upton.

STEAM   American

NA NA HEY HEY KISS HIM GOODBYE *Fontana 1667* [*USA*] *Fontana TF 1058* [*UK*]. Steam, a group of six men then in their early twenties, came into prominence in late 1969 with this disc which was released in September. The song was written by G. de Carlo, D. Frashuer and Paul Leka (discoverer of the group, also their manager and producer). It was No 1 in the USA for two weeks and 16 weeks in the bestsellers, and received a Gold Disc award for million sale from RIAA on 8 December 1969. It reached No 20 in the Soul charts with an eight-week chart run.

Five of the group had been together since their early teens, and all lived in Connecticut, practising in each other's houses. The group at that time consisted of Hank Schorz (guitar, organ, piano, drums); Mike Daniels (bass); Bill Steer (vocalist); Tom Zuke (rhythm guitar); Jay Babins (lead guitar).

In 1969, Ray Corries (drums, bass and vocalist) was added to the group. Schorz then became lead vocalist. The recording was made at Mercury Sound Studios in New York.

In 1983, Bananarama had a British Top 10 hit with this song.

STEPPENWOLF   American

ROCK ME *Dunhill 4182* [*USA*]. Written by John Kay of the group, this comes from the film *Candy* for which the group sang the songs.

The disc was released in February 1969 and was No 7 for two weeks in the US charts with 10 weeks in the bestsellers. A million sale was reported in May.

RAY STEVENS   American

GITARZAN *Monument 1131* [*USA*]. Multi-instrumentalist and songwriter Ray Stevens, specialist in novelty songs, had a big hit with this humorous record. It was written by him and Bill Everett. The disc was released at the end of March 1969 and reached No 7 for two weeks in the US charts with 13 weeks in the bestsellers, with million sale by 16 June and a Gold Disc award from RIAA. Ray's first million seller was **Ahab the Arab** (see 1962).

TEE SET   Dutch

MA BELLE AMIE *Tee Set Records/Delta TS 1329* [*Netherlands*] *Colossus 107* [*USA*]. Tee Set were another Dutch group who, like the Cats and Shocking Blue, broke onto the international scene in 1969. On 12 July 1969 the three Dutch groups all entered the Dutch Top 40. Shocking Blue were in at No 17 (with **Venus**), the Cats entered at No 31, and Tee Set crept into the charts at No 40 with **Ma Belle Amie**. The following week it leapt to No 20, making the

Top 10 on 9 August. It peaked at No 6 on 23 August, and eventually sold 100,000 copies in the Netherlands.

Released on the Discostar label, it was also a hit in neighbouring Belgium, and on other independent labels in Switzerland (No 2), Germany, Austria, Denmark and Italy. In the Netherlands the Tee Set label was released via Delta, which later joined with Negram and became part of EMI Bovema. **Ma Belle Amie** would probably have remained a Continental hit if Jerry Ross, head of the American record company Colossus, had not heard it at a disco in Zürich. He secured rights for North and South America, and heavily promoted the record. In America it reached No 4 in *Cash Box*, and No 5 in *Billboard* with 12 weeks in the Hot 100. This American success gave it an opening in other English-speaking territories. It was No 1 in South Africa, No 3 in Canada, and a Top 10 hit in Australia and New Zealand. It also reached No 6 in Brazil. It was not a hit in Britain, where it was released by Major Minor.

Tee Set had started in 1966 with covers of English hits. They then moved on to writing their own material. This song was written by Tee Set lead singer Peter Tetteroo and group member Hans van Eyk. The other group members were Perry Lever, Franklin Madjid and Herman van Boeyen. The record was produced by Peter Tetteroo, and sold a million copies globally.

THE TEMPTATIONS   *American*

I CAN'T GET NEXT TO YOU *Gordy 7093 [USA] Tamla Motown TMG 722 [UK]*. This was the Temptations' 27th hit record, and reached No 1 for two weeks in the pop charts, with 17 weeks on the Hot 100. It was No 1 in the Soul charts for 5 weeks, with 15 weeks in the Soul Top 50. In Britain it went to No 13, with a nine-week chart run in early 1970.

The song was written by Norman Whitfield and Barrett Strong, and recorded at the Motown studios in Detroit.

B.J. THOMAS   *American*

RAINDROPS KEEP FALLING ON MY HEAD *Scepter 12265 [USA] Wand WN 1 [UK]*. A sparkling ballad written by Hal David (words) and Burt Bacharach (music), it was sung by B.J. Thomas for the film *Butch Cassidy and The Sundance Kid*. The disc was released in October 1969 and by the end of the year became No 1 for three weeks, with a Gold Disc award from RIAA for million sale (December). By the end of January 1970, sales were estimated at two million in the USA alone. It stayed in the US bestsellers for 22 weeks.

Release in Britain was on the Wand label on 5 December 1969 and it reached No 38. The song received an Oscar for 'Best Film Song' of the year, and the disc sold over three million.

THREE DOG NIGHT   *American*

ONE *Dunhill 4191 [USA]*. **One** was written by artist-songwriter Harry Nilsson who first

recorded it. Three Dog Night's disc was released in May 1969 and went to No 1 for a week in the US charts with 16 weeks in the bestsellers, and sold the million by 23 July plus an RIAA Gold Disc award, the first for the group.

This West Coast band comprised vocalists Danny Hutton (born in Buncrana, Donegal, Ireland), Cory Wells (from New York) and Chuck Negron (from New York) backed by four exceptional musicians, Joe Sherman (bass), Jimmy Greenspoon (organ), Mike Alsup (lead guitar) and Floyd Sneed (drums).

Three Dog Night is an Eskimo term meaning 'extreme cold'.

EASY TO BE HARD *Dunhill 4203 [USA]*. Yet another song from the musical *Hair* by Gerome Ragni and James Rado (words) with Galt MacDermot (music) to sell a million on disc. Three Dog Night's recording was released in August 1969 and reached No 1 for two weeks in the USA and stayed in the bestsellers for 13 weeks.

ELI'S COMING *Dunhill 4215 [USA]*. The third million seller in a row for Three Dog Night was taken from their album **Suitable for Framing**. It was released in October 1969, achieving No 7 for two weeks in the US charts with 14 weeks in the bestsellers. The recording is a version of the familiar song written by Laura Nyro.

VANITY FAIR   *British*

EARLY IN THE MORNING *Page One POF 142 [UK] Page One 21027 [USA]*. **Early in the Morning** was originally recorded by Cliff Richard, who had a big hit with it in the Far East, reaching No 1 in Japan. He had it in mind for a future British release, but because of other material he wanted to put out first Vanity Fair had covered it before Cliff was ready to release it. Cliff's original version also had selective Continental release, and was a hit in the Netherlands.

Vanity Fair's group name was taken from the ninteenth-century novel by Thackeray.

Early in the Morning was released on 20 June and reached No 7 for two weeks in Britain

with 12 weeks in the bestsellers. Release in the USA was in November 1969 and it achieved No 9 for two weeks in early 1970 with 13 weeks in the bestsellers, by which time the disc had sold a million globally.

The song was written by Mike Leander and Eddie Seago.

Vanity Fair consisted of Dick Allix, born 3 June 1945 in Gravesend, Kent, drums; Trevor Brice, born 12 February 1945 in Strood, Kent, lead vocalist, pianist; Tony Goulden, born 21 November 1944 in Rochester, Kent, lead and 12-string guitar, also vocals; Tony Jarrett, born 4 September 1944 in Rochester, Kent, bass guitar and vocals; Barry Landemann, born 25 October 1947 in Woodbridge, Suffolk, piano.

THE VENTURES   *American*

HAWAII FIVE-O *Liberty 56068 [USA]*. The theme from the successful TV series of the same title was written by Mort Stevens. It achieved No 4 and stayed in the US bestseller charts for four weeks.

By 1969 the Ventures became exceedingly popular in Japan, following a number of tours there. Their discs were put out by EMI's Toshiba Records and became big sellers. By 1971 they had made nine tours, and many of their compositions of a Japanese flavour were recorded by native artists, including **Kyoto Doll**, **Kyoto Boy** (both by Yuko Nagisa), **Hokkaido Skies** (Chiyo Okumura) and **Stranger in Midosuji** (Fifi Ouyang), each selling over a million.

THE WHO   *British*

TOMMY (Double Album) *Track 613-013/4 [UK] US Decca 7205 [USA]*. The Who were formed in London in 1964, consisting of Peter Townshend (lead guitar) born 19 May 1945, Chiswick, London; Keith Moon (drums) born 23 August 1947, Wembley, London; John Entwhistle (bass guitar, trumpet, French horn, piano) born 9 October 1945, Chiswick, London; Roger Daltrey (lead singer, guitar, harp) born 1 March 1945, Hammersmith, London.

Townshend, son of a dance-band saxophonist, met the other three in Acton County Grammar School, and their early local success came from imitations of US blues and rock'n'roll performers. Later, they were the pioneers of pop-art costumes and in their act began literally breaking things up, smashing instruments during their performance. Their fans went berserk at this most violent stage act in the business. They made a successful tour with the Beatles and in the summer of 1967 they built up a big reputation in the USA at the Monterey Pop Festival, and also toured the States. Their singles successes in Britain were **My Generation** (No 3 for three weeks, 1965) on Brunswick label; **I'm a Boy** (No 2 for two weeks, 1966) on Reaction label; **Pictures of Lily** (No 4 for two weeks, 1967) on Track label; **Happy Jack** (No 3 for week, 1967) on Track label; **Pinball Wizard** (No 4 for one week, 1969) on Track label.

In April 1969, the group's double album of **Tommy** was released. Composed by Peter

Townshend with contributions by Who members John Entwhistle and Keith Moon, this 'rock' opera about a deaf, dumb and blind boy proved to be one of the most ambitious rock ventures ever undertaken. The Who included excerpts from it on their 1969 US tour, and the album (released there May 1969) became a big seller, and received a Gold Disc award for million dollar sales from RIAA by December 1969. It reached No 1 for three weeks.

The million sale was reached in August. The album was 110 weeks in the US bestsellers. In Britain it reached No 2 for two weeks in June 1969.

The double album's contents were: **Overture; It's a Boy: 1921; Amazing Journey; Sparks; Eyesight for the Blind** (written by Sonny Boy Williamson); **Miracle Cure; Sally Simpson, I'm Free, Welcome; Tommy's Holiday Camp; We're not Gonna Take It; Christmas, Cousin Kevin; Acid Queen; Underture; Do You Think It's All Right?; Fiddle About; Pinball Wizard; There's a Doctor; Go to the Mirror; Tommy Can You Hear Me?; Smash the Mirror; Sensation.**

It was later made into a film starring Tina Turner. Keith Moon died in London in 1978.

THE WINSTONS   American

COLOR HIM FATHER *Metromedia 117 [USA].* A highly polished performing unit, the Winstons got their big break when they were heard by the Impressions in their home, Washington, D.C. They toured America as a back-up band for the Impressions and were soon touring on their own as a name act. They were signed with Metromedia Records in Atlanta, Georgia, and **Color Him Father** was their debut disc for the label. It became an overnight hit and rose to No 6 for two weeks in the US charts with 13 weeks in the Hot 100. It was No 2 for 5 weeks in the R&B charts with a 12-week chart run. It won a Gold Disc from the RIAA on 24 July 1969. The song, written by lead singer Richard Spencer, is a soft soul ballad.

The group were Richard Spencer (lead singer, tenor sax) formerly with the Otis Redding band; Phil Tolotta (organist and second lead singer); Quincy Mattison (lead guitar and vocalist) also with Otis Redding and Arthur Conley, backing Conley on his **Sweet Soul Music** hit; Ray Maritano (alto sax and

vocalist) a graduate of Berklee School of Music and played sax in the US Air Force Band; Sonny Peckrol (bass guitar and vocalist) first began performing in teen clubs while at high school; G.C. Coleman (drummer and vocalist) also worked with Otis Redding and was drummer for two years for Tamla Motown principally with the Marvelettes.

Grammy Award (1969) for 'Best Rhythm-and-Blues Song'.

DAVID ALEXANDER WINTER   Dutch

OH LADY MARY *Riviera-CED 121 252 [France].* Dutch-born singer Winter was triumphant at the 1969 Antibes Song Festival and was discovered by Riviera Records (an affiliate of the Barclay group). This disc was released in April 1969 and by September sold 750,000 and the million by November in France, where it was No 1 for five weeks and in the Top 10 for around six months. It was also a hit in Italy (No 4). The song was written by Carli and Bukey, and also became a hit in 1970 for Germany's Peter Alexander (No 1 for four weeks).

STEVIE WONDER   American

I DON'T KNOW WHY/MY CHERIE AMOUR *Tamla 54180 [USA] Tamla Motown TMG 690 [UK].* Most records listed as double A sides had both sides in the charts at the same time, whether charting independently or both listed together as one entry. In this case, **I Don't Know Why** was the original A side. It entered the *Billboard* Hot 100 at No 77 on 15 February, and the *Cash Box* Top 100 at No 53 the following week. While it leapt up the lower end of the charts fairly quickly (based mainly on radio plays rather than sales), it stalled when it reached the Top 40. It peaked at No 41 with five weeks in *Cash Box* and at No 39 with seven weeks in *Billboard.* The side was produced by Stevie Wonder and D. Hunter, and also made No 16 in the R&B charts with a six-week chart run.

Coming off the No 1 album **For Once in My Life**, this was a considerable disappointment. Motown therefore decided to flip the record and began promoting the B side. This worked, and on 31 May **My Cherie Amour** entered the charts. It made No 4 in *Billboard,* with 14 weeks on the Hot 100. It did better in *Cash Box,* where it peaked at No 3 during a 16-week chart run. This side also did better on the R&B charts, reaching No 4 with 13 weeks in the *Billboard* R&B Top 50. (though in the *Cash Box* R&B Top 50 it peaked at No 13). **My Cherie Amour** was written by Stevie Wonder, Hank Cosby and Sylvia Moy, and produced by Hank Cosby.

It was a similar story in England. **I Don't Know Why** made the charts in March, but only reached No 14 with 11 weeks in the Top 50. **My Cherie Amour** followed it into the charts in July, reaching No 4 with 15 more weeks in the charts. It won Stevie Wonder his first Silver Disc on 12 June.

YESTER-ME, YESTER-YOU, YESTERDAY *Tamla 54188 [USA] Tamla Motown TMG 717 [UK].* The third million seller in a row for Stevie

Wonder, his sixth overall, came with **Yester-Me, Yester-You, Yesterday**. It was written by Ronald Miller and Bryan Wells, and was produced at the Motown studios in Detroit by John Bristol. It entered the American charts in October 1969, reaching No 7 during a chart life of 14 weeks. It went to No 5 with 11 weeks on the R&B charts.

It gave Wonder his first British No 1, going to the top of two of the three national charts for one week on 6 December. It was 13 weeks in the Top 50, and won Stevie Wonder his second British Silver Disc in a row on 31 December. Though a pop No 1, the record failed to make the British R&B charts, which by the end of 1969 had been reduced to a Top 10.

1969 was a good year on the singles front for Wonder, with two releases both making the Top 10 on both sides of the Atlantic and selling a million copies each. Wonder also released two albums that year. The first was **For Once in My Life**, which had two Top 10 singles on it. It reached No 50 with 18 weeks on the album charts. It made the album Top 200 in January 1969, and was followed onto the charts in October by **My Cherie Amour**, which contained both Wonder's 1969 singles million sellers. That reached No 34, with 20 weeks on the charts. In Britain **My Cherie Amour** made the LP charts for two weeks, reaching No 17. It was also a No 1 album on the UK R&B LP Top 10.

TAMMY WYNETTE   American

TAMMY'S GREATEST HITS (Album) *Epic 26486 [USA].* Tammy Wynette was born on 5 May 1942 in Red Bay, Alabama, the daughter of a talented musical family, and began to take music seriously in high school, singing and playing the piano. She later worked with Country Boy Eddie on a Birmingham TV show, wrote a number of songs, and made a successful appearance on Porter Wagoner's TV show which led to singing engagements in the South. She made a visit to Nashville to try to get Epic Records interested in some songs written by a friend but ended up with Epic's producer Billy Sherrill signing her to a disc contract. Within a few weeks, her first single **Apartment No 9** was a hit with country music fans (1967) and instantly a favourite on most American country, pop and Top 40 stations.

She was the winner of the Country Music Association of America's 'Top Female Vocalist' award for 1967, 1968, 1969 and 1970. **I Don't Wanna Play House** won her a Grammy award, 1967, for 'Best Country-and-Western Solo Vocal Performance (Female)', and likewise **Stand by Your Man** for 1969. Tammy's heavy schedule of personal appearances with her then famous husband George Jones, included 'Kraft Music Hall', 'Johnny Cash Show', 'Mike Douglas Show' and 'Joey Bishop Show'.

She became the first female singer with a solely country repertoire to sell an album in excess of one million dollars, with an RIAA Gold Disc award April 1970. By October 1971 it was also the first for a female country singer to sell a million units, for which she received a Platinum Disc award. Her producer was Glenn

up. His earliest musical influences were the American rock'n'roll singers like Elvis Presley whose music poured over the US border from American radio stations, and from Canadian radio as well. In the early sixties he turned to folk music, and he and his group the Squires became one of the leading folk outfits in Winnipeg.

In 1966 he headed south for California, intending to make his name as a folk singer. Instead he joined Buffalo Springfield, helped shape their sound with his powerful lead guitar work, and wrote some of their most successful numbers. In 1968 Buffalo Springfield disbanded, and Neil Young began working on solo projects. In 1969, he agreed to join fellow former-Buffalo man Steve Stills, ex-Byrd David Crosby and Graham Nash of the British group the Hollies, and transformed Crosby, Stills and Nash into Crosby, Stills, Nash and Young. What appealed to him about the new group was that he could continue with his solo work, for the group was a fairly loose arrangement. In fact, Young left the band after making one studio and one live album, plus a hits package. However, out of eight albums made by Crosby, Stills and Nash, it was the three made with Young that topped the American charts.

The first fruit of his solo efforts was not a success, but the second album did make the charts. **Everybody Knows This is Nowhere** entered the charts in June 1969, and reached No 34 during its 98 weeks on the album Top 200. It won an RIAA Gold Disc for million dollar sales on 16 October 1970, and was awarded a Platinum Disc for million unit sales on 13 October 1986. In making the album, Young had teamed up with Los Angeles band Crazy Horse. They were originally a trio consisting of Danny Whitten (guitar), Billy Talbot (bass guitar) and Ralph Molina (drums). Young brought in the renowned musician and arranger Jack Nitzsche, who had worked for Phil Spector and more recently with the Rolling Stones.

In Britain this album did not make the charts, but subsequent albums did. **After the Goldrush** (1970) made the British Top 10, while the follow-up **Harvest** (1972) went to No 1. That albums also gave him his only No 1 in America.

On the singles front, **Cinnamon Girl** from the **Everybody Knows This is Nowhere** album was his first American hit in 1970. His only Top 10 single was **Heart of Gold**, which went to No 1 in 1972, selling over a million copies in the USA alone. In Britain he has had only two solo single hits, with **Heart of Gold** just making the Top 10 in 1972, and **Four Strong Winds** a minor hit in 1979.

The contents of the **Everybody Knows** album included: **Everybody Knows This Is Nowhere**; **Down By The River**; **Cowgirl In The Sand**; **Cinnamon Girl**; and **Running Dry (Requiem for the Rockets)**. All the songs were written by Neil Young.

Sutton, the songwriter husband of Lynn Anderson, a top country-and-western singer.

The contents of the album were: **Stand by Your Man**, by Tammy Wynette and Billy Sherrill (1968); **Lonely Street**, by K. Fowder, C. Below and W.S. Stevenson; **D-I-V-O-R-C-E**, by B. Braddock and C. Putman (1968); **Gentle on My Mind**, by John Hartford (1967); **Take Me to Your World**, by Glenn Sutton and Billy Sherrill (1968); **Almost Persuaded**, by Glenn Sutton and Billy Sherrill (1966); **Your Good Girl's Gonna Go Bad**, by Glenn Sutton and Billy Sherrill (1967); **Apartment No 9**, by J. Payeheck and B. Austin (1967); **Hey, Good Lookin'**, by Hank Williams (1951); **I Don't Wanna Play House**, by Glenn Sutton and Billy Sherrill (1967); **My Arms Stay Open Late**, by J. Lomas and C. Putnam; **There Goes My Everything**, by Dallas Frazier (1965).

This album stayed in the US bestseller national charts for 61 weeks and reached No 37. It was released in Britain under the title **The Best of Tammy Wynette** (CBS label).

NEIL YOUNG   *Canadian*

EVERYBODY KNOWS THIS IS NOWHERE (Album) *Reprise 6349 [USA]*. Neil Young was born in Toronto, Ontario, Canada, on 12 November 1945. While a child his family moved to Winnipeg, which is where he grew

SAORI YUKI   *Japanese*

YOAKE-No SKAT (Scat in the dark) *Express ETP-10096 [Japan]*. Released in Japan in April 1969, this disc was a tremendous hit and sold two million in two months. It was No 1 for 10 weeks and stayed in the Top 10 for four months.

The Express label is a subsidiary of Toshiba Records, EMI's Japanese company.

ZAGER AND EVANS   *American*

IN THE YEAR 2525 (Exordium and Terminus) *RCA Victor 0174 [USA] RCA Victor 1860 [UK]*. Denny Zager and Rick Evans, two country guitarists from Lincoln, Nebraska, were once part of a group called the Eccentrics, but they decided to become a duo and spent much time on songs and rehearsing an act. They had performed on-and-off together since 1960. Rick Evans wrote this song around 1964.

In November 1968 the duo borrowed $500 and set off for Odessa, Texas, to record the song. They formed their own record company, Truth Records, had an initial pressing of 1,000 recordings, and sold copies to record shops from the back of their car whenever they could get it played by the local radio stations. The disc soon received constant airplay, and a further 10,000 copies were pressed and sold. Buoyed by this regional success, the duo sent copies to all the major disc companies in New York. The copy sent to RCA came to the attention of their executive producer, Ernie Altschuler, who immediately traced them to Zeplin, Missouri, where they were then playing. He signed them to an exclusive contract. RCA then put considerable promotional weight behind the disc, released in June 1969, and after four weeks it was No 1, remaining in that position for six weeks and selling over a million in less than two months, with an RIAA Gold Disc award on 8 July.

The disc was released in Britain in July 1969, where it was No 1 for three weeks with 13 weeks in the bestsellers, sold over 250,000 and had further big sales abroad. Soon after the single's release in the USA, RCA issued an album combining **In the Year 2525** with nine of Rick Evans other songs titled **2525 (Exordium and Terminus)**.

The single sold four million (two million in the USA and two million abroad).

THE ZOMBIES   *British*

TIME OF THE SEASON *Date 1628 [USA]*. Written by Rod Argent of the group this was taken from their album of the same title and issued as a single in January 1969. It reached No 1 for a week in the USA with 13 weeks in the bestsellers, and sold a million by 11 April with a Gold Disc award by RIAA. The group had its first million seller in 1964.

APPENDICES

BRITISH NUMBER ONE SINGLES

BRITISH NUMBER ONE SINGLES

Date	Title and Artist	Label	Weeks at No 1				
			NME	RR	RM	D	MM

1960

Date	Title and Artist	Label	NME	RR	RM	D	MM
Jan 2	What Do You Want to Make Those Eyes at Me For? EMILE FORD/CHECKMATES	Pye	4	·	3	4	4
23	Why[1] ANTHONY NEWLEY	Decca	4	·	6	5	6
30	Starry Eyed[1] MICHAEL HOLLIDAY	Columbia	1	·	–	1	–
Mar 5	Poor Me ADAM FAITH	Parlophone	2	1	1	1	1
12	Running Bear JOHNNY PRESTON	Mercury	1	2	2	2	2
26	My Old Man's a Dustman LONNIE DONEGAN	Pye	4*	4	5*	3	3
Apr 23	Stuck On You/Fame and Fortune ELVIS PRESLEY	RCA Victor	–	–	–	1	1
23	Do You Mind? ANTHONY NEWLEY	Decca	1	1	–	1	1
30	Cathy's Clown EVERLY BROTHERS	Warner Bros	9	7	9	7	9
June 25	Three Steps to Heaven EDDIE COCHRAN	London	–	2	–	–	–
25	Mama/Robot Man CONNIE FRANCIS	MGM	–	–	–	2	–
July 2	Good Timin' JIMMY JONES	MGM	3	3	4	2	3
23	Please Don't Tease[2] CLIFF RICHARD/SHADOWS	Columbia	4	3	3	4	4
23	Shakin' All Over[2] JOHNNY KIDD/PIRATES	HMV	–	1	–	–	–
Aug 20	Apache[2] SHADOWS	Columbia	6	5	6	6	4
Sep 24	Mess of Blues/Girl of My Best Friend ELVIS PRESLEY	RCA Victor	–	–	–	–	1
Oct 1	Tell Laura I Love Her RICKY VALENCE	Columbia	2	3	2	3	2
15	Only the Lonely ROY ORBISON	London	3	2	3	2	3
Nov 5	It's Now Or Never ELVIS PRESLEY	RCA Victor	9*	8*	9*	7*	8*
Dec 24	I Love You/'D' in Love CLIFF RICHARD/SHADOWS	Columbia	–	1	–	2	1

1961

Date	Title and Artist	Label	NME	RR	RM	D	MM
Jan 7	I Love You/'D' in Love CLIFF RICHARD/SHADOWS	Columbia	–	1	–	1	1
7	Poetry in Motion JOHNNY TIULOTSEN	London	3	2	3	1	2
28	Are You Lonesome Tonight? ELVIS PRESLEY	RCA Victor	5	4	4	5*	5
Feb 25	Sailor PETULA CLARK	Pye	–	1	–	2	–
25	Walk Right Back/Ebony Eyes EVERLY BROTHERS	Warner Bros.	3	3	4	2	3
Mar 25	Wooden Heart ELVIS PRESLEY	RCA Victor	3+	6	4+	4+	6
Apr 8	Are You Sure? ALLISONS	Fontana	2+	–	2	2	–
29	You're Driving Me Crazy TEMPERENCE SEVEN	Parlophone	1	1	2	–	1
May 6	Blue Moon MARCELS	Pye Internat.	2	2	2	3	2
20	Runaway DEL SHANNON	London	4+	3	2+	4	6+
20	On the Rebound FLOYD CRAMER	RCA Victor	–	1	–	–	–
27	Surrender ELVIS PRESLEY	RCA Victor	4*	4	5*	3	3
July 15	A Girl Like You CLIFF RICHARD/SHADOWS	Columbia	–	–	–	1	–
15	Temptation EVERLY BROTHERS	Warner Bros.	1	2	4	1	1
22	We'll I Ask You EDEN KANE	Decca	2	1	1	1	1
Aug 5	You Don't Know HELEN SHAPIRO	Columbia	4+	3	2	2	2
26	Johnny Remember Me JOHN LEYTON	Top Rank	5+	4+	5	7	6
Sep 23	Wild in the Country ELVIS PRESLEY	RCA Victor	1	–	–	–	–
23	Reach For the Stars/Climb Ev'ry Mountain SHIRLEY BASSEY	Columbia	–	1	–	–	–
30	Kon-Tiki SHADOWS	Columbia	–	1	1	–	1
Oct 7	Michael (Row The Boat) HIGHWAYMEN	HMV	1	1	1	2	1
14	Walking Back to Happiness HELEN SHAPIRO	Columbia	4	3	4	3	4
Nov 11	His Latest Flame/Little Sister ELVIS PRESLEY	RCA Victor	3	4	3	4	3
Dec 2	Take Good Care of My Baby BOBBY VEE	London	1	–	1	–	–
2	Tower of Strength FRANKIE VAUGHAN	Philips	4	3	4	4	3
30	Moon River DANNY WILLIAMS	HMV	1	1	–	–	–

Date	Title and Artist	Label	Weeks at No 1 NME	RR	RM	D	MM
	Stranger on the Shore — ACKER BILK	Columbia	–	–	–	–	1

1962

Date	Title and Artist	Label	NME	RR	RM	D	MM
Jan 6	Stranger On The Shore — MR ACKER BILK	Columbia	1	–	2	1	1
6	Moon River — DANNY WILLIAMS	HMV	–	1	–	–	–
13	The Young Ones — CLIFF RICHARD/SHADOWS	Columbia	6*	6*	5	5*	6*
Feb 17	Rock-A-Hula Baby/Can't Help Falling In Love — ELVIS PRESLEY	RCA Victor	–	4	4	3	4
24	Let's Twist Again — CHUBBY CHECKER	Columbia	2	–	·	–	–
Mar 10	March Of The Siamese Children — KENNY BALL/HIS JAZZMEN	Pye Jazz	1		·	2	–
Mar 17	Wonderful Land — SHADOWS	Columbia	9	8	·	7	8
May 12	Nut Rock[3][4] — B. BUMBLE/STINGERS	Top Rank	1	1	·	1	1
19	Good Luck Charm — ELVIS PRESLEY	RCA Victor	5	5	·	7	6
June 23	Come Outside — MIKE SARNE/WENDY RICHARD	Parlophone	2	2	·	–	1
July 7	Picture Of You — JOE BROWN	Piccadilly	1	–	·	1	1
14	I Can't Stop Loving You — RAY CHARLES	HMV	1	2	·	1	1
21	I Remember You — FRANK IFIELD	Columbia	8	7	·	5	8
Aug 25	Speedy Gonzales — PAT BOONE	London	–	–	·	2	–
Sep 8	She's Not You — ELVIS PRESLEY	RCA Victor	3	3	·	4	2
Oct 6	Telstar — TORNADOS	Decca	5	5	·	5	6
Nov 10	Lovesick Blues/She Taught Me How To Yodel — FRANK IFIELD	Columbia	5	5	·	5	5
Dec 15	Return To Sender — ELVIS PRESLEY	RCA Victor	2	3	·	2	1
29	The Next Time/Bachelor Boy — CLIFF RICHARD/SHADOWS	Columbia	1	–	·	1	1

1963

Date	Title and Artist	Label	NME	RR	RM	D	MM
Jan 5	The Next Time/Bachelor Boy[5] — CLIFF RICHARD/SHADOWS	Columbia	–	3		4	4
5	Dance On — SHADOWS	Columbia	3	1		–	–
26	Diamonds — JET HARRIS/TONY MEEHAN	Decca	4	3		2	4
Feb 16	The Wayward Wind[6] — FRANK IFIELD	Columbia	1	3		1	–
23	Please Please Me[6] — BEATLES	Parlophone	2	–		2	2

Date	Title and Artist	Label	NME	RR	D	MM
Mar 9	Summer Holiday/Dancing Shoes — CLIFF RICHARD/SHADOWS	Columbia	3	2	3	3
30	Foot Tapper — SHADOWS	Columbia	1	1	1	1
Apr 6	How Do You Do It? — GERRY/PACEMAKERS	Columbia	3	4	4	3
27	From Me To You — BEATLES	Parlophone	5	7	5	6
June 1	Do You Want To Know A Secret? — BILLY J KRAMER/DAKOTAS	Parlophone	2	–	1	1
15	I Like It — FREDDIE/DREAMERS	Columbia	4	4	5	4
July 13	I'm Confessin' — FRANK IFIELD	Columbia	3	2	2	3
Aug 3	Devil In Disguise — ELVIS PRESLEY	RCA Victor	–	1	–	–
3	Sweets For My Sweet — SEARCHERS	Pye	3	2	3	2
24	Bad To Me — BILLY J KRAMER/DAKOTAS	Parlophone	2	3	2	2
Sep 7	She Loves You[7] — BEATLES	Parlophone	6+	6+	5+	7+
Oct 5	Do You Love Me? — BRIAN POOLE/TREMELOES	Decca	3	3	3	2
26	You'll Never Walk Alone — GERRY/PACEMAKERS	Columbia	4	4	5	4
Dec 7	I Want To Hold Your Hand — BEATLES	Parlophone	4+	3	4+	4+

1964

Date	Title and Artist	Label	NME	RR	D	MM
Jan 4	I Want To Hold Your Hand — BEATLES	Parlophone	2	2	1	1
11	Glad All Over — DAVE CLARK FIVE	Columbia	2	2	2	3
25	The Hippy Hippy Shake — SWINGING BLUE JEANS	HMV	–	–	1	–
Feb 1	Needles And Pins — SEARCHERS	Pye	3	3	3	3
22	Diane — BACHELORS	Decca	–	2	–	–
22	Anyone Who Had A Heart — CILLA BLACK	Parlophone	4	2	3	4
Mar 14	Bits And Pieces — DAVE CLARK FIVE	Columbia	–	–	1	–
21	Little Children — BILLY J KRAMER/DAKOTAS	Parlophone	1	2	1	1
28	Can't Buy Me Love — BEATLES	Parlophone	4*	3	3*	3*
Apr 18	A World Without Love — PETER & GORDON	Columbia	2	2	2	2
May 2	Don't Throw Your Love Away — SEARCHERS	Pye	1	2	2	2
16	Juliet — FOUR PENNIES	Philips	2	1	2	2
30	You're My World — CILLA BLACK	Parlophone	3	3	3	3
June 20	It's Over — ROY ORBISON	London	2	2	2	2

Date	Title and Artist	Label	NME	RR	D	MM
July 4	The House Of The Rising Sun ANIMALS	Columbia	2	1	2	1
11	It's All Over Now ROLLING STONES	Decca	–	1	–	1
18	A Hard Day's Night BEATLES	Parlophone	4*	3	4*	4*
Aug 15	Do Wah Diddy Diddy MANFRED MANN	HMV	2	2	2	2
29	Have I The Right HONECOMES	Pye	2	2	3	3
Sep 12	You Really Got Me KINKS	Pye	1	2	–	1
19	I'm Into Something Good HERMAN'S HERMITS	Columbia	3	2	3	2
Oct 10	Oh, Pretty Woman ROY ORBISON	London	3	3+	3	4+
24	(There's) Always Something There To Remind Me[8] SANDIE SHAW	Pye	2	3	2	1
Nov 14	Baby Love SUPREMES	Stateside	1	2	2	3
21	Little Red Rooster ROLLING STONES	Decca	2*	1	1	–
Dec 5	I Feel Fine BEATLES	Parlophone	4*	3	4*	4*

1965

Date	Title and Artist	Label	NME	RR	D	MM
Jan 2	I Feel Fine BEATLES	Parlophone	2	2	2	2
16	Yeh, Yeh GEORGIE FAME	Columbia	1	2	1	1
23	Go Now MODDY BLUES	Decca	2	1	2	1
30	You've Lost That Lovin' Feeling RIGHTEOUS BROTHERS	London	1	2	1	2
Feb 13	Tired Of Waiting For You KINKS	Pye	1	1	1	1
20	I'll Never Find Another You SEEKERS	Columbia	2	2	2	2
Mar 6	It's Not Unusual TOM JONES	Decca	1	1	1	1
13	The Last Time ROLLING STONES	Decca	4	3	4	3
Apr 10	The Minute You're Gone[9] CLIFF RICHARD	Columbia	1	1	–	1
10	For Your Love[9] YARDBIRDS	Columbia	1	–	–	–
10	Concrete And Clay[9] UNIT 4 + 2	Decca	–	1	1	–
17	Ticket To Ride BEATLES	Parlophone	5*	3	4*	5*
May 15	King Of The Road ROGER MILLER	Philips	–	1	–	–
15	A World Of Our Own SEEKERS	Columbia	–	–	1	–
22	Where Are You Now JACKIE TRENT	Pye	1	1	1	1
29	Long Live Love SANDIE SHAW	Pye	2	3	3	2

Date	Title and Artist	Label	NME	RR	D	MM
June 12	The Price Of Love EVERLEY BROTHERS	Warner Bros.	1	–	–	–
12	Crying In The Chapel[10] ELVIS PRESLEY	RCA Victor	2	2+	2	3
26	I'm Alive[10] HOLLIES	Parlophone	2	3+	2	2
July 17	Mr Tambourine Man BYRDS	CBS	2	2	2	2
31	Help! BEATLES	Parlophone	4*	3	4*	4*
Aug 28	I Got You Babe SONNY AND CHER	Atlantic	1	2	2	2
Sep 4	(I Can't Get No) Satisfaction ROLLING STONES	Decca	3	2	2	2
25	Make It Easy On Yourself WALKER BROTHERS	Philips	–	1	1	1
25	Tears KEN DODD	Columbia	6	5	5	5
Nov 6	Get Off Of My Cloud ROLLING STONES	Decca	3	3	3	2
20	The Carnival Is Over SEEKERS	Columbia	1	3	2	4
27	1-2-3 LEN BARRY	Brunswick	1	–	–	–
Dec 11	Day Tripper/We Can Work It Out BEATLES	Parlophone	3*	2	3*	2

1966

Date	Title and Artist	Label	NME	RR	D	MM
Jan 1	Day Tripper/We Can Work It Out BEATLES	Parlophone	2	3	2	2
15	Keep On Running SPENCER DAVIS GROUP	Fontana	3	1	2	2
29	Michelle OVERLANDERS	Pye	1	3	2	2
Feb 12	These Boots Were Made For Walkin' NANCY SINATRA	Reprise	1	4	1	1
19	Nineteenth Nervous Breakdown ROLLING STONES	Decca	3	–	3	3
Mar 12	I Can't Let Go[11] HOLLIES	Parlophone	2	–	–	–
12	Sha La La La Lee SMALL FACES	Decca	–	–	1	1
19	The Sun Ain't Gonna Shine Anymore[11] WALKER BROTHERS	Philips	4	4	4	3
Apr 9	Somebody Help Me SPENCER DDAVIS GROUP	Fontana	1	2	1	2
23	You Don't Have To Say You Love Me DUSTY SPRINGFIELD	Philips	2	1	2	2
May 7	Pretty Flamingo MANFRED MANN	HMV	3	3	3	3
28	Paint It Black ROLLING STONES	Decca	1	1	–	1
June 4	Strangers In The Night FRANK SINATRA	Reprise	3	3	3	2
18	Paperback Writer BEATLES	Parlophone	2	2	2	4*

Date	Title and Artist	Label	NME	RR	D	MM
July 9	Sunny Afternoon KINKS	Pye	2	2	2	–
16	Get Away GEORGIE FAME	Columbia	–	1	–	2
23	Out Of Time CHRIS FARLOWE	Immediate	2	1	2	1
Aug 6	With A Girl Like You TROGGS	Fontana	2	2	2	2
20	Yellow Submarine/ Eleanor Rigby BEATLES	Parlophone	4	4	3	3
Sep 10	All Or Nothing SMALL FACES	Decca	1	1	2	2
24	Distant Drums JIM REEVES	RCA Victor	5	5	4	2
Oct 8	I'm A Boy WHO	Reaction	–	–	–	2
22	Reach Out — I'll Be There FOUR TOPS	Tamla Motown	3	3	4	3
Nov 12	Good Vibrations BEACH BOYS	Capitol	2	2	2	3
Dec 3	Green Green Grass Of Home TOM JONES	Decca	5	5	4	5
31	Morningtown Ride SEEKERS	Columbia	–	–	1	–

1967

Date	Title and Artist	Label	NME	RR	D	MM
Jan 7	Green Green Grass Of Home TOM JONES	Decca	2	2	2	2
21	I'm A Believer MONKEES	RCA Victor	4	4	4	4
Feb 18	This is My Song[12] PETULA CLARK	Pye	2	2	2	1
25	Release Me[13] ENGLEBERT HUMPERDINCK	Decca	6	6	5	3+
Mar 4	Penny Lane/Strawberry Fields Forever[13] BEATLES	Parlophone	–	–	–	3
Apr 8	This Is My Song[12] HARRY SECOMBE	Philips	–	–	1	–
8	Somethin' Stupid FRANK & NANCY SINATRA	Reprise	1	2	2	2
22	Puppet On A String SANDIE SHAW	Pye	4	3	3	4
May 20	Silence Is Golden TREMELOES	CBS	3	3	3	3
June 10	A Whiter Shade Of Pale PROCUL HARUM	Deram	5	6	6	5
July 15	Alternate Title MONKEES	RCA Victor	–	–	–	1
15	All You Need Is Love BEATLES	Parlophone	4*	3	2	3
Aug 5	San Francisco SCOTT McKENZIE	CBS	4	4	4	3
Sep 2	The Last Waltz[14] ENGLEBERT HUMPERDINCK	Decca	6	5	·	7
Oct 14	Massachusetts BEE GEES	Polydor	3	4	·	3
Nov 11	Baby Now That I've Found You FOUNDATIONS	Pye	3	2	·	2

Date	Title and Artist	Label	NME	RR	D	MM
25	Let The Heartaches Begin LONG JOHN BALDRY	Pye	1	2	·	2
Dec 9	Hello Goodbye BEATLES	Parlophone	4	4	·	4

1968

Date	Title and Artist	Label	NME	RR	D	MM
Jan 6	Hellow Goodbye BEATLES	Parlophone	2	3		1
13	Magical Mystery Tour (2EPs) BEATLES	Parlophone	–	–		1
20	Ballad Of Bonnie And Clyde GEORGIE FAME	CBS	1	1		1
27	Everlasting Love LOVE AFFAIR	CBS	3	2		3
Feb 17	Mighty Quinn MANFRED MANN	Fontana	2	2		2
Mar 2	Cinderella Rockefella ESTHER & ABI OFARIM	Philips	4	3		4
23	The Legend Of Xanadu DAVE DEE, DOZY, BEAKY, MICH & TITCH	Fontana	–	1		–
30	Delilah TOM JONES	Decca	–	–		2
30	Lady Madonna BEATLES	Parlophone	2	2		–
Apr 13	Congratulations CLIFF RICHARD	Columbia	1	2		–
13	What A Wonderful World LOUIS ARMSTRONG	HMV	4	4		5
May 18	Young Girl UNION GAP	CBS	5	4		4
June 15	Jumpin' Jack Flash ROLLING STONES	Decca	2	2		3
July 6	Baby Come Back EQUALS	President	3	3		3
27	I Pretend DES O'CONNOR	Columbia	–	1		–
27	Mony Mony TOMMY JAMES/SHONDELLES	Major Minor	4	3+		5
Aug 17	Fire ARTHUR BROWN	Track	–	1		–
24	Help Yourself TOM JONES	Decca	2	–		–
31	Do It Again BEACH BOYS	Capitol	–	1		–
31	This Guy's In Love HERB ALPERT	A&M	–	–		1
Sep 7	I Just Gotta Get A Message To You BEE GEES	Polydor	1	1		1
14	Hey Jude BEATLES	Apple	3	2		4*
28	Those Were The Days MARY HOPKIN	Apple	5	6		5
Nov 9	With A Little Help From My Friends JOE COCKER	Regal Zonophone	1	1		1
16	The Good, The Bad And The Ugly HUGO MONTENEGRO	RCA Victor	1	4		3
16	Eloise BARRY RYAN	MGM	2	–		1

Date		Title and Artist	Label	Weeks at No 1 NME RR MM		
Dec	7	Lily The Pink SCAFFOLD	Parlophone	4	3	2

1969

Date		Title and Artist	Label	NME	RR	MM
Jan	4	Lily The Pink[15] SCAFFOLD	Parlophone	1	1	1
	4	Ob-La-Di Ob-La-Da MARMALADE	CBS	2	3	3
	25	Albatross FLEETWOOD MAC	Blue Horizon	3	1	2
Feb	8	Blackberry Way MOVE	Regal Zonophone	1	1	1
	15	Half As Nice AMEN CORNER	Immediate	1	2	2
Mar	1	Where Do You Go To PETER SARSTEDT	United Artists	4	4	4
	29	I Heard It Through The Grapevine MARVIN GAYE	Tamla Motown	3	3	3
Apr	19	Israelites DESMOND DEKKER	Pyramid	2	1	1
	26	Get Back BEATLES	Apple	5	6*	5
June	7	Dizzy TOMMY ROE	Stateside	2	1	2
	14	The Ballad Of John And Yoko BEATLES	Apple	2	3	3
July	5	Something In The Air THUNDERCLAP NEWMAN	Track	2	3	1
	19	In The Ghetto ELVIS PRESLEY	RCA Victor	1	—	1
	26	Honkey Tonk Women ROLLING STONES	Decca	5	5	5
Aug	30	In The Year 2525 ZAGER & EVANS	RCA Victor	3	3	3
Sep	20	Bad Moon Rising CREEDENCE CLEARWATER REVIVAL	Liberty	3	3	3
Oct	11	Je T'Aime...Moi Non Plus JANE BIRKIN & SERGE GAINSBOURG	Major Minor	—	1	—
	11	I'll Never Fall In Love Again BOBBIE GENTRY	Capitol	3	1	3
	25	Sugar Sugar ARCHIES	RCA Victor	4+	8	6
Nov	15	Oh Well FLEETWOOD MAC	Reprise	1	—	—
Dec	6	Yester-Me, Yester-You, Yesterday STEVIE WONDER	Tamla Motown	1	—	1
	13	Ruby, Don't Take Your Love To Town KENNY ROGERS/FIRST EDITION	Reprise	1	—	—
Dec	20	Two Little Boys[16] ROLF HARRIS	Columbia	2	2	2

KEY

* Entered the chart at No 1 the first week of releeast.
+ Weeks at the top were not consecutive

1 Anthony Newley's **Why** reached No 1 in *Record Mirror* on 23 January, one to two weeks ahead of topping the other charts. As that is the earliest date it topped one of the five national charts, that is the date given in the above table. However, in both the charts where Michael Holliday's **Starry Eyed** went to No 1, Anthony Newley followed him to the top and did not precede him.

2 In the *Record Retailer* charts, Cliff Richard went to No 1 for one week, was then replaced for one week by Johnny Kidd, who was in turn replaced by Cliff going back to the top spot again for two more weeks. On August 20 the Shadows knocked Cliff off the top with **Apache**, just as they did in all the other charts. In fact, three of the Shadows' five chart-toppers knocked Cliff Richard off the No 1 spot.

3 On 24 March *Record Mirror* ceased compiling a chart of their own. From that date on they used the *Record Retailer* Top 50.

4 In *NME* chart, B. Bumble's one week at the top was as No 1 equal with the Shadows' **Wonderful Land** in its ninth week at the top. This is the only occasion in the entire history of the charts that two instrumental disc have tied for first place.

5 At No 1 at the end of 1962. In some charts both sides of this record charted as two separate entries. In one of these, the *Cash Box* British charts, both sides each went to No 1. This is the only time in the history of the charts that both sides of the same record have independently gone to the top, thus giving Cliff the unique achievement of two No 1s from one record. *Cash Box* compiled their British Top 20 by averaging out the other charts listed above with their own limited sampling to iron out the differences between then.

6 These two records were No 1 equal in the *NME* on 20 Feburary, with **Please Please Me** having a second week at the top, this time on its own, the week after.

7 **She Loves You** had a four week run at the top in September, 5 weeks in the *Melody Maker*. **Do You Love Me** and **You'll Never Walk Alone** then both went to the top, and at the end of November **She Loves You** returned to the No 1 slot. It was only knocked off the top by the Beatles' next release, **I Want To Hold Your Hand**, which entered the charts at No 1 the first week of release.

8 Sandie Shaw went to No 1 in all charts except the *NME* on 31 October. In the *Record Retailer* and *Meledy Maker* charts, Roy Orbison returned to the top after Sandie for one final week at No 1.

9 In the *NME* Cliff Richard and the Yardbirds were No 1 equal on 10 April. In the Top 50 compiled by *Record Retailer*. Unit 4 + 2 were No 1 on 10 April. They were replaced on 17th April by Cliff Richard, while the Beatles (who entered the other three charts at No 1 first week of release that week) went to No 1 on 24 April.

10 Elvis Presley went to No 1 in *Melody Maker* on 12 June, and in the other three charts on 19 June. In *Record Retailer* he was replaced after one week by the Hollies, who in turn were replaced after one week by Elvis. He had this second week at the top on 3 July. The Hollies were back at No 1 on 10 July for two more weeks.

11 On 19 March, both the Hollies and the Walker Brothers were at No 1 equal in the *NME*.

12 The only occcasion in the sixties where two versions of the same song both went to No 1.

13 In *Melody Maker* Englebert Humperdinck went to No 1 on 25 February. After only one week he was replaced by the Beatles on 4 March. (This was the date on which he topped the other three charts.) Englebert returned to the top for another two weeks on 25 March.

14 On 26 August *Disc* and *Melody Maker*, for long owned by the same company, both began using the same charts. From this date on there were only three British charts.

15 Also No 1 at the end of 1968. In the *Record Retailer* chart, Scaffold were No 1 for the last week of December 1968. They then dropped down to No 3 for the first week of 1969, with Marmalade going to No 1. Scaffold were back at the top for another week on 11 January. Marmalade replace them at the top for the second time on 18 January, and stayed at No 1 for the following week.

16 **Two Little Boys** also had four weeks at No 1 in January 1970, making a total of six weeks at the top for Rolf Harris.

AMERICAN NUMBER ONE SINGLES

Date	Title and Artist	Label	BB	CB	V	RV

1960

Date	Title and Artist	Label	BB	CB	V	RV
Jan 2	Why FRANKIE AVALON	Chancellor	1	3	1	–
9	El Paso MARTY ROBBINS	CBS-Columbia	2	–	–	–
16	Uh! Oh! NUTTY SQUIRRELLS	Hanover	–	–	1	–
23	Running Bear JOHNNY PRESTON	Mercury	3	3	3	–
Feb 13	Teen Angel MARK DINNING	MGM	2	2	1	–
20	Theme From A Summer Place PERCY FAITH	CBS-Columbia	9	8	9	–
Apr 23	Greenfields BROTHERS FOUR	CBS-Columbia	–	–	2*	–
23	Stuck On You ELVIS PRESLEY	RCA Victor	4	4	2	–
May 21	Cathy's Clown EVERLY BROTHERS	Warner Bros.	5	5	5	–
June 25	Everybody's Somebody's Fool CONNIE FRANCIS	MGM	2	3	2	–
July 9	Alley-Oop HOLLYWOOD ARGYLES	Lute	1	1	2	–
23	I'm Sorry BRENDA LEE	US Decca	3	2	1	–
30	Itsy Bitsy Teenie Weenie Yellow Polkadot Bikini BRIAN HYLAND	Leader	1	1	2	–
Aug 13	It's Now Or Never ELVIS PRESLEY	RCA Victor	5	4	6	–
Sep 10	The Twist[1] CHUBBY CHECKER	Parkway	1	4	1	–
Oct 1	My Heart Has A Mind Of Its Own CONNIE FRANCIS	MGM	2	1	4	–
15	Mr Custer LARRY VERNE	Era	1	–	–	–
15	Save The Last Dance For Me DRIFTERS	Atlantic	3+	6	–	–
29	I Want To Be Wanted BRENDA LEE	US Decca	1	–	4	–
Nov 19	Georgia On My Mind RAY CHARLES	ABC Paramount	1	–	–	–
26	Stay MAURICE WILLIAMS/ZODIACS	Herald	1	–	–	–
26	Last Date FLOYD CRAMER	RCA Victor	–	–	1	–
26	Are You Lonesome Tonight?[2] ELVIS PRESLEY	RCA Victor	5	5	3	–
Dec 3	Poetry In Motion JOHNNY TILLOTSEN	Cadence	–	–	1	–

1961

Date	Title and Artist	Label	BB	CB	V	RV
Jan 7	Are You Lonesome Tonight? ELVIS PRESLEY	RCA Victor	1	–	1	–
7	Wonderland By Night BERT KAEMPFERT	US Decca	3	1	2	2
14	Exodus FERRANTE & TEICHER	United Artists	–	2	–	1
28	Will You Love Me Tomorrow SHIRELLES	Scepter	2	2	–	–
28	Calcutta! LAWRENCE WELK	Dot	2	4	5	6
Mar 4	Pony Time CHUBBY CHECKER	Parkway	3	1	2	–
18	Surrender ELVIS PRESLEY	RCA Victor	2	2	3	3
Apr 1	Blue Moon MARCELS	Colpix	3	3	3	3
22	Runaway DEL SHANNON	Big Top	4	3+	4	4
May 6	Mother-In-Law ERNIE K-DOE	Minit	1	3+	–	1
27	Running Scared[3] ROY ORBISON	Monument	1	1	2+	–
27	100 Pounds of Clay GENE McDANIELS	Liberty	–	–	–	1
27	Travellin' Man[3] RICKY NELSON	Imperial	2+	3	2+	3
June 24	Rain Drops DEE CLARK	Vee Jay	–	–	1	–
24	Moody River PAT BOONE	Dot	1	–	1	–
July 1	Quarter To Three GARY US BONDS	Legrand	2	3	4	4
15	Tossing And Turning BOBBY LEWIS	Beltone	7	4	2+	4
Aug 12	Michael HIGHWAYMEN	United Artists	2	4	4+	4
Sep 2	Wooden Heart[4] JOE DOWELL	Smash	1	–	–	–
16	Take Good Care Of My Baby BOBBY VEE	Liberty	3	3	4+	2
Oct 7	Crying ROY ORBISON	Monument	–	1	–	1
14	Hit The Road Jack RAY CHARLES	ABC Paramount	2	1	2+	–
28	Runaround Sue DION	Laurie	2	2	2+	3
Nov 4	Big Bad John JIMMY DEAN	CBS-Columbia	5	5	5	6
Dec 9	The Lion Sleeps Tonight TOKENS	RCA Victor	2	4	2	3
16	Please Mr Postman MARVELETTES	Tamla	1	–	–	–

1962

Date	Title and Artist	Label	BB	CB	V	RV
Jan 6	The Lion Sleeps Tonight TOKENS	RCA Victor	1	–	3	1
6	The Twist[6] CHUBBY CHECKER	Parkway	2	4	1	3
27	Peppermint Twist JOEY DEE/STARLIGHTERS	Roulette	3	–	1	–
Feb 3	The Duke Of Earl GENE CHANDLER	Vee Jay	3	5	4	5
Mar 10	Hey Baby BRUCE CHANNEL	Smash	3	4	4	3
31	Don't Break The Heart That Loves You CONNIE FRANCIS	MGM	1	–	–	–
Apr 7	Slow Twistin' CHUBBY CHECKER	Parkway	–	1	–	–
7	Johnny Angel[7] SHELLEY FABARES	Colpix	2	1	–	1

Date	Title and Artist	Label	BB	CB	V	RV
7	Good Luck Charm ELVIS PRESLEY	RCA Victor	2	1	4	3
28	Mashed Potatoe Time DEE DEE SHARP	Cameo	–	1	–	1
May 5	Soldier Boy SHIRELLERS	Sceptor	3	2	1	2
12	Stranger On The Shore MR. ACKER BILK	Atco	1	1	4	2
26	I Can't Stop Loving You RAY CHARLES	ABC-Paramount	5	5	4	5
June 30	The Stripper DAVID ROSE	MGM	1	2	–	1
July 7	Roses Are Red BOBBY VINTON	Epic	4	4	5	5
Aug 11	Breaking Up Is Hard To Do NEIL SEDAKA	RCA Victor	2	1	1	1
18	The Loco-Motion LITTLE EVA	Dimension	1	3	4	2
Sep 1	Sheila TOMMY ROE	ABC-Paramount	2	–	–	–
8	Sherry FOUR SEASONS	Vee Jay	5	6	5	5
15	Ramblin' Rose[8] NAT KING COLE	Capitol	–	–	1	1
Oct 20	The Monster Mash BOBBY 'BORIS' PICKETT/CRYPT KICKERS	Garpax	2	3	1	2
Nov 3	He's A Rebel CRYSTALS	Philles	2	–	2	1
10	Big Girls Don't Cry FOUR SEASONS	Vee Jay	5	5	5	6
Dec 15	Return To Sender ELVIS PRESLEY	RCA Victor	–	1	–	1
22	Limbo Rock CHUBBY CHECKER	Parkway	–	1	–	–
22	Telstar TORNADOS	London	2	1	2	1

1963

Date	Title and Artist	Label	BB	CB	V	RV
Jan 5	Telstar TORNADOS	London	1	2	2	1
12	Got Away Little Girl STEVE LAWRENCE	CBS-Columbia	2	2	1	3
26	The Night Has A Thousand Eyes BOBBY VEE	Epic	–	–	1	–
26	Walk Right In ROOFTOP SINGERS	Vanguard	2	1	1	1
Feb 2	Hey Paula[9] PAUL & PAULA	Philips	3	4	3+	4
Mar 2	Walk Like A Man FOUR SEASONS	Vee Jay	3	2	2	2
23	Our Day Will Come RUBY/ROMANTICS	Kapp	1	1	1	1
30	End Of The World SKEETA DAVIS	RCA Victor	–	–	1	1
30	He's So Fine CHIFFONS	Laurie	4	4	3	3
Apr 27	Can't Get Used To Losing You ANDY WILLIAMS	CBS-Columbia	–	1	1	–
27	I Will Follow Him LITTLE PEGGY MARCH	RCA Victor	3	3	4	3
May 18	If You Wanna Be Happy JIMMY SOUL	S.P.Q.R.	2	1	2	2
June 1	It's My Party LESLIE GORE	Mercury	2	2	4	3

Date	Title and Artist	Label	BB	CB	V	RV[11]
15	Sukiyaki KYU SAKAMOTO	Capitol	3	4	1	2
July 6	Blue on Blue BOBBY VINTON	Epic	–	–	–	1
6	Easier Said Than Done ESSEX	Roulette	2	2	4	2
20	Surf City JAN & DEAN	Liberty	2	1	–	1
Aug 3	So Much In Love TYMES	Parkway	1	–	–	1
3	Fingertips (Part 2) LITTLE STEVIE WONDER	Tamla	3	4	3	3
31	Hello Mudduh, Hello Fadduh! ALLAN SHERMAN	Warner Bros.	–	1	–	1
31	Candy Girl FOUR SEASONS	Vee Jay	–	–	1	–
31	My Boyfriend's Back ANGELS	Smash	3	2	1	2
Sep 14	Blue Velvet BOBBY VINTON	Epic	3	3	5	2
Oct 5	Sally Go Round the Roses JAYNETTS	Tuff	–	–	–	1
12	Be My Baby RONETTES	Philles	–	1	1	–
12	Sugar Shack JAMES GILMER/FIREBALLS	Dot	5	3	4	5
Nov 9	Deep Purple NINO TEMPO/APRIL STEVENS	Atco	1	2	–	1
23	I'm Leaving It Up To You DALE & GRACE	Michelle	2	1	2	1
30	Dominique SINGING NUN	Philips	4	5	4	4
Dec 28	Louis Louis[10] KINGSMEN	Wand	–	–	–	1

1964

Date	Title and Artist	Label	BB	CB	V	RV
Jan 4	Dominique SINGING NUN	Philips	–	–	2	–
4	There! I've Said It Again BOBBY VINTON	Epic	4	1	3	–
11	Louis Louis KINGSMEN	Wand	–	2	–	–
25	I Want To Hold Your Hand BEATLES	Capitol	7	8	4	–
Mar 7	She Loves You BEATLES	Swan	2	2	5	–
Apr 4	Twist And Shout BEATLES	Tollie	–	1	1	–
4	Can't Buy Me Love BEATLES	Capitol	5	5	2	–
May 2	Hello, Dolly! LOUIS ARMSTRONG	Kapp	1	1	3	3
16	My Guy MARY WELLS	Motown	2	1	–	–
23	Love Me Do BEATLES	Tollie	1	1	1	1
30	Chapel Of Love DIXIE CUPS	Red Bird	3	3	3	4
June 20	A World Without Love PETER & GORDON	Capitol	1	1	2	–
July 4	I Get Around BEACH BOYS	Capitol	2	1	1	2
11	Memphis JOHNNY RIVERS	Imerpial	–	–	1	–
11	Rag Doll FOUR SEASONS	Philips	2	2	3	2

Date	Title and Artist	Label	BB	CB	V	RW
25	A Hard Day's Night BEATLES	Capitol	2	3	4	2
Aug 15	Everybody Loves Somebody DEAM MARTIN	Reprise	1	1	–	–
22	Where Did Our Love Go SUPREMES	Motown	2	2	–	2
Sep 5	The House Of The Rising Sun ANIMALS	MGM	3	3	4	3
26	Bread and Butter NEWBEATS	Hickory	–	–	–	1
26	Oh, Pretty Woman ROY ORBISON	Monument	3	3	4	1
Oct 17	Do Wah Diddy Diddy MANFRED MANN	Ascot	2	2	–	2
31	We'll Sing In The Sunsine GALE GARNETT	RCA Victor	–	1	–	–
31	Last Kiss J FRANK WILSON/CAVALIERS	Josie	–	1	1	2
31	Baby Love SUPREMES	Motown	4	2	5	4
Nov 28	Leader Of The Pack SHANGRI LAS	Red Bird	1	1	–	1
Dec 5	She's Not There ZOMBIES	Parrot	–	1	–	–
5	Ringo LORNE GREENE	RCA Victor	1	1	–	–
12	Mr Lonely BOBBY VINTON	Epic	1	–	3	2
19	Come See About Me[12] SUPREMES	Motown	1	1	–	1
19	I Feel Fine[12] BEATLES	Capitol	1	1	–	–

1965

Date	Title and Artist	Label	BB	CB	V	RW
Jan 2	I Feel Fine BEATLES	Capitol	2	3	3	2
16	Come See About Me SUPREMES	Motown	1	–	–	1
23	Love Potion No 9 SEARCHERS	Kapp	–	–	–	1
23	Downtown PETULA CLARK	Warner Bros.	2	2	4	1
Feb 6	You've Lost That Loving Feeling RIGHTEOUS BROTHERS	Philles	2	3	–	3
20	This Diamond Ring GARY LEWIS/PLAYBOYS	Liberty	2	1	2	2
Mar 6	My Girl TEMPTATIONS	Gordy	1	–	–	–
6	Eight Days A Week BEATLES	Capitol	2	3	3+	3
27	The Birds And The Bees JEWEL AKENS	Era	–	–	1	–
27	Stop! In The Name Of Love SUPREMES	Motown	2	1	2	1
Apr 10	I'm Telling You Now FREDDIE/DREAMERS	Tower	2	2	1	2
24	Game Of Love WAYNE FONTANA/MINDBENDESS	Fontana	1	1	–	1
May 1	Mrs Brown You've Got A Loveley Daughter HERMAN'S HERMITS	MGM	3	4	5	3
22	Ticket To Ride BEATLES	Capitol	1	1	–	1
29	Help Me Rhonda[13] BEACH BOYS	Capitol	2	1	2	2
June 5	Back In My Arms Again[13] SUPREMES	Motown	1	1	–	–
12	Woolly Bully SAM THE SHAM/PHAROAHS	MGM	–	–	–	1

Date	Title and Artist	Label	BB	CB	V	RW
19	Crying In The Chapel ELVIS PRESLEY	RCA Victor	–	–	1	–
19	I Can't Help Myself FOUR TOPS	Motown	2+	2	3	1
26	Mr Tambourine Man BYRDS	CBS-Columbia	1	1	–	1
July 10	(I Can't Get No) Satisfaction ROLLING STONES	London	4	4	3	3
Aug 7	I'm Henry VIII, I Am HERMAN'S HERMITS	MGM	1	1	2	3
14	I Got You Babe SONNY & CHER	Atco	3	2	2	3
28	Help! BEATLES	Capitol	3	3	4	1
Sep 18	Like A Rolling Stone BOB DYLAN	CBS-Columbia	–	1	–	–
25	Eve Of Destruction BARRY McGUIRE	Dunhill	1	1	–	2
Oct 2	Catch Us If You Can DAVE CLARK FIVE	Epic	–	–	1	–
2	Hang On Sloopy McCOYS	Bang	1	1	1	2
9	Yesterday BEATLES	Capitol	4	3+	3	2
23	A Lovers Concerto TOYS	Dyno Voice	–	1	–	2
Nov 6	Get Off Of My Cloud ROLLING STONES	London	2	2	4	–
20	I Hear A Symphony SUPREMES	Motown	2	1	2	3
27	1-2-3 LEN BARRY	US Decca	–	1	–	–
Dec 4	Turn! Turn! Turn! BYRDS	CBS-Columbia	3	1	2	2
11	Let's Hang On FOUR SEASONS	Philips	–	1	–	1
18	A Taste Of Honey HERB ALPERT/TIJUANA BRASS	A&M	–	1	–	–
25	Over And Over DAVE CLARK FIVE	Epic	1	1	–	1

1966

Date	Title and Artist	Label	BB	CB	V	RW
Jan 1	The Sounds Of Silence[14] SIMON & GRAFUNKEL	CBS/Columbia	2+	1	5	2
1	I Got You JAMES BROWN	King	–	–	–	1
8	We Can Work It Out[14] BEATLES	Capitol	3+	4	1	2
Feb 5	My Love[15] PETULA CLARK	Warner Bros.	2	–	2	1
5	Barbara Ann[15] BEACH BOYS	Capitol	–	1	–	2
12	Lightnin' Strikes LOU CHRISTIE	MGM	1	2	–	1
26	These Boots Are Made For Walkin NANCY SINATRA	Reprise	1	1	2	1
Mar 5	The Ballad Of The Green Berets S/SGT BARRY SADLER	RCA Victor	5	4	5	3
Apr 2	Nineteenth Nervous Breakdown ROLLING STONES	London	–	1	–	–

Date	Title and Artist	Label	BB	CB	V	RW
2	Nowhere Man BEATLES	Capitol	–	–	–	2
9	Daydream LOVIN' SPOONFUL	Kama Sutra	–	1	–	–
9	(You're My) Soul And Inspiration RIGHTEOUS BROTHERS	Verve	3	2	3	2
30	Good Lovin' YOUNG RASCALS	Atlantic	1	1	–	2
May 7	Monday, Monday MAMAS & PAPAS	Dunhill	3	3	5	2
28	When A Man Loves A Woman PERCY SLEDGE	Atlantic	2	1	1	2
June 4	A Groovy Kind Of Love MINDBENDERS	Fontana	–	1	–	1
11	Paint It Black ROLLING STONES	London	2	1	2	1
18	Strangers In The Night[16] FRANK SINATRA	Reprise	1	1	1	1
25	Paperback Writer[16] BEATLES	Capitol	2+	2	1	1
July 9	Hanky Panky TOMMY JAMES/SHONDELLS	Roulette	2	2	3	2
23	Wild Thing[17] TROGGS	Atco/Fontana	2	1	1	2
30	They're Coming To Take Me Away, Ha-Haaa! NAPOLEON XIV	Warner Bros.	–	1	–	1
Aug 6	Little Red Riding Hood SAM THE SHAM/PHARAOHS	MGM	–	1	–	1
13	Summer In The City LOVIN' SPOONFUL	Kama Sutra	3	2	3	1
27	Sunny BOBBY HEBB	Philips	–	1	–	1
Sep 3	See You In September[18] HAPPENINGS	BT Puppy	–	–	1	1
3	Sunshine Superman[18] DONOVAN	Epic	1	1	1	1
10	Yellow Submarine[18] BEATLES	Capitol	–	1	1	1
10	You Can't Hurry Love SUPREMES	Motown	2	1	2	2
24	Cherish ASSOCIATION	Valiant	3	3	3	2
Oct 15	Reach Out I'll Be There FOUR TOPS	Motown	2	1	–	–
22	96 Tears ?/MYSTERIANS	Cameo	1	1	2	1
29	Last Train To Clarksville MONKEES	Colgems	1	2	–	2
Nov 12	Poor Side Of Town JOHNNY RIVERS	Imperial	1	1	1	1
19	You Keep Me Hangin' On[19] SUPREMES	Motown	2	1	–	2+
19	Good Vibrations[19] BEACH BOYS	Capitol	1	1	3+	1
26	Winchester Cathedral[19] NEW VAUDEVILLE BAND	Fontana	3+	1	3+	1
Dec 17	Mellow Yellow DONOVAN	Epic	–	–	–	2
24	I'm A Believer[20] MONKEES	Colgems	1	2	1	1
24	That's Life[20] FRANK SINATRA	Reprise	–	–	–	1

AMERICAN NUMBER ONE SINGLES

1967

Date	Title and Artist	Label	BB	CB	V	RW
Jan 7	I'm A Believer[20] MONKEES	Colgems	6	6	6	4
7	Snoopy Vs The Red Baron[20] ROYAL GUARDSMEN	Laurie	–	–	–	1
Feb 11	Georgie Girl SEEKERS	Capitol	–	1	–	1
18	Kind Of A Drag BUCKINGHAMS	USA	2	–	2	1
25	Ruby Tuesday ROLLING STONES	London	1	2+	–	1
Mar 4	Love Is Here And Now You're Gone SUPREMES	Motown	1	1	2	2
18	Penny Lane BEATLES	Capitol	1	2	1	2
25	Happy Together TURTLES	White Whale	3	2	3	2
Apr 15	Somethin' Stupid FRANK & NANCY SINATRA	Reprise	4	2+	6	3+
24	A Little Bit You, A Little Bit Me MONKEES	Colgems	–	2	–	1
May 13	The Happening SUPREMES	Motown	1	1	–	1
20	Groovin' YOUNG RASCALS	Atlantic	4+	3+	5	2
June 3	I Got Rhythm HAPPENINGS	B T Puppy	–	1	–	–
3	Respect ARETHA FRANKLIN	Atlantic	2	2	–	3
27	She'd Rather Be With Me TURTLES	White Whale	–	–	–	1
July 1	Windy ASSOCIATION	Warner Bros.	4	3+	5	2
15	A Little Bit Of Soul MUSIC EXPLOSION	Laurie	–	–	–	1
15	Can't Take My Eyes Off You FRANKIE VALLI	Philips	–	2+	–	2
29	Light My Fire DOORS	Elektra	3	1	3	1
Aug 12	All You Need Is Love BEATLES	Capitol	1	2	–	2
26	Ode To Billy Joe BOBBIE GENTRY	Capitol	4	4	5	4
Sep 23	The Letter BOX TOPS	Mala	4	3	4	4
Oct 14	Never My Love ASSOCIATION	Warner Bros.	–	1	–	–
21	To Sir With Love LULU	Epic	5	3	5	3
Nov 11	Soul Man SAM & DAVE	Stax	–	1	–	1
18	Incense And Peppermints STRAWBERRY ALARM CLOCK	Uni	1	1	–	2
25	The Rain, The Park And Other Things COWSILLS	MGM	–	1	–	–
Dec 2	Daydream Believer MONKEES	Colgems	4	4	4	3
23	Hello Goodbye BEATLES	Capitol	1	1	1	2

1968

Date	Title and Artist	Label	BB	CB	V	RW
Jan 6	Hello Goodbye BEATLES	Capitol	2	1	2	2
13	I Heard It Through The Grapevine GLADYS KNIGHT/PIPS	Soul	–	1	–	–
20	Chain Of Fools ARETHA FRANKLIN	Atlantic	–	1	–	–
20	Judy In Disguise (With Glasses) JOHN FRED/PLAYBOY BAND	Paula	2	1	2	2
Feb 3	Bend Me, Shape Me AMERICAN BREED	Acta	–	–	–	1
3	Green Tambourine LEMON PIPERS	Buddah	1	1	2	1
10	Love Is Blue PAUL MAURIAT	Philips	5	7	4	3
Mar 9	Valley Of The Dolls DIONNE WARWICK	Scepter	–	–	–	2
16	(Sittin' On) The Dock Of The Bay OTIS REDDING	Volt	4	–	4	–
23	Simon Says 1910 FRUITGUM COMPANY	Buddah	–	–	–	1
30	Valleri MONKEENS	Colgems	–	2	–	2
Apr 13	Young Girl UNION GAP	CBS/Columbia	–	1	–	1
13	Honey BOBBY GOLDSBORO	United Artists	5	4	5	5
May 18	Tighten Up ARCHIE BELL/DRELLS	Atlantic	2	1	2	1
25	Mrs Robinson SIMON & GARFUNKEL	CBS/Columbia	3	4	3	3
June 22	This Guy's In Love With You HERB ALPERT	A&M	4	4	4	4
July 20	Jumpin' Jack Flash ROLLING STONES	London	–	1	1	–
20	Grazing In The Grass HUGH MASEKELA	Uni	2	1	1	3
Aug 3	Lady Willpower[21] UNION GAP	CBS/Columbia	–	1	–	1
3	Hello, I Love You[21] DOORS	Elektra	2	1	3	1
10	Classical Gas[21] MASON WILLIAMS	Warner Bros.	–	1	–	–
17	People Got To Be Free RASCALS	Atlantic	5	3	4	2
Sep 7	Harper Valley PTA JEANNIE C. RILEY	Plantation	1	1	1	3
21	Hey Jude BEATLES	Apple	9	7	9+	4
Oct 26	Those Were The Days[22] MARY HOPKINS	Apple	–	2	1	4
Nov 23	Love Child DIANA ROSS/SUPREMES	Motown	2	3	1	4
Dec 14	For Once In My Life[23] STEVIE WONDER	Tamla	–	1	–	1
14	I Heard It Through The Grapevine[23] MARVIN GAYE	Tamla	3	2	3	1

1969

Date	Title and Artist	Label	BB	CB	V	RM
Jan 4	I Heard It Through The Grapevine MARVIN GAYE	Tamla	4	3	4	–
4	I'm Gonna Make You Love Me DIANA ROSS/SUPREMES/TEMPTATIONS	Motown	–	1	–	3
25	Soulful Strut YOUNG HOLT UNLIMITED	Brunswick	–	–	–	1
Feb 1	Crimson And Clover TOMMY JAMES/SHONDELLS	Roulette	2	1	2	2
8	Touch Me DOORS	Elektra	–	1	–	–
15	Everyday People SLY/FAMILY STONE	Epic	4	2	4	1
22	Build Me Up Buttercup FOUNDATIONS	Uni	–	2	–	2
Mar 8	You Showed Me TURTLES	White Whale	–	–	–	1
15	Proud Mary CREEDENCE CLEARWATER REVIVAL	Fantasy	–	–	–	1
15	Dizzy TOMMY ROE	ABC	4	2	4	2
29	Time Of The Seasons ZOMBIES	Date	–	1	–	–
Apr 5	Aquarius/Let The Sun Shine In 5TH DIMENSION	Soul City	6	5	6	4
May 3	Hair COWSILLS	MGM	–	2	–	3
24	Get Back BEATLES	Apple	5	5	5	4
June 21	Bad Moon Rising CREEDENCE CLEARWATER REVIVAL	Fantasy	–	–	–	1
28	In The Ghetto ELVIS PRESLEY	RCA Victor	–	1	–	1
28	Love Theme From Romeo And Juliet HENRY MANCINI	RCA Victor	2	2	2	1
July 12	One THREE DOG NIGHT	Dunhill	–	–	–	1
12	In The Year 2525[24] ZAGR & EVANS	RCA Victor	6	4	6	4
Aug 9	Crystal Blue Persuasion[24] TOMMY JEAMS/SHONDELLS	Roulette	–	–	–	1
16	Honky Tonk Women ROLLING STONES	London	4	4	4	3
Sep 6	A Boy Named Sue JOHNNY CASH	CBS/Columbia	–	–	–	1
13	Sugar Sugar ARCHIES	Calendar	4	4	4	3
Oct 4	Easy To Be Hard THREE DOG NIGHT	Dunhill	–	–	–	2
11	Little Woman BOBBY SHERMAN	Metromedia	–	1	–	–
18	I Can't Get Next To You TEMPTATIONS	Gordy	2	–	2	–
18	Jean OLIVER	Crewe	–	–	–	1
18	Suspicious Minds ELVIS PRESLEY	RCA Victor	1	2	2	2
Nov 1	Wedding Bell Blues[25] 5TH DIMENSION	Soul City	3	3	2	1
22	Come Together BEATLES	Apple	1	3	1	5

Date	Title and Artist	Label	Weeks at No 1 BB CB V RM			
			BB	CB	V	RM
Dec 6	Na Na Hey Hey Kiss Him Goodbye STEAM	Fontana	2	–	1	1
13	And When I Die BLOOD, SWEAT & TEARS	CBS/Columbia	–	1	–	–
20	Leaving On A Jet Plane PETER, PAUL & MARY	Warner Bors./ 7 Arts	1	1	–	2
20	Someday We'll Be Together DIANA ROSS/SUPREMES	Motown	1	1	2	–

KEY

* As of the week ending 23 April, *Variety* changed the basis of its chart compilation from record sales (as in Britain) to sales and radio airplay which was already the basis of the *Billboard* and *Cash Box* charts. It meant an expansion of the chart from a Top 25 to a Top 100, bringing the *Variety* chart into line with *Billboard* and *Cash Box*.

+ Weeks at No 1 were not consecutive.

1 Chubby Checker took **The Twist** back up to No 1 in January 1962, the only time that a record has reached the top on two separate chart runs.

2 Elvis Presley's **Are You Lonesome Tonight?** went to No 1 in *Cash Box* on 26 November and is therefore so dated above. In *Variety* Floyd Cramer was No 1 that week, followed by Johnny Tillotsen, Elvis followed him to the top on 10 December, so even in *Variety* Elvis had the last No 1 of the year. He was also at the top in all three charts in January 1961, so his total number of weeks at No 1 is greater than that shown above.

3 In *Billboard* Ricky Nelson went to No 1 for one week, followed by Orbison, with Nelson returning to the top the week after that. In *Cash Box* Roy Orbison went to No 1 for one week, and was followed by Ricky Nelson who was No 1 for three weeks in a row. In *Variety* Roy Orbison spent one week at No 1 followed by Ricky Nelson for one week. Orbison then returned to the top for a second week, to be replaced by Ricky Nelson a second time.

4 In *Variety* the Highwaymen had three separate runs at No 1 with **Michael**. In *Billboard* the Highwaymen followed Joe Dowell to the top.

5 The Marvelettes followed the Tokens to No 1 in *Billboard*. They were in turn followed at the top by the Tokens, though a week later than in the other two charts. Thus the Tokens were the last No 1 of the year (and the Christmas No 1) in *Billboard* as well as in the other two papers.

6 In the *Variety* charts, Chubby Checker followed Joey Dee to the top. **The Twist** had previously gone to No 1 in 1960, and is the only record to go to the top during two separate chart runs.

7 In *Cash Box* and *Record World* Shelley Fabares followed Elvis Presley to the top.

8 Nat King Cole went to No 1 the week before the Four Seasons. In *Record Vendor* he went to No 1 on 8 September, and the Four Seasons on 15 September. In the *Variety* Top 50 they went to the top the week ending 22 September.

9 In *Variety* Paul & Paula followed Bobby Vee to the top on 2 February. They were replaced at No 1 the following week by the Rooftop Singers, with Paul & Paula returning to No 1 for two more weeks the week ending 16 February.

10 In *Record Vendor* Skeeta Davis went to No 1 on 23 March followed by Ruby and the Romantics the following week.

11 *Record Vendor* ceased publication at the end of 1963. It returned as *Record World* in May 1964.

12 In the *Billboard* charts the Supremes went to No 1 for one week on 19 December, followed the next week by the Beatles. Both records went to No 1 in January 1965. In *Cash Box* the Beatles went to No 1 on 19 December, for one week. They were followed by the Supremes, also for one week. The Beatles were back at the top for the first week of

1965. The Supremes did not make No 1 with **Come See About Me** in *Variety*.

13 In *Billboard* the Beach Boys followed the Beatles to No 1, and were then followed to the top by the Supremes. In *Cash Box* it was the other way round, with the Supremes followed by the Beach Boys.

14 In *Record World* Simon and Garfunkel followed the Beatles to No 1.

15 In *Record World* the Beach Boys went to No 1 on 5 February, and two weeks later were followed to the top by Petula Clark.

16 In *Cash Box*, *Record World* and *Variety*, Frank Sinatra went to No 1 for one week, followed by the Beatles. In *Billboard* the Beatles went to No 1 on 25 June, were then replaced the following week by Sinatra, and came back to the top for one week final week on 9 July.

17 As a result of some confusion as to who was the Troggs' licensee in America, both Atco and Fontana released the record.

18 In *Record World* Donovan went to No 1 on 3 September, followed one week later by the Beatles, and the week after that (17 September) by the Happenings.

19 These three records all made No 1, but in a different order in each chart. In the *Billboard* Hot 100, the Supremes went to No 1 for two weeks on 19 November. They were replaced on 3 December by the New Vaudeville Band. After only one week at the top they were replaced by the Beach Boys, who had only one week at the top (on 10 December) before the New Vaudeville Band returned to No 1 for two more weeks. In *Cash Box* the Beach Boys were first to go to No 1, for one week on 19th November. They were followed by the New Vaudeville Band for one week with **Winchester Cathedral**. On 3 December the Supremes went to the top for one week with the New Vaudeville Band returning to the top for two final weeks on 10 December. In *Variety* the Supremes did not make the top. The Beach Boys went to No 1 the week ending 19 November and after two weeks were replaced by the New Vaudeville Band. They remained at No 1 for one week, 3rd December, and were then replaced by the Beach Boys who had a third week at the top on 10 December. The following week the New Vaudeville Band returned to No 1 for two more weeks. In *Record World* the Supremes went to No 1 on 19 November, followed by the Beach Boys. A week after that, on 3 December, the Supremes went back up to No 1 for a second and final week. On 10 December the New Vaudeville Band went to No 1 for one week.

20 In *Record World* on 25 December 1966, Frank Sinatra and the Monkees were tied at No 1. On 7 January 1967 the Royal Guardsmen went to No 1 for one week, and on 14 January the Monkees returned to the top for a further four weeks.

21 The Doors went to No 1 in *Billboard* and *Variety* on 3 August and are therefore listed ahead of Mason Williams who topped the *Cash Box* chart on 10 August. However in *Cash Box*, the only chart where all three of these records went to No 1, the order was Union Gap on 3 August, Mason Williams on 10 August and the Doors on 17 August.

22 Mary Hopkin made No 1 in *Variety* on 13 November, in the middle of the Beatles' run at the top with **Hey Jude**.

23 In *Record World* Marvin Gaye went to No 1 before Stevie Wonder.

24 In *Record World*, Zager and Evans went to No 1 on 19 July where they stayed for four weeks. On their last week at the top, 9 August, they were tied for first place with Tommy James and the Shondells.

25 In *Record World*, the 5th Dimension went to No 1 for one week on 22 November, when they were No 1 equal with the Beatles who were at the top for the third of their five consecutive weeks at the top.

Date	Title and Artist	Label	No.
	1960		
Jan 16	What Do You Want? ADAM FAITH	Parlophone	1
30	Put Your Hand on My Shoulder PAUL ANKA	Columbia	2
30	Snow Coach RUSS CONWAY	Columbia	2
30	Little White Bull TOMMY STEELE	Decca	1
Feb 13	Why ANTHONY NEWLEY	Decca	1
13	Starry Eyed MICHAEL HOLLIDAY	Columbia	1
13	Seven Little Girls AVONS	Columbia	1
20	A Voice in the Wilderness CLIFF RICHARD/SHADOWS	Columbia	3
27	Sea of Love MARTY WILDE	Philips	3
27	Rawhide FRANKIE LAINE	Philips	1
27	Heartaches by the Number GUY MITCHELL	Philips	1
Mar 12	Way Down Yonder in New Orleans FREDDY CANNON	Top Rank	1
26	Poor Me ADAM FAITH	Parlophone	2
May 7	Fall in Love with You CLIFF RICHARD/SHADOWS	Columbia	4
21	Cathy's Clown EVERLY BROTHERS	Warner Bros.	2
June 11	Do You Mind? ANTHONY NEWLEY	Decca	2
25	Handy Man JIMMY JONES	MGM	1
Aug 13	Please Don't Tease CLIFF RICHARD/SHADOWS	Columbia	5
Sep 3	Apache SHADOWS	Columbia	1
10	A Mess of Blues ELVIS PRESLEY	RCA Victor	2
24	Because They're Young DUANE EDDY	London	2
Oct 8	Theme From a Summer Place PERCY FAITH	Philips	1
15	Tell Laura I Love Her RICKY VALENCE	Columbia	1
15	Good Timin' JIMMY JONES	MGM	1
22	Nine Times Out of Ten CLIFF RICHARD/SHADOWS	Columbia	6
29	It's Now Or Never* ELVIS PRESLEY	RCA Victor	3
Nov 5	As Long as He Needs Me SHIRLEY BASSEY	Columbia	1
26	My Old Man's a Dustman LONNIE DONEGAN	Pye	2
Dec 17	He'll Have To Go JIM REEVES	RCA Victor	1
24	I Love You/'D' in Love CLIFF RICHARD/SHADOWS	Columbia	7
24	Rocking Goose JOHNNY/HURRICANES	London	2
24	Save the Last Dance for Me DRIFTERS	London	1
31	Little Donkey NINA & FREDERICK	Columbia	1

Date	Title and Artist	Label	No.
	1961		
Jan 7	Strawberry Fair ANTHONY NEWLEY	Decca	3
7	Poetry In Motion JOHNNY TILLOTSEN	London	1
14	Lonely Pup ADAM FAITH	Parlophone	3
14	My Heart Has A Mind Of Its Own CONNIE FRANCIS	MGM	2
14	Goodness Gracious Me SOPHIA LOREN/PETER SELLERS	Parlophone	1
21	Man Of Mystery/The Stranger SHADOWS	Columbia	2
Feb 11	Sailor PETULA CLARK	Pye	1
18	Are You Sure? ALLISONS	Fontana	1
18	Walk Right Back/Ebony Eyes EVERLY BROTHERS	Warner Bros.	3
Apr 8	Theme For A Dream CLIFF RICHARD/SHADOWS	Columbia	8
22	A Scottish Soldier ANDY STEWART	Top Rank	1
29	F.B.I. SHADOWS	Columbia	3
June 24	Runaway DEL SHANNON	London	1
Aug 5	But I Do CLARENCE 'FROGMAN' HENRY	Pye International	1
19	Half Way To Paradise BILLY FURY	Decca	1
26	You Don't Know HELEN SHAPIRO	Columbia	1
Sep 2	Johnny Remember Me JOHN LEYTON	Top Rank	1
9	Well I Ask You EDEN KANE	Decca	1
Oct 28	Wild Wind JOHN LEYTON	Top Rank	2
Nov 4	Walking Back To Happiness HELEN SHAPIRO	Columbia	2
11	When The Girl In Your Arms Is The Girl In Your Heart/Got A Funny Feeling CLIFF RICHARD/SHADOWS	Columbia	9
18	Reach For The Stars/Climb Ev'ry Mountain SHIRLEY BASSEY	Columbia	2
Dec 16	Tower Of Strength FRANKIE VAUGHAN	RCA Victor	1
16	Big Bad John JIMMY DEAN	Philips	1
23	Moon River DANNY WILLIAMS	HMV	1
23	Take Good Care Of My Baby BOBBY VEE	London	1
30	The Time Has Come ADAM FAITH	Parlophone	4
30	Are You Lonesome Tonight?[1] ELVIS PRESLEY	RCA Victor	4
30	Wooden Heart ELVIS PRESLEY	RCA Victor	5
30	Surrender ELVIS PRESLEY	RCA Victor	6
30	Wild In The Country ELVIS PRELSEY	RCA Victor	7
30	His Latest Flame/Little Sister ELVIS PRELSEY	RCA Victor	8

255

Date		Title and Artist	Label	No.
		1962		
Jan	6	Midnight In Moscow KENNY BALL/HIS JAZZMEN	Pye Jazz	1
	6	Johnny Will PAT BOONE	London	1
	13	The Young Ones* CLIFF RICHARD/SHADOWS	Columbia	10
	13	Stranger On The Shore MR ACKER BILK	Columbia	1
	20	Let There Be Drums SANDY NELSON	London	1
	27	I'd Never Find Another You BILLY FURY	Decca	2
Feb	17	Rock-A-Hula Baby ELVIS PRESLEY	RCA Victor	9
	17	G.I. Blues (L.P.)[2] ELVIS PRESLEY	RCA Victor	8
	24	Let's Twist Again CHUBBY CHECKER	Columbia	1
	24	Happy Birthday Sweet Sixteen NEIL SEDAKA	RCA Victor	2
Mar	31	Wonderful Land SHADOWS	Columbia	4
Apr	7	Walk On By LEROY VAN DYKE	Mercury	1
	21	Tell Me What He Said HELEN SHAPIRO	Columbia	3
May	5	March Of The Siamese Children KENNY BALL/HIS JAZZMEN	Pye Jazz	2
	19	I'm Looking Out The Window/Do You Wanna Dance?[3] CLIFF RICHARD/SHADOWS	Columbia	11
June	9	Good Luck Charm ELVIS PRESLEY	RCA Victor	10
	14	Come Outside MIKE SARNE/WENDY RICHARD	Parlophone	1
	14	Picture Of You JOE BROWN	Piccadilly	1
	28	I Can't Stop Loving You RAY CHARLES	HMV	1
	28	I Remember You FRANK IFIELD	Columbia	1
Aug	11	Speedy Gonzales PAT BOONE	London	2
Sep	15	Roses Are Red RONNIE CARROLL	Philips	1
	22	Guitar Tango SHADOWS	Columbia	5
	22	Things BOBBY DARIN	London	3
Oct	13	Telstar TORNADOS	Decca	1
Nov	3	The Locomotion LITTLE EVA	London	1
	3	Lovesick Blues FRANK IFIELD	Columbia	2
	3	It'll Be Me CLIFF RICHARD/SHADOWS	Columbia	12
Dec	22	She's Not You ELVIS PRESLEY	RCA Victor	11
	22	Return To Sender ELVIS PRESLEY	RCA Victor	12
	22	Bobby's Girl SUSAN MAUGHAN	Philips	1
	22	Dance On* SHADOWS	Columbia	6

Date		Title and Artist	Label	No.
	22	Sun Arise ROLF HARRIS	Columbia	1
	29	Venus In Blue Jeans MARK WYNTER	Pye	1
	29	The Next Time/Bachelor Boy* CLIFF RICHARD	Columbia	13
		1963		
Jan	5	Guitar Man DUANE EDDY	RCA Victor	3
	5	Sheila TOMMY ROE	HMV	1
Feb	2	The Wayward Wind FRANK IFIELD	Columbia	3
	2	Diamonds JET HARRIS/TONY MEEHAN	Decca	1
Mar	9	Summer Holiday/Dancing Shoes CLIFF RICHARD/SHADOWS	Columbia	14
Apr	6	Let's Dance CHRIS MONTEZ	London	1
	13	Please Please Me BEATLES	Parlophone	1
	27	How Do You Do It GERRY/PACEMAKERS	Columbia	1
	27	Foot Tapper SHADOWS	Columbia	7
	27	From A Jack To A King NED MILLER	London	1
May	4	From Me To You BEATLES	Parlophone	2
	4	Deck Of Cards WINK MARTINDALE	London	1
June	15	Nobody's Darlin' But Mine FRANK IFIELD	Columbia	4
July	6	I Like It GERRY/PACEMAKERS	Columbia	2
	13	Ramblin' Rose NAT 'KING' COLE	Capitol	1
Aug	3	Devil In Disguise ELVIS PRESLEY	RCA Victor	13
	3	I'm Confessin' FRANK IFIELD	Columbia	5
	3	In Dreams ROY ORBISON	London	2
	10	Atlantis SHADOWS	Columbia	8
	17	Take These Chains From My Heart RAY CHARLES	HMV	2
	24	Twist And Shout (E.P.)[4] BEATLES	Parlophone	3
	24	That's What Love Will Do JOE BROWN	Piccadilly	2
	24	Sweets For My Sweet SEARCHERS	Pye	1
	31	Bad To Me BILLY J KRAMER/DAKOTAS	Parlophone	1
Sep	7	She Loves You BEATLES	Parlophone	4
	14	Lucky Lips CLIFF RICHARD/SHADOWS	Columbia	15
	14	The Frightened City SHADOWS	Columbia	9
Oct	19	Do You Love Me BRIAN POOLE/TREMELOES	Decca	1
	26	You'll Never Walk Alone GERRY/PACEMAKERS	Columbia	3

Date	Title and Artist	Label	No.
26	It's All In The Game CLIFF RICHARD/SHADOWS	Columbia	16
Nov 9	Then He Kissed Me CRYSTALS	London	1
23	Blue Bayou/Mean Woman Blues ROY ORBISON	London	3
Dec 7	I Want To Hold Your Hand* BEATLES	Parlophone	5
14	The Beatles Hits (E.P.) BEATLES	Parlophone	6
14	Don't Talk To Him CLIFF RICHARD/SHADOWS	Columbia	17
14	You Were Made For Me FREDDIE/DREAMERS	Columbia	1
14	I (Who Have Nothing) SHIRLEY BASSEY	Columbia	3
21	Glad All Over DAVE CLARK FIVE	Columbia	1

1964

Date	Title and Artist	Label	No.
Jan 4	I Only Want To Be With You DUSTY SPRINGFIELD	Philips	1
4	Dominique SINGING NUN	Philips	1
4	Twenty Four Hours From Tulsa GENE PITNEY	United Artists	1
4	Maria Elena LOS INDIOS TABAJARAS	RCA Victor	1
11	For Goodness Sale SWINGING BLUE JEANS	HMV	1
11	Sugar And Spice SEARCHERS	Pye	2
Feb 1	I'm The One GERRY/PACEMAKERS	Columbia	4
15	Diane BACHELORS	Decca	1
15	Anyone Who Had A Heart CILLA BLACK	Parlophone	1
29	Bits And Pieces DAVE CLARK FIVE	Columbia	2
29	Needles And Pins SEARCHERS	Pye	3
Mar 14	Little Children BILLY J KRAMER/DAKOTAS	Parlophone	2
14	I Think Of You MERSEYBEATS	Fontana	1
21	Not Fade Away ROLLING STONES	Decca	1
21	All My Loving (E.P.) BEATLES	Parlophone	7
28	Just One Look HOLLIES	Parlophone	1
Apr 4	I Love You Because JIM REEVES	RCA Victor	2
11	I Believe BACHELORS	Decca	2
11	A World Without Love PETER & GORDON	Columbia	1
18	Don't Throw Your Love Away* SEARCHERS	Pye	4
25	Can't Buy Me Love BEATLES	Parlophone	8
May 2	My Boy Lollipop MILLIE	Fontana	1
23	Juliet FOUR PENNIES	Philips	1

Date	Title and Artist	Label	No.
23	You're My World CILLA BLACK	Parlophone	2
June 6	It's Over ROY ORBISON	London	4
July 4	The House Of The Rising Sun ANIMALS	Columbia	1
4	Someone, Someone BRIAN POOLE/TREMELOES	Decca	2
11	It's All Over Now ROLLING STONES	Decca	2
18	A Hard Day's Night* BEATLES	Parlophone	9
25	Hold Me P J PROBY	Decca	1
Aug 1	Do Wah Diddy Diddy MANFRED MANN	HMV	1
8	I Won't Forget You JIM REEVES	RCA Victor	3
15	Call Up The Groups BARRON KNIGHTS	Columbia	1
29	Have I The Right HONEYCOMBES	Pye	1
29	I Just Don't Know What To Do With Myself DUSTY SPRINGFIELD	Philips	2
Sep 12	Five By Five (E.P.) ROLLING STONES	Decca	3
19	I Wouldn't Trade You For The World BACHELORS	Decca	3
Oct 3	I'm Into Something Good HERMAN'S HERMITS	Columbia	1
10	Oh, Pretty Woman ROY ORBISON	London	5
10	Where Did Our Love Go SUPREMES	Stateside	1
10	Rag Doll FOUR SEASONS	Philips	1
10	The Wedding JULIE ROGERS	Mercury	1
10	You Really Got Me KINKS	Pye	1
24	Always Something There To Remind Me SANDIE SHAW	Pye	1
Nov 21	All Day And All Of The Night KINKS	Pye	2
Dec 5	I Feel Fine* BEATLES	Parlophone	10
5	Baby Love SUPREMES	Stateside	2
12	Little Red Rooster ROLLING STONES	Decca	4
12	I'm Gonna Be Strong GENE PITNEY	Stateside	2
19	Walk Away MATT MONRO	Parlophone	1
19	Walk Tall VAL DOONICAN	Decca	1
19	Downtown PETULA CLARK	Pye	2
19	When You Walk In The Room SEARCHERS	Pye	5
19	There's A Heartache Following Me JIM REEVES	RCA Victor	4
26	Somewhere P J PROBY	Liberty	2
26	I Understand FREDDIE/DREAMERS	Columbia	2

Date	Title and Artist	Label	No.
26	No Arms Can Ever Hold You BACHELORS	Decca	4

1965

Date	Title and Artist	Label	No.
Jan 2	Yeh, Yeh GEORGIE FAME	Columbia	1
2	Pretty Paper ROY ORBISON	London	6
2	Girl Don't Come SANDIE SHAW	Pye	2
9	I Could Easily Fall CLIFF RICHARD/SHADOWS	Columbia	18
9	Terry TWINKLE	Decca	1
23	Go Now MOODY BLUES	Decca	1
Feb 6	You've Lost That Lovin' Feeling RIGHTEOUS BROTHERS	London	1
6	Tired Of Waiting For You KINKS	Pye	3
6	Cast Your Fates To The Wind SOUNDS ORCHESTRAL	Piccadilly	1
13	Long Tall Sally (EP) BEATLES	Parlophone	11
27	I'll Never Find Another You SEEKERS	Columbia	1
Mar 6	It's Not Unusual TOM JONES	Decca	1
20	The Last Time ROLLING STONES	Decca	5
27	Silhouettes HERMAN'S HERMITS	Columbia	2
May 1	Ticket To Ride BEATLES	parlophone	12
1	The Minute You're Gone CLIFF RICHARD	Columbia	19
8	Pop Goe The Workers BARRON KNIGHTS	Columbia	2
29	Catch The Wind DONOVAN	Pye	1
June 19	Long Live Love SANDIE SHAW	Pye	3
19	A World Of Our Own SEEKERS	Columbia	2
19	He's In Town ROCKIN' BERRIES	Piccadilly	1
26	Crying In The Chapel ELVIS PRESLEY	RCA Victor	14
July 31	Help!* BEATLES	Parlophone	13
Aug 7	I'm Alive HOLLIES	Parlophone	2
7	Mr Tambourine Man BYRDS	CBS	1
21	You've Got Your Troubles FORTUNES	Decca	1
28	I've Got You Babe SONNY & CHER	Atlantic	1
Sep 4	Tossing And Turning IVY LEAGUE	Piccadilly	1
30	The Beatles No 1 (E.P.) BEATLES	Parlophone	14
Oct 9	Tears KEN DODD	Columbia	1
16	Make It Easy On Yourself WALKER BROTHERS	Philips	1

Date	Title and Artist	Label	No.
16	A Walk In The Black Forest HORST JANKOWSKI	Mercury	1
Nov 6	Almost There ANDY WILLIAMS	CBS	1
13	Get Off Of My Cloud ROLLING STONES	Decca	6
13	Yesterday Man CHRIS ANDREWS	Decca	1
27	The Carnival Is Over SEEKERS	Columbia	3
Dec 4	Here It Comes Again FORTUNES	Decca	2
11	Day Tripper/We Can Work It Out* BEATLES	Parlophone	15
18	Wind Me Up CLIFF RICHARD	Columbia	20
18	The River KEN DODD	Columbia	2
18	My Generation WHO	Brunswick	1
18	1-2-3 LEN BARRY	Brunswick	1
18	Zorba's Dance MARCELLO MINERBI	Durium	1
18	(I Can't Get No) Satisfaction ROLLING STONES	Decca	7

1966

Date	Title and Artist	Label	No.
Jan 15	Keep On Running SPENCER DAVIS GROUP	Fontana	1
22	A Girl Like You CLIFF RICHARD/SHADOWS	Columbia	21
22	My Ship Is Coming In WALKER BROTHERS	Philips	2
Feb 12	These Boots Are Made For Walking NANCY SINATRA	Reprise	1
19	You Were On My Mind CRISPIAN ST. PETERS	Decca	1
19	Nineteenth Nervous Breakdown ROLLING STONES	Decca	8
19	Michelle OVERLANDERS	Pye	1
26	Spanish Flea HERB ALPERT/TIJUANA BRASS	Pye International	1
Mar 12	Sha La La La Lee SMALL FACES	Decca	1
12	A Groovy Kind Of Love MINDBENDERS	Fontana	1
Apr 9	My Love PETULA CLARK	Pye	3
9	The Sun Ain't Gonna Shine Anymore WALKER BROTHERS	Philips	3
23	Make The World Go Away EDDY ARNOLD	RCA Victor	1
May 7	You Don't Have To Say You Love Me DUSTY SPRINGFIELD	Philips	3
28	Pretty Flamingo MANFRED MANN	HMV	2
June 4	Constantly CLIFF RICHARD	Columbia	22
4	Paint It Black ROLLING STONES	Decca	9
11	Strangers In The Night FRANK SINATRA	Reprise	1
11	Daydream LOVIN' SPOONFUL	Pye International	1

Date		Title and Artist	Label	No.
	11	Hold Tight DAVE DEE, DOZY, BEAKY, MICK & TITCH	Fontana	1
	25	Paperback Writer BEATLES	Parlophone	16
Aug	20	Wild Thing TROGGS	Fontana	1
	27	With A Girl Like You TROGGS	Fontana	2
Sep	3	Yellow Submarine/Eleanor Rigby BEATLES	Parlophone	17
	3	Sunny Afternoon KINKS	Pye	4
Oct	8	Distant Drums JIM REEVES	RCA Victor	5
Nov	12	Reach Out I'll Be There FOUR TOPS	Tamla Motown	1
Dec	2	Green Green Grass Of Home TOM JONES	Decca	2
	2	Good Vibrations BEACH BOYS	Capitol	1
	24	Morningtown Ride SEEKERS	Columbia	4
	24	What Should I Be VAL DOONICAN	Decca	2
	31	On The Beach CLIFF RICHARD/SHADOWS	Columbia	23

1967

Date		Title and Artist	Label	No.
Jan	1	Bend It DAVE DEE, DOZY, BEAKY, MICK & TITCH	Fontana	2
	1	I'm A Believer* MONKEES	RCA Victor	1
	1	Sunshine Superman DONOVAN	Pye	2
	1	Gimme Some Lovin' SPENCER DAVIS GROUP	Fontana	2
	1	Semi-Detached Suburban Mr James MANFRED MANN	Fontana	3
	1	Winchester Cathedral NEW VAUDEVILLE BAND	Fontana	1
Feb	18	This Is My Song PETULA CLARK	Pye	4
	25	Penny Lane/Strawberry Fields Forever* BEATLES	Parlophone	18
	25	Release Me ENGLEBERT HUMPERDINCK	Decca	1
	25	Let's Spend The Night Together/Ruby Tuesday ROLLING STONES	Decca	10
Apr	22	Pupet On A String SANDIE SHAW	Pye	4
	22	Something Stupid5 FRANK & NANCY SINATRA	Reprise	2/2
May	13	A Little Bit Me, A Little Bit You MONKEES	RCA Victor	2
	13	This Is My Song HARRY SECOMBE	Philips	1
	20	I Left My Heart In San Francisco TONY BENNETT	CBS	1
June	3	Silence Is Golden TREMELOES	Decca	1
	10	A Whiter Shade Of Pale PROCUL HARUM	Deram	1
	17	There Goes My Everything ENGLEBERT HUMPERDINCK	Decca	2

Date		Title and Artist	Label	No.
July	22	All You Need Is Love BEATLES	Parlophone	19
Aug	12	San Francisco SCOTT McKENZIE	CBS	1
Sep	2	Just Loving You ANITA HARRIS	CBS	1
	9	The Last Waltz ENGLEBERT HUMPERDINCK	Decca	3
	9	I'll Never Fall In Love Again TOM JONES	Decca	3
Oct	28	Massachusetts BEE GEES	Polydor	1
Nov	25	Baby, Now That I've Found You FOUNDATIONS	Pye	1
	25	Hole In My Shoe TRAFFIC	Island	1
Dec	2	Hello Goodbye* BEATLES	Parlophone	20
	16	Let The Heartaches Begin LONG JOHN BALDRY	Pye	1
	23	Magical Mystery Tour (2 EPs) BEATLES	Parlophone	21
	23	There Must Be A Way FRANKIE VAUGHAN	Columbia	2

1968

Date		Title and Artist	Label	No.
Jan	1	If The Whole World Stopped Loving VAL DOONICAN	Pye	3
	1	Careless Hands DES O'CONNOR	Columbia	1
	1	Something's Gotten Hold Of My Heart GENE PITNEY	Stateside	3
	13	I'm Coming Home TOM JONES	Decca	4
	13	Daydream Believer MONKEES	RCA Victor	3
	20	Ballad Of Bonnie And Clyde GEORGIE FAME	CBS	2
Feb	3	Am I That Easy To Forget ENGLEBERT HUMPERDINCK	Decca	4
	3	Everlasting Love LOVE AFFAIR	CBS	1
	24	Help Yourself TOM JONES	Decca	5
	24	She Wears My Ring SOLOMAN KING	Columbia	1
Mar	2	Mighty Quinn MANFRED MANN	Fontana	4
	2	Cinderella Rockafella ESTHER & ABI OFARIM	Philips	1
	16	Legend Of Xanadu DAVE DEE, DOZY, BEAKY, MICK AND TITCH	Fontana	3
	16	Judy In Disguise JOHN FREED/PLAYBOY BAND	Pye International	1
	23	Delilah TOM JONES	Decca	6
	30	Lady Madonna BEATLES	Parlophone	22
Apr	27	Congratulations CLIFF RICHARD	Columbia	24
	27	World BEE GEES	Polydor	2
	27	What A Wonderful World LOUIS ARMSTRONG	HMV	1
May	18	A Man Without Love ENGLEBERT HUMPERDINCK	Decca	5

Date	Title and Artist	Label	No.
18	Simon Says 1910 FRUITGUM COMPANY	Pye	1
25	Young Girl UNION GAP	CBS	1
June 1	If I Only Had Time JOHN ROWLES	MCA	1
22	Honey BOBBY GOLDSBORO	United Artists	1
Aug 10	Baby Come Back EQUALS	President	1
24	I Pretend DES O'CONNOR	Columbia	2
Sep 14	This Guy's In Love HERB ALPERT	A&M	2
14	Hey Jude BEATLES	Apple	23
14	I've Gotta Get A Message To You BEE GEES	Polydor	3
14	Mony Mony TOMMY JAMES/SHONDELLS	Major Minor	1
Oct 5	Those Were The Days MARY HOPKIN	Apple	1
Dec 7	The Good, The Bad And The Ugly HUGO MONTENEGRO	RCA Victor	1
26	Build Me Up Buttercup FOUNDATIONS	Pye	2
26	Lily The Pink SCAFFOLD	Parlophone	1

1969

Date	Title and Artist	Label	No.
Jan 11	One, Two, Three O'Leary DES O'CONNOR	Columbia	3
11	Ain't Got No — I Got Life NINA SIMONE	RCA Victor	1
18	Albatross FLEETWOOD MAC	Blue Horzion	1
Feb 1	Urban Spaceman BONZO DOG DO DAH BAND	Liberty	1
1	Ob-La-Di Ob-La-Da MARMALADE	CBS	1
1	Where Do You Go To PETER SARSTEDT	United Artists	1
Apr 26	Israelites DESMOND DEKKER/ACES	Pyramid	1
May 3	Get Back BEATLES	Apple	24
3	I Heard It Through The Grapevine MARVIN GAYE	Tamla Motown	1
June 7	Gentle On My Mind DEAN MARTIN	Reprise	1
14	In The Bad, Bad Old Days FOUNDATIONS	Pye	3
July 12	The Balland Of John And Yoko BEATLES	Apple	25
Aug 2	Honky Tonk Women ROLLING STONES	Decca	11
16	Something In The Air THUNDERCLAP NEWMAN	Track	1
Sep 13	In The Ghetto ELVIS PRESLEY	RCA Victor	15
20	In The Year 2525 ZAGER & EVANS	RCA Victor	1
Oct 25	Bad Moon Rising CREEDENCE CLEARWATER REVIVAL	Liberty	1
Dec 6	Don't Forget To Remember BEE GEES	Polydor	4

Date	Title and Artist	Label	No.
6	Saved By The Bell ROBIN GIBB	Polydor	1
6	My Cherie Amour STEVIE WONDER	Tamla Motown	1
13	Yester-Me, Yester-You, Yesterday STEVIE WONDER	Tamla Motown	2
20	Sugar Sugar ARCHIES	RCA Victor	1
31	Two Little Boys ROLF HARRIS	Columbia	2

KEY (above)

The final column on the right shows the total number of Silver Discs awarded to the artist up to, and including, the above award.

* Immediate Silver Disc for advance orders of 250,000 or more by date of release.

1 Decca had decided not to claim Silver Discs for Elvis Presley records, claiming that Elvis did not need the publicity. After an outcry from Presley fans they changed their mind and at the end of December five Elvis records were submitted for awards and received them at the same time. Most would have qualified for a Silver Disc on the day of release for advance orders of over a quarter of a million copies.
2 **G. I. Blues** was the first album in Britain to sell over 250,000 copies.
3 Cliff Richard and the Shadows' **I'm Looking Out the Window/Do You Wanna Dance** was the 100th Silver Disc awarded. Cliff and the Shadows had also won the 50th Silver Disc, for **I Love You/D In Love** in 1960.
4 **Twist And Shout** was the first EP in Britain to sell over 250,000 copies.
5 This was Frank and Nancy Sinatra's first Silver Disc as a duo, but the second award that each had received. Both had won a Silver Disc for one solo recording before.

KEY

The following is a list of all albums to be awarded a Gold Disc by the RIAA for sales of over one million dollars worth at factory prices. The date given is that of certification by the RIAA. Many albums did not qualify for a Gold Disc until after the year of their release. They are listed under the year that the award was made, and not under the year of release. The number in the right-hand column shows the total number of Gold albums that the artist had been awarded up to that time.

* Subsequently awarded an RIAA Platinum Disc for sales of over one million copies. (Not all Gold Disc albums that went on to sell a million copies were put forward for Platinum certification by the record company concerned.)

1 The Philadelphia Orchestra conducted by Eugene Ormandy also appeared on the Mormon Tabernacle Choir album *The Lord's Prayer*.
2 The Young Rascals became the Rascals, and are the same group.
3 Janis Joplin was lead singer with Big Brother and the Holding Company.

Date		Title and Artist	Label	No.

1960

Date		Title and Artist	Label	No.
Jan	19	The Student Prince MARIO LANZA	RCA Victor	1
Feb	12	Pat's Great Hits PAT BOONE	Dot	1
	17	60 Years Of Music America Loves Best VARIOUS ARTISTS	RCA Victor	1
	17	Elvis ELVIS PRESLEY	RCA Victor	1
Apr	18	The Kingston Trio KINGSTON TRIO	Capitol	1
	18	The Kingston Trio At Large KINGSTON TRIO	Capitol	2
	21	Heavenly* JOHNNY MATHIS	CBS-Columbia	2
	21	More Sing Along With Mitch MITCH MILLER	CBS-Columbia	2
May	5	Warm JOHNNY MATHIS	CBS-Columbia	3
Oct	24	From The Hungry I KINGSTON TRIO	Capitol	3
	24	Here We Go Again KINGSTON TRIO	Capitol	4
	24	Love Is The Thing NAT 'KING' COLE	Capitol	1
Dec	7	Merry Christmas* JOHNNY MATHIS	CBS-Columbia	4
	7	Christmas Sing Along MITCH MILLER	CBS-Columbia	3
	7	Still More! Sing Along With Mitch MITCH MILLER	CBS-Columbia	4
	7	The Sound Of Music ORIGINAL CAST	CBS-Columbia	1

1961

Date		Title and Artist	Label	No.
June	16	Calcutta! LAWRENCE WELK	Dot	1
	22	Sold Out KINGSTON TRIO	Capitol	5
	22	Come Dance With Me FRANK SINATRA	Capitol	1
Sep	28	The Glenn Miller Story GLENN MILLER ORCHESTRA	RCA Victor	1
	18	Song Hits From Theatreland MANTOVANI	London	1
	18	Film Encores Volume 1 MANTOVANI	London	2
	18	Christmas Carols MANTOVANI	London	3
	18	Gems Forever MANTOVANI	London	4
	18	Strauss Waltzes MANTOVANI	London	5
Oct	10	Spirituals ERNIE FORD	Capitol	2
	16	Belafonte At Carnegie Hall HARRY BELAFONTE	RCA Victor	1
	17	Elvis' Golden Records* ELVIS PRESLEY	RCA Victor	2
Nov	22	Tchaikovsky: Piano Concerto No 1 VAN CLIBURN	RCA Victor	1
Dec	7	Encore Of Golden Hits PLATTERS	Mercury	1
	21	Blue Hawaii ELVIS PRESLEY	RCA Victor	3

1962

Date		Title and Artist	Label	No.
Jan	12	More Johnny's Greatest Hits JOHNNY MATHIS	CBS-Columbia	5
	12	Party Sing Along With Mitch MITCH MILLER	CBS-Columbia	5
	12	Holiday Sing Along With Mitch MITCH MILLER	CBS-Columbia	6
	12	West Side Story ORIGINAL CAST	CBS-Columbia	1
Feb	9	Camelot ORIGINAL CAST	CBS-Columbia	1
	9	Flower Drum Song ORIGINAL CAST	CBS-Columbia	1
	16	Sail Along Silvery Moon BILLY VAUGHN	Dot	1
	16	Blue Hawaii BILLY VAUGHN	Dot	2
	16	Theme From A Summer Place BILLY VAUGHN	Dot	3
Mar	1	The Button-Down Mind Of Bob Newhart BOB NEWHART	Warner Bros.	1
	7	Sentimental Sing Along With Mitch MITCH MILLER	CBS-Columbia	7
	7	Memories Sing Along With Mitch MITCH MILLER	CBS-Columbia	8
	8	Saturday Night Sing Along With Mitch MITCH MILLER	CBS-Columbia	9
June	12	Star Carol ERNIE FORD	Capitol	3
	22	Nearer The Cross ERNIE FORD	Capitol	4
	21	Songs For Swinging Lovers FRANK SINATRA	Capitol	2
	21	This Is Sinatra FRANK SINATRA	Capitol	3
	21	Frank Sinatra Sings For Only The Lonely FRANK SINATRA	Capitol	4
	21	Nice 'n' Easy FRANK SINATRA	Capitol	5
	27	Judy At Carnegie Hall JUDY GARLAND	Capitol	1
	27	Music For Lovers Only JACKIE GLEASON	Capitol	1
	27	Music, Martini's And Memories JACKIE GLEASON	Capitol	2
	27	String Along KINGSTON TRIO	Capitol	6
July	6	Happy Times! Sing Along With Mitch MITCH MILLER	CBS-Columbia	10
	19	Modern Sounds In Country And Western Music RAY CHARLES	ABC Paramount	1
	19	'S Marvelous RAY CONNIFF	CBS-Columbia	1
	19	Concert In Rhythm RAY CONNIFF	CBS-Columbia	2
	19	Memories Are Made Of This RAY CONNIFF	CBS-Columbia	3
	19	So Much In Love RAY CONNIFF	CBS-Columbia	4
Oct	30	Breakfast At Tiffany's HENRY MANCINI	RCA Victor	2
Dec	4	Bouquet PERCY FAITH	CBS-Columbia	1

Date	Title and Artist	Label	No.
4	Swing Softly JOHNNY MATHIS	CBS-Columbia	6
4	Open Fire, Two Guitars JOHNNY MATHIS	CBS-Columbia	7
4	Faithfully JOHNNY MATHIS	CBS-Columbia	8
10	Peter, Paul And Mary* PETER, PAUL & MARY	Warner Bros.	1
10	My Son The Folk Singer ALLAN SHERMAN	Warner Bros.	1
18	The First Family VAUGHN MEADER	Cadence	1

1963

Date	Title and Artist	Label	No.
Jan 7	The Glorious Sound Of Christmas[1] PHILADELPHIA ORCHESTRA	CBS-Columbia	1
7	West Side Story* FILM SOUNDTRACK	CBS-Columbia	1
Feb 5	Tchaikovsky: 1812 Festival Overture ANTAL DORATI	Mercury	1
Mar 12	Season's Greetings From Perry Como PERRY COMO	RCA Victor	1
12	G.I. Blues ELVIS PRESLEY	RCA Victor	4
12	Exodus FILM SOUNDTRACK	RCA Victor	1
22	Viva PERCY FAITH	CBS-Columbia	2
27	The Music Man FILM SOUNDTRACK	Warner Bros.	1
Apr 19	Time Out DAVE BRUBECK QUARTET	CBS-Columbia	1
July 11	I Left My Heart In San Francisco TONNY BENNETT	CBS-Columbia	1
Aug 13	Belafonte HARRY BELAFONTE	RCA Victor	2
13	Calypso HARRY BELAFONTE	RCA Victor	3
13	Belafonte Returns To Carnegie Hall HARRY BELAFONTE	RCA Victor	4
13	Girls, Girls, Girls ELVIS PRESLEY	RCA Victor	5
13	Elvis' Christmas Album ELVIS PRESLEY	RCA Victor	6
23	Jump Up Calypso HARRY BELAFONTE	RCA Victor	5
27	Moving PETER, PAUL & MARY	Warner Bros.	2
Sep 3	Exodus MANTOVANI	London	6
19	Days Of Wine And Roses ANDY WILLIAMS	CBS-Columbia	1
Oct 14	Moon River And Other Great Movie Themes ANDY WILLIAMS	CBS-Columbia	2
21	Christmas With Conniff RAY CONNIFF	CBS-Columbia	5
21	Handel's Messiah PHILADELPHIA ORCHESTRA	CBS-Columbia	2
21	The Lord's Prayer MORMAN TABERNACLE CHOIR	CBS-Columbia	1
21	Porgy And Bess FILM SOUNDTRACK	CBS-Columbia	1
Nov 6	Folk Song Sing Along MITCH MILLER	CBS-Columbia	11

Date	Title and Artist	Label	No.
13	In The Wind PETER, PAUL & MARY	Warner Bros.	3
Dec 17	The Singing Nun SINGING NUN	Philips	1

1964

Date	Title and Artist	Label	No.
Jan 8	My Fair Lady* ORIGINAL CAST	CBS-Columbia	1
15	Ramblin' Rose NAT 'KING' COLE	Capitol	2
15	The King And I FILM SOUNDTRACK	Capitol	1
15	Carousel FILM SOUNDTRACK	Capitol	1
15	John FitzGerald Kennedy — A Memorial Album (Broadcast by WMCA New York) ED BROWN	Premier	1
Feb 3	Meet The Beatles! BEATLES	Capitol	1
Apr 4	Honey In The Horn AL HIRT	RCA Victor	1
13	The Beatles' Second Album BEATLES	Capitol	2
May 12	The Second Barbra Streisand Album BARBRA STREISAND	CBS-Columbia	1
June 2	Hello, Dolly! ORIGINAL CAST	RCA Victor	1
Aug 10	Hello, Dolly! LOUIS ARMSTRONG	Kapp	1
17	The Wonderful World Of Andy Williams ANDY WILLIAMS	CBS-Columbia	3
19	Victory At Sea Volume One ROBERT RUSSELL BENNETT	RCA Victor	1
19	Christmas Hymns And Carols ROBERT SHAW	RCA Victor	1
24	Something New BEATLES	Capitol	3
Sep 4	Unforgettable NAT 'KING' COLE	Capitol	3
4	The Best Of The Kingston Trio KINGSTON TRIO	Capitol	7
21	Funny Girl ORIGINAL CAST	Capitol	1
Oct 16	Ramblin' NEW CHRISTY MINSTRELS	CBS-Columbia	1
16	The Barbra Streisand Album BARBRA STREISAND	CBS-Columbia	2
Nov 2	Johnny Horton's Greatest Hits* JOHNNY HORTON	CBS-Columbia	1
Dec 16	Cotton Candy AL HIRT	RCA Victor	2
18	My Fair Lady FILM SOUNDTRACK	CBS-Columbia	1
18	The Andy Williams Christmas Album* ANDY WILLIAMS	CBS-Columbia	4
18	Call Me Irresponsible ANDY WILLIAMS	CBS-Columbia	5
31	The Beatles' Story BEATLES	Capitol	4
31	Beatles '65 BEATLES	Capitol	5
31	Mary Poppins FILM SOUNDTRACK	Buena Vista	1

Date		Title and Artist	Label	No.

1965

Date		Title and Artist	Label	No.
Jan	21	Glad All Over DAVE CLARK FIVE	Epic	1
	21	Peter, Paul And Mary, In Concert PETER, PAUL & MARY	Warner Bros.	4
	29	Everybody Loves Somebody DEAN MARTIN	Reprise	1
Feb	11	Ring Of Fire JOHNNY CASH	CBS-Columbia	1
	11	Wonderland Of Golden Hits ANDRE KOSTELANETZ	CBS-Columbia	1
	18	All Summer Long BEACH BOYS	Capitol	1
	18	The Beach Boys Concert BEACH BOYS	Capitol	2
	20	Sugar Lips AL HIRT	RCA Victor	3
Mar	23	People BARBRA STREISAND	CBS-Columbia	3
	30	The Sound Of Music FILM SOUNDTRACK	RCA Victor	1
Apr	26	Trini Lopez At PJ's TRINI LOPEZ	Warner Bros.	1
June	16	Getz/Gilberto STAN GETZ & JOAO GILBERTO	Verve	1
July	1	Beatles VI BEATLES	Capitol	6
	30	Dear Heart ANDY WILLIAMS	CBS-Columbia	6
Aug	23	Help! BEATLES	Capitol	7
	31	Introducing Herman's Hermits HERMAN'S HERMITS	MGM	1
	31	Herman's Hermits On Tour HERMAN'S HERMITS	MGM	2
Sep	1	Return Of Roger Miller ROGER MILLER	Smash	1
	1	More Golden Hits PLATTERS	Mercury	2
	17	Great Songs From My Fair Lady ANDY WILLIAMS	CBS-Columbia	7
	21	Gunfighter Ballads And Trail Songs* MARTY ROBINS	CBS-Columbia	1
	30	Look At Us SONNY & CHER	Atlantic	1
Oct	1	The Beach Boys Today BEACH BOYS	Capitol	3
	5	The Pink Rantha HENRY MANCINI	RCA Victor	3
	12	Out Of Our Heads ROLLING STONES	London	1
	28	Fidler On the Roof ORIGINAL CAST	RCA Victor	1
Nov	15	Surfin' USA BEACH BOYS	Capitol	4
	15	Surfer Girl BEACH BOYS	Capitol	5
	15	Sinatra's Sinatra FRANK SINATRA	Reprise	6
	30	Welcome To The LBJ Ranch VARIOUS ARTISTS	Capitol	1
Dec	2	The Door Is Still Open To My Heart DEAN MARTIN	Reprise	2
	2	My Name Is Barbra BARBRA STREISAND	CBS-Columbia	4
	15	Whipped Cream And Other Delights HERB ALPERT/TIJUANA BRASS	A&M	1

Date		Title and Artist	Label	No.
	15	Going Places HERB ALPERT/TIJUANA BRASS	A&M	2
	24	Rubber Soul BEATLES	Capitol	8

1966

Date		Title and Artist	Label	No.
Jan	4	My Name Is Barbra, Two* BARBRA STREISAND	CBS-Columbia	5
	11	The Best Of Herman's Hermits HERMAN'S HERMITS	MGM	3
	15	December's Children (And Everybodies) ROLLING STONES	London	2
	29	Joan Baez JOAN BAEZ	Vanguard	1
	29	Joan Baez, Volume 2 JOAN BAEZ	Vanguard	2
	29	Joan Baez In Concert JOAN BAEZ	Vanguard	3
Feb	2	Summer Days BEACH BOYS	Capitol	6
	6	September Of My Years FRANK SINATRA	Reprise	7
	6	A Man And His Music FRANK SINATRA	Reprise	8
	11	Golden Hits ROGER MILLER	Smash	2
	17	Ballads Of The Green Berets STAFF SGT. BARRY SADLER	RCA Victor	1
Mar	24	Roy Orbison's Greatest Hits ROY ORBISON	Monument	1
Apr	5	Young People's Living Language: Spanish TUITION RECORD	YPLL	1
	5	Young People's Living Language: French TUITION RECORD	YPLL	2
	20	Color Me Barbra BARBRA STREISAND	CBS-Columbia	6
	25	I'm The One Who Loves You DEAN MARTIN	Reprise	3
	27	Big Hits (High Tide And Green Grass) ROLLING STONES	London	3
May	4	Oliver ORIGINAL CAST	RCA Victor	1
	9	The Lonely Bull HERB ALPERT/TIJUANA BRASS	A&M	3
	9	Herb Alpert's Tijuana Brass Vol. 2 HERB ALPERT/TIJUANA BRASS	A&M	4
	9	South Of The Border HERB ALPERT/TIJUANA BRASS	A&M	5
	9	What Now My Love HERB ALPERT/TIJUANA BRASS	A&M	6
	12	My World EDDY ARNOLD	RCA Victor	1
	16	South Pacific ORIGINAL CAST	CBS-Columbia	1
June	10	If You Can Believe Your Eyes & Ears MAMAS & PAPAS	Dunhill	1
July	8	Yesterday And Today BEATLES	Capitol	9
	20	The Best Of Jim Reeves JIM REEVES	RCA Victor	1
	28	The Best Of The Animals ANIMALS	MGM	1

Date		Title and Artist	Label	No.
Aug	4	Gold Vault Of Hits FOUR SEASONS	Philips	1
	4	Roger And Out ROGER MILLER	Smash	3
	9	Aftermath ROLLING STONES	London	4
	11	Dr. Zhivago FILM SOUNDTRACK	MGM	1
	16	Strangers In The Night FRANK SINATRA	Reprise	9
	16	Think Ethnic SMOTHERS BROTHERS	Mercury	1
	22	Revolver BEATLES	Capitol	10
	24	The Dave Clark Five's Greatest Hits DAVE CLARK FIVE	Epic	2
Sep	20	Somewhere My Love* RAY CONNIFF	CBS-Columbia	6
	27	The Shadow Of Your Smile ANDY WILLIAMS	CBS-Columbia	8
Oct	11	The Best Of Al Hirt AL HIRT	RCA Victor	4
	14	Bill Cosby Is A Very Funny Fellow, Right!* BILL COSBY	Warner Bros.	1
	14	I Started Out As A Child* BILL COSBY	Warner Bros.	2
	14	Why Is There Air? BILL COSBY	Warner Bros.	3
	14	Wonderfulness* BILL COSBY	Warner Bros.	4
	27	Perry Como Singes Merry Christmas Music PERRY COMO	RCA Camden	2
	27	Favourites In Hi Fi JEANETTE MACDONALD & NELSON EDDY	RCA Victor	1
	27	The Monkees MONKEES	Colgems	1
Nov	1	Elvis Presley ELVIS PRESLEY	RCA Victor	4
	1	Elvis' Golden Records, Volume 2 ELVIS PRESLEY	RCA Victor	5
	1	Elvis' Golden Records, Volume 3 ELVIS PRESLEY	RCA Victor	6
	7	Boots NANCY SINATRA	Reprise	1
	11	Dean Martin Hits Again DEAN MARTIN	Reprise	4
	28	Soul And Inspiration RIGHTEOUS BROTHERS	Verve	1
Dec	1	The Mamas And The Papas MAMAS & PAPAS	Dunhill	2
	12	Bobby Vinton's Greatest Hits BOBBY VINTON	Epic	1
	21	Little Deuce Coupe BEACH BOYS	Capitol	7
	21	Shut Down, Volume 2 BEACH BOYS	Capitol	8
	21	Winchester Cathedral NEW VAUDEVILLE BAND	Fontana	1
	30	Spanish Eyes AL MARTINO	Capitol	1

1967

Date		Title and Artist	Label	No.
Jan	6	More Of The Monkees MONKEES	Colgems	2

Date		Title and Artist	Label	No.
	6	Just Like us PAUL REVERE/RAIDERS	CBS-Columbia	1
	19	S.R.O. HERB ALPERT/TIJUANA BRASS	A&M	7
	19	Got Live If You Want It ROLLING STONES	London	5
	20	Songs Of The Fabulous Fifties ROGER WILLIAMS	Kapp	1
	20	Till ROGER WILLIAMS	Kapp	2
	20	More Songs Of The Fabulous Fifties ROGER WILLIAMS	Kapp	3
	20	Roger Williams' Greatest Hits ROGER WILLIAMS	Kapp	4
Feb	7	Yakety Sax BOOTS RANDOLF	Monument	1
	7	That's Life FRANK SINATRA	Reprise	10
	16	Lou Rawls Live! LOU RAWLS	Capitol	1
	22	The Two Sides Of The Smothers Brothers SMOTHERS BROTHERS	Mercury	2
	24	Between The Buttons ROLLING STONES	London	6
Mar	20	Midnight Ride PAUL REVERE/RAIDERS	CBS-Columbia	2
Apr	7	Thoroughly Modern Millie FILM SOUNDTRACK	US Decca	1
	10	An Evening With Belafonte HARRY BELAFONTE	RCA Victor	6
	10	The Best Of Mancini HENRY MANCINI	RCA Victor	4
	12	The Best Of The Beach Boys BEACH BOYS	Capitol	9
	17	Spirit Of '67 PAUL REVERE/RAIDERS	CBS-Columbia	3
	17	Winchester Cathedral LAWRENCE WELK	Dot	2
	20	The Mamas And The Papas Deliver MAMAS & PAPAS	Dunhill	3
May	14	Mame ORIGINAL CAST	CBS-Columbia	1
	19	My Cup Runneth Over ED AMES	RCA Victor	1
	19	Headquarters MONKEES	Colgems	3
June	1	Stranger On The Shore MR ACKER BILK	Atco	1
	13	I Never Loved A Man The Way I Love You ARETHA FRANKLIN	Atlantic	1
	15	Sergeant Pepper's Lonely Heart's Club Band BEATLES	Capitol	11
	28	The Man Of La Mancha ORIGINAL CAST	Kapp	1
	30	Revenge BILL COSBY	Warner Bros.	5
July	6	Parsley, Sage, Rosemary And Thyme* SIMON & GARFUNKEL	CBS-Columbia	1
	6	Born Free ANDY WILLIAMS	CBS-Columbia	9
	7	The Best Of The Lovin' Spoonful LOVIN' SPOONFUL	Kama Sutra	1
	14	I Walk The Line JOHNNY CASH	CBS-Columbia	2

Date	Title and Artist	Label	No.
14	Themes For Young Lovers PERCY FAITH	CBS-Columbia	4
24	Surrealistic Pillow JEFFERSON AIRPLANE	RCA Victor	1
Aug 16	Flowers ROLLING STONES	London	7
22	A Man And A Woman FILM SOUNDTRACK	United Artists	1
24	Ebb Tide EARL GRANT	US Decca	1
24	Blue Midnight BERT KAEMPFERT	US Decca	1
25	Sounds Like HERB ALPERT/TIJUANA BRASS	A&M	8
25	Bringing It All Back Home BOB DYLAN	CBS-Columbia	1
25	Highway 61 Revisited BOB DYLAN	CBS-Columbia	2
25	Blonde On Blonde BOB DYLAN	CBS-Columbia	3
25	Sergio Mendes And Brasil '66 SERGIO MENDES/BRASIL '66	A&M	1
25	Paul Revere And The Raiders' Greatest Hits PAUL REVERE/RAIDERS	CBS-Columbia	4
25	Sound Of Silence SIMON & GARFUNKEL	CBS-Columbia	2
Sep 11	The Doors* DOORS	Elektra	1
13	Second Vault Of Golden Hits FOUR SEASONS	Philips	2
Oct 9	Ode To Billy Joe BOBBIE GENTRY	Capitol	1
17	Tony Bennett's Greatest Hits Vol. 3 TONY BENNETT	CBS-Columbia	2
Nov 2	Pisces, Aquarius, Capricorn & Jones, Ltd. MONKEES	Colgems	4
27	Along Comes The Association ASSOCIATION	Warner Bros.	1
27	Sinatra At The Sands FRANK SINATRA	Reprise	1
Dec 6	Release Me ENGLEBERT HUMPERDINCK	Parrot	1
6	Their Satanic Majesties' Request ROLLING STONES	London	8
8	Herb Alpert's Ninth HERB ALPERT/TIJUANA BRASS	A&M	9
15	Magical Mystery Tour BEATLES	Capitol	12
15	We Wish You A Merry Christmas RAY CONNIFF	CBS-Columbia	7
21	The Button Down Mind Strikes Back BOB NEWHART	Warner Bros.	2
28	Insight Out ASSOCIATION	Warner Bros.	2

1968

Date	Title and Artist	Label	No.
Jan 5	Bob Dylan's Greatest Hits* BOB DYLAN	CBS-Columbia	4
5	Jim Nabors Sings Love Me With All Of Your heart JIM NABORS	CBS-Columbia	1
12	Strange Days DOORS	Elektra	2

Date	Title and Artist	Label	No.
Feb 2	Dream With Dean DEAN MARTIN	Reprise	5
7	Guantanamera SANDPIPERS	A&M	1
9	Farewell To The First Golden Era MAMAS & PAPAS	Dunhill	4
16	How Great Thou Art ELVIS PRESLEY	RCA Victor	7
26	Distant Drums JIM REEVES	RCA Victor	2
27	Blooming Hits PAUL MAURIAT	Philips	1
Mar 6	The Best Of Buck Owens BUCK OWENS	Capitol	1
13	The Byrds' Greatest Hit* BYRDS	CBS-Columbia	1
13	Doctor Dolittle FILM SOUNDTRACK	20th Century Fox	1
19	John Wesley Harding BOB DYLAN	CBS-Columbia	5
19	Are You Experienced?* JIMI HENDRIX	Reprise	1
19	Houston DEAN MARTIN	Reprise	6
19	Welcome To My World DEAN MARTIN	Reprise	7
27	The Graduate SIMON & GARFUNKEL	CBS-Columbia	3
28	The Best Of Eddy Arnold EDDY ARNOLD	RCA Victor	2
Apr 6	Ray Charles Greatest Hits RAY CHARLES	ABC Paramount	2
6	Modern Sounds In Country And Western Music, Volume 2 RAY CHARLES	ABC Paramount	3
9	Loving You ELVIS PRESLEY	RCA Victor	8
12	The Turtles' Golden Hits TURTLES	White Whale	1
17	The Birds, The Bees And The Monkees MONKEES	Colgems	5
17	Gigi FILM SOUNDTRACK	MGM	1
18	Bookends* SIMON & GARFUNKEL	CBS-Columbia	4
May 2	Somewhere There's A Someone DEAN MARTIN	Reprise	8
7	Nashville Skyline* BOB DYLAN	CBS-Columbia	5
8	Songs I Sing On The Jackie Gleeson Show FRANK FONTAINE	ABC Paramount	1
8	Persuasive Percussion ENOCH LIGHT	Command	1
14	Love, Andy ANDY WILLIAMS	CBS-Columbia	10
17	Doris Day's Greatest Hits DORIS DAY	CBS-Columbia	1
22	Disraeli Gears CREAM	Atco	1
23	Merry Christmas ANDY WILLIAMS	CBS-Columbia	11
July 2	Glenn Miller And His Orchestra GLENN MILLER	RCA Victor	2
12	To Russell, My Brother, Whom I Slept With BILL COSBY	Warner Bros.	6

Date	Title and Artist	Label	No.
19	The Beat Of The Brass HERB ALPERT/TIJUANA BRASS	A&M	10
22	Wheels Of Fire CREAM	Atco	2
22	Groovin' YOUNG RASCALS	Atlantic	1
23	Vanilla Fudge VANILLA FUDGE	Atlantic	1
29	Collections YOUNG RASCALS	Atlantic	2
30	Somewhere My Love ROGER WILLIAMS	Kapp	5
Aug 6	Waiting For The Sun* DOORS	Elektra	3
14	The Good, The Bad And The Ugly FILM SOUNDTRACK	United Artists	1
23	Aretha — Lady Soul ARETHA FRANKLIN	Atlantic	2
Sep 4	Look Around SERGIO MENDES/BRASIL '66	A&M	2
4	The Young Rascals[2] YOUNG RASCALS	Atlantic	3
4	Time Peace/The Rascals Greatest Hits[2] RASCALS	Atlantic	4
17	Camelot* FILM SOUNDTRACK	Warner Bros.	1
Oct 4	Feliciano JOSE FELICIANO	RCA Victor	1
10	Axis: Bold As Love* JIMI HENDRIX	Reprise	2
15	Cheap Thrills*[3] BIG BROTHER & THE HOLDING COMPANY	CBS-Columbia	1
17	Gentle On My Mind GLEN CAMPBELL	Capitol	1
17	By The Time I Get To Phoenix GLEN CAMPBELL	Capiotl	2
30	Johnny Cash At Folsom Prison* JOHNNY CASH	CBS-Columbia	3
30	My Love Forgive Me ROBERT GOULET	CBS-Columbia	1
Nov 1	Honey ANDY WILLIAMS	CBS-Columbia	12
13	The Songs And Comedy Of The Smothers Brothers SMOTHERS BROTHERS	Mercury	3
18	Wichita Lineman GLEN CAMPBELL	Capitol	3
18	Electric Ladyland* JIMI HENDRIX	Reprise	3
25	The Kinks Greatest Hits KINKS	Reprise	1
27	Honey BOBBY GOLDSBORO	United Artists	1
27	The Dean Martin Christmas Album DEAN MARTIN	Reprise	9
27	Steppenwolf STEPPENWOLF	Dunhill	1
Dec 3	Fresh Cream CREAM	Atco	3
3	Aretha Now ARETHA FRANKLIN	Atlantic	3
3	In-A-Gadda-Da-Vida IRON BUTTERFLY	Atco	1
4	The Time Has Come CHAMBERS BROTHERS	CBS-Columbia	1
5	Walt Disney Presents Jungle Book FILM SOUNDTRACK	Disneyland	1

Date	Title and Artist	Label	No.
6	The Beatles (The White Album) BEATLES	Apple	13
16	The Christmas Album HERB ALPERT/TIJUANA BRASS	A&M	11
23	Beggars Banquette ROLLING STONES	London	9
23	Funny Girl BARBRA STREISAND	CBS-Columbia	7
30	The Sea SAN SEBASTIAN STRINGS	Warner Bros.	1

1969

Date	Title and Artist	Label	No.
Jan 2	The Story Of Mary Poppins STORYTELLER LP	Disneyland	1
17	The Christmas Song NAT 'KING' COLE	Capitol	4
17	The Lettermen!!!...And Live LETTERMEN	Capitol	1
20	Wildflowers JUDY COLLINS	Elektra	1
27	Album 1700 PETER, PAUL & MARY	Warner Bros.	5
29	Bobbie Gentry And Glen Campbell BOBBIE GENTRY & GLEN CAMPBELL	Capitol	2 & 4
Feb 2	Who Will Answer? ED AMES	RCA Victor	2
3	Dean Martin's Greatest Hits! Vol. 1 DEAN MARTIN	Reprise	10
5	Yellow Submarine BEATLES	Apple	14
12	Steppenwolf The Second STEPPENWOLF	Dunhill	2
18	Boots With Strings BOOTS RANDOLPH	Monument	2
24	Dionne Warwick's Greatest Motion Picture Hits DIONNE WARWICK	Scepter	1
27	The Last Waltz ENGLEBERT HUMPERDINCK	Parrot	2
27	A Man Without Love ENGLEBERT HUMPERDINCK	Parrot	3
Mar 3	The Association's Greatest Hits* ASSOCIATION	Warner Bros.	3
3	Wonderland By Night BERT KAEMPFERT	US Decca	2
3	Bert Kaempfert's Greatest Hits BERT KAEMPFERT	US Decca	3
4	Wednesday Morning, 3 A.M. SIMON & GARFUNKEL	CBS-Columbia	5
10	Sing We Now Of Christmas HARRY SIMEONE CHORALE	20th Century Fox	1
21	200 MPH BILL COSBY	Warner Bros.	7
25	It Must Be Him RAY CONNIFF	CBS-Columbia	8
25	Hair ORIGINAL CAST	RCA Victor	1
25	Young Girl GARY PUCKETT/UNION GAP	CBS-Columbia	1
28	The Great Caruso MARIO LANZA	RCA Victor	2
Apr 9	His Hand In Mine ELVIS PRESLEY	RCA Victor	9
10	Blood, Sweat And Tears* BLOOD, SWEAT & TEARS	CBS-Columbia	1

Date		Title and Artist	Label	No.
	21	Goodbye CREAM	Atco	4
	21	Freedom Suite RASCALS	Atlantic	5
	22	Donovan's Greatest Hits DONOVAN	Epic	1
	24	Soulin' LOU RAWLS	Capitol	2
	24	2001: A Space Odyssey FILM SOUNDTRACK	MGM	1
May	5	The Best Of The Lettermen LETTERMEN	Capitol	2
	7	The Tom Jones Fever Zone TOM JONES	Parrot	1
	7	Help Yourself TOM JONES	Parrot	2
	26	Equinox SERGIO MENDES/BRASIL '66	A&M	3
	26	Fool On The Hill SERGIO MENDES/BRASIL '66	A&M	4
	26	A Day In The Life WES MONTGOMERY	A&M	1
	29	Harper Valley PTA JEANNIE C. RILEY	Plantation	1
June	4	This Is Tome Jones TOME JONES	Parrot	3
	11	The Very Best Of Connie Francis CONNIE FRANCIS	MGM	1
	13	The Best Of Herman's Hermits Vol. 2 HERMAN'S HERMITS	MGM	4
	13	There's A Kind Of Hush All Over The World HERMAN'S HERMITS	MGM	5
July	3	Tom Jones Live TOM JONES	Parrot	4
	3	Romeo And Juliet FILM SOUNDTRACK	Capitol	1
	14	The Age Of Aquarius FIFTH DIMENSION	Soul City	1
	22	Led Zeppelin LED ZEPPELIN	Atlantic	1
	22	Elvis (TV Special) ELVIS PRESLEY	RCA Victor	10
	24	Johnny Cash's Greatest Hits* JOHNNY CASH	CBS-Columbia	4
	25	Oliver FILM SOUNDTRACK	Colgems	1
	27	Ball IRON BUTTERFLY	Atco	2
Aug	5	The Soft Parade* DOORS	Elektra	4
	12	Johnny Cash At San Quentin* JOHNNY CASH	CBS-Columbia	5
	14	Switched On Bach* WALTER CARLOS	CBS-Columbia	1
	15	Three Dog Night THREE DOG NIGHT	Dunhill	1
	18	Tommy WHO	US Decca	1
	19	Blind Faith BLIND FAITH	Atco	1
	20	Happy Heart ANDY WILLIAMS	CBS-Columbia	13
	30	Gentle On My Mind DEAN MARTIN	Reprise	11

Date		Title and Artist	Label	No.
Sep	9	Music From 'A Fistful Of Dollars' & 'For A Few Dollars More' & 'The Good, The Bad And The Ugly' HUGO MONTENGRO	RCA Victor	1
	9	Through The Past, Darkly (Big Hits Volume 2) ROLLING STONES	London	10
	12	A Warm Shade Of Ivory HENRY MANCINI	RCA Victor	5
	29	Alice's Restaurant* ARLO GUTHRIE	Reprise	1
	29	Golden Greats GARY LEWIS	Liberty	1
	29	Realization JOHNNY RIVERS	United Artisats	1
	30	Crosby, Stills And Nash CROSBY, STILLS & NASH	Atlantic	1
Oct	8	Who Knows Where The Time Goes JUDDY COLLINS	Elektra	2
	10	Golden Instrumentals BILLY VAUGHN	Dot	4
	14	Smash Hits* JIMI HENDRIX	Reprise	4
	27	Abbey Road BEATLES	Apple	15
	27	Tom Jones — Live At Las Vegas TOM JONES	Parrot	5
Nov	10	The Best Of The Bee Gees BEE GEES	Atco	1
	10	The Best Of Cream CREAM	Atco	5
	10	Led Zeppelin II LED ZEPPELIN	Atlantic	2
	24	The Green, Green, Grass Of Home TOM JONES	Parrot	6
	24	Let It Bleed ROLLING STONES	London	11
	26	The Band BAND	Capitol	1
Dec	2	The Child Is Father To The Man BLOOD, SWEAT & TEARS	CBS-Columbia	2
	2	Santana* SANTANA	CBS-Columbia	1
	3	I Got Dem Ol' Kozmic Blues Again Mama JANIS JOPLIN	CBS-Columbia	1
	4	Stand!* SLY/FAMILY STONE	Epic	1
	12	Hot Buttered Soul ISAAC HAYES	Enterprise	1
	12	From, Memphis To Vegas/From Vegas To Memphis ELVIS PRESLEY	RCA Victor	11
	12	Cycles FRANK SINATRA	Reprise	12
	12	Suitable For Framing THREE DOG NIGHT	Dunhill	2
	17	Chicago Transit Authority* CHICAGO	CBS-Columbia	1
	24	Honey RAY CONNIFF	CBS-Columbia	9
	24	The Buddy Holly Story BUDDY HOLLY/CRICKETS	Coral	1

AWARD WINNERS

This appendix gives the winners of the main sections in the annual popularity polls of the British pop papers, the US Grammy winners, and top records by chart performance and sales in Britain and America.

TOP BRITISH MALE SINGER

Year	NME	MM	RM	D
1960	Cliff Richard	Cliff Richard	—	—
1961	Cliff Richard	Cliff Richard	—	—
1962	Cliff Richard	Cliff Richard	—	—
1963	Cliff Richard	Cliff Richard	—	—
1964	Cliff Richard	Cliff Richard	Cliff Richard	—
1965	Cliff Richard	Cliff Richard	Cliff Richard	Cliff Richard
1966	Cliff Richard	Tom Jones	Cliff Richard	Cliff Richard
1967	Tom Jones	Cliff Richard	Tom Jones	Tom Jones
1968	Tom Jones	Tom Jones	Tom Jones	Tom Jones
1969	Tom Jones	Tom Jones	—	Tom Jones

TOP BRITISH FEMALE SINGER

Year	NME	MM	RM	D
1960	Shirley Bassey	Shirely Bassey	—	—
1961	Helen Shapiro	Shirley Bassey	—	—
1962	Helen Shapiro	Helen Shapiro	—	—
1963	Kathy Kirby	Susan Maughan	—	—
1964	Dusty Springfield	Cilla Black	Cilla Black	—
1965	Dusty Springfield	Sandie Shaw	Sandie Shaw	Sandie Shaw
1966	Dusty Springfield	Dusty Springfield	Dusty Springfield	Dusty springfield
1967	Lulu	Dusty Springfield	Dusty Springfield	Lulu
1968	Lulu	Julie Driscol	Lulu	Lulu
1969	Lulu	Christine Perfect	—	Cilla Black

TOP BRITISH VOCAL PERSONALITY

Year	NME
1960	Lonnie Donegan
1961	Adam Faith
1962	Joe Brown
1963	Joe Brown
1964	Cliff Richard
1965	John Lennon
1966	Cliff Richard
1967	Cliff Richard
1968	Cliff Richard
1969	Cliff Richard

TOP WORLD MUSICAL PERSONALITY

NME
Duane Eddy
Elvis Presley
Elvis Presley
Elvis Presley
Elvis Presley
Elvis Presley
Elvis Presley
Elvis Presley
Elvis Presley
Elvis Presley

TOP BRITISH VOCAL GROUP

Year	NME	MM	RM	D
1960	King Brothers	Polka Dots	—	—
1961	Springfields	King Brothers	—	—
1962	Springfields	Springfields	—	—
1963	Beatles	Beatles	—	—
1964	Beatles	Beatles	Rolling Stones	—
1965	Beatles	Beatles	Beatles	Beatles
1966	Beatles	Beatles	Beatles	Beatles
1967	Beatles	Beatles	Beatles	Beatles
1968	Beatles	Beatles	Beatles	Beatles
1969	Beatles	Beatles	Beatles	Beatles

TOP WORLD VOCAL GROUP

Year	NME	MM	RM	D
1960	Everly Brothers	—	—	—
1961	Everly Brothers	—	—	—
1962	Everly Brothers	—	—	—
1963	Beatles	Four Seasons	—	—
1964	Beatles	Beatles	Beatles	—
1965	Beatles	Beatles	Beatles	Beatles
1966	Beach Boys	Beatles	Beach Boys	Beatles
1967	Beatles	Beatles	Beatles	Beatles
1968	Beatles	Beatles	Beatles	Beatles
1969	Beatles	Beatles	—	Beatles

TOP BRITISH/WORLD INSTRUMENTAL GROUP

Year	NME	MM	RM	D
1960	Shadows	—	—	—
1961	Shadows	Shadows	—	—
1962	Shadows	Shadows	—	—
1963	Shadows	Shadows	—	—
1964	Shadows	Shadows	Shadows	—
1965	Shadows	Shadows	Shadows	—
1966	Shadows	Shadows	Shadows	—
1967	Shadows	Shadows	Shadows	—
1968	Shadows	Shadows	Shadows	—
1969	Shadows	Shadows	—	—

TOP WORLD MALE SINGER

Year	NME	MM	RM	D
1960	Elvis Presley	—	—	—
1961	Elvis Presley	—	—	—
1962	Elvis Presley	—	—	—
1963	Cliff Richard	Elvis Presley	—	—
1964	Elvis Presley	Elvis Presley	Elvis Presley	—
1965	Elvis Presley	Elvis Presley	Elvis Presley	Gene Pitney
1966	Elvis Presley	Elvis Presley	Elvis Presley	Elvis Presley
1967	Elvis Presley	Otis Redding	Elvis Presley	Scott Walker
1968	Elvis Presley	Bob Dylan	Elvis Presley	Scott Walker
1969	Elvis Presley	Bob Dylan	—	Elvis Presley

TOP WORLD FEMALE SINGER

Year	NME	MM	RM	D
1960	Connie Francis	—	—	—
1961	Connie Francis	—	—	—
1962	Breda Lee	—	—	—
1963	Brenda Lee	Brenda Lee	—	—
1964	Brenda Lee	Mary Wells	Brenda Lee	—
1965	Dusty Springfield	Brenda Lee	Brenda Lee	Dusty Springfield
1966	Dusty Springfield	Dusty Springfield	Cher	Dusty Springfield
1967	Dusty Springfield	Dusty Springfield	Dusty Springfield	Dusty Springfield
1968	Lulu	Aretha Franklin	Dusty Springfield	Aretha Franklin
1969	Dusty Springfield	Janis Joplin	—	Lulu

TOP WORLD INSTRUMENTALIST

Year	NME	MM	RM	D
1965	—	Burt Bacharach	—	—
1966	—	Herb Alpert	—	—
1967	—	Jimi Hendrix	Hank B. Marvin	Jimi Hendrix
1968	—	Eric Clapton	Mason Williams	Jimi Hendrix
1969	—	Eric Clapton	—	Eric Clapton

TOP BRITISH INSTRUMENTALIST

Year	NME	MM	RM	D
1960	Russ Conway	Bert Weedon	—	—
1961	Bert Weedon	Bert Weedon	—	—
1962	Jet Harris	Acker Bilk	—	—
1963	Jet Harris	Jet Harris	—	—
1964	—	Hank B. Marvin	—	—
1965	—	Hank B. Marvin	—	—
1966	—	Hank B. Marvin	—	—
1967	—	Eric Clapton	—	Hank B. Marvin
1968	—	Eric Clapton	—	Hank B. Marvin
1969	—	Eric Clapton	—	Eric Clapton

TOP NEW SINGER (BRITISH)

Year	NME	MM	RM	D
1960	Emile Ford	—	—	—
1961	John Leyton	—	—	—
1962	Frank Ifield	Helen Shapiro	—	—
1963	Gerry Marsden	Billy J. Kramer	—	—
1964	Mick Jagger	Lulu	—	—
1965	Donovan	Donovan	Donovan	Wayne Fontana
1966	Stevie Winwood	—	Chris Farlowe	Cat Stevens
1967	Engelbert Humperdinck	—	—	—
1968	Mary Hopkin	Julie Driscol	Mary Hopkin	Mary Hopkin
1969	Clodagh Rodgers	—	—	—

TOP NEW GROUP (BRITISH)

Year	NME	MM	RM	D
1964	Rolling Stones	—	—	—
1965	Seekers	—	—	—
1966	Spencer Davis Group	Troggs	—	—
1967	Bee Gees	Procul Harum	—	Herd
1968	Love Affair	—	—	—
1969	Jethro Tull	Blind Faith	—	—

BEST DRESSED SINGER (WORLD)

Year	NME	MM	RM	D
1964	—	—	Cliff Richard	—
1965	—	—	Cliff Richard	—
1966	—	—	—	Cliff Richard
1967	—	—	—	Cliff Richard
1968	—	—	Elvis Presley	Cliff Richard
1969	—	—	—	Cliff Richard

TOP BRITISH ARTISTS

Year	MR VALENTINE	MISS VALENTINE	WORLD FEMALE GROUP
1964	—	—	Crystals
1965	—	—	Supremes
1966	Scott Walker	Dusty Springfield	Supremes
1967	Scott Walker	Lulu	Supremes
1968	Scott Walker	Lulu	Supremes
1969	Cliff Richard	Lulu	Supremes

The Mr and Miss Valentine sections came from the *Disc* polls, and the World Female Group section from *Record Mirror*.

TOP BRITISH DISC JOCKEY

Year	NME	MM	RM	D
1960	David Jacobs	David Jacobs	—	—
1961	David Jacobs	David Jacobs	—	—
1962	David Jacobs	David Jacobs	—	—
1963	David Jacobs	David Jacobs	—	—
1964	Jimmy Savile	Jimmy Savile	Jimmy Savile	—
1965	Jimmy Savile	Jimmy Savile	Jimmy Savile	Jimmy Savile
1966	Jimmy Savile	Jimmy Savile	Jimmy Savile	Jimmy Savile
1967	Jimmy Savile & Tony Blackburn tied	Jimmy Savile	—	Simon Dee
1968	Jimmy Savile	John Peel	John Peel	Kenny Everett
1969	Jimmy Savile	John Peel	—	Tong Blackburn

TOP BRITISH TV POP SHOW

Year	NME	MM	RM
1960	—	Boy Meets Girl (ABC)	—
1961	—	Juke Box Jury (BBC)	—
1962	—	Thank Your Luck Stars (ABC)	—
1963	—	Lucky Stars Summer Spin (ABC)	—
1964	Ready Steady Go (ITV)	Ready Steady Go (ITV)	—
1965	Top Of The Pops (BBC)	Ready Steady Go (ITV)	Top Of The Pops (BBC)
1966	Top Of The Pops (BBC)	Top Of The Pops (BBC)	Top Of The Pops (BBC)
1967	Top Of The Pops (BBC)	Top Of The Pops (BBC)	Top Of The Pops (BBC)
1968	Top Of The Pops (BBC)	Top Of The Pops (BBC)	Top Of The Pops (BBC)
1969	Top Of The Pops (BBC)	Colour Me Pop (BBC)	—

SINGLE OF THE YEAR

Year	Title and Artist	Label	Poll
1960	Apache SHADOWS	Columbia	NME
	Living Doll CLIFF RICHARD/SHADOWS	Columbia	MM
1961	Johnny Remember Me JOHN LEYTON	Top Rank	NME
	Apache+ SHADOWS	Columbia	MM
	Portrait Of My love* MATT MONRO	Parlophone	MM

269

1962	I Remember You	Columbia	NME
	FRANK IFIELD		
	The Young Ones*	Columbia	MM
	CLIFF RICHARD/SHADOWS		
	Stranger On The Shore+	Columbia	MM
	ACKER BILK		
1963	She Loves You	Parlophone	NME
	BEATLES		
	She Love You*	Parlophone	MM
	BEATLES		
	Diamonds+	Decca	MM
	JET HARRIS & TONY MEEHAN		
1964	House Of The Rising Sun	Columbia	NME
	ANIMALS		
	It's Over*	London	MM
	ROY ORBISON		
	The Rise And Fall Of Flingle Bunt+	Columbia	MM
	SHADOWS		
1965	Satisfaction	Decca	NME
	ROLLING STONES		
	Crying In The Chapel	RCA	RM
	ELVIS PRESLEY		
	Ticket To Ride*	Parlophone	MM
	BEATLES		
	Cast Your Fates To The Wind+	Piccadilly	MM
	SOUNDS ORCHESTRAL		
1966	Eleanor Rigby	Parlophone	NME
	BEATLES		
	Love Letters	RCA	RM
	ELVIS PRESLEY		
	Good Vibrations	Capitol	D
	BEACH BOYS		
	Paperback Writer*	Parlophone	MM
	BEATLES		
	The War Lord+	Columbia	MM
	SHADOWS		
1967	A White Shade Of Pale	Deram	AP
	PROCUL HARUM		
1968	Hey Jude	Parlophone	NME, D
	BEATLES		
	Jumping Jack Flash	Decca	MM
	ROLLING STONES		
	US Mail	RCA	RM
	ELVIS PRESLEY		
1969	Honky Tonk Women	Decca	NME
	ROLLING STONES		
	Get Back	Apple	MM, D
	BEATLES		

The above lists the discs that were voted 'Record Of The Year' in the various polls. The polls are identified by the initials of the paper in the last column. AP = All Polls. For most of the decade *Melody Maker* had separate polls for vocal records (indicated *) and instrumentals (indicated +)

ALBUM OF THE YEAR

Year	Title and Artist	Label	Poll
1966	Revolver	Parlophone	D
	BEATLES		
1967	Sgt Pepper's Lonely Hearts Club Band	Parlophone	D, MM
	BEATLES		
1968	The Beatles (2 LPs) (The White Album)	Parlophone	D
	BEATLES		
	John Wesley Harding	CBS	MM
	BOB DYLAN		
1969	Abbey Road	Apple	D
	BEATLES		
	Goodbye	Polydor	MM
	CREAM		

The above tables show the results of the main sections of the four weekly pop papers that were published in Britain throughout the decade. Not all sections have been used, and individual polls did not always run the same sections each year. There was no *Record Mirror* poll in 1969, probably because the paper had just been taken over at the time the poll would normally have taken place.

TOP SINGLES ARTIST IN BRITAIN

Year	Artist	Label(s)	Company
1960	Cliff Richard	Columbia	EMI
1961	Elvis Presley	RCA	Decca
1962	Elvis Presley	RCA	Decca
1963	Beatles	Parlophone	EMI
1964	Beatles	Parlophone	EMI
1965	Rolling Stones	Decca	Decca
1966	Beach Boys	Capitol	EMI
1967	Engelbert Humperdinck	Decca	Decca
1968	Tom Jones	Decca	Decca
1969	Fleetwood Mac	Immediate, Blue Horizon, Reprise	Various

The above list is from the *New Musical Express*, which calculated a table of the most popular stars based on an inverse points ratio. They gave 30 points for the No 1 record each week, down to one point for the No 30 disc. The list shows the artist and label for each year, and the record company owning the label (or releasing the label under license in the case of RCA.) The domination of Britain's two biggest record companies can be seen.

A points system based on the *Record Retailer* Top 50 is the basis of the top record for each year shown below. This tends to measure consistency, but has only an indirect relationship to sales. Acts like the Beatles, who sold very large quantities of records in a short space of time, were under-represented in these tables. An alternative way of measuring success is to start with those records that have spent longest at No 1, going down the charts comparing length of time spent at No 2, No 3 etc as a tie-breaker. That is what the Guinness team of Paul Gambaccini and Tim and Jo Rice have done in their *UK Top 1000 Singles* book, and the top record for each year according to this system is also given. Neither system necessarily identifies the biggest selling record of the year.

TOP CHART SINGLE IN BRITAIN

Year	Title and Artist	Label	Source
1960	Cathy's Clown EVERLY BROTHERS	Warner Bros.	RR
	It's Now Or Never ELVIS PRESLEY	RCA Victor	G
1961	Runaway DEL SHANNON	London	RR
	Wooden Heart ELVIS PRESLEY	RCA Victor	G
1962	Stranger On The Shore ACKER BILK	Columbia	RR
	Wonderful Land THE SHADOWS	Columbia	G
1963	From Me To You BEATLES	Parlophone	RR
	From Me To You BEATLES	Parlophone	G
1964	I Love You Because JIM REEVES	RCA Victor	RR
	You're My World CILLA BLACK	Parlophone	G
1965	I'll Never Find Another You THE SEEKERS	Columbia	RR
	Tears KEN DODD	Columbia	G
1966	Distant Drums JIM REEVES	RCA Victor	RR
	Distant Drums JIM REEVES	RCA Victor	G
1967	Release Me ENGELBERT HUMPERDINCK	Decca	RR
	Release Me ENGELBERT HUMPERDINCK	Decca	G
1968	What A Wonderful World LOUIS ARMSTRONG	HMV	RR
	Those Were The Days MARY HOPKIN	Apple	G
1969	My Way FRANK SINATRA	Reprise	RR
	Sugar Sugar THE ARCHIES	RCA Victor	G

TOP CHART SINGLE IN AMERICA

Year	Title and Artist	Label	Source
1960	Theme From A Summer Place PERCY FAITH	CBS/Columbia	CB W
1961	Exodus FERRANTE & TEICHER	United Artists	CB
	Tossing And Turning BOBBY LEWIS	Beltone	W
1962	Limbo Rock CHUBBY CHECKER	Parkway	CB
	I Can't Stop Loving You RAY CHARLES	ABC	W
1963	Limbo Rock CHUBBY CHECKER	Parkway	CB
	Sugar Shack JIMMY GILMER	Dot	W
1964	I Want To Hold Your Hand BEATLES	Capitol	CB W
1965	Back In My Arms Again SUPREMES	Motown	CB
	Satisfaction ROLLING STONES	London	W
1966	The Ball Of The Green Berets STAFF SGT BARRY SADLER	RCA Victor	CB
	I'm A Believer MONKEES	Colgems	W
1967	The Letter BOX TOPS	Mala	CB
	To Sir With Love LULU	Epic	W
1968	Hey Jude BEATLES	Apple	CB W
1969	Sugar Sugar ARCHIES	Calendar	CB
	Aquarius/Let The Sun Shine In 5TH DIMENSION	Soul City	W

A similar system to that used above is used with the American pop charts. Here the *Cash Box* Top 100 charts are used. (*Billboard* also did an annual survey, but theirs did not cover the whole year, ending in November.) The American chart expert Joel Whitburn provides the alternative system, similar to that used by the Guinness authors.

TOP CHART ALBUM IN BRITAIN

Year	Title and Artist	Label	Source
1960	South Pacific SOUNDTRACK	RCA Victor	RR
1961	G.I. Blues ELVIS PRESLEY	RCA Victor	RR
1962	The Young Ones CLIFF RICHARD/SHADOWS	Columbia	RR
1963	Please Please Me BEATLES	Parlophone	RR
1964	West Side Story SOUNDTRACK	Philips	RR
1965	Beatles For Sale BEATLES	Parlophone	RR
1966	The Sound Of Music SOUNDTRACK	RCA Victor	RR
1967	The Sound Of Music SOUNDTRACK	RCA Victor	RR
1968	The Sound Of Music SOUNDTRACK	RCA Victor	RR
1969	The Best Of The Seekers SEEKERS	Columbia	RR

Film soundtracks were very popular. Both the Elvis Presley and Cliff Richard LPs were also film soundtracks.

TOP CHART ALBUM IN AMERICA

Year	Title and Artist	Label	Source
1960	The Sound Of Music ORIGINAL BROADWAY CAST	CBS/Columbia	CB
1961	Camelot ORIGINAL BROADWAY CAST	CBS/Columbia	CB
1962	West Side Story SOUNDTRACK	CBS/Columbia	CB
1963	West Side Story SOUNDTRACK	CBS/Columbia	CB
1964	Meet The Beatles BEATLES	Capitol	CB
1965	Beatles For Sale BEATLES	Capitol	CB
1966	The Sound Of Music SOUNDTRACK	RCA Victor	CB
1967	Dr. Zhivago SOUNDTRACK	MGM	CB
1968	Disraeli Gears CREAM	Atco	CB
1969	Hair ORIGINAL CAST	RCA Victor	CB

TOP R&B CHART SINGLE IN AMERICA

Year	Title and Artist	Label	Source
1960	Kiddio BROOK BENTON	Mercury	BB
1961	Tossing And Turning BOBBY LEWIS	Beltone	BB
1962	Soul Twist KING CURTIS	Enjoy	BB
1963	Part Time Lover LITTLE JOHNNY TAYLOR	Galaxy	BB
1964	My Guy MARY WILSON	Motown	BB
1965	I Can't Help Myself FOUR TOPS	Motown	BB
1966	Hold On! I'm Coming SAM & DAVE	Stax	BB
1967	Respect ARETHA FRANKLIN	Atlantic	BB
1968	Say It Loud, I'm Black And I'm Proud JAMES BROWN	King	BB
1969	What Does It Take To Win Your Love? JUNIOR WALKER	Soul	BB

TOP C&W CHART SINGLE IN AMERICA

Year	Title and Artist	Label	Source
1960	Please Help Me I'm Falling HANK LOCKLIN	RCA Victor	BB
1961	I Fall To Pieces PATSY CLINE	US Decca	BB
1962	Wolverton Mountain CLAUD KING	CBS/Columbia	BB
1963	Still BILL ANDERSON	US Decca	BB
1964	My Heart Skips A Beat BUCK OWENS	Capitol	BB
1965	What's He Doing In My World EDDY ARNOLD	RCA Victor	BB
1966	Almost Persuaded DAVID HOUSTON	Epic	BB
1967	All The Time JACK GREEN	US Decca	BB
1968	Folsom Prison Blues JOHNNY CASH	CBS/Columbia	BB
1969	My Life BILL ANDERSON	US Decca	BB

NATIONAL ASSOCIATION OF RECORDING MERCHANDISERS AWARDS

Each year the members of NARAS give awards for what they believe to have been the biggest selling records in America in a number of categories. The awards are not based on actual sales figures from record companies, which are confidential, but on the observations of NARM members.

BIGGEST SELLING SINGLE IN AMERICA

Year	Title and Artist	Label
1960	Are You Lonesome Tonight? ELVIS PRESLEY	RCA Victor
1961	Big Bad John JIMMY DEAN	CBS/Columbia
1962	I Can't Stop Loving You RAY CHARLES	ABC-Paramount
1963	Dominique THE SINGING NUN	Philips
	Blue Velvet BOBBY VINTON	Epic
1964	I Want To Hold Your Hand BEATLES	Capitol
1965	Mrs Brown You've Got A Lovely Daughter HERMAN'S HERMITS	MGM
1966	I'm A Believer MONKEES	Colgems
1967	Daydream Believer MONKEES	Colgems
1968	Hey Jude BEATLES	Apple
1969	Sugar Sugar ARCHIES	Calendar

BIGGEST SELLING ALBUM IN AMERICA

Year	Title and Artist	Label
1960	Sixty Years Of Music, Vol 2 VARIOUS ARTISTS	RCA Victor
1961	Blue Hawaii ELVIS PRESLEY	RCA Victor
1962	First Family VAUGHN MEADER	Cadence
1963	Peter, Paul and Mary PETER, PAUL AND MARY	Warner Bros.
1964	Meet The Beatles BEATLES	Capitol
1965	Whipped Cream And Other Delights HERB ALPERT	A&M
1966	The Monkees MONKEES	Colgems
1967	Sgt. Pepper's Lonely Hearts Club Band BEATLES	Capitol
1968	The Beatles (2 LPs) (The White Album) BEATLES	Apple
1969	Abbey Road BEATLES	Apple

BIGGEST SELLING ARTIST IN AMERICA

Year	Male Singer	Female Singer	Group
1960	Elvis Presley	Connie Francis	Kingston Trio
1961	Elvis Presley	Connie Francis	Mitch Miller And The Gang
1962	Elvis Presley	Brenda Lee	Kingstone Trio/Peter, paul and Mary
1963	Andy Williams	Barbra Streisand	Peter, Paul And Mary
1964	Andy Williams	Barbra Streisand	Beatles
1965	Elvis Presley	Barbra Streisand	Beatles, Beach Boys and Supremes
1966	Dean Martin	Barbra Streisand	Herman's Hermits, Monkees and Rolling Stones
1967	Dean Martin	Aretha Franklin	Beatles and Monkees
1968	Glen Campbell	Aretha Franklin	Beatles
1969	Tom Jones	Dionne Warwick	Beatles

AMERICAN NATIONAL ACADEMY OF RECORDING ARTS AND SCIENCES GRAMMY WINNERS

Each year the members of NARAS select what they believe to have been the best of a wide selection of music available in America. Over the years NARAS changed some of the categories, so not all sections existed throughout the decade. The winners of the main categories are given below.

BEST SINGLE

Year	Title and Artist	Label
1960	Theme From A Summer Place PERCY FAITH	CBS/Columbia
1961	Moon River HENRY MANCINI	RCA Victor
1962	I Left My Heart In San Francisco TONY BENNETT	CBS/Columbia
1963	The Days Of Wine And Roses HENRY MANCINI	RCA Victor
1964	The Girl From Ipanema STAN GETZ/ASTRUD GILBERTO	Verve
1965	A Taste Of Honey HERB ALPERT	A&M
1966	Stranger In The Night FRANK SINATRA	Reprise
1967	Up, Up And Away 5TH DIMENSION	Soul City
1968	Mrs. Robinson SIMON & GARFUNKEL	CBS/Columbia
1969	Aquarius/Let The Sunshine In 5TH DIMENSION	Soul City

BEST ALBUM

Year	Title and Artist	Label
1960	Button Down Mind Of Bob Newhart BOB NEWHART	Warner Bros.
1961	Judy At Carnegy Hall JUDY GARLAND	Capitol
1962	The First Family VAUGHN MEADER	Cadence
1963	The Barbra Streisand Album BARBRA STREISAND	CBS/Columbia
1964	Getz/Gilberto STAN GETZ/ASTRUD GILBERTO	Verve
1965	September Of My Years FRANK SINATRA	Reprise
1966	Sinatra: A Man And His Music FRANK SINATRA	Reprise
1967	Sgt Pepper's Lonely Hearts Club Band BEATLES	Capitol
1968	By The Time I Get To Phoenix GLENN CAMPBELL	Capitol
1969	Blood, Sweat And Tears BLOOD, SWEAT AND TEARS	CBS/Columbia

BEST SONG

Year	Title	Writer(s)
1960	Theme From Exodus	Ernest Gold
1961	Moon River	Henry Mancini and Johnny Mercer
1962	What Kind Of Fool Am I?	Leslie Briscussi and Anthony Newley
1963	The Days Of Wine And Roses	Henry Mancini and Johnny Mercer
1964	Hello, Dolly!	Jerry Herman
1965	The Shadow Of Your Smile	Paul Webster and Johnny Mandel
1966	Michelle	John Lennon and Paul McCartney
1967	Up, Up And Away	Jim Webb
1968	Little Green Apples	Bobby Russell
1969	Games People Play	Joe South

BEST VOCAL PERFORMANCE, MALE

Year	Title and Artist	Label
1960	Georgia On My Mind RAY CHARLES	ABC-Paramount
1961	Lollipops And Roses JACK JONES	Kapp
1962	I Left My Heart In San Francisco TONY BENNETT	CBS/Columbia
1963	Wives And Lovers JACK JONES	Kapp
1964	Hello, Dolly! LOUIS ARMSTRONG	Kapp
1965	It Was A Very Good Year FRANK SINATRA	Reprise
1966	Strangers In The Night FRANK SINATRA	Reprise
1967	By The Time I Get To Phoenix GLEN CAMPBELL	Capitol
1968	Light My Fire JOSE FELICIANO	RCA Victor
1969	Everybody's Talkin' HARRY NILSSON	United Artists

BEST VOCAL PERFORMANCE, FEMALE

Year	Title and Artist	Label
1960	Mack The Knife ELLA FITZGERALD	Verve
1961	Judy At Carnegy Hall (LP) JUDY GARLAND	Capitol
1962	Ella Swings Brightly (LP) ELLA FITZGERALD	Verve
1963	The Barbra Streisand Album (LP) BARBRA STREISAND	CBS/Columbia
1964	People BARBRA STREISAND	CBS/Columbia
1965	My Name Is Barbra (LP) BARBRA STREISAND	CBS/Columbia
1966	If He Walked Into My Life EYDIE GORMÉ	CBS/Columbia
1967	Ode To Billie Joe BOBBIE GENTRY	Capitol
1968	Do You Know The Way To San José DIONNE WARWICK	Scepter
1969	Is That All There Is? PEGGY LEE	Capitol

BEST VOCAL PERFORMANCE, GROUP OR DUO

Year	Title and Artist	Label
1960	We Got Us EYDIE GORMÉ/STEVE LAWRENCE	ABC-Paramount
1961	High Flying LAMBERT, HENDRICKS AND ROSS	CBS/Columbia
1962	If I Had A Hammer PETER, PAUL AND MARY	Warner Bros.
1963	Blowin' In The Wind PETER, PAUL AND MARY	Warner Bros.
1964	A Hard Day's Night BEATLES	Capitol
1965	We Dig Mancini THE ANITA KERR SINGERS	RCA Victor
1966	A Man And A Woman THE ANITA KERR SINGERS	Warner Bros.
1967	Up, Up And Away 5TH DIMENSION	Soul City

1968	Mrs. Robinson SIMON AND GARFUNKEL	CBS/Columbia
1969	Aquarius/Let The Sunshine In 5TH DIMENSION	Soul City

BEST R&B RECORDING

Year	Title and Artist	Label
1960	Let The Good Times Roll RAY CHARLES	Altantic
1961	Hit The Road Jack RAY CHARLES	ABC-Paramount
1962	I Can't Stop Loving You RAY CHARLES	ABC-Paramount
1963	Busted RAY CHARLES	ABC-Paramount
1964	How Glad I Am NANCY WILSON	Capitol
1965	Papa's Got A Brand New Bag JAMES BROWN	King
1966	Crying Time RAY CHARLES	ABC-Paramount
1967	Respect ARETHA FRANKLIN	Atlantic

This section was discontinued from 1968.

BEST COUNTRY AND WESTERN PERFORMANCE

Year	Title and Artist	Label
1960	El Passo MARTY ROBBINS	CBS/Columbia
1961	Big Bad John JIMMY DEAN	CBS/Columbia
1962	Funny Way Of Laughin' BURL IVES	US Decca
1963	Detroit City BOBBY BARE	RCA Victor
1964	No award made.	
1965	No award made.	
1966	Almost Persuaded DAVID HUSTON	Epic
1967	Gentle On My Mind GLEN CAMPBELL	Capitol

This section was discontinued from 1968.

BEST FOLK PERFORMANCE

Year	Title and Artist	Label
1960	Swing Dat Hammer HARRY BELAFONTE	RCA Victor
1961	At Home And Abroad BELAFONTE FOLK SINGERS	RCA Victor
1962	If I Had A Hammer PETER, PAUL AND MARY	Warner Bros.
1963	Blowin' In The Wind PETER, PAUL AND MARY	Warner Bros.
1964	We'll Sing In The Sunshine GALE GARNETT	RCA Victor
1965	An Evening With Belafonte and Makeba (LP) HARRY BELAFONTE/MIRIAM MAKEBA	RCA Victor
1966	Blues In The Street CORTELIA CLARK	RCA Victor
1967	Gentle On My Mind JOHN HARTFORD	RCA Victor
1968	Both Sides Now JUDY COLLINS	Elektra
1969	Clouds JONI MITCHELL	Warn Bros.

BEST NEW ARTIST

1960	Bob Newhart
1961	Peter Nero
1962	Robert Goulet
1963	The Swingle Singers
1964	Beatles
1965	Tom Jones
1966	No award made
1967	Bobbie Gentry
1968	Jose Feliciano
1969	Crosby, Stills and Nash

INDEX OF ARTISTS

Artists are listed followed by the year in which their million selling record(s) were released in brackets, and the page number for each entry.

1910 Fruitgum Company (1968) 206; (1969) 234

Aces, The — *see* Desmond Dekker
Adamo (1969) 220
Aken, Jewel (1965) 117
Allisons, The (1961) 37
Alpert, Herb (1962) 54; (1965) 117, 118; (1966) 144; (1968) 195
American Breed, The (1967) 168
Andrews, Chris (1965) 118
Andrews, Julie (1961) 37; (1964) 93; (1965) 117
Angels, The (1963) 72
Animals, The (1964) 94; (1966) 144
Anka, Paul (1960) 15; (1964) 94
Anthony, Richard (1962) 54
Antoine (1968) 195
Aphrodite's Child (1968) 195
Apollo 11 Astronauts (1969) 220
Archies, the (1969) 220, 221
Armstrong, Louis (1964) 94; (1967) 168
Association, The (1966) 145; (1967) 168; (1968) 196
Aznavour, Charles (1963) 72

Bachelors, the (1964) 95
Ball, Kenny (1961) 37
Ballard, Hank (1960) 15;
Bano, Al (1967) 168
Bare, Bobby (1963) 72; (1964) 95
Barouch, Pierre (1966) 144
Barry, Joe (1961) 37
Barry, Len (1965) 118
Barth, Belle (1960) 15;
Bass, Fontella (1965) 118
Bassey, Shirley (1964) 95
Beach Boys, The (1963) 72; (1964) 95; (1965) 119; (1966) 145;
Beatles, The (1961) 48; (1962) 54; (1963) 73, 74, 75; (1964) 96, 97, 98; (1965) 119, 120, 121; (1966) 146, 147; (1967) 168, 169, 170; (1968) 196; (1969) 221, 222
Bee Gees, The (1967) 170; (1968) 197
Bell, Archie, and the Drells (1968) 197
Bendix, Ralf (1961) 37
Bennett, Tony (1962) 55
Benton, Brook (1960) 32; (1961) 37; (1969) 222
Big Brother and the Holding Company (1968) 197
Bilk, Acker (1961) 38
Birkin, Jane, and Serge Gainsbourg (1969) 223
Black, Bill (1960) 15, 16;
Black, Cilla (1964) 98, 99
Black, Jeanne (1960) 16;
Black, Roy (1966) 147; (1969) 223
Blaine, Marcie (1962) 55
Bland, Bobby (1963) 75

Blood Sweat And Tears (1969) 223, 224
Blue Diamonds, The (1960) 16;
Blue Flames, The — *see* Georgie Fame
Bonds, Gary 'US' (1961) 38
Bonney, Graham (1966) 147
Booker T and the MGs (1962) 55
Boone, Pat (1961) 38; (1962) 55
Box Tops, The (1967) 170; (1968) 197
Boyce, Tommy, and Bobby Heart (1967) 170
Bravos, Los (1966) 152
Brooklyn Bridge, The (1968) 197
Brossart, Naomi (1962) 61
Brothers Four, The (1960) 16
Brown, Arthur (1968) 197
Brown, Charles (1960) 16
Brown, James (1965) 121, 122; (1967) 171
Brubeck, Dave (1961) 38
Bruhl, Heidi (1960) 16
Bryant, Anita (1960) 16
Buckinghams, The (1966) 147
Bue, Papa (1960) 17
Buffalo Springfield (1967) 171
Burnette, Johnny (1960) 17
Burton, Richard (1961) 37
Butler, Jerry (1961) 39; (1969) 224
Byrd, Charlie (1962) 59
Byrds, The (1965) 122; (1967) 171

Campbell, Glen (1968) 197; (1969) 224
Cannon, Freddy (1962) 55; (1965) 122
Carlos, Walter, and Benjamin Folkman (1968) 198
Carr, Vikki (1967) 171
Carter, Clarence (1968) 198
Carter, Mel (1965) 122
Cascades, The (1963) 75
Caselli, Caterina (1966) 147
Cash, Johnny (1963) 75; (1967) 171; (1968); 198; (1969) 224
Cavaliers, The — *see* J. Frank Wilson
Celentano, Adriano (1967) 171
Chairmen Of The Board (1969) 224
Chandler, Gene (1962) 55
Channel, Bruce (1962) 56
Charles, Ray (1960) 17; (1961) 39; (1962) 56; (1963) 76
Checker, Chubby (1960) 17; (1961) 39; (1962) 56
Chicago Transit Authority (1969) 225
Chiffons, The (1963) 76
Christie, Lou (1962) 56; (1963) 76; (1965) 122
Cinquetti, Gigliola (1964) 99
Clanton, Jimmy (1962) 56
Clark, Dee (1961) 39
Clark, Petula (1961) 39; (1962) 56, 57; (1964) 99; (1965) 123; (1967) 171
Classics IV (1967) 172; (1968) 199; (1969) 225
Cole, Nat 'King' (1962) 57
Como, Perry (1960) 18
Conley, Arthur (1967) 172

Conniff, Ray (1966) 147
Contours, The (1962) 57
Cooke, Sam (1960) 18; (1962) 57
Cosby, Bill (1964) 99, 100; (1965) 123; (1966) 148; (1967) 172; (1969) 225
Costa, Don (1960) 18
Cousins, The (1961) 39
Cowsills, The (1967) 172; (1969) 225
Cramer, Floyd (1960) 18; (1961) 39
Crazy World Of Arthur Brown, The (1968) 197
Cream (1967) 172, 173 (1968) 199
Creedence Clearwater Revival (1968) 199; (1969) 225, 226
Crewe, Bob (1966) 148
Croiselle, Nicole (1966) 144
Crosby, Stills And Nash (1969) 227
Crystals, The (1961) 39; (1962) 57; (1963) 77
Cuff Links, The (1969) 227
Cyrkle, The (1966) 148

Dakotas, The — *see* Billy J. Kramer
Dale And Grace (1963) 77
Darin, Bobby (1960) 18; (1962) 58
Darren, James (1961) 39
Dave and Grace (1963) 77
Dave Clark Five (1963) 76, 77; (1964) 99; (1965) 123
Dave Dee, Dozy, Beaky, Mick and Tich (1966) 149; (1968) 199
Davis, Sammy (1962) 58
Davis, Skeeta (1962) 58
Davis, Tyrone (1968) 199
Davis Group, Spencer (1966) 148; (1967) 173
Daytonas, The — *see* Ronny
De Shannon, Jackie (1969) 227
Dean, Jimmy (1961) 40
Dee, Joey (1961) 40; (1962) 58
Deep Purple (1968) 199
Dekker, Desmond (1969) 227
Delfonics, The (1968) 199
Dells, The (1969) 227
Detroit Wheels, The — *see* Mitch Ryder
Deutscher, Drafi (1965) 123
Diamond, Neil (1966) 149; (1969) 228
Dick and Deedee (1961) 40
Dion (1961) 40; (1968) 199
Dixie Cups, The (1964) 100
Dodd, Ken (1965) 123
Domino, Fats (1960) 18
Donegan, Lonnie (1960) 18
Donovan (1966) 149, 150
Doors, The (1967) 173; (1968) 200; (1969) 228
Dorsey, Lee (1961) 40
Doud, Earl (1965) 124
Dourakine, Dimitri (1969) 228
Dovells, The (1961) 40
Dowell, Joe (1961) 41
Drake, Pete (1964) 100
Drifters, The (1960) 19; (1963) 78

Dudley, Dave (1963) 78
Dylan, Bob (1965) 124; (1967) 174; (1969) 228

Easybeats, The (1966) 150
Eddy, Duane (1960) 19; (1962) 58
Elledge, Jimmy (1961) 41
Ellis, Shirley (1965) 125
Enchanters, The — see Garnet Nimms
Equals, The (1968) 200
Essex, The (1963) 78
Eva, Little (1962) 61
Everly Brothers, The (1960) 19; (1961) 41

Fabares, Shelley (1962) 58
Fabric, Bent (1962) 58
Faith, Percy (1960) 19
Fame, Georgie (1964) 100; (1967) 174
Fardon, Don (1968) 200
Feliciano, Jose (1968) 200
Ferrante and Teicher (1960) 20; (1961) 41;
   (1969) 228
Fifth Dimension, The (1967) 174; (1968) 201;
   (1969) 228
Film Soundtrack (Camelot) (1967) 168
   (Doctor Zhivago) (1966) 144
   (Easy Rider) (1969) 220
   (Goldfinger) (1964) 93
   (Un Homme Et Une Femme) (1966) 144
   (Mary Poppines) (1964) 93
   (My Fair Lady) (1964) 93
   (Romeo And Juliet) (1969) 220
   (The Sound Of Music) (1965) 117
   (West Side Story) (1961) 37
Finnegan, Larry (1962) 59
Fireballs, The — see Jimmy Gilmer
Fleetwood Mac (1968) 201; (1969) 229
Flying Machine (1969) 229
Folk Crusaders, The (1967) 174
Folkman, Benjamin, and Walter Carlos (1968)
   198
Fontana, Wayne (1965) 125
Foundations, The (1967) 174; (1968) 202
Four Seasons, The (1962) 59; (1963) 78; (1964)
   100; (1965) 125
Four Tops, The (1964) 100; (1965) 125; (1966)
   150;
Foxx, Innez (1963) 78
Francis, Connie (1960) 20; (1961) 41
Franklin, Aretha (1967) 175, 176; (1968) 202
Fred, John, and his Playboy Band (1967) 176
Freddie and The Dreamers (1963) 78; (1964)
   100
Freddy (1960) 20; (1961) 41; (1962) 59; (1964)
   100
Friends Of Distinction (1969) 229
Froboess, Conny (1962) 59

Gainsbourg, Serge, and Jane Birkin (1969)
   223
Garland, Judy (1961) 41
Garnett, Gale (1964) 100
Gaye, Marvin (1968) 202
Gene and Debbe (1967) 176
Gentry, Bobbie (1967) 176
Gentrys, The (1965) 126
Gerry and the Pacemakers (1964) 101
Getz, Stan (1962) 59; (1964) 102
Gibb, Robin (1969) 229
Gilberto, Astrud (1964) 102
Gilmer, Jimmy (1963) 78
Gitte (1963) 79
Goldsboro, Bobby (1964) 102; (1965) 126;
   (1966) 150; (1968) 203
Gore, Lesley (1963) 79

Gorme, Eydie (1963) 79
Granata, Rocco (1960) 21
Grant, Earl (1961) 42
Grass Roots, The (1967) 176; (1968) 203
Greaves, R. B. (1969) 229
Green, Garland (1969) 229
Greene, Lorne (1964) 102
Guess Who (1969) 229, 230
Guthrie, Arlo (1967) 177

Haggard, Merle (1969) 230
Hallyday, Johnny (1961) 42
Happenings, The (1966) 150; (1967) 177
Hardy, Francoise (1962) 59
Harris, Anita (1967) 177
Harris, Jet, and Tony Meehan (1963) 79
Harris, Richard (1968) 203
Harris, Rolf (1960) 21; (1969) 230
Harrison, Rex (1964) 93
Hart, Bobby, and Tommy Boyce (1967) 170
Hawkins, Edwin (1969) 230
Hebb, Bobby (1966) 150
Heintje (1967) 177; (1968) 203
Hendrix, Jimi (1967) 178; (1968) 203
Hepburn, Audrey (1964) 93
Herman's Hermits (1964) 102; (1965) 126, 127;
   (1966) 151; (1967) 178
Highwaymen, The (1961) 42
Hinton, Joe (1964) 103
Hirt, Al (1963) 80; (1964) 103
Hollies, The (1966) 151; (1967) 178, 179;
   (1969) 231
Holloway, Stanley (1964) 93
Hollywood Argyles, The (1960) 21
Holm, Michael (1969) 231
Holman, Eddie (1969) 231
Honeycombs, The (1964) 103
Hooker, John Lee (1963) 80
Hopkin, Mary (1968) 204
Horton, Johnny (1960) 21; (1961) 42
Humperdinck, Engelbert (1967) 179
Hyland, Brian (1960) 21; (1962) 60

Ifield, Frank (1962) 60
Indios Tabajaras, Los (1963) 81
Intruders, The (1968) 204
Iron Butterfly (1968) 204
Isley Brothers, The (1962) 60; (1969) 231

Jackson Five, The (1969) 231
Jaggerz (1969) 232
James, Tommy, and the Shondells (1966) 152;
   (1967) 180; (1968) 204; (1969) 232
Jan and Dean (1963) 80
Jan and Kjeld (1960) 21
Jankowski, Horst (1965) 128
Jarre, Maurice (1966) 144
Jay and the Americans (1968) 205
Jay and the Techniques (1967) 180
Jefferson Airplane (1967) 180
Jimi Hendrix Experience, The (1967) 178;
   (1968) 203
Johnson, Marv (1960) 22
Jones, Casey (1965) 128
Jones, Jimmy (1960) 22
Jones, Tom (1965) 128, 129; (1966) 152; (1967)
   180; (1968) 205; (1969) 232
Jurgens, Udo (1966) 152

Kaempfert, Bert (1960) 22; (1965) 129
Kayama, Yuzo (1965) 129
Keith (1966) 152
Kennedy, President John F. (1963) 72
Kenner, Chris (1961) 42
Kim, Andy (1969) 232

King, B. B. (1969) 232
King, Claude (1962) 60
King, Jonathan (1965) 129
Kingsmen, The (1963) 80
Kinks, The (1964) 103; (1965) 129;
Knight, Gladys (1961) 42; (1967) 180; (1968)
   205
Kramer, Billy J. (1964) 104

Launchers, The — see Yuzo Kayama
Lawrence, Steve (1962) 60
Leali, Fausto (1967) 180
Led Zeppelin (1969) 233
Lee, Brenda (1960) 22; (1962) 60; (1963) 80;
Lee, Dicky (1962) 61
Lee, Leapy (1968) 205
Lemon Pipers, The (1967) 180
Lennon, John (1969) 235
Lester, Ketty (1962) 61
Lewis, Barbara (1965) 129
Lewis, Bobby (1961) 43
Lewis, Gary (1964) 104
Lewis, Ramsey (1965) 129, 130; (1966) 152
Lindsay, Mark (1969) 233
Little Eva (1962) 61
Little Tony (1967) 181
Locklin, Hank (1960) 22
Lolita (1960) 22
Lopez, Trini (1963) 80
Los Bravos (1966) 152
Los Indios Tabajaras (1963) 81
Lovin' Spoonful, The (1966) 153
Luc-Gabrielle, Sister — see The Singing Nun
Lulu (1967) 181
Lundberg, Victor (1967) 181

MacDermot, Galt (1968) 195
Mack, Lonnie (1963) 81
Mahina Stars (1964) 104
Maki, Karumen (1969) 233
Malmquist, Siv (1964) 104
Mamas and the Papas, The (1965) 130; (1966)
   154; (1967) 181
Mancini, Henry (1961) 43; (1969) 233
Mann, Manfred (1964) 104, 105; (1968) 205
Mantovani (1960) 23; (1961) 43
Mao Tse Tung (1966) 162
Marcels, The (1961) 43
March, Little Peggy (1963) 81
Marketts, The (1963) 81
Mar-Keys, The (1961) 43
Marmalade (1968) 205; (1969) 233
Martha and the Vandellas (1963) 81; (1964)
   105
Martin, Dean (1964) 105
Martino, Al (1965) 131
Marvelettes, The (1961) 43
Masekela, Hugh (1968) 206
Matsuo, Kazuko (1964) 104
Mauriat, Paul (1967) 181, 182
Mayuzumi, Jun (1968) 206
McCoys, The (1965) 130
McDaniels, Gene (1961) 43
McGuire, Barry (1965) 130
McKenzie, Scott (1967) 181
Meader, Vaughn (1962) 61
Meehan, Tony, and Jet Harris (1963) 79
Mel and Tim (1969) 233
Mercy (1969) 234
Midnighters, The — see Hank Ballard
Miller, Mitch (1960) 23
Miller, Ned (1962) 61
Miller, Roger (1964) 105; (1965) 131
Millie (1964) 105

Mimms, Garnet (1963) 82
Mina (1962) 61
Minagawa, Osamu (1969) 234
Minami, Haruo (1964) 105
Mindbenders, The (1965) 125; (1966) 154
Miracles, The (1961) 43; (1962) 62; (1963) 82; (1965) 131; (1967) 182
Monkees, The (1966) 154, 155; (1967) 182; (1968) 206
Monte, Lou (1962) 62
Montenegro, Hugo (1968) 206
Montez, Chris (1962) 62
Moody Blues, The (1964) 105; (1967) 183
Moore, Melba (1968) 195
Morandi, Gianni (1964) 106; (1969) 234
More, Bob (1961) 44
Moriyama, Ryoko (1969) 234
Moroder, Giorgio (1969) 234
Morricone, Ennio (1964) 94
Morrison, Dorothy Coombs (1969) 230
Morrison, Van (1967) 183
Music Explosion, The (1967) 183
Mouskouri, Nana (1961) 44

Napoleon XIV (1966) 155
Nelson, Ricky (1961) 44
Nelson, Sandy (1961) 44
Neville, Aaron (1966) 155
New Christie Minstrels, The (1963) 82
New Vaudeville Band, The (1966) 156
Newbeats, The (1964) 106
Ninomiya, Yukiko (1965) 131
Nobles, Cliff (1968) 206

Ofarim, Esther and Abi (1968) 207
Ohio Express, The (1968) 207
O'Kaysions, The (1968) 207
Okumura, Chiyo (1966) 156
Oliver (1969) 234, 235
Orbison, Roy (1960) 23, 24; (1961) 44; (1962) 62; (1963) 82; (1964) 106, 107
Original Theatre and Film Soundtrack albums — see under Film Soundtrack and Theatre Cast
Orlons, The (1962) 62; (1963) 82
Outsiders, The (1966) 156

Parker, Robert (1966) 156
Paul and Paula (1962) 62
Pavone, Rita (1963) 82, 83;
Peppermint Rainbow (1968) 207
Pericoli, Emilio (1961) 44
Peter and Gordon (1964) 107; (1965) 131; (1966) 156
Peter, Paul and Mary (1962) 63; (1963) 83; (1964) 107; (1967) 184; (1969) 235
Pharaohs, The — see Sam the Sham
Phillips, Esther (1962) 63
Pickett, Bobby 'Boris' (1962) 63
Pickett, Wilson (1955) 131; (1966) 156; (1967) 184
Pinky and the Killers (1968) 207
Pips, The — see Gladys Knights and the Pips
Pitney, Gene (1961) 45; (1962) 63; (1963) 83; (1965) 132
Plastic Ono Band, The (1969) 235
Playboys, The — see Gary Lewis
Plimpton, Shelley (1968) 195
Poppy Family, The (1969) 235
Posey, Sandy (1966) 156, 157
Pravo, Patty (1968) 207
Presley, Elvis (1960) 24, 25; (1961) 45; (1962) 63; (1963) 83; (1964) 107; (1965) 132; (1966) 157; (1968) 207; (1969) 235, 236

Preston, Johnny (1960) 26
Pride, Charley (1969) 236
Procul Harum (1967) 184
Puckett, Garry — see The Union Gap
Purify, James and Bobby (1966) 157

Question Mark and the Mysterians (1966) 157
Quinn, Freddy — see Freddy

Rado, James (1968) 195
Ragni, Gerome (1968) 195
Ramsey Lewis Trio (1965) 129, 130; (1966) 152
Rascals, The (see also The Young Rascals) (1968) 208
Rawls, Lou (1969) 236
Redding, Otis (1968) 208
Rich, Charlie (1960) 26
Richard, Cliff (1960) 26, 27, 28; (1961) 46, 47; (1962) 63, 64; (1963) 83, 84; (1964) 107; (1965) 132; (1968) 208
Righteous Brothers, The (1966) 157
Riley, Jeannie C. (1968) 208, 209
Rios, Miguel (1969) 237
Rios, Waldo De Los (1969) 237
Rivers, Johnny (1966) 157
Roberts, Rocky, and the Airedales (1967) 184
Robin, Alen (1965) 124
Robinson, Smokey, and the Miracles — see The Miracles
Roe, Tommy (1962) 64; (1966) 157; (1968) 209; (1969) 237
Rogers, Kenny (1969) 237
Rokes, The (1967) 185
Rolling Stones, The (1964) 107, 108; (1965) 133, 134; (1966) 157, 158; (1967) 185, 186; (1968) 209; (1969) 237, 238
Ronettes, The (1963) 84
Ronny and The Daytonas (1964) 108
Rooftop Singers, The (1963) 85
Rose, Dave (1962) 64
Ross, Diana — see The Supremes
Rosso, Nini (1965) 134
Royal Guardsmen, The (1966) 158
Rush, Merrilee (1968) 209
Ryan, Barry (1968) 210; (1969) 238
Rydell, Bobby (1960) 28, 29; (1963) 85
Ryder, Mitch (1965) 134

Sadler, Staff Sgt Barry (1966) 159
Sakamoto, Kyu (1962) 65
Sam and Dave (1966) 159; (1967) 186; (1968) 210
Sam the Sham (1965) 134; (1966) 159
Santana (1969) 238
Scaffold, The (1968) 210
Scott, Jack (1960) 29
Scott, Linda (1961) 48
Searchers, The (1964) 109
Seekers, The (1965) 134, 135; (1966) 159
Shadows, The (see also Cliff Richard) (1960) 29; (1961) 48; (1962) 65
Shadows of Night, The (1966) 160
Shangri-Las, The (1964) 110
Shannon, Del (1961) 48; (1964) 110
Shapiro, Helen (1961) 48
Sharp, Dee Dee (1962) 66
Shaw, Sandie (1967) 186
Sheila (1963) 85
Sheridan, Tony (1961) 48
Sherman, Allan (1962) 66; (1963) 85
Sherman, Bobby (1969) 239
Shirelles, The (1960) 29; (1962) 66
Shocking Blue (1969) 239
Shondell, Troy (1961) 49

Simon and Garfunkel (1965) 135; (1966) 160; (1968) 210
Simon, Joe (1969) 240
Sinatra, Frank (1966) 160; (1968) 210; (1969) 240
Sinatra, Frank and Nancy (1967) 186
Sinatra, Nancy (1966) 160, 161
Singing Nun, The (1963) 85, 86
Sir Douglas Quintet Plus Two (1968) 211
Sledge, Percy (1966) 161
Sly and the Family Stone (1968) 211; (1969) 240
Small Faces, The (1967) 186
Smith (1969) 240
Smith, O. C. (1968) 211
Smith, Ray (1960) 30
Smith, Whistling Jack (1967) 187
Soeur Sourire — see The Singing Nun
Solo, Bobby (1964) 110
Sonny and Cher (1965) 135, 136; (1967) 187
Soul, Jimmy (1963) 86
Soul Survivors, The (1967) 187
Sounds Orchestral (1964) 110
Soundtracks — see Film Soundtracks
Spanky and Our Gang (1967) 187
Spencer Davis Group (1966) 148; (1967) 173
Spiders, The (1966) 161
Spiral Staircase, The (1969) 240
Springfield, Dusty (1963) 86; (1966) 161
Springfields, The (1962) 66
Stafford, Terry (1964) 110
Starlighters, The (1961) 40; (1962) 58
Starr, Lucille (1964) 110
Status Quo (1968) 211
Steam (1969) 240
Steppenwolf (1968) 212; (1969) 240
Stevens, April (1963) 87
Stevens, Connie (1960) 30
Stevens, Ray (1962) 66; (1969) 240
Strawberry Alarm Clock, The (1967) 187
Streisand, Barbra (1965) 136; (1967) 187; (1968) 212
String-A-Longs, The (1961) 49
Supremes, The (1964) 111; (1965) 137; (1966) 161; (1967) 188; (1968) 212; (1969) 238
Surfaris, The (1963) 87

Taylor, Johnny (1968) 213
Tee Set (1969) 240
Tempo, Nino (1963) 87
Temptations, The (1965) 137; (1968) 212, 213; (1969) 241
Tempters, The (1968) 213
Tex, Joe (1964) 111; (1967) 188
Theatre Cast (Camelot (1961) 37
(Fiddler On The Roof) (1964) 93
(Hair) (1968) 195
(Man Of La Mancha) (1966) 144
(The Sound of Music (1960) 15
Thomas, B. J. (1966) 161; (1968) 213; (1969) 241
Thompson, Sue (1961) 49
Three Dog Night (1969) 241
Three Meckys, The (1968) 213
Tijuana Brass — see Herb Alpert
Tillotson, Johnny (1960) 30
Tokens, The (1961) 49
Tornados, The (1962) 66
Toys, The (1965) 138
Tremeloes, The (1967) 188, 189
Triumphs, The (1966) 161
Troggs, The (1966) 162; (1967) 189
Turner, Ike and Tina (1960) 30

Turtles, The (1967) 189
Tymes, The (1963) 87

Union Gap, The (1967) 189; (1968) 213, 214
Upchurch, Philip (1961) 50

Valli, Frankie (1967) 190
Van Dyke, Dick (1964) 93
Van Dyke, Leroy (1961) 50
Vandellas, The — *see* Martha and the
   Vandellas
Vanity Fair (1969) 241
Various Artists (All Star Festival LP) (1963) 72
   (Famous Original Hits LP) (1965) 117
   (Stunde Der Stars LP) (1969) 220
   (World Star Festival LP) 220
Vaughn, Billy (1961) 50
Vee, Bobby (1960) 30, 31; (1961) 50; (1962) 67;
   (1967) 190
Ventures, The (1960) 31; (1961) 50; (1964) 111;
   (1969) 241
Verne, Larry (1960) 32

Viking Jazz Band, The (1960) 17
Vinton, Bobby (1962) 67; (1963) 87; (1968) 214
Vogues, The (1968) 214

Walker Brothers, The (1965) 138
Ward, Dale (1963) 87
Warner, Neil (1966) 144
Warwick, Dionne (1963) 87; (1964) 112; (1967)
   190
Washington, Dinah (1960) 32
We Five (1965) 138
Welk, Lawrence (1960) 32
Wells, Mary (1963) 88; (1964) 112
Wendland, Gerhard (1962) 67
Whistling Jack Smith (1967) 187
Who, The (1969) 241
Williams, Andy (1962) 67; (1963) 88
Williams, Mason (1968) 214
Williams, Maurice (1960) 32
Wilson, J. Frank (1964) 112
Wilson, Jackie (1960) 32

Winstons, The (1969) 242
Winter, David Alexander (1969) 242
Wonder, Stevie (1963) 88; (1965) 138; (1967)
   190; (1968) 214; (1969) 242
Wood, Brenton (1967) 190
Wood, Natalie (1961) 37
Wynette, Tammy (1968) 214; (1969) 242

Yardbirds, The (1965) 138
Yoshikawa, Jacky (1966) 162; (1967) 190
Young, Faron (1961) 50
Young-Holt Unlimited (1968) 214
Young, Neil (1969) 243
Young Rascals, The (*see also* the Rascals)
   (1966) 162; (1967) 190
Youngbloods, The (1967) 190
Yuki, Saori (1969) 243

Zager and Evans (1969) 243
Zodiacs, The (1960) 32
Zombies, The (1964) 112; (1969) 243

INDEX OF TITLES

This index lists the title of every million selling record of the sixties, followed by the name of the artist and the year of release in brackets, and then the page number. Titles are listed alphabetically excluding 'a' and 'the'. Foreign language titles are listed under both their original title and the English translation.

1 2 3 (LEN BARRY, 1965) 118

1 2 3 Red Light (THE 1910 FRUITGUM COMPANY, 1968) 206

13 Smash Hits (LP) (TOM JONES, 1968) 205

96 Tears (QUESTION MARK, 1966) 157

98.6 (KEITH, 1966) 152

A Chi (FAUSTO LEALI, 1967) 180
Abbey Road (LP) (THE BEATLES, 1969) 222
Abraham Martin And John (DION, 1968) 199
Action (FREDDY CANNON, 1965) 122
Aftermath (LP) (THE ROLLING STONES, 1966) 157
Age Of Aquarius, The (LP) (FIFTH DIMENSION, 1969) 228
Ahab The Arab (RAY STEVENS, 1962) 66
Ain't No Way (ARETHA FRANKLIN, 1968) 102
Ain't That Lovin' You Baby? (ELVIS PRESLEY, 1964) 107
Al Di La (EMILIO PERICOLI, 1961) 44
Albatross (FLEETWOOD MAC, 1968) 201
Album 1700 (LP) (PETER, PAUL AND MARY, 1967) 184
Alice's Restaurant (LP) (ARLO GUTHRIE, 1967) 177
All Alone Am I (BRENDA LEE, 1962) 60
All In White (ROY BLACK, 1966) 147
All Star Festival (LP) (VARIOUS ARTISTS, 1963) 72
All The Boys And Girls (FRANCOISE HARDY, 1962) 59
All You Need Is Love (THE BEATLES, 1967) 169
Alley Cat (BENT FARBIC, 1962) 58
Alley-Oop (THE HOLLYWOOD ARGYLES, 1960) 21
An Open Letter To My Teenage Son (VICTOR LUNDBERG, 1967) 181
And When I Die (BLOOD, SWEAT AND TEARS, 1967) 224
Andy Williams Christmas Album, The (LP) (ANDY WILLIAMS, 1963) 88
Angel Of The Morning (MERRILEE RUSH, 1968) 209
Any Way You Want It (THE DAVE CLARK FIVE, 1964) 99
Anyone Who Had A Heart (DIONNE WARWICK, 1963) 87
Anyone Who Had A Heart (CILLA BLACK, 1964) 98
Anything That's Part Of You (ELVIS PRESLEY, 1962) 63

Aoi Hitomi (JACKY YOSHIKAWA, 1966) 162
Apache (THE SHADOWS, 1960) 29
Apartment, Theme From The (FERRANTE AND TEICHER, 1960) 20
Apples, Peaches, Pumpkin Pie (Ready Or Not) (JAY AND THE TECHNIQUES, 1967) 180
Aquarius/Let The Sun Shine In (FIFTH DIMENSION, 1969) 228
Are You Experienced? (LP) (JIMI HENDRIX, 1967) 178
Are You Lonesome Tonight (ELVIS PRESLEY, 1960) 25
Are You Sure? (THE ALLISONS, 1961) 37
Arizona (MARK LINDSAY, 1969) 233
As Tears Go By (THE ROLLING STONES, 1965) 133
Ask Me (ELVIS PRESLEY, 1964) 107
Axis: Bold As Love (LP) (JIMI HENDRIX, 1967) 178

Baby Come Back (THE EQUALS, 1968) 200
Baby I Love You (ARETHA FRANKLIN, 1967) 175
Baby I Love You (ANDY KIM, 1969) 232
Baby I Need Your Love (THE FOUR TOPS, 1964) 100
Baby I'm Yours (BARBARA LEWIS, 1965) 129
Baby It's You (SMITH, 1969) 240
Baby Love (THE SUPREMES, 1964) 111
Baby Now That I've Found You (THE FOUNDATIONS, 1967) 174
Baby Roo (CONNIE FRANCIS, 1961) 41
Baby (You Got What It Takes) (DINAH WASHINGTON AND BROOK BENTON, 1960) 32
Babysitter Boogie (RALF BENDIX, 1961) 37
Bachelor Boy (CLIFF RICHARD AND THE SHADOWS, 1962) 64
Back In My Arms Again (THE SUPREMES, 1965) 137
Backfield In Motion (MEL AND TIM, 1969) 233
Bad Moon Rising (CREEDENCE CLEARWATER REVIVAL, 1969) 225
Bad To Me (BILLY J. KRAMER AND THE DAKOTAS, 1964) 104
Ballad Of Bonnie And Clyde, The (GEORGIE FAME, 1967) 174
Ballad Of John And Yoko, The (THE BEATLES, 1969) 221
Ballad Of The Green Berets, The (STAFF SGT BARRY SADLER, 1966) 159
Ballad Of The Green Berets, The (LP) (STAFF SGT BARRY SADLER, 1966) 159
Ballo Del Mattone, Il (RITA PAVONE, 1963) 83
Bambola, La (PATTY PRAVO, 1968) 207
Banjo Boy (JAN AND KJELD, 1960) 21
Barbara Ann (THE BEACH BOYS, 1965) 119
Barefootin' (ROBERT PARKER, 1966) 156
Bayou Country (LP) (CREEDENCE CLEARWATER REVIVAL, 1969) 225
Be My Baby (THE RONETTES, 1963) 84
Be True To Your School (THE BEACH BOYS,

1963) 73
Bearings, The (ANTOINE, 1968) 195
Beat Goes On, The (SONNY AND CHER, 1967) 187
Beat Of The Brass, The (LP) (HERB ALPERT, 1968) 195
Beatles, The (2 LPs) (THE BEATLES, 1968) 196
Beatles For Sale (LP) (THE BEATLES, 1964) 98
Beatles Second Album, The (LP) (THE BEATLES, 1964) 97
Beatles '65 (LP) (THE BEATLES, 1964) 98
Beautiful Morning, A (THE RASCALS, 1968) 208
Because (THE DAVE CLARK FIVE, 1964) 99
Because They're Young (DUANE EDDY, 1960) 19
Beggars Banquet (LP) (THE ROLLING STONES, 1968) 209
Bend It (DAVE DEE, DOZY, BEAKY, MICK AND TICH, 1966) 149
Bend Me, Shape Me (THE AMERICAN BREED, 1967) 168
Best Of Bill Cosby, The (LP) (BILL COSBY, 1969) 225
Best Of Charley Pride, The (LP) (CHARLEY PRIDE, 1969) 236
Best Of Herman's Hermits, The (LP) (HERMAN'S HERMITS, 1965) 127
Best Of The Animals, The (THE ANIMALS, 1966) 144
Between The Buttons (LP) (THE ROLLING STONES, 1967) 185
Beyond The Sea (BOBBY DARIN, 1960) 18
Big Bad John (JIMMY DEAN, 1961) 40
Big Girls Don't Cry (THE FOUR SEASONS, 1962) 59
Big Hits (High Tide And Green Grass) (LP) (THE ROLLING STONES, 1966) 158
Bill Cosby Is A Very Funny Fellow, Right? (LP) (BILL COSBY, 1964) 99
Birds And The Bees, The (JEWEL AKENS, 1965) 117
Bits And Pieces (THE DAVE CLARK FIVE, 1964) 99
Black Cat Tango (OSAMU MINAGAWA, 1969) 234
Black Is Black (LOS BRAVOS, 1966) 152
Blame It On The Bossa Nova (EYDIE GORME, 1963) 79
Blood Sweat And Tears (LP) (BLOOD, SWEAT AND TEARS, 1969) 223
Blooming Hits (LP) (PAUL MAURIAT, 1967) 182
Blowin' In The Wind (PETER, PAUL AND MARY, 1963) 83
Blue Angel (ORY ORBISON, 1960) 24
Blue Bayou (ROY ORBISON, 1963) 82
Blue Chateau (JACKY YOSHIKAWA AND HIS BLUE COMETS, 1967) 190
Blue Eyes (JACKY YOSHIKAWA, 1966) 162
Blue Hawaii (LP) (ELVIS PRESLEY, 1961) 45
Blue Moon (THE MARCELS, 1961) 43
Blue Velvet (BOBBY VINTON, 1963) 87
Bob Dylan's Greatest Hits (LP) (BOB DYLAN, 1967) 174

Bobby's Gril (MARCIE BLAINE, 1962) 55
Boll Weevil Song (BROOK BENTON, 1961) 37
Bookends (LP) (SIMON AND GARFUNKEL, 1968) 210
Born A Woman (SANDY POSEY, 1966) 156
Born To Be Wild (STEPPENWOLF, 1968) 212
Born To Lose (RAY CHARLES, 1962) 56
Bossa Nova Baby (ELVIS PRESLEY, 1963) 83
Boy Named Sue, A (JOHNNY CASH, 1969) 224
Bread And Butter (THE NEWBEATS, 1964) 106
Breakfast At Tiffany's (LP) (HENRY MANCINI, 1961) 43
Breaking Up Is Hard To Do (NEIL SEDAKA, 1962) 65
Brick Dance, The (RITA PAVONE, 1963) 83
Bristol Stomp (THE DOVELLS, 1961) 40
Brown Eyed Girl (VAN MORRISON, 1967) 183
Build Me Up Buttercup (THE FOUNDATIONS, 1968) 202
Bus Stop (THE HOLLIES, 1966) 151
Busted (RAY CHARLES, 1963) 76
Byrds' Greatest Hits, The (LP) (THE BYRDS, 1967) 171

Calcutta (LAWRENCE WELK, 1960) 32
California Dreamin' (THE MAMAS AND THE PAPAS, 1965) 130
Call On Me (BOBBY BLAND, 1963) 75
Camelot (LP) (FILM SOUNDTRACK, 1967) 168
Camelot (LP) (ORIGINAL THEATRE CAST, 1961) 37
Can I Change My Mind? (TYRONE DAVIS, 1968) 199
Candy Man (ROY ORBISON, 1961) 44
Can't Buy Me Love (THE BEATLES, 1964) 96
Can't Get Used To Losing You (ANDY WILLIAMS, 1963) 88
Can't Help Falling In Love (ELVIS PRESLEY, 1961) 45
Can't Take My Eyes Off You (FRANKIE VALLI, 1967) 190
Can't You Hear My Heart Beat? (HERMAN'S HERMITS, 1965) 126
Can't You See That She's Mine? (THE DAVE CLARK FIVE, 1964) 99
Careless Love (RAY CHARLES, 1962) 56
Carnival Is Over, The (THE SEEKERS, 1965) 135
Carrie Anne (THE HOLLIES, 1967) 179
Casatschok (DIMITRI DOURAKINE, 1969) 228
Cast Your Fates To The Wind (SOUNDS ORCHESTRAL, 1964) 110
Catch Us If You Can (THE DAVE CLARK FIVE, 1965) 123
Cathy's Clown (THE EVERLY BROTHERS, 1960) 19
Chain Gang (SAM COOKE, 1960) 18
Chain Of Fools (ARETHA FRANKLIN, 1967) 176
Chapel Of Love (THE DIXIE CUPS, 1964) 100
Chariot (PETULA CLARK, 1962) 57
Cheap Thrills (LP) (BIG BROTHER AND THE HOLDING COMPANY WITH JANIS JOPLIN, 1968) 197
Cherish (THE ASSOCIATION, 1966) 145
Cherry, Cherry (NEIL DIAMOND, 1966) 149
Chewy Chewy (THE OHIO EXPRESS, 1968) 207
Chicago Transit Authority (2 LPs) (CHICAGO TRANSIT AUTHORITY, 1969) 225
Chokin' Kind, The (JOE SIMON, 1969) 240
Christmas Album, A (LP) (BARBRA STREISAND, 1967) 187
Christmas With Heintje (LP) (HEINTJE, 1968) 203
Chug-A-Lug (ROGER MILLER, 1964) 105
Cinderella Rockefella (ESTHER AND ABI OFARIM, 1968) 207

Clapping Song, The (SHIRLEY ELLIS, 1965) 125
Classical Gas (MASON WILLIAMS, 1968) 214
Cloud Nine (THE TEMPTATIONS, 1968) 213
Cold Sweat — Part 1 (JAMES BROWN, 1967) 171
Collection Of Beatles Oldies, A (LP) (THE BEATLES, 1966) 147
Colour Him Father (THE WINSTONS, 1969) 242
Come Back When You Grow Up (BOBBY VEE AND THE STRANGERS, 167) 190
Come See About Me (THE SUPREMES, 1964) 111
Come Together (THE BEATLES, 1969) 222
Commotion (CREEDENCE CLEARWATER REVIVAL, 1969) 226
Congratulations (CLIFF RICHARD, 1968) 208
Cotton Candy (AL HIRT, 1964) 103
Cowboys To Girls (THE INTRUDERS, 1968) 204
Crazy Heart (LITTLE TONY, 1967) 181
Creedence Clearwater Revival (LP) (CREEDENCE CLEARWATER REVIVAL, 1968) 199
Crimson And Clover (TOMMY JAMES AND THE SHONDELLS, 1968) 204
Crosby Stills And Nash (LP) (CROSBY STILLS AND NASH, 1969) 227
Cry Baby (GARNET MIMMS AND THE ENCHANTERS, 1963) 82
Cry Like A Baby (THE BOX TOPS, 1968) 197
Cry With Me (THE ROKES, 1967) 185
Crying (ROY ORBISON, 1961) 44
Crying In The Chapel (ELVIS PRESLEY, 1965) 132
Crystal Blue Persuasion (TOMMY JAMES AND THE SHONDELLS, 1969) 232
Cuore (RITA PAVONE, 1963) 83
Cuore Matto (LITTLE TONY, 1967) 181

D In Love (CLIFF RICHARD AND THE SHADOWS, 1960) 28
Da Do Ron Ron (THE CRYSTALS, 1963) 77
Dance On (THE SHADOWS, 1962) 65
Dance With Me In The Morning (GERHARD WENDLAND, 1962) 67
(Dance With The) Guitar Man (DUANE EDDY, 1962) 58
Dancing In The Street (MARTHA AND THE VANDELLAS, 1964) 105
Dancing Shoes (CLIFF RICHARD AND THE SHADOWS, 1963) 84
Dandelion (THE ROLLING STONES, 1967) 185
Dang Me (ROGER MILLER, 1964) 105
Day Tripper (THE BEATLES, 1965) 121
Daydream (THE LOVIN' SPOONFUL, 1966) 153
Daydream Believer (THE MONKEES, 1967) 182
Days Of Future Past (LP) (THE MOODY BLUES, 1967) 183
Days Of Wine And Roses (ANDY WILLIAMS, 1963) 88
Days Of Wine And Roses (LP) (ANDY WILLIAMS, 1963) 88
Dear One (LARRY FINNEGAN, 1962) 59
December's Children (And Everybody's) (LP) (THE ROLLING STONES, 1965) 134
Dedicated To The One I Love (THE MAMAS AND THE PAPAS, 1967) 181
Deep Purple (NINO TEMPO AND APRIL STEVENS, 1963) 87
Deine Schonstes Geschenk (ROY BLACK, 1969) 223
Delaware (PERRY COMO, 1960) 18
Delilah (TOM JONES, 1968) 205
Desafinado (Slightly Out Of Tune) (STAN GETZ AND CHARLIE BYRD, 1962) 59
Detroit City (BOBBY BARE, 1963) 72
Devil In Disguise, (You're The) (ELVIS PRESLEY, 1963) 83

Devil Or Angel (BOBBY VEE, 1960) 30
Diamonds (JET HARRIS AND TONY MEEHAN, 1963) 79
Diana Ross And The Supremes' Greatest Hits (LP) (THE SUPREMES, 1967) 188
Diana Ross Presents The Jackson Five (LP) (THE JACKSON FIVE, 1969) 231
Diane (THE BACHELORS, 1964) 95
Dimples (JOHN LEE HOOKER, 1963) 80
Ding A Ling (BOBBY RYDELL, 1960) 29
Disraeli Gears (LP) (CREAM, 1967) 172
Dizzy (TOMMY ROE, 1968) 209
Do Wah Diddy Diddy (MANFRED MANN, 1964) 104
Do You Love Me? (THE DAVE CLARK FIVE, 1963) 76
Do You Wanna Dance? (CLIFF RICHARD AND THE SHADOWS, 1962) 64
Do You Want To Know A Secret? (THE BEATLES, 1964) 97
Dock Of The Bay, The (OTIS REDDING, 1968) 208
Doctor Zhivago (LP) (FILM SOUNDTRACK conducted by MAURICE JARRE, 1966) 144
Doggin' Around (JACKIE WILSON, 1960) 32
Dominique (THE SINGING NUN, 1963) 85
Don't Be Cruel (BILL BLACK, 1960) 16
Don't Come Knockin' (FATS DOMINO, 1960) 18
Don't Cry Daddy (ELVIS PRESLEY, 1969) 236
Don't Ha Ha (CASEY JONES, 1965) 128
Don't Hang Up (THE ORLONS, 1962) 62
Don't Let The Sun Catch You Crying (GERRY AND THE PACEMAKERS, 1964) 101
Don't Talk To Him (CLIFF RICHARD AND THE SHADOWS, 1963) 84
Don't Worry Baby (THE BEACH BOYS, 1964) 95
Doors, The (LP) (THE DOORS, 1967) 173
Down On The Corner (CREEDENCE CLEARWATER REVIVAL, 1969) 226
Downtown (PETULA CLARK, 1964) 99
Dream Baby (ROY ORBISON, 1962) 62
Dreamin' (JOHNNY BURNETTE, 1960) 17
Du Sollst Nicht Weinen (HEINTJE, 1968) 203
Duke Of Earl (GENE CHANDLER, 1962) 55

Early Beatles, The (LP) (THE BEATLES, 1965) 120
Early In The Morning (VANITY FAIR, 1969) 241
Easier Said Than Done (THE ESSEX, 1963) 78
Easy Rider (LP) (FILM SOUNDTRACK, 1969) 220
Easy To Be Hard (THREE DOG NIGHT, 1969) 241
Ebb Tide (EARL GRANT, 1961) 42
Ebony Eyes (THE EVERLY BROTHERS, 1961) 41
Eight Days A Week (THE BEATLES, 1965) 119
Eleanor Rigby (THE BEATLES, 1966) 146
Electric Ladyland (2 LPs) (THE JIMI HENDRIX EXPERIENCE, 1968) 203
Eli's Coming (THREE DOG NIGHT, 1969) 241
Eloise (BARRY RYAN, 1968) 210
Emerald — No Densetsu (THE TEMPTERS, 1968) 213
End Of Our Road, The (GLADYS KNIGHT AND THE PIPS, 1968) 205
End Of The World, The (SKEETER DAVIS, 1962) 58
Eve Of Destruction, The (BARRY McGUIRE, 1965) 130
Even The Bad Times Are Good (THE TREMELOES, 1967) 189
Every Beat Of My Heart (GLADYS KNIGHT AND THE PIPS, 1961) 42
Every Time (PAUL ANKA AND ENNIO MORRICONI, 1964) 94

Everybody Is A Star (SLY AND THE FAMILY STONE, 1969) 240

Everybody Knows This Is Nowhere (LP) (NEIL YOUNG, 1969) 243

Everybody Loves Somebody (DEAN MARTIN, 1964) 105

Everybody's Somebody's Fool (CONNIE FRANCIS, 1960) 20

Everyday People (SLY AND THE FAMILY STONE, 1968) 211

Everyone's Gone To The Moon (JONATHAN KING, 1965) 129

Expresso Bongo (EP) (CLIFF RICHARD AND THE SHADOWS, 1960) 26

Expressway To Your Heart (THE SOUL SURVIVORS, 1967) 187

Fall In Love With You (CLIFF RICHARD AND THE SHADOWS, 1960) 27

Falling (ROY ORBISON, 1963) 82

Fame And Fortune (ELVIS PRESLEY, 1960) 24

Famous Original Hits (LP) (VARIOUS ARTISTS, 1965) 117

FBI (THE SHADOWS, 1961) 48

Fiddler On The Roof (LP) (ORIGINAL THEATRE CAST, 1964) 93

Finger Poppin' Time (HANK BALLARD, 1960) 15

Fingertips, Part Two (STEVIE WONDER, 1963) 88

Fire (THE CRAZY WORLD OF ARTHUR BROWN, 1968) 197

First Family, The (LP) (VAUGHN MEADER AND NAOMI BROSSART, 1962) 61

First Man On The Moon (APOLLO 11 ASTRONAUTS AND HUGH DOWNES, 1969) 220

Five Hundred Miles Away From Home (EP) (RICHARD ANTHONY, 1962) 54

Five Hundred Miles Away From Home (BOBBY BARE, 1963) 72

Fly, The (CHUBBY CHECKER, 1961) 39

Fool In Love, A (IKE AND TINA TURNER, 1960) 30

Football Match, The (RITA PAVONE, 1963) 82

For Once In My Life (STEVIE WONDER, 1968) 214

For What It's Worth (Stop, Hey What's That Sound?) (BUFFALO SPRINGFIELD, 1967) 171

For Your Love (THE YARDBIRDS, 1965) 138

Forever (PETE DRAKE, 1964) 100

Forever With You (YUZO KAYAMA, 1965) 129

Forget Him (BOBBY RYDELL, 1963) 85

Fortunate Son (CREEDENCE CLEARWATER REVIVAL, 1969) 226

Four Strong Winds (BOBBY BARE, 1964) 95

Frank Sinatra's Greatest Hits! (LP) (FRANK SINATRA, 1968) 210

Frankie And Johnny (ELVIS PRESLEY, 1966) 157

French Song, The (LUCILLE STARR, 1964) 110

Friday On My Mind (THE EASYBEATS, 1966) 150

From A Jack To A King (NED MILLER, 1962) 61

From Me To You (THE BEATLES, 1963) 74

Fun, Fun, Fun (THE BEACH BOYS, 1964) 95

Funky Broadway (WILSON PICKETT, 1967) 184

Funny Girl (LP) (BARBRA STREISAND, 1968) 212

Funny (How Time Slips Away) (JIMMY ELLEDGE, 1961) 41

Funny (How Time Slips Away) (JOE HINTON, 1964) 103

Galveston (GLEN CAMPBELL, 1969) 224

Game Of Love (WAYNE FONTANA AND THE MINDBENDERS, 1965) 125

Ganz In Weiss (ROY BLACK, 1966) 147

Gee Whiz It's You (CLIFF RICHARD AND THE SHADOWS, 1961) 46

Gen Alte Schau Me Net So Teppart An (THE THREE MECKYS, 1968) 213

Genius Of Jankowski, The (LP) (HORST JANKOWSKI, 1965) 128

Georgia On My Mind (RAY CHARLES, 1960) 17

Georgy Girl (THE SEEKERS, 1966) 159

Get Back (THE BEATLES, 1969) 221

Get Off Of My Cloud (THE ROLLING STONES, 1965) 133

Get Together (THE YOUNGBLOODS, 1967) 190

G.I. Blues (LP) (ELVIS PRESLEY, 1960) 25

Gimme Little Sign (BRENTON WOOD, 1967) 190

Gimme Some Lovin' (THE SPENCER DAVIS GROUP, 1966) 148

Girl From Ipanema, The (ASTRUD GILBERTO AND STAN GETZ, 1964) 102

Girl Like You, A (CLIFF RICHARD AND THE SHADOWS, 1961) 46

Girl Watcher (THE O'KAYSIONS, 1968) 207

Gitarzan (RAY STEVENS, 1969) 240

Give Me Just A Little More Time (CHAIRMEN OF THE BOARD, 1969) 224

Give Peace A Chance (THE PLASTIC ONO BAND (JOHN LENNON), 1969) 235

Glad All Over (THE DAVE CLARK FIVE, 1963) 77

Glen Campbell — Live (2 LPs) (GLEN CAMPBELL, 1969) 224

Gloria (THE SHADOWS OF NIGHT, 1966) 160

Go Away Little Girl (THE HAPPENINGS, 1966) 150

Go Away Little Girl (STEVE LAWRENCE, 1962) 60

Go Now (THE MOODY BLUES, 1964) 105

Going In Circles (FRIENDS OF DISTINCTION, 1969) 229

Going Places (LP) (HERB ALPERT, 1965) 118

Going To A Go-Go (THE MIRACLES, 1965) 131

Goldfinger (SHIRLEY BASSEY, 1964) 95

Goldfinger (LP) (ORIGINAL FILM SOUNDTRACK, 1964) 93

Gone, Forgotten, All Over (FREDDY, 1964) 100

Good Lovin' (THE YOUNG RASCALS, 1966) 162

Good Luck Charm (ELVIS PRESLEY, 1962) 63

Good Morning Starshine (OLIVER, 1969) 234

Good The Bad And The Ugly, The (HUGO MONTENEGRO, 1968) 206

Good Timin' (JIMMY JONES, 1960) 22

Good Vibrations (THE BEACH BOYS, 1966) 145

Goodbye Cruel World (JAMES DARREN, 1961) 39

Got A Funny Feeling (CLIFF RICHARD AND THE SHADOWS, 1961) 46

Got Live If You Want It (LP) (THE ROLLING STONES, 1966) 158

Grazin' In The Grass (FRIENDS OF DISTINCTION, 1969) 229

Grazing In The Grass (HUGH MASEKELA, 1968) 206

Greatest Hits (LP) (THE ASSOCIATION, 1968) 196

Greatest Hits — Volume 1 (LP) (JOHNNY CASH, 1967) 171

Green Fields (BROTHERS FOUR, 1960) 16

Green, Green (THE NEW CHRISTIE MINSTRELS, 1963) 82

Green Green Grass Of Home (TOM JONES, 1966) 152

Green Onions (BOOKER T. AND THE MGs, 1962) 55

Green River (CREEDENCE CLEARWATER REVIVAL, 1969) 226

Green River (LP) (CREEDENCE CLEARWATER REVIVAL, 1969) 226

Green Tambourine (THE LEMON PIPERS, 1967) 180

Groovin' (THE YOUNG RASCALS, 1967) 190

Groovy Kind Of Love, A (THE MINDBENDERS, 1966) 154

GTO (RONNY AND THE DAYTONAS, 1964) 108

Guitar Man, (Dance With The) (DUANE EDDY, 1962) 58

Gypsy Cried, The (LOU CHRISTIE, 1962) 56

Hair (THE COWSILLS, 1969) 225

Hair (LP) (ORIGINAL THEATRE CAST, MELBA MOORE, 1968) 195

Handy Man (JIMMY JONES, 1960) 22

Hang On Sloopy (THE RAMSEY LEWIS TRIO, 1965) 130

Hang On Sloopy (THE McCOYS, 1965) 130

Hanky Panky (TOMMY JAMES, 1966) 152

Happening, The (THE SUPREMES, 1967) 188

Happy Together (THE TURTLES, 1967) 189

Hard Day's Night, A (THE BEATLES, 1964) 97

Hard Day's Night, A (FILM SOUNDTRACK LP) (THE BEATLES, 1964) 97

Hard Day's Night, A (LP) (THE BEATLES, 1964) 98

Harper Valley PTA (JEANNIE C. RILEY, 1968) 208

Harper Valley PTA (LP) (JEANNIE C. RILEY, 1968) 209

Hats Off To Larry (DEL SHANNON, 1961) 48

Have I The Right? (THE HONEYCOMBS, 1964) 103

Have You Seen Your Mother, Baby, Standing In The Shadows? (THE ROLLING STONES, 1966) 158

Hawaii Five-O (THE VENTURES, 1969) 241

He Ain't Heavy — He's My Brother (THE HOLLIES, 1969) 231

Headquarters (LP) (THE MONKEES, 1967) 182

Heart (RITA PAVONE, 1963) 83

Heatwave (MARTHA AND THE VANDELLAS, 1963) 81

Heidschi Bumbeidschi (LP) (HEINTJE, 1968) 203

Heintje (LP) (HEINTJE, 1968) 203

Heisser Sand (MINA, 1962) 61

He'll Have To Stay (JEANNE BLACK, 1960) 16

Hello Dolly (LOUIS ARMSTROING, 1964) 94

Hello Goodbye (THE BEATLES, 1967) 169

Hello I Love You (THE DOORS, 1968) 200

Hello Mary Lou (RICKY NELSON, 1961) 44

Hello Muddah, Hello Faddah (ALLAN SHERMAN, 1963) 85

Hello Walls (FARON YOUNG, 1961) 50

Help! (THE BEATLES, 1965) 120

Help! (LP) (THE BEATLES, 1965) 120

Help! (FILM SOUNTRACK LP) (THE BEATLES, 1965) 120

Help Me Rhonda (THE BEACH BOYS, 1965) 119

Here Comes My Baby (THE TREMELOES, 1967) 188

He's A Rebel (THE CRYSTALS, 1962) 57

He's So Fine (THE CHIFFONS, 1963) 76

Hey! Baby (BRUCE CHANNEL, 1962) 56

Hey Jude (THE BEATLES, 1968) 196

Hey Paula (PAUL AND PAULA, 1962) 62

Hey There Lonely Girl (EDDIE HOLMAN, 1969) 231

Himno A La Alegria (MIGUEL RIOS AND WALDO DE LOS RIOS, 1969) 237

His Hand In Mine (LP) (ELVIS PRESLEY, 1961) 45

His Latest Flame, (Marie's The Name) (ELVIS PRESLEY, 1961) 45

Hit The Road Jack (RAY CHARLES, 1961) 39
Hokkaido Skies (CHIYO OKUMURA, 1966) 156
Hold Me, Thrill Me, Kiss Me (MEL CARTER, 1965) 122
Hold On I'm Comin' (SAM AND DAVE, 1966) 159
Hold What You've Got (JOE TEX, 1964) 111
Holly Holy (NEIL DIAMOND, 1969) 228
Homme Et Une Femme, Un (LP) (FILM SOUNDTRACK, 1966) 144
Honey (BOBBY GOLDSBORO, 1968) 203
Honey In The Horn (LP) (AL HIRT, 1963) 80
Honky Tonk Women (THE ROLLING STONES, 1969) 237
Hooked On A Feeling (B. J. THOMAS, 1968) 213
Horse, The (CLIFF NOBLE AND CO., 1968) 206
Hot Sand (MINA, 1962) 61
Hour Of The Stars (LP) (VARIOUS ARTISTS, 1969) 220
House Of The Rising Sun (THE ANIMALS, 1964) 94
House That Jack Built, The (ARETHA FRANKLIN, 1968) 202
Hurt (FAUSTO LEALI, 1967) 180
Hush (DEEP PURPLE, 1968) 199

I Believe (THE BACHELORS, 1964) 95
I Can't Get Next To You (THE TEMPTATIONS, 1969) 241
(I Can't Get No) Satisfaction (THE ROLLING STONES, 1965) 133
I Can't Help Myself (THE FOUR TOPS, 1965) 125
I Can't Stop Loving You (RAY CHARLES, 1962) 56
I Could Easily Fall (In Love With You) (CLIFF RICHARD AND THE SHADOWS, 1964) 107
I Don't Know Why (STEVIE WONDER, 1969) 242
I Don't Want To Spoil The Party (THE BEATLES, 1965) 199
I Feel Fine (THE BEATLES, 1964) 98
I Feel So Bad (ELVIS PRESLEY, 1961) 45
I Get Around (THE BEACH BOYS, 1964) 95
I Got Rhythm (THE HAPPENINGS, 1967) 177
I Got You Babe (SONNY AND CHER, 1965) 135
I Got You (I Feel Good) (JAMES BROWN, 1965) 122
I Gotta Know (ELVIS PRESLEY, 1960) 25
I Hear A Symphony (THE SUPREMES, 1965) 137
I Heard It Through The Grapevine (MARVIN GAYE, 1968) 202
I Heard It Through The Grapevine (GLADYS KNIGHT AND THE PIPS, 1967) 180
I Left My Heart In San Francisco (TONY BENNETT, 1962) 55
I Like It Like That (THE DAVE CLARK FIVE, 1965) 123
I Like It Like That, Part 1 (CHRIS KENNER, 1961) 42
I Love How You Love Me (BOBBY VINTON, 1968) 214
I Love You (CLIFF RICHARD AND THE SHADOWS, 1960) 28
I Never Loved A Man (The Way I Loved You) (ARETHA FRANKLIN, 1967) 175
I Only Live Twice (THE FOLK CRUSADERS, 1967) 174
I Only Want To Be With You (DUSTY SPRINGFIELD, 1963) 86
I Remember You (FRANK IFIELD, 1962) 60
I Say A Little Prayer (ARETHA FRANKLIN, 1968) 202
I Say A Little Prayer (DIONNE WARWICK, 1967) 190

I Second That Emotion (SMOKEY ROBINSON AND THE MIRACLES, 1967) 182
I Started Out As A Child (LP) (BILL COSBY, 1964) 100
I Thank You (SAM AND DAVE, 1968) 210
I Think We're Alone Now (TOMMY JAMES AND THE SHONDELLS, 1967) 180
I Understand (FREDDIE AND THE DREAMERS, 1964) 100
I Want To Hold Your Hand (THE BEATLES, 1963) 75
I Want To Marry A Cowboy (GITTE, 1963) 79
I Want You Back (THE JACKSON FIVE, 1969) 231
I Was Made To Love Her (STEVIE WONDER, 1967) 190
I Was Kaiser Bill's Batman (WHISTLING JACK SMITH, 1967) 187
I Will Follow Him (LITTLE PEGGY MARCH, 1963) 81
I Wish It Would Rain (THE TEMPTATIONS, 1968) 213
I Wonder What She's Doing Tonight? (TOMMY BOYCE AND BOBBY HART, 1967) 170
Ich Will Einen Cowboy Als Mann (GITTE, 1963) 79
If I Can Dream (ELVIS PRESLEY, 1968) 207
If I Didn't Have A Dime (To Play The Jukebox) (GENE PITNEY, 1962) 63
If I Embarrass You, Tell Your Friends (LP) (BELLE BARTH, 1960) 15
If I Had a Hammer (TRINI LOPEZ, 1963) 80
If You Can Believe Your Eyes and Ears (LP) (THE MAMAS AND THE PAPAS, 1966) 154
If You Wanna Be Happy (JIMMY SOUL, 1963) 86
Il Ballo Del Mattone (RITA PAVONE, 1963) 83
Il Silenzio (NINI ROSSO, 1965) 134
I'll Never Fall In Love Again (TOM JONES, 1967) 180
I'll Never Find Another You (THE SEEKERS, 1965) 134
I'm A Believer (THE MONKEES, 1966) 155
I'm A Fool To Care (JOE BARRY, 1961) 37
I'm A Man (THE SPENCER DAVIS GROUP, 1967) 173
I'm Gonna Make You Love Me (DIANA ROSS AND THE SUPREMES AND THE TEMPTATIONS, 1968) 212
I'm Henry VIII I Am (HERMAN'S HERMITS, 1965) 127
I'm Hurtin' (ROY ORBISON, 1960) 24
I'm Into Something Good (HERMAN'S HERMITS, 1964) 102
I'm Leaving It Up To You (DALE AND GRACE, 1963) 77
I'm Looking Out The Window (CLIFF RICHARD AND THE SHADOWS, 1962) 64
I'm Not Old Enough To Love You (GIGLIOLA CINQUETTI, 1964) 99
I'm So Lonely I could Cry (B. J. THOMAS, 1966) 161
I'm Sorry (BRENDA LEE, 1960) 22
I'm Telling You Now (FREDDIE AND THE DREAMERS, 1963) 78
I'm Your Puppet (JAMES AND BOBBY PURIFY, 1966) 157
In-A-Gadda-Da-Vida (LP) (IRON BUTTERFLY, 1968) 204
In Crowd, The (RAMSEY LEWIS TRIO, 1965) 129
In Dreams (ROY ORBISON, 1963) 82
In Ginocchio Da Te (GIANNI MORANDI, 1964) 106
In My Little Corner Of The World (ANITA BRYANT, 1960) 16

In My Room (THE BEACHBOYS, 1963) 73
In The Ghetto (ELVIS PRESLEY, 1969) 235
In The Midnight Hour (WILSON PICKETT, 1965) 131
In The Sun (AL BANO, 1967) 168
In The Wind (LP) (PETER, PAUL AND MARY, 1963) 83
In The Year 2525 (ZAGER AND EVENS, 1969) 243
Incense And Peppermints (THE STRAWBERRY ALARM CLOCK, 1967) 187
Indian Giver (1910 FRUITGUM COMPANY, 1969) 234
Indian Reservation (The Lament Of The Cherokee) (DON FARDON, 1968) 200
Introducing...The Beatles (LP) (THE BEATLES, 1964) 96
Israelites (DESMOND DEKKER AND THE ACES, 1969) 227
It Hurts Me (ELVIS PRESLEY, 1964) 107
It Mek (DESMOND DEKKER AND THE ACES, 1969) 227
It Must Be Him (VIKKI CARR, 1967) 171
Italia Mia (LP) (MANTOVANI, 1961) 43
Itchycoo Park (THE SMALL FACES, 1967) 186
It'll Be Me (CLIFF RICHARD AND THE SHADOWS, 1962) 64
It's All In The Game (CLIFF RICHARD AND THE SHADOWS, 1963) 84
It's All Over Now (THE ROLLING STONES, 1964) 107
It's My Party (LESLEY GORE, 1963) 79
It's Not Unsual (TOM JONES, 1965) 128
It's Now Or Never (ELVIS PRESLEY, 1960) 25
It's Over (ROY ORBISON, 1964) 106
It's Raining (GIANI MORANDI, 1969) 234
It's Too Late (BOBBY GOLDSBORO, 1966) 150
It's Your Thing (THE ISLEY BROTHERS, 1969) 231
Itsy, Bitsy, Teenie, Weenie, Yellow Polka Dot Bikini (BRIAN HYLAND, 1960) 21
I've Gotta Get A Message To You (THE BEE GEES, 1968) 197
I've Told Every Little Star (LINDA SCOTT, 1961) 48

Jam Up Jelly Tight (TOMMY ROE, 1969) 237
Java (AL HIRT, 1963) 80
Jazz Samba (LP) (STAN GETZ AND CHARLIE BYRD, 1962) 59
Je T'Aime...Moi Non Plus (JANE BIRKIN AND SERGE GAINSBOURG, 1969) 223
Jealous Kind Of Fella (GARLAND GREEN, 1969) 229
Jealous Of You (CONNIE FRANCIS, 1960) 20
Jean (OLIVER, 1969) 235
Jenny Take A Ride (MITCH RYDER, 1965) 134
J'Entends Siffler Le Train (EP) (RICHARD ANTHONY, 1962) 54
Jingle Jangle (THE ARCHIES, 1969) 221
John Fitzgerald Kennedy — A Memorial Album (PRESIDENT JOHN KENNEDY, 1963) 72
Johnny Angel (SHELLEY FABARES, 1962) 58
Johnny Cash At Folsom Prison (LP) (JOHNNY CASH, 1968) 198
Johnny Cash At San Quentin (LP) (JOHNNY CASH, 1969) 224
Johnny Horton's Greatest Hits (LP) (JOHNNY HORTON, 1961) 42
Josephine (BILL BLACK, 1960) 16
Judy At Carnegie Hall (2 LPs) (JUDY GARLAND, 1961) 41
Judy In Disguise (With Glasses) (JOHN FRED AND HIS PLAYBOY BAND, 1967) 176

Jumpin' Jack Flash (THE ROLLING STONES, 1968) 209

Junge, Komm Rald Wieder (FREDDY, 1962) 59

Just A Little Bit Better (HERMAN'S HERMITS, 1965) 127

Just Loving You (ANITA HARRIS, 1967) 177

Just Tell Her Jim Said Hello (ELVIS PRESLEY, 1962) 63

Kaette Kita Yopparai (THE FOLK CRUSADERS, 1967) 174

Keep On Dancing (THE GENTRYS, 1965) 126

Keep Searchin' (We'll Follow The Sun) (DEL SHANNON, 1964) 110

Keep The Ball Rollin' (JAY AND THE TECHNIQUES, 1967) 180

Kennedy, John Fitzgerald — A Memorial Album (LP) (JOHN KENNEDY, 1963) 72

Kili Watch (THE COUSINS, 1961) 39

Kimi To Itsumadeo (YUZO KAYAMA, 1965) 129

Kind Of A Drag (THE BUCKINGHAMS, 1966) 147

King Of The Road (ROGER MILLER, 1965) 131

Kinijirareta Koi (RYOKO MORIYAMA, 1969) 234

Kissin' Cousins (ELVIS PRESLEY, 1964) 107

Koi No Kisetsu (PINKY AND THE KILLERS, 1968) 207

Kon-Tiki (THE SHADOWS, 1961) 48

Kuro Neko No Tango (OSAMU MINAGAWA, 1969) 234

L'Amour Est Blue (PAUL MAURIAT, 1967) 181

La Bambola (PATTY PRAVO, 1968) 207

La Coppia Piu' Bella Del Mondo (ADRIANO CELENTANO, 1967) 171

La La La (If I Had You) (BOBBY SHERMAN, 1969) 239

La La La (Means I Love You) (THE DELFONICS, 1968) 199

La Mama (CHARLES ANZAVOUR, 1963) 72

La Paloma (FREDDY, 1961) 41

La Partita Di Pallone (RITA PAVONE, 1963) 82

La Tramontana (ANTOINE, 1968) 195

Lacrima Sur Viso, Una (BOBBY SOLO, 1964) 110

Lady Godiva (PETER AND GORDON, 1966) 156

Lady Jane (THE ROLLING STONES, 1966) 158

Lady Madonna (THE BEATLES, 1968) 196

Lady Willpower (UNION GAP, 1968) 213

Land Of A Thousand Dances (WILSON PICKETT, 1966) 156

Last Date (FLOYD CRAMER, 1960) 18

Last Kiss (J. FRANK WILSON AND THE CAVALIERS, 1964) 112

Last Night (THE MAR-KEYS, 1961) 43

Last Time, The (THE ROLLING STONES, 1965) 133

Last Train To Clarksville (THE MONKEES, 1966) 154

Last Waltz, The (ENGLEBERT HUMPERDINCK, 1967) 179

Laughing (GUESS WHO, 1969) 230

Lazy Day (SPANKY AND OUR GANG, 1967) 187

Leader Of The Pack (THE SHANGRI-LAS, 1964) 110

Leah (ROY ORBISON, 1962) 62

Leaving On A Jet Plane (PETER, PAUL AND MARY, 1969) 235

L'Ecole Est Finie (SHEILA, 1963) 85

Led Zeppelin (LP) (LED ZEPPELIN, 1969) 233

Led Zeppelin 2 (LP) (LED ZEPPELIN, 1969) 233

Legend Of The Emerald (THE TEMPTERS, 1968) 213

Legend Of Xanadu, The (DAVE DEE, DOZY, BEAKY, MICK AND TICH, 1968) 199

Let It Bleed (LP) (THE ROLLING STONES, 1969) 238

Let There Be Drums (SANDY NELSON, 1961) 44

Let Yourself Go (FRIENDS OF DISTINCTION, 1969) 229

Let's Dance (CHRIS MONTEZ, 1962) 62

Let's Go, Let's Go, Let's Go (HANK BALLARD, 1960) 15

Let's Hang On (THE FOUR SEASONS, 1965) 125

Let's Live For Today (THE GRASS ROOTS, 1967) 176

Let's Spend The Night Together (THE ROLLING STONES, 1967) 185

Let's Twist Again (CHUBBY CHECKER, 1961) 39

Let's Twist Again (JOHNNY HALLIDAY, 1961) 42

Letter, The (THE BOX TOPS, 1967) 170

Letter From Sherry, A (DALE WARD, 1963) 87

Liebeskummer Lohnt Sich Nicht (SIV MALMQUIST, 1964) 104

Light My Fire (THE DOORS, 1967) 173

Light My Fire (JOSE FELICIANO, 1968) 200

Lightnin's Strikes (LOU CHRISTIE, 1965) 122

Like A Rolling Stone (BOB DYLAN, 1965) 124

Li'l Red Riding Hood (SAM THE SHAM, 1966) 159

Lily The Pink (THE SCAFFOLD, 1968) 210

Limbo Rock (CHUBBY CHECKER, 1962) 56

Lion Sleeps Tonight, The (THE TOKENS, 1961) 49

Listen People (HERMAN'S HERMITS, 1966) 151

Little Arrows (LEAPY LEE, 1968) 205

Little Bit Me A Little Bit You, A (THE MONKEES, 1967) 182

Little Bit O'Soul, A (THE MUSIC EXPLOSION, 1967) 183

Little Bitty Girl (BOBBY RYDELL, 1960) 28

Little Children (BILLY J. KRAMER AND THE DAKOTAS, 1964) 104

Little Deuce Coupe (THE BEACH BOYS, 1963) 73

Little Green Apples (O. C. SMITH, 1968) 211

Little Ole Man (Uptight — Everything's Alright) (BILL COSBY, 1967) 172

Little Sister (ELVIS PRESLEY, 1961) 45

Little Things (BOBBY GOLDSBORO, 1965) 126

Little Woman (BOBBY SHERMAN, 1969) 239

Living Loving Maid (She's Just A Woman) (LED ZEPPELIN, 1969) 233

Locomotion (LITTLE EVA, 1962) 61

Lodi (CREEDENCE CLEARWATER REVIVAL, 1969) 225

Lonely Bull, The (HERB ALPERT AND HIS TIJUANA BRASS, 1962) 54

Lonely Bull, The (LP) (HERB ALPERT AND HIS TIJUANA BRASS, 1962) 54

Lonely Weekends (CHARLIE RICH, 1960) 26

Look At Us (LP) (SONNY AND CHER, 1965) 136

Looking Through The Eyes Of Love (GENE PITNEY, 1965) 132

Looky Looky (GIORGIO MORODER, 1969) 234

Losing You (BRENDA LEE, 1963) 80

Louie Louie (THE KINGSMEN, 1963) 80

Love (Can Make You Happy) (MERCY, 1969) 234

Love Child (DIANA ROSS AND THE SUPREMES, 1968) 212

Love Forever (YUZO KAYAMA, 1965) 129

Love Is All Around (THE TROGGS, 1967) 189

Love Is Blue (PAUL MAURIAT, 1967) 181

Love Is Here And Now You're Gone (THE SUPREMES, 1967) 188

Love Is Love (BARRY RYAN, 1969) 238

Love Letters (KETTY LESTER, 1962) 61

Love Letters (ELVIS PRESLEY, 1966) 157

Love Me Do (THE BEATLES, 1962) 54

Love Problems Are Not Worthwhile (SIV MALMQUIST, 1964) 104

Love Theme From 'Romeo And Juliet' (HENRY MANCINI, 1969) 233

Lover's Concerto, A (THE TOYS, 1965) 138

Lovesick Blues (FRANK IFIELD, 1962) 60

Lucky Lips (CLIFF RICHARD AND THE SHADOWS, 1963) 84

Ma Belle Amie (TEE SET, 1969) 240

MacArthur Park (RICHARD HARRIS, 1968) 203

Magic Carpet Ride (STEPPENWOLF, 1968) 212

Magical Mystery Tour (LP) (THE BEATLES, 1967) 169

Magical Mystery Tour (Double EP) (THE BEATLES, 1967) 170

Majestic, The (DION, 1961) 40

Make It Easy On Yourself (THE WALKER BROTHERS, 1965) 138

Malaguena (CONNIE FRANCIS, 1960) 20

Mama (CONNIE FRANCIS, 1960) 20

Mama (HEINTJE, 1967) 177

Mama, La (CHARLES AZNAVOUR, 1963) 72

Mamas And The Papas, The (LP) (THE MAMAS AND THE PAPAS, 1966) 154

Man And A Woman, A (LP) (FILM SOUNDTRACK, 1966) 144

Man Of La Mancha (LP) (ORIGINAL THEATRE CAST, 1966) 144

Man Who Shot Liberty Valance, The (GENE PITNEY, 1962) 63

Mantovani Plays Music From Exodus And Other Great Themes (LP) (MANTOVANI, 1960) 23

Many Tears Ago (CONNIE FRANCIS, 1960) 20

Marble Stone And Iron Break (DRAFI DEUTSCHER, 1965) 123

Maria Elena (LOS INDIOS TABAJARAS, 1963) 81

(Marie's The Name) His Latest Flame (ELVIS PRESLEY, 1961) 45

Marina (ROCCO GRANATA, 1960) 21

Marmor Stein Und Eisen Bricht (DRAFI DEUTSCHER, 1965) 123

Mary Poppins (LP) (ORIGINAL FILM SOUNDTRACK/JULIE ANDREWS/DICK VAN DYKE, 1964) 93

Mashed Potato Time (DEE DEE SHARP, 1962) 66

Massachusetts (THE BEE GEES, 1967) 170

Matsunoki Kouta (YUKIKO NINOMIYA, 1965) 131

Mean Woman Blues (ROY ORBISON, 1963) 82

Meet The Beatles (LP) (THE BEATLES, 1964) 96

Mellow Yellow (DONOVAN, 1966) 150

Memories Sing Along With Mitch (LP) (MITCH MILLER, 1960) 23

Memphis (LONNIE MACK, 1963) 81

Mendocino (MICHAEL HOLM, 1969) 231

Mendocino (THE SIR DOUGLAS QUINTET PLUS TWO, 1968) 211

Merci Cherie (UDO JURGENS, 1966) 152

Mess Of Blues, A (ELVIS PRESLEY, 1960) 24

Mexico (BOB MOORE, 1961) 44

Michael (Row The Boat Ashore) (THE HIGHWAYMEN, 1961) 42

Mickey's Monkey (THE MIRACLES, 1963) 82

Midnight Confessions (THE GRASS ROOTS, 1968) 203

Midnight Cowboy (FERRANTE AND TEICHER, 1969) 228

Midnight In Moscow (KENNY BALL, 1961) 37

Mighty Joe (SHOCKING BLUE, 1969) 239

Mighty Quinn (MANFRED MANN, 1968) 205

Minute You're Gone, The (CLIFF RICHARD, 1965) 132

Mirage (TOMMY JAMES AND THE SHONDELLS, 1967) 180

Mister Custer (LARRY VERNE, 1960) 32

Mockingbird (INNEZ FOXX, 1963) 78

Modern Sounds In Country and Western Music, Volume 1 (LP) (RAY CHARLES, 1962) 56

Monday Monday (THE MAMAS AND THE PAPAS, 1966) 154

Monkees, The (LP) (THE MONKEES, 1966) 154

Monsieur (PETULA CLARK, 1962) 56

Monster Mash (BOBBY 'BORIS' PICKETT, 1962) 63

Mony Mony (TOMMY JAMES AND THE SHONDELLS, 1968) 204

Moody River (PAT BOONE, 1961) 38

Moon River (JERRY BUTLER, 1961) 39

Moon River and Other Great Movie Themes (LP) (ANDY WILLIAMS, 1962) 67

More Of The Monkees (LP) (THE MONKEES, 1967) 182

More Today Than Yesterday (THE SPIRAL STAIRCASE, 1969) 240

Most Beautiful Couple In The World, The (ADRIANO CELENTANO, 1967) 171

Most Of The Animals, The (THE ANIMALS, 1966) 144

Mother's Little Helper (THE ROLLING STONES, 1966) 158

Mountain's High, The (DICK AND DEEDEE, 1961) 40

Move Two Mountains, (You've Got To) (MARV JOHNSON, 1960) 22

Moving (LP) (PETER, PAUL AND MARY, 1963) 83

Mr Tambourine Man (THE BYRDS, 1965) 122

Mrs Brown You've Got A Lovely Daughter (HERMAN'S HERMITS, 1965) 127

Mrs Robinson (SIMON AND GARFUNKEL, 1968) 210

Music To Watch Girls By (THE BOB CREWE GENERATION, 1966) 148

Mustang Sally (WILSON PICKETT, 1966) 156

My Bonnie (TONY SHERIDAN AND THE BEATLES, 1961) 48

My Boy Lollipop (MILLIE, 1964) 105

My Boyfriend's Back (THE ANGELS, 1963) 72

My Cherie Amour (STEVIE WONDER, 1969) 242

My Fair Lady (LP) (ORIGINAL FILM SOUNDTRACK AND AUDREY HEPBURN AND REX HARRISON, 1964) 93

My Girl (THE TEMPTATIONS, 1965) 137

My Guy (MARY WELLS, 1964) 112

My Heart Has A Mind Of Its Own (CONNIE FRANCIS, 1960) 20

My Home Town (PAUL ANKA, 1960) 15

My Love (PETULA CLARK, 1965) 123

My Mammy (THE HAPPENINGS, 1967) 177

My Name Is Barbra, Two (LP) (BARBRA STREISAND, 1965) 136

My Old Man's A Dustman (LONNIE DONEGAN, 1960) 18

My Son The Folk Singer (LP) (ALLAN SHERMAN, 1962) 66

My Song (ARETHA FRANKLIN, 1968) 202

My Way (FRANK SINATRA, 1969) 240

My World Is Empty Without You (THE SUPREMES, 1966) 161

Na Na Hey Hey Kiss Him Goodbye (STEAM, 1969) 240

Nashville Skyline (LP) (BOB DYLAN, 1969) 228

Needles And Pins (THE SEARCHERS, 1964) 109

Nel Sole (AL BANO, 1967) 168

Nessuno Mi Puo Guidicare (CATERINA CASELLI, 1966) 147

Never My Love (THE ASSOCIATION, 1967) 168

Never On Sunday (DON COSTA, 1960) 18

New York Mining Disaster 1941 (Have You Seen My Wife, Mr Jones?) (THE BEE GEES, 1967) 170

Next Time, The (CLIFF RICHARD AND THE SHADOWS, 1962) 64

Night (JACKIE WILSON, 1960) 32

Night Has A Thousand Eyes, The (BOBBY VEE, 1962) 67

Nights In White Satin (THE MOODY BLUES, 1967) 183

Nine Times Out Of Ten (CLIFF RICHARD AND THE SHADOWS, 1960) 28

Nineteenth Nervous Breakdown (THE ROLLING STONES, 1966) 157

96 Tears (QUESTION MARK, 1966) 157

98.6 (KEITH, 1966) 152

No Milk Today (HERMAN'S HERMITS, 1967) 178

No One (CONNIE FRANCIS, 1961) 41

No One Can Judge Me (CATERINA CASELLI, 1966) 147

No Time (GUESS WHO, 1969) 230

Nobody I Know (PETER AND GORDON, 1964) 107

Non Ho L'Eta (Per Amarti) (GIGLIOLA CINQUETTI, 1964) 99

Non Son Degna Di Te (GIANNI MORANDI, 1964) 106

Norman (SUE THOMPSON, 1961) 49

North To Alaska (JOHNNY HORTON, 1960) 21

Not Good Enough For You (GIANNI MORANDI, 1964) 106

Nothing But A Heartache (THE SUPREMES, 1965) 137

Nowhere Man (THE BEATLES, 1966) 146

Ob-La-Di Ob-La-Da (THE BEATLES, 1968) 196

Ob-La-Di Ob-La-Da (MARMALADE, 1968) 205

Ode To Billie Joe (BOBBIE GENTRY, 1967) 176

Ogni Volta (PAUL ANKA AND ENNIO MORRICONI, 1964) 94

On A Carousel (THE HOLLIES, 1967) 178

Oh Happy Day (THE EDWIN HAWKINS SINGERS, 1969) 230

Oh Lady Mary (DAVID ALEXANDER WINTER, 1969) 242

Oh Pretty Woman (ROY ORBISON, 1964) 107

Oh Well (FLEETWOOD MAC, 1969) 229

Oh What A Night (THE DELLS, 1969) 227

Okie From Muskogee (MERLE HAGGARD, 1969) 230

On My Knees To You (GIANNI MORANDI, 1964) 106

On The Rebound (FLOYD CRAMER, 1961) 39

One (THREE DOG NIGHT, 1969) 241

One Broken Heart For Sale (ELVIS PRESLEY, 1963) 83

One Hundred Pounds Of Clay (GENE McDANIELS, 1961) 43

One Mint Julep (RAY CHARLES, 1961) 39

One Two Three (LEN BARRY, 1965) 118

1 2 3 Red Light (THE 1910 FRUITGUM COMPANY, 1968) 206

Only Love Can Break A Heart (GENE PITNEY, 1962) 63

Only The Lonely (ROY ORBISON, 1960) 23

Only The Strong Survive (JERRY BUTLER, 1969) 224

Orange Blossom Special (BILLY VAUGHN, 1961) 50

Out Of Limits (THE MARKETTS, 1963) 81

Out Of Our Heads (LP) (THE ROLLING STONES, 1965) 133

Over And Over (THE DAVE CLARK FIVE, 1965) 123

Over You (UNION GAP, 1968) 214

Ozashiki Kouta (MAHINA STARS AND KAZUKO MATSUO, 1964) 104

Paint It Black (THE ROLLING STONES, 1966) 158

Palisades Park (FREDDY CANNON, 1962) 55

Paloma, La (FREDDY, 1961) 41

Papa's Got A Brand New Bag — Part 1 (JAMES BROWN, 1965) 121

Paper Roses (ANITA BRYANT, 1960) 16

Paperback Writer (THE BEATLES, 1966) 146

Parsley, Sage, Rosemary And Thyme (LP) (SIMON AND GARFUNKEL, 1966) 160

Partita di Pallone, La (RITA PAVONE, 1963) 82

Patches (DICKEY LEE, 1962) 61

Penny Lane (THE BEATLES, 1967) 168

People Got To Be Free (THE RASCALS, 1968) 208

Pepino The Italian Mouse (LOU MONTE, 1962) 62

Peppermint Twist Part 1 (JOEY DEE AND THE STARLIGHTERS, 1961) 40

Perfidia (THE VENTURES, 1961) 50

Peter, Paul and Mary (LP) (PETER, PAUL AND MARY, 1962) 63

Peter, Paul And Mary In Concert (LP) (PETER, PAUL AND MARY, 1964) 107

Petit Bonheur (ADAMO, 1969) 220

Piangi Con Me (THE ROKES, 1967) 185

Pictures Of Matchstick Men (STATUS QUO, 1968) 211

Pisces, Aquarius, Capricorn And Jones Ltd (LP) (THE MONKEES, 1967) 182

Playboy (GENE AND DEBBE, 1967) 176

Pleasant Valley Sunday (THE MONKEES, 1967) 182

Please Come Home For Christmas (CHARLES BROWN, 1960) 16

Please Don't Stop Loving Me (ELVIS PRESLEY, 1966) 157

Please Don't Tease (CLIFF RICHARD AND THE SHADOWS, 1960) 27

Please Help Me, I'm Falling (HANK LOCKLIN, 1960) 22

Please Mr Postman (THE MARVELETTES, 1961) 43

Please Please Me (THE BEATLES, 1963) 73

Please Please Me (LP) (THE BEATLES, 1963) 73

Poetry In Motion (JOHNNY TILLOTSEN, 1960) 30

Pony Time (CHUBBY CHECKER, 1961) 39

Popeye The Hitch Hiker (CHUBBY CHECKER, 1962) 56

Positively 4th Street (BOB DYLAN, 1965) 124

Presidential Years, the (JOHN KENNEDY, 1963) 72

Proud Mary (CREEDENCE CLEARWATER REVIVAL, 1969) 225

PS I Love You (THE BEATLES, 1962) 54

Puff (The Magic Dragon) (PETER, PAUL AND MARY, 1963) 83

Puppet On A String (SANDIE SHAW, 1967) 186

Puppy Love (PAUL ANKA, 1960) 15

Put A Little Love In Your Heart (JACKIE DE SHANNON, 1969) 227

Quarter To Three (GARY 'US' BONDS, 1961) 38

Rag Doll (THE FOUR SEASONS, 1964) 100

Rain And Tears (APHRODIE'S CHILD, 1968) 195

Rain, The Park And Other Things, The (THE COWSILLS, 1967) 172

Raindrops (DEE CLARK, 1961) 39

Raindrops Keep Falling On My Head (B. J. THOMAS, 1969) 241

Rainy Night In Georgia (BROOK BENTON, 1969) 222

Ramblin' Rose (NAT 'KING' COLE, 1962) 57

Ramblin' Rose (LP) (NAT 'KING' COLE, 1962) 57

Ramona (THE BLUE DIAMONDS, 1960) 16

Rapper, The (JAGGERZ, 1969) 232

Reach Out I'll Be There (THE FOUR TOPS, 1966) 150

Red Roses For A Blue Lady (BERT KAEMPFERT, 1965) 129

Red Rubber Ball (THE CYRKLE, 1966) 148

Reflections (THE SUPREMES, 1967) 188

Reflections Of My Life (MARMALADE, 1969) 233

Release Me (ESTHER PHILLIPS, 1962) 63

Release Me (ENGLEBERT HUMPERDINCK, 1967) 179

Release Me (LP) (ENGLEBERT HUMPERDINCK, 1967) 179

Remember (Walkin' In The Sand) (THE SHANGRI-LAS, 1964) 110

Rescue Me (FONTELLA BASS, 1965) 118

Respect (ARETHA FRANKLIN, 1967) 175

Return To Sender (ELVIS PRESLEY, 1962) 63

Revenge (LP) (BILL COSBY, 1967) 172

Revolver (LP) (THE BEATLES, 1966) 147

Rhythm Of The Rain (THE CASCADES, 1963) 75

Ride! (DEE DEE SHARP, 1962) 66

Ring Of Fire (JOHNNY CASH, 1963) 75

Ring Of Gold (HEIDI BRUHL, 1960) 16

Ringo (LORNE GREENE, 1964) 102

Robot Man (CONNIE FRANCIS, 1960) 20

Rock-A-Hula Baby (ELVIS PRESLEY, 1961) 45

Rock Me (STEPPENWOLF, 1969) 240

Rockin' Little Angel (RAY SMITH, 1960) 30

Romeo (PETULA CLARK, 1961) 39

Romeo And Juliet (LP) (FILM SOUNDTRACK, 1969) 220

Roses Are Red (My Love) (BOBBY VINTON, 1962) 67

Rubber Ball (BOBBY VEE, 1960) 31

Rubber Soul (LP) (THE BEATLES, 1965) 121

Rubberneckin' (ELVIS PRESLEY, 1969) 236

Ruby Don't Take Your Love To Town (KENNY ROGERS AND THE FIRST EDITION, 1969) 237

Ruby Tuesday (THE ROLLING STONES, 1967) 185

Run To Him (BOBBY VEE, 1961) 50

Runaround Sue (DION, 1961) 40

Runaway (DEL SHANNON, 1961) 48

Running Bear (JOHNNY PRESTON, 1960) 26

Running Scared (ROY ORBISON, 1961) 44

Sad Movies (Make Me Cry) (SUE THOMPSON, 1961) 49

Sad Sunset (THE SPIDERS, 1966) 161

Sailor (LOLITA, 1960) 22

San Francisco (Be Sure To Wear Some Flowers In Your Hair) (SCOTT McKENZIE, 1967) 181

Santana (LP) (SANTANA, 1969) 238

Satisfaction (THE ROLLING STONES, 1965) 133

Save All Your Lovin' For Me (BRENDA LEE, 1962) 60

Save The Last Dance For Me (THE DRIFTERS, 1960) 19

Saved By The Bell (ROBIN GIBB, 1969) 229

Scat In The Dark (SAORI YUKI, 1969) 243

Scende La Poggia (GIANI MORANDI, 1969) 234

Schlafe Mein Prinzchen (PAPA BUE, 1960) 17

School Is Over (SHEILA, 1963) 85

Sealed With A Kiss (BRIAN HYLAND, 1962) 60

Secret Agent Man (JOHNNY RIVERS, 1966) 157

See Saw (ARETHA FRANKLIN, 1968) 202

See The Funny Little Clown (BOBBY GOLDSBORO, 1964) 102

See You In September (THE HAPPENINGS, 1966) 150

Seemann (LOLITA, 1960) 22

Sentimental Singalong With Mitch (LP) (MITCH MILLER, 1960) 23

Sergeant Pepper's Lonely Hearts Club Band (LP) (THE BEATLES, 1967) 169

Sha La La (MANFRED MANN, 1964) 105

She Loves You (THE BEATLES, 1963) 74

She'd Rather Be With Me (THE TURTLES, 1967) 189

Sheila (TOMMY ROE, 1962) 64

Sherry (THE FOUR SEASONS, 1962) 59

She's A Woman (THE BEATLES, 1964) 98

She's Not There (THE ZOMBIES, 1964) 112

She's Not You (ELVIS PRESLEY, 1962) 63

Shop Around (THE MIRACLES, 1961) 43

Shout, Part 1 (JOEY DEE AND THE STARLIGHTERS, 1962) 58

Shut Down (THE BEACH BOYS, 1963) 73

Silence, The (NINI ROSSO, 1965) 134

Silence Is Golden (THE TREMELOES, 1967) 189

Silhouettes (HERMAN'S HERMITS, 1965) 127

Silver Threads And Golden Needles (THE SPRINGFIELDS, 1962) 66

Simon Says (THE 1910 FRUITGUM COMPANY, 1968) 206

Since You've Been Gone (ARETHA FRANKLIN, 1968) 202

Singing Nun, The (LP) (THE SINGING NUN, 1963) 86

Single Girl (SANDY POSEY, 1966) 157

(Sittin' On) The Dock Of The Bay (OTIS REDDING, 1968) 208

Six Days On The Road (DAVE DUDLEY, 1963) 78

Sixteen Reasons (CONNIE STEVENS, 1960) 30

Skinny Legs And All (JOE TEX, 1967) 188

Slip Away (CLARENCE CARTER, 1968) 198

Sloop John B (THE BEACH BOYS, 1966) 145

Slow Twistin' (CHUBBY CHECKER, 1962) 56

Smash Hits (LP) (THE JIMI HENDRIX EXPERIENCE, 1968) 203

Smile A Little Smile For Me (FLYING MACHINE, 1969) 229

Snoopy Versus The Red Baron (THE ROYAL GUARDSMEN, 1966) 158

So Much In Love (THE TYMES, 1963) 87

So You Love Me? (THE CONTOURS, 1962) 57

Soft Parade, The (LP) (THE DOORS, 1969) 228

Soldier Boy (THE SHIRELLES, 1962) 66

Some Kinda Fun (CHRIS MONTEZ, 1962) 62

Someday We'll Be Together (DIANA ROSS AND THE SUPREMES, 1969) 238

Somethin' Stupid (FRANK AND NANCY SINATRA, 1967) 186

Something (THE BEATLES, 1969) 222

Something New (LP) (THE BEATLES, 1964) 98

Sometimes I Feel Like A Lonely Baby (KARUMEN MAKI, 1969) 233

Somewhere My Love (LP) (RAY CONNIFF, 1969) 147

Son Come Home Soon (FREDDY, 1962) 59

Song Of Joy (MIGUEL RIOS AND WALDO DE LOS RIOS, 1969) 237

Soul And Inspiration (THE RIGHTEOUS BROTHERS, 1966) 157

Soul Man (SAM AND DAVE, 1967) 186

Soulful Strut (YOUNG—HOLT UNLIMITED, 1968) 214

Sound Of Music, The (LP) (FILM SOUNDTRACK JULIE ANDREWS, 1965) 117

Sound Of Music, The (LP) (ORIGINAL THEATRE CAST, 1960) 15

Sound Of Silence, The (SIMON AND GARFUNKEL, 1965) 135

South Of The Border (LP) (HERB ALPERT, 1965) 117

South Street (THE ORLONS, 1963) 82

Spanish Eyes (AL MARTINO, 1965) 131

Spanish Flea (HERB ALPERT, 1965) 118

Speedy Gonzales (PAT BOONE, 1962) 55

Spinning Wheel (BLOOD, SWEAT AND TEARS, 1969) 224

Spooky (CLASSICS IV, 1967) 172

SRO (LP) (HERB ALPERT, 1966) 144

Stand (LP) (SLAY AND THE FAMILY STONE, 1969) 240

Stand By Your Man (TAMMY WYNETTE, 1968) 214

Standing In The Shadows Of Love (THE FOUR TOPS, 1966) 150

Stasera Mi Butto (ROCKY ROBERTS AND THE AIREDALES, 1967) 184

Stay (MAURICE WILLIAMS AND THE ZODIACS, 1960) 32

Stoned Soul Picnic (THE FIFTH DIMENSION, 1968) 201

Stop! In The Name Of Love (THE SUPREMES, 1965) 137

Stop, Stop, Stop (THE HOLLIES, 1966) 151

Stormy (CLASSICS IV, 1968) 199

Stranger On The Shore (ACKER BILK, 1961) 38

Strangers In The Night (FRANK SINATRA, 1966) 160

Strawberry Fields Forever (THE BEATLES, 1967) 168

Stripper, The (DAVE ROSE, 1962) 64

Stuck On You (ELVIS PRESLEY, 1960) 24

Stunde Der Stars (LP) (VARIOUS ARTISTS, 1969) 220

Sugar Lips (AL HIRT, 1964) 103

Sugar Shack (JIMMY GILMER AND THE FIREBALLS, 1963) 78

Sugar Sugar (THE ARCHIES, 1969) 220

Sugar Town (NANCY SINATRA, 1966) 161

Sukiaki (KYU SAKAMOTO, 1962) 65

Summer Holiday (CLIFF RICHARD AND THE SHADOWS, 1963) 84

Summer Holiday (LP) (CLIFF RICHARD AND THE SHADOWS, 1963) 83

Summer In The City (THE LOVIN' SPOONFUL, 1966) 153

Summer Place, Theme From A (PERCY FAITH, 1960) 19

Sunday Will Never Be The Same (SPANKY AND OUR GANG, 1967) 187

Sunny (BOBBY HEBB, 1966) 150

Sunshine Of Your Love (CREAM, 1967) 173

Sunshine Superman (DONOVAN, 1966) 149

Super Girl (GRAHAM BONEY, 1966) 147

Surf City (JAN AND DEAN, 1963) 80

Surfer Girl (THE BEACH BOYS, 1963) 73

Surfin' USA (THE BEACHBOYS, 1963) 73

Surrealist Pillow (LP) (JEFFERSON AIRPLANE, 1967) 180

Surrender (ELVIS PRESLEY, 1961) 45

Suspicion (TERRY STAFFORD, 1964) 110

Suspicious Minds (ELVIS PRESLEY, 1969) 235

Sweet Caroline (NEIL DIAMOND, 1969) 228

Sweet Cherry Wine (TOMMY JAMES AND THE SHONDELLS, 1969) 232

Sweet Pea (TOMMY ROE, 1966) 157

Sweet Soul Music (ARTHUR CONLEY, 1967) 172

(Sweet, Sweet Baby) Since You've Been Gone (ARETHA FRANKLIN, 1968) 202

Swingin' School (BOBBY RYDELL, 1960) 29

Switched On Bach (LP) (WALTER CARLOS AND BENJAMIN FOLKMAN, 1968) 198

Take A Letter Maria (R. B. GREAVES, 1969) 229

Take Five (DAVE BRUBECK QUARTET, 1961) 38

Take Good Care Of My Baby (BOBBY VEE, 1961) 50

Take These Chains From My Heart (RAY CHARLES, 1963) 76

Tammy's Greatest Hits (LP) (TAMMY WYNETTE, 1969) 242

Tanze Mit Mir In Den Morgen (GERHARD WENDLAND, 1962) 67

Tapioka Tundra (THE MONKEES, 1968) 206

TCB (Taking Care of Business) (LP) (DIANA ROSS AND THE SUPREMES AND THE TEMPTATIONS, 1968) 212

Tear On Your Face, A (BOBBY SOLO, 1964) 110

Teardrops On Your Letter (HANK BALLARD, 1960) 15

Tears (KEN DODD, 1965) 123

Teddy (CONNIE FRANCIS, 1960) 20

Tell It Like It Is (AARON NEVILLE, 1966) 155

Telstar (THE TORNADOS, 1962) 66

Tenshi No Yuwaku (JUN MAYUZUMI, 1968) 206

Thank You (Falettin Me Be Mice Elf Again) (SLY AND THE FAMILY STONE, 1969) 240

Thank You Girl (THE BEATLES, 1964) 97

That's All You Gotta Do (BRENDA LEE, 1960) 22

That's The Way Love Is (BOBBY BLAND, 1963) 75

Their Satanic Majesty's Request (LP) (THE ROLLING STONES, 1967) 186

Theme For A Dream (CLIFF RICHARD AND THE SHADOWS, 1961) 46

Theme From 'A Summer Place' (PERCY FAITH, 1960) 19

Theme From 'The Appartment' (FERRANTE AND TEICHER, 1960) 20

Then He Kissed Me (THE CRYSTALS, 1963) 77

There Goes My Everything (ENGLEBERT HUMPERDINCK, 1967) 179

There! I've Said It Again (BOBBY VINTON, 1963) 87

There's A Kind Of Hush (HERMAN'S HERMITS, 1967) 178

There's No Other (Like My Baby) (THE CRYSTALS, 1961) 39

These Boots Are Made For Walkin' (NANCY SINATRA, 1966) 160

These Eyes (GUESS WHO, 1969) 229

They Remind Me Too Much Of You (ELVIS PRESLEY, 1963) 83

They're Coming To Take Me Away Ha-Haaa! (NAPOLEON XIV, 1966) 155

Things (BOBBY DARIN, 1962) 58

Think (ARETHA FRANKLIN, 1968) 202

Thirteen Smash Hits (LP) (TOM JONES, 1968) 205

This Diamond Ring (GARY LEWIS AND THE PLAYBOYS, 1964) 104

This Guy's In Love With You (HERB ALPERT, 1968) 195

This Is My Song (PETULA CLARK, 1967) 171

This Is Tom Jones (LP) (TOM JONES, 1969) 232

This Magic Moment (JAY AND THE AMERICANS, 1968) 205

This Time (We're Really Breaking Up) (TROY SHONDELL, 1961) 49

Those Were The Days (MARY HOPKIN, 1968) 204

Thoughts Of Chairman Mao, The (LP) (MAO TSE TUNG, 1966) 162

Thrill Is Gone, The (B. B. KING, 1969) 232

Through The Past Darkly — Big Hits Volume Two (LP) (THE ROLLING STONES, 1969) 238

Ticket To Ride (THE BEATLES, 1965) 119

Tie Me Kangeroo Down Sport (ROLF HARRIS, 1960) 21

Tighten Up (ARCHIE BELL AND THE DRELLS, 1968) 197

Time Is On My Side (THE ROLLING STONES, 1964) 108

Time Of The Seasons (THE ZOMBIES, 1969) 243

Time Won't Let Me (THE OUTSIDERS, 1966) 156

Tired Of Waiting For You (THE KINKS, 1965) 129

To Sir With Love (LULU, 1967) 181

Together (CONNIE FRANCIS, 1961) 41

Tokiniwa Haha No Naiko No Yohni (KARUMEN MAKI, 1969) 233

Tokyo Gorin Ondo (HARUO MINAMI, 1964) 105

Tokyo Olympic Song (HARUO MINAMI, 1964) 105

Tom Jones Fever Zone, The (LP) (TOM JONES, 1968) 205

Tom Jones Live In Las Vegas (LP) (TOM JONES, 1969) 232

Tommy (2 LPs) (THE WHO, 1969) 241

Tonight (FERRANTE AND TEICHER, 1961) 41

Tonight I Fell In Love (THE TOKENS, 1961) 49

Tonight I'll Jump (ROCKY ROBERTS AND THE AIREDALES, 1967) 184

Tonight's The Night (THE SHIRELLES, 1960) 29

Too Many Rules (CONNIE FRANCIS, 1961) 41

Too Weak To Fight (CLARENCE CARTER, 1968) 198

Tossin' And Turnin' (BOBBY LEWIS, 1961) 43

Touch Me (THE DOORS, 1968) 200

Tous Les Garcons Et Les Filles (FRANCOISE HARDY, 1962) 59

Town Without Pity (GENE PITNEY, 1961) 45

Traces (CLASSICS IV, 1969) 225

Tracks Of My Tears (THE MIRACLES, 1965) 131

Tracy (THE CUFF LINKS, 1969) 227

Travelin' Man (RICKY NELSON, 1961) 44

True Love Ways (PETER AND GORDON, 1965) 131

Turn Around Look At Me (THE VOGUES, 1968) 214

Turn! Turn! Turn! (THE BYRDS, 1965) 122

Twenty Four Hours From Tulsa (GENE PITNEY, 1963) 83

Twist, The (HANK BALLARD, 1960) 15

Twist, The (CHUBBY CHECKER, 1960) 17

Twist And Shout (THE BEATLES, 1964) 96

Twist And Shout (EP) (THE BEATLES, 1963) 74

Twist And Shout (THE ISLEY BROTHERS, 1962) 60

Twistin' The Night Away (SAM COOKE, 1962) 57

Two Faces Have I (LOU CHRISTIE, 1963) 76

Two Little Boys (ROLF HARRIS, 1969) 230

Two Little Italians (CONNY FROBOESS, 1962) 59

Two Lovers (MARY WELLS, 1963) 88

Ueo Muite Aruko (KYU SAKAMOTO, 1962) 65

Un Homme Et Une Femme (LP) (FILM SOUNDTRACK, 1966) 144

Una Lacrima Sul Viso (BOBBY SOLO, 1964) 110

Under Foreign Stars (FREDDY, 1960) 20

Undun (GUESS WHO, 1969) 230

Unpermitted Love (RYOKO MORIYAMA, 1969) 234

Unter Freemden Sternen (FREDDY, 1960) 20

Up On The Roof (THE DRIFTERS, 1963) 78

Up Tight (Everything's All Right) (LITTLE STEVIE WONDER, 1965) 138

Up, Up And Away (THE FIFTH DIMENSION, 1967) 174

Uptown (THE CRYSTALS, 1962) 57

Valleri (THE MONKEES, 1968) 206

Valley Of The Dolls (DIONNE WARWICK, 1967) 190

Venus (SHOCKING BLUE, 1969) 239

Venus In Blue Jeans (JIMMY CLANTON, 1962) 56

Vergangen, Vergessen, Vorueber (FREDDY, 1964) 100

Viens Dancer Le Twist (JOHNNY HALLIDAY, 1961) 42

Viva Las Vegas (ELVIS PRESLEY, 1964) 107

Voice In The Wilderness, A (CLIFF RICHARD AND THE SHADOWS, 1960) 27

Volare (BOBBY RYDELL, 1960) 29

Wade In The Water (THE RAMSEY LEWIS TRIO, 1966) 152

Wah-Watusi, The (THE ORLONS, 1962) 62

Waiting For The Sun (LP) (THE DOORS, 1968) 200

Walk, Don't Run (THE VENTURES, 1960) 31

Walk, Don't Run '64 (THE VENTURES, 1964) 111

Walk In The Black Forest, A (HORST JANKOWSKI, 1965) 128

Walk Like A Man (THE FOUR SEASONS, 1963) 78

Walk On By (LEROY VAN DYKE, 1961) 50

Walk On By (DIONNE WARWICK, 1964) 112

Walk Right Back (THE EVERLY BROTHERS, 1961) 41

Walk Right In (THE ROOFTOP SINGERS, 1963) 85

Walking Back To Happiness (HELEN SHAPIRO, 1961) 48

Walkin' To New Orleans (FATS DOMINO, 1960) 18

Wanderer, The (DION, 1961) 40

We Can Work It Out (THE BEATLES, 1965) 121

We Love You (THE ROLLING STONES, 1967) 185

We Will Never Part (HEIDI BRUHL, 1960) 16

Wedding Bell Blues (FIFTH DIMENSION, 1969) 228

Weihnachten Mit Heintje (LP) (HEINTJE, 1968) 203

Weisse Rosen Aus Athen (NANA MOUSKOURI, 1961) 44

Welcome To The LBJ Ranch (LP) (EARL DOUD AND ALEN ROBIN, 1965) 124

We'll Sing In The Sunshine (GALE GARNETT, 1964) 100

West Side Story (LP) (ORIGINAL FILM SOUNDTRACK, 1961) 37

What A Wonderful World (LOUIS ARMSTRONG, 1967) 168

What In The World's Come Over You? (JACK SCOTT, 1960) 29

What Kind Of Fool Am I? (SAMMY DAVIS JR., 1962) 58

What Now My Love? (HERB ALPERT, 1965) 118

What Now My Love? (LP) (HERB ALPERT, 1966) 144

What'd I Say? (ELVIS PRESLEY, 1964) 107

What's New Pussycat? (TOM JONES, 1965) 129

Wheels (THE STRING-A-LONGS, 1961) 49

Wheels (BILLY VAUGHN, 1961) 50

When A Man Loves A Woman (PERCY SLEDGE, 1966) 161

When The Girl In Your Arms Is The Girl In Your Heart (CLIFF RICHARD AND THE SHADOWS, 1961) 46
When The Saints Go Marching In (TONY SHERIDAN AND THE BEATLES, 1961) 48
Where Did Our Love Go (THE SUPREMES, 1964) 111
Where The Boys Are (CONNIE FRANCIS, 1961) 41
Which Way You Goin' Billy? (THE POPPY FAMILY, 1969) 235
Whipped Cream And Other Delights (LP) (HERB ALPERT, 1965) 11
White Album, The (2 LPs) (THE BEATLES, 1968) 196
White Room (CREAM, 1968) 199
White Rose Of Athens (NANA MOUSKOURI, 1961) 44
White Silver Sands (BILL BLACK, 1960) 15
Whiter Shade Of Pale, A (PROCUL HARUM, 1967) 184
Whole Lotta Love (LED ZEPPELIN, 1969) 233
Who's Making Love? (JOHNNY TAYLOR, 1968) 213
Why Is There Air? (LP) (BILL COSBY, 1965) 123
Wild In The Country (ELVIS PRESLEY, 1961) 45
Wild One (BOBBY RYDELL, 1960) 28
Wild Thing (THE TROGGS, 1966) 162
Will You Be Staying After Sunday? (PEPPERMINT RAINBOW, 1968) 207
Will You Love Me Tomorrow (THE SHIRELLES, 1960) 29
Willie And The Hand Jive (CLIFF RICHARD AND THE SHADOWS, 1960) 27
Willie And The Poor Boys (LP) (CREEDENCE CLEARWATER REVIVAL, 1969) 226
Winchester Cathedral (THE NEW VAUDEVILLE BAND, 1966) 156
Wind Me Up (Let Me Go) (CLIFF RICHARD, 1965) 132
Windy (THE ASSOCIATION, 1967) 168
Wipe Out (THE SURFARIS, 1963) 87
Wir Wollen Neimals Auseinandergeh'n (HEIDI BRUHL, 1960) 16

Witchcraft (ELVIS PRESLEY, 1963) 83
Witchita Lineman (GLEN CAMPBELL, 1968) 197
With A Girl Like You (THE TROGGS, 1966) 162
With The Beatles (LP) (THE BEATLES, 1963) 74
Without Love (There Is Nothing) (TOM JONES, 1969) 232
Wolverton Mountain (CLAUDE KING, 1962) 60
Woman, Woman (THE UNION GAP, 1967) 189
Wonderful Land (THE SHADOWS, 1962) 65
Wonderful World (SAM COOKE, 1960) 18
Wonderful World (HERMAN'S HERMITS, 1965) 127
Wonderfulness (LP) (BILL COSBY, 1966) 148
Wonderland By Night (BERT KAEMPFERT, 1960) 22
Wooden Heart (JOE DOWELL, 1961) 41
Wooden Heart (ELVIS PRESLEY, 1960) 25
Wooly Bully (SAM THE SHAM, 1965) 134
Words (THE BEE GEES, 1968) 197
Words (THE MONKEES, 1967) 182
Working For The Man (ROY ORBISON, 1962) 62
World (THE BEE GEES, 1967) 170
World Of Our Own, A (THE SEEKERS, 1965) 135
World Star Festival (LP) (VARIOUS ARTISTS, 1969) 220
World Without Love, A (PETER AND GORDON, 1964) 107
Worst That Could Happen, The (THE BROOKLYN BRIDGE, 1968) 197
Wunderland Bei Nacht (BERT KAEMPFERT, 1960) 22

Ya Ya (LEE DORSEY, 1961) 40
Yeh Yeh (GEORGIE FAME AND THE BLUE FLAMES, 1964) 100
Yellow Submarine (THE BEATLES, 1966) 146
Yellow Submarine (LP) (THE BEATLES, 1969) 221
Yes It Is (THE BEATLES, 1965) 119
Yesterday (THE BEATLES, 1965) 120
Yesterday...And Today (LP) (THE BEATLES, 1966) 146
Yesterday Man (CHRIS ANDREWS, 1965) 118

Yester-Me, Yester-You, Yesterday (STEVIE WONDER, 1969) 242
Yoako-No Skat (SAORI YUKI, 1969) 243
You Can't Hurry Love (THE SUPREMES, 1966) 161
You Can't Sit Down, Part 2 (PHILIP UPCHURCH COMBO, 1961) 50
You Don't Have To Say You Love Me (DUSTY SPRINGFIELD, 1966) 161
You Don't Know (HELEN SHAPIRO, 1961) 48
You Don't Know Me (RAY CHARLES, 1962) 56
You Don't Own Me (LESLEY GORE, 1963) 79
You Keep Me Hangin' On (THE SUPREMES, 1966) 161
You Really Got Me (THE KINKS, 1964) 103
You Shouldn't Cry (HEINTJE, 1968) 203
You Were Made For Me (FREDDIE AND THE DREAMERS, 1963) 78
You Were On My Mind (WE FIVE, 1965) 138
Young Girl (UNION GAP, 1968) 213
Young Ones, The (CLIFF RICHARD AND THE SHADOWS, 1962) 63
Young Ones, The (LP) (CLIFF RICHARD AND THE SHADOWS, 1961) 46
Your Good Thing (Is About To End) (LOU RAWLS, 1969) 236
(You're My) Soul And Inspiration (THE RIGHTEOUS BROTHERS, 1966) 157
You're My World (CILLA BLACK, 1964) 99
(You're The) Devil In Disguise (ELVIS PRESLEY, 1963) 83
You're Sixteen (JOHNNY BURNETTE, 1960) 17
(You've Got To) Move Two Mountains (MARV JOHNSON, 1960) 22
You've Made Me So Very Happy (BLOOD, SWEAT AND TEARS, 1969) 224
You've Really Got A Hold On Me (THE MIRACLES, 1962) 62
Yuhi Ga Naiteiru (THE SPIDERS, 1966) 161
Yummy Yummy Yummy (THE OHIO EXPRESS, 1968) 207

Zwei Kleine Italiener (CONNY FROBOESS, 1962) 59